ECONOMICS

The McGraw-Hill Series in Economics

ELEVENTH EDITION

Economics

David C. Colander
Middlebury College

McGraw Hill Education

ECONOMICS, ELEVENTH EDITION

Published by McGraw-Hill Education, 2 Penn Plaza, New York, NY 10121. Copyright ©2020 by McGraw-Hill Education. All rights reserved. Printed in the United States of America. Previous editions ©2017, 2013, and 2010. No part of this publication may be reproduced or distributed in any form or by any means, or stored in a database or retrieval system, without the prior written consent of McGraw-Hill Education, including, but not limited to, in any network or other electronic storage or transmission, or broadcast for distance learning.

Some ancillaries, including electronic and print components, may not be available to customers outside the United States.

This book is printed on acid-free paper.

3 4 5 6 7 8 9 LWI 21 20

ISBN 978-1-260-22558-7 (bound edition)
MHID 1-260-22558-5 (bound edition)
ISBN 978-1-260-50694-5 (loose-leaf edition)
MHID 1-260-50694-0 (loose-leaf edition)

Director: *Anke Weekes*
Senior Product Developer: *Christina Kouvelis*
Marketing Manager: *Bobby Pearson*
Lead Content Project Manager, core: *Christine Vaughan*
Senior Content Project Manager, assessment: *Bruce Gin*
Senior Buyer: *Laura Fuller*
Designer: *Egzon Shaqiri*
Content Licensing Specialist: *Melissa Homer*
Cover Image: *©amiak/Shutterstock*
Compositor: *Aptara®, Inc.*

All credits appearing on page or at the end of the book are considered to be an extension of the copyright page.

Library of Congress Cataloging-in-Publication Data

Names: Colander, David C., author.
Title: Economics / David C. Colander, Middlebury College.
Description: Eleventh edition. | New York, NY : McGraw-Hill Education, [2020]
Identifiers: LCCN 2018046218| ISBN 9781260225587 (alk. paper) | ISBN 1260225585 (alk. paper)
Subjects: LCSH: Economics.
Classification: LCC HB171.5 .C788 2020 | DDC 330—dc23 LC record available at https://lccn.loc.gov/2018046218

The Internet addresses listed in the text were accurate at the time of publication. The inclusion of a website does not indicate an endorsement by the authors or McGraw-Hill Education, and McGraw-Hill Education does not guarantee the accuracy of the information presented at these sites.

mheducation.com/highered

About the Author

Courtesy of David Colander

David Colander is Distinguished College Professor at Middlebury College. He has authored, coauthored, or edited over 40 books and over 200 articles on a wide range of economic topics.

He earned his BA at Columbia College and his MPhil and PhD at Columbia University. He also studied at the University of Birmingham in England and at Wilhelmsburg Gymnasium in Germany. Professor Colander has taught at Columbia University, Vassar College, the University of Miami, and Princeton University as the Kelley Professor of Distinguished Teaching. He has also been a consultant to Time-Life Films, a consultant to Congress, a Brookings Policy Fellow, and Visiting Scholar at Nuffield College, Oxford.

Professor Colander has been president of both the History of Economic Thought Society and the Eastern Economics Association. He has also served on the editorial boards of *The Journal of Economic Perspectives, The Journal of Economic Education, The Journal of Economic Methodology, The Journal of the History of Economic Thought, The Journal of Socio-Economics,* and *The Eastern Economic Journal.* He has been chair of the American Economic Association Committee on Electronic Publishing, a member of the AEA Committee on Economic Education, and is currently the associate editor for content of *The Journal of Economic Education.*

He is married to a pediatrician, Patrice. In their spare time, the Colanders designed and built an oak post-and-beam house on a ridge overlooking the Green Mountains to the east and the Adirondacks to the west. The house is located on the site of a former drive-in movie theater. (They replaced the speaker poles with fruit trees and used the I-beams from the screen as support for the second story of the carriage house and the garage.) They now live in both Florida and Vermont.

Preface

Economics is about ideas, not models. The goal of this text is to convey to students the ideas that make up modern economics. The ideas are both about the way the economy works, and about how to design policy to make the economy work better.

How This Book Differs from Others

Ideas are nuanced; models are not. From its beginning, this book has provided a nuanced narrative that emphasizes both ideas and models. Its distinctive features have been its conversational style and its inclusion of different views within mainstream economics. It doesn't offer a cookie cutter presentation of material, but instead offers a blend of logical model building and nuanced discussion of applying the models. The writing style is conversational, designed to allow the student to feel a connection with me—the writer—to make it clear that I am a human being, not a machine. This approach is particularly welcomed as students spend more and more time learning material online.

Even while spending a lot of time online, students seek personal connections. It still makes my day when students whom I've never met in person write me thanking me for making the course fun and for relating to them. I'm delighted with the reception this book has received, and the loyal following who have used, and continue to use, the book.

While the book is consciously mainstream, it differs from most other top books in its tone. It presents economic theory more as a changing heuristic than as an unchanging scientific theory. So, while the discussion of the models is the same as in other books, the discussion of the application of the models is different. I emphasize the difficulties of applying the models while most principles books gloss over them.

Nuanced Economics: Teaching More Than Models

Recent economic pedagogy has shifted away from seeing textbooks as a narrative, to seeing them as a compilation of models that can be presented in separable building blocks or modules. This modularization of the teaching of economic principles involves dividing economic knowledge into learning objectives, sub learning objectives, and sub-sub learning objectives.

This building block approach makes lots of sense as long as one remembers that you also need mortar and

architectural blueprints to hold the building blocks together. That mortar and those blueprints are embedded in the text's narrative. Unfortunately, mortar and blueprints don't fit nicely into building block modules captured by learning objectives. Mortar and blueprints require conceptualization that goes beyond the standard models—conceptualization that brings the big picture into focus. And, because there are a variety of architectural blueprints, there is not a single, but a variety of, big pictures; models highlight only one of those blueprints.

The study of such issues is the grist for "big think" economics that characterizes this book where nuance is integrated into understanding, and students see the importance of mortar. Consideration of such issues often goes under the heading of critical thought. To learn to think critically students have to be presented with some questions without definitive answers, but ones upon which, when addressed creatively, economic models can shed light. My book contains lots of such questions.

My approach to models follows the approach Alfred Marshall used back when he first introduced the supply/demand model into the principles course. Marshall emphasized that economics was an approach to problems, not a body of confirmed truths. In my view, the modeling method, not the models, is the most important element of an economic understanding. In my presentation of models, I carefully try to guide students in the modeling method, rather than having them memorize truths from models. I carefully emphasize the limitations of the models and the assumptions that underlie them, and am constantly urging students to think beyond the models. This approach pushes the students a bit harder than the alternative, but it is, in my view, the best pedagogical approach; it is the critical thinking approach.

When taking a critical thinking approach two principles stand out: (1) Institutions and history are important in policy discussions and (2) good economics is open to dealing with various viewpoints. Let me discuss each of these principles briefly.

Institutions and History Are Important to Understand Policy

If you open up Adam Smith's *Wealth of Nations*, John Stuart Mill's *Principles of Political Economy*, or Alfred Marshall's *Principles of Economics*, you will see economic analysis placed in historical and institutional context. The modern textbook template moved away from that, and in previous editions, I have tried to return the principles of economics toward that broader template, presenting models in a historical and institutional context. This edition continues that emphasis on institutions and history. Modern work in game theory and strategic decision making is making it clear that the implications of economic reasoning depend on the institutional setting. To understand economics requires an understanding of existing institutions and the historical development of those institutions. In a principles course we don't have time to present much about history and institutions, but that does not preclude us from letting students know that these issues are important. And that's what I try to do.

When I say that institutions and history are important, I am talking especially about economic policy. This text and the accompanying supplements are not designed for future economics majors. Most principles students aren't going to go on in economics. I write for students who will probably take only one or two economics courses in their lifetime. These students are interested in policy, and what I try to present to them is modern economic reasoning relevant to policy questions.

Because I think policy is so important in explaining how to apply economic reasoning, I utilize a distinction made by J. N. Keynes (John Maynard Keynes' father) and Classical economists generally. That distinction is between theorems—the deductive conclusions of models—and precepts—the considered judgments of economists about the policy implications of the models. I make it clear to students that models do not tell us what to do about policy—they give us theorems. Only when we combine the models' results with our understanding of institutions, our understanding of the social context, and our understanding of the normative goals we want to achieve, can we arrive at policy conclusions embodied in precepts.

Openness to Various Views

While I present modern economics, I present it in such a way that is open to many different points of view. I don't present the material as "the truth" but simply as the conventional wisdom. Learning conventional wisdom is a useful hurdle for all students to jump over. To encourage students to question conventional wisdom, at the end of each chapter I include a set of questions—Questions from Alternative Perspectives—written by economists from a variety of different perspectives. These include Post-Keynesian, Feminist, Austrian, Radical, Institutionalist, and Religious perspectives. Each is described further in the "Distinguishing Features" section that follows the preface. The Radical questions come from the Dollars and Sense Collective, a group with whom I've worked to coordinate their readers (www.dollarsandsense.org/bookstore.html) with this text. I also often integrate Austrian ideas into my class; I find that *The Free Market* (www.mises.org) is a provocative resource.

I often pair an article in *The Free Market* with one in *Dollars and Sense* in my assignments to students for supplementary reading. Having students read both Radical and Austrian views, and then integrate those views into more middle-of-the-road views is, for me, a perfect way to teach the principles course. (If I have a lot of radicals and libertarians in the class, I assign them articles that advocate more middle-of-the-road views.)

Integrating Nuance into the Learning Platform

Changes in technology are changing the medium through which ideas are conveyed and the way students learn. Students today don't know a time without the Internet and social media, which provide them with access to a broad range of digital resources and instant feedback. Technology has changed the way they learn, and if we are to reach them, we have to present material in ways that fit their learning style. They want to be able to access their courses anywhere, anytime—at a coffee shop in the afternoon, in their dorm room late at night, or at lunch hour at work. They still want material that speaks to them, but it has to speak to them in their language at the time they want to listen. Modern learning is blended learning in which online presentations, review, testing of material, and feedback are seamlessly blended with the narrative of the text. This revision is designed to improve what the publisher calls the learning platform in both the content presented and in the delivery of that content.

I think of this book as consisting of both the text and the delivery system for the text. For the book to succeed, the online delivery system has to deliver the material to students in a manner that they can access both online and in the physical book. The new reality of accessing books online has driven important changes in the last edition, and in this edition. Specifically, while the content and pedagogical approach described above remain largely the same, the delivery is different.

In the last two editions the learning platform was refined, and all of the content, including end-of-chapter questions, was made to line up directly with learning objectives. These learning objectives serve as the organizational structure for the material. The learning objectives themselves were broken down into further learning objectives associated with concepts that are presented in bite-sized portions of the text as part of the SmartBook offer.

This now allows students the opportunity to master concepts that support the larger picture no matter how they access it in the Colander learning platform. Within McGraw-Hill's Connect and SmartBook platforms, students can learn the core building blocks online with instant feedback; instructors can assess student learning data and know what their students understand, and what they don't. With that information, they can devote class time to those issues with which students are having problems.

In the previous two editions, the end-of-chapter material was also restructured for online delivery: All of the standard questions and problems were made autogradable and integrated with the online experience. Such integration allows students to move seamlessly between homework problems and portions of the narrative to get the information they need, when they need it. This is a significant advance in pedagogy. Now, even professors in large lecture classes can assign questions and exercises at the end of chapters and provide feedback to students at the point of need.

While the new learning platforms made the teaching of the building blocks easier, they presented a challenge for my approach that emphasized the nuance of interpretation as a key element of what students were to learn. That discussion of nuance was scattered throughout the text; it wasn't a building block to be learned in one place. Rather it was mortar to be learned over the course of the entire semester. This learning goal did not come through in the learning platform as strongly as it did in the text itself. While the modular learning platform worked well in teaching a building block approach to models, it didn't work so well helping students understand the context of the models. It provided the building blocks but not the mortar. So the previous versions of my online learning platforms emphasized models a bit more than I would have liked and context a bit less.

The nuance material was still there, but it was not integrated into the learning platform as much as I thought it should be. In previous editions, I did what I could to account for that. Specifically I added aspects of the book that allowed professors who wanted to emphasize nuance to do so. These included two sets of end-of-chapter questions, Issues to Ponder and Questions from Alternative Perspectives, which have no "correct" answer, but instead are designed to get the students to think. In a learning environment that blends both online and in-person experiences, these are the questions that can form the basis for rich classroom discussions that engage the students with broad issues as much as the online material engages them with the building blocks.

In this edition I go a step further in integrating nuance into the course. Specifically, I have essentially made

nuance its own general learning objective—a learning objective that relates to the entire book. So in addition to the learning objectives specific to individual chapters, there is a general learning objective that is relevant to all chapters. The general learning objective—the mortar that holds the building blocks together—is: *Know that to relate models to the real world, you need to use a nuanced approach.*

For professors who want to include this learning objective in their course, I have written a prologue to the student found on pages P-1 to P-5, just before Chapter 1. In it I discuss the need for context and nuance in applying the models, and introduce students to two methodological tools that philosophers use to move from models to policy positions. This prologue, what you might think of as Chapter 0, serves as the mortar and blueprint to guide students in thinking critically about the models and their application. This short prologue, which can be assigned along with Chapter 1, presents a general discussion of the problem of context and nuance and introduces the general learning objective.

Students are reminded of this general learning objective throughout the book in chapter discussions of nuanced issues, which are highlighted in SmartBook and probes that focus on nuance. I also provide professors with some guidance and suggestions on how to integrate a discussion of values and ethics into the course, along with a list of Connect questions and material in SmartBook that deal with integrating values into the analysis. These are to be found in the Instructor's website for the book. For those who want to emphasize critical thought and nuance in the course, it is much easier to do so than before.

Specific Content Changes to This Edition

Any new edition provides the possibility to update discussions and I have done so throughout the book, both in updating references to events, and in examples. On a mundane level I changed examples and products being discussed. For example, there was an earlier discussion of the supply and demand for CDs, which at one point in the past seemed reasonable. CDs have gone the way of buggy whips, and so the discussion was changed to chocolate, which has a longer shelf life—there will always be demand for 80 percent dark chocolate, at least from me.

I also reviewed all the boxes, eliminating or updating those that were outdated, replacing them with new boxes that capture some of the new ideas being discussed. For example, in Chapter 3 I added a box on polycentric government and the ideas of economist

Elinor Ostrom, and in Chapter 8W I updated the discussion of the farm program.

I did the same with discussions in the text, adding updates where needed. That led to substantial changes in some chapters. For example, President Trump's changing the narrative on trade meant some significant changes in Chapter 10 on trade were needed. I replaced the opening discussion of trade to include Trump's criticism of free trade agreements and updated the discussion of WTO trade negotiations and U.S. trade policy to account for the Trump presidency. The growing importance of platform monopolies and network externalities led to substantial changes in Chapter 14 and the discussion of antitrust policy in Chapter 15. Chapter 17 on labor also was modified to account for developments in the information revolution. I also added discussions of artificial intelligence and deep learning in both the micro and macro chapters. These developments will likely have significant implications for the economy in the coming decade, as AI and deep learning do to mental labor what the Industrial Revolution did to physical labor.

Because of the changing nature of the macro problem facing the economy, macro examples were updated more frequently than micro examples. In this edition the discussion of the macro economy is from the perspective of 2018. The economy is strong, but there is continuing concern that the growth is not sustainable. The monetary policy discussion involved substantial changes since the Fed is no longer using unconventional monetary policy, but is instead trying to unwind its balance sheet as it returns to a conventional monetary policy.

The use of fiscal policy also changed, with the tax cut and spending increase, even as the economy was doing well, showing how politics generally trumps economics in driving fiscal policy. Another change in the macro chapters involved discussions of cryptocurrencies and how they are not currencies, since they don't meet the definition of money, but are instead crypto assets, almost designed to be blown into bubbles. I discuss how blockchain technology might be revolutionary, but the hype around cryptocurrency is more like Tulipmania and how the real revolution in currency is more likely to come through new digital currencies such as M-Pesa.

Finally, there were a number of changes to allow the introduction of nuanced understanding as a separate learning objective. I added a discussion of Adam Smith's impartial spectator tool, and how in assessing policy, one must go beyond how it will benefit oneself, and concentrate on how it can be judged from society's point of view. I encourage students to discuss contentious policy issues with others who approach the issues differently as a way of advancing the discussion.

Enjoy!

In summary, this book differs from others in its distinctive blend of nuance and no-nonsense modeling. Working with models doesn't involve nuance; it involves knowing the models and their assumptions—questions about models are right or wrong—and nuanced discussion of applying the models where there are inevitably gray areas where critical thought is needed. Seeing students navigate this gray area and arrive at a nuanced understanding of economic principles gives me enormous joy. I hope it does for you as well.

People to Thank

Let me conclude this preface by thanking the hundreds of people who have offered suggestions, comments, kudos, and criticism on this project since its inception. This book would not be what it is without their input. So many people have contributed to this text in so many ways that I cannot thank everyone. So, to all the people who helped—many, many thanks. I specifically want to thank the eleventh edition reviewers, whose insightful comments kept me on track. Reviewers include:

Catherine M. Chambers
University of Central Missouri

Frankie P. Albritton Jr.
Seminole State College

Paul Chambers
University of Central Missouri

B. Andrew Chupp
Georgia Institute of Technology

Diane Cunningham
Los Angeles Valley College

Gregory E. DeFreitas
Hofstra University

John P. Finnigan
Marist College

Bernhard Georg Gunter
American University

Benjamin Leyden
University of Virginia

Victoria Miller
Akin Technical College

ABM E. Nasir
North Carolina Central University

Christina Ann Robinson
Central Connecticut State University

William Shambora
Ohio University

Mark Griffin Smith
Colorado College

Don Uy-Barreta
De Anza College

Kenneth Woodward
Saddleback College

In addition to the comments of the formal reviewers listed above, I have received helpful suggestions, encouragement, and assistance from innumerable individuals via e-mails, letters, symposia, and focus groups. Their help made this edition even stronger than its predecessor. They include James Wetzel, Virginia Commonwealth University; Dmitry Shishkin, Georgia State University;

Amy Cramer, Pima Community College–West; Andrea Terzi, Franklin College; Shelby Frost, Georgia State University; Doris Geide-Stevenson, Weber State University; James Chasey, Advanced Placement Economics Teaching Consultant and Homewood-Flossmoor High School (ret.); David Tufte, Southern Utah University; Eric Sarpong, Georgia State University; Jim Ciecka, DePaul University; Fran Bradley, George School; Ron Olive, University of Massachusetts–Lowell; Rachel Kreier, Hofstra University; Kenneth Elzinga, University of Virginia; Ben Leyden, University of Virginia; Poul Thøis Madse, Danmarks Medie—OG Journalistehojskole; Rich Tarmey, Colorado Mountain College; Michael Mandelberg, Stuart Webber, Trinity Lutheran College; Bob Rogers, Ashland University; Zackery Hansen, Southern Utah University; and Matt Gaffney, Missouri State University.

I want to give a special thank-you to the supplement authors and subject matter experts including Jennifer Rester Savoie, Pearl River Community College; Susan Bell, Seminole State University; Per Norander, University of North Carolina at Charlotte; Frankie P. Albritton Jr., Seminole State University; and Kenneth Woodward, Saddleback College. They all did an outstanding job.

I'd also like to thank the economists who wrote the alternative perspective questions. These include Ann Mari May of the University of Nebraska–Lincoln, John Miller of Wheaton College, Dan Underwood of Peninsula College, Ric Holt of Southern Oregon University, and Bridget Butkevich of George Mason University. I enjoyed working with each of them, and while their views often differed substantially, they were all united in wanting questions that showed economics as a pluralist field that encourages students to question the text from all perspectives.

I have hired numerous students to check aspects of the book, to read over my questions and answers to questions, and to help proofread. For this edition, these include Reid Smith, Amelia Pollard and Zhewei Yang. I thank them all.

A special thank-you for this edition goes to two people. The first is Jenifer Gamber, whose role in the book cannot be overestimated. She helped me clarify its vision by providing research, critiquing expositions and often improving them, and being a good friend. She has an amazing set of skills, and I thank her for using them to improve the book. The second is Christina Kouvelis, senior product developer, who came into this project and with her hard work, dedication, and superb ability made it possible to get the book done on time. She and Jenifer are two amazing women.

Next, I want to thank the entire McGraw-Hill team, including Terri Schiesl, managing director; Anke Weekes, director; Christine Vaughan, lead content project manager; Bruce Gin, senior assessment project manager; Egzon Shaqiri, designer; Bobby Pearson, marketing manager; Julia Blankenship, marketing specialist; and Doug Ruby, director of digital content. All of them have done a superb job, for which I thank them sincerely.

Finally, I want to thank Pat, my wife, and my sons, Kasey and Zach, for helping me keep my work in perspective, and for providing a loving environment in which to work.

Distinguishing Features

Margin Comments

Located throughout the text in the margin, these key take-aways underscore and summarize the importance of the material, at the same time helping students focus on the most relevant topics critical to their understanding.

Margin Questions

These self-test questions are presented in the margin of the chapter to enable students to determine whether the preceding material has been understood and to reinforce understanding before students read further. Answers to Margin Questions are found at the end of each chapter.

Web Notes

This feature extends the text discussion onto the web. Web Notes are denoted within the margins, and are housed within Connect and featured in SmartBook.

Nuance Prologue and Questions

Nuanced aspects of economics are presented throughout the book, and in a Prologue for the Student. In SmartBook, nuance questions have been added that directly relate to applying the models and the problems of integrating values into the analysis. A guide to these questions can be found on the Instructor Resource website.

Issues to Ponder

Each chapter ends with a set of Issues to Ponder questions that are designed to encourage additional economic thinking and application.

Questions from Alternative Perspectives

The end-of-chapter material includes a number of questions that ask students to assess economics from alternative perspectives. Specifically, six different approaches are highlighted: Austrian, Post-Keynesian, Institutionalist, Radical, Feminist, and Religious. Below are brief descriptions of each group.

Austrian Economists

Austrian economists believe in methodological individualism, by which they mean that social goals are best met through voluntary, mutually beneficial interactions. Lack of information and unsolvable incentive problems undermine the ability of government to plan, making the market the best method for coordinating economic activity. Austrian economists oppose state intrusion into private property and private activities. They are not economists from Austria; rather, they are economists from anywhere who follow the ideas of Ludwig von Mises and Friedrich Hayek, two economists who were from Austria.

Austrian economists are sometimes classified as conservative, but they are more appropriately classified as libertarians, who believe in liberty of individuals first and in other social goals second. Consistent with their views, they are often willing to support what are sometimes considered radical ideas, such as legalizing addictive drugs or eliminating our current monetary system—ideas that most mainstream economists would oppose. Austrian economists emphasize the uncertainty in the economy and the inability of a government controlled by self-interested politicians to undertake socially beneficial policy.

Institutionalist Economists

Institutionalist economists argue that any economic analysis must involve specific considerations of institutions. The lineage of Institutionalist economics begins with the pioneering work of Thorstein Veblen, John R. Commons, and Wesley C. Mitchell. Veblen employed evolutionary analysis to explore the role of institutions in directing and retarding the economic process. He saw human behavior driven by cultural norms and conveyed the way in which they were with sardonic wit and penetrating insight, leaving us with enduring metaphors such as the leisure class and conspicuous consumption. Commons argued that institutions are social constructs that improve general welfare. Accordingly, he established cooperative investigative programs to support pragmatic changes in the legal structure of government. Mitchell was a leader in developing economics as an empirical study; he was a keen observer of the business cycle and argued that theory must be informed by systematic attention to empirical data, or it was useless.

Contemporary Institutionalists employ the founders' "trilogy"—empirically informed, evolutionary analysis, directed toward pragmatic alteration of institutions shaping economic outcomes—in their policy approach.

Radical Economists

Radical economists believe substantial equality-preferring institutional changes should be implemented in our economic system. Radical economists evolved out of Marxian economics. In their analysis, they focus on the lack of equity in our current economic system and on institutional changes that might bring about a more equitable system. Specifically, they see the current economic system as one in which a few people—capitalists and high-level managers—benefit enormously at the expense of many people who struggle to make ends meet in jobs that are unfulfilling or who even go without work at times. They see the fundamental instability and irrationality of the capitalist system at the root of a wide array of social ills that range from pervasive inequality to alienation, racism, sexism, and imperialism. Radical economists often use a class-oriented analysis to address these issues and are much more willing to talk about social conflict and tensions in our society than are mainstream economists.

A policy favored by many Radicals is the establishment of worker cooperatives to replace the corporation. Radicals argue that such worker cooperatives would see that the income of the firm is more equitably allocated. Likewise, Radical economists endorse policies, such as universal health care insurance, that conform to the ethic of "putting people before profits."

Feminist Economists

Feminist economics offers a substantive challenge to the content, scope, and methodology of mainstream economics. Feminist economists question the boundaries of what we consider economics to be and examine social arrangements surrounding provisioning. Feminist economists have many different views, but all believe that in some way traditional economic analysis misses many important issues pertaining to women.

Feminist economists study issues such as how the institutional structure tends to direct women into certain types of jobs (generally low-paying jobs) and away from other types of jobs (generally high-paying jobs). They draw our attention to the unpaid labor performed by women throughout the world and ask, "What would GDP look like if women's work were given a value and included?" They argue for an expansion in the content of economics to include women as practitioners and as worthy of study and for the elimination of the masculine bias in mainstream economics. Is there such a bias? To see it, simply compare the relative number of women in your economics class to the relative number of women at your school. It is highly likely that your class has relatively more men. Feminist economists want you to ask why that is, and whether anything should be done about it.

Religious Economists

Religion is the oldest and, arguably, the most influential institution in the world—be it Christianity, Islam, Judaism, Buddhism, Hinduism, or any of the many other religions in the world. Modern science, of which economics is a part, emphasizes the rational elements of thought. It attempts to separate faith and normative issues from rational analysis in ways that some religiously oriented economists find questionable. The line between a religious and nonreligious economist is not hard and fast; all economists bring elements of their ethical considerations into their analysis. But those we call "religious economists" integrate the ethical and normative issues into economic analysis in more complex ways than the ways presented in the text.

Religiously oriented economists have a diversity of views; some believe that their views can be integrated reasonably well into standard economics, while others see the need for the development of a distinctive faith-based methodology that focuses on a particular group of normative concerns centered on issues such as human dignity and caring for the poor.

Post-Keynesian Economists

Post-Keynesian economists believe that uncertainty is a central issue in economics. They follow J. M. Keynes' approach more so than do mainstream economists in emphasizing institutional imperfections in the economy and the importance of fundamental uncertainty that rationality cannot deal with. They agree with Institutionalists that the study of economics must emphasize and incorporate the importance of social and political structure in determining market outcomes.

While their view about the importance of uncertainty is similar to the Austrian view, their policy response to that uncertainty is quite different. They do not see uncertainty as eliminating much of government's role in the economy; instead, they see it leading to policies in which government takes a larger role in guiding the economy.

Supplements

McGraw-Hill has established a strong history of top-rate supplements to accompany this text, and this eleventh edition strives to carry on the tradition of excellence. The following ancillaries are available for quick download and convenient access via the Instructor Resource material available through McGraw-Hill Connect®.

Solutions Manual

Prepared by Jenifer Gamber and me, this manual provides answers to all end-of-chapter questions—the Questions and Exercises, Questions from Alternative Perspectives, and Issues to Ponder.

Test Banks

The test bank contains more than 5,600 quality multiple choice and true-false questions for instructors to draw from in their classrooms. Jenifer Gamber and I have worked diligently to make sure that the questions are clear and useful. Each question is categorized by learning objective, level of difficulty, economic concept, AACSB learning categories, and Bloom's Taxonomy objectives. Questions were reviewed by professors and students alike to ensure that each one was effective for classroom use. All of the test bank content is available for assigning within Connect.

A computerized test bank is available via TestGen, a complete, state-of-the-art test generator and editing application software that allows instructors to quickly and easily select test items. Instructors can then organize, edit, and customize questions and answers to rapidly generate tests for paper or online administration. With both quick-and-simple test creation and flexible and robust editing tools, TestGen is a complete test generator system for today's educators.

An essay-only test bank, organized by chapter, will be available via the Instructor Resource material available within Connect.

PowerPoint Presentations

Jennifer Rester Savoie of Pearl River Community College worked tirelessly to revise the PowerPoint slide program, animating graphs and emphasizing important concepts. Each chapter has been scrutinized to ensure an accurate, direct connection to the text.

Problem Sets

Additional problem sets accompany each chapter, which can be assigned to students either for practice or assessment. They are also included as extra assessment content available within Connect.

Assurance of Learning Ready

Many educational institutions today are focused on the notion of *assurance of learning,* an important element of some accreditation standards. *Economics, 11/e* is designed specifically to support your assurance of learning initiatives with a simple yet powerful solution.

Instructors can use Connect to easily query for learning outcomes/objectives that directly relate to the learning objectives of the course. You can then use the reporting features of Connect to aggregate student results in similar fashion, making the collection and presentation of assurance of learning data simple and easy.

AACSB Statement

McGraw-Hill Global Education is a proud corporate member of AACSB International. Understanding the importance and value of AACSB accreditation, the author of *Economics, 11/e* has sought to recognize the curricula guidelines detailed in the AACSB standards for business accreditation by connecting questions in the test bank and end-of-chapter material to the general knowledge and skill guidelines found in the AACSB standards.

It is important to note that the statements contained in *Economics, 11/e* are provided only as a guide for the users of this text. The AACSB leaves content coverage and assessment within the purview of individual schools, the mission of the school, and the faculty. While *Economics, 11/e* and the teaching package make no claim of any specific AACSB qualification or evaluation, we have within *Economics, 11/e* labeled selected questions according to the general knowledge and skills areas.

McGraw-Hill Customer Care Contact Information

At McGraw-Hill, we understand that getting the most from new technology can be challenging. That's why our services don't stop after you purchase our products. You can e-mail our Product Specialists 24 hours a day to get product training online. Or you can search our knowledge bank of Frequently Asked Questions on our support website. For Customer Support, call **800-331-5094** or visit **www.mhhe.com/ support.** One of our Technical Support Analysts will be able to assist you in a timely fashion.

![McGraw Hill Education logo] **connect®** | Students—study more efficiently, retain more and achieve better outcomes. Instructors—focus on what you love—teaching.

SUCCESSFUL SEMESTERS INCLUDE CONNECT

FOR INSTRUCTORS

You're in the driver's seat.

Want to build your own course? No problem. Prefer to use our turnkey, prebuilt course? Easy. Want to make changes throughout the semester? Sure. And you'll save time with Connect's auto-grading too.

65%
Less Time Grading

They'll thank you for it.

Adaptive study resources like SmartBook® help your students be better prepared in less time. You can transform your class time from dull definitions to dynamic debates. Hear from your peers about the benefits of Connect at **www.mheducation.com/highered/connect**

Make it simple, make it affordable.

Connect makes it easy with seamless integration using any of the major Learning Management Systems—Blackboard®, Canvas, and D2L, among others—to let you organize your course in one convenient location. Give your students access to digital materials at a discount with our inclusive access program. Ask your McGraw-Hill representative for more information.

Solutions for your challenges.

A product isn't a solution. Real solutions are affordable, reliable, and come with training and ongoing support when you need it and how you want it. Our Customer Experience Group can also help you troubleshoot tech problems—although Connect's 99% uptime means you might not need to call them. See for yourself at **status.mheducation.com**

Effective, efficient studying.

Connect helps you be more productive with your study time and get better grades using tools like SmartBook, which highlights key concepts and creates a personalized study plan. Connect sets you up for success, so you walk into class with confidence and walk out with better grades.

©Shutterstock/wavebreakmedia

> **"**I really liked this app—it made it easy to study when you don't have your text-book in front of you.**"**
>
> —Jordan Cunningham,
> Eastern Washington University

Study anytime, anywhere.

Download the free ReadAnywhere app and access your online eBook when it's convenient, even if you're offline. And since the app automatically syncs with your eBook in Connect, all of your notes are available every time you open it. Find out more at **www.mheducation.com/readanywhere**

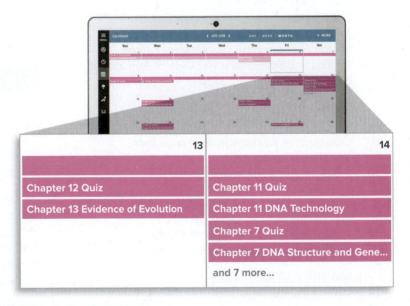

No surprises.

The Connect Calendar and Reports tools keep you on track with the work you need to get done and your assignment scores. Life gets busy; Connect tools help you keep learning through it all.

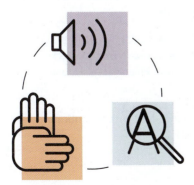

Learning for everyone.

McGraw-Hill works directly with Accessibility Services Departments and faculty to meet the learning needs of all students. Please contact your Accessibility Services office and ask them to email accessibility@mheducation.com, or visit **www.mheducation.com/about/accessibility.html** for more information.

Brief Contents

Contents

PART II

MICROECONOMICS

THE POWER OF TRADITIONAL ECONOMIC MODELS

PART III

MACROECONOMICS

MACROECONOMIC BASICS

List of Boxes

A REMINDER

THINKING LIKE A MODERN ECONOMIST

Some Useful Tools in Moving from Models to the Real World

The study of economics is generally divided into two separate fields: positive economics and normative economics. *Positive economics* is the study of what is and how the economy works. It is the science of economics; it follows scientific methodology, focuses on facts and logic, and tries to be as value-free as possible. The majority of any principles of economics course involves teaching you the methods and tools of positive economics. For example, you will learn the supply/demand model and its implications. One of the conclusions of that model is that if supply increases, price will fall. In good positive economics, given the assumptions, that is the only right answer. No in between. No nuance.

Policy makers, however, aren't especially interested in whether price will fall in an abstract model; they are interested in what will happen in the real world. More specifically, they want to know what will be the impact of a particular policy. Is it a good or a bad policy? Policy analysis extends economics into the arena of *normative economics*—the study of the goals of the economy. Normative economics involves an explicit discussion of what is meant by "good" and by "bad" according to the values of a society. Normative economics follows a humanist and philosophical methodology that relies on logical thought experiments, reflection, and discussion among practitioners to move toward a consensus on values. Because normative economics incorporates often poorly understood and highly uncertain values and sensibilities into the analysis, its methodology requires a much more nuanced understanding of how the models relate to reality than scientific methodology provides.

Many economic policy discussions pirouette around the normative difficulties of specifying goals by simply assuming that the goal is to get as much output as possible from as few inputs as possible—the more stuff the better. Sounds reasonable. But what if who gets what, and how he or she gets it, matters (as it generally does)? What if, for example, a policy results in Person A getting an extra 100 stuffs, while Person B loses 50 stuffs? There's more stuff overall, but Person B has less. Person B might not think the policy is fair. So fairness needs to be considered. Alternatively, say Person B needs a kidney or he will die. Person A has an extra one, and so sells her kidney to Person B. While the number of kidneys hasn't changed, they are allocated in a way that keeps more people alive. That's good, right? Not necessarily. Many people find it immoral to sell kidneys. Should such morality guide policy? U.S. society has decided that it should; selling organs is illegal in the United States. Applied policy has to deal with these and hundreds of similar questions of values and morality.

Normative and positive economics are often presented as distinct areas, as if values can be excluded from positive economics. Philosophers have pointed out that, regardless of how hard we try, we can never do purely positive analysis. Values are just too entangled in the way we look at the world—how we interpret data, the assumptions we make, and the emphasis

we give to different lines of reasoning. For example, if you believe that putting a price on something—such as in the kidney example—undermines the relationship among individuals, then the supply/demand model is not the correct model for analyzing the effect of a policy that involves kidneys because the supply/demand model doesn't allow for a consideration of such questions. So, just by using a model you have already made certain implicit moral judgments that influence your policy conclusions.

Even if we could do pure positive economics, as soon as we move into policy analysis, we have to deal with values, and thus must include an explicit consideration of values. Policy involves achieving normatively determined goals. Because policy involves using insights from positive analysis to achieve goals determined in normative analysis, policy analysis cannot be classified as either completely normative or completely positive. It is a bit of both. As you'll soon read in Chapter 1, I place policy in the netherworld between normative and positive economics—in the *art of economics*— the application of the knowledge gained in positive economics to the goals of economics determined in normative economics.

The Tools of Normative Economies

In this prologue I want to introduce you to two tools that economists have developed to deal with questions about integrating values into the analysis. They are the impartial spectator tool and the devil's advocate tool. The **impartial spectator tool** is *a thought experiment in which a person strives to see the world apart from her own position in it.* An impartial spectator basically tries to maintain a neutral position. Doing so is extremely difficult. That's where the devil's advocate tool comes in. The **devil's advocate tool** is *a tool that helps a person take seriously the arguments of people with whom he or she is least likely to agree so that a person can be as impartial as possible.* These two philosophical tools are meant to help economists deal with the nuance inherent in applied policy, and help policy economists arrive at policies that capture society's shared values.

The Impartial Spectator Tool

The impartial spectator tool comes from 18th-century Scottish moral philosopher and economist Adam Smith. In his *Theory of Moral Sentiments* Smith argued that when trying to come to a position on a policy, an economist should not support or reject a policy on the basis of the benefit or cost it will provide himself. Instead, he should decide on the basis of his estimate of whether the policy will benefit society as a whole. Is it a policy that individuals from all walks of life would generally accept if they studied it carefully with an economists' understanding of how the world works? The impartial spectator tool is designed to address such issues.

The impartial spectator tool requires that individuals place themselves behind a veil of ignorance, and from that position ask: Would I support this position if I were in each of the many different positions people hold in the world? Having considered the policy from many different positions, how would I best resolve differences of opinions? The goal is to arrive at what the individual would argue is a reasonable consensus of people from all different walks of life. If done correctly, and if people can really place themselves behind this veil of ignorance, then a person's support for a policy will be disconnected from whether that policy will benefit him or her. For example, a poor person might favor a work requirement on food assistance for healthy individuals, while a rich person might oppose that work requirement.

The Devil's Advocate Tool

Thinking through a problem on its own based on the impartial spectator tool will lead you only so far in arriving at defensible normative goals. To further narrow down the set of normative goals, you also have to subject your values to the strongest challenge possible. You do this with the devil's advocate tool. The devil's advocate tool challenges the policy economist to search out and discuss her views with others who hold different views, and to argue with them, not in order to win the argument, but in order to better understand those opposing positions, and her own. Free and open speech—no safe zones—are central to the devil's advocate tool.

Probably the economist who developed the most nuanced use of these tools was 19th-century British moral philosopher and economist John Stuart Mill. In his book *On Liberty,* which provided the normative foundation to his principles of economics book, he wrote the following:

> He who knows only his own side of the case, knows little of that. His reasons may be good, and no one may have been able to refute them. But if he is equally unable to refute the reasons on the opposite side; if he does not so much as know what they are, he has no ground for preferring either opinion. . . . He must be able to hear them from persons who actually believe them; who defend them in earnest, and do their very utmost for them. He must know them in their most plausible and persuasive form; . . . So essential is this discipline to a real understanding of moral and human subjects, that if opponents of all important truths do not exist, it is indispensable to imagine them, and supply them with the strongest arguments which the most skilful devil's advocate can conjure up. (Mill 1859/1947: 35–36)

Mill's support of the market was based on both deeply held values about the importance of individual freedom, as well as positive analysis. Mill also strongly advocated for women's rights and argued against slavery when many noneconomist elite in British society supported slavery, and saw advocating for women's rights as heresy. Even though Mill strongly favored the market and was considered a laissez-faire advocate, he also favored significant government action to create and maintain the freedom of opportunity for all that he felt was necessary for fair and functioning markets.

Similarly, today, many economists advocate for progressive values and sensibilities in their policies, even as they advocate for the market. Where progressive pro-market economists often disagree with other progressive advocates is in how best to achieve progressive goals. Economists have found that often policies that on the surface are designed to achieve seemingly desirable progressive goals, in practice, end up helping a small group of people quite different than the intended beneficiaries. There are unintended consequences. To avoid these unintended consequences, progressive pro-market economists often see policies designed to protect competition, and to prevent government policy from being captured by vested interests, as the most effective means of achieving progressive goals.

The Importance of Nuance

The material in this course focuses on positive economics—learning the models. But throughout I will also discuss the problems with interpreting, applying, and integrating values into the models. Such discussion will inevitably involve problems of nuance. So as you read, keep in mind the need for nuance and the importance of values whenever you are relating the models you learn to real-world problems.

I consider the need for nuance in applied policy thinking so important that you should consider it a general learning objective that relates to the entire book: *Know that to relate models to the real world, you need to use a nuanced approach.* To ensure that you learn this principle, you will find questions that address issues of nuance incorporated within the end-of-chapter materials. If you're using Connect, you'll be asked nuance questions that are based on that material in SmartBook that addresses this general learning objective. The goal is to keep in focus the issues involved with applying the models and with interpreting the goals of economic policy even as you are learning the models.

Alternative Perspectives in Economics

One of the choices I made when approaching this product was to concentrate almost exclusively on the consensus or mainstream view. I strongly believe that focusing on that mainstream view is the best way to introduce students to economics. However, I also strongly believe that all students should be aware of the diverse views among economists and know that the mainstream view is not the only view out there. Numerous economists see the mainstream presentation as misleading, or as diverting the discussion away from other, more relevant, moral issues. These economists are generally called heterodox economists and are classified into groups, including Austrian, Post-Keynesian, Institutionalist, Radical, Feminist, and Religious economists. (The "Distinguishing Features" section of the preface has a brief description of these groups.)

These heterodox groups fall on various sides of the ideological perspective, and in their work they often raise normative questions that standard economics avoids. Some believe that the conventional analysis is unfair to the market; others believe that the conventional analysis is unfair to government-focused policy. Still others believe that the conventional analysis misses what is truly important in life.

These alternative perspectives are often not presented in principles courses. If the goal were only to teach positive economics, that makes sense. Alternative perspectives distract from the models. But if the goal is also to teach how the models are interpreted and used (which I believe it should be), then leaving out alternative perspectives is problematic because alternative perspectives provide the devil's advocate arguments needed to firm up one's own arguments.

To integrate these alternative perspectives into the course, at the end of every chapter I present a set of questions from alternative perspectives. These questions challenge the conventional economics presented in the text from different perspectives. My suggestion is that you use these questions as devil's advocate's assistants. If you are progressive and somewhat anti-market, focus on answering the Austrian questions. If you are pro-market, focus on answering the Radical questions. If you are STEM focused, look at the Institutionalist and Religious questions. And if you are male, focus on answering the Feminist questions. Alternatively, get a study partner whose policy views are as different from your own as you can find. Work collaboratively with her to study the material—explain what she finds objectionable, and how it differs from what you find objectionable.

Conclusion

Economic policy is a moral endeavor. How to integrate normative issues is a question that economists have struggled with from the beginning of economics. Conventional economics deals with this by focusing on the less value-laden scientific aspects of economics embedded in models. That's what most of the book will teach you. But that leaves students on their own to struggle with adding values back into the analysis to arrive at a policy conclusion. The goal of this prologue, and of the nuance discussions throughout the text, is to assist you in integrating values back into the analysis so you can arrive at supportable policy positions. In doing so you should:

- *Be impartial:* You should think of yourself as an impartial spectator, a position that involves placing yourself in other people's shoes. Analyze the policy from those other perspectives, and see if your answer would remain convincing to you when standing in others' shoes. (If you are poor you might favor progressive taxation, but if you're rich will you also favor them?) If you can't convince yourself standing in other people's shoes, explore why you can't and modify your support for the policy accordingly.

- *Be skeptical:* Start with being skeptical of your views and others. Unless you have studied an issue, do not take strong policy stands. Instead be open to arguments from all points of view. Take a firm position on policy only once you have gone through this process of reflection, discussion, and challenge.

- *Be reasonable:* Choose a tentative policy position that seems reasonable to you. Think hard about it, doing research of views on all sides. After you have taken a side, to add nuance to the consideration, think hard about how someone could object to your proposal, and develop responses. If you can't develop responses to those objections that satisfy yourself, modify your proposal to account for those objections.

- *Be creative:* When there seem to be irreconcilable differences in values about a policy, be creative and see if you can design a policy that avoids the difference in values. Think of how you can come to a solution to the problem you are dealing with. For example, if one person favors a proportional tax and another favors a progressive tax as a matter of policy, is there a way to achieve the equivalence of a progressive tax by other means—for example by making the tax proportional in both income and wealth, rather just in terms of income.

- *Be humble:* Present your reasoning to others who are actually in the other shoes, and see if your answer convinces them. If not, explore with them why, and modify your support for the policy accordingly.

- *Be open to challenge:* If you can't find individuals representing different views, make the arguments for them, playing the role of the devil's advocate. Challenge the argument at each level.

ECONOMICS

PART I

Introduction: Thinking Like an Economist

Part I is an introduction, and an introduction to an introduction seems a little funny. But other sections have introductions, so it seemed a little funny not to have an introduction to Part I; and besides, as you will see, I'm a little funny myself (which, in turn, has two interpretations; I'm sure you will decide which of the two is appropriate). It will, however, be a very brief introduction, consisting of questions you may have had and some answers to those questions.

Some Questions and Answers

Why study economics?
Because it's neat and interesting and helps provide insight into events that are constantly going on around you.

Why is this book so big?
Because there's a lot of important information in it and because the book is designed so your teacher can pick and choose. You'll likely not be required to read all of it, especially if you're on the quarter system. But once you start it, you'll probably read it all anyhow. (Would you believe?)

Why does this book cost so much?
To answer this question, you'll have to read the book.

Will this book make me rich?
No.

Will this book make me happy?
It depends.

This book doesn't seem to be written in a normal textbook style. Is this book really written by a professor?
Yes, but he is different. He misspent his youth working on cars; he married his high school sweetheart after they met again at their 20th high school reunion, and they remain happily married today, still totally in love. Twenty-five years after graduating from high school, his wife went back to medical school and got her MD because she was tired of being treated poorly by doctors. Their

five kids make sure he doesn't get carried away in the professorial cloud.

Will the entire book be like this?
No, the introduction is just trying to rope you in. Much of the book will be hard going. Learning happens to be a difficult process: no pain, no gain. But the author isn't a sadist; he tries to make learning as pleasantly painful as possible.

What do the author's students think of him?
Weird, definitely weird—and hard. But fair, interesting, and sincerely interested in getting us to learn. (Answer written by his students.)

So there you have it. Answers to the questions that you might never have thought of if they hadn't been put in front of you. I hope they give you a sense of me and the approach I'll use in the book. There are some neat ideas in it. Let's now briefly consider what's in the first five chapters.

A Survey of the First Five Chapters

This first section is really an introduction to the rest of the book. It gives you the background necessary so that the later chapters make sense. Chapter 1 gives you an overview of the entire field of economics as well as an introduction to my style. Chapter 2 focuses on the production possibility curve, comparative advantage, and trade. It explains how trade increases production possibilities but also why, in the real world, free trade and no government regulation may not be the best policy. Chapter 3 gives you some history of economic systems and introduces you to the institutions of the U.S. economy. Chapters 4 and 5 introduce you to supply and demand, and show you not only the power of those two concepts but also the limitations.

Now let's get on with the show.

CHAPTER 1

Economics and Economic Reasoning

In my vacations, I visited the poorest quarters of several cities and walked through one street after another, looking at the faces of the poorest people. Next I resolved to make as thorough a study as I could of Political Economy.

—Alfred Marshall

After reading this chapter, you should be able to:

LO1-1 Define *economics* and identify its components.

LO1-2 Discuss various ways in which economists use economic reasoning.

LO1-3 Explain real-world events in terms of economic forces, social forces, and political forces.

LO1-4 Explain how economic insights are developed and used.

LO1-5 Distinguish among positive economics, normative economics, and the art of economics.

©Ingram Publishing

When an artist looks at the world, he sees color. When a musician looks at the world, she hears music. When an economist looks at the world, she sees a symphony of costs and benefits. The economist's world might not be as colorful or as melodic as the others' worlds, but it's more practical. If you want to understand what's going on in the world that's really out there, you need to know economics.

I hardly have to convince you of this fact if you keep up with the news. You will be bombarded with stories of unemployment, interest rates, how commodity prices are changing, and how businesses are doing. The list is endless. So let's say you grant me that economics is important. That still doesn't mean that it's worth studying. The real question then is: How much will you learn? Most of what you learn depends on you, but part depends on the teacher and another part depends on the textbook. On both these counts, you're in luck; since your teacher chose this book for your course, you must have a super teacher.[1]

What Economics Is

Economics is *the study of how human beings coordinate their wants and desires, given the decision-making mechanisms, social customs, and political realities of the society.* One of the key words in the definition of the term *economics* is *coordination.* Coordination can mean many things. In the study of economics, coordination refers to how the three central problems facing any economy are solved. These central problems are:

1. What, and how much, to produce.

2. How to produce it.

3. For whom to produce it.

How hard is it to make the three decisions? Imagine for a moment the problem of living in a family: the fights, arguments, and questions that come up. "Do I have to do the dishes?" "Why can't I have piano lessons?" "Bobby got a new sweater. How come I didn't?" "Mom likes you best." Now multiply the size of the family by millions. The same fights, the same arguments, the same questions—only for society the questions are millions of times more complicated. In answering these questions, economies find that inevitably individuals want more than is available, given how much they're willing to work. That means that in our economy there is a problem of **scarcity**—*the goods available are too few to satisfy individuals' desires.*

Scarcity

Scarcity has two elements: our wants and our means of fulfilling those wants. These can be interrelated since wants are changeable and partially determined by society. The way we fulfill wants can affect those wants. For example, if you work on Wall Street, you will probably want upscale and trendy clothes. In Vermont I am quite happy wearing Levi's and flannel; in Florida I am quite happy in shorts.

The degree of scarcity is constantly changing. The quantity of goods, services, and usable resources depends on technology and human action, which underlie production. Individuals' imagination, innovativeness, and willingness to do what needs to be done can greatly increase available goods and resources. Who knows what technologies are in our future—nanites or micromachines that change atoms into whatever we want could conceivably eliminate scarcity of goods we currently consume. But they would not eliminate scarcity entirely since new wants are constantly developing.

So, how does an economy deal with scarcity? The answer is coercion. In all known economies, coordination has involved some type of coercion—limiting people's wants and increasing the amount of work individuals are willing to do to fulfill those wants. The reality is that many people would rather play than help solve society's problems. So the basic economic problem involves inspiring people to do things that other people want them to do, and not to do things that other people don't want them to do. Thus, an alternative definition of economics is: the study of how to get people to do things they're not wild about doing (such as studying) and not to do things they are wild

> Three central coordination problems any economy must solve are what to produce, how to produce it, and for whom to produce it.

> The coordination questions faced by society are complicated.

> The quantity of goods, services, and usable resources depends on technology and human action.

---

[1]This book is written by a person, not a machine. That means that I have my quirks, my odd sense of humor, and my biases. All textbook writers do. Most textbooks have the quirks and eccentricities edited out so that all the books read and sound alike—professional but dull. I choose to sound like me—sometimes professional, sometimes playful, and sometimes stubborn. In my view, that makes the book more human and less dull. So forgive me my quirks—don't always take me too seriously— and I'll try to keep you awake when you're reading this book at 3 a.m. the day of the exam. If you think it's a killer to read a book this long, you ought to try writing one.

about doing (such as eating all the ice cream they like), so that the things some people want to do are consistent with the things other people want to do.

Microeconomics and Macroeconomics

Economic theory is divided into two parts: microeconomic theory and macroeconomic theory. Microeconomic theory considers economic reasoning from the viewpoint of individuals and firms and builds up to an analysis of the whole economy. **Microeconomics** is *the study of individual choice, and how that choice is influenced by economic forces.* Microeconomics studies such things as the pricing policies of firms, households' decisions on what to buy, and how markets allocate resources among alternative ends.

As we build up from microeconomic analysis to an analysis of the entire economy, everything gets rather complicated. Many economists try to uncomplicate matters by taking a different approach—a macroeconomic approach—first looking at the aggregate, or whole, and then breaking it down into components. **Macroeconomics** is *the study of the economy as a whole*. It considers the problems of inflation, unemployment, business cycles, and growth. Macroeconomics focuses on aggregate relationships such as how household consumption is related to income and how government policies can affect growth.

Consider an analogy to the human body. A micro approach analyzes a person by looking first at each individual cell and then builds up. A macro approach starts with the person and then goes on to his or her components—arms, legs, fingernails, feelings, and so on. Put simply, microeconomics analyzes from the parts to the whole; macroeconomics analyzes from the whole to the parts.

Microeconomics and macroeconomics are very much interrelated. What happens in the economy as a whole is based on individual decisions, but individual decisions are made within an economy and can be understood only within its macro context. For example, whether a firm decides to expand production capacity will depend on what the owners expect will happen to the demand for their products. Those expectations are determined by macroeconomic conditions. Because microeconomics focuses on individuals and macroeconomics focuses on the whole economy, traditionally microeconomics and macroeconomics are taught separately, even though they are interrelated.

A Guide to Economic Reasoning

People trained in economics think in a certain way. They analyze everything critically; they compare the costs and the benefits of every issue and make decisions based on those costs and benefits. For example, say you're trying to decide whether a policy to eliminate terrorist attacks on airlines is a good idea. Economists are trained to put their emotions aside and ask: What are the costs of the policy, and what are the benefits? Thus, they are open to the argument that security measures, such as conducting body searches of every passenger or scanning all baggage with bomb-detecting machinery, might not be the appropriate policy because the costs might exceed the benefits. To think like an economist involves addressing almost all issues using a cost/benefit approach. Economic reasoning also involves abstracting from the "unimportant" elements of a question and focusing on the "important" ones by creating a simple model that captures the essence of the issue or problem. How do you know whether the model has captured the important elements? By collecting empirical evidence and "testing" the model—matching the predictions of the model with the empirical evidence—to see if it fits. Economic reasoning—how to think like a modern economist, making decisions on the basis of costs and benefits—is the most important lesson you'll learn from this book.

The book *Freakonomics* gives examples of the economist's approach. It describes a number of studies by University of Chicago economist Steve Levitt that unlock

---

Microeconomics is the study of how individual choice is influenced by economic forces.

Macroeconomics is the study of the economy as a whole. It considers the problems of inflation, unemployment, business cycles, and growth.

Q-1 Classify the following topics as primarily macroeconomic or microeconomic:

1. The impact of a tax increase on aggregate output.
2. The relationship between two competing firms' pricing behavior.
3. A farmer's decision to plant soy or wheat.
4. The effect of trade on economic growth.

Economic reasoning is making decisions on the basis of costs and benefits.

Economic Knowledge in One Sentence: TANSTAAFL

Once upon a time, Tanstaafl was made king of all the lands. His first act was to call his economic advisers and tell them to write up all the economic knowledge the society possessed. After years of work, they presented their monumental effort: 25 volumes, each about 400 pages long. But in the interim, King Tanstaafl had become a very busy man, what with running a kingdom of all the lands and all. Looking at the lengthy volumes, he told his advisers to summarize their findings in one volume.

Despondently, the economists returned to their desks, wondering how they could summarize what they'd been so careful to spell out. After many more years of rewriting, they were finally satisfied with their one-volume effort and tried to make an appointment to see the king. Unfortunately, affairs of state had become even more pressing than before, and the king couldn't take the time to see them. Instead he sent word to them that he couldn't be bothered with a whole volume, and ordered them, under threat of death (for he had become a tyrant), to reduce the work to one sentence.

The economists returned to their desks, shivering in their sandals and pondering their impossible task. Thinking about their fate if they were not successful, they decided to send out for one last meal. Unfortunately, when they were collecting money to pay for the meal, they discovered they were broke. The disgusted delivery person took the last meal back to the restaurant, and the economists started down the path to the beheading station. On the way, the delivery person's parting words echoed in their ears. They looked at each other and suddenly they realized the truth. "We're saved!" they screamed. "That's it! That's economic knowledge in one sentence!" They wrote down the sentence and presented it to the king, who thereafter fully understood all economic problems. (He also gave them a good meal.) The sentence?

There **A**in't **N**o **S**uch **T**hing **A**s **A** **F**ree **L**unch— **TANSTAAFL**

seemingly mysterious observations with basic economic reasoning. For example, Levitt asked the question: Why do drug dealers on the street tend to live with their mothers? The answer he arrived at was that they couldn't afford to live on their own; most earned less than $5 an hour. Why, then, were they dealing drugs and not working a legal job that, even for a minimum wage job, paid over $7 an hour? The answer to that is determined through cost/benefit analysis. While their current income was low, their potential income as a drug dealer was much higher since, given their background and existing U.S. institutions, they were more likely to move up to a high position in the local drug business (and *Freakonomics* describes how it is a business) and earn a six-figure income than they were to move up from working as a Taco Bell technician to an executive earning a six-figure income in corporate America. Levitt's model is a very simple one—people do what is in their best interest financially—and it assumes that people rely on a cost/benefit analysis to make decisions. Finally, he supports his argument through careful empirical work, collecting and organizing the data to see if they fit the model. His work is a good example of "thinking like a modern economist" in action.

Economic reasoning, once learned, is infectious. If you're susceptible, being exposed to it will change your life. It will influence your analysis of everything, including issues normally considered outside the scope of economics. For example, you will likely use economic reasoning to decide the possibility of getting a date for Saturday night, and who will pay for dinner. You will likely use it to decide whether to read this book, whether to attend class, whom to marry, and what kind of work to go into after you graduate. This is not to say that economic reasoning will provide all the answers. As you will see throughout this book, real-world questions are inevitably complicated, and economic reasoning simply provides a framework within which to approach a question. In the economic way of thinking, every choice has costs and benefits, and decisions are made by comparing them.

Marginal Costs and Marginal Benefits

The relevant costs and relevant benefits to economic reasoning are the expected *incremental,* or additional, costs incurred and the expected *incremental* benefits that result from a decision. Economists use the term *marginal* when referring to additional or incremental. Marginal costs and marginal benefits are key concepts.

A **marginal cost** is *the additional cost to you over and above the costs you have already incurred.* That means not counting **sunk costs**—*costs that have already been incurred and cannot be recovered*—in the relevant costs when making a decision. Consider, for example, attending class. You've already paid your tuition; it is a sunk cost. So the marginal (or additional) cost of going to class does not include tuition.

Similarly with marginal benefit. A **marginal benefit** is *the additional benefit above what you've already derived.* The marginal benefit of reading this chapter is the *additional* knowledge you get from reading it. If you already knew everything in this chapter before you picked up the book, the marginal benefit of reading it now is zero.

The Economic Decision Rule

Comparing marginal (additional) costs with marginal (additional) benefits will often tell you how you should adjust your activities to be as well off as possible. Just follow the **economic decision rule:**

> *If the marginal benefits of doing something exceed the marginal costs, do it.*
>
> *If the marginal costs of doing something exceed the marginal benefits, don't do it.*

As an example, let's consider a discussion I might have with a student who tells me that she is too busy to attend my classes. I respond, "Think about the tuition you've spent for this class—it works out to about $60 a lecture." She answers that the book she reads for class is a book that I wrote, and that I wrote it so clearly she fully understands everything. She goes on:

> I've already paid the tuition and whether I go to class or not, I can't get any of the tuition back, so the tuition is a sunk cost and doesn't enter into my decision. The marginal cost to me is what I could be doing with the hour instead of spending it in class. I value my time at $75 an hour [people who understand everything value their time highly], and even though I've heard that your lectures are super, I estimate that the marginal benefit of attending your class is only $50. The marginal cost, $75, exceeds the marginal benefit, $50, so I don't attend class.

I congratulate her on her diplomacy and her economic reasoning, but tell her that I give a quiz every week, that students who miss a quiz fail the quiz, that those who fail all the quizzes fail the course, and that those who fail the course do not graduate. In short, she is underestimating the marginal benefits of attending my classes. Correctly estimated, the marginal benefits of attending my class exceed the marginal costs. So she should attend my class.

Economics and Passion

Recognizing that everything has a cost is reasonable, but it's a reasonableness that many people don't like. It takes some of the passion out of life. It leads you to consider possibilities like these:

- Saving some people's lives with liver transplants might not be worth the additional cost. The money might be better spent on nutritional programs that would save 20 lives for every 2 lives you might save with transplants.
- Maybe we shouldn't try to eliminate all pollution because the additional cost of doing so may be too high. To eliminate all pollution might be to forgo too much of some other worthwhile activity.

Web Note 1.1

Costs and Benefits

If the marginal benefits of doing something exceed the marginal costs, do it. If the marginal costs of doing something exceed the marginal benefits, don't do it.

Q-2 Say you bought a share of Oracle for $100 and a share of Cisco for $10. The price of each is currently $15. Assuming taxes are not an issue, which would you sell if you needed $15?

Web Note 1.2

Blogonomics

Economic reasoning is based on the premise that everything has a cost.

- Providing a guaranteed job for every person who wants one might not be a worthwhile policy goal if it means that doing so will reduce the ability of an economy to adapt to new technologies.

You get the idea. This kind of reasonableness is often criticized for being coldhearted. But, not surprisingly, economists disagree; they argue that their reasoning leads to a better society for the majority of people.

Economists' reasonableness isn't universally appreciated. Businesses love the result; others aren't so sure, as I discovered some years back when my then-girlfriend told me she was leaving me. "Why?," I asked. "Because," she responded, "you're so, so . . . reasonable." It took me many years after she left to learn what she already knew: There are many types of reasonableness, and not everyone thinks an economist's reasonableness is a virtue. I'll discuss such issues later; for now, let me simply warn you that, for better or worse, studying economics will lead you to view questions in a cost/benefit framework.

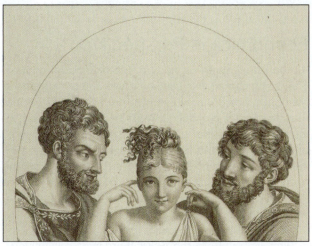

Opportunity costs have always made choice difficult, as we see in the early-19th-century engraving *One or the Other.*

©Heritage Images/Houlton Archive/Getty Images

Opportunity Cost

Putting economists' cost/benefit rules into practice isn't easy. To do so, you have to be able to choose and measure the costs and benefits correctly. Economists have devised the concept of opportunity cost to help you do that. **Opportunity cost** is *the benefit that you might have gained from choosing the next-best alternative.* To obtain the benefit of something, you must give up (forgo) something else—namely, the next-best alternative. The opportunity cost is the market value of that next-best alternative; it is a cost because in choosing one thing, you are precluding an alternative choice. The TANSTAAFL story in the earlier Added Dimension box embodies the opportunity cost concept because it tells us that there is a cost to everything; that cost is the next-best forgone alternative.

Let's consider some examples. The opportunity cost of going out once with Natalie (or Nathaniel), the most beautiful woman (attractive man) in the world, is the benefit you'd get from going out with your solid steady, Margo (Mike). The opportunity cost of cleaning up the environment might be a reduction in the money available to assist low-income individuals. The opportunity cost of having a child might be two boats, three cars, and a two-week vacation each year for five years, which are what you could have had if you hadn't had the child. (Kids really are this expensive.)

Examples are endless, but let's consider two that are particularly relevant to you: what courses to take and how much to study. Let's say you're a full-time student and at the beginning of the term you had to choose five courses. Taking one precludes taking some other, and the opportunity cost of taking an economics course may well be not taking a course on theater. Similarly with studying: You have a limited amount of time to spend studying economics, studying some other subject, sleeping, or partying. The more time you spend on one activity, the less time you have for another. That's opportunity cost.

Notice how neatly the opportunity cost concept takes into account costs and benefits of all other options and converts these alternative benefits into costs of the decision you're now making. One of the most useful aspects of the opportunity cost concept is that it focuses on two aspects of costs of a choice that often might be forgotten— implicit costs and illusionary sunk costs. **Implicit costs** are *costs associated with a decision that often aren't included in normal accounting costs.*

For example, in thinking about whether it makes sense to read this book, the *next-best value* of the time you spend reading it should be one of the costs that you consider.

Q-3 Can you think of a reason why a cost/benefit approach to a problem might be inappropriate? Can you give an example?

Opportunity cost is the basis of cost/ benefit economic reasoning; it is the benefit that you might have gained from choosing the next-best alternative.

Web Note 1.3

Opportunity Cost

Economics in Perspective

All too often, students study economics out of context. They're presented with sterile analysis and boring facts to memorize, and are never shown how economics fits into the larger scheme of things. That's bad; it makes economics seem boring—but economics is not boring. Every so often throughout this book, sometimes in the appendixes and sometimes in these boxes, I'll step back and put the analysis in perspective, giving you an idea from whence the analysis sprang and its historical context. In educational jargon, this is called *enrichment*.

I begin here with economics itself.

First, its history: In the 1500s there were few universities. Those that existed taught religion, Latin, Greek, philosophy, history, and mathematics. No economics. Then came the *Enlightenment* (about 1700), in which reasoning replaced God as the explanation of why things were the way they were. Pre-Enlightenment thinkers would answer the question "Why am I poor?" with "Because God wills it." Enlightenment scholars looked for a different explanation. "Because of the nature of land ownership" is one answer they found.

Such reasoned explanations required more knowledge of the way things were, and the amount of information expanded so rapidly that it had to be divided or categorized for an individual to have hope of knowing a subject. Soon philosophy was subdivided into science and philosophy. In the 1700s, the sciences were split into natural sciences and social sciences. The amount of knowledge kept increasing, and in the late 1800s and early 1900s social science itself split into subdivisions: economics, political science, history, geography, sociology, anthropology, and psychology. Many of the insights about how the economic system worked were codified in Adam Smith's *The Wealth of Nations,* written in 1776. Notice that this is before economics as a subdiscipline developed, and Adam Smith could also be classified as an anthropologist, a sociologist, a political scientist, and a social philosopher.

Throughout the 18th and 19th centuries, economists such as Adam Smith, Thomas Malthus, John Stuart Mill, David Ricardo, and Karl Marx were more than economists; they were social philosophers who covered all aspects of social science. These writers were subsequently called *Classical economists.* Alfred Marshall continued in that classical tradition, and his book, *Principles of Economics,* published in the late 1800s, was written with the other social sciences much in evidence. But Marshall also changed the questions economists ask; he focused on those questions that could be asked in a graphical supply/demand framework.

This book falls solidly in the Marshallian tradition. It presents economics as a way of thinking—as an engine of analysis used to understand real-world phenomena. But it goes beyond Marshall, and introduces you to a wider variety of models and thinking than the supply and demand models that Marshall used.

Marshallian economics is primarily about policy, not theory. It sees institutions as well as political and social dimensions of reality as important, and it shows you how economics ties in to those dimensions.

Often, it isn't because it is an implicit, not normally measured cost. Similarly with firms—owners often think that they are making a profit from a business, but if they add the value of their time to their cost, which economists argue they should, then their profit often becomes a loss. They might have earned more simply by taking a job somewhere else. Implicit costs should be included in opportunity costs. Sunk costs, however, are often included in making decisions, but should not be. These costs are called illusionary sunk costs—costs that show up in financial accounts but that economists argue should not be considered in a choice because they are already spent. They will not change regardless of what the person making the decision chooses. For example, once you have bought a book (that can't be resold), what you paid for that book is sunk. Following economic reasoning, that sunk cost shouldn't enter into your decision on whether to read it. An important role of the opportunity cost concept is to remind you that *the costs relevant to decisions are often different from the measured costs.*

The relevance of opportunity cost isn't limited to your individual decisions. Opportunity costs are also relevant to government's decisions, which affect everyone in society. A common example is what is called the guns-versus-butter debate. The

The costs relevant to decisions are often different from the measured costs.

resources that a society has are limited; therefore, its decision to use those resources to have more guns (more weapons) means that it will have less butter (fewer consumer goods). Thus, when society decides to spend $50 billion more on an improved health care system, the opportunity cost of that decision is $50 billion not spent on helping the homeless, paying off some of the national debt, or providing for national defense.

The opportunity cost concept has endless implications. It can even be turned upon itself. For instance, thinking about alternatives takes time; that means that there's a cost to being reasonable, so it's only reasonable to be somewhat unreasonable. If you followed that argument, you've caught the economic bug. If you didn't, don't worry. Just remember the opportunity cost concept for now; I'll infect you with economic thinking in the rest of the book.

Economic Forces, Social Forces, and Political Forces

The opportunity cost concept applies to all aspects of life and is fundamental to understanding how society reacts to scarcity. When goods are scarce, those goods must be rationed. That is, a mechanism must be chosen to determine who gets what.

Economic and Market Forces

Let's consider some specific real-world rationing mechanisms. Dormitory rooms are often rationed by lottery, and permission to register in popular classes is often rationed by a first-come, first-registered rule. Food in the United States, however, is generally rationed by price. If price did not ration food, there wouldn't be enough food to go around. All scarce goods must be rationed in some fashion. These rationing mechanisms are examples of **economic forces,** *the necessary reactions to scarcity*.

One of the important choices that a society must make is whether to allow these economic forces to operate freely and openly or to try to rein them in. A **market force** is *an economic force that is given relatively free rein by society to work through the market*. Market forces ration by changing prices. When there's a shortage, the price goes up. When there's a surplus, the price goes down. Much of this book will be devoted to analyzing how the market works like an invisible hand, guiding economic forces to coordinate individual actions and allocate scarce resources. The **invisible hand** is *the price mechanism, the rise and fall of prices that guides our actions in a market*.

Social and Political Forces

Societies can't choose whether or not to allow economic forces to operate—economic forces are always operating. However, societies can choose whether to allow market forces to predominate. **Social forces**—*forces that guide individual actions even though those actions may not be in an individual's selfish interest,* and **political forces**—*legal directives that direct individuals' actions*—play a major role in deciding whether to let market forces operate. Economic reality is determined by a contest among these various forces.

Let's consider a historical example in which social forces prevented an economic force from becoming a market force: the problem of getting a date for Saturday night back when people actually dated (or called the pairing off of two individuals a "date"). If a school (or a society) had significantly more heterosexual people of one gender than the other (let's say more men than women), some men would find themselves without a date—that is, men would be in excess supply—and would have to find something else to do, say study or go to a movie by themselves. An "excess supply" person could solve the problem by paying someone to go out with him or her, but that would have changed the nature of the date in unacceptable ways. It would be revolting to the person who offered payment and to the person who was offered payment. That unacceptability is an

Q-4 John, your study partner, has just said that the opportunity cost of studying this chapter is about 1/38 the price you paid for this book, since the chapter is about 1/38 of the book. Is he right? Why or why not?

Q-5 Ali, your study partner, states that rationing health care is immoral—that health care should be freely available to all individuals in society. How would you respond?

When an economic force operates through the market, it becomes a market force.

Economic reality is controlled by three forces:
1. Economic forces (the invisible hand).
2. Social forces.
3. Political forces.

Social, cultural, and political forces can play a significant role in the economy.

Winston Churchill and Lady Astor

There are many stories about Nancy Astor, the first woman elected to Britain's Parliament. A vivacious, fearless American woman, she married into the English aristocracy and, during the 1930s and 1940s, became a bright light on the English social and political scenes, which were already quite bright.

One story told about Lady Astor is that she and Winston Churchill, the unorthodox genius who had a long and distinguished political career and who was Britain's prime minister during World War II, were sitting in a pub having a theoretical discussion about morality. Churchill suggested that as a thought experiment Lady Astor ponder the following question: If a man were to promise her a huge amount of money—say a million pounds—for the privilege, would she sleep with him? Lady Astor did ponder the question for a while and finally answered, yes, she

Lady Astor
©Bettmann/Getty Images

would, if the money were guaranteed. Churchill then asked her if she would sleep with him for five pounds. Her response was sharp: "Of course not. What do you think I am—a prostitute?" Churchill responded, "We have already established that fact; we are now simply negotiating about price."

One moral that economists might draw from this story is that economic incentives, if high enough, can have a powerful influence on behavior. But an equally important moral of the story is that noneconomic incentives also can be very strong. Why do most people feel it's wrong to sell sex for money, even if they might be willing to do so if the price were high enough? Keeping this second moral in mind will significantly increase your economic understanding of real-world events.

Q-6 Your study partner, Joan, states that market forces are always operative. Is she right? Why or why not?

©Rachel Epstein/PhotoEdit

example of the complex social and cultural norms that guide and limit our activities. People don't try to buy dates because social forces prevent them from doing so.[2]

Often political and social forces work together against the invisible hand. For example, in the United States there aren't enough babies to satisfy all the couples who desire them. Babies born to particular sets of parents are rationed—by luck. Consider a group of parents, all of whom want babies. Those who can, have a baby; those who can't have one, but want one, try to adopt. Adoption agencies ration the available babies. Who gets a baby depends on whom people know at the adoption agency and on the desires of the birth mother, who can often specify the socioeconomic background (and many other characteristics) of the family in which she wants her baby to grow up. That's the economic force in action; it gives more power to the supplier of something that's in short supply.

If our society allowed individuals to buy and sell babies, that economic force would be translated into a market force. The invisible hand would see to it that the quantity of babies supplied would equal the quantity of babies demanded at some price. The market, not the adoption agencies, would do the rationing.[3]

---

[2]Pairing habits of young adults have changed in ways that have made "dating" somewhat of a historical social convention. The new social conventions that guide such pairing functions do not eliminate the problem of excess individuals, but they do obscure it and create multiple dimensions of "excess." Thinking about how they do so is a useful exercise.

[3]Even though it's against the law, some babies are nonetheless "sold" on a semilegal market, also called a gray market. Recently, the "market price" for a healthy baby was about $30,000. If selling babies were legal (and if people didn't find it morally repugnant to have babies in order to sell them), the price would be much lower because there would be a larger supply of babies. (It was not against the law to sell human eggs in the early 2000s, and one human egg was sold for $50,000. The average price was much lower; it varied with donor characteristics such as SAT scores and athletic accomplishments.)

Most people, including me, find the idea of selling babies repugnant. But why? It's the strength of social forces reinforced by political forces. One can think of hundreds of examples of such social and political forces overriding economic forces.

What is and isn't allowable differs from one society to another. For example, in North Korea, many private businesses are against the law, so not many people start their own businesses. In the United States, until the 1970s, it was against the law to hold gold except in jewelry and for certain limited uses such as dental supplies, so most people refrained from holding gold. Ultimately a country's laws and social norms determine whether the invisible hand will be allowed to work.

Social and political forces are active in all parts of your life. You don't practice medicine without a license; you don't sell body parts or certain addictive drugs. These actions are against the law. But many people do sell alcohol; that's not against the law if you have a permit. You don't charge your friends interest to borrow money (you'd lose friends); you don't charge your children for their food (parents are supposed to feed their children); many sports and media stars don't sell their autographs (some do, but many consider the practice tacky); you don't lower the wage you'll accept in order to take a job from someone else (you're no scab). The list is long. You cannot understand economics without understanding the limitations that political and social forces place on economic actions.

In summary, what happens in a society can be seen as the reaction to, and interaction of, three sets of forces: (1) economic forces, (2) political and legal forces, and (3) social and cultural forces. Economics has a role to play in sociology and politics, just as sociology and politics have roles to play in economics.

People don't charge friends interest to borrow money.
©Syda Productions/Shutterstock

What happens in society can be seen as a reaction to, and interaction of, economic forces with other forces.

Using Economic Insights

Economic insights are based on generalizations, called theories, about the workings of an abstract economy as well as on contextual knowledge about the institutional structure of the economy. In this book I will introduce you to economic theories and models. Theories and models tie together economists' terminology and knowledge about economic institutions. Theories are inevitably too abstract to apply in specific cases, and thus a theory is often embodied in an **economic model**—*a framework that places the generalized insights of the theory in a more specific contextual setting*—or in an **economic principle**—*a commonly held economic insight stated as a law or principle.* To see the importance of principles, think back to when you learned to add. You didn't memorize the sum of 147 and 138; instead, you learned a principle of addition. The principle says that when adding 147 and 138, you first add $7 + 8$, which you memorized was 15. You write down the 5 and carry the 1, which you add to $4 + 3$ to get 8. Then add $1 + 1 = 2$. So the answer is 285. When you know just one principle, you know how to add millions of combinations of numbers.

Theories, models, and principles are continually "brought to the data" to see if the predictions of the model match the data. Increases in computing power and new statistical techniques have given modern economists a far more rigorous set of procedures to determine how well the predictions fit the data than was the case for earlier economists. This has led to a stronger reliance on quantitative empirical methods in modern economics than in earlier economics.

Modern empirical work takes a variety of forms. In certain instances, economists study questions by running controlled laboratory experiments. That branch of economics is called **experimental economics**—*a branch of economics that studies the economy*

Web Note 1.4

Hip Hop Economics

through controlled experiments. These include laboratory experiments—experiments in which individuals are brought into a computer laboratory and their reactions to various treatments are measured and analyzed; field experiments—experiments in which treatments in the real world are measured and analyzed; computer experiments—experiments in which simulated economies are created within the computer and results of various policies are explored; and natural experiments—naturally occurring events that approximate a controlled experiment where something has changed in one place but has not changed somewhere else.

An example of a natural experiment occurred when New Jersey raised its minimum wage and neighboring state Pennsylvania did not. Economists Alan Kruger and David Card compared the effects on unemployment in both states and found that increases in the minimum wage in New Jersey did not significantly affect employment. This led to a debate about what the empirical evidence was telling us. The reason is that in such natural experiments, it is impossible to hold "other things constant," as is done in laboratory and field experiments, and thus the empirical results in economics are more subject to dispute.

While economic models are less general than theories, they are still usually too general to apply in specific cases. Models lead to **theorems** *(propositions that are logically true based on the assumptions in a model).* To arrive at policy **precepts** *(policy rules that conclude that a particular course of action is preferable),* theorems must be combined with knowledge of real-world economic institutions and value judgments determining the goals for which one is striving. In discussing policy implications of theories and models, it is important to distinguish precepts from theorems.

Economic analysis changes as technology changes. In recent years, data availability and computational power have increased exponentially, and this has changed the way economists study problems. Economists fresh out of graduate school are much more likely than older economists to "let the data speak," which means to use computing power to look for stable statistical relationships in the data and then use those relationships to guide their policy. Modern economists are highly involved with the development of systems that can perform tasks that people previously believed required human intelligence such as the ability to learn from the past, find meaning, and reason, known as artificial intelligence and deep learning systems. In many ways, the algorithmic approach to problems underlying these systems reflects economists'—such as Herbert Simon and Friedrich von Hayek—theories of how an economy works and how systems process information.

Theories, models, and principles must be combined with a knowledge of real-world economic institutions to arrive at specific policy recommendations.

The Invisible Hand Theorem

Knowing a theory gives you insight into a wide variety of economic phenomena even though you don't know the particulars of each phenomenon. For example, much of economic theory deals with the *pricing mechanism* and how the market operates to coordinate *individuals' decisions.* Economists have come to the following theorems:

> *When the quantity supplied is greater than the quantity demanded, price has a tendency to fall.*
> *When the quantity demanded is greater than the quantity supplied, price has a tendency to rise.*

Using these generalized theorems, economists have developed a theory of markets that leads to the further theorem that, under certain conditions, markets are efficient. That is, the market will coordinate individuals' decisions, allocating scarce resources efficiently. **Efficiency** means *achieving a goal as cheaply as possible.* Economists call

Q-7 There has been a superb growing season and the quantity of tomatoes supplied exceeds the quantity demanded. What is likely to happen to the price of tomatoes?

this theorem the **invisible hand theorem**—*a market economy, through the price mechanism, will tend to allocate resources efficiently.*

Theories, and the models used to represent them, are enormously efficient methods of conveying information, but they're also necessarily abstract. They rely on simplifying assumptions, and *if you don't know the assumptions, you don't know the theory.* The result of forgetting assumptions could be similar to what happens if you forget that you're supposed to add numbers in columns. Forgetting that, yet remembering all the steps, can lead to a wildly incorrect answer. For example,

If you don't know the assumptions, you don't know the theory.

147

+138

1,608 is wrong.

Knowing the assumptions of theories and models allows you to progress beyond gut reaction and better understand the strengths and weaknesses of various economic theories and models. Let's consider a central economic assumption: the assumption that individuals behave rationally—that what they choose reflects what makes them happiest, given the constraints. If that assumption doesn't hold, the invisible hand theorem doesn't hold.

Presenting the invisible hand theorem in its full beauty is an important part of any economics course. Presenting the assumptions on which it is based and the limitations of the invisible hand is likewise an important part of the course. I'll do both throughout the book.

Economic Theory and Stories

Economic theory, and the models in which that theory is presented, often developed as a shorthand way of telling a story. These stories are important; they make the theory come alive and convey the insights that give economic theory its power. In this book I present plenty of theories and models, but they're accompanied by stories that provide the context that makes them relevant.

Theory is a shorthand way of telling a story.

At times, because there are many new terms, discussing theories takes up much of the presentation time and becomes a bit oppressive. That's the nature of the beast. As Albert Einstein said, "Theories should be as simple as possible, but not more so." When a theory becomes oppressive, pause and think about the underlying story that the theory is meant to convey. That story should make sense and be concrete. If you can't translate the theory into a story, you don't understand the theory.

Economic Institutions

To know whether you can apply economic theory to reality, you must know about economic institutions—laws, common practices, and organizations in a society that affect the economy. Corporations, governments, and cultural norms are all examples of economic institutions. Many economic institutions have social, political, and religious dimensions. For example, your job often influences your social standing. In addition, many social institutions, such as the family, have economic functions. I include any institution that significantly affects economic decisions as an economic institution because you must understand that institution if you are to understand how the economy functions.

To apply economic theory to reality, you've got to have a sense of economic institutions.

Economic institutions sometimes seem to operate in ways quite different than economic theory predicts. For example, economic theory says that prices are determined by supply and demand. However, businesses say that they set prices by rules of thumb—often by what are called cost-plus-markup rules. That is, a firm determines what its costs are, multiplies by 1.4 or 1.5, and the result is the price it sets. Economic

Economists and Market Solutions

Economic reasoning is playing an increasing role in government policy. Consider the regulation of pollution. Pollution became a policy concern in the 1960s as books such as Rachel Carson's *Silent Spring* were published. In 1970, in response to concerns about the environment, the Clean Air Act was passed. It capped the amount of pollutants (such as sulfur dioxide, carbon monoxide, nitrogen dioxides, lead, and hydrocarbons) that firms could emit. This was a "command-and-control" approach to regulation, which brought about a reduction in pollution, but also brought about lots of complaints by firms that either found the limits costly to meet or couldn't afford to meet them and were forced to close.

©Design Pics/Kelly Redinger

Enter economists. They proposed an alternative approach, called cap-and-trade, that achieved the same overall reduction in pollution but at a lower overall cost. In the plan they proposed, government still set a pollution cap that firms had to meet, but it gave individual firms some flexibility. Firms that reduced emissions by less than the required limit could buy pollution permits from other firms that reduced their emissions by more than their limit. The price of the permits would be determined in an "emissions permit market." Thus, firms that had a low cost of reducing pollution would have a strong incentive to reduce pollution by more than their limit in order to sell these permits, or rights to pollute, to firms that had a high cost of reducing pollution and therefore could reduce their pollution by less than what was required. The net reduction was the same, but the reduction was achieved at a lower cost.

In 1990 Congress adopted economists' proposal and the Clean Air Act was amended to include tradable emissions permits. An active market in emissions permits developed, and it is estimated that the tradable permit program has lowered the cost of reducing sulfur dioxide emissions by $1 billion a year while, at the same time, reducing emissions by more than half, to levels significantly below the cap. Other cap-and-trade programs have developed as well. You can read more about the current state of tradable emissions at www.epa.gov/airmarkets.

---

theory says that supply and demand determine who's hired; experience suggests that hiring is often done on the basis of whom you know, not by market forces.

These apparent contradictions have two complementary explanations. First, economic theory abstracts from many issues. These issues may account for the differences. Second, there's no contradiction; economic principles often affect decisions from behind the scenes. For instance, supply and demand pressures determine what the price markup over cost will be. In all cases, however, to apply economic theory to reality—to gain the full value of economic insights—you've got to have a sense of economic institutions.

Economic Policy Options

Economic policies are *actions (or inaction) taken by government to influence economic actions*. The final goal of the course is to present the economic policy options facing our society today. For example, should the government restrict mergers between firms? Should it run a budget deficit? Should it do something about the international trade deficit? Should it decrease taxes?

I saved this discussion for last because there's no sense talking about policy options unless you know some economic terminology, some economic theory, and something about economic institutions. Once you know something about them, you're in a position to consider the policy options available for dealing with the economic problems our society faces.

Policies operate within institutions, but policies also can influence the institutions within which they operate. Let's consider an example: welfare policy and the institution of the two-parent family. In the 1960s, the United States developed a variety of policy initiatives designed to eliminate poverty. These initiatives provided income to single parents with children, and assumed that family structure would be unchanged by these policies. But family structure changed substantially, and, very likely, these policies played a role in increasing the number of single-parent families. The result was the programs failed to eliminate poverty. Now this is not to say that we should not have programs to eliminate poverty, nor that two-parent families are always preferable to one-parent families; it is only to say that we must build into our policies their effect on institutions.

To carry out economic policy effectively, one must understand how institutions might change as a result of the economic policy.

Q-8 True or false? Economists should focus their policy analysis on institutional changes because such policies offer the largest gains.

Objective Policy Analysis

Good economic policy analysis is objective; that is, it keeps the analyst's value judgments separate from the analysis. Objective analysis does not say, "This is the way things should be," reflecting a goal established by the analyst. That would be subjective analysis because it would reflect the analyst's view of how things should be. Instead, objective analysis says, "This is the way the economy works, and if society (or the individual or firm for whom you're doing the analysis) wants to achieve a particular goal, this is how it might go about doing so." Objective analysis keeps, or at least tries to keep, an individual's subjective views— value judgments—separate. That doesn't mean that policy analysis involves no value judgments; policy analysis necessarily involves value judgments. But an objective researcher attempts to make the value judgments being used both transparent and not his own, but instead value judgments an "impartial spectator" (using Adam Smith's terminology) would use.

To make clear the distinction between objective and subjective analysis, economists have divided economics into three categories: *positive economics, normative economics,* and the *art of economics*. **Positive economics** is *the study of what is, and how the economy works*. It explores the pure theory of economics, and it discovers agreed-upon empirical regularities, often called empirical facts. Economic theorists then relate their theories to those facts. Positive economics asks such questions as: How does the market for hog bellies work? How do price restrictions affect market forces? These questions fall under the heading of economic theory.

Positive economics is the study of what is, and how the economy works.

As I stated above, economic theory does not provide definitive policy recommendations. It is too abstract and makes too many assumptions that don't match observed behavior. In positive economic theory, one looks for empirical facts and develops *theorems*—propositions that logically follow from the assumptions of one's model. Theorems and agreed-upon empirical facts are almost by definition beyond dispute and serve as the foundation for economic science. But these theorems don't tell us what policies should be followed.

Q-9 John, your study partner, is a free market advocate. He argues that the invisible hand theorem tells us that the government should not interfere with the economy. Do you agree? Why or why not?

To decide on policy, economists integrate normative judgments with insights from positive economics. **Normative economics** is *the study of what the goals of the economy should be*. Normative economics asks such questions as: What should the distribution of income be? What should tax policy be designed to achieve? In discussing such questions, economists must carefully delineate whose goals they are discussing. One cannot simply assume that one's own goals for society are society's goals. For example, let's consider an ongoing debate in economics. Some economists are worried about climate change; they believe that high consumption in rich societies is causing climate change and that the high consumption is a result of

Normative economics is the study of what the goals of the economy should be.

interdependent wants—people want something only because other people have it—but having it isn't necessarily making people happier. These economists argue that society's normative goal should include a much greater focus on the implications of economic activities for climate change, and the distribution of income, than is currently the case. Discussion of these goals falls under the category of normative economics.

In debating normative issues, economists defer to philosophers for guidance on what the goals of society should be. But that hasn't always been the case. The founder of economics, Adam Smith, was himself a moral philosopher, and economic policy analysis developed within a utilitarian moral philosophy that saw the normative goal of policy as being "the greatest good for the greatest number." This goal required economists to consider policy in terms of the consequences of that policy, not on the basis of its inherent morality. It also required them to consider policy not from a perspective that was good for any particular group, but from the perspective of a fair composite of society. When conducting policy analysis they had to bend over backwards to maintain impartiality.

Focus on such impartiality led early economists to argue against both slavery and the oppression of women at a time when those positions were highly unpopular and seen as radical. It also led them to argue in favor of the significant coordination of society by the market, which they felt would bring about greater happiness for a greater number than would the alternative of significant government coordination. Their support of markets was based on their moral philosophy, not just their science.

Adam Smith was part of this moral tradition, and before he wrote his economic treatise, *The Wealth of Nations,* he wrote a philosophical treatise, *The Theory of Moral Sentiments,* which provided a normative foundation for his economics. In it, Smith created a tool that he argued was useful in shedding light on what was meant by the vague and somewhat contradictory "greatest good for the greatest number." That tool was the **impartial spectator tool** in which *each person places himself in the position of a third-person examiner and judges a situation from everyone's perspective, not just his own.* Then, having done that, he does his best to come to a policy that he could argue would achieve the greatest good for the greatest number.

Economists did not expect people to arrive at definitive policy conclusions based on this tool. But they did see the tool as providing a framework within which people could discuss policy in terms of what was best for society as a whole, not what was best for themselves, or their friends. This tool would focus arguments about policy on their impact on people in the community, rather than on abstract debates about the morality of policy, which generally led nowhere. That approach to morality was an important part of policy economics, and was how economists moved from the theorems developed in science to policy precepts.

Some economists hoped that they would be able to determine the goals of policy scientifically, but they quickly decided that that was impossible. They came to believe that *utility*—a general measure of people's welfare used in policy analysis—is neither scientifically measurable nor comparable between individuals. It is for that reason that economic science does not lead to any particular policy conclusions. To move to policy conclusions, one must supplement science with moral philosophical insights developed in self-reflective considerations and heartfelt discussions with others about what is meant by the greatest good for the greatest number. Policy economists have to picture themselves as walking in the shoes of every person everywhere, not just their own.

The **art of economics,** also called political economy, is *the application of the knowledge learned in positive economics to achieve the goals one has determined in normative economics.* It looks at such questions as: To achieve the goals that society

To use the impartial spectator tool, each person places himself in the position of a third-person examiner and judges a situation from everyone's perspective, not just his own

The art of economics is the application of the knowledge learned in positive economics to achieve the goals determined in normative economics.

Economics and Climate Change

A good example of the central role that economics plays in policy debates is the debate about climate change. Almost all scientists are now convinced that climate change is occurring and that human activity such as the burning of fossil fuel is one of the causes. The policy question is what to do about it. To answer that question, most governments have turned to economists. The first part of the question that economists have

©AP Photo/Alden Pellett

considered is whether it is worth doing anything, and in a well-publicized report commissioned by the British government, economist Nicholas Stern argued that, based upon his cost/benefit analysis, yes it is worth doing something. The reason: Because the costs of not doing anything would likely reduce output by 20 percent in the future, and those costs (appropriately weighted for when they occur) are less than the benefits of policies that can be implemented.

The second part of the question is: What policies to implement? The policies he recommended were policies that changed incentives—specifically, policies that raised the costs of emitting greenhouse gases and decreased the

costs of other forms of production. Those recommended policies reflected the economist's opportunity cost framework in action: If you want to change the result, change the incentives that individuals face.

There is considerable debate about Stern's analysis—both with the way he conducted the cost/benefit analysis and with his policy recommendations. Such debates are inevitable when the data are incomplete and numerous judgments need to be made. I suspect that these debates will continue over the coming years with economists on various sides of the debates. Economists are generally not united in their views about complicated policy issues since they differ in their normative views and in their assessment of the problem and of what politically can be achieved; that's because policy is part of the art of economics, not part of positive economics. But the framework of the policy debate about climate change is the economic framework. Thus, even though political forces will ultimately choose what policy is followed, you must understand the economic framework to take part in the debate.

---

wants to achieve, how would you go about it, given the way the economy works?[4] Most policy discussions fall under the art of economics. The art of economics branch is specifically about policy; it is designed to arrive at *precepts,* or guides for policy. Precepts are based on theorems and empirical facts developed in positive economics and goals developed in normative economics. The art of economics requires economists to assess the appropriateness of theorems to achieving the normative goals in the real world. Whereas once the assumptions are agreed upon, theorems derived from models are not debatable, precepts are debatable, and economists that use the same theorems can hold different precepts. For example, a model may tell us that rent controls (a legal maximum on rent) will cause a shortage of housing. That does not mean that rent controls are necessarily bad policies, since rent controls may also have some desirable effects. The precept that rent controls are bad policy is based upon a judgment about the importance of those other effects, and one's normative judgments

[4]This three-part distinction was made back in 1891 by a famous economist, John Neville Keynes, father of John Maynard Keynes, the economist who developed macroeconomics. This distinction was instilled into modern economics by Milton Friedman and Richard Lipsey in the 1950s. They, however, downplayed the art of economics, which J. N. Keynes had seen as central to understanding the economist's role in policy. In his discussion of the scope and method of economics, Lionel Robbins used the term *political economy* rather than Keynes' term *the art of economics.*

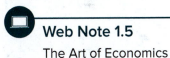

Web Note 1.5
The Art of Economics

Q-10 Tell whether the following five statements belong in positive economics, normative economics, or the art of economics.

1. We should support the market because it is efficient.

2. Given certain conditions, the market achieves efficient results.

3. Based on past experience and our understanding of markets, if one wants a reasonably efficient result, markets should probably be relied on.

4. The distribution of income should be left to markets.

5. Markets allocate income according to contributions of factors of production.

about the benefits and costs of the policy. In this book, when I say that economists tend to favor a policy, I am talking about precepts, which means that alternative perspectives are possible even among economists.

In each of these three branches of economics, economists separate their own value judgments from their objective analysis as much as possible. The qualifier "as much as possible" is important, since some value judgments inevitably sneak in. We are products of our environment, and the questions we ask, the framework we use, and the way we interpret the evidence all involve value judgments and reflect our backgrounds.

Maintaining objectivity is easiest in positive economics, where you are working with abstract models to understand how the economy works. Maintaining objectivity is harder in normative economics. You must always be objective about whose normative values you are using. It's easy to assume that all of society shares your values, but that assumption is often wrong.

Maintaining objectivity is hardest in the art of economics because it can suffer from the problems of both positive and normative economics. Because noneconomic forces affect policy, to practice the art of economics we must make judgments about how these noneconomic forces work. These judgments are likely to reflect our own value judgments. So we must be exceedingly careful to be as objective as possible in practicing the art of economics.

Policy and Social and Political Forces

When you think about the policy options facing society, you'll quickly discover that the choice of policy options depends on much more than economic theory. Politicians, not economists, determine economic policy. To understand what policies are chosen, you must take into account historical precedent plus social, cultural, and political forces. In an economics course, I don't have time to analyze these forces in as much depth as I'd like. That's one reason there are separate history, political science, sociology, and anthropology courses.

While it is true that these other forces play significant roles in policy decisions, specialization is necessary. In economics, we focus the analysis on the invisible hand, and much of economic theory is devoted to considering how the economy would operate if the invisible hand were the only force operating. But as soon as we apply theory to reality and policy, we must take into account political and social forces as well.

An example will make my point more concrete. Most economists agree that holding down or eliminating tariffs (taxes on imports) and quotas (numerical limitations on imports) makes good economic sense. They strongly advise governments to follow a policy of free trade. Do governments follow free trade policies? Almost invariably they do not. Politics leads society in a different direction. If you're advising a policy maker, you need to point out that these other forces must be taken into account, and how other forces should (if they should) and can (if they can) be integrated with your recommendations.

Conclusion

Tons more could be said to introduce you to economics, but an introduction must remain an introduction. As it is, this chapter should have:

1. Introduced you to economic reasoning.
2. Surveyed what we're going to cover in this book.
3. Given you an idea of my writing style and approach.

We'll be spending long hours together over the coming term, and before entering into such a commitment it's best to know your partner. While I won't know you, by the end of this book you'll know me. Maybe you won't love me as my mother does, but you'll know me.

This introduction was my opening line. I hope it also conveyed the importance and relevance of economics. If it did, it has served its intended purpose. Economics is tough, but tough can be fun.

Summary

- The three coordination problems any economy must solve are what to produce, how to produce it, and for whom to produce it. In solving these problems, societies have found that there is a problem of scarcity. *(LO1-1)*

- Economics can be divided into microeconomics and macroeconomics. Microeconomics is the study of individual choice and how that choice is influenced by economic forces. Macroeconomics is the study of the economy as a whole. It considers problems such as inflation, unemployment, business cycles, and growth. *(LO1-1)*

- Economic reasoning structures all questions in a cost/benefit framework: If the marginal benefits of doing something exceed the marginal costs, do it. If the marginal costs exceed the marginal benefits, don't do it. *(LO1-2)*

- Sunk costs are not relevant in the economic decision rule. *(LO1-2)*

- The opportunity cost of undertaking an activity is the benefit you might have gained from choosing the next-best alternative. *(LO1-2)*

- "There ain't no such thing as a free lunch" (TANSTAAFL) embodies the opportunity cost concept. *(LO1-2)*

- Economic forces, the forces of scarcity, are always working. Market forces, which ration by changing prices, are not always allowed to work. *(LO1-3)*

- Economic reality is controlled and directed by three types of forces: economic forces, political forces, and social forces. *(LO1-3)*

- Under certain conditions, the market, through its price mechanism, will allocate scarce resources efficiently. *(LO1-4)*

- Theorems are propositions that follow from the assumptions of a model; precepts are the guides for policies based on theorems, normative judgments, and empirical observations about how the real world differs from the model. *(LO1-4)*

- Economics can be subdivided into positive economics, normative economics, and the art of economics. Positive economics is the study of what is, normative economics is the study of what should be, and the art of economics relates positive to normative economics. *(LO1-5)*

Key Terms

art of economics	efficiency	marginal benefit	positive economics
economic decision rule	experimental economics	marginal cost	precepts
economic force	impartial spectator tool	market force	scarcity
economic model	implicit costs	microeconomics	social forces
economic policy	invisible hand	normative economics	sunk cost
economic principle	invisible hand theorem	opportunity cost	theorems
economics	macroeconomics	political forces	

Questions and Exercises McGraw Hill connect

1. Why does the textbook author focus on coordination rather than on scarcity when defining economics? (*LO1-1*)

2. State whether the following are primarily microeconomic or macroeconomic policy issues: (*LO1-1*)
   a. Should U.S. interest rates be lowered to decrease the amount of unemployment?
   b. Will the fact that more and more doctors are selling their practices to managed care networks increase the efficiency of medical providers?
   c. Should the current federal income tax be lowered to reduce unemployment?
   d. Should the federal minimum wage be raised?
   e. Should Sprint and Verizon both be allowed to build local phone networks?
   f. Should commercial banks be required to provide loans in all areas of the territory from which they accept deposits?

3. List two microeconomic and two macroeconomic problems. (*LO1-1*)

4. Calculate, using the best estimates you can: (*LO1-2*)
   a. Your opportunity cost of attending college.
   b. Your opportunity cost of taking this course.
   c. Your opportunity cost of attending yesterday's lecture in this course.

5. List one recent choice you made and explain why you made the choice in terms of marginal benefits and marginal costs. (*LO1-2*)

6. You rent a car for $29.95. The first 100 miles are free, but each mile thereafter costs 10 cents. You plan to drive it 200 miles. What is the marginal cost of driving the car? (*LO1-2*)

7. Economists Henry Saffer of Kean University, Frank J. Chaloupka of the University of Illinois at Chicago, and Dhaval Dave of Bentley College estimated that the government must spend $4,170 on drug control to deter one person from using drugs and that the cost one drug user imposes on society is $897. Based on this information alone, should the government spend the money on drug control? (*LO1-2*)

8. What is the opportunity cost of buying a $20,000 car? (*LO1-2*)

9. Suppose you currently earn $60,000 a year. You are considering a job that will increase your lifetime earnings by $600,000 but that requires an MBA. The job will mean also attending business school for two years at an annual cost of $50,000. You already have a bachelor's degree, for which you spent $160,000 in tuition and books. Which of the above information is relevant to your decision on whether to take the job? (*LO1-2*)

10. Suppose your college has been given $5 million. You have been asked to decide how to spend it to improve your college. Explain how you would use the economic decision rule and the concept of opportunity costs to decide how to spend it. (*LO1-2*)

11. Give two examples of social forces and explain how they keep economic forces from becoming market forces. (*LO1-3*)

12. Give two examples of political or legal forces and explain how they might interact with economic forces. (*LO1-3*)

13. Individuals have two kidneys, but most of us need only one. People who have lost both kidneys through accident or disease must be hooked up to a dialysis machine, which cleanses waste from their bodies. Say a person who has two good kidneys offers to sell one of them to someone whose kidney function has been totally destroyed. The seller asks $30,000 for the kidney, and the person who has lost both kidneys accepts the offer. (*LO1-3*)
   a. Who benefits from the deal?
   b. Who is hurt?
   c. Should a society allow such market transactions? Why?

14. What is an economic model? What besides a model do economists need to make policy recommendations? (*LO1-4*)

15. Does economic theory prove that the free market system is best? Why? (Difficult) (*LO1-4*)

16. Distinguish between theorems and precepts. Is it possible for two economists to agree about theorems but disagree about precepts? Why or why not? (*LO1-4*)

17. What is the difference between normative and positive statements? (*LO1-5*)

18. State whether the following statements belong in positive economics, normative economics, or the art of economics. (*LO1-5*)
   a. In a market, when quantity supplied exceeds quantity demanded, price tends to fall.
   b. When determining tax rates, the government should take into account the income needs of individuals.
   c. Given society's options and goals, a broad-based tax is generally preferred to a narrowly based tax.
   d. California currently rations water to farmers at subsidized prices. Once California allows the trading of water rights, it will allow economic forces to be a market force.

Questions from Alternative Perspectives

1. Is it possible to use objective economic analysis as a basis for government planning? *(Austrian)*

2. In "Rational Choice with Passion: Virtue in a Model of Rational Addiction," Andrew M. Yuengert of Pepperdine University argues that there is a conflict between reason and passion.
   a. What might that conflict be?
   b. What implications does it have for applying the economic model? *(Religious)*

3. Economic institutions are "habits of thought" that organize society.
   a. In what way might patriarchy be an *institution* and how might it influence the labor market?
   b. Does the free market or patriarchy better explain why 98 percent of secretaries are women and 98 percent of automobile mechanics are men? *(Feminist)*

4. In October of 2004, the supply of flu vaccine fell by over 50 percent when a major producer of the vaccine was shut down. The result was that the vaccine had to be rationed, with a priority schedule established: young children, people with weakened immunity, those over 65, etc. taking priority.
   a. Compare and contrast this allocation outcome with a free market outcome.
   b. Which alternative is more just? *(Institutionalist)*

5. The textbook model assumes that individuals have enough knowledge to follow the economic decision rule.
   a. How did you decide which college you would attend?
   b. Did you have enough knowledge to follow the economic decision rule?
   c. For what type of decisions do you not use the economic decision rule?
   d. What are the implications for economic analysis if most people don't follow the economic decision rule in many aspects of their decisions? *(Post-Keynesian)*

6. Radical economists believe that all of economics, like all theorizing or storytelling, is value-laden. Theories and stories reflect the values of those who compose them and tell them. For instance, radicals offer a different analysis than most economists of how capitalism works and what ought to be done about its most plaguing problems: inequality, periodic economic crises with large-scale unemployment, and the alienation of the workers.
   a. What does the radical position imply about the distinction between positive economics and normative economics that the text makes?
   b. Is economics value-laden or objective and is the distinction between positive and normative economics tenable or untenable? *(Radical)*

Issues to Ponder

1. At times we all regret decisions. Does this necessarily mean we did not use the economic decision rule when making the decision?

2. Economist Steven Landsburg argues that if one believes in the death penalty for murderers because of its deterrent effect, using cost/benefit analysis we should execute computer hackers—the creators of worms and viruses—because the deterrent effect in cost saving would be greater than the deterrent effect in saving lives. Estimates are that each execution deters eight murders, which, if one valued each life at about $7 million, saves about $56 million; he estimates that executing hackers would save more than that per execution, and thus would be the economic thing to do.
   a. Do you agree or disagree with Landsburg's argument? Why?
   b. Can you extend cost/benefit analysis to other areas?

3. Adam Smith, who wrote *The Wealth of Nations,* and who is seen as the father of modern economics, also wrote *The Theory of Moral Sentiments*. In it he argued that society would be better off if people weren't so selfish and were more considerate of others. How does this view fit with the discussion of economic reasoning presented in the chapter?

4. A *Wall Street Journal* article asked readers the following questions. What's your answer?
   a. An accident has caused deadly fumes to enter the school ventilation system where it will kill five children. You can stop it by throwing a switch, but doing so will kill one child in another room. Do you throw the switch?
   b. Say that a doctor can save five patients with an organ transplant that would end the life of a patient who is sick, but not yet dead. Does she do it?
   c. What is the difference between the two situations described in *a* and *b*?
   d. How important are opportunity costs in your decisions?

5. Economics is about strategic thinking, and the strategies can get very complicated. Suppose Marge kisses Mike and asks whether he liked it. She'd like Mike to answer "yes" and she'd like that answer to be truthful. But Mike knows that, and if he likes Marge, he may well say that he liked the kiss even if he didn't. But Marge knows that, and thus might not really believe that Mike liked the kiss—he's just saying "yes" because that's what Marge wants to hear. But Mike knows that Marge knows that, so sometimes he has to convey a sense that he didn't like it, so that

Marge will believe him when he says that he did like it. But Marge knows that . . . You get the picture.

  a. Should you always be honest, even when it hurts someone?

  b. What strategies can you figure out to avoid the problem of not believing the other person?

6. Go to two stores: a supermarket and a convenience store.

  a. Write down the cost of a gallon of milk in each.

  b. The prices are most likely different. Using the terminology used in this chapter, explain why that is the case and why anyone would buy milk in the store with the higher price.

  c. Do the same exercise with shirts or dresses in Walmart (or its equivalent) and Saks (or its equivalent).

7. About 100,000 individuals in the United States are waiting for organ transplants, and at an appropriate price many individuals would be willing to supply organs. Given those facts, should human organs be allowed to be bought and sold?

8. Name an economic institution and explain how it affects economic decision making or how its actions reflect economic principles.

9. Tyler Cowen, an economist at George Mason University, presents an interesting case that pits the market against legal and social forces. The case involves payola—the payment of money to disc jockeys for playing a songwriter's songs. He reports that Chuck Berry was having a hard time getting his music played because of racism. To counter this, he offered a well-known disc jockey, Alan Freed, partial songwriting credits, along with partial royalties, on any Chuck Berry song of his choice. Freed chose *Maybellene,* which he played and promoted. It went on to be a hit, Chuck Berry went on to be a star, and Freed's estate continues to receive royalties.

  a. Should such payments be allowed? Why?

  b. How did Freed's incentives from the royalty payment differ from Freed's incentives if Chuck Berry had just offered him a flat payment?

  c. Name two other examples of similar activities—one that is legal and one that is not.

10. Name three ways a limited number of dormitory rooms could be rationed. How would economic forces determine individual behavior in each? How would social or legal forces determine whether those economic forces become market forces?

11. Prospect theory suggests that people are hurt more by losses than they are uplifted by gains of a corresponding size. If that is true, what implications would it have for economic policy?

12. Is a good economist always objective? Explain your answer.

13. Why are modern economists more likely to "let the data speak" than are earlier economists?

Answers to Margin Questions

1. (1) Macroeconomics; (2) Microeconomics; (3) Microeconomics; (4) Macroeconomics. (*LO1-1*)

2. Since the price of both stocks is now $15, it doesn't matter which one you sell (assuming no differential capital gains taxation). The price you bought them for doesn't matter; it's a sunk cost. Marginal analysis refers to the future gain, so what you expect to happen to future prices of the stocks—not past prices—should determine which stock you decide to sell. (*LO1-2*)

3. A cost/benefit analysis requires that you put a value on a good, and placing a value on a good can be seen as demeaning it. Consider love. Try telling an acquaintance that you'd like to buy his or her spiritual love, and see what response you get. (*LO1-2*)

4. John is wrong. The opportunity cost of reading the chapter is primarily the time you spend reading it. Reading the book prevents you from doing other things. Assuming that you already paid for the book, the original price is no longer part of the opportunity cost; it is a sunk cost. Bygones are bygones. (*LO1-2*)

5. Whenever there is scarcity, the scarce good must be rationed by some means. Free health care has an opportunity cost in other resources. So if health care is not rationed, to get the resources to supply that care, other goods would have to be more tightly rationed than they currently are. It is likely that the opportunity cost of supplying free health care would be larger than most societies would be willing to pay. (*LO1-3*)

6. Joan is wrong. Economic forces are always operative; market forces are not. (*LO1-3*)

7. According to the invisible hand theorem, the price of tomatoes will likely fall. (*LO1-4*)

8. False. While such changes have the largest gain, they also may have the largest cost. The policies economists should focus on are those that offer the largest net gain—benefits minus costs—to society. (*LO1-5*)

9. He is wrong. The invisible hand theorem is a positive theorem and does not tell us anything about what policy to adopt. To do so would be to violate Hume's dictum that a "should" cannot be derived from an "is." This is not to say that government should or should not interfere; whether government should interfere is a very difficult question. (*LO1-5*)

10. (1) Normative; (2) Positive; (3) Art; (4) Normative; (5) Positive. (*LO1-5*)

The Production Possibility Model, Trade, and Globalization

> No one ever saw a dog make a fair and deliberate exchange of one bone for another with another dog.
>
> —Adam Smith

©Glowimages/Getty Images

After reading this chapter, you should be able to:

LO2-1 Demonstrate trade-offs with a production possibility curve.

LO2-2 Relate the concepts of comparative advantage and efficiency to the production possibility curve.

LO2-3 State how, through comparative advantage and trade, countries can consume beyond their individual production possibilities.

LO2-4 Explain how globalization is guided by the law of one price.

Every economy must solve three main coordination problems:

1. What, and how much, to produce.
2. How to produce it.
3. For whom to produce it.

In Chapter 1, I suggested that you can boil down all economic knowledge into the single phrase "There ain't no such thing as a free lunch." There's obviously more to economics than that, but it's not a bad summary of the core of economic reasoning—it's relevant for an individual, for nonprofit organizations, for governments, and for nations. Oh, it's true that once in a while you can snitch a sandwich, but what economics tells you is that if you're offered something that approaches free-lunch status, you should also be on the lookout for some hidden cost.

Economists have a model, the production possibility model, that conveys the trade-offs society faces. This model is important for understanding not only the trade-offs society faces but also why people specialize in what they do and trade for the goods they need. Through specialization and trade, individuals, firms, and countries can achieve greater levels of output than they could otherwise achieve.

The Production Possibility Model

The production possibility model can be presented both in a table and in a graph. (The appendix to this chapter has a discussion of graphs in economics.) I'll start with the table and then move from that to the graph.

A Production Possibility Curve for an Individual

Let's consider a study-time/grades example. Say you have exactly 20 hours a week to devote to two courses: economics and history. (So maybe I'm a bit optimistic.) Grades are given numerically and you know that the following relationships exist: If you study 20 hours in economics, you'll get a grade of 100; 18 hours, 94; and so forth.[1]

Let's say that the best you can do in history is a 98 with 20 hours of study a week; 19 hours of study guarantees a 96, and so on. The production possibility table in Figure 2-1(a) shows the highest combination of grades you can get with various allocations of the 20 hours available for studying the two subjects. One possibility is getting a 70 in economics and a 78 in history.

Notice that the opportunity cost of studying one subject rather than the other is reflected in the production possibility table, which lists the trade-offs between two choices. The information in the table comes from experience: We are assuming that you've discovered that if you transfer an hour of study from economics to history, you'll lose 3 points on your grade in economics and gain 2 points in history. Assuming studying economics is your next-best alternative, the opportunity cost of a 2-point rise in your history grade is a 3-point decrease in your economics grade.

The information in the production possibility table also can be presented graphically in a diagram called a production possibility curve. A **production possibility curve (PPC)** is *a curve measuring the maximum combination of outputs that can be obtained from a given number of inputs*. It gives you a visual picture of the trade-off embodied in a decision.

A production possibility curve is created from a production possibility table by mapping the table in a two-dimensional graph. I've taken the information from the table in Figure 2-1(a) and mapped it into Figure 2-1(b). The history grade is mapped, or plotted, on the horizontal axis; the economics grade is on the vertical axis.

As you can see from the bottom row of Figure 2-1(a), if you study economics for all 20 hours and study history for 0 hours, you'll get grades of 100 in economics and 58 in history. Point *A* in Figure 2-1(b) represents that choice. If you study history for all 20 hours and study economics for 0 hours, you'll get a 98 in history and a 40 in economics. Point *E* represents that choice. Points *B, C,* and *D* represent three possible choices between these two extremes. The slope of the PPC provides a measure of the opportunity cost of a choice; increasing your grade in economics by 3 points will have an opportunity cost of 2 points on your history grade.

Q-1 In the graph below, what is the opportunity cost of producing an extra unit of good *X* in terms of good *Y*?

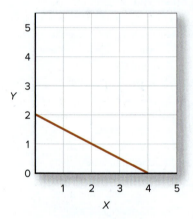

The production possibility curve is a curve measuring the maximum combination of outputs that can be obtained from a given number of inputs.

---

[1]Throughout the book I'll be presenting numerical examples to help you understand the concepts. The numbers I choose are often arbitrary. After all, you have to choose something. As an exercise, you might choose different numbers than I did, numbers that apply to your own life, and work out the argument using those numbers.

FIGURE 2-1 (A AND B)   A Production Possibility Table and Curve for Grades in Economics and History

The production possibility table (**a**) shows the highest combination of grades you can get with only 20 hours available for studying economics and history. The information in the production possibility table in (**a**) can be plotted on a graph, as is done in (**b**). The grade received in economics is on the vertical axis, and the grade received in history is on the horizontal axis.

Hours of Study in History	Grade in History	Hours of Study in Economics	Grade in Economics
20	98	0	40
19	96	1	43
18	94	2	46
17	92	3	49
16	90	4	52
15	88	5	55
14	86	6	58
13	84	7	61
12	82	8	64
11	80	9	67
10	78	10	70
9	76	11	73
8	74	12	76
7	72	13	79
6	70	14	82
5	68	15	85
4	66	16	88
3	64	17	91
2	62	18	94
1	60	19	97
0	58	20	100

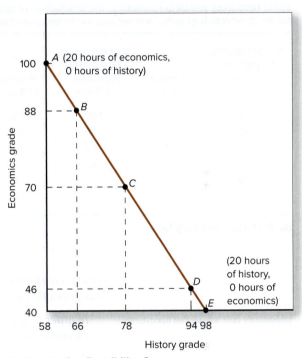

(a) Production Possibility Table

(b) Production Possibility Curve

Notice that the production possibility curve slopes downward from left to right. That means that there is an inverse relationship (a trade-off) between grades in economics and grades in history. The better the grade in economics, the worse the grade in history, and vice versa.

To summarize, the production possibility curve demonstrates that:

1. There is a limit to what you can achieve, given the existing institutions, resources, and technology.

2. Every choice you make has an opportunity cost. You can get more of something only by giving up something else.

The slope of the production possibility curve tells you the trade-off between the cost of one good in terms of another.

Increasing Opportunity Costs of the Trade-Off

In the study-time/grade example, the cost of one grade in terms of the other remained constant; you could always trade 2 points on your history grade for 3 points on your economics grade. This assumption of an unchanging trade-off made the production possibility curve a straight line. Although this made the example easier, is it realistic? Probably not, especially if we are using the PPC to describe the choices that a society makes. For many of the choices society must make, the perceived opportunity costs of

are providing online competition for traditional colleges. Similarly, online stores are proliferating. As Internet technology becomes built into our economy, we can expect more specialization, more division of labor, and the economic growth that follows.

The Benefits of Trade

Web Note 2.2

Gains from Trade

Voluntary trade is a win-win proposition.

The reason why markets make people better off follows from a very simple argument: When people freely enter into a trade, both parties can be expected to benefit from the trade; otherwise, why would they have traded in the first place? So when the butcher sells you meat, he's better off with the money you give him, and you're better off with the meat he gives you. Voluntary trade is a win-win proposition.

When there is competition in trading, such that individuals are able to pick the best trades available to them, each individual drives the best bargain he or she can. The end result is that both individuals in the trade benefit as much as they possibly can, given what others are willing to trade. This argument for the benefits from trade underlies the general policy of **laissez-faire**—*an economic policy of leaving coordination of individuals' actions to the market.* (*Laissez-faire,* a French term, means "Let events take their course; leave things alone.") Laissez-faire is not a theorem in economics; it is a precept because it extends the implications of a model to reality and draws conclusions about the real world. It is based on normative judgments, judgments about the relevance of the model, and assumptions upon which the model is based.

Q-6 What argument underlies the general laissez-faire policy argument?

Let's consider a numerical example of the gains that accrue to two countries when they trade. I use an international trade example so that you can see that the argument holds for international trade as well as domestic trade. Let's say that the two countries are Pakistan and Belgium, and that Pakistan has a comparative advantage in producing textiles, while Belgium has a comparative advantage in producing chocolate. Specifically, Pakistan can produce 4,000 yards of textiles a day or 1 ton of chocolate a day, or any proportional combination in between. Pakistan's production possibility curve is shown in Figure 2-7(a). Similarly, in a given day, Belgium can produce either 1,000 yards of textiles or 4 tons of chocolate, or any proportion in between. Its production possibility curve is shown in Figure 2-7(b).

In the absence of trade, the most each country can consume is some combination along its production possibility curve. Say Pakistan has chosen to produce and consume 2,000 yards of textiles and 0.5 ton of chocolate [point *A* in Figure 2-7(a)], while Belgium has chosen to produce and consume 500 yards of textiles and 2 tons of chocolate [point *D* in Figure 2-7(b)].

Let's now consider what would happen if each specialized, doing what it does best, and then traded with the other for the goods it wants. This separates the production and consumption decisions. Because Pakistan can produce textiles at a lower cost in terms of chocolate, it makes sense for Pakistan to specialize in textiles, producing 4,000 yards [point *C* in Figure 2-7(a)]. Similarly, it makes sense for Belgium to specialize in chocolate, producing 4 tons [point *F* in Figure 2-7(b)]. By specializing, the countries together produce 4 tons of chocolate and 4,000 yards of textiles. If the countries divide production so that each country gets 2,000 yards of fabric and 2 tons of chocolate, Pakistan can consume at point *B* and Belgium at point *E*. Both are consuming beyond their production possibility curves without trade. This tells us an important principle about trade: *Trade lets countries consume beyond their* "no-trade" *production possibility curve.* It is primarily these gains that lead to economists' support of free trade and their opposition to barriers to trade.

Specialization and trade create gains that make all better off.

Q-7 Steve can bake either 4 loaves of bread or 8 dozen cookies a day. Sarah can bake either 4 loaves of bread or 4 dozen cookies a day. Show, using production possibility curves, that Steve and Sarah would be better off specializing in their baking activities and then trading, rather than baking only for themselves.

The pressure to find comparative advantages is never-ending, in part because comparative advantage can change. Two hundred years ago, the United States had

FIGURE 2-7 (A AND B)   **The Gains from Trade**

Trade makes those involved in the trade better off. If each country specializes and takes advantage of its comparative advantage, each can consume a combination of goods beyond its production possibility curve. In the example shown, Pakistan can consume at point B and Belgium at point E.

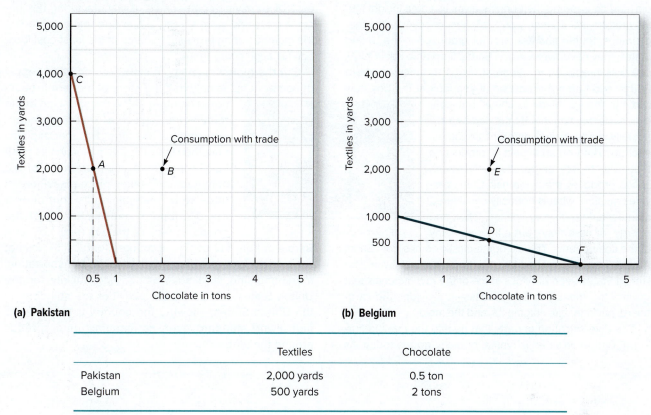

(a) Pakistan

(b) Belgium

	Textiles	Chocolate
Pakistan	2,000 yards	0.5 ton
Belgium	500 yards	2 tons

a comparative advantage in producing textiles. It was rich in natural resources and labor, and it had a low-cost source of power (water). As the cost of U.S. labor went up, and as trade opportunities widened, that comparative advantage disappeared. As it did, the United States moved out of the textile industry. Countries with cheaper labor, such as Bangladesh, today have the comparative advantage in textiles. As firms have relocated textile production to Bangladesh, total costs have fallen. The gains from trade show up as higher pay for Bangladeshi workers and lower-priced cloth for U.S. consumers. Of course, trade is a two-way street. In return for Bangladesh's textiles, the United States sends computer software and airplanes, products that would be highly expensive, indeed almost impossible, for Bangladesh to produce on its own. So Bangladeshi consumers, on average, are also made better off by the trade.

That same process of changing comparative advantage that the United States experienced long ago is going on in China today. As Chinese wages rise relative to other less developed countries (wages have been going up about 10 percent a year for the past decade in China), China is moving out of low-skilled labor-intensive industries and into higher-skilled industries. This moves the nature of Chinese competition up the value chain, providing more competition for U.S. college students going into the job market.

Q-8 True or false? Two countries can achieve the greatest gains from trade by each producing the goods for which it has a comparative advantage and then trading those goods.

Made in China?

Barbie and her companion Ken are as American as apple pie, and considering their origins gives us some insight into the modern U.S. economy and its interconnection with other countries. Barbie and Ken are not produced in the United States; they never were. When Barbie first came out in 1959, she was produced in Japan. Today, it is unclear where Barbie and Ken are produced. If you look at the box they come in, it says "Made in China," but look-

©AP Photo/Ariana Cubillos

ing deeper we find that Barbie and Ken are actually made in five different countries, each focusing on an aspect of production that reflects its comparative advantage. Japan produces the nylon hair. China provides much of what is normally considered manufacturing—factory spaces, labor, and energy for assembly—but it imports many of the components. The oil for the plastic comes from Saudi Arabia. That oil is refined into plastic pellets in Taiwan. The United States even provides some of the raw materials that go into the manufacturing process—it provides the cardboard, packing, paint pigments, and the mold.

The diversification of parts that go into the manufacturing of Barbie and Ken is typical of many goods today. As the world economy has become more integrated, the process of supplying components of manufacturing has become more and more spread out, as firms have divided up the manufacturing process in search of the least-cost location for each component.

But the global diversity in manufacturing and supply of components is only half the story of modern production. The other half is the shrinking of the relative importance of that manufacturing, and it is this other half that explains how the United States maintains its position in the world when so much of the manufacturing takes place elsewhere. It does so by maintaining its control over the distribution and marketing of the goods. In fact, of the $15 retail cost of a Barbie or Ken, $12 can be accounted for by activities not associated with manufacturing—design, transportation, merchandising, and advertising. And, luckily for the United States, many of these activities are still done in the United States, allowing the country to maintain its high living standard even as manufacturing spreads around the globe.

Globalization and the Law of One Price

There is much more to be said about both trade and the gains from trade, and later chapters will explore trade in much more detail. But let me briefly discuss the relationship of the theory of comparative advantage to globalization.

Globalization

Web Note 2.3

Brexit

The global economy increases the number of competitors for the firm.

Globalization is *the increasing integration of economies, cultures, and institutions across the world.* In a globalized economy, firms think of production and sales at a global level. They produce where costs are lowest, and sell across the world at the highest price they can get. A globalized world is a world in which economies of the world are highly integrated. Globalization has two effects on firms. The first is positive; because the world economy is so much larger than the domestic economy, the rewards for winning globally are much larger than the rewards for winning domestically. The second effect is negative; it is much harder to win, or even to stay in business, competing in a global market. A company may be the low-cost producer in a particular country yet may face foreign competitors that can undersell it. The global economy increases the number of competitors for the firm. Consider the automobile industry. Three companies are headquartered in the United States, but more than 40 automobile companies operate worldwide. Today, China produces

The Developing Country's Perspective on Globalization

This book is written from a U.S. point of view. From that perspective, the relevant question is: Can the United States maintain its high wages relative to the low wages in China, India, and other developing countries? I suspect that most U.S. readers hope that it can. From a developing country's perspective, I suspect that the hope is that it cannot; their hope is that their wage rates catch up with U.S. wage rates. Judged from a developing country's perspective, the question is: Is it fair that U.S. workers don't work as hard as we do but earn much more?

The market does not directly take fairness into account. The market is interested only in who can produce a good or service at the lowest cost. This means that in a competitive economy, the United States can maintain its high wages only to the degree that it can produce sufficient goods and services more cheaply than low-wage countries can at the market exchange rate. It must keep the amount it imports roughly equal to the amount it exports.

Developing countries recognize that, in the past, the United States has had a comparative advantage in creativity and innovation, and they are doing everything they can to compete on these levels as well as on basic production levels. They are actively trying to develop such skills in their population and to compete with the United States not only in manufacturing and low-tech jobs but also in research, development, finance, organizational activities, artistic activities, and high-tech jobs. Right now companies in China and India are working to challenge U.S. dominance in all high-tech and creativity fields. (For example, they too are working on nanotechnology.) To do this, they are trying to entice top scientists and engineers to stay in their country, or to return home if they have been studying or working in the United States. Since more than 50 percent of all PhDs given in science, engineering, and economics go to non-U.S. citizens (in economics, it is about 60 percent), many observers believe that the United States cannot assume its past dominance in the innovative and high-tech fields will continue forever. Eventually forces will be set in motion that will eliminate any trade imbalance, although those forces can sometimes take a long time to materialize.

more than twice as many automobiles as does the United States. U.S. automakers face stiff competition from foreign automakers; unless they meet that competition, they will not survive.

These two effects are, of course, related. When you compete in a larger market, you have to be better to survive, but if you do survive the rewards are greater.

Globalization increases competition by allowing greater specialization and division of labor, which, as Adam Smith first observed in *The Wealth of Nations,* increases growth and improves the standard of living for everyone. Thus, in many ways globalization is simply another name for increased specialization. Globalization allows (indeed, forces) companies to move operations to countries with a comparative advantage. As they do so, they lower costs of production. Globalization leads to companies specializing in smaller portions of the production process because the potential market is not just one country but the world. Such specialization can lead to increased productivity as firms get better and better at producing through practice, what economists call *learning by doing.*

In a globalized economy, production will shift to the lowest-cost producer. Globalization scares many people in the United States because, with wages so much lower in many developing countries than in the United States, they wonder whether all jobs will move offshore: Will the United States be left producing anything? Economists' answer is: Of course it will. Comparative advantage, by definition, means that if one country has a comparative advantage in producing one set of goods, the other country has to have a comparative advantage in the other set of goods. The real questions are: In what

Q-9 How does globalization reduce the costs of production?

Q-10 Is it likely that all U.S. jobs one day will have moved abroad? Why or why not?

goods will the United States have comparative advantages? and: How will those comparative advantages come about?

One reason people have a hard time thinking of goods in which the United States has a comparative advantage is that they are thinking in terms of labor costs. They ask: Since wages are lower in China, isn't it cheaper to produce all goods in China? The answer is no; production requires many more inputs than just labor. Technology, natural resources, institutional structure, specialized types of knowledge, and entrepreneurial know-how are also needed to produce goods, and the United States has significant advantages in these other factors. It is these advantages that result in higher U.S. wages compared to other countries.

The United States has excelled particularly in goods that require creativity and innovation. The United States has remained the leader of the world economy and has kept a comparative advantage in many goods even with its high relative wages, in part because of continual innovation. For example, the Internet started in the United States, which is why the United States is the location of so many information technology firms. The United States also has led the way in biotechnology innovation. Similarly, the creative industries, such as film, art, and advertising, have flourished in the United States. These industries are dynamic, high-profit, high-wage industries. (One of the reasons companies choose to locate in the United States is that the United States has such a great comparative advantage in these other aspects of production.) As long as U.S. production maintains a comparative advantage in innovation, the United States will be able to specialize in goods that allow firms to pay higher wages.

Web Note 2.4
Trade and Wages

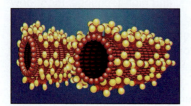

Nanotechnology—dynamic industry of the future?
©McGraw-Hill Education

Exchange Rates and Comparative Advantage

There is, however, reason to be concerned. If innovation and creativity don't develop new industries in which the United States has a comparative advantage fast enough, as the current dynamic industries mature and move to low-wage countries, at current exchange rates (the value of a currency relative to the value of foreign currencies), the United States will not maintain comparative advantages in sufficient industries to warrant the relative wage differentials that exist today. In that case, U.S. demand for foreign goods and services will be higher than foreign demand for U.S. goods and services. For the last 20 years that has been the case. To bring them into equilibrium, the U.S. wage premium (the higher pay that U.S. workers receive compared to equivalent foreign workers) will have to decline to regain our comparative advantages. Since nominal wages (the wages that you see in your paycheck) in the United States are unlikely to fall, this will most likely occur through a decline in the U.S. exchange rate, large increases in foreign wages, or both. Either of these will make foreign products imported into the United States more expensive and U.S. products cheaper for foreigners, and eventually (over 30 or 40 years) will balance the comparative advantages and trade flows.

The Law of One Price

Many Americans do not like the "exchange rate answer," but in terms of policy, it is probably the best the United States can hope for. If the United States tries to prevent outsourcing (production moving to other countries) with trade restrictions. U.S.-based companies will find that they can no longer compete internationally, and the United States will be in worse shape than if it had allowed outsourcing.

The reality is that competition, combined with transferable technology and similar institutions, drives wages and prices of similar factors and goods toward equality. This reality often goes by the name of the **law of one price**—*the wages of workers in one country will not differ significantly from the wages of (equal) workers in another institutionally similar country.* As we will discuss in a later chapter, the debate is about what an "equal" worker is and what an equivalent institutional structure is.

Because of a variety of historical circumstances, the United States has been able to avoid the law of one price in wages since World War I. One factor has been the desire of foreigners to increase their holding of U.S. financial assets by trillions of dollars, which has let the United States consume more goods than it produces. Another is that the United States' institutional structure, technology, entrepreneurial labor force, and nonlabor inputs have given the United States sufficiently strong comparative advantages to offset the higher U.S. wage rates. The passage of time and modern technological changes have been eroding the United States' comparative advantages based on institutional structure and technology. To the degree that this continues to happen, to maintain a balance in the comparative advantages of various countries, the wages of workers in other countries such as India and China will have to move closer to the wages of U.S. workers.

Slowly they are doing just that. Manufacturing wages in the United States have been flat for the past 20 years while Chinese manufacturing wages have been increasing each of those years, often by double digits. That increase has significantly decreased the gap between Chinese manufacturing wages and U.S. manufacturing wages. Low-cost manufacturing competition has shifted to other countries such as Vietnam and Bangladesh.

> The law of one price states that wages of workers in one country will not differ significantly from the wages of (equal) workers in another institutionally similar country.

Globalization and the Timing of Benefits of Trade

One final comment about globalization and the U.S. economy is in order. None of the above discussion contradicts the proposition that trade makes both countries better off. Thus, the discussion does not support the position taken by some opponents to trade and globalization that foreign competition is hurting the United States and that the United States can be made better off by imposing trade restrictions. Instead, the discussion is about the timing of the benefits of trade. Many of the benefits of trade already have been consumed by the United States during the years that the United States has been running trade deficits (importing more than it is exporting). The reality is that the United States has been living better than it could have otherwise precisely because of trade. It also has been living much better than it otherwise could because it is paying for some of its imports with IOUs promising payment in the future rather than with exports today. But there is no free lunch, and when these IOUs are presented for payment, the United States will have to pay for some of the benefits that it already has consumed.

> The reality is that the United States has been living better than it could have otherwise precisely because of trade and outsourcing.

Conclusion

While the production possibility curve model does not give unambiguous answers as to what government's role should be in regulating trade, it does serve a very important purpose. It is a geometric tool that summarizes a number of ideas in economics: trade-offs, opportunity costs, comparative advantage, efficiency, and how trade leads to

The production possibility curve represents the tough choices society must make.

efficiency. These ideas are all essential to economists' conversations. They provide the framework within which those conversations take place. Thinking of the production possibility curve (and picturing the economy as being on it) directs you to think of the trade-offs involved in every decision.

Look at questions such as: Should we save the spotted owl or should we allow logging in the western forests? Should we expand the government health care system or should we strengthen our national defense system? Should we emphasize policies that allow more consumption now or should we emphasize policies that allow more consumption in the future? Such choices involve difficult trade-offs that can be pictured by the production possibility curve.

Not everyone recognizes these trade-offs. For example, politicians often talk as if the production possibility curve were nonexistent. They promise voters the world, telling them, "If you elect me, you can have more of everything." When they say that, they obscure the hard choices and increase their probability of getting elected.

Economists continually point out that seemingly free lunches often involve significant hidden costs.

Economists do the opposite. They promise little except that life is tough, and they continually point out that seemingly free lunches often involve significant hidden costs. Alas, political candidates who exhibit such reasonableness seldom get elected. Economists' reasonableness has earned economics the nickname *the dismal science*.

Summary

- The production possibility curve measures the maximum combination of outputs that can be obtained from a given number of inputs.   (*LO2-1*)

- In general, in order to get more and more of something, we must give up ever-increasing quantities of something else.   (*LO2-1*)

- Trade allows people to use their comparative advantage and shift out society's production possibility curve.   (*LO2-2*)

- The rise of markets coincided with significant increases in output. Specialization, trade, and competition have all contributed to the increase.   (*LO2-2*)

- Points inside the production possibility curve are inefficient, points along the production possibility curve are efficient, and points outside are unattainable.   (*LO2-2*)

- By specializing in producing those goods for which one has a comparative advantage (lowest opportunity cost), one can produce the greatest amount of goods with which to trade. Doing so, countries can increase consumption.   (*LO2-3*)

- Globalization is the increasing integration of economies, cultures, and institutions across the world.   (*LO2-4*)

- Because many goods are cheaper to produce in countries such as China and India, production that formerly took place in the United States is now taking place in foreign countries.   (*LO2-4*)

- If the United States can maintain its strong comparative advantage in goods using new technologies and innovation, the jobs lost by production moving outside the United States can be replaced with other high-paying jobs. If it does not, then some adjustments in relative wage rates or exchange rates must occur.   (*LO2-4*)

- Business's tendency to shift production to countries where it is cheapest to produce is guided by the law of one price.   (*LO2-4*)

Key Terms

comparative advantage
efficiency
globalization

inefficiency
laissez-faire
law of one price

production possibility
curve (PPC)

productive efficiency

Questions and Exercises   Mc Graw Hill Education connect

1. Show how a production possibility curve would shift if a society became more productive in its output of widgets but less productive in its output of wadgets. (*LO2-1*)

2. Show how a production possibility curve would shift if a society became more productive in the output of both widgets and wadgets. (*LO2-1*)

3. Design a grade production possibility table and curve that demonstrates a rising trade-off as the grade in each subject rises. (*LO2-1*)

4. In two hours JustBorn Candies can produce 30,000 Peeps or 90,000 Mike and Ikes or any combination in between. (*LO2-2*)
   a. What is the trade-off between Peeps and Mike and Ikes?
   b. Draw a production possibility curve that reflects this trade-off.
   c. Identify and label three points: efficient production, inefficient production, impossible.
   d. Illustrate what would happen if JustBorn Candies developed a technology that increased productivity equally for both products.

5. How does the theory of comparative advantage relate to production possibility curves? (*LO2-2*)

6. A country has the following production possibility table: (*LO2-2*)

Resources Devoted to Clothing	Output of Clothing	Resources Devoted to Food	Output of Food
100%	20	0%	0
80	16	20	5
60	12	40	9
40	8	60	12
20	4	80	14
0	0	100	15

   a. Draw the country's production possibility curve.
   b. What's happening to the trade-off between food and clothing?

   c. Say the country gets better at the production of food. What will happen to the production possibility curve?
   d. Say the country gets equally better at producing both food and clothing. What will happen to the production possibility curve?

7. If neither of two countries has a comparative advantage in either of two goods, what are the gains from trade? (*LO2-3*)

8. Does the fact that the production possibility model tells us that trade is good mean that in the real world free trade is necessarily the best policy? Explain. (*LO2-3*)

9. Suppose the United States and Japan have the following production possibility tables: (*LO2-3*)

Japan		United States	
Bolts of Cloth	Tons of Wheat	Bolts of Cloth	Tons of Wheat
1,000	0	500	0
800	100	400	200
600	200	300	400
400	300	200	600
200	400	100	800
0	500	0	1,000

   a. Draw each country's production possibility curve.
   b. In what good does the United States have a comparative advantage?
   c. Is there a possible trade that benefits both countries?
   d. Demonstrate your answer graphically.

10. What effect has globalization had on the ability of firms to specialize? How has this affected the competitive process? (*LO2-4*)

11. If workers in China and India become as productive as U.S. workers, what adjustments will allow the United States to regain its competitiveness? (*LO2-4*)

12. State the law of one price. How is it related to the movement of manufacturing out of the United States? (*LO2-4*)

Questions from Alternative Perspectives

1. Why might government be less capable than the market to do good? *(Austrian)*

2. The text makes it look as if maximizing output is the goal of society.
   a. Is maximizing output the goal of society?
   b. If the country is a Christian country, should it be?
   c. If not, what should it be? *(Religious)*

3. It has been said that "capitalism robs us of our sexuality and sells it back to us."
   a. Does sex sell?
   b. Is sex used to sell goods from Land Rovers to tissue paper?
   c. Who, if anyone, is exploited in the use of sex to sell commodities?
   d. Are both men and women exploited in the same ways? *(Feminist)*

4. Thorstein Veblen wrote that *vested interests* are those seeking "something for nothing." In this chapter, you learned how technology shapes the economy's production possibilities over time so that a country becomes increasingly good at producing a subset of goods.
   a. In what ways have vested interests used their influence to bias the U.S. economy toward the production of military goods at the expense of consumer goods?
   b. What are the short-term and long-term consequences of that bias for human welfare, in the United States and abroad? *(Institutionalist)*

5. Writing in 1776, Adam Smith was concerned with not only the profound effects of the division of labor on productivity (as your textbook notes) but also its stultifying effect on the human capacity. In *The Wealth of Nations,* Smith warned that performing a few simple operations over and over again could render any worker, no matter his or her native intelligence, "stupid and ignorant."
   a. Does the division of labor in today's economy continue to have both these effects?
   b. What are the policy implications? *(Radical)*

Issues to Ponder

1. When all people use economic reasoning, inefficiency is impossible because if the benefit of reducing that inefficiency were greater than the cost, the inefficiency would be eliminated. Thus, if people use economic reasoning, it's impossible to be on the interior of a production possibility curve. Is this statement true or false? Why?

2. If income distribution is tied to a particular production technique, how might that change one's view of alternative production techniques?

3. Research shows that after-school jobs are highly correlated with decreases in grade point averages. Those who work 1 to 10 hours get a 3.0 GPA and those who work 21 hours or more have a 2.7 GPA. Higher GPAs are, however, highly correlated with higher lifetime earnings. Assume that a person earns $8,000 per year for working part-time in college, and that the return to a 0.1 increase in GPA gives one a 10 percent increase in one's lifetime earnings with a present value of $80,000.
   a. What would be the argument for working rather than studying harder?
   b. Is the assumption that there is a trade-off between working and grades reasonable?

4. Lawns produce no crops but occupy more land (40 million acres) in the United States than any single crop, such as corn. This means that the United States is operating inefficiently and hence is at a point inside the production possibility curve. Right? If not, what does it mean?

5. Groucho Marx is reported to have said "The secret of success is honesty and fair dealing. If you can fake those, you've got it made." What would likely happen to society's production possibility curve if everyone could fake honesty? Why? (*Hint:* Remember that society's production possibility curve reflects more than just technical relationships.)

6. Say that the hourly cost to employers per German industrial worker is $43. The hourly cost to employers per U.S. industrial worker is $39, while the average cost per Taiwanese industrial worker is $10.
   a. Give three reasons why firms produce in Germany rather than in a lower-wage country.
   b. Germany has an agreement with other EU countries that allows people in any EU country, including Greece and Italy, which have lower wage rates, to travel and work in any EU country, including high-wage countries. Would you expect a significant movement of workers from Greece and Italy to Germany right away? Why or why not?
   c. Workers in Thailand are paid significantly less than workers in Taiwan. If you were a company CEO, what other information would you want before you decided where to establish a new production facility?

Answers to Margin Questions

1. You must give up 2 units of good *Y* to produce 4 units of good *X*, so the opportunity cost of *X* is ½ *Y*. (*LO2-1*)

2. If no resource had a comparative advantage, the production possibility curve would be a straight line connecting the points of maximum production of each product as in the graph below.

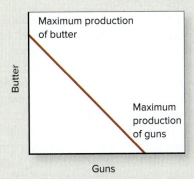

At all points along this curve, the trade-off between producing guns and butter is equal. (*LO2-2*)

3. Points *A* and *C* are along the production possibility curve, so they are points of efficiency. Point *B* is inside the production possibility curve, so it is a point of inefficiency. Point *D* is to the right of the production possibility curve, so it is unattainable. (*LO2-2*)

4. Remind them of the importance of cultural forces. Until recently, in Saudi Arabia, women's right to drive was limited. (*LO2-2*)

5. The production possibility curve shifts in along the butter axis as in the graph below. (*LO2-2*)

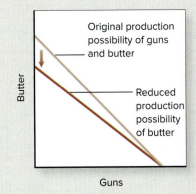

6. The argument that underlies the general laissez-faire policy argument is that when there is competition in trade, individuals are able to pick the best trades available to them and the end result is that both parties to the trade benefit as much as they possibly can. (*LO2-3*)

7. Steve's and Sarah's production possibility curves are shown in the figure below. If they specialize, they can, combined, produce 4 loaves of bread and 8 dozen cookies, which they can split up. Say that Steve gets 2 loaves of bread and 5 dozen cookies (point *A*). This puts him beyond his original production possibility curve, and thus is an improvement for him. That leaves 2 loaves of bread and 3 dozen cookies for Sarah (point *B*), which is beyond her original production possibility curve, which is an improvement for her. Both are better off than they would have been without trade. (*LO2-3*)

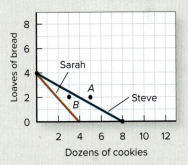

8. True. By producing the good for which it has a comparative advantage, a country will have the greatest amount of goods with which to trade and will reap the greatest gains from trade. (*LO2-3*)

9. Globalization allows more trade and specialization. That specialization lowers costs of production since it allows the lowest-cost producer to produce each good. (*LO2-4*)

10. No. By definition, if one country has a comparative advantage in producing one set of goods, the other country has a comparative advantage in the production of the other set. Jobs will be needed to support this production. Additionally, many jobs cannot be moved abroad effectively because they require physical proximity to the point of sale. (*LO2-4*)

Graphish: The Language of Graphs

A picture is worth 1,000 words. Economists, being efficient, like to present ideas in **graphs,** *pictures of points in a coordinate system in which points denote relationships between numbers.* But a graph is worth 1,000 words only if the person looking at the graph knows the graphical language: *Graphish,* we'll call it. (It's a bit like English.) Graphish is usually written on graph paper. If the person doesn't know Graphish, the picture isn't worth any words and Graphish can be babble.

I have enormous sympathy for students who don't understand Graphish. A number of my students get thrown for a loop by graphs. They understand the idea, but Graphish confuses them. This appendix is for them, and for those of you like them. It's a primer in Graphish.

Two Ways to Use Graphs

In this book I use graphs in two ways:

1. To present an economic model or theory visually, showing how two variables interrelate.

2. To present real-world data visually. To do this, I use primarily bar charts, line charts, and pie charts.

Actually, these two ways of using graphs are related. They are both ways of presenting visually the *relationship* between two things.

Graphs are built around a number line, or axis, like the one in Figure A2-1(a). The numbers are generally placed in order, equal distances from one another. That number line allows us to represent a number at an appropriate point on the line. For example, point *A* represents the number 4.

The number line in Figure A2-1(a) is drawn horizontally, but it doesn't have to be; it also can be drawn vertically, as in Figure A2-1(b).

How we divide our axes, or number lines, into intervals is up to us. In Figure A2-1(a), I called each interval 1; in Figure A2-1(b), I called each interval 10. Point *A* appears after 4 intervals of 1 (starting at 0 and reading from left to right), so it represents 4. In Figure A2-1(b), where each interval represents 10, to represent 5, I place point *B* halfway in the interval between 0 and 10.

So far, so good. Graphish developed when a vertical and a horizontal number line were combined, as in Figure A2-1(c). When the horizontal and vertical number lines are put together, they're called *axes.* (Each line is an axis. *Axes* is the plural of *axis.*) I now have a **coordinate system**—*a two-dimensional space in which one point represents two numbers.* For example, point *A* in Figure A2-1(c) represents the numbers (4, 5)—4 on the horizontal number line and 5 on the vertical number line. Point *B* represents the numbers (1, 20). (By convention, the horizontal numbers are written first.)

Being able to represent two numbers with one point is neat because it allows the relationships between two numbers to be presented visually instead of having to be expressed verbally, which is often cumbersome. For example, say the cost of producing 6 units of something is $4 per

---

FIGURE A2-1 (A, B, AND C)   **Horizontal and Vertical Number Lines and a Coordinate System**

(a) Horizontal Number Line

(b) Vertical Number Line

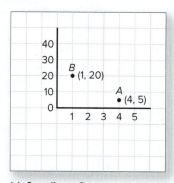

(c) Coordinate System

FIGURE A2-2 (A, B, C, AND D) A Table and Graphs Showing the
Relationships between Price and Quantity

	Price per Pen	Quantity of Pens Bought per Day
A	$3.00	4
B	2.50	5
C	2.00	6
D	1.50	7
E	1.00	8

(a) Price/Quantity Table

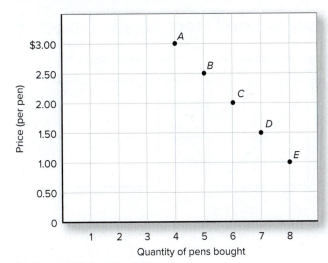

(b) From a Table to a Graph (1)

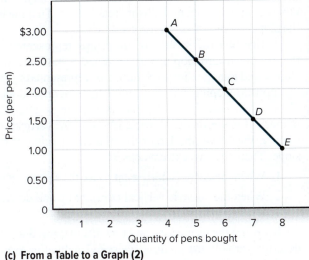

(c) From a Table to a Graph (2)

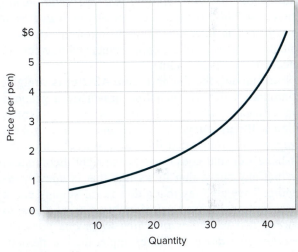

(d) Nonlinear Curve

unit and the cost of producing 10 units is $3 per unit. By putting both these points on a graph, we can visually see that producing 10 costs less per unit than does producing 6.

Another way to use graphs to present real-world data visually is to use the horizontal line to represent time. Say that we let each horizontal interval equal a year, and each vertical interval equal $100 in income. By graphing your income each year, you can obtain a visual representation of how your income has changed over time.

Using Graphs in Economic Modeling

I use graphs throughout the book as I present economic models, or simplifications of reality. A few terms are

often used in describing these graphs, and we'll now go over them. Consider Figure A2-2(a), which lists the number of pens bought per day (column 2) at various prices (column 1).

We can present the table's information in a graph by combining the pairs of numbers in the two columns of the table and representing, or plotting, them on two axes. I do that in Figure A2-2(b).

By convention, when graphing a relationship between price and quantity, economists place price on the vertical axis and quantity on the horizontal axis.

I can now connect the points, producing a line like the one in Figure A2-2(c). With this line, I interpolate the numbers between the points (which makes for a nice

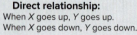
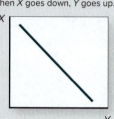
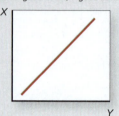
visual presentation). That is, I make the **interpolation assumption**—*the assumption that the relationship between variables is the same between points as it is at the points.* The interpolation assumption allows us to think of a line as a collection of points and therefore to connect the points into a line.

Even though the line in Figure A2-2(c) is straight, economists call any such line drawn on a graph a *curve.* Because it's straight, the curve in A2-2(c) is called a **linear curve**—*a curve that is drawn as a straight line.* Notice that this curve starts high on the left-hand side and goes down to the right. Economists say that any curve that looks like that is *downward-sloping.* They also say that a downward-sloping curve represents an **inverse relationship**—*a relationship between two variables in which when one goes up, the other goes down.* In this example, the line demonstrates an inverse relationship between price and quantity—that is, when the price of pens goes up, the quantity bought goes down.

Figure A2-2(d) presents a **nonlinear curve**—*a curve that is drawn as a curved line.* This curve, which really is curved, starts low on the left-hand side and goes up to the right. Economists say any curve that goes up to the right is *upward-sloping.* An upward-sloping curve represents a **direct relationship**—*a relationship in which when one variable goes up, the other goes up too.* The direct relationship I'm talking about here is the one between the two variables (what's measured on the horizontal and vertical lines). *Downward-sloping* and *upward-sloping* are terms you need to memorize if you want to read, write, and speak Graphish, keeping graphically in your mind the image of the relationships they represent.

Slope

One can, of course, be far more explicit about how much the curve is sloping upward or downward by defining it in terms of **slope**—*the change in the value on the vertical axis divided by the change in the value on the horizontal axis.* Sometimes the slope is presented as "rise over run":

$$\text{Slop} = \frac{\text{Rise}}{\text{Run}} = \frac{\text{Change in value on vertical axis}}{\text{Change in value on horizontal axis}}$$

Slopes of Linear Curves

In Figure A2-3, I present five linear curves and measures of their slopes. Let's go through an example to show how we can measure slope. To do so, we must pick two points. Let's use points *A* (6, 8) and *B* (7, 4) on curve *a.* Looking at these points, we see that as we move from 6 to 7 on the horizontal axis, we move from 8 to 4 on the vertical axis. So when the number on the vertical axis falls by 4, the number on the horizontal axis increases by 1. That means the slope is −4 divided by 1, or −4.

Notice that the inverse relationships represented by the two downward-sloping curves, *a* and *b*, have negative slopes, and that the direct relationships represented by the two upward-sloping curves, *c* and *d*, have positive slopes. Notice also that the flatter the curve, the smaller the numerical value of the slope; and the more vertical, or steeper, the curve, the larger the numerical value of the slope. There are two extreme cases:

1. When the curve is horizontal (flat), the slope is zero.
2. When the curve is vertical (straight up and down), the slope is infinite (larger than large).

Knowing the term *slope* and how it's measured lets us describe verbally the pictures we see visually. For example, if I say a curve has a slope of zero, you should picture in your mind a flat line; if I say "a curve with a slope of minus one," you should picture a falling line that makes a 45° angle with the horizontal and vertical axes. (It's the hypotenuse of an isosceles right triangle with the axes as the other two sides.)

Slopes of Nonlinear Curves

The preceding examples were of *linear (straight) curves.* With *nonlinear curves*—the ones that really do curve—the slope of the curve is constantly changing. As a result, we must talk about the slope of the curve at a particular point, rather than the slope of the whole curve. How can a point have a slope? Well, it can't really, but it can almost, and if that's good enough for mathematicians, it's good enough for us.

FIGURE A2-3   Slopes of Curves

The slope of a curve is determined by rise over run. The slope of curve *a* is shown in the graph. The rest are shown below:

	Rise	÷	Run	=	Slope
b	−1		+2		−0.5
c	1		1		1
d	4		1		4
e	1		1		1

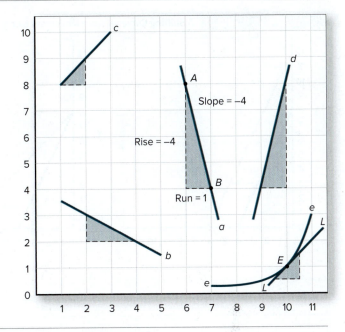

Defining the slope of a nonlinear curve is a bit more difficult. The slope at a given point on a nonlinear curve is determined by the slope of a linear (or straight) line that's tangent to that curve. (A line that's tangent to a curve is a line that just touches the curve, and touches it only at one point in the immediate vicinity of the given point.) In Figure A2-3, the line *LL* is tangent to the curve *ee* at point *E*. The slope of that line, and hence the slope of the curve at the one point where the line touches the curve, is +1.

Maximum and Minimum Points

Two points on a nonlinear curve deserve special mention. These points are the ones for which the slope of the curve is zero. I demonstrate those in Figure A2-4(a) and (b). At point *A* we're at the top of the curve, so it's at a maximum point; at point *B* we're at the bottom of the curve, so it's at a minimum point. These maximum and minimum points are often referred to by economists, and it's important to realize that the value of the slope of the curve at each of these points is zero.

There are, of course, many other types of curves, and much more can be said about the curves I've talked about. I won't do so because, for purposes of this course, we won't need to get into those refinements. I've presented as much Graphish as you need to know for this book.

FIGURE A2-4 (A AND B)   A Maximum and a Minimum Point

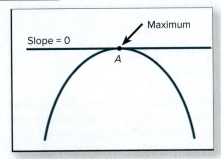

(a) **Maximum Point**

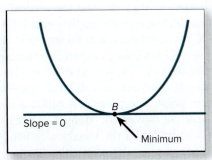

(b) **Minimum Point**

FIGURE A2-5 (A, B, AND C)   A Shifting Curve versus a Movement along a Curve

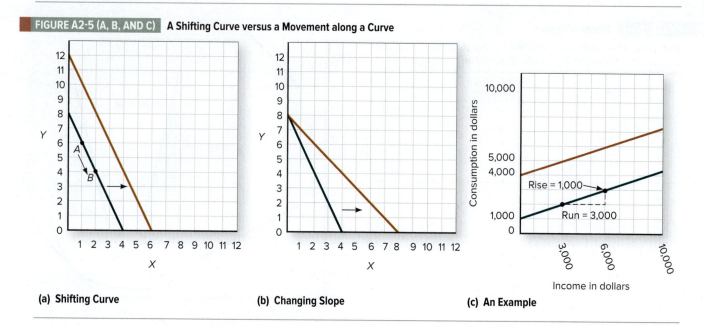

(a) Shifting Curve   (b) Changing Slope   (c) An Example

Equations and Graphs

Sometimes economists depict the relationships shown in graphs using equations. Since I present material algebraically in the appendixes to a few chapters, let me briefly discuss how to translate a linear curve into an equation. Linear curves are relatively easy to translate because all linear curves follow a particular mathematical form: $y = mx + b$, where y is the variable on the vertical axis, x is the variable on the horizontal axis, m is the slope of the line, and b is the vertical-axis intercept. To write the equation of a curve, look at that curve, plug in the values for the slope and vertical-axis intercept, and you've got the equation.

For example, consider the blue curve in Figure A2-5(a). The slope (rise over run) is −2 and the number where the curve intercepts the vertical axis is 8, so the equation that depicts this curve is $y = -2x + 8$. It's best to choose variables that correspond to what you're measuring on each axis, so if price is on the vertical axis and quantity is on the horizontal axis, the equation would be $p = -2q + 8$. This equation is true for any point along this line. Take point A (1, 6), for example. Substituting 1 for x and 6 for y into the equation, you see that $6 = -2(1) + 8$, or $6 = 6$. At point B, the equation is still true: $4 = -2(2) + 8$. A move from point A to point B is called a *movement along a curve*. A movement along a curve does not change the relationship of the variables; rather, it shows how a change in one variable affects the other.

Sometimes the relationship between variables will change. The curve will shift, change slope, or both shift and change slope. These changes are reflected in changes to the m and b variables in the equation. Suppose the vertical-axis intercept rises from 8 to 12, while the slope remains the same. The equation becomes $y = -2x + 12$; for every value of y, x has increased by 4. Plotting the new equation, we can see that the curve has *shifted* to the right, as shown by the orange line in Figure A2-5(a). If instead the slope changes from −2 to −1, while the vertical-axis intercept remains at 8, the equation becomes $y = -x + 8$. Figure A2-5(b) shows this change graphically. The original blue line stays anchored at 8 and rotates out along the horizontal axis to the new orange line.

Here's an example for you to try. The lines in Figure A2-5(c) show two relationships between consumption and income. Write the equation for the blue line.

The answer is $C = \frac{1}{3}Y + \$1,000$. Remember, to write the equation you need to know two things: the vertical-axis intercept ($1,000) and the slope ($\frac{1}{3}$). If the intercept changes to $4,000, the curve will shift up to the orange line as shown.

Presenting Real-World Data in Graphs

The previous discussion treated the Graphish terms that economists use in presenting models that focus on hypothetical relationships. Economists also use graphs in presenting actual economic data. Say, for example, that you want to show how exports have changed over time. Then you would place years on the horizontal

FIGURE A2-6 (A, B, AND C) Presenting Information Visually

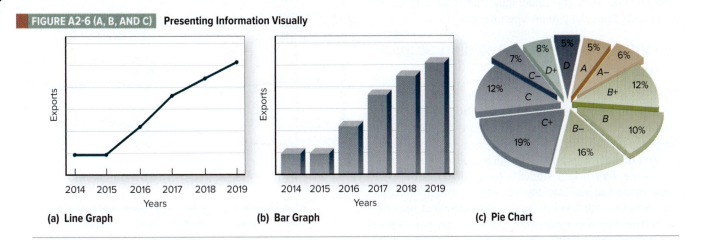

(a) Line Graph   (b) Bar Graph   (c) Pie Chart

axis (by convention) and exports on the vertical axis, as in Figure A2-6(a) and (b). Having done so, you have a couple of choices: You can draw a **line graph**—*a graph where the data are connected by a continuous line;* or you can make a **bar graph**—*a graph where the area under each point is filled in to look like a bar*. Figure A2-6(a) shows a line graph and Figure A2-6(b) shows a bar graph.

Another type of graph is a **pie chart**—*a circle divided into "pie pieces," where the undivided pie represents the total amount and the pie pieces reflect the percentage of the whole pie that the various components make up*. This type of graph is useful in visually presenting how a total amount is divided. Figure A2-6(c) shows a pie chart, which happens to represent the division of grades on a test I gave. Notice that 5 percent of the students got A's.

There are other types of graphs, but they're all variations on line and bar graphs and pie charts. Once you understand these three basic types of graphs, you shouldn't have any trouble understanding the other types.

Interpreting Graphs about the Real World

Understanding Graphish is important because, if you don't, you can easily misinterpret the meaning of graphs. For example, consider the two graphs in Figure A2-7(a) and (b). Which graph demonstrates the larger rise in income? If you said **(a)**, you're wrong. The intervals in the vertical axes differ, and if you look carefully you'll see that the curves in both graphs represent the same combination of points. So when considering graphs,

FIGURE A2-7 (A AND B) The Importance of Scales

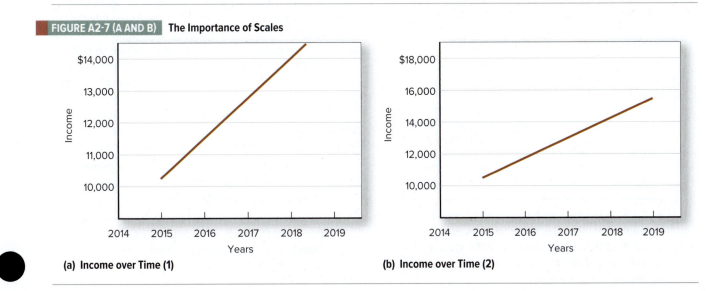

(a) Income over Time (1)   (b) Income over Time (2)

always make sure you understand the markings on the axes. Only then can you interpret the graph.

Quantitative Literacy: Avoiding Stupid Math Mistakes

The data of economics are often presented in graphs and tables. Numerical data are compared by the use of percentages, visual comparisons, and simple relationships based on quantitative differences. Economists who have studied the learning process of their students have found that some very bright students have some trouble with these presentations. Students sometimes mix up percentage changes with level changes, draw incorrect implications from visual comparisons, and calculate quantitative differences incorrectly. This is not necessarily a math problem—at least in the sense that most economists think of math. The mistakes are in relatively simple stuff—the kind of stuff learned in fifth, sixth, and seventh grades. Specifically, as reported in "Student Quantitative Literacy: Is the Glass Half-Full or Half-Empty?" (Robert Burns, Kim Marie McGoldrick, Jerry L. Petr, and Peter Schuhmann, 2002 University of North Carolina at Wilmington Working Paper), when the professors gave a test to students at a variety of schools, they found that a majority of students missed the following questions:

1. What is 25 percent of 400?
   a. 25   b. 50   c. 100
   d. 400   e. none of the above

2. Consider Figure A2-8, where U.S. oil consumption and U.S. oil imports are plotted for 1990–2000. Fill in the blanks to construct a true statement: U.S. domestic oil consumption has been steady while imports have been _____; therefore U.S. domestic oil production has been _____.
   a. rising; rising   b. falling; falling
   c. rising; falling   d. falling; rising

3. Refer to the following table to select the true statement.

Economic Growth in Poland Percent Increase in GDP, 1990–1994				
1990	1991	1992	1993	1994
−11.7	−7.8	−1.5	4.0	3.5

   a. GDP in Poland was larger in 1992 than in 1991.
   b. GDP in Poland was larger in 1994 than in 1993.
   c. GDP in Poland was larger in 1991 than in 1992.
   d. GDP in Poland was larger in 1993 than in 1994.
   e. Both b and c are true.

FIGURE A2-8

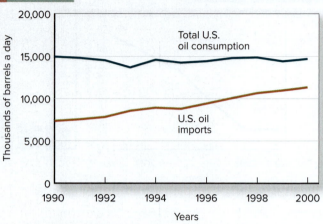

4. If U.S. production of corn was 60 million bushels in 2018 and 100 million bushels in 2019, what was the percentage change in corn production from 2018 to 2019?
   a. 40   b. 60   c. 66.67
   d. 100   e. 200

The reason students got these questions wrong is unknown. Many of them had had higher-level math courses, including calculus, so it is not that they weren't trained in math. I suspect that many students missed the questions because of carelessness: the students didn't think about the question carefully before they wrote down the answer.

Throughout this book we will be discussing issues assuming a quantitative literacy sufficient to answer these questions. Moreover, questions using similar reasoning will be on exams. So it is useful for you to see whether or not you fall in the majority. So please answer the four questions given above now if you haven't done so already.

Now that you've answered them, I give you the correct answers upside-down in the footnote at the bottom of the page.[1]

If you got all four questions right, great! You can stop reading this appendix now. If you missed one or more, read the explanations of the correct answers carefully.

1. The correct answer is c. To calculate a percentage, you multiply the percentage times the number. Thus, 25 percent of 400 is 100.

2. The correct answer is c. To answer it you had to recognize that U.S. consumption of oil comes from U.S. imports and U.S. production. Thus, the

1-c; 2-c; 3-e; 4-c.

distance between the two lines represents U.S. production, which is clearly getting smaller from 1990 to 2000.

3. The correct answer is e. The numbers given to you are percentage changes, and the question is about levels. If the percentage change is positive, as it is in 1993 and 1994, the level is increasing. Thus, 1994 is greater (by 3.5 percent) than 1993, even though the percentage change is smaller than in 1993. If the percentage change is negative, as it is in 1992, the level is falling. Because income fell in 1992, the level of income in 1991 is greater than the level of income in 1992.

4. The correct answer is c. To calculate percentage change, you first need to calculate the change, which in this case is $100 - 60$, or 40. So corn production started at a base of 60 and rose by 40. To calculate the percentage change that this represents, you divide the amount of the rise, 40, by the base, 60. Doing so gives us $40/60 = 2/3 = .6667$, which is 66.67 percent.

Now that I've given you the answers, I suspect that most of you will recognize that they are the right answers. If, after reading the explanations, you still don't follow the reasoning, you should look into getting some extra help in the course either from your teacher, from your TA, or from some program the college has. If, after reading the explanations, you follow them and believe that if you had really thought about them you would have gotten them right, then the next time you see a chart or a table of numbers being compared *really think about them*. Be a bit slower in drawing inferences since they are the building blocks of economic discussions. If you want to do well on exams, it probably makes sense to practice some similar questions to make sure that you have concepts down.

A Review

Let's now review what we've covered.

- A graph is a picture of points on a coordinate system in which the points denote relationships between numbers.
- A downward-sloping line represents an inverse relationship or a negative slope.
- An upward-sloping line represents a direct relationship or a positive slope.
- Slope is measured by rise over run, or a change of y (the number measured on the vertical axis) over a change in x (the number measured on the horizontal axis).
- The slope of a point on a nonlinear curve is measured by the rise over the run of a line tangent to that point.
- At the maximum and minimum points of a nonlinear curve, the value of the slope is zero.
- A linear curve has the form $y = mx + b$.
- A shift in a linear curve is reflected by a change in the b variable in the equation $y = mx + b$.
- A change in the slope of a linear curve is reflected by a change in the m variable in the equation $y = mx + b$.
- In reading graphs, one must be careful to understand what's being measured on the vertical and horizontal axes.

Key Terms

bar graph	graph	line graph	pie chart
coordinate system	interpolation assumption	linear curve	slope
direct relationship	inverse relationship	nonlinear curve	

Questions and Exercises

1. Create a coordinate space on graph paper and label the following points:
   a. $(0, 5)$ b. $(-5, -5)$
   c. $(2, -3)$ d. $(-1, 1)$

2. Graph the following costs per unit, and answer the questions that follow.

Horizontal Axis: Output	Vertical Axis: Cost per Unit
1	$30
2	20
3	12
4	6
5	2
6	6
7	12
8	20
9	30

a. Is the relationship between cost per unit and output linear or nonlinear? Why?
b. In what range in output is the relationship inverse? In what range in output is the relationship direct?
c. In what range in output is the slope negative? In what range in output is the slope positive?
d. What is the slope between 1 and 2 units?

3. Within a coordinate space, draw a line with:
   a. Zero slope.   b. Infinite slope.
   c. Positive slope.   d. Negative slope.

4. Calculate the slope of lines *a* through *e* in the following coordinate system:

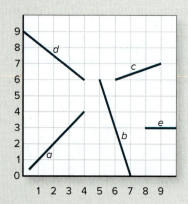

5. Given the following nonlinear curve, answer the following questions:

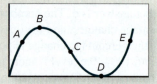

a. At what point(s) is the slope negative?
b. At what point(s) is the slope positive?
c. At what point(s) is the slope zero?
d. What point is the maximum? What point is the minimum?

6. Draw the graphs that correspond to the following equations:
   a. $y = 3x - 8$
   b. $y = 12 - x$
   c. $y = 4x + 2$

7. Using the equation $y = 3x + 1,000$, demonstrate the following:
   a. The slope of the curve changes to 5.
   b. The curve shifts up by 500.

8. State what type of graph or chart you might use to show the following real-world data:
   a. Interest rates from 1929 to 2019.
   b. Median income levels of various ethnic groups in the United States.
   c. Total federal expenditures by selected categories.
   d. Total costs of producing between 100 and 800 shoes.

Economic Institutions

> Nobody can be a great economist who is only an economist—and I am even tempted to add that the economist who is only an economist is likely to become a nuisance if not a positive danger.
>
> —Friedrich Hayek

CHAPTER 3

©Spencer Platt/Getty Images

After reading this chapter, you should be able to:

LO3-1 Define *market economy* and compare and contrast socialism with capitalism.

LO3-2 Describe the role of businesses and households in a market economy.

LO3-3 List and discuss the various roles of government.

LO3-4 Explain why global policy issues differ from national policy issues.

The powerful U.S. economy generates a high standard of living and sense of economic well-being (compared to most other countries) for almost all those living in the United States. The reason why is often attributed to its use of markets, and to the wonders of a market economy. To some degree, that's true, but simply saying markets are the reason for the strength of the U.S. economy obscures as much information as it conveys. First, it misses the point that other countries have markets too, but many of those have much lower standards of living. Second, it conveys a sense that markets exist independently of social and cultural institutions, and that's just not correct. Markets are highly developed social constructs that are part of a country's social and economic institutions. Markets are based on **institutions,** which Nobel Prize–winning economist Douglass North defines as *"the formal and informal rules that constrain human economic behavior."* Institutions include laws that protect ownership of property and the legal system to enforce and interpret laws. They also include political institutions that develop those laws, the cultural traits of society that guide people's tastes and behaviors, and the many organizational structures such as corporations, banks, and nonprofit organizations that make up our economy. To understand markets, you need to understand institutions. In a principles course, we don't have time to develop a full analysis of institutions, but what we can do is to provide an overview of U.S. economic institutions and a brief discussion of why they are important. That's what we do in this chapter.

We begin by looking at the U.S. economic system in historical perspective, considering how it evolved and how it relates to other historical economic systems. Then we consider some of the central institutions of the modern U.S. economy and how they influence the way in which the economy works.

Economic Systems

The U.S. economy is a **market economy**—*an economic system based on private property and the market in which, in principle, individuals decide how, what, and for whom to produce.* In a market economy, individuals follow their own self-interest, while market forces of supply and demand are relied on to coordinate those individual pursuits. Businesses, guided by prices in the market, produce goods and services that they believe people want and that will earn a profit for the business. Prices in the market guide businesses in deciding what to produce. Distribution of goods is to each individual according to his or her ability, effort, inherited property, and luck.

Reliance on market forces doesn't mean that political, social, and historical forces play no role in coordinating economic decisions. These other forces do influence how the market works. For example, for a market to exist, government must allocate and defend **private property rights**—*the control a private individual or firm has over an asset.* The concept of private ownership must exist and must be accepted by individuals in society. When you say "This car is mine," you mean that it is unlawful for someone else to take it without your permission. If someone takes it without your permission, he or she is subject to punishment through the government-enforced legal system.

How Markets Work

Markets work through a system of rewards and payments. If you do something, you get paid for doing that something; if you take something, you pay for that something. How much you get is determined by how much you give. This relationship seems fair to most people. But there are instances when it doesn't seem fair. Say someone is unable to work. Should that person get nothing? How about Joe down the street, who was given $10 million by his parents? Is it fair that he gets lots of toys, like Corvettes and skiing trips to Aspen, and doesn't have to work, while the rest of us have to work 40 hours a week and maybe go to school at night?

I'll put off those questions about fairness at this point—they are very difficult questions. For now, all I want to present is the concept of fairness that underlies a market economy: "Them that works, gets; them that don't, starve."[1] In a market economy, individuals are encouraged to follow their own self-interest.

---

[1]How come the professor gets to use rotten grammar but screams when he sees rotten grammar in your papers? Well, that's fairness for you. Actually, I should say a bit more about writing style. All writers are expected to know correct grammar; if they don't, they don't deserve to be called writers. Once you know grammar, you can individualize your writing style, breaking the rules of grammar where the meter and flow of the writing require it. In college you're still proving that you know grammar, so in papers handed in to your teacher, you shouldn't break the rules of grammar until you've proved to the teacher that you know them. Me, I've done lots of books, so my editors give me a bit more leeway than your teachers will give you.

In market economies, individuals are free to do whatever they want as long as it's legal. The market is relied on to see that what people want to get, and want to do, is consistent with what's available. Price is the mechanism through which people's desires are coordinated and goods are rationed. If there's not enough of something to go around, its price goes up; if more of something needs to get done, the price given to individuals willing to do it goes up. If something isn't wanted or doesn't need to be done, its price goes down. In a market economy, fluctuations in prices play a central role in coordinating individuals' wants.

Fluctuations in prices play a central role in coordinating individuals' wants in a market economy.

What's Good about the Market?

Is the market a good way to coordinate individuals' activities? Much of this book will be devoted to answering that question. The answer that I, and most U.S. economists, come to is: Yes, it is a reasonable way. True, it has problems; the market can be unfair, mean, and arbitrary, and sometimes it is downright awful. Why then do economists support it? For the same reason that Oliver Wendell Holmes supported democracy—it is a lousy system, but, based on experience with alternatives, it is better than all the others we've thought of.

The primary debate among economists is not about using markets; it is about how markets should be structured, and whether they should be modified and adjusted by government regulation. Those are much harder questions, and on these questions, opinions differ enormously.

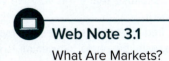

Web Note 3.1
What Are Markets?

The primary debate among economists is not about using markets but about how markets are structured.

Capitalism and Socialism

The view that markets are a reasonable way to organize society has not always been shared by all economists. Throughout history strong philosophical and practical arguments have been made against markets. The philosophical argument against the market is that it brings out the worst in people—it glorifies greed. It encourages people to beat out others rather than to be cooperative. As an alternative some economists have supported socialism. In theory, **socialism** is *an economic system based on individuals' goodwill toward others, not on their own self-interest, and in which, in principle, society decides what, how, and for whom to produce.* The concept of socialism developed in the 1800s as a description of a hypothetical economic system to be contrasted with the predominant market-based economic system of the time, which was called capitalism. **Capitalism** is defined as *an economic system based on the market in which the ownership of the means of production resides with a small group of individuals called capitalists.*

Q-2 Which would be more likely to attempt to foster individualism: socialism or capitalism?

You can best understand the idea behind theoretical socialism by thinking about how decisions are made in a family. In most families, benevolent parents decide who gets what, based on the needs of each member of the family. When Sabin gets a new coat and his sister Sally doesn't, it's because Sabin needs a coat while Sally already has two coats that fit her and are in good condition. Victor may be slow as molasses, but from his family he still gets as much as his superefficient brother Jerry gets. In fact, Victor may get more than Jerry because he needs extra help.

Q-3 Are there any activities in a family that you believe should be allocated by a market? What characteristics do those activities have?

Markets have little role in most families. In my family, when food is placed on the table, we don't bid on what we want, with the highest bidder getting the food. In my family, every person can eat all he or she wants, although if one child eats more than a fair share, that child gets a lecture from me on the importance of sharing. "Be thoughtful; be considerate; think of others first" are lessons that many families try to teach.

In theory, socialism was an economic system that tried to organize society in the same way as most families are organized, trying to see that individuals get what they need. Socialism tried to take other people's needs into account and adjust people's own

Socialism is, in theory, an economic system that tried to organize society in the same way as most families are organized—all people contribute what they can and get what they need.

ADDED DIMENSION

Tradition and Today's Economy

In a tradition-based society, such as a feudal society, the social and cultural forces create an inertia (a tendency to resist change) that predominates over economic and political forces.

"Why did you do it that way?"

"Because that's the way we've always done it."

Tradition-based societies had markets, but they were peripheral, not central, to economic life. In feudal times, what was produced, how it was produced, and for whom it was produced were primarily decided by tradition.

In today's U.S. economy, the market plays the central role in economic decisions. But that doesn't mean that tradition is dead. As I said in Chapter 1, tradition still plays a significant role in today's society, and, in many aspects of society, tradition still overwhelms the invisible hand. Consider the following:

1. The persistent view that women are more responsible than men for home production and are primarily consumers rather than producers.

Source: National Archives and Records Administration (NWDNS-179-WP-1563)

2. The raised eyebrows when a man is introduced as a nurse, secretary, homemaker, or member of any other profession conventionally identified as women's work.

3. Society's unwillingness to permit the sale of individuals or body organs.

4. Parents' willingness to care for their children without financial compensation.

Each of these tendencies reflects tradition's influence in Western society. Some are so deeply rooted that we see them as self-evident. Some of tradition's effects we like; others we don't—but we often take them for granted. Economic forces may work against these traditions, but the fact that they're still around indicates the continued strength of tradition in our market economy.

---

wants in accordance with what's available. In socialist economies, individuals were urged to look out for the other person; if individuals' inherent goodness does not make them consider the general good, government would make them. In contrast, a capitalist economy expected people to be selfish; it relied on markets and competition to direct that selfishness to the general good.[2]

As I stated above, the term *socialism* originally developed as a description of a hypothetical, not an actual, economic system. Actual socialist economies came into being only in the early 1900s, and when they developed they differed enormously from the hypothetical socialist economies that writers had described earlier. The introduction of socialism in practice was closely associated with communism, which reflected the ideas of Karl Marx. Specifically, it was the Communist Party that introduced socialism into Russia, and later China. This has created a political connection between socialism and communism in which communism is the political economic system that follows socialist ideals.

In practice, socialist governments have taken a strong role in guiding the economy. Socialism became known as an economic system based on government ownership of the means of production, with economic activity governed by central planning. In a centrally planned socialist economy, sometimes called a command economy,

Q-4 What is the difference between socialism in theory and socialism in practice?

---

[2]As you probably surmised, the above distinction is too sharp. Even capitalist societies wanted people to be selfless, but not too selfless. Children in capitalist societies were generally taught to be selfless at least in dealing with friends and family. The difficulty parents and societies face is finding a balance between the two positions: selfless but not too selfless; selfish but not too selfish.

government planning boards set society's goals and then directed individuals and firms as to how to achieve those goals.

For example, if government planning boards decided that whole-wheat bread was good for people, they directed firms to produce large quantities and priced it exceptionally low. Planners, not prices, coordinated people's actions. The results were often not quite what the planners desired. Bread prices were so low that pig farmers fed bread to their pigs even though pig feed would have been better for the pigs and bread was more costly to produce. At the low price, the quantity of bread demanded was so high that there were bread shortages; consumers had to stand in long lines to buy bread for their families.

As is often the case, over time the meaning of the word *socialism* expanded and evolved further. It was used to describe the market economies of Western Europe, which by the 1960s had evolved into economies that had major welfare support systems and governments that were very much involved in their market economies. For example, Sweden, even though it relied on markets as its central coordinating institution, was called a socialist economy because its taxes were high and it provided a cradle-to-grave welfare system.

When the Union of Soviet Socialist Republics (USSR) broke apart in 1991, Russia and the countries that evolved out of the USSR adopted a market economy as their organizing framework. China, which is ruled by the Communist Party, also adopted many market institutions. As they did, the terms *capitalism* and *socialism* fell out of favor. People today talk little about the differences in economic systems such as capitalism and socialism; instead they talk about the differences in institutions. Most economies today are differentiated primarily by the degree to which their economies rely on markets, not whether they are a market, capitalist, or socialist economy.

The term *socialism,* however, still shows up in the news. China, for example, continues to call itself a socialist country, even though it is relying more and more heavily on markets to organize production, and is sometimes seen as more capitalistic than many Western economies. Another example of the interest in socialism can be found in the rhetoric of Venezuelan President Hugo Chávez, and his successor, Nicolás Maduro, who attempted to transform Venezuela into what they called "21st-century socialism." They defined 21st-century socialism as government ownership, or at least control, of major resources, and an economy dominated by business cooperatives owned and operated by workers supported by government loans and contracts. Their hope was that this 21st-century socialism would serve as a new economic model of egalitarianism for the entire world. Most observers were doubtful, and, as of 2018, the Venezuelan economy was floundering. President Maduro stayed in power by dismantling democratic institutions and giving himself almost dictatorial powers. The bottom line is that economic systems, and the institutions that make them up, are constantly evolving, and will likely continue to evolve.[3]

Revolutionary shifts that give rise to new economic systems are not the only way economic systems change. Systems also evolve internally, as I discussed above. For example, the U.S. economy is and has always been a market economy, but it has changed over the years, evolving with changes in social customs, political forces, and the strength of markets. In the 1930s, during the Great Depression, the U.S. economy integrated a number of what might be called socialist institutions into its existing institutions. Distribution of goods was no longer, even in theory, only according to ability; need also played a role. Governments began to play a larger role in the economy, taking control over some of the *how, what,* and *for whom* decisions. From the 1980s until the 2010s the process was reversed. The United States became even more market-oriented and the government tried to pull back its involvement in the market in favor of private

People today talk little about differences in economic systems; instead they talk about differences in institutions.

---

[3]The appendix to this chapter traces the development of economic systems.

enterprise. That movement slowed with the financial crisis of 2007, but increased again with the election of Donald Trump as president in 2016. Which direction the future will take remains to be seen, but we can expect institutions to continue to change.

Economic Institutions in a Market Economy

Q-5 Into what three sectors are market economies generally broken up?

Now that we have put the U.S. economic system in historical perspective, let's consider some of its main components. The U.S. economy can be divided into three sectors: businesses, households, and government, as Figure 3-1 shows. Households supply labor and other factors of production to businesses and are paid by businesses for doing so. The market where this interaction takes place is called a *factor market*. Businesses produce goods and services and sell them to households and government. The market where this interaction takes place is called the *goods market*.

Each of the three sectors is interconnected; moreover, the entire U.S. economy is interconnected with the world economy. Notice also the arrows going out to and coming in from both business and households. Those arrows represent the connection of an economy to the world economy. It consists of interrelated flows of goods (exports and imports) and money (capital flows). Finally, consider the arrows connecting government with households and business. Government taxes business and households. It buys goods and services from business and buys labor services from households. Then, with some of its tax revenue, it provides services (for example, roads and education) to both business and households and gives some of its tax revenue directly back to individuals. In doing so, it redistributes income. But government also serves a second function. It oversees the interaction of business and households in the goods and factor markets. Government, of course, is not independent. The United States, for instance, is a democracy, so households vote to determine who shall govern. Similarly, governments are limited not only by what voters want but also by their relationships with other countries. They are part of an international community of countries, and they must keep up relations with other countries in the world. For example, the United States is a

---

FIGURE 3-1 **Diagrammatic Representation of a Market Economy**

This circular-flow diagram of the economy is a good way to organize your thinking about the aggregate economy. As you can see, the three sectors—households, government, and business—interact in a variety of ways.

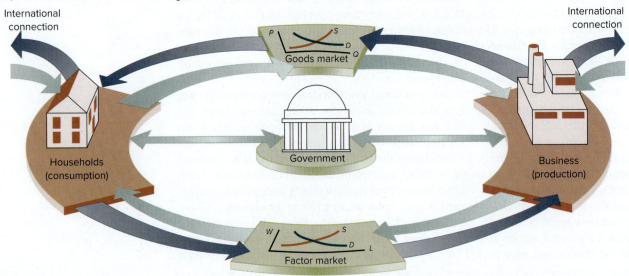

member of many international organizations and has signed international treaties in which it has agreed to limit its domestic actions, such as its ability to tax imports.

Now let's look briefly at the individual components.

Business

President Calvin Coolidge once said "The business of America is business." That's a bit of an overstatement, but business is responsible for over 80 percent of U.S. production. (Government is responsible for the other 20 percent.) In fact, anytime a household decides to produce something, it becomes a business. **Business** is simply the name given to *private producing units in our society.*

Businesses in the United States decide *what* to produce, *how* much to produce, and *for whom* to produce it. They make these central economic decisions on the basis of their own self-interest, which is influenced by market incentives. Anyone who wants to can start a business, provided he or she can come up with the required cash and meet the necessary regulatory requirements. Each year, about 700,000 businesses are started.

Don't think of business as something other than people. Businesses are ultimately made up of a group of people organized together to accomplish some end. Although corporations account for about 80 percent of all sales, in terms of numbers of businesses, most are one- or two-person operations. Home-based businesses are easy to start. All you have to do is say you're in business, and you are. However, some businesses require licenses, permits, and approvals from various government agencies.

Whatever the business, actually starting one is inevitably more difficult than one initially imagined. Succeeding in running a business requires hard work and an almost fanatical dedication; that's why **entrepreneurship** *(the ability to organize and get something done)* is such an important part of business. It is the market's ability to align entrepreneurial activities with the general benefit of society that gives the market its power.

WHAT DO U.S. FIRMS PRODUCE? Producing physical goods is only one of society's economic tasks. Another task is to provide services (activities done for others). Services do not involve producing a physical good. When you get your hair cut, you buy a service, not a good. Much of the cost of the physical goods we buy actually is not a cost of producing the good, but is a cost of one of the most important services: distribution, which includes payments associated with having the good where you want it when you want it. After a good is produced, it has to be transported to consumers, either indirectly through retailers or directly to consumers. If the good isn't at the right place at the right time, it can often be useless.

Let's consider an example: hot dogs at a baseball game. How many of us have been irked that a hot dog that costs 40 cents to fix at home costs $6.00 at a baseball game? The reason why the price can differ so much is that a hot dog at home isn't the same as a hot dog at a game and you are willing to pay the extra $5.60 to have the hot dog when and where you want it. *Distribution*—getting goods where you want them when you want them—is as important as production and is a central component of a service economy.

The importance of the service economy can be seen in modern technology companies. They provide information and methods of handling information, not physical goods. Google and Facebook produce no physical product but they provide central services to our lives. As the U.S. economy has evolved, the relative importance of services has increased. Today, services make up approximately 80 percent of the U.S. economy, compared to 20 percent in 1947, and services are likely to continue to rise in importance in the future.

Web Note 3.2

Starting a Business

Businesses in the United States decide *what* to produce, *how* much to produce, and *for whom* to produce it.

Entrepreneurship is an important part of business.

©Joyce Vincent/Shutterstock

Although b
produce, th
sovereignt

Q-6 Tru
States, the
only social
started. Wl

Q-7 Are
United Sta
what are n

FIGURE 3

The cha
propriet

Source: St

REAL-WORLD APPLICATION

What Government Are We Talking About?

In thinking about the role of government in economic policy we often will talk about government as a single entity. In fact, government has many different competing branches and structures, with different branches and structures of government having quite different agendas. This means that the question of government versus the market misses an important element of the policy debate: Which branch and structure of government is one talking about?

A polycentric government—one with many different bases of power—is quite different from a monocentric government. The United States is an example of a polycentric government. The federal government is comprised of three branches of government (executive, legislative, and

judicial) that don't always see issues in the same way. For example, President Trump's initial executive order to ban people from certain countries from traveling to the United States in early 2017 was declared unconstitutional by several federal judges. Their rulings led Trump to revise the order, which eventually was deemed constitutional by the Supreme Court. The United States is also polycentric in having both federal and state governments that can, and do, see issues differently. Another aspect of government that is important to integrate into one's thinking about government's role is the degree to which government is responsive to people's desires. One will likely have different views about the role for an authoritarian dictatorship and a well-functioning democracy.

Government as a Referee

Even if government spending made up only a small proportion of total expenditures, government would still be central to the study of economics. The reason is that, in a market economy, government sets the rules of interaction between households and businesses, and acts as a referee, enforcing the rules and changing them when it sees fit. Government decides whether economic forces will be allowed to operate freely.

Some examples of U.S. laws regulating the interaction between households and businesses today are:

Web Note 3.4

Laws or Contracts?

1. Businesses are not free to hire and fire whomever they want. They must comply with equal opportunity and labor laws. For example, closing a plant requires 60 days' notice for many kinds of firms.

2. Many working conditions are subject to government regulation: safety rules, wage rules, overtime rules, hours-of-work rules, and the like.

3. Businesses cannot meet with other businesses to agree on prices they will charge.

4. In some businesses, workers must join a union to work at certain jobs.

Most of these laws evolved over time. Up until the 1930s, household members, in their roles as workers and consumers, had few rights. Businesses were free to hire and fire at will and, if they chose, to deceive and take advantage of consumers. Over time, new laws to curb business abuses have been passed, and government agencies have been formed to enforce these laws. Some people think the pendulum has swung too far the other way. They believe businesses are saddled with too many regulatory burdens.

One big question that I'll address throughout this book is: What referee role should the government play in an economy? For example, should government use its taxing powers to redistribute income from the rich to the poor? Should it allow mergers between companies? Should it regulate air traffic? Should it regulate prices? Should it attempt to stabilize fluctuations of aggregate income?

Specific Roles for Government

In its role as both an actor and a referee, government plays a variety of specific roles in the economy. These include:

1. Providing a stable set of institutions and rules.
2. Promoting effective and workable competition.
3. Correcting for externalities.
4. Ensuring economic stability and growth.
5. Providing public goods.
6. Adjusting for undesirable market results.

PROVIDE A STABLE SET OF INSTITUTIONS AND RULES   A basic role of government is to provide a stable institutional framework that includes the set of laws specifying what can and cannot be done as well as a mechanism to enforce those laws. For example, if someone doesn't pay you, you can't go take what you are owed; you have to go through the government court system. Where governments don't provide a stable institutional framework, as often happens in developing and transitional countries, economic activity is difficult; usually such economies are stagnant. Continued civil unrest in Syria, Iraq, Libya, and Yemen over the past decade has hurt their economies, and some economists suggest that reestablishing peace could double growth in the region.

PROMOTE EFFECTIVE AND WORKABLE COMPETITION   In a market economy, the pressure to monopolize—for one firm to try to control the market—and competition are always in conflict; the government must decide what role it is to play in protecting or promoting competition. Thus, when Microsoft gained monopolistic control of the computer operating system market with Windows, the U.S. government took the company to court and challenged that monopoly.

What makes this a difficult function for government is that most individuals and firms believe that competition is far better for the other guy than it is for themselves, that their own monopolies are necessary monopolies, and that competition facing them is unfair competition. For example, most farmers support competition, but these same farmers also support government farm subsidies (payments by government to producers based on production levels) and import restrictions. Likewise, most firms support competition, but these same firms also support tariffs, which protect them from foreign competition. Most professionals, such as architects and engineers, support competition, but they also support professional licensing, which limits the number of competitors who can enter their field. As you will see when reading the newspapers, there are always arguments for limiting entry into fields. The job of the government is to determine whether these arguments are strong enough to overcome the negative effects those limitations have on competition.

CORRECT FOR EXTERNALITIES   When two people freely enter into a trade or agreement, they both believe that they will benefit from the trade. But unless they're required to do so, traders are unlikely to take into account any effect that an action may have on a third party. Economists call *the effect of a decision on a third party not taken into account by the decision maker* an **externality.** An externality can be positive (in which case society as a whole benefits from the trade between the two parties) or negative (in which case society as a whole is harmed by the trade between the two parties).

The government may be able to help correct for externalities.

©overcrew/Getty Images

An example of a positive externality is education. When someone educates herself or himself, all society benefits, since better-educated people usually make better citizens and are better equipped to figure out new approaches to solving problems—approaches that benefit society as a whole. An example of a negative externality involves the burning of coal, which puts sulfur dioxide, carbon dioxide, and fine particulates into the air. Sulfur dioxide contributes to acid rain, carbon dioxide contributes to global warming, and fine particulates damage people's lungs. This means that burning coal has an externality associated with it—an effect of an action that is not taken into account by market participants.

When there are externalities, there is a potential role for government to adjust the market result through taxes, subsidies, or regulation. Throughout this book we will be considering the advantages and disadvantages of each.

ENSURE ECONOMIC STABILITY AND GROWTH   In addition to providing general stability, government has the potential role of providing economic stability. Most people would agree that if it's possible, government should prevent large fluctuations in the level of economic activity, maintain a relatively constant price level, and provide an economic environment conducive to economic growth. These aims, which became the goals of the U.S. government in 1946 when the Employment Act was passed, are generally considered macroeconomic goals. They're justified as appropriate aims for government to pursue because they involve **macroeconomic externalities** (*externalities that affect the levels of unemployment, inflation, or growth in the economy as a whole*).

> A macroeconomic externality is the effect of an individual decision that affects the levels of unemployment, inflation, or growth in an economy as a whole but is not taken into account by the individual decision maker.

Here's how a macro externality could occur. When individuals decide how much to spend, they don't take into account the effects of their decision on others; thus, there may be too much or too little spending. Too little spending often leads to unemployment. But in making their spending decision, people don't take into account the fact that spending less might create unemployment. So their spending decisions can involve a macro externality. Similarly, when people raise their price and don't consider the effect on inflation, they too might be creating a macro externality.

PROVIDE PUBLIC GOODS   Another role for government is to supply public goods. A **public good** is *a good that if supplied to one person must be supplied to all and whose consumption by one individual does not prevent its consumption by another individual*. In contrast, a **private good** is *a good that, when consumed by one individual, cannot be consumed by another individual*. An example of a private good is an apple; once I eat that apple, no one else can consume it. An example of a public good is national defense, which, if supplied to one, will also protect others. In order to supply defense, governments must require people to pay for it with taxes, rather than leaving it to the market to supply it.

ADJUST FOR UNDESIRABLE MARKET RESULTS   A controversial role for government is to adjust the results of the market when those market results are seen as socially undesirable. Government redistributes income, taking it away from some individuals and giving it to others whom it sees as more deserving or more in need. In doing so, it attempts to see that the outcomes of trades are fair. Determining what's fair is a difficult philosophical question that economists can't answer. That question is for the people, through the government, to decide.

An example of this role involves having government decide what's best for people, independently of their desires. The market allows individuals to decide. But what if people don't know what's best for themselves? Or what if they do know but don't act on that knowledge? For example, people might know that addictive drugs are bad for them, but because of peer pressure, or because they just don't care, they may take drugs anyway. Government action prohibiting such activities through laws or high taxes may then be warranted. *Goods or activities that government believes are bad for people even though they choose to use the*

Our International Competitors

The world economy is often divided into three main areas or trading blocs: the Americas, Europe and Africa, and East Asia. These trading blocs are shown in the map below.

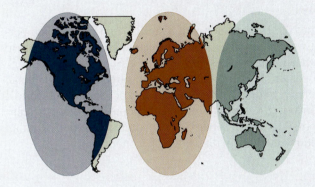

Each area has a major currency. In the Americas, it is the dollar; in Europe, it is the euro; and in East Asia, it is the Japanese yen. These areas are continually changing; by 2013 the EU had expanded to 28 countries, incorporating many of the countries of Eastern Europe. China's economy has been growing fast and, given the size of its population, is likely to overtake Japan as the key Asian economy in the coming decades.

The accompanying table gives you a sense of the similarities and differences in the economies of the United States, China, and the European Union.

	United States	China	European Union
Area (square miles)	3,537,438	3,705,407	1,691,588
Population	327 million	1.4 billion	516 million
GDP*	$19.9 trillion	$23.1 trillion	$20.0 trillion
Percentage of world output	15%	18%	16%
GDP per capita	$61,000	$17,000	$39,000
Natural resources	Coal, copper, lead, and others	Coal, iron ore	Coal, iron ore, natural gas, fish, and others
Exports as a percentage of GDP	12%	20%	14%
Imports as a percentage of GDP	15%	17%	15%
Currency value (as of Sept. 2018)	Dollar ($1 = $1)	Yuan (¥6.83 = $1)	Euro (€0.86 = $1)

*Calculated using purchasing power parity.

Source: *CIA World Factbook* (www.cia.gov) and current exchange rate tables. EU trade figures adjusted to exclude intra-EU trade. Currency changes can affect GDP figures.

---

goods or engage in the activities are called **demerit goods or activities.** Illegal drugs are a demerit good and using addictive drugs is a demerit activity.

Alternatively, there are some activities that government believes are good for people, even if people may not choose to engage in them. For example, government may believe that going to the opera or contributing to charity is a good activity. But in the United States only a small percentage of people go to the opera, and not everyone in the United States contributes to charity. Similarly, government may believe that whole-wheat bread is more nutritious than white bread. But many consumers prefer white bread. Goods like whole-wheat bread and activities like contributing to charity are known as **merit goods or activities**—*goods and activities that government believes are good for you even though you may not choose to engage in the activities or to consume the goods.* Government sometimes provides support for them through subsidies or tax benefits.

> With merit and demerit goods, individuals are assumed to be doing what is not in their self-interest.

Market Failures and Government Failures

The reasons for government intervention are often summed up in the phrase *market failure.* **Market failures** are *situations in which the market does not lead to a desired result.* In the real world, market failures are pervasive—the market is always failing in

Q-9   If there is an externality, does that mean that the government should intervene in the market to adjust for that externality?

one way or another. But the fact that there are market failures does not mean that government intervention will improve the situation. There are also **government failures**—*situations in which the government intervenes and makes things worse*. Government failures are pervasive in the real world—the government is always failing in one way or another. So real-world policy makers usually end up choosing which failure—market failure or government failure—will be least problematic.

Global Institutions

So far in this chapter we've put the U.S. economy in historical and institutional perspective. In this last section, we briefly put it into perspective relative to the world economy. By doing so, we gain a number of insights into the U.S. economy. The U.S. economy makes up about 15 percent of world output and consumption, a percentage that is much larger than its relative size by geographic area (6 percent of the world's landmass) or by population (just over 4 percent of the world population). It is becoming more integrated; it is impossible to talk about U.S. economic institutions without considering how those institutions integrate with the world economy.

Global Corporations

Consider corporations. Most large corporations today are not U.S., German, or Japanese corporations; they are **global corporations** *(corporations with substantial operations on both the production and sales sides in more than one country)*. Just because a car has a Japanese or German name doesn't mean that it was produced abroad. Many Japanese and German companies now have manufacturing plants in the United States, and many U.S. firms have manufacturing plants abroad. When goods are produced by global corporations, corporate names don't always tell much about where a good is produced. As global corporations' importance has grown, most manufacturing decisions are made in reference to the international market, not the U.S. domestic market. This means that the consumer sovereignty that guides decisions of firms is becoming less and less U.S. consumer sovereignty, and more and more global consumer sovereignty.

Global corporations are corporations with substantial operations on both the production and sales sides in more than one country.

Global corporations offer enormous benefits for countries. They create jobs; they bring new ideas and new technologies to a country; and they provide competition for domestic companies, keeping them on their toes. But global corporations also pose a number of problems for governments. One is their implication for domestic and international policy. A domestic corporation exists within a country and can be dealt with using policy measures within that country. A global corporation exists within many countries. If it doesn't like the policies in one country—say taxes are too high or regulations too tight—it can shift its operations to other countries. A global corporation has no global government to regulate it.

Web Note 3.5

Global 500

Coordinating Global Issues

Global economic issues differ from national economic issues because national economies have governments to referee disputes among players in the economy; global economies do not—no international government exists. Some argue that we need a global government to oversee global businesses. But that argument has not been heeded. The closest institution there is to a world government is the United Nations (UN), which, according to critics, is simply a debating society. It has no ability to tax and no ability to impose its will separate from the political and military power of its members. When the United States opposes a UN mandate, it can, and often does, ignore it. Hence, international problems must be dealt with through negotiation, consensus, bullying, and concessions.

Governments, however, have developed a variety of international institutions to promote negotiations and coordinate economic relations among countries. Besides the United

Nations, these include the World Bank, the World Court, and the International Monetary Fund (IMF). These organizations have a variety of goals. For example, the World Bank, a multinational, international financial institution, works with developing countries to secure low-interest loans, channeling such loans to them to foster economic growth. The International Monetary Fund, a multinational, international financial institution, is concerned primarily with monetary issues. It deals with international financial arrangements. When developing countries encountered financial problems in the 1980s and had large international debts that they could not pay, the IMF helped work on repayment plans.

Countries also have developed global and regional organizations whose job it is to coordinate trade among countries and reduce trade barriers. On the international level, the World Trade Organization (WTO) works to reduce trade barriers among countries. On the regional level, there are the European Union (EU), which is an organization of European countries that developed out of a trade association devoted to reducing trade barriers among member countries; the North American Free Trade Agreement (NAFTA), an organization devoted to reducing trade barriers between the United States, Mexico, and Canada; and Mercosur, an organization devoted to reducing trade barriers among North, Central, and South American countries.

In addition to these formal institutions, there are informal meetings of various countries. These include the Group of Seven, which meets to promote negotiations and to coordinate economic relations among countries. The seven are Japan, Germany, Britain, France, United States, Canada, and Italy.

Since governmental membership in international organizations is voluntary, their power is limited. When the United States doesn't like a World Court ruling, it simply states that it isn't going to follow the ruling. When the United States is unhappy with what the United Nations is doing, it withholds some of its dues. Other countries do the same from time to time. Other member countries complain but can do little to force compliance. It doesn't work that way domestically. If you decide you don't like U.S. policy and refuse to pay your taxes, you'll wind up in jail.

What keeps nations somewhat in line when it comes to international rules is a moral tradition: Countries want to (or at least want to look as if they want to) do what's "right." Countries will sometimes follow international rules to keep international opinion favorable to them. But perceived national self-interest often overrides international scruples.

> Governments have developed international institutions to promote negotiations and coordinate economic relations among countries. Some are: the UN; the World Bank; the World Court; and the International Monetary Fund.

> Countries have developed global and regional organizations to coordinate trade and reduce trade barriers. Some are: the WTO; the EU; and NAFTA.

> Since governmental membership in international organizations is voluntary, their power is limited.

> **Q-10** If the United States chooses not to follow a World Court decision, what are the consequences?

Conclusion

This has been a whirlwind introduction to economic institutions and their role in the economy. Each of them—business, households, and government—is important, and to understand what happens in the economy, one must have a sense of how these institutions work and the role they play. In the remainder of the book we won't discuss institutions much as we concentrate on presenting economic analysis. I rely on you to integrate the analysis with institutions as you apply the economic analysis and reasoning that you learn to the real world.

Summary

- A market economy is an economic system based on private property and the market. It gives private property rights to individuals and relies on market forces to solve the *what, how,* and *for whom* problems. (*LO3-1*)

- In a market economy, price is the mechanism through which people's desires are coordinated and goods are rationed. The U.S. economy today is a market economy. (*LO3-1*)

- The predominant market-based system during the early 1900s was capitalism, an economic system based on the market in which the ownership of production resided with a small group of individuals called capitalists.   *(LO3-1)*

- In principle, under socialism society solves the *what, how,* and *for whom* problems in the best interest of the individuals in society. It is based on individuals' goodwill toward one another.   *(LO3-1)*

- In practice, socialism was an economic system based on government ownership of the means of production, with economic activity governed by central planning. Socialism in practice was sometimes called a command economy.   *(LO3-1)*

- A diagram of the U.S. market economy shows the connections among businesses, households, and government. It also shows the U.S. economic connection to other countries.   *(LO3-2)*

- In the United States, businesses make the *what, how,* and *for whom* decisions.   *(LO3-2)*

- Although businesses decide what to produce, they succeed or fail depending on their ability to meet consumers' desires. That's consumer sovereignty.   *(LO3-2)*

- The three main forms of business are corporations, sole proprietorships, and partnerships. Each has its advantages and disadvantages.   *(LO3-2)*

- Although households are the most powerful economic institution, they have assigned much of their power to government and business. Economics focuses on households' role as the supplier of labor.   *(LO3-2)*

- Government plays two general roles in the economy: (1) as a referee and (2) as an actor.   *(LO3-3)*

- Six roles of government are to (1) provide a stable set of institutions and rules, (2) promote effective and workable competition, (3) correct for externalities, (4) ensure economic stability and growth, (5) provide public goods, and (6) adjust for undesirable market results.   *(LO3-3)*

- To understand the U.S. economy, one must understand its role in the world economy.   *(LO3-4)*

- Global corporations are corporations with significant operations in more than one country. They are increasing in importance.   *(LO3-4)*

- Global economic issues differ from national economic issues because national economies have governments. The global economy does not.   *(LO3-4)*

Key Terms

business	externality	market economy	private property right
capitalism	global corporation	market failure	profit
consumer sovereignty	government failure	merit good or activity	public good
corporation	households	partnership	socialism
demerit good or activity	institutions	private good	sole proprietorship
entrepreneurship	macroeconomic externality		

Questions and Exercises ■ connect

1. In a market economy, what is the central coordinating mechanism?   *(LO3-1)*

2. In a centrally planned socialist economy, what is the central coordinating mechanism?   *(LO3-1)*

3. How does a market economy solve the *what, how,* and *for whom* to produce problems?   *(LO3-1)*

4. How does a centrally planned socialist economy solve the *what, how,* and *for whom* to produce problems?   *(LO3-1)*

5. Is capitalism or socialism the better economic system? Why?   *(LO3-1)*

6. Why does an economy's strength ultimately reside in its people?   *(LO3-2)*

7. Why is entrepreneurship a central part of any business?   *(LO3-2)*

8. List the three major forms of business.   *(LO3-2)*
   a. What form is most common?
   b. What form accounts for the largest proportion of sales?

9. You're starting a software company in which you plan to sell software to your fellow students. What form of business organization would you choose? Why?   *(LO3-2)*

10. What are the two largest categories of state and local government expenditures?   (LO3-3)

11. What are the six roles of government listed in the text?   (LO3-3)

12. Say the government establishes rights to pollute so that without a pollution permit you aren't allowed to emit pollutants into the air, water, or soil. Firms are allowed to buy and sell these rights. In what way will this correct for an externality?   (LO3-3)

13. Give an example of a merit good, a demerit good, a public good, and a good that involves an externality.   (LO3-3)

14. Name two international organizations that countries have developed to coordinate economic actions.   (LO3-4)

15. What are two organizations that countries can use to coordinate economic relations and reduce trade barriers?   (LO3-4)

16. Why are international organizations limited in their effectiveness?   (LO3-4)

Questions from Alternative Perspectives

1. Friedrich Hayek, the man quoted at the start of the chapter, is an Austrian economist who won a Nobel Prize in Economics. He argued that government intervention is difficult to contain. Suppose central planners have decided to financially support all children with food vouchers, free day care, and public school.
   a. What problems might this create?
   b. How might this lead to further interference by central planners into family choices? *(Austrian)*

2. In *The Social Contract,* Jean-Jacques Rousseau argued that "no State has ever been founded without a religious basis [but] the law of Christianity at bottom does more harm by weakening than good by strengthening the constitution of the State." What does he mean by that, and is he correct? *(Religious)*

3. In economics, a household is defined as a group of individuals making joint decisions as though acting as one person.
   a. How do you think decisions are actually made about things like consumption and allocation of time within the household?
   b. Does bargaining take place?
   c. If so, what gives an individual power to bargain effectively for his or her preferences?

   d. Do individuals act cooperatively within the family and competitively everywhere else?
   e. Does this make sense? *(Feminist)*

4. This chapter emphasized the importance of the relationship between how the economic system is organized and value systems. Knowing that how I raise my child will greatly shape how he or she will ultimately fit into the social and economic process, should I raise my child to be selfless, compassionate, and dedicated to advancing the well-being of others, knowing she will probably be poor; or shall I raise her to be self-centered, uncaring, and greedy to increase her chances to acquire personal fortune? Which decision is just and why? *(Institutionalist)*

5. The text discusses consumer sovereignty and suggests that it guides the market choices.
   a. Is consumer sovereignty a myth or reality in today's consumer culture?
   b. Do consumers "direct" the economy as suggested by the text, or has invention become the mother of necessity, as Thorstein Veblen once quipped?
   c. If the consumer is not sovereign, then who is and what does that imply for economics? *(Radical)*

Issues to Ponder

1. What arguments can you give for supporting a socialist organization of a family and a market-based organization of the economy?

2. Economists Edward Lazear and Robert Michael calculated that the average family spends two and a half times as much on each adult as they do on each child.
   a. Does this mean that children are deprived and that the distribution is unfair?
   b. Do you think these percentages change with family income? If so, how?

   c. Do you think that the allocation would be different in a family in a command economy than in a capitalist economy? Why?

3. One of the specific problems socialist economies had was keeping up with capitalist countries technologically.
   a. Can you think of any reason inherent in a centrally planned economy that would make innovation difficult?
   b. Can you think of any reason inherent in a capitalist economy that would foster innovation?

   c. Joseph Schumpeter, a famous Harvard economist of the 1930s, predicted that as firms in capitalist societies grew in size, they would innovate less. Can you suggest what his argument might have been?

   d. Schumpeter's prediction did not come true. Modern capitalist economies have had enormous innovations. Can you provide explanations as to why?

4. Tom Rollins founded a company called Teaching Co. He taped lectures at the top universities, packaged the lectures on DVD, and sold them for between $20 and $230 per series.

   a. Discuss whether such an idea could be expanded to include college courses that one could take at home.

   b. What are the technical, social, and economic issues involved?

   c. If it is technically possible and cost-effective, will the new venture be a success?

5. Go to a store in your community.

   a. Ask what limitations the owners faced in starting their business.

   b. Were these limitations necessary?

   c. Should there have been more or fewer limitations?

   d. Under what heading of reasons for government intervention would you put each of the limitations?

   e. Ask what kinds of taxes the business pays and what benefits it believes it gets for those taxes.

   f. Is it satisfied with the existing situation? Why? What would it change?

6. A market system is often said to be based on consumer sovereignty—the consumer determines what's to be produced. Yet business decides what's to be produced. Can these two views be reconciled? How? If not, why?

7. How might individuals disagree about the government's role in intervening in the market for merit, demerit, and public goods?

8. Discuss the concepts of market failure and government failure in relation to operas.

9. You've set up the rules for a game and started the game but now realize that the rules are unfair. Should you change the rules?

10. In trade talks with Australia, the United States proposed that Australia cannot regulate the amount of foreign content on new media without first consulting the United States. Actor Bridie Carter of *McLeod's Daughters* argued against adopting the trade agreement, arguing the agreement trades away Australia's cultural identity. This highlights one of the effects of globalization: the loss of variety based on cultural differences. How important should such cultural identity issues be in trade negotiations?

Answers to Margin Questions

1. He is wrong. Property rights are required for a market to operate. Once property rights are allocated, the market will allocate goods, but the market cannot distribute the property rights that are required for the market to operate. (*LO3-1*)

2. Capitalism places much more emphasis on fostering individualism. Socialism tries to develop a system in which the individual's needs are placed second to society's needs. (*LO3-1*)

3. Most families allocate basic needs through control and command. The parents do (or try to do) the controlling and commanding. Generally parents are well-intentioned, trying to meet their perception of their children's needs. However, some family activities that are not basic needs might be allocated through the market. For example, if one child wants a go-cart and is willing to do extra work at home in order to get it, go-carts might be allocated through the market, with the child earning vouchers that can be used for such nonessentials. (*LO3-1*)

4. In theory, socialism is an economic system based on individuals' goodwill. In practice, socialism involved central planning and government ownership of the primary means of production. (*LO3-1*)

5. Market economies are generally broken up into businesses, households, and government. (*LO3-2*)

6. False. In the United States, individuals are free to start any type of business they want, provided it doesn't violate the law. The invisible hand sees to it that only those businesses that customers want earn a profit. The others lose money and eventually go out of business, so in that sense only businesses that customers want stay in business. (*LO3-2*)

7. As can be seen in Figure 3-2, most businesses in the United States are sole proprietorships, not corporations. Corporations, however, generate the most revenue. (*LO3-2*)

8. The two largest expenditure categories for the federal government are health and education and income security. (*LO3-3*)

9. Not necessarily. The existence of an externality creates the possibility that government intervention might help. But there are also government failures in which the government intervenes and makes things worse. (*LO3-3*)

10. The World Court has no enforcement mechanism. Thus, when a country refuses to follow the court's decisions, the country cannot be directly punished except through indirect international pressures. (*LO3-4*)

The History of Economic Systems

In Chapter 1, I made the distinction between market and economic forces: Economic forces have always existed—they operate in all aspects of our lives—but market forces have not always existed. Markets are social creations societies use to coordinate individuals' actions. Markets developed, sometimes spontaneously, sometimes by design, because they offered a better life for at least some—and usually a large majority of—individuals in a society.

To understand why markets developed, it is helpful to look briefly at the history of the economic systems from which our own system descended.

Feudal Society: Rule of Tradition

Let's go back in time to the year 1000 when Europe had no nation-states as we now know them. (Ideally, we would have gone back further and explained other economic systems, but, given the limited space, I had to draw the line somewhere—an example of a trade-off.) The predominant economic system at that time was feudalism. There was no coordinated central government, no unified system of law, no national patriotism, no national defense, although a strong religious institution simply called the Church fulfilled some of these roles. There were few towns; most individuals lived in walled manors, or "estates." These manors "belonged to" the "lord of the manor." (Occasionally the "lord" was a lady, but not often.) I say "belonged to" rather than "were owned by" because most of the empires or federations at that time were not formal nation-states that could organize, administer, and regulate ownership. No documents or deeds gave ownership of the land to an individual. Instead, tradition ruled, and in normal times nobody questioned the lord's right to the land. The land "belonged to" the lord because the land "belonged to" him—that's the way it was.

Without a central nation-state, the manor served many functions a nation-state would have served had it existed. The lord provided protection, often within a walled area surrounding the manor house or, if the manor was large enough, a castle. He provided administration and decided disputes. He also decided *what* would be done, *how* it would be done, and *who* would get what, but these decisions were limited. In the same way that the land belonged to the lord because that's the way it always had been, what people did and how they did it were determined by what they always had done. Tradition ruled the manor more than the lord did.

Problems of a Tradition-Based Society

Feudalism developed about the 8th and 9th centuries and lasted until about the 15th century, though in isolated countries such as Russia it continued well into the 19th century, and in all European countries its influence lingered for hundreds of years (as late as about 150 years ago in some parts of Germany). Such a long-lived system must have done some things right, and feudalism did: It solved the *what, how,* and *for whom* problems in an acceptable way.

But a tradition-based society has problems. In a traditional society, because someone's father was a baker, the son also must be a baker, and because a woman was a homemaker, she wouldn't be allowed to be anything but a homemaker. But what if Joe Blacksmith Jr., the son of Joe Blacksmith Sr., is a lousy blacksmith and longs to knead dough, while Joe Baker Jr. would be a superb blacksmith but hates making pastry? Tough. Tradition dictated who did what. In fact, tradition probably arranged things so that we will never know whether Joe Blacksmith Jr. would have made a superb baker.

As long as a society doesn't change too much, tradition operates reasonably well, although not especially efficiently, in holding the society together. However, when a society must undergo change, tradition does not work. Change means that the things that were done before no longer need to be done, while new things do need to get done. But if no one has traditionally done these new things, then they don't get done. If the change is important but a society can't figure out some way for the new things to get done, the society falls apart. That's what happened to feudal society. It didn't change when change was required.

The life of individuals living on the land, called *serfs,* was difficult, and feudalism was designed to benefit the lord. Some individuals in feudal society just couldn't take life on the manor, and they set off on their own. Because there was no organized police force, they were unlikely to be caught and forced to return to the manor. Going hungry, being killed, or both, however, were frequent fates of an escaped serf. One place to which serfs could safely escape, though, was a town or city—the remains of what in Roman times had been thriving and active cities. These cities, which had been decimated by plagues, plundering bands, and starvation in the preceding centuries, nevertheless remained an escape hatch for runaway serfs

73

because they relied far less on tradition than did manors. City dwellers had to live by their wits; many became merchants who lived predominantly by trading. They were middlemen; they would buy from one group and sell to another.

Trading in towns was an alternative to the traditional feudal order because trading allowed people to have an income independent of the traditional social structure. Markets broke down tradition. Initially merchants traded using barter (exchange of one kind of good for another): silk and spices from the Orient for wheat, flour, and artisan products in Europe. But soon a generalized purchasing power (money) developed as a medium of exchange. Money greatly expanded the possibilities of trading because its use meant that goods no longer needed to be bartered. They could be sold for money, which could then be spent to buy other goods.

In the beginning, land was not traded, but soon the feudal lord who just had to have a silk robe but had no money was saying, "Why not? I'll sell you a small piece of land so I can buy a shipment of silk." Once land became tradable, the traditional base of the feudal society was undermined. Tradition that can be bought and sold is no longer tradition—it's just another commodity.

From Feudalism to Mercantilism

Toward the end of the Middle Ages (mid-15th century), markets went from being a sideshow, a fair that spiced up people's lives, to being the main event. Over time, some traders and merchants started to amass fortunes that dwarfed those of the feudal lords. Rich traders settled down; existing towns and cities expanded and new towns were formed. As towns grew and as fortunes shifted from feudal lords to merchants, power in society shifted to the towns. And with that shift came a change in society's political and economic structure.

As these traders became stronger politically and economically, they threw their support behind a king (the strongest lord) in the hope that the king would expand their ability to trade. In doing so, they made the king even stronger. Eventually, the king became so powerful that his will prevailed over the will of the other lords and even over the will of the Church. As the king consolidated his power, nation-states as we know them today evolved. *The government became an active influence on economic decision making.*

As markets grew, feudalism evolved into mercantilism. The evolution of feudal systems into mercantilism occurred in the following way: As cities and their markets grew in size and power relative to the feudal manors and the traditional economy, a whole new variety of possible economic activities developed. It was only natural that individuals began to look to a king to establish a new tradition that would determine who would do what. Individuals in particular occupations organized into groups called *guilds,* which were similar to strong labor unions today. These guilds, many of which had financed and supported the king, now expected the king and his government to protect their interests.

As new economic activities, such as trading companies, developed, individuals involved in these activities similarly depended on the king for the right to trade and for help in financing and organizing their activities. For example, in 1492, when Christopher Columbus had the wild idea that by sailing west he could get to the East Indies and trade for their riches, he went to Spain's Queen Isabella and King Ferdinand for financial support.

Since many traders had played and continued to play important roles in financing, establishing, and supporting the king, the king was usually happy to protect their interests. The government doled out the rights to undertake a variety of economic activities. By the late 1400s, Western Europe had evolved from a feudal to a mercantilist economy.

The mercantilist period was marked by the increased role of government, which could be classified in two ways: by the way it encouraged growth and by the way it limited growth. Government legitimized and financed a variety of activities, thus encouraging growth. But government also limited economic activity in order to protect the monopolies of those it favored, thus limiting growth. So mercantilism allowed the market to operate, but it kept the market under its control. The market was not allowed to respond freely to the laws of supply and demand.

From Mercantilism to Capitalism

Mercantilism provided the source for major growth in Western Europe, but mercantilism also unleashed new tensions within society. Like feudalism, mercantilism limited entry into economic activities. It used a different form of limitation—politics rather than social and cultural tradition—but individuals who were excluded still felt unfairly treated.

The most significant source of tension was the different roles played by craft guilds and owners of new businesses, who were called industrialists or capitalists (businesspeople who have acquired large amounts of money and use it to invest in businesses). Craft guild members were artists in their own crafts: pottery, shoemaking, and the like. New business owners destroyed the art of production by devising machines to replace hand production. Machines produced goods cheaper and faster than craftsmen.[1] The result was an increase in supply and a downward pressure on the price, which was set by the government. Craftsmen didn't want to be replaced by machines. They argued that machine-manufactured goods didn't have the same quality as handcrafted goods, and that the new machines would disrupt the economic and social life of the community.

Industrialists were the outsiders with a vested interest in changing the existing system. They wanted the freedom to conduct business as they saw fit. Because of the enormous cost advantage of manufactured goods over crafted goods, a few industrialists overcame government opposition and succeeded within the mercantilist system. They earned their fortunes and became an independent political power.

Once again, the economic power base shifted, and two groups competed with each other for power—this time, the guilds and the industrialists. The government had to decide whether to support the industrialists (who wanted government to loosen its power over the country's economic affairs) or the craftsmen and guilds (who argued for strong government limitations and for maintaining traditional values of workmanship). This struggle raged in the 1700s and 1800s. But during this time, governments themselves were changing. This was the Age of Revolutions, and the kings' powers were being limited by democratic reform movements—revolutions supported and financed in large part by the industrialists.

The Need for Coordination in an Economy

Craftsmen argued that coordination of the economy was necessary, and the government had to be involved. If government wasn't going to coordinate economic activity, who would? To answer that question, a British moral philosopher named Adam Smith developed the concept of the invisible hand, in his famous book *The Wealth of Nations* (1776), and used it to explain how markets could coordinate the economy without the active involvement of government.

As stated in Chapter 2, Smith argued that the market's invisible hand would guide suppliers' actions toward the general good. No government coordination was necessary.

With the help of economists such as Adam Smith, the industrialists' view won out. Government pulled back from its role in guiding the economy and adopted a laissez-faire policy.

The Industrial Revolution

The invisible hand worked; capitalism thrived. Beginning about 1750 and continuing through the late 1800s, machine production increased enormously, almost totally replacing hand production. This phenomenon has been given a name, the Industrial Revolution. The economy grew faster than ever before. Society was forever transformed. New inventions changed all aspects of life. James Watt's steam engine (1769) made manufacturing and travel easier. Eli Whitney's cotton gin (1793) changed the way cotton was processed. James Kay's flying shuttle (1733),[2] James Hargreaves' spinning jenny (1765), and Richard Arkwright's power loom (1769), combined with the steam engine, changed the way cloth was processed and the clothes people wore.

The need to mine vast amounts of coal to provide power to run the machines changed the economic and physical landscapes. The repeating rifle changed the nature of warfare. Modern economic institutions replaced guilds. Stock markets, insurance companies, and corporations all became important. Trading was no longer financed by government; it was privately financed (although government policies, such as colonial policies giving certain companies monopoly trading rights with a country's colonies, helped in that trading). The Industrial Revolution, democracy, and capitalism all arose in the middle and late 1700s. By the 1800s, they were part of the institutional landscape of Western society. Capitalism had arrived.

Welfare Capitalism
From Capitalism to ~~Socialism~~

Capitalism was marked by significant economic growth in the Western world. But it was also marked by human abuses—18-hour workdays; low wages; children as young as five years old slaving long hours in dirty, dangerous factories and mines—to produce enormous wealth for an elite few. Such conditions and inequalities led to criticism of the capitalist or market economic system.

Marx's Analysis

The best-known critic of this system was Karl Marx, a German philosopher, economist, and sociologist who wrote

---

[1]Throughout this section I use *men* to emphasize that these societies were strongly male-dominated. There were almost no businesswomen. In fact, a woman had to turn over her property to a man upon her marriage, and the marriage contract was written as if she were owned by her husband!

[2]The invention of the flying shuttle frustrated the textile industry because it enabled workers to weave so much cloth that the spinners of thread from which the cloth was woven couldn't keep up. This challenge to the textile industry was met by offering a prize to anyone who could invent something to increase the thread spinners' productivity. The prize was won when the spinning jenny was invented.

in the 1800s and who developed an analysis of the dynamics of change in economic systems. Marx argued that economic systems are in a constant state of change, and that capitalism would not last. Workers would revolt, and capitalism would be replaced by a socialist economic system.

Marx saw an economy marked by tensions among economic classes. He saw capitalism as an economic system controlled by the capitalist class (businessmen). His class analysis was that capitalist society is divided into capitalist and worker classes. He said constant tension between these economic classes causes changes in the system. The capitalist class made large profits by exploiting the proletariat class—the working class—and extracting what he called surplus value from workers who, according to Marx's labor theory of value, produced all the value inherent in goods. Surplus value was the additional profit, rent, or interest that, according to Marx's normative views, capitalists added to the price of goods. What standard economic analysis sees as recognizing a need that society has and fulfilling it, Marx saw as exploitation.

Marx argued that this exploitation would increase as production facilities became larger and larger and as competition among capitalists decreased. At some point, he believed, exploitation would lead to a revolt by the proletariat, who would overthrow their capitalist exploiters.

By the late 1800s, some of what Marx predicted had occurred, although not in the way that he thought it would. Production moved from small to large factories. Corporations developed, and classes became more distinct from one another. Workers were significantly differentiated from owners. Small firms merged and were organized into monopolies and trusts (large combinations of firms). The trusts developed ways to prevent competition among themselves and ways to limit entry of new competitors into the market. Marx was right in his predictions about these developments, but he was wrong in his prediction about society's response to them.

The Revolution That Did Not Occur

Western society's response to the problems of capitalism was not a revolt by the workers. Instead, governments stepped in to stop the worst abuses of capitalism. The hard edges of capitalism were softened.

Evolution, not revolution, was capitalism's destiny. The democratic state did not act, as Marx argued it would, as a mere representative of the capitalist class. Competing pressure groups developed; workers gained political power that offset the economic power of businesses.

In the late 1930s and the 1940s, workers dominated the political agenda. During this time, capitalist economies developed an economic safety net that included government-funded programs, such as public welfare and unemployment insurance, and established an extensive set of regulations affecting all aspects of the economy. Today, depressions are met with direct government policy. Antitrust laws, regulatory agencies, and social programs of government softened the hard edges of capitalism. Laws were passed prohibiting child labor, mandating a certain minimum wage, and limiting the hours of work. Capitalism became what is sometimes called welfare capitalism.

Due to these developments, government spending now accounts for about a fifth of all spending in the United States, and for more than half in some European countries. Were an economist from the late 1800s to return from the grave, he'd probably say socialism, not capitalism, exists in Western societies. Most modern-day economists wouldn't go that far, but they would agree that our economy today is better described as a welfare capitalist economy than as a capitalist, or even a market, economy. Because of these changes, the U.S. and Western European economies are a far cry from the competitive "capitalist" economy that Karl Marx criticized. Markets operate, but they are constrained by the government.

The concept *capitalism* developed to denote a market system controlled by one group in society, the capitalists. Looking at Western societies today, we see that domination by one group no longer characterizes Western economies. Although in theory capitalists control corporations through their ownership of shares of stock, in practice corporations are controlled in large part by managers. There remains an elite group who control business, but *capitalist* is not a good term to describe them. Managers, not capitalists, exercise primary control over business, and even their control is limited by laws or the fear of laws being passed by governments.

Governments, in turn, are controlled by a variety of pressure groups. Sometimes one group is in control; at other times, another. Government policies similarly fluctuate. Sometimes they are proworker, sometimes proindustrialist, sometimes progovernment, and sometimes prosociety.

From Feudalism to Socialism

You probably noticed that I crossed out *Socialism* in the previous section's heading and replaced it with *Welfare Capitalism.* That's because capitalism did not evolve to socialism as Karl Marx predicted it would. Instead, Marx's socialist ideas took root in feudalist Russia, a society that the Industrial Revolution had in large part bypassed. Since socialism arrived at a different place and a different time than Marx predicted it would, you shouldn't be surprised to read that socialism arrived in a different way than Marx predicted. The proletariat did not revolt to establish socialism. Instead, World War I, which the Russians were losing, crippled Russia's feudal economy and government. A small group of socialists overthrew the czar (Russia's king) and took over the government in 1917. They quickly pulled Russia out of the war, and then set out to organize a socialist society and economy.

Russian socialists tried to adhere to Marx's ideas, but they found that Marx had concentrated on how capitalist economies operate, not on how a socialist economy should be run. Thus, Russian socialists faced a huge task with little guidance. Their most immediate problem was how to increase production so that the economy could emerge from feudalism into the modern industrial world. In Marx's analysis, capitalism was a necessary stage in the evolution toward the ideal state for a very practical reason. The capitalists exploit the workers, but in doing so capitalists extract the necessary surplus—an amount of production in excess of what is consumed. That surplus had to be extracted in order to provide the factories and machinery upon which a socialist economic system would be built. But since capitalism did not exist in Russia, a true socialist state could not be established immediately. Instead, the socialists created *state socialism*—an economic system in which government sees to it that people work for the common good until they can be relied upon to do that on their own.

Socialists saw state socialism as a transition stage to pure socialism. This transition stage still exploited the workers; when Joseph Stalin took power in Russia in the late 1920s, he took the peasants' and small farmers' land and turned it into collective farms. The government then paid farmers low prices for their produce. When farmers balked at the low prices, millions of them were killed.

Simultaneously, Stalin created central planning agencies that directed individuals on what to produce and how to produce it, and determined for whom things would be produced. During this period, *socialism* became synonymous with *central economic planning,* and Soviet-style socialism became the model of socialism in practice.

Also during this time, Russia took control of a number of neighboring states and established the Union of Soviet Socialist Republics (USSR), the formal name of the Soviet Union. The Soviet Union also installed Soviet-dominated governments in a number of Eastern European countries. In 1949 most of China, under the rule of Mao Zedong, adopted Soviet-style socialist principles.

Since the late 1980s, the Soviet socialist economic and political structure has fallen apart. The Soviet Union as a political state broke up, and its former republics became autonomous. Eastern European countries were released from Soviet control. Now they faced a new problem: transition from socialism to a market economy. Why did the Soviet socialist economy fall apart? Because workers lacked incentives to work; production was inefficient; consumer goods were either unavailable or of poor quality; and high Soviet officials were exploiting their positions, keeping the best jobs for themselves and moving themselves up in the waiting lists for consumer goods. In short, the parents of the socialist family (the Communist Party) were no longer acting benevolently; they were taking many of the benefits for themselves.

These political and economic upheavals in Eastern Europe and the former Soviet Union suggest the kind of socialism these societies tried did not work. However, that failure does not mean that socialist goals are bad; nor does it mean that no type of socialism can ever work. The point is that all systems have problems, and it is likely that the political winds of change will lead to new forms of economic organization being tried as the problems of the existing system lead to political demands for change. Venezuela's recent attempt to establish a new form of socialism is an example. Given past experience with socialist systems, however, most economists believe that any future workable "new socialist" system will include important elements of market institutions.

Supply and Demand

> Teach a parrot the terms *supply* and *demand* and you've got an economist.
>
> —Thomas Carlyle

©Neil Roy Johnson/Shutterstock

Supply and demand. Supply and demand. Roll the phrase around in your mouth; savor it like a good wine. *Supply* and *demand* are the most-used words in economics. And for good reason. They provide a good off-the-cuff answer for any economic question. Try it.

Why are bacon and oranges so expensive this winter? *Supply and demand.*

Why are interest rates falling? *Supply and demand.*

Why can't I find decent wool socks anymore? *Supply and demand.*

The importance of the interplay of supply and demand makes it only natural that, early in any economics course, you must learn about supply and demand. Let's start with demand.

Demand

People want lots of things; they "demand" much less than they want because demand means a willingness and ability to pay. Unless you are willing and able to pay for it, you may *want* it, but you don't *demand* it. For example, I want to own a Ferrari. But, I must admit, I'm not willing to do what's necessary to own one. If I really wanted one, I'd mortgage everything I own, increase my income by doubling the number of hours I work, not buy anything else, and get that car. But I don't do any of those things, so at the going price, $650,000, I do not demand a Ferrari. Sure, I'd buy one if it cost $30,000, but from my actions it's clear that, at $650,000, I don't demand it. This points to an important aspect of demand: The quantity you demand at a low price differs from the quantity you demand at a high price. Specifically, the quantity you demand varies inversely—in the opposite direction—with price.

Prices are the tool by which the market coordinates individuals' desires and limits how much people demand. When goods become scarce, the market reduces the quantity people demand; as their prices go up, people buy fewer goods. As goods become abundant, their prices go down, and people buy more of them. The invisible hand—the price mechanism—sees to it that what people demand (do what's necessary to get) matches what's available.

The Law of Demand

The ideas expressed above are the foundation of the **law of demand:**

> *Quantity demanded rises as price falls, other things constant.*

Or alternatively:

> *Quantity demanded falls as price rises, other things constant.*

This law is fundamental to the invisible hand's ability to coordinate individuals' desires; as prices change, people change how much they're willing to buy.

What accounts for the law of demand? If the price of something goes up, people will tend to buy less of it and buy something else instead. They will *substitute* other goods for goods whose relative price has gone up. If the price of Netflix falls but the price of more cable channels stays the same, you're likely to drop some cable channels and subscribe to Netflix.

To see that the law of demand makes intuitive sense, just think of something you'd really like but can't afford. If the price is cut in half, you—and other consumers—become more likely to buy it. Quantity demanded goes up as price goes down.

Just to be sure you've got it, let's consider a real-world example: demand for vanity—specifically, vanity license plates. When the North Carolina state legislature increased the vanity plates' price from $30 to $40, the quantity demanded fell from 60,334 to 31,122. Assuming other things remained constant, that is the law of demand in action.

The Demand Curve

A **demand curve** is *the graphic representation of the relationship between price and quantity demanded.* Figure 4-1 shows a demand curve.

The law of demand states that the quantity of a good demanded is inversely related to the good's price.

Web Note 4.1

Markets without Money

When price goes up, quantity demanded goes down. When price goes down, quantity demanded goes up.

Q-1 Why does the demand curve slope downward?

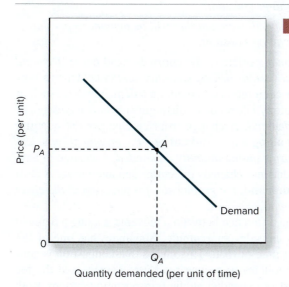

FIGURE 4-1 A Sample Demand Curve

The law of demand states that the quantity demanded of a good is inversely related to the price of that good, other things constant. As the price of a good goes up, the quantity demanded goes down, so the demand curve is downward-sloping.

As you can see, the demand curve slopes downward. That's because of the law of demand: As the price goes up, the quantity demanded goes down, other things constant. In other words, price and quantity demanded are inversely related.

Notice that in stating the law of demand, I put in the qualification "other things constant." That's three extra words, and unless they were important I wouldn't have included them. But what does "other things constant" mean? Say that over two years, both the price of cars and the number of cars purchased rise. That seems to violate the law of demand, since the number of cars purchased should have fallen in response to the rise in price. Looking at the data more closely, however, we see that individuals' income has also increased. Other things didn't remain the same.

The increase in price works as the law of demand states—it decreases the number of cars bought. But the rise in income increases the quantity demanded at every price. That increase in demand outweighs the decrease in quantity demanded that results from a rise in price, so ultimately more cars are sold. If you want to study the effect of price alone—which is what the law of demand refers to—you must make adjustments to hold income constant. Because other things besides price affect demand, the qualifying phrase "other things constant" is an important part of the law of demand.

The other things that are held constant include individuals' tastes, prices of other goods, and even the weather. Those other factors must remain constant if you're to make a valid study of the effect of an increase in the price of a good on the quantity demanded. In practice, it's impossible to keep all other things constant, so you have to be careful when you say that when price goes up, quantity demanded goes down. It's likely to go down, but it's always possible that something besides price has changed.

Shifts in Demand versus Movements along a Demand Curve

To distinguish between the effects of price and the effects of other factors on how much of a good is demanded, economists have developed the following precise terminology—terminology that inevitably shows up on exams. The first distinction is between demand and quantity demanded.

> **Demand** refers to *a schedule of quantities of a good that will be bought per unit of time at various prices, other things constant.*

> **Quantity demanded** refers to *a specific amount that will be demanded per unit of time at a specific price, other things constant.*

In graphical terms, the term *demand* refers to the entire demand curve. *Demand* tells us how much will be bought *at various prices*. *Quantity demanded* tells us how much will be bought at a specific price; it refers to a point on a demand curve, such as point *A* in Figure 4-1. This terminology allows us to distinguish between *changes in quantity demanded* and *shifts in demand*. A change in price changes the quantity demanded. It refers to a **movement along a demand curve**—*the graphical representation of the effect of a change in price on the quantity demanded.* A change in anything other than price that affects demand changes the entire demand curve. A shift factor of demand causes a **shift in demand,** *the graphical representation of the effect of anything other than price on demand.*

To make sure you understand the difference between a movement along a demand curve and a shift in demand, let's consider an example. Singapore has one of the world's highest numbers of cars per mile of road. This means that congestion is considerable. Singapore adopted two policies to reduce road use: It increased the fee charged to use roads and it provided an expanded public transportation system. Both

---

"Other things constant" places a limitation on the application of the law of demand.

Q-2 The uncertainty caused by terrorist attacks makes consumers reluctant to spend on luxury items. This reduces _____. Should the missing words be *demand for luxury goods* or *quantity of luxury goods demanded*?

Change in price causes a movement along a demand curve; a change in a shift factor causes a shift in demand.

FIGURE 4-2 (A AND B)   **Shift in Demand versus a Change in Quantity Demanded**

A rise in a good's price results in a reduction in quantity demanded and is shown by a movement up along a demand curve from point *A* to point *B* in (**a**). A change in any other factor besides price that affects demand leads to a shift in the entire demand curve, as shown in (**b**).

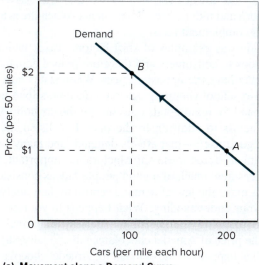

(a) Movement along a Demand Curve

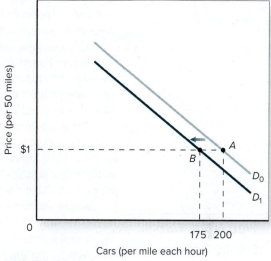

(b) Shift in Demand

policies reduced congestion. Figure 4-2(a) shows that increasing the toll charged to use roads from $1 to $2 per 50 miles of road reduces quantity demanded from 200 to 100 cars per mile every hour (a movement along the demand curve). Figure 4-2(b) shows that providing alternative methods of transportation such as buses and subways shifts the demand curve for roads in to the left so that at every price, demand drops by 25 cars per mile every hour.

Some Shift Factors of Demand

Important shift factors of demand include:

1. Society's income.
2. The prices of other goods.
3. Tastes.
4. Expectations.
5. Taxes and subsidies.

Web Note 4.2

Influencing Demand

Let's consider a couple of them. First, income. From our example above of the "other things constant" qualification, we saw that a rise in income increases the demand for goods. For most goods this is true. As individuals' income rises, they can afford more of the goods they want, such as steaks, computers, or clothing. These are normal goods. For other goods, called inferior goods, an increase in income reduces demand. An example is urban mass transit. A person whose income has risen tends to stop riding the bus to work because she can afford to buy a car and rent a parking space.

Next, let's consider the price of other goods. Because people make their buying decisions based on the price of related goods, demand will be affected by the prices of other goods. Suppose the price of jeans rises from $25 to $35, but the price of khakis

Q-3 Explain the effect of each of
the following on the demand for new
computers:

1. The price of computers falls by
    30 percent.

2. Total income in the economy rises.

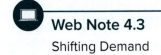

Web Note 4.3

Shifting Demand

remains at $25. Next time you need pants, you're apt to try khakis instead of jeans. They are substitutes. When the price of a substitute rises, demand for the good whose price has remained the same will rise. Or consider another example. Suppose the price of movie tickets falls. What will happen to the demand for popcorn? You're likely to increase the number of times you go to the movies, so you'll also likely increase the amount of popcorn you purchase. The lower cost of a movie ticket increases the demand for popcorn because popcorn and movies are complements. When the price of a good declines, the demand for its complement rises.

Let's consider taxes and subsidies as examples of shift factors. Taxes levied on consumers increase the cost of goods to consumers and therefore reduce demand for those goods. Subsidies to consumers have the opposite effect. When states host tax-free weeks during August's back-to-school shopping season, consumers load up on products to avoid sales taxes. Demand for retail goods rises during the tax holiday.

There are many other shift factors in addition to the ones I've listed. In fact anything—except the price of the good itself—that affects demand (and many things do) is a shift factor. While economists agree these shift factors are important, they believe that no shift factor influences how much of a good people buy as consistently as its price. That's why economists make the law of demand central to their analysis.

Before we move on let's test your understanding: What happens to your demand curve for Amedei chocolates in the following examples: First, let's say Valentine's Day is coming up. Next, let's say that the price of Amedei chocolates falls. Finally, say that you won $1 million in a lottery. What happens to the demand for Amedei chocolates in each case? If you answered: It shifts out to the right; it remains unchanged; and it shifts out to the right—you've got it.

The Demand Table

As I emphasized in Chapter 2, introductory economics depends heavily on graphs and graphical analysis—translating ideas into graphs and back into words. So let's graph the demand curve.

Figure 4-3(a), a demand table, describes Alice's demand for Amazon Prime movies. For example, at a price of $4, Alice will rent (buy the use of) six movies per week, and at a price of $1 she will rent nine.

Four points about the relationship between the number of movies Alice rents and the price of renting them are worth mentioning. First, the relationship follows the law of demand: As the rental price rises, quantity demanded decreases. Second, quantity demanded has a specific *time dimension* to it. In this example, demand refers to the number of movie rentals per week. Without the time dimension, the table wouldn't provide us with any useful information. Nine movie rentals per year is quite different from nine movie rentals per week. Third, the analysis assumes that Alice's movie rentals are interchangeable—the ninth movie rental doesn't significantly differ from the first, third, or any other movie rental. The fourth point is already familiar to you: The analysis assumes that everything else is held constant.

From a Demand Table to a Demand Curve

Figure 4-3(b) translates the demand table in Figure 4-3(a) into a demand curve. Point *A* (quantity = 9, price = $1.00) is graphed first at the (9, $1.00) coordinates. Next we plot points *B, C, D,* and *E* in the same manner and connect the resulting dots with a solid line. The result is the demand curve, which graphically conveys the same information that's in the demand table. Notice that the demand curve is downward-sloping, indicating that the law of demand holds.

FIGURE 4-3 (A AND B) **From a Demand Table to a Demand Curve**

The demand table in (a) is translated into a demand curve in (b). Each combination of price and quantity in the table corresponds to a point on the curve. For example, point A on the graph represents row A in the table: Alice demands nine movie rentals at a price of $1. A demand curve is constructed by plotting all points from the demand table and connecting the points with a line.

	Price (per movie)	Movie Rentals Demanded (per week)
A	$1.00	9
B	2.00	8
C	4.00	6
D	6.00	4
E	8.00	2

(a) A Demand Table

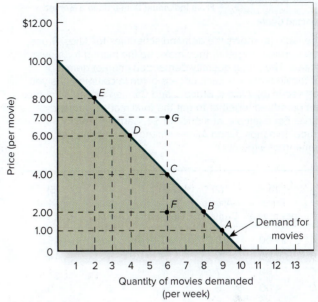

(b) A Demand Curve

The demand curve represents the *maximum price* that an individual will pay for various quantities of a good; the individual will happily pay less. For example, say Amazon Prime offers Alice six movie rentals at a price of $2 each [point F of Figure 4-3(b)]. Will she accept? Sure; she'll pay any price within the shaded area to the left of the demand curve. But if Amazon Prime offers her six rentals at $7 each (point G), she won't accept. At a price of $7 apiece, she's willing to rent only three movies.

> The demand curve represents the maximum price that an individual will pay.

Individual and Market Demand Curves

Normally, economists talk about market demand curves rather than individual demand curves. A **market demand curve** is *the horizontal sum of all individual demand curves*. Firms don't care whether individual A or individual B buys their goods; they only care that *someone* buys their goods.

Adding individual demand curves together to create a market demand curve is a good graphical exercise. I do that in Figure 4-4. In it I assume that the market consists of three buyers, Alice, Bruce, and Carmen, whose demand tables are given in Figure 4-4(a). Alice and Bruce have demand tables similar to the demand tables discussed previously. At a price of $6 each, Alice rents four movies; at a price of $4, she rents six. Carmen is an all-or-nothing individual. She rents one movie as long as the price is equal to or less than $2; otherwise she rents nothing. If you plot Carmen's demand curve, it's a vertical line. However, the law of demand still holds: As price increases, quantity demanded decreases.

The quantity demanded by each consumer is listed in columns 2, 3, and 4 of Figure 4-4(a). Column 5 shows total market demand; each entry is the horizontal sum of the entries in columns 2, 3, and 4. For example, at a price of $6 apiece (row F), Alice demands four movie rentals, Bruce demands one, and Carmen demands zero, for a total market demand of five movie rentals.

> **Q-4** Derive a market demand curve from the following two individual demand curves:

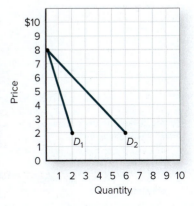

FIGURE 4-4 (A AND B) From Individual Demands to a Market Demand Curve

The table **(a)** shows the demand schedules for Alice, Bruce, and Carmen. Together they make up the market for movie rentals. Their total quantity demanded (market demand) for movie rentals at each price is given in column 5. As you can see in **(b)**, Alice's, Bruce's, and Carmen's demand curves can be added together to get the total market demand curve. For example, at a price of $4, Carmen demands 0, Bruce demands 3, and Alice demands 6, for a market demand of 9 (point *D*).

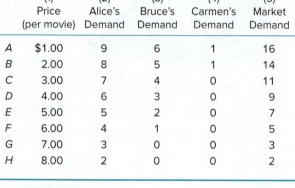

	(1) Price (per movie)	(2) Alice's Demand	(3) Bruce's Demand	(4) Carmen's Demand	(5) Market Demand
A	$1.00	9	6	1	16
B	2.00	8	5	1	14
C	3.00	7	4	0	11
D	4.00	6	3	0	9
E	5.00	5	2	0	7
F	6.00	4	1	0	5
G	7.00	3	0	0	3
H	8.00	2	0	0	2

(a) A Demand Table

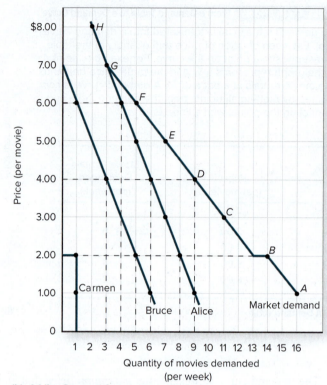

(b) Adding Demand Curves

Figure 4-4(b) shows three demand curves: one each for Alice, Bruce, and Carmen. The market, or total, demand curve is the horizontal sum of the individual demand curves. To see that this is the case, notice that if we take the quantity demanded at $2 by Alice (8), Bruce (5), and Carmen (1), they sum to 14, which is point *B* (14, $2) on the market demand curve. We can do that for each price. Alternatively, we can simply add the individual quantities demanded, given in the demand tables, prior to graphing [which we do in column 5 of Figure 4-4(a)], and graph that total in relation to price. Not surprisingly, we get the same total market demand curve.

In practice, of course, firms don't measure individual demand curves, so they don't sum them up in this fashion. Instead, they statistically estimate market demand. Still, summing up individual demand curves is a useful exercise because it shows you how the market demand curve is the sum (the horizontal sum, graphically speaking) of the individual demand curves, and it gives you a good sense of where market demand curves come from. It also shows you that, even if individuals don't respond to small changes in price, the market demand curve can still be smooth and downward-sloping. That's because, for the market, the law of demand is based on two phenomena:

1. At lower prices, existing demanders buy more.

2. At lower prices, new demanders (some all-or-nothing demanders like Carmen) enter the market.

For the market, the law of demand is based on two phenomena:

1. At lower prices, existing demanders buy more.

2. At lower prices, new demanders enter the market.

Supply

In one sense, supply is the mirror image of demand. Individuals control the factors of production—inputs, or resources, necessary to produce goods. Individuals' supply of these factors to the market mirrors other individuals' demand for those factors. For example, say you decide you want to rest rather than weed your garden. You hire someone to do the weeding; you demand labor. Someone else decides she would prefer more income instead of more rest; she supplies labor to you. You trade money for labor; she trades labor for money. Her supply is the mirror image of your demand.

For a large number of goods and services, however, the supply process is more complicated than demand. For many goods there's an intermediate step: Individuals supply factors of production to firms.

Let's consider a simple example. Say you're a taco technician. You supply your labor to the factor market. The taco company demands your labor (hires you). The taco company combines your labor with other inputs such as meat, cheese, beans, and tables, and produces tacos (production), which it supplies to customers in the goods market. For produced goods, supply depends not only on individuals' decisions to supply factors of production but also on firms' ability to transform those factors of production into usable goods.

The supply process of produced goods is generally complicated. Often there are many layers of firms—production firms, wholesale firms, distribution firms, and retailing firms—each of which passes on in-process goods to the next layer of firms. Real-world production and supply of produced goods is a multistage process.

The supply of nonproduced goods is more direct. Individuals supply their labor in the form of services directly to the goods market. For example, an independent contractor may repair your washing machine. That contractor supplies his labor directly to you.

Thus, the analysis of the supply of produced goods has two parts: an analysis of the supply of factors of production to households and to firms and an analysis of the process by which firms transform those factors of production into usable goods and services.

Supply of produced goods involves a much more complicated process than demand and is divided into analysis of factors of production and the transformation of those factors into goods.

The Law of Supply

There's a law of supply that corresponds to the law of demand. The **law of supply** states:

Quantity supplied rises as price rises, other things constant.

Or alternatively:

Quantity supplied falls as price falls, other things constant.

Price determines quantity supplied just as it determines quantity demanded. Like the law of demand, the law of supply is fundamental to the invisible hand's (the market's) ability to coordinate individuals' actions.

The law of supply is based on a firm's ability to switch from producing one good to another, that is, to substitute. When the price of a good a person or firm supplies rises, individuals and firms can rearrange their activities in order to supply more of

The law of supply is based on substitution and the expectation of profits.

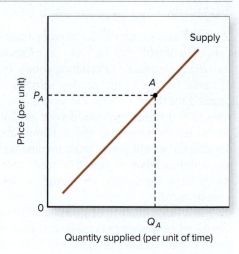

FIGURE 4-5 **A Sample Supply Curve**

The supply curve demonstrates graphically the law of supply, which states that the quantity supplied of a good is directly related to that good's price, other things constant. As the price of a good goes up, the quantity supplied also goes up, so the supply curve is upward-sloping.

that good to the market. They want to supply more because the opportunity cost of *not* supplying the good rises as its price rises. For example, if the price of corn rises and the price of soybeans has not changed, farmers will grow less soybeans and more corn, other things constant.

With firms, there's a second explanation of the law of supply. Assuming firms' costs are constant, a higher price means higher profits (the difference between a firm's revenues and its costs). The expectation of those higher profits leads it to increase output as price rises, which is what the law of supply states.

The Supply Curve

A **supply curve** is *the graphical representation of the relationship between price and quantity supplied.* A supply curve is shown in Figure 4-5.

The supply curve represents the set of *minimum* prices an individual seller will accept for various quantities of a good. The market's invisible hand stops suppliers from charging more than the market price. If suppliers could escape the market's invisible hand and charge a higher price, they would gladly do so. Unfortunately for them, and fortunately for consumers, a higher price encourages other suppliers to begin selling movies. Competing suppliers' entry into the market sets a limit on the price any supplier can charge.

Notice how the supply curve slopes upward to the right. That upward slope captures the law of supply. It tells us that the quantity supplied varies *directly*—in the same direction—with the price.

As with the law of demand, the law of supply assumes other things are held constant. If the price of soybeans rises and quantity supplied falls, you'll look for something else that changed—for example, a drought might have caused a drop in supply. Your explanation would go as follows: Had there been no drought, the quantity supplied would have increased in response to the rise in price, but because there was a drought, the supply decreased, which caused price to rise.

As with the law of demand, the law of supply represents economists' off-the-cuff response to the question "What happens to quantity supplied if price rises?" If the law seems to be violated, economists search for some other variable that has changed. As was the case with demand, these other variables that might change are called shift factors.

Shifts in Supply versus Movements along a Supply Curve

The same distinctions in terms made for demand apply to supply.

> **Supply** refers to *a schedule of quantities a seller is willing to sell per unit of time at various prices, other things constant.*

> **Quantity supplied** refers to *a specific amount that will be supplied at a specific price.*

In graphical terms, supply refers to the entire supply curve because a supply curve tells us how much will be offered for sale at various prices. "Quantity supplied" refers to a point on a supply curve, such as point *A* in Figure 4-5.

The second distinction that is important to make is between the effects of a change in price and the effects of shift factors on how much is supplied. Changes in price cause changes in quantity supplied; such changes are represented by a **movement along a supply curve**—*the graphical representation of the effect of a change in price on the quantity supplied.* If the amount supplied is affected by anything other than price, that is, by a shift factor of supply, there will be a **shift in supply**—*the graphical representation of the effect of a change in a factor other than price on supply.*

To make that distinction clear, let's consider an example: the supply of gasoline. In August 2017, Hurricane Harvey hit the Gulf Coast region of the United States and disrupted gasoline refinery production in the United States. U.S. production of gasoline at refineries in the Gulf Coast fell by about 30 percent. This disruption reduced the amount of gasoline U.S. producers were offering for sale *at every price,* thereby shifting the supply of U.S. gasoline to the left from S_0 to S_1, and the quantity of gasoline that would be supplied at the \$2.35 price fell from point *A* to point *B* in Figure 4-6. But the price did not stay at \$2.35. It rose to \$2.55. In response to the higher price, other areas in the United States increased their quantity supplied (from point *B* to point *C* in Figure 4-6). That increase *due to the higher price* is called a movement along the supply curve. So if a change in quantity supplied occurs because of a higher price, it is called a *movement along the supply curve;* if a change in supply occurs because of one of the shift factors (i.e., for any reason other than a change in price), it is called a *shift in supply.*

Q-5 Assume that the price of gasoline rises, causing the demand for hybrid cars to rise. As a result, the price of hybrid cars rises. This makes _____ rise. Should the missing words be *the supply* or *the quantity supplied*?

A change in price causes a movement along a supply curve; a change in a shift factor causes a shift in supply.

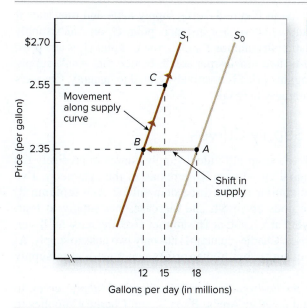

12 15   18
Gallons per day (in millions)

FIGURE 4-6 Shifts in Supply versus Movement along a Supply Curve

A *shift in supply* results when the shift is due to any cause other than a change in price. It is a shift in the entire supply curve (see the arrow from *A* to *B*). A *movement along a supply curve* is due to a change in price only (see the arrow from *B* to *C*). To differentiate the two, movements caused by changes in price are called *changes in the quantity supplied,* not changes in supply.

Shift Factors of Supply

Shift factors of supply are similar to those for demand. Examples include:

1. Price of inputs.
2. Technology.
3. Expectations.
4. Taxes and subsidies.

Other factors besides price that affect how much will be supplied include the price of inputs used in production, technology, expectations, and taxes and subsidies. The analysis of how these affect supply parallels the analysis of the law of demand, so we will only consider technology, leaving the analysis of other shift factors to you.

Advances in technology change the production process, reducing the number of inputs needed to produce a good, and thereby reducing its cost of production. A reduction in the cost of production increases profits and leads suppliers to increase production. Advances in technology increase supply.

Remember, as was the case with demand, a shift factor of supply is anything other than its price that affects supply. It shifts the entire supply curve. A change in price causes a movement along the supply curve.

Q-6 Explain the effect of each of the following on the supply of romance novels:

1. The price of paper rises by 20 percent.
2. Government provides a 10 percent subsidy to book producers.

To be sure you understand shifts in supply, explain what is likely to happen to your supply curve for labor in the following cases: (1) You suddenly decide that you absolutely need a new car. (2) You win a million dollars in the lottery. And finally, (3) the wage you earn doubles. If you came up with the answers: Shift out to the right, shift in to the left, and no change—you've got it down. If not, it's time for a review.

Do we see such shifts in the supply curve often? Yes. A good example is computers. For the past 30 years, technological changes have continually shifted the supply curve for computers out to the right.

The Supply Table

Remember Figure 4-4(a)'s demand table for movie rentals? In Figure 4-7(a), we follow the same reasoning to construct a supply table for three hypothetical movie suppliers. Each supplier follows the law of supply: When price rises, each supplies more, or at least as much as each did at a lower price.

From a Supply Table to a Supply Curve

Figure 4-7(b) takes the information in Figure 4-7(a)'s supply table and translates it into a graph of each supplier's supply curve. For instance, point C_A on Ann's supply curve corresponds to the information in columns 1 and 2, row C. Point C_A is at a price of $2 per movie and a quantity of two movies per week. Notice that Ann's supply curve is upward-sloping, meaning that price is positively related to quantity. Charlie's and Barry's supply curves are similarly derived.

Individual and Market Supply Curves

The market supply curve is derived from individual supply curves in precisely the same way that the market demand curve was. To emphasize the symmetry, I've made the three suppliers quite similar to the three demanders. Ann (column 2) will supply two at $2; if price goes up to $4, she increases her supply to four. Barry (column 3) begins supplying at $2, and at $6 supplies five, the most he'll supply regardless of how high price rises. Charlie (column 4) has only two units to supply. At a price of $7 he'll supply that quantity, but higher prices won't get him to supply any more.

The **market supply curve** is *the horizontal sum of all individual supply curves.* In Figure 4-7(a) (column 5), we add together Ann's, Barry's, and Charlie's supplies to

FIGURE 4-7 (A AND B) From Individual Supplies to a Market Supply

As with market demand, market supply is determined by adding all quantities supplied at a given price. Three suppliers—Ann, Barry, and Charlie—make up the market of movie suppliers. The total market supply is the sum of their individual supplies at each price, shown in column 5 of **(a)**.

Each of the individual supply curves and the market supply curve have been plotted in **(b)**. Notice how the market supply curve is the horizontal sum of the individual supply curves.

Quantities Supplied	(1) Price (per movie)	(2) Ann's Supply	(3) Barry's Supply	(4) Charlie's Supply	(5) Market Supply
A	$0.00	0	0	0	0
B	1.00	1	0	0	1
C	2.00	2	1	0	3
D	3.00	3	2	0	5
E	4.00	4	3	0	7
F	5.00	5	4	0	9
G	6.00	6	5	0	11
H	7.00	7	5	2	14
I	8.00	8	5	2	15

(a) A Supply Table

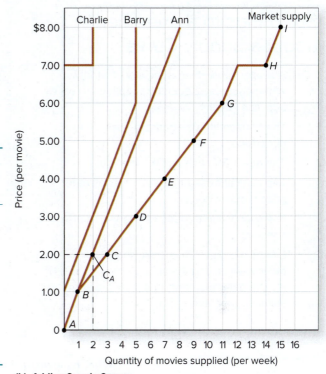

(b) Adding Supply Curves

arrive at the market supply curve, which is graphed in Figure 4-7(b). Notice that each point corresponds to the information in columns 1 and 5 for each row. For example, point *H* corresponds to a price of $7 and a quantity of 14.

The market supply curve's upward slope is determined by two different sources: As price rises, existing suppliers supply more and new suppliers enter the market. Sometimes existing suppliers may not be willing to increase their quantity supplied in response to an increase in prices, but a rise in price often brings brand-new suppliers into the market. For example, a rise in teachers' salaries will have little effect on the number of hours current teachers teach, but it will increase the number of people choosing to be teachers.

The law of supply is based on two phenomena:

1. At higher prices, existing suppliers supply more.
2. At higher prices, new suppliers enter the market.

The Interaction of Supply and Demand

Thomas Carlyle, the English historian who dubbed economics "the dismal science," also wrote this chapter's introductory tidbit. "Teach a parrot the terms *supply* and *demand* and you've got an economist." In earlier chapters, I tried to convince you that economics is *not* dismal. In the rest of this chapter, I hope to convince you that, while supply and demand are important to economics, parrots don't make good economists. If students think that when they've learned the terms *supply* and *demand* they've learned economics, they're mistaken. Those terms are just labels for the ideas behind supply and demand, and it's the ideas that are important. What matters about supply and demand isn't the labels but how the concepts interact. For instance, what happens if a freeze kills the blossoms on the orange trees? If price doesn't change, the quantity of oranges supplied isn't expected to equal the quantity demanded. But in the real

If students think that when they've learned the terms *supply* and *demand* they've learned economics, they're mistaken.

Six Things to Remember about a Supply Curve

- A supply curve follows the law of supply. When price rises, quantity supplied increases, and vice versa.
- The horizontal axis—quantity—has a time dimension.
- The quality of each unit is the same.
- The vertical axis—price—assumes all other prices remain constant.
- The supply curve assumes everything else is constant.
- Effects of price changes are shown by movements along the supply curve. Effects of nonprice determinants of supply are shown by shifts of the entire supply curve.

world, prices do change, often before the frost hits, as expectations of the frost lead people to adjust. It's in understanding the interaction of supply and demand that economics becomes interesting and relevant.

Equilibrium

When you have a market in which neither suppliers nor consumers collude and in which prices are free to move up and down, the forces of supply and demand interact to arrive at an equilibrium. The concept of equilibrium comes from physics—classical mechanics. **Equilibrium** is *a concept in which opposing dynamic forces cancel each other out.* For example, a hot-air balloon is in equilibrium when the upward force exerted by the hot air in the balloon equals the downward pressure exerted on the balloon by gravity. In supply/demand analysis, equilibrium means that the upward pressure on price is exactly offset by the downward pressure on price. **Equilibrium quantity** is *the amount bought and sold at the equilibrium price.* **Equilibrium price** is *the price toward which the invisible hand drives the market.* At the equilibrium price, quantity demanded equals quantity supplied.

What happens if the market is not in equilibrium—if quantity supplied doesn't equal quantity demanded? You get either excess supply or excess demand, and a tendency for prices to change.

Bargain hunters can get a deal when there is excess supply.

EXCESS SUPPLY   If there is **excess supply** (a surplus), *quantity supplied is greater than quantity demanded,* and some suppliers won't be able to sell all their goods. Each supplier will think: "Gee, if I offer to sell it for a bit less, I'll be the lucky one who sells my goods; someone else will be stuck with goods they can't sell." But because all suppliers with excess goods will be thinking the same thing, the price in the market will fall. As that happens, consumers will increase their quantity demanded. So the movement toward equilibrium caused by excess supply is on both the supply and demand sides.

EXCESS DEMAND   The reverse is also true. Say that instead of excess supply, there's **excess demand** (a shortage)—*quantity demanded is greater than quantity supplied.* There are more consumers who want the good than there are suppliers selling the good. Let's consider what's likely to go through demanders' minds. They'll likely call long-lost friends who just happen to be sellers of that good and tell them it's good to talk to them and, by the way, don't they want to sell that . . . ? Suppliers will be rather pleased that so many of their old friends have remembered them, but they'll also likely see the connection between excess demand and their friends' thoughtfulness. To stop their phones from ringing all the time, they'll likely raise their price. The reverse is true for excess supply. It's amazing how friendly suppliers become to potential consumers when there's excess supply.

PRICE ADJUSTS   This tendency for prices to rise when the quantity demanded exceeds the quantity supplied and for prices to fall when the quantity supplied exceeds the quantity demanded is a central element to understanding supply and demand. So remember:

> *When quantity demanded is greater than quantity supplied, prices tend to rise.*
>
> *When quantity supplied is greater than quantity demanded, prices tend to fall.*

Two other things to note about supply and demand are (1) the greater the difference between quantity supplied and quantity demanded, the more pressure there is for prices to rise or fall, and (2) when quantity demanded equals quantity supplied, the market is in equilibrium.

People's tendencies to change prices exist as long as quantity supplied and quantity demanded differ. But the change in price brings the laws of supply and demand into play. As price falls, quantity supplied decreases as some suppliers leave the business (the law of supply). And as some people who originally weren't really interested in buying the good think, "Well, at this low price, maybe I do want to buy," quantity demanded increases (the law of demand). Similarly, when price rises, quantity supplied will increase (the law of supply) and quantity demanded will decrease (the law of demand).

Whenever quantity supplied and quantity demanded are unequal, price tends to change. If, however, quantity supplied and quantity demanded are equal, price will stay the same because no one will have an incentive to change.

Prices tend to rise when there is excess demand and fall when there is excess supply.

When quantity demanded exceeds quantity supplied, a line may form.

©Ned Snowman/Shutterstock

The Graphical Interaction of Supply and Demand

Figure 4-8 shows supply and demand curves for movie rentals and demonstrates the force of the invisible hand. Let's consider what will happen to the price of movies in three cases:

1. When the price is $7 each.
2. When the price is $3 each.
3. When the price is $5 each.

1. When price is $7, quantity supplied is seven and quantity demanded is only three. Excess supply is four. Individual consumers can get all they want, but most suppliers can't sell all they wish; they'll be stuck with movies that they'd like to rent. Suppliers will tend to offer their goods at a lower price and demanders, who see plenty of suppliers out there, will bargain harder for an even lower price. Both these forces will push the price as indicated by the down arrows in Figure 4-8.

Now let's start from the other side.

2. Say price is $3. The situation is now reversed. Quantity supplied is three and quantity demanded is seven. Excess demand is four. Now it's consumers who can't get what they want and suppliers who are in the strong bargaining position. The pressures will be on price to rise in the direction of the up arrows in Figure 4-8.

3. At $5, price is at its equilibrium: Quantity supplied equals quantity demanded. Suppliers offer to sell five and consumers want to buy five, so there's no pressure on price to rise or fall. Price will tend to remain where it is (point *E* in Figure 4-8). Notice that the equilibrium price is where the supply and demand curves intersect.

What Equilibrium Isn't

It is important to remember two points about equilibrium. First, equilibrium isn't a state of the world. It's a characteristic of the model—the framework you use to look at the world. The same situation could be seen as an equilibrium in one framework and as

Equilibrium isn't a state of the world. It's a characteristic of the model.

The Interaction of Supply and Demand

Combining Ann's supply from Figure 4-7 and Alice's demand from Figure 4-4, let's see the force of the invisible hand. When there is excess demand, there is upward pressure on price. When there is excess supply, there is downward pressure on price. Understanding these pressures is essential to understanding how to apply economics to reality.

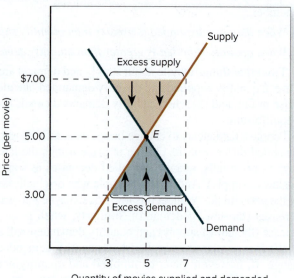

Price (per movie)	Quantity Supplied	Quantity Demanded	Surplus (+)/ Shortage (−)
$7.00	7	3	+4
5.00	5	5	0
3.00	3	7	−4

a disequilibrium in another. Say you're describing a car that's speeding along at 100 miles an hour. That car is changing position relative to objects on the ground. Its movement could be, and generally is, described as if it were in disequilibrium. However, if you consider this car relative to another car going 100 miles an hour, the cars could be modeled as being in equilibrium because their positions relative to each other aren't changing.

Second, equilibrium isn't inherently good or bad. It's simply a state in which dynamic pressures offset each other. Some equilibria are good—a market in competitive equilibrium is one in which people can buy the goods they really want at the best possible price. Other equilibria are awful. Say two countries are engaged in a nuclear war against each other and both sides are blown away. An equilibrium will have been reached, but there's nothing good about it.

Equilibrium is not inherently good or bad.

Political and Social Forces and Equilibrium

Understanding that equilibrium is a characteristic of the model, not of the real world, is important in applying economic models to reality. For example, in the preceding description, I said equilibrium occurs where quantity supplied equals quantity demanded. In a model where economic forces are the only forces operating, that's true. In the real world, however, other forces—political and social forces—are operating. These will likely push price away from that supply/demand equilibrium. Were we to consider a model that included all these forces—political, social, and economic—equilibrium would be likely to exist where quantity supplied isn't equal to quantity demanded. For example:

- Farmers use political pressure to obtain prices for their crops that are higher than supply/demand equilibrium prices.

- Social pressures often offset economic pressures and prevent unemployed individuals from accepting work at lower wages than currently employed workers receive.

FIGURE 4-9 (A AND B)   Shifts in Supply and Demand

If demand increases from D_0 to D_1, as shown in (a), the quantity of movie rentals that was demanded at a price of $4.50, 8, increases to 10, but the quantity supplied remains at 8. This excess demand tends to cause prices to rise. Eventually, a new equilibrium is reached at the price of $5, where the quantity supplied and the quantity demanded are 9 (point B).

If supply of movie rentals decreases, then the entire supply curve shifts inward to the left, as shown in (b), from S_0 to S_1. At the price of $4.50, the quantity supplied has now decreased to 6 movies, but the quantity demanded has remained at 8 movies. The excess demand tends to force the price upward. Eventually, an equilibrium is reached at the price of $5 and quantity 7 (point C).

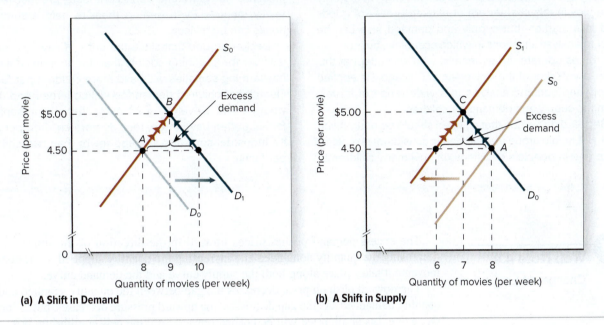

(a) A Shift in Demand   (b) A Shift in Supply

- Existing firms conspire to limit new competition by lobbying Congress to pass restrictive regulations and by devising pricing strategies to scare off new entrants.
- Renters often organize to pressure local government to set caps on the rental price of apartments.

If social and political forces were included in the analysis, they'd provide a counter–pressure to the dynamic forces of supply and demand. The result would be an equilibrium with continual excess supply or excess demand if the market were considered only in reference to economic forces. Economic forces pushing toward a supply/demand equilibrium would be thwarted by social and political forces pushing in the other direction.

Shifts in Supply and Demand

Supply and demand are most useful when trying to figure out what will happen to equilibrium price and quantity if either supply or demand shifts. Figure 4-9(a) deals with an increase in demand. Figure 4-9(b) deals with a decrease in supply.

Let's consider again the supply and demand for movie rentals. In Figure 4-9(a), the supply is S_0 and initial demand is D_0. They meet at an equilibrium price of $4.50 per movie and an equilibrium quantity of 8 movies per week (point A). Now say that the demand for movie rentals increases from D_0 to D_1. At a price of $4.50, the quantity of movie rentals supplied will be 8 and the quantity demanded will be 10; excess demand of 2 exists.

Q-7 Demonstrate graphically the effect of a heavy frost in Florida on the equilibrium quantity and price of oranges.

The Supply and Demand for Children

In Chapter 1, I distinguished between an economic force and a market force. Economic forces are operative in all aspects of our lives; market forces are economic forces that are allowed to be expressed through a market. My examples in this chapter are of market forces—of goods sold in a market—but supply and demand also can be used to analyze situations in which economic, but not market, forces operate. An economist who was adept at this was Gary Becker of the University of Chicago. He applied supply and demand analysis to a wide range of issues, even the supply and demand for children.

Becker didn't argue that children should be bought and sold. But he did argue that economic considerations play a large role in people's decisions on how many children to have. In farming communities, children can be productive early in life; by age six or seven, they can work on a farm. In an advanced industrial community, children provide pleasure but generally don't contribute productively to family income. Even getting them to help around the house can be difficult.

Becker argued that since the price of having children is lower for a farming society than for an industrial society, farming societies will have more children per family. Quantity of children demanded will be larger. And that's what we find. Developing countries that rely primarily on farming often have three, four, or more children per family. Industrial societies average fewer than two children per family.

Web Note 4.4

Changes in Equilibrium

Q-8 Demonstrate graphically the likely effect of an increase in the price of gas on the equilibrium quantity and price of hybrid cars.

Web Note 4.5

Explaining Oil Prices

The excess demand pushes prices upward in the direction of the small arrows, decreasing the quantity demanded and increasing the quantity supplied. As it does so, movement takes place along both the supply curve and the demand curve.

The upward push on price decreases the gap between the quantity supplied and the quantity demanded. As the gap decreases, the upward pressure decreases, but as long as that gap exists at all, price will be pushed upward until the new equilibrium price ($5) and new quantity (9) are reached (point *B*). At point *B*, quantity supplied equals quantity demanded. So the market is in equilibrium. Notice that the adjustment is twofold: The higher price brings about equilibrium by both increasing the quantity supplied (from 8 to 9) and decreasing the quantity demanded (from 10 to 9).

Figure 4-9(b) begins with the same situation that we started with in Figure 4-9(a); the initial equilibrium quantity and price are eight movies per week at $4.50 per movie (point *A*). In this example, however, instead of demand increasing, let's assume supply decreases—say because some suppliers change what they like to do and decide they will no longer supply movies. That means that the entire supply curve shifts inward to the left (from S_0 to S_1). At the initial equilibrium price of $4.50, the quantity demanded is greater than the quantity supplied. Two more movies are demanded than are supplied. (Excess demand = 2.)

This excess demand exerts upward pressure on price. Price is pushed in the direction of the small arrows. As the price rises, the upward pressure on price is reduced but will still exist until the new equilibrium price, $5, and new quantity, seven, are reached. At $5, the quantity supplied equals the quantity demanded. The adjustment has involved a movement along the demand curve and the new supply curve. As price rises, quantity supplied is adjusted upward and quantity demanded is adjusted downward until quantity supplied equals quantity demanded where the new supply curve intersects the demand curve at point *C*, an equilibrium of seven and $5.

Here is an exercise for you to try. Demonstrate graphically how the price of computers could have fallen dramatically in the past 20 years, even as demand increased. (*Hint:* Supply has increased even more, so even at lower prices, far more computers have been supplied than were being supplied 20 years ago.)

A Limitation of Supply/Demand Analysis

Supply and demand are tools, and, like most tools, they help us enormously when used appropriately. Used inappropriately, however, they can be misleading. Throughout the book I'll introduce you to the limitations of the tools, but let me discuss an important one here.

In supply/demand analysis, other things are assumed constant. If other things change, then one cannot directly apply supply/demand analysis. Sometimes supply and demand are interconnected, making it impossible to hold other things constant. Let's take an example. Say we are considering the effect of a fall in the wage rate on unemployment. In supply/demand analysis, you would look at the effect that fall would have on workers' decisions to supply labor, and on business's decision to hire workers. But there are also other effects. For instance, the fall in the wage lowers people's income and thereby reduces demand for goods. That reduction in demand for goods may feed back to firms and reduce the firms' demand for workers, which might further reduce the demand for goods. If these ripple effects do occur, and are important enough to affect the result, they have to be added for the analysis to be complete. A complete analysis always includes the relevant feedback effects.

There is no single answer to the question of which ripples must be included. There is much debate among economists about which ripple effects to include, but there are some general rules. Supply/demand analysis, used without adjustment, is most appropriate for questions where the goods are a small percentage of the entire economy. That is when the other-things-constant assumption will most likely hold. As soon as one starts analyzing goods that are a large percentage of the entire economy, the other-things-constant assumption is likely not to hold true. The reason is found in the **fallacy of composition**—*the false assumption that what is true for a part will also be true for the whole.*

Consider a lone supplier who lowers the price of his or her good. People will substitute that good for other goods, and the quantity of the good demanded will increase. But what if all suppliers lower their prices? Since all prices have gone down, why should consumers switch? The substitution story can't be used in the aggregate. There are many such examples.

An understanding of the fallacy of composition is of central relevance to macroeconomics. In the aggregate, whenever firms produce (whenever they supply), they create income (demand for their goods). So in macro, when supply changes, demand changes. This interdependence is one of the primary reasons we have a separate macroeconomics. In macroeconomics, the other-things-constant assumption central to microeconomic supply/demand analysis often does not hold.

It is to account for these interdependencies that we separate macro analysis from micro analysis. In macro we use curves whose underlying foundations are much more complicated than the supply and demand curves we use in micro, and in modern economics there is an active debate about how more complex structural models can extend our understanding of how markets operate.

One final comment: The fact that supply and demand may be interdependent does not mean that you can't use supply/demand analysis; it simply means that you must modify its results with the interdependency that, if you've done the analysis correctly, you've kept in the back of your head. Using supply and demand analysis is generally a step in any good economic analysis, but you must remember that it may be only a step.

Q-9 When determining the effect of a shift factor on price and quantity, in which of the following markets could you likely assume that other things will remain constant?

1. Market for eggs.
2. Labor market.
3. World oil market.
4. Market for luxury boats.

The fallacy of composition is the false assumption that what is true for a part will also be true for the whole.

Q-10 Why is the fallacy of composition relevant for macroeconomic issues?

It is to account for interdependency between aggregate supply decisions and aggregate demand decisions that we have a separate micro analysis and a separate macro analysis.

Conclusion

Throughout the book, I'll be presenting examples of supply and demand. So I'll end this chapter here because its intended purposes have been served. What were those intended purposes? First, I exposed you to enough economic terminology and economic thinking to allow you to proceed to my more complicated examples. Second, I have set your mind to work putting the events around you into a supply/demand framework. Doing that will give you new insights into the events that shape all our lives. Once you incorporate the supply/demand framework into your way of looking at the world, you will have made an important step toward understanding the economic way of thinking.

Summary

- The law of demand states that quantity demanded rises as price falls, other things constant. (*LO4-1*)

- The law of supply states that quantity supplied rises as price rises, other things constant. (*LO4-2*)

- Factors that affect supply and demand other than price are called shift factors. Shift factors of demand include income, prices of other goods, tastes, expectations, and taxes on and subsidies to consumers. Shift factors of supply include the price of inputs, technology, expectations, and taxes on and subsidies to producers. (*LO4-1, LO4-2*)

- A change in quantity demanded (supplied) is a movement along the demand (supply) curve. A change in demand (supply) is a shift of the entire demand (supply) curve. (*LO4-1, LO4-2*)

- The laws of supply and demand hold true because individuals can substitute. (*LO4-1, LO4-2*)

- A market demand (supply) curve is the horizontal sum of all individual demand (supply) curves. (*LO4-1, LO4-2*)

- When quantity supplied equals quantity demanded, prices have no tendency to change. This is equilibrium. (*LO4-3*)

- When quantity demanded is greater than quantity supplied, prices tend to rise. When quantity supplied is greater than quantity demanded, prices tend to fall. (*LO4-3*)

- When the demand curve shifts to the right (left), equilibrium price rises (declines) and equilibrium quantity rises (falls). (*LO4-3*)

- When the supply curve shifts to the right (left), equilibrium price declines (rises) and equilibrium quantity rises (falls). (*LO4-3*)

- In the real world, you must add political and social forces to the supply/demand model. When you do, equilibrium is likely not going to be where quantity demanded equals quantity supplied. (*LO4-4*)

- In macro, small side effects that can be assumed away in micro are multiplied enormously and can significantly change the results. To ignore them is to fall into the fallacy of composition. (*LO4-4*)

Key Terms

demand
demand curve
equilibrium
equilibrium price
equilibrium quantity
excess demand

excess supply
fallacy of composition
law of demand
law of supply
market demand curve
market supply curve

movement along a
  demand curve
movement along a supply
  curve
quantity demanded
quantity supplied

shift in demand
shift in supply
supply
supply curve

Questions and Exercises ■ connect

1. State the law of demand. Why is price inversely related to quantity demanded?   (*LO4-1*)

2. You're given the following individual demand tables for comic books: (*LO4-1*)

Price	John	Liz	Alex
$ 2	4	36	24
4	4	32	20
6	0	28	16
8	0	24	12
10	0	20	8
12	0	16	4
14	0	12	0
16	0	8	0

   a. Determine the market demand table.
   b. Graph the individual and market demand curves.
   c. If the current market price is $4, what is the total market quantity demanded? What happens to total quantity demanded if price rises to $10?
   d. Say that an advertising campaign increases demand by 50 percent. What will happen to the individual and market demand curves?

3. List four shift factors of demand and explain how each affects demand.   (*LO4-1*)

4. Distinguish the effect of a shift factor of demand on the demand curve from the effect of a change in price on the demand curve.   (*LO4-1*)

5. State the law of supply. Why is price directly related to quantity supplied?   (*LO4-2*)

6. Mary has just stated that normally, as price rises, supply will increase. Her teacher grimaces. Why?   (*LO4-2*)

7. List four shift factors of supply and explain how each affects supply.   (*LO4-2*)

8. Derive the market supply curve from the following two individual supply curves.   (*LO4-2*)

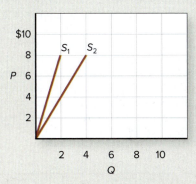

9. You're given the following demand and supply tables: (*LO4-3*)

	Demand		
P	D_1	D_2	D_3
$30	20	5	10
40	15	3	7
50	10	0	5
60	5	0	0

	Supply		
P	S_1	S_2	S_3
$30	0	4	11
40	0	8	17
50	10	12	18
60	10	15	20

   a. Draw the market demand and market supply curves.
   b. Label equilibrium price and quantity.
   c. What is excess supply/demand at price $30? Price $60?

10. It has just been reported that eating red meat is bad for your health. Using supply and demand curves, demonstrate the report's likely effect on the equilibrium price and quantity of steak sold in the market.   (*LO4-3*)

11. Why does the price of airline tickets rise during the summer months? Demonstrate your answer graphically.   (*LO4-3*)

12. Why does sales volume rise during weeks when states suspend taxes on sales by retailers? Demonstrate your answer graphically assuming that the retailer pays the tax.   (*LO4-3*)

13. What is the expected impact of increased security measures imposed by the federal government on airline fares and volume of travel? Demonstrate your answer graphically.   (*LO4-3*)

14. Explain what a sudden popularity of "Economics Professor" brand casual wear would likely do to prices of that brand.   (*LO4-3*)

15. In a flood, usable water supplies ironically tend to decline because the pumps and water lines are damaged. What will a flood likely do to prices of bottled water?   (*LO4-3*)

16. OPEC announces it will increase oil production by 20 percent. What is the effect on the price of oil? Demonstrate your answer graphically.   (*LO4-3*)

17. Draw hypothetical supply and demand curves for tea. Show how the equilibrium price and quantity will be affected by each of the following occurrences: *(LO4-3)*
    a. Bad weather wreaks havoc with the tea crop.
    b. A medical report implying tea is bad for your health is published.
    c. A technological innovation lowers the cost of producing tea.
    d. Consumers' income falls. (Assume tea is a normal good.)

18. You're a commodity trader and you've just heard a report that the winter wheat harvest will be 2 billion bushels, a 40 percent jump, rather than an expected 30 percent jump.   *(LO4-3)*
    a. What would you expect would happen to wheat prices?
    b. Demonstrate graphically the effect you suggested in part *a*.

19. In the United States, say gasoline costs consumers about $2.50 per gallon. In Italy, say it costs consumers about $6 per gallon. What effect does this price differential likely have on: *(LO4-3)*
    a. The size of cars in the United States and in Italy?
    b. The use of public transportation in the United States and in Italy?
    c. The fuel efficiency of cars in the United States and in Italy?
    d. What would be the effect of raising the price of gasoline in the United States to $5 per gallon?

20. Assume that Argentina imposes a 20 percent tax on natural gas exports.   *(LO4-3)*
    a. Demonstrate the likely effect of that tax on gas exports using supply and demand curves.
    b. What does it likely do to the price of natural gas in Argentina?

21. In most developing countries, there are long lines of taxis at airports, and these taxis often wait two or three hours for a customer. What does this tell you about the price in that market? Demonstrate with supply and demand analysis.   *(LO4-3)*

22. Define the fallacy of composition. How does it affect the supply/demand model?   *(LO4-4)*

23. In which of the following three markets are there likely to be the greatest feedback effects: market for housing, market for wheat, market for manufactured goods?   *(LO4-4)*

24. State whether "other things constant" is likely to hold in the following supply/demand analyses: *(LO4-4)*
    a. The impact of an increase in the demand for pencils on the price of pencils.
    b. The impact of an increase in the supply of labor on the quantity of labor demanded.
    c. The impact of an increase in aggregate savings on aggregate expenditures.
    d. The impact of a new method of producing tires on the price of tires.

Questions from Alternative Perspectives

1. In a centrally planned economy, how might central planners estimate supply or demand? *(Austrian)*

2. In the late 19th century, Washington Gladden said, "He who battles for the Christianization of society, will find their strongest foe in the field of economics. Economics is indeed the dismal science because of the selfishness of its maxims and the inhumanity of its conclusions."
   a. Evaluate this statement.
   b. Is there a conflict between the ideology of capitalism and the precepts of Christianity?
   c. Would a society that emphasized a capitalist mode of production benefit by a moral framework that emphasized selflessness rather than selfishness? *(Religious)*

3. Economics is often referred to as the study of choice.
   a. In U.S. history, have men and women been equally free to choose the amount of education they receive even within the same family?
   b. What other areas can you see where men and women have not been equally free to choose?
   c. If you agree that men and women have not had equal rights to choose, what implications does that have about the objectivity of economic analysis? *(Feminist)*

4. Knowledge is derived from a tautology when something is true because you assume it is true. In this chapter, you have learned the conditions under which supply and demand explain outcomes. Yet, as your text author cautions, these conditions may not hold. How can you be sure if they ever hold? *(Institutionalist)*

5. Do you think consumers make purchasing decisions based on general rules of thumb instead of price?
   a. Why would consumers do this?
   b. What implication might this have for the conclusions drawn about markets? *(Post-Keynesian)*

6. Some economists believe that imposing international labor standards would cost jobs. In support of this argument, one economist said, "Either you believe labor demand curves are downward-sloping, or you don't." Of course, not to believe that demand curves are negatively sloped would be tantamount to declaring yourself an economic illiterate. What else about the nature of labor demand curves might help a policy maker design policies that could counteract the negative effects of labor standards employment? *(Radical)*

Issues to Ponder

1. Oftentimes, to be considered for a job, you have to know someone in the firm. What does this observation tell you about the wage paid for that job?

2. In the early 2000s, the demand for housing increased substantially as low interest rates increased the number of people who could afford homes.
   a. What was the likely effect of this on housing prices? Demonstrate graphically.
   b. In 2005, mortgage rates began increasing. What was the likely effect of this increase on housing prices? Demonstrate graphically.
   c. In a period of increasing demand for housing, would you expect housing prices to rise more in Miami suburbs, which had room for expansion and fairly loose laws about subdivisions, or in a city such as San Francisco, which had limited land and tight subdivision restrictions?

3. When the U.S. postal service honored rodeo star Bill Pickett with a stamp, it mistakenly put a picture of rodeo rider Ben Pickett, not the rodeo star Bill Pickett, on the stamp. It printed 150,000 sheets with the wrong image. Recognizing its error, it recalled the stamp, but it found that 183 sheets had already been sold.
   a. What would the recall likely do to the price of the 183 sheets that were sold?
   b. When the government recognized that it could not recall all the stamps, it decided to issue the remaining ones. What would that decision likely do?
   c. What would the holders of the misprinted sheets likely do when they heard of the government's decision?

4. What would be the effect of a 75 percent tax on lawsuit punitive awards that was proposed by then California governor Arnold Schwarzenegger in 2004 on:
   a. The number of punitive awards. Demonstrate your answer using supply and demand curves.
   b. The number of pretrial settlements.

5. Why is a supply/demand analysis that includes only economic forces likely to be incomplete?

Answers to Margin Questions

1. The demand curve slopes downward because price and quantity demanded are inversely related. As the price of a good rises, people switch to purchasing other goods whose prices have not risen by as much.   (*LO4-1*)

2. *Demand for luxury goods.* The other possibility, *quantity of luxury goods demanded,* is used to refer to movements along (not shifts of) the demand curve.   (*LO4-1*)

3. (1) The decline in price will increase the quantity of computers demanded (movement down along the demand curve). (2) With more income, demand for computers will rise (shift of the demand curve out to the right).   (*LO4-1*)

4. When adding two demand curves, you sum them horizontally, as in the accompanying diagram.   (*LO4-1*)

5. *The quantity supplied* rises because there was a movement along the supply curve. The supply curve itself remains unchanged.   (*LO4-2*)

6. (1) The supply of romance novels declines since paper is an input to production (supply shifts in to the left). (2) The supply of romance novels rises since the subsidy decreases the cost to the producer (supply shifts out to the right).   (*LO4-2*)

7. A heavy frost in Florida will decrease the supply of oranges, increasing the price and decreasing the quantity demanded, as in the accompanying graph.   (*LO4-3*)

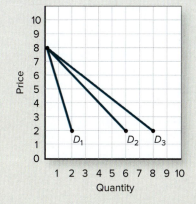

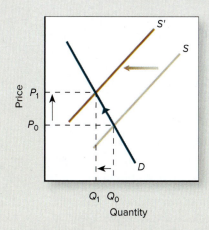

8. An increase in the price of gas will likely increase the demand for hybrid cars, increasing their price and increasing the quantity supplied, as in the accompanying graph. (*LO4-3*)

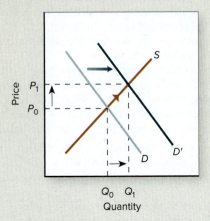

9. Other things are most likely to remain constant in the egg and luxury boat markets because each is a small percentage of the whole economy. Factors that affect the world oil market and the labor market will have ripple effects that must be taken into account in any analysis. (*LO4-4*)

10. The fallacy of composition is relevant for macroeconomic issues because it reminds us that, in the aggregate, small effects that are immaterial for micro issues can add up and be material. (*LO4-4*)

Using Supply and Demand

It is by invisible hands that we are bent and tortured worst.

—Nietzsche

CHAPTER 5

©Robert Ingelhart/Getty Images

After reading this chapter, you should be able to:

LO5-1 Apply the supply and demand model to real-world events.

LO5-2 Demonstrate the effect of a price ceiling and a price floor on a market.

LO5-3 Explain the effect of excise taxes and tariffs on a market.

LO5-4 Explain the effect of quantity restrictions on a market.

LO5-5 Explain the effect of a third-party-payer system on equilibrium price and quantity.

Supply and demand give you a lens through which to view the economy. That lens brings into focus issues that would otherwise seem like a muddle. In this chapter, we use the supply/demand lens to consider real-world events.

Real-World Supply and Demand Applications

Let's begin by giving you an opportunity to apply supply/demand analysis to real-world events. Below are three events. After reading each, try your hand at explaining what happened, using supply and demand curves. To help you in the process Figure 5-1 provides some diagrams. *Before* reading my explanation, try to match the shifts to the examples. In each, be careful to explain which curve, or curves, shifted and how those shifts affected equilibrium price and quantity.

1. A drought in California leads farmers to leave 500,000 acres of land fallow. As a result the price of fresh produce such as avocados from California rises. Market: Avocados in the United States.

2. The expansion of hydraulic fracking to extract oil and natural gas in the United States increases the demand for sand, a key ingredient in the fracking process. As a result the price of sand rises. Market: Sand in the United States.

FIGURE 5-1 (A, B, AND C)

In this exhibit, three shifts of supply and demand are shown. Your task is to match them with the events listed in the text.

Answers: 1–b; 2–a; 3–c.

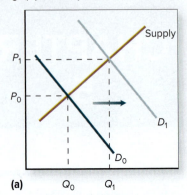

(a)

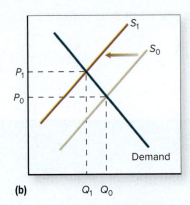

(b)

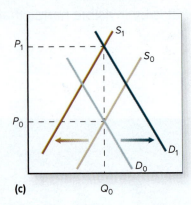

(c)

3. A growing middle class in China and India has increased the demand for many food products, particularly edible oils such as soy and palm. At the same time, to meet the increasing demand for ethanol, U.S. farmers have chosen to grow less soy (from which soy oil is made) and more corn (from which ethanol is made). The result? Dramatic increases in the price of edible oil worldwide. Market: Global edible oils.

Now that you've matched them, let's see if your analysis matches mine.

DROUGHT   Weather is a shift factor of supply. A drought reduces the productivity of land, shifting the supply curve for avocados to the left, as shown in Figure 5-1(b). At the original price (shown by P_0), quantity demanded exceeds quantity supplied and the invisible hand of the market pressures the price to rise until quantity demanded equals quantity supplied (shown by P_1).

Q-1   True or false? If supply rises, price will rise.

HYDRAULIC FRACKING   Sand is the key ingredient in the fracking process. As the use of hydraulic fracking technology expanded, U.S. oil and gas producers increased their demand for sand. Figure 5-1(a) shows that the demand curve for sand shifted from D_0 to D_1. At the original price P_0, sellers were running out of sand and raised their price.

Web Note 5.1

Fair Trade Coffee

EDIBLE OILS   Increases in the size of the middle class in developing countries such as China and India increased the demand for food and edible oils used to prepare those foods. This is represented by a shift in the demand for edible oils out to the right from D_0 to D_1. At the same time, increases in the price of crude oil led U.S. farmers to grow less soy and more corn, which shifted the supply curve for edible oils from S_0 to S_1. The result was a dramatic increase in the price of edible oils, shown in Figure 5-1(c) as an increase from P_0 to P_1.

Anything that affects demand or supply other than the price of the good will shift the curves.

     Now that we've been through some examples, let's review. Remember: Anything that affects demand and supply other than price of the good will shift the curves. Changes in the price of the good result in movements along the curves. Another thing to recognize is that when both curves are shifting, you can get a change in price but little change in quantity, or a change in quantity but little change in price.

Supply and Demand in Action

Sorting out the effects of the shifts of supply or demand or both can be confusing. Here are some helpful hints to keep things straight:

- Draw the initial demand and supply curves and label them. The equilibrium price and quantity is where these curves intersect. Label them.

- If only price has changed, no curves will shift and a shortage or surplus will result.

- If a nonprice factor affects demand, determine the direction demand has shifted and add the new demand curve. Do the same for supply.

- Equilibrium price and quantity is where the new demand and supply curves intersect. Label them.

- Compare the initial equilibrium price and quantity to the new equilibrium price and quantity.

See if you can describe what happened in the three graphs below.

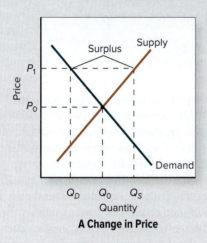

A Change in Price

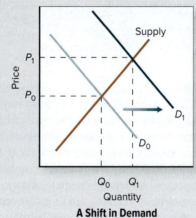

A Shift in Demand

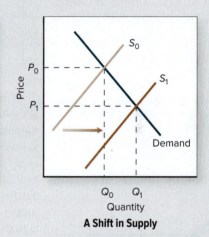

A Shift in Supply

To test your understanding Table 5-1 gives you six generic results from the interaction of supply and demand. Your job is to decide what shifts produced those results. This exercise is a variation of the one with which I began the chapter. It goes over the same issues, but this time without the graphs. On the left-hand side of Table 5-1, I list combinations of movements of observed prices and quantities, labeling them 1–6. On the right I give six shifts in supply and demand, labeling them *a–f*.

You are to match the shifts with the price and quantity movements that best fit each described shift, using each shift and movement only once. My recommendation to you is to draw the graphs that are described in *a–f*, decide what happens to price and quantity, and then find the match in 1–6.

Q-2 Say a hormone has been discovered that increases cows' milk production by 20 percent. Demonstrate graphically what effect this discovery would have on the price and quantity of milk sold in a market.

If you don't confuse your "shifts of" with your "movements along," supply and demand provide good off-the-cuff answers for many economic questions.

TABLE 5-1

Price and Quantity Changes			Shifts in Supply and Demand
1.	$P\uparrow$	$Q\uparrow$	*a.* No change in demand. Supply shifts in.
2.	$P\uparrow$	$Q\downarrow$	*b.* Demand shifts out. Supply shifts in.
3.	$P\uparrow$	$Q?$	*c.* Demand shifts in. No change in supply.
4.	$P\downarrow$	$Q?$	*d.* Demand shifts out. Supply shifts out.
5.	$P?$	$Q\uparrow$	*e.* Demand shifts out. No change in supply.
6.	$P\downarrow$	$Q\downarrow$	*f.* Demand shifts in. Supply shifts out.

TABLE 5-2 Diagram of Effects of Shifts of Demand and Supply on Price and Quantity

This table provides a summary of the effects of shifts in supply and demand on equilibrium price and equilibrium quantity. Notice that when both curves shift, the effect on either price or quantity depends on the relative size of the shifts.

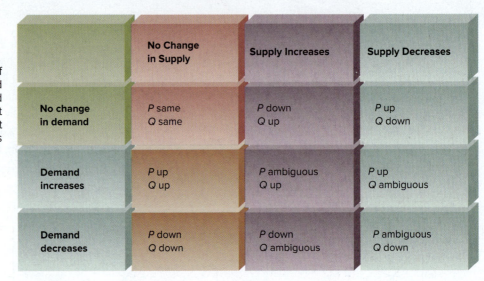

	No Change in Supply	Supply Increases	Supply Decreases
No change in demand	P same Q same	P down Q up	P up Q down
Demand increases	P up Q up	P ambiguous Q up	P up Q ambiguous
Demand decreases	P down Q down	P down Q ambiguous	P ambiguous Q down

Q-3 If both demand and supply shift in to the left, what happens to price and quantity?

Web Note 5.2

Economics of Chocolate

Q-4 If price and quantity both fell, what would you say was the most likely cause?

Now that you've worked them, let me give you the answers I came up with. They are: 1–*e;* 2–*a;* 3–*b;* 4–*f;* 5–*d;* 6–*c.* How did I come up with the answers? I did what I suggested you do—took each of the scenarios on the right and predicted what happens to price and quantity. For case *a,* supply shifts in to the left and there is a movement up along the demand curve. Since the demand curve is downward-sloping, the price rises and quantity declines. This matches number 2 on the left. For case *b,* demand shifts out to the right. Along the original supply curve, price and quantity would rise. But supply shifts in to the left, leading to even higher prices but lower quantity. What happens to quantity is unclear, so the match must be number 3. For case *c,* demand shifts in to the left. There is movement down along the supply curve with lower price and lower quantity. This matches number 6. For case *d,* demand shifts out and supply shifts out. As demand shifts out, we move along the supply curve to the right and price and quantity rise. But supply shifts out too, and we move out along the new demand curve. Price declines, erasing the previous rise, and the quantity rises even more. This matches number 5.

I'll leave it up to you to confirm my answers to *e* and *f.* Notice that when supply and demand both shift, the change in either price or quantity is uncertain—it depends on the relative size of the shifts. As a summary, I present a diagrammatic of the combinations in Table 5-2.

Government Intervention: Price Ceilings and Price Floors

People don't always like the market-determined price. If the invisible hand were the only factor that determined prices, people would have to accept it. But it isn't; social and political forces also determine price. For example, when prices fall, sellers look to government for ways to hold prices up; when prices rise, buyers look to government for ways to hold prices down. Let's now consider the effect of such actions in the supply/demand model.[1] Let's start with an example of the price being held down.

---

[1]Modern economists use many different models. No model precisely fits reality, and when I discuss a real-world market as fitting a model, I am using pedagogical license. As I have emphasized in previous chapters, the propositions that come out of a model are theorems–logical conclusions given the assumptions. To extend the theorem to a policy precept requires considering which assumptions of the model fit the situation one is describing.

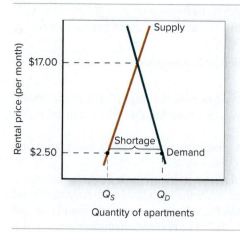

FIGURE 5-2 Rent Control in Paris

A price ceiling imposed on housing rent in Paris during World War II created a shortage of housing when World War II ended and veterans returned home. The shortage would have been eliminated if rents had been allowed to rise to $17 per month.

Price Ceilings

When government wants to hold prices down, it imposes a **price ceiling**—*a government-imposed limit on how high a price can be charged*. That limit is generally below the equilibrium price. (A price ceiling that is above the equilibrium price will have no effect at all.) From Chapter 4, you already know the effect of a price that is below the equilibrium price—quantity demanded will exceed quantity supplied and there will be excess demand. Let's now look at an example of **rent control**—*a price ceiling on rents, set by government*—and see how that excess demand shows up in the real world.

Rent controls exist today in a number of American cities as well as other cities throughout the world. Many of the laws governing rent were first instituted during the two world wars in the first half of the 20th century. Consider Paris, for example. In World War II, the Paris government froze rent to ease the financial burden of those families whose wage earners were sent to fight in the war. When the soldiers returned at the end of the war, the rent control was continued; removing it would have resulted in an increase in rents from $2.50 to $17 a month, and that was felt to be an unfair burden for veterans.

Figure 5-2 shows this situation. The below-market rent set by government created an enormous shortage of apartments. Initially this shortage didn't bother those renting apartments, since they got low-cost apartments. But it created severe hardships for those who didn't have apartments. Many families moved in with friends or extended families. Others couldn't find housing at all and lived on the streets. Eventually the rent controls started to cause problems even for those who did have apartments. The reason is that owners of buildings cut back on maintenance. More than 80 percent of Parisians had no private bathrooms and 20 percent had no running water. Since rental properties weren't profitable, no new buildings were being constructed and existing buildings weren't kept in repair. It was even harder for those who didn't have apartments.

Since the market price was not allowed to ration apartments, alternative methods of rationing developed. People paid landlords bribes to get an apartment, or watched the obituaries and then simply moved in their furniture before anyone else did. Eventually the situation got so bad that rent controls were lifted.

The system of rent controls is not only of historical interest. Below I list some phenomena that existed in past years in New York City.

1. A couple paid $450 a month for a two-bedroom Park Avenue apartment with a solarium and two terraces, while another individual paid $3,500 a month for a studio apartment shared with two roommates.

2. The vacancy rate for apartments in New York City was 1.2 percent. Anything under 5 percent is considered a housing emergency.

 Web Note 5.3

Rent Control

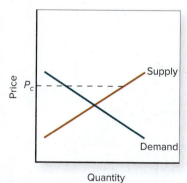

Q-5 What is the effect of the price ceiling, P_c, shown in the graph below on price and quantity?

Q-6 What is the effect of the price
ceiling, P_c, shown in the graph below on
price and quantity?

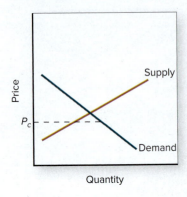

With price ceilings, existing goods are
no longer rationed entirely by price.
Other methods of rationing existing
goods arise called nonprice rationing.

3. The actor Mia Farrow paid $2,900 a month (a fraction of the market-clearing
rent) for 10 rooms on Central Park West. It was an apartment her mother first
leased 70 years ago.

4. Would-be tenants made payments, called key money, to current tenants or
landlords to get apartments.

Your assignment is to explain how these phenomena might have come about,
and to demonstrate, with supply and demand, the situation that likely caused them.
(*Hint:* New York City had rent control.)

Now that you have done your assignment (you have, haven't you?), let me give you
my answers so that you can check them with your answers.

The situation is identical to that presented above in Figure 5-2. Take the first item.
The couple lived in a rent-controlled apartment while the individual with roommates did
not. If rent control were eliminated, rent on the Park Avenue apartment would rise and
rent on the studio would most likely decline. Item 2: The housing emergency was a result
of rent control. Below-market rent resulted in excess demand and little vacancy. Item 3:
That Mia Farrow rented a rent-controlled apartment was the result of nonprice rationing.
Instead of being rationed by price, other methods of rationing arose. These other methods of rationing scarce resources are called *nonprice rationing*. In New York City, strict
rules determined the handing down of rent-controlled apartments from family member
to family member. Item 4: New residents searched for a long time to find apartments to
rent, and many discovered that illegal payments to landlords were the only way to obtain
a rent-controlled apartment. Key money is a black market payment for a rent-controlled
apartment. Because of the limited supply of apartments, individuals were willing to
pay far more than the controlled price. Landlords used other methods of rationing the
limited supply of apartments—instituting first-come, first-served policies, and, in practice, selecting tenants based on gender, race, or other personal characteristics, even
though such discriminatory selection was illegal. In some cases in New York City the
rent was so far below the market that developers paid thousands of dollars—in one case
$400,000—to a tenant to vacate an apartment so the developer could buy the building
from the landlord, tear it down, and replace it with a new non-rent-controlled building.

If rent controls had only the bad effects described above, no community would
institute them. They are, however, implemented with good intentions—to cope with
sudden increases in demand for housing that would otherwise cause rents to explode
and force many poor people out of their apartments. The negative effects occur over
time as buildings begin to deteriorate and the number of people looking to rent and
unable to find apartments increases. As this happens, people focus less on the original
renters and more on new renters excluded from the market and on the inefficiencies of
price ceilings. Since politicians tend to focus on the short run, we can expect rent
control to continue to be used when demand for housing suddenly increases.

Price Floors

Sometimes political forces favor suppliers, sometimes consumers. So let us now go
briefly through a case in which the government is trying to favor suppliers by attempting to prevent the price from falling below a certain level. **Price floors**—*government-
imposed limits on how low a price can be charged*—do just this. The price floor is
generally above the existing price. (A price floor below equilibrium price would have
no effect.) When there is an effective price floor, quantity supplied exceeds quantity
demanded and the result is excess supply.

An example of a price floor is the minimum wage. Both individual states and the
federal government impose **minimum wage laws**—*laws specifying the lowest wage a
firm can legally pay an employee.* The U.S. federal government first instituted a

Q-7 What is the effect of the price
floor, P_f, shown in the graph below, on
price and quantity?

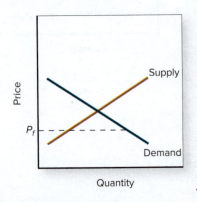

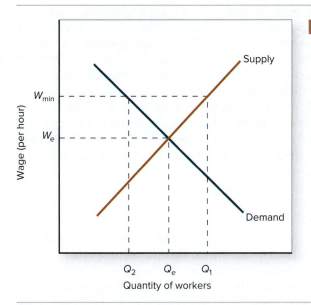

FIGURE 5-3 A Minimum Wage

A minimum wage, W_{min}, above equilibrium wage, W_e, helps those who are able to find work, shown by Q_2, but hurts those who would have been employed at the equilibrium wage but can no longer find employment, shown by $Q_e - Q_2$. A minimum wage also hurts producers who have higher costs of production and consumers who may face higher product prices.

minimum wage of 25 cents per hour in 1938 as part of the Fair Labor Standards Act. It has been raised many times since. As of 2018 the federal minimum wage was $7.25 per hour. Twenty-nine states had minimum wages higher than the federal minimum, and a number of cities had a $15 minimum wage. Only a small percentage of workers (about 1.6 percent of hourly paid workers) receive the minimum wage, almost all of whom are unskilled and/or part-time. The market-determined equilibrium wage for most full-time adult workers is generally above the minimum wage.

The effect of a minimum wage on the unskilled labor market is shown in Figure 5-3. The government-set minimum wage is above equilibrium, as shown by W_{min}. At the market-determined equilibrium wage W_e, the quantity of labor supplied and demanded equals Q_e. At the higher minimum wage, the quantity of labor supplied rises to Q_1 and the quantity of labor demanded declines to Q_2. There is an excess supply of workers (a shortage of jobs) represented by the difference $Q_1 - Q_2$. This represents people who are looking for work but cannot find it.

Who wins and who loses from a minimum wage? The minimum wage improves the wages of the Q_2 workers who are able to find work. Without the minimum wage, they would have earned W_e per hour. The minimum wage hurts those, however, who cannot find work at the minimum wage but who are willing to work, and would have been hired, at the market-determined wage. These workers are represented by the distance $Q_e - Q_2$ in Figure 5-3. The minimum wage also hurts firms that now must pay their workers more, increasing the cost of production, and consumers to the extent that firms are able to pass that increase in production cost on in the form of higher product prices.

All economists agree that the above analysis is logical and correct. But they disagree about whether governments should have minimum wage laws. One reason is that the empirical effects of minimum wage laws are relatively small; in fact, some studies have found them to be negligible. (There is, however, much debate about these estimates, since "other things" never remain constant.) A second reason is that some real-world labor markets are not sufficiently competitive to fit the supply/demand model. A third reason is that the minimum wage affects the economy in ways that some economists see as desirable and others see as undesirable. I point this out to remind you that the supply/demand framework is a tool to be used to analyze issues. It does not provide final answers about policy. (In microeconomics, economists explore the policy issues

Web Note 5.4

Minimum Wage

The minimum wage helps some people and hurts others.

Economists disagree about whether government should have minimum wage laws.

©Dan Holm/Shutterstock

of interferences in markets much more carefully.) There is nothing in economic theory that says that minimum wage laws are bad and should not be supported. Such laws have costs and benefits; what economics says is that the decision on whether to impose them should be based on a careful analysis of those costs and benefits.

Because the federal minimum wage is low, and not binding for most workers, a movement called the living-wage movement has begun. The living-wage movement focuses on local governments, calling on them to establish a minimum wage at a *living wage*— a wage necessary to support a family at or above the federally determined poverty line. Hundreds of cities have established living-wage laws at varying levels, often about $15 an hour. The analysis of these living-wage laws is the same as that for minimum wages.

Government Intervention: Excise Taxes and Tariffs

Web Note 5.5

Taxing Marijuana

A tax on suppliers shifts the supply curve up by the amount of the tax.

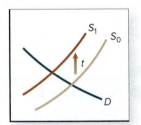

Q-8   Your study partner, Umar, has just stated that a tax on demanders of $2 per unit will raise the equilibrium price consumers pay from $4 to $6. How do you respond?

Let's now consider an example of a tax on goods. An **excise tax** is *a tax that is levied on a specific good.* The luxury tax on expensive cars that the United States imposed in 1991 is an example. A **tariff** is *an excise tax on an imported good.* We can see the effect that excise taxes and tariffs will have on prices and quantities by considering the impact of taxes in the supply/demand model: A tax on suppliers shifts the supply curve up by the amount of the tax; a tax on demanders shifts the demand curve down by the amount of the tax.

To lend some sense of reality, let's take the example of when the United States taxed the suppliers of expensive boats. We show that case in Figure 5-4. The price of a boat before the luxury tax was $60,000, and 600 boats were sold at that price. Now the government taxes suppliers $10,000 for every luxury boat sold. What will the new price of the boat be, and how many will be sold?

If you were about to answer "$70,000," be careful. Ask yourself whether I would have given you that question if the answer were that easy. By looking at the supply and demand curves in Figure 5-4, you can see why $70,000 is the wrong answer.

To sell 600 boats, suppliers must be fully compensated for the tax. So the tax of $10,000 on the supplier shifts the supply curve up from S_0 to S_1. However, at $70,000, consumers are not willing to purchase 600 boats. They are willing to purchase only 420 boats. Quantity supplied exceeds quantity demanded at $70,000. Suppliers lower their prices until quantity supplied equals quantity demanded at $65,000, the new equilibrium price.

The new equilibrium price is $65,000, not $70,000. The reason is that at the higher price, the quantity of boats people demand is less. Some people choose not to buy boats and others find substitute vehicles or purchase their boats outside the United States. The tax

---

FIGURE 5-4   **The Effect of an Excise Tax**

An excise tax on suppliers shifts the entire supply curve up by the amount of the tax. Since at a price equal to the original price plus the tax there is excess supply, the price of the good rises by less than the tax.

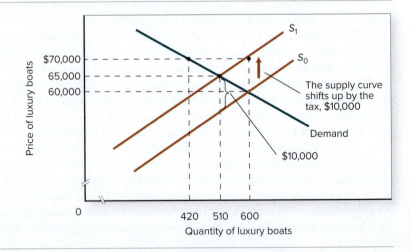

causes a movement up along a demand curve to the left. Excise taxes reduce the quantity of goods demanded. That's why boat manufacturers were up in arms after the tax was imposed and why the revenue generated from the tax was less than expected. Instead of collecting $10,000 × 600 ($6 million), revenue collected was only $10,000 × 510 ($5.1 million). (The tax was repealed three years after it was imposed.)

A tariff has the same effect on the equilibrium price and quantity as an excise tax. The difference is that only foreign producers sending goods into the United States pay the tax. An example is the 30 percent tariff imposed on steel imported into the United States in the early 2000s. The government instituted the tariff because U.S. steelmakers were having difficulty competing with lower-cost foreign steel. The tariff increased the price of imported steel, making U.S. steel more competitive to domestic buyers. As expected, the price of imported steel rose by over 15 percent, to about $230 a ton, and the quantity imported declined. Tariffs don't hurt just the foreign producer. Tariffs increase the cost of imported products to domestic consumers. In the case of steel, manufacturing companies such as automakers faced higher production costs. The increase in the cost of steel lowered production in those industries and increased the cost of a variety of goods to U.S. consumers.

Government Intervention: Quantity Restrictions

Another way in which governments often interfere with, or regulate, markets is with licenses, which limit entry into a market. For example, to be a doctor you need a license; to be a vet you need a license; and in some places to be an electrician, a financial planner, or a cosmetologist, or to fish, you need a license. There are many reasons for licenses, and we will not consider them here. Instead, we will simply consider what effect licenses have on the price and quantity of the activity being licensed. Specifically, we'll look at a case where the government issues a specific number of licenses and holds that number constant. The example we'll take is licenses to drive a taxi. In New York City, these are called taxi medallions because the license is an aluminum plate attached to the hood of a taxi. Taxi medallions were established in 1937 as a way to increase the wages of licensed taxi drivers. Wages of taxi drivers had fallen from $26 a week in 1929 to $15 a week in 1933. As wages fell, the number of taxi drivers fell from 19,000 to about 12,000. The remaining 12,000 taxi drivers successfully lobbied New York City to grant drivers with current licenses who met certain requirements permanent rights to drive taxis—medallions. (It wasn't until the early 2000s that the number of medallions was increased slightly.) The restriction had the desired effect. As the economy grew, demand for taxis grew (the demand for taxis shifted out) as shown in Figure 5-5(a) and because the supply of taxis remained at about 12,000, the wages of the taxi drivers owning medallions increased.

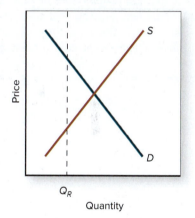

Q-9 What is the effect of the quantity restrictions, Q_R, shown in the graph below, on equilibrium price and quantity?

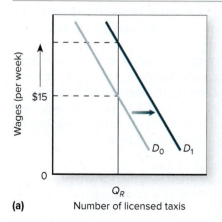

(a)

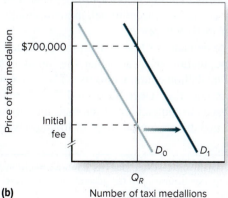

(b)

FIGURE 5-5 (A AND B) **Quantity Restrictions in the Market for Taxi Licenses**

When the demand for taxi services increased, because the number of taxi licenses was limited to 12,000, wages increased to above $15 an hour, as **(a)** shows. Because taxi medallions were limited in supply, as demand for taxi services rose, so did the demand for medallions. Their price rose significantly, as **(b)** shows.

Uber, Lyft, and Taxi Pricing

Recently, the taxi business has been in flux because of the development of companies such as Uber and Lyft that match individuals who need rides with private drivers willing to provide them on demand. The innovation over traditional taxi services is that the finding of the ride is handled on smartphone apps. Apart from these characteristics, Uber and Lyft function essentially just like taxi services—people hire drivers for transportation from one location to another. So allowing Uber and Lyft to operate in a city is equivalent to increasing the number of taxi medallions in the city. Allowing more taxi drivers adds more competition, holding the prices of taxi services down and lowering the value of the taxi medallions. (Prices of NYC taxi medallions fell from $1.3 million before Uber was active to about $180,000 in 2018.) It is not surprising that existing taxi companies and drivers don't like the new entrants.

©Mr.Whiskey/Shutterstock

Existing taxi services have lobbied against these new companies, arguing that Uber should be subject to the same regulations that they are. Because they aren't, they have a significant cost advantage that allows them to undercut traditional taxi prices. Some municipalities, such as Las Vegas, have agreed with that argument and passed laws forbidding Uber to operate there. These fights will likely continue.

One pricing innovation that Uber has implemented that existing taxi services do not use—in large part because the regulatory commissions do not let them use it—is "surge pricing." Surge pricing means that at certain times when taxis are in high demand—when it is raining, or on holidays such as New Year's Eve—Uber raises its rates, sometimes to seven times as high as its regular rates. This means that only those who are willing and able to pay such high prices are able to get a ride. Many in the lay public do not like surge pricing, but it is a pricing feature that economists have urged for many years—an efficient market means that as demand rises, price rises, reducing the quantity demanded to the available quantity supplied. With surge pricing, taxis are available for those who really want a taxi and are willing to pay. Economists call this practice peak and off-peak pricing.

Issuing taxi medallions had a secondary effect. Because New York City also granted medallion owners the right to sell their medallions, a market in medallions developed. Those fortunate enough to have been granted a medallion by the city found that they had a valuable asset. A person wanting to drive a taxi, and earn those high wages, had to buy a medallion from an existing driver. This meant that while new taxi drivers would earn a higher wage once they had bought a license, their wage after taking into account the cost of the license would be much lower.

Quantity restrictions tend to increase price.

As the demand for taxis rose, the medallions became more and more valuable. The effect on the price of medallions is shown in Figure 5-5(b). The quantity restriction, Q_R, means that any increases in demand lead only to price increases. Although the initial license fee was minimal, increases in demand for taxis quickly led to higher and higher medallion prices.

The demand for taxi medallions continued to increase each year as the New York City population grew more than the supply increased. The result was that the price of a taxi medallion continued to rise. That rise continued until Uber and Lyft entered the picture (see the "Uber, Lyft, and Taxi Pricing" Real-World Application box) and increased the competition. Their entering lowered the price of medallions. Not surprisingly, taxi drivers are pushing for limitations on both Uber and Lyft.[2]

---

[2]As is usually the case, the analysis is more complicated in real life. New York issues both individual and corporate licenses. But the general reasoning carries through: Effective quantity restrictions increase the value of a license.

Third-Party-Payer Markets

As a final example for this chapter, let's consider third-party-payer markets. In **third-party-payer markets,** *the person who receives the good differs from the person paying for the good.* An example is the health care market, where many individuals have insurance. They generally pay a co-payment for health care services and an HMO or other insurer pays the remainder. Medicare and Medicaid are both third-party payers. Figure 5-6 shows what happens in the supply/demand model when there is a third-party-payer market and a small co-payment. In the normal case, when the individual demander pays for the good, equilibrium quantity is where quantity demanded equals quantity supplied—in this case at an equilibrium price of $25 and an equilibrium quantity of 10.

Under a third-party-payer system, the person who chooses how much to purchase doesn't pay the entire cost. Because the co-payment faced by the consumer is much lower, quantity demanded is much greater. In this example with a co-payment of $5, the consumer demands 18. Given an upward-sloping supply curve, the seller requires a higher price, in this case $45 for each unit supplied to provide that quantity. Assuming the co-payment is for each unit, the consumer pays $5 of that price for a total out-of-pocket cost of $90 ($5 times 18). The third-party payer pays the remainder, $40, for a cost of $720 ($40 times 18). Total spending is $810. This compares to total spending of only $250 (25 times 10) if the consumer had to pay the entire price. Notice that with a third-party-payer system, total spending, represented by the large shaded rectangle, is much higher than total spending if the consumer paid, represented by the small darker rectangle.

The third-party-payer system describes much of the health care system in the United States today. Typically, a person with health insurance makes a fixed co-payment for an office visit, regardless of procedures and tests provided. Given this payment system, the insured patient has little incentive to limit the procedures offered by the doctor. The doctor charges the insurance company, and the insurance company pays. The rise in health care costs over the past decades can be attributed in part to the third-party-payer system.

A classic example of how third-party-payer systems can affect choices is a case where a 70-year-old man spent weeks in a hospital recovering from surgery to address abdominal bleeding. The bill, to be paid by Medicare, was nearing $275,000 and the patient wasn't recovering as quickly as expected. The doctor finally figured out that the

In third-party-payer markets, equilibrium quantity and total spending are much higher.

Q-10 If the cost of textbooks were included in tuition, what would likely happen to their prices? Why?

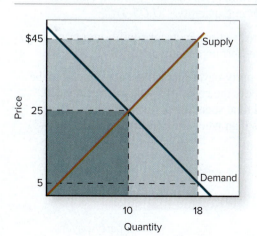

FIGURE 5-6 **Third-Party-Payer Markets**

In a third-party-payer system, the person who chooses the product doesn't pay the entire cost. Here, with a co-payment of $5, consumers demand 18 units. Sellers require $45 per unit for that quantity. Total expenditures, shown by the entire shaded region, are much greater compared to total spending when the consumer pays the entire cost, shown by just the dark shaded region.

patient's condition wasn't improving because ill-fitting dentures didn't allow him to eat properly. The doctor ordered the hospital dentist to fix the dentures, but the patient refused the treatment. Why? The patient explained: "Seventy-five dollars is a lot of money." The $75 procedure wasn't covered by Medicare.

Third-party-payer systems are not limited to health care. (Are your parents or the government paying for part of your college education? If you were paying the full amount, would you be demanding as much college education as you currently are?) Anytime a third-party-payer system exists, the quantity demanded will be higher than it otherwise would be. Market forces will not hold down costs as much as they would otherwise because the person using the service doesn't have an incentive to hold down costs. Of course, that doesn't mean that there are no pressures. The third-party payers—parents, employers, and government—will respond to this by trying to limit both the quantity of the good individuals consume and the amount they pay for it. For example, parents will put pressure on their kids to get through school quickly rather than lingering for five or six years, and government will place limitations on what procedures Medicare and Medicaid patients can use. The goods will be rationed through social and political means. Such effects are not unexpected; they are just another example of supply and demand in action.

Conclusion

I began this chapter by pointing out that supply and demand are the lens through which economists look at reality. It takes practice to use that lens, and this chapter gave you some practice. Focusing the lens on a number of issues highlighted certain aspects of those issues. The analysis was simple but powerful and should, if you followed it, provide you with a good foundation for understanding the economist's way of thinking about policy issues.

Summary

- By minding your Ps and Qs—the shifts of and movements along curves—you can describe almost all events in terms of supply and demand. (*LO5-1*)

- A price ceiling is a government-imposed limit on how high a price can be charged. Price ceilings below market price create shortages. (*LO5-2*)

- A price floor is a government-imposed limit on how low a price can be charged. Price floors above market price create surpluses. (*LO5-2*)

- Taxes and tariffs paid by suppliers shift the supply curve up by the amount of the tax or tariff. They raise the equilibrium price (inclusive of tax) and decrease the equilibrium quantity. (*LO5-3*)

- Quantity restrictions increase equilibrium price and reduce equilibrium quantity. (*LO5-4*)

- In a third-party-payer market, the consumer and the one who pays the cost differ. Quantity demanded, price, and total spending are greater when a third party pays than when the consumer pays. (*LO5-5*)

Key Terms

excise tax	price ceiling	rent control	third-party-payer
minimum wage law	price floor	tariff	market

Questions and Exercises ■ connect

1. Say that the equilibrium price and quantity both rose. What would you say was the most likely cause? *(LO5-1)*

2. Say that equilibrium price fell and quantity remained constant. What would you say was the most likely cause? *(LO5-1)*

3. The technology has been developed so that road use can be priced by computer. A computer in the surface of the road picks up a signal from your car and automatically charges you for the use of the road. How would this affect bottlenecks and rush-hour congestion? *(LO5-1)*

4. Demonstrate the effect on price and quantity of each of the following events: *(LO5-1)*
   a. In a recent popularity test, Elmo topped Cookie Monster in popularity (this represents a trend in children's tastes). Market: cookies.
   b. The Atkins Diet that limits carbohydrates was reported to be very effective. Market: bread.

5. Suppose oil production in Libya is interrupted by political unrest. At the same time, the demand for oil by China continues to rise. *(LO5-1)*
   a. Demonstrate the impact on the quantity of oil bought and sold.
   b. Oil production in Libya returns to its original levels. What is the likely effect on equilibrium oil price and quantity? Demonstrate your answer graphically.

6. Kennesaw University Professor Frank A. Adams III and Auburn University Professors A. H. Barnett and David L. Kaserman recently estimated the effect of legalizing the sale of cadaverous organs, which currently are in shortage at zero price. What are the effects of the following two possibilities on the equilibrium price and quantity of transplanted organs if their sale were to be legalized? Demonstrate your answers graphically. *(LO5-1)*
   a. Many of those currently willing to donate the organs of a deceased relative at zero price are offended that organs can be bought and sold and therefore withdraw from the donor program.
   b. People are willing to provide significantly more organs.

7. In 2014, a drought in the Midwest raised grain prices, leading to a decline in the size of cattle herds. Ultimately, the price of ground beef rose from about $3 a pound to over $4 by 2015. Demonstrate graphically the effect of the drought on equilibrium price and quantity in the ground beef market. *(LO5-1)*

8. Demonstrate graphically the effect of an effective price ceiling. *(LO5-2)*

9. Demonstrate graphically why rent controls might increase the total payment that new renters pay for an apartment. *(LO5-2)*

10. Demonstrate graphically the effect of a price floor. *(LO5-2)*

11. Graphically show the effects of a minimum wage on the number of unemployed. *(LO5-2)*

12. Taxes can be levied on consumers or producers. *(LO5-3)*
   a. Demonstrate the effect of a $4 per-unit tax on suppliers on equilibrium price and quantity.
   b. Demonstrate the effect of a $4 per-unit tax on consumers on equilibrium price and quantity.
   c. How does the impact on equilibrium prices (paid by consumers and received by producers) and quantity differ between a and b?

13. Draw the supply and demand curves associated with the tables below. *(LO5-3)*

Price	Q_S	Q_D
$0.00	50	200
0.50	100	175
1.00	150	150
1.50	200	125
2.00	250	100

   a. What is equilibrium price and quantity?
   b. What is equilibrium price and quantity with a $0.75 per-unit tax levied on suppliers? Demonstrate your answer graphically.
   c. How does your answer to b change if the tax were levied on consumers, not suppliers? Demonstrate your answer graphically.
   d. What conclusion can you draw about the difference between levying a tax on suppliers and consumers?

14. Quotas are quantity restrictions on imported goods. Demonstrate the effect of a quota on the price of imported goods. *(LO5-4)*

15. The city of Pawnee issues a fixed number of fishing licenses each year. *(LO5-4)*
   a. Using the accompanying graph, demonstrate the effect of a limit of 100 fishing licenses at a cost of $20 per license.
   b. Is there excess supply or demand for licenses? Label the excess supply or demand on the graph.
   c. What is the maximum amount a person would be willing to pay on the black market for a license?
   d. How much would Pawnee need to charge to eliminate the excess supply or demand?

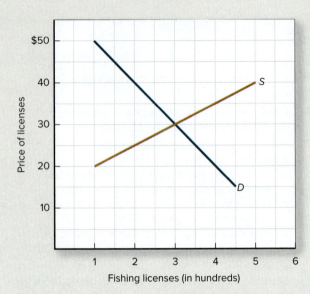

16. In what ways is the market for public postsecondary education an example of a third-party-payer market? What's the impact of this on total educational expenditures? *(LO5-5)*

17. You're given the following supply and demand tables: *(LO5-5)*

	Demand		Supply	
P	**Q**		**P**	**Q**
$ 0	1,200		$ 0	0
2	900		2	0
4	600		4	150
6	300		6	300
8	0		8	600
10	0		10	600
12	0		12	750
14	0		14	900

a. What is equilibrium price and quantity in a market system with no interferences?

b. If this were a third-party-payer market where the consumer pays $2, what is the quantity demanded? What is the price charged by the seller?

c. What is total spending in the two situations described in *a* and *b*?

Questions from Alternative Perspectives

1. Some economists believe minimum wages create distortions in the labor market. If you are an employer and unable to hire the one willing and able to work for the lowest wage, how else might you choose a worker? Is this fair? Why or why not? *(Austrian)*

2. On average, women are paid less than men. What are the likely reasons for that? Should the government intervene with a law that requires firms to pay equal wages to those with comparable skills? *(Feminist)*

3. Biological evolution occurs very slowly; cultural evolution occurs less slowly, but still slowly compared to institutional and market evolution.
   a. Give some examples of these observations about the different speeds of adjustment.
   b. Explain the relevance of these observations to economic reasoning. *(Institutionalist)*

4. Most religions argue that individuals should not fully exploit market positions. For example, the text makes it sound as if allowing prices to rise to whatever level clears

the market is the best policy to follow. That means that if, for example, someone were stranded in the desert and were willing to pay half his or her future income for life for a drink of water, charging him or her that price would be appropriate. Is it appropriate? Why or why not? *(Religious)*

5. Rent control today looks far different from the rent freeze New York City enacted after World War II. Most rent controls today simply restrict annual rent increases and guarantee landlords a "fair return" in return for maintaining their properties.
   a. How would the economic effects of today's rent controls differ from the rent control programs depicted in your textbook?
   b. Do you consider them an appropriate mechanism to address the disproportionate power that landlords hold over tenants?
   c. If not, what policies would you recommend to address that inequity and the lack of affordable housing in U.S. cities? *(Radical)*

Issues to Ponder

1. In the late 1990s, the television networks were given $70 billion worth of space on public airways for broadcasting high-definition television rather than auctioning it off.

   a. Why do airways have value?
   b. After the airway had been given to the network, would you expect that the broadcaster would produce high-definition television?

2. About 10,000 tickets for the Men's Final Four college basketball games at the St. Louis Edward Jones Dome are to be sold in a lottery system for between $110 and $130 apiece. Typically applications exceed available tickets by 100,000. A year before the game, scalpers already offer to sell tickets for between $200 and $2,000 depending on seat location, even though the practice is illegal.
   a. Demonstrate the supply and demand for Final Four tickets. How do you know that there is an excess demand for tickets at $130?
   b. Demonstrate the scalped price of between $200 and $2,000.
   c. What would be the effect of legalizing scalping on the resale value of Final Four tickets?

3. In some states and localities "scalping" is against the law, although enforcement of these laws is spotty.
   a. Using supply/demand analysis and words, demonstrate what a weakly enforced antiscalping law would likely do to the price of tickets.
   b. Using supply/demand analysis and words, demonstrate what a strongly enforced antiscalping law would likely do to the price of tickets.

4. In 1938 Congress created a Board of Cosmetology in Washington, D.C., to license beauticians. To obtain a license, people had to attend a cosmetology school. In 1992 this law was used by the board to close down a hair-braiding salon specializing in cornrows and braids operated by unlicensed Mr. Uqdah, even though little was then taught in cosmetology schools about braiding and cornrows.
   a. What possible reason can you give for why this board exists?
   b. What options might you propose to change the system?
   c. What will be the political difficulties of implementing those options?

5. In the Oregon health care plan for rationing Medicaid expenditures, therapy to slow the progression of AIDS and treatment for brain cancer were covered, while liver transplants and treatment for infectious mononucleosis were not covered.
   a. What criteria do you think were used to determine what was covered and what was not covered?
   b. Should an economist have opposed the Oregon plan because it involves rationing?
   c. How does the rationing that occurs in the market differ from the rationing that occurs in the Oregon plan?

6. Airlines and hotels have many frequent-flyer and frequent-visitor programs in which individuals who fly the airline or stay at the hotel receive bonuses that are the equivalent to discounts.
   a. Give two reasons why these companies have such programs rather than simply offering lower prices.
   b. Can you give other examples of such programs?
   c. What is a likely reason why firms whose employees receive these benefits do not require their employees to give the benefits to the firm?

7. The U.S. government supports the U.S. price of sugar by limiting sugar imports into the United States. Restricting imports is effective because the United States consumes more sugar than it produces.
   a. Using supply/demand analysis, demonstrate how import restrictions increase the price of domestic sugar.
   b. What other import policy could the government implement to have the same effect as the import restriction?
   c. Under the Uruguay Round of the General Agreement on Tariffs and Trade, the United States agreed to permit at least 1.25 million tons of sugar to be imported into the United States. How does this affect the U.S. sugar price support program?

8. Apartments in New York City are often hard to find. One of the major reasons is rent control.
   a. Demonstrate graphically how rent controls could make apartments hard to find.
   b. Often one can get an apartment if one makes a side payment to the current tenant. Can you explain why?
   c. What would be the likely effect of eliminating rent controls?
   d. What is the political appeal of rent controls?

9. At one time, angora goat wool (mohair) was designated as a strategic commodity (it used to be utilized in some military clothing). Because of that, for every dollar's worth of mohair sold to manufacturers, ranchers used to receive $3.60.
   a. Demonstrate graphically the effect of eliminating this designation and subsidy.
   b. Why was the program likely kept in existence for so long?
   c. Say that a politician has suggested that the government should pass a law that requires all consumers to pay a price for angora goat wool high enough so that the sellers of that wool would receive $3.60 more than the market price. Demonstrate the effect of the law graphically. Would consumers support it? How about suppliers?

10. Supply/demand analysis states that equilibrium occurs where quantity supplied equals quantity demanded, but in U.S. agricultural markets quantity supplied almost always exceeds quantity demanded. How can this be?

11. Nobel Prize–winning economist Bill Vickrey suggested that automobile insurance should be paid as a tax on gas, rather than as a fixed fee per year per car. How would that change likely affect the number of automobiles that individuals own?

12. The United States imposes substantial taxes on cigarettes but not on loose tobacco. When the tax went into effect, what effect did it likely have for cigarette rolling machines?

13. At one time in Japan, doctors both prescribed and sold the drugs to the patient, receiving a 25 percent markup. In the United States, doctors prescribe drugs, but, generally, they do not sell them.
   a. Which country likely prescribed the most drugs? Why?
   b. How would a plan to limit the price of old drugs, but not new drugs to allow for innovation, likely affect the drug industry?

c. How might a drug company in the United States encourage a doctor in the United States, where doctors receive nothing for drugs, to prescribe more drugs?

14. In the early 2000s, Whole Foods Market Inc. switched to a medical care plan that had a high deductible, which meant that employees were responsible for the first $1,500 of care, whereas after that they received 80 percent coverage.

The firm also put about $800 in an account for each employee to use for medical care. If employees did not use this money, they could carry it over to the next year.
a. What do you expect happened to medical claim costs?
b. What do you believe happened to hospital admissions?
c. Demonstrate graphically the reasons for your answers in a and b.

Answers to Margin Questions

1. False. When supply rises, supply shifts out to the right. Price falls because demand slopes downward. (LO5-1)

2. A discovery of a hormone that will increase cows' milk production by 20 percent will increase the supply of milk, pushing the price down and increasing the quantity demanded, as in the accompanying graph. (LO5-1)

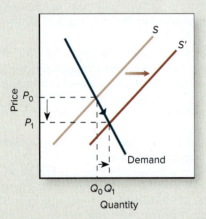

3. Quantity decreases but it is unclear what happens to price. (LO5-1)

4. It is likely demand shifted in and supply remained constant. (LO5-1)

5. Since the price ceiling is above the equilibrium price, it will have no effect on the market-determined equilibrium price and quantity. (LO5-2)

6. The price ceiling will result in a lower price and quantity sold. There will be excess demand $Q_D - Q_S$. (LO5-2)

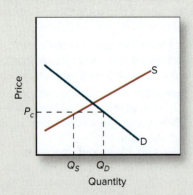

7. Since the price floor is below the equilibrium price, it will have no effect on the market-determined equilibrium price and quantity. (LO5-2)

8. I would respond that the tax will most likely raise the price by less than $2 since the tax will cause the quantity demanded to decrease. This will decrease quantity supplied, and hence decrease the price the suppliers receive. In the diagram below, Q falls from Q_0 to Q_1 and the price the supplier receives falls from $4 to $3, making the final price $5, not $6. (LO5-3)

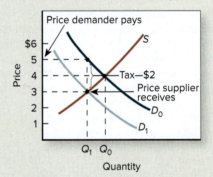

9. Given the quantity restriction, equilibrium quantity will be Q_R and equilibrium price will be P_0, which is higher than the market equilibrium price of P_e. (LO5-4)

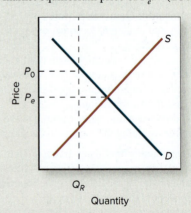

10. Universities would probably charge the high tuition they do now, but they would likely negotiate with publishers for lower textbook prices because they are both demanding and paying for the textbook. (LO5-5)

Algebraic Representation of Supply, Demand, and Equilibrium

In this chapter and in the previous chapter, I discussed demand, supply, and the determination of equilibrium price and quantity in words and graphs. These concepts also can be presented in equations. In this appendix I do so, using straight-line supply and demand curves.

The Laws of Supply and Demand in Equations

Since the law of supply states that quantity supplied is positively related to price, the slope of an equation specifying a supply curve is positive. (The quantity intercept term is generally less than zero since suppliers are generally unwilling to supply a good at a price less than zero.) An example of a supply equation is

$$Q_S = -5 + 2P$$

where Q_S is units supplied and P is the price of each unit in dollars per unit. The law of demand states that as price rises, quantity demanded declines. Price and quantity are negatively related, so a demand curve has a negative slope. An example of a demand equation is

$$Q_D = 10 - P$$

where Q_D is units demanded and P is the price of each unit in dollars per unit.

Determination of Equilibrium

The equilibrium price and quantity can be determined in three steps using these two equations. To find the equilibrium price and quantity for these particular demand and supply curves, you must find the quantity and price that solve both equations simultaneously.

Step 1: Set the quantity demanded equal to quantity supplied:

$$Q_S = Q_D \rightarrow -5 + 2P = 10 - P$$

Step 2: Solve for the price by rearranging terms. Doing so gives:

$$3P = 15$$
$$P = \$5$$

Thus, equilibrium price is $5.

FIGURE A5-1 **Supply and Demand Equilibrium**

The algebra in this appendix leads to the same results as the geometry in the chapter. Equilibrium occurs where quantity supplied equals quantity demanded.

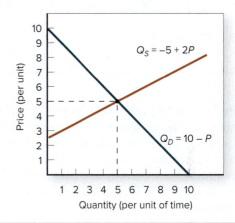

Step 3: To find equilibrium quantity, you can substitute $5 for P in either the demand or supply equation. Let's do it for supply: $Q_S = -5 + (2 \times 5) = 5$ units. I'll leave it to you to confirm that the quantity you obtain by substituting $P = \$5$ in the demand equation is also 5 units.

The answer could also be found graphically. The supply and demand curves specified by these equations are depicted in Figure A5-1. As you can see, demand and supply intersect; quantity demanded equals quantity supplied at a quantity of 5 units and a price of $5.

Movements along a Demand and Supply Curve

The demand and supply curves above represent schedules of quantities demanded and supplied at various prices. Movements along each can be represented by selecting various prices and solving for quantity demanded and supplied. Let's create a supply and demand table using the above equations—supply: $Q_S = -5 + 2P$; demand: $Q_D = 10 - P$.

P	$Q_S = -5 + 2P$	$Q_D = 10 - P$
$0	-5	10
1	-3	9
2	-1	8
3	1	7
4	3	6
5	5	5
6	7	4
7	9	3
8	11	2
9	13	1
10	15	0

As you move down the rows, you are moving up along the supply schedule, as shown by increasing quantity supplied, and moving down along the demand schedule, as shown by decreasing quantity demanded. Just to confirm your equilibrium quantity and price calculations, notice that at a price of $5, quantity demanded equals quantity supplied.

Shifts of a Demand and Supply Schedule

What would happen if suppliers changed their expectations so that they would be willing to sell more goods at every price? This shift factor of supply would shift the entire supply curve out to the right. Let's say that at every price, quantity supplied increases by 3. Mathematically the new equation would be $Q_S = -2 + 2P$. The quantity intercept increases by 3. What would you expect to happen to equilibrium price and quantity? Let's solve the equations mathematically first.

Step 1: To determine equilibrium price, set the new quantity supplied equal to quantity demanded:

$$10 - P = -2 + 2P$$

Step 2: Solve for the equilibrium price:

$$12 = 3P$$
$$P = \$4$$

Step 3: To determine equilibrium quantity, substitute P in either the demand or supply equation:

$$Q_D = 10 - (1 \times 4) = 6 \text{ units}$$
$$Q_S = -2 + (2 \times 4) = 6 \text{ units}$$

Equilibrium price declined to $4 and equilibrium quantity rose to 6, just as you would expect with a rightward shift in a supply curve.

Now let's suppose that demand shifts out to the right. Here we would expect both equilibrium price and equilibrium quantity to rise. We begin with our original supply and demand curves—supply: $Q_S = -5 + 2P$; demand: $Q_D = 10 - P$. Let's say at every price, the quantity demanded rises by 3. The new equation for demand would be $Q_D = 13 - P$. You may want to solve this equation for various prices to confirm that at every price, quantity demanded rises by 3. Let's solve the equations for equilibrium price and quantity.

Step 1: Set the quantities equal to one another:

$$13 - P = -5 + 2P$$

Step 2: Solve for equilibrium price:

$$18 = 3P$$
$$P = \$6$$

Step 3: Substitute P in either the demand or supply equation:

$$Q_D = 13 - (1 \times 6) = 7 \text{ units}$$
$$Q_S = -5 + (2 \times 6) = 7 \text{ units}$$

Equilibrium price rose to $6 and equilibrium quantity rose to 7 units, just as you would expect with a rightward shift in a demand curve.

Just to make sure you've got it, I will do two more examples. First, suppose the demand and supply equations for wheat per year in the United States can be specified as follows (notice that the slope is negative for the demand curve and positive for the supply curve):

$$Q_D = 500 - 2P$$
$$Q_S = -100 + 4P$$

P is the price in dollars per thousand bushels and Q is the quantity of wheat in thousands of bushels. Remember that the units must always be stated. What are the equilibrium price and quantity?

Step 1: Set the quantities equal to one another:

$$500 - 2P = -100 + 4P$$

Step 2: Solve for equilibrium price:

$$600 = 6P$$
$$P = \$100$$

Step 3: Substitute P in either the demand or supply equation:

$$Q_D = 500 - (2 \times 100) = 300$$
$$Q_S = -100 + (4 \times 100) = 300$$

Equilibrium quantity is 300 thousand bushels.

As my final example, take a look at Alice's demand curve depicted in Figure 4-4(b) in Chapter 4. Can you write an equation that represents the demand curve in that figure? It is $Q_D = 10 - 2P$. At a price of zero, the quantity of movie rentals Alice demands is 10, and for every increase in price of \$1, the quantity she demands falls by 2. Now look at Ann's supply curve shown in Figure 4-7(b) in Chapter 4. Ann's supply curve mathematically is $Q_S = 2P$. At a zero price, the quantity Ann supplies is zero, and for every \$1 increase in price, the quantity she supplies rises by 2. What are the equilibrium price and quantity?

Step 1: Set the quantities equal to one another:

$$10 - 2P = 2P$$

Step 2: Solve for equilibrium price:

$$4P = 10$$
$$P = \$2.5$$

Step 3: Substitute P in either the demand or supply equation:

$$Q_D = 10 - (2 \times 2.5) = 5, \text{ or}$$
$$Q_S = 2 \times 2.5 = 5 \text{ movies per week}$$

Ann is willing to supply five movies per week at \$2.50 per rental and Alice demands five movies at \$2.50 per movie rental. Remember that in Figure 4-8 in Chapter 4, I showed you graphically the equilibrium quantity and price of Alice's demand curve and Ann's supply curve. I'll leave it up to you to check that the graphic solution in Figure 4-8 is the same as the mathematical solution we came up with here.

Price Ceilings and Price Floors

Let's now consider a price ceiling and price floor. We start with the supply and demand curves:

$$Q_S = -5 + 2P$$
$$Q_D = 10 - P$$

This gave us the solution

$$P = 5$$
$$Q = 5$$

Now, say that a price ceiling of \$4 is imposed. Would you expect a shortage or a surplus? If you said "shortage," you're doing well. If not, review the chapter before continuing with this appendix. To find out how much the shortage is, we must find out how much will be supplied and how much will be demanded at the price ceiling. Substituting \$4 for price in both equations lets us see that $Q_S = 3$ units and $Q_D = 6$ units. There will be a shortage of three units. Next, let's consider a price floor of \$6. To determine the surplus, we follow the same exercise. Substituting \$6 into the two equations gives a quantity supplied of seven units and a quantity demanded of four units, so there is a surplus of three units.

Taxes and Subsidies

Next, let's consider the effect of a tax of \$1 placed on the supplier. That tax would decrease the price received by suppliers by \$1. In other words,

$$Q_S = -5 + 2(P - 1)$$

Multiplying the terms in parentheses by 2 and collecting terms results in

$$Q_S = -7 + 2P$$

This supply equation has the same slope as in the previous case, but a new intercept term—just what you'd expect. To determine the new equilibrium price and quantity, follow steps 1 to 3 discussed earlier. Setting this new equation equal to demand and solving for price gives

$$P = 5\tfrac{2}{3}$$

Substituting this price into the demand and supply equations tells us equilibrium quantity:

$$Q_S = Q_D = 4\tfrac{1}{3} \text{ units}$$

Of that price, the supplier must pay \$1 in tax, so the price the supplier receives net of tax is \$4⅔.

Next, let's say that the tax were put on the demander rather than on the supplier. In that case, the tax increases the price for demanders by \$1 and the demand equation becomes

$$Q_D = 10 - (P + 1), \text{ or}$$
$$Q_D = 9 - P$$

Again solving for equilibrium price and quantity requires setting the demand and supply equations equal to one another and solving for price. I leave the steps to you. The result is

$$P = 4\tfrac{2}{3}$$

This is the price the supplier receives. The price demanders pay is \$5⅔. The equilibrium quantity will be 4⅓ units.

These are the same results we got in the previous cases showing that, given the assumptions, it doesn't matter who actually pays the tax: The effect on equilibrium price and quantity is identical no matter who pays it.

Quotas

Finally, let's consider the effect of a quota of 4⅓ placed on the market. Since a quota limits the quantity supplied, as long as the quota is less than the market equilibrium quantity, the supply equation becomes

$$Q_S = 4\tfrac{1}{3}$$

where Q_S is the actual amount supplied. The price that the market will arrive at for this quantity is determined by the demand curve. To find that price, substitute the quantity 4⅓ into the demand equation ($Q_D = 10 - P$):

$$4\tfrac{1}{3} = 10 - P$$

and solve for P:

$$P = 5\tfrac{2}{3}$$

Since consumers are willing to pay \$5⅔, this is what suppliers will receive. The price that suppliers would have been willing to accept for a quantity of 4⅓ is \$4⅔. This can be found by substituting the amount of the quota in the supply equation:

$$4\tfrac{1}{3} = -5 + 2P$$

and solving for P:

$$2P = 9\tfrac{1}{3}$$
$$P = 4\tfrac{2}{3}$$

Notice that this result is very similar to the tax. For demanders it is identical; they pay \$5⅔ and receive 4⅓ units. For suppliers, however, the situation is much preferable; instead of receiving a price of \$4⅔, the amount they received with the tax, they receive \$5⅔. With a quota, suppliers receive the "implicit tax revenue" that results from the higher price.

Questions and Exercises

1. Suppose the demand and supply for milk are described by the following equations: $Q_D = 600 - 100P$; $Q_S = -150 + 150P$, where P is price in dollars, Q_D is quantity demanded in millions of gallons per year, and Q_S is quantity supplied in millions of gallons per year.
   a. Create demand and supply tables corresponding to these equations.
   b. Graph supply and demand and determine equilibrium price and quantity.
   c. Confirm your answer to b by solving the equations mathematically.

2. Beginning with the equations in question 1, suppose a growth hormone is introduced that allows dairy farmers to offer 125 million more gallons of milk per year at each price.
   a. Construct new demand and supply curves reflecting this change. Describe with words what happened to the supply curve and to the demand curve.
   b. Graph the new curves and determine equilibrium price and quantity.
   c. Determine equilibrium price and quantity by solving the equations mathematically.

   d. Suppose the government set the price of milk at \$3 a gallon. Demonstrate the effect of this regulation on the market for milk. What is quantity demanded? What is quantity supplied?

3. Write demand and supply equations that represent demand, D_0, and supply, S_0, in Figure A5-1 in this appendix.
   a. Solve for equilibrium price and quantity mathematically. Show your work.
   b. Rewrite the demand equation to reflect an increase in demand of 3 units. What happens to equilibrium price and quantity?
   c. Rewrite the supply equation to reflect a decrease in supply of 3 units at every price level. What happens to equilibrium price and quantity using the demand curve from b?

4. a. How is a shift in demand reflected in a demand equation?
   b. How is a shift in supply reflected in a supply equation?
   c. How is a movement along a demand (supply) curve reflected in a demand (supply) equation?

5. Suppose the demand and supply for wheat are described by the following equations: $Q_D = 10 - P$; $Q_S = 2 + P$,

where P is the price in dollars, Q_D is quantity demanded in millions of bushels per year, and Q_S is quantity supplied in millions of bushels per year.
a. Solve for equilibrium price and quantity of wheat.
b. Would a government-set price of $5 create a surplus or a shortage of wheat? How much? Is $5 a price ceiling or a price floor?

6. Suppose the U.S. government imposes a $1-per-gallon-of-milk tax on dairy farmers. Using the demand and supply equations from question 1:
a. What is the effect of the tax on the supply equation? The demand equation?
b. What are the new equilibrium price and quantity?
c. How much do dairy farmers receive per gallon of milk after the tax? How much do demanders pay?

7. Repeat question 6 assuming the tax is placed on the buyers of milk. Does it matter who pays the tax?

8. Repeat question 6 assuming the government pays a subsidy of $1 per gallon of milk to farmers.

9. Suppose the demand for movies is represented by $Q_D = 15 - 4P$, and the supply of movies is represented by $Q_S = 4P - 1$. Determine if each of the following is a price floor, price ceiling, or neither. In each case, determine the shortage or surplus.
a. $P = \$3$
b. $P = \$1.50$
c. $P = \$2.25$
d. $P = \$2.50$

PART II

Microeconomics

> In my vacations, I visited the poorest quarters of several cities and walked through one street after another, looking at the faces of the poorest people. Next I resolved to make as thorough a study as I could of Political Economy.

You may remember having already seen this quotation from Alfred Marshall. It began the first chapter. I chose this beginning for two reasons. First, it gives what I believe to be the best reason to study economics. Second, the quotation is from a hero of mine, one of the economic giants of all times. His *Principles of Economics* was the economists' bible in the late 1800s and early 1900s. How important was Marshall? It was Marshall who first used the supply and demand curves as an engine of analysis.

I repeat this quotation here because, for Marshall, economics was microeconomics, and it is his vision of economics that underlies this book's approach to microeconomics. For Marshall, economics was an art that was meant to be applied—used to explain why things were the way they were, and what we could do about them. He had little use for esoteric theory that didn't lead to a direct application to a real-world problem. Reflecting on the state of economics in 1906, Marshall wrote to a friend:

> I had a growing feeling in the later years of my work at the subject that a good mathematical theorem dealing with economic hypotheses was very unlikely to be good economics: and I went more and more on the rules—(1) Use mathematics as a shorthand language, rather than as an engine of inquiry. (2) Keep to them until you have done. (3) Translate into English. (4) Then illustrate by examples that are important in real life. (5) Burn the mathematics. (6) If you can't succeed in (4), burn (3). This last I did often. (From a letter from Marshall to A. L. Bowley, reprinted in A. C. Pigou, *Memorials of Alfred Marshall*, p. 427.)

Marshall didn't feel this way about mathematical economics because he couldn't do mathematics. He was trained as a formal mathematician, and he was a good one. But, for him, mathematics wasn't economics, and the real world was too messy to have applied to it much of the fancy mathematical economic work that some of his fellow economists were doing. Marshall recognized the influence of market, political, and social forces and believed that all three had to be taken into account in applying economic reasoning to reality.

You won't see much highfalutin mathematical economics in these microeconomic chapters. The chapters follow the Marshallian methodology and present the minimum of formal theory necessary to apply the concepts of economics to the real world, and then they do just that: start talking about real-world issues.

Section I, The Power of Traditional Economic Models (Chapters 6, 7, 8, and 8W), develops the supply/demand model and shows you how it can be used to analyze policy issues. Section II, International Economic Policy Issues (Chapters 9 and 10), extends economic reasoning to international issues. Section III, Production and Cost Analysis (Chapters 11 and 12), shows the foundation of cost analysis and how it relates to firms.

Section IV, Market Structure (Chapters 13–16), introduces you to various market structures, and antitrust policy.

Section V, Factor Markets (Chapters 17, 17W, and 18), looks at a particular set of markets—factor markets. These markets play a central role in determining the distribution of income. These chapters won't tell you how to get rich (you'll have to wait for the sequel for that), but they will give you new insights into how labor markets work.

Section VI, Choice and Decision Making (Chapters 19 and 20), presents both the traditional and modern theories of choice, including the game theoretic foundations of modern economic thinking and its relation to some new developments in behavioral economics.

Section VII, Modern Economic Thinking (Chapters 21–23), discusses some new developments that are changing the nature of modern microeconomics.

CHAPTER 6

Describing Supply and Demand: Elasticities

After reading this chapter, you should be able to:

LO6-1 Use *elasticity* to describe the responsiveness of quantities to changes in price and distinguish five elasticity terms.

LO6-2 Explain the importance of substitution in determining elasticity of supply and demand.

LO6-3 Relate price elasticity of demand to total revenue.

LO6-4 Define and calculate income elasticity and cross-price elasticity of demand.

LO6-5 Explain how the concept of *elasticity* makes supply and demand analysis more useful.

©Jesse Allen/National Aeronautics and Space Administration

It was reported that during Hurricane Harvey in 2017, some stores raised their price of bottled water from $9 a case to $99 a case. That's more than a 10-fold increase! They did it because the demand for bottled water increased and the supply decreased. The increase in price rationed the water to those who were willing to pay and discouraged people from hoarding water, just to be on the safe side. Because around the time of the hurricane the quantity of bottled water demanded was not responsive to price, a small increase in the price would not have significantly decreased the quantity demanded. The large increase did. In economic terminology, the demand for water was highly price inelastic, which means that to significantly affect quantity demanded, the price had to rise a lot.

As you can see, information about elasticity is extremely important to firms in making their pricing decisions, and to economists in their study of the economy. That's one reason why grocery stores like shoppers to use their preferred-customer cards. These cards provide the stores with data about shopper behavior such as how sensitive shoppers are to price changes. Whenever a firm is thinking of changing its prices, it has a strong interest in elasticity.

Price Elasticity

The most commonly used elasticity concept is price elasticity of demand and supply. **Price elasticity of demand** is *the percentage change in quantity demanded divided by the percentage change in price:*

$$E_D = \frac{\text{Percentage change in quantity demanded}}{\text{Percentage change in price}}$$

Price elasticity of supply is *the percentage change in quantity supplied divided by the percentage change in price:*

$$E_S = \frac{\text{Percentage change in quantity supplied}}{\text{Percentage change in price}}$$

Let's consider some numerical examples. Say the price of a good rises by 10 percent and, in response, quantity demanded falls by 20 percent. The price elasticity of demand is 2 (−20 percent/10 percent). Notice that I said 2, not −2. Because quantity demanded is inversely related to price, the calculation for the price elasticity of demand comes out negative. Despite this fact, economists talk about price elasticity of demand as a positive number. (Those of you who remember some math can think of elasticity as an *absolute value* of a number, rather than a simple number.) Using this convention makes it easier to remember that a *larger* number for price elasticity of demand means quantity demanded is *more responsive* to price.

To make sure you have the idea down, let's consider two more examples. Say that when price falls by 5 percent, quantity supplied falls by 2 percent. In this case, the price elasticity of supply is 0.4 (2 percent/5 percent). And, finally, say the price goes up by 10 percent and in response the quantity demanded falls by 15 percent. Price elasticity of demand is 1.5 (15 percent/10 percent).

> Price elasticity is the percentage change in quantity divided by the percentage change in price.

> **Q-1** If when price rises by 4 percent, quantity supplied rises by 8 percent, what is the price elasticity of supply?

What Information Price Elasticity Provides

Price elasticity of demand and supply tells us exactly how quantity responds to a change in price. A price elasticity of demand of 0.3 tells us that a 10 percent rise in price will lead to a 3 percent decline in quantity demanded. If the elasticity of demand were a larger number, say 5, the same 10 percent rise in price will lead to a 50 percent decline in quantity demanded. As elasticity increases, quantity responds more to price changes.

Classifying Demand and Supply as Elastic or Inelastic

It is helpful to classify elasticities by relative responsiveness. Economists usually describe supply and demand by the terms *elastic* and *inelastic*. Formally, demand or supply is **elastic** if *the percentage change in quantity is greater than the percentage change in price* ($E > 1$). Conversely, demand or supply is **inelastic** if *the percentage change in quantity is less than the percentage change in price* ($E < 1$). In the last two examples, an elasticity of demand of 0.3 means demand is inelastic ($E_D < 1$), and an elasticity of demand of 5 means demand is elastic ($E_D > 1$).

> Elastic: $E > 1$
> Inelastic: $E < 1$

The commonsense interpretation of these terms is the following: An *inelastic* supply means that the quantity supplied doesn't change much with a change in price. For example, say the price of land rises. The amount of land supplied won't change much, so the supply of land is inelastic. An *elastic* supply means that quantity supplied changes by a larger percentage than the percentage change in price. For example, say the price of pencils doubles. What do you think will happen to the quantity of pencils supplied? I suspect it will more than double, which means that the supply of pencils is elastic.

The same terminology holds with demand. Consider a good such as Hulu, which has a close substitute, Netflix. If Hulu's price rises, the quantity demanded will fall a lot as people shift to the substitute (Netflix). So the demand for Hulu would be highly elastic. Alternatively, consider table salt, which has no close substitute, at least at current prices. Demand for table salt is highly inelastic. That is, a rise in the price of table salt does not result in a large decline in quantity demanded.

> **Q-2** If price elasticity of demand is greater than 1, what would we call demand: elastic or inelastic?

Elasticity Is Independent of Units

Before continuing, notice that elasticity measures the percentage, not the unit, change in variables. Using percentages allows us to measure responsiveness independent of units, making comparisons among different goods easier. Say a $1 increase in the price of a $1,000 computer decreases the quantity demanded by 1, from 10 to 9. Say also that a $1 increase in the price of a pen, from $1 to $2, decreases quantity demanded by 1—from 10,000 to 9,999. Using unit changes, the $1 price increase reduced the quantities demanded for both pens and computers by 1. But such a comparison of unit changes is not very helpful. To see that, ask yourself if you were planning on raising your price, which good you'd rather be selling.

The computer price increased by 1/1,000 of its original price, a relatively small percentage increase, and quantity demanded declined by 1/10 of original sales, a large percentage decline. The percentage decline in quantity demanded exceeded the percentage rise in price, so your total revenue (Price × Quantity) would decrease. The percentage increase in price of pens was relatively large— 100 percent—and the percentage decline in quantity demanded was relatively small—1/100 of 1 percent. So if you raise the price of pens, total revenue increases. Clearly, if you're raising your price in these examples, you'd rather be selling pens than computers.

By using percentages, this is made clear: With computers, a 0.1 percent increase in price decreases quantity demanded by 10 percent, so the elasticity is 100. With pens, a 100 percent increase in price decreases quantity demanded by 0.01 percent—an elasticity of 0.0001.

Calculating Elasticities

To see that you've got the analysis down, calculate price elasticity of demand or supply in the following three real-world examples:

Case 1: When Orange County, Florida, raised the price of its toll roads by 14 percent, the number of motorists using toll roads fell by only 1.8 percent.

Case 2: When gasoline prices rose by 10 percent in Washington, D.C., the quantity of gasoline demanded there fell by 40 percent.

Case 3: When the minimum wage in Vermont rose by 11 percent, the quantity of labor supplied for relevant jobs increased by about 1.7 percent.

In the first case, price elasticity of demand is 0.13. The quantity of motorists using toll roads in Orange County did not change much when the toll was increased. Elasticity was less than 1, so demand was inelastic. In the second case, price elasticity of demand is 4. The quantity of gas demanded in Washington, D.C., responded by a lot to a relatively small change in gas prices. Elasticity was greater than 1, so demand was elastic. The price elasticity of supply in the third case is 0.16. The quantity of labor supplied did not respond much to the change in wage. Elasticity was less than 1, so supply was inelastic.

Web Note 6.1

Price Elasticity of Gas Demand

Let's now calculate some elasticities graphically. Let's begin by determining the price elasticity of demand between points *A* and *B* in Figure 6-1(a).

The demand curve in the figure is a hypothetical demand for WolfPack Simulation Software. You can see that as the price of the software rises from $20 to $26, the quantity demanded falls from 14,000 to 10,000 units a year. To determine the price elasticity of demand, we need to determine the percentage change in quantity and the percentage change in price. In doing so, there is a small problem that is sometimes called the *endpoint problem:* The percentage change differs depending on whether you

FIGURE 6-1 (A AND B) Graphs of Elasticities

In **(a)** we are calculating the elasticity of the demand curve between *A* and *B*. We essentially calculate the midpoint and use that midpoint to calculate percentage changes. This gives us a percentage change in price of 26 percent and a percentage change in quantity of 33 percent, for an elasticity of 1.27. In **(b)** the percentage change in price is 10.53 percent and the percentage change in quantity is 1.87 percent, giving an elasticity of 0.18.

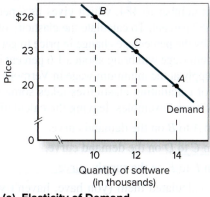

(a) **Elasticity of Demand**

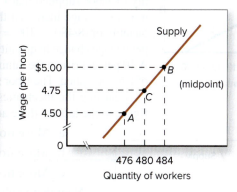

(b) **Elasticity of Supply**

view the change as a rise or a decline. For example, say you calculate the rise in price from $20 to $26, starting from $20. That gives you a percentage increase in price of $[(20 - 26)/20] \times 100 = 30$ percent. If, however, you calculate that same change in price, $6, as a fall in price from $26 to $20, the percentage decrease in price is $[(26 - 20)/26] \times 100 = 23$ percent. The easiest way to solve this problem is to use the average of the two end values to calculate percentage change. In our example, instead of using 20 or 26 as a starting point, you use $(20 + 26)/2$, or 23. So the percentage change in price is

Economists use the average of the two end values to get around the endpoint problem.

$$\frac{P_2 - P_1}{\frac{1}{2}(P_1 + P_2)} = \frac{(26 - 20)}{23} \times 100 = 26 \text{ percent}$$

Similarly, the percentage change in quantity is

$$\frac{Q_2 - Q_1}{\frac{1}{2}(Q_1 + Q_2)} = \frac{(10 - 14)}{12} \times 100 = -33 \text{ percent}$$

Having done this, we can calculate elasticity as usual by dividing the percentage change in quantity by the percentage change in price:[1]

$$\text{Elasticity} = \frac{\text{Percentage change in quantity}}{\text{Percentage change in price}} = \frac{-33}{26} = 1.27$$

The elasticity of demand between points *A* and *B* is approximately 1.3. This means that a 10 percent increase in price will cause a 13 percent fall in quantity demanded. Thus, demand between *A* and *B* is elastic.

[1] I drop the negative sign because, as discussed earlier, economists talk about price elasticity of demand as a positive number.

Q-3 What is t elasticity betwe the graph below

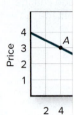

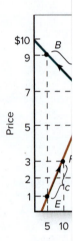

Q-4 Your stu just stated that curve is inelasti

Thinking Like a Modern Economist

Why Do So Many Prices End in 99 Cents?

The traditional economic assumption is that a 1 percent change in price, say from $1.01 to $1.00, is the close equivalent to a similar 1 percent change in price, say from $1.00 to 99 cents. Both should have almost identical effects. Behavioral economists have found that that is not the case; people react more to a fall in price from $1.00 to 99 cents than they do to a fall in price from $1.01 to $1.00. That's why we see so many prices that end in 99 cents. People perceive a $4.00 price as much higher than a $3.99 price, and they buy much more at $3.99. So the elasticity is much greater for price declines from $1.00 to $0.99 than from $1.01 to $1.00. This is a predictably irrational behavior.

Another predictably irrational behavior involves a zero price—when goods are free. People seem to react quite differently to a zero price than to other prices. In

©Erica S. Leeds

an experiment, behavioral economists Kristina Shampanies and Dan Ariely offered to sell people one of two chocolates—a ritzy Lindt Chocolate truffle for 15 cents or a Hershey Kiss for 1 cent. Seventy-three percent chose the truffle and 27 percent chose the Kiss. Then they reduced the price of both chocolates by a penny—the Lindt chocolate to 14 cents and the Kiss to FREE. The effect on demand was enormous. Now only 31 percent chose the Lindt and 69 percent chose the Hershey Kiss. A zero price seems to have a big effect on the quantity demanded.

Firms know that people react to zero prices in this manner, and they try to take advantage of it all the time. For example, they offer "free" goods that aren't really free; *buy one and get one free* sells a lot more goods than cutting price by 50 percent.

Five Terms to Describe Elasticity

Five elasticity terms are:
1. Perfectly elastic ($E = \infty$).
2. Elastic ($E > 1$).
3. Unit elastic ($E = 1$).
4. Inelastic ($E < 1$).
5. Perfectly inelastic ($E = 0$).

As a review, the five terms to describe elasticity along a curve are listed here from most to least elastic:

1. *Perfectly elastic:* Quantity responds enormously to changes in price ($E = \infty$).
2. *Elastic:* The percentage change in quantity exceeds the percentage change in price ($E > 1$).
3. *Unit elastic:* The percentage change in quantity is the same as the percentage change in price ($E = 1$).
4. *Inelastic:* The percentage change in quantity is less than the percentage change in price ($E < 1$).
5. *Perfectly inelastic:* Quantity does not respond at all to changes in price ($E = 0$).

Now that you have seen that elasticity changes along straight-line supply and demand curves, the first point—that elasticity is related to but not the same as slope—should be clear. Whereas elasticity changes along a straight-line curve, slope does not.

Substitution and Elasticity

The most important determinant of price elasticity of demand is the number of substitutes for the good.

Now that you know how to measure elasticity, let's consider some of the factors that are likely to make demand more or less elastic, that is, more or less responsive to price.

How responsive quantity demanded will be to changes in price can be summed up in one word: substitution. As a general rule, the more substitutes a good has, the more elastic is its demand.

Geometric Tricks for Estimating Price Elasticity

There are a couple of useful tricks to determine whether a point on a straight-line supply or demand curve is elastic or inelastic. The trick with demand is the following: (1) Determine where the demand curve intersects the price and quantity axes. (2) At a point midway between the origin and the quantity line intersection, draw a vertical line back up to the demand curve. The point where it intersects the demand curve will have an elasticity of 1; it will be unit elastic; all points to the left of that line (in the graph below, at a price above $4) will be elastic, and all points to the right of that (a price below $4) will be inelastic.

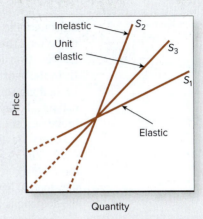

To determine whether a straight-line supply curve is elastic or inelastic you simply extend it to one of the axes, as in the following graph. The point at which this extension intersects the axes indicates the elasticity of the supply curve.

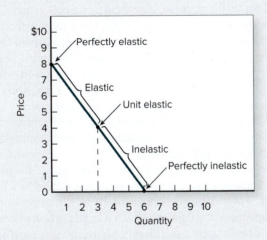

- If the extension intersects the vertical (price) axis, as does S_1, all points on the supply curve have an elasticity greater than 1; the supply curve is elastic.
- If the extension intersects the horizontal (quantity) axis, as does S_2, all points on the supply curve have an elasticity less than 1; the supply curve is inelastic.
- If the extension intersects the two axes at the origin, the supply curve has an elasticity of 1; the supply curve has unit elasticity.

If you combine these tricks with a knowledge that a perfectly elastic supply or demand curve is horizontal and crosses the price axis, and a perfectly inelastic supply or demand curve is vertical and crosses the quantity axis, you can even remember which is which. If a straight-line supply curve crosses the quantity axis, all points on it are inelastic; if it crosses the price axis, all points on it are elastic. Similarly, the top half of the demand curve (the part that crosses the price axis) is elastic; the bottom half (the part that crosses the quantity axis) is inelastic.

The reasoning is as follows: If a good has substitutes, a rise in the price of that good will cause the consumer to shift consumption to those substitute goods. Put another way, when a satisfactory substitute is available, a rise in that good's price will have a large effect on the quantity demanded. For example, I think a Whopper is a satisfactory substitute for a Big Mac. If most people agree with me, when the price of Big Macs rises people will switch from Big Macs to Whoppers. The demand for Big Macs would be very elastic.

Substitution and Demand

The number of substitutes a good has is affected by several factors. Four of the most important are:

1. The time period being considered.
2. The degree to which a good is a luxury.

Whoppers and Big Macs can be substitutes.
©Tony Freeman/PhotoEdit

131

3. The market definition.

4. The importance of the good in one's budget.

These four reasons are derivatives of the substitution factor. Let's consider each to see why.

The more substitutes, the more elastic the demand and the more elastic the supply.

1. *The time period being considered:*   The larger the time interval considered, or the longer the run, the more elastic is the good's demand. There are more substitutes in the long run than in the short run. That's because the long run provides more alternatives. Consider when the price of rubber went up significantly during World War II. In the short run, rubber had few substitutes; the demand for rubber was inelastic. In the long run, however, the rise in the price of rubber stimulated research for alternatives. Today automobile tires, which were made of all rubber when World War II broke out, are made from almost entirely synthetic materials. In the long run, demand was very elastic.

2. *The degree to which a good is a luxury:*   The less a good is a necessity, the more elastic is its demand. Because by definition one cannot do without necessities, they tend to have fewer substitutes than do luxuries. Insulin for a diabetic is a necessity; the demand is highly inelastic. Chocolate Ecstasy cake, however, is a luxury. A variety of other luxuries can be substituted for it (for example, cheesecake or a ball game).

Q-5   What are four important factors affecting the number of substitutes a good has?

3. *The market definition:*   As the definition of a good becomes more specific, demand becomes more elastic. If the good we're talking about is broadly defined (say, transportation), it has few substitutes and demand will be inelastic. If you want to get from A to B, you need transportation. If the definition of the good is narrowed—say, to "transportation by bus"—there are more substitutes. Instead of taking a bus, you can walk, ride your bicycle, or drive your car. In that case, demand is more elastic.

4. *The importance of the good in one's budget:*   Demand for goods that represent a large proportion of one's budget is more elastic than demand for goods that represent a small proportion of one's budget. Goods that cost very little relative to your total expenditures aren't worth spending a lot of time figuring out whether there's a good substitute. An example is pencils. Their low price means most people would buy just as many even if the price doubled. Their demand is inelastic. It is, however, worth spending lots of time looking for substitutes for goods that take a large portion of one's income. The demand for such goods tends to be more elastic. Many colleges have discovered this as they tried to raise tuition when other colleges did not. The demand curve they faced was elastic.

How Substitution Factors Affect Specific Decisions

Let's consider how some of the substitution factors affect a specific decision. Let's say you've been hired by two governments (the city of Washington, D.C., and the U.S. government) to advise them about the effect that raising the gas tax by 10 percent will have on tax revenues. You look at the three factors that affect elasticity of demand.

Q-6   In the long run, would you expect demand to be more or less elastic?

In your report to the two governments, you would point out that in the short run demand is less elastic than in the long run, since people aren't going to trade in their gas-guzzling cars for fuel-efficient cars immediately in response to a 10 percent rise in gas taxes—partly because they can't afford to, partly because they don't want to, and partly because not that many fuel-efficient cars are available to buy at the moment. When the time comes, however, that they would ordinarily purchase a new car, they're likely to switch to cars that are more fuel-efficient than their old cars, and to switch as much as they can to forms of transportation that are more fuel-efficient than cars. In the long run the demand will be far more elastic.

In the long run, demand generally becomes more elastic.

The second point you'd note is that gasoline is generally considered a necessity, although not all driving is necessary. However, since gasoline is only a small part of the cost of driving a car, demand will probably tend to be inelastic.

The third factor (how specifically the good is defined) requires special care. It makes your recommendations for the government of the city of Washington, D.C., and the U.S. government quite different from each other. For the U.S. government, which is interested in the demand for gasoline in the entire United States, gasoline has a relatively inelastic demand. The general rule of thumb is that a 1-cent rise in tax will raise tax revenues by $1 billion. That inelasticity can't be carried over to the demand for gasoline in a city such as Washington, D.C. Because of the city's size and location, people in Washington have a choice. A large proportion of the people who buy gas in Washington can as easily buy gas in the adjacent states of Maryland or Virginia. Gasoline in Washington is a narrowly defined good and therefore has a quite elastic demand. A rise in price will mean a large fall in the quantity of gas demanded.

I mention this point because someone forgot about it when the city of Washington, D.C., raised the tax on a gallon of gasoline by 8 cents, a rise at that time of about 10 percent (this was case 2 in our discussion of calculating elasticities). In response, monthly gasoline sales in Washington fell from 16 million gallons to less than 11 million gallons, a 40 percent decrease! The demand for gas in Washington was not inelastic, as it was for the United States as a whole; it was very elastic ($E_D = 4$). Washingtonians went elsewhere to buy gas.

The fact that smaller geographic areas have more elastic demands limits how highly state and local governments can tax goods relative to their neighboring localities or states. Where there are tax differences, new stores open all along the border and existing stores expand to entice people to come over that border and save on taxes. For example, the liquor tax is higher in Vermont than in New Hampshire, so it isn't surprising that right across the border from Vermont, New Hampshire has a large number of liquor stores. Here's one final example: If you look at license plates in Janzen Beach, Oregon (right across the Washington state border), you'll see a whole lot of Washington license plates. Why? If you answered that it likely has something to do with differential sales taxes in Washington and Oregon, you've got the idea.

Elasticity, Total Revenue, and Demand

Knowing elasticity of demand is useful to firms because from it they can tell whether the total revenue will go up or down when they raise or lower their prices. The total revenue a supplier receives is the price he or she charges times the quantity he or she sells. (Total revenue equals total quantity sold multiplied by the price of the good.) Elasticity tells sellers what will happen to total revenue if their price changes. Specifically:

- If demand is elastic ($E_D > 1$), a rise in price lowers total revenue. (Price and total revenue move in opposite directions.)

- If demand is unit elastic ($E_D = 1$), a rise in price leaves total revenue unchanged.

- If demand is inelastic ($E_D < 1$), a rise in price increases total revenue. (Price and total revenue move in the same direction.)

The relationship between elasticity and total revenue is no mystery. There's a very logical reason why they are related, which can be seen most neatly by recognizing that total revenue ($P \times Q$) is represented by the area under the demand curve at that price and quantity. For example, at point E on the demand curve in Figure 6-3(a), the total revenue at price $4 and quantity 6 is the area designated by the A and B rectangles, $24.

If we increase price to $6, quantity demanded decreases to 4, so total revenue is still $24. Total revenue has remained constant, so the demand curve from point E to point F is unit elastic. The new total revenue is represented by the A and C rectangles. The difference between the old total revenue (A and B) and the new total revenue (A and C) is the difference between the rectangles B and C. Comparing these rectangles provides us with a visual method of estimating elasticities.

Web Note 6.2

Product Discounts

Q-7 If demand is inelastic and a firm raises price, what happens to total revenue?

FIGURE 6-3 (A, B, AND C)   **Elasticity and Total Revenue**

Total revenue is measured by the rectangle produced by extending lines from the demand curve to the price and quantity axes. The change in total revenue resulting from a change in price can be estimated by comparing the sizes of the before and after rectangles. If price is being raised, total revenue increases by rectangle *C* and decreases by rectangle *B*. As you can see, the effect of a price rise on total revenue differs significantly at different points on a demand curve; (**a**) shows an almost unitary elastic range, (**b**) shows an inelastic range, and (**c**) shows an elastic range.

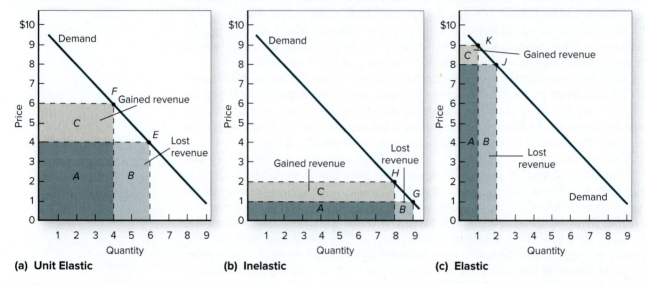

Figure 6-3(b) shows an inelastic range; Figure 6-3(c) shows a highly elastic range. While in Figure 6-3(b) the slope of the demand curve is the same as in Figure 6-3(a), we begin at a different point on the demand curve (point *G*). If we raise our price from $1 to $2, quantity demanded falls from 9 to 8. The gained area (rectangle *C*) is much greater than the lost area (rectangle *B*). In other words, total revenue increases significantly, so the demand curve between points *H* and *G* is highly inelastic.

In Figure 6-3(c) the demand curve is again the same, but we begin at still another point, *J*. If we raise our price from $8 to $9, quantity demanded falls from 2 to 1. The gained area (rectangle *C*) is much smaller than the lost area (rectangle *B*). In other words, total revenue decreases significantly, so the demand curve from points *J* to *K* is highly elastic.

Total Revenue along a Demand Curve

With elastic demands, a rise in price decreases total revenue. With inelastic demands, a rise in price increases total revenue.

The way in which elasticity changes along a demand curve and its relationship to total revenue can be seen in Figure 6-4. When output is zero, total revenue is zero; similarly, when price is zero, total revenue is zero. That accounts for the two endpoints of the total revenue curve in Figure 6-4(b). Let's say we start at a price of zero, where demand is perfectly inelastic. As we increase price (decrease quantity demanded), total revenue increases significantly. As we continue to do so, the increases in total revenue become smaller until finally, after output of Q_0, total revenue actually starts decreasing. It continues decreasing at a faster and faster rate until finally, at zero output, total revenue is zero.

As an example of where such calculations might come in handy, recall the vanity license plates that we used to illustrate the law of demand in Chapter 4. A rise in the price of vanity plates of about 29 percent, from $30 to $40, decreased the quantity demanded about 64 percent, from 60,334 to 31,122, so the price elasticity of demand was about $0.64/0.29 = 2.2$. Since demand was elastic, total revenue fell. Specifically, total revenue fell from $1,810,020 ($30 × 60,334) to $1,244,880 ($40 × 31,122).

Web Note 6.3

Elasticity and Cartels

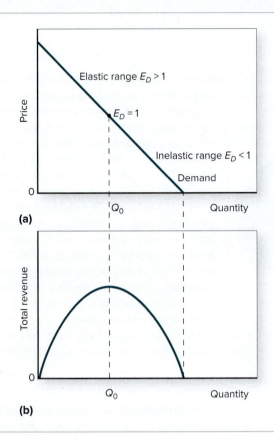

(a)

(b)

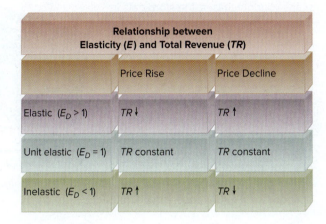

FIGURE 6-4 (A AND B)   How Total Revenue Changes

Total revenue is at a maximum when elasticity equals 1, as you can see in (a) and (b). When demand is elastic, total revenue decreases with an increase in price. When demand is inelastic, total revenue increases with an increase in price.

Relationship between Elasticity (*E*) and Total Revenue (*TR*)		
	Price Rise	Price Decline
Elastic ($E_D > 1$)	$TR \downarrow$	$TR \uparrow$
Unit elastic ($E_D = 1$)	TR constant	TR constant
Inelastic ($E_D < 1$)	$TR \uparrow$	$TR \downarrow$

Income and Cross-Price Elasticity

There are many elasticity concepts besides the price elasticity of demand and the price elasticity of supply. Since these other elasticities can be useful in specifying the effects of shift factors on the demand for a good, I will introduce you to two of them: income elasticity of demand and cross-price elasticity of demand.

Income Elasticity of Demand

The most commonly used of these other elasticity terms is *income elasticity of demand*. **Income elasticity of demand** is defined as *the percentage change in demand divided by the percentage change in income.* Put another way,

$$\text{Income elasticity of demand} = \frac{\text{Percentage change in demand}}{\text{Percentage change in income}}$$

It tells us the responsiveness of demand to changes in income. (Notice I used *demand,* not *quantity demanded,* to emphasize that in response to a change in anything but the price of that good, the entire demand curve shifts; there's no movement along the demand curve.) An increase in income generally increases one's consumption of almost all goods, although the increase may be greater for some goods than for others. **Normal goods**—*goods whose consumption increases with an increase in income*— have income elasticities greater than zero.

Normal goods are sometimes divided into luxuries and necessities. A **luxury** is *a good that has income elasticity greater than 1*—its percentage increase in demand is greater than the percentage increase in income. For example, say your income goes up 10 percent and you buy 20 percent more songs from iTunes. The income elasticity of iTunes music is 2;

Income elasticity of demand shows the responsiveness of demand to changes in income.

Q-8 If a good's consumption increases with an increase in income, what type of good would you call it?

Empirically Measuring Elasticities

Where do firms get the information they need to calculate elasticities? Think of the grocery store where you can get a special buyer's card; the checkout clerk scans it and you get all the discounts. And the card is free! Those grocery stores are not just being nice. When the clerk scans your purchases, the store gets information that is forwarded to a central processing unit that can see how people react to different prices. This information allows firms to fine-tune their pricing—raising prices on goods for which the demand is inelastic and lowering prices on goods for which the demand is elastic.

Alternatively, think of the warranty cards that you send in when you buy a new computer or a new TV. The information goes into the firms' databases and is used by their economists in future price-setting decisions.

©Aleksandra Gigowska/Shutterstock

How do stores use this information? One way is that they develop user profiles, and run promotions on items such as laundry products, carbonated soft drinks, cereal, and several other items for which consumers are most responsive to price (i.e., the demand is elastic). This attracts shoppers to their store. Then, the stores place high-profit novelty items that consumers generally do not compare across stores, but for which demand is inelastic, in prominent in-store displays. It's not quite a bait-and-switch strategy, but it is a strategy to lure shoppers into a store for a "deal" but still end up selling higher-priced products than their competitors. Another way stores calculate the elasticity of demand for goods is to initially charge different prices in different stores, and then, once they have determined the elasticity, they choose a price that maximizes total profit.

---

thus, iTunes music is a luxury good. Economist Robert Fogel estimates income elasticity for health care to be 1.6 and, therefore, it is a luxury. Alternatively, say your income goes up by 100 percent and your demand for shoes goes up by 50 percent. Your income elasticity for shoes would be 0.5. Shoes are a **necessity**—*a good that has an income elasticity between 0 and 1.* The consumption of a necessity rises by a smaller proportion than the rise in income. Economists estimate the income elasticity of all food to be 0.2; food is a necessity.

It is even possible that an increase in income can cause a *decrease* in the consumption of a particular good. Unlike normal goods, which have a positive income elasticity of demand, these goods have a negative income elasticity of demand. The term applied to such goods is **inferior goods**—*goods whose consumption decreases when income increases.* In some circumstances, potatoes could be an example of an inferior good. As income goes up, people might so significantly shift their consumption toward meat and away from potatoes that their total consumption of potatoes decreases. A recent study by a Stanford economist found tortillas to be an inferior good in Mexico.

Income elasticity for most goods is different in the short run than in the long run. The income elasticity for foreign travel, for example, is estimated to be 0.2 in the short run and 3.0 in the long run. Short-run decisions to travel abroad may be motivated by factors other than income such as business trips or family emergencies. Foreign travel decisions in the long run are likely to be part of vacation plans, and people choose from a variety of locations, both domestic and foreign. In the short run, people often save high proportions of their increases in income, so most goods, other than impulse goods, such as furniture, have low short-run income elasticities. To avoid this problem, economists generally focus on long-run income elasticities.

Cross-Price Elasticity of Demand

Cross-price elasticity of demand is another frequently used elasticity concept. It tells us the responsiveness of demand to the change in prices of related goods.

💻 **Web Note 6.4**

Inferior Goods

Q-9 Label each of the following goods as a luxury, necessity, or inferior good. Income elasticity is given for each.

a. Dental services: 1.6

b. Beer: 0.8

c. Baloney: −0.15

Cross-price elasticity of demand is defined as *the percentage change in demand divided by the percentage change in the price of a related good.* Put another way,

Cross-price elasticity of demand shows the responsiveness of demand to changes in prices of related goods.

$$\text{Cross-price elasticity of demand} = \frac{\text{Percentage change in demand}}{\text{Percentage change in price of a related good}}$$

Let's consider an example. Say the price of Apple iPhones rises. What is likely to happen to the demand for Android phones? It is likely to rise, so the cross-price elasticity between the two is positive. Positive cross-price elasticities of demand mean the goods are **substitutes**—*goods that can be used in place of one another.* When the price of a good goes up, the demand for the substitute goes up. Another example is the demand for beef and pork, with an estimated cross-price elasticity of 0.1. When the price of beef rises, consumers will switch to pork.

Most goods are substitutes for one another, so most cross-price elasticities are positive. But not all. To see that, let's consider another example: Say the price of hot dogs rises; what is likely to happen to the demand for ketchup? If you're like me and use lots of ketchup on your hot dogs, as you cut your consumption of hot dogs, you will also cut your consumption of ketchup. Ketchup and hot dogs are not substitutes but rather complements. **Complements** are *goods that are used in conjunction with other goods.* A fall in the price of a good will increase the demand for its complement. The cross-price elasticity of complements is negative. As practice, list pairs of goods that are complements, make another list of substitutes, and compare lists with a study partner. On the list might be name and generic brands of the same product. If you've identified these as substitutes, you're on the right track.

Web Note 6.5

Calculating Elasticity

Substitutes have positive cross-price elasticities; complements have negative cross-price elasticities.

Some Examples

To make sure you've got these concepts down, see Figure 6-5, which demonstrates two examples. In Figure 6-5(a), income has risen by 20 percent, increasing demand at price P_0 from 20 to 26. To determine the income elasticity, we must first determine the percentage change in demand. We calculate the percentage change in demand to be $6/[(20 + 26)/2] = (6/23) \times 100 = 26$ percent. The percentage change in income is 20, so the income elasticity is 26/20, or 1.3.

In Figure 6-5(b), a 33 percent fall in the price of pork has caused the demand for beef to fall by 3.8 percent—from 108 to 104 at a price of P_0. The cross-price elasticity of demand is $3.8/33 = 0.12$.

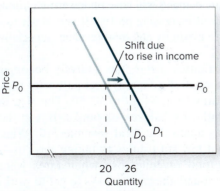

(a) Calculating Income Elasticity

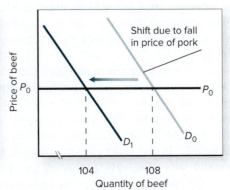

(b) Calculating Cross-Price Elasticity

FIGURE 6-5 (A AND B) **Calculating Elasticities**

Shift factors, such as income or the price of another good, shift the entire demand curve. To calculate these elasticities, we see how much demand will shift at a constant price and then calculate the relevant elasticities.

A REMINDER ✔

A Review of Various Elasticity Terms

Income elasticity of demand is defined as *the percentage change in demand divided by the percentage change in income.*

$$\text{Income elasticity of demand} = \frac{\text{Percentage change in demand}}{\text{Percentage change in income}}$$

Cross-price elasticity of demand is defined as *the percentage change in demand divided by the percentage change in the price of a related good.*

$$\text{Cross-price elasticity of demand} = \frac{\text{Percentage change in demand}}{\text{Percentage change in price of a related good}}$$

Complement: Cross-price elasticity of demand is negative.

Substitute: Cross-price elasticity of demand is positive.

Normal good: Income elasticity of demand is positive.

Luxury: Income elasticity is greater than 1.

Necessity: Income elasticity is less than 1.

Inferior good: Income elasticity of demand is negative.

The Power of Supply/Demand Analysis

Now that you've got the elasticity terms down, let's consider some examples that demonstrate the power of supply/demand analysis when it is combined with the concept of elasticity. Let's start with some easy cases.

When Should a Supplier Not Raise Price?

First, let's say a firm is trying to increase its profits and hires you to tell it whether it should raise or lower its price. The firm knows that it faces an inelastic demand. Should it raise its price?

I hope your answer was: Definitely yes. How can I be so sure the correct answer is yes? Because I remembered the discussion of the relationship between price elasticity of demand and total revenue. With an inelastic demand, the percentage change in quantity is less than the percentage change in price, so total revenue must increase with an increase in price. Total costs also will decrease, so profits—total revenues minus total costs—also must increase.

Along those same lines, consider a university president thinking of raising tuition. Say that raising tuition by 10 percent will decrease the number of students by 1 percent. What's the price elasticity? The percentage change in quantity is 1 percent; the percentage change in price is 10. Dividing the percentage change in quantity by the percentage change in price, we have an elasticity of 0.1. That's an inelastic demand ($E_D < 1$), so raising tuition will increase the university's total revenue.

But if a 10 percent rise in tuition will decrease the enrollment by 25 percent, the elasticity will be large (2.5). In response to an increase in tuition, the university's total revenue will decrease significantly. When you have an elastic demand, you should hesitate to increase price. To make sure you're following the argument, explain the likely effect an elastic demand will have on lowering tuition. (Your argument should involve the *possibility* of increasing profit.) If you're not following the argument, go back to the section on elasticity and total revenue, especially Figure 6-3.

When the long-run and short-run elasticities differ, the analysis becomes somewhat more complicated. Consider the case of a local transit authority that, faced with a budget crisis, increased its fares from $1.50 to $2.50. The rise in revenue during the first year helped the authority balance its books. But in the two years following, ridership declined so much that total revenue fell. What happened? In the short run, commuters had few substitutes to taking the bus—demand was relatively inelastic, so that total revenue rose when fares were increased. But, as time went on, commuters found alternative ways to get to work. Long-run demand was more elastic in this case, so much so that total revenue declined.

Q-10 A firm faces an elastic demand for its product. It has come to an economist to advise it on whether to lower its price. The answer she gives is: Maybe. Why is this the right answer?

138

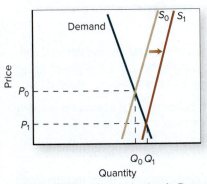
(a) Inelastic Supply and Inelastic Demand

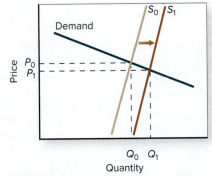
(b) Inelastic Supply and Elastic Demand

FIGURE 6-6 (A AND B) **Effects of Shifts in Supply on Price and Quantity**

In (**a**), supply intersects demand where demand is inelastic and the quantity effects are relatively small. In (**b**), demand is more elastic and the quantity effects are much larger. In general the effects of shifts in supply on equilibrium quantity and price are determined by the elasticity of demand.

Elasticity and Shifting Supply and Demand

Let's now turn to shifts in supply and demand. Knowing the elasticity of the supply and demand curves allows us to be more specific about the effects of shifts in supply and demand.

Figure 6-6 demonstrates the relative effects of supply shifts on equilibrium price and quantity under different assumptions about elasticity. As you can see, the more elastic the demand, the greater the effect of a supply shift on quantity, and the smaller the effect on price. Going through a similar exercise for demand shifts with various supply elasticities is also a useful exercise. If you do so, you will see that the more elastic the supply, the greater the effect of a demand shift on quantity, and the smaller the effect on price.

To be sure that you have understood elasticity, consider the following three observations about price and quantity and match them with the three descriptions of supply and demand:

a. Price rises significantly; quantity hardly changes at all.

b. Price remains almost constant; quantity increases enormously.

c. Price falls significantly; quantity hardly changes at all.

1. Demand is highly elastic; supply shifts out.

2. Supply is highly inelastic; demand shifts out.

3. Demand is highly inelastic; supply shifts out.

The answers are: a–2; b–1; c–3.

Conclusion

I'll stop the exercises here. As you can see, the elasticity concept is important. Economists use it all the time when discussing supply and demand.

However, the elasticity concept is not easy to remember, or to calculate, so working with it takes some practice. It becomes a bit less forbidding if you remember that elasticity is what your shorts lose when they've been through the washer and dryer too many times. If a relationship is elastic, price (for price elasticity) exerts a strong pull on quantity. If it's inelastic, there's little pull on quantity.

Summary

- Elasticity is defined as percentage change in quantity divided by percentage change in some variable that affects demand (or supply) or quantity demanded (or supplied). The most common elasticity concept used is price elasticity.   *(LO6-1)*

$$E_D = \frac{\text{Percentage change in quantity demanded}}{\text{Percentage change in price}}$$

$$E_S = \frac{\text{Percentage change in quantity supplied}}{\text{Percentage change in price}}$$

- Elasticity is a better descriptor than is slope because it is independent of units of measurement.   *(LO6-1)*

- To calculate percentage changes in prices and quantities, use the average of the end values.   *(LO6-1)*

- Five elasticity terms are *elastic* ($E > 1$); *inelastic* ($E < 1$); *unit elastic* ($E = 1$); *perfectly inelastic* ($E = 0$); and *perfectly elastic* ($E = \infty$).   *(LO6-1)*

- The more substitutes a good has, the greater its elasticity.   *(LO6-2)*

- Factors affecting the number of substitutes in demand are (1) time period considered, (2) the degree to which the good is a luxury, (3) the market definition, and (4) the importance of the good in one's budget.   *(LO6-2)*

- The most important factor affecting the number of substitutes for supply is time. As the time interval lengthens, supply becomes more elastic.   *(LO6-2)*

- Elasticity changes along straight-line demand and supply curves. Demand becomes less elastic as we move down along a demand curve.   *(LO6-3)*

- When a supplier raises price, if demand is inelastic, total revenue increases; if demand is elastic, total revenue decreases; if demand is unit elastic, total revenue remains constant.   *(LO6-3)*

- Other important elasticity concepts are income elasticity and cross-price elasticity of demand.   *(LO6-4)*

$$\text{Income elasticity of demand} = \frac{\text{Percentage change in demand}}{\text{Percentage change in income}}$$

$$\text{Cross-price elasticity of demand} = \frac{\text{Percentage change in demand}}{\text{Percentage change in price of a related good}}$$

- Knowing elasticities allows us to be more precise about the qualitative effects that shifts in demand and supply have on prices and quantities.   *(LO6-5)*

- The more elastic the demand, the greater the effect of a supply shift on quantity and the smaller the effect on price.   *(LO6-5)*

- The more elastic the supply, the greater the effect of a demand shift on quantity and the smaller the effect on price.   *(LO6-5)*

Key Terms

complement
cross-price elasticity of
    demand
elastic
income elasticity of
    demand

inelastic
inferior good
luxury
necessity
normal good

perfectly elastic
perfectly inelastic
price elasticity of
    demand

price elasticity of supply
substitute
unit elastic

Questions and Exercises ■ connect

1. Determine the price elasticity of demand if, in response to an increase in price of 10 percent, quantity demanded decreases by 20 percent. Is demand elastic or inelastic?   *(LO6-1)*

2. A firm has just increased its price by 5 percent over last year's price, and it found that quantity sold remained the same.   *(LO6-1)*

   a. What is its price elasticity of demand?
   b. How would you calculate it?
   c. What additional information would you search for before you did your calculation?

3. When tolls on the Dulles Airport Greenway were reduced from $1.75 to $1.00, traffic increased from 10,000 to

26,000 trips a day. Assuming all changes in quantity were due to the change in price, what is the price elasticity of demand for the Dulles Airport Greenway? (*LO6-1*)

4. One football season Domino's Pizza, a corporate sponsor of the Washington Redskins (a football team), offered to reduce the price of its $8 medium-size pizza by $1 for every touchdown scored by the Redskins during the previous week. Until that year, the Redskins weren't scoring many touchdowns. Much to the surprise of Domino's, in one week in 1999, the Redskins scored six touchdowns. (Maybe they like pizza.) Domino's pizzas were selling for $2 a pie! The quantity of pizzas demanded soared the following week from 1 pie an hour to 100 pies an hour. What was price elasticity of demand for Domino's pizza? (*LO6-1*)

5. Which has greater elasticity: a supply curve that goes through the origin with slope of 1 or a supply curve that goes through the origin with slope of 4? (*LO6-1*)

6. Calculate the elasticity of the designated ranges of supply and demand curves on the following graph. (*LO6-1*)

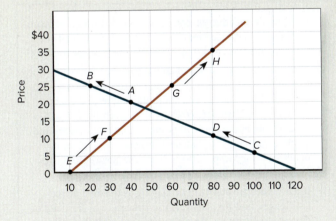

7. Which of the pairs of goods would you expect to have a greater price elasticity of demand? (*LO6-2*)
   a. Cars, transportation.
   b. Housing, leisure travel.
   c. Rubber during World War II, rubber during the entire 20th century.

8. Economists have estimated the following transportation elasticities. For each pair, explain possible reasons why the elasticities differ. (*LO6-2*)
   a. Elasticity of demand for buses is 0.23 during peak hours and 0.42 during off-peak hours.
   b. Elasticity of demand for buses is 0.7 in the short run and 1.5 in the long run.
   c. Elasticity of demand for toll roads is 4.7 for low-income commuters and 0.63 for high-income commuters.

9. Kean University Professor Henry Saffer and Bentley University Professor Dave Dhaval estimated that if the alcohol industry increased the prices of alcoholic beverages by 100 percent underage drinking would fall

by 28 percent and underage binge drinking would fall by 51 percent. (*LO6-2*)
   a. What is the elasticity of demand of underage drinking and binge drinking?
   b. What might explain the difference in elasticities?

10. A newspaper recently lowered its price from $5.00 to $3.00. As it did, the number of newspapers sold increased from 240,000 to 280,000. (*LO6-3*)
    a. What was the newspaper's elasticity of demand?
    b. Given that elasticity, did it make sense for the newspaper to lower its price?
    c. What would your answer be if much of the firm's revenue came from advertising and the higher the circulation, the more it could charge for advertising?

11. Once a book has been written, would an author facing an inelastic demand curve for the book prefer to raise or lower the book's price? Why? (*LO6-3*)

12. University of Richmond Professor Erik Craft analyzed the states' pricing of vanity plates. He found that in California, where vanity plates cost an average of $28.75, the elasticity of demand was 0.52. In Massachusetts, where vanity plates cost $50, the elasticity of demand was 3.52. (*LO6-3*)
    a. Assuming vanity plates have zero production cost and his estimates are correct, was each state collecting the maximum revenue it could from vanity plates? Explain your reasoning.
    b. What recommendation would you have for each state to maximize revenue?
    c. If these estimates are correct, which state was most likely to be following a politically unsupportable policy?
    d. Assuming the demand curves were linear, graphically demonstrate your reasoning in *a* and *b*.

13. How is elasticity related to the revenue from a sales tax? (*LO6-3*)

14. Suppose average movie ticket prices are $8.50 and attendance is 1.2 billion. The price of tickets rises to $9.50 and attendance rises to 1.4 billion. (*LO6-3*)
    a. What happened to total revenue?
    b. If you were to estimate elasticity from these figures, what would your estimate be?
    c. What provisos would you offer about your estimate of elasticity?

15. Which of the following producers would you expect to support a tax on beer? Which would not? Explain your answer. (*LO6-4*)
    a. Producers of hard liquor. Cross-price elasticity with beer: −0.11.
    b. Producers of wine. Cross-price elasticity with beer: 0.23.

16. For each of the following goods, state whether it is a normal good, a luxury, a necessity, or an inferior good. Explain your answers. (*LO6-4*)
    a. Vodka.   d. Perfume.
    b. Table salt.   e. Beer.
    c. Furniture.   f. Sugar.

17. For each of the following pairs of goods, state whether the cross-price elasticity is likely positive, negative, or zero. Explain your answers. *(LO6-4)*
    a. Lettuce, carrots.
    b. Housing, furniture.
    c. Nike sneakers, Puma sneakers.
    d. Jeans, formal suits.

18. When the price of ketchup rises by 18 percent, the demand for hot dogs falls by 2 percent. *(LO6-4)*
    a. Calculate the cross-price elasticity of demand.
    b. Are the goods complements or substitutes?
    c. In the original scenario, what would have to happen to the demand for hot dogs for us to conclude that hot dogs and ketchup are substitutes?

19. Calculate the income elasticities of demand for the following: *(LO6-4)*
    a. Income rises by 20 percent; demand rises by 10 percent.

b. Income rises from $30,000 to $40,000; demand increases (at a constant price) from 17 to 20.

20. Would you expect a shift in supply to have a greater effect on equilibrium quantity in the short run or in the long run? Explain your answer. *(LO6-5)*

21. Would a shift in demand have a greater effect on the percentage change in equilibrium quantity for a straight-line supply curve that intersects the quantity axis or the price axis? *(LO6-5)*

22. For each of the following assume that the supply curve shifts while the demand curve remains constant. What is the direction of the supply shift and relative elasticity of demand? *(LO6-5)*
    a. Price remains nearly constant. Quantity increases enormously.
    b. Price falls enormously. Quantity does not change.
    c. Price rises slightly. Quantity remains nearly constant.

Questions from Alternative Perspectives

1. The text tells us that there are long-run elasticities and short-run elasticities.
   a. How long is the long run and how long is the short run?
   b. What meaning do the elasticity measures have if you don't know those lengths? *(Austrian)*

2. In this chapter, we learn that most new cars aren't sold at their list price but are sold at a discount and that this allows dealerships to charge more to customers with inelastic demand. At the same time, studies have shown that retail car dealerships systematically offer substantially better prices on identical cars to white men than they do to blacks or women. (Source: Ian Ayres, "Fair Driving: Gender and Race Discrimination in Retail Car Negotiations," *Harvard Law Review* 104 (1991): 817–72.)
   a. Why do you think this happens?
   b. In this example, does the fact that customers have different elasticities allow for racial or sexual discrimination? *(Feminist)*

3. Early economists made a distinction between needs and wants. Needs were economists' concern; wants were of far less importance.
   a. Is such a distinction useful?
   b. Would making such a distinction change the nature of economic analysis?

c. Does the fact that the book makes no distinction between luxuries and necessities other than in their elasticity of demand reflect a bias in economic analysis? *(Religious)*

4. In the chapter, you saw that an increase in Vermont's minimum wage stimulated a small quantity response.
   a. What does this tell you about the nature of the labor market in Vermont? *(Hint:* Think carefully and critically about the conditions shaping worker options and their responses to changes in wages.)
   b. What policy implications does your answer to *a* suggest? *(Institutionalist)*

5. If elasticities are constantly changing as the time period gets longer, how do managers use a measure of elasticity of demand to determine the price they charge? If they don't use elasticities, how do they set price? *(Post-Keynesian)*

6. Price elasticity is not just a technical economic concept. It also reflects the distribution of economic power—the bargaining power and economic opportunities of buyers and sellers.
   a. When suppliers (for example, landlords or energy companies) hold disproportionate power over buyers, or consumers (for example, employers in low-wage labor markets) hold disproportionate power over sellers, what meaning do elasticities have?
   b. Should anything be done about those inequities? *(Radical)*

Issues to Ponder

1. In the box "Geometric Tricks for Estimating Price Elasticity," there are three statements about the elasticities of straight-line supply curves. One of those statements is that supply curves intersecting the quantity axis are inelastic. Can you prove that that is true by algebraic manipulation of the elasticity formula?

2. In the 1960s, coffee came in 1-pound cans. Today, most coffee comes in 11-ounce cans.
   a. Can you think of an explanation why?
   b. Can you think of other products besides coffee whose standard size has shrunk? (Often the standard size is supplemented by a "supersize" alternative.)

3. Why would an economist be more hesitant about making an elasticity estimate of the effect of an increase in price of 1 percent than an increase in price of 50 percent?

4. A major cereal producer decides to lower price from $3.60 to $3 per 15-ounce box.
   a. If quantity demanded increases by 18 percent, what is the price elasticity of demand?
   b. If, instead of lowering its price, the cereal producer increases the size of the box from 15 to 17.8 ounces, what would you expect that the response will be? Why?

5. Economists have estimated the demand elasticity for motor fuel to be between 0.4 and 0.85.
   a. If the price rises 10 percent and the initial quantity sold is 10 million gallons, what is the range of estimates of the new quantity demanded?
   b. In carrying out their estimates, they came up with different elasticity estimates for rises in price than for falls in price, with an increase in price having a larger elasticity than a decrease in price. What hypothesis might you propose for their findings?

6. Demand for "prestige" college education is generally considered to be highly inelastic. What does this suggest about tuition increases at prestige schools in the future?

Why don't colleges raise tuition by amounts even greater than they already do?

7. In 2004, Congress allocated over $20 billion to fight illegal drugs. About 60 percent of the funds was directed at reducing the supply of drugs through domestic law enforcement and interdiction. Some critics of this approach argue that supply-side approaches to reduce the drug supply actually help drug producers.
   a. Demonstrate graphically the effect of supply-side measures on the market for illegal drugs.
   b. Explain how these measures affect drug producers. (*Hint:* Consider the elasticity of demand.)
   c. Demonstrate the effect of demand-side measures such as treatment and prevention on the market for illegal drugs.
   d. How does the shift in demand affect the profitability of producers?

8. In the discussion of elasticity and raising and lowering prices, the text states that if you have an elastic demand, you should hesitate to raise your price, and that lowering price can *possibly* increase profits (total revenue minus total cost). Why is the word *possibly* used?

9. Colleges have increasingly used price sensitivity to formulate financial aid. The more eager the student, the less aid he or she can expect to get. Use elasticity to explain this phenomenon. Is this practice justified?

10. If there were only two goods in the world, can you say whether they would be complements or substitutes? Explain your answer.

Answers to Margin Questions

1. Price elasticity of supply = Percentage change in quantity supplied divided by percentage change in price = 8/4 = 2. (*LO6-1*)

2. If price elasticity of demand is greater than 1, by definition demand is elastic. (*LO6-1*)

3. The percentage change in quantity is 100 (8/8 × 100) and the percentage change in price is 100 (2/2 × 100). Elasticity, therefore, is approximately 1 (100/100). (*LO6-1*)

4. I tell her that she is partially right (for the bottom part of the curve), but that elasticity on a straight-line demand curve changes from perfectly elastic at the vertical-axis intersection to perfectly inelastic at the horizontal-axis intersection. (*LO6-1*)

5. Four factors affecting the number of substitutes in demand are (1) time period considered, (2) the degree to which the good is a luxury, (3) the market definition, and (4) importance of the good in one's budget. (*LO6-2*)

6. I would expect demand to be more elastic in the long run because people have more time to find substitutes and change their behavior. (*LO6-2*)

7. If demand is inelastic, total revenue increases with an increase in price. (*LO6-3*)

8. If consumption increases with an increase in income, the good is a normal good. (*LO6-4*)

9. a. Luxury.
   b. Necessity.
   c. Inferior good. (*LO6-4*)

10. With an elastic demand, lowering price will increase total revenue because it will increase sales by more than the change in price. But producing more also will increase costs, so information about total revenue is not enough to answer the question. (*LO6-5*)

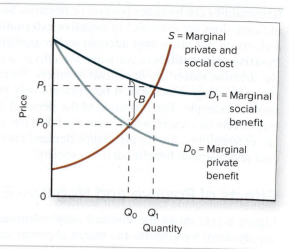

FIGURE 8-2 A Positive Externality

When there is a positive externality, the marginal social benefit will be above the marginal private benefit and the market price will be too low to maximize social welfare.

Since a negative externality represents an additional cost to society, the marginal social cost curve represented by S_1 lies above the marginal private cost curve represented by S_0. The distance between the two curves represents the additional cost of the externality. For example, at quantity Q_0, the private marginal cost faced by the firm is P_0. The marginal cost from the externality at quantity Q_0 is shown by distance C. The optimal price and quantity for society, that combination that equates marginal social cost and marginal social benefit, are P_1 and Q_1. When the externality is not taken into account, the supply/demand equilibrium is at too high a quantity, Q_0, and at too low a price, P_0.

Q-1 Why does the existence of an externality prevent the market from working properly?

Notice that the market solution results in a level of steel production that exceeds the level that equates the marginal social costs with the marginal social benefits. If the market is to maximize welfare, some type of government intervention may be needed to reduce production from Q_0 to Q_1 and raise price from P_0 to P_1.

Figure 8-2 demonstrates the case where there are positive externalities, that is, when the production of a good *benefits* people not involved in the trade. An example is education. Consider a person who is working and takes a class at night. He or she will bring the knowledge from class back to co-workers through day-to-day interaction on projects. The co-workers will be learning the material from the class indirectly. They are outside the initial decision to take the class, but they benefit nonetheless.

In the case of positive externalities, the market will not provide enough of the good. Figure 8-2 shows this case graphically. Now we have to differentiate the marginal private benefit from the marginal social benefit. The **marginal social benefit** equals *the marginal private benefit of consuming a good plus the benefits of the positive externalities resulting from consuming that good*. The vertical distance between D_0 and D_1 is the additional benefit that others receive at each quantity. At quantity Q_0, the market equilibrium, the marginal benefit of the externality is shown by distance B. At this quantity, the marginal social benefit exceeds the marginal social cost. The market provides too little of the good. The optimal price and quantity for society are P_1 and Q_1, respectively. Again, some type of intervention to increase quantity may be warranted.

Q-2 If a positive externality exists, does that mean that the market works better than if no externality exists?

Positive externalities result in the marginal private benefit being below the marginal social benefit.

Alternative Methods of Dealing with Externalities

Externalities can be dealt with via
1. Direct regulation.
2. Incentive policies.
3. Voluntary solutions.

Ways to deal with externalities include (1) direct regulation, (2) incentive policies (tax incentive policies and market incentive policies), and (3) voluntary solutions.

Common Resources and the Tragedy of the Commons

Individuals tend to overuse commonly owned goods. Let's consider an example—say that grazing land is held in common. Individuals are free to bring their sheep to graze on the land. What is likely to happen? Each grazing sheep will reduce the amount of grass for other sheep. If individuals don't have to pay for grazing, when deciding how much to graze their sheep they will not take into account the cost to others of their sheep's grazing. The result may be overgrazing—killing the grass and destroying the grazing land. This is known as the *tragedy of the commons*. A more contemporary example of the tragedy of the commons is fishing. The sea is a common resource; no one owns it, and whenever people catch fish, they reduce the number of fish that others can catch. The result will likely be overfishing.

The tragedy of the commons is an example of the problems posed by externalities. Catching fish imposes a negative externality—fewer fish for others to catch. Because of the negative effect on others, the social cost of catching a fish is greater than the private cost. Overfishing has been

©MIXA/Getty Images

a problem in the United States and throughout the world. Thus, the tragedy of the commons is caused by individuals not taking into account the negative externalities of their actions.

Why doesn't the market solve the externality problem? Some economists argue that in the tragedy of the commons examples it would, if given a chance. The problem is a lack of property rights (lack of ownership). If rights to all goods were defined, the tragedy of the commons would disappear. In the fishing example, if someone owned the sea, he or she would charge individuals to fish. By charging for fishing rights, the owner would internalize the externality and thus avoid the tragedy of the commons.

Nobel Prize–winning political economist Elinor Ostrom has studied common resources in a number of cultures, and has found that different societies have used a wide variety of institutional arrangements to deal with the tragedy of the commons. Her work has shown that there is no single answer to these problems, and that the answer chosen needs to reflect cultural mores of the society.

Direct Regulation

In a program of **direct regulation,** *the amount of a good people are allowed to use is directly limited by the government.* Let's consider an example. Say we have two individuals, Ms. Thrifty, who uses 10 gallons of gasoline a day, and Mr. Big, who uses 20 gallons a day. Say we have decided that we want to reduce total daily gas consumption by 10 percent, or 3 gallons. The regulatory solution might require both individuals to reduce consumption by some specified amount. Likely direct regulatory strategies would require an equal quantity reduction (each consumer reducing consumption by 1.5 gallons) or an equal percentage reduction (each consumer reducing consumption by 10 percent).

Both of those strategies would reduce consumption, but neither would be **efficient** (*achieving a goal at the lowest cost in total resources without consideration as to who pays those costs*). This is because direct regulation does not take into account that the costs of reducing consumption may differ among individuals. Say, for example, that Ms. Thrifty could almost costlessly reduce consumption by 3 gallons while Mr. Big would find it very costly to reduce consumption by even 0.5 gallon. In that case, either regulatory solution would be **inefficient** (*achieving a goal in a more costly manner than necessary*). It would be less costly (more efficient) to have Ms. Thrifty undertake

Q-3 It is sometimes said that there is a trade-off between fairness and efficiency. Explain one way in which that is true and one way in which that is false.

most of the reduction. A policy that would automatically make the person who has the lower cost of reduction *choose* (as opposed to being *required*) to undertake the most reduction would achieve the same level of reduction at a lower cost. In this case, the efficient policy would get Ms. Thrifty to choose to undertake the majority of the reduction.

Incentive Policies

Economists tend to like incentive policies to deal with externalities.

Two types of incentive policies would each get Ms. Thrifty to undertake the larger share of reduction. One is to tax consumption; the other is to issue certificates to individuals who reduce consumption and to allow them to trade those certificates with others.

TAX INCENTIVE POLICIES   Let's say that the government imposes a tax on gasoline consumption of 50 cents per gallon. This would be an example of a **tax incentive program** *(a program using a tax to create incentives for individuals to structure their activities in a way that is consistent with the desired ends).* Since Ms. Thrifty can almost costlessly reduce her gasoline consumption, she will likely respond to the tax by reducing gasoline consumption, say, by 2.75 gallons. She pays only $3.63 in tax but undertakes most of the conservation. Since Mr. Big finds it very costly to reduce his consumption of gasoline, he will likely respond by reducing gasoline consumption by very little, say by 0.25 gallon. He pays $9.88 in tax but does little of the conservation.

Q-4 In what sense is the tax incentive approach to externalities fair?

In this example, the tax has achieved the desired end in a more efficient manner than would the regulatory solution—the person for whom the reduction is least costly cuts consumption the most. Why? Because the incentive to reduce is embodied in the price, and individuals are forced to choose how much to change their consumption. The tax has made them internalize the externality. The solution also has a significant element of fairness about it. The person who conserves the most pays the least tax.

Let's now consider how the tax incentive solution will solve the problem in our earlier example of steel production. Figure 8-3 shows the situation. Say the government determines that the additional cost to society of producing steel equals C. If the government sets the pollution tax on steel production at C, the firm will reduce its output to Q_1 on its own. Such taxes on externalities are often called **effluent fees—** *charges imposed by government on the level of pollution created.* The efficient tax

---

FIGURE 8-3 **Regulation through Taxation**

If the government sets a tax sufficient to take into account a negative externality, individuals will respond by reducing the quantity of the pollution-causing activity supplied to a level that individuals would have supplied had they included the negative externality in their decision.

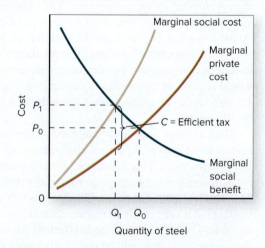

equals the additional cost imposed on society and not taken into account by the decision maker. With such a tax, the cost the suppliers face is the social cost of supplying the good. With the tax, the invisible hand guides the traders to equate the marginal social cost to the marginal social benefit and the equilibrium is socially optimal.

MARKET INCENTIVE POLICIES   A second incentive policy that gets individuals to internalize an externality is a **market incentive plan** (*a plan requiring market participants to certify that they have reduced total consumption—not necessarily their own individual consumption—by a specified amount*). Such a program would be close to the regulatory solution but involves a major difference. If individuals choose to reduce consumption by more than the required amount, they will be given a marketable certificate that they can sell to someone who has chosen to reduce consumption by less than the required amount. By buying that certificate, the person who has not personally reduced consumption by the requisite amount will have met the program's requirements. Let's see how the program would work with Mr. Big and Ms. Thrifty.

In our example, Mr. Big finds it very costly to reduce consumption while Ms. Thrifty finds it easy. So we can expect that Mr. Big won't reduce consumption much and will instead buy certificates from Ms. Thrifty, who will choose to undertake significant reduction in her consumption to generate the certificates, assuming she can sell them to Mr. Big for a high enough price to make that reduction worth her while. So, as was the case in the tax incentive program, Ms. Thrifty undertakes most of the conservation—but she reaps a financial benefit for it.

Obviously there are enormous questions about the administrative feasibility of these types of proposals, but what's important to understand here is not the specifics of the proposals but the way in which incentive policies are *more efficient* than the regulatory policy. As I stated before, *more efficient* means *less costly* in terms of resources, with no consideration paid to who is bearing those costs. Incorporating the incentive into a price and then letting individuals choose how to respond to that incentive lets those who find it least costly undertake most of the adjustment.

More and more, governments are exploring incentive policies for solving problems. Sin taxes (taxes on goods government believes to be harmful) are an example of the tax incentive approach. (These will be discussed further in Chapter 23, "Microeconomic Policy, Economic Reasoning, and Beyond.") Marketable permits for pollution and for CO_2 emissions are an example of the marketable certificate approach. You can probably see more examples discussed in the news.

> Incentive policies are more efficient than direct regulatory policies.

Voluntary Reductions

A third alternative method of dealing with externalities is to make the reduction voluntary, leaving individuals free to choose whether to follow a socially optimal or a privately optimal path. Let's consider how a voluntary program might work in our Mr. Big and Ms. Thrifty example. Let's say that Ms. Thrifty has a social conscience and undertakes most of the reduction while Mr. Big has no social conscience and reduces consumption hardly at all. It seems that this is a reasonably efficient solution. But what if the costs were reversed and Mr. Big had the low cost of reduction and Ms. Thrifty had the high cost? Then the voluntary solution would not be so efficient. Of course, it could be argued that when people do something voluntarily, it makes them better off. So one could argue that even when Ms. Thrifty has a high cost of reduction and voluntarily undertakes most of the reduction, she also has a high benefit from reducing her consumption.

The largest problem with voluntary solutions is that a person's willingness to do things for the good of society generally depends on that person's belief that others will

Web Note 8.2

Free Riders and Union Shops

Q-5 What are two reasons to be dubious of solutions based on voluntary action that is not in people's self-interest?

also be helping. If a socially conscious person comes to believe that a large number of other people won't contribute, he or she will often lose that social conscience: Why should I do what's good for society if others won't? This is an example of the **free rider problem** *(individuals' unwillingness to share in the cost of a public good),* which economists believe will often limit, and eventually undermine, social actions based on voluntary contributions. A small number of free riders will undermine the social consciousness of many in the society and eventually the voluntary policy will fail.

Economists believe that a small number of free riders will undermine the social consciousness of many in the society and that eventually a voluntary policy will fail.

There are exceptions. During times of war and extreme crisis, voluntary programs are often successful. For example, during World War II the war effort was financed in part through successful voluntary programs. But generally the results of voluntary programs for long-term social problems that involve individuals significantly changing their actions haven't been positive.

The Optimal Policy

An **optimal policy** is *one in which the marginal cost of a policy equals the marginal benefit of that policy.* If a policy isn't optimal (that is, the marginal cost exceeds the marginal benefit or the marginal benefit exceeds the marginal cost), resources are being wasted because the savings from reducing expenditures on a program will be worth more than the gains that would be lost from reducing the program, or the benefit from spending more on a program will exceed the cost of expanding the program.

If a policy isn't optimal, resources are being wasted because the savings from reducing expenditures on a program will be worth more than the gains that will be lost from reducing the program.

Let's consider an example of this latter case. Say the marginal benefit of a program significantly exceeds its marginal cost. That would seem good. But that would mean that we could expand the program by decreasing some other program or activity whose marginal benefit doesn't exceed its marginal cost, with a net gain in benefits to society. To spend too little on a beneficial program is as inefficient as spending too much on a nonbeneficial program.

This concept of optimality carries over to economists' view of most problems. For example, some environmentalists would like to completely rid the world of pollution. Most economists believe that doing so is costly and that since it's costly, one would want to take into account those costs. That means that society should reduce pollution only to the point where the marginal cost of reducing pollution equals the marginal benefit. That point is called the *optimal level of pollution*—the amount of pollution at which the marginal benefit of reducing pollution equals the marginal cost. To reduce pollution below that level would make society as a whole worse off.

Some environmentalists want to rid the world of all pollution, while most economists want to reduce pollution to the point where the marginal cost of reducing pollution equals the marginal benefit.

Public Goods

A **public good** is *a good that is nonexclusive (no one can be excluded from its benefits) and nonrival (consumption by one does not preclude consumption by others).* As I discussed in Chapter 3, in reality there is no such thing as a pure public good, but many of the goods that government provides—education, defense, roads, and legal systems—have public-good aspects to them. Probably the closest example we have of a pure public good is national defense. A single individual cannot protect himself or herself from a foreign invasion without protecting his or her neighbors as well. Protection for one person means that many others are also protected. Governments generally provide goods with significant public aspects to them because private businesses will not supply them, unless they transform the good into a mostly private good.

A public good is a good that is nonexclusive and nonrival.

What is and is not considered a public good depends on technology. Consider roads—at one point roads were often privately supplied since with horses and

Is It Time to Start Paying for Driving on Roads?

Economists have long suggested that the best way to handle road congestion is through a method called dynamic pricing—charging higher prices for the use of roads during peak times when there is significant congestion. Advances in scanner technology have made this possible. Prices are continually changed by a computer algorithm that measures supply and demand, and sets the price to achieve the desired balance. An example is Rt. 66 in Washington, D.C., where dynamic pricing was put in place in express lanes in late 2017. The algorithm adjusted price every few minutes to keep average speed at 45 miles per hour. To drive 10 miles on it at the peak time cost as much as $44. These super-high tolls eliminated the congestion, but drew lots of complaints that only the rich could afford the roads, and that normal people were being prevented from using public roads.

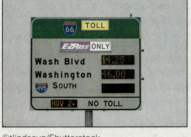

©tlindsayg/Shutterstock

Over time, as drivers figure out ways to leave a bit earlier or a bit later to avoid the super-high tolls, and as more drivers carpool and split the cost, the normal tolls will fall and there will be less congestion. If the program is successful, and it has been in other places, you will likely see significant increases in dynamic pricing of roads in the future. To drive in downtown New York City during certain times of the day may cost more than $100, and to cross bridges may cost $30 or $40. Deciding routes to find the right combination of desired speed and tolls will become a job unto itself.

Of course, pricing technology is not the only technology that is changing. Simultaneously we will likely be switching to self-driving cars, and these cars will likely have an app that requires us to just put in our driving and cost preferences; the car will take care of the rest.

buggies the road owners could charge tolls relatively easily. Then, with the increased speed of the automobile, collecting tolls on most roads became too time-consuming. At that point the nonexclusive public-good aspect of roads became dominant—once a road was built, it was most efficiently supplied to others at a zero cost—and government became the provider of most roads. Today, with modern computer technology, sensors that monitor road use can be placed on roads and in cars. Charging for roads has once again become more feasible. In the future we may again see more private provision of roads. Some economists have even called for privatization of existing roads, and private roads are being built in many states and countries.

Web Note 8.3

Charging for Roads

The Market Value of a Public Good

One of the reasons that pure public goods are sufficiently interesting to warrant a separate discussion is that the supply/demand model can be modified to neatly contrast the efficient quantity of a private good with the efficient quantity of a public good. The key to understanding the difference is to recognize that once a pure public good is supplied to one individual, it is simultaneously supplied to all, whereas a private good is supplied only to the individual who purchased it. For example, if the price of an apple is 50 cents, the efficient purchase rule is for individuals to buy apples until the marginal benefit of the last apple consumed is equal to 50 cents. The analysis focuses on the individual. If the equilibrium price is 50 cents, the marginal benefit of the last apple sold in the market is equal to 50 cents. That benefit is paid for by one individual and is enjoyed by one individual.

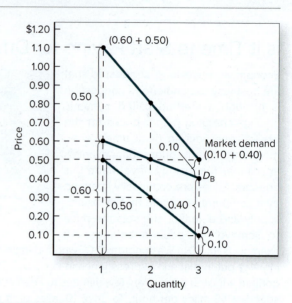

FIGURE 8-4   **The Market Value of a Public Good**

Since a public good is enjoyed by many people without diminishing its value to others, the market demand curve is constructed by adding the marginal benefit each individual receives from the public good at each quantity. For example, the value of the first unit to the market is $1.10, the sum of individual A's value ($0.50) and individual B's value ($0.60).

Now consider a public good. Say that the marginal benefit of an additional missile for national defense is 50 cents to one individual and 25 cents to another. In this case the value of providing one missile provides 75 cents (25 + 50) of total social benefit. With a public good the focus is on the group. The societal benefit in the case of a public good is the *sum* of the individual benefits (since each individual gets the benefit of the good). With private goods, we count only the benefit to the person buying the good since only one person gets it.

The above reasoning can be translated into supply and demand curves. The market demand curve represents the marginal benefit of a good to society. As we saw in Chapter 4, in the case of a private good, the market demand curve is the *horizontal sum* of the individual demand curves. The total amount of a private good supplied is split up among many buyers. While the market demand curve for a private good is constructed by adding all the quantities demanded at every price, the market demand curve in the case of public goods is the *vertical sum* of the individual demand curves at every quantity. The quantity of the good supplied is not split up; the full benefit of the total output is received by everyone.

Figure 8-4 gives an example of a public good. In it we assume that society consists of only two individuals—A and B, with demand curves D_A and D_B. To arrive at the market demand curve for the public good, we vertically add the price that each individual is willing to pay for each unit since both receive a benefit when the good is supplied. Thus, at quantity 1 we add $0.60 to $0.50. We arrive at $1.10, the marginal benefit of providing the first missile. By adding together the willingness to pay by individuals A and B for quantities 2 and 3, we generate the market demand curve for missiles. Extending this example from two individuals to the economy as a whole, you can see that, even though the benefit of a public good is small to each person, the total benefit is large. With about 330 million people in the United States, the benefit of that missile would be $165 million even if each person valued it on average at 50 cents.

Adding demand curves vertically is easy to do in textbooks, but not in practice. With private-good demand curves, individuals reveal their demand when they buy a good. If they don't buy it, it wasn't worth the price. Since public goods are free of charge, individuals do not purchase public goods; their demand is not revealed by their

With private goods you sum demand curves horizontally; with public goods you sum them vertically.

Q-6   Why is it so difficult for government to decide the efficient quantity of a public good to provide?

actions. Government must guess how much people are willing to pay. If a public good is to be financed by a tax on the citizens who benefit from it, individuals have an incentive to conceal their willingness to pay for it. The self-interested citizen wants to benefit from the public good without bearing the cost of providing it. Similarly, if people think they will not be taxed but will benefit from the public good, they have an incentive to exaggerate their willingness to pay. That is, people have an incentive to be free riders.

Excludability and the Costs of Pricing

The public-/private-good differentiation is seldom clear-cut since many goods are somewhat public and somewhat private in nature, with the degree of publicness in large part determined by available technology. As technology changes, the degree of publicness of a good changes. For example, radio signals were previously classified as public goods because it was technologically impossible to exclude listeners, but when encoded satellite broadcasting was developed, exclusion became relatively easy. Today companies such as SiriusXM Radio supply radio broadcasts as private goods.

The public-/private-good differentiation is seldom clear-cut.

To capture the complicated nature of goods, economist Paul Romer suggested that instead of categorizing goods as purely public or private, it is better to divide them by their degree of publicness and privateness, which means by their degree of rivalry in consumption, and their degree of excludability in pricing. This division gives us the following categories:

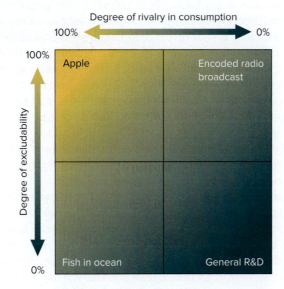

True private goods, such as an apple (if you eat it, no one else can, and you can easily exclude others from consuming it), which are both rival in consumption and 100 percent excludable, are in the upper-left corner; they are most efficiently supplied privately. True public goods, such as basic research and development (sometimes called the development of general-purpose technology), which are nonrival in consumption and 0 percent excludable, are in the lower-right corner; they must be supplied publicly. Goods in other positions in the box can be provided either publicly or privately. How they are supplied depends on political decisions made by the government. An example of a debate about how to supply a good that is somewhat excludable is music. It is nonrival in consumption (after you've listened to a song, that song is still available to others to hear) but is excludable (those not owning FLAC files or concert tickets cannot listen), although the ease of excludability depends on the nature and level of enforcement of the property rights for music. For example, in 2000 music-sharing services, such as Napster, developed that allowed people to share music with others for free. The music industry strongly objected, arguing that such sharing violated copyright laws. They went to court and forced Napster to shut down. Eventually, other music-sharing services such as SoundCloud, Spotify, and iTunes developed that paid copyright holders a portion of their revenues, arriving at a new institutional equilibrium, which will likely remain until technology once again changes.

Informational and Moral Hazard Problems

The final case of market failure I want to address is caused by imperfect information. The perfectly competitive model assumes that individuals have perfect information about what they are buying. So, if they voluntarily buy a good, it is a reasonable presumption that they expect that they are making themselves better off by doing so. But what if buyers don't know everything there is to know about the product or service—that is, they don't have perfect information? Say someone convinces you that he is selling an expensive diamond and you buy it, only to find out later that it is actually just glass. Alternatively, say someone convinces you her used car is a cherry (in perfect condition). You buy it only to discover later that it is a lemon (faulty) and won't run no matter what you do to it.

Real-world markets often involve deception, cheating, and inaccurate information. For example, car dealers often know about defects in the cars they sell but do not always reveal those defects to consumers. Another example occurs when consumers who want health insurance do not reveal their health problems to the insurance company. In both cases, it is in the interest of the knowledgeable person not to reveal information that the other person or firm would need to know to make an informed decision about the transaction. Hence, imperfect information can be a cause of market failure.

Markets in goods where there is a lack of information or when buyers and sellers don't have equal information may not work well. Let's consider the used-car example more carefully to make the point. Let's say that owners of used cars know everything about their cars, but buyers know nothing. If sellers are profit maximizers, they will reveal as little as possible about the cars' defects; they will reveal as much as they can about the cars' good qualities.

To make the example specific, let's say also that only two types of used cars are offered for sale: "lemons" that are worth $4,000 and "cherries" that are worth $8,000. The market initially consists of equal quantities of lemons and cherries. Say also that the buyers cannot distinguish between lemons and cherries. What will happen? Individuals, knowing that they have a 50 percent chance of buying a lemon, may well offer around $6,000 (the average of $4,000 and $8,000). Given that price, individuals with cherries will be very hesitant to sell and individuals with lemons will be eager to sell. Eventually, buyers will recognize that the sellers of cherries have left the market. In the end only lemons will be offered for sale, and buyers will offer only $4,000 with the expectation that cars offered will be lemons. The result is a market failure: The market for cherries—good used cars—has disappeared.

Such a market failure is called an **adverse selection problem**—*a problem that occurs when buyers and sellers have different amounts of information about the good for sale and use that information to the detriment of the other*. In the case of adverse selection, only lemons—those with the most problems—remain in the market. Take the example of medical insurance. Insurance providers need to make a profit. To do so, they set rates that reflect their estimate of the costs of providing health care. The problem is that individuals have better information about their health than do the insurance

Imperfect information can be a cause of market failure.

Adverse selection problems can occur when buyers and sellers have different amounts of information about the good for sale.

providers. Health insurers want a diverse group to spread out the costs, but they face a greater demand among those with the worst health problems. Seeing that their customers have more health problems than average, medical insurance providers raise the rates. Those who are in good health find those charges to be too high and reduce the quantity of health insurance they purchase. The providers are therefore left with a group with an even higher incidence of health problems and higher medical costs than the general population. Less than the desired amount of low-cost insurance exists for people in good health. In addition to the adverse selection problem there is also a **moral hazard problem**—*a problem that arises when people don't have to bear the negative consequences of their actions.* In insurance this means that individuals tend to change their behavior to the detriment of the insurer because they have insurance. Put simply, people with insurance tend to be less careful, because the consequences of not being careful are reduced. So not only do those with more medical problems choose to be insured, but once insured they will be less careful.

Q-7 How would you expect medical insurance rates to change if medical insurers could use information contained in DNA to predict the likelihood of major medical illnesses?

Signaling and Screening

Informational problems can be partially resolved by signaling. **Signaling** refers to *an action taken by an informed party that reveals information to an uninformed party that offsets the false signal that caused the adverse selection problem in the first place.* Take the lemon problem with used cars. The adverse selection problem occurred because the individual's act of selling the used car provided a signal to the buyer that the car was a lemon. Lowering the offering price of a car would provide an even stronger signal that the car is a lemon—buyers reasonably would equate low prices with low quality. But the false signal can be partially offset by a seller warranty—a guarantee to the buyer that the car is not a lemon. That's why many used cars come with warranties. The warranty offers a signal to the buyer that the car is not a lemon.

Signaling refers to an action taken by an informed party that reveals information to an uninformed party and thereby partially offsets adverse selection.

In other cases it is harder to offset a false signal. Consider the plight of an unemployed worker. This person may be an excellent worker who, because she is unemployed, is willing to work for a low wage because she really needs the job. However, if she offers to work for a low wage, the firm may think that she must not be a very good worker. The knowledge that the firm may think that way may prevent her from offering to work at a low wage. So she remains unemployed even though, if there were full information, there is a wage at which she would like to work and at which the firm would like to hire her.

The informational problem can also be partially resolved by screening. **Screening** refers to *an action taken by the uninformed party that induces the informed party to reveal information.* Whereas signaling is an action taken by the informed party, screening is an action taken by the uninformed party. Take the car example. The person buying the car could ask the seller's permission to take the car to a mechanic. If the seller says "no," the car is likely a lemon. Another example is asking job applicants for references even if a company isn't going to contact them.

Policies to Deal with Informational Problems

What should society do about informational problems that lead to market failures? One answer is to regulate the market and see that individuals provide the right information. An example of regulation is government licensing of individuals in the market, requiring those with licenses to reveal full information about the good being sold. Government has set up numerous regulatory commissions and passed laws that require full disclosure of information. The Federal Trade Commission, the Consumer Product Safety Commission, the Occupational Safety and Health Administration, the Food and

Web Note 8.4

Licensure

Drug Administration, and state licensing boards are all examples of regulatory solutions designed to partially offset informational market failures.

But these regulatory solutions have problems of their own. The commissions and their regulations introduce restrictions that can slow down the economic process and prevent trades that people want to make. Consider as an example the Food and Drug Administration (FDA). It restricts what drugs may be sold until sufficient information about the drugs' effects can be disclosed. The FDA testing and approval process can take 5 to 10 years, is extraordinarily costly, and raises the price of drugs. The delays have caused some people to break the law by buying the drugs before they are approved.

A MARKET IN INFORMATION   Economists who lean away from government regulation suggest that the problem presented by the information examples above is not really a problem of market failure but instead a problem of the lack of a market. They propose an alternative way to deal with informational problems—let the market deal with the problem. Information is valuable and is an economic product in its own right. Left on their own, markets will develop to provide the information that people need and are willing to pay for. (For example, a large number of consumer rating and review websites provide such information.) In the car example, the buyer can hire a mechanic who can test the car with sophisticated diagnostic techniques and determine whether it is likely a cherry or a lemon. Firms can offer guarantees that will provide buyers with assurance that they can either return the car or have it fixed if the car is a lemon. There are many variations of such market solutions. If the government regulates information, these markets may not develop; people might rely on government instead of markets. Thus, the informational problem can be seen as a problem of government regulation, not a problem of the market.

> *Informational problems may be a problem of the lack of a market.*

LICENSING OF DOCTORS   Let's consider another informational problem that contrasts the market approach with the regulatory approach: medical licensing.[1] Currently all doctors in the United States are required to be licensed to practice, but this was not always the case.

In the early 1800s, medical licenses were not required by law, so anyone who wanted to could set up shop as a physician. Today, however, it is illegal to practice medicine without a license. Licensing of doctors can be justified by informational problems since individuals often don't have an accurate way of deciding whether a doctor is good. Licensing requires that all doctors have at least a minimum competency. Because people see the license framed and hanging on the doctor's office wall, they have the *information* that a doctor must be competent.

A small number of economists, of whom Milton Friedman is the best known, have proposed that licensure laws be eliminated, leaving the medical field unlicensed. Specifically, critics of medical licensure raise these questions:

> *Some economists argue that licensure laws were established to restrict supply, not to help the consumer.*

Why, if licensed medical training is so great, do we even need formal restrictions to keep other types of medicine from being practiced?

Whom do these restrictions benefit: the general public or the doctors who practice mainstream medicine?

What have been the long-run effects of licensure?

---

[1]The arguments presented here about licensing doctors also apply to dentists, lawyers, college professors, cosmetologists (in some states, cosmetologists must be licensed), and other professional groups.

Licensure and Surgery

Surgery should be the strongest case for licensure. Would you want an untrained butcher to operate on you? Of course not. But opponents of licensure point out that it's not at all clear how effectively licensure prevents butchery. Ask a doctor, "Would you send your child to any board-certified surgeon picked at random?" The honest answer you'd get is "No way. Some of them are

©Morsa Images/Getty Images

butchers." How do they know that? Being around hospitals, they have access to information about various surgeons' success and failure rates; they've seen them operate and know whether or not they have manual dexterity.

Advocates of the informational alternative suggest that you ask yourself, "What skill would I want in a surgeon?" A likely answer would be "Manual dexterity. Her fingers should be magic fingers." Does the existing system of licensure ensure that everyone who becomes a surgeon has magic fingers? No. To become licensed as a surgeon requires a grueling seven-year residency after four years of medical school, but manual dexterity, as such, is never explicitly tested or checked!

The informational alternative wouldn't necessarily eliminate the seven-year surgical residency. If the public believed that a seven-year residency was necessary to create skilled surgeons, many potential surgeons would choose that route. But there would be other ways to become a surgeon. For example, in high school, tests could be given for manual dexterity. Individuals with superb hand/eye coordination could go to a one-year technical college to train to be "heart technicians," who would work as part of a team doing heart surgery.

Clearly open-heart surgery is the extreme case, and most people will not be convinced that it can be performed by unlicensed medical personnel. But what about minor surgery? According to informational alternative advocates, many operations could be conducted more cheaply and better (since people with better manual dexterity would be doing the work) if restrictive licensing were ended. Or, if you don't accept the argument for human medical treatments, how about for veterinarians? For cosmetologists? For plumbers? Might the informational alternatives work in these professions?

Even the strongest critics of licensure agree that, in the case of doctors, the informational argument for government intervention is strong. But the question is whether licensure is the right form of government intervention. Why doesn't the government simply provide the public with information about doctors' training and about which treatments work and which don't? That would give the freest rein to *consumer sovereignty* (the right of the individual to make choices about what is consumed and produced). The same argument applies to pharmaceuticals. Some people believe laetril is an effective cancer treatment even when scientific studies have shown it is not. If people have the necessary information but still choose to treat cancer with laetrile, why should the government tell them they can't?

If the informational alternative is preferable to licensure, why didn't the government choose it? Friedman argues that government didn't follow that path because the licensing was done as much for the doctors as for the general public. Licensure has led to a monopoly position for doctors. They can restrict supply and increase price and thereby significantly increase their incomes.

Let's now take a closer look at the informational alternative that critics say would be preferable.

Q-8 Who would benefit and who would lose if an informational alternative to licensing doctors were used?

THE INFORMATIONAL ALTERNATIVE TO LICENSURE   The informational alternative would allow anyone to practice medicine but would have the government certify doctors' backgrounds and qualifications. The government would require that doctors' backgrounds be made public knowledge. Each doctor would have to post the following information prominently in his or her office:

1. Grades in college.
2. Grades in medical school.
3. Success rate for various procedures.
4. References.
5. Medical philosophy.
6. Charges and fees.

According to supporters of the informational alternative, these data would allow individuals to make informed decisions about their medical care. Like all informed decisions, they would be complicated. For instance, doctors who only take patients with minor problems can show high "success rates," while doctors who are actually more skilled but who take on problem patients may have to provide more extensive information so people can see why their success rates shouldn't be compared to those of the doctors who take just easy patients. But despite the problems, supporters of the informational alternative argue that it's better than the current situation.

Current licensure laws don't provide any of this information to the public. All a patient knows is that a doctor has managed to get through medical school and has passed the medical board exams (which are, after all, only sets of multiple-choice questions). The doctor may have done all this 30 years ago, possibly by the skin of his or her teeth, but, once licensed, a doctor is a doctor for life. (A well-known doctor joke is the following: What do you call the person with the lowest passing grade point average in medical school? Answer: Doctor.) The informational alternative would provide much more useful data to the public than the current licensing procedure does. There are, of course, arguments on both sides. A key issue of debate is whether people have the ability to assess the information provided. Supporters of licensing argue that people do not have that ability; supporters of the informational alternative argue that they do.

Government Failure and Market Failures

The above three types of market failure—externalities, public goods, and informational problems—give you a good sense of how markets can fail. They could be extended almost infinitely; all real-world markets in some way fail. But the point was to provide you not only with a sense of the way in which markets fail but also with a sense that economists know that markets fail and many of them support markets and oppose regulation anyway. Simply to point out a market failure is not necessarily to call for government to step in and try to rectify the situation. Why? The reason can be called *government failure,* which we defined above as happening when the government intervention in the market to improve the market failure actually makes the situation worse.

Q-9 Would an economist necessarily believe that we should simply let the market deal with a pollution problem?

Why are there government failures? Let's briefly list some important reasons:

1. *Government doesn't have an incentive to correct the problem.* Government reflects politics, which reflects individuals' interests in trying to gain more for themselves. Political pressures to benefit some group or another will often dominate over doing the general good.

2. *Governments don't have enough information to deal with the problem.* Regulating is a difficult business. To intervene effectively, even if it wants to,

Climate Change, Global Warming, and Economic Policy

An issue in which almost all the dimensions of economic policy analysis come into play is global warming. The issue is enormous, and a recent expert consensus estimate of the cost of global warming in terms of lost income was a 1 percent decline in global economic activity, which for the United States comes out to about $200 billion, or $610 per person per year.

©Carl De Souza/AFP/Getty Images

As discussed in the box in Chapter 1 on market solutions, the framework within which the debate is taking place is the economic framework. Economists have done numerous studies of the costs and benefits of various policies, which have led to a consensus that global warming and the accompanying climate change should be seen as an issue of market failure, that is, that the market places no price on emitting carbon dioxide gas into the atmosphere even though emissions impose a cost on society.

The policy problems of dealing with climate change are formidable. The first is a major free rider problem. Because there is no world government that can force countries to comply with any global effort to address carbon emissions, any policy has to be voluntary, making it easy for one country to opt out (free ride). President Trump's pulling the United States out of the Paris Accord was seen by many as free riding by the United States. A second problem is that climate change is not bad for all areas. Some countries and areas within countries may actually benefit from climate change. For example, significant global warming will likely extend the growing season in northern countries and make areas that previously were almost uninhabitable because of the cold more pleasant. The costs of global warming are highly concentrated in low-lying coastal areas. This diversity of costs and benefits makes arriving at a voluntary agreement much less likely.

A third problem is that the largest expected benefits to stopping climate change are in the future, while many of the costs are *now,* and people tend to discount future costs and benefits. A fourth problem is the lack of a clear cost/benefit analysis for various policy alternatives and the uncertainty of the success of various technologies. Cost estimates of various policies to become largely free of fossil fuel emissions by 2100 vary from 1 percent to 16 percent of total world output. (Were a cost-competitive fuel-cell-powered car or a fusion nuclear reactor developed, the use of fossil fuel would decrease significantly, and the cost estimate would be much less.)

All these problems suggest that the debate about climate change policy will likely be a lively one. Over the coming years, we can expect to see three types of policies implemented: (1) the lowest-cost/highest-benefit policies that are easy to implement, such as more use of energy-efficient lightbulbs, improved insulation standards on new buildings, and reduced standby power requirements on electronic devices; (2) the politically high-profile policies instituted on a state or country basis, rather than on a global basis, that don't really do much to solve the problem but that sound good in a sound bite; and (3) those policies that do not make much sense in an economic framework but that help certain firms and geographic areas, and that make sense within a political framework.

Many economists believe that increased corn-based ethanol production is an example; the carbon dioxide emissions from producing ethanol from corn are almost as great as the reduction in carbon dioxide emissions resulting from the use of ethanol as a fuel, but the programs significantly help farmers, so they have political support. Despite calls for change, the requirement that refiners use a certain portion of renewable fuels such as ethanol has remained.

government must have good information, but just as the market often lacks adequate information, so does the government.

3. *Intervention in markets is almost always more complicated than it initially seems.* Almost all actions have unintended consequences. Government attempts to offset market failures can prevent the market from dealing with the problem more effectively. The difficulty is that generally the market's ways of dealing with problems work only in the long run. As government deals with

Web Note 8.5

Unintended Consequences

the short-run problems, it eliminates the incentives that would have brought about a long-run market solution.

Q-10 If one accepts the three reasons for market failure, why might one still oppose government intervention?

4. *The bureaucratic nature of government intervention does not allow fine-tuning.* When the problems change, the government solution often responds far more slowly. An example is the Interstate Commerce Commission, which continued to exist years after its regulatory job had been eliminated.

5. *Government intervention leads to more government intervention.* Given the nature of the political process, opening the door in one area allows government to enter into other areas where intervention is harmful. Even in those cases where government action may seem to be likely to do some good, it might be best not to intervene, if that intervention will lead to additional government action in cases where it will not likely do good.

The above list is only a brief introduction to government failures. Much more could be said about each of them. But exploring them would take us away from economics and into political science. The important point to remember is that government failures exist and must be taken into account before making any policy recommendation. That's why real-world economic policy falls within the art of economics, and policy conclusions cannot be drawn from the models of positive economics.

Conclusion

As a textbook writer, I wish I could say that some conclusions can be drawn about whether the government should, or should not, enter into the economy. I certainly have views about particular instances (in case you haven't guessed, I'm a highly opinionated individual), but to lay out arguments and information that would convince a reasonable person to agree with me would take an entire book for each area in which government might intervene.

What I can do in this textbook is stimulate your interest in discovering for yourself the information and the subtleties of the debates for and against government intervention. Just about every time you read, hear, or are asked the question "Should the government intervene in a market?" the answer is "It depends." If your first impulse is to give any answer other than that one, you may have trouble maintaining the appropriate objectivity when you start considering the costs and benefits of government intervention.

Should the government intervene in the market? It depends.

Summary

- An externality is the effect of a decision on a third party that is not taken into account by the decision maker. Positive externalities provide benefits to third parties. Negative externalities impose costs on third parties. *(LO8-1)*

- The markets for goods with negative externalities produce too much of the good for too low a price. The markets for goods with positive externalities produce too little of the good for too great a price. *(LO8-1)*

- Economists generally prefer incentive-based programs to regulatory programs because incentive-based programs are more efficient. An example of an incentive-based program is to tax the producer of a good that results in a negative externality by the amount of the externality. *(LO8-2)*

- Voluntary solutions are difficult to maintain for long periods of time because people have an incentive to be free riders—to enjoy the benefits of others' volunteer efforts without putting forth effort themselves.   (*LO8-2*)

- An optimal policy is one in which the marginal cost of a policy equals its marginal benefit.   (*LO8-2*)

- Public goods are nonexclusive and nonrival. It is difficult to measure the benefits of public goods because people do not reveal their preferences by purchasing them in the marketplace.   (*LO8-3*)

- Theoretically, the market value of a public good can be calculated by summing the value that each individual places on every quantity. This is vertically summing individual demand curves.   (*LO8-3*)

- Individuals have an incentive to withhold information that will result in a lower price if one is a seller and a higher price if one is a consumer. Because of this incentive to withhold information, the markets for some goods disappear. Such market failures are known as adverse selection problems.   (*LO8-4*)

- The health insurance market suffers from both adverse selection problems and moral hazard problems.   (*LO8-4*)

- Licensure and full disclosure are two solutions to the informational problem.   (*LO8-4*)

- Government intervention may worsen the problem created by the market failure. Government failure occurs because: (1) governments don't have an incentive to correct the problem, (2) governments don't have enough information to deal with the problem, (3) intervention is more complicated than it initially seems, (4) the bureaucratic nature of government precludes fine-tuning, and (5) government intervention often leads to more government intervention.   (*LO8-5*)

Key Terms

adverse selection problem
direct regulation
efficient
effluent fee
externality

free rider problem
government failure
inefficient
marginal social benefit
marginal social cost

market failure
market incentive plan
moral hazard problem
negative externality
optimal policy

positive externality
public good
screening
signaling
tax incentive program

Questions and Exercises connect

1. State three reasons for a potentially beneficial role of government intervention.   (*LO8-1*)

2. Is the marginal social benefit of a good that exhibits positive externalities greater or less than the private social benefit of that good? Why?   (*LO8-1*)

3. How would an economist likely respond to the statement "There is no such thing as an acceptable level of pollution"?   (*LO8-1*)

4. Would a high tax on oil significantly reduce the amount of pollution coming from the use of oil? Why or why not?   (*LO8-2*)

5. The marginal cost, marginal social cost, and demand for fish are represented by the curves in the graph below. Suppose that there are no restrictions on fishing.   (*LO8-1*)
   a. Assuming perfect competition, demonstrate graphically what the catch is going to be, and at what price it will be sold.

b. What are the socially efficient price and output?

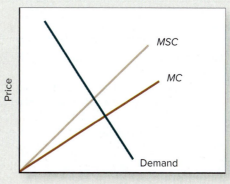

6. Which is more efficient: a market incentive program or a direct regulatory program? Why?   (*LO8-2*)

7. There's a gas shortage in Gasland. You're presented with two proposals that will achieve the same level of reduction in the use of gas. Proposal A would force everybody to reduce their gas consumption by 5 percent. Proposal B would impose a 50-cent tax on the consumption of a gallon of gas, which would also achieve a 5 percent reduction. Consumers of gas can be divided into two groups—one group whose demand is elastic and another group whose demand is inelastic. (*LO8-2*)
   a. How will the proposals affect each group?
   b. Which group would support a regulatory policy?
   c. Which would support a tax policy?

8. Economists Don Fullerton and Thomas C. Kinnaman studied the effects of the Charlottesville, Virginia, change from charging a flat fee for garbage collection to charging $0.80 per 32-gallon bag and found the following results:
The weight of garbage collected fell by 14 percent.
The volume of garbage collected fell by 37 percent.
The weight of recycling rose by 16 percent. (*LO8-2*)
   a. Why did recycling increase and garbage collection decrease?
   b. Why did the weight of garbage fall by less than the volume of garbage collected?
   c. Demonstrate, using supply and demand curves, the effect of the change in pricing on the volume of garbage collected.

9. List the public-good aspects (if any) of the following goods: safety, street names, and a steak dinner. (*LO8-3*)

10. Why are both nonexcludability and nonrivalry important elements of public goods? (*LO8-3*)

11. Why are voluntary contributions to provide for public goods such as city parks unlikely to lead to an efficient quantity of parks in a city? (*LO8-3*)

12. Use the table below, which shows the demand for a public good in an economy consisting of two households, A and B, to answer a to d below. (*LO8-3*)

Price	$0.00	$0.50	$1.00	$1.50	$2.00	$2.50	$3.00
Quantity A	12	10	8	6	4	2	0
demanded B	4	3	2	1	0	0	0

   a. Graph the individual demand curves and the market demand curve.
   b. What would make you doubt that the table is an accurate reporting of the individual demand curves?
   c. If the marginal cost of providing 1 unit of the good is $2.00, what is the socially optimal amount of the public good?

   d. Given the free rider problem, is your answer to c most likely an underestimate or an overestimate?

13. If you are willing to pay $5,000 for a used car that is a "cherry" and $1,000 for a used car that is a "lemon," how much will you be willing to offer to purchase a car if there is a 50 percent chance that the car is a lemon? If owners of cherry cars want $4,000 for their cherries, how will your estimate of the chance of getting a cherry change? (*LO8-4*)

14. Give three examples of signaling in the real world. (*LO8-4*)

15. Automobile insurance companies offer low-premium contracts with high deductibles and high-premium contracts with low deductibles. How is this an example of screening? (*LO8-4*)

16. What is the adverse selection problem? (*LO8-4*)

17. If neither buyers nor sellers could distinguish between "lemons" and "cherries" in the used-car market, what would you expect to be the mix of lemons and cherries for sale? (*LO8-4*)

18. Automobile insurance companies charge lower rates to married individuals than they do to unmarried individuals. What economic reason is there for such a practice? Is it fair? (*LO8-4*)

19. An advanced degree is required to teach at most colleges. In what sense is this a form of restricting entry through licensure? (*LO8-4*)

20. Who would benefit and who would lose if an informational alternative to licensing doctors were introduced? (*LO8-4*)

21. What is the effect of the moral hazard problem on insurance premiums? Explain your answer. (*LO8-4*)

22. The total cost of government regulations in the U.S. manufacturing sector was estimated by the National Association of Manufacturers to be about $2 trillion in 2012, or $15,400 per family. (*LO8-5*)
   a. Do the findings mean that the United States had too many regulations?
   b. How would an economist decide which regulations to keep and which to do away with?

23. When Ben wears his red shirt, it bothers Sally, who hates the color red. Since Ben's wearing of a red shirt imposes a cost on Sally, it involves an externality. Would it therefore be correct to have the government intervene and forbid Ben to wear a red shirt? (*LO8-5*)

24. True or false? Burning fossil fuels contributes to climate change. Thus, it makes sense for the government to place a tax on the burning of fossil fuels. Why? (*LO8-5*)

Questions from Alternative Perspectives

1. The book titles this chapter "Market Failure versus Government Failure."
   a. Does the fact that the author spends most of the chapter discussing market failure rather than government failure suggest an ideological bias in the book?
   b. If so, how would you characterize that bias? *(Austrian)*

2. In the late 19th century, Washington Gladden said, "He who battles for the Christianization of society will find their strongest foe in the field of economics. Economics is indeed the dismal science because of the selfishness of its maxims and the inhumanity of its conclusions."
   a. Evaluate this statement.
   b. Is there a conflict between the ideology of the market and the precepts of Christianity?
   c. Would a society that emphasized a market mode of production benefit from having a moral framework that emphasized selflessness rather than selfishness? *(Religious)*

3. Institutional economists define economics as the study of how people use institutions to socially interact in the process of extracting materials from the biophysical world to produce and exchange goods and services to reproduce culture and better the human condition. If you accept this definition of economics, under what conditions is government intervention in the market acceptable? *(Institutionalist)*

4. Post-Keynesians suggest that contractual agreements might be a way to deal with asymmetric information.
   a. Name a business or consumer transaction where asymmetric information might occur.
   b. How could a contractual agreement overcome the problems of asymmetric information in that market?
   c. Would that contractual agreement arise without government intervention? *(Post-Keynesian)*

5. Water privatization in South Africa has been guided by what the World Bank calls the "cost recovery" approach: Water should be made available to people only if the company providing it can recover its costs plus a profit. In 1995, private companies began taking over the provision of water in South Africa. By the early 2000s some cities saw water prices increase fourfold, millions of people had their water cut off, and outbreaks of cholera returned for the first time in decades. Since then, many cities have re-municipalized their water supplies.
   a. Which of your textbook's list of market failures apply to the privatization of water utilities in South Africa?
   b. Is the failure so serious that it makes the private provision of water bad public policy?
   c. If not, why not? If so, what policies would make more economic sense? *(Radical)*

Issues to Ponder

1. Most economists believe that the federal gasoline tax should be raised to $1 per gallon or higher. What do you suppose were their reasons?

2. In his book *At the Hand of Man*, Raymond Bonner argues that Africa should promote hunting, charging large fees for permits to kill animals (for example, $7,500 for a permit to shoot an elephant).
   a. What are some arguments in favor of this proposal?
   b. What are some arguments against?

3. Suppose an air-quality law is passed that requires 3.75 percent of all the cars sold to emit zero pollution.
   a. What would be the likely impact of this law?
   b. Can you think of any way in which this law might actually increase pollution rather than decrease it?
   c. How might an economist suggest modifying this law to better achieve economic efficiency?

4. Economist Robert W. Turner suggested three market failures that could justify government provision of national parks. What three failures did he likely discuss and what is the cause of the failure?

5. Should government eliminate the Food and Drug Administration's role in restricting which drugs may be marketed? Why or why not?

6. Financial analysts are not currently required to be licensed. Should they be licensed? Why or why not?

7. Scientists have identified a gene that accounts for 5 percent of thrill-seeking behavior. People with this gene are likely to take more risks such as smoking and bungee jumping in search of the next thrill. Provide two arguments—one for and one against—requiring people to undergo testing to find out if they have this gene before a company agrees to provide life insurance.

8. List five ways you are affected on a daily basis by government intervention in the market. For what reason might government be involved? Is that reason justified?

9. Would a high tax on oil significantly reduce the total amount of pollution in the environment?

10. A debate about dairy products concerns the labeling of milk produced from cows that have been injected with the

hormone BST, which significantly increases milk production. Since the FDA has determined that this synthetically produced copy of a milk hormone is indistinguishable from the hormone produced naturally by the cow, and also has determined that milk from cows treated with BST is indistinguishable from milk from untreated cows, some people have argued that no labeling requirement is necessary. Others argue that the consumer has a right to know.

a. Where do you think most dairy farmers stand on this labeling issue?

b. If consumers have a right to know, should labels inform them of other drugs, such as antibiotics, normally given to cows?

c. Do you think dairy farmers who support BST labeling also support the broader labeling law that would be needed if other drugs were included? Why?

Answers to Margin Questions

1. An externality is an effect of a decision not taken into account by the decision maker. When there are externalities, the private cost no longer necessarily reflects the social cost, and therefore the market may not work properly. (*LO8-1*)

2. No. The existence of a positive externality does not mean that the market works better than if no externality existed. It means that the market is not supplying a sufficient amount of the resource or activity, and insufficient supply can be as inefficient as an oversupply. (*LO8-1*)

3. Because efficiency does not take into account who pays the costs, there may be a trade-off between fairness and efficiency. For example, a tax on gasoline would be efficient, but because the poor tend to drive older, less fuel-efficient cars, they will end up paying more of the tax, which some may believe to be unfair. The tax could be seen as both fair and efficient because consumers choose to reduce their gas use based on the new price, so the solution is efficient. The solution has an element of fairness in it since those causing the pollution are those paying more. (*LO8-2*)

4. The tax incentive approach to deal with externalities is fair in the following sense: Individuals whose actions result in more pollution pay more. Individuals whose actions result in less pollution pay less. In some broader sense this may not be fair if one takes into account the initial positions of those polluting. For example, people who live in less-populated states often have to drive farther to work and would pay a higher tax than others. (*LO8-2*)

5. Voluntary actions that are not in people's self-interest may not work in large groups because individuals will rely on others to volunteer. There is also a potential lack of efficiency in voluntary solutions since the person who voluntarily reduces consumption may not be the person who faces the least cost of doing so. (*LO8-2*)

6. It is difficult for government to decide the efficient quantity of a public good because public goods are not purchased by individuals in markets. Therefore, individuals do not reveal the value they place on public goods. Individuals also face incentives to overstate the value they place on public goods if they do not have to pay for them, and to understate the value if they do have to share the cost. (*LO8-3*)

7. Since adverse selection is a problem in the medical insurance industry, with fuller information, I would expect that average medical rates would decline since the adverse selection problem would disappear. Medical insurers would be able to offer lower-cost insurance to people who are less likely to get sick and who perhaps choose not to be covered at today's high rates. (*LO8-4*)

8. If an informational alternative to licensing doctors were introduced, existing doctors would suffer a significant monetary loss, and students who would likely go on to medical school in existing institutions would face lower potential incomes when they entered practice. Those who benefit would likely be (1) those who did not want to go through an entire medical school schedule but were willing to learn a specialty that required far less education and in which they had a particular proclivity to do well and (2) consumers, who would get more for less. (*LO8-4*)

9. An economist would not necessarily believe that we should simply let the market deal with the pollution problem. Pollution clearly involves externalities. Where economists differ from many laypeople is in how to handle the problem. An economist is likely to look more carefully into the costs, try to build price incentives into whatever program is designed, and make the marginal private cost equal the marginal social cost. (*LO8-5*)

10. One can accept all three explanations for market failure and still oppose government intervention if one believes that government intervention will cause worse problems than the market failure causes. (*LO8-5*)

Politics and Economics: The Case of Agricultural Markets

American farmers have become welfare addicts, protected and assisted at every turn by a network of programs paid for by their fellow citizens. If Americans still believe in the virtue of self-reliance, they should tell Washington to get out of the way and let farmers practice it.

—Stephen Chapman

CHAPTER 8W

This web chapter can be found in McGraw-Hill Connect®

Source: Jeff Vanuga, USDA Natural Resources Conservation Service

After reading this chapter, you should be able to:

LO8W-1 Explain the good/bad paradox in farming and how it can be avoided.

LO8W-2 Explain how a price support system works and show the distributional consequences of four alternative methods of price support.

LO8W-3 Discuss real-world pressures politicians face when designing agricultural policy.

Comparative Advantage, Exchange Rates, and Globalization

After reading this chapter, you should be able to:

LO9-1 Explain the principle of comparative advantage.

LO9-2 Explain why economists' and laypeople's views of trade differ.

LO9-3 Summarize the sources of U.S. comparative advantage and discuss some concerns about the future of the U.S. economy.

LO9-4 Discuss how exchange rates are determined and what their role is in equalizing trade flows.

©Steve Allen/Brand X Pictures/Getty Images

If economists had a mantra, it would be "Trade is good." Trade allows specialization and division of labor and thereby promotes economic growth. Much of economists' support for trade comes from their theory of comparative advantage. In this chapter we consider how the theory of comparative advantage relates to the U.S. economy. We also explore the role exchange rates play in the theory of comparative advantage and international trade.

The Principle of Comparative Advantage

The reason countries trade is the same reason that people trade: Trade can make both better off. The reason that this is true is the principle of comparative advantage that was introduced in Chapter 2. It is, however, important enough to warrant an in-depth review. The basic idea of the principle of **comparative advantage** is that *as long as the relative opportunity costs of producing goods (what must be given up of one good in order to get another good) differ among countries, then there are potential gains from trade.* Let's review this principle by considering the story of I.T., an imaginary international trader, who convinces two countries to enter into trades by giving both countries some of the advantages of trade; he keeps the rest for himself.

The Gains from Trade

Here's the situation. On his trips to the United States and Saudi Arabia, I.T. noticed that the two countries did not trade. He also noticed that the opportunity cost of producing a ton of food in Saudi Arabia was 10 barrels of oil and that the opportunity cost for the United States of producing a ton of food was 1/10 of a barrel of oil. At the time, the United States' production was 60 barrels of oil and 400 tons of food, while Saudi Arabia's production was 400 barrels of oil and 60 tons of food.

The choices for the United States can be seen in Figure 9-1(a), and the choices for Saudi Arabia can be seen in Figure 9-1(b). The tables give the numerical choices, and the figures translate those numerical choices into graphs.

The principle of comparative advantage states that as long as the relative opportunity costs of producing goods differ among countries, then there are potential gains from trade.

FIGURE 9-1 (A AND B) Comparative Advantage: The United States and Saudi Arabia

Looking at tables **(a)** and **(b)**, you can see that if Saudi Arabia devotes all its resources to oil, it can produce 1,000 barrels of oil, but if it devotes all of its resources to food, it can produce only 100 tons of food. For the United States, the story is the opposite: Devoting all of its resources to oil, the United States can produce only 100 barrels of oil—10 times less than Saudi Arabia—but if it devotes all of its resources to food, it can produce 1,000 tons of food—10 times more than Saudi Arabia. Assuming resources are comparable, Saudi Arabia has a comparative advantage in the production of oil, and the United States has a comparative advantage in the production of food. The information in the tables is presented graphically below each table. These are the countries' production possibility curves. Each point on each country's curve corresponds to a row on that country's table.

Percentage of Resources Devoted to Oil	Oil Produced (barrels)	Food Produced (tons)	Row
100%	100	0	A
80	80	200	B
60	60	400	C
40	40	600	D
20	20	800	E
0	0	1,000	F

United States' Production Possibility Table

Percentage of Resources Devoted to Oil	Oil Produced (barrels)	Food Produced (tons)	Row
100%	1,000	0	A
80	800	20	B
60	600	40	C
40	400	60	D
20	200	80	E
0	0	100	F

Saudi Arabia's Production Possibility Table

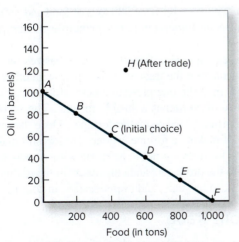

(a) United States' Production Possibility Curve

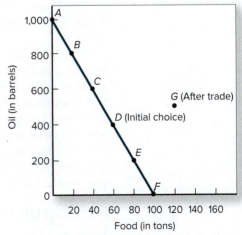

(b) Saudi Arabia's Production Possibility Curve

Q-1 If the opportunity cost of oil for food were the same for both the United States and Saudi Arabia, what should I.T. do?

These graphs represent the two countries' production possibility curves. Each combination of numbers in the table corresponds to a point on the curve. For example, point B in each graph corresponds to the entries in row B, columns 2 and 3, in the relevant table.

Let's assume that the United States has chosen point C (production of 60 barrels of oil and 400 tons of food) and Saudi Arabia has chosen point D (production of 400 barrels of oil and 60 tons of food).

Now I.T., who understands the principle of comparative advantage, comes along and offers the following deal to the United States:

If you produce 1,000 tons of food and no oil [point F in Figure 9-1(a)] and give me 500 tons of food while keeping 500 tons for yourself, I'll guarantee you 120 barrels of oil, double the amount you're now getting. I'll put you on point H, which is totally beyond your current production possibility curve. You'll get more oil and have more food. It's an offer you can't refuse.

I.T. then flies off to Saudi Arabia, to which he makes the following offer:

If you produce 1,000 barrels of oil and no food [point A in Figure 9-1(b)] and give me 500 barrels of oil while keeping 500 barrels for yourself, I guarantee you 120 tons of food, double the amount of food you're now getting. I'll put you on point G, which is totally beyond your current production possibility curve. You'll get more oil and more food. It's an offer you can't refuse.

Both countries accept; they'd be foolish not to. So the two countries' final consumption positions are as follows:

	Oil (barrels)	Food (tons)
Total production	1,000	1,000
U.S. consumption	120	500
U.S. gain in consumption	+60	+100
Saudi consumption	500	120
Saudi gain in consumption	+100	+60
I.T.'s profit	380	380

For arranging the trade, I.T. makes a handsome profit of 380 tons of food and 380 barrels of oil. I.T. has become rich because he understands the principle of comparative advantage.

Now obviously this hypothetical example significantly overemphasizes the gains a trader makes. Generally the person arranging the trade must compete with other traders and offer both countries a better deal than the one presented here. But the person who first recognizes a trading opportunity often makes a sizable fortune. The second and third persons who recognize the opportunity make smaller fortunes. Once the insight is generally recognized, the possibility of making a fortune is gone. Traders still make their normal returns, but the instantaneous fortunes are not to be made without new insights. In the long run, benefits of trade go to the producers and consumers in the trading countries, not the traders, but the long run can be years, and even decades, in coming.

Dividing Up the Gains from Trade

As the above story suggests, when countries avail themselves of comparative advantage, there are high gains of trade to be made. Who gets these gains is unclear. The principle of comparative advantage doesn't determine how those gains of trade will be divided up among the countries involved and among traders who make the trade possible. While there are no definitive laws determining how real-world gains from trade will be apportioned, economists have developed some insights into how those gains are likely to be divided up. The first insight concerns how much the trader gets. The general rule is:

The more competition that exists among traders, the less likely it is that the trader gets big gains of trade; more of the gains from trade will go to the citizens in the two countries, and less will go to the traders.

What this insight means is that where entry into trade is unimpaired, most of the gains of trade will pass from the trader to the countries. Thus, the trader's big gains from trade occur in markets that are newly opened or if the product is unique and cannot be easily copied.

This insight isn't lost on trading companies. Numerous import/export companies exist whose business is discovering possibilities for international trade in newly opened markets. Individuals representing trading companies go around hawking projects or goods to countries. For example, at the end of the 1999 NATO bombing campaign in Kosovo, what the business world calls the *import/export contingent* flew to Kosovo with offers of goods and services to sell. Many of those same individuals were in Iran as the United States lifted sanctions in 2016, and were also waiting to set up deals with Cuba as U.S. relations with Cuba thawed.

A second insight is:

Once competition prevails, smaller countries tend to get a larger percentage of the gains of trade than do larger countries.

The reason, briefly, is that more opportunities are opened up for smaller countries by trade than for larger countries. The more opportunities, the larger the relative gains. Say, for instance, that the United States begins trade with Mali, a small country in Africa. Enormous new consumption possibilities are opened up for Mali—prices of all types of goods will fall. Assuming Mali has a comparative advantage in fish, before international trade began, cars were probably extraordinarily expensive in Mali, while fish were cheap. With international trade, the price of cars in Mali falls substantially, so Mali gets the gains. Because the U.S. economy is so large compared to Mali's, the U.S. price of fish doesn't change noticeably. Mali's fish are just a drop in the bucket. The price ratio of cars to fish doesn't change much for the United States, so it doesn't get much of the gains of trade. Mali gets almost all the gains from trade.

There's an important catch to this gains-from-trade argument. The argument holds only if competition among traders prevails. That means that Mali residents are sold cars at the same price (plus shipping costs) as U.S. residents. International traders in small countries often have little competition from other traders and keep large shares of the gains from trade for themselves. In the earlier food/oil example, the United States and Saudi Arabia didn't get a large share of the benefits. It was I.T. who got most of the benefits. Since the traders often come from the larger country, the smaller country doesn't get this share of the gains from trade; the larger country's international traders do.

A third insight is:

Gains from trade go to the countries producing goods that exhibit economies of scale.

Trade allows an increase in production. If there are economies of scale, that increase can lower the average cost of production of a good. Hence, an increase in production can lower the price of the good in the producing country. The country producing the good with the larger economies of scale has its costs reduced by more, and hence gains more from trade than does its trading partner.

Three determinants of the terms of trade are:

1. The more competition, the less the trader gets.
2. Smaller countries get a larger proportion of the gain than larger countries.
3. Countries producing goods with economies of scale get a larger gain from trade.

Q-2 In what circumstances would a small country not get the larger percentage of the gains from trade?

Why Economists and Laypeople Differ in Their Views of Trade

The comparative advantage model conveys a story with the theme of "trade is good"; trade benefits both parties to the trade. This story doesn't fit much of the lay public's view of trade, nor its fear of outsourcing. If trade is good, why do so many people oppose it, and what accounts for the difference between economists' view of trade and the lay public's view? I suggest four reasons.

Gains Are Often Stealth

Gains from trade are often stealth gains.

One reason for the difference is that laypeople often do not recognize the gains of trade—the gains are often stealth gains such as a decline in prices—while they easily identify the loss of jobs caused by the trade adjustments as countries shift production to take advantage of trade. For example, consider the price of clothing: A shirt today costs far less in real terms (in terms of the number of hours you have to work to buy it) than it did a decade or two ago. Much of the reason for that is trade. But how many people attribute that fall in the price of shirts to trade? Not many; they just take it for granted. But the reality is that much of our current lifestyle in the United States has been made possible by trade.

Much of our current lifestyle is made possible by trade.

Opportunity Cost Is Relative

A second reason for the difference between the lay view of trade and economists' view is that the lay public often believes that since countries such as China have lower wages, they must have a comparative advantage in just about everything so that if we allow free trade, eventually we will lose all U.S. jobs. This belief is a logical contradiction; by definition comparative advantage refers to relative cost. If one country has a comparative advantage in one set of goods, the other country must have a comparative advantage in another set.

The comparative advantage model assumes that a country's imports and exports are equal.

That said, economists also must admit that the lay public does have a point. The comparative advantage model assumes that a country's imports and exports are equal. That is, its **balance of trade**—*the difference between the value of exports and the value of imports*—is zero. But U.S. imports and exports are not equal. Currently, the United States imports much more than it exports; it pays for the excess of imports over exports with IOUs. As long as foreign countries are willing to accept U.S. promises to pay sometime in the future, they can have a comparative advantage in the production of many more goods than the United States.[1] Currently, people in other countries finance the U.S. trade deficit by buying U.S. assets. Once the other countries decide that it is no longer in their interests to finance the U.S. trade deficit, economic forces such as the adjustment of exchange rates will be set in motion to restore a more equal division of comparative advantages.

Trade Is Broader Than Manufactured Goods

Q-3 What are four reasons for the difference between laypeople's and economists' views of trade?

A third reason accounting for the difference between the lay view of trade and the economists' view is that laypeople often think of trade as trade in just manufactured goods. Trade is much broader, and includes the services that traders provide. Countries can have comparative advantages in trade itself, and the gains the trader makes can account for the seeming differences in countries' comparative advantages.

---

[1]One could make the model fit reality if one thinks of the United States as having a comparative advantage in producing IOUs that other people will accept.

Notice in my example that the international traders who brought the trade about benefited significantly from trade. I included traders because trade does not take place on its own—markets and trade require entrepreneurs, people who see the opportunity for a trade and do what is needed to make the trade possible. The market is not about abstract forces; it is about real people working to improve their position. Many of the gains from trade do not go to the countries producing or consuming the good but rather to the trader. And the gains that traders get can be enormous.

Consider, for example, $200 sneakers that the "with-it" students wear. Those sneakers are likely made in China, costing about $8 to make. So much of the benefits of trade do not go to the producer or the consumer; they go to the trader. However, not all of the difference is profit. The trader has other costs, such as the costs of transportation and advertising—someone has to convince you that you need those "with-it" sneakers. (Just do it, right?) A portion of the benefits of the trade accrues to U.S. advertising firms, which can pay more to creative people who think up those crazy ads.

The United States currently has a large comparative advantage in facilitating trade, and many trade companies are U.S.-based. These companies buy many of the goods and services that support trade from their home country—the United States. What this means is that goods manufactured in China, India, and other Asian countries are creating demand for advertising, management, and distribution, and are therefore creating jobs and income in the United States. That's one reason for the large increase in service jobs in the U.S. economy. These are jobs that laypeople often do not associate with trade.

Trade with China and India has been generating jobs in the United States.

Trade Has Distributional Effects

A fourth reason most economists see international trade differently than do most laypeople involves distributional issues. The economists' model doesn't take into account trade's effect on the distribution of income. Most laypeople, however, are extremely concerned with the distribution of income, which means that they look at the effects of trade differently. The problem is that while trade tends to benefit society as a whole, the benefits are often highly unevenly distributed. In the short run (which can last for 10 or 20 years), trade can hurt some a lot. Specifically, when trade is opened among countries, as it has been during the period of globalization, those producers whose goods are both tradable and internationally competitive benefit; those producers whose goods are both tradable and not internationally competitive lose. On the consumer's side, most people generally benefit since they now can get tradable goods at the lower international prices.

For the United States, this has meant that with globalization many people who worked in manufacturing either lost their jobs or saw their wages fall to make U.S. production competitive. The same was true for those holding less-skilled jobs that could be outsourced. Blue-collar America has been hard-hit by globalization. The problems facing these groups have been multiplied by immigration of workers who were willing to work at physically difficult jobs for lower wages than Americans were willing to work for. This immigration is another aspect of globalization that put further downward pressure on wages in those sectors.

On the high end of the income distribution were people with intellectual property rights who suddenly had billions more people to whom to sell their products. Their income shot up; instead of being multimillionaires, they were now billionaires. Similarly, demand for the services of those in high-tech and managerial and organizational jobs increased enormously because their work could not (yet) be duplicated in low-wage countries. Both finance and high-level management fell into these categories. So while the share of U.S. jobs in the manufacturing sector fell from 25 percent in the 1970s to 8 percent more recently, the share of U.S. jobs in the professional service sector rose from 7 percent to 24 percent. The income going to that sector also rose

Web Note 9.1

Blue-Collar America

Four reasons economists and laypeople differ in their views of trade are:

1. Gains are often stealth.
2. Opportunity cost is relative.
3. Trade is broader than manufactured goods.
4. Trade has distributional effects.

significantly. Finance in the economy rose from about 4 percent of the economy in the 1980s to about 9 percent more recently, and the financial sector accounted for much of the profits in the U.S. economy. Salaries in the financial sector went up to astronomical levels, even as manufacturing wages were falling. Put another way, the international traders and those associated with them (those who got many of the gains from trade in our comparative advantage example) thrived as a result of globalization. The gains from trade from which to take their share of the trade grew. So with every switch of business from the United States to China, U.S. international traders benefited.

Q-4 Why has globalization caused employment and wages to decline in the manufacturing sector but not in the education, government, and health care sectors?

Workers in the education, health care, and government sectors also felt little or no downward pressure on their wages from globalization, because these sectors produce goods and services that cannot be easily traded on the global market and so face less foreign competition. They are nontradables. In fact, wages in these sectors grew, just as they did in the financial sector. Employment in the government, education, and health industries rose significantly, while manufacturing jobs fell. Whereas workers in the tradable sector would lose their jobs if their wages didn't fall, workers in these nontradable sectors faced no global competition, so they could both raise their wages and keep their jobs.

People in these nontradable sectors benefited not just as producers but also as consumers—earning more and buying manufactured and tradable agricultural goods such as televisions, tablets, automobiles, shirts, shoes, and grapes—at lower and lower prices. Thus, the workers in these sectors got the gains of trade as consumers—lower prices—and kept their jobs and higher wages.

In contrast, manufacturing wages in the United States, adjusted for inflation, have not risen for 40 years; lower-paid individuals in these sectors have been able to keep up their consumption only by borrowing and by increasing workloads (e.g., as in more two-income families). When you put all these effects together, you can see that globalization has played a major role in increasing the income disparity in the United States. It has created a group of haves—those who work in nontradable and trade-organization sectors—and of have nots—those who work in sectors facing brutal global competition. Much of the lay public's concern about globalization and international trade is rooted in these distributional effects of globalization. True, on average, trade may have benefited the United States, but that is of little comfort to those whose pay has fallen, and who have lost a job, because of increased foreign competition.

These distributional effects within the United States are important, and it is true that economists' comparative advantage model doesn't focus on them. Instead it focuses on the aggregate effects of trade. From a global, aggregate perspective, the many U.S. workers who have been hurt by trade are counterbalanced by the billions of people in developing countries who have been pulled out of poverty by trade. U.S. jobs that are outsourced to developing countries often go to people who earn one-tenth of what a U.S. worker earns, and those jobs sometimes mean that the job holders in those countries can feed their families. On a global perspective, trade is the way global income equality comes about. Trade also leads to greater world economic growth. That world growth increases income and wealth abroad, thereby creating additional demand for U.S. goods. Two billion consumers whose incomes are increasing offer many new growth opportunities for U.S. firms. Trade expands the total pie, and even when a country gets a smaller proportion of the new total pie, the absolute amount it gets can increase.

Sources of U.S. Comparative Advantage

The concentrated nature of the costs of trade and the dispersed nature of the benefits present a challenge for policy makers.

When thinking about how the theory of comparative advantage relates to the current debate about outsourcing—what jobs are outsourced and what jobs are created in the United States—it is important to remember that comparative advantage is not determined by wages alone. Many other factors enter into comparative advantage, and these other factors give the United States a comparative advantage in a variety of goods and services. Some of those other sources of U.S. comparative advantage include:

1. *Skills of the U.S. labor force:* Our educational system and experience in production (learning by doing) have created a U.S. workforce that is highly productive, which means that it can be paid more and still be competitive.

2. *U.S. governmental institutions:* The United States has a stable, relatively non-corrupt government, which is required for effective production. These institutions give firms based in the United States a major comparative advantage.

3. *U.S. physical and technological infrastructure:* The United States has probably the best infrastructure for production in the world. This infrastructure includes extensive road systems, telecommunications networks, and power grids.

4. *English as the international language of business:* U.S. citizens learn English from birth. Chinese and Indian citizens must learn it as a second language. One is seldom as comfortable or productive working in one's second language as in one's first language.

5. *Wealth from past production:* The United States is extraordinarily wealthy, which means that the United States is the world's largest consumer. Production that supports many aspects of consumption cannot be easily transferred geographically, and thus the United States will maintain a comparative advantage in producing geographically tied consumption goods, such as gourmet dining.

6. *U.S. natural resources:* The United States is endowed with many resources: rich farmland, a pleasant and varied climate, beautiful scenery for tourism, minerals, and water. These give it comparative advantages in a number of areas.

7. *Cachet:* The United States continues to be a cultural trendsetter. People all over the world want to watch U.S. movies, want to have U.S. goods, and are influenced by U.S. advertising agencies to favor U.S. goods. As long as that is the case, the United States will have a comparative advantage in goods tied to that cachet.

8. *Inertia:* It takes time and costs money to change production. Companies will not move production to another country for a small cost differential. The difference has to be large, it has to be expected to continue for a long time, and it must be large enough to offset the risk of the unknown. Thus, the United States has an advantage over other potential places for production simply because the situation is known.

9. *U.S. intellectual property rights:* Currently, U.S. companies and individuals hold a large number of intellectual property rights, which require other countries that use their patented goods or methods to pay U.S. patent holders. Every time someone (legally) buys the Windows operating system for his or her computer, a portion of the purchase price covers a payment to a U.S. company. America's culture of embracing new ideas and questioning authority cultivates an environment of innovation that will likely continue to generate new intellectual property rights.

10. *A relatively open immigration policy:* Many of the brightest, most entrepreneurial students of developing countries immigrate and settle in the United States. They create jobs and help maintain U.S. comparative advantages in a number of fields, especially high-technology fields. More than 50 percent of the engineering degrees, for example, go to foreign students, many of whom remain in the United States.

The United States has numerous sources of comparative advantage.

Web Note 9.2

Immigration Programs

Combined, these other sources of comparative advantage will maintain the United States' competitiveness in a variety of types of production for the coming decades.

Some Concerns about the Future

The above discussion of the sources of U.S. comparative advantage should have made those of you who are U.S. citizens feel a bit better about the future of the U.S. economy; the United States is not about to lose all its jobs to outsourcing. But that does not mean that there are not real issues of concern. The typical layperson's concern that the comparative advantage story does not capture what is going on with trade and outsourcing has some real foundations, and deserves to be considered seriously.

Inherent and Transferable Sources of Comparative Advantages

When David Ricardo first made the comparative advantage argument in the early 1800s, he was talking about an economic environment that was quite different from today's. His example was Britain and Portugal, with Britain producing wool and Portugal producing wine. What caused their differing costs of production was climate; Britain's climate was far less conducive to growing grapes than Portugal's but more conducive to raising sheep. Differing technologies or labor skills in the countries did not play a key role in their comparative advantages, and it was highly unlikely that the climates, and therefore comparative advantages, of the countries could change. Put another way, both countries had inherent sources of comparative advantages, which we will call **inherent comparative advantages**—*comparative advantages that are based on factors that are relatively unchangeable,* rather than transferable sources of comparative advantages, which we will call **transferable comparative advantages**—*comparative advantages based on factors that can change relatively easily.*

As the theory of comparative advantage developed, economists applied it to a much broader range of goods whose sources of comparative advantage were not due to climate. For example, some countries had land, specific resources, capital, types of labor, or technology as sources of comparative advantage. Extending the analysis to these other sources of comparative advantage makes sense, but it is important to keep in mind that only some of these comparative advantages are inherent; others are transferable. Comparative advantages due to resources or climate are unlikely to change; comparative advantages that depend on capital, technology, or education, however, can change. In fact, we would expect them to change.

The Law of One Price

Whether a country can maintain a much higher standard of living than another country in the long run depends in part on whether its sources of comparative advantage are transferable or inherent. Saudi Arabia will maintain its comparative advantage in producing oil, but the United States' comparative advantage based on better education is likely to be more fleeting. In cases where sources of comparative advantage are not inherent, economic forces will push to eliminate that comparative advantage. The reason is the *law of one price*—in a competitive market, there will be pressure for equal factors to be priced equally. If factor prices aren't equal, firms can reduce costs by redirecting production to countries where factors are priced lower. Even seemingly inherent comparative advantages can be changed by technology. Consider oil. Technological developments in extracting shale oil in countries such as the United States have reduced Saudi Arabia's comparative advantage in oil. Alternatively, the development of cost-effective fuel cells might leave Saudi Arabia with a comparative advantage in oil but not necessarily with a comparative advantage in producing energy.

When markets are working, any country with a comparative advantage due only to transferable capital and technology will lose that comparative advantage as capital and technology spread to other countries. Ultimately, in the case of transferable comparative

Inherent comparative advantages are based on factors that are relatively unchangeable.

Transferable comparative advantages are based on factors that can change relatively easily.

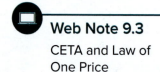

Web Note 9.3

CETA and Law of One Price

Law of one price: In a competitive market, there will be pressure for equal factors to be priced equally.

Q-5 Will transferable or inherent comparative advantages be more impacted by the law of one price? Why?

advantage, production will shift to the lower-wage country that has equivalent institutional structures. This is the law of one price in action: The same good—including equivalent labor—must sell for the same price, unless trade is restricted or other differences exist. That is what's happening now with the United States and outsourcing. Skills needed in the information technology sector, for example, are transferable. Because an information technology professional with three to five years' experience earns about $85,000 in the United States and only $30,000 in India, those jobs are moving abroad. As long as wages differ, and the workers' productivities in countries are comparable, transferable comparative advantages of U.S. production will continue to erode until costs of production in different countries equalize. As they erode, production and jobs will be moved abroad.

Transferable comparative advantages will tend to erode over time.

The question, therefore, is not: Why is outsourcing to China and India occurring today? The questions are: Why didn't it happen long ago? And how did U.S. productivity, and hence the U.S. standard of living, come to so exceed China's and India's productivity? Or alternatively: How did the United States get in its current high-wage position, and is it likely to maintain that position into the indefinite future?

How the United States Gained and Is Now Losing Sources of Comparative Advantage

To better understand the current U.S. position, let's look at it historically. The United States developed its highly favorable position from the 1920s until the late 1940s when the two world wars directed production toward the United States. Those wars, the entrepreneurial spirit of the U.S. population, U.S. institutions conducive to production, and the flow of technology and capital (financial assets) into the United States gave the United States a big boost both during the two world wars and after. Coming out of World War II, at the then-existing exchange rates, the United States had a major cost advantage in producing a large majority of goods, just as China has a cost advantage in producing the large majority of goods today.

Such cost advantages in a majority of areas of production are not sustainable because the balance of trade will be highly imbalanced. In the absence of specific policy by governments, or large private flows of capital to pay for those imports, eventually that imbalance will right itself. After World War II, the trade balance that favored the United States was maintained temporarily by U.S. companies, which invested heavily in Europe, and by the U.S. government, which transferred funds to Europe with programs such as the Marshall Plan—a program to aid Europe in rebuilding its economy. These flows of capital financed Europe's **trade deficits**—*when imports exceed exports*—and allowed the United States to run large **trade surpluses**—*when exports exceed imports*—just as current flows of capital into the United States from a variety of countries, and the explicit policy of buying U.S. bonds by Chinese and Japanese central banks, are financing the U.S. trade deficits now, and allowing large Chinese trade surpluses with the United States.

In the absence of specific policy by governments, or large private flows of capital, eventually any large trade imbalance will right itself.

Methods of Equalizing Trade Balances

Capital flows that sustain trade imbalances eventually stop, and when they do, adjustments in sources of comparative advantages must take place so that the trade surplus countries—such as China today—become less competitive (lose sources of comparative advantage) and the trade deficit countries—in this case, the United States—become more competitive (gain sources of comparative advantage). This adjustment can occur in a number of ways. The two most likely adjustments today are that wages in China rise relative to wages in the United States, or the U.S. exchange rate (discussed in the next section) falls. Both adjustments will make Chinese goods relatively more expensive and U.S. goods relatively cheaper, just as these adjustments did with countries such as Japan, Taiwan, and Korea in previous decades. Neither of these is

Q-6 What are two likely adjustments that will reduce the trade deficit between China and the United States?

especially pleasant for the United States, which is why we will likely hear continued calls for trade restrictions in the coming decade.

Unfortunately, as I will discuss in a later chapter, the trade restriction policies that governments can undertake will generally make things worse. In a globalized free trade economy, the U.S. wage advantage can be maintained only to the degree that the total cost of production of a good in the United States (with all the associated costs) is no more expensive than the total cost of producing that same good abroad (with all the associated costs). The degree to which production shifts because of lower wages abroad depends on how transferable the U.S. comparative advantages are that we listed above. Some of them are generally nontransferable, and thus will support sustained higher relative U.S. wages. English as the language of business; the enormous wealth of the United States; inertia; and U.S. political, social, and capital infrastructure will keep much production in the United States, and will maintain a comparative advantage for U.S. production even with significantly higher U.S. wages.

But in the coming decades, we can expect a narrowing of the wage gap between the United States and China and India. Given these strong market forces that cannot be prevented without undermining the entire international trading system, about the only available realistic strategy for the United States is to adapt to this new situation. Its best strategy is to work toward maintaining existing comparative advantages through investment in education and infrastructure, while continuing to provide an environment conducive to innovation so that it develops comparative advantages in new industries.

> The U.S. wage advantage can be maintained only to the degree that total cost of production of a good in the United States is no more than the total cost of that same good abroad.

Determination of Exchange Rates and Trade

As mentioned above, transferable sources of comparative advantage aren't the only way to eliminate trade imbalances. Exchange rates are another. An **exchange rate** is *the rate at which one country's currency can be traded for another country's currency*. The market for foreign currencies is called the foreign exchange (forex) market. It is this market that determines the exchange rates that newspapers report daily in tables such as the table below, which shows the cost of various currencies in terms of dollars and the cost of dollars in terms of those currencies.

Web Note 9.4

Exchange Rate Data

Exchange Rates, June 2018

	U.S. $ Equivalent	Currency per U.S. $
Argentina (peso)	0.040	24.98
Canada (dollar)	0.769	1.30
China (yuan)	0.156	6.39
Denmark (krone)	0.158	6.31
European Union (euro)	1.176	0.85
Israel (shekel)	0.280	3.57
Japan (yen)	0.009	109.75
Pakistan (rupee)	0.009	116.11
Philippines (peso)	0.019	52.60
Russia (ruble)	0.016	62.38
Saudi Arabia (riyal)	0.267	3.75
U.K. (pound)	1.333	0.75

The second column in this table reports the price of foreign currencies in terms of dollars. For example, 1 Argentinean peso costs about 4 cents. The third column tells

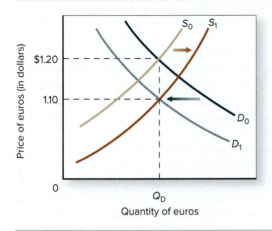

FIGURE 9-2 **The Supply of and Demand for Euros**

As long as you keep quantities and prices of *what* straight, the determination of exchange rates is easy. Just remember that if you're talking about the supply of and demand for euros, the price will be measured in dollars and the quantity will be in euros.

you the price of dollars in terms of the foreign currency. For example, 1 U.S. dollar costs 24.98 Argentinean pesos.

People exchange currencies to buy goods or assets in other countries. For example, an American who wants to buy stock of a company that trades on the EU stock exchange first needs to buy euros with dollars. If the stock costs 150 euros, he will need to buy 150 euros. With an exchange rate of $1.20 for 1 euro, he will need to pay $180 to buy 150 euros ($1.20 × 150). Only then can he buy the stock.

Let's now turn to a graphical analysis of the foreign exchange (forex) market. At first glance, the graphical analysis of foreign exchange rates seems simple: You have an upward-sloping supply curve and a downward-sloping demand curve. But what goes on the axes? Obviously price and quantity, but what price? And what quantity? Because you are talking about the prices of currencies relative to each other, you have to specify which currencies you are using.

Figure 9-2 presents the supply of and demand for euros in terms of dollars. Notice that the quantity of euros goes on the horizontal axis and the dollar price of euros goes on the vertical axis. When you are comparing currencies of only two countries, the supply of one currency equals the demand for the other currency. To demand one currency, you must supply another. In this figure, I am assuming that there are only two trading partners: the United States and the European Union. This means that the supply of euros is equivalent to the demand for dollars. The Europeans who want to buy U.S. goods or assets need dollars, so they supply euros to buy dollars. Let's consider an example. Say a European wants to buy a jacket made in the United States. She has euros, but the U.S. producer wants dollars. So, to buy the jacket, she or the U.S. producer must somehow exchange euros for dollars. She is *supplying* euros in order to *demand* dollars. (The actual transaction is conducted by banks that have traders who buy and sell currencies as needed.)

The supply curve of euros is upward-sloping because the more dollars European citizens get for their euros, the cheaper U.S. goods and assets become for them and the greater the quantity of euros they want to supply to buy those goods. Say, for example, that the dollar price of 1 euro rises from $1.10 to $1.20. That means that the price of a dollar to a European has fallen from 0.91 euro to 0.83 euro. For a European, a good that cost $100 now falls in price from 91 euros to 83 euros. U.S. goods are cheaper, so the Europeans buy more U.S. goods and more dollars, which means they supply more euros.

The demand for euros comes from Americans who want to buy European goods or assets. The demand curve is downward-sloping because the lower the dollar price of euros, the more euros U.S. citizens want to buy, using the same reasoning I just described.

To demand one currency, you must supply another currency.

Q-7 Show graphically the effect on the price of euros of an increase in the demand for dollars by Europeans.

The market is in equilibrium when the quantity supplied equals the quantity demanded. In my example, when supply is S_0 and demand is D_0, equilibrium occurs at a dollar price of $1.20 for 1 euro.

Suppose forces shift the supply and demand for euros; for example, say people lose faith in the euro, leading them to want to hold their assets in dollar-denominated assets. The supply of euros rises from S_0 to S_1. At the same time, Americans also lose faith in the euro and decide to buy fewer euros. This shifts the demand for euros from D_0 to D_1. Combined, the two shifts lead to a fall in the price of the euro as shown in Figure 9-2, decreasing the price from $1.20 to $1.10.

Because one euro buys fewer dollars, we say the euro has depreciated in value. A **currency depreciation** is *a change in the exchange rate so that one currency buys fewer units of a foreign currency.* For example, when the dollar price of euros falls from $1.20 to $1.10, the euro is depreciating; 1 euro buys fewer dollars. The dollar, on the other hand, appreciated in value because 1 dollar can be exchanged for more euros. A **currency appreciation** is *a change in the exchange rate so that one currency buys more units of a foreign currency.*

Q-8 If one dollar can be exchanged for more euros, has the dollar appreciated or depreciated?

Exchange Rates and Trade

The exchange rate plays an important role in the demand for a country's domestic goods. We can see that by considering both the domestic supply of tradable goods—those goods that can be produced in one country and sold in another—and the international supply of tradable goods on the same graph. We do so in Figure 9-3. For simplicity we assume that the world supply of goods is perfectly elastic (horizontal) at P_1. That is, foreign countries are willing to sell as much as is demanded at a single price. With free trade, if domestic producers of tradable goods want to sell any goods, they must match this world price. If consumers can buy all the goods they want at the world price, why pay more?

Domestic supply of tradable goods is determined by the wage and the productivity of workers in the United States—as quantity supplied rises, suppliers have to charge higher prices to cover higher costs of production. The supply curve, therefore, reflects the comparative advantages of U.S. producers with respect to world producers. It is

---

FIGURE 9-3   How International Trade Is Affected by Exchange Rates

The exchange rate plays an important role in international trade. If the world price of goods is less than the domestic price of tradable goods, domestic producers must match the world price level. If the world price level is P_1, domestic producers will sell Q_1 and domestic consumers demand Q_2. The difference is made up by imports shown by the difference between Q_2 and Q_1. A country will have a zero trade balance (net imports will be zero) when the world price level equals the domestic price level, P_0.

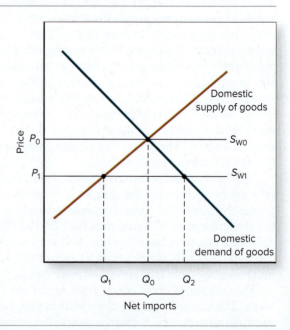

upward-sloping because as output increases, the cost of production rises relative to the cost of world production. If the world supply is S_{W1}, the United States has a comparative advantage for goods up until Q_1, where the domestic supply intersects the world supply. World producers have a comparative advantage in the production of goods to the right of Q_1.

Trade for an economy that faces global competition needs to take into account world supply, which is horizontal at the world price for tradable goods.[2] If the world supply curve intersects domestic supply and demand at the domestic equilibrium price, as it does when the world supply curve is S_{W0}, imports will be exactly offset by exports. If the world price is below the domestic equilibrium, as it is when the world supply curve is S_{W1}, a country is running a trade deficit. In this figure the world price is P_1, which results in a trade deficit of $Q_2 - Q_1$. Indefinite trade deficits are not sustainable. A decrease in the domestic economy's exchange rates, relative declines in wages, or improvements in comparative advantage can eliminate the trade deficit.

Q-9 If the world supply of goods is at the domestic price level, what will be the level of net imports? Explain your answer.

Let's consider how exchange rate adjustment can eliminate a U.S. trade deficit with China. (We are using China to represent the rest of the world.)

Exchange rates affect a trade balance through their impact on comparative advantages. The reason is that as the exchange rate changes, the price of a country's goods to people in other countries changes. In the case of U.S. dollars and Chinese yuan, if the dollar depreciates, U.S. citizens will pay more dollars for each good they buy from China, which means that the relative price of foreign goods rises. So, a depreciation of the domestic country's currency will shift the world supply curve up, making it easier for U.S. producers to compete. Similarly, an appreciation will shift the world supply curve down, making it harder for a country to compete globally.

Depreciation of a domestic country's currency will shift the world supply curve up. An appreciation will shift the world supply curve down.

In theory, the exchange rate adjustment can bring two countries' comparative advantages into alignment, eliminating any trade imbalance. The assumption that exchange rates will adjust to bring trade into balance underlies the story economists tell about comparative advantages. That story assumes that comparative advantages net out so the trade deficit of both countries is zero.

Some Complications in Exchange Rates

If the supply and demand for currencies applied only to tradable goods, trade among countries would generally be in balance, and countries would have roughly equal sectors of comparative advantages in producing goods. However, that doesn't always happen. A major reason why is that the demand for a country's currency reflects not only the demand for a country's produced goods but also the demand for its assets.

When the demand for a country's assets is high, the value of its currency will also be high. With a higher exchange rate, the world price of produced goods will be low and the domestic country will have a comparative advantage in relatively fewer sectors compared to other countries. That has been the case in the United States over the past 30 years, and is one of the reasons so much manufacturing production has fared so poorly.

Another source of differences in comparative advantage is what is called the **resource curse**—*the paradox that countries with an abundance of resources tend to have lower economic growth and more unemployment than countries with fewer natural resources.* The reason for the curse is that the country that has a comparative

---

[2]This is a discussion for a composite good made up of a weighted combination of all goods in an economy. Actual trade is in many different types of goods and services, and this position is consistent with significant imports and exports of particular goods, as long as in the aggregate they balance out. It is the trade balance, not total trade, that is captured by the graph.

Q-10 How can the discovery of a highly valuable resource lead to the appreciation of a currency and loss of comparative advantage in other goods?

When one sector of an economy gains a comparative advantage, other sectors must lose their comparative advantage or there will be a trade imbalance.

advantage in resources finds that the demand for its resources pushes its exchange rate up. A higher exchange rate reduces the comparative advantage of other tradable goods, shifting the world supply curve, and hence domestic production of these goods, down. In terms of Figure 9-3, world supply for goods other than resources falls from S_{W0} to S_{W1} and domestic production falls from Q_0 to Q_1. The resource curse also tends to reduce employment because a decline in employment in these other goods is not offset by an increase in employment in the resource sector. While the production of the resource often pays well, it does not require large numbers of workers. Because the Netherlands experienced this phenomenon when it discovered offshore oil, it is also sometimes called the Dutch disease.

The resource curse is not always caused by natural resources. It happens whenever there is a large increase in global demand for one sector of an economy's goods. When one sector of an economy gains a comparative advantage, other sectors must lose their comparative advantage or there will be a trade imbalance. This happened in the United States during the rise in globalization in the technology, business organization, and finance sectors. Globalization increased the demand for people who provided logistical support, marketing, and financial expertise. These were high-paying jobs and, on average, it was an enormous boon to the U.S. economy. But that increase in demand meant that the low-wage U.S. workers in other tradable goods industries lost their comparative advantage. So while total income in the United States rose, income and employment in the low-wage manufacturing tradable sector fell, causing significant hardship and unemployment in these sectors.

Conclusion

International trade, and changing comparative advantages, has become more and more important for the United States in recent decades. With international transportation and communication becoming faster and easier, and with other countries' economies growing, the U.S. economy will inevitably become more interdependent with the other economies of the world. Ultimately, this international trade will improve the lives of most Americans, and even more so for the world. However, the path there will likely be very difficult for those U.S. citizens in the tradable goods sector.

Summary

- According to the principle of comparative advantage, as long as the relative opportunity costs of producing goods (what must be given up in one good in order to get another good) differ among countries, there are potential gains from trade. *(LO9-1)*

- Three insights into the terms of trade are:
  1. The more competition exists in international trade, the less the trader gets and the more the involved countries get.
  2. Once competition prevails, smaller countries tend to get a larger percentage of the gains from trade than do larger countries.
  3. Gains from trade go to countries that produce goods that exhibit economies of scale. *(LO9-1)*

- Economists and laypeople differ in their views on trade. *(LO9-2)*

- The gains from trade in the form of low consumer prices tend to be widespread and not easily recognized, while the costs in jobs lost tend to be concentrated and readily identifiable. *(LO9-2)*

- The United States has comparative advantages based on its skilled workforce, its institutions, and its language, among other things. *(LO9-3)*

- Inherent comparative advantages are based on factors that are relatively unchangeable. They are not subject to the law of one price. *(LO9-3)*

- Transferable comparative advantages are based on factors that can change relatively easily. The law of one price can eliminate these comparative advantages.   (*LO9-3*)

- Concerns about trade for the United States are that U.S. relative wages will decline and the value of the dollar will decline as well.   (*LO9-3*)

- The prices of currencies—foreign exchange rates—can be analyzed with the supply and demand model in the same way as any other good can be. An appreciation of the dollar occurs when a single dollar can buy more foreign currency. A depreciation of the dollar occurs when a single dollar buys less foreign currency.   (*LO9-4*)

- An appreciation of a currency will shift the world supply of a good down and increase that country's imports.   (*LO9-4*)

- The depreciation of a country's currency makes that country's goods more competitive.   (*LO9-4*)

- The resource curse occurs when significant amounts of natural resources are discovered. This raises foreign demand for the resource, raising the value of the domestic country's currency, making other sectors less competitive. A variation of the resource curse is one reason for a greater inequality of income distribution in the United States.   (*LO9-4*)

Key Terms

balance of trade	currency depreciation	resource curse	transferable comparative
comparative	exchange rate	trade deficit	advantage
advantage	inherent comparative	trade surplus	
currency appreciation	advantage		

Questions and Exercises   connect

1. Will a country do better importing or exporting a good for which it has a comparative advantage? Why?   (*LO9-1*)

2. Widgetland has 60 workers. Each worker can produce 4 widgets or 4 wadgets. Each resident in Widgetland currently consumes 2 widgets and 2 wadgets. Wadgetland also has 60 workers. Each can produce 3 widgets or 12 wadgets. Wadgetland's residents each consume 1 widget and 8 wadgets. Is there a basis for trade? If so, offer the countries a deal they can't refuse.   (*LO9-1*)

3. Suppose there are two states that do not trade: Iowa and Nebraska. Each state produces the same two goods: corn and wheat. For Iowa the opportunity cost of producing 1 bushel of wheat is 3 bushels of corn. For Nebraska the opportunity cost of producing 1 bushel of corn is 3 bushels of wheat. At present, Iowa produces 20 million bushels of wheat and 120 million bushels of corn, while Nebraska produces 20 million bushels of corn and 120 million bushels of wheat.   (*LO9-1*)
   a. Explain how, with trade, Nebraska can end up with 40 million bushels of wheat and 120 million bushels of corn while Iowa can end up with 40 million bushels of corn and 120 million bushels of wheat.
   b. If the states ended up with the numbers given in *a,* how much would the trader get?

4. Suppose that two countries, Machineland and Farmland, have the following production possibility curves: (*LO9-1*)

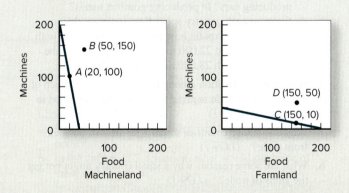

   a. Explain how these two countries can move from points *A* and *C,* where they currently are, to points *B* and *D*.
   b. If possible, state by how much total production for the two countries has risen.
   c. If you were a trader, how much of the gains from trade would you deserve for discovering this trade?
   d. If the per-unit cost of production falls as output rises, how would the analysis change?

Answers to Margin Questions

1. He should walk away because there is no basis for trade. *(LO9-1)*

2. The percentage of gains from trade that goes to a country depends upon the change in the price of the goods being traded. If trade led to no change in prices in a small country, then that small country would get no gains from trade. Another case in which a small country gets a small percentage of the gains from trade would occur when its larger trading partner was producing a good with economies of scale and the small country was not. In a third case, if the traders who extracted most of the surplus or gains from trade come from the larger country, then the smaller country would end up with few of the gains from trade. *(LO9-1)*

3. Four reasons for the difference are: (1) gains from trade are often stealth gains, (2) comparative advantage is determined by more than wages, (3) nations trade more than just manufactured goods, and (4) trade has distributional effects. *(LO9-2)*

4. The manufacturing sector produces tradable goods, which has made it vulnerable to international trade. Foreign producers can produce these goods at a lower cost, putting downward pressure on wages and employment. Production in the education, health care, and government sectors is less tradable, making it less subject to pressure from globalization. *(LO9-2)*

5. Transferable comparative advantage will be more affected because it is an advantage that is not tied to a particular country. Countries where prices are higher will face outflow of capital and technology to bring prices back in balance. This will transfer comparative advantage from the high-price countries to low-price countries. *(LO9-3)*

6. Two likely adjustments that will reduce the trade deficit are a fall in the value of the dollar (U.S. exchange rate) and a rise in Chinese wages relative to U.S. wages. *(LO9-3)*

7. An increase in the demand for dollars is the equivalent to an increase in the supply of euros, so an increase in the demand for dollars pushes down the price of euros in terms of dollars, as in the following diagram. *(LO9-4)*

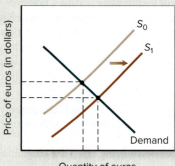

8. It appreciated because one dollar can buy more euros. Alternatively stated, it takes fewer dollars to buy the same number of euros. *(LO9-4)*

9. There would be no imports since the price of imports is the same as the price of domestic goods. American consumers would be indifferent between buying foreign and domestic goods. *(LO9-4)*

10. The discovery of the resource will increase the demand for the domestic currency, which leads to an appreciation of the currency. This appreciation makes domestic goods more expensive to foreigners, which leads to a loss in the comparative advantage in those goods. *(LO9-4)*

International Trade Policy

> Manufacturing and commercial monopolies owe their origin not to a tendency imminent in a capitalist economy but to governmental interventionist policy directed against free trade.
>
> —Ludwig von Mises

CHAPTER 10

©Mike Nelson/AFP/Getty Images

After reading this chapter, you should be able to:

LO10-1 Summarize some important data of trade.

LO10-2 Explain policies countries use to restrict trade.

LO10-3 Summarize the reasons for trade restrictions and why economists generally oppose trade restrictions.

LO10-4 List two international organizations and two trade agreements that support free trade.

Based on the theory of comparative advantage, most economists oppose trade restrictions. Politicians, and the public, are far more dubious. With the election of Donald Trump as president, free trade came under attack. He argued that free trade agreements that the United States had signed were a bad deal for America, and that he was going to pull America out. In this chapter we consider such issues. We start by considering the pattern and nature of trade, then we discuss the variety of trade restrictions that governments can impose, and why most economists would advise President Trump against pulling out of the United States' previous trade deals.

The Nature and Patterns of Trade

Let's begin with some numbers to get a sense of the nature and dimensions of international trade.

Increasing but Fluctuating World Trade

In 1928, the ratio of world trade to U.S. GDP was almost 60 percent. In 1935, that ratio had fallen to less than 30 percent. In 1950 it was only 20 percent.

Then it started rising. Today it is about 220 percent, with world trade amounting to about $42 trillion. As you can see, international trade has been growing, but with significant fluctuations in that growth.

There are two reasons why world trade fluctuates: (1) When output rises, international trade rises, and when output falls, international trade falls; and (2) countries impose trade restrictions from time to time. These two reasons often reinforce each other; for example, decreases in world income during the Depression of the 1930s caused a large decrease in trade and that decrease was exacerbated by a worldwide increase in trade restrictions.

Differences in the Importance of Trade

The importance of international trade to countries' economies differs widely, as we can see in the table below, which presents the importance of the shares of exports (the value of goods and services sold abroad) and imports (the value of goods and services purchased abroad) for various countries.

	Total Output*	Exports to GDP Ratio	Imports to GDP Ratio
Netherlands	$ 945	96%	87%
Germany	421	46	39
Canada	1,799	31	33
Italy	2,182	30	33
France	2,925	30	33
United Kingdom	2,936	28	31
Japan	5,167	16	16
United States	20,413	12	15

*Numbers in billions

Source: *World Development Indicators*, The World Bank and the International Monetary Fund.

Among the countries listed, the Netherlands has the highest exports compared to total output; the United States has the lowest. The Netherlands' imports are also the highest as a percentage of total output. U.S. exports are the lowest. The relationship between a country's imports and its exports is no coincidence. For most countries, imports and exports roughly equal one another, though in any particular year that equality can be rough indeed. For the United States in recent years, imports have generally significantly exceeded exports, which means that a trade imbalance can continue for a long time. But that situation can't continue forever, as I'll discuss.

What and with Whom the United States Trades

The majority of U.S. exports and imports involve significant amounts of manufactured goods. This isn't unusual, since much of international trade is in manufactured goods.

The primary trading partners of the United States are Canada, Mexico, the European Union, and the Pacific Rim countries.

Figure 10-1 shows the regions with which the United States trades. Exports to Canada and Mexico make up the largest percentage of total U.S. exports to individual countries. Among the various regions, the largest regions to which the U.S. exports are the Pacific Rim and the European Union. Countries from which the United States imports major quantities include China, Canada, and Mexico and the regions of the European Union and the Pacific Rim. Thus, the countries we export to are also the countries we import from.

FIGURE 10-1 (A AND B) **U.S. Exports and Imports by Region**

Major regions that trade with the United States include Canada, Mexico, the European Union, and the Pacific Rim.

Source: U.S. Census Bureau, FT900: *U.S. International Trade in Goods and Services* (www.census.gov).

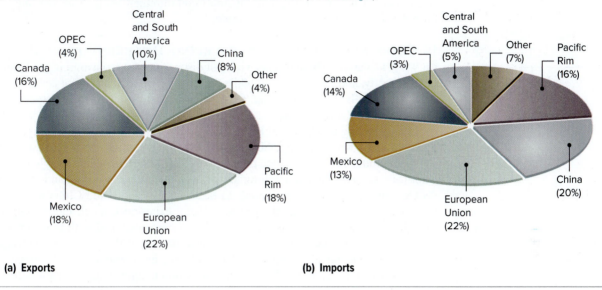

(a) Exports

(b) Imports

THE CHANGING NATURE OF TRADE The nature of trade is continually changing, both in terms of the countries with which the United States trades and the goods and services traded. For example, U.S. imports from China, India, and other East Asian countries have increased substantially in recent years. In the late 1980s goods from China accounted for 2.5 percent of all U.S. merchandise imports. Today they account for 20 percent. Imports from India have increased 20-fold over that time— from 0.1 percent to 2 percent of all goods imported.

The kind of goods and services the United States imports also has changed. Thirty years ago, the goods the United States imported from China and India were primarily basic manufacturing goods and raw commodities. Technologically advanced goods were produced here in the United States. Today we are importing high-tech manufactured goods from these countries, and they are even developing their own new products that require significant research and development.

The change in the nature of the goods that a country produces and exports up the technological ladder is typical for developing countries. It characterized Japan, Korea, and Singapore in the post–World War II era, and today characterizes China and India. As this movement up the technological ladder has occurred, foreign companies that had been subcontractors for U.S. companies become direct competitors of the U.S. companies. For example, the automaker Kia and the electronics producer Samsung have developed into major global firms, and in the future you can expect numerous Chinese companies to become household names.

We can expect the nature of trade to change even more in the future as numerous technological changes in telecommunications continue to reduce the cost of both voice and data communications throughout the world and expand the range of services that can be provided by foreign countries. Production no longer needs to occur in the geographic area where the goods are consumed. For example, financial accounting, compositing (typesetting) of texts, and research can now be done almost anywhere, and transferred with the click of a mouse. The customer service calls for a U.S. company

Q-1 How has the nature of U.S. imports from China changed in recent years?

We can expect the nature of trade to change even more in the future.

can be answered almost anywhere, in countries such as India, which has a sizable well-educated, English-speaking population, and much lower wage rates. India even trains its employees to speak with a Midwest U.S. accent to make it less apparent to customers that the call is being answered in India. This trade in services is what the press often refers to as *outsourcing,* but it is important to remember that outsourcing is simply a description of some aspects of trade.

IS CHINESE AND INDIAN OUTSOURCING DIFFERENT FROM PREVIOUS OUTSOURCING?   There has been a lot of discussion about outsourcing to China and India recently, and thus it is worthwhile to consider what is, and what is not, different about trade with China and India. First, what isn't different is the existence of outsourcing. Manufacturers have used overseas suppliers for years. What is different about outsourcing to China and India today compared to earlier outsourcing to Japan, Singapore, and Korea in the 1980s and 1990s is the potential size of that outsourcing. China and India have a combined population of 2.7 billion people, a sizable number of whom are well educated and willing to work for much lower wages than U.S. workers. As technology opens up more areas to trade, and as India and China move up the technology ladder, U.S.-based firms will likely experience much more competition than they have experienced to date. How U.S. companies deal with this competition will be a key economic policy issue for the next decade. If they develop new technologies and new industries in which the United States has comparative advantages, then the United States' future can be bright. If they don't, significant, difficult adjustment will need to occur.

> How U.S. companies deal with new high-tech competition will likely be the defining economic policy issue for the next decade.

The rising competitiveness of Asian economies with the U.S. economy is manifested in the large deficit the United States is running on its balance of trade, as shown in Figure 10-2. A trade deficit means that U.S. imports exceed U.S. exports. The United States has been running trade deficits since the 1970s, and in 2006 the U.S. trade deficit reached over $800 billion. It has decreased slightly since then, but it remains high. The U.S. trade deficit means that the United States is consuming a lot more than it is producing, and paying for current consumption with promises to pay in the future.

Debtor and Creditor Nations

> Running a trade deficit isn't necessarily bad.

Running a trade deficit isn't necessarily bad. In fact, while you're doing it, it's rather nice. If you were a country, you probably would be running a trade deficit now since, most likely, you're consuming (importing) more than you're producing (exporting).

FIGURE 10-2   The U.S. Trade Balance

The United States has been running trade deficits since the 1970s, as you can see in the figure.

Source: U.S. Department of Commerce, Bureau of Economic Analysis, *International Transactions* (www.bea.gov).

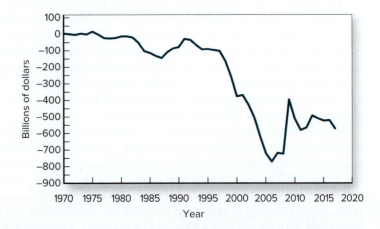

International Issues in Perspective

Since the 1970s, international issues have become increasingly important for the U.S. economy. That statement would be correct even if the reference period went back as far as the late 1800s. The statement would not be correct if the reference period were earlier than the late 1800s. In the 1600s, 1700s, and most of the 1800s, international trade was vital to the American economy—even more vital than now. The American nation grew from colonial possessions of England, France, and Spain. These "new world" colonial possessions were valued for their gold, agricultural produce, and natural resources. From a European standpoint, international trade was the colonies' reason for being.*

A large portion of the U.S. government's income during much of the 1800s came from tariffs. Technology was imported from abroad, and international issues played a central role in wars fought on U.S. soil. Up until the 1900s, no one would have studied the U.S. economy independently of international issues. Not only was there significant international trade; there was also significant immigration. The United States is a country of immigrants.

Only in the late 1800s did the United States adopt an isolationist philosophy in both politics and trade. So in reference to that isolationist period, the U.S. economy has become more integrated with the world economy. However, in a broader historical perspective, that isolationist period was an anomaly, and today's economy is simply returning international issues to the key role they've usually played.

Another aspect of trade that is important not to forget is that international trade has social and cultural dimensions. While much of the chapter deals with specifically economic issues, we must also remember the cultural and social implications of trade.

Let's consider an example from history. In the Middle Ages, Greek ideas and philosophy were lost to Europe when hordes of barbarians swept over the continent. These ideas and that philosophy were rediscovered in the Renaissance only as a by-product of trade between the Italian merchant cities and the Middle East. (The Greek ideas that had spread to the Middle East were protected from European upheavals.) *Renaissance* means rebirth: a rebirth in Europe of Greek learning. Many of our traditions and sensibilities are based on those of the Renaissance, and that Renaissance was caused, or at least significantly influenced, by international trade. Had there been no trade, our entire philosophy of life might have been different.

In economics courses we do not focus on these broader cultural issues but instead focus on relatively technical issues such as the reasons for trade and the implications of tariffs. But keep in the back of your mind these broader implications as you go through the various components of international economics. They add a dimension to the story that otherwise might be forgotten.

_____

*The Native American standpoint was, I suspect, somewhat different.

How can you do that? By living off past savings, getting support from your parents or a spouse, or borrowing.

Countries have the same options. They can live off foreign aid, past savings, or loans. The U.S. economy is currently financing its trade deficit by selling off assets—financial assets such as stocks and bonds, or real assets such as real estate and corporations. Since the assets of the United States total many trillions of dollars, it can continue to run trade deficits of a similar size for years to come, but in doing so it is reducing its wealth from what it would have been each year.

The United States has not always run a trade deficit. Following World War II it ran trade surpluses—an excess of exports over imports—with other countries, so it was an international lender. Thus, it acquired large amounts of foreign assets. Because of the large trade deficits the United States has run since the 1980s, now the United States is a large debtor nation. The United States has borrowed significantly more from abroad than it has lent abroad.

As the United States has gone from being a large creditor nation to being the world's biggest debtor nation, international considerations have been forced on the United

Web Note 10.1

Who Holds U.S. Debt?

Q-2 Will a debtor nation necessarily be running a trade deficit?

States. The cushion of being a creditor—of having a flow of interest income—has been replaced by the trials of being a debtor and having to pay out interest every year without currently getting anything for the payment of that interest by the debtor nation.

One way countries try to reduce trade deficits is to reduce imports by restricting trade. That was clearly one of the goals that President Trump had when he talked tough on trade. These trade restrictions can keep a country from having to face the adjustments associated with improving its comparative advantage either by reducing wages or, as we saw in an earlier chapter, by allowing its currency to depreciate.

Varieties of Trade Restrictions

Three policies used to restrict trade are:

1. Tariffs (taxes on internationally traded goods).
2. Quotas (quantity limits placed on imports).
3. Regulatory trade restrictions (government-imposed procedural rules that limit imports).

The policies countries can use to restrict trade include tariffs and quotas, voluntary restraint agreements, sanctions, regulatory trade restrictions, and nationalistic appeals. I'll consider each in turn and also review the geometric analysis of each.

Tariffs and Quotas

A **tariff** is *an excise tax on an imported (internationally traded) good.* (Tariffs are also called *customs duties.*) Tariffs are the most-used and most-familiar type of trade restriction. Tariffs operate in the same way a tax does: They make imported goods relatively more expensive than they otherwise would have been, and thereby encourage the consumption of domestically produced goods. On average, U.S. tariffs raise the price of imported goods by less than 3 percent. Figure 10-3(a) presents average tariff rates for industrial goods for a number of countries and Figure 10-3(b) shows the tariff rates imposed by the United States since 1920.

Q-3 How are tariffs like taxes? Demonstrate with a supply and demand curve.

Probably the most infamous tariff in U.S. history is the Smoot-Hawley Tariff of 1930, which raised tariffs on imported goods to an average of 60 percent. It was passed at the height of the Great Depression in the United States in the hope of protecting American jobs. It didn't work. Other countries responded with similar tariffs. Partly as

---

FIGURE 10-3 (A AND B)   Selected Tariff Rates

The tariff rates in (a) will be continually changing as the changes negotiated by the World Trade Organization come into effect. In (b) you see tariff rates for the United States since 1920.

Source: The World Bank (www.worldbank.org).

Country	Tariff	Country	Tariff
Argentina	13.6%	Norway	6.6%
Australia	2.5	Philippines	6.3
Canada	4.2	Singapore	0.2
Colombia	5.7	South Africa	7.6
European Union	5.1	Sri Lanka	9.3
India	13.4	Thailand	11.0
Indonesia	6.9	United States	3.5
Japan	4.0	Venezuela	12.9
Mexico	7.1	Zimbabwe	16.8

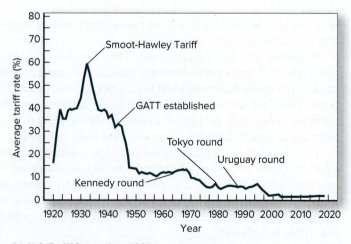

(a) Tariff Rates by Country

(b) U.S. Tariff Rates since 1920

a result of these trade wars, international trade plummeted from $60 billion in 1928 to $25 billion in 1938, unemployment worsened, and the international depression deepened. These effects of the tariff convinced many, if not most, economists that free trade is preferable to trade restrictions.

The dismal failure of the Smoot-Hawley Tariff was the main reason the **General Agreement on Tariffs and Trade (GATT),** *a regular international conference to reduce trade barriers,* was established in 1947 immediately following World War II. In 1995 GATT was replaced by the **World Trade Organization (WTO),** *an organization whose functions are generally the same as GATT's were—to promote free and fair trade among countries.* Unlike GATT, the WTO is a permanent organization with an enforcement system (albeit weak). Since its formation, rounds of negotiations have resulted in a decline in worldwide tariffs. The latest round of negotiations, begun in 2002, did not lead to an agreement, and were essentially abandoned in 2016. With President Trump's election in 2016, economists' focus moved to saving existing trade agreements, not adding new ones.

A **quota** is *a quantity limit placed on imports.* Quotas have the same effect on equilibrium price and quantity as do the quantity restrictions discussed in Chapter 5, and their effect in limiting trade is similar to the effect of a tariff. Both increase price and reduce quantity. Tariffs, like all taxes on suppliers, shift the supply curve up by the amount of the tax, as Figure 10-4 shows. A tariff, T, raises equilibrium price from P_0 to P_1 by an amount that is less than the tariff, and equilibrium quantity declines from Q_0 to Q_1. With a quota, Q_1, the equilibrium price also rises to P_1.

There is, however, a difference between tariffs and quotas. In the case of the tariff, the government collects tariff revenue (the tariff, T, times the quantity imported) represented by the shaded region. In the case of a quota, the government collects no revenue. The benefit of the increase in price goes to the importer as additional corporate revenue. So which of the two do you think import companies favor? The quota, of course—it means more profits as long as your company is the one to receive the rights to fill the quotas. In fact, once quotas are instituted, firms compete intensely to get them.

Tariffs affect trade patterns. For example, since the 1960s the United States has imposed a tariff on light trucks from Japan. The result is that the United States imports few light trucks from Japan. You will see Japanese-named trucks, but most of these are produced in the United States. Many similar examples exist, and by following the tariff structure, you can gain a lot of insight into patterns of trade.

The issues involved with tariffs and quotas can be seen in a slightly different way by assuming that the country being considered is small relative to the world economy and that imports compete with domestic producers. The small-country assumption means that the supply from the world to this country is perfectly elastic (horizontal) at the world price, $2, as in Figure 10-5(a).

The world price of the good is unaffected by this country's supply. This assumption allows us to distinguish the world supply from domestic supply. In the absence of any trade restrictions, the world price of $2 would be the domestic price. Domestic low-cost suppliers would supply 100 units of the good at $2. The remaining 100 units demanded are being imported.

In Figure 10-5(a) I show the effect of a tariff of 50 cents placed on all imports. Since the world supply curve is perfectly elastic, all of this tax, shown by the shaded region, is borne by domestic consumers. Price rises to $2.50 and quantity demanded falls to 175. With a tariff, the rise in price will increase domestic quantity supplied from 100 to 125 and will reduce imports to 50. Now let's compare this situation with a quota of 50, shown in Figure 10-5(b). Under a quota of 50, the final price would be the same, but higher revenue would accrue to foreign and domestic producers rather than to the government. One final difference: Any increase in demand under

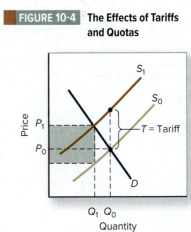

FIGURE 10-4 The Effects of Tariffs and Quotas

Q-4 Why do importers prefer a quota to a tariff? Why does government prefer a tariff?

FIGURE 10-5 (A AND B)   **Tariffs and Quotas When the Domestic Country Is Small**

This exhibit shows the effects of a tariff in **(a)** and of a quota in **(b)** when the domestic country is small. The small-country assumption means that the world supply is perfectly elastic, in this case at $2.00 a unit. With a tariff of 50 cents, world supply shifts up by 50 cents. Domestic quantity demanded falls to 175 and domestic quantity supplied rises to 125. Foreign suppliers are left supplying the difference, 50 units. The domestic government collects revenue shown in the shaded area. The figure in **(b)** shows how the same result can be achieved with a quota of 50. Equilibrium price rises to $2.50. Domestic firms produce 125 units and consumers demand 175 units. The difference between the tariff and the quota is that, with a tariff, the domestic government collects the revenue from the higher price. With a quota, the benefits of the higher price accrue to the foreign and domestic producers.

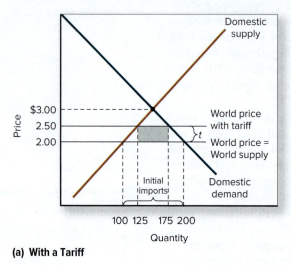

(a) With a Tariff

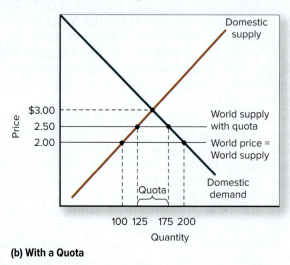

(b) With a Quota

a quota would result in higher prices because it would have to be filled by domestic producers. Under a tariff, any increase in demand would not affect price.

Voluntary Restraint Agreements

Voluntary restraint agreements are often not all that voluntary.

Imposing new tariffs and quotas is specifically ruled out by the WTO, but foreign countries know that WTO rules are voluntary and that, if a domestic industry brought sufficient political pressure on its government, the WTO rules would be forgotten. To avoid the imposition of new tariffs on their goods, countries often voluntarily restrict their exports. That's why Japan has, at times, agreed informally to limit the number of cars it exports to the United States.

The effect of such voluntary restraint agreements is similar to the effect of quotas: They directly limit the quantity of imports, increasing the price of the good and helping domestic producers. For example, when the United States encouraged Japan to impose "voluntary" quotas on exports of its cars to the United States, Toyota benefited from the quotas because it could price its limited supply of cars higher than it could if it sent in a large number of cars, so profit per car would be high. Since they faced less competition, U.S. car companies also benefited. They could increase their prices because Toyota had done so. As Chinese car companies develop in the next decade, we can expect similar pushes for Chinese voluntary restraints.

Sanctions

A sanction, sometimes called an embargo, is a restriction on imports or exports of a country's goods.

A **sanction,** sometimes called an embargo, is *a restriction on the imports or exports of a country's goods.* Sanctions are usually established for international political reasons rather than for primarily economic reasons. An example was the U.S. embargo of trade with Iran instituted in 2010 to put pressure on Iran to not develop a nuclear bomb; it was not imposed for economic reasons. That embargo led Iran in 2015 to negotiate limits on its nuclear activity in exchange for lifting the trade sanctions. In 2017 the United States imposed new, although limited, sanctions on Iran in an attempt to curb its ballistic missile program.

Regulatory Trade Restrictions

Tariffs, quotas, and sanctions are the primary *direct* methods to restrict international trade. There are also indirect methods that restrict trade in not-so-obvious ways; these are called **regulatory trade restrictions** *(government-imposed procedural rules that limit imports)*. One type of regulatory trade restriction has to do with protecting the health and safety of a country's residents. For example, a country might restrict imports of all vegetables grown where certain pesticides are used, knowing full well that all other countries use those pesticides. The effect of such a regulation would be to halt the import of vegetables. Another example involves building codes. U.S. building codes require that plywood have fewer than, say, three flaws per sheet. Canadian building codes require that plywood have fewer than, say, five flaws per sheet. The different building codes are a nontariff barrier that makes trade in building materials between the United States and Canada difficult.

A second type of regulatory restriction involves making import and customs procedures so intricate and time-consuming that importers simply give up. For example, at one time France required all imported electronics to be individually inspected in Toulouse. Since Toulouse is a provincial city, far from any port and outside the normal route for imports after they enter France, the inspection process took months. That requirement essentially prevented imported electronics from taking market share from French companies.

Some regulatory restrictions are imposed for legitimate reasons; others are designed simply to make importing more difficult and hence protect domestic producers from international competition. It's often hard to tell the difference. A good example of this difficulty are EU trade regulations that disallow all imports of meat from animals that are fed growth-inducing hormones. As the box "Hormones and Economics" details, the debate about this issue has continued for decades.

Nationalistic Appeals and "Buy Domestic" Requirements

Finally, nationalistic appeals can help restrict international trade. "Buy American" campaigns are examples. Many Americans, given two products of equal appeal, except that one is made in the United States and one is made in a foreign country, would buy the U.S. product. To get around this tendency, foreign and U.S. companies often go to great lengths to get a MADE IN THE U.S.A. classification on goods they sell in the United States. For example, components for many autos are made in Japan but shipped to the United States and assembled in Ohio or Tennessee so that the finished car can be called an American product. These "Buy American" policies can even be requirements. For example, the U.S. government stimulus package of 2009 included a "Buy American" clause that required any public works project funded by the package to use only American-made products.

Reasons for and against Trade Restrictions

Let's now turn to a different question: If trade is beneficial, as the theory of comparative advantage tells us it is, why do countries restrict trade?

Web Note 10.2
Sugar Regulations

Q-5 How might a country benefit from having an inefficient customs agency?

Some regulatory restrictions are imposed for legitimate reasons; others are designed simply to make importing more difficult.

Web Note 10.3
Buy American

Companies find ways to get around "Buy American" trade policies.

©Africa Studio/Shutterstock

Hormones and Economics

Trade restrictions, in practice, are often much more complicated than they seem in textbooks. Seldom does a country say, "We're limiting imports to protect our home producers." Instead the country explains the restrictions in a more politically acceptable way. Consider the fight between the European Union (EU) and the United States over U.S. meat exports. In 1988 the EU, in line with Union-wide internal requirements, banned imports of any meat from animals treated with growth-inducing hormones, which U.S. meat producers use extensively. The result: The EU banned the meat exported from the United States.

©Pixtal/Age fotostock

The EU claimed that it had imposed the ban only because of public health concerns. The United States claimed that the ban was actually a trade restriction, pointing out that its own residents ate this kind of meat with confidence because a U.S. government agency had certified that the levels of hormones in the meat were far below any danger level.

The United States retaliated against the EU by imposing 100 percent tariffs on Danish and West German hams, Italian tomatoes, and certain other foods produced by EU member nations. The EU threatened to respond by placing 100 percent tariffs on $100 million worth of U.S. walnuts and dried fruits, but instead entered into bilateral meetings with the United States. Those meetings allowed untreated meats into the EU for human consumption and treated meats that would be used as dog food. In response, the United States removed its retaliatory tariffs on hams and tomatoes, but retained its tariffs on many other goods. In the 1990s, Europe's dog population seemed to be growing exponentially as Europe's imports of "dog food" increased by leaps and bounds. In 1996 the United States asked the WTO to review the EU ban. It did

so in 1997, finding in favor of the United States. The EU appealed and in 1999 the WTO stood by its earlier ruling and the United States reimposed the 100 percent tariffs. Since then, the EU has stood firm and has conducted studies that, it says, show the use of growth hormones to be unsafe, but the WTO continues to rule that they are safe. In 2004, the EU replaced its ban on U.S. beef with a provisional ban until it collected more information. It argued that making its ban provisional, not permanent, met the WTO rules. The United States disagreed and continued its retaliatory tariffs. In January 2009, for example, the U.S. government placed a 300 percent tariff on Roquefort cheese as one of its retaliatory measures but quickly removed it temporarily.

In 2013 a partial compromise was reached; the EU significantly increased the amount of non-hormone-treated U.S. beef that could be imported from the United States and the United States removed many of the retaliatory tariffs. With that compromise, the issue was supposed to be resolved. But in 2016, the United States claimed that Europe had reneged on its part of the deal, and that it was going to retaliate with tariffs on European goods. As of 2018, the debate was continuing, and was made all the more confusing by Brexit (Britain's decision to pull out of the European Union), and by President Trump's "America First" approach to trade in which he disregarded previous trade agreements and imposed tariffs on various goods from other countries, including U.S. allies.

Which side was right in this dispute? The answer is far from obvious. Both the United States and the EU have potentially justifiable positions. As I said, trade restrictions are more complicated in reality than in textbooks.

Unequal Internal Distribution of the Gains from Trade

One reason countries restrict trade is that the gains of trade are not equally distributed. In the example of the argument for trade discussed in a previous chapter, I.T. persuaded Saudi Arabia to specialize in the production of oil rather than food, and persuaded the United States to produce more food than oil. That means, of course, that some U.S. oil workers will have to become farmers, and in Saudi Arabia some farmers will have to become oil producers.

Often people don't want to make radical changes in the kind of work they do—they want to keep on producing what they're already producing. So when these people see the same kinds of goods that they produce coming into their country from abroad, they lobby to prevent the foreign competition.

Had I.T. been open about the difficulties of trading, he would have warned the countries that change is hard. It has very real costs that I.T. didn't point out when he made his offers. Economists generally favor free trade because the costs of trade are temporary, whereas gains from trade are permanent. Once the adjustment has been made, the costs will be gone but the benefits will remain.

For most goods, the benefits for the large majority of the population so outweigh the costs to some individuals that, decided on a strict cost/benefit basis, international trade is still a deal you can't refuse. The table below lists economists' estimates of the cost to consumers of saving a job in some industries through trade restrictions.

Industry	Cost of Production (per job saved)
Luggage	$1,285,078
Sugar	826,104
Dairy	685,323
Canned tuna	257,640
Apparel	199,241

Source: Estimates by economists W. Michael Cox and Richard Alm.

With benefits so outweighing costs, it would seem that transition costs could be forgotten. But they can't.

Benefits of trade are generally widely scattered among the entire population. In contrast, costs of free trade often fall on small groups of people who loudly oppose the particular free trade that hurts them. This creates a political push against free trade.

It isn't only in the United States that the push for trade restrictions focuses on the small costs and not on the large benefits. For example, the European Union (EU) places large restrictions on food imports from nonmember nations. If the EU were to remove those barriers, food prices in EU countries would decline significantly—it is estimated that meat prices alone would fall by about 65 percent. Consumers would benefit, but farmers would be hurt. The farmers, however, have the political clout to see that the costs are considered and the benefits aren't. The result: The EU places high duties on foreign agricultural products.

The cost to society of relaxing trade restrictions has led to a number of programs to assist those who are hurt. Such programs are called **trade adjustment assistance programs**—*programs designed to compensate losers for reductions in trade restrictions.*

Governments have tried to use trade adjustment assistance to facilitate free trade, but they've found that it's enormously difficult to limit the adjustment assistance to those who are actually hurt by international trade. As soon as people find that there's assistance for people injured by trade, they're likely to try to show that they too have been hurt and deserve assistance. Losses from free trade become exaggerated and magnified. Instead of only a small portion of the gains from trade being needed for trade adjustment assistance, much more is demanded—often even more than the gains.

Telling people who claim to be hurt that they aren't really being hurt isn't good politics. That's why offering trade adjustment assistance as a way to relieve the pressure to restrict trade is a deal many governments can refuse.

Benefits of trade are generally widely scattered among the entire population. In contrast, costs of free trade often fall on specific small groups.

Q-6 Who is likely to be more vocal when lobbying government to impose trade restrictions: producers or consumers? Explain your answer.

Telling people who claim to be hurt that they aren't really being hurt isn't good politics.

Haggling by Companies over the Gains from Trade

Many naturally advantageous bargains aren't consummated because each side is pushing for a larger share of the gains from trade than the other side thinks should be allotted.

To see how companies haggling over the gains of trade can restrict trade, let's reconsider the original deal that I.T. proposed in an earlier chapter explaining comparative advantage. I.T. got 380 tons of food and 380 barrels of oil. The United States got an additional 100 tons of food and 60 barrels of oil. Saudi Arabia got an additional 100 barrels of oil and 60 tons of food.

Suppose the Saudis had said, "Why should we be getting only 100 barrels of oil and 60 tons of food when I.T. is getting 380 barrels of oil and 380 tons of food? We want an additional 300 tons of food and another 300 barrels of oil, and we won't deal unless we get them." Similarly, the United States might have said, "We want an additional 300 tons of food and an additional 300 barrels of oil, and we won't go through with the deal unless we get them." If either the U.S. or the Saudi Arabian company that was involved in the trade for its country (or both) takes this position, I.T. might just walk—no deal. Tough bargaining positions can make it almost impossible to achieve gains from trade.

The side that drives the hardest bargain gets the most gains from the bargain, but it also risks making the deal fall through. Such strategic bargaining goes on all the time. **Strategic bargaining** means *demanding a larger share of the gains from trade than you can reasonably expect.* If you're successful, you get the lion's share; if you're not successful, the deal falls apart and everyone is worse off.

Strategic bargaining can lead to higher gains from trade for the side that drives the hardest bargain, but it also can make the deal fall through.

Haggling by Countries over Trade Restrictions

Another type of trade bargaining that often limits trade is bargaining between countries. Trade restrictions and the threat of trade restrictions play an important role in that kind of haggling. Sometimes countries must go through with trade restrictions that they really don't want to impose, just to make their threats credible.

Once one country has imposed trade restrictions, other countries attempt to get those restrictions reduced by threatening to increase their own restrictions. Again, to make the threat credible, sometimes countries must impose or increase trade restrictions simply to show they're willing to do so. For example, China allowed significant illegal copying of U.S. software without paying royalties. The United States put pressure on China to stop such copying and felt that China was not responding effectively. To force compliance, the United States made a list of Chinese goods that it threatened with 100 percent tariffs unless China complied. The United States did not want to put on these restrictions but felt that it would have more strategic bargaining power if it threatened to do so. Hence the name **strategic trade policies**—*threats to implement tariffs to bring about a reduction in tariffs or some other concession from the other country.* President Trump pushed strategic hard bargaining to its limits, as he tried to extract better trading rules with all U.S. trading partners.

Ultimately, strategic bargaining power depends on negotiators' skills and the underlying gains from trade that a country would receive. A country that would receive only a small portion of the gains from trade is in a much stronger bargaining position than a country that would receive significant gains. It's easier for the former to walk away from trade. Economists' concern about President Trump's "America First" policy, which was a policy of trying to improve the bargain the United States struck in previous trade deals, is that other countries will retaliate with a "Their Country First" policy, and make any deal impossible. In that case, no country is first and all lose.

Q-7 True or false? In strategic trade bargaining, it is sometimes reasonable to be unreasonable. Explain.

Strategic trade policies are threats to implement tariffs to bring about a reduction in tariffs or some other concession from the other country.

Trump Trade Policy and Antiglobalization Forces

President Trump doesn't like many of the trade agreements that the United States has entered in the past. He argues that they are bad deals. He isn't alone. Whenever the World Trade Organization or a similar type of organization promoting free trade hosts a meeting, protests (sometimes violent ones) are held by a loosely organized collection of groups opposing globalization. The goals of these groups are varied. Some argue that trade hurts developed countries such as the United States; others argue that it hurts developing countries by exploiting poor workers so that Westerners can buy luxuries cheaply. Still others argue that trade exerts a subtler Western economic imperialism in which globalization spreads Western cultural values and undermines developing countries' social structures. Others agree with Trump and argue that trade takes away jobs in the United States. Each of these arguments has some appeal, although making them simultaneously is difficult because doing so says that voluntary trade hurts both parties involved in the trade. Until recently these arguments have had little impact on the views of most policy makers and economists, who when they weigh the costs and benefits of freer trade come out on the side of free trade.

©Paul Conklin/PhotoEdit

Supporting free trade does not mean that globalization has no costs. Globalization does have costs, but many of the costs are really the result of technological changes. The reality is that technological developments, such as those in telecommunications and transportation, are pushing countries closer together. This has been going on for centuries, and will inevitably involve difficult social and cultural changes, regardless of whether trade is free or not. Restricting trade might temporarily slow these changes but is unlikely to stop them.

Most empirical studies have found that, with regard to material goods, the workers in developing countries involved in trade are generally better off than those not involved in trade. That's why most developing countries work hard to encourage companies to move production facilities to their countries. From a worker's perspective, earning $4 a day can look quite good when the alternative is earning $3 a day. Would the worker rather earn $10 a day? Of course, but higher wages in a given country reduce the likelihood firms will locate production there.

Many economists are sympathetic to various antiglobalization arguments, but they often become frustrated at the lack of clarity of the antiglobalization groups' views, including those of President Trump. To oppose something is not enough; to effect positive change, one must both (1) understand how the thing one opposes works and (2) have a realistic plan for a better alternative. President Trump's approach is more of a disruptive approach, which gets people to consider issues that otherwise would not be raised. He believes that because foreign countries gain more from trade with the United States than the United States gains from them, such a disruptive approach puts the United States in a better bargaining position. Critics argue that the better bargaining position is only a small gain, and that this small gain is more than outweighed by the loss of trust and cooperation that a disruptive approach brings about.

The potential problem with strategic trade policies is that they can backfire. One rule of strategic bargaining is that the other side must believe that you'll go through with your threat. Thus, strategic trade policy can lead a country that actually supports free trade to impose trade restrictions, just to show how strongly it believes in free trade.

Specialized Production

My discussion of comparative advantage took as a given that one country was inherently more productive than another country in producing certain goods. But when one looks at trading patterns, it's often not at all clear why particular countries have a productive advantage in certain goods. There's no inherent reason for Switzerland to specialize in the production of watches or for South Korea to specialize in the production of cars. Much in trade cannot be explained by inherent comparative advantages due to resource endowments. If they don't have inherent advantages, why are countries and places often so good at producing what they specialize in? Two important explanations are *learning by doing* and *economies of scale*.

Learning by doing means becoming better at a task the more you perform it.

LEARNING BY DOING   **Learning by doing** means *becoming better at a task the more often you perform it.* Take watches in Switzerland. Initially production of watches in Switzerland may have been a coincidence; the person who started the watch business happened to live there. But then people in the area became skilled in producing watches. Their skill made it attractive for other watch companies to start up. As additional companies moved in, more and more members of the labor force became skilled at watchmaking and word went out that Swiss watches were the best in the world. That reputation attracted even more producers, so Switzerland became the watchmaking capital of the world. Had the initial watch production occurred in Austria, not Switzerland, Austria might be the watch capital of the world.

When there's learning by doing, it's much harder to attribute inherent comparative advantage to a country. One must always ask: Does country A have an inherent comparative advantage, or does it simply have more experience? Once country B gets the experience, will country A's comparative advantage disappear? If it will, then country B has a strong reason to limit trade with country A in order to give its own workers time to catch up as they learn by doing.

In economies of scale, costs per unit of output go down as output increases.

ECONOMIES OF SCALE   In determining whether an inherent comparative advantage exists, a second complication is **economies of scale**—*the situation in which costs per unit of output fall as output increases.* Many manufacturing industries (such as steel and autos) exhibit economies of scale. The existence of significant economies of scale means that it makes sense (that is, it lowers costs) for one country to specialize in one good and another country to specialize in another good. But who should specialize in what is unclear. Producers in a country can, and generally do, argue that if only the government would establish barriers, they would be able to lower their costs per unit and eventually sell at lower costs than foreign producers.

Q-8 Is it efficient for a country to maintain a trade barrier in an industry that exhibits economies of scale?

Most countries recognize the importance of learning by doing and economies of scale. A variety of trade restrictions are based on these two phenomena. The most common expression of the learning-by-doing and economies-of-scale insights is the **infant industry argument,** which is that *with initial protection, an industry will be able to become competitive.* Countries use this argument to justify many trade restrictions. They argue, "You may now have a comparative advantage, but that's simply because you've been at it longer, or are experiencing significant economies of scale. We need trade restrictions on our _____ industry to give it a chance to catch up. Once an infant industry grows up, then we can talk about eliminating the restrictions."

The infant industry argument says that with initial protection, an industry will be able to become competitive.

This infant industry argument also has been used to justify tariffs on new high-tech products such as solar panels. U.S. firms have pushed for tariffs on Chinese solar panels so that they can develop the technology here in the United States rather than have the technology developed in China.

Macroeconomic Costs of Trade

The comparative advantage argument for free trade assumes that a country's resources are fully utilized. When countries don't have full employment, imports can decrease domestic aggregate demand and increase unemployment. Exports can stimulate domestic aggregate demand and decrease unemployment. Thus, when an economy is in a recession, there is a strong macroeconomic reason to limit imports and encourage exports. These macroeconomic effects of free trade play an important role in the public's view of imports and exports. When a country is in a recession, pressure to impose trade restrictions increases substantially. We saw this in 2009 when, faced with the job losses due to the serious recession, there was significant pressure to design programs to keep spending in the United States where it would create jobs and not be spent on imports that would create jobs for other countries.

National Security

Countries often justify trade restrictions on grounds of national security. These restrictions take two forms:

1. Export restrictions on strategic materials and defense-related goods.
2. Import restrictions on defense-related goods. For example, in a war we don't want to be dependent on oil from abroad.

For a number of goods, national security considerations make sense. For example, the United States restricts the sale of certain military items to countries that may be fighting the United States someday. The problem is where to draw the line about goods having a national security consideration. Should countries protect domestic agriculture? All high-technology items, since they might be useful in weapons? All chemicals? Steel? When a country makes a national security argument for trade, we must be careful to consider whether a domestic political reason may be lurking behind that argument.

International Politics

International politics frequently provides another reason for trade restrictions. Currently the United States restricts trade with Venezuela, North Korea, and Iran in an attempt to influence their political decisions. Essentially, the argument is: Trade helps you, so we'll hurt you by stopping trade until you do what we want. So what if it hurts us too? It'll hurt you more than it hurts us. President Trump has pushed this approach to trade negotiations further than any previous U.S. president, and in 2018 he was threatening to pull out of many of the trade agreements the United States had previously agreed to.

Increased Revenue Brought In by Tariffs

A final argument made for one particular type of trade restriction—a tariff—is that tariffs bring in revenues. In the 19th century, tariffs were the U.S. government's primary source of revenue. They are less important as a source of revenue today for many developed countries because those countries have instituted other forms of taxes. However, tariffs remain a primary source of revenue for many developing countries. They're relatively easy to collect and are paid by people rich enough to afford imports. These countries justify many of their tariffs with the argument that they need the revenues.

Why Economists Generally Oppose Trade Restrictions

Each of the preceding arguments for trade restrictions has some validity, but most economists discount them and support free trade. The reason is that, in their considered judgment, the harm done by trade restrictions outweighs the benefits. This is true even though, from the U.S. perspective, transferable comparative advantages are likely to place significant pressures on firms to outsource U.S. jobs abroad, and hold down U.S. wages in the coming decades. Most economists believe that the United States will be better off if it allows free trade.

Reasons for restricting trade include:

1. Unequal internal distribution of the gains from trade.
2. Haggling by companies over the gains from trade.
3. Haggling by countries over trade restrictions.
4. Specialized production: learning by doing and economies of scale.
5. Macroeconomic aspects of trade.
6. National security.
7. International politics.
8. Increased revenue brought in by tariffs.

Economists generally oppose trade restrictions because:

1. From a global perspective, free trade increases total output.
2. International trade provides competition for domestic companies.
3. Restrictions based on national security are often abused or evaded.
4. Trade restrictions are addictive.

FREE TRADE INCREASES TOTAL OUTPUT   Economists' first argument for free trade is that, viewed from a global perspective, free trade increases total output. From a national perspective, economists agree that particular instances of trade restrictions may actually help one nation even as most other nations are hurt. But they argue that the country imposing trade restrictions can benefit *only if the other country doesn't retaliate* with trade restrictions of its own. Retaliation is the rule, not the exception, however, and when there is retaliation, trade restrictions cause both countries to lose. Thus, if the United States were to place a tariff on goods from China, those aspects of production that depend on Chinese goods would be hurt, and, as I discussed above, there are many such goods. Moreover, China would likely place tariffs on goods from the United States, hurting both countries. Such tariffs would cut overall production, making both countries worse off.

INTERNATIONAL TRADE PROVIDES COMPETITION   A second reason most economists oppose trade restrictions is that trade restrictions reduce international competition. International competition is desirable because it forces domestic companies to stay on their toes. If trade restrictions on imports are imposed, domestic companies don't work as hard and therefore become less efficient.

For example, in the 1950s and 1960s, the United States imposed restrictions on imported steel. U.S. steel industries responded to this protection by raising their prices and channeling profits from their steel production into other activities. By the 1970s, the U.S. steel industry was using outdated equipment to produce overpriced steel. Instead of making the steel industry stronger, restrictions made it a flabby, uncompetitive industry.

In the 1980s and 1990s, the U.S. steel industry became less and less profitable. Larger mills closed or consolidated, while nonunion minimills, which made new steel out of scrap steel, did well. By the late 1990s, minimills accounted for 45 percent of total U.S. steel production. In 2002 it looked as if a number of larger mills were going to declare bankruptcy, and enormous pressure was placed on the federal government to bail them out by taking over their pension debt and instituting tariffs. The U.S. government responded by imposing 20 to 30 percent tariffs on foreign steel imports. Most economists opposed the tariffs and pointed out that they were unlikely to lead to a rebuilding of the U.S. steel industry because other countries had a comparative advantage in steel production. Moreover, other countries would retaliate with tariffs on U.S. goods. Despite their opposition, the tariffs were instituted. Major U.S. trading partners—including EU countries, Japan, and China—responded by threatening to implement tariffs on U.S. goods. The following year the U.S. government withdrew the tariffs. Today, U.S. steel companies produce only a small fraction of the world's steel, and almost all of that is from recycled steel.

The benefits of international competition are not restricted to mature industries like steel; they can also accrue to young industries wherever they appear. Economists dispose of the infant industry argument by referencing the historical record. In theory the argument makes sense. But very few of the infant industries protected by trade restrictions have ever grown up. What tends to happen instead is that infant industries become dependent on the trade restrictions and use political pressure to keep that protection. As a result, they often remain immature and internationally uncompetitive. Most economists would support the infant industry argument only if the trade restrictions included definite conditions under which the restrictions would end.

Very few of the infant industries protected by trade restrictions have ever grown up.

RESTRICTIONS BASED ON NATIONAL SECURITY ARE OFTEN ABUSED OR EVADED   Most economists agree with the national security argument for export restrictions on goods that are directly war-related. Selling bombs to Iran, whom the

United States has called a member of the Axis of Evil, doesn't make much sense. Economists point out that the argument is often carried far beyond goods directly related to national security. For example, in the 1980s the United States restricted exports of sugar-coated cereals to the Soviet Union purportedly for reasons of national security. Sugar-frosted flakes may be great, but they were unlikely to help the Soviet Union in a war.

Another argument that economists give against the national security rationale is that trade restrictions on military sales can often be evaded. Countries simply have another country buy the goods for them. Such third-party sales—called *transshipments*—are common in international trade and limit the effectiveness of any absolute trade restrictions for national security purposes.

Economists also argue that by fostering international cooperation, international trade makes war less likely—a significant contribution to national security.

TRADE RESTRICTIONS ARE ADDICTIVE   Economists' final argument against trade restrictions is: Yes, some restrictions might benefit a country, but almost no country can limit its restrictions to the beneficial ones. Trade restrictions are addictive—the more you have, the more you want. Thus, a majority of economists take the position that the best response to such addictive policies is "Just say no."

Yes, some restrictions might benefit a country, but almost no country can limit its restrictions to the beneficial ones.

Institutions Supporting Free Trade

As I have stated throughout the text, economists generally like markets and favor trade being as free as possible. They argue that trade allows specialization and the division of labor. When each country follows its comparative advantage, production is more efficient and the production possibility curve shifts out. These views mean that most economists, liberal and conservative alike, generally oppose international trade restrictions.

Despite political pressures to restrict trade, governments have generally tried to follow economists' advice and have entered into a variety of international agreements and organizations. The most important is the World Trade Organization (WTO), which has over 150 members and is the successor to the General Agreement on Tariffs and Trade (GATT). You will still occasionally see references to GATT, even though the WTO has taken its place. One of the differences between the WTO and GATT is that the WTO includes some enforcement mechanisms.

The push for free trade has a geographic dimension, which includes **free trade associations**—*groups of countries that have reduced or eliminated trade barriers among themselves.* The European Union (EU) is the most famous free trade association. All barriers to trade among the EU's member countries were removed in 1992, and over the next 20 years the EU expanded significantly. In 1993, the United States and Canada agreed to enter into a similar free trade union, and they, together with Mexico, created the North American Free Trade Association (NAFTA).

Until Donald Trump's election as president, the United States was negotiating two new trade agreements—the Transatlantic Trade and Investment Partnership (TTIP) and the Trans-Pacific Partnership (TPP). The TTIP would lower tariffs and trade restrictions between European countries and the United States; the TPP would lower tariffs and restrictions for 12 countries bordering on the Pacific, including the United States, Japan, Australia, and Canada. Talks for the TPP began in 2005, but it was only in 2015 that they were agreed upon by the heads of state. The U.S. Congress was slow to approve the TPP, and with President Trump's election, these deals were essentially abandoned. The focus was on what other trade deals the United States would pull out of.

Web Note 10.4
Thumbs Up or Down?

Q-9 What are two important international economic organizations?

Q-10 What are two important trade associations?

Dumping

The WTO allows countries to impose trade restrictions on imports if they can show that the goods are being dumped. *Dumping* is selling a good in a foreign country at a lower price than in the country where it's produced. On the face of it, who could complain about someone who wants to sell you a good cheaply? Why not just take advantage of the bargain price? The first objection is the learning-by-doing argument. To stay competitive, a country must keep on producing. Dumping by another country can force domestic producers out of business. Having eliminated the competition, the foreign producer has the field to itself and can raise the price. Thus, dumping can be a form of predatory pricing.

The second argument against dumping involves the short-term macroeconomic and political effects it can have on the importing country. Even if one believes that dumping is not a preliminary to predatory pricing, it can displace workers in the importing country, causing political pressure on that government to institute trade restrictions. If that country's economy is in a recession, the resulting unemployment will have substantial macroeconomic repercussions, so pressure for trade restrictions will be amplified.

Determining whether dumping is taking place is extremely difficult; countries have different institutional structures, and determining costs of producing a good is complicated. Thus, invariably, there is legitimate debate about where dumping has occurred, and often politics, not economics, dominates the debate. In 2018, President Trump imposed steep tariffs on washing machines and solar panels, arguing that countries such as Korea and China were dumping these products on the American market. Some analysts argued that the solar panel tariffs may end up costing American jobs since most employment in that industry is in installation.

President Trump's aggressive strategic trade bargaining, in which he tries to negotiate better trading terms for the United States with the threat of tariffs if other countries don't give in highlights some issues that are not often discussed in introductory courses, but which are important in understanding modern debates about trade. The issues bring home the fact that free trade is more complicated than it sometimes seems.

The first issue involves free trade associations—do they lead to freer trade or do they lead to more restrictions in trade? Economists have mixed views. While economists see free trade between regional countries as beneficial, they also suggest that such regional free trade associations may impose significant trade restrictions on nonmember countries and thus reduce free trade. Economists also believe that bilateral negotiations between member nations tend to replace multilateral efforts among members and nonmembers. Whether the net effect of these bilateral negotiations is positive or negative is subject to debate.

The second issue involves intellectual property rights. Trade requires the harmonization of laws and regulatory structures among trading partners, so that all firms involved in trade face similar regulations. For example, production of food must meet similar regulatory requirements. (The box "Hormones and Economics" on page 216 captured such a regulatory issue.)

The division of the gains from trade depends on how these regulatory issues are resolved. In today's economy, laws governing intellectual property rights are especially important. In negotiating freer trade agreements the United States has required other countries to accept U.S. intellectual property rights laws that give enormous rights and advantages to patent, copyright, and trademark holders and restrict activities by competing companies in other countries. The result is to limit those countries' firms' ability to compete with U.S. firms.

Had current intellectual property rights laws existed when the United States was founded (and had the less restrictive laws that existed then been enforced), it is unlikely that the U.S. economy would have grown anywhere near as fast as it did. Significant portions of U.S. production at the time involved copying European technologies without paying for their use, improving upon those technologies, and selling their goods back to Europe. Current free trade agreements restrict that type of competition, and thus reduce elements of trade and growth.

Whether the positive effects of recent free trade agreements are stronger than the negative effects (and just how positive should be interpreted) is again subject to debate, as Harvard economist, Dani Rodrik, has recently pointed out. The bottom line: Free trade is more nuanced than can be presented in a principles course, so be careful about extending simple arguments to complicated issues.

Conclusion

The difficulties that globalization and trade bring to a country—the effect on income distribution, and the wrenching structural changes it requires—lead many laypeople to support trade restrictions such as tariffs, quotas, and indeed anything to protect domestic jobs. Such policies might alleviate some short-run problems, but they ultimately will be unlikely to work. Not only will other countries retaliate; they will also take advantage of trade. So if the United States closes off trade with China, other countries will emerge as competitors.

The problem comes when we don't face up to those problems and don't deal with the political problems that an expansion of trade creates. The United States has avoided dealing with these problems for the last 20 years, and the problems have built up. One problem is the enormous increase in income inequality in the United States, with those workers facing global competition losing out, and those protected from it (or being in a position to take advantage of it) gaining. In short, the large trade deficits run up over the past 20 years have given us great benefits, but they also have had costs.

Summary

- The nature of trade is continually changing. The United States is importing more and more high-tech goods and services from India and China and other East Asian countries. (*LO10-1*)

- Outsourcing is a type of trade. Outsourcing is a larger phenomenon today compared to 30 years ago because China and India are so large that enormous outsourcing is possible. (*LO10-1*)

- Trade restrictions include tariffs and quotas, sanctions, voluntary restraint agreements, regulatory trade restrictions, and nationalistic appeals. (*LO10-2*)

- Tariffs and quotas raise the price and reduce the quantity of goods. The difference is who gets the revenue that results from higher price. (*LO10-2*)

- Reasons that countries impose trade restrictions include unequal internal distribution of the gains from trade, haggling by companies over the gains from trade, haggling by countries over trade restrictions, learning by doing and economies of scale, macroeconomic costs of trade, national security, international political reasons, and increased revenue brought in by tariffs. (*LO10-3*)

- Economists generally oppose trade restrictions because of the history of trade restrictions and their understanding of the advantages of free trade. (*LO10-3*)

- Two organizations that support free trade are GATT and the WTO. Two important trade associations are the EU and NAFTA. (*LO10-4*)

Key Terms

economies of scale
free trade association
General Agreement on
  Tariffs and Trade
  (GATT)

infant industry argument
learning by doing
quota
regulatory trade
  restriction

sanction
strategic bargaining
strategic trade policy
tariff

trade adjustment
  assistance program
World Trade Organization
  (WTO)

Questions and Exercises   connect

1. How important is international trade in terms of its relationship to total U.S. production? What does this suggest about the importance of trade policies relative to other countries? (*LO10-1*)

2. Which countries are the two greatest trading partners for the United States? With which countries is trade rapidly increasing? (*LO10-1*)

3. Demonstrate graphically how the effects of a tariff differ from the effects of a quota. (*LO10-2*)

4. How do the effects of voluntary restraint agreements differ from the effects of a tariff? (*LO10-2*)

5. The world price of textiles is P_w, as in the accompanying figure of the domestic supply and demand for textiles.

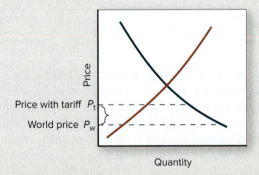

Quantity

The government imposes a tariff t to protect the domestic producers. For this tariff: (*LO10-2*)
   a. Label the revenue gains to domestic producers.
   b. Label the revenue to government.
   c. Label the costs to domestic producers.
   d. Are the gains to domestic producers greater than the costs? Why?

6. In 1964 President Lyndon B. Johnson imposed the Chicken Tax—a 25 percent tax on all imported light

trucks in retaliation for a tariff placed by Germany on chickens imported from the United States. The light-truck tariff hurt Volkswagen van sales. Were these tariffs good or bad from the following perspectives? (*LO10-2*)
   a. The U.S. government.
   b. German consumers of chickens.
   c. U.S. chicken producers.
   d. U.S. light-truck producers.
   e. Economists.

7. On January 1, 2005, quotas on clothing imports to the United States first instituted in the 1960s to protect the U.S. garment industry were eliminated. (*LO10-2*)
   a. Demonstrate graphically how this change affected equilibrium price and quantity of imported garments.
   b. Demonstrate graphically how U.S. consumers benefited from the end of the quota system.
   c. What was the likely effect on profits of foreign companies that sold clothing in the U.S. market?

8. What are three reasons countries restrict trade? Are they justified? (*LO10-3*)

9. Why would a country have trade assistance programs? What makes them difficult to implement? (*LO10-3*)

10. How would a credible threat of trade restrictions lead to lower trade restrictions? (*LO10-3*)

11. How are economies of scale, comparative advantage, and trade restrictions related? (*LO10-3*)

12. Name three reasons economists support free trade. (*LO10-3*)

13. What is the relationship between GATT and the WTO? (*LO10-4*)

Questions from Alternative Perspectives

1. Frederic Bastiat wrote that "government is the great fiction through which everybody endeavors to live at the expense of everybody else." Is this a correct way to understand the fight about tariffs? *(Austrian)*

2. Frederic Bastiat wrote: "It seems to me that this is theoretically right, for whatever the question under discussion—whether religious, philosophical, political, or economic; whether it concerns prosperity, morality, equality, right, justice, progress, responsibility, cooperation, property, labor, trade, capital, wages, taxes, population, finance, or government—at whatever point on the scientific horizon I begin my researches, I invariably reach this one conclusion: The solution to the problems of human relationships is to be found in liberty." What is problematic with this view? *(Radical)*

3. Frederic Bastiat wrote, "When goods do not cross borders, soldiers will." Discuss. *(Religious)*

4. Who has benefited most from free trade? Who has been hurt most by it? Does that match the positions the various groups have about their support for free trade? Which group do economists align themselves with? Why? *(Post-Keynesian)*

5. The text presents free trade as advantageous for developing countries. However, in its period of most rapid development, the half century following the Civil War, the United States imposed tariffs on imports that averaged around 40 percent, a level higher than those in all but one of today's developing economies.
   a. Why did so many of today's industrialized countries not follow those policies as they were developing?
   b. What does this insight into economic history suggest about the doctrine of free trade and whose interests it serves? *(Radical)*

Issues to Ponder

1. How does considering trade in the broader cultural context change one's analysis?

2. One of the basic economic laws is "the law of one price." It says that given certain assumptions one would expect that if free trade is allowed, the price of goods in countries should converge.
   a. Can you list what three of those assumptions likely are?
   b. Should the law of one price hold for labor also? Why or why not?
   c. Should it hold for capital more so or less so than for labor? Why?

3. Suggest an equitable method of funding trade adjustment assistance programs.
   a. Why is it equitable?
   b. What problems might a politician have in implementing such a method?

4. When the United States placed a temporary price floor on tomatoes imported from Mexico, a U.S. trade representative said, "The agreement will provide strong relief to the tomato growers in Florida and other states, and help preserve jobs in the industry." What costs did Americans bear from the price floor?

5. Mexico exports many vegetables to the United States. These vegetables are grown using chemicals that are not allowed in U.S. vegetable agriculture. Should the United States restrict imports of Mexican vegetables? Why or why not?

6. The U.S. government taxes U.S. companies for their overseas profits, but it allows them to deduct from their U.S. taxable income the taxes that they pay abroad and interest on loans funding operations abroad, with no limits on the amount deducted.
   a. Is it possible that the overseas profit tax produces no net revenue?
   b. What would you suggest to the government about this tax if its purpose were to increase corporate income tax revenue?
   c. Why might the government keep this tax even if it were not collecting any net revenue?

7. In the 1930s Clair Wilcox of Swarthmore College organized a petition by economists "that any measure which provided for a general upward revision of tariff rates be denied passage by Congress, or if passed, be vetoed." It was signed by one-third of all economists in the United States at the time, of all political persuasions. A month later, the Smoot-Hawley Tariff was passed.
   a. Why did economists oppose the tariff?
   b. Demonstrate the effect of the tariff on the price of goods.
   c. How would the tariff help the economy if other countries did not institute a retaliatory tariff?
   d. What would be the effect on the macroeconomy if other countries did institute a retaliatory tariff?

8. If you were economic adviser to a country that was following your advice about trade restrictions and that country fell into a recession, would you change your advice? Why, or why not?

When the productivity curves are falling, the corresponding cost curves are rising.

point of the marginal cost curve (output = 12) is at the same level of output as the maximum point on the marginal productivity curve. When the productivity curves are falling, the corresponding cost curves are rising. Why is that the case? Because as productivity falls, costs per unit increase; and as productivity increases, costs per unit decrease.

THE RELATIONSHIP BETWEEN THE MARGINAL COST AND AVERAGE COST CURVES

Now that we've considered the shapes of each cost curve, let's consider some of the important relationships among them—specifically the relationships between the marginal cost curve on the one hand and the average variable cost and average total cost curves on the other. These general relationships are shown graphically in Figure 11-4.

Let's first look at the relationship between marginal cost and average total cost. In the green shaded and yellow shaded areas (areas A and B) at output below Q_1, even though marginal cost is rising, average total cost is falling. Why? Because, in areas A and B, the marginal cost curve is below the average total cost curve. At point B, where average total cost is at its lowest, the marginal cost curve intersects the average total cost curve. In area C, above output Q_1, where average total cost is rising, the marginal cost curve is above the ATC curve.

The positioning of the marginal cost curve is not happenstance. The position of marginal cost relative to average total cost tells us whether average total cost is rising or falling.

Web Note 11.5

Marginal Costs in the Information Economy

Q-8 If marginal costs are increasing, what is happening to average total costs?

If $MC > ATC$, then ATC is rising.

If $MC = ATC$, then ATC is at its low point.

If $MC < ATC$, then ATC is falling.

FIGURE 11-4

The Relationship of Marginal Cost Curve to Average Variable Cost and Average Total Cost Curves

The marginal cost curve goes through the minimum points of both the average variable cost curve and the average total cost curve. Thus, there is a small range where average total costs are falling and average variable costs are rising.

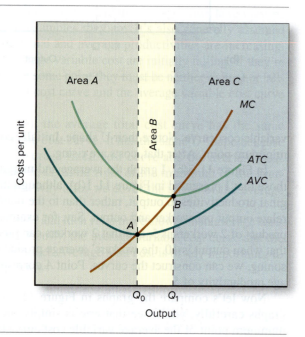

To understand why this is, think of it in terms of your grade point average. If you have a B average and you get a C on the next test (that is, your marginal grade is a C), your grade point average will fall below a B. Your marginal grade is below your average grade, so your average grade is falling. If you get a C+ on the next exam (that is, your marginal grade is a C+), *even though your marginal grade has risen from a C to a C+,* your grade point average will fall. Why? Because your marginal grade is still below your average grade. To make sure you understand the concept, explain the next two cases:

1. If your marginal grade is above your average grade, your average grade will rise.

2. If your marginal grade and average grade are equal, the average grade will remain unchanged.

Marginal and average reflect a general relationship that also holds for marginal cost and average variable cost.

If $MC > AVC$, then AVC is rising.

If $MC = AVC$, then AVC is at its low point.

If $MC < AVC$, then AVC is falling.

Q-9 If marginal costs are decreasing, what must be happening to average variable costs?

Q-10 Why does the marginal cost curve intersect the average variable cost curve at the minimum point?

This relationship is best seen in the yellow shaded area (area *B*) of Figure 11-4, when output is between Q_0 and Q_1. In this area, the marginal cost curve is above the average variable cost curve, so average variable cost is rising; but the *MC* curve is below the average total cost curve, so average total cost is falling. The intuitive explanation for the relationship in this area is that average total cost includes average variable cost, but it also includes average fixed cost, which is falling. As long as short-run marginal cost is only slightly above average variable cost, the average total cost will continue to fall. Put another way: Once marginal cost is above average variable cost, as long as average variable cost doesn't rise by more than average fixed cost falls, average total cost will still fall.

Intermission

At this point I'm going to cut off the chapter, not because we're finished with the subject, but because there's only so much that anyone can absorb in one chapter. It's time for a break.

Those of you with significant others, go out and do something significant. Those of you with parents bearing the cost of this education, give them a call and tell them that you appreciate their expenditure on your education. Think of the opportunity cost of that education to them; it's not peanuts. Those of you who are married should go out and give your spouse a big kiss; tell him or her that the opportunity cost of being away for another minute was so high that you couldn't control yourself. Those of you with kids, go out and read them a Dr. Seuss book. (*The Cat in the Hat* is a good one.) Let's face it—Seuss is a better writer than I, and if you've been conscientious about this course, you may not have paid your kids enough attention. We'll return to the grind in the next chapter.

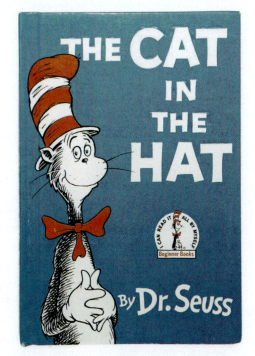

©Julie Clopper/Shutterstock

A Review of Costs

Term	Definition	Equation
Marginal cost	The additional cost resulting from a 1-unit increase in output.	$MC = \Delta TC$
Total cost	The sum of all costs of inputs used by a firm in production.	$TC = FC + VC$
Average total cost	Total cost per unit of production.	$ATC = AFC + AVC$ $= TC/Q$
Fixed cost	Cost that is already spent and cannot be recovered. It exists only in the short run.	FC
Average fixed cost	Fixed costs per unit of production.	$AFC = FC/Q$
Variable cost	Costs that vary with production.	VC
Average variable cost	Variable costs per unit of production.	$AVC = VC/Q$

Summary

- Accounting profit is explicit revenue less explicit cost. Economists include implicit revenue and cost in their determination of profit. *(LO11-1)*

- Implicit revenue includes the increases in the value of assets owned by the firm. Implicit costs include the opportunity cost of time and capital provided by the owners of the firm. *(LO11-1)*

- In the long run, a firm can choose among all possible production techniques; in the short run, the firm is constrained in its choices. *(LO11-2)*

- The law of diminishing marginal productivity states that as more and more of a variable input is added to a fixed input, the additional output the firm gets will eventually be decreasing. *(LO11-2)*

- Costs are generally divided into fixed costs, variable costs, and total costs. *(LO11-3)*

- $TC = FC + VC; MC =$ Change in $TC; AFC = FC/Q;$ $AVC = VC/Q; ATC = AFC + AVC.$

- The average variable cost curve and marginal cost curve are mirror images of the average product curve and the marginal product curve, respectively.   (*LO11-4*)

- The law of diminishing marginal productivity causes marginal and average costs to rise.   (*LO11-4*)

- If $MC > ATC$, then ATC is rising.
  If $MC = ATC$, then ATC is constant.
  If $MC < ATC$, then ATC is falling.

- The marginal cost curve goes through the minimum points of the average variable cost curve and average total cost curve.   (*LO11-4*)

Key Terms

average fixed cost	firm	marginal costs	profit
average product	fixed costs	marginal product	short-run decision
average total cost	law of diminishing	production	total cost
average variable cost	marginal productivity	production function	total revenue
economic profit	long-run decision	production table	variable costs

Questions and Exercises ■ connect

1. What costs and revenues do economists include when calculating profit that accountants don't include? Give an example of each.   (*LO11-1*)

2. Peggy-Sue's cookies are the best in the world, or so I hear. She has been offered a job by Cookie Monster, Inc. to come to work at $130,000 per year. Currently, she is producing her own cookies, and she has revenues of $260,000 per year. Her costs are $40,000 for labor, $15,000 for rent, $35,000 for ingredients, and $5,000 for utilities. She has $100,000 of her own money invested in the operation, which, if she leaves, can be sold for $400,000 that she can invest at 1 percent per year.   (*LO11-1*)
   a. Calculate her accounting and economic profits.
   b. Advise her as to what she should do.

3. Economan has been infected by the free enterprise bug. He sets up a firm on extraterrestrial affairs. The rent of the building is $4,000, the cost of the two secretaries is $50,000, and the cost of electricity and gas comes to $5,000. There's a great demand for his information, and his total revenue amounts to $100,000. By working in the firm, though, Econo-man forfeits the $55,000 he could earn by working for the Friendly Space Agency and the $4,000 he could have earned as interest had he saved his

   funds instead of putting them in this business.   (*LO11-1*)
   a. What is his profit or loss by an accountant's definitions?
   b. What is his profit or loss by an economist's definitions?

4. What distinguishes the short run from the long run?   (*LO11-2*)

5. What is the difference between marginal product and average product?   (*LO11-2*)

6. Explain how studying for an exam is subject to the law of diminishing marginal productivity.   (*LO11-2*)

7. Find $TC, AFC, AVC, AC,$ and MC from the following table: (*LO11-3*)

Units	FC	VC
0	$100	$ 0
1	100	40
2	100	60
3	100	70
4	100	85
5	100	130

8. For each of the following indicate what costs are being calculated: *(LO11-3)*
   a. *FC + VC*
   b. *TC/Q*
   c. *FC/Q*
   d. *VC/Q*
   e. *AFC + AVC*

9. Classify each of the following as fixed or variable costs: *(LO11-3)*
   a. Outsourced payroll services.
   b. Leased offices.
   c. Company-owned building.
   d. Payroll taxes.

10. Which of the costs discussed in the chapter is the most important when a firm is deciding how much to produce? *(LO11-3)*

11. Explain how each of the following will affect the average fixed cost, average variable cost, average total cost, and marginal cost curves faced by a steel manufacturer: *(LO11-3)*
    a. New union agreement increases hourly pay.
    b. Local government imposes an annual lump-sum tax per plant.
    c. Federal government imposes a "stack tax" on emission of air pollutants by steel mills.
    d. New steelmaking technology increases productivity of every worker.

12. Graph the following table: *(LO11-4)*

Number of Workers	Total Output
0	0
1	20
2	60
3	150
4	260
5	350
6	420
7	455
8	420
9	375
10	300

   a. What is marginal product and average product at each level of production?
   b. Graph marginal product and average product.
   c. Label the areas of increasing marginal productivity, diminishing marginal productivity, and diminishing absolute productivity.

13. If average product is falling, what is happening to short-run average variable cost? *(LO11-4)*

14. If marginal cost is increasing, what do we know about average cost? *(LO11-4)*

15. A firm has fixed costs of $100 and variable costs of the following: *(LO11-4)*

Output	1	2	3	4	5	6	7	8	9
Variable costs	$35	75	110	140	175	215	260	315	390

   a. Show *AFC, ATC, AVC,* and *MC* in a table.
   b. Graph the *AFC, ATC, AVC,* and *MC* curves.
   c. Explain the relationship between the *MC* curve and the *AVC* and *ATC* curves.
   d. Say fixed costs dropped to $50. Which curves shifted? Why?

16. If average productivity falls, will marginal cost necessarily rise? How about average cost? *(LO11-4)*

17. An economic consultant is presented with the following total product table and asked to derive a table for average variable costs. The price of labor is $10 per hour. *(LO11-4)*

Labor	TP
1	5
2	15
3	30
4	36
5	40

   a. Help him do so.
   b. Show that the graphs of the average productivity curve and average variable cost curve are mirror images of each other.
   c. Show the marginal productivity curve for labor inputs between 1 and 5.
   d. Show that the marginal productivity curve and marginal cost curve are mirror images of each other.

18. Say that a firm has fixed costs of $100 and constant average variable costs of $25. *(LO11-4)*
    a. Show *AFC, VC, AVC,* and *MC* in a table.
    b. Graph the *AFC, ATC, AVC,* and *MC* curves.
    c. Explain why the curves have the shapes they do.
    d. What law is not operative for this firm?

19. Say a firm has $100 in fixed costs and its average variable costs increase by $5 for each unit, so that the cost of 1 is $25, the cost of 2 is $30, the cost of 3 is $35, and so on. *(LO11-4)*
    a. Show *VC, AFC, AVC,* and *MC* in a table.
    b. Graph the *AFC, ATC, AVC,* and *MC* curves associated with these costs.
    c. Explain how costs would have to increase in order for the curves to have the "normal" shapes of the curves presented in the text.

Questions from Alternative Perspectives

1. The text presents very detailed cost tables when it considers the decisions of firms.
   a. Do entrepreneurs have such cost tables available to them when they enter a business?
   b. If not, how do they gather such information?
   c. If such information is gathered through trial and error, what implications does that have for government intervention in the marketplace? *(Austrian)*

2. Say that a drug firm could increase its profit by marketing a drug that it knows might have serious side effects. Say also that it knows that it can never be prosecuted for doing so.
   a. Would it?
   b. Should it? *(Religious)*

3. The analysis in the book suggests that firms hire inputs so that they hold costs as low as possible. Yet, as Gloria Steinem has pointed out, looking at reality one sees men selling refrigerators and women selling men's underwear.
   a. Do you believe that that allocation of jobs reflects firms trying to minimize costs because of the relative expertise of women and men?
   b. If not, what does it reflect? *(Feminist)*

4. The text does not emphasize firms' role in shaping the tastes and preferences of consumers even though this is a very important role with firms spending about $185 billion a year on advertising. If it is true that firms are shaping consumer preferences, whose welfare are people maximizing when they make consumption decisions? *(Institutionalist)*

5. Walmart, the nation's largest retailer, has perfected a "just-in-time" competitive strategy. This retail giant relies on bar codes for instant inventory, distribution centers that purchase supplies at the last minute and deliver only when needed, a small core of suppliers that Walmart can pressure for large discounts, routinized work that requires on average seven hours of training, and part-time workers who often work full-time hours without getting corresponding benefits. How does this "just-in-time" approach change the mix of fixed and variable costs to the advantage of Walmart? *(Radical)*

Issues to Ponder

1. "There is no long run; there are only short and shorter runs." Evaluate that statement.

2. If you increase production to an infinitely large level, the average variable cost and the average total cost will merge. Why?

3. When cell phones were first introduced, bandwidth was limited, which led to economically interesting pricing structures. One by Sprint offered customers 4,000 free minutes for $39.99 a month. The fine print revealed a catch. Only 350 of those minutes were anytime minutes; the remaining were restricted to evening and weekend usage. If you went over your allotted time, you were charged 35 cents per minute for any additional minutes.
   a. What was your marginal cost? Graph it.
   b. What would your average variable cost curve for peak time usage have looked like?
   c. If you did not keep track of your usage, how would you figure your marginal cost?
   d. Why did firms offer such confusing plans?
   e. Were firms that charged this way in favor of or against portability of phone numbers?
   f. Why are these offers no longer prevalent?

4. Say that neither labor nor machines are fixed but there is a 50 percent quick-order premium paid for both workers and machines for their delivery in the short run. Once you buy them, they cannot be returned, however. What do your short-run marginal cost and short-run average total cost curves look like?

5. If machines are variable and labor fixed, how will the general shapes of the short-run average cost curve and marginal cost curve change?

Answers to Margin Questions

1. Accounting profit measures explicit costs and revenues; economic profit includes implicit costs and revenues as well. *(LO11-1)*

2. Normally the marginal productivity curve and average productivity curve are both inverted U shapes. *(LO11-2)*

3. Firms are likely to operate on the downward-sloping portion of the marginal productivity curve because on the upward-sloping portion, firms could increase workers' output by hiring more workers. A firm will continue to hire more workers at least to the point where diminishing marginal productivity sets in.   (*LO11-2*)

4. Average variable costs would be $40.   (*LO11-3*)

5. As you can see in the graph, both of these curves are U-shaped and the marginal cost curve goes through the average cost curve at the minimum point of the average cost curve.   (*LO11-4*)

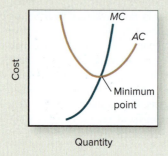

6. The distance between the average total cost and the average variable cost is determined by the average fixed cost at that quantity. As quantity increases, the average fixed cost decreases, so the two curves get closer and closer together.   (*LO11-4*)

7. Since the average productivity and marginal productivity of workers are the mirror images of average costs and marginal costs, and when the marginal costs and average costs intersect the two are equal, it follows that the average productivity and marginal productivity of workers must also be equal at that point.   (*LO11-4*)

8. It is impossible to say what is happening to average total costs on the basis of what is happening to marginal costs. It is the magnitude of marginal costs relative to average total costs that is important.   (*LO11-4*)

9. It is impossible to say because it is the magnitude of marginal cost relative to average variable cost that determines what is happening to average variable cost.   (*LO11-4*)

10. The marginal cost curve intersects the average variable cost curve at the minimum point because once the marginal cost exceeds average variable costs, the average variable costs must necessarily begin to rise, and vice versa.   (*LO11-4*)

Production and Cost Analysis II

©D. Hurst/Alamy Stock Photo

Welcome back from your intermission. I hope you've reestablished your relationship with the real world and are ready to return, with renewed vigor, to the world of economics. When we took our intermission in the last chapter, we had worked our way through the various short-run costs. The short run is a time period in which some inputs are fixed. In the first part of this chapter, we consider firms' long-run decisions and the determinants of the long-run cost curves. Then, in the second part, we'll talk about applying cost analysis to the real world.

Firms have many more options in the long run than they do in the short run. They can change any input they want. Plant size is not given; neither is the technology available given.

To make their long-run decisions, firms look at the costs of the various inputs and the technologies available for combining those inputs, and then decide which combination offers the lowest cost.

Say you're opening a hamburger stand. One decision you'll have to make is what type of stove to buy. You'll quickly discover that many different types are available. Some use more gas than others but cost less to buy; some are electric; some are self-cleaning and hence use less labor; some are big; some are little; some use microwaves; some use convection. Some have long-term guarantees; some have no guarantees. Each has a colorful brochure telling you how wonderful it is. After studying the various detailed specifications and aspects of the production technology, you choose the stove that has the combination of characteristics that you believe best fits your needs.

Next you decide on workers. Do you want bilingual workers, college-educated workers, part-time workers, experienced workers . . . ? You get the idea: Even simple production decisions involve complicated questions. These decisions are made on the basis of the expected costs, and expected usefulness, of inputs.

Technical Efficiency and Economic Efficiency

When choosing among existing technologies in the long run, firms are interested in the lowest cost, or most economically efficient, methods of production. They consider all technically efficient methods and compare their costs. The terms *economically efficient* and *technically efficient* differ in meaning. **Technical efficiency** means that *a production process uses as few inputs as possible to produce a given level of output*. When there are multiple inputs, many different production processes can be technically efficient. For example, say that to produce 100 bushels of wheat, one production process uses 10 workers and 1 acre and another production process uses 1 worker and 100 acres; say also that these are the lowest number of inputs you can use with those production processes. Which of these two production techniques is more efficient? Both are technically efficient since neither involves less of both inputs. (A production process that uses 11 workers and 1 acre would be technically inefficient.) But that doesn't mean that both of these production processes are equally economically efficient. That question can't be answered unless you know the relative costs of the two inputs.

If renting an acre of land costs $100 and each worker costs $10, our answer likely will be different than if land rents for $10 an acre and each worker costs $100. The **economically efficient** method of production is *the method that produces a given level of output at the lowest possible cost*. With land at $100 an acre, you will use the production process that uses lots of workers and less land. With land at $10 an acre, you will use the production process that uses fewer workers but more land. Thus, all economically efficient production processes are technically efficient, but not all technically efficient production processes are economically efficient.

In long-run production decisions, firms will look at all available production technologies and choose the technology that, given the available inputs and their prices, is the economically efficient way to produce. These choices will reflect the prices of the various factors of production. Those prices, in turn, will reflect the factors' relative scarcities.

Consider the use of land by firms in the United States and in Japan. The United States has large amounts of land (7.5 acres) per person, so the price of land is lower than in Japan, which has only 0.73 acre per person. An acre of rural land that might cost $3,000 in the United States might cost $25,000 in Japan. Because of this difference in the price of inputs, production techniques use much more labor per acre of land in Japan than in the United States. Similarly with Bangladesh: Labor is more abundant and capital is scarcer, so production techniques in Bangladesh use much more labor per unit of capital than in the United States. Whereas Bangladesh would use hundreds of workers and very little machinery to build a road, the United States would use three or four people along with three machines. Both countries are being economically efficient, but because costs of inputs differ, the economically efficient method of production differs. Summarizing: The economically efficient method of production is the technically efficient method of production that has the lowest cost. (For a further, graphical analysis of economic efficiency, see the Appendix at the end of this chapter.)

The Shape of the Long-Run Cost Curve

In the last chapter, we saw that the law of diminishing marginal productivity accounted for the shape of the short-run average cost curve. The firm was adding more of a variable input to a fixed input. The law of diminishing marginal productivity doesn't apply

Web Note 12.1

Cheap Labor

Q-1 True or false? If a process is economically efficient, it is also technically efficient. Explain your answer.

Q-2 Why does Bangladesh use production techniques that require more workers per acre of land than do the techniques used in the United States?

Economies of Scale and 3D Printing

Technology is continually changing and as it does, so does the cost structure of production. Consider 3D printing, also called additive manufacturing, in which a three-dimensional part is created with a computer that directs a machine to fuse together liquid or powder in a predetermined shape. This is a significant advance over injection molding or machining. Machining a part requires enormous work, cutting down the raw material into the part you want. Injection molding is similarly work-intensive. The production of such parts can be

©cookelma/Getty Images

automated using templates and molds, but with both of those manufacturing processes, the fixed setup costs are high. So, automating the process makes sense only when you want to produce a large quantity. If you need only a few of the parts, you produce them by hand at a high cost.

3D printing changes that. With 3D printing you can simply enter the specifications of the part you want into the computer, and hit the Print button. Out comes the part, the same way that printed paper comes out when you print using a laser printer, except in three dimensions. (It's a bit more complicated, but you get the idea.) Once you have your part specifications, the second unit is no cheaper to print than the first; the economies of scale are reduced because your cost structure has shifted from one with large fixed costs to one with much lower fixed costs. So, even if the variable costs of 3D printing are much higher than the variable costs of more traditional methods of manufacturing, for many parts that you need on demand, or that you need only a relatively small number of, 3D printing can significantly reduce costs. Many of the parts that make up airplanes and the parts used in specialized medical equipment are now made using 3D printing.

to the long run since, in the long run, all inputs are variable. The most important determinants of what is economically efficient in the long run are economies and diseconomies of scale. Let's consider each of these in turn and see what effect they will have on the shape of the long-run average cost curve.

The shape of the long-run cost curve is due to the existence of economies and diseconomies of scale.

Economies of Scale

We say that production exhibits **economies of scale** *when long-run average total costs decrease as output increases.* For example, if producing 40,000 high-definition TVs costs a firm $16 million ($400 each), but producing 200,000 costs the firm $40 million ($200 each), between 40,000 and 200,000 units, production exhibits significant economies of scale. One can also say that there are increasing returns to scale.

In real-world production processes, at low levels of production, economies of scale are extremely important because many production techniques require a certain minimum level of output to be useful. For example, say you want to produce a pound of steel. You can't just build a mini blast furnace, stick in some coke and iron ore, and come out with a single pound of steel. The smallest technically efficient blast furnaces have a production capacity measured in tons per hour, not pounds per year. The cost of the blast furnace is said to be an **indivisible setup cost** *(the cost of an indivisible input for which a certain minimum amount of production must be undertaken before the input becomes economically feasible to use).*

In the production of steel, the cost of a blast furnace is an indivisible setup cost that requires a minimum level of production to be economically feasible.

Indivisible setup costs are important because they create many real-world economies of scale: As output increases, the costs per unit of output decrease. As an example, consider this book. Preparing the book for publishing is an indivisible setup cost; it is a cost that must be incurred if any production is to take place, but it

FIGURE 12-1 (A AND B)   **A Typical Long-Run Average Total Cost Table and Curve**

In the long run, average costs initially fall because of economies of scale; then they are constant for a while, and finally they tend to rise due to diseconomies of scale.

Quantity	Total Costs of Labor	Total Costs of Machines	Total Costs $= TC_L + TC_M$	Average Total Costs $= TC/Q$
11	$381	$254	$ 635	$58
12	390	260	650	54
13	402	268	670	52
14	420	280	700	50
15	450	300	750	50
16	480	320	800	50
17	510	340	850	50
18	549	366	915	51
19	600	400	1,000	53
20	666	444	1,110	56

(a) Long-Run Production Table

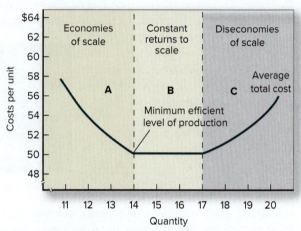

(b) Long-Run Average Cost Curve

Q-3 Why are larger production runs often cheaper per unit than smaller production runs?

is not a cost that increases with the number of books produced. That means that the more copies of the book that are produced, the lower the cost per book. That's why it costs more per book to produce a textbook for an upper-level, low-enrollment course than it does for a lower-level, high-enrollment course. The same amount of work goes into both (both need to be written, edited, and composited), and the printing costs differ only slightly. The actual production or print-run costs of printing a book (the costs to print and bind the book after it is all prepared) are only about $3 to $10 per book. The other costs are indivisible setup costs. Prices of produced goods, including books, reflect their costs of production. As you move to upper-level academic courses, where print runs are smaller, you'll likely discover that the books are smaller and less colorful but are priced the same as, or more than, this introductory text.

In the long-run planning decisions about the cost of producing this book, the expected number of copies to be sold was an important element. That figure influenced the number of books produced, which in turn affected the expected cost per unit. This will be the case anytime there are economies of scale. With economies of scale, cost per unit of a small production run is higher than cost per unit of a large production run.

Figure 12-1(a) demonstrates a long-run production table; Figure 12-1(b) shows the related typical shape of a long-run average cost curve. (Notice that there are no fixed costs. Because we're in the long run, all costs are variable.) Economies of scale account for the downward-sloping part. Cost per unit of output is decreasing.

Because of the importance of economies of scale, businesspeople often talk of a minimum efficient level of production. What they mean by minimum efficient level of production is that, given the price at which they expect to be able to sell a good, the indivisible setup costs are so high that production runs of less than a certain size don't make economic sense. Thus, the **minimum efficient level of production** is *the amount of production that spreads out setup costs sufficiently for a firm to undertake*

In the long run, all inputs are variable, so only economies of scale can influence the shape of the long-run cost curve.

Travels of a T-Shirt and Economies of Scale

The T-shirt said "MADE IN CHINA," but when economist Pietra Rivoli, in her delightful book *The Travels of a T-Shirt in the Global Economy,* tracked down the process of making the T-shirt that she bought in Florida, she discovered that it's a lot more complicated than that. True, the company that sewed the shirt was in Shanghai, China. But guess where the cotton for the shirt came from? West Texas, USA, at a farm like the Reinsch family farm that is highlighted in Rivoli's book.

Source: USDA/Photo by David Nance

Now here's an exam question for you: Why, if China's labor cost is 1/20 that of U.S. labor costs, is the cotton for a T-shirt grown in the United States, shipped across the ocean to China to be woven and sewn into a T-shirt, and shipped back again to the United States to be sold?

Answer: Economies of scale (and some U.S. subsidies, but you aren't expected to know that yet). In fact, until recently, the United States had been the world leader in the production of cotton. The size of the average farm in the United States is about 440 acres compared to 8 acres in Africa and 2.5 acres in China. The Reinsch's farm is 1,000 acres and can produce about 500,000 pounds of cotton, enough for 1.3 million T-shirts. Size makes a difference; cotton farmers outside the United States almost exclusively handpick their cotton. Because U.S. farmers have such large farms, they can use large machinery to do all the picking, and thereby take advantage of economies of scale, countering the much higher labor costs in the United States. Other countries are responding. For example, China is converting its small farms to large-scale farming, and replacing labor with machines. As they do, U.S. producers of cotton will continue to lose their comparative advantage.

---

production profitably. At this point, the market has expanded to a size large enough for firms to take advantage of economies of scale. In a perfectly competitive market, the minimum efficient level of production for a firm thinking of entering the market is where the average total costs are at a minimum.

Diseconomies of Scale

Notice that on the right side of Figure 12-1(b) the long-run average cost curve is upward-sloping. Average cost is increasing. We say that production exhibits **diseconomies of scale** *when long-run average total costs increase as output increases.* For example, if producing 200,000 high-definition TVs costs the firm $40 million ($200 each) and producing 400,000 high-definition TVs costs the firm $100 million ($250 each), there are diseconomies of scale associated with choosing to produce 400,000 rather than 200,000. One also can say there are decreasing returns to scale. Diseconomies of scale usually, but not always, start occurring as firms get large. It is important to remember that diminishing marginal productivity is not the cause of diseconomies of scale.

Diseconomies of scale could not occur if production relationships were only technical relationships. If that were the case, the same technical process could be used over and over again at the same per-unit cost. In reality, however, production relationships have social dimensions, which introduce the potential for important diseconomies of scale into the production process in two ways:

1. As the size of the firm increases, monitoring costs generally increase.
2. As the size of the firm increases, team spirit or morale generally decreases.

Diminishing marginal productivity refers to the decline in productivity caused by increasing units of a variable input being added to a fixed input. Diseconomies of scale refer to the decreases in productivity that occur when there are equal percentage increases of all inputs (no input is fixed).

Q-4 If production involved only technical relationships and had no social dimension, what would the long-run average total cost curve look like?

253

Holacracy, Diseconomies of Scale, and Zappos

Companies are continually searching for ways to avoid diseconomies of scale, and there are hundreds of management fads that claim to avoid them, which have come (and gone). One recent fad is holacracy (the term is a play on the word *bureaucracy*), which is a decentralized organizational structure in which roles are defined around work, not people; authority is distributed to teams; decisions are made locally; and everyone is bound (the CEO and maintenance person alike) by the same set of highly visible rules.

One company to recently adopt this structure is the shoe company Zappos, an online shoe and clothing

©mikewaters/123RF

company. Leaders at Zappos argue that the holacracy structure is far more efficient than other methods of organization. Many observers have their doubts about whether the holacracy organizational structure will make Zappos more efficient and, if it does, whether it can be adapted to more traditional companies. Most companies have found that a blend of top-down and bottom-up control inevitably evolves into the system firms actually use. But if holacracy is successful at Zappos, we will expect other firms to adopt it, since they are always looking for ways to improve efficiency.

Monitoring costs are *the costs incurred by the organizer of production in seeing to it that the employees do what they're supposed to do.* If you're producing something yourself, the job gets done the way you want it done; monitoring costs are zero. However, as the scale of production increases, you have to hire people to help you produce. This means that if the job is to be done the way you want it done, you have to monitor (supervise) your employees' performance. The cost of monitoring can increase significantly as output increases; it's a major contributor to diseconomies of scale. Most big firms have several layers of bureaucracy devoted simply to monitoring employees. The job of middle managers is, to a large extent, monitoring.

As firms become larger, monitoring costs increase and achieving team spirit is more difficult.

The other social dimension that can contribute to diseconomies of scale is the loss of **team spirit** (*the feelings of friendship and being part of a team that bring out people's best efforts*). Most types of production are highly dependent on team spirit. When the team spirit or morale is lost, production slows considerably. The larger the firm is, the more difficult it is to maintain team spirit.

Another important reason why diseconomies of scale can come about is that the bigger things get, the more checks and balances are needed to ensure that all the various components of production are coordinated. The larger the organization, the more checks and balances and the more paperwork.

Some large firms manage to solve these problems and avoid diseconomies of scale. But problems of monitoring and loss of team spirit often limit the size of firms. They underlie diseconomies of scale in which less additional output is produced for a given increase in inputs, so that per-unit costs of output increase.

Constant Returns to Scale

Sometimes in a range of output, a firm does not experience either economies of scale or diseconomies of scale. In this range, there are **constant returns to scale** *where long-run average total costs do not change with an increase in output.* Constant returns to scale are shown by the flat portion of the average total cost curve in Figure 12-1(b). Constant returns to scale occur when production techniques can be replicated again and again to increase output. This occurs before monitoring costs rise and team spirit is lost.

The long-run and the short-run average cost curves have similar U shapes. But it's important to remember that the reasons why they have this U shape are quite different. The assumption of initially increasing and then eventually diminishing marginal productivity (as a variable input is added to a fixed input) accounts for the shape of the short-run average cost curve. Economies and diseconomies of scale account for the shape of the long-run average total cost curve; initially economies of scale drive average costs down, then diseconomies of scale drive average costs up.

Q-5 Why is the short-run average cost curve a U-shaped curve?

Q-6 Why is the long-run average total cost curve generally considered to be a U-shaped curve?

The Importance of Economies and Diseconomies of Scale

Economies and diseconomies of scale play important roles in real-world long-run production decisions. Economies of scale are an important reason why firms attempt to expand their markets either at home or abroad. If they can make and sell more at lower per-unit costs, they will make more profit. Diseconomies of scale prevent a firm from expanding and can lead corporate raiders to buy the firm and break it up in the hope that the smaller production units will be more efficient, thus eliminating some of the diseconomies of scale.

Economies and diseconomies of scale play important roles in real-world long-run production decisions.

Envelope Relationship

Since in the long run all inputs are flexible, while in the short run some inputs are not flexible, long-run cost will always be less than or equal to short-run cost at the same level of output. To see this, let's consider a firm that had planned to produce 100 units but now adjusts its plan to produce more than 100. We know that in the long run the firm chooses the lowest-cost method of production. In the short run, it faces an additional constraint: All expansion must be done by increasing only the variable input. That constraint must increase average cost (or at least not decrease it) compared to what average cost would have been had the firm planned to produce that level to begin with. If it didn't, the firm would have chosen that new combination of inputs in the long run. Additional constraints increase cost. The *envelope relationship* is the relationship between long-run and short-run average total costs. It tells us that, at the planned output level, short-run average total cost equals long-run average total cost, but at all other levels of output, short-run average total cost is higher than long-run average total cost. This relationship is shown in Figure 12-2.

The envelope relationship tells us that at the planned output level, short-run average total cost equals long-run average total cost, but at all other levels of output, short-run average total cost is higher than long-run average total cost.

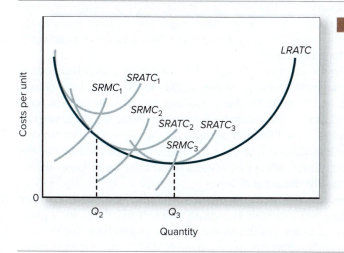

FIGURE 12-2 Envelope of Short-Run Average Total Cost Curves

The long-run average total cost curve is an envelope of the short-run average total cost curves. Each short-run average total cost curve touches the long-run average total cost curve at only one point. (*SR* stands for short run; *LR* stands for long run.)

Why Are Textbooks So Long?

Understanding costs and their structure will help you understand why intro economics textbooks are so long—and why their length is to your advantage.

The majority of the costs of a book are fixed costs in relation to the length of the book. The initial costs in terms of length are about 20 percent of the total price of the book. So increasing the length of the book increases costs slightly. But the longer length allows the writer to include more issues that some professors want and many professors require to even consider using the book. That means that greater length can allow publishers to sell more books, allowing the fixed costs to be divided over more output. This decrease in fixed cost per unit can lower average total cost more than increasing the length of the book increases average total costs per unit. So if the added length increases the number of users, the additional length can lower the average cost of the book.

©McGraw-Hill Education/Mark Dierker, photographer

Length does lower the costs of the book—up to a point. Textbook publishers are continually looking for that point. They direct authors to shorten their books but also to include almost all issues that various groups want. The latter direction—in favor of inclusion—often takes precedence, which is why textbooks are so long.

This doesn't mean that textbooks will continue to become longer. Recently, print economics textbooks have become smaller because students began to complain that the texts were getting too heavy to carry. But even shorter print textbooks are on the way out. E-books are replacing print textbooks and with e-books weight doesn't matter. The role of publishing companies is changing from providing textbooks to providing: (1) large amounts of content, which professors can customize as they see fit; and (2) online learning systems that deliver content in the most efficient manner.

Why it is called an envelope relationship should be clear from the figure. Each short-run average total cost curve touches (is tangent to) the long-run average total cost curve at one, and only one, output level; at all other output levels, short-run average cost exceeds long-run average cost. The long-run average total cost curve is an envelope of short-run average total cost curves.

The intuitive reason why the short-run average total cost curves always lie above or tangent to the long-run average cost curve is simple. In the short run, you have chosen a plant; that plant is fixed, and its costs for that period are part of your average fixed costs. Changes must be made within the confines of that plant. In the long run, you can change everything, choosing the combination of inputs in the most efficient manner. The more options you have to choose from, the lower the costs of production. Put another way: Additional constraints always raise costs (or at least won't lower them). So in the long run, costs must be the same or lower.

Another insight to note about this envelope relationship is the following: When there are economies of scale and you have chosen an efficient plant size for a given output, your short-run average costs will fall as you increase production. Technically, this must be the case because the short-run marginal cost (*SRMC*) curve goes through

Additional constraints always raise costs (or at least won't lower them).

the minimum point of the short-run average total cost (*SRATC*) curve, and the minimum point of the *SRATC* curve is to the right of the efficient level of production in the long run. That means that at output Q_2, $SRMC_2$ has to be below $SRATC_2$ and short-run average total cost has to be falling. Intuitively, what's happening is that at output Q_2, your fixed costs are high. Now demand increases and you increase production. Your average fixed costs are high; your marginal costs are low; and initially the fall in average fixed costs more than offsets the increased marginal cost. Once marginal cost exceeds *SRATC,* that no longer is the case.[1]

Only when the firm is at the minimum point of the long-run average total cost (*LRATC*) curve (at output Q_3) is the $SRATC_3$ curve tangent to the *LRATC* curve at a point where the *SRMC* curve intersects both the curves. For large markets, this point is the least-cost production level of a firm.

Entrepreneurial Activity and the Supply Decision

In this chapter and the preceding one, we have discussed the technical nature of costs and production. In the next chapter, we will formally relate costs of production to the supply of goods. As a bridge between the two chapters, let's consider the entrepreneur, who establishes the relationship between costs and the supply decision, and discuss some of the problems of using cost analysis in the real world.

In thinking about the connection between cost and supply, one fundamental insight is that the revenue received for a good must be greater than the planned cost of producing it. Otherwise why would anyone supply it? The difference between the expected price of a good and the expected average total cost of producing it is the supplier's expected economic profit per unit. It's profit that underlies the dynamics of production in a market economy.

Cost curves do not become supply curves through some magic process. To move from cost to supply, entrepreneurial initiative is needed. An **entrepreneur** is *an individual who sees an opportunity to sell an item at a price higher than the average cost of producing it.* The entrepreneur is the organizer of production and the one who visualizes the demand and convinces the individuals who own the factors of production that they want to produce that good. Businesses work hard at maintaining the entrepreneurial spirit in their employees. The greater the difference between price and average total cost, the greater the entrepreneur's incentive to tackle the organizational problems and supply the good.

The role of the entrepreneur is not easily captured in models but should not be underestimated. Entrepreneurs are the visionaries who turn new technologies into usable goods and services. They are the hidden element of supply that is essential to the continued growth of an economy. While financial reward plays a role in entrepreneurial effort, it is not always the central motivation. People are motivated by many desires, including recognition, fame, and just the pleasure of seeing something done efficiently and well.

The expected price must exceed the average total costs of supplying the good for a good to be supplied.

Web Note 12.2

Entrepreneurship

Q-7 Why is the role of the entrepreneur central to the production process in the economy?

---

[1]The above reasoning depends on the curves being smooth (i.e., having no kinks), a standard assumption of the model. If we give up the smoothness assumption, the *SRATC* curve could be kinked and the *SRMC* curve could be discontinuous. In that case, the *SRATC* curve might be tangent to the *LRATC* curve from the left, but not from the right, and it might not decrease. This would make movement from the long to the short run a discrete jump, whereas the existing model and smoothness assumption make it a smooth continuous movement. So if your intuition doesn't lead you to understand the model, you are probably thinking of a model with different assumptions. You'll be in good company, too. When an economist by the name of Jacob Viner first created this model, his intuition led him to a different result because his intuition was basing the analysis on different assumptions than he was using in his formal model.

In recent years there has been an increase in social entrepreneurship.

In recent years we have seen an increase in social entrepreneurship—where entrepreneurs turn their focus on achieving social, rather than just economic, ends. These social entrepreneurs are blending profit motives with other motives into the charters of the corporations, making them *for-benefit,* not *for-profit,* corporations. Novo Nordisk is an example. It is a pharmaceutical company whose goal is more than just profit. Instead of a profit bottom line, it has what it calls a triple bottom line. It tries to be financially responsible (profitable), socially responsible (valuable to patients and employees), and environmentally responsible (minimal environmental footprint). For-benefit corporations provide a way in which people can join together to simultaneously fulfill their social goals as well as their material welfare goals. Advocates argue that for-benefit corporations will become a new "fourth sector" in the U.S. economy.

Using Cost Analysis in the Real World

All too often, students walk away from an introductory economics course thinking that cost analysis is a relatively easy topic. Memorize the names, shapes, and relationships of the curves, and you're home free. In the textbook model, that's right. In real life, it's not, because actual production processes are marked by economies of scope, learning by doing and technological change, many dimensions, unmeasured costs, joint costs, indivisible costs, uncertainty, asymmetries, and multiple planning and adjustment periods with many different short runs. And this is the short list!

Economies of Scope

Web Note 12.3

Increasing the Scope

The cost of production of one product often depends on what other products a firm is producing. Economists say that in the production of two goods, there are **economies of scope** *when the costs of producing products are interdependent so that it's less costly for a firm to produce one good when it's already producing another.* For example, once a firm has set up a large marketing department to sell cereal, the department might be able to use its expertise in marketing a different product—say, dog food. A firm that sells gasoline can simultaneously use its gas station attendants to sell soda, milk, and incidentals. The minimarts so common along our highways and neighborhood streets developed because gasoline companies became aware of economies of scope.

Economies of scope play an important role in firms' decisions about what combination of goods to produce. They look for both economies of scope and economies of scale. When you read about firms' mergers, think about whether the combination of their products will generate economies of scope. Many otherwise unexplainable mergers between seemingly incompatible firms can be explained by economies of scope.

Q-8 What is the difference between an economy of scope and an economy of scale?

By allowing firms to segment the production process, globalization has made economies of scope even more important to firms in their production decisions. Low-cost labor in other countries has led U.S. firms to locate their manufacturing processes in those countries and to concentrate domestic activities on other aspects of production. As I have stressed throughout this book, production is more than simply manufacturing; the costs of marketing, advertising, and distribution are often larger components of the cost of a good than are manufacturing costs. Each of these involves special knowledge and expertise, and U.S. companies are specializing in the marketing, advertising, and distribution aspects of the production process. By concentrating on those aspects, and by making themselves highly competitive by taking advantage of low-cost manufacturing elsewhere, U.S. firms become more competitive and expand, increasing

Thinking Like a Modern Economist

Social Norms and Production

The traditional economic model presents the production decision as a cost-based decision. The firm calculates the cost of inputs and chooses the lowest-price input. Modern economists believe that these costs are important, but they also believe that a number of other elements come into play. They are working to devise models that incorporate them. One of the most important of those other elements is social norms, and the choices a firm makes so that it fits the social norms of society. Behavioral economist Dan Ariely argues that social norms play a far greater role in a firm's decisions than the traditional economic model includes.

He argues both that firms should include social norms in their decision making and that economists should develop new models of the firms that incorporate social norms in their decision process. He writes:

> If corporations started thinking in terms of social norms, they would realize that these norms build loyalty and—more important— make people want to extend themselves to the degree that corporations need today: to be flexible, concerned, and willing to pitch in. That's what a social relationship delivers.

demand for U.S. labor. Often they expand into new areas, taking advantage of economies of scope in distribution and marketing.

Consider Nike—it produces shoes and sportswear, right? Wrong. It is primarily a U.S. marketing and distribution company; it outsources its production to affiliate companies. Nike expanded its product line from just shoes to a broader line of sports clothing in order to take advantage of economies of scope in its marketing and distribution specialties.

Nike is only one of many examples. The large wage differentials in the global economy are causing firms to continually reinvent themselves—to shed aspects of their business where they do not have a comparative advantage, and to add new businesses where their abilities can achieve synergies and economies of scope.

Learning by Doing and Technological Change

The production terminology that we've been discussing is central to the standard economic models. In the real world, however, other terms and concepts are also important. The production techniques available to real-world firms are constantly changing because of *learning by doing* and *technological change*. These changes occur over time and cannot be accurately predicted.

Unlike events in the standard economic model, all events in the real world are influenced by the past; people learn by doing. But to keep the model simple, learning by doing isn't a part of the traditional economic model. **Learning by doing** simply means that *as we do something, we learn what works and what doesn't, and over time we become more proficient at it.* Practice may not make perfect, but it certainly makes better and more efficient. Many firms estimate that output per unit of input will increase by 1 or 2 percent a year, even if inputs or technologies do not change, as employees learn by doing.

The concept of learning by doing emphasizes the importance of the past in trying to predict performance. Let's say a firm is deciding between two applicants for the job of managing its restaurant. One was a highly successful student but has never run

Q-9 Does learning by doing cause the average cost curve to be downward-sloping?

Many firms estimate worker productivity to grow 1 to 2 percent a year because of learning by doing.

The nature of production has changed considerably in the last 85 years. The picture on the left shows a 1933 production line in which people did the work as the goods moved along the line. The picture on the right shows a modern production line. Robots do much of the work.

a restaurant; the other was an OK student who has run a restaurant that failed. Which one does the firm hire? The answer is unclear. The first applicant may be brighter, but the lack of experience will likely mean that the person won't be hired. Businesses give enormous weight to experience. So this firm may reason that in failing, the second applicant will have learned lessons that make her the better candidate. U.S. firms faced such a choice when they were invited to expand into the new market economies of Eastern Europe in the early 1990s. Should they hire the former communist managers who had failed to produce efficiently, or should they hire the reformers? (Generally they decided on the former communist managers, hoping they had learned by failing.)

Technological change is *an increase in the range of production techniques that leads to more efficient ways of producing goods as well as the production of new and better goods.* That is, technological change offers an increase in the known range of production. For example, at one point automobile tires were made from rubber, clothing was made from cotton and wool, and buildings were made of wood. As a result of technological change, many tires are now made from petroleum distillates, much clothing is made from synthetic fibers (which in turn are made from petroleum distillates), and many buildings are constructed from steel.

The standard long-run model takes technology as a given. From our experience, we know that technological change affects firms' decisions and production. Technological change can fundamentally alter the nature of production costs.

In some industries, technological change is occurring so fast that it overwhelms all other cost issues. The digital electronics industry is a good example. The expectation of technological change has been built into the plans of firms in that industry. The industry has followed Moore's law, which states that the cost of computing will fall by half every 18 months. Indeed, that has happened since the computer was first offered to the mass retail market. With costs falling that fast because of learning by doing and technological change, all other cost components are overwhelmed, and, instead of costs increasing as output rises significantly, as might be predicted because of diseconomies of scale, costs keep going down and we get more powerful products for the same or possibly even a lower price.

Technological change can fundamentally alter the nature of production costs.

Web Note 12.4

Moore's Law

Increased computational power (decreased cost) has affected other industries as well. Technological change has been so dramatic that we no longer talk about changes in a good, but rather the development of entirely new goods and ways of doing things. Consider consumer goods. Telephone landlines have been replaced by cell phones, which in turn have been replaced by smartphones that are effectively computers with voice and messaging capabilities. VCRs have been replaced by wireless video streaming. Music isn't played from CDs as it once was, but is streamed online, chosen by you or for you by programs such as Spotify. You don't buy paper books but download bits and bytes transformed into online multimedia products, which have written components.

Computational technology has also revolutionized automobiles, making them more reliable and of much higher quality per dollar spent. In the 1960s, I could work on my own car, changing the points or modifying the carburetor. Modern cars have no such parts; they have been replaced by electronic parts. When a car isn't running right, its owner must now take it to a garage, which hooks up the car to a diagnostic computer that reports what is wrong. No more lifting the hood. Soon, gas engines will be replaced by much simpler-to-repair electric engines.

It is not only the engine in the car that is changing. So too is the driving. Driverless cars are on the road, and many expect that in the coming decade, they will be the norm. Automobiles have fundamentally changed; they are much more efficient and reliable and their price has fallen because of the introduction of computer technology. As these examples point out, technological change drives costs down and can overwhelm diseconomies of scale, causing prices to fall more and more.

Don't think of technological change as occurring only in high-tech industries. Consider chicken production. The price of chickens has fallen enormously over the past 50 years. Why? Because of technological change. At one time, chickens were raised in farmyards. They walked around, ate scraps and feed, and generally led a chicken's life. Walking around had definite drawbacks—it took space (which cost money); it made standardization (a requirement of taking advantage of economies of scale) difficult, which prevented lowering costs; it used energy, which meant more feed per pound of chicken; and sometimes it led to disease, since chickens walked in their own manure.

The technological change was to put the chickens in wire cages so that the manure falls through to a conveyor belt and is transferred outside. Another conveyor belt feeds the chickens food laced with antibiotics to prevent disease. Soft music is played to keep them calm (they burn fewer calories). Once they reach the proper weight, they are slaughtered in a similar automated process. How the chickens feel about this technological change is not clear. (When I asked them, all they had to say was *cluck*.)

This method of raising chickens will likely be replaced in the next couple of decades by another technological change—genetic engineering that will allow chicken parts to be produced directly from single cells. Only the breasts and drumsticks will be produced (and wings if you live in Buffalo) as what is known as "in vitro meat." All low-efficiency, low-profit-margin parts such as necks, feet, and heads will be eliminated from the "efficient chicken."

In many businesses, the effect of learning by doing and technological change on prices is built into the firm's pricing structure. If they expect their costs to fall with more experience, or if they expect technological advances to lower costs in the future, businesses might bid low for a big order to give themselves the chance to lower their costs through learning by doing or technological change.

Technological change and learning by doing are intricately related. The efficient chicken production we now have did not come about overnight. It occurred over a

Technological change occurs in all industries, not only high-tech industries.

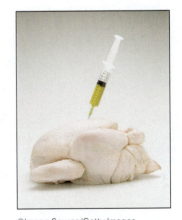

©Image Source/Getty Images

Technological change and learning by doing are intricately related.

20-year period as firms learned how to do it. Chickens respond to Mozart better than to hip-hop. That had to be learned. Similarly, genetic reproduction of chicken parts will evolve as scientists and firms learn more about cloning and DNA.

Many Dimensions

The only dimension of output in the standard model is how much to produce. Many, if not most, decisions that firms make are not the one-dimensional decisions of the traditional model, such as "Should we produce more or less?" They're multidimensional questions such as "Should we change the quality? Should we change the wrapper? Should we improve our shipping speed? Should we increase our inventory?" Each of these questions relates to a different dimension of the production decision and each has its own marginal costs. Thus, there isn't just one marginal cost; there are 10 or 20 of them. Good economic decisions take all relevant margins into account.

The reason that the traditional model is important is that each of these questions can be analyzed by applying the same reasoning used in the traditional model. But you must remember, *in applying the analysis, it's the reasoning, not the specific model, that's important.*

Good economic decisions take all relevant margins into account.

Unmeasured Costs

If asked "In what area of decision making do businesses most often fail to use economic insights?" most economists would say costs. The relevant costs are generally not the costs you'll find in a firm's accounts.

Why the difference? Economists operate conceptually; they include in costs exactly what their theory says they should. They include all opportunity costs. Accountants who have to measure firms' costs in practice and provide the actual dollar figures take a much more pragmatic approach; their concepts of costs must reflect only explicit costs—those costs that are reasonably precisely measurable.

To highlight the distinction, let me review the difference between explicit and implicit costs (discussed in the previous chapter) and introduce another difference—how economists and accountants measure depreciation of capital.

ECONOMISTS INCLUDE OPPORTUNITY COST   First, say that a business produces 1,000 widgets[2] that sell at $4 each for a total revenue of $4,000. To produce these widgets, the business had to buy $1,200 worth of widgetgoo, which the owner has hand-shaped into widgets. An accountant would say that the total cost of producing 1,000 widgets was $1,200 and that the firm's profit was $2,800. That's because an accountant uses explicit costs that can be measured.

Economic profit is different. An economist, looking at that same example, would point out that the accountant's calculation doesn't take into account the time and effort that the owner put into making the widgets. While a person's time involves no explicit cost in money, it does involve an opportunity cost, the forgone income that the owner could have made by spending that time working in another job. If the business takes 400 hours of the person's time and the person could have earned $8 an hour working for someone else, then the person is forgoing $3,200 in income. Economists include

Q-10 As the owner of the firm, Jim pays himself $1,000. All other expenses of the firm add up to $2,000. What would an economist say are the total costs for Jim's firm?

---

[2]What's a widget? It's a wonderful little gadget that's the opposite of a wadget. (No one knows what they look like or what they are used for.) Why discuss widgets? For the same reason that scientists discuss fruit flies—their production process is simple, unlike most real-world production processes.

that implicit cost in their concept of cost. When that implicit cost is included, what looks like a $2,800 profit becomes a $400 economic loss.

ECONOMIC DEPRECIATION VERSUS ACCOUNTING DEPRECIATION   **Depreciation** is *a measure of the decline in value of an asset that occurs over time.* Say a firm buys a machine for $10,000 that's meant to last 10 years. After 1 year, machines like that are in short supply, so instead of falling, its value rises to $12,000. An accountant, looking at the firm's costs that year, would use historical cost (what the machine cost in terms of money actually spent) depreciated at, say, 10 percent per year, so the machine's depreciation for each of its 10 years of existence would be $1,000. An economist would say that since the value of the machine is rising, the machine has no depreciation; it has appreciation and provides a revenue of $2,000 to the firm. The standard model avoids such messy, real-world issues of measuring depreciation costs and instead assumes that all costs are measurable in a single time period.

The Standard Model as a Framework

The standard model can be expanded to include these real-world complications. Modern production is data-intensive, and, as computing and information processing costs fall, cost accounting and production decisions are becoming more and more integrated with the economist's analysis. Just about every industry has industry-specific software that tailors economic analysis to its particular needs. For example, Robert Kaplan of the Harvard Business School argues that cost accounting systems based on traditional concepts of fixed and variable costs lead firms consistently to make the wrong decisions. He argues that in today's manufacturing, direct labor costs have fallen substantially—in many industries to only 2 or 3 percent of the total cost—and overhead costs have risen substantially. This change in costs facing firms requires a much more careful division among types of overhead costs, and a recognition that what should and should not be assigned as a cost to a particular product differs with each decision.

I don't discuss these real-world complications because I suspect that even with its simplifications, the standard model has been more than enough to learn in an introductory course. Learning the standard model, however, provides you with only the rudiments of cost analysis, in the same way that learning the rules of mechanics provides you with only the basics of mechanical engineering. In addition to a knowledge of the laws of mechanics, building a machine requires years of experience. Similarly for economics and cost analysis. Introductory economics provides you with a superb framework for starting to think about real-world cost measurement, but it can't make you an expert cost analyst.

> Despite its limitations, the standard model provides a good framework for cost analysis.

Conclusion

We've come to the end of our discussion of production, cost, and supply. The two chapters we spent on them weren't easy; there's tons of material here, and, quite frankly, it will likely require at least two or three reads and careful attention to your professor's lecture before your mind can absorb it. So if you're planning to sleep through a lecture, the ones on these chapters aren't the ones for that.

These chapters will provide a framework for considering costs, and as long as you remember that it is only a framework, it will allow you to get into interesting real-world issues. But you've got to know the basics to truly understand those issues. So, now that you've come to the end of these two chapters, unless you really feel comfortable with the analysis, it's probably time to review them from the beginning. (Sorry, but remember, there ain't no such thing as a free lunch.)

Summary

- An economically efficient production process must be technically efficient, but a technically efficient process need not be economically efficient. (*LO12-1*)

- The long-run average total cost curve is U-shaped. Economies of scale initially cause average total cost to decrease; diseconomies eventually cause average total cost to increase. (*LO12-2*)

- Production is a social, as well as a technical, phenomenon; that's why concepts like team spirit are important—and that's why diseconomies of scale occur. (*LO12-2*)

- The marginal cost and short-run average cost curves slope upward because of diminishing marginal productivity. The long-run average cost curve slopes upward because of diseconomies of scale. (*LO12-2*)

- There is an envelope relationship between short-run average cost curves and long-run average cost curves. The short-run average cost curves are always above the long-run average cost curve. (*LO12-2*)

- An entrepreneur is an individual who sees an opportunity to sell an item at a price higher than the average cost of producing it. (*LO12-3*)

- Once we start applying cost analysis to the real world, we must include a variety of other dimensions of costs that the traditional model does not cover. (*LO12-4*)

- Costs in the real world are affected by economies of scope, learning by doing and technological change, the many dimensions to output, and unmeasured costs such as opportunity costs. (*LO12-4*)

Key Terms

constant returns to scale	economically efficient	indivisible setup cost	monitoring costs
depreciation	economies of scale	learning by doing	team spirit
diseconomies of scale	economies of scope	minimum efficient level of production	technical efficiency
	entrepreneur		technological change

Questions and Exercises ■ connect

1. What is the difference between technical efficiency and economic efficiency? (*LO12-1*)

2. One farmer can grow 1,000 bushels of corn on 1 acre of land with 200 hours of labor and 20 pounds of seed. Another farmer can grow 1,000 bushels of corn on 1 acre of land with 100 hours of labor and 20 pounds of seed. (*LO12-1*)
   a. Could both methods be technically efficient?
   b. Is it possible that both of these production processes are economically efficient?

3. A dressmaker can sew 800 garments with 160 bolts of fabric and 3,000 hours of labor. Another dressmaker can sew 800 garments with 200 bolts of fabric and

   2,000 hours of identical labor. Fabric costs $80 a bolt and labor costs $10 an hour. (*LO12-1*)
   a. Is it possible for both methods to be technically efficient? Why or why not?
   b. Is it possible for both methods to be economically efficient? Why or why not?

4. A student has just written on an exam that, in the long run, fixed cost will make the average total cost curve slope downward. Why will the professor mark it incorrect? (*LO12-2*)

5. Why could diseconomies of scale never occur if production relationships were only technical relationships? (*LO12-2*)

6. In the early 2000s carmakers began to design vehicles' chassis, engines, and transmissions so that different models could be produced on the same assembly line. Within the first year of implementing the plan, Ford cut production costs by $240 per car. (*LO12-2*)
   a. What cost concept was Ford taking advantage of to produce its savings?
   b. What effect did the plan likely have on Ford's short-run average total cost curve?

7. Draw a long-run average total cost curve. (*LO12-2*)
   a. Why does it slope downward initially?
   b. Why does it eventually slope upward?
   c. How would your answers to *a* and *b* differ if you had drawn a short-run cost curve?
   d. How large is the fixed-cost component of the long-run cost curve?
   e. If there were constant returns to scale everywhere, what would the long-run cost curve look like?

8. Sea lions have been depleting the stock of steelhead trout. One idea to scare sea lions off the Washington State coast is to launch fake killer whales, predators of sea lions. The cost of making the first whale is $16,000—$5,000 for materials and $11,000 for the mold. The mold can be reused to make additional whales, so additional whales would cost $5,000 apiece. (*LO12-2*)
   a. Make a table showing the total cost and average total cost of producing 1 to 10 fake killer whales.
   b. Does production of fake whales exhibit diseconomies of scale, economies of scale, or constant returns to scale?

   c. What is the fixed cost of producing fake whales?
   d. What is the variable cost of producing fake whales?

9. Why are long-run costs always less than or equal to short-run costs? (*LO12-2*)

10. Draw a short-run marginal cost curve, short-run average cost curve, and long-run average total cost curve for an efficient firm producing where there are diseconomies of scale. (*LO12-2*)

11. Where along the long-run average total cost curve will an efficient firm try to produce in the long run? (*LO12-2*)

12. What is the role of the entrepreneur in translating cost of production into supply? (*LO12-3*)

13. Your average total cost is $30; the price you receive for the good is $15. Should you keep on producing the good? Why? (*LO12-3*)

14. True or false? Because entrepreneurs are motivated by opportunities to sell an item at a price higher than the average cost of producing it, they do not start for-benefit firms. Explain your answer. (*LO12-3*)

15. A student has just written on an exam that technological change will mean that the cost curve is downward-sloping. Why did the teacher mark it wrong? (*LO12-4*)

16. How does learning by doing affect average total costs? (*LO12-4*)

17. If a firm is experiencing learning by doing, what is likely true about the long-run average total cost curve? Explain your answer. (*LO12-4*)

Questions from Alternative Perspectives

1. The text presents costs as if a firm could look them up in a book.
   a. How do you believe a firm's true costs are revealed?
   b. Is this an optimal method of finding out costs? (*Austrian*)

2. The chapter points out that "businesses give enormous weight to experience," or learning by doing. Empirical evidence suggests that, in surveys and applications, women tend to report the nature of their jobs in far less detail than do men.
   a. How might this contribute to differences in "experience" between men and women?
   b. In what other ways might women's real-world experiences be undervalued when they go to look for jobs? (*Feminist*)

3. Adam Smith argued that at birth most people were similarly talented, and that differences in individual abilities, and hence productivity, are largely the effect of the division of labor, not its cause. What implications does that insight have for economic policy, and for the way we

should treat others who receive less income than we do? (*Religious*)

4. Firms have an incentive to "externalize" their costs, that is, to make others face the opportunity costs of their actions while firms reduce their own accounting costs.
   a. Give some examples of firms doing this.
   b. What implications for policy does it have? (*Institutionalist*)

5. A major survey conducted by economists David Levine and Laura Tyson found that "in most reported cases the introduction of substantive shop floor participation (job redesign and participatory work groups) leads to some combination of an increase in satisfaction, commitment, quality and productivity, and a reduction in turnover and absenteeism." Despite that evidence of real cost savings of participatory work groups, only a few U.S. corporate employers (for instance, Xerox and Scott Paper) have taken this high road to labor relations, while many continue to pursue the low road Walmart-like approach to cost saving. Why is that? (*Radical*)

Issues to Ponder

1. A pair of shoes that wholesales for $28.79 has approximately the following costs:

Manufacturing labor	$ 2.25
Materials	4.95
Factory overhead, operating expenses, and profit	8.50
Sales costs	4.50
Advertising	2.93
Research and development	2.00
Interest	.33
Net income to producer	3.33
Total	$28.79

   a. Which of these costs would likely be a variable cost?
   b. Which would likely be a fixed cost?
   c. If output were to rise, what would likely happen to average total costs? Why?

2. What inputs do you use in studying this book? What would the long-run average total cost and marginal cost curves for studying look like? Why?

3. If you were describing the marginal cost of an additional car driving on a road, what costs would you look at? What is the likely shape of the marginal cost curve?

4. A major issue of contention at many colleges concerns the cost of meals that is rebated when a student does not sign up for the meal plan. The administration usually says that it should rebate only the marginal cost of the food alone, which it calculates at, say, $1.25 per meal. Students say that the marginal cost should include more costs, such as the saved space from fewer students using the facilities and the reduced labor expenses on food preparation. This can raise the marginal cost to $6.00.
   a. Who is correct, the administration or the students?
   b. How might your answer to *a* differ if this argument were being conducted in the planning stage, before the dining hall is built?
   c. If you accept the $1.25 figure of a person not eating, how could you justify using a higher figure of about $6.00 for the cost of feeding a guest at the dining hall, as many schools do?

5. When economist Jacob Viner first developed the envelope relationship, he told his draftsman to make sure that all the marginal cost curves went through both (1) the minimum point of the short-run average cost curve and (2) the point where the short-run average total cost curve was tangent to the long-run average total cost curve. The draftsman told him it couldn't be done. Viner told him to do it anyhow. Why was the draftsman right?

6. The cost of setting up a steel mill is enormous. For example, a Gary, Indiana, hot-strip mill would cost an estimated $1.5 billion to build. Using this information and the cost concepts from the chapter, explain the following quotation: "To make operations even marginally profitable, big steelmakers must run full-out. It's like a car that is more efficient at 55 miles an hour than in stop-and-go traffic at 25."

Answers to Margin Questions

1. True. Since an economically efficient method of production is that method that produces a given level of output at the lowest possible cost, it also must use as few inputs as possible. It is also technically efficient. (*LO12-1*)

2. Bangladesh uses more labor-intensive techniques than does the United States because the price of labor is much lower in Bangladesh relative to the United States. Production in both countries is economically efficient. (*LO12-1*)

3. Larger production runs are generally cheaper per unit than smaller production runs because of indivisible setup costs, which do not vary with the size of the run. (*LO12-2*)

4. Because the same technical process could be used over and over again at the same cost, the long-run average cost curve would never become upward-sloping. (*LO12-2*)

5. The short-run average cost curve initially slopes downward because of increasing marginal productivity and large average fixed costs, and then begins sloping upward because of diminishing marginal productivity, giving it a U shape. (*LO12-2*)

6. The long-run average total cost curve is generally considered to be U-shaped because initially there are economies of scale and, for large amounts of production, there are diseconomies of scale. (*LO12-2*)

7. Economic activity does not just happen. Some dynamic, driven individual must instigate production. That dynamic individual is called an entrepreneur. (*LO12-3*)

8. Economies of scale are economies that occur because of increases in the amount of one good a firm is producing. Economies of scope occur when producing different types of goods lowers the cost of each of those goods. (*LO12-4*)

9. No. Learning by doing causes a shift in the cost curve because it is a change in the technical characteristics of production. It does not cause the cost curve to be downward-sloping—it causes it to shift downward. *(LO12-4)*

10. An economist would say that he doesn't know what total cost is without knowing what Jim could have earned if he had undertaken another activity instead of running his business. Just because he paid himself $1,000 doesn't mean that $1,000 is his opportunity cost. *(LO12-4)*

APPENDIX

Isocost/Isoquant Analysis

In the long run, a firm can vary more than one factor of production. One of the decisions firms face in this long run is which combination of factors of production to use. Economic efficiency involves choosing those factors to minimize the cost of production.

In analyzing this choice of which combination of factors to use, economists have developed a graphical technique called *isocost/isoquant analysis*. In this technique, the analyst creates a graph placing one factor of production, say labor, on one axis and another factor, say machines, on the other axis, as I have done in Figure A12-1. Any point on that graph represents a combination of machines and labor that can produce a certain amount of output, say 8 pairs of earrings. For example, point *A* represents 3 machines and 4 units of labor being used to produce 8 pairs of earrings. Any point in the blue shaded area represents more of one or both factors and any point in the brown shaded area represents less of one or both factors.

The Isoquant Curve

The firm's problem is to figure out how to produce its output—let's say it has chosen an output of 60 pairs of earrings—at as low a cost as possible. That means somehow we must show graphically the combinations of machines and labor that can produce 60 pairs of earrings as cheaply as possible. We do so with what is called an isoquant curve. An **isoquant curve** is *a curve that represents combinations of factors of production that result in equal amounts of output*. (*Isoquant* is a big name for an "equal quantity.") At all points on an isoquant curve, the firm can produce the same amount of output. So, given a level of output, a firm can find out what combinations of the factors of production will produce that output. Suppose a firm can produce 60 pairs of earrings with the following combination of labor and machines:

	Labor	Machines	Pairs of Earrings
A	3	20	60
B	4	15	60
C	6	10	60
D	10	6	60
E	15	4	60
F	20	3	60

This table shows the technical limits of production. It shows that the firm can use, for example, 3 units of labor and 20 machines or 20 units of labor and 3 machines to produce 60 pairs of earrings. The isoquant curve is a graphical representation of the table. I show the isoquant curve for producing 60 pairs in Figure A12-2. Points *A* to *F* represent rows A to F in the table.

To be sure you understand it, let's consider some points on the curve. Let's start at point *A*. At point *A*, the

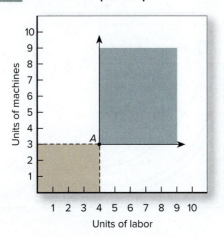

FIGURE A12-1   The Isocost/Isoquant Graph

FIGURE A12-2   **Isoquant Curve for 60 Pairs of Earrings**

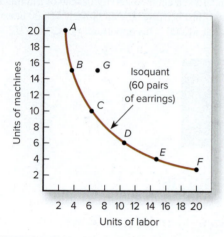

firm is producing 60 pairs of earrings using 20 machines and 3 workers. If the firm wants to reduce the number of machines by 5, it must increase the number of units of labor by 1 to keep output constant. Doing so moves the firm to point *B*. At point *B*, the firm is also producing 60 pairs of earrings, but is doing it with 15 machines and 4 workers. Alternatively, if the firm were at point *D,* and it wants to reduce the number of machines from 6 to 4, it must increase the number of units of labor from 10 to 15 to keep output constant at 60. At any point on this isoquant curve, the firm is being technically efficient—it is using as few resources as possible to produce 60 pairs of earrings. It would never want to produce 60 at a point like *G* because that point uses more inputs. It is a technically inefficient method of production.

The numbers in the production table and the shape of the curve were not chosen randomly. They were chosen to be consistent with the law of diminishing marginal productivity, which means the curve is bowed inward. That is because as the firm increases the use of one factor more and more, it must use fewer and fewer units of the other factor to keep output constant. This reflects the technical considerations embodied in the law of diminishing marginal productivity. Thus, the chosen numbers tell us that if a firm wants to keep output constant, as it adds more and more of one factor (and less of the other factor), it has to use relatively more of that factor. For example, initially it might add 1 machine to replace 1 worker, holding output constant. If it continues, it will have to use 1.5 machines, then 2 machines, and so on.

The rate at which one factor must be added to compensate for the loss of another factor, to keep output constant, is called the **marginal rate of substitution.** To say

that there is diminishing marginal productivity is to say that there is a diminishing marginal rate of substitution. It is because the table assumes a diminishing marginal rate of substitution that the isoquant curve is bowed inward.

Graphically, the slope of the isoquant curve is the marginal rate of substitution. To be exact, the absolute value of the slope at a point on the isoquant curve equals the ratio of the marginal productivity of labor to the marginal productivity of machines:

$$|\text{Slope}| = \frac{MP_{\text{labor}}}{MP_{\text{machines}}} = \begin{matrix}\text{Marginal} \\ \text{rate of} \\ \text{substitution}\end{matrix}$$

With this equation, you can really see why the isoquant is downward-sloping. As the firm moves from point *A* to point *F,* it is using more labor and fewer machines. Because of the law of diminishing marginal productivity, as the firm moves from *A* to *F,* the marginal productivity of labor decreases and the marginal productivity of machines increases. The slope of the isoquant falls since the marginal rate of substitution is decreasing.

Let's consider a specific example. Say in Figure A12-2 the firm is producing at point *B*. If it cuts its input by 5 machines but also wants to keep output constant, it must increase labor by 2 (move from point *B* to point *C*). So the marginal rate of substitution of labor for machines between points *B* and *C* must be 5/2, or 2.5.

The firm can complete this exercise for many different levels of output. Doing so will result in an **isoquant map,** *a set of isoquant curves that shows technically efficient combinations of inputs that can produce different levels of output.* Such a map for output levels of 40, 60, and 100 is shown in Figure A12-3.

Each curve represents a different level of output. Isoquant I is the lowest level of output, 40, and isoquant III is the highest level of output. When a firm chooses

FIGURE A12-3   **An Isoquant Map**

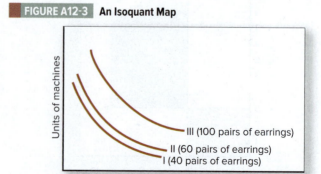

an output level, it is choosing one of those isoquants. The chosen isoquant represents the technically efficient combinations of resources that can produce the desired output.

The Isocost Line

So far I have only talked about technical efficiency. To move to economic efficiency, we have to bring in the costs of production. We do so with the **isocost line**—*a line that represents alternative combinations of factors of production that have the same costs.* (*Isocost* is a fancy name for "equal cost.") Each point on the isocost line represents a combination of factors of production that, in total, cost the firm an equal amount.

To draw the isocost line, you must know the cost per unit of each input as well as the amount the firm has chosen to spend on production. Say labor costs $5 a unit, machinery costs $3 a unit, and the firm has chosen to spend $60. What is the greatest number of earrings it can produce with that $60? To answer that question, we need to create a curve representing the various amounts of inputs a firm can get with that $60. We do so in the following manner. Say the firm decides to spend the entire $60 on labor. Since labor costs $5 a unit, it can buy 12 units of labor. This alternative is represented by point *A* in Figure A12-4.

Alternatively, since machines cost $3 a unit, if the firm chooses to spend all of the $60 on machines, it can buy 20 machines (point *B* in Figure A12-4). This gives us two points on the isocost curve. Of course, the assumption of diminishing marginal rates of substitution makes it highly unlikely that the firm would want to produce at either of these points. Instead, it would likely use some

combination of inputs. But these extreme points are useful nonetheless because by connecting them (the line that goes from *A* to *B* in Figure A12-4), we can see the various combinations of inputs that also cost $60.

To see that this is indeed the case, say the firm starts with 20 machines and no labor. If the firm wants to use some combination of labor and machinery, it can give up some machines and use the money it saves by using fewer machines to purchase units of labor. Let's say it gives up 5 machines, leaving it with 15. That means it has $15 to spend on labor, for which it can buy 3 units of labor. That means 15 machines and 3 units of labor is another combination of labor and machines that cost the firm $60. This means that point *C* is also a point on the isocost line. You can continue with this exercise to prove to yourself that the line connecting points *A* and *B* does represent various combinations of labor and machinery the firm can buy with $60. Thus, the line connecting *A* and *B* is the $60 isocost line.

To see that you understand the isocost line, it is useful to go through a couple of examples that would make it shift. For example, what would happen to the isocost line if the firm chooses to increase its spending on production to $90? To see the effect, we go through the same exercise as before: If it spent it all on labor, it could buy 18 units of labor. If it spent it all on machines, it could buy 30 units of machinery. Connecting these points will give us a curve to the right of and parallel to the original curve. It has the same slope because the relative prices of the factors of production, which determine the slope, have not changed.

Now ask yourself, What happens to the isocost line if the price of labor rises to $10 a unit? If you said the isocost curve becomes steeper, shifting along the labor axis to point *D* while remaining anchored along the machinery axis until the slope is $-10/3$, you've got it. In general, the absolute value of the slope of the isocost curve is the ratio of the price of the factor of production on the *x*-axis to the price of the factor of production on the *y*-axis. That means that as the price of a factor rises, the endpoint of the isocost curve shifts in on the axis on which that factor is measured.

Choosing the Economically Efficient Point of Production

Now let's move on to a consideration of the economically efficient combination of resources to produce 60 pairs of earrings with $60. To do that, we must put the isoquant cost curve from Figure A12-2 and the isocost curve from Figure A12-4 together. We do so in Figure A12-5.

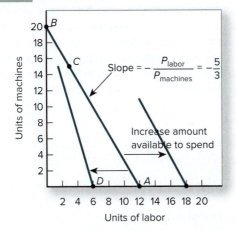

FIGURE A12-4 **Isocost Curves**

Units of machines (y-axis): 2, 4, 6, 8, 10, 12, 14, 16, 18, 20
Units of labor (x-axis): 2, 4, 6, 8, 10, 12, 14, 16, 18, 20

$$\text{Slope} = -\frac{P_{labor}}{P_{machines}} = -\frac{5}{3}$$

Increase amount available to spend

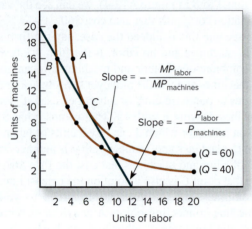

The problem for the firm is to produce as many pairs of earrings as possible with the $60 it has to spend. Or, put another way, given a level of production it has chosen, it wants to produce at the least-cost combination of the factors of production.

Let's now find the least-cost combination of inputs to produce 60 pairs of earrings. Let's say that, initially, the firm chooses point A on its isoquant curve—that's at 15 machines and 4 workers. That produces 60 pairs of earrings, but has a cost of $45 + $20 = $65. The firm can't produce 60 pairs of earrings unless it is willing to spend more than $60. If it fires a worker to bring its cost in line, moving it to point B, it moves down to a lower isoquant—it is producing only 40 pairs.

If the firm has a less-than-competent manager, that manager will conclude that you can't produce 60 for $60. But say the firm has an efficient manager—one who has taken introductory economics. As opposed to *reducing* the number of workers as the other manager did, she *increases* the number of workers to 6 and reduces the number of machines to 10. Doing so still produces 60 pairs of earrings, since C is a point on the isoquant curve, but the strategy reduces the cost from $65 at point A to $60 (10 machines at $3 = $30 and 6 workers at

$5 = $30). So she is producing 60 pairs of earrings at a cost of $60. She is operating at the economically efficient point—point C.

Let's talk about the characteristics of point C. Point C is the point where the isoquant curve is tangent to the isocost curve—the point at which the slope of the isoquant curve $(-MP_L/MP_M)$ equals the slope of the isocost curve $(-P_L/P_M)$. That is, $-MP_L/MP_M = -P_L/P_M$. This can be rewritten as

$$MP_L/P_L = MP_M/P_M$$

What this equation says is that when the additional output per dollar spent on labor equals the additional output per dollar spent on machines, the firm is operating efficiently. It makes sense. If the additional output per dollar spent on labor exceeded the additional output per dollar spent on machines, the firm would do better by increasing its use of labor and decreasing its use of machines.

Point C represents the combination of labor and machines that will result in the highest output given the isocost curve facing the firm. To put it in technical terms, the firm is operating at an economically efficient point where the marginal rate of substitution equals the ratio of the factor prices. Any point other than C on the isocost curve will cost $60 but produce fewer than 60 pairs of earrings. Any other point than C on the isoquant curve will produce 60 pairs of earrings but cost more than $60. Only C is the economically efficient point given the factor costs.

To see that you understand the analysis, say that the price of labor falls to $3 and you still want to produce 60. What will happen to the amount of labor and machines you hire? Alternatively, say that the price of machines rises to $5 and you want to spend only $60. What will happen to the amount of labor and machines you hire?

If your answers are (1) you hire more workers and fewer machines and (2) you reduce production using fewer machines and, maybe, less labor, you've got the analyses down. If you didn't give those answers, I suggest rereading this appendix, if it is to be on the exam, and working through the questions and exercises.

Key Terms

isocost line   isoquant map   marginal rate of substitution
isoquant curve

Questions and Exercises

1. What happens to the marginal rate of substitution as a firm increases the use of one input, keeping output constant? What accounts for this?

2. Draw an isocost curve for a firm that has $100 to spend on producing jeans. Input includes labor and materials. Labor costs $8 and materials cost $4 a unit. How does each of the following affect the isocost curve? Show your answer graphically.
   a. Production budget doubles.
   b. Cost of materials rises to $10 a unit.
   c. Cost of labor and materials each rises by 25 percent.

3. Show, using isocost/isoquant analysis, how firms in the United States use relatively less labor and relatively more land than Japan for the production of similar goods, yet both are behaving with economic efficiency.

4. Demonstrate the difference between economic efficiency and technical efficiency, using isocost/isoquant analysis.

5. Draw a hypothetical isocost curve and an isoquant curve tangent to the isocost curve. Label the combination of inputs that represents an economically efficient use of resources.
   a. How does a technological innovation affect your analysis?
   b. How does the increase in the price of the input on the x-axis affect your analysis?

6. Show graphically the analysis of the example in Figure A12-5 if the price of labor falls to $3. Demonstrate that the firm can increase production given the same budget.

7. Show graphically the analysis of the example in Figure A12-5 if the price of machines rises to $5. Demonstrate that the firm must reduce production if it keeps the same budget.

Perfect Competition

> There's no resting place for an enterprise in
> a competitive economy.
>
> —Alfred P. Sloan

©Bart Sadowski/Shutterstock

The concept *competition* is used in two ways in economics. One way is as a process. *Competition as a process* is a rivalry among firms and is prevalent throughout our economy. It involves one firm trying to figure out how to take away market share from another firm. An example is my publishing firm giving me a contract to write a great book like this in order for the firm to take market share away from other publishing firms that are also selling economics text-books. The other use of *competition* is as a *perfectly competitive market structure*. It is this use that is the subject of this chapter.

Perfect Competition as a Reference Point

Although perfect competition has highly restrictive assumptions, it provides us with a reference point for thinking about various market structures and competitive processes. Why is such a reference point important? Think of the following analogy.

In physics when you study the laws of gravity, you initially study what would happen in a vacuum. Perfect vacuums don't exist, but talking about what would happen if you dropped an object in a perfect vacuum makes the analysis easier. So too with economics. Our equivalent of a perfect vacuum is perfect competition. In perfect competition, the invisible hand of the market operates unimpeded. In this chapter, we'll consider how perfectly competitive markets work and see how to apply the cost analysis developed in the previous two chapters.

Conditions for Perfect Competition

A **perfectly competitive market** is *a market in which economic forces operate unimpeded.* For a market to be called *perfectly competitive,* it must meet some stringent conditions. Some of them are: Both buyers and sellers are price takers. The number of firms is large. There are no barriers to entry. Firms' products are identical. There is complete information. Selling firms are profit-maximizing entrepreneurial firms. These and other similar conditions are needed to ensure that economic forces operate instantaneously and are unimpeded by political and social forces.

For perfect competition:
1. Both buyers and sellers are price takers.
2. There are no barriers to entry.
3. Firms' products are identical.

To give you a sense of these conditions, let's consider some of these conditions a bit more carefully.

1. *Both buyers and sellers are price takers.* A **price taker** is *a firm or individual who takes the price determined by market supply and demand as given.* When you buy toothpaste, you go to the store and find that the price of toothpaste is, say, $2.33 for the medium-size tube; you're a price taker. The firm, however, is a price maker since it set the price at $2.33. So even though the toothpaste industry is highly competitive, it's not a perfectly competitive market. In a perfectly competitive market, market supply and demand determine the price; both firms and consumers take the market price as given.

2. *There are no barriers to entry.* **Barriers to entry** are *social, political, or economic impediments that prevent firms from entering a market.* They might be legal barriers such as patents for products or processes. Barriers might be technological, such as when the minimum efficient level of production allows only one firm to produce at the lowest average total cost. Or barriers might be created by social forces, such as when bankers will lend only to individuals with specific racial characteristics. Perfect competition can have no barriers to entry.

3. *Firms' products are identical.* This requirement means that each firm's output is indistinguishable from any other firm's output. Corn bought by the bushel is relatively homogeneous. One kernel is indistinguishable from any other kernel. In contrast, you can buy 30 different brands of many goods—soft drinks, for instance: Pepsi, Coke, 7UP, and so on. They are all slightly different from one another and thus not identical.

Generally these conditions aren't met and firms are less than perfectly competitive.

Q-1 Why is the assumption of no barriers to entry important for the existence of perfect competition?

Web Note 13.1

Barriers to Entry

Demand Curves for the Firm and the Industry

The market demand curve is downward-sloping, but each individual firm in a competitive industry is so small that it perceives that its actions will not affect the price it can get for its product. Price is the same no matter how much the firm produces. Think of an individual firm's actions as removing one piece of sand from a beach. Does that lower the level of the beach? For all practical, and even most impractical, purposes, we can assume it doesn't. Similarly for a perfectly competitive firm. That is why we consider the demand curve facing the firm to be perfectly elastic (horizontal).

The price the firm can get is determined by the market, and the competitive firm takes the market price as given. This difference in perception is extremely important. It means that firms will increase their output in response to an increase in market demand even though that increase in output will cause the market price to fall and can

Q-2 How can the demand curve for the market be downward-sloping but the demand curve for a competitive firm be perfectly elastic?

make all firms collectively worse off. But since, by the assumptions of perfect competition, they don't act collectively, each firm follows its self-interest. Let's now consider that self-interest in more detail.

The Profit-Maximizing Level of Output

The goal of a firm is assumed to be maximizing profits—to get as much for itself as possible. So when it decides what quantity to produce, it will continually ask, "How will profit change with changes in the quantity I produce?" Since profit is the difference between total revenue and total cost, what happens to profit in response to a change in output is determined by **marginal revenue (MR),** *the change in total revenue associated with a change in quantity,* and **marginal cost (MC),** *the change in total cost associated with a change in quantity.* That's why marginal revenue and marginal cost are key concepts in determining the profit-maximizing or loss-minimizing level of output of any firm.

To determine the profit-maximizing output, all you need to know is MC and MR. Firms maximize profits where MC = MR.

To emphasize the importance of *MR* and *MC,* those are the only cost and revenue figures shown in Figure 13-1. Notice that we don't illustrate profit at all. We'll calculate profit later. All we want to determine now is the profit-maximizing level of output. To do this, you need only know *MC* and *MR.* Specifically, a firm maximizes profit when *MC = MR.* To see why, let's look at *MC* and *MR* more closely.

Marginal Revenue

For a competitive firm, MR = P.

Let's first consider marginal revenue. Since a perfect competitor accepts the market price as given, marginal revenue is simply the market price. In the example shown in Figure 13-1, if the firm increases output from 2 to 3, its revenue rises by $35 (from $70 to $105). So its marginal revenue is $35, the price of the good. Since at a price of $35 it can sell as much as it wants, for a competitive firm, *MR = P.* Marginal revenue is given in column 1 of Figure 13-1(a). As you can see, *MR* equals $35 for all levels of output.

FIGURE 13-1 (A AND B) **Marginal Cost, Marginal Revenue, and Price**

The profit-maximizing output for a firm occurs where marginal cost equals marginal revenue. Since for a competitive firm *P = MR,* its profit-maximizing output is where *MC = P.* At any other output, it is forgoing profit.

(1) Price = MR	(2) Quantity Produced	(3) Marginal Cost
$35.00	0	
35.00	1	$28.00
35.00	2	20.00
35.00	3	16.00
35.00	4	14.00
35.00	5	12.00
35.00	6	17.00
35.00	7	22.00
35.00	8	30.00
35.00	9	40.00
35.00	10	54.00

(a) MC/Price Table

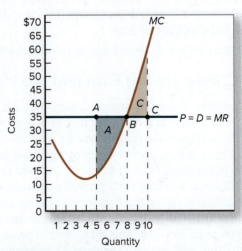

(b) MC/Price Graph

The Internet and the Perfectly Competitive Model

As I have emphasized throughout the book, one of the most difficult skills to learn involves applying the models to the real world—determining whether the model captures sufficient aspects of reality so that it can be used as a framework for looking at a problem. This is made more difficult by rapidly changing technologies. Consider the Internet and the perfectly competitive model. The Internet is eliminating, or at least significantly reducing, the spatial dimension of competition, allowing individuals and firms to compete globally rather than just locally. When you see a price on the Internet, you don't care where the supplier is physically located (as long as you do not have to pay shipping fees). Thus, the Internet is making the economy more closely resemble the perfectly competitive model. With the Internet, entry and exit are much easier than in traditional brick-and-mortar business, making markets more like perfectly competitive markets.

But even as the Internet makes the economy more like a perfectly competitive market in the spatial dimension, it makes it less like it in other dimensions. The competitive

©Jonathan Weiss/Shutterstock

model assumes consumers and producers have complete information. While that has never been true as long as information was equally incomplete to all, economists felt that the model was often close enough. With the Internet that assumption is more problematic. Credit cards, frequent-buyer cards, and Internet programs mine online search and buying patterns and provide producers huge amounts of information about consumers. Using data analytics and deep-learning algorithms, large producers and firms such as Amazon that provide platforms for markets are gaining all types of information about consumers and producers. Data analytic specialists tell me that they know what people will do sooner than people know themselves. They can predict what you will do, and how you will react to different offers. Such data allow firms to price-discriminate—charging different prices to different people, making the economy less like the perfectly competitive model. On balance, most economists see the economy as becoming more competitive, but see the unequal distribution of information as an issue to keep an eye on.

Marginal Cost

Now let's move on to marginal cost. I'll be brief since I discussed marginal cost in detail in an earlier chapter. Marginal cost is the change in total cost that accompanies a change in output. Figure 13-1(a) shows marginal cost in column 3. Notice that initially in this example, marginal cost is falling, but after the fifth unit of output, it's increasing. This is consistent with our discussion in earlier chapters.

Notice also that the marginal cost figures are given for movements from one quantity to another. That's because marginal concepts tell us what happens when there's a change in something, so marginal concepts are best defined between numbers. The numbers in column 3 are the marginal costs. So the marginal cost of increasing output from 1 to 2 is $20, and the marginal cost of increasing output from 2 to 3 is $16. The marginal cost right at 2 (which the marginal cost graph shows) would be between $20 and $16, at approximately $18.

Profit Maximization: $MC = MR$

As I noted above, to maximize profit, a firm should produce where marginal cost equals marginal revenue. Looking at Figure 13-1(b), we see that a firm following that rule will produce at an output of 8, where $MC = MR = \$35$. Now let me try to convince you that 8 is indeed the profit-maximizing output. To do so, let's consider three different possible quantities the firm might look at.

Q-3 What are the two things you must know to determine the profit-maximizing output?

Let's say that initially the firm decides to produce 5 widgets, placing it at point A in Figure 13-1(b). The firm receives $35 for each widget, so the marginal revenue for producing the fifth unit is $35. The marginal cost of doing so is $12. By producing 5 rather than 4 units, profit has increased by $23 ($35 − $12). So it makes sense to have produced 5 units rather than 4. Notice that we don't know total profit, just the change in total profit as we change production levels. Should the firm increase production to 6? Again, marginal revenue is $35. This time marginal cost is $17. Profit increases by $18. Again it makes sense to increase production. As long as $MC < MR$, it makes sense to increase production. The blue shaded area (A) represents the entire increase in profit the firm can get by increasing output beyond 5 units.

Now let's say that the firm decides to produce 10 widgets, placing it at point C. Here the firm gets $35 for each widget. The marginal cost of producing that 10th unit is $54. So, $MC > MR$. If the firm decreases production by 1 unit, its cost decreases by $54 and its revenue decreases by $35. Profit increases by $19 ($54 − $35 = $19), so at point C, it makes sense to decrease output. This reasoning holds true as long as the marginal cost is above the marginal revenue. The reddish shaded area (C) represents the increase in profits the firm can get by decreasing output.

At point B (output = 8) the firm gets $35 for each widget, and its marginal cost is $35, as you can see in Figure 13-1(b). The marginal cost of increasing output by 1 unit is $40 and the marginal revenue of selling 1 more unit is $35, so its profit falls by $5. If the firm decreases output by 1 unit, its MC is $30 and its MR is $35, so its profit falls by $5. Either increasing or decreasing production will decrease profit, so at point B, an output of 8, the firm is maximizing profit.

Profit-maximizing condition for a competitive firm: $MC = MR = P$.

Since MR is just market price, we can state the **profit-maximizing condition** of a competitive firm as $MC = MR = P$. So, if $MR > MC$, increase production; if $MR < MC$, decrease production. If $MR = MC$, the firm is maximizing profit.

If marginal revenue does not equal marginal cost, a firm can increase profit by changing output.

You should commit this profit-maximizing condition to memory. You should also be sure that you understand the intuition behind it. If marginal revenue isn't equal to marginal cost, a firm obviously can increase profit by changing output. If that isn't obvious, the marginal benefit of an additional hour of thinking about this condition will exceed the marginal cost (whatever it is), meaning that you should... right, you guessed it . . . study some more.

The Marginal Cost Curve Is the Supply Curve

Now let's consider again the definition of the supply curve as a schedule of quantities of goods that will be offered to the market at various prices. Notice that the upward-sloping portion of the marginal cost curve fits that definition. It tells how much the firm will supply at a given price. Figure 13-2 shows the various quantities the firm will supply at different market prices beginning at the upward-sloping portion at point A. If the price is $35, we showed that the firm would supply 8 (point C). If the price had been $19.50, the firm would have supplied 6 (point B); if the price had been $61, the firm would have supplied 10 (point D). Because the marginal cost curve tells us how much of a produced good a firm will supply at a given price, *the marginal cost curve is the firm's supply curve.* The MC curve tells the competitive firm how much it should produce at a given price. (As you'll see later, there's an addendum to this statement. Specifically, the marginal cost curve is the firm's supply curve only if price exceeds average variable cost.)

Because the marginal cost curve tells us how much of a produced good a firm will supply at a given price, the marginal cost curve is the firm's supply curve.

Firms Maximize Total Profit

Q-4 Why do firms maximize total profit rather than profit per unit?

Notice that when you talk about maximizing profit, you're talking about maximizing *total profit,* not profit per unit. Profit per unit would be maximized at a much lower

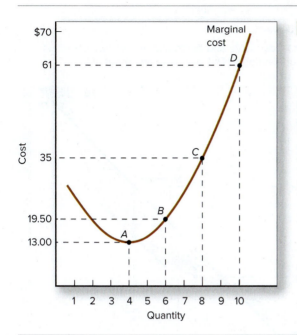

FIGURE 13-2 **The Marginal Cost Curve Is a Firm's Supply Curve**

Since the marginal cost curve tells the firm how much to produce, the marginal cost curve is the perfectly competitive firm's supply curve. This exhibit shows four points on a firm's supply curve; as you can see, the quantity the firm chooses to supply depends on the price. For example, if market price is $19.50, the firm produces 6 units.

output level than is total profit. Profit-maximizing firms don't care about profit per unit; as long as an increase in output will increase total profits, a profit-maximizing firm should increase output. That's difficult to grasp, so let's consider a concrete example.

Say two people are selling T-shirts that cost $4 each. One sells 2 T-shirts at a price of $6 each and makes a profit per shirt of $2. His total profit is $4. The second person sells 8 T-shirts at $5 each, making a profit per unit of only $1 but selling 8. Her total profit is $8, twice as much as the fellow who had the $2 profit per unit. In this case, $5 (the price with the lower profit per unit), not $6, yields more total profit.

An alternative method of determining the profit-maximizing level of output is to look at the total revenue and total cost curves directly. Figure 13-3 shows total cost and total revenue for the firm we're considering so far. The table in Figure 13-3(a) shows total revenue in column 2, which is just the number of units sold times market price. Total cost is in column 3. Total cost is the cumulative sum of the marginal costs from Figure 13-1(a) plus a fixed cost of $40. Total profit (column 4) is the difference between total revenue and total cost. Looking down column 4 of Figure 13-3(a), you can quickly see that the profit-maximizing level of output is 8, since total profit is highest at an output of 8. This is also where $MR = MC$.

In Figure 13-3(b) we plot the firm's total revenue and total cost curves from the table in Figure 13-3(a). The total revenue curve is a straight line; each additional unit sold increases revenue by the same amount, $35. The total cost curve is bowed upward at most quantities, reflecting the increasing marginal cost at different levels of output. The firm's profit is represented by the distance between the total revenue curve and the total cost curve. For example, at output 5, the firm makes $45 in profit.

Total profit is maximized where the vertical distance between total revenue and total cost is greatest. In this example, total profit is maximized at output 8, just as in the alternative approach. At that output, marginal revenue (the slope of the total revenue curve) and marginal cost (the slope of the total cost curve) are equal.

FIGURE 13-3 (A AND B)   Determination of Profits by Total Cost and Total Revenue Curves

The profit-maximizing output level also can be seen by considering the total cost curve and the total revenue curve. Profit is maximized at the output where total revenue exceeds total cost by the largest amount. This occurs at an output of 8.

(1) Quantity	(2) Total Revenue	(3) Total Cost	(4) Total Profit
0	$ 0	$ 40	$-40
1	35	68	-33
2	70	88	-18
3	105	104	1
4	140	118	22
5	175	130	45
6	210	147	63
7	245	169	76
8	280	199	81
9	315	239	76
10	350	293	57

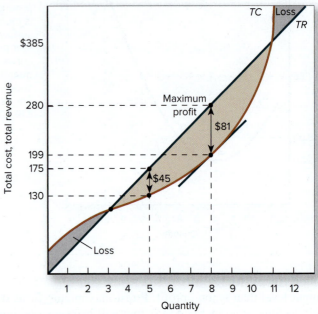

(a) Total Revenue and Total Cost Table

(b) Total Revenue and Total Cost Curves

Total Profit at the Profit-Maximizing Level of Output

Marginal cost is all that is needed to determine a competitive firm's supply curve.

In the initial discussion of the firm's choice of output, given price, I carefully presented only marginal cost and price. We talked about maximizing profit, but nowhere did I mention what profit, average total cost, average variable cost, or average fixed cost was. I mentioned only marginal cost and price to emphasize that marginal cost is all that's needed to determine a competitive firm's supply curve (and a competitive firm is the only firm that has a supply curve) and to determine the output that will maximize profit. Now that you know that, let's turn our attention more closely to profit.

Determining Profit from a Table of Costs and Revenue

Profit is determined by total revenue minus total cost.

The $P = MR = MC$ condition tells us how much output a competitive firm should produce to maximize profit. It does not tell us the profit the firm makes. *Profit is determined by total revenue minus total cost.* Table 13-1 expands Figure 13-1(a) and presents a table of all the costs relevant to the firm. Going through the columns and reminding yourself of the definition of each is a good review of the two previous chapters. If the definitions don't come to mind immediately, you need a review. If you don't know the definitions of *MC, AVC, ATC, FC,* and *AFC,* go back and reread those chapters.

The firm is interested in maximizing profit. Looking at Table 13-1, you can quickly see that the profit-maximizing position is 8, as it was before, since at an output of 8, total profit (column 10) is highest.

TABLE 13-1 **Costs Relevant to a Firm**

(1) Price = Marginal Revenue	(2) Quantity Produced	(3) Total Fixed Cost	(4) Average Fixed Cost	(5) Total Variable Cost	(6) Average Variable Cost	(7) Total Cost	(8) Marginal Cost	(9) Average Total Cost	(10) Total Revenue	(11) Total Profit
$35.00	0	$40.00	—	0	—	$ 40.00		—	0	$−40.00
35.00	1	40.00	$40.00	$ 28.00	$28.00	68.00	$28.00	$68.00	$ 35.00	−33.00
35.00	2	40.00	20.00	48.00	24.00	88.00	20.00	44.00	70.00	−18.00
35.00	3	40.00	13.33	64.00	21.33	104.00	16.00	34.67	105.00	1.00
35.00	4	40.00	10.00	78.00	19.50	118.00	14.00	29.50	140.00	22.00
35.00	5	40.00	8.00	90.00	18.00	130.00	12.00	26.00	175.00	45.00
35.00	6	40.00	6.67	107.00	17.83	147.00	17.00	24.50	210.00	63.00
35.00	7	40.00	5.71	129.00	18.43	169.00	22.00	24.14	245.00	76.00
35.00	8	40.00	5.00	159.00	19.88	199.00	30.00	24.88	280.00	81.00
35.00	9	40.00	4.44	199.00	22.11	239.00	40.00	26.56	315.00	76.00
35.00	10	40.00	4.00	253.00	25.30	293.00	54.00	29.30	350.00	57.00

Using the $MC = MR = P$ rule, you can also see that the profit-maximizing level of output is 8. Increasing output from 7 to 8 has a marginal cost of $30, which is less than $35, so it makes sense to do so. Increasing output from 8 to 9 has a marginal cost of $40, which is more than $35, so it does not make sense to do so. The output 8 is the profit-maximizing output. At that profit-maximizing level of output, the profit the firm earns is $81, which is calculated by subtracting total cost of $199 from total revenue of $280. Notice also that average total cost is lowest at an output of about 7, and the average variable cost is lowest at an output of about 6.[1] Thus, the profit-maximizing position (which is 8) is *not* necessarily a position that minimizes either average variable cost or average total cost. It is only the position that maximizes total profit.

Determining Profit from a Graph

These relationships can be seen in a graph. In Figure 13-4(a) I add the average total cost and average variable cost curves to the graph of marginal cost and price first presented in Figure 13-1. Notice that the marginal cost curve goes through the lowest points of both average cost curves. (If you don't know why, it would be a good idea to go back and review the previous chapters.)

The profit-maximizing output can be determined in a table (as in Table 13-1) or in a graph (as in Figure 13-4).

FIND OUTPUT WHERE $MC = MR$ The way you find profit graphically is first to find the point where $MC = MR$ (point *A*). That intersection determines the quantity the firm will produce if it wants to maximize profit. Why? Because the vertical distance between a point on the marginal cost curve and a point on the marginal revenue curve represents the additional profit the firm can make by changing output. For example, if it increases production from 6 to 7, its marginal cost is $22 and its marginal revenue is $35. By increasing output it can increase profit by $13 (from $63 to $76). The same reasoning holds true for any output less than 8. For outputs higher than 8, the opposite reasoning holds true. Marginal cost exceeds marginal revenue, so it pays to decrease

Q-5 If the firm described in Figure 13-4 is producing 4 units, what would you advise it to do, and why?

---

[1] I say "about 6" and "about 7" because the table gives only whole numbers. The actual minimum point occurs at 5.55 for average variable cost and 6.55 for average total cost. The nearest whole numbers to these are 6 and 7.

FIGURE 13-4 (A, B, AND C) **Determining Profits Graphically**

The profit-maximizing output depends *only* on where the *MC* and *MR* curves intersect. The total amount of profit or loss that a firm makes depends on the price it receives and its average total cost of producing the profit-maximizing output. This exhibit shows the case of (**a**) a profit, (**b**) zero profit, and (**c**) a loss.

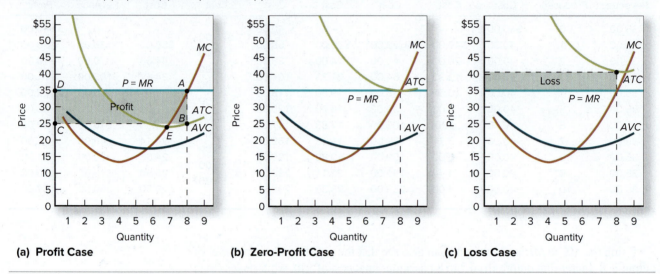

(a) **Profit Case**   (b) **Zero-Profit Case**   (c) **Loss Case**

output. So, to maximize profit, the firm must see that marginal revenue equals marginal costs, which occurs where the two curves intersect.

FIND PROFIT PER UNIT WHERE $MC = MR$ After having determined the profit-maximizing quantity, drop a vertical line down to the horizontal axis and see what average total cost is at that output level (point *B*). Next extend a line back to the vertical axis (point *C*). That tells us that the average total costs per unit are $25. Next go up the price axis to the price that the firm receives (point *D*). For a competitive firm, that price is the marginal revenue as well as its average revenue, since the price is constant. The difference between this price and average cost is profit per unit. Connecting these points gives us the shaded rectangle, *ABCD,* which is the total profit earned by the firm (the total quantity times the profit per unit).

Notice that at the profit-maximizing position, the profit per unit isn't at its highest because average total cost is *not* at its minimum point. Profit per unit of output would be highest at point *E*. A common mistake that students make is to draw a line up from point *E* when they are finding profits. That is wrong. It is important to remember: *To determine maximum profit, you must first determine what output the firm will choose to produce by seeing where* MC *equals* MR *and then determine the average total cost at that quantity by dropping a line down to the* ATC *curve.* Only then can you determine what maximum profit will be.

ZERO PROFIT OR LOSS WHERE $MC = MR$ Notice also that as the curves in Figure 13-4(a) are drawn, *ATC* at the profit-maximizing position is below the price, so the firm makes a profit. The choice of short-run average total cost curves was arbitrary and doesn't affect the firm's profit-maximizing condition: $MC = MR$. It could have been assumed that fixed cost was higher, which would have shifted the *ATC* curve up. In Figure 13-4(b) it's assumed that fixed cost is $81 higher than in Figure 13-4(a). Instead of $40, it's $121. The appropriate average total cost curve for a fixed cost of

When the ATC curve is below the marginal revenue curve, the firm makes a profit. When the ATC curve is above the marginal revenue curve, the firm incurs a loss.

Thinking Like a Modern Economist

Profit Maximization and Real-World Firms

Most real-world firms do not have profit as their only goal. The reason is that, in the real world, the decision maker's income is part of the cost of production. For example, a paid manager has an incentive to hold down costs but has little incentive to hold down his income, which, for the firm, is a cost. Alternatively, say that a firm is a worker-managed firm. If workers receive a share of the profits, they'll push for higher profits, but they'll also see to it that in the process of maximizing profits they don't hurt their own interest—maximizing their wages. In short, real-world firms will hold down the costs of factors of production *except* the cost of the decision maker.

In real life, this problem of the lack of incentives to hold down costs is important. For example,

©Comstock Images/Alamy

firms' managerial expenses often balloon even as firms are cutting "costs." Similarly, CEOs and other high-ranking officers of the firm often have enormously high salaries. How and why the lack of incentives to hold down costs affects the economy is best seen by first considering the nature of an economy with incentives to hold down all costs. That's why we use as our standard model the traditional profit-maximizing firm. (*Standard model* means the model that economists use as our basis of reasoning; from it, we branch out.) Using what are called game theory models, modern economists work with firms to devise incentive-compatible contracts that align the goals of decision makers in the firm with the goals of the owners of firms.

$121 is drawn in Figure 13-4(b). Notice that in this case economic profit is zero and the marginal cost curve intersects the minimum point of the average total cost curve at an output of 8 and a price of $35. (Remember from the last chapter that even though economic profit is zero, all resources, including entrepreneurs, are being paid their opportunity cost.)

In Figure 13-4(c), fixed cost is even higher. Profit-maximizing output is still 8, but now at an output of 8 average total cost is $41 and the firm is making an economic loss of $6 on each unit sold. The loss is given by the shaded rectangle. In this case, the profit-maximizing condition is actually a loss-minimizing condition. So $MC = MR = P$ is both a *profit-maximizing condition* and a *loss-minimizing condition*.

I draw these three cases to emphasize to you that determining the profit-maximizing output level doesn't depend on fixed cost or average total cost. It depends only on where marginal cost equals price.

Q-6 What is wrong with the following diagram?

The Shutdown Point

Earlier I stated the supply curve of a competitive firm is its marginal cost curve. More specifically, the supply curve is the part of the marginal cost curve that is above the average variable cost curve. Considering why this is the case should help the analysis stick in your mind.

Let's consider Figure 13-5(a)—a reproduction of Figure 13-4(c)—and the firm's decision at various prices. At a price of $35, it's incurring a loss of $6 per unit. If it's making a loss, why doesn't it shut down? The answer lies in the fixed costs. There's

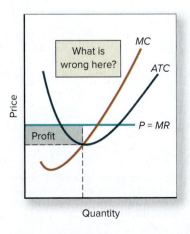

FIGURE 13-5 The Shutdown
Decision and Long-Run Equilibrium

A firm should continue to produce
as long as price exceeds average
variable cost. Once price falls
below that, it will do better by
temporarily shutting down and
saving the variable costs. This
occurs at point A in (a). In (b), the
long-run equilibrium position for
a firm in a competitive industry is
shown. In that long-run equilibrium,
only normal profits are made.

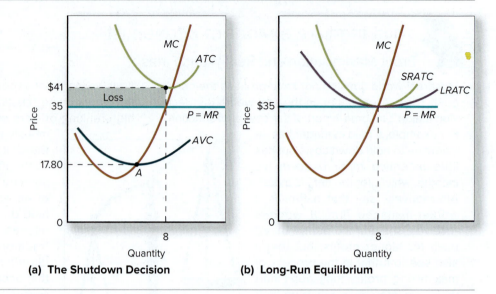

(a) The Shutdown Decision   **(b) Long-Run Equilibrium**

no use crying over spilt milk. In the short run, a firm knows these fixed costs are sunk
costs; it must pay them regardless of whether or not it produces. The firm considers
only the costs it can save by stopping production, and those costs are its variable costs.
As long as a firm is covering its variable costs, it pays to keep on producing. By producing, its loss is $48; if it stopped producing, its loss would be all the fixed costs
($169). So it makes a smaller loss by producing.

However, once the price falls below average variable costs (below $17.80), it will
pay to shut down [point A in Figure 13-5(a)]. In that case, the firm's loss from producing would be more than $169, and it would do better to simply stop producing tempo-
rarily and avoid paying the variable cost. Thus, the point at which price equals *AVC* is
the **shutdown point** *(that point below which the firm will be better off if it temporarily
shuts down than it will if it stays in business)*. When price falls below the shutdown
point, the average variable cost the firm can avoid paying by shutting down exceeds
the price it would get for selling the good. When price is above average variable cost,
in the short run a firm should keep on producing even though it's making a loss. As
long as a firm's total revenue is covering its total variable cost, temporarily producing
at a loss is the firm's best strategy because it's making a smaller loss than it would
make if it were to shut down.

Q-7 In the early 2000s, many airlines
were making losses, yet they continued
to operate. Why?

The shutdown point is the point below
which the firm will be better off if it shuts
down than it will if it stays in business.

If *P* > minimum of *AVC*, the firm will
continue to produce in the short run.
If *P* < minimum of *AVC*, the firm will
shut down.

Short-Run Market Supply and Demand

Most of the preceding discussion focused on supply and demand analysis of a firm.
Now let's consider supply and demand in an industry. We've already discussed industry demand. Even though the demand curve faced by the firm is perfectly elastic, the
industry demand curve is downward-sloping.

How about the industry supply curve? We previously demonstrated that the supply curve for a competitive firm is that portion of a firm's marginal cost curve that is
above the average variable cost curve. To discuss the industry supply curve, we must
use a market supply curve. In the short run when the number of firms in the market
is fixed, the **market supply curve** is just *the horizontal sum of all the firms' marginal cost curves, taking account of any changes in input prices that might occur*. To
move from individual firms' marginal cost curves or supply curves to the market

The market supply curve is the horizontal
sum of all the firms' marginal cost curves,
taking account of any changes in input
prices that might occur.

supply curve, we add the quantities all firms will supply at each possible price. Since all firms in a competitive market have identical marginal cost curves, a quick way of summing the quantities is to multiply the quantities from the marginal cost curve of a representative firm at each price by the number of firms in the market. As the short run evolves into the long run, the number of firms in the market can change. As more firms enter the market, the market supply curve shifts to the right because more firms are supplying the quantity indicated by the representative marginal cost curve. Likewise, as the number of firms in the market declines, the market supply curve shifts to the left. Knowing how the number of firms in the market affects the market supply curve is important to understanding long-run equilibrium in perfectly competitive markets.

Long-Run Competitive Equilibrium: Zero Profit

The analysis of the competitive firm consists of two parts: the short-run analysis just presented and the long-run analysis. In the short run, the number of firms is fixed and the firm can either earn economic profit or incur economic loss. In the long run, firms enter and exit the market and neither economic profits nor economic losses are possible. In the long run, firms make zero economic profit. Thus, in the long run, only the zero-profit equilibrium shown in Figure 13-5(b) is possible. As you can see, at that long-run equilibrium, the firm is at the minimum of both the short-run and the long-run average total cost curves.

Why can't firms earn economic profit or make economic losses in the long run? Because of the entry and exit of firms: If there are economic profits, firms will enter the market, shifting the market supply curve to the right. As market supply increases, the market price will decline and reduce profits for each firm. Firms will continue to enter the market and the market price will continue to decline until the incentive of economic profits is eliminated. At that price, all firms are earning zero profit. Similarly, if the price is lower than the price necessary to earn a profit, firms incurring losses will leave the market and the market supply curve will shift to the left. As market supply shifts to the left, market price will rise. Firms will continue to exit the market and market price will continue to rise until all remaining firms no longer incur losses and earn zero profit. Only at zero profit do entry and exit stop.

Zero profit does not mean that entrepreneurs get nothing for their efforts. The entrepreneur is an input to production just like any other factor of production. In order to stay in the business, the entrepreneur must receive his opportunity cost, or **normal profit** *(the amount the owners of a business would have received in the next-best alternative).* That normal profit is built into the costs of the firm; economic profits are profits above normal profits.

Another aspect of the zero-profit position deserves mentioning. What if one firm has superefficient workers or machinery? Won't the firm make a profit in the long run? The answer is, again, no. In a long-run competitive market, other firms will see the value of those workers and machines and will compete to get them for themselves. As firms compete for the superefficient factors of production, the prices of those specialized inputs will rise until all profits are eliminated. Those factors will receive what are called rents for their specialized ability. For example, say the average worker receives $400 per week, but Sarah, because she's such a good worker, receives $600. So $200 of the $600 she receives is a rent for her specialized ability. Either her existing firm matches that $600 wage or she will change employment.

The zero-profit condition is enormously powerful; it makes the analysis of competitive markets far more applicable to the real world than can a strict application of the assumption of perfect competition. If economic profit is being made, firms will enter and compete that profit away. Price will be pushed down to the average total cost

Since profits create incentives for new firms to enter, output will increase, and the price will fall until zero profits are being made.

Web Note 13.2

Shutdown and Exit

Q-8 If a competitive firm makes zero profit, why does it stay in business?

The zero-profit condition is enormously powerful; it makes the analysis of competitive markets far more applicable to the real world than would otherwise be the case.

Finding Output, Price, and Profit

To find a competitive firm's price, level of output, and profit given a firm's marginal cost curve and average total cost curve, use the following four steps:

1. Determine the market price at which market supply and demand curves intersect. This is the price the competitive firm accepts for its products.

2. Draw the horizontal marginal revenue (MR) curve at the market price.

3. Determine the profit-maximizing level of output by finding the level of output where the MR and MC curves intersect.

4. Determine profit by subtracting average total costs at the profit-maximizing level of output from the price and multiplying by the firm's output.

If you are demonstrating profit graphically, find the point at which MC = MR. Extend a line down to the ATC curve. Extend a line from this point to the vertical axis. To complete the box indicating profit, go up the vertical axis to the market price.

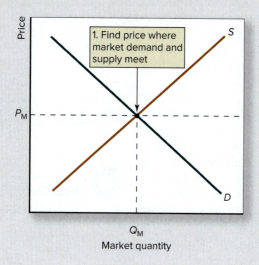

1. Find price where market demand and supply meet

Market quantity

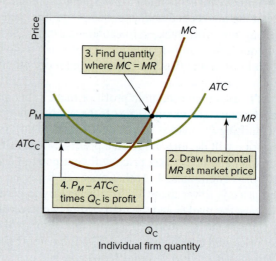

3. Find quantity where MC = MR

2. Draw horizontal MR at market price

4. $P_M - ATC_C$ times Q_C is profit

Individual firm quantity

of production as long as there are no barriers to entry. As we'll see in later chapters, in their analysis of whether markets are competitive, many economists focus primarily on whether barriers to entry exist.

Adjustment from the Short Run to the Long Run

Now that we've been through the basics of the perfectly competitive supply and demand curves, we're ready to consider the two together and to see how the adjustment to long-run equilibrium will likely take place for the firm and in the market.

An Increase in Demand

First, in Figure 13-6 (a and b), let's consider a market that's in equilibrium but that suddenly experiences an increase in demand. Figure 13-6(a) shows the market reaction. Figure 13-6(b) shows a representative firm's reaction. Originally market equilibrium occurs at a price of $7 and market quantity supplied of 700 thousand units [point A in (a)], with each of 70 firms producing 10 thousand units [point a in (b)]. Firms are making zero profit because they're in long-run equilibrium. If demand increases from

FIGURE 13-6 (A AND B)   **Market Response to an Increase in Demand**

Faced with an increase in demand, which it sees as an increase in price and hence profits, a competitive firm will respond by increasing output (from *A* to *B*) in order to maximize profit. The market response is shown in (**a**); the firm's response is shown in (**b**). As all firms increase output and as new firms enter, price will fall until all profit is competed away. Thus, the long-run market supply curve will be perfectly elastic, as is S_{LR} in (**a**). The final equilibrium will be the original price but a higher output. The original firms return to their original output (*A*), but since there are more firms in the market, the market output increases to *C*.

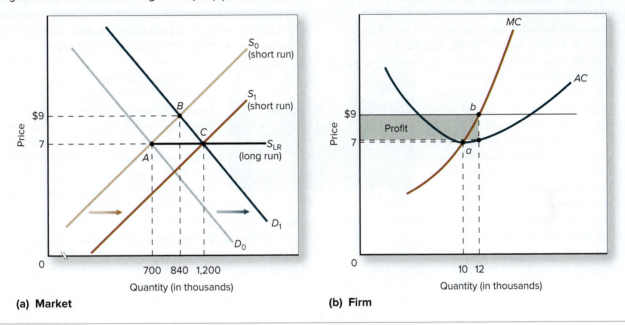

(a) Market   **(b) Firm**

D_0 to D_1, the firms will see the market price increasing and will increase their output until they're once again at a position where $MC = P$. This occurs at point *B* at a market output of 840 thousand units in (a) and at point *b* at a firm output of 12 thousand in (b). In the short run, each of the 70 existing firms makes an economic profit [the shaded area in Figure 13-6(b)]. Price has risen to $9, but average cost is only $7.10, so if the price remains $9, each firm is making a profit of $1.90 per unit. But price cannot remain at $9 since new firms will have an incentive to enter the market.

As new firms enter, if input prices remain constant, the short-run market supply curve shifts from S_0 to S_1 and the market price returns to $7. The entry of 50 new firms provides the additional output in this example, bringing market output to 1.2 million units sold for $7 apiece. The final equilibrium will be at a higher market output but at the same price.

Q-9 If berets suddenly became the "in" thing to wear, what would you expect to happen to the price in the short run? In the long run?

Long-Run Market Supply

The long-run market supply curve is a schedule of quantities supplied when firms are no longer entering or exiting the market. This occurs when firms are earning zero profit. In this case, the long-run supply curve is created by extending to the right the line connecting points *A* and *C* in Figure 13-6(a). Since equilibrium price remains at $7, the long-run supply curve is perfectly elastic. The long-run supply curve is horizontal because factor prices are constant and there are constant returns to scale. That is, factor prices do not increase as industry output increases. Economists call this market a *constant-cost industry*. Two other possibilities exist: an *increasing-cost industry* (in which factor prices rise as more firms enter the market and existing firms

In the long run, firms earn zero profits.

The Shutdown Decision and the Relevant Costs

The previous two chapters emphasized that it is vital to choose the costs relevant to the decision at hand. Discussing the shutdown decision gives us a chance to demonstrate the importance of those choices. Say the firm leases the office it operates in. The rental cost of that office is a fixed cost for most decisions, since the rent must be paid whether or not the office is used. However, if the firm can end the rental contract, and thereby save the rental cost, the office is not a fixed cost. But neither is it a normal variable cost. Since the firm can end the rental contract and save the cost only if it shuts down, that rental cost of the office is an *indivisible setup cost*. For the shutdown decision, the rent is a variable cost. For other decisions about changing quantity, it's a fixed cost.

The moral: The relevant cost can change with the decision at hand, so when you apply the analysis to real-world situations, be sure to think carefully about what the *relevant cost* is.

©Bob Krist/Corbis Documentary/Getty Images

Consider the problem facing GM and other U.S. auto producers before they were reorganized after a government bailout in 2008. In their contracts with their workers, they had agreed to pay their workers whether they worked or not, making labor costs, in large part, fixed. This meant that GM actually saved much less when cutting production than it would if it did not have to pay idle workers. The implication of these contracts was that when demand fell, GM had a strong incentive to keep on producing, and then to sell the cars at a loss. Why sell at a loss? Because the loss was less than if GM had shut down production. GM ultimately restructured its contracts when the government bailed out the company. This restructuring changed many of its fixed costs to variable costs, so that its production can respond more quickly to changes in demand.

---

expand production) and a *decreasing-cost industry* (in which factor prices fall as industry output expands), but we will leave a discussion of those to upper-level courses.

There are two aspects of long-run equilibrium that you should remember. The first is that in long-run equilibrium, zero profit is being made. Long-run equilibrium is defined by zero economic profit. The second is that the long-run supply curve is more elastic than the short-run supply curve. That's because output changes are much less costly in the long run than in the short run. *In the short run, the price does more of the adjusting. In the long run, more of the adjustment is done by quantity.*

An Example in the Real World

The perfectly competitive model and the reasoning underlying it are extremely powerful. With them you have a simple model to use as a first approach to predict the effect of an event, or to explain why an event occurred. For example, consider Walmart's decision to close more than 60 of its Sam's Club stores after experiencing years of losses.

Figure 13-7 shows what happened. Initially, Walmart saw the losses it was suffering as temporary. In the years prior to the shutdown decision, Walmart's cost curves looked like those in Figure 13-7. Since price exceeded average variable cost, Walmart continued to produce even though it was making a loss.

But after years of losses, Walmart's perspective changed. The company moved from the short run to the long run. Walmart began to believe that demand at these Sam's Club stores wasn't temporarily low but rather permanently low. It began to ask: What costs are truly fixed and what costs are simply indivisible costs that we can save

Q-10 In the early 2000s, demand for burkas (the garment the Taliban had required Afghani women to wear) declined when the Taliban were ousted. In the short run, what would you expect to happen to the price of burkas? How about in the long run?

Web Note 13.3

Is It Perfect Competition or Not?

A Summary of a Perfectly Competitive Industry

Four things to remember when considering a perfectly competitive industry are:

1. The profit-maximizing condition for perfectly competitive firms is $MC = MR = P$.

2. To determine profit or loss at the profit-maximizing level of output, subtract the average total cost at that level of output from the price and multiply the result by the output level.

3. Firms will shut down production if price falls below the minimum of their average variable costs.

4. A perfectly competitive firm is in long-run equilibrium only when it is earning zero economic profit, or when price equals the minimum of long-run average total costs.

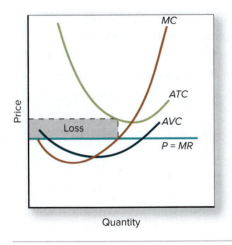

FIGURE 13-7 A Real-World Example: A Shutdown Decision

Supply/demand analysis can be applied to a wide variety of real-world examples. This exhibit shows one, but there are many more. As you experience life today, a good exercise is to put on your supply/demand glasses and interpret everything you see in a supply/demand framework.

if we close down completely, selling our buildings and reducing our overhead? Since in the long run all costs are variable, the *ATC* became its relevant *AVC*. Walmart recognized that prices had fallen below these long-run average costs. At that point, it shut down those stores for which $P < AVC$.

There are hundreds of other real-world examples to which the perfectly competitive model adds insight. That's one reason why it's important to keep it in the back of your mind.

Conclusion

We've come to the end of the presentation of perfect competition. It was tough going, but if you went through it carefully, it will serve you well, both as a basis for later chapters and as a reference point for how real-world economies work. But like many good things, a complete understanding of the chapter doesn't come easy.

©igor kisselev/Alamy Stock Photo

Summary

- The necessary conditions for perfect competition include: Buyers and sellers are price takers, there are no barriers to entry, and firms' products are identical. *(LO13-1)*

- The profit-maximizing position of a competitive firm is where marginal revenue equals marginal cost. *(LO13-2)*

- The supply curve of a competitive firm is its marginal cost curve. Only competitive firms have supply curves. *(LO13-2)*

- To find the profit-maximizing level of output for a perfect competitor, find that level of output where $MC = MR$. Profit is price less average total cost times output at the profit-maximizing level of output. *(LO13-3)*

- In the short run, competitive firms can make a profit or loss. In the long run, they make zero profits. *(LO13-3)*

- Profit equals total revenue less total cost. Graphically, profit is the vertical distance between the price of the good and the *ATC* curve at the profit-maximizing level of output times that level of output. *(LO13-3)*

- The shutdown price for a perfectly competitive firm is a price below average variable cost. *(LO13-3)*

- The short-run market supply curve is the horizontal summation of the marginal cost curves for all firms in the market. An increase in the number of firms in the market shifts the market supply curve to the right, while a decrease shifts it to the left. *(LO13-3)*

- Perfectly competitive firms make zero profit in the long run because if profit were being made, new firms would enter and the market price would decline, eliminating the profit. If losses were being made, firms would exit and the market price would rise. *(LO13-3)*

- The long-run supply curve is a schedule of quantities supplied where firms are making zero profit. *(LO13-4)*

- The slope of the long-run supply curve depends on what happens to factor prices when output increases. *(LO13-4)*

- Constant-cost industries have horizontal long-run supply curves. *(LO 13-4)*

Key Terms

barriers to entry
marginal cost *(MC)*
marginal revenue *(MR)*

market supply
  curve
normal profit

perfectly competitive
  market
price taker

profit-maximizing
  condition
shutdown point

Questions and Exercises   connect

1. Why must buyers and sellers be price takers for a market to be perfectly competitive? *(LO13-1)*

2. List three conditions for perfect competition. *(LO13-1)*

3. If the conditions for perfect competition are generally not met, why do economists use the model? *(LO13-1)*

4. You're thinking of buying one of two firms. One has a profit margin of $8 per unit; the other has a profit margin of $4 per unit. Which should you buy? Why? (Difficult) *(LO13-2)*

5. A perfectly competitive firm sells its good for $20. If marginal cost is four times the quantity produced, how much does the firm produce? Why? (Difficult) *(LO13-2)*

6. Draw marginal cost, marginal revenue, and average total cost curves for a typical perfectly competitive firm and indicate the profit-maximizing level of output and total profit for that firm. Is the firm in long-run equilibrium? Why or why not? *(LO13-3)*

7. State what is *wrong* with each of the graphs. (*LO13-3*)

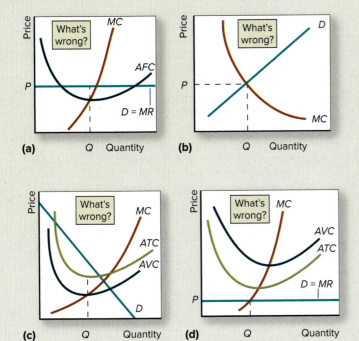

(a)

(b)

(c)

(d)

8. What will be the effect of a technological development that reduces marginal costs in a competitive market on short-run price, quantity, and profit? (*LO13-3*)

9. Draw marginal cost, marginal revenue, and average total cost curves for a typical perfectly competitive firm in long-run equilibrium and indicate the profit-maximizing level of output and total profit for that firm. (*LO13-3*)

10. Each of 10 firms in a given industry has the costs given in the left-hand table. The market demand schedule is given in the right-hand table. (*LO13-3*)

Quantity	Total Cost
0	$12
1	24
2	27
3	31
4	39
5	53
6	73

Price	Quantity Demanded
$24	0
20	10
16	20
12	30
8	40
4	50
0	60

a. What is the market equilibrium price and the price each firm gets for its product?
b. What is the equilibrium market quantity and the quantity each firm produces?

c. What profit is each firm making?
d. Below what price will firms begin to exit the market?

11. Graphically demonstrate the quantity and price of a perfectly competitive firm. (*LO13-3*)
a. Why is a slightly larger quantity not preferred?
b. Why is a slightly lower quantity not preferred?
c. Label the shutdown point in your diagram.
d. You have just discovered that shutting down means that you would lose your land zoning permit, which is required to start operating again. How does that change your answer to *c*?

12. How is a firm's marginal cost curve related to the market supply curve? (*LO13-3*)

13. Draw the *ATC*, *AVC*, and *MC* curves for a typical firm. Label the price at which the firm would shut down temporarily and the price at which the firm would exit the market in the long run. (*LO13-3*)

14. Under what cost condition is the shutdown point the same as the point at which a firm exits the market? (*LO13-3*)

15. A profit-maximizing firm is producing where $MR = MC$ and has an average total cost of $4, but it gets a price of $3 for each good it sells. (*LO13-3*)
a. What would you advise the firm to do?
b. What would you advise the firm to do if you knew average variable costs were $3.50?

16. A farmer is producing where $MC = MR$. Say that half of the cost of producing wheat is the rental cost of land (a fixed cost) and half is the cost of labor and machines (a variable cost). If the average total cost of producing wheat is $8 and the price of wheat is $6, what would you advise the farmer to do? ("Grow something else" is not allowed.) (*LO13-3*)

17. Based on the following table: (*LO13-4*)

Output	Price	Total Cost
0	$10	$ 31
1	10	40
2	10	45
3	10	48
4	10	55
5	10	65
6	10	80
7	10	100
8	10	140
9	10	220
10	10	340

a. What is the profit-maximizing output?
b. What will happen to the market price in the long run?

18. Why is the long-run market supply curve horizontal in a constant-cost industry? (*LO13-4*)

19. Use the accompanying graph, which shows the marginal cost and average total cost curves for the shoe store Zapateria, a perfectly competitive firm.   *(LO13-4)*
    a. How many pairs of shoes will Zapateria produce if the market price of shoes is $70 a pair?
    b. What is the total profit Zapateria will earn if the market price of shoes is $70 a pair?
    c. Should Zapateria expect more shoe stores to enter this market? Why or why not?
    d. What is the long-run equilibrium price in the shoe market assuming it is a constant-cost industry?

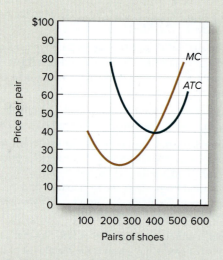

20. A *Wall Street Journal* headline states: "A Nation of Snackers Snubs Old Favorite: The Beloved Cookie." As U.S. consumers adopted more carbohydrate-conscious diets, the number of cookie boxes sold declined 5.4 percent that year, the third consecutive year of decline.   *(LO13-4)*
    a. Assuming the cookie industry is perfectly competitive, demonstrate using market supply and demand curves the effect of this decline in demand on equilibrium price and quantity in the short run.
    b. Assuming a cookie firm was in equilibrium before the change in demand, and it is a constant-cost industry, demonstrate the effect of the decline on equilibrium price for an individual cookie firm in the short run.
    c. How might your answer to *a* change if you are considering the long run?

Questions from Alternative Perspectives

1. The book presents the perfectly competitive model as the foundation for economic analysis.
    a. How well does the theory of perfect competition reflect the real world?
    b. What role, if any, does the government have in promoting perfectly competitive markets?
    c. What is the danger in the government's intervening to promote competitive markets? *(Austrian)*

2. This chapter discusses perfect competition as a benchmark to think about the economy.
    a. Can labor market discrimination—hiring someone on the basis of race or gender rather than capability—exist in a perfectly competitive industry?
    b. Can the elimination of discrimination increase efficiency? *(Feminist)*

3. Perfect competition is analytically elegant.
    a. What percentage of an economy's total production do you think is provided by perfectly competitive firms?

    b. Based on your answer to *a*, why does the text spend so much time on perfect competition? *(Institutionalist)*

4. The perfectly competitive model assumes that firms know when marginal revenue equals marginal costs.
    a. If a firm doesn't have this information, can it produce at the profit-maximizing level of output?
    b. If firms don't have such knowledge, how might the theory of perfect competition be changed to better reflect reality? *(Post-Keynesian)*

5. As the chapter points out, the Internet has made the U.S. economy more competitive by lowering barriers to entry and exit from industries.
    a. To what extent is the Internet itself competitive?
    b. Can competitive conditions develop from information technology, a technology that was created initially by centralized planning, that depends on agreed-upon rules to conduct business, and that has notoriously low marginal costs? (Think of the cost of listening to a song off the Internet.) *(Radical)*

Issues to Ponder

1. If a firm is owned by its workers but otherwise meets all the qualifications for a perfectly competitive firm, will its price and output decisions differ from the price and output decisions of a perfectly competitive firm? Why?

2. The milk industry has a number of interesting aspects. Provide economic explanations for the following:
   a. Fluid milk is 87 percent water. It can be dried and reconstituted so that it is almost indistinguishable from fresh milk. What is a likely reason that such reconstituted milk is not produced?
   b. The United States has regional milk-marketing regulations whose goals are to make each of the regions self-sufficient in milk. What is a likely reason for this?
   c. A U.S. senator from a milk-producing state has been quoted as saying, "I am absolutely convinced . . . that simply bringing down dairy price supports is not a way to cut production." Is it likely that he is correct? What is a probable reason for his statement?

3. A California biotechnology firm submitted a tomato that will not rot for weeks to the U.S. Food and Drug Administration. It designed such a fruit by changing the genetic structure of the tomato. What effect will this technological change have on:
   a. The price of tomatoes?
   b. Farmers who grow tomatoes?
   c. The geographic areas where tomatoes are grown?
   d. Where tomatoes are generally placed on salad bars in winter?

4. Hundreds of music stores have been closing in the face of stagnant demand for CDs because of new competition by online music vendors.
   a. How would price competition from these new sources cause a retail store to close?
   b. In the long run, will CDs remain a viable product? If so, how?

5. In 2018, Sears closed 275 of its stores.
   a. Demonstrate graphically the relationship between ATC, AVC, and price faced by Sears stores when they decided to close.
   b. Assuming the market is perfectly competitive and is a constant-cost industry, what will happen in this market in the long run? Demonstrate with market supply and demand curves.

Answers to Margin Questions

1. Without the assumption of no barriers to entry, firms could make a profit by raising price; hence, the demand curve they face would not be perfectly elastic and, hence, perfect competition would not exist. *(LO13-1)*

2. The competitive firm is such a small portion of the total market that it can have no effect on price. Consequently it takes the price as given, and, hence, its perceived demand curve is perfectly elastic. *(LO13-1)*

3. To determine the profit-maximizing output of a competitive firm, you must know price and marginal cost. *(LO13-2)*

4. Firms are interested in getting as much for themselves as they possibly can. Maximizing total profit does this. Maximizing profit per unit might yield very small total profits. *(LO13-2)*

5. If the firm in Figure 13-4 were producing 4 units, I would explain to it that the marginal cost of increasing output is only $12 and the marginal revenue is $35, so it should significantly expand output until 8, where the marginal cost equals the marginal revenue, or price. *(LO13-3)*

6. The diagram is drawn with the wrong profit-maximizing output and, hence, the wrong profit. Output is determined where marginal cost equals price, and profit is the difference between the average total cost and price at that output, not at the output where marginal cost equals average total cost. The correct diagram is shown here. *(LO13-3)*

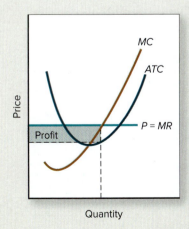

7. The marginal cost for airlines is significantly below average total cost. Since they're recovering their average variable cost, they continue to operate. In the long run, if this continues, some airlines will be forced out of business. *(LO13-3)*

8. The costs for a firm include the normal costs, which in turn include a return for all factors of production. Thus, it is worthwhile for a competitive firm to stay in business, since it is doing better than, or at least as well as, it could in any other activity. *(LO13-3)*

9. Suddenly becoming the "in" thing to wear would cause the demand for berets to shift out to the right, pushing the price up in the short run. In the long run, the market is probably not perfectly competitive and it would likely push the price down because there probably are considerable economies of scale in the production of berets. *(LO13-4)*

10. A decline in demand pushed the short-run price of these burkas down. In the long run, however, once a number of burka makers go out of business, the price of burkas should eventually move back to approximately where it was before the decline, assuming a constant-cost industry. *(LO13-4)*

Monopoly and Monopolistic Competition

> Monopoly is business at the end of its journey.
>
> —Henry Demarest Lloyd

©Julia Ewan/The Washington Post/Getty Images

After reading this chapter, you should be able to:

LO14-1 Summarize how and why the decisions facing a monopolist differ from the collective decisions of competing firms.

LO14-2 Determine a monopolist's price, output, and profit graphically and numerically.

LO14-3 Show graphically the welfare loss from monopoly.

LO14-4 Explain why there would be no monopoly without barriers to entry.

LO14-5 Explain how monopolistic competition differs from monopoly and perfect competition.

In the last chapter we considered perfect competition. We now move to the other end of the spectrum: monopoly. **Monopoly** is *a market structure in which one firm makes up the entire market.* It is the polar opposite of competition. It is a market structure in which the firm faces no competitive pressure from other firms.

Monopolies exist because of barriers to entry into a market that prevent competition. These can be legal barriers (as in the case where a firm has a patent that prevents other firms from entering); sociological barriers, where entry is prevented by custom or tradition; natural barriers, where the firm has a unique ability to produce what other firms can't duplicate; technological barriers, where the size of the market can support only one firm; or positive network externalities, where increases in a firm's size increase the value of the firm's product to consumers. This final barrier is of particular relevance today with the enormous growth of network businesses such as Facebook. For such firms, the bigger the firm gets, the harder it is for other firms to compete with it.

The Key Difference between a Monopolist and a Perfect Competitor

A key question we want to answer in this chapter is: How does a monopolist's decision differ from the collective decision of competing firms (i.e., from the competitive solution)? Answering that question brings out a key difference

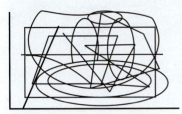

Doodle Number 27: Contemplating Costs

between a competitive firm and a monopoly. Since a competitive firm is too small to affect the price, it does not take into account the effect of its output decision on the price it receives. A competitive firm's marginal revenue (the additional revenue it receives from selling an additional unit of output) is the given market price. A monopolistic firm takes into account that its output decision can affect price; its marginal revenue is not its price. A monopolistic firm will reason: "If I increase production, the price I can get for each unit sold will fall, so I had better be careful about how much I increase production."

Let's consider an example. Say your drawings in the margins of this book are seen by a traveling art critic who decides you're the greatest thing since Rembrandt, or at least since Andy Warhol. Carefully he tears each page out of the book, mounts the pages on special paper, and numbers them: Doodle Number 1 (Doodle While Contemplating Demand), Doodle Number 2 (Doodle While Contemplating Production), and so on.

All told, he has 100. He figures, with the right advertising and if you're a hit on the art circuit, he'll have a monopoly in your doodles. He plans to sell them for $20,000 each: He gets 50 percent; you get 50 percent. That's $1 million for you. You tell him, "Hey, man! I can doodle my way through the entire book. I'll get you 500 doodles. Then I get $5 million and you get $5 million."

The art critic has a pained look on his face. He says, "You've been doodling when you should have been studying. Your doodles are worth $20,000 each only if they're rare. If there are 500, they're worth $1,000 each. And if it becomes known that you can turn them out that fast, they'll be worth nothing. I won't be able to limit quantity at all, and my monopoly will be lost. So obviously we must figure out some way that you won't doodle anymore—and study instead. Oh, by the way, did you know that the price of an artist's work goes up significantly when he or she dies? Hmm?" At that point you decide to forget doodling and to start studying, and to remember always that increasing production doesn't necessarily make suppliers better off.

As we saw in the last chapter, competitive firms do not take advantage of that insight. Each individual competitive firm, responding to its self-interest, is not doing what is in the interest of the firms collectively. In competitive markets, as one supplier is pitted against another, consumers benefit. In monopolistic markets, the firm faces no competitors and does what is in its best interest. Monopolists can see to it that the monopolists, not the consumers, benefit; perfectly competitive firms cannot.

Q-1 Why should you study rather than doodle?

Monopolists see to it that monopolists, not consumers, benefit.

A Model of Monopoly

How much should the monopolistic firm choose to produce if it wants to maximize profit? To answer that we have to consider more carefully the effect that changing output has on the total profit of the monopolist. That's what we do in this section. First, we consider a numerical example; then we consider that same example graphically. The relevant information for our example is presented in Table 14-1.

Determining the Monopolist's Price and Output Numerically

Table 14-1 shows the price, total revenue, marginal revenue, total cost, marginal cost, average total cost, and profit at various levels of production. It's similar to the table in the last chapter where we determined a competitive firm's output. The big difference is that marginal revenue changes as output changes and is not equal to the price. Why?

First, let's remember the definition of marginal revenue: Marginal revenue is the change in total revenue associated with a change in quantity. In this example, if a

TABLE 14-1 **Monopolistic Profit Maximization**

(1) Quantity	(2) Price	(3) Total Revenue	(4) Marginal Revenue	(5) Total Cost	(6) Marginal Cost	(7) Average Total Cost	(8) Profit
0	$36	$ 0		$ 47			$ −47
			$ 33		$ 1		
1	33	33		48		$48.00	−15
			27		2		
2	30	60		50		25.00	10
			21		4		
3	27	81		54		18.00	27
			15		8		
4	24	96		62		15.50	34
			9		16		
5	21	105		78		15.60	27
			3		24		
6	18	108		102		17.00	6
			−3		40		
7	15	105		142		20.29	−37
			−9		56		
8	12	96		198		24.75	−102
			−15		80		
9	9	81		278		30.89	−197

monopolist increases output from 4 to 5, the price it can charge falls from $24 to $21 and its revenue increases from $96 to $105, so marginal revenue is $9. Marginal revenue of increasing output from 4 to 5 for the monopolist reflects two changes: a $21 gain in revenue from selling the 5th unit and a $12 decline in revenue because the monopolist must lower the price on the previous 4 units it produces by $3 a unit, from $24 to $21. This highlights the key characteristic of a monopolist—its output decision affects its price. Because an increase in output lowers the price on all previous units, a monopolist's marginal revenue is always below its price. Comparing columns 2 and 4, you can confirm that this is true.

> A monopolist's marginal revenue is always below its price.

Now let's see if the monopolist will increase production from 4 to 5 units. The marginal revenue of increasing output from 4 to 5 is $9, and the marginal cost of doing so is $16. Since marginal cost exceeds marginal revenue, increasing production from 4 to 5 will reduce total profit and the monopolist will not increase production. If it decreases output from 4 to 3, where *MC* < *MR*, the revenue it loses ($15) exceeds the reduction in costs ($8). It will not reduce output from 4 to 3. Since it cannot increase total profit by increasing output to 5 or decreasing output to 3, it is maximizing profit at 4 units.

As you can tell from the table, profits are highest ($34) at 4 units of output and a price of $24. At 3 units of output and a price of $27, the firm has total revenue of $81 and total cost of $54, yielding a profit of $27. At 5 units of output and a price of $21, the firm has a total revenue of $105 and a total cost of $78, also for a profit of $27. The highest profit it can make is $34, which the firm earns when it produces 4 units. This is its profit-maximizing level.

> **Q-2** In Table 14-1, explain why 4 is the profit-maximizing output.

Determining Price and Output Graphically

The monopolist's output decision also can be seen graphically. Figure 14-1 graphs the table's information into a demand curve, a marginal revenue curve, and a marginal cost curve. The marginal cost curve is a graph of the change in the firm's total cost as it changes output. It's the same curve as we saw in our discussion of perfect competition. The marginal revenue curve tells us the change in total revenue when quantity changes. It is graphed by plotting and connecting the points given by quantity and marginal revenue in Table 14-1.

The marginal revenue curve for a monopolist is new, so let's consider it a bit more carefully. It tells us the additional revenue the firm will get by expanding output. It is a

FIGURE 14-2 (A, B, C, AND D)   Finding the Monopolist's Price and Output

Determining a monopolist's price and output can be tricky. The text discusses the steps shown in this figure. To make sure you understand, try to go through the steps on your own, and then check your work with the text.

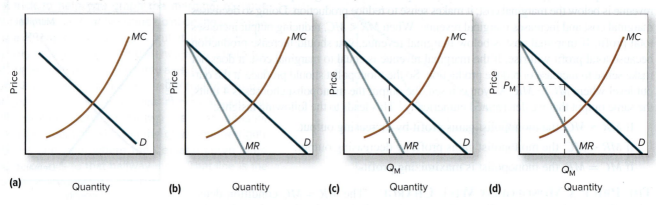

(a)   Quantity   (b)   Quantity   (c)   Quantity   (d)   Quantity

The second step is to determine where $MC = MR$. Having found that point, we extend a line up to the demand curve and down to the quantity axis to determine the output the monopolist chooses, Q_M. We do this in Figure 14-2(c). Finally we see where the quantity line intersects the demand curve. Then we extend a horizontal line from that point to the price axis, as in Figure 14-2(d). This determines the price the monopolist will charge, P_M.

Profits and Monopoly

The monopolist's profit can be determined only by comparing average total cost to price. So before we can determine profit, we need to add another curve: the average total cost curve. As we saw with a perfect competitor, it's important to follow the correct sequence when finding profit:

- First, draw the firm's marginal revenue curve.
- Second, determine the output the monopolist will produce by the intersection of the marginal cost and marginal revenue curves.
- Third, determine the price the monopolist will charge for that output. (Remember, the price it will charge depends on the demand curve.)
- Fourth, determine the monopolist's profit (loss) by subtracting average total cost from average revenue (P) at that level of output and multiplying by the chosen output.

If price exceeds average total cost at the output it chooses, the monopolist will make a profit. If price equals average total cost, the monopolist will make no profit (but it will make a normal return). If price is less than average cost, the monopolist will incur a loss: Total cost exceeds total revenue.

A MONOPOLIST MAKING A PROFIT   I consider the case of a monopolist making a profit in Figure 14-3, going through the steps slowly. The monopolist's demand, marginal cost, and average total cost curves are presented in Figure 14-3(a). Our first step is to draw the marginal revenue curve, which has been added in Figure 14-3(b). The second step is to find the output level at which marginal cost equals marginal revenue. From that point, draw a vertical line to the horizontal (quantity) axis. That intersection tells us the monopolist's output, Q_M in Figure 14-3(b). The third step is to find what price the monopolist will charge at that output. We do so by extending the vertical line to

Q-5 Indicate the profit that the monopolist shown in the graph below earns.

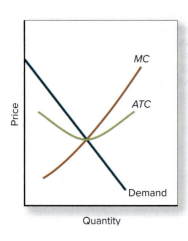

the demand curve (point *A*) and then extending a horizontal line over to the price axis. Doing so gives price, P_M. Our fourth step is to determine the average total cost at that quantity. We do so by seeing where our vertical line at the chosen output intersects the average total cost curve (point *B*). That tells us the monopolist's average cost at its chosen output.

To determine profit, we extend lines from where the quantity line intersects the demand curve (point *A*) and the average total cost curve (point *B*) to the price axis in Figure 14-3(c). The resulting shaded rectangle in Figure 14-3(c) represents the monopolist's profit.

A Monopolist Breaking Even and Making a Loss

A monopolist doesn't always make a profit. In Figure 14-4 we consider two other average total cost curves to show you that a monopolist may make a loss or no profit as well as an economic profit. In Figure 14-4(a) the monopolist is making zero profit; in Figure 14-4(b) it's making a loss. Whether a firm is making a profit, zero profit, or a loss depends on average total costs relative to price. So clearly, in the short run, a monopolist can be making either a profit or a loss, or it can be breaking even.

Most of you, if you've been paying attention, will say, "Sure, in the model monopolists might not make a profit, but in the real world monopolists are making a killing." And it is true that numerous monopolists make a killing. But many more monopolists just break even or lose money. Each year the U.S. Patent Office issues about 325,000 patents. A **patent** is *legal protection of a technical innovation that gives the person holding it sole right to use that innovation*—in other words, it gives the holder a monopoly to produce a good. Most patented goods make a loss; in fact, the cost of getting the patent often exceeds the revenues from selling the product.

Let's consider an example—the self-stirring pot, a pot with a battery-operated stirrer attached to its lid. The stirrer was designed to prevent the bottom of the pot from burning. The inventor tried to get the Home Shopping Network to sell it. Unfortunately

---

FIGURE 14-3 (A, B, AND C)   Determining Profit for a Monopolist

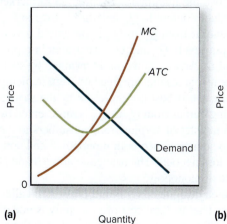

(a)

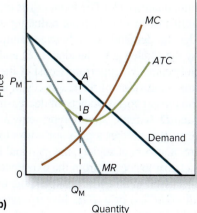

(b)

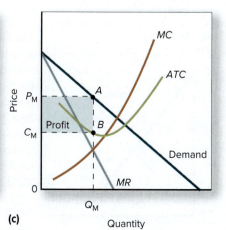

(c)

FIGURE 14-4 (A AND B) **Other Monopoly Cases**

Depending on where the *ATC* curve falls, a monopolist can make a profit, break even [as in (**a**)], or make a loss [as in (**b**)] in the short run. In the long run, a monopolist who is making a loss will go out of business.

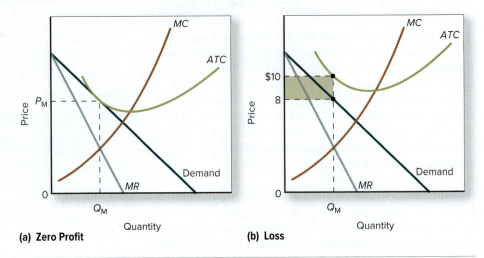

(a) Zero Profit

(b) Loss

for the inventor, HSN considered the cost (even after economies of scale were taken into account) far higher than what people would be willing to pay and therefore decided not to include the pot in its offerings. The inventor had a monopoly on the production and sale of the self-stirring pot, but only a loss to show for it. Examples like this can be multiplied by the thousands. The reality for many monopolies is that their costs exceed their revenues, so they make a loss.

Welfare Loss from Monopoly

As we saw above, monopolists aren't guaranteed a profit. Thus, profits can't be the primary reason that the economic model we're using sees monopoly as bad. If not because of profits, then what standard is the economic model using to conclude that monopoly is undesirable? One reason can be seen by looking at consumer and producer surplus for the normal monopolist equilibrium and perfectly competitive equilibrium.

The Normal Monopolist

The welfare loss from monopoly is a triangle, as is shown in the graph below. It is not the loss that most people consider. Most people are often interested in normative losses that the graph does not capture.

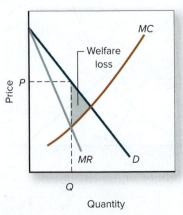

Producer and consumer surplus for both monopoly and perfect competition is shown in Figure 14-5. In a competitive equilibrium, the total consumer and producer surplus is the area below the demand curve and above the marginal cost curve up to market equilibrium quantity Q_C. The monopolist reduces output to Q_M and raises price to P_M. The benefit lost to society from reducing output from Q_C to Q_M is measured by the area under the demand curve between output levels Q_C and Q_M. That area is represented by the shaded areas labeled *A*, *B*, and *D*. Area *A*, however, is regained by society. Society gains the opportunity cost of the resources that are freed up from reducing production—the value of the resources in their next-best use indicated by the shaded area *A*. So the net cost to society of decreasing output from Q_C to Q_M is represented by areas *B* and *D*. (Area *C* simply represents a transfer of surplus from consumers to the monopolist. It is neither a gain nor a loss to society. Since both monopolist and consumer are members of society, the gain and loss net out.) The triangular areas *B* and *D* are the net cost to society from the existence of monopoly.

As discussed in an earlier chapter, the area designated by *B* and *D* is often called the *deadweight loss* or *welfare loss triangle*. That welfare cost of monopoly is one of the reasons economists oppose monopoly. That cost can be summarized as follows: Because monopolies charge a price that is higher than marginal cost, people's decisions

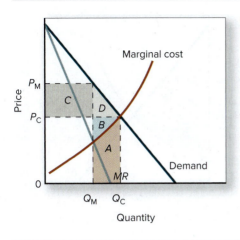

FIGURE 14-5 **The Welfare Loss from Monopoly**

The welfare loss from a monopoly is represented by the triangles *B* and *D*. The rectangle *C* is a transfer from consumer surplus to the monopolist. The area *A* represents the opportunity cost of diverted resources. This is not a loss to society since the resources will be used in producing other goods.

don't reflect the true cost to society. Price exceeds marginal cost. Because price exceeds marginal cost, people's choices are distorted; they choose to consume less of the monopolist's output and more of some other output than they would if markets were competitive. That distinction means that the marginal cost of increasing output is lower than the marginal benefit of increasing output, so there's a welfare loss.

Q-6 Why is area *C* in Figure 14-5 not considered a loss to society from monopoly?

The Price-Discriminating Monopolist

So far we've considered monopolists that charge the same price to all consumers. Let's consider what would happen if our monopolist suddenly gained the ability to **price-discriminate**—*to charge different prices to different individuals or groups of individuals* (for example, students as compared to businesspeople). If a monopolist can identify groups of customers who have different elasticities of demand, separate them in some way, and limit their ability to resell its product between groups, it can charge each group a different price. Specifically, it could charge consumers with less elastic demands a higher price and individuals with more elastic demands a lower price. By doing so, it will increase total profit. Suppose, for instance, Megamovie knew that at $10 it would sell 1,000 movie tickets and at $5 a ticket it would sell 1,500 tickets. Assuming Megamovie could show the film without cost, it would maximize profits by charging $10 to 1,000 moviegoers, earning a total profit of $10,000. If, however, it could somehow attract the additional 500 viewers at $5 a ticket without reducing the price to the first 1,000 moviegoers, it could raise its profit by $2,500, to $12,500. As you can see, the ability to price-discriminate allows a monopolist to increase its profit.

When a monopolist price-discriminates, it charges individuals high up on the demand curve higher prices and those low on the demand curve lower prices.

Web Note 14.1

Divide and Conquer

We see many examples of price discrimination in the real world:

1. *Movie theaters give discounts to senior citizens and children.* Movie theaters charge senior citizens and children a lower price because they have a more elastic demand for movies.

2. *Airlines charge more to fly on Fridays and Sundays.* Businesspeople who work far from home fly out on Sunday and back on Friday. Their demand is inelastic. Tourists and leisure travelers are far more flexible in their travel plans and can fly any day of the week. Tuesday, Wednesday, and Saturday flights are typically the cheapest.

Automobiles are seldom sold at list price.

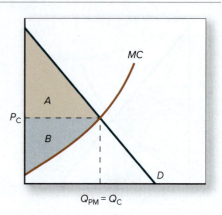

FIGURE 14-6 **A Price-Discriminating Monopolist**

A price-discriminating monopolist produces the same output as the combination of all firms in a competitive market. Total surplus is maximized in both cases. The difference is that the price-discriminating monopolist captures all of the surplus represented by areas *A* and *B*, while all firms in the perfectly competitive market capture only area *B*.

3. *Tracking consumer information and pricing accordingly.* Two people buying something on the Internet are not necessarily presented with the same price. Firms collect data about individuals with tracking devices called cookies, which are deposited on buyers' computer hard drives, and offer prices according to their estimated elasticity of demand. Thus, when you are searching the Internet for something to buy, you might be presented with a different price than someone else visiting the same site.

It might seem unfair for a monopolist to charge different people different prices, but doing so eliminates welfare loss from monopoly. The reason is that for a price-discriminating monopolist, the marginal revenue curve is the demand curve. So it will produce where $MC = MR = D$; in other words, it will produce the same output as would be produced in a perfectly competitive market. You can see this in Figure 14-6. The monopolist chooses to produce Q_{PM}. Since the supply curve in a perfectly competitive market is the sum of all marginal cost curves and equilibrium is where the supply and demand curves intersect, output in a competitive market will also be Q_{PM}. Both are producing where quantity supplied equals quantity demanded and there is no welfare loss.

What could be seen as unfair is what happens to consumer and producer surplus. In a perfectly competitive market, consumers pay and producers receive one price, P_C. Consumer surplus is the area above market price (area *A*) and producer surplus is the area below market price above the marginal cost curve (area *B*). For a price-discriminating monopolist, because it can charge what consumers are willing to pay, all consumer surplus is captured by the monopolist. Producer surplus for a price-discriminating monopolist is areas *A* and *B*.

Q-7 Why does a price-discriminating monopolist make a higher profit than a normal monopolist?

Barriers to Entry and Monopoly

The standard model of monopoly just presented is simple, but, like many simple things, it hides some issues. One issue the standard model of monopoly hides is in this question: What prevents other firms from entering the monopolist's market? You should be able to answer that question relatively quickly. If a monopolist exists, it must exist due to some type of barrier to entry (a social, political, or economic impediment that prevents firms from entering the market). Three important barriers to entry are natural ability, economies of scale, and government restrictions. In the absence of barriers to entry, the monopoly would face competition from other firms, which would erode its monopoly profit. Studying how these barriers to entry are established enriches the standard model and lets us distinguish different types of monopoly.

Web Note 14.2

Diamonds Are Forever

If there were no barriers to entry, profit-maximizing firms would always compete away monopoly profits.

Can Price Controls Increase Output and Lower Market Price?

In an earlier chapter, you learned how effective price ceilings and floors reduce output and reduce the welfare of society. With any type of price control in a competitive market, some trades that individuals would like to have made are prevented. Thus, with competitive markets, price controls of any type are seen as generally bad (though they might have some desirable income distribution effects).

When there is monopoly, the argument is not so simple. The monopoly price is higher than the marginal cost and society loses out; monopolies create their own deadweight loss. In the monopoly case, price controls can actually lower price, increase output, and reduce deadweight loss. Going through the reasoning why provides a good review of the tools.

The figure below shows you the argument.

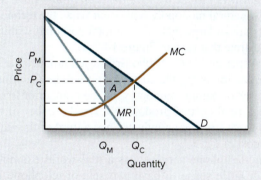

The monopoly sets its quantity where $MR = MC$. Output is Q_M and price is P_M; the welfare loss is the blue shaded triangle A. Now say that the government comes in and places a price ceiling on the monopolist at the competitive price, P_C. Since the monopolist is compelled by law to charge price P_C, it no longer has an incentive to restrict output. Put another way, the price ceiling—the dashed line P_C—becomes the monopolist's demand curve and marginal revenue curve. (Remember, when the demand curve is horizontal, the marginal revenue curve is identical to the demand curve.) Given the law, the monopolist's best option still is to produce where $MC = MR$, but that means

charging price P_C and increasing output to Q_C. As you can see from the figure, the price ceiling causes output to rise and price to fall.

If, when there is monopoly, price controls can increase efficiency, why don't economists advocate price controls more than they do? Let's review four reasons why.

1. For price controls to increase output and lower price, the price has to be set within the right price range—below the monopolist's price and above the price where the monopolist's marginal cost and marginal revenue curves intersect. It is unclear politically that such a price will be chosen. Even if regulators could pick the right price initially, markets may change. Demand may increase or decrease, putting the controlled price outside the desired range.

2. All markets are dynamic. The very existence of monopoly profits will encourage other firms in other industries to try to break into that market, keeping the existing monopolist on its toes. Because of this dynamic element, in some sense no market is ever a pure textbook monopoly.

3. Price controls create their own deadweight loss in the form of rent seeking. Price controls do not eliminate monopoly pressures. The monopolist has a big incentive to regain its ability to set its own price and will lobby hard to remove price controls. Economists see resources spent to regain their monopoly price as socially wasteful.

4. Economists distrust government. Governments have their own political agendas—there is no general belief among economists that governments will try to set the price at the competitive level. Once one opens up the price control gates in cases of monopoly, it will be difficult to stop government from using price controls in competitive markets.

The arguments are, of course, more complicated, and will be discussed in more detail in later chapters, but this should give you a good preview of some of the policy arguments that occur in real life.

Natural Ability

A barrier to entry that might exist is that a firm is better at producing a good than anyone else. It has unique abilities that make it more efficient than all other firms. The barrier to entry in such a case is the firm's natural ability. The defense attorneys in an antitrust case against Microsoft argued that it was Microsoft's superior products that led to its capture of 90 percent of the market.

Monopolies based on ability usually don't provoke the public's ire. Often in the public's mind such monopolies are "just monopolies." The standard economic model doesn't distinguish between a "just" and an "unjust" monopoly. The just/unjust distinction raises the question of whether a firm has acquired a monopoly based on its ability or on certain unfair tactics such as initially pricing low to force competitive companies out of business but then pricing high. Many public debates over monopoly focus on such normative issues, about which the economists' standard model has nothing to say.

Natural Monopolies

An alternative reason why a barrier to entry might exist is that there are significant economies of scale. If sufficiently large economies of scale exist, it would be inefficient to have two producers since if each produced half of the output, neither could take advantage of the economies of scale. Such industries are called natural monopolies. A **natural monopoly** is *an industry in which a single firm can produce at a lower cost than can two or more firms.* A natural monopoly will occur when the technology is such that indivisible setup costs are so large that average total costs fall within the range of possible outputs. I demonstrate that case in Figure 14-7(a).

> In a natural monopoly, a single firm can produce at a lower cost than can two or more firms.

If one firm produces Q_1, its cost per unit is C_1. If two firms each produce half that amount, $Q_{1/2}$, so that their total production is Q_1, the cost per unit will be C_2, which is significantly higher than C_1. In cases of natural monopoly, as the number of firms in the industry increases, the average total cost of producing a fixed number of units increases. For example, if each of three firms in an industry had a third of the market, each firm would have an average cost of C_3.

Until the 1990s local landline telephone service was a real-world example of such a natural monopoly. It made little sense to have two sets of telephone lines going into people's houses. Cell phones and smartphones changed that and undermined

---

FIGURE 14-7 (A AND B)   **A Natural Monopolist**

The graph in **(a)** shows the average cost curve for a natural monopoly. One firm producing Q_1 would have a lower average cost than a combination of firms would have. For example, if three firms each produced $Q_{1/3}$, the average cost for each would be C_3.

The graph in **(b)** shows that a natural monopolist would produce Q_M and charge a price P_M. It would earn a profit shown by the orange shaded box. If the monopolist were required to charge a price equal to marginal cost, P_C, it would incur a loss shown by the blue shaded box.

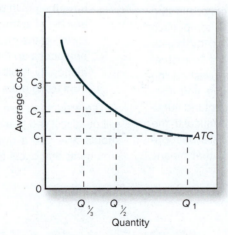

(a) Average Cost for Natural Monopolist

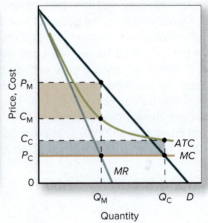

(b) Profit of Natural Monopolist

Monopolizing Monopoly

Have you ever played Monopoly? Probably you have. And in the process, you have made money for Parker Brothers, the firm that has the monopoly on Monopoly. How the firm got it is an interesting story of actual events following games and vice versa. The beginnings of the Monopoly game go back to a Quaker woman named Lizzie Magie, who was part of the one-tax movement of populist economist Henry George. That movement, which was a central populist idea in the late 1800s, wanted to put a tax on all land rent to finance government. George argued that there would be no need for an income tax; the tax on the land monopoly would finance it all. Lizzie Magie created a game, called the Landlord's Game, as a way of teaching George's ideas, and showing how monopoly caused problems. She patented the game in 1904.

A new invention would have undercut your most profitable item. You bought the invention and kept it off the market.

COLLECT $75 FROM TREASURER

NEW INVENTION R.I.P

© 1977, 1985, 1989, 2005 by Ralph Anspach, Patent 4138881

©Ralph Anspach

Despite the patent, people copied the game with her approval, since her desire was to spread George's ideas. As the game spread, it kept changing form and rules, and eventually acquired the property names associated with Atlantic City, which the game now uses, and came to be called Monopoly. A number of variations of the game developed.

In the 1930s Charles Darrow was taught the game and had some friends write up the rules, which they copyrighted. (They couldn't patent the game because they didn't invent it.) In 1935 Darrow made an agreement with Parker Brothers, a firm that sold games, that gave the firm the right to produce this monopoly game in exchange for royalties. As Parker Brothers discovered the history of the monopoly game and of the particular games that preceded it, Parker Brothers bought the rights to the previous games so that the firm would secure its full rights to Monopoly. It paid the various people between $500 and $10,000 for those rights. In 1974, an economics professor, Ralph Anspach, created an "Anti-Monopoly" game that pitted monopolists against competitors. To protect its monopoly, in 1974 Parker Brothers sued Anspach. In 1985 after suits and countersuits they came to an agreement. Anspach assigned the rights to the "Anti-Monopoly" trademark to Parker Brothers, but kept the rights to use it under license.

the landline monopoly. That often happens; natural monopolies are only natural given a technology.

A natural monopoly also can occur when a single industry standard is more efficient than multiple standards, even when that standard is owned by one firm. An example is the operating system for computers. A single standard is much more efficient than multiple standards because the communication among computer users is easier.

From a welfare standpoint, natural monopolies are different from other types of monopolies. In the case of a natural monopoly, even if a single firm makes some monopoly profit, the price it charges may still be lower than the price two firms making normal profit would charge because its average total costs will be lower. In the case of a natural monopoly, not only is there no welfare loss from monopoly, but there can actually be a welfare gain since a single firm producing is so much more efficient than many firms producing. Such natural monopolies are often organized as public utilities. For example, most towns have a single water department supplying water to residents.

Figure 14-7(b) shows the profit-maximizing level of output and price that a natural monopolist would choose. To show the profit-maximizing level of output, I've added a marginal cost curve that is below the average total cost curve. (If you don't know why this must be the case, a review of costs is in order.) A natural monopolist uses the same $MC = MR$ rule that a monopolist uses to determine output. The natural monopolist will produce Q_M and charge a price P_M. Average total costs are C_M and the natural monopolist earns a profit shown by the orange shaded box.

Normative Views of Monopoly

Many laypeople's views of government-created monopoly reflect the same normative judgments that Classical economists made. Classical economists considered, and much of the lay public considers, such monopolies unfair and inconsistent with liberty. Monopolies prevent people from being free to enter whatever business they want and are undesirable on normative grounds. In this view, government-created monopolies are simply wrong.

This normative argument against government-created monopoly doesn't extend to all types of government-created monopolies. The public accepts certain types of government-created monopoly that it believes have over-riding social value. An example is patents. To encourage research and development of new products, government gives out patents for a wide variety of innovations, such as genetic engineering, Xerox machines, and cans that can be opened without a can opener.

A second normative argument against monopoly is that the public doesn't like the income distributional effects of monopoly. Although, as we saw in our discussion of monopoly, monopolists do not always earn an economic profit, they often do, which means that the monopoly might transfer income in a way that the public (whose

normative views help determine society's policy toward monopoly) doesn't like. This distributional effect of monopoly based on normative views of who deserves income is another reason many laypeople oppose monopoly: They believe it transfers income from "deserving" consumers to "undeserving" monopolists.

A third normative reason people oppose government-created monopoly that isn't captured by the standard model of monopoly is that the possibility of government-created monopoly encourages people to spend a lot of their time in political pursuits trying to get the government to favor them with a monopoly, and less time doing "productive" things. It causes *rent-seeking* activities in which people spend resources to gain monopolies for themselves.

Each of these arguments probably plays a role in the public's dislike of monopoly. As you can see, these real-world arguments blend normative judgments with objective analysis, making it difficult to arrive at definite conclusions. Most real-world problems require this blending, making applied economic analysis difficult. The economist must interpret the normative judgments about what people want to achieve and explain how public policy can be designed to achieve those desired ends.

Q-8 Why is the competitive price impossible for an industry that exhibits strong economies of scale?

Where a natural monopoly exists, the perfectly competitive solution is impossible, since average total costs are not covered where $MC = P$. A monopolist required by government to charge the competitive price P_C, where $P = MC$, will incur a loss shown by the blue shaded box because marginal cost is always below average total cost. Either a government subsidy or some output restriction is necessary in order for production to be feasible. In such cases, monopolies are often preferred by the public as long as they are regulated by government. I will discuss the issues of regulating natural monopolies in the chapter on real-world competition.

Network and Platform Monopolies

Web Note 14.3

The Best Monopoly in America

The standard textbook presentation of monopoly is done in reference to firms that produce a specific good and earn their revenues from selling a product. That's an enormous simplification. Much of the debate about monopoly today involves *platform businesses,* firms that provide people with a platform, or underlying infrastructure, that facilitates interaction among people. Platform businesses are more complicated than textbook monopolies since their business model involves not just one, but multiple activities and sources of income. Platform businesses often do not charge for the platform they provide; rather, they earn their revenues from selling ad space to other businesses, and by selling data about people who use their platform to firms so that they can better target their advertising.

The Dark Side of Amazon

Amazon is a great company—innovative and efficient. It has added enormous competition throughout the economy. But it has a dark side that comes along with its monopoly position. One aspect of that dark side involves how it uses the data it collects on you every time you visit its site. By tracking sales, Amazon knows what is selling and what isn't, and it often uses those data to decide where it should develop a competing product. To many this is an unfair advantage.

©kay roxby/Shutterstock

The best sellers on Amazon can expect that Amazon will undercut them with a competing product, transferring profits from those sellers who use the Amazon platform to Amazon itself. Small firms find it very hard to compete with Amazon. The bigger Amazon gets, the more it can take advantage of people and firms that sell goods on its platform, which discourages the entry of new sellers.

For a firm with its market power, Amazon has not made significant profits. Instead it has chosen to invest in future growth to expand its market share. So, as of 2018, it was not exploiting its monopoly position as much as it could. But its stock sells for a lot. The reason why is that investors know that Amazon is gaining strong monopoly positions in numerous areas and expect that at some point in the future it will start monetizing that monopoly position.

Examples of platform firms are Facebook and Google. Both firms provide services that connect people to one another. But they also collect data on their users. Every time you search on Google, you provide Google with data, and every time you "friend" someone, post an update, play a game, or click on an advertisement on Facebook, it is collecting data about you that it can exploit, or sell to other firms. A standard saying is that if you cannot figure out how a company whose service you are using is earning its revenue, it's likely you are not the customer; "you" are the product.

If you cannot figure out how a company whose service you are using is earning its revenue, it's likely you are not the customer; "you" are the product.

Amazon, which connects buyers and sellers for a fee in what it calls the "Amazon Marketplace," is also a platform business. Amazon does more than provide the marketplace; it also provides logistics. It will store, pack, and ship other firms' products at its fulfillment centers. It also sells goods on its own. Platform monopolies make their money both from the fees they charge for their platform and from exploiting the data and information they gain in the process of selling goods or making the market. Thus, the firms that use the Amazon Marketplace platform can also have Amazon as their partner, and be competing against Amazon, which creates potential problems of fairness.

Because it is often more efficient for people to gather on a single rather than multiple competing platforms, there is a natural push for platform businesses to gain a significant share of the market and become platform monopolies. This tendency is the result of what is often called **first-mover advantage**—*benefits gained from being the first to gain a significant share of a market*. First-mover advantage operates in a number of markets.

The first-mover advantage for a platform business is the virtuous cycle that is created as more and more people use the platform. The value created by the platform derives from the network of connections that are created; the larger the network, the more valuable the service. These benefits are known as a **network externality**—*when greater use of a product increases the benefit of that product to everyone without them paying for it*. Social networks such as Facebook exhibit network externalities. If you were the only person in the world on Facebook, it would be pretty useless. As the number of people on Facebook increases, Facebook's value to communication grows enormously. Another example of a product with network externalities is the Windows operating system. It is of much more use to you if many other people use it too, because you can then easily communicate with other Windows users and purchase software based on that platform. With network externalities, platform firms experience a virtuous circle of growth—the bigger they get, the more helpful they are to the people who use them, the more valuable they become, and the more difficult it becomes for new firms to enter the market, or for smaller firms to expand.

Platform monopolies create different problems for policy than do standard monopolies, and how public policy should deal with these firms is still very much in debate. Like natural monopolies, it may make sense to allow platform firms to grow into monopolies due to gains in efficiency. But in setting up the rules of competition, care must be taken to ensure that there will be countervailing power, if a competitive outcome is to be attained.

Platform businesses clearly provide enormous dynamic drive for the economy, but they are also amassing significant power, both in their ability to earn profits and to affect society. Will platform businesses make those decisions with only their profits in mind or will they take into account the public interest? Even if they consider the public interest, the question is how they perceive that interest. An example of the questions posed can be seen in Facebook's treatment of Russian entities that posted fake news during the 2016 U.S. presidential election. Facebook's primary criterion with regard to ads was the financial bottom line, not the social bottom line. Politicians didn't like that and expressed concern, and after the election Facebook changed its procedures, claiming that it was now more focused on the social bottom line.

In summary, platform monopolies offer enormous advantages and gains to the economy. But they create new problems that some argue reduce competition both in the market for platforms, and in the products that are bought and sold on these platforms. Dealing with these problems effectively will be a major concern of public policy in the next decade.

Platform monopolies offer enormous advantages and gains to the economy. But they create new problems.

Monopolistic Competition

So far I have introduced you to the two extremes of market structure: perfect competition and monopoly. Most real-world market structures fall somewhere between the two—in what is called monopolistic competition and oligopoly. In this section I discuss monopolistic competition. In the next chapter I discuss oligopoly.

Characteristics of Monopolistic Competition

Monopolistic competition is *a market structure in which there are many firms selling differentiated products and few barriers to entry.*

The four distinguishing characteristics of monopolistic competition are:

1. Many sellers.
2. Differentiated products.
3. Multiple dimensions of competition.
4. Easy entry of new firms in the long run.

Let's consider each in turn.

MANY SELLERS   When there are only a few sellers, it's reasonable to explicitly take into account your competitors' reaction to the price you set. When there are many sellers, it isn't. In monopolistic competition, firms don't take into account rivals' reactions. Here's an example. There are many types of soap: Dove, Irish Spring, Yardley's Old English, and so on. So when Dove decides to run a sale, it won't spend a lot of time thinking about Yardley's reaction. There are so many firms that one firm can't concern itself with the reaction of any specific firm. The soap industry is characterized by monopolistic competition.

PRODUCT DIFFERENTIATION   The "many sellers" characteristic gives monopolistic competition its competitive aspect. Product differentiation gives it its monopolistic aspect. In a monopolistically competitive market, the goods that are sold aren't homogeneous, as in perfect competition; they are differentiated slightly. Irish Spring soap is slightly different from Ivory, which in turn is slightly different from Yardley's Old English.

Web Note 14.4
Product Differentiation

So in one sense each firm has a monopoly in the good it sells. But that monopoly is fleeting; it is based on advertising to convince people that one firm's good is different from the goods of competitors. The good may or may not really be different. Bleach differs little from one brand to another, yet buying Clorox makes many people feel that they're getting pure bleach. I generally don't buy it; I generally buy generic bleach. Ketchup, however, while made from the same basic ingredients, differs among brands (in my view). For me, only Heinz ketchup is real ketchup. (However, recently, my wife switched and put Hunt's ketchup in a Heinz bottle, and pointed out to me that I didn't notice. She's right; I didn't notice. But I still want Heinz ketchup; it's what my mother gave me, and seeing the Heinz bottle and believing that there is Heinz ketchup in it makes me feel good—so much for my economist's rationality.)

Because a monopolistic competitor has some monopoly power, advertising to increase that monopoly power (and hence increase the firm's profits) makes sense as long as the marginal benefit of advertising exceeds the marginal cost. Despite the fact that their goods are similar but differentiated, to fit economists' monopolistically competitive model, firms must make their decisions as if they had no effect on other firms.

MULTIPLE DIMENSIONS OF COMPETITION   In perfect competition, price is the only dimension on which firms compete; in monopolistic competition, competition takes many forms. Product differentiation reflects firms' attempt to compete on perceived attributes; advertising is another form competition takes. Other dimensions of competition include service and distribution outlets. These multiple dimensions of competition make it much harder to analyze a specific industry, but the alternative methods of competition follow the same two general decision rules as price competition:

In monopolistic competition, competition takes many forms.

- Compare marginal costs and marginal benefits; and
- Change that dimension of competition until marginal costs equal marginal benefits.

EASE OF ENTRY OF NEW FIRMS IN THE LONG RUN   The last condition a monopolistically competitive market must meet is that entry must be relatively easy; that is, there must be no significant entry barriers. Barriers to entry create the potential for long-run economic profit and prevent competitive pressures from pushing price down to average total cost. In monopolistic competition, if there were long-run economic profits, other firms would enter until no economic profit existed.

Advertising and Monopolistic Competition

While firms in a perfectly competitive market have no incentive to advertise (since they can sell all they want at the market price), monopolistic competitors have a strong incentive. That's because their products are differentiated from the others; advertising plays an important role in providing that differentiation.

GOALS OF ADVERTISING

Goals of advertising include shifting the firm's demand curve to the right and making it more inelastic.

GOALS OF ADVERTISING   Goals of advertising include shifting the firm's demand curve to the right. Advertising works by providing consumers with information about the firm's product and by making people want only a specific brand. That allows the firm to sell more, to charge a higher price, or to enjoy a combination of the two.

When many firms are advertising, the advertising might be done less to shift the demand curve out than to keep the demand curve where it is—to stop consumers from shifting to a competitor's product. In either case, firms advertise to move the demand curve further out than it would be if the firms weren't advertising.

Advertising has another effect; it shifts the average total cost curve up. Thus, in deciding how much to advertise, a firm must consider advertising's effect on both revenue and cost. It is advantageous to the firm if the marginal revenue of advertising exceeds the marginal cost of advertising.

Q-9 Why do monopolistically competitive firms advertise while perfect competitors do not?

DOES ADVERTISING HELP OR HURT SOCIETY?   Our perception of products (the degree of trust we put in them) is significantly influenced by advertising. Think of the following pairs of goods:

Web Note 14.5

Brand Names

Rolex	Cheerios	Clorox bleach	Bayer
Timex	Oat Circles	generic bleach	generic aspirin

Each of these names conveys a sense of what it is and how much trust we put in the product, and that determines how much we're willing to pay for it. For example, most people would pay more for Cheerios than for Oat Circles. Each year firms in the United States spend about $220 billion on advertising. A 30-second commercial during the Super Bowl can cost more than $5 million. That advertising increases firms' costs but also differentiates their products.

Are we as consumers better off or worse off with differentiated products? That's difficult to say. There's a certain waste in much of the differentiation. That waste shows up in the graph by the fact that monopolistic competitors don't produce at the minimum point of their average total cost curve. But there's also a sense of trust that we get from buying names we know and in having goods that are slightly different from one another. I'm a sophisticated consumer who knows that there's little difference between generic aspirin and Bayer aspirin. Yet sometimes I buy Bayer aspirin even though it costs more.

Edward Chamberlin who, together with Joan Robinson, was the originator of the description of monopolistic competition believed that the difference between the cost of a perfect competitor and the cost of a monopolistic competitor was the cost of what he called "differentness."[3] If consumers are willing to pay that cost, then it's not a waste but, rather, it's a benefit to them.

We must be careful about drawing any implications from this analysis. Average total cost for a monopolistically competitive firm includes the cost of advertising and product differentiation.

There's often little difference between name brand and generic products.

©Sheila Fitzgerald/Shutterstock

---

[3]Joan Robinson, a Cambridge, England, economist, called this the theory of imperfect competition, rather than the theory of monopolistic competition.

Whether we as consumers are better off with as much differentiation as we have, or whether we'd all be better off if all firms produced a generic product at a lower cost, is debatable.

Output, Price, and Profit of a Monopolistic Competitor

Although a full analysis of the multiple dimensions of monopolistic competition cannot be compressed into two dimensions, a good introduction can be gained by considering it within the standard two-dimensional (price, quantity) graph.

To do so we simply consider the characteristics of monopolistic competition and see what implication they have for the analysis. The firm has some monopoly power; therefore, a monopolistic competitor faces a downward-sloping demand curve. The downward-sloping demand curve means that in making decisions about output, the monopolistic competitor will, as will a monopolist, face a marginal revenue curve that is below price. At its profit-maximizing output, marginal cost will be less than price (not equal to price as it would be for a perfect competitor). We consider that case in Figure 14-8(a).

The monopolistic competitor faces the demand curve D, marginal revenue curve MR, and marginal cost curve MC. This demand curve is its portion of the total market demand curve. Using the $MC = MR$ rule discussed in the last chapter, you can see that the firm will choose output level Q_M (because that's the level of output at which marginal revenue intersects marginal cost). Having determined output, we extend a dotted line up to the demand curve and see that the firm will set a price equal to P_M. This price exceeds marginal cost. So far all we've done is reproduce the monopolist's decision.

Where does the competition come in? Competition implies zero economic profit in the long run. [If there's profit, a new competitor will enter the market, decreasing the existing firms' demand (shifting it to the left).] In long-run equilibrium, a perfect competitor makes only a normal profit. Economic profits are determined by ATC, not by MC, so the competition part of monopolistic competition tells us where the average total cost curve must be at the long-run equilibrium output. It must be equal to price, and it will be equal to price only if the ATC curve is tangent to (just touching) the demand curve at the output the firm chooses. We add that average total cost curve to

Q-10 How does the equilibrium for a monopoly differ from that for a monopolistic competitor?

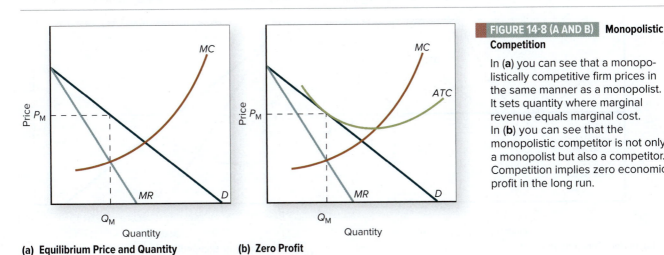

(a) **Equilibrium Price and Quantity**   (b) **Zero Profit**

FIGURE 14-8 (A AND B) **Monopolistic Competition**

In (**a**) you can see that a monopolistically competitive firm prices in the same manner as a monopolist. It sets quantity where marginal revenue equals marginal cost. In (**b**) you can see that the monopolistic competitor is not only a monopolist but also a competitor. Competition implies zero economic profit in the long run.

the *MC, MR,* and demand curves in Figure 14-8(b). Profit or loss, I hope you remember, is determined by the difference between price and average total cost at the quantity the firm chooses.

To give this condition a little more intuitive meaning, let's say, for instance, that the monopolistically competitive firm is making a profit. This profit would set two adjustments in motion. First, it would attract new entrants. Some of the firm's customers would then defect, and its portion of the market demand curve would shift to the left. Second, to try to protect its profits, the firm would likely increase expenditures on product differentiation and advertising to offset that entry to shift the demand curve back to the right. (There would be an All New, Really New, Widget campaign.) These expenditures would shift its average total cost curve up. These two adjustments would continue until the profits disappeared and the new demand curve was tangent to the new average total cost curve. A monopolistically competitive firm can make no long-run economic profit.

Comparing Monopoly, Monopolistic Competition, and Perfect Competition

If both the monopolistic competitor and the perfect competitor make zero economic profit in the long run, it might seem that, in the long run at least, they're identical. They aren't, however. The perfect competitor perceives its demand curve as perfectly elastic, and the zero economic profit condition means that it produces at the minimum of the average total cost curve where the marginal cost curve equals price. We demonstrate that case in Figure 14-9(a).

The monopolistic competitor faces a downward-sloping demand curve for its differentiated product. It produces where the marginal cost curve equals the marginal revenue curve, and not where *MC* equals price. In equilibrium, price

---

FIGURE 14-9 (A AND B) **A Comparison of Perfect and Monopolistic Competition**

The perfect competitor perceives its demand curve as perfectly elastic, and zero economic profit means that it produces at the minimum of the *ATC* curve, as represented in (**a**). A monopolistic competitor, on the other hand, faces a downward-sloping demand curve and produces where marginal cost equals marginal revenue, as represented in (**b**). In long-run equilibrium, the *ATC* curve is tangent to the demand curve at that level, which is *not* at the minimum point of the *ATC* curve. The monopolistic competitor sells Q_M at price P_M. A perfect competitor with the same marginal cost curve would produce Q_C at price P_C.

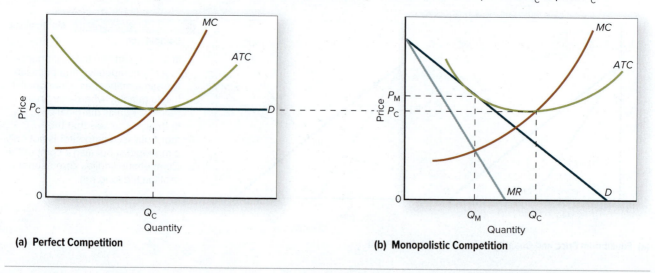

(a) Perfect Competition   **(b) Monopolistic Competition**

exceeds marginal cost. The average total cost curve of a monopolistic competitor is tangent to the demand curve at the profit-maximizing level of output, which cannot be at the minimum point of the average total cost curve since the demand curve is sloping downward. The minimum point of the average total cost curve (where a perfect competitor produces) is at a higher output (Q_C) than that of the monopolistic competitor (Q_M). I demonstrate the monopolistically competitive equilibrium in Figure 14-9(b) to allow you to compare monopolistic competition with perfect competition.

The perfect competitor in long-run equilibrium produces at a point where $MC = P = ATC$. At that point, ATC is at its minimum. A monopolistic competitor produces at a point where $MC = MR$. Price is higher than marginal cost. For a monopolistic competitor in long-run equilibrium:

$$(P = ATC) \geq (MC = MR)$$

At that point, ATC is *not* at its minimum.

What does this distinction between a monopolistically competitive industry and a perfectly competitive industry mean in practice? It means that for a monopolistic competitor, since increasing output lowers average cost, increasing market share is a relevant concern. If only the monopolistic competitor could expand its market, it could raise its profit. For a perfect competitor, increasing output offers no benefit in the form of lower average cost. A perfect competitor would have no concern about market share (the firm's percentage of total sales in the market).

Finally, let's think about the difference between monopolistic competition and monopoly. They are almost the same, except for one important difference. For a monopolist, the average total cost curve can be, *but need not be,* at a position below price so that the monopolist can make a long-run economic profit. In contrast, the average total cost curve for a monopolistic competitor must be tangent to the demand curve at the price and output chosen by the monopolistic competitor. No long-run economic profit is possible, which means that a monopolistic competitor is simply a monopolist that makes zero profit.

For a monopolistic competitor in long-run equilibrium, $(P = ATC) \geq (MC = MR)$

An important difference between a monopolist and a monopolistic competitor is in the position of the average total cost curve in long-run equilibrium.

Conclusion

We've come to the end of the presentation of the formal models of perfect competition, monopoly, and monopolistic competition. As you can see, the real world gets very complicated very quickly. I'll show you just how complicated in the chapter on real-world competition and technology. But don't let the complicated real world get you down on the theories presented here. It's precisely because the real world is so complicated that we need some framework, like the one presented in this chapter. That framework lets us focus on specific issues—and hopefully the most important.

Working through the models takes a lot of effort, but it's effort well spent. In Chapter 1, I quoted Einstein: "A theory should be as simple as possible, but not more so." This chapter's analysis isn't simple; it takes repetition, working through models, and doing thought experiments to get it down pat. But it's as simple as possible. Even so, it's extremely easy to make a foolish mistake, as I did in my PhD oral examination when I was outlining an argument on the blackboard. ("*What did you say the output would be for this monopolist, Mr. Colander?*") As I learned then, it takes long hours of working through the models again and again to get them right.

Summary

- A monopolist takes into account how its output affects price; a perfect competitor does not.   (*LO14-1*)

- The price a monopolist charges is higher than the competitive market price due to the restriction of output; a monopolist can make a profit in the long run.   (*LO14-2*)

- A monopolist's profit-maximizing output is where marginal revenue equals marginal cost.   (*LO14-2*)

- A monopolist can charge the maximum price consumers are willing to pay for the quantity the monopolist produces.   (*LO14-2*)

- To determine a monopolist's profit, first determine its output (where $MC = MR$). Then determine its price and average total cost at that output level. The difference between price and average total cost at the profit-maximizing level of output is profit per unit. Multiply this by output to find total profit.   (*LO14-2*)

- Because monopolists reduce output and charge a price that is higher than marginal cost, monopolies create a welfare loss to society.   (*LO14-3*)

- If a monopolist can (1) identify groups of customers who have different elasticities of demand, (2) separate them in some way, and (3) limit their ability to resell its product between groups, it can price-discriminate.   (*LO14-3*)

- A price-discriminating monopolist earns more profit than a normal monopolist because it can charge a higher price to those with less elastic demands and a lower price to those with more elastic demands.   (*LO14-3*)

- Price discrimination eliminates welfare loss from monopoly.   (*LO14-3*)

- Three important barriers to entry are natural ability, economies of scale, and government restrictions.   (*LO14-4*)

- Natural monopolies exist in industries with strong economies of scale. Because their average total costs are always falling, it is more efficient for one firm to produce all the output.   (*LO14-4*)

- The competitive price is impossible in a natural monopoly because marginal cost is always below average total cost. No firm would enter an industry where not even normal (zero economic) profit can be made.   (*LO14-4*)

- Platform monopolies and network externalities are becoming increasingly important in the economy. (*LO14-4*)

- Monopolistic competition is characterized by (1) many sellers, (2) differentiated products, (3) multiple dimensions of competition, and (4) ease of entry for new firms.   (*LO14-5*)

- Monopolistic competitors differ from perfect competitors in that the former face a downward-sloping demand curve.   (*LO14-5*)

- A monopolistic competitor differs from a monopolist in that a monopolistic competitor makes zero economic profit in long-run equilibrium.   (*LO14-5*)

Key Terms

first-mover advantage	monopoly	network externality	price-discriminate
monopolistic competition	natural monopoly	patent	

Questions and Exercises ■ connect

1. What is the key difference between a monopolist and a perfect competitor?   (*LO14-1*)

2. Does a monopolist take market price as given? Why or why not?   (*LO14-1*)

3. Why is marginal revenue below average revenue for a monopolist?   (*LO14-2*)

4. State what's wrong with the following graphs: (LO14-2)

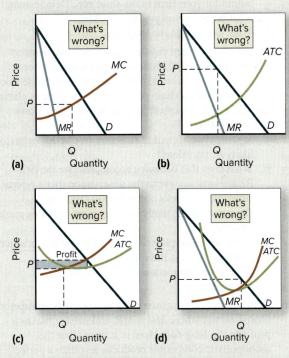

(a)

(b)

(c)

(d)

5. Say you place a lump-sum tax (a tax that is treated as a fixed cost) on a monopolist. How will that affect its output and pricing decisions? (LO14-2)

6. A monopolist is selling fish. But if the fish don't sell, they rot. What will be the likely elasticity at the point on the demand curve at which the monopolist sets the price? (Difficult) (LO14-2)

7. Demonstrate graphically the profit-maximizing positions for a perfect competitor and a monopolist. How do they differ? (LO14-2)

8. True or false? Monopolists differ from perfect competitors because monopolists make a profit. Why? (LO14-2)

9. A monopolist with a straight-line demand curve finds that it can sell 2 units at $12 each or 12 units at $2 each. Its fixed cost is $20 and its marginal cost is constant at $3 per unit. (LO14-2)
   a. Draw the MC, ATC, MR, and demand curves for this monopolist.
   b. At what output level would the monopolist produce?
   c. At what output level would a perfectly competitive firm produce?

10. Demonstrate the welfare loss created by a monopoly. (LO14-3)

11. Will the welfare loss from a monopolist with a perfectly elastic marginal cost curve be greater or less than the welfare loss from a monopolist with an upward-sloping marginal cost curve? (LO14-3)

12. What three things must a firm be able to do to price-discriminate? (LO14-3)

13. The Government Accounting Office reported that airlines block new carriers at major airports. (LO14-4)
    a. What effect does such blocking have on fares and the number of flights at those airports?
    b. How much are airlines willing to spend to control the use of gates to block new carriers?

14. How is efficiency related to the number of firms in an industry characterized by strong economies of scale? (LO14-4)

15. During the 2001 anthrax scare, the U.S. government threatened to disregard Bayer's patent of ciprofloxacin, the most effective drug to fight anthrax, and license the production of the drug to American drug companies to stockpile the drug in case of an anthrax epidemic. While the policy would lower costs to the U.S. government of stockpiling the drug, it also would have other costs. What are those costs? (Difficult) (LO14-4)

16. Econocompany is under investigation by the U.S. Department of Justice for violating antitrust laws. The government decides that Econocompany has a natural monopoly and that, if it is to keep the government's business, it must sell at a price equal to marginal cost. Econocompany says that it can't do that and hires you to explain to the government why it can't. (LO14-4)
    a. Explain why in reference to the following graph.
    b. What price would it charge if it were unregulated?
    c. What price would you advise that it should be allowed to charge?

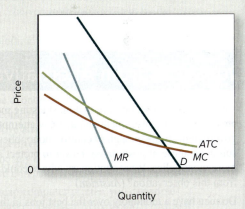

17. What is the first-mover advantage and how does it affect platform monopolies? (LO14-4)

18. What are the benefits of platform monopolies? What are the costs? (LO14-4)

19. What are the ways in which a firm can differentiate its product from that of its competitors? What is the overriding objective of product differentiation? (LO14-5)

20. What are the "monopolistic" and the "competitive" elements of monopolistic competition? (LO14-5)

demand curve and bisects the quantity axis at one-half the value of the quantity-axis intercept of the demand curve. The marginal revenue curve, because it bisects the quantity axis at one-half the value of the quantity-axis intercept of the accompanying demand curve, must fall twice as fast as the market demand curve. That is, its slope is twice the slope of the market demand curve.

Knowing that its slope is twice the market demand curve slope, you can write the marginal revenue curve with the same price-axis intercept as the demand curve and a slope of two times the slope of the demand curve. (*Warning:* This works only with linear demand curves.) The price-axis intercept of the demand curve is the value of P where Q equals 0: 112. The quantity-axis intercept of the demand curve is the value of Q where P equals 0: 28. So, the marginal revenue curve has a price-axis intercept at 112 and a quantity-axis intercept at 14. Mathematically, such a curve is represented by:

$$P = 112 - (112/14)P$$

or

$$P = 112 - 8Q$$

Now that we've determined the monopolist's marginal revenue curve, we can determine its equilibrium quantity by setting $MR = MC$ and solving for Q. Doing so gives us:

$$112 - 8Q = 2Q + 4$$
$$-10Q = -108$$
$$Q = 10.8$$

The monopolist then charges the price consumers are willing to pay for that quantity. Mathematically, substitute 10.8 into the demand equation and solve for price:

$$P = 112 - 4(10.8)$$
$$P = \$68.80$$

Comparing the price and quantity produced by a monopolist and those of a competitive industry shows that the monopolist charges a higher price and produces a lower output.

Questions and Exercises

1. The market demand curve is $Q_D = 50 - P$. The marginal cost curve is $MC = 4Q + 6$.
   a. Assuming the marginal cost curve is for a competitive industry as a whole, find the profit-maximizing level of output and price.
   b. Assuming the marginal cost curve is for only one firm that comprises the entire market, find the profit-maximizing level of output and price.
   c. Compare the two results.

2. The market demand curve is $Q_D = 160 - 4P$. A monopolist's total cost curve is $TC = 6Q^2 + 15Q + 50$.
   a. Find the profit-maximizing level of output and price for a monopolist.
   b. Find its average cost at that level of output.
   c. Find its profit at that level of output.

3. Suppose fixed costs for the monopolist in question 2 increase by 52.
   a. Find the profit-maximizing level of output and price for a monopolist.
   b. Find its average cost at that level of output.
   c. Find its profit at that level of output.

4. The market demand curve is $Q_D = 12 - \frac{1}{3}P$. Costs do not vary with output.
   a. Find the profit-maximizing level of output and price for a monopolist.
   b. Find the profit-maximizing level of output and price for a competitive industry.

Oligopoly and Antitrust Policy

In business, the competition will bite you if you keep running; if you stand still, they will swallow you.

—Victor Kiam

©Anton Havelaar/123RF

In previous chapters we discussed competition, monopoly, and a blend of the two—monopolistic competition. In this chapter we discuss another blend: **oligopoly**—*a market structure in which there are only a few firms and firms explicitly take other firms' likely response into account.*

The Distinguishing Characteristics of Oligopoly

The central element of oligopoly is that there are a small number of firms in an industry so that, when making decisions, a firm must take into account the expected reaction of other firms. Oligopolistic firms are mutually interdependent and can be collusive or noncollusive.

This mutual interdependence is the big difference between monopolistic competition and oligopoly. In oligopoly, firms explicitly take other firms' actions into account. In monopolistic competition, there are so many firms that individual firms tend not to explicitly take into account rival firms' likely responses to their decisions. Collusion is difficult. In oligopoly there are fewer firms, and each firm is more likely to explicitly engage in **strategic decision making**—*taking explicit account of a rival's expected response to a decision you are making.* In oligopolies all decisions, including pricing decisions, are strategic decisions. Also, in oligopolies, collusion is much easier. Thus, one distinguishes between monopolistic competition and oligopoly by whether or not firms explicitly take into account competitors' reactions to their decisions.

Why is the distinction important? Because it determines whether economists can model and predict the price and output of an industry. Nonstrategic decision making can be predicted relatively accurately if individuals behave rationally. Strategic decision making is much more difficult to predict, even if people behave rationally. What one person does depends on what he or she expects other people to do, which in turn depends on what others expect the one person to do. Consistent with this distinction, economists' model of monopolistic competition has a definite prediction. A model of monopolistic competition will tell us: Here's how much will be produced and here's how much will be charged. Economists' models of oligopoly don't have a definite prediction. There are no unique price and output decisions at which an oligopoly will rationally arrive; there are a variety of rational oligopoly decisions, and a variety of oligopoly models.

Most industries in the United States have some oligopolistic elements. If you ask almost any businessperson whether he or she directly takes into account rivals' likely response, the answer you'll get is "In certain cases, yes; in others, no."

Most retail stores that you deal with are oligopolistic in your neighborhood or town, although, if the market is seen to extend beyond your neighborhood, they may be quite competitive. For example, how many grocery stores do you shop at? Do you think they keep track of what their competitors are doing? You bet. They keep a close eye on their competitors' prices and set their own accordingly.

Models of Oligopoly Behavior

No single general model of oligopoly behavior exists. The reason is that an oligopolist can decide on pricing and output strategy in many possible ways, and there are no compelling grounds to characterize any of them as *the* oligopoly strategy. Although there are five or six formal models, I'll focus on two informal models of oligopoly behavior that give you insight into real-world problems. The two models we'll consider are the cartel model and the contestable market model. These should give you a sense of how real-world oligopolistic pricing takes place.

Why, you ask, can't economists develop a simple formal model of oligopoly? The reason lies in the interdependence of oligopolists. Since there are few competitors, what one firm does specifically influences what other firms do, so an oligopolist's plan must always be a contingency or strategic plan. If my competitors act one way, I'll do X, but if they act another way, I'll do Y. Strategic interactions have a variety of potential outcomes rather than a single outcome such as in the formal models we discussed. An oligopolist spends enormous amounts of time guessing what its competitors will do, and it develops a strategy of how it will act accordingly. As we will discuss in Chapter 20, an entire theory called game theory has developed that considers interdependent decisions. The appendix to Chapter 20 shows how game theory can be applied to oligopoly decisions.

The Cartel Model

A **cartel** is *a combination of firms that acts as if it were a single firm;* a cartel is a shared monopoly. If oligopolies can limit entry by other firms, they have a strong incentive to cartelize the industry and to act as a monopolist would, restricting output to a level that maximizes profit for the combination of firms. Thus, the **cartel model of oligopoly** is *a model that assumes that oligopolies act as if they were monopolists that have assigned output quotas to individual member firms of the oligopoly so that*

Oligopolistic firms are mutually interdependent.

Oligopolies take into account the reactions of other firms; monopolistic competitors do not.

Q-1 Your study partner, Jean, has just said that monopolistic competitors use strategic decision making. How would you respond?

If oligopolies can limit the entry of other firms and form a cartel, they increase the profits going to the combination of firms in the cartel.

total output is consistent with joint profit maximization. All firms follow a uniform pricing policy that serves their collective interest.

Since a monopolist makes the most profit that can be squeezed from a market, cartelization is the best strategy for an oligopoly. It requires each oligopolist to hold its production below what would be in its own interest were it not to collude with the others. Such explicit formal collusion is against the law in the United States, but informal collusion is allowed and oligopolies have developed a variety of methods to collude implicitly. Thus, the cartel model has some relevance.

The model has some problems, however. For example, various firms' interests often differ, so the collective interest of the firms in the industry isn't clear. In many cases a single firm, often the largest or dominant firm, takes the lead in pricing and output decisions, and the other firms (which are often called *fringe firms*) follow suit, even though they might have preferred to adopt a different strategy.

This dominant-firm cartel model works only if the smaller firms face barriers to entry or the dominant firm has significantly lower cost conditions. If that were not the case, the smaller firms would pick up an increasing share of the market, eliminating the dominant firm's monopoly. An example of such a dominant-firm market was the copier market in the 1960s and 1970s, in which Xerox set the price and other firms followed. That copier market also shows the temporary nature of such a market. As the firms became more competitive on cost and quality, Xerox's market share fell and the company lost its dominant position. The copier market is far more competitive today than it used to be.

In other cases the various firms meet—sometimes only by happenstance, at the golf course or at a trade association gathering—and arrive at a collective decision. In the United States, meetings for this purpose are illegal, but they do occur. In yet other cases, the firms engage in **implicit collusion**—*multiple firms make the same pricing decisions even though they have not explicitly consulted with one another.* They "just happen" to come to a collective decision.

IMPLICIT PRICE COLLUSION

Implicit price collusion, in which firms just happen to charge the same price but didn't meet to discuss price strategy, isn't against the law. Oligopolies often operate as close to the fine edge of the law as they can. For example, many oligopolistic industries allow a price leader to set the price, and then the others follow suit. The airline and steel industries take that route. Firms just happen to charge the same price or very close to the same price.

It isn't only in major industries that you see such implicit collusion. In small towns, you'll notice that most independent carpenters charge the same price. There's no explicit collusion, but were a carpenter to offer to work for less than the others, he or she would feel unwelcome at the local breakfast restaurant.

Or let's take another example: the Miami fish market, where sport fishermen sell their catch at the dock. When I lived in Miami, I often went to the docks to buy fresh fish. There were about 20 stands, all charging the same price. Price fluctuated, but it was by subtle agreement, and close to the end of the day the word would go out that the price could be reduced.

I got to know some of the sellers and asked them why they priced like that when it would be in their individual interest to set their own price. Their answer: "We like our boat and don't want it burned." They may have been talking in hyperbole, but social pressures play an important role in stabilizing prices in an oligopoly.

CARTELS AND TECHNOLOGICAL CHANGE

Even if all firms in the industry cooperate, other firms, unless they are prevented from doing so, can always enter the market with a technologically superior new product at the same price or with the same good at

Web Note 15.1
Price Fixing

Q-2 Why is it difficult for firms in an industry to maintain a cartel?

In some cases, firms collude implicitly—they just happen to make the same pricing decisions. This is not illegal.

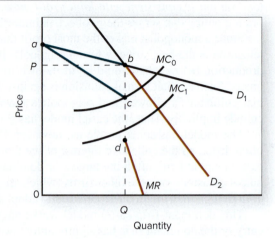

FIGURE 15-1 **The Kinked Demand Curve**

One explanation for why prices are sticky is that firms face a kinked demand curve. When we draw the relevant marginal revenue curve for the kinked demand, we see that the corresponding *MR* curve is discontinuous. It has a gap in it. Shifts in marginal costs between *c* and *d* will not change the price or the output that maximizes profits.

a lower price. It is important to remember that technological changes are constantly occurring, and that a successful cartel with high profits will provide incentives for significant technological change, which can eliminate demand for its monopolized product.

WHY ARE PRICES STICKY?

Informal collusion happens all the time in U.S. businesses. One characteristic of informal collusive behavior is that prices tend to be sticky—they don't change frequently. Informal collusion is an important reason why prices are sticky. But it's not the only reason.

Another possible reason is that firms don't collude, but do have certain expectations of other firms' reactions, which changes their perceived demand curves. Specifically, they perceive that the demand curve they face is kinked. This kinked demand curve is used especially to explain why firms often do not use lower-price strategies to increase sales.

Let's go through the reasoning behind the kinked demand curve. If a firm increases its price, and the firm believes that other firms won't go along, its perceived demand curve for increasing price will be very elastic (D_1 in Figure 15-1). It will lose lots of business to the other firms that haven't raised their price. The relevant portions of its demand curve and its marginal revenue curve are shown in blue in Figure 15-1.

If it decreases its price, however, the firm assumes that all other firms would immediately match that decrease, so it would gain very few, if any, additional sales. A large fall in price would result in only a small increase in sales, so its demand is relatively inelastic (D_2 in Figure 15-1). This less elastic portion of the demand curve and the corresponding marginal revenue curve are shown in red in Figure 15-1.

Notice that when you put these two curves together, you get a rather strange demand curve (it's kinked) and an even stranger marginal revenue curve (one with a gap). I didn't make a mistake in drawing the curves; that's the way they come out given the assumptions. When the demand curve has a kink, the marginal revenue curve must have a gap. Shifts in marginal cost (such as MC_0 to MC_1) will not change the firm's profit maximization position. A large shift in marginal cost is required before firms will change their price. Why should this be the case? The intuitive answer lies in the reason behind the kink. If the firm raises its price, other firms won't go along, so it will lose lots of market share. However, when the firm lowers price, other firms will go along and the firm won't gain market share. Thus, the firm has strong reasons not to change its price in either direction.

Q-3 Is the demand curve as perceived by an oligopolist likely to be more or less elastic for a price increase or a price decrease?

When the demand curve has a kink, the marginal revenue curve must have a gap.

I should emphasize that the kinked demand curve is not a theory of oligopoly pricing. It does not say why the original price is what it is; the kinked demand curve is simply a theory of sticky prices.

The Contestable Market Model

A second model of oligopoly is the contestable market model. The **contestable market model** is *a model of oligopoly in which barriers to entry and barriers to exit, not the structure of the market, determine a firm's price and output decisions.* Thus, it emphasizes entry and exit conditions, and says that the price that an oligopoly will charge will exceed the cost of production only if new firms cannot exit and enter the market. The higher the barriers, the more the price exceeds cost. Without barriers to entry or exit, the price an oligopolist sets will be equal to the competitive price. Thus, an industry that structurally looks like an oligopoly could set competitive prices and output levels.

In the contestable market model of oligopoly, pricing and entry decisions are based only on barriers to entry and exit, not on market structure. Thus, even if the industry contains only one firm, it could still be a competitive market if entry is open.

Comparison of the Contestable Market Model and the Cartel Model

Because of the importance of social pressures in determining strategies of oligopolies, no one "oligopolistic model" exists. Oligopolies with a stronger ability to collude (that is, more social pressures to prevent entry) are able to get closer to a monopolist solution. Equilibrium of oligopolies with weaker social pressures and less ability to prevent new entry is closer to the perfectly competitive solution. That's as explicit as we can be.

An oligopoly model can take two extremes: (1) the cartel model, in which an oligopoly sets a monopoly price, and (2) the contestable market model, in which an oligopoly with no barriers to entry sets a competitive price. Thus, we can say that an oligopoly's price will be somewhere between the competitive price and the monopolistic price. Other models of oligopolies give results in between these two.

Q-4 What are the two extremes an oligopoly model can take?

Much of what happens in oligopoly pricing is highly dependent on the specific legal structure within which firms interact. In Japan, where large firms are specifically allowed to collude, we see Japanese goods that do not face international competition selling for a much higher price than those same Japanese goods sell for in the United States. For example, before increased international competition, Japanese televisions sold in Japan cost as much as twice the amount as the same televisions in the United States. From the behavior of Japanese firms, we get a sense of what pricing strategy U.S. oligopolists would follow in the absence of the restrictions placed on them by law.

NEW ENTRY AS A LIMIT ON THE CARTELIZATION STRATEGY One of the things that limits oligopolies from acting as a cartel is the threat from outside competition. The threat will tend to be more effective if this outside competitor is much larger than the firms in the oligopoly.

One of the things that limits oligopolies from acting as a cartel is the threat from outside competition.

For example, small-town banks have a tendency to collude (implicitly, of course), offering lower interest to savers and charging higher interest to borrowers than big banks charge, even though their average costs aren't significantly higher. When I ask small-town banks why this is, they tell me that my perceptions are faulty and that I should mind my own business. But if a big bank, which couldn't care less about increasing the wealth of a small-town banker, enters the town and establishes a branch office, interest rates to savers seem to go up and interest rates to borrowers seem to go down. The big bank can add significant competition—competition that couldn't come from within the town.

Strategic Competition between Uber and Lyft

Many of the new dynamic companies in our economy do not produce products, but rather provide platforms for markets to work. Uber and Lyft—ride-sharing companies that connect people who are looking for a driver to take them somewhere to people who are willing to drive people where they want to go—are examples of platform businesses. Buyers and sellers are connected through an app on smartphones. Essentially, Uber and Lyft are taxi companies that have been set up to avoid many of the rules and regulations that taxis face. Currently, rides using Uber and Lyft are generally cheaper than taxis. Customers can order rides and pay for them almost hassle-free with an app on their smartphone.

©Roman Tiraspolsky/Shutterstock

As of 2018, competition between Uber and Lyft was fierce. Although both were losing money, both had extremely high stock valuations. The reason why is that investors were predicting that eventually both companies would be able to use their market power to provide high profits in the future. Much of the market power of companies is based on inertia; customers become accustomed to a particular app and, once they are comfortable using it, stick with it even when prices rise.

While the enormous competition between Uber and Lyft is currently holding their fares down, this will not likely remain the case. There is strong pressure for the two companies to merge, or to implicitly collude and develop a tacit agreement to share the market. Economists see signs pointing to a likely merger. For example, the two companies have designed their apps to appear similar, which will make a merger easier. Competition can be fierce just before a merger as each tries to gain a strategic advantage in the eventual merger. The greater a company's market share at the time of the merger, the better the company will make out in the agreement.

The specific results of strategic competition are hard to predict; a small change (such as a CEO's offhand comment) can significantly change the results. Economists have developed a tool, game theory, to study this interaction. We will explore this tool in a later chapter.

On a national scale, the outside competition comes from international firms.

On a national scale, the outside competition often comes from international firms. For example, implicit collusion among U.S. automobile firms led to foreign firms' entry into the U.S. automobile market. There are many such examples of this outside competition breaking down cartels with no barriers to entry. Thus, a cartel with no barriers to entry faces a long-run demand curve that's very elastic. This means that its price will be very close to its marginal cost and average cost. This is the same prediction that came from the contestable market theory.

PLATFORM MONOPOLIES AND CONTESTABLE MARKETS As we discussed in the last chapter, many of the large, dynamic new companies are platform monopolies, whose product advantages are driven by network externalities—the bigger they are, the more valuable their services are to consumers, and the stronger are their monopoly positions. This not only creates a strong push toward monopoly, but also says that a monopoly can better serve customers' needs. So, platform monopolies tend to be natural monopolies. Competition, if it is going to come, will come from new technologies that change the nature of the market and open the new market to competition. This means that once a platform is established, there will be strong barriers to entry, which provide existing firms with significant market power. At first, competition might be fierce as firms fight for who will win the battle to become the monopoly, but once the dominant firms are established, the competition will decrease. (See the "Strategic Competition between Uber and Lyft" box.)

A Comparison of Various Market Structures

Structure / Characteristics	Monopoly	Oligopoly	Monopolistic Competition	Perfect Competition
Number of Firms	One	Few	Many	Almost infinite
Barriers to Entry	Significant	Significant	Few	None
Pricing Decisions	$MC = MR$	Strategic pricing, between monopoly and perfect competition	$MC = MR$	$MC = MR = P$
Output Decisions	Most output restriction	Output somewhat restricted	Output restricted somewhat by product differentiation	No output restriction
Interdependence	Only firm in market, not concerned about competitors	Interdependent strategic pricing and output decision	Each firm acts independently	Each firm acts independently
Profit	Possibility of long-run economic profit	Some long-run economic profit possible	No long-run economic profit possible	No long-run economic profit possible
P and MC	$P > MC$	$P > MC$	$P > MC$	$P = MC$

Classifying Industries and Markets in Practice

An industry seldom fits neatly into one category or another. Inevitably, numerous arbitrary decisions must be made as to what the appropriate market is, and whether the industry comes closest to the characteristics of one or the other market structure. So to classify actual industries, a variety of procedures and measures have been developed, and in this section we review those procedures and measures.

To see the problems that arise in classifying industries, consider the banking industry. There are about 5,000 commercial banks in the United States, and banking is considered reasonably competitive. However, a particular small town may have only one or two banks, so there will be a monopoly or oligopoly with respect to banks in that town. Is the United States or the town the relevant market? The same argument exists when we think of international competition. Many firms sell in international markets and, while a group of firms may compose an oligopoly in the United States, the international market might be more accurately characterized by monopolistic competition.

Web Note 15.2

Porter's Five Forces

Another dimension of the classification problem concerns deciding what is to be included in an industry. If you define the industry as "the transportation industry," there are many firms. If you define it as "the urban transit industry," there are fewer firms; if you define it as "the commuter rail industry," there are still fewer firms. Similarly with the geographic dimension of industry. There's more competition in the global market than in the local market. The narrower the definition, the fewer the firms.

One of the ways in which economists classify markets in practice is by cross-price elasticities (the responsiveness of a change in the demand for a good to a change in the price of a related good). Industrial organization economist F. M. Sherer has suggested the following rule of thumb: When two goods have a cross-price elasticity greater than or equal to 3, they can be regarded as belonging to the same market.

The North American Industry Classification System

The **North American Industry Classification System (NAICS)** is *an industry classification that categorizes industries by type of economic activity and groups firms with like production processes.* In the NAICS, all firms are placed into 20 broadly defined two-digit sectors. These two-digit sectors are further subdivided into three-digit subsectors, four-digit industry groupings, five-digit industries, and six-digit national industry groupings. Each subgrouping becomes more and more narrowly defined. Table 15-1 lists the 20 sectors and shows some subgroupings for one sector, Information, to give you an idea of what's included in each.

When economists talk about industry structure, they generally talk about industries in the four- to six-digit subsector groupings in the United States. This is a convention.

Q-5 Which would have more output: the two-digit industry 21 or the four-digit industry 2111? Explain your reasoning.

TABLE 15-1 **Industry Groupings in the North American Industry Classification System**

Two-Digit Sectors	Three- to Five-Digit Subsectors
11 Agriculture, forestry, fishing, and hunting	
21 Mining	
22 Utilities	
23 Construction	
31–33 Manufacturing	
42 Wholesale trade	
44–45 Retail trade	
48–49 Transportation and warehousing	51 Information
51 Information	511 Publishing Industries (except Internet)
52 Finance and insurance	5111 Newspaper, Periodical, Book, and Directory Publishers
53 Real estate and rental and leasing	51111 Newspaper Publishers
54 Professional, scientific, and technical services	
55 Management of companies and enterprises	
56 Administrative and support, and waste management and remediation services	
61 Educational services	
62 Health care and social assistance	
71 Arts, entertainment, and recreation	
72 Accommodation and food services	
81 Other services (except public administration)	
92 Public administration	

Source: U.S. Census Bureau (www.census.gov/eos/www/naics).

Economists are often called on to give expert testimony in court cases, and if an economist wants to argue that an industry is more competitive than its opponents say it is, he or she challenges this convention of using a four- to six-digit classification of industry, asserting that the classification is arbitrary (which it is) and that the relevant market should be the two- to three-digit classification.

Empirical Measures of Industry Structure

To empirically measure industry structure, economists use one of two methods: the concentration ratio or the Herfindahl index.

A **concentration ratio** is *the value of sales by the top firms of an industry stated as a percentage of total industry sales.* The most commonly used concentration ratio is the four-firm concentration ratio. For example, a four-firm concentration ratio of 60 percent tells you that the top four firms in the industry produce 60 percent of the industry's output. The higher the ratio, the closer the industry is to an oligopolistic or monopolistic type of market structure.

The **Herfindahl index** is *an index of market concentration calculated by adding the squared value of the individual market shares of all the firms in the industry.* For example, say that 10 firms in the industry each have 10 percent of the market:

$$\text{Herfindahl index} = 10^2 + 10^2 + 10^2 + 10^2 + 10^2 + 10^2 + 10^2 + 10^2 + 10^2 + 10^2$$
$$= 1,000$$

The Herfindahl index is a method used by economists to classify how competitive an industry is.

The Herfindahl index weights the largest firms in the industry more heavily than does the concentration ratio because it squares market shares.

The two measures can differ because of their construction, but generally if the concentration ratio is high, so is the Herfindahl index. Table 15-2 presents the four-firm concentration ratio and the Herfindahl index of selected industries.

Because it squares market shares, the Herfindahl index gives more weight to firms with large market shares than does the concentration ratio measure.

The Herfindahl index plays an important role in government policy; it is used as a rule of thumb by the U.S. Department of Justice in determining whether an industry is sufficiently competitive to allow a merger between two large firms. If the Herfindahl index is less than 1,000, the Department of Justice generally assumes the industry is

Q-6 If the four-firm concentration ratio of an industry is 60 percent, what is the highest Herfindahl index that industry could have? What is the lowest?

TABLE 15-2   **Empirical Measures of Industry Structure**

Industry	Four-Firm Concentration Ratio	Herfindahl Index
Poultry	46	773
Soft drinks	52	896
Breakfast cereal	78	2,999
Women's and misses' dresses	21	186
Book printing	38	492
Stationery	51	976
Soap and detergent	38	664
Men's footwear	44	734
Women's footwear	64	1,556
Pharmaceuticals	34	506
Computer and peripheral equipment	49	1,183
Radio, TV, wireless broadcasting	42	583
Burial caskets	73	2,965

Source: *Census of Manufacturers* (http://factfinder2.census.gov).

sufficiently competitive, and it doesn't look more closely at the merger. This policy may change in the future.

Conglomerate Firms and Bigness

Neither the four-firm concentration ratio nor the Herfindahl index gives us a picture of corporations' bigness.

Neither the four-firm concentration ratio nor the Herfindahl index gives us a picture of corporations' bigness. That's because many corporations are conglomerates—companies that span a variety of unrelated industries. For example, a conglomerate might produce both shoes and automobiles.

To see that concentration ratios are not an index of bigness, say the entire United States had only 11 firms, each with a 9 percent share of each industry. Both indexes would classify the U.S. economy as unconcentrated, but many people would seriously doubt whether that were the case. Little work has been done on classifying conglomerates or in determining whether they affect an industry's performance.

Oligopoly Models and Empirical Estimates of Market Structure

To see how empirical measures of market structure relate to oligopoly models, let's consider the cartel and contestable market models of oligopoly. The cartel model fits best with these empirical measurements of market concentration because it assumes that the structure of the market (the number of firms) is directly related to the price a firm charges. It predicts that oligopolies charge higher prices than do monopolistic competitors, who in turn charge higher prices than competitive firms charge.

Q-7 The Herfindahl index is 1,500. Using a contestable market approach, what would you conclude about this industry?

The contestable market model gives far less weight to the empirical estimates of market structure. According to the model, markets that structurally look highly oligopolistic could actually be highly competitive—much more so than markets that structurally look less competitive. This contestable market model view of judging markets by performance, not structure, has had many reincarnations. Close relatives of it have previously been called the *barriers-to-entry* model, the *stay-out pricing* model, and the *limit-pricing* model. These models provide a view of competition that doesn't depend on market structure.

Q-8 The Herfindahl index is 1,500. Using a structural analysis of markets approach, what would you conclude about this industry?

To see the implications of the contestable market approach, let's consider an oligopoly with a four-firm concentration ratio of 60 percent and a Herfindahl index of 1,500. Using the structural approach, we would say that, because of the multiplicity of oligopoly models, we're not quite sure what price firms in this industry would charge, but that it seems reasonable to assume that there would be some implicit collusion and that the price would be closer to a monopolist price than to a competitive price. If that same market had a four-firm concentration ratio of 30 percent and a Herfindahl index of 700, the industry would be more likely to have a competitive price.

A contestable market model advocate would disagree, arguing that barriers to entry and exit are what's important. If no significant barriers to entry exist in the first case but significant barriers to entry exist in the second case, the second case would be more monopolistic than the first. An example is the Miami fish market mentioned earlier, where there were 20 sellers (none with a large percentage of the market) and significant barriers to entry (only fishers from the pier were allowed to sell fish there and the slots at the pier were limited). Because of those entry limitations, the pricing and output decisions would be close to the monopolistic price. If you took that same structure but had free entry, you'd get much closer to competitive decisions.

As I presented the two views, I emphasized the differences in order to make the distinction clear. However, I must also point out that there's a similarity in the two views. Often barriers to entry are the reason there are only a few firms in an industry.

And when there are many firms, that suggests that there are few barriers to entry. In such situations, which make up the majority of cases, the two approaches come to the same conclusion.

Antitrust Policy

Now that we've gone over the four major market structures in theory, and the way in which industries are classified in practice, let's consider government's role in affecting market structure. That role goes under the name antitrust policy in the United States and competition policy in some other countries.

Judgment by Performance or Structure?

Antitrust policy is *the government's policy toward the competitive process.* It's the government's rulebook for carrying out its role as referee. In volleyball, for instance, the rulebook would answer such questions as: When should a foul be called? When has a person caught and thrown rather than hit the ball over the net? In business a referee is needed for such questions as: When can two companies merge? What competitive practices are legal? When is a company too big? To what extent is it fair for two companies to coordinate their pricing policies? When is a market sufficiently competitive or too monopolistic?

The United States has seen wide swings in economists' prescriptions concerning such questions, depending on which of the two views of competition has held sway. The two competing views are:

1. **Judgment by performance:** *We should judge the competitiveness of markets by the performance (behavior) of firms in that market.*

2. **Judgment by structure:** *We should judge the competitiveness of markets by the structure of the industry.*

Two examples illustrate the difference.

At different times, U.S. antitrust law has been based on two competing views: judgment by performance and judgment by structure.

STANDARD OIL: JUDGING MARKET COMPETITIVENESS BY PERFORMANCE In the late 1880s, a number of trusts (cartels) in the railroad, steel, tobacco, and oil industries were created by what were sometimes called *robber barons* (organizers of trusts who engaged in the exploitation of natural resources and other unethical behavior). The trusts were seen as making enormous profits, preventing competition, and in general bullying everyone in sight. One such cartel was the Standard Oil Trust, created by John D. Rockefeller, which used its monopoly power to close refineries, raise prices, and limit the production of oil. In response the U.S. Congress passed the *Sherman Antitrust Act of 1890*—a law designed to regulate the competitive process.

In 1908 the government brought a lawsuit against Standard Oil for violating the Sherman Antitrust Act. In 1911 the U.S. Supreme Court handed down its opinion. It was determined that Standard Oil controlled 90 percent of the market and thus was definitely a monopoly. However, the Court decided that the monopolistic market structure did not violate the Sherman Antitrust Act. To be guilty of antitrust violations there had to be evidence that the firm used its monopoly power to its benefit, and the court found that Standard Oil was indeed guilty of "unfair business practices." The resolution was to break up Standard Oil, which made the distinction between judgment by performance and judgment by structure academic. In 1914 the Sherman Antitrust Act was clarified and strengthened with the *Clayton Antitrust Act,* which identified specific practices as illegal and monopolistic.

The structure/performance distinction was important in a case involving U.S. Steel in 1920. Here the Supreme Court ruled that although U.S. Steel controlled a majority

The outcome of the Standard Oil case was determined by performance. The ALCOA case was determined by market structure.

Nefarious Business Practices

The U.S. antitrust laws concern far more than mergers and market structure; they also place legal restrictions on certain practices of businesses such as price-fixing. In a secretly recorded comment during a price-fixing meeting, the former president of Archer Daniels Midland (ADM), a major supplier of food and grain, stated, "Our competitors are our friends and our customers are our enemies."

By law, firms are not allowed to *explicitly* collude in order to fix prices above the competitive level. A key aspect of the law is the explicit nature of the collusion that is disallowed. Airlines, gas stations, and firms in many other industries have prices that generally move in tandem—when one firm changes its price, others seem to follow.

©ADRIAN DENNIS/AFP/Getty Images

Such practices would suggest that these firms are implicitly colluding, but they are not violating the law unless there is explicit collusion.

To prove explicit collusion is difficult—there must be a smoking gun, and there is seldom sufficient evidence of explicit collusion to prosecute businesses. There are exceptions, however. In 1996, ADM was caught red-handed when one of its former officials gave prosecutors tapes of meetings in which price-fixing occurred. Meeting secretly around the world, in countries like Mexico, France, Canada, and Japan, ADM executives tried to fix prices of lysine, a feed additive, and citric acid. One of ADM's officials, working undercover for the FBI, secretly recorded these meetings. Faced with the taped evidence against it, ADM agreed to pay $100 million in fines—the largest criminal antitrust fine in history up to that year. Since that time, fines have risen to even greater sums, with LG, Sharp, and Hitachi paying a fine of $860 million for price-fixing. The largest fines, however, have been paid by banks who were fined $5.8 billion for fixing interest rates.

of the market and was therefore a structural monopoly, it was not a monopoly in performance. That is, it had not used unfair business practices to become a monopolist or once it was a monopolist, and thus it was not in violation of antitrust law. Unlike Standard Oil, U.S. Steel was not required to break up into small companies.

THE ALCOA CASE: JUDGING MARKET COMPETITIVENESS BY STRUCTURE

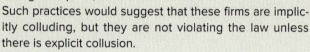

Q-9 How was market competitiveness judged in the Standard Oil and ALCOA cases?

Judgment by performance was the primary criterion governing antitrust policy until 1945, when the U.S. courts changed their interpretation of the law with the Aluminum Company of America (ALCOA) case. ALCOA was the only producer of aluminum in the United States, a position it built by using its knowledge of the market to expand its capacity before any competitors had a chance to enter the market. Like U.S. Steel, it had not used unfair business practices to become a monopolist. This time, however, the courts focused on the structure of the market and ruled ALCOA to be in violation of antitrust laws, even though it was not guilty of monopoly behavior.

JUDGING MARKETS BY STRUCTURE AND PERFORMANCE: THE REALITY

Both judgment by structure and judgment by performance have their problems.

Both judgment by structure and judgment by performance have their problems. Judgment by structure seems unfair on a gut level. After all, in economics the purpose of competition is to motivate firms to produce better goods than their competitors are producing, and to do so at lower cost. If a firm is competing so successfully that all the other firms leave the industry, the successful firm will be a monopolist, and on the basis of judgment by structure will be guilty of antitrust violations. Under the judgment-by-structure criterion, a firm is breaking the law if it does what it's supposed to be doing: producing the best product it can at the lowest possible cost.

Supporters of the judgment-by-structure criterion recognize this problem but nonetheless favor the structure criterion. An important reason for this is practicality.

Judgment by performance requires that each action of a firm be analyzed on a case-by-case basis. Doing that is enormously time-consuming and expensive. In some interpretations, actions of a firm might be considered appropriate competitive behavior; in other interpretations, the same actions might be considered inappropriate. For example, say that an automobile company requires that in order for its warranty to hold, owners of its warranted vehicles must use only the company's parts and service centers. Is this requirement of the automobile company intended to create a monopoly position for its parts and service center divisions or to ensure proper maintenance? The answer depends on the context of the action.

The problem is that judging each case contextually is beyond the courts' capabilities. There are so many firms and so many actions that the courts can't judge all industries on their performance. To solve this problem the courts limit the cases they look at using market share, even though it is firms' performance that will ultimately be judged.

Judging by market structure also has difficulties. As you saw in the discussion of monopolistic competition, it's difficult to determine the relevant geographic market (local, national, or international) and the relevant industry (three-digit or five-digit NAICS code) necessary to identify the structural competitiveness of any industry.

The Role of Antitrust in Today's Economy

Antitrust enforcement has followed the political winds. While discussions of policy are often framed within economics, they generally reflect prevailing ideology and politics. For example, in the 1980s under Republican president Reagan, the United States undertook less antitrust enforcement; in the 1990s under Democratic president Clinton, it undertook more; in the 2000s under Republican president Bush (W) less; in the 2010s under Democratic president Obama more; and, if the pattern holds, we can expect less enforcement under Republican president Trump. As you can see, there is a pattern.

But despite the pattern, over the past decades the long-run trend has been a reduction in the number of antitrust cases brought before the courts. There are three causes for the decline in antitrust enforcement: (1) antitrust laws are known and prevent monopoly actions from occurring, (2) globalization has changed American ideology, and (3) the rate of technological change has increased.

A century of experience has taught businesses what the law allows, which means that antitrust laws work as a preventive measure. Often the threat of an antitrust case is sufficient, so no enforcement is necessary. An example occurred in 2015 when Comcast Cable abandoned a proposed merger with Time Warner Cable when the Justice Department stated that it would likely oppose the merger on antitrust grounds.

Another reason is a change in American ideology. Whereas in the 1950s and 1960s the prevailing ideology saw big business as "bad," starting in the 1980s big business became seen as a combination of good and bad. When antitrust policy was developed in the last century, antitrust and competition were thought of in terms of national policy. The concern was about the power of U.S. firms within the U.S. market. Policy makers were less concerned about imports because the United States was the low-cost producer of many goods, and because trade barriers made global competition difficult. That changed starting in the 1980s when the era of globalization began. Technological revolutions in communication and shipping and a political commitment to globalization meant that the United States was no longer the relevant market; the world was. The bigger the market, the more competition there is.

Competition is now thought of in terms of international policy. For example, U.S.-based Apple, which produces about one-third of all smartphones sold in the United States, faces competition from South Korean multinational firm Samsung, which produces another third of phones sold in the U.S. market. Foreign competition provides competition for Apple; as big as Apple is, there is less need for antitrust enforcement to ensure competition. As big business faces significant international competition, the U.S. market structure has become less of an indicator of monopoly power.

Globalization also means that other countries can provide the antitrust enforcement. While U.S. antitrust authorities have been less active, other countries' antitrust agencies have been more aggressive, and global companies must now take into account likely antitrust implications of multiple jurisdictions, such as China and the European Union (EU). For example, Google recently faced antitrust litigation in the EU because European antitrust authorities felt that Google's search engine favored its comparative shopping service, even though that search engine had passed muster with U.S. antitrust authorities.

Web Note 15.3

Google and the EU

A final reason why antitrust enforcement has declined is that technologies have become more complicated, making the issues in antitrust enforcement so complicated that it can take years to sort them out. Often, by the time a remedy to a supposed offense is determined, the technologies involved and the relevant markets have changed and the remedy is no longer relevant. Examples go back to the 1980s, when a case was brought against IBM. By the time the courts had made their decision, the advent of personal computers had made IBM mainframes obsolete; IBM had lost its monopoly in computers because of technological change. In the 1990s, it was Microsoft's turn. By the time the case against it was decided, Microsoft was being upstaged by Google and Apple. Put simply, the mechanics of antitrust enforcement are just too slow to operate in the fast-changing business environment.

Q-10 True or false? Google exploits its monopoly position by charging high prices to consumers.

COMPLICATIONS FROM STRUCTURAL CHANGES   While the ability of the current regulatory structure to deal with antitrust issues has declined, the need for regulation has not. The issues underlying the concern for monopoly power remain. Companies with market power can take advantage of consumers and the public in ways that many would consider unfair. Antitrust laws are government's response to that concern. Current antitrust laws simply aren't sufficient to address those concerns. Most observers now agree that if we want effective antitrust we need new laws, or at least a major revision of existing laws.

Much of the discussion of antitrust has involved how to make existing antitrust laws relevant to the new companies that are driving our economy such as Facebook, Google, Uber, and Amazon. The issue isn't that these new companies are charging high prices. Often, they are providing much of what they do for "free." Who can complain about that? The concern comes from their other practices, specifically what platform businesses are doing with the data and information they collect about their customers, and how competition should be encouraged in an economy undergoing an information revolution.

These large platform businesses have developed valuable composite pictures of each of their users that they can sell and use to design ads to get people to respond just the way they want, taking advantage of consumers' weaknesses and behavioral regularities. This information can put consumers, and competitors, at an unfair disadvantage. The massive amount of consumer information gathered by existing firms serves as a barrier to entry for potential new competitors since they do not have the data to target ads nearly as well. The data also allow existing firms to see future competition and to stomp on it; they know which new potential platforms are popular long before anyone else does.

Essentially, they have inside information that allows them to buy up potential competitors before those firms become large enough to be serious competitors. For example, Facebook bought Instagram, WhatsApp, and tbh. Google bought Waze. And when a company doesn't want to be bought up? They can deal with that too. Snapchat refused Facebook's takeover bid; Facebook created a snap clone, which it tied to Facebook's Messenger, undermining Snapchat's momentum.

NEW TYPES OF ANTITRUST REMEDIES

Such actions change the competitive landscape. So, the same issues of structure and performance exist today that existed in the 1890s when the Sherman Act was passed, but they play out in quite different ways. Thus, it isn't surprising that the suggested remedies are likely to be somewhat different. Let's consider a few of them.

First, breaking up the companies is far less likely to be the solution since the value of platform businesses to consumers rises with the market share of the business. Breaking them up would decrease the benefit of the service to consumers. Second, technology changes quickly and antitrust remedies involving breaking up a company move slowly. Modern antitrust remedies need to be thought of in a dynamic context in which new technologies are continually challenging older technologies.

Web Note 15.4

Antitrust Today

Increasing competition involves facilitating technological change that challenges existing producers and their products. For firms like Google and Facebook, antitrust laws will likely deal with rules about how to treat the data. One remedy that has been proposed is to let consumers retain ownership over their records, allowing them to move data collected on their behavior to new firms if they want, or to pay to keep the platform from collecting data from them at all. Thus, a person might be given the option of paying, say, 0.0001 cent for each search on Google, with the guarantee that any record of that search is erased. Alternatively, for a fixed fee—perhaps $20—a consumer could have all the data that a company has collected on her erased.

Another proposal involves requiring platform marketplaces such as Amazon to be responsible for the legality of the goods and the conduct of the firms using their platform. Similarly, social network and search companies could be made responsible for the content of posts, and for the ads that appear on their site. Preferences to their own apps, which the EU found Google guilty of, might be dealt with by oversight committees that have the technical background and expertise to make informed decisions.

None of these solutions is simple, and each has its own problems. But the business of modern business is not simple; it is highly technical, and antitrust policy must deal with that complexity.

The business of modern business is not simple.

Conclusion

We've come to the end of our discussion of market structure and government policy toward the competitive process. What conclusion should we reach? That's a tough question because the problem has so many dimensions. What we can say is that market structure is important, and generally more competition is preferred to less competition. We can also say that, based on experience, government-created and protected monopolies have not been the optimal solution, especially when industries are experiencing technological change. Neither is traditional antitrust policy. It is just too slow, and is not designed to deal with the highly technical issues that need to be considered.

So, the future will likely not be about antitrust enforcement with the current regulatory structure, but about *changing* the regulatory structure. That is never easy.

Summary

- The two distinguishing characteristics of an oligopolistic market are (1) there are a small number of firms and (2) firms engage in strategic decision making.   (*LO15-1*)

- A contestable market theory of oligopoly judges an industry's competitiveness more by performance and barriers to entry than by structure. Cartel models of oligopoly concentrate on market structure.   (*LO15-2*)

- An oligopolist's price will be somewhere between the competitive price and the monopolistic price.   (*LO15-2*)

- Industries are classified by economic activity in the North American Industry Classification System (NAICS). Industry structures are measured by concentration ratios and Herfindahl indexes.   (*LO15-3*)

- A concentration ratio is the sum of the market shares of individual firms with the largest shares in an industry.   (*LO15-3*)

- A Herfindahl index is the sum of the squares of the individual market shares of all firms in an industry.   (*LO15-3*)

- Antitrust policy is the government's policy toward the competitive process.   (*LO15-4*)

- There is a debate about whether markets should be judged on the basis of structure or on the basis of performance.   (*LO15-4*)

- Judgment by performance means judging the competitiveness of markets by the behavior of firms in that market. Judgment by structure means judging the competitiveness of markets by how many firms operate in the industry and their market shares.   (*LO15-4*)

- Antitrust enforcement has declined over the past 40 years due to changes in ideology, the advent of globalization, and advances in technology. Structural changes in the economy have not eliminated the need for antitrust policy; they have changed the type of policies required to ensure competition.   (*LO15-4*)

Key Terms

antitrust policy	contestable market model	judgment by structure	oligopoly
cartel	Herfindahl index	North American	strategic decision
cartel model of oligopoly	implicit collusion	Industry Classification	making
concentration ratio	judgment by performance	System (NAICS)	

Questions and Exercises   ■ connect

1. What distinguishes oligopoly from monopolistic competition?   (*LO15-1*)

2. Is an oligopolist more or less likely to engage in strategic decision making compared to a monopolistic competitor?   (*LO15-1*)

3. What is the difference between the contestable market model and the cartel model of oligopoly?   (*LO15-2*)

4. How are the contestable market model and the cartel model of oligopoly related?   (*LO15-2*)

5. Robert Crandell, former CEO of American Airlines, phoned the former Braniff Airways CEO and said, "Raise your fares 20 percent and I'll raise mine the next morning."   (*LO15-2*)
   a. Why would he do this?

   b. If you were the Braniff Airways CEO, would you have gone along?
   c. Why should Crandell not have done this?

6. Kellogg's, which controls 32 percent of the breakfast cereal market, cut the prices of some of its best-selling brands of cereal to regain market share lost to Post, which controls 20 percent of the market. General Mills has 24 percent of the market. The price cuts were expected to trigger a price war. Based on this information, what market structure best characterizes the market for breakfast cereal?   (*LO15-2*)

7. At one time Mattel proposed acquiring Fisher-Price for $1.2 billion. At the time, Mattel was a major player in the

toy industry with 11 percent of the market. Fisher-Price had 4 percent. The other two large firms were Tyco, with a 5 percent share, and Hasbro, with a 15 percent share. In the infant/preschool toy market, Mattel had an 8 percent share and Fisher-Price had a 27 percent share, the largest. The other two large firms were Hasbro, with a 25 percent share, and Rubbermaid, with a 12 percent share. (*LO15-3*)

a. What were the approximate Herfindahl and four-firm concentration ratios for these industries? (Assume all other firms in each industry had 1 percent of the market each.)

b. If you were Mattel's economist, which industry definition would you suggest using in court if you were challenged by the government?

c. Give an argument why the merger might decrease competition.

d. Give an argument why the merger might increase competition.

8. Which industry is more highly concentrated: one with a Herfindahl index of 1,200 or one with a four-firm concentration ratio of 55 percent? (*LO15-3*)

9. The pizza market is divided as follows: (*LO15-3*)

Pizza Hut	20.7%
Domino's	17.0
Little Caesars	6.7
Pizza Inn/Pantera's	2.2
Round Table	2.0
All others	51.4

a. How would you describe its market structure?

b. What is the approximate Herfindahl index?

c. What is the four-firm concentration ratio?

10. If you were an economist for a firm that wanted to merge, would you argue that the three-digit or five-digit NAICS industry is the relevant market? Why? (*LO15-3*)

11. Suppose you are an economist for Mattel, manufacturer of the Barbie doll, which was making an unsolicited bid to take over Hasbro, manufacturer of the G.I. Joe doll. (*LO15-4*)

a. Would you argue that the relevant market is dolls, preschool toys, or all toys including video games? Why?

b. Would your answer change if you were working for Hasbro?

12. What is the difference between judgment by performance and judgment by structure? (*LO15-4*)

13. Is a contestable model or cartel model more likely to judge an industry by performance? Explain your answer. (*LO15-4*)

14. Distinguish the basis of judgment for the Standard Oil and the ALCOA cases. (*LO15-4*)

15. Demonstrate graphically how regulating the price of a monopolist can both increase quantity and decrease price. (Difficult) (*LO15-4*)

a. Why did the regulation have the effect it did?

b. How relevant to the real world do you believe this result is in the contestable markets view of the competitive process?

c. How relevant to the real world do you believe this result is in the cartel view of the competitive process?

16. Discuss the effect of antitrust policy in the: (*LO15-4*)

a. Monopolistic competition model.

b. Cartel model of oligopoly.

c. Contestable market model of oligopoly.

17. What are three reasons fewer antitrust cases have been brought before the courts? (*LO15-4*)

18. How do platform businesses change the nature of antitrust policy? (*LO15-4*)

Questions from Alternative Perspectives

1. In the past two chapters you have learned much about market power: how it is used, the efficiency implications, and how society has responded. Yet this power remains, albeit minimally checked from time to time. The economist Thorstein Veblen would not be surprised by this. He would argue that firms use market power because they can. How do monopolists use "power" to manipulate outcomes? (*Institutionalist*)

2. Alexis de Tocqueville once stated, "The Americans have applied to the sexes the great principle of political economy which governs the manufacturers of our age, by carefully dividing the duties of men from those of women, in order that the great work of society may be the better carried on."

a. Do you agree with his statement?

b. What problems might his argument have? (*Feminist*)

3. In which market structure would women likely be most successful? Why? (*Feminist*)

4. Does market structure determine firm behavior or does firm behavior determine market structure? (*Post-Keynesian*)

(*Continued*)

5. A recent study of mergers and acquisitions found that 83 percent of the deals achieved did not result in positive shareholder returns. Some resulted in losses.
   a. If such mergers are not especially profitable, why do they occur?
   b. U.S. antitrust policy has changed dramatically since the 1960s when the government regularly blocked mergers among companies in the same industry. Today, the federal government is much less active; it allows almost all mergers. Is this new approach justified, or has government just given in to the powers that be?
   c. What antitrust policies would work best in today's U.S. economy? *(Radical)*

Issues to Ponder

1. A firm is convinced that if it lowers its price, no other firm in the industry will change price; however, it believes that if it raises its price, some other firms will match its increase, making its demand curve more inelastic. The current price is $8 and its marginal cost is constant at $4.
   a. Sketch the general shape of the firm's *MR, MC,* and demand curves and show why there are two possible equilibria.
   b. If there are two equilibria, which of the two do you think the firms will arrive at? Why?
   c. If the marginal cost falls to $3, what would you predict would happen to price?
   d. If the marginal cost rises to $5, what would you predict would happen to price?
   e. Do a survey of five or six firms in your area. Ask them how they believe other firms would respond to their increasing or decreasing price. Based on that survey, discuss the relevance of this kinked demand model compared to the one presented in the book.

2. Private colleges of the same caliber generally charge roughly the same tuition. Would you characterize these colleges as a cartel type of oligopoly?

3. When Mattel proposed acquiring Fisher-Price, the infant/preschool toy market four-firm concentration ratio was 72 percent. With 8 percent of the market, Mattel was the fourth-largest firm in that market. Mattel proposed to buy Fisher-Price, the market leader with 27 percent.
   a. Why would Mattel want to buy Fisher-Price?
   b. What arguments can you think of in favor of allowing this acquisition?
   c. What arguments can you think of against allowing this acquisition?
   d. How do you think the four-firm concentration ratio for the entire toy industry would compare to this infant/preschool toy market concentration ratio?

4. How would the U.S. economy likely differ today if Standard Oil had not been broken up?

5. American Airlines offered a 50-percent-off sale and cut fares. Continental Airlines and Northwest Airlines sued American Airlines over this action.
   a. What was the likely basis of the suit?
   b. How does the knowledge that Continental and Northwest were in serious financial trouble play a role in the suit?

6. You're working at the Department of Justice. Ms. Ecofame has just developed a new index, the Ecofame index, which she argues is preferable to the Herfindahl index. The Ecofame index is calculated by cubing the market share of the top 10 firms in the industry.
   a. Calculate an Ecofame guideline that would correspond to the Department of Justice guidelines.
   b. State the advantages and disadvantages of the Ecofame index as compared to the Herfindahl index.

7. What did Adam Smith mean when he wrote, "Seldom do businessmen of the same trade get together but that it results in some detriment to the general public"?

Answers to Margin Questions

1. I would respond that monopolistic competitors, by definition, do not take into account the expected reactions of competitors to their decisions; therefore, they cannot use strategic decision making. I would tell Jean she probably meant, "*Oligopolies* use strategic decision making." *(LO15-1)*

2. Maintaining a cartel requires firms to make decisions that are not in their individual best interests. Such decisions are hard to enforce unless there is an explicit enforcement mechanism, which is difficult in a cartel. *(LO15-2)*

3. The demand curve perceived by an oligopolist is more elastic above the current price because it believes that others will not follow price increases. If it increased price, its quantity demanded would fall by a lot. The opposite is true below the current price. The demand curve below current

price is less elastic. Price declines would be matched by competitors and the oligopolist would see little change in quantity demanded with a price decline. (*LO15-2*)

4. The two extremes an oligopoly model can take are (1) a cartel model, which is the equivalent of a monopoly, and (2) a contestable market model, which, if there are no barriers to entry, is the equivalent of a competitive industry. (*LO15-2*)

5. The smaller the number of digits, the more inclusive the classification. Therefore, the two-digit industry would have significantly more output. (*LO15-3*)

6. The highest Herfindahl index for this industry would occur if one firm had the entire 60 percent, and all other firms had an infinitesimal amount, making the Herfindahl index slightly over 3,600. The lowest Herfindahl index this industry could have would occur if each of the top four firms had 15 percent of the market, yielding a Herfindahl index of 900. (*LO15-3*)

7. The contestable market approach looks at barriers to entry, not structure. Therefore, we can conclude nothing about the industry from the Herfindahl index. (*LO15-3*)

8. In a market with a Herfindahl index of 1,500, the largest firm would have, at most, slightly under 38 percent of the market. The least concentrated such an industry could be would be if seven firms each had between 14 and 15 percent of the market. In either of these two cases, the industry would probably be an oligopolistic industry and could border on monopoly. (*LO15-3*)

9. The Court decided that Standard Oil had engaged in systematic abuse and unfair business practices, and therefore was guilty of antitrust violations and must be broken up. It was judged by performance. In the ALCOA case, the Supreme Court decided the structure of the market, not the company's performance, was the appropriate standard by which to judge cases. (*LO15-4*)

10. False. Google actually provides a free search engine to individuals. The concern about Google primarily relates to its other practices, such as its use of the data it collects on individuals. (*LO15-4*)

CHAPTER 16

Real-World Competition and Technology

> It is ridiculous to call this an industry. This is rat eat rat; dog eat dog. I'll kill 'em, and I'm going to kill 'em before they kill me. You're talking about the American way of survival of the fittest.
>
> —Ray Kroc (founder of McDonald's)

After reading this chapter, you should be able to:

LO16-1 Explain what is meant by "competition is for losers."

LO16-2 Define the monitoring problem and state its implications for economics.

LO16-3 Discuss why competition should be seen as a process, not a state.

LO16-4 Summarize how firms protect monopoly.

LO16-5 Name two implications of network externalities for the economic process.

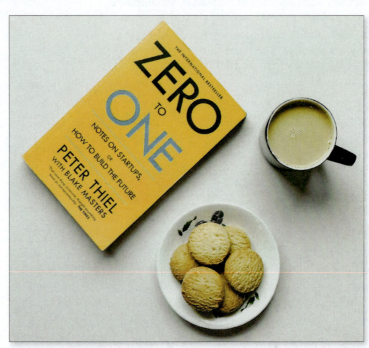

©Jagdish Choudhary/Shutterstock

In earlier chapters we've seen some nice, neat models, but as we discussed, often these models don't fit reality directly. Real-world markets aren't perfectly monopolistic; they aren't perfectly competitive either. They're somewhere between the two. The monopolistic competition and oligopoly models in previous chapters come closer to reality and provide some important insights into the "in-between" markets, but, like any abstraction, they, too, fail to capture aspects of the actual nature of competition.

In this chapter, I give you a sense of what actual firms, markets, and competition are like. This chapter also discusses an issue that is very much in the news—technology—and relates it to the models we developed earlier and shows how economists' modern models differ from the traditional textbook models.

Competition Is for Losers

Let's start with the bottom line of Internet mogul Peter Thiel's book, *Zero to One*. His bottom line is: Competition is for losers. Thiel puts it this way: "Tolstoy famously opens *Anna Karenina* by observing: 'All happy families are alike; each unhappy family is unhappy in its own way.' Business is the opposite. All happy companies are different: Each one earns a monopoly by solving a unique problem. All failed companies are the same: They failed to escape competition."

Thiel argues that the goal of all businesses is, and should be, to create a monopoly for itself, and that successful businesses are constantly working toward that end. Building a monopoly is difficult; other companies are simultaneously building up their own monopolies, some directly affecting you, and others affecting you in only a roundabout way. If you don't continually improve and integrate new technology, you die. So in your business strategy, you are constantly thinking about how to fight off competition and how to strengthen your monopoly.

Thiel contrasts this view of competition with the view of competition that students get from introductory economics books (like the previous chapters in this book). The textbook view is built around structure—competition on one end and monopoly on the other, with monopolistic competition and oligopoly between the two. It is all very static and classifiable. Thiel's view of the world turns monopolistic competition inside out. There is only one market structure—what might be called dynamic monopoly. All firms find themselves moving toward the *zero* "competition" end, or the *one* "monopoly" end (hence the title of his book, *Zero to One*).

This process view of competition is not unique to Thiel. All types of economists, including me, view competition as a process, and discussions of the competitive process have a long history in economics. The problem we teachers of introductory economics have is discussions of the competitive process don't easily fit into neat simple models, and the introductory economics course is built around neat simple models that can be drawn on whiteboards. The process view of competition in which the market is seen as composed of dynamic monopolies—firms trying to move from zero to one—can't be captured in such models. So, in this chapter we get out of the formal modeling mode, think about competition as the dynamic process that it is, and then relate that thinking back to our models.

The Goals of Real-World Firms and the Monitoring Problem

Introducing the concept of dynamic monopoly requires talking about what constitutes the driving force of most businesses. What drives most people to start businesses is not only profits; it is solving problems and achieving goals. Successful businesses solve problems for their customers, and they do it at a lower cost than their competitors; they are benefiting society. How do you know? Because customers are voluntarily paying them for their product. Benefiting society makes one feel good. The profits are nice, but for most entrepreneurs whom I know, it is not profit at all cost—it is profit consistent with feeling good about themselves, and the freedom that being in charge provides them to make the decisions. What this means is that for dynamic monopolies, even those run by a single individual, profit maximization is not an especially good assumption to capture their goals. It certainly is not the profit goal that the standard model highlights—short-run profit.

In a dynamic context, short-run profit is not the focus—if anything long-run profit is. So even if firms are profit maximizers, their primary concern is not short-run profit, but rather long-run profit. This means that even if they can, they may not

Q-1 What is meant by the phrase "competition is for losers"?

Discussions of the competitive process don't easily fit into neat simple models.

Q-2 Why isn't profit maximization an especially good assumption to make about real-world firms?

Who Controls Corporations?

When a corporation is formed, it issues stock, which is sold or given to individuals. Ownership of stock entitles you to vote in the election of a corporation's directors, so in theory holders of stock control the company. In practice, however, in most large corporations, ownership is separated from control of the firm. Most stockholders have little input into the decisions a corporation makes. Instead, most corporations are controlled by their managers, who often run them for their own benefit as well as for the owners'. The reason is that the owners' control of management is limited.

A large percentage of most corporations' stock is not even controlled by the owners; instead, it is controlled by financial institutions such as mutual funds (financial institutions that invest individuals' money for them) and by pension funds (financial institutions that hold people's money for them until it is to be paid out to them upon their retirement). Thus, ownership of corporations is another step removed from individuals. Studies have shown that 80 percent of the largest

©Stephen Brashear/Getty Images

200 corporations in the United States are essentially controlled by managers and have little effective stockholder control.

Why is the question of who controls a firm important? Because economic theory assumes the goal of business owners is to maximize profits, which would be true of corporations if stockholders made the decisions. Managers don't have the same incentives to maximize profits that owners do. There's pressure on managers to maximize profits, but that pressure can often be weak or ineffective. An example of how firms deal with this problem involves stock options. Many companies give their managers stock options—rights to buy stock at a low price—to encourage them to worry about the price of their company's stock. But these stock options dilute the value of company ownership, decrease profits per share, and can give managers an incentive to overstate profits through accounting gimmicks, as happened at Enron, Xerox, and a number of other firms in the early 2000s.

take full advantage of a potential monopolistic situation in order to strengthen their long-run position. For example, many stores have liberal return policies: "If you don't like it, you can return it for a full refund." Similarly, many firms spend millions of dollars improving their reputations or building up a brand. Most firms want to be known as good citizens. Such expenditures on reputation and goodwill can increase long-run profit, even if they reduce short-run profit. Amazon didn't make any profits in its first decade.

The difficulties with the profit-maximizing assumption are multiplied when firms get larger and are no longer run by a single individual. Most real-world production doesn't take place in owner-operated businesses; it takes place in large corporations with eight or nine levels of management, thousands of stockholders whose stock is often held in trust for them, and a board of directors, chosen by management, overseeing the company by meeting 8 to 10 times a year. Those who get the profit are not those who make the decisions about what the firm does. Signing a proxy statement is as close as most stockholders get to directing the company they "own" to maximize profit.

Economic theory tells us that, unless someone is seeing to it that they do, self-interested decision makers have little incentive to hold down their pay. But their pay is a cost of the firm. And if their pay isn't held down, the firm's profit will be lower than otherwise. Most firms put some pressure on managers to make at least a predesignated level of profit. (If you ask managers, they'll tell you that they face enormous pressure.) So the profit motive certainly plays a role—but to say that profit plays a role is not to say that firms maximize profit. Having dealt with many companies, I'll go out on a

Most real-world production doesn't take place in owner-operated businesses; it takes place in large corporations.

Why Are CEOs Paid So Much?

CEOs are paid more today than they were 30 years ago—a lot more. Today, CEOs' pay at top companies is about 250 times that of what an average worker receives, while 30 years ago, CEOs received only 40 times as much. Why the change? Some have suggested that it's just that CEOs are greedy. That's probably true, but it doesn't explain why CEOs are paid so much more today than before, unless they've become a lot greedier, which is unlikely; they've always been greedy. So we have to look elsewhere for an answer.

©Fuse/Corbis/Getty Images

One thing that's changed in the past 30 years is the bargaining power of workers. Workers' pay is now being held down by competition and outsourcing. (If workers ask for a raise, the company responds "No way" and threatens to shift production to China; the workers are forced to give in to save their jobs.) But CEOs' pay is not restrained by outsourcing. (At least not yet.) This means that back in the 1980s, high CEO compensation created labor unrest; today, it does not.

Economists Xavier Gabaix and Augustin Landier of New York University have argued that the rise in CEOs' pay is the result of supply and demand forces. They argue that, today, unconstrained supply and demand forces determine pay of CEOs, whereas back in the 1980s, the bargaining considerations of workers partially prevented supply and demand forces from fully operating.

To explain why CEOs are paid so much more today than they were earlier, they argue that the demand for top CEOs has increased significantly in recent years because there are more large firms today than there were 30 years ago, making small differences in CEO performance matter a lot. They further argue that CEO talent is in short supply, which means that the supply curve for top-rate CEOs is highly inelastic, just like the supply curve for top football players, who also get very high pay. Replacing a top CEO with a CEO ranked 250th, they calculate, would reduce a company's market value by 0.016 percent, which for a large firm they calculated to be about $60 million. This means that today large firms are competing for the highly inelastic supply of high-quality CEOs, and the high demand pushes the pay up. So their answer to the question of why CEOs are paid so much more now is that the number of large firms has increased, which has shifted out the demand for CEOs enormously.

This explanation, if correct, offers a policy suggestion for those who feel that the CEOs aren't deserving of their high pay: Make the income tax more progressive. A high tax on an inelastic supply will not decrease the quantity supplied significantly, so if one makes the income tax more progressive, it will have little effect on the quantity of CEO effort supplied and thus will have minimal negative effects on efficiency.

limb and say that there are enormous wastes and inefficiencies in many U.S. businesses.

This structure presents a problem in applying the model to the real world. The textbook economic model assumes that individuals are utility maximizers—that they're motivated by self-interest. Then, in the textbook model of the firm, the assumption is made that firms, composed of self-interest-seeking individuals, are profit-seeking firms, without explaining how self-interest-seeking individuals who manage real-world corporations will find it in their interest to maximize profit for the firm. Economists recognize this problem, which was introduced in an earlier chapter. It's an example of the **monitoring problem**—*the need to oversee employees to ensure that their actions are in the best interest of the firm.*

Monitoring is required because employees' incentives differ from the owner's incentives, and it's costly to see that the employee does the owner's bidding. The monitoring problem is now a central problem focused on by economists who specialize in

The monitoring problem is that employees' incentives differ from the owner's incentives.

343

industrial organization. They study internal structures of firms and look for a contract that managers can be given: an **incentive-compatible contract** in which *the incentives of each of the two parties to the contract are made to correspond as closely as possible.* The specific monitoring problem relevant to firm structure is that often owners find it too costly to monitor the managers to ensure that managers do what's in the owners' interest. And self-interested managers are interested in maximizing the firm's profit only if the structure of the firm requires them to do so.

When appropriate monitoring doesn't take place, high-level managers can pay themselves very well. For example, in 2017 the CEO of Charter Communications was paid $98 million. But are salaries such as this too high? That's a difficult question.

One way to arrive at an answer is to compare U.S. managers' salaries with those in Japan, where the control of firms is different. Banks in Japan have significant control over the operations of firms, and they closely monitor firms' performance. The result is that, in Japan, high-level managers on average earn about one-fifth of what their U.S. counterparts make, while wages of low-level workers are comparable to those of low-level workers in the United States. Given Japanese companies' success in competing with U.S. companies, this suggests that high managerial pay in the United States reflects a monitoring problem inherent in the structure of corporations common to all third-party-payer systems. There are, of course, other perspectives. Considering what some sports, film, and music stars receive places the high salaries of U.S. managers in a different light.

What Do Real-World Firms Maximize?

If firms don't maximize profit, what do they maximize? What are their goals? The answer again is: It depends.

Real-world firms often have a set of complicated goals that reflect the organizational structure and incentives built into the system. Clearly, profit is one of their goals. Firms spend a lot of time designing incentives to get managers to focus on profit.

But often intermediate goals become the focus of firms. For example, many real-world firms focus on growth in sales; at other times they institute a cost-reduction program to increase long-run profit. At still other times they may simply take it easy and not push hard at all, enjoying the position they find themselves in—being what British economist Joan Robinson called **lazy monopolists**—*firms that do not push for efficiency, but merely enjoy the position they are already in.* This term describes many, but not all, real-world corporations. When Robinson coined the term, firms faced mostly domestic competition. Today, with firms facing more and more global competition, firms are a bit less lazy than they were.

The Lazy Monopolist and X-Inefficiency

Lazy monopolists are not profit maximizers; they see to it that they make enough profit so that the stockholders aren't squealing, but they don't push as hard as they could to hold down their costs. They perform as efficiently as is consistent with keeping their jobs. The result is what economists call **X-inefficiency** (*firms operating far less efficiently than they could technically*). Such firms have monopoly positions, but they don't make large monopoly profits. Instead, their costs rise because of inefficiency; they may simply make a normal level of profit or, if X-inefficiency becomes bad enough, a loss.

The standard model avoids dealing with the monitoring problem by assuming that the owner of the firm makes all the decisions. The owners of firms who receive the profit, and only the profit, would like to see that all the firm's costs are held down. Unfortunately, very few real-world firms operate that way. In reality, owners seldom

Self-interested managers are interested in maximizing firm profit only if the structure of the firm requires them to do so.

Web Note 16.1

Executive Compensation

Q-3 Why would most economists be concerned about third-party-payer systems in which the consumer and the payer are different?

Although profit is one goal of a firm, often firms focus on other intermediate goals such as cost and sales.

Q-4 Why doesn't a manager have the same incentive to hold down costs as an owner does?

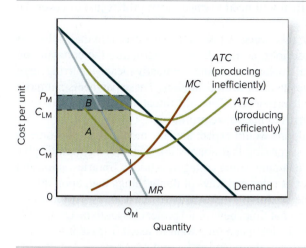

FIGURE 16-1 True Cost Efficiency and the Lazy Monopolist

A monopolist producing efficiently would have costs C_M and would produce at price P_M and quantity Q_M. A lazy monopolist, in contrast, would let costs rise until the minimum level of profit is reached—in this example at C_{LM}. Profit for the monopolist is represented by the entire shaded area, whereas profit for the lazy monopolist is squeezed down to area B.

make operating decisions. They hire or appoint managers to make those decisions. The managers they hire don't have that same incentive to hold down costs. Therefore, it isn't surprising to many economists that managers' pay is usually high and that high-level managers see to it that they have "perks" such as chauffeurs, jet planes, ritzy offices, and assistants to do as much of their work as possible.

The equilibrium of a lazy monopolist is presented in Figure 16-1. A monopolist would produce at price P_M and quantity Q_M. Average total cost would be C_M, so the monopolist's profit would be the entire shaded rectangle (areas A and B). The lazy monopolist would allow costs to increase until the firm reached a minimally acceptable level of profit. In Figure 16-1, costs rise to C_{LM}. The profit of the lazy monopolist is area B. The remainder of the potential profit is eaten up in cost inefficiencies.

What places a limit on firms' laziness is the degree of competitive pressures they face. All economic institutions must earn sufficient revenue to cover costs, so all economic institutions have a limit on how lazy and inefficient they can get—a limit imposed by their monopoly position. They can translate the monopoly profit into X-inefficiency, thereby benefiting the managers and workers in the firm, but once they've done so, they can't be more inefficient. They would go out of business.

The competitive pressures a firm faces limit its laziness.

HOW COMPETITION LIMITS THE LAZY MONOPOLIST If all individuals in the industry are lazy, then laziness becomes the norm and competitive pressures don't reduce their profits. Laziness is relative, not absolute. But if a new firm comes in all gung-ho and hardworking, or if an industry is opened up to international competition, the lazy monopolists can be squeezed and must undertake massive restructuring to make themselves competitive. Many U.S. firms have been undergoing such restructuring in order to make themselves internationally competitive.

A second way in which competitive pressure is placed on a lazy monopolist is by a **corporate takeover,** in which *another firm or a group of individuals issues a tender offer (that is, offers to buy up the stock of a company) to gain control and to install its own managers.* In recent years many of these takeovers were done by private equity firms, which are firms that are not listed on the stock exchange. Most of these private equity firms are primarily investment vehicles, whose expertise is in finance, not in production. They buy up firms that have not been performing well financially and push them to improve their financial payout by becoming more efficient. Usually such tender offers are financed by large amounts of debt, which means that if the takeover

A corporate takeover, or simply the threat of a takeover, can improve a firm's efficiency.

is successful, the private equity firm will need to make large profits just to cover the interest payments on the debt.

Q-5 In what way does the threat of a corporate takeover place competitive pressures on a firm?

Managers generally don't like takeovers. A takeover may cost them their jobs and the perks that go along with those jobs, so they'll often restructure the company on their own as a preventive measure. Such restructuring frequently means incurring large amounts of debt to finance a large payment to stockholders. These payments put more pressure on management to operate efficiently. Thus, the threat of a corporate takeover places competitive pressure on firms to maximize profits.

Were profit not a motive at all, one would expect the lazy monopolist syndrome to take precedence. In fact, it's not surprising that nonprofit organizations often display lazy monopolist tendencies. For example, some colleges, schools, libraries, jails, and nonprofit hospitals have a number of rules and ways of doing things that, upon reflection, benefit the employees of the institution rather than the customers. At most colleges, students aren't polled about what time they would prefer classes to meet; instead, the professors and administrators decide when they want to teach. I leave it to you to figure out whether your college exhibits these tendencies and whether you'd prefer that your college, library, or hospital change to a for-profit institution. Studying these incentive-compatible problems is what management courses are all about.

MOTIVATIONS FOR EFFICIENCY OTHER THAN THE PROFIT INCENTIVE   I'm not going to discuss management theory here other than to stimulate your thinking about the problem. However, I'd be remiss in presenting you this broad outline of the monitoring problem without mentioning that the drive for profit isn't the only drive that pushes for efficiency. Some individuals derive pleasure from efficiently run organizations. Such individuals don't need to be monitored. Thus, if administrators are well intentioned, they'll hold down costs even if they aren't profit maximizers. In such cases, monitoring (creating an organization and structure that gives people profit incentives) can actually reduce efficiency! It's amazing to some economists how some nonprofit organizations operate as efficiently as they do—some libraries and colleges fall into that category. Their success is built on their employees' pride in their jobs, not on their pure self-interest.

Individuals have complicated motives; some simply have a taste for efficiency.

Most economists don't deny that such inherently efficient individuals exist, and that most people derive some pleasure from efficiency, but they believe that it's hard to maintain that push for efficiency year in, year out, when some of your colleagues are lazy monopolists enjoying the fruits of your efficiency. Most people derive some pleasure from efficiency, but, based on their observation of people's actions, economists believe that holding down costs without the profit motive takes stronger willpower than most people have.

The Fight between Competitive and Monopolistic Forces

Even if all the assumptions for perfect competition could hold true, it's unlikely that real-world markets would be perfectly competitive. The reason is that perfect competition assumes that individuals accept a competitive institutional structure—political and social forces that support competition—even though changing that structure could result in significant gains for sellers or buyers. The simple fact is that *self-interest-seeking individuals don't like competition for themselves* (although they do like it for others), and when competitive pressures get strong and the invisible hand's push turns to shove, individuals often shove back, using either social or political means. That's why you can understand real-world competition only if you understand how the invisible hand, social forces, and political pressures push against each other to create real-world economic institutions. Real-world competition should be seen as a process—a fight between the forces of monopolization and the forces of competition.

Competition is a process—a fight between the forces of monopolization and the forces of competition.

How Monopolistic Forces Affect Perfect Competition

Let's consider some examples. During the Depression of the 1930s, competition was pushing down prices and wages. What was the result? Individuals socially condemned firms for unfair competition, and numerous laws were passed to prevent it. Unions were strengthened politically and given monopoly powers so they could resist the pressure to push down wages. The Robinson-Patman Act was passed, making it illegal for large retailers to lower prices to the detriment of local mom-and-pop stores. Individual states passed similar laws, and in the 1990s it was under one of these that Wal-Mart Stores, Inc. lost a court case in which it was accused of charging too-low prices in its pharmacies.

As another example, consider agricultural markets, which have many of the conditions for almost perfect competition. To my knowledge, not one country in the world allows a competitive agricultural market to exist. The United States has myriad laws, regulations, and programs that prevent agricultural markets from working competitively. U.S. agricultural markets are characterized by price supports, acreage limitations, and quota systems. Thus, where perfectly competitive markets could exist, they aren't allowed to. An almost infinite number of other examples can be found. Our laws and social values and customs simply do not allow perfect competition to work because government emphasizes other social goals besides efficiency. When competition negatively affects these other goals (which may or may not be goals that most people in society hold), government prevents competition from operating.

The United States has myriad laws, regulations, and programs that prevent agricultural markets from working competitively.

Economic Insights and Real-World Competition

The extreme rarity of perfectly competitive markets *should not* make you think that economics is irrelevant to the real world. Far from it. In fact, the movement away from perfectly competitive markets could have been predicted by economic theory.

Consider Figure 16-2. Competitive markets will exist only if suppliers or consumers don't collude. If the suppliers producing 0L can get together and restrict entry, preventing suppliers who would produce LM from entering the industry, the remaining

Q-6 Explain, using supply and demand curves, why most agricultural markets are not perfectly competitive.

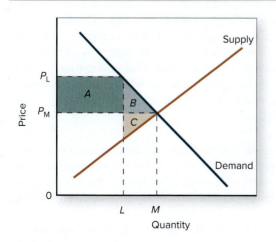

FIGURE 16-2 Movement Away from Competitive Markets

Where suppliers of 0L can restrict suppliers of LM from entering the market, they can raise the price of the good from P_M to P_L, giving the suppliers of 0L area A in additional income. The suppliers kept out of the market lose area C. The consumers, however, lose both areas A and B. Often the costs of organizing for consumers are higher than the costs for the suppliers, so consumers accept the market restrictions.

suppliers can raise their price from P_M to P_L, giving them the shaded area A in additional income. If the cost of their colluding and preventing entry is less than that amount, economic theory predicts that these individuals will collude. The suppliers kept out of the market lose only area C, so they don't have much incentive to fight the restrictions on entry. Consumers lose the areas A plus B, so they have a strong incentive to fight. However, often their cost of organizing a protest is higher than the suppliers' cost of collusion, so consumers accept the restrictions.

Suppliers introducing restrictions on entry seldom claim that the reason for the restrictions is to increase their incomes. Usually they couch the argument for restrictions in terms of the general good, but, while their reasons are debatable, the net effect of restricting entry into a market is to increase suppliers' income to the detriment of consumers.

How Competitive Forces Affect Monopoly

Don't think that because perfect competition doesn't exist, competition doesn't exist. In the real world, competition is fierce; the invisible hand is no weakling. It holds its own against other forces in the economy.

Q-7 Why is it almost impossible for a perfect monopoly to exist?

Competition is so strong that it makes the other extreme (perfect monopolies) as rare as perfect competition. For a monopoly to last, other firms must be prevented from entering the market. In reality it's almost impossible to prevent entry, and therefore it's almost impossible for perfect monopoly to exist. Monopoly profits send out signals to other firms that want to get some of that profit for themselves.

BREAKING DOWN MONOPOLY   To get some of the profit, firms will break down a monopoly through political or economic means. If the monopoly is a legal monopoly, high profit will lead potential competitors to lobby to change the law underpinning that monopoly. If the law can't be changed—say, the monopolist has a patent (which, as I discussed in the chapter on monopoly, is a legal right to be the sole supplier of a good)—potential competitors will generally get around the obstacle by developing a slightly different product or by working on a new technology that avoids the monopoly but satisfies the relevant need.

Say, for example, that you've just discovered the proverbial better mousetrap. You patent it and prepare to enjoy the life of a monopolist. But to patent your mousetrap, you must submit to the patent office the technical drawings of how your better mousetrap works. That gives all potential competitors (some of whom have better financing and already existing distribution systems) a chance to study your idea and see if they can think of a slightly different way (a way sufficiently different to avoid being accused of infringing on your patent) to achieve the same end. They often succeed—so in some cases firms don't apply for patents on new products because the information in the patent application spells out what's unique about the product. That information can help competitors more than the monopoly provided by the patent would hurt them. Instead many firms try to establish an initial presence in the market and rely on inertia to protect what little monopoly profit they can extract.

Establishing an initial presence in a market can be more effective than obtaining a patent when trying to extract monopoly profit.

REVERSE ENGINEERING   Going to the patent office isn't the only way competitors gather information about competing products. One of the other ways routinely used by firms is called **reverse engineering**—*the process of a firm buying other firms' products, disassembling them, figuring out what's special about them, and then copying them within the limits of the law.*

Variations on reverse engineering go on in all industries. Consider the clothing industry. One firm I know of directs its workers to go to top department stores on their lunch hour and buy the latest fashions. The workers bring the clothes back and, that afternoon, the garment makers dismantle each garment into its component parts, make a pattern of each part, and sew up the original again. The next day the worker who chose that garment returns it to the department store, saying, "I don't really like it."

Meanwhile the firm has e-mailed the patterns to its Hong Kong office, and two weeks later its shipment of garments comes in—garments that are almost, but not perfectly, identical to the ones the workers bought. The firm sells this shipment to other department stores at one-fourth the cost of the original.

If you ask businesspeople, they'll tell you that competition is fierce and that profit opportunities are fleeting—which is a good sign that competition does indeed exist in the U.S. economy.

Competition: Natural and Platform Monopolies

The view one takes of the fight between competitive and monopolistic forces influences one's view of what government policy should be in relation to natural monopolies—industries whose average total cost is falling as output increases. We saw in the chapter on monopolies that natural monopolies can make large profits and that consequently there have been significant calls for government regulation of these monopolies to prevent their "exploitation" of the consumer.

Over the past decade, economists and policy makers have become less supportive of such regulation. They argue that even in these cases of natural monopoly, competition works in other ways. High monopoly profits lead to research on alternative ways of supplying the product, such as sending TV signals through electrical lines or sending phone messages by satellite. New technologies provide competition to existing firms. When this technological competition doesn't work fast enough, people direct their efforts toward government, and political pressure is brought to bear either to control the monopoly through regulation or to break up the monopoly.

New technologies can compete with and undermine natural monopolies.

Natural monopolies are especially important for today's economy because many of the dynamic companies, such as Google, Facebook, Airbnb, Microsoft, and Amazon, are platform monopolies that have significant natural monopoly elements. These platform monopolies provide a virtual marketplace for trades to take place. Replacing physical marketplaces with virtual marketplaces increases competition in the goods traded within the market enormously, but it also gives the provider of the market a monopoly that it can exploit. Since the more people that use the market the more useful it is, as platform monopolies get bigger, their monopolistic position increases, making them natural monopolies.

Over time monopolies often lose their monopolies and become forgotten.

©Idealink Photography/Alamy Stock Photo

REGULATING NATURAL MONOPOLIES In the past, the pressure to regulate natural monopolies has been strong. Regulated natural monopolies have been given the exclusive right to operate in an industry but, in return, they've had to agree to have the price they charge and the services they provide regulated. Regulatory boards control the price that natural monopolies charge so that it will be a "fair price," which they generally define as a price that includes all costs plus a normal return on capital investment (a normal profit, but no economic profit). Most states have a number of regulatory boards.

When firms are allowed to pass on all cost increases to earn a normal profit on those costs, they have little or no incentive to hold down costs. In such cases, X-inefficiency develops with a passion, and such monopolies look for capital-intensive

Web Note 16.2

Net Neutrality

When firms are allowed to pass on all cost increases to earn a normal profit on those costs, they have little or no incentive to hold down costs.

projects that will increase their rate bases. To fight such tendencies, regulatory boards must screen every cost and determine which costs are appropriate and which aren't—an almost impossible job. For example, nuclear power is an extremely capital-intensive method of producing electric power, and regulated electric companies favored nuclear power plants until they were told that some nuclear power plant construction costs could not be passed on.

Once regulation gets so specific that it's scrutinizing every cost, the regulatory process becomes extremely bureaucratic, which itself increases the cost. Moreover, to regulate effectively, the regulators must have independent information and must have a sophisticated understanding of economics, cost accounting, and engineering. Often regulatory boards are made up of volunteer laypeople who start with little expertise; they are exhausted or co-opted by the political infighting they have had to endure by the time they develop some of the expertise they need. As is often the case in economics, there's no easy answer to the problem.

It is because of the problems with regulation that more and more economists argue that even in the case of natural and platform monopolies, no explicit regulation is desirable, and that society would be better off relying on direct competitive forces guided by broader regulatory guidelines emphasizing free entry into the industry. They argue that regulated monopolies inevitably inflate their costs so much and are so inefficient and lazy that a monopoly right should never be granted.

DEREGULATING NATURAL MONOPOLIES In the 1980s and 1990s, such views led to the deregulation and competitive supply of both electric power and telephone services. Regulators are making these markets competitive by breaking down the layers of the industry into subindustries and deregulating those subindustries that can be competitive. For example, the electricity industry can be divided into the power generating industry, the power line industry, and the power grid industry. By dividing up the industry, regulators can carve out the part that has the characteristics of a natural monopoly and open the remaining parts to competition.

Let's take a closer look at the electrical industry. It used to be that electricity was supplied by independent local firms, each providing electricity for its own local customers. Today, however, electricity is supplied through a large grid that connects many regions of the country. With this grid, electricity generated in one area can easily be sent all over the country, and suppliers can compete for customers in a variety of regions. The grid makes competition in power supply feasible, and many states have adopted provisions to open their electricity markets to multiple providers.

The power line industry, however, is not competitive. It would be extremely costly for each company to run a separate power line into your house. That is, the power line industry exhibits *economies of scale*. Because of the economies of scale, the power line industry is the natural monopoly aspect of electrical power supply. The deregulation of electricity involves splitting off the production of electricity from the maintenance of the line—and choosing an appropriate charge for electric line maintenance. While in the newspapers you will likely read that the electrical power industry is being deregulated, that is not quite correct. Only those portions of the market where competition is likely to exist are being deregulated.

How Firms Protect Their Monopolies

The image I've presented of competition being motivated by profits is a useful one. It shows how a market economy adjusts to ever-changing technology and demands in the real world. Competition is a dynamic, not a static, force.

Q-8 What is the problem with regulations that set prices relative to costs?

Web Note 16.3

Regulating Natural Monopolies

Economies of scale can create natural monopolies.

Firms do not sit idly by and accept competition. They fight it. How do monopolies fight real-world competition? By spending money on maintaining their monopoly. By advertising. By lobbying. By producing products that are difficult to copy. By not taking full advantage of their monopoly position, which means charging a low price that discourages entry. Often firms could make higher short-run profits by charging a higher price, but they forgo the short-run profits in order to strengthen their long-run position in the industry.

Firms do not sit idly by and accept competition. They fight it.

Cost/Benefit Analysis of Creating and Maintaining Monopolies

Preventing real-world competition costs money. Monopolies are expensive to create and maintain. Economic theory predicts that if firms have to spend money on creating and protecting their monopoly, they're going to "buy" less monopoly power than if it were free. How much will they buy? They will buy monopoly power until the marginal cost of such power equals the marginal benefit. Thus, they'll reason:

Q-9 What decision rule does a firm use when deciding whether to create or maintain a monopoly?

- Does it makes sense for us to hire a lobbyist to fight against this law that will reduce our monopoly power? Here is the probability that a lobbyist will be effective, here is the marginal cost, and here is the marginal benefit.

- Does it make sense for us to buy this machine? If we do, we'll be the only one to have it and are likely to get this much business. Here is the marginal cost, and here is the marginal benefit.

- Does it make sense for us to advertise to further our market penetration? Here are the likely various marginal benefits; here are the likely marginal costs.

Examples of firms spending money to protect or create monopolies are in the news all the time. The farm lobby fights to keep quotas and farm support programs. Drug companies spend a lot of resources to discover new drugs they can patent. A vivid example of the length to which firms will go to create a monopoly position is Owens Corning's fight to trademark its hue of pink Fiberglas. Owens Corning, a company that makes insulation, spent more than $200 million to advertise and promote its color "pink" and millions more in the court to protect its right to sole use of that hue. Owens Corning weighed the costs and benefits and believed that its pink provided sufficient brand recognition to warrant spending millions to protect it.

Establishing Market Position

Some economists, such as Robert Frank at Cornell University, have argued that today's economy is becoming more and more like a monopoly economy. Modern competition, he argues, is a winner-take-all competition. In such a competition, the winner (established because of brand loyalty, patent protection, or simply consumer laziness) achieves a monopoly and can charge significantly higher prices than its costs without facing competition. The initial competition, focusing on establishing market position, is intense.

In winner-take-all markets, the initial competition is focused on establishing market position.

To see how important establishing a market position is in today's economy, consider the initial public offering (IPO) of new Internet firms that are often highly valued by Wall Street. Many of these firms have no profits and no likelihood of profits for a number of years, but they sell at extraordinarily high stock prices. Why? The reasoning is that these companies are spending money to establish brand names. As their names become better known, they will establish a monopoly position, and eventually their monopoly positions will be so strong that they can't help but make a profit. With the dot-com stock market crash in the early 2000s, this argument was shown to be wrong

Branding

One of the important ways in which firms try to maintain a monopoly position is called *branding*. U.S. firms spend about $220 billion a year to advertise their products, trying to produce brand names and create a pleasant image in the minds of consumers. Here are a few food-related brand names. I'm sure you know about most, but a couple are still in the process of forming brand recognition.

©The McGraw-Hill Companies, Inc./Jill Braaten, photographer

- *Coffee:* When you think of coffee, you think of Starbucks and inexpensive extravagance. You might not be able to afford a Lexus, but you can afford a Starbucks cup of coffee.

- *Chicken:* Perdue doesn't produce any chicken, but it does do a lot of advertising, and it brands the chickens it sells, so when you think of chicken, you think of Perdue.

- *Bananas:* A banana is a banana is a banana, but only if you haven't been influenced by Miss Chiquita. At its peak, the Chiquita banana jingle was played 376 times a day on radio stations across the United States.

- *Steak:* Most steaks are currently sold generically. Firms such as Omaha Steaks are trying to change that. Don't just buy a steak—buy an Omaha steak.

- *Water:* Firms take water from the tap (or possibly from a spring), run it through some filters, and sell the image of purity by creating a nice-sounding name—Dasani, Vermont Pure . . . Well, it's better for you than soda.

- *Pork:* Pork tends to be associated with pigs and does not carry a "good-for-you" image. A national association of pork producers is trying to change that image: "Pork—the other white meat."

for most Internet firms. For one or two lucky firms that established their brands, it was true. The problem is that most people have no way of deciding which firms will be successful.

Platform Monopolies and Technology

Web Note 16.4

Network Economies

As I have emphasized, many of the most important modern monopolies are platform monopolies that exhibit network externalities. Network externalities have two implications for the economic process. First, they increase the likelihood that an industry becomes a winner-take-all industry. Second, the market might not gravitate toward the most efficient standard technology. Technological standards are important particularly for platform monopolies because network externalities involve the interaction among individuals and processes. Many examples of the development of industry standards exist. Some are television broadcast standards (they differ in the United States and Europe, which is why U.S. TVs cannot be used in Europe), building standards (there is a standard size of doors), and electrical current standards (220 or 110; AC or DC).

Network externalities lead to market standards and affect market structure.

Standards and Winner-Take-All Industries

Q-10 True or false? Industry standards tend to reduce competition in a market with network externalities.

Early in the development of new products, there may be two or three competing technological standards, any one of which could be a significant improvement over what existed before. As network externalities broaden the use of a product, the need for a single standard becomes more important and eventually one standard wins out. The firm that gets its standard accepted as the industry standard gains an enormous advantage over the other firms. This firm will dominate the market. The Google search engine is an example of how getting your product accepted as the standard can do wonders for the firm. Facebook is another example. By getting people to accept Facebook as their social network, it undermines the development of alternative social networks.

Once a standard develops, even if other firms try to enter with a better technological standard, they will have a hard time competing because everyone is already committed to the existing industry standard. Deviating from that standard will reduce the benefits of the network externality.

Firms in an industry developing a standard will have a strong incentive to be the first to market with the product; they will be willing to incur large losses initially in their attempt to set the industry standard. The first-mover advantage, discussed in an earlier chapter, helps explain why the stock of small technology companies sell for extremely high prices even though they are having large losses. The large losses are created because the firms are spending money to gain market share so that their products would become the industry standard. If the firm is successful in getting its product accepted as the standard, the demand for the product will rise and it will have enormous profits in the future.

The first-mover advantage helps explain the high stock prices of start-up technology companies.

Technological Lock-In

Economists debate the degree to which standards can be inefficient and yet be maintained by the first-mover advantage. Some economists argue that the inefficiency can be quite large; others argue that it is small. One aspect of the debate has centered around the QWERTY keyboard on computers. Research by Stanford economist Paul David showed that the arrangement of the keys in the QWERTY keyboard was designed to slow down people's typing so that the keys would not stick on the early mechanical typewriters. As the technology of typewriters improved, the need to slow down typing soon ended, but because the QWERTY keyboard was introduced first, it had become the standard. Other, more efficient, keyboards have been proposed but not adopted. The QWERTY keyboard has remained, even with its built-in inefficiencies. David suggested that QWERTY is a metaphor for **technological lock-in**—*when prior use of a technology makes the adoption of subsequent technologies difficult.*

QWERTY is a metaphor for technological lock-in.

David's technological lock-in argument suggests that many of our institutions and technologies may be inefficient. Other economists argue that the QWERTY keyboard was not that inefficient and if it had been, other keyboards would have been adopted. I am not sure who is right in this debate, but it may soon be made obsolete by another technological development: voice recognition software, which will make keyboarding a relic of the past.

The QWERTY debate is a part of a larger debate about the competitive process and government involvement in that process. The issues are somewhat the same as they were in the earlier discussion of government regulation of natural monopolies. Many economists see government involvement as necessary to protect the economy and the consumer. They advocate what economist Brian Arthur calls "a nudging hand" approach, in which the government keeps the competition fair.

Other economists see monopoly as part of the competitive process—something that will be eliminated as competitive forces act against it. Standards will develop, but they will be temporary. If the standards are sufficiently inefficient, they will be replaced, or an entirely new product will come along that makes the old standard irrelevant. For such economists, neither natural monopoly nor technological lock-in is a reason for government interference. Government interference, even the nudging hand, would slow or stop the competitive process and make society worse off.

Modern debates about policy regarding competition take dynamic issues into account, but still leave open a debate about what the role of government should be.

Who is right? My own view leans toward the competitive process view with a nudge here or there, but one cannot be dogmatic about it; each case must be decided on its own merits. Moreover, even in those cases where explicit regulation is not called for, the government must set up appropriate rules and property rights to see that the competitive playing field is reasonably level.

Conclusion

The stories of competition and monopoly have no end. Both are continuous processes. Monopolies create competition. Out of the competitive struggle, other monopolies emerge, only to be beaten down by competition. Technology is a big part of that struggle. Individuals and firms, motivated by self-interest, try to use the changes brought by technology to their benefit. By doing so, they change both the nature of the economy and the direction of technological change itself.

Summary

- The phrase "competition is for losers" refers to the belief that the goal of all businesses is to become monopolists. Successful firms are constantly thinking about how to strengthen their monopoly positions.   (*LO16-1*)

- The goals of real-world firms extend beyond profits both because entrepreneurs have a variety of motives, and because firms face complex monitoring problems.   (*LO16-2*)

- The monitoring problem arises because the incentives faced by managers are not always to maximize the profit of the firm. Economists have helped design incentive-compatible contracts to help alleviate the monitoring problem.   (*LO16-2*)

- Monopolists facing no competition can become lazy and not hold down costs as much as they are able. X-inefficiency refers to firms operating less efficiently than they could technically.   (*LO16-2*)

- X-inefficiency can be limited by the threat of competition or takeovers. Corporate takeovers often mean change in management.   (*LO16-2*)

- The competitive process involves a continual fight between monopolization and competition. Suppliers

are willing to pay an amount equal to the additional profit gained from the restriction. Consumers are willing to pay an amount equal to the additional cost of products to avoid a restriction. Consumers, however, face a higher cost of organizing their efforts.   (*LO16-3*)

- Firms compete against patents that create monopolies by making slight modifications to existing patents and engaging in reverse engineering to copy other firms' products within the limits of the law.   (*LO16-3*)

- The U.S. government is deregulating natural monopolies by dividing the firms into various subindustries, carving out those parts that exhibit the characteristics of a natural monopoly, and opening the remaining parts to competition.   (*LO16-3*)

- Firms will spend money on monopolization until the marginal cost equals the marginal benefit. They protect their monopolies by such means as advertising, lobbying, and producing products that are difficult for other firms to copy.   (*LO16-4*)

- Two implications of network externalities for the economic process are that they (1) increase the likelihood of a winner-take-all industry and (2) might lead to less-than-efficient technological standards.   (*LO16-4*)

Key Terms

corporate takeover	lazy monopolist	reverse engineering	X-inefficiency
incentive-compatible contract	monitoring problem	technological lock-in	

Questions and Exercises connect

1. True or false? It is obvious that all for-profit businesses in the United States will maximize profit. Why? *(LO16-2)*

2. Describe the monitoring problem. How does an incentive-compatible contract address the monitoring problem? *(LO16-2)*

3. Define *X-inefficiency.* Can a perfect competitor be X-inefficient? Explain why or why not. *(LO16-2)*

4. Some analysts have argued that competition will eliminate X-inefficiency from firms. Will it? Why? *(LO16-2)*

5. True or false? If it were easier for consumers to collude than for suppliers to collude, there would often be shortages of goods. Why? *(LO16-3)*

6. Demonstrate graphically the net gain to producers and the net loss to consumers if suppliers are able to restrict their output to Q_r in the accompanying graph. Demonstrate the net deadweight loss to society. *(LO16-3)*

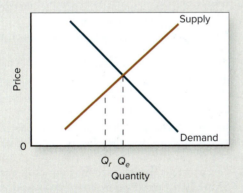

7. Up to how much is the monopolist depicted in the accompanying graph willing to spend to protect its market position? Demonstrate your answer graphically. *(LO16-4)*

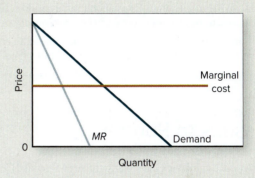

8. True or false? Platform monopolies should be broken up to improve competition. Why? *(LO16-4)*

9. True or false? Monopolies are bad; patents give firms monopoly; therefore, patents are bad. Why? *(LO16-4)*

10. Taking into consideration changing technologies, why might the competitive process not lead to the most efficient outcome? *(LO16-5)*

11. How do network externalities increase the winner-take-all nature of a market? *(LO16-5)*

12. True or false? Technically competent firms will succeed. Why? *(LO16-5)*

Questions from Alternative Perspectives

1. Some economists have compared managers to politicians.
   a. How do the incentives facing managers resemble those of politicians?
   b. How do they differ?
   c. What does your answer say about the relative value of each to society? *(Austrian)*

2. Think of the pay of various groups in society.
   a. How does the compensation awarded to heads of religious organizations compare to the salary of CEOs in profit-making organizations?
   b. What is the explanation for this difference?
   c. Should there be a difference? *(Religious)*

3. How many of the 10 highest-paid CEOs are women? (To find out, you can go to the *paywatch* source,

https://aflcio.org/paywatch, on the web.) What is the likely reason for your finding? *(Feminist)*

4. While some assets, such as forests, can provide benefits to society in perpetuity, some firms see forests as consumable assets. One example occurred when corporate raider James Goldsmith forcibly acquired Crown Zellerbach in Washington State. After doing so, he cut all of Crown Zellerbach's trees, including one 12,000-acre clear-cut, and then sold off all the company's remaining assets piecemeal, a practice called "junk bond forestry." What does this suggest about the long-term environmental sustainability of free market decisions? *(Institutionalist)*

(Continued)

5. Because the future is inherently uncertain, firms often follow "rules of thumb" to make decisions such as how much capital (factories and machinery for production) to buy and how to price their products. Examples are financial ratios and markup pricing.
   a. Does this behavior make sense?
   b. How does uncertainty that firms face encourage firms to use "rules of thumb"?
   c. What implications for economic analysis does firms' use of rules of thumb have? *(Post-Keynesian)*

6. Large corporations spend tremendous sums in an effort to influence public policy. Some corporations fund "citizens'" groups to push policies that the corporations want. Giant drug companies fund scientists to prove that the companies' drugs work. Large businesses even hire economists to come up with theories that show why huge businesses and mega-mergers could be beneficial (or at least not harmful).
   a. What are some likely results if corporations control "the marketplace of ideas"?
   b. What, if anything, should be done about this control? *(Radical)*

Issues to Ponder

1. Airlines and hotels have many frequent-flyer and frequent-visitor programs in which individuals who fly the airline or stay at the hotel receive bonuses that are the equivalent of discounts.
   a. Give two reasons why these companies have such programs rather than simply offering lower prices.
   b. Can you give other examples of such programs?
   c. What is a likely reason why firms don't monitor these programs?
   d. Should the benefits of these programs be taxable?

2. Are managers and high-level company officials paid high salaries because they're worth it to the firm, or because they're simply extracting profit from the company to give to themselves? How would you tell whether you're correct?

3. True or false? Nonprofit colleges must be operating relatively efficiently. Otherwise for-profit colleges would force existing colleges out of business. Why?

4. Author Charles Murray has argued that museums actually inhibit rather than foster the appreciation of art. He points out that the technology exists to make essentially "perfect" copies of any major artwork that even the best-trained artistic eye could not differentiate from the original.
   a. What would the introduction of this technology do to art museums?
   b. If that is true, why do you believe that the technology is not used?
   c. How are reproductions of music symphonies handled legally?
   d. What would the prohibition of making recordings of music performances do to the demand for musicians and for symphony halls?
   e. Why are music symphonies handled differently from art?

5. Find a prescription drug that you, someone in your family, or a friend normally takes.
   a. What is the price you (they) pay for it?
   b. What is the lowest online U.S. price for that drug? (Costco is a good place to look.)
   c. If the online price (with shipping) is cheaper, why don't you (they) buy it online?
   d. With that price information, will you (they) buy the drug online in the future?
   e. What does this process tell you about the competitiveness of the drug market?

6. In the early 2000s, the wholesale price of the generic drug fluoxetine (the generic for Prozac) was $3.60 per 100.
   a. Given that the cost of dispensing this drug was about $5 to $10 per prescription, how much would you expect the drug to sell for?
   b. A prescription for 100 tablets of fluoxetine sold for $54 at DrugStore.com and sold for similar prices at other pharmacies. What would you conclude about the market structure, given that information?
   c. At Pharmnet.com one could buy 100 fluoxetine tablets for $26. If this was true, what can we say about drug market imperfections?

7. Why would a company want to sacrifice short-run profits to establish market position?

8. The title of an article in *The Wall Street Journal* was "Pricing of Products Is Still an Art, Often Having Little Link to Costs." In the article, the following cases were cited:
   • Vodka pricing: All vodkas are essentially indistinguishable—colorless, tasteless, and odorless—and the cost of producing vodka is independent of brand name, yet prices differ substantially.
   • Perfume: A $100 bottle of perfume may contain $4 to $6 worth of ingredients.

- Jeans and "alligator/animal" shirts: The "plain pocket" jeans and the Lacoste knockoffs often cost 40 percent less than the brand-name items, yet the knockoffs are essentially identical to the brand-name items.
  a. Do these differences undermine economists' analysis of pricing? Why or why not?
  b. What does each of these examples likely imply about fixed costs and variable costs?
  c. What do they likely imply about costs of production versus costs of selling?
  d. As what type of market would you characterize each of the above examples?

9. Soft-drink companies pay universities for the exclusive "pouring rights" to sell their products on campus. In a recent deal, UCLA signed a contract with Pepsi for $1.5 million per year limiting on-campus soft-drink sales to only Pepsi.
   a. Why would Pepsi agree to pay such a fee?
   b. What would likely happen if there were no pouring rights on campus?
   c. Is the sale of pouring rights beneficial to students or harmful to them?

10. Monsanto Corporation lost its U.S. patent protection for its highly successful herbicide Roundup in the year 2000. What do you suppose was Monsanto's strategy for Roundup in the short run? In the long run?

11. One of the things that is slowing the development of nanotechnology is the legal morass of patents that anyone working with new ideas must deal with. Some have argued that the government should give prizes for new discoveries, such as was offered for the first private flight in space, or as was offered by Napoleon for the discovery of how to store vegetables for long periods, rather than award patents, such as are awarded to drugs.
    a. What is the advantage of prizes over patents?
    b. What is the cost?

Answers to Margin Questions

1. Real-world firms are fighting to create and maintain monopolies. According to Peter Thiel, the winners are those that have a monopoly and face little competition because they are better than the other firms. Only the "losers" face significant competition. (*LO16-1*)

2. Firms are not interested in just short-run profits. They are also interested in long-run profits. So a firm might sacrifice short-run profits for higher long-run profits. Also, those making the decisions for the firm are not always those who own the firm. (*LO16-2*)

3. Most economists are concerned about third-party-payer systems because of the problems of monitoring. It is the consumers who have the strongest incentive to make sure that they are getting value for their money. Any third-party-payer system reduces the consumers' vigilance and therefore puts less pressure on holding down costs. (*LO16-2*)

4. A manager does not have the same incentive to hold down costs as an owner does because when an owner holds down costs, the owner's profits are increased, but when a manager holds down costs, the increased profits accrue to the owner, not the manager. Thus, the manager has less direct motivation to hold down costs than an owner does. This is especially true if the costs being held down are the manager's perks and pay. (*LO16-2*)

5. The threat of a corporate takeover places competitive pressures on firms because it creates the possibility that the managers will be replaced and lose all their perks and above-market-equilibrium pay. (*LO16-2*)

6. Most agricultural markets are not perfectly competitive because the gains to producers from moving away from competitive markets are fairly large and, for small deviations from competitive markets, the costs are fairly small to those suppliers and consumers who are kept out. This can be seen in the accompanying graph.

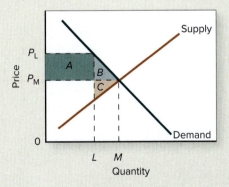

If suppliers producing $0L$ got together and limited supply to L, they could push the price up to P_L and could gain the rectangle A for themselves. Consumers and suppliers who are kept out of the market lose triangles B and C respectively, which, in the diagram, not only are each smaller than A but also when combined are smaller than A. Of course, the area A is lost to the consumers, but the costs of organizing those consumers to fight and protect competition are often prohibitively large.   (*LO16-3*)

7. It is almost impossible for perfect monopoly to exist because preventing entry is nearly impossible. Monopoly profits are a signal to potential entrants to get the barriers to entry removed.   (*LO16-3*)

8. The problem with regulation that sets prices relative to costs is that this removes the incentive for firms to hold down costs and can lead to X-inefficiency. While, in theory, regulators could scrutinize every cost, in

practice that is impossible—there would have to be a regulatory board duplicating the work that a firm facing direct market pressure undertakes in its normal activities.   (*LO16-3*)

9. If the additional benefits of creating or maintaining a monopoly exceed the cost of doing so, do it. If they don't, don't.   (*LO16-4*)

10. True. It is difficult for new firms to challenge and establish a market standard because a new standard will not benefit as much from the network externalities established by the existing standard.   (*LO16-5*)

Work and the Labor Market

> Work banishes those three great evils: boredom, vice, and poverty.
>
> —Voltaire

©iStockphoto.com/kupicoo

Most of us earn our living by working. We supply labor (get a job) and get paid for doing things that other people tell us they want done. Even before we get a job, work is very much a part of our lives. We spend a large portion of our school years preparing for work. Probably many of you are taking this economics course because you've been told that it will help prepare you for a job—or that it will get you more pay than you're getting in your present job. For you, this course is investment in human capital (skills embodied in workers through experience, education, and on-the-job training). If work in the marketplace isn't already familiar to you, once you get out of school it will become so (unless you're sitting on a hefty trust fund or marry somebody who is).

Your job will likely occupy at least a third of your waking hours. To a great extent, it will define you. When someone asks, "What do you do?" you won't answer, "I clip coupons, go out on dates, visit my children…" Instead you'll answer, "I work for the Blank Company" or "I'm an economist" or "I'm a teacher." Defining ourselves by our work means that work is more than the way we get income. It's a part of our social and cultural makeup. If we lose our jobs, we lose part of our identity.

There's no way I can discuss all the social, political, cultural, and economic dimensions of work and labor in one chapter, but it's important to begin by at least pointing them out in order to put my discussion of labor markets in perspective. A **labor market** is *a factor market in which individuals supply labor services for wages to other individuals and to firms that need (demand)*

Other Factors of Production

The factors of production are sometimes classified as land, labor, and capital, and income from these factors is rent, wages, and interest and profits, respectively. We focus on labor because it is the most important source of income for most of you, and given the limited time in a principles course, choices have to be made. (Opportunity cost rears its head. You can find a discussion of these other factors in the online Chapter 17W, "Nonwage and Asset Income: Rents, Profits, and Interest," among the library resources in McGraw-Hill Connect®.) I should, however, note a couple of issues about these other factors of production. First, land as a factor of production depends on property rights. How property rights are determined

and structured plays an important role in the amount of rent and the distribution of that rent. Whereas most people would agree that people deserve the fruits of their labor, there is less agreement about rent.

Second, capital is much more difficult to analyze than labor or land. In fact, capital is one of the most difficult aspects of economics, and we do not have a good theory of the rate of interest or profit income that is the result of capital. The modern theory of capital focuses on human capital, intellectual capital, and social capital as well as financial and physical capital. A full analysis of these various elements and the income that derives from their use is far beyond an introductory course.

labor services. Because social and political pressures are particularly strong in labor markets, we can understand the nature of such markets only by considering how social and political forces interact with economic forces to determine our economic situation.

If the invisible hand were the only force operating, wages would be determined entirely by supply and demand. There's more to it than that, as you'll see, but it shouldn't surprise you that my discussion of the invisible hand and the labor market is organized around the concepts of supply and demand.

The Supply of Labor

The labor supply choice facing an individual (that is, the decisions of whether, how, and how much to work) can be seen as a choice between nonmarket activities and legal market activities. Nonmarket activities include sleeping, dating, studying, playing, cooking, cleaning, gardening, and black market trading. Legal market activities include taking some type of paid job or working for oneself, directly supplying products or services to consumers.

Economists focus on the incentive effect when considering an individual's choice of whether and how much to work.

Many considerations are involved in individuals' choices of whether and how much to work and at what kind of job to work. Social background and conditioning are especially important, but the factor economists focus on is the **incentive effect** (*how much a person will change his or her hours worked in response to a change in the wage rate*). The incentive effect is determined by the value of supplying one's time to legal market activities relative to the value of supplying one's time to nonmarket activities. The normal relationship is:

The higher the wage, the higher the quantity of labor supplied.

This relationship between the wage rate and the quantity of labor supplied is shown in the figure in the margin. The wage rate is measured on the vertical axis; the quantity of labor supplied is measured on the horizontal axis. As you can see, the supply curve's upward slope indicates that as the wage rate increases, the quantity of labor supplied increases. Why is that the normal relationship? Because work involves opportunity cost. By working one hour more, you have one hour less to devote to nonmarket activities, which often are simply called *leisure*. Alternatively, if you devote the hour to nonmarket activities, you lose one hour's worth of income from working.

The supply curve for labor is upward-sloping; the higher the wage, the higher the quantity of labor supplied.

Say, for example, that by working you make $10 per hour. If you decide to work two hours less, you'll have $20 less to spend but two hours more available for other activities (including spending the smaller amount of money). When the wage rises, say to $12 per hour, an hour of leisure has a higher opportunity cost. As the cost of leisure goes up, you buy less of it, meaning that you work more.

As I noted in my general discussions of supply and demand, the incentive effects represented by the market supply curve come from individuals' either/or decisions to enter, or leave, the labor market and from individuals' decisions to work more, or fewer, hours. Given the institutional constraints in the labor market, which require many people to work a fixed number of hours if they work at all, much of the incentive effect of higher wages influences the either/or decisions of individuals. This affects the labor force participation rate (the number of people employed or looking for work as a percentage of people able to work) rather than adjusting the number of hours worked. For example, when wages rise, retired workers may find it worthwhile to go back to work, and many teenagers may choose to find part-time jobs.

Real Wages and the Opportunity Cost of Work

The upward-sloping supply curve of labor tells you that, other things equal, as wages go up, the quantity of labor supplied goes up. But if you look at the historical record, you will see that over the last century, real wages in the United States increased substantially, but the average number of hours worked per person fell. This difference is partly explained by the income effect. Higher incomes make people richer, and richer people can afford to choose more leisure. (See the box "Income and Substitution Effects.")

Given that people are far richer today than they were 100 years ago, it isn't surprising that they work less. What's surprising is that they work as much as they do—eight hours a day rather than the two or so hours a day that would be enough to give people the same income they had a century ago.

The explanation for why people haven't reduced their hours of work more substantially can be found in how leisure has changed. A century ago, conversation was an art. People could use their time for long, leisurely conversations. Letter writing was a skill all educated people had, and cooking dinner was a three-hour event. If today people were satisfied with leisure consisting of long conversations, whittling, and spending quality time with their families rather than skiing, golfing, or traveling, they could get by with working perhaps only four or five hours per day instead of eight hours. But that isn't the case.

Today leisurely dinners, conversations about good books, and witty letters have been replaced by "efficient" leisure: a fast-food supper, a home video, and the instant analysis of current events. Microwave ovens, frozen dinners, Pop-Tarts, smartphones, the Internet—the list of gadgets and products designed to save time is endless. All these gadgets that increase the "efficiency" of leisure (increase the marginal utility per hour of leisure spent) cost money, which means people today must work more to enjoy their leisure! In the United States, one reason people work hard is so that they can play hard (and expensively).

The fast pace of modern society has led a number of people to question whether we, as a society, are better off working hard to play hard. Are we better off or simply more harried? Most economists don't try to answer this normative question; but they do point out that people are choosing their harried lifestyle, so to argue that people are worse off, one must argue that people are choosing something they don't really want. That may be true, but it's a tough argument to prove.

Q-1 Under the usual conditions of supply, what would you expect would happen to the amount of time you study if the wage of your part-time job rises?

Modern gadgets increase the efficiency of leisure but cost money, which means people must work more to enjoy their leisure.

Economists do not try to answer the normative question of whether people are better off today, working hard to play hard, or simply are more harried.

Income and Substitution Effects

Because labor income is such an important component of most people's total income, when wages change other things often do not stay equal, and at times the effect can seem strange. For example, say that you earn $10 an hour and you decide to work eight hours per day. Suddenly demand for your services goes up and you find that you can receive $40 an hour. Will you decide to work more hours? According to the economic decision rule, you will, but you also might decide that at $40 an hour you'll work only six hours a day—$240 a day is enough; the rest of the day you want leisure time to spend your money. In such a case, a higher wage means working less, and the measured supply curve of labor would be backward-bending.

Does this violate the economic decision rule? The answer is no, because other things—specifically your income—do not remain equal. The higher wage makes you decide to work more—as the economic decision rule says; but the effect of the higher wage is overwhelmed by the effect of the higher income that allows you to decide to work less.

To distinguish between these two effects, economists have given them names. The decision by a worker to work more hours when his or her pay goes up is called the *substitution effect*. A worker substitutes work for leisure because the price of leisure has risen. The decision to work fewer hours when your pay goes up, based on the fact that you're richer and therefore can live a better life, is called the *income effect*.

It's possible that the income effect can exceed the substitution effect, and a wage increase can cause a person to work less, but that possibility does not violate the economic decision rule, which refers to the substitution effect only.

The Supply of Labor and Nonmarket Activities

In addition to leisure, labor supply issues and market incentives play an important role in other nonmarket activities. For example, a whole set of illegal activities, such as selling illegal drugs, are alternatives to taking a legal job.

Web Note 17.1

Who Works?

Let's say that an 18-year-old street kid figures he has only two options: He can either work at a minimum wage job or deal drugs illegally. Let's say that dealing drugs risks getting arrested or shot, but it also means earning $50 or $75 an hour. Given that choice, many risk takers opt to sell drugs. When an emergency room doctor asked a shooting victim in New York City why he got involved in selling drugs, he responded, "I'm not going to work for chump change. I make $3,000 a week, tax-free. What do they pay you, sucker?" The doctor had to admit that even he wasn't making that kind of money.

As we discussed in Chapter 1, most low-level drug dealers don't earn anywhere near that pay, but dealing drugs offers a few the chance to advance and earn that and more. For middle-class individuals who have prospects for good jobs, the cost of being arrested can be high—an arrest can destroy their future prospects. For poor street kids with little chance of getting a good job, an arrest makes little difference to their future. For them the choice is heavily weighted toward selling drugs. This is especially true for the entrepreneurial types—the risk takers—the movers and shakers who might have become the business leaders of the future. I've asked myself what decision I would have made had I been in their position. And I suspect I know the answer.

Prohibiting certain drugs leads to potentially high income from selling those drugs and has significant labor market effects. The incentive effects that prohibition has on the choices of jobs facing poor teenagers is a central reason why some economists support the legalization of currently illegal drugs.

Income Taxation, Work, and Leisure

Q-2 Why do income taxes reduce your incentive to work?

It is after-tax income, not before-tax income, that determines how much you work. Why? Because after-tax income is what you give up by not working. The government, not you, forgoes what you would have paid in taxes if you had worked. This means that when the government raises your marginal tax rate (the tax you pay on an additional dollar of income), your incentive to work falls. Really high marginal tax rates—say 60 or 70 percent—can significantly reduce individuals' incentive to work and earn income.

One main reason why the U.S. government reduced marginal income tax rates in the 1980s was to reduce the negative incentive effects of high taxes. Whereas in the 1950s and 1960s the highest federal U.S. marginal income tax rate was 70 percent, today the highest federal marginal income tax rate is about 40 percent. European countries, which have significantly higher marginal tax rates than the United States, are currently struggling with the problem of providing incentives for people to work.

European countries, which have relatively high marginal tax rates, are struggling with the problem of providing incentives for people to work.

Reducing the marginal tax rate in the United States hasn't completely eliminated the problem of significant negative incentive effects on individuals' work effort. The reason is that the amount people receive from many government redistribution programs is tied to earned income. When your earned income goes up, your benefits from these programs go down.

Say, for example, that you're getting welfare and you're deciding whether to take a $10-an-hour job. Income taxes and Social Security taxes reduce the amount you take home from the job by 20 percent, to $8 an hour. But you also know that the Welfare Department will reduce your welfare benefits by 50 cents for every dollar you take home. This means that you lose another $4 per hour, so the marginal tax rate on your $10-an-hour job isn't 20 percent; it's 60 percent. By working an hour, you've increased your net income by only $4. When you consider the transportation cost of getting to and from work, the expense of getting new clothes to wear to work, the cost of child care, and other job-associated expenses, the net gain in income is often minimal. Your implicit marginal tax rate is almost 100 percent! At such rates, there's an enormous incentive either not to work or to work off the books (get paid in cash so you have no recorded income that the government can easily trace).

Taxes reduce the amount you take home and the incentive to work.

©JohnKwan/Shutterstock

The negative incentive effect can sometimes be even more indirect. For example, college scholarships are generally given on the basis of need. A family that earns more gets less in scholarship aid; the amount by which the scholarship is reduced as a family's income increases acts as a marginal tax on individuals' income. Why work hard to provide for yourself if a program will take care of you if you don't work hard? Hence, the irony in any need-based assistance program is that it reduces the people's incentive to prevent themselves from being needy. These negative incentive effects on labor supply that accompany any need-based program present a public policy dilemma for which there is no easy answer.

Q-3 What is the irony of any need-based program?

The Elasticity of the Supply of Labor

Exactly how these various incentives affect the amount of labor an individual supplies is determined by the elasticity of the individual's labor supply curve.

The elasticity of the market supply curve is determined by the elasticity of individuals' supply curves and by individuals entering and leaving the labor force. Both of these, in turn, are determined by individuals' opportunity cost of working. If a large number of people are willing to enter the labor market when wages rise, then the market labor supply will be highly elastic even if individuals' supply curves are inelastic.

The elasticity of supply also depends on the type of market being discussed. For example, the elasticity of the labor supply facing one firm of many in a small town will likely be far greater than the elasticity of the labor supply facing all firms combined in that town. If only one firm raises its wage, it will attract workers away from other firms; if all the firms in town raise their wages, any increase in labor must come from increases in labor force participation, increases in hours worked per person, or immigration (the movement of new workers into the town's labor market).

Elasticity of market supply depends on:

1. Individuals' opportunity cost of working.
2. The type of market being discussed.
3. The elasticity of individuals' supply curves.
4. Individuals entering and leaving the labor market.

Existing workers prefer inelastic labor supplies because that means an increase in demand for labor will raise their wage by more. Employers prefer elastic supplies because that means an increase in demand for labor doesn't require large wage increases. These preferences can be seen in news reports about U.S. immigration laws, their effects, and their enforcement. Businesses such as hotels and restaurants often oppose strict immigration laws. Their reason is that jobs such as janitor, hotel house-keeper, and busperson are frequently filled by new immigrants or undocumented workers who have comparatively low wage expectations.

Because of the importance of the elasticity of labor supply, economists have spent a great deal of time and effort estimating it. Their best estimates of labor supply elasticities to market activities are about 0.1 for heads of households and 1.1 for secondary workers in households. These elasticity figures mean that a wage increase of 10 percent will increase the quantity of labor supplied by 1 percent for heads of households (an inelastic supply) and 11 percent for secondary workers in households (an elastic supply). Why the difference? Institutional factors. Hours of work are only slightly flexible. Since most heads of households are employed, they cannot significantly change their hours worked. Many secondary workers in households are not employed, and the higher elasticity reflects new secondary workers entering the labor market.

Immigration and the International Supply of Labor

Web Note 17.2

Leaving Home

International limitations on the flow of people, and hence on the flow of labor, play an important role in elasticities of labor supply. In many industries, wages in developing countries are 1/10th or less the wages in the United States and Europe. This large wage differential means that many people from those low-wage countries would like to move to the United States and Europe to earn the higher wages. Because they cannot always meet the legal immigration restrictions that limit the flow, many people come into the United States and Europe illegally. Although it fluctuates, about 1 million legal and illegal immigrants enter the United States each year. Illegal immigrants take a variety of jobs at lower wages and worse conditions than U.S. citizens and legal immigrants are willing to take. The result is that the actual supply of labor is more elastic than the measured supply, especially in those jobs that cannot be easily policed.

The Derived Demand for Labor

The demand for labor follows the basic law of demand:

> The higher the wage, the lower the quantity of labor demanded.

This relationship between the wage rate and the quantity of labor demanded is shown in the graph in the margin. Its downward slope shows that as the wage rate falls, the quantity of labor demanded rises. The reason for this relationship differs between the demand for labor by self-employed individuals and the demand for labor by firms.

When individuals are self-employed (work for themselves), the demand for their labor is the demand for the product or service they supply—be it cutting hair, shampooing rugs, or filling teeth. You have an ability to do something, you offer to do it at a certain price, and you see who calls. You determine how many hours you work, what price you charge, and what jobs you take. The income you receive depends on the demand for the good or service you supply and your decision about how much labor you want to supply. In analyzing self-employed individuals, we can move directly from demand for the product to demand for labor.

When a person is not self-employed, determining the demand for labor isn't as direct. It's a two-step process: Consumers demand products from firms; firms, in turn,

The higher the wage, the lower the quantity of labor demanded.

demand labor and other factors of production. The demand for labor by firms is a **derived demand**—*the demand for factors of production by firms, which depends on consumers' demands.* In other words, it's derived from consumers' demand for the goods that the firm sells. Thus, you can't think of demand for a factor of production such as labor separately from demand for goods. Firms translate consumers' demands into a demand for factors of production.

Derived demand is the demand for factors of production by firms, which depends on consumers' demands.

Factors Influencing the Elasticity of Demand for Labor

The elasticity of the derived demand for labor, or for any other input, depends on a number of factors. One of the most important is (1) *the elasticity of demand for the firm's good.* The more elastic the demand for a firm's goods, the more elastic the derived demand. Other factors influencing the elasticity of derived demand include (2) *the relative importance of labor in the production process* (the more important the factor, the less elastic is the derived demand); (3) *the possibility, and cost, of substitution in production* (the easier substitution is, the more elastic is the derived demand); and (4) *the degree to which marginal productivity falls with an increase in labor* (the faster productivity falls, the less elastic is the derived demand).

Four factors that influence the elasticity of demand for labor are:

1. *The elasticity of demand for the firm's good.*
2. *The relative importance of labor in the production process.*
3. *The possibility, and cost, of substitution in production.*
4. *The degree to which marginal productivity falls with an increase in labor.*

Each of these relationships follows from the definition of *elasticity* (the percentage change in quantity divided by the percentage change in price) and a knowledge of production. To be sure you understand, ask yourself the following question: If all I knew about two firms was that one was a perfect competitor and the other was a monopolist, which firm would I say is likely to have the more elastic derived demand for labor? If your answer wasn't automatically "the competitive firm" (because its demand curve is perfectly elastic and hence more elastic than a monopolist's), I would suggest that at this point you review the discussion of factors influencing demand elasticity in the chapter on elasticities and relate that to this discussion. The two discussions are similar and serve as good reviews for each other.

Q-4 Name at least two factors that influence the elasticity of a firm's derived demand for labor.

Labor as a Factor of Production

The traditional factors of production are land, labor, capital, and entrepreneurship. When economists talk of the labor market, they're talking about two of these factors: labor and entrepreneurship. **Entrepreneurship** is *labor that involves high degrees of organizational skills, concern, oversight responsibility, and creativity.* It is a type of creative labor.

Entrepreneurship is labor that involves high degrees of organizational skills, concern, oversight responsibility, and creativity.

The reason for distinguishing between labor and entrepreneurship is that an hour of work is not simply an hour of work. If high degrees of organizational skill, concern, oversight responsibility, and creativity are exerted (which is what economists mean by *entrepreneurship*), one hour of such work can be the equivalent of days, weeks, or even years of nonentrepreneurial labor. That's one reason why pay often differs between workers doing what seems to be the same job. It's also why one of the important decisions a firm makes is what type of labor to hire. Should the firm try to hire high-wage entrepreneurial labor or low-wage nonentrepreneurial labor?

In the appendix to this chapter, I formally develop the firm's derived demand. Here in the chapter itself I will simply point out that the demand for labor follows the basic law of demand—the lower the price, the higher the quantity demanded. Figure 17-1 shows a demand-for-labor curve combined with a supply-of-labor curve. As you would expect, equilibrium is at wage W_e and quantity supplied Q_e.

Shift Factors of Demand

Factors that shift the demand curve for labor will put pressure on the equilibrium wage to change. Let's consider some examples. Say the cost of a competing factor of

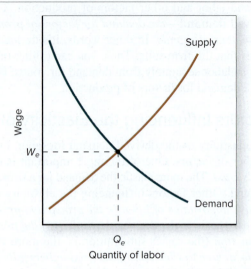

FIGURE 17-1 Equilibrium in the Labor Market

When the supply and demand curves for labor are placed on the same graph, the equilibrium wage, W_e, is where the quantity supplied equals quantity demanded. At this wage, Q_e laborers are supplied.

production, such as a machine that also could do the job, rises. That would shift the demand for this factor out to the right, and in doing so put pressure on the wage to rise.

Alternatively, say a new technology develops that requires skills different from those currently being used—for instance, requiring knowing how to use a computer rather than knowing how to use a slide rule. The demand for individuals knowing how to use slide rules will decrease, and their wage will tend to fall.

Another example: Say an industry becomes more monopolistic. What will that do to the demand for labor in that industry? Since monopolies produce less output, the answer is that it would decrease the demand for workers because the industry would hire fewer of them. The demand for workers would shift in and wages would tend to fall.

Finally, say the demand for the firm's good increases. It's clear that the firm's demand for labor will also increase. The way in which these shift factors work is developed in more detail in the appendix to this chapter.

Q-5 What would happen to a firm's demand for labor if its product became more popular?

TECHNOLOGY AND THE DEMAND FOR LABOR   How will a change in technology affect the demand for labor? This question has often been debated, and it has no unambiguous answer. What economists do know is that the simple reasoning often used by laypeople when they argue that new technology will decrease the demand for labor is wrong. That simplistic reasoning is as follows: "Technology makes it possible to replace workers with machines, so it will decrease the demand for labor." This is sometimes called *Luddite reasoning* because it's what drove the Luddites (19th-century English weavers) to go around smashing machines in early-19th-century England.

What's wrong with Luddite reasoning? First, look at history. Technology has increased enormously, yet the demand for labor has not decreased; instead it has increased as output has increased. In other words, Luddite reasoning doesn't take into account the fact that technological change generally increases total output and therefore total employment. A second problem with Luddite reasoning is that people build and maintain the machines, so increased demand for machines increases the demand for labor.

Luddite reasoning isn't *all* wrong. Technology can decrease the demand for certain skills. The computer has decreased demand for calligraphers; the automobile

Luddite reasoning has its problems.

reduced demand for carriage makers. New technology changes the types of labor demanded. If you have the type of labor that will be made technologically obsolete, you will be hurt by technological change. However, technological change hasn't reduced the overall demand for labor; it has instead led to an increase in total output and a need for even more laborers to produce that output. What technological change has done is change the composition of labor demand while at the same time increasing total labor demand.

The changes in the type of labor demanded and hence the relative pay can be significant, as we have seen in the last few decades with a decline in manufacturing labor. The Industrial Revolution significantly changed the nature of physical labor done by humans. Machines do the heavy lifting, with humans doing what might be called the scutwork—shoveling up the dirt that the backhoe left behind. That process of technological change is ongoing, and we are seeing an increase in the use of robots to do many repetitive tasks that blue-collar workers formerly did. Thus, demand for general manufacturing labor will likely continue to decline. But that decrease has been accompanied by an increase in demand for service industry labor, and demand for labor associated with designing, building, and repairing robots and computers, or partaking in activities that fill up people's free time because all physical and mental work can be done more efficiently by robots or computers.

The fast-developing information revolution of the 20th and 21st centuries is doing to mental jobs what the Industrial Revolution did to physical jobs. Machines are now replacing routine mental labor (labor that involves a repetition of some action) with computer algorithms that can do the jobs humans did faster and better. In many ways this is just a continuation of changes that have been taking place for decades; knowing how to add, multiply, and spell used to be skills that were highly valued, and millions of jobs involved using those skills. Ever since the advent of desktop calculators in the 1960s, pocket calculators in the 1970s, and desktop computers in the 1980s those skills have become far less important; calculators and automated spell checkers can do much of the work.

What is now changing is both the speed and acceleration of those changes. The information revolution is extending beyond the routine mental jobs and is now affecting what we previously considered nonroutine mental labor involving high levels of creativity, which were thought to have been uniquely human. Algorithms are being designed that can do what we thought only humans could do: write books, diagnose disease, and create music and art. This subbranch of the information revolution might be called the algorithm revolution, where an algorithm is essentially an artificial brain.

To date, most algorithms are devoted to specific tasks that assist humans. But they are becoming more and more sophisticated so that visionaries are now envisioning general-purpose algorithms that are better than human brains. The defeat of human competitors in the game Go by computers signals that future. (See the box: "Are Humans Obsolete?")

What does this mean for human labor? People will still likely work, but it is not clear whether these jobs of the future will be good jobs—ones that people find fulfilling and that pay wages that society finds acceptable. It is likely that a large majority of the jobs of the future will be mental scut jobs—cleaning up around the heavy mental work that is being done by the algorithm. These jobs will likely have relatively low pay, especially when compared to the pay of the people who design and control the algorithms. Income could become far less equal than it currently is. Designers of algorithms will likely be extremely well compensated. Individuals with jobs associated with algorithms and protecting the wealth of the rich—jobs in finance and certain branches of law—will also do extremely well. Others—which includes the majority of

The fast-developing information revolution of the 20th and 21st centuries is doing to mental jobs what the Industrial Revolution did to physical jobs.

Web Note 17.3

Artificial Intelligence

Are Humans Obsolete?

On May 23, 2017, a momentous event occurred: Google's AlphaGo beat the best human Go player in the world. Why was this momentous? After all, computer algorithms had already won on *Jeopardy!* and in chess. Why was Go different? The reason is that Go is a highly intuitive game for which humans were believed to be uniquely adapted; Go requires intuition and imagination, as well as rote computing power. If computer algorithms can win at Go, they can do just about any of the mental work that people do, only quicker and better. Computers can also do art, music, and emotional counseling better. Bottom line: If AlphaGo can do what humans have traditionally done, humans could be made obsolete. Not immediately, of course. The algorithmic component of the information revolution will take decades, even centuries.

©AlphaGo

The evolution will likely go something like this: An increasing number of specific job algorithms will be designed to replace humans in specific facets of life. These algorithms will likely be designated by names. For example, general physicians will be replaced by Algorithm Doc-1; surgeons by Algorithm Doc-97; and life coaches specializing in males 35–40 by Algorithm-LC-M35-40. Simultaneously general-purpose algorithms will be created that can do multiple types of jobs—overall planning and supervision whose function will be to control and coordinate the specific algorithms. Individuals will assist the algorithms handling small issues not worth designing an algorithm for.

As discussed in the text, the problem is not that there won't be enough jobs for humans. Based on past experience, there will be jobs for everyone. The question is: Will the jobs be jobs that people want at pay levels that people, and society as a whole, are willing to accept? That is far from clear. The information revolution is creating a few highly paid jobs, and a large number of relatively low-paid and not especially intellectually fulfilling jobs.

The policy issues associated with these changes go far beyond economics. They are as much or more social and psychological as they are economic issues. Economics alone cannot deal with them. What economics can do is let society know that forces are pushing in that direction and suggest policies that might alleviate them to some degree.

college graduates—will not do so well. Just as general manual labor became poorly compensated in the United States during the 1980s, general mental labor will likely become poorly compensated in the coming decades. Combine that low pay with the anomie and lack of purpose that comes when one knows that one's job could be done better by an algorithm, and you see that technology presents policy concerns for society even if it does not reduce the number of jobs.

INTERNATIONAL COMPETITIVENESS AND A COUNTRY'S DEMAND FOR LABOR   Many of the issues in the demand for labor concern one firm's or industry's demand for labor relative to another firm's or industry's demand. When we're talking about the demand for labor by the country as a whole—an issue fundamentally important to many of the policy issues being discussed today—we have to consider the country's overall international competitiveness. A central determinant of a country's competitiveness is the relative wage of labor in that country compared to the relative wage of labor in other countries.

Wages vary considerably among countries. For example, in 2018 workers in the manufacturing industry earned an average of about $40 an hour in the United States, $50 an hour in Germany, and $8 an hour in Mexico. Multinational corporations are continually making decisions about where to place production facilities, and labor costs—wage rates—play an important role in these decisions.

But why produce in the United States when the hourly rate in Taiwan, for example, is only 1/3 that in the United States? Or in Mexico, where the hourly rate is only about 1/5 that in the United States? The reasons are complicated, but include (1) differences in workers—U.S. workers may be more productive; (2) transportation costs—producing in the country to which you're selling keeps transportation costs down; (3) potential trade restrictions; and (4) compatibility of production techniques with social institutions—production techniques must fit with a society's social institutions. If they don't, production will fall significantly.

Number (5) is the *focal point phenomenon*—a situation where a company chooses to move, or expand, production to another country because other companies have already moved or expanded there. A company can't consider all places, and it costs a lot of money to explore a country's potential as a possible host country. For example, Japanese businesses know what to expect when they open a plant in the United States; they don't know in many other countries. So the United States and other countries that Japanese businesses have knowledge about become focal points. They are considered as potential sites for business, while other, possibly equally good, countries are not. Combined, these reasons lead to a "follow-the-leader" system in which countries fall in and out of global companies' production plans. The focal point countries expand and develop; the others don't.

As I have discussed in a number of chapters, the outsourcing that is currently occurring is a reflection of the relative cost differential that firms calculate as they are deciding where to place production units. Initially, that cost differential included large setup costs, making U.S. production cost-effective in many industries despite lower wages elsewhere. As firms have spent the setup costs to establish production facilities abroad, that cost differential relevant to their decisions is increasing, which means that U.S.-based production will continue to experience strong pressure to move offshore in the coming decade. Unless offset by new jobs in other industries, the resulting increase in demand for foreign-based workers and decrease in demand for U.S.-based workers will likely put upward pressure on foreign wages and keep strong downward pressure on U.S. wages, limiting wage increases.

> Other factors besides wages play an important role in a firm's decision on where to locate.

> **Q-6** Name two factors besides relative wages that determine the demand for labor in one country compared to another.

Determination of Wages

Supply and demand forces strongly influence wages, but they do not fully determine wages. Real-world labor markets are filled with examples of individuals or firms that resist these supply and demand pressures through organizations such as labor unions, professional associations, and agreements among employers. But, as I've emphasized throughout the book, supply/demand analysis is a useful framework for considering such resistance.

For example, say that you're advising a firm's workers on how to raise their wages. You point out that if workers want to increase their wages, they must figure out some way either to increase the demand for their services or to limit the labor supplied to the firm. One way to limit the number of workers the firm will hire (and thus keep existing workers' wages high) is to force the firm to pay an above-equilibrium wage, as in Figure 17-2(a). Say that in their contract negotiations the workers get the firm to agree to pay a wage of W_1. At wage W_1, the quantity of labor supplied is Q_S and the quantity of labor demanded is Q_D. The difference, $Q_S - Q_D$, represents the number of people who want jobs at wage W_1 but will not be employed. In such a case, jobs must be rationed. Whom you know, where you come from, or the color of your skin may play a role in whether you get a job with that firm.

As a second example, consider what would happen if U.S. immigration laws were liberalized. If you say the supply curve of labor would shift out to the right and the

> Supply and demand forces strongly influence wages, but they do not fully determine wages.

> **Web Note 17.4**
> Wage Determination

FIGURE 17-2 (A AND B) The Labor Market in Action

In **(a)** you can see the effect of an above-equilibrium wage: If workers force the firm to pay them a wage of W_1, more workers will be supplied (Q_S) than demanded (Q_D). With an excess supply of labor, jobs must be rationed. In **(b)** you can see the effect of an increase in the supply of labor. Assuming the demand for labor remains the same, the increase in the supply of labor will cause the wage level to drop from W_0 to W_1.

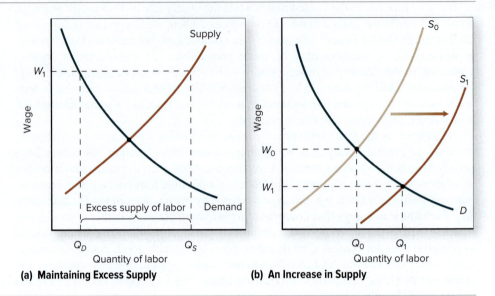

(a) Maintaining Excess Supply

(b) An Increase in Supply

Q-7 How could an increase in the supply of labor lead to an increase in the demand for labor?

wage level would drop, you're right, as shown in Figure 17-2(b). In it the supply of labor increases from S_0 to S_1. In response, the wage falls from W_0 to W_1 and the quantity of labor demanded increases from Q_0 to Q_1.

In analyzing the effect of such a major change in the labor supply, however, remember that the supply and demand framework is relevant only if the change in the supply of labor doesn't also affect the demand for labor. In reality, a liberalization of U.S. immigration laws might increase the demand for products, thereby increasing the demand for labor and raising wages. When you look at the overall effect of a change, you will often find that the final result is less clear-cut. That's why it's important always to remember the assumptions behind the model you're using. Those assumptions often add qualifications to the simple "right" answer.

Imperfect Competition and the Labor Market

Just as product markets can be imperfectly competitive, so too can labor markets. For example, there might be a **monopsony** *(a market in which a single firm is the only buyer)*. An example of a monopsony is a "company town" in which a single firm is the only employer. Whereas a monopolist takes into account the fact that if it sells more it will lower the market price, a monopsonist takes into account the fact that it will raise the market prices if it buys more. Thus, it buys less and pays less than would a market with an equivalent number of competitive buyers.

A monopsony is a market in which a single firm is the only buyer.

Alternatively, laborers might have organized together in a union that allows workers to operate as if there were only a single seller. In effect, the union could operate as a monopoly. Alternatively again, there might be a **bilateral monopoly** *(a market with only a single seller and a single buyer)*. Let's briefly consider these three types of market imperfections.

A monopsonist takes into account the fact that hiring another worker will increase the wage rate it must pay all workers.

MONOPSONY When there's only one buyer of labor services, it makes sense for that buyer to take into account the fact that if it hires another worker, the equilibrium wage will rise and it will have to pay more to all workers. The choice facing a monopsonist can be seen in Figure 17-3, in which the supply curve of labor is upward-sloping so that the **marginal factor cost** *(the additional cost to a firm of hiring another*

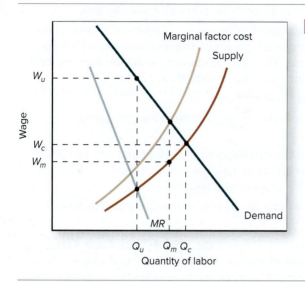

FIGURE 17-3 Monopsony, Union Power, and the Labor Market

A monopsonist hires fewer workers and pays them less than would a set of competitive firms. The monopsonist determines the quantity of labor, Q_m, to hire at the point where the marginal factor cost curve intersects the demand curve. The monopsonist pays a wage of W_m. A union has a tendency to push for a higher wage, W_u, and a lower quantity of workers, Q_u.

worker) is above the supply curve since the monopsonist takes into account the fact that hiring another worker will increase the wage rate it must pay to all workers.

Instead of hiring Q_c workers at a wage of W_c, as would happen in a competitive labor market, the monopsonist hires Q_m workers and pays them a wage of W_m. (A good exercise to see that you understand the argument is to show that where there's a monopsonist, a minimum wage simultaneously can increase employment and raise the wage.)

UNION MONOPOLY POWER   When a union exists, it will have an incentive to act as a monopolist, restricting labor supply to increase its members' wages. To do so it must have the power to restrict both supply and union membership. A union would have a strong tendency to act like a monopolist and to move to an equilibrium somewhat similar to the monopsonist case, except for one important difference. The wage the union would set wouldn't be below the competitive wage; instead, the wage would be above the competitive wage at W_u, as in Figure 17-3. Faced with a wage of W_u, competitive firms will hire Q_u workers. Thus, with union monopoly power, the benefits of restricting supply accrue to the union members, not to the firm as in the monopsonist case.

BILATERAL MONOPOLY   As our final case, let's consider a bilateral monopoly in which a monopsonist faces a union with monopoly power. In this case, we can say that the equilibrium wage will be somewhere between the monopsonist wage W_m and the union monopoly power wage W_u. The equilibrium quantity will be somewhere between Q_u and Q_m in Figure 17-3. Where in that range the wage and equilibrium quantity will be depends on the two sides' negotiating skills and other noneconomic forces.

A bilateral monopoly is a market in which a single seller faces a single buyer.

Political and Social Forces and the Labor Market

Let's now consider some real-world characteristics of U.S. labor markets. For example:

1. English teachers are paid close to what economics teachers are paid even though the quantity of English teachers supplied significantly exceeds the quantity of English teachers demanded, while the quantity of economics teachers supplied is approximately equal to the quantity demanded.

2. On average, women earn about 85 cents for every $1 earned by men.

3. Certain types of jobs are undertaken primarily by members of a single ethnic group. For example, a large percentage of construction workers on high-rise buildings are Mohawk people. They have an uncanny knack for keeping their balance on high, open building frames.

4. Firms often pay higher than "market" wages.

5. Firms often don't lay off workers even when demand for their products decreases.

6. It often seems that there are two categories of jobs: dead-end jobs and jobs with potential for career advancement. Once in a dead-end job, a person finds it almost impossible to switch to a job with potential.

7. The rate of unemployment among blacks is nearly twice as high as the rate among whites.

To understand real-world labor markets, one must broaden the analysis.

Supply/demand analysis alone doesn't explain these phenomena. Each of them can, however, be explained as the result of market, political, and social forces. Thus, to understand real-world labor markets, it is necessary to broaden the analysis of labor markets to include other forces that limit the use of the market. These include legal and social limitations on the self-interest-seeking activities of firms and individuals. Let's consider a couple of the central issues of interaction among these forces and see how they affect the labor market.

Fairness and the Labor Market

People generally have an underlying view of what's fair. That view isn't always consistent among individuals, but it's often strongly held. The first lesson taught in a personnel or human resources course is that people aren't machines. They're human beings with feelings and emotions. If they feel good about a job, if they feel they're part of a team, they will work hard; if they feel they're being taken advantage of, they can be highly disruptive.

On some assembly-line jobs, it is relatively easy to monitor effort, so individuals can be—and in the past often were—treated like machines. Their feelings and emotions were ignored. Productivity was determined by the speed of the assembly line; if workers couldn't or wouldn't keep up the pace, they were fired.

EFFICIENCY WAGES   Most modern jobs, however, require workers to make decisions and to determine how best to do a task. Today's managers are aware that workers' emotional state is important to whether they make sound decisions and do a good job. So most firms, even if they don't really care about anything but profit, will try to keep their workers happy. It's in their own interest to do so. That might mean paying workers more than the going market wage, not laying them off even if layoffs would make sense economically, providing day care so the workers aren't worried about their children, or keeping wage differentials among workers small to limit internal rivalry. Such actions can often make long-run economic sense, even though they might cost the firm in the short run. They are common enough that they have acquired a name—**efficiency wages** *(wages paid above the going market wage to keep workers happy and productive).*

Q-8 Why might efficiency wages make sense in the long run?

Views of fairness also enter into wage determination through political channels. Social views of fairness influence government, which passes laws to implement those views. Minimum wage laws, comparable worth laws, and antidiscrimination laws are examples.

Nonwage Income and Property Rights

The four traditional categories of income are wages, rent, profits, and interest. Wages, discussed in the text, are determined by economic factors (the forces of supply and demand), with strong influences by political and social forces, which often restrict entry or hold wages higher than what they would be in a truly competitive market.

The same holds true for nonwage income: payments for use of land (rent), capital (profit), and financial assets (interest). The forces of supply and demand also determine these forms of income. But, as we have emphasized, supply and demand are not necessarily the end of the story. Supply and demand determine price and income, given an institutional structure that includes property rights (the rights given to people to use specified property) and the contractual legal system (the set of laws that govern economic behavior of the society). If you change property rights, you change the distribution of income. Thus, in a larger sense, supply and demand don't determine the distribution of income; the distribution of property rights does.

The system of property rights and the contractual legal system that underlie the U.S. economy evolved over many years. Many people believe that property rights were unfairly distributed to begin with; if you believe that, you'll also believe that the distribution of income and the returns to those property rights are unfair. In other words, you can favor markets but object to the underlying property rights. Many political fights about income distribution concern fights over property rights, not fights over the use of markets.

Such distributional fights have been going on for a long time. In feudal times, much of the land was held communally; it belonged to everyone, or at least everyone used it. It was common land—a communally held resource.

As the economy evolved into a market economy, that land was appropriated by individuals, and these individuals became landholders who could determine the use of the land and could receive rent for allowing other individuals to use that land. Supply and demand can explain how much rent will accrue to a landholder; it cannot explain the initial set of property rights.

For many issues, such as ownership of land, questions about the underlying property rights are in large part academic for Western societies. The property rights that exist, and the contractual legal system under which markets operate, are given. You're not going to see somebody going out and introducing a new alternative set of property rights in which the ownership of property is transferred to someone else. The government may impose shifts at the margin; for example, new zoning laws—laws that set limits on the use of one's property—will modify property rights and create fights about whether society has the right to impose such laws. But there will be no wholesale change in property rights. That's why most economic thinking simply takes property rights as given.

For other areas, such as intellectual property rights, which are being affected by technological change, assuming unchanging property rights does not make sense. Technological change forces the underlying property rights to change, and how they change plays a big role in how technological change affects the distribution of income. Property rights determine how the benefits of technological change are spread among the population. In recent years, institutional economists have redirected their analysis to look more closely at the underlying legal and philosophical basis of supply and demand. As they do so, they are extending and modifying the economic theory of income distribution.

COMPARABLE WORTH LAWS   Let's consider one of those, **comparable worth laws,** which are *laws mandating comparable pay for comparable work*—that is, mandatory "fairness." The problem in implementing these laws is in defining what is comparable. Do you define comparable work by the education it requires, by the effort the worker puts out, or by other characteristics? Similarly with pay: Compensation has many dimensions and it is not at all clear which are the relevant ones, or whether the political system will focus on the relevant ones.

Economists who favor comparable worth laws point out that social and intrafirm political issues are often the determining factors in setting pay. In fact, firms often have their own implicit or explicit comparable worth systems built into their structure.

For example, seniority, not productivity, often determines pay. Bias against women and minorities and in favor of high-level management is sometimes built into firms' pay-setting institutions. In short, within firms, pay structure is influenced by, but is not determined by, supply and demand forces. Comparable worth laws are designed to affect those institutional biases and thus are not necessarily any less compatible with supply and demand forces than are current pay-setting institutions.

The federal government is not the only government agency that establishes labor laws. State and local governments also do. For example, recently a number of local governments have established "living wage" laws, which are a type of minimum wage law that requires specified employers to pay a "living wage." "Living wage" is most often defined as that wage that would allow one worker, working 40 hours a week, to support a family of four at the poverty level. The analysis of these laws is similar to that of the minimum wage.

Discrimination and the Labor Market

Web Note 17.5

Faculty Hiring Bias

Q-9 True or false? Economic theory argues that discrimination should be eliminated. Why?

Discrimination exists in all walks of life: On average, women are paid less than men, and blacks are often directed into lower-paying jobs. Economists have done a lot of research to understand discrimination and what can be done about it. The first problem is to determine how people are treated differently and get an idea of how much of the difference is caused by discrimination. Let's consider discrimination against women.

On average, women receive somewhere around 85 percent of the pay that men receive. That has increased from about 60 percent in the 1970s. This persistent pay gap suggests that discrimination is occurring. The economist's job is to figure out how much of this is statistically significant and, of the portion that is caused by discrimination, what the nature of that discrimination is.

Analyzing the data, economists have found that somewhat more than half of the pay difference can be explained by causes other than discrimination, such as length of time on the job. But that still leaves a relatively large difference that can be attributed to discrimination.

Three Types of Direct Demand-Side Discrimination

Three types of demand-side discrimination are:

1. Discrimination based on individual characteristics that will affect job performance.
2. Discrimination based on correctly perceived statistical characteristics of the group.
3. Discrimination based on individual characteristics that don't affect job performance or are incorrectly perceived.

In analyzing discrimination, it's important to distinguish three types. The three types are: (1) discrimination based on individual characteristics that will affect job performance, (2) discrimination based on correctly perceived statistical characteristics of the group, and (3) discrimination based on individual characteristics that don't affect job performance or are incorrectly perceived. Let's look first at demand-side discrimination based on relevant individual characteristics. Firms commonly make decisions about employees based on individual characteristics that will affect job performance. For example, restaurants might discriminate against (avoid hiring) applicants with sourpuss personalities. Another example might be a firm hiring more young salespeople because its clients like to buy from younger rather than older employees. If that characteristic can be an identifying factor for a group of individuals, the discrimination becomes more visible.

The second type of demand-side discrimination is discrimination based on group characteristics. This occurs when firms make employment decisions about individuals because they are members of a group who on average have particular characteristics that affect job performance. A firm may correctly perceive that young people in general have a lower probability of staying on a job than do older people and therefore may discriminate against younger people.

Why Do Women Earn Less Than Men?

The pay gap between women and men involves ongoing research, and economists are studying it from many different angles. All agree; the pay gap exists, but the question is: Why? To the extent that it is the result of gender discrimination, what type of discrimination is driving it? A recent study of wages of men and women in Denmark suggests that a significant portion of wage differentials in Denmark has to do with institutional supply-side discrimination, not with demand-side discrimination. By that we mean that the pay gap isn't because companies discriminate against women. Rather, it's because in most marriages, women take most of the responsibility for caring for the children in the family.

©fullempty/Shutterstock

Specifically, the researchers found that the pay differential between men and women before the women had children was almost nonexistent. However, when the women had children, their wages fell behind both women who remained childless and behind men who had children. Upon having children, women earned lower wages, worked fewer hours, and were more likely not to work at all than men who had children. When men had children, their pay did not fall behind; men with children did not work fewer hours, and their pay remained roughly equal to the pay of women who did not have children. So we can blame it on the kids. The earnings fall wasn't temporary. While the earnings of women with children did rise as their children grew, their earnings never fully recovered, accounting for much of the pay gap between women and men in Denmark.

While some of the drop in earnings is likely due to demand-side discrimination, the evidence suggests that in Denmark the pay gap is more likely tied up with institutional supply-side discrimination. Within the family, women, not men, end up as the primary caregiver. Some of that may be a matter of personal preference. Caring for children is rewarding for both men and women, and people are willing to give up income to do so. In the study, the women who grew up in households where the mother worked more than the father experienced less of a drop in income upon becoming mothers, suggesting women who grew up in households where home responsibilities were shared more equitably followed their parents' preferences. Still, such preferences didn't account for the entire differential.

One can see the institutional supply-side discrimination in reactions to parental leave policy. Two and a half years after Australia's Labor government offered a parental leave program, only 1 father for every 500 mothers chose to take it. In the United States, 76 percent of men take less than a week off when their baby is born and 96 percent are back at work after two weeks or less. If this is the cause of the pay gap, it leaves two policy options: (1) We can accept the pay differential as capturing differences in preferences; or (2) policy can be designed to change, or impose, different preferences on people. Sweden is following the latter. In Sweden, men are required to take at least a three-month leave after having a child or they will lose the benefit.

The third type of demand-side discrimination is discrimination based on irrelevant individual characteristics. This discrimination is based either on individual characteristics that do not affect job performance or on incorrectly perceived statistical characteristics of groups. A firm might not hire people over age 50 because the supervisor doesn't like working with older people, even though older people may be just as productive as, or even more productive than, younger people.

Of the three types, discrimination based on irrelevant individual characteristics will be easiest to eliminate; it doesn't have an economic motivation. In fact, discrimination based on individual characteristics that don't affect job performance is costly to a firm. Competing firms will hire these people and be in a better competitive position because they did so. Market forces will work toward eliminating this type of discrimination.

An example of the success of a firm's policy to reduce discrimination is the decision by McDonald's to create a special program to hire workers with learning disabilities. Individuals who have learning disabilities often make good employees. They tend to have lower turnover rates and follow procedures better than do many of the more transient employees McDonald's hires. Moreover, through its advertising, McDonald's helped change some negative stereotypes about people with disabilities. So in this case market forces and political forces are working together.

Q-10 Why is discrimination based on characteristics that affect job performance difficult to eliminate?

If the discrimination is of either of the first two types (that is, based on characteristics that do affect job performance, either directly or statistically), the discrimination will be harder to eliminate. In these cases, not discriminating can be costly to the firm, so political forces to eliminate discrimination will be working against market forces to keep discrimination.

Whenever discrimination saves the firm money, the firm will have an economic incentive to use subterfuges to get around an antidiscrimination law. These subterfuges will make the firm appear to be complying with the law, even when it isn't. An example would be a firm that finds some other reason besides age to explain why it isn't hiring an older person.

Institutional Discrimination

Institutional discrimination is discrimination in which the structure of the job makes it difficult or impossible for certain groups of individuals to succeed. Institutional discrimination does not come from the demand side, but is built into the institutional structure. Consider colleges and universities. To succeed in the academic market, one must devote an enormous amount of effort during one's 20s and 30s to pursuing one's career. But these are precisely the years when, given biology and culture, many women have major family responsibilities, presenting an obstacle for women to succeed. Were academic institutions different—say, a number of positions at universities were designed for high-level, part-time work during this period—these obstacles for women to advance their careers could be reduced.

Requiring peak time commitment when women are also facing peak family responsibilities is the norm for many companies, too. Thus, women face significant institutional discrimination.

Institutions can have built-in discrimination.

Whether this institutional discrimination is embedded in the firm's structure or in the family is an open question. For example, sociologists have found that in personal relationships women tend to move to be with their partners more than men move to be with their partners. In addition, women in two-parent relationships generally do much more work around the house and take a greater responsibility for child rearing than men do even when both are employed.

How important are these sociological observations? In discussing discrimination I ask the members of my class if they expect their personal relationships with their partners to be fully equal. The usual result is the following: 80 percent of the women expect a fully equal relationship; 20 percent expect their partner's career to come first. Eighty percent of the men expect their own careers to come first; 20 percent expect an equal relationship. I then point out that somebody's expectations aren't going to be fulfilled. Put simply, most observers believe that the institutional discrimination that occurs in interpersonal relationships is significant.

Economists have made adjustments for these sociological factors, and have found that institutional factors explain a portion of the lower pay that women receive but that other forms of workplace discrimination also explain a portion.

Whether prejudice should be allowed to affect the hiring decision is a normative question for society to settle. In answering these normative questions, our society has passed laws making it illegal for employers to discriminate on the basis of race, religion, sex, age, disability, or national origin. The reason society has made it illegal is its ethical belief in equal opportunity for all, or at least most, individuals.

The Evolution of Labor Markets

Now that we've briefly considered how noneconomic forces can influence labor markets, let's turn our attention to how labor markets developed.

Labor markets as we now know them developed in the 1700s and 1800s. Given the political and social rules that operated at that time, the invisible hand was free to push wage rates down to subsistence level. Workweeks were long and working conditions were poor. Laborers began to turn to other ways—besides the market—of influencing their wage. One way was to use political power to place legal restrictions on employers in their relationship with workers. A second way was to organize together—to unionize. Let's consider each in turn.

Evolving Labor Laws

Over the years, government has responded to workers' political pressure with numerous laws that limit what can and what cannot be done in the various labor markets. For example, in many areas of production, laws limit the number of normal hours a person can work in a day to eight. The laws also prescribe the amount of extra pay an employee must receive when working more than the normal number of hours. (Generally it's time-and-a-half.) Similarly, the number and length of workers' breaks are defined by law (one break every four hours).

Laws play an important role in the structure of labor markets.

Child labor laws mandate that a person must be at least 16 years old to be hired. The safety and health conditions under which a person can work are regulated by laws. (For example, on a construction site, all workers are required to wear hard hats.) Workers can be fired only for cause, and employers must show that they had cause to fire a worker. (For example, a 55-year-old employee cannot be fired simply because he or she is getting older.) Employers must not allow sexual harassment in the workplace. (Bosses can't make sexual advances to employees, and firms must make a good-faith attempt to see that employees don't sexually harass their co-workers.)

Combined, these laws play an enormously important role in the functioning of the labor market.

The Labor Market and You

This chapter is meant to give you a sense of how the labor market works. But what does it all mean for those of you who'll soon be getting a job or are in the process of changing jobs? I'll try to answer that question in this last section.

Table 17-1 shows a variety of useful statistics about the labor market. Let's consider how some of them might affect you. For example, consider relative pay of jobs requiring a college degree compared to jobs requiring only a high school diploma. Jobs requiring a college degree pay significantly more, on average, than do jobs requiring only a high school diploma. In recent years the income gap between the two groups has noticeably increased. So the answer to the question of whether it's worthwhile to stick college out for another couple of years and get a degree is probably yes.

Next, consider the salaries of PhDs compared to the salaries of MBAs. A PhD is a person who has gone to graduate school after college, usually for a number of years, and earned an advanced degree called a Doctorate of Philosophy—even though one can earn a PhD in many subjects besides philosophy (such as economics). As you can see, PhDs' starting salaries are lower than salaries of MBAs (masters of business administration) and professionals with other kinds of advanced degrees. Does this mean that PhDs are discriminated against? Not necessarily. It's possible that PhDs' lower pay suggests that PhDs derive a "psychic income" from their work in addition to the amount of money they earn.

Since PhDs are often quite smart, their willingness to accept psychic income as a substitute for higher pay suggests that there's much more to consider in a job than the

TABLE 17-1 (A AND B) Some Typical Starting Salaries

Occupation	Private or Public
Physician assistant	$85,000
Dentist	73,000
Actuarial analyst	50,000
Management analyst	46,000
Economist	44,000
Secondary school teacher	40,000
Technical maintenance	24,000
Administrative assistant	24,000
Radio announcer	24,000
Maintenance and grounds	22,000
Flight attendant	21,000
Taco technician	18,000
Retail sales associate	16,000

Sources: Author's estimates based on various sources (pay varies significantly by region).

(a) Some Typical Starting Salaries of BAs

Degree	Annual Salary*
Law (3 years)	
Major firms	$160,000
Small firms	62,500
Engineering	
Bachelor's degree	75,000
Master's degree	85,000
Business	
Bachelor's degree	45,000
Master's (MBA) degree (2 years)	90,000
MD (4 years and 3-year internship)	135,000
PhD (5 years)	
In economics	90,000
In humanities	65,000

*These figures are rough estimates based on data from various published sources and informal surveys of author.

(b) Starting Salaries for Selected Professional Degrees

salary. What's most important about a job isn't the wage, but whether you like what you're doing and the life that job provides. (Of course, their lower salaries also could imply that PhDs really aren't so smart.)

So my suggestion to you is definitely to finish college, especially if you enjoy it. (And with books like this, how could you help but enjoy it?) But go to graduate school only if you really enjoy learning. In picking your job, first and foremost pick a job that you enjoy (as long as it pays you enough to live on). Among jobs you like, choose a job in a field in which the supply of labor is limited, or the demand for labor is significantly increasing. Either of those trends is likely to lead to higher wages. After all, if you're doing something you like, you might as well get paid as much as possible for it.

Jobs in which the supply will likely be limited are those in which social or political forces have placed restrictions on entry or those requiring special abilities. If you have some special ability, try to find a job you enjoy in which you can use that ability. You might also look for a job in which entry is restricted, but beware: Jobs that are restricted in supply must be rationed, so while such jobs pay higher wages, you may need personal connections to obtain one of them.

I'm sure most of you are aware that your choice of jobs is one of the most important choices you'll be making in your life. So I'm sure you feel the pressure. But you should also know that a job, unlike marriage, isn't necessarily supposed to be for life. There's enormous flexibility in the U.S. labor market. Many people change jobs six or seven times in their lifetimes. So while the choice is important, a poor choice can be remedied; don't despair if the first job you take isn't perfect. Good luck.

Conclusion

We've come to the end of our discussion about the labor market. As I said at the beginning, most people are defined by their job. Thus the labor market is important, and economic forces play a central role in its operation. But it is also important to remember, precisely because work is so significant to us all, that the labor market is not governed by economic forces alone. Cultural, political, and social forces are central issues in labor markets and in how economic forces play out. So whenever you consider issues involving labor markets, think supply and demand, but also think of people fighting against those forces with political and social pressures to see that economic forces work for, not against, them.

Summary

- Incentive effects are important in labor supply decisions. The higher the wage, the higher the quantity supplied.   (*LO17-1*)

- Elasticity of market supply of labor depends on (1) individuals' opportunity cost of working, (2) the type of market being discussed, (3) the elasticity of individuals' supply curves, and (4) individuals entering and leaving the labor market.   (*LO17-1*)

- The demand for labor by firms is derived from the demand by consumers for goods and services. It follows the basic law of demand—the higher the wage, the lower the quantity demanded.   (*LO17-2*)

- Elasticity of market demand for labor depends on (1) the elasticity of demand for the firm's good, (2) the relative importance of labor in production, (3) the possibility and cost of substitution in production, and (4) the degree to which marginal productivity falls with an increase in labor.   (*LO17-2*)

- Technological advances and changes in international competitiveness shift the demand for labor. Both have reduced demand for some types of labor and increased demand for other types. The net effect has been an increase in the demand for labor.   (*LO17-2*)

- A monopsony is a market in which a single firm is the only buyer. A monopsonist hires fewer workers at a lower wage compared to a competitive firm.   (*LO17-3*)

- A bilateral monopoly is a market in which there is a single seller and a single buyer. The wage and number of workers hired in a bilateral monopoly depend on the relative strength of the union and the monopsonist.   (*LO17-3*)

- Firms are aware of workers' well-being and will sometimes pay efficiency wages to keep workers happy and productive.   (*LO17-3*)

- Views of fairness in the labor market have led to laws that mandate comparable pay for comparable work.   (*LO17-4*)

- Discrimination may be based on (1) relevant individual characteristics, (2) relevant group characteristics, or (3) irrelevant individual characteristics. The easiest to eliminate is discrimination based on irrelevant individual characteristics. The others are motivated by market incentives.   (*LO17-4*)

- Labor laws have evolved and will continue to evolve.   (*LO17-5*)

Key Terms

bilateral monopoly	efficiency wages	incentive effect	marginal factor cost
comparable worth laws	entrepreneurship	labor market	monopsony
derived demand			

Questions and Exercises   connect

1. Why are social and political forces more active in the labor market than in most other markets?   (*LO17-1*)

2. Economist Edward Prescott observed that while Americans worked 5 percent fewer hours per week than the French in the 1970s, they worked 50 percent more hours per week in the early 2000s. He found that taxes accounted for nearly all of the difference. What was his likely argument?   (*LO17-1*)

3. How is opportunity cost related to the supply of labor?   (*LO17-1*)

4. Using the economic decision rule and opportunity cost, explain why an increase in the wage rate increases quantity of labor supplied?   (*LO17-1*)

5. Is an increase in the marginal income tax rate reflected by a shift in the after-tax supply of labor or a movement along the supply curve when the pretax wage rate is on the vertical axis? Explain your answer.   (*LO17-1*)

6. Using the concept of opportunity cost, explain why welfare programs might increase the number of poor.   (*LO17-1*)

7. If th
   supp
   labo

8. List
   dem

9. List
   dem

10. The
    salaı
    morе
    a. E
       s
    b. V
       a
       n

11. Ecoı
    ket f
    dem
    tity s
    a. V
       s
    b. V
    c. V
       tl
       e

12. Dem
    law.
    bad i

13. As te
    large
    perfc
    entir
    the r

14. New
    place
    can t
    mark

15. The
    you (
    this ı
    Obeı
    ture?

16. "Eiġ
    Ame
    Walı
    to bu
    a. C
       ra
    b. V
       n
    c. V
       cc

17. Shov
    incre

b. If not all the teachers' students were required to take the test, how would the program have to treat students who did not take the exam?

c. What would be the most likely way in which the program would change what teachers did?

6. Why might it be inappropriate to discuss the effect of immigration policy using supply and demand analysis?

7. Why is unemployment nearly twice as high among black Americans as among white Americans? What should be done about the situation?

8. Give four reasons why women earn less than men. Which reasons do you believe are most responsible for the wage gap?

9. Interview three married female and three married male professors at your college, asking them what percentage of work in the professor's household each adult household member does.
   a. Assuming your results can be extended to the population at large, what can you say about the existence of institutional discrimination?
   b. If gender-related salary data for individuals at your college are available, determine whether women or men of equal rank and experience receive higher average pay.
   c. Relate your findings in *a* and *b*.

10. In an article in the *Journal of Human Resources* titled "The Economic Reality of the Beauty Myth," economists Susan Averett and Sanders Korenman found that family income of obese women is about 17 percent lower than that of women who are of recommended weight. The differential was less for men than for women.
    a. What conclusions can you draw from these findings?
    b. Do the findings necessarily mean that there is a "beauty" discrimination?
    c. What might explain the larger income penalty for women?

11. More than half of agricultural workers in the United States are undocumented immigrants. Some Americans support strong enforcement of immigration laws that limit the number of workers from Central and South America coming to the United States so that U.S. citizens can get those jobs, while others argue that without them, the jobs that they take will be left unfilled. Who is right?

Answers to Margin Questions

1. Under usual conditions of supply, one would expect that if the wage of my part-time job rises, the quantity of labor I supply in that part-time job also rises. Institutional constraints such as tax considerations or company rules might mean that the quantity of labor I supply doesn't change. However, under the usual conditions of supply, I will study less if the wage of my part-time job rises. (*LO17-1*)

2. Taxes reduce the opportunity cost, or relative price, of nonwork activities. So you will substitute leisure for labor as marginal tax rates increase. (*LO17-1*)

3. The irony of any need-based program is that such a program reduces people's incentive to prevent themselves from becoming needy. (*LO17-1*)

4. Some factors that influence the elasticity of a firm's derived demand for labor include (1) the elasticity of demand for the firm's good; (2) the relative importance of labor in the production process; (3) the possibility, and cost, of substitution in production; and (4) the degree to which marginal productivity falls with an increase in labor. (*LO17-2*)

5. The demand for laborers at that firm would shift out to the right. (*LO17-2*)

6. Differences among countries in productivity, transportation costs, trade restrictions, and social institutions all determine the relative demand for labor in one country compared to another country. (*LO17-2*)

7. If the increase in labor supply leads to an increase in the demand for products in general, the increase in labor supply also will lead to an increase in labor demand. (*LO17-3*)

8. Firms might pay workers higher-than-competitive wages in the long run to cultivate worker loyalty and get workers to work harder. (*LO17-3*)

9. False. Economic theory does not argue that discrimination should be eliminated. Economic theory tries to stay positive. Discrimination is a normative issue. If one's normative views say that discrimination should be eliminated, economic theory might be useful to help do that most efficiently. (*LO17-4*)

10. Whenever discrimination saves the firm money, the firm will be pressured to discriminate to lower costs to remain competitive. (*LO17-4*)

Derived Demand

This appendix considers the issues of derived demand in more detail. Although it focuses on the derived demand for labor, you should note that the formal analysis of the firm's derived demand for labor presented in the chapter is quite general and carries over to the derived demand for capital and for land. Firms translate consumers' demands for goods into derived demands for any and all of the factors of production. Let's start our consideration by looking at the firm's decision to hire.

The Firm's Decision to Hire

What determines a firm's decision to hire someone? The answer is simple. A profit-maximizing firm hires someone if it thinks there's money to be made by doing so. Unless there is, the firm won't hire the person. So for a firm to decide whether to hire someone, it must compare the worker's **marginal revenue product (*MRP*)** *(the marginal revenue it expects to earn from selling the additional worker's output)* with the wage that it expects to pay the additional worker. For a competitive firm (for which $P = MR$), that marginal revenue product equals the worker's **value of marginal product (*VMP*)**—the worker's **marginal physical product (*MPP*)** *(the additional units of output that hiring an additional worker will bring about)* times the price (*P*) at which the firm can sell the additional product.

Marginal revenue product $= MPP \times P$

Say, for example, that by hiring another worker a firm can produce an additional 6 widgets an hour, which it can sell at $2 each. That means the firm can pay up to $12 per hour and still expect to make a profit. Notice that a key question for the firm is: How much additional product will we get from hiring another worker? A competitive firm can increase its profit by hiring another worker as long as the value of the worker's marginal product (which also equals her marginal revenue product) (*MPP* × *P*) is higher than her wage.

To see whether you understand the principle, consider the example in Figure A17-1(a). Column 1 shows the number of workers, all of whom are assumed to be identical. Column 2 shows the total output of those workers. Column 3 shows the marginal physical product of an additional worker. This number is determined by looking at the change in the total product due to this person's work. For example, if the firm is currently employing 30 workers and it hires one more, the firm's total product or output will rise from 294 to 300, so the marginal product of moving from 30 to 31 workers is 6.

Notice that workers' marginal product decreases as more workers are hired. Why is this? Remember the assumption of fixed capital: More and more workers are working with the same amount of capital and there is diminishing marginal productivity.

Column 4 shows **labor productivity**—*the average output per worker,* which is a statistic commonly referred to in economic reports. It's determined by dividing the total output by the number of workers. Column 5 shows the additional worker's marginal revenue product, which, since the firm is assumed to be competitive, is determined by multiplying the price the firm receives for the product it sells ($2) by the worker's marginal physical product.

Column 5, the marginal revenue product, is of central importance to the firm. It tells the firm how much additional money it will make from hiring an additional worker. That marginal revenue product represents a competitive firm's demand for labor.

Figure A17-1(b) graphs the firm's derived demand for labor, based on the data in column 5 of Figure A17-1(a). The resulting curve is the firm's **derived demand curve for labor,** which *shows the maximum amount of labor, measured in labor-hours, that a firm will hire.* To see this, let's assume that the wage is $9 and that the firm is hiring 30 workers. If it hires another worker so it has 31 workers, workers' marginal revenue product of $12 exceeds their wage of $9, so the firm can increase profits by doing so. It increases output and profits since the additional revenue the firm gets from increasing workers from 30 to 31 is $12 and the additional cost the firm incurs is the wage of $9.

Now say the firm has hired 4 additional workers so it has 34 workers. As the firm hires more workers, the marginal product of workers declines. As you can see from the graph in Figure A17-1(b), the marginal revenue product of decreasing from 34 to 33 workers is $6. Since the workers' marginal revenue product of $6 is less than their wage of $9, now the firm can increase profits by laying

FIGURE A17-1 (A AND B)   **Determining How Many Workers to Hire and the Firm's Derived Demand for Labor**

The marginal revenue product is any firm's demand curve for labor. Since for a competitive firm $P = MR$, a competitive firm's derived demand curve for labor is its value of the marginal product curve ($P \times MPP$). This curve tells us the additional revenue the firm gets from having an additional worker. From the chart in (**a**) we can see that when the firm increases from 27 to 28 workers, the marginal product per hour for each worker is 9. If the product sells for $2, then marginal revenue product is $18, which is one point on the demand curve for labor [point A in (**b**)]. When the firm increases from 34 to 35 workers, the value of the marginal product decreases to $4. This is another point on the firm's derived demand curve [point B in (**b**)]. By connecting the two points, as I have done in (**b**), you can see that the firm's derived demand curve for labor is downward-sloping.

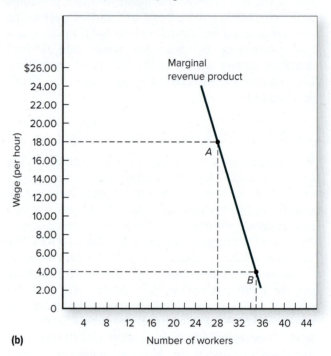

(1) Number of Workers	(2) Total Product per Hour	(3) Marginal Physical Product per Hour	(4) Average Product per Hour	(5) Marginal Revenue Product (MRP)
27	270	9.00	10.00	$18
28	279	8.00	9.96	16
29	287	7.00	9.90	14
30	294	6.00	9.80	12
31	300	5.00	9.68	10
32	305	4.00	9.53	8
33	309	3.00	9.36	6
34	312	2.00	9.18	4
35	314		8.97	

(a)

(b)

off some workers. Doing so decreases output but increases profit because it significantly increases the average product of the remaining workers.

Only when a worker's wage of $9 equals the marginal revenue product does the firm have no incentive to change the number of employees. In this example, the wage ($9) equals workers' marginal revenue product at 32 workers. When the firm is hiring 32 workers, either hiring another worker or laying off 1 worker will decrease profits. Decreasing from 32 to 31 workers loses $10 in revenue, but increasing from 32 to 33 workers gains $8 in revenue but costs $9 in wages. Since the marginal revenue product curve tells the firm, given a wage, how many workers it should hire, *the marginal revenue product curve is the firm's demand curve for labor.*

The fact that the demand curve for labor is downward-sloping means that as more workers are hired, workers' marginal product falls. This might tempt you to think that the last worker hired is inherently less productive than the

first worker hired. But that simply can't be because, by assumption, the workers are identical. Thus, the marginal product of any worker must be identical to the marginal product of any other worker, given that a specified number of workers are working. What the falling marginal product means is that *when 30 rather than 25 workers are working*, the marginal product of any one of those 30 workers is less than the marginal product of any one of 25 of those workers when only 25 are working. When the other inputs are constant, hiring an additional worker lowers the marginal product not only of the last worker but also of any of the other workers.

To understand what's going on here, you must remember that when marginal product is calculated, all other inputs are held constant—so if a firm hires another worker, that worker will have to share machines or tools with other workers. When you share tools, you start running into significant bottlenecks, which cause production to fall. That's why the marginal product of workers goes down when a new worker is hired. This assumption that all other factors of production are held constant is an important one. If all other factors of production are increased, it is not at all clear that workers' productivity will fall as output increases.

Why does a firm hire another worker if doing so will lead to a fall in other workers' productivity and, possibly, a fall in the average productivity of all workers? Because the firm is interested in total profit, not productivity. As long as hiring an extra worker increases revenue by more than the worker costs, the firm's total profit increases. A profit-maximizing firm would be crazy not to hire another worker, even if by doing so it lowers the marginal product of the workers.

The economic model of labor markets assumes that marginal productivities can be determined relatively easily. In reality they can't. They require guesses and estimates that are often influenced by a worker's interaction with the person doing the guessing and estimating. Thus, social interaction plays a role in determining wages. If you get along with the manager, his estimate of your marginal productivity is likely to be higher than if you don't. And for some reason, managers' estimates of their own marginal productivity tend to be high. In part because of difficulties in estimating marginal productivities, actual pay can often differ substantially from marginal productivities.

Factors Affecting the Demand for Labor

There are many technical issues that determine how the demand for products is translated through firms into a demand for labor (and other factors of production), but we need not go into them in detail. I will, however, state three general principles:

1. Changes in the demand for a firm's product will be reflected in changes in its demand for labor.
2. The structure of a firm plays an important role in determining its demand for labor.
3. A change in the other factors of production that a firm uses will change its demand for labor.

Let's consider each of these principles in turn.

Changes in the Firm's Demand

The first principle is almost self-evident. An increase in the demand for a product leads to an increase in demand for the laborers who produce that product. The increase in demand pushes the price up, raising the marginal revenue product of labor (which, you'll remember, for a competitive firm is the price of the firm's product times the marginal physical product of labor).

The implications of this first principle, however, are not so self-evident. Often people think of firms' interests and workers' interests as being counter to one another, but this principle tells us that in many ways they are not. What benefits the firm also benefits its workers. Their interests are in conflict only when it comes to deciding how to divide up the total revenues among the owners of the firm, the workers, and the other inputs. Thus, it's not uncommon to see a firm and its workers fighting each other at the bargaining table, but also working together to prevent imports that might compete with the firm's product or to support laws that may benefit the firm.

An example of such cooperation occurred when union workers at a solar energy firm helped fight for an extension of government subsidies for solar energy. Why? Because their contract included a clause that if the solar energy subsidy bill passed, the union workers' wages would be significantly higher than if it didn't. This cooperation between workers and firms has led some economists to treat firms and workers as a single entity, out to get as much as they can as a group. These economists argue that it isn't helpful to separate out factor markets and goods markets. They argue that bargaining power models, which combine factor and goods markets, are the best way to analyze at what level wages will be set. In other words, the cost of labor to a firm should be modeled as if it is determined at the same time that its price and profitability are determined, not separately.

The Structure of the Firm and Its Demand for Labor

The way in which the demand for products is translated into a demand for labor is determined by the structure of the firm. For example, let's consider the difference between a monopolistic industry and a competitive industry. For both, the decision about whether to hire is based on whether the wage is below or above the marginal revenue product. But the firms that make up the two industries calculate their marginal revenue products differently.

The price of a competitive firm's output remains constant regardless of how many units it sells. Thus, its marginal revenue product equals the value of the marginal product. To calculate its marginal revenue product we simply multiply the price of the firm's product by the worker's marginal physical product. For a competitive firm:

Marginal revenue product of a worker =

Value of the worker's marginal product =

$MPP \times$ Price of product

The price of a monopolist's product decreases as more units are sold since the monopolist faces a downward-sloping demand curve. The monopolist takes that into account. That's why it focuses on marginal revenue rather than price. As it hires more labor and produces more output, the price it charges for its product will fall. Thus, for a monopolist:

Marginal revenue product of a worker =

$MPP \times$ Marginal revenue

Since a monopolist's marginal revenue is always less than price, a monopolistic industry will always hire fewer workers than a comparable competitive industry, which is consistent with the result we discussed in the chapter on monopoly: a monopolistic industry will always produce less than a competitive industry, other things equal.

To ensure that you understand the principle, let's consider the example in Table A17-1, a table of prices, wages, marginal revenues, marginal physical products, and marginal revenue products for a firm in a competitive industry and a monopolistic industry.

A firm in a competitive industry will hire up to the point where the wage equals $MPP \times P$ (columns 5 × 3). This occurs at 6 workers. Hiring either fewer or more workers would mean a loss in profits for a firm in a competitive industry.

Now let's compare the competitive industry with an equivalent monopolistic industry. Whereas the firm in the competitive industry did not take into account the effect an increase in output would have on prices, the monopolist will. It takes into account the fact that to sell the additional output of an additional worker, it must lower the price of the good. The relevant marginal revenue product for the monopolist appears in column 7. At 6 workers, the worker's wage rate of $2.85 exceeds the worker's marginal revenue product of $1.95, which means that the monopolist would hire fewer than 6 workers—5 full-time workers and 1 part-time worker.

As a second example of how the nature of firms affects the translation of demand for products into demand for labor, consider what would happen if workers rather than independent profit-maximizing owners controlled the firms. You saw before that whenever another worker is hired, other inputs constant, the marginal physical product of all similar workers falls. That can contribute to a reduction in existing workers' wages. The profit-maximizing firm doesn't take into account that effect on existing workers' wages. It wants to hold its costs down. If existing workers are making the decisions about hiring, they'll take that wage decline into account. If they believe that hiring more workers will lower their own wage, they have an incentive to see that new workers aren't hired. Thus, like the monopolist, a worker-controlled firm will hire fewer workers than a competitive profit-maximizing firm.

There aren't many worker-controlled firms in the United States, but a number of firms include existing workers' welfare in their decision processes. Moreover, with the growth of the team concept, in which workers are seen as part of a team with managers, existing workers' input into managerial decision making is increasing. In many U.S. firms, workers have some say in whether additional workers will be hired and at what wage they will be hired. Other firms have an implicit understanding or a written contract with existing workers that restricts hiring and firing decisions.

According to Glassdoor, the top five companies to work for in 2018 based on employee reviews were:

1. Facebook.

2. Bain & Company.

3. Boston Consulting Group.

4. In-N-Out Burger.

5. Google.

Among the reasons Google is on the list is its climbing wall and nap pods. (And its pay includes significant bonuses of stock options.)

Why do firms consider workers' welfare? They do so to be seen as "good employers," which makes it easier for them to hire in the future. Given the strong social and legal

TABLE A17-1 **The Effect of Monopoly and Firm Structure on the Demand for Labor**

(1) Number of Workers	(2) Wage	(3) Price (P)	(4) Marginal Revenue (Monopolist) (MR)	(5) Marginal Physical Product (MPP)	(6) Marginal Revenue Competitive (MPP × P)	(7) Product Monopolist (MPP × MR)
5	$2.85	$1.00	$0.75	5	$5.00	$3.75
6	2.85	0.95	0.65	3	2.85	1.95
7	2.85	0.90	0.55	1	0.90	0.55

limitations on firms' hiring and firing decisions, one cannot simply apply marginal productivity theory to the real world. One must first understand the institutional and legal structures of the labor market. However, the existence of these other forces doesn't mean that the economic forces represented by marginal productivity don't exist. Rather, it means that firms struggle to find a wage policy that accommodates both economic and social forces in their wage-setting process. For example, in 2007, when automakers were struggling financially, the United Autoworkers Union negotiated multi-tier wage contracts with auto companies. The companies continued to pay their existing workers a higher wage, but paid new workers a lower wage, even though old and new workers were doing identical jobs. These multitier wage contracts were the result of the interactions of the social and market forces. The multitiered wage contracts created social unease within the workforce and within eight years, when automakers were faring better financially, they were eliminated.

Changes in Other Factors of Production

A third principle determining the derived demand for labor is the amount of other factors of production that the firm has. Given a technology, an increase in other factors of production will increase the marginal physical product of existing workers. For example, let's say that a firm buys more machines so that each worker has more machines with which to work. The workers' marginal physical product increases, and the cost per unit of output for the firm decreases. The net effect on the demand for labor is unclear; it depends on how much the firm increases output, how much the firm's price is affected, and how easily one type of input can be substituted for another—or whether it must be used in conjunction with others.

While we can't say what the final effect on demand will be, we can determine the firm's **cost minimization condition**—*where the ratio of marginal product to the price of an input is equal for all inputs.*[1] When a firm is

_____

[1] This condition was explicitly discussed in terms of isocost/isoquant analysis in the appendix to Chapter 12.

using resources as efficiently as possible, and hence is minimizing costs, the marginal product of each factor of production divided by the price of that factor must equal that of all the other factors. Specifically, the *cost minimization condition* is

$$\frac{MP_l}{w} = \frac{MP_m}{P_m} = \frac{MP_x}{P_x}$$

where

$w =$ Wage rate

$l =$ Labor

$m =$ Machines

$x =$ Any other input

If this cost minimization condition is not met, the firm could hire more of the input with the higher marginal product relative to price, and less of other inputs, and produce the same amount of output at a lower cost.

Let's consider a numerical example. Say the marginal product of labor is 20 and the wage is $4, while the marginal product of machines is 30 and the rental price of machines is $4. You're called in to advise the firm. You say, "Fire one worker, which will decrease output by 20 and save $4; spend that $4 on machines, which will increase output by 30." Output has increased by 10 while costs have remained constant. As long as the marginal products divided by the prices of the various inputs are unequal, you can make such recommendations to lower cost.

Conclusion

Changes in these factors make demand for labor shift around a lot. This shifting introduces uncertainty into people's lives and into the economic system. Often people attempt to build up institutional barriers to reduce uncertainty—through either social or political forces. Thus, labor markets function under an enormous volume of regulations and rules. We need to remember that while economic factors often lurk behind the scenes to determine pay and hiring decisions, these are often only part of the picture.

Key Terms

cost minimization
   condition
derived demand curve
   for labor

labor productivity
marginal physical
   product (*MPP*)

marginal revenue
   product (*MRP*)

value of marginal product
   (*VMP*)

Questions and Exercises

1. Using the information in Figure A17-1, answer the following questions:
   a. If the market wage were $7 an hour, how many workers would the firm hire?
   b. If the price of the firm's product fell to $1, how would your answer to *a* change?

2. If firms were controlled by workers, would they likely hire more or fewer workers? Why?

3. In the 1980s and the 1990s farmers switched from small square bales, which they hired students on summer break to stack for them, to large round bales, which can be handled almost entirely by machines. What is the likely reason for the switch?

4. Should teachers be worried about the introduction of computer- and video-based teaching systems? Why or why not?

5. A competitive firm gets $3 per widget. A worker's average product is 4 and marginal product is 3. What is the maximum the firm should pay the worker?

6. How would your answer to question 5 change if the firm were a monopolist?

7. Fill in the following table for a competitive firm that has a $2 price for its goods.

8. Your manager comes in with three sets of proposals for a new production process. Each process uses three inputs: land, labor, and capital. Under proposal A, the firm would be producing an output where the *MPP* of land is 30, labor is 42, and capital is 36. Under proposal B, at the output produced the *MPP* would be 20 for land, 35 for labor, and 96 for capital. Under proposal C, the *MPP* would be 40 for land, 56 for labor, and 36 for capital. Inputs' cost per hour is $5 for land, $7 for labor, and $6 for capital.
   a. Which proposal would you adopt?
   b. If the price of labor rises to $14, how will your answer change?

Number of Workers	TP	MPP	AP	MRP
1	10		____	
		____		____
2	19			
		8		____
3	____		____	
				____
4	____		8.5	
		____		$12
5	____		____	

Design elements: Web Note icon: ©McGraw-Hill Education; Real-World Application icon: ©McGraw-Hill Education; A Reminder icon: ©McGraw-Hill Education; Added Dimension icon: ©McGraw-Hill Education; Thinking Like a Modern Economist icon: ©NeydtStock/Shutterstock

Nonwage and Asset Income: Rents, Profits, and Interest

> The first man to fence in a piece of land, saying "This is mine," and who found people simple enough to believe him, was the real founder of civil society.
>
> —Jean-Jacques Rousseau

©Brian A Jackson/Shutterstock

This web chapter can be found in McGraw-Hill Connect®

Chapter Outline

After reading this chapter, you should be able to:

LO17W-1 Distinguish rent from other types of income and explain the relationship between rent seeking and property rights.

LO17W-2 Define *profit* and explain its relationship to entrepreneurship.

LO17W-3 Define *interest* and demonstrate how it is used in determining present value.

LO17W-4 Explain the marginal productivity theory of income distribution.

Who Gets What?
The Distribution of Income

"God must love the poor," said Lincoln, "or he wouldn't have made so many of them." He must love the rich, or he wouldn't divide so much mazuma among so few of them.

—H. L. Mencken

After reading this chapter, you should be able to:

LO18-1 Explain how income, wealth, and poverty are measured, and how their real-world measures changed over time.

LO18-2 Summarize the socio-economic tensions that high income and wealth inequalities can cause.

LO18-3 Explain why there are so many philosophical debates about equality and fairness, and summarize some of the debates.

LO18-4 Discuss the practical and theoretical problems of redistributing income.

(Top) ©Comstock/Stockbyte/Getty Images; (bottom) ©Design Pics/Con Tanasiuk RF

In 2017, Ginni Rometty, president and CEO of IBM, earned $96 million (base pay plus stock options); that's about $1.9 million per week. Assuming she worked 70 hours per week (you have to work hard to earn that kind of money), that's more than $26,374 per hour.

Today, the average family doctor earns $190,000 per year; that's $3,654 per week. Assuming she works 70 hours per week (she's conscientious, makes house calls, and spends time with her hospitalized patients), that's $52 per hour.

Joe Smith, a cashier in a fast-food restaurant, earns $12 per hour. But to earn enough for his family to be able to eat, he works a lot of overtime, for which he is paid time-and-a-half, or $18 per hour. So he makes about $53,040 per year, or $1,020 per week, by working 70 hours per week.

Hama Manout, a peasant in the Central African Republic, earns $400 a year; that's $7.69 per week. Assuming he works 70 hours per week (you have to work hard when you are truly poor just to keep from starving), that's a little over 10 cents per hour.

Are such major differences typical of how income is distributed among people in general? Are such differences fair? And if they're unfair, what can be done about them? This chapter addresses such issues. (I should warn you, however: If you're looking for answers, this chapter won't provide them; it will simply make the assumptions on both sides clear.)

The issues addressed in these questions play a fundamentally important role in policy debates today. The reason why is that in the last 40 years the income distribution in the United States has changed considerably. Many formerly middle-income people have moved into the upper-income levels; their wealth and their control of real assets have grown considerably. But simultaneously, many lower-income people's income has stagnated or fallen. This change is bringing income distribution issues to center stage in modern policy debates.

Measuring the Distribution of Income, Wealth, and Poverty

There are several different ways to look at income distribution. In the 1800s, economists were concerned with how income was divided among the owners of businesses (for whom profits were the source of income), the owners of land (who received rent), and workers (who earned wages). That concern reflected the relatively sharp distinctions among social classes that existed in capitalist societies at that time. Landowners, workers, and owners of businesses were separate groups, and few individuals moved from one group to another.

Time has changed that. Today workers, through their pension plans and investments in financial institutions, are owners of over 50 percent of all the shares issued on the New York Stock Exchange. Landowners as a group receive a relatively small portion of total income. Companies are run not by capitalists, but by managers who are, in a sense, workers. In short, the social lines have blurred.

This blurring of the lines between social classes doesn't mean that we can forget the question "Who gets what?" It simply means that our interest in who gets what has a different focus. We no longer focus on classification of income by source. Instead we look at how total income is distributed among income groups. How much income do the top 5 percent get? How much do the top 15 percent get? How much do the bottom 10 percent get? Share distribution of income is *the relative division of total income among income groups.*

A second distributional issue economists are concerned with is the socioeconomic distribution of income *(the allocation of income among relevant socioeconomic groupings)*. How much do black people get relative to white people? How much do older people get compared to younger people? How much do women get compared to men?

The Lorenz Curve

To get a sense of the distribution of income in the United States consider Figure 18-1. It ranks people by their income and tells how much the richest 20 percent (a quintile) and the poorest 20 percent receive. For example, the poorest 20 percent might get 5 percent of the income and the richest 20 percent might get 40 percent. In it you can see that the 20 percent of Americans receiving the lowest level of income got 3.1 percent

Web Note 18.1
Executive Pay

The share distribution of income is the relative division of total income among income groups.

The socioeconomic distribution of income is the relative division or allocation of total income among relevant socioeconomic groups.

FIGURE 18-1 (A AND B)   **A Lorenz Curve of U.S. Income**

If income were perfectly equally distributed, the Lorenz curve would be a diagonal line. In (**b**) we see the U.S. Lorenz curve based on the numbers in (**a**) compared to a Lorenz curve reflecting a perfectly equal distribution of income.

Source: *Current Population Reports*, U.S. Bureau of the Census, 2018 (www.census.gov).

Income Quintile	Percentage of Total Family Income	Cumulative Percentage of Total Family Income
Lowest fifth	3.1%	3.1%
Second fifth	8.2	11.3
Third fifth	14.3	25.6
Fourth fifth	23.0	48.6
Highest fifth	51.5	100.0

(a)

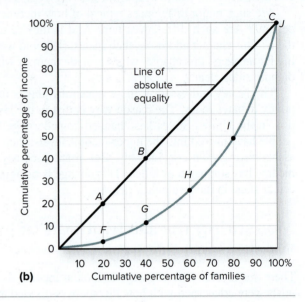

(b)

A Lorenz curve is a geometric representation of the share distribution of income among families in a given country at a given time.

Q-1 When drawing a Lorenz curve, what do you put on the two axes?

of the total income. The top 20 percent of Americans received 48.6 percent of the total income. The ratio of the income of the top 20 percent compared to the income of the bottom 20 percent was about 16:1.

The same information can be seen graphically in what is called a **Lorenz curve**—*a geometric representation of the share distribution of income among families in a given country at a given time.* The Lorenz curve measures the cumulative percentage of *families* on the horizontal axis, arranged from poorest to richest, and the cumulative percentage of *family income* on the vertical axis. Since the figure presents cumulative percentages (all of the families with income below a certain level), both axes start at zero and end at 100 percent.

A perfectly equal distribution of income would be represented by a diagonal line like the one in Figure 18-1(b). That is, the poorest 20 percent of the families would have 20 percent of the total income (point *A*); the poorest 40 percent of the families would have 40 percent of the income (point *B*); and 100 percent of the families would have 100 percent of the income (point *C*). An unequal distribution of income is represented by a Lorenz curve that's below the diagonal line. All real-world Lorenz curves are below the diagonal because in the real world income is always distributed unequally.

The blue line in Figure 18-1(b) represents a Lorenz curve of the U.S. income distribution presented in Figure 18-1(a)'s table. From Figure 18-1(a) you know that, in 2017, the bottom 20 percent of the families in the United States received 3.1 percent of the income. Point *F* in Figure 18-1(b) represents that combination of percentages (20 percent and 3.1 percent). To find what the bottom 40 percent received, we must add the income percentage of the bottom 20 percent and the income percentage of the next 20 percent. Doing so gives us 11.3 percent [3.1 plus 8.2 percent from column 2 of Figure 18-1(a)]. Point *G* in Figure 18-1(b) represents the combination of percentages (40 percent and 11.3 percent). Continuing this process for points *H*, *I*, and *C*, you get a Lorenz curve that shows the share distribution of income in the United States in 2017.

Chapter 18 ■ Who Gets What? The Distribution of Income

393

U.S. Income Distribution over Time

Lorenz curves are most useful in visual comparisons of income distribution over time and between countries. Figure 18-2 presents Lorenz curves for the United States in 1929, 1970, and 2017. They show that from 1929 to 1970 the share distribution of income became more equal. (The curve for 1970 is closer to being a diagonal line than the curve for 1929.) Income of the bottom fifth of families rose by a much higher proportion than did income of the top fifth. That was a continuation of a trend that had begun in the 1920s. In the 1970s that trend stopped and began to reverse. As you can see, from 1970 to 2017 income distribution became less equal. (The curve for 2017 is further from being diagonal than is the curve for 1970.) The income of the bottom fifth of families fell by over 10 percent, while the income of the top fifth rose significantly.

Important reasons for the initial increase in equality are the redistribution measures instituted by the U.S. government between the 1930s and the 1970s, including welfare programs, unemployment insurance, Social Security, progressive taxation (taxation of higher income at higher rates, lower income at lower rates), and improved macroeconomic performance of the economy.

The trend back toward greater inequality starting in the 1970s was caused by a fall in the real income of the poor, when their wage increases didn't keep up with price increases. Part of the reason was globalization; another part is that taxes have become less progressive, government funding for social programs has fallen, and the wages of unskilled and medium-skilled workers have been squeezed by an influx of immigrants into the United States who are willing to work for low wages.

While wages have fluctuated with the business cycle since then, the trend toward greater inequality continued until about 2017 when pressures pushing for rising inequality seemed to be decreasing.

The distribution of income over time is not only affected by business cycles, government policy, and competitive pressures; it is also affected by demographic and technological factors. Many families have relatively low income in their early years, relatively higher income in their middle years, and then relatively low income again in their retirement years. The Lorenz curve reflects these differences, so even if lifetime income were equally distributed, income in any one year would not be. Moreover,

From 1929 to 1970, income inequality in the United States decreased. From 1970 to 2017, it increased.

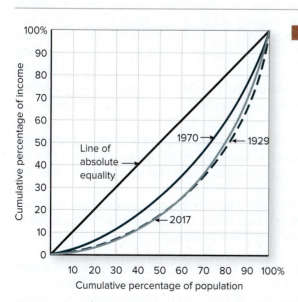

FIGURE 18-2 **Lorenz Curves for the United States: 1929, 1970, and 2017**

The amount of inequality of income distribution has fluctuated in the United States. Until about 1970, it decreased; since then it has increased.

Source: *Current Population Reports*, U.S. Bureau of the Census (www.census.gov).

when the percentages of these groups change, the Lorenz curve will change. For example, as the baby-boom generation retires and no longer works, their collective income will fall. That decline in overall income relative to the income of the smaller number of working families will affect the Lorenz curve.

The effect of technology is a bit different; that effect is easiest to convey with an example. Before the development of radio, TV, records, tapes, CDs, MP3 players, and online, on-demand music stores such as Spotify, the number of people who could listen to a performer was limited by how many people could fit in a concert hall. Without recordings or broadcasting to satisfy the demand for entertainment, that meant lots of local singers could earn a decent, but not phenomenal, wage. As recording, broadcasting, and transportation technology progressed, the number of people who could listen to a performance was nearly unlimited and "superstars" were born. The "almost superstars" lost out and were destined to sing for low wages at weddings, bar mitzvah parties, and church recitals, while the superstars became multimillionaires. Similar changes occurred in sports and other performance activities. The point of the example is that technology can significantly influence income distribution. University of Chicago economist Kevin Murphy argues that as global competition continues to grow, and as telecommunications networks expand, the pressure for income inequality to increase will continue.

Technology has played a role in increasing income inequality.

Defining Poverty

Much of the government's concern with income distribution has centered on the poorest group—those in poverty. Defining poverty is not easy. Do we want to define it as an absolute amount of real income that does not change over time? If poverty were defined as an *absolute* amount of real income, few in the United States would be in poverty today; just about all of today's poor have higher real incomes than did the middle class 50 or 60 years ago. Or do we want to define it as a *relative* concept that rises as the average income in the society rises? For example, anyone with an income of less than one-fifth of the average income could be defined as living in poverty. If that relative concept of poverty were chosen, then the proportion of people classified as poor would always be the same.

Poverty can be defined as a relative or absolute concept.

Q-2 Is the U.S. definition of poverty an absolute or a relative definition?

THE OFFICIAL DEFINITION OF POVERTY   The United States uses a definition of poverty that is a combination of a relative and an absolute measure. Thus, it satisfies neither those who favor an absolute measure nor those who favor a relative measure, and there are calls to increase and calls to decrease the **poverty threshold**—*the income below which a family is considered to live in poverty.* The official definition of poverty is the following:

> A family is in poverty if its income is equal to or less than three times an average family's minimum food expenditures as calculated by the U.S. Department of Agriculture.

Poverty is defined by the U.S. government as an income equal to or less than three times an average family's minimum food expenditures as calculated by the U.S. Department of Agriculture.

The minimum weekly food budget includes 4 eggs, 1½ pounds of meat, 3 pounds of potatoes, about 4 pounds of vegetables, and other foods; the cost is about $39 per person per week. By the latest calculations, that means that for a family of four, the poverty line is $25,283.

As Table 18-1 shows, using the official poverty measure, the number of people in poverty decreased in the 1960s and then began increasing in the 1970s. In 2017, 39.7 million Americans lived below the poverty threshold.

DEBATES ABOUT THE DEFINITION OF POVERTY   The minimum food budget used to determine the poverty line was determined in the 1960s and has not been recalculated to account for rising standards of living. Thus, it is in principle an absolute

TABLE 18-1   **Number and Percentage of Persons in Poverty**

	Number of People (in millions)	Percentage of Population	Poverty Income of Family of 4* (in current dollars)
1960	39.9	22.2%	$ 3,022
1970	24.4	12.6	3,986
1980	29.3	13.0	8,351
1990	33.6	13.5	13,254
2000	31.6	11.3	17,463
2010	46.2	15.1	22,113
2015	43.1	13.5	24,036
2016	40.6	12.7	24,339
2017	39.7	12.3	24,858

*Family of 4 with 2 related children.

Source: *Current Population Reports*, U.S. Bureau of the Census (www.census.gov).

measure. Starting in 1969, however, the amount needed to buy that food is adjusted by the rate of inflation rather than by the rise in the price of the originally selected foods. Since food prices have risen by less than the rise in the general price level, the poverty threshold has gone up by more than it would have had food prices been used. That means the definition includes significant aspects of relativity; had a purely absolute measure been used, the poverty rate would be considerably lower.

Those who favor a relative measure of poverty argue that our current poverty measure is too low. They point out that food is now closer to one-seventh of a family's total budget, so food is no longer a good basis for determining the poverty level. Households spend much more now on housing, utilities, health care, and expenses related to work. A poverty threshold that takes different expenses into account raises the poverty threshold and raises the poverty rate from about 12 percent to 21 percent, with millions more people on the poverty roll.

Those who favor an absolute measure of poverty argue that the current measure is too high. They point out that U.S. poverty figures do not include in-kind (noncash) transfers such as food stamps and housing assistance. Nor does the current poverty measure take into account underreporting of income, or the savings people have. (Many elderly people may have low incomes but significant wealth, which they could choose to spend.) If we make adjustments for in-kind transfers and underreporting of income, the official number of people in poverty decreases to about 60 percent of the official number. University of Texas economist Daniel Slesnick takes it further and points out that, since the price of food has increased at less than the rate of inflation, a much lower level of expenditures than the amount used to calculate the poverty threshold will provide a "nutritionally adequate diet." Slesnick calculated that when one takes the decrease in the relative price of food into account, the number of people in poverty would have fallen to one-seventh the official count.

The moral of this debate: Like most economic statistics, poverty statistics should be used with care.

THE COSTS OF POVERTY AND SOCIAL MOBILITY   People who favor policies aimed at achieving equality of income argue that poverty brings significant costs to society. One is that society suffers when some of its people are in poverty, just as the entire family suffers when one member doesn't have enough to eat. Most people derive pleasure from knowing that others are not in poverty.

There are arguments that the poverty line is both too high and too low.

Like most economic statistics, poverty statistics should be used with care.

Web Note 18.2

Poverty and Achievement

The Gini Coefficient

A second measure economists use to talk about the degree of income inequality is the Gini coefficient of inequality. The Gini coefficient is derived from the Lorenz curve by comparing the area between (1) the Lorenz curve and the diagonal (area *A*) and (2) the total area of the triangle below the diagonal (areas *A* and *B*). That is:

Gini coefficient = Area *A*/(Areas *A* + *B*)

A Gini coefficient of zero would be perfect equality, since area *A* is 0 if income is perfectly equally distributed. The highest the Gini coefficient can go is 1. So all Gini coefficients must be between 0 and 1. The lower the Gini coefficient, the closer the income distribution is to being equal. The Gini coefficient for the United States was 0.415 in 2016.

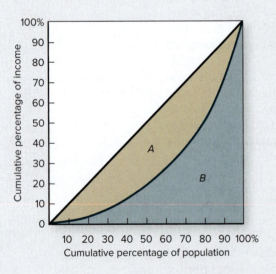

The following table gives Gini coefficients for a number of other countries. The Gini coefficients for transitional economies such as the Slovak Republic have risen over the last few years because they are now market economies and their incomes are less equally distributed.

Gini Coefficients for Selected Countries	
Algeria	.353
Bangladesh	.324
Brazil	.497
Canada	.321
China	.465
Czech Republic	.250
Germany	.270
Greece	.367
Guatemala	.530
Hungary	.282
Indonesia	.368
Iran	.445
Latvia	.345
Norway	.268
Panama	.507
Philippines	.444
Romania	.273
Slovak Republic	.237
South Africa	.625
Thailand	.445
United States	.415

Source: CIA, *The World Factbook*, www.cia.gov.

Another cost of poverty is that it increases incentives for crime. People with little income have little to lose. As people's incomes increase they have more to lose by committing crimes, and therefore fewer crimes are committed. Consistent with this argument, the crime rate has largely declined in the 1990s and early 2000s, as the economy grew. When the economy entered a severe recession in 2008, crime rates were expected to rise. They didn't. Instead they fell, and continued to fall, bringing into question the importance of poverty for crime.

While crime rates didn't rise, general dissatisfaction with the income distribution did. The sense of fairness that previously existed is giving way to increasing concern about the lack of fairness. Some observers argued that an economic system that led to such large inequalities in income, and left millions without a job or source of income, was unfair. Their complaints often concerned a lack of opportunity for many, and a sense of entitlement of a few. Our society was founded on the belief that if one worked hard one would be rewarded with increasing income and better job prospects for one's children than one's parents had. That belief is being tested, with continued high unemployment and the pressure of globalization holding down wages of jobs in the tradable sectors.

Before, most people accepted that individuals who worked hard could escape poverty, and individuals who didn't work hard would end up, or remain, in poverty. While everyone knew that the poor had it harder, and the rich easier, the United States was seen as a meritocracy, where hard work and ability were key to advancing both economically and socially. In the 1960s and 1970s, studies found that the United States had significant upward and downward mobility, confirming this belief. Recent studies, however, have questioned this view.

Specifically, a recent study by economist Bernt Bratsberg and his colleagues discovered that income mobility has significantly declined in the United States, and that now, the United States has less mobility than Europe. They determined this by ranking countries on a scale of 0 to 1, with 0 meaning perfect mobility (a child's income bears no relation to its parent's income) and 1 meaning no mobility (a child's income is identical to its parent's income). They found that, for sons, Sweden scored a .2, Britain scored a .36, and the United States scored a .54, suggesting that the United States had only about half as much social mobility as did Sweden and Britain. The situation was worse at the bottom; children born to a family in the bottom fifth of the U.S. income distribution were the least likely to move up. Other studies have confirmed this finding; it is harder for people today to surpass their parents on the income scale than it was a generation ago, and it is much harder for someone in the United States compared to someone in Europe to move up the income scale.

International Dimensions of Income Inequality

When considering income distribution, we usually are looking at conditions within a single country. For example, an American among the richest 5 percent of the U.S. population earns approximately 30 times what an American who is among the poorest 20 percent of the American people gets.

There are other ways to look at income. We might judge income inequality in the United States relative to income inequality in other countries. Is the U.S. distribution of income more or less equal than another country's? We could also look at how income is distributed among countries. Even if income is relatively equally distributed within countries, it may be unequally distributed among countries.

Web Note 18.3

Income Distribution Data

COMPARING INCOME DISTRIBUTION ACROSS COUNTRIES Figure 18-3 gives us a sense of how the distribution of income in the United States compares to that in other countries. We see that the United States has significantly more income inequality than Sweden, but somewhat less than Brazil (and many other developing and newly industrialized countries).

An important reason why the United States has more income inequality than Sweden is that Sweden's tax system is more progressive. Sweden has a top marginal tax rate on the highest incomes of 60 percent, compared to about 40 percent in the United States. Given this difference, it isn't surprising that Sweden has less income inequality.

The United States has less income inequality than most developing countries but more income inequality than many developed countries.

INCOME DISTRIBUTION AMONG COUNTRIES When we consider the distribution of world income, the picture becomes even more unequal than the picture we see within countries. The reason is clear: Income is highly unequally distributed among countries. The average per capita income of the richest countries in the world is more

Q-3 How does the income distribution in the United States compare with that in other countries?

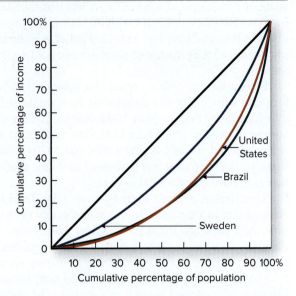

FIGURE 18-3 **U.S. Income Distribution Compared to That of Other Countries**

Among countries of the world, the United States has neither the most equal nor the most unequal distribution of income.

Sources: *Income and Poverty in the United States*, United States Census Bureau and World Bank. 2018. *World Development Indicators 2018*. Washington, DC: World Bank. doi:10.1596/978 -1-4648 -0683 -4. License: Creative Commons Attribution CC BY 3.0 IGO

than 100 times the average income of the poorest countries of the world. Thus, a Lorenz curve of world income would show much more inequality than the Lorenz curve for a particular country. Worldwide, income inequality is enormous. A minimum level of income in the United States would be a wealthy person's income in a poor country like Bangladesh.

THE TOTAL AMOUNT OF INCOME IN VARIOUS COUNTRIES   To gain a better picture of income distribution problems, you need to consider not only the division of income but also the total amounts of income in various countries. Figure 18-4 presents per capita income (gross national income) for various countries. Looking at the enormous differences of income among countries, we must ask which is more important: the distribution of income or the absolute level of income. Which would you rather be: one of four members in a family that has an income of $3,000 a year, which places you in the top 10 percent of Bangladesh's income distribution, or one of four members of a family with an income of $12,000 (four times as much), which places you in the bottom 10 percent of the income earners in the United States?

The Distribution of Wealth

In considering equality, two measures are often used: *equality of wealth* and *equality of income*. Because of space limitations, my focus will be on income, but I want to mention wealth. **Wealth** is *the value of the things individuals own less the value of what they owe*. It is a *stock* concept representing the value of assets such as houses, buildings, and machines. For example, a farmer who owns a farm with a net worth of $5 million is wealthy compared to an investment banker with a net worth of $225,000.

  Income is *payments received plus or minus changes in value in a person's assets in a specified time period*. In contrast to wealth, income is a *flow* concept. It's a stream through time. That farmer with the $5 million net worth might have an income of $20,000 a year while the investment banker with $1 million net worth might have an income of $300,000 a year. The farmer, with $5 million worth of assets, is wealthier than the investment banker, but the investment banker has a higher income.

Wealth is the value of assets individuals own less the value of what they owe.

Income is payments received plus or minus changes in value of a person's assets in a specified time period.

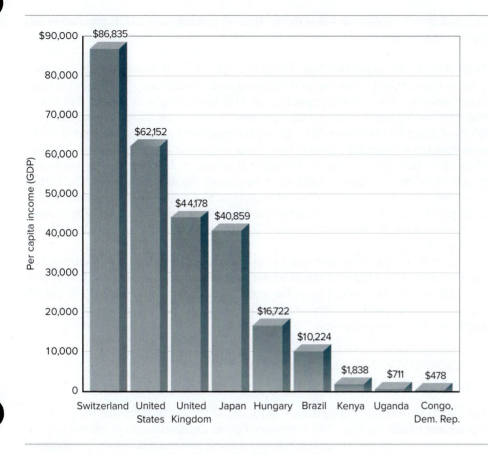

FIGURE 18-4 **Per Capita Income (Gross National Income) in Various Countries**

Income is unequally distributed among the countries of the world.

Source: World Economic Outlook Database, April 2016, International Monetary Fund (www.imf-org, accessed June 20, September 25, 2018).

A LORENZ CURVE OF THE DISTRIBUTION OF WEALTH

Figure 18-5 compares the Lorenz curve for wealth in the United States with the Lorenz curve for income in the United States. You can see that wealth in the United States is more unequally

In the United States, wealth is significantly more unequally distributed than is income.

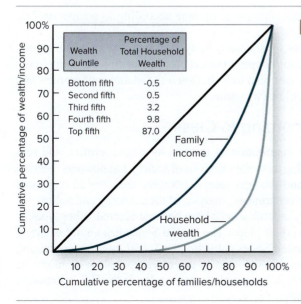

FIGURE 18-5 **Wealth Distribution in the United States and Wealth Compared to Income**

Wealth is much more unequally distributed than income in the United States. In fact, the lowest 40 percent of the population has no wealth; they have borrowed as much as they own.

Sources: *Income and Poverty in the United States,* United States Census Bureau; and *Survey of Consumer Finances,* Board of Governors of the Federal Reserve System.

Wealth Quintile	Percentage of Total Household Wealth
Bottom fifth	-0.5
Second fifth	0.5
Third fifth	3.2
Fourth fifth	9.8
Top fifth	87.0

distributed than income and that the bottom 40 percent of the U.S. population has close to zero wealth.

HOW MUCH WEALTH DO THE WEALTHY HAVE?   Relative comparisons such as those depicted by Lorenz curves don't give you a sense of how much wealth it takes to be "wealthy." The following numbers provide you with a better sense. Bill Gates, who founded Microsoft and became the richest person in the United States, had a net worth of about $90 billion in 2017. Six of the wealthiest people in the United States were people who founded platform businesses, each with net worth over $40 billion. Most of us have little chance of joining that group; in fact, most of us have little possibility of becoming one of the top 5 percent of the wealthholders in the United States, which would require total wealth of at least $2.4 million. Once there was a time when people's ultimate financial goal was to be a millionaire. In the 2000s, the ultimate financial goal for the wealthiest people is to be a billionaire. The millionaire's club is no longer highly exclusive.

Of course, people in the club don't always stay there; the club is constantly changing. For example, a number of families who were in the club earlier are no longer in it. Many billionaires lost billions when the world stock market collapsed in 2008 and fell off the list of the world's wealthiest people. Today, some of these people and families might only be multimillionaires.

Socioeconomic Dimensions of Income and Wealth Inequality

The share distribution of inequality is only one of the dimensions that inequality of income and wealth can take. As I mentioned before, the distribution of income according to source of income (wages, rents, and profits) was once considered important. Today's focus is on the distribution of income based on race, ethnic background, geographic region, and other socioeconomic factors such as gender and type of job.

Income Distribution According to Socioeconomic Characteristics

Table 18-2 gives an idea of the distribution of income according to socioeconomic characteristics.

You can see that income differs substantially by type of job, leading some economists to argue that a new professional/nonprofessional class distinction is arising in the United States. Substantial differences also exist between the incomes of women and men, and between white people and black people.

Income Distribution According to Class

Early economists focused on the distribution of income by wages, profits, and rent because that division corresponded to their class analysis of society. Landowners received rent, capitalists received profit, and workers received wages. Tensions among these classes played an important part in economists' analyses of the economy and policy.

Even though class divisions by income source have become blurred, other types of socioeconomic classes have taken their place. The United States has a kind of upper class. In fact, a company in the United States publishes the *Social Register,* containing the names and pedigrees of about 25,000 socially prominent people who might be categorized "upper class." Similarly, it is possible to further divide the U.S. population into a middle class and a lower class.

Billionaires often lose a billion here, gain a billion there; sometimes they even become multibillionaires. Seldom do they become poor.

The millionaire's club is no longer highly exclusive.

The United States has socioeconomic classes with some mobility among classes. This is not to say such classes should exist; it is only to say that they do exist.

TABLE 18-2 **Various Socioeconomic Income Distribution Designations**

Median Income, 2017 By Occupational Category	Male	Female
Financial analysts	$82,680	$71,188
Management	$81,796	$60,996
Healthcare practitioners and technical	$69,732	$55,536
Protective services	$46,488	$35,880
Installation, maintenance, and repair	$45,916	$38,272
Sales and office	$43,368	$34,944
Construction and extraction	$41,392	$41,704
Production	$39,988	$29,328
Production, transportation, and material moving	$38,272	$28,340
Office and administrative support	$38,220	$35,932
Personal care and service	$31,824	$26,156
Farming, fishing, and forestry	$30,420	$24,492
Building and grounds cleaning and maintenance	$29,796	$24,076
Food preparation and serving	$26,104	$23,868

By Age, 2017	Median Individual Income
15–24	$12,193
25–34	35,455
35–44	42,823
45–54	43,985
55–64	37,635
Over 65	24,224

By Race, 2017	Median Individual Income
White	$40,601
Asian	38,698
Black	23,431
Hispanic origin	20,937

By Sex	Median Income 1990	2000	2010	2017
Male	$20,293	$28,343	$32,205	$40,396
Female	10,070	16,063	20,775	25,486

Source: *Current Population Reports, Consumer Income,* U.S. Bureau of the Census (www.census.gov).

Class divisions are no longer determined solely by income source. For example, upper-class people do not necessarily receive their income from rent and profits. CEOs of major companies are generally considered upper class, and they receive much of their income as payment for their services. Today we have "upper-class" people who derive their income from wages and "lower-class" people who derive their meager income from profits (usually in the form of pensions, which depend on profits from the investment of pension funds in stocks and bonds). Of course, once people become rich, they earn interest and profits on their wealth as well as income from wages.

What has made the most difference in today's class structure in the United States compared to its class structure in earlier periods and to the structure in today's developing countries is the tremendous growth in the relative size of the middle class. Economists used to see the class structure as a pyramid. From a base composed of a large lower class, the pyramid tapered upward through a medium-size middle class to a peak occupied by the upper class [Figure 18-6(a)]. The class structure is still pyramidal in most developing countries. However, in the United States in the 1960s and 1970s, the middle class grew, and the geometric portrayal of the U.S. class structure changed from a pyramid in Figure 18-6(a) to the diamond shape in Figure 18-6(b) with a small upper class, a large middle class, and a small lower class. In the last 30 years, that diamond geometric portrayal has become less appropriate; the middle class itself became split. Some in the middle class have done well and moved into the upper middle class, while others have done poorly, expanding the number at the bottom.

If your job was in a tradable sector such as manufacturing, or was a service that could be outsourced, globalization pushed your wage down or left you unemployed.

In the United States, the middle class is the largest class.

FIGURE 18-6 (A, B, AND C)   **The Class System as a Pyramid, a Diamond, and a Pentagon**

The class structure in developing countries is a pyramid; in the United States the class structure is more like a pentagon.

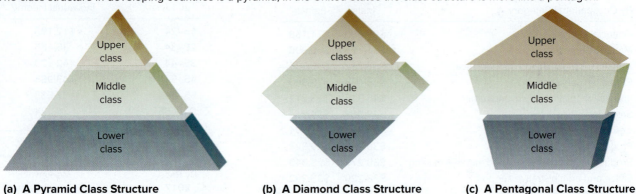

(a) **A Pyramid Class Structure**   (b) **A Diamond Class Structure**   (c) **A Pentagonal Class Structure**

Class structure today in the United States has a pentagonal shape.

Those in nontradable sectors such as government workers or semiskilled service workers such as teachers, whose jobs could not be outsourced or easily replaced with immigrant workers, remained in the middle class. This process, which is continuing, is expanding the lower class to include many formerly in the middle class. Exacerbating the division between the rich and the poor is that those in the lower class are less likely to move up the ladder into the middle class and those in the upper class are also less likely to move down the ladder into the middle class, splitting the upper from the lower class.

Today, the pentagonal shape shown in Figure 18-6(c) seems a more appropriate description of the class structure in the United States. The middle class is still relatively large, but the bottom, what some have described as an underclass—a group of people at the bottom who are just getting along and, while they may temporarily escape poverty, are always on the edge of the poverty line—has gotten larger too. This bottom group includes a disproportionate percentage of blacks, and has been expanded by a significant number of undocumented immigrants. These, combined with those formerly in the middle class who lost their "middle-class" jobs, have expanded the bottom group. And the difference is significant. Median wealth of white households, for example, is about 20 times that of black and Hispanic households. The typical Hispanic and black household has about $6,000 in wealth, whereas the typical white family has over $100,000. With the decline of social mobility in the United States, the lower class and their children have only a slight chance of entering into the middle class.

Q-4   How have distributional fights about income changed over time?

Whatever the best geometric portrayal of the class system, the increase in the relative size of the middle class in developed countries has significantly blurred the distinction between capitalists and workers. In early capitalist society, the distributional fight (the fight over relative income shares) was largely between workers and capitalists. In modern market-based societies, the distributional fight is among various types of individuals. Union workers are pitted against nonunion workers; salaried workers are pitted against workers paid by the hour; government workers are pitted against manufacturing workers. The old are pitted against the young; women are pitted against men; blacks are pitted against Hispanics and Asians, and all three groups are pitted against whites. Such a system exacerbates what is sometimes called class warfare. In the past few years blacks and Hispanics have faced more job losses and housing foreclosures than whites. Nevertheless, according to Pew Research, blacks and Hispanics were more optimistic about their future prospects than whites.

Income Distribution and Fairness

People's acceptance of the U.S. economic system is based not only on what the distribution of income is but also on what people think it should be and what they consider fair. It is to that question that we now turn. Judgments about whether the distribution of income is fair, or should be changed, are normative ones, based on the values the analyst applies to the situation. Value judgments necessarily underlie all policy prescriptions.

Value judgments necessarily underlie all policy prescriptions.

Philosophical Debates about Equality and Fairness

Depending on one's values, any income distribution can be justified. For example, Friedrich Nietzsche, the 19th-century German philosopher, argued that society's goal should be to support its supermen—its best and brightest. Lesser individuals' duty should be to work for the well-being of these supermen. Bertrand de Juvenal, a 20th-century philosopher, has argued that a high level of income inequality is necessary to sustain the arts, beauty, education, and civilization. He and others say that a world of equally distributed income would be a world without beauty. Even if we don't personally own beautiful, expensive homes, or aren't devoted opera fans, these philosophers argue that our lives are improved because some people do own such homes and because opera performances exist. Inequality creates diversity that enriches the lives of everyone.

Other philosophers disagree strongly. They argue that equality itself is the overriding goal. That view is embodied in the Declaration of Independence: "We hold these truths to be self-evident, that all men are created equal." And for many people the inherent value of equality is not open to question—it is simply self-evident.

Q-5 Is it self-evident that greater equality of income would make the society a better place to live? Why?

Believing that equality is an overriding goal does not necessarily imply that income should be equally distributed. For example, John Rawls (a Harvard University professor who believed that equality is highly desirable and that society's goal should be to maximize the welfare of the least well-off) agreed that to meet that goal some inequality is necessary. Rawls argued that if, in pursuing equality, you actually make the least well-off worse off than they otherwise would have been, then you should not pursue equality any further. For example, say under one policy there would be perfect equality and everyone would receive $10,000 per year. Under another policy, the least well-off person receives $12,000 per year and all others receive $40,000. Rawls argued that the second policy is preferable to the first even though it involves more inequality.

Economists, unlike philosophers, are not concerned about justifying any particular distribution of income. In their objective role, economists limit themselves to explaining the effects that various policies will have on the distribution of income; they let the policy makers judge whether those effects are desirable.

However, in order to judge economic policies, you, in your role as a citizen who elects policy makers, must make certain judgments about income distribution because all real-world economic policies have distribution effects. Accordingly, a brief discussion of income distribution and fairness is in order.

Fairness and Equality

The U.S. population has a strong general tendency to favor equality—equality is generally seen as fair. Most people, including me, share that view. However, in some instances equality of income is not directly related to people's view of fairness. For example, consider this distribution of income between John and Fred:

Q-6 You are dividing a pie among five individuals. What would be a fair distribution of that pie?

John gets $50,000 a year.

Fred gets $12,000 a year.

Think a minute. Is that fair?

What Should Be the Goal of Economic Policy?

Today, most discussions of economic policy focus on a goal of increasing income: Policies that achieve higher income are good; policies that do not are bad. Historically, that has not always been the goal. In the 1800s the economic policy focused on basic goods—distinguishing necessities from luxuries. Only policies that increased basic goods were good; the welfare implications of policies that increased luxuries were much more problematic.

The 1930s marked a major change in how economic policy was conceived. Economics began focusing much more on the utility of all goods, downplaying the distinction between luxuries and basic goods. With this change, the goal of economic policy focused much more on total income, regardless of how that income was divided. The division of goods into necessities and luxuries was seen as adding a normative element to policy that was outside the purview of positive economics.

Recently, Nobel Prize–winning economist Amartya Sen has argued against that utilitarian approach, pointing out that normative elements are unavoidable in policy analysis. He argues that using income as a measure of welfare is not the best approach and has suggested replacing it with a "capabilities" measure. For Sen, the goal of economic policy should be to increase a society's capabilities, which he defines as an individual's freedom within that society to achieve a particular life. For Sen, capabilities are best measured by basic indicators such as life expectancy, literacy, and infant mortality rates—not by income. Poor ratings on such indicators impede people from leading good and happy lives. Sen's work is controversial, but it is important in reminding us that the goals of economic policy should always be kept in mind and that we should not simply accept the goal as being an increase in total income.

The answer I'm hoping for is that you don't yet have enough information to make the decision.

Here's some more information. Say that John gets that $50,000 for holding down three jobs, while Fred gets his $12,000 for sitting around doing nothing. At this point, many of us would argue that it's possible John should be getting even more than $50,000 and Fred should be getting less than $12,000.

But wait! What if we discover that Fred is an invalid and unless his income increases to $15,000 a year he will die? Most of us would change our minds again and argue that Fred deserves more, regardless of how much John works.

But wait! How about if, after further digging, we discover that Fred is an invalid because he squandered his health on alcohol, drugs, and fried foods? In that case some people would likely change their minds again as to whether Fred deserves more.

By now you should have gotten my point. Looking only at a person's income masks many dimensions that most people consider important in making value judgments about fairness.

Fairness as Equality of Opportunity

When most people talk about believing in equality of income, they often mean they believe in equality of opportunity for comparably endowed individuals to earn income. If equal opportunity of equals leads to inequality of income, then the inequality of income is fair. Unfortunately, there's enormous latitude for debate on what constitutes equal opportunity of equals.

In the real world, needs differ, desires differ, and abilities differ. Should these differences be considered relevant differences in equality? You must answer that question before you can judge any economic policy because to make a judgment on whether an economic policy should or should not be adopted, you must make a judgment about whether a policy's effect on income is fair. In making those judgments, most people rely on their immediate gut reaction. I hope what you have gotten out of the discussion

Fairness has many dimensions and it is often difficult to say what is fair and what isn't.

Three problems in determining whether an equal income distribution is fair are:

1. *People don't start from equivalent positions.*
2. *People's needs differ.*
3. *People's efforts differ.*

about John and Fred and equality of opportunity is the resolve to be cautious about trusting your gut reactions. The concept of fairness is crucial and complicated, and it deserves deeper consideration than just a gut reaction.

The concept of fairness is crucial and complicated, and it deserves deeper consideration than just a gut reaction.

The Problems of Redistributing Income

Let's now say that we have considered all the issues discussed so far in this chapter and have concluded that some redistribution of income from the rich to the poor is necessary if society is to meet our ideal of fairness. How do we go about redistributing income?

First, we must consider what programs exist and what their negative side effects might be. The side effects can be substantial and can subvert the intention of the program so that far less money is available overall for redistribution and inequality is reduced less than we might expect.

Three Important Side Effects of Redistributive Programs

Three important side effects that economists have found in programs to redistribute income are:

1. A tax may result in people working less (a switch from labor to leisure).
2. People may attempt to avoid or evade taxes, leading to a decrease in measured income.
3. Redistributing money may cause people to make themselves look as if they're more needy than they really are.

Three side effects of redistribution of income are:
1. The labor/leisure incentive effect.
2. The avoidance and evasion incentive effect.
3. The incentive effect to look more needy than you are.

All economists believe that people will change their behavior in response to changes in taxation and income redistribution programs. These responses, called *incentive effects of taxation,* are important and must be taken into account in policy making. But economists differ significantly on the size of incentive effects, and empirical evidence doesn't resolve the question. Some economists believe that incentive effects are so high that little taxation for redistribution should take place. They argue that when the rich do well, the total pie is increased so much that the spillover benefits to the poor are greater than the proceeds the poor would get from redistribution. For example, supporters of this view argue that the growth in capitalist economies was made possible by entrepreneurs. Because those entrepreneurs invested in new technology, income in society grew. Moreover, those entrepreneurs paid taxes. The benefits resulting from entrepreneurial action spilled over to the poor, making the poor far better off than any redistribution would. The fact that some of those entrepreneurs became rich is irrelevant because their actions made all of society better off.

Q-7 When determining the effects of programs that redistribute income, can one reasonably assume that other things will remain constant?

Other economists believe that there should be significant taxation for redistribution. While they agree that sometimes the incentive effects are substantial, they see the goal of equality overriding these effects.

Politics, Income Redistribution, and Fairness

We began this discussion of income distribution and fairness by assuming that our value judgments should determine the way in which taxes are structured—that if our values lead us to the conclusion that the poor deserve more income, we could institute policies that would get more to the poor. Reality doesn't necessarily work that way. Often politics, not value judgments, play a central role in determining what taxes individuals will pay. The group that can deliver the most votes will elect lawmakers who will enact tax policies that benefit that group at the expense of groups with fewer votes.

Often politics, not value judgments, play a central role in determining what taxes an individual will pay.

On the surface, the democratic system of one person/one vote would seem to suggest that the politics of redistribution would favor the poor, but it doesn't. One would

Income Distribution Policy, Fairness, and the Takeaway Principle

Discussions of income distribution policy often focus on *re*distribution policy—how do you redistribute income that has already been earned. What economists have found is that redistributing income is very hard. Once people feel that income belongs to them, because they have "earned" it, they don't like anyone taking it away. They become like a dog with a treasured bone.

One way around this problem is to focus not on redistribution policy, but on *distribution* policy—how income is first distributed—a policy that is designed to affect the structure of society that underlies the distribution of income rather than trying to adjust the distribution of income after it is first received through tax policy or through a government program. Income distribution policy is designed to change the institutional structure so that it generates a more equal distribution of income, so that income flows to all are more equal from the start. Because the policy results in a more equal distribution of income directly, nothing has to be taken away from people for the final distribution to be more equal. Let me give two examples of distribution policy.

The first example involves the structure of intellectual property rights. Currently, in an effort to promote innovation, the United States grants monopoly rights for long periods of time to people who design new technologies by issuing patents and copyrights. There is enormous debate about whether the incentives to advance technology created by patents are important, and whether holders of these rights are the ones who actually do the innovating. Patent holders might just be those positioned to take advantage of the system.

Economists Michael Boldrin and David Levine argue that patents serve little social purpose, and that they do little to stimulate technological growth. But even if patents do serve some purpose, there is little debate that they create enormous income for the small group of people who own them. The U.S. patent and copyright system creates monopoly positions and makes the distribution of income less equal than it otherwise would be, exacerbating existing income inequality. If patent and copyright terms were shorter, or nonexistent, so that discoveries, and discoveries of efficient means of production, quickly moved into the public domain, the U.S. income distribution would be much more equal.

The second example involves licensing and restrictions on entry into different types of work. Many professions place limitations on who is allowed to work in that profession that go far beyond what is needed for public safety. Essentially, the limitations are designed to increase the pay of those already in the field, which also means that they decrease the pay for those who would like, and are able, to do the work but who are not allowed to do so. If these restrictions were reduced, income would be more equally distributed without any need to redistribute income by government through tax policy.

Policies designed to increase equality by changing the institutional structure are not easy to implement, but implementing them is likely easier than trying to change the structure through direct redistribution policy since they don't require taking income away from people after they have already earned it.

expect that the poor would use their votes to make sure income was redistributed to them from the rich. Why don't they? The answer is complicated.

One reason is that many of the poor don't vote because they assume that one vote won't make much difference. As a result, poor people's total voting strength is reduced. A second reason is that the poor aren't seen by most politicians as a solid voting bloc. There's no organization of the poor that can deliver votes to politicians. A third reason is that those poor people who do vote often cast their votes with other issues in mind. An anti-income-redistribution candidate might have a strong view on abortion as well, and for many the abortion view is the one that decides their vote.

A fourth reason is that elections require financing. Much of that financing comes from the rich. The money is used for advertising and publicity aimed at convincing the poor that it's actually in their best interests to vote for a person who supports the rich. People are often influenced by that kind of biased publicity.

Reasonable-sounding arguments can be made to support just about any position, and the rich have the means to see that the arguments supporting their positions get the

Chapter 18 ▪ Who Gets What? The Distribution of Income

407

publicity. Of course, some of their arguments are also correct. The issues are usually sufficiently complicated that a trained economist must study them for a long time to determine which arguments make sense.

Income Redistribution Policies

The preceding discussion should have provided you with a general sense of the difficulty of redistributing income. Let's now consider briefly how income redistribution policies and programs have worked in the real world. In considering this, it is helpful to keep in mind that government has two direct methods and one indirect method to redistribute income. The direct methods are (1) *taxation* (policies that tax the rich more than the poor) and (2) *expenditures* (programs that help the poor more than the rich). The indirect method involves establishing, changing, and protecting property rights. Let's first consider direct methods.

Web Note 18.4

Basic Income Program

Direct methods of redistribution are taxation and expenditure programs.

TAXATION TO REDISTRIBUTE INCOME   The U.S. federal government gets its revenue from a variety of taxes. The three largest sources of revenue are the personal income tax, the corporate income tax, and the Social Security tax.

State and local governments get their revenue from income taxes, sales taxes, and property taxes. The rates vary among states.

Tax systems can be progressive, proportional (sometimes called *flat rate*), or regressive. A **progressive tax** is one in which *the average tax rate increases with income.* (A progressive income tax schedule might tax individuals at a rate of 15 percent for income up to $20,000; at 25 percent for income between $20,000 and $40,000; and at 35 percent for every dollar earned over $40,000.) It redistributes income from the rich to the poor. A **proportional tax** is one in which *the average rate of tax is constant regardless of income level.* Such a tax might be 25 percent of every dollar earned. It is neutral in regard to income distribution. A **regressive tax** is one in which *the average tax rate decreases as income increases.* It redistributes income from poor to rich. The United States has chosen a somewhat progressive income tax, while the Social Security tax is a proportional tax up to a specified earned income.

Q-8   True or false? A progressive tax is preferable to a proportional tax. Why?

Federal Income Taxes   In the early 1940s, the federal personal income tax was made highly progressive, with a top tax rate of 90 percent on the highest incomes. The degree of progressivity went down significantly through various pieces of legislation after World War II until 1986, when the income tax system was amended to provide for an initial rate of 15 percent and a top rate of 28 percent. (The U.S. income tax also has an earned income tax credit where heads of households earning below a certain amount get a tax credit from government, reducing their taxes, and sometimes providing them with an income subsidy.)

The changes did not reduce the actual progressivity of the personal income tax as much as they seemed to because the 1986 reforms eliminated many of the loopholes in the U.S. Tax Code. Some loopholes had allowed rich people to legally reduce their reported incomes and to pay taxes on those lower incomes at lower rates. The top personal income tax rate on high-income individuals today is 37 percent.

Whereas the personal income tax is progressive, the Social Security tax is initially proportional. All individuals pay the same tax rate on wage income (7.65 percent for employer and 7.65 percent for employee; 15.3 percent for self-employed) up to a cap of $128,400 in 2018. Above that income cap, no Social Security tax is due (except for the Medicare portion, which has no cap on the amount to which it is applied). At this income cap, the Social Security tax becomes regressive: Higher-income individuals pay a lower percentage of their total income in Social Security taxes than do lower-income individuals. (They also receive relatively less in Social Security benefits, compared to what they put in. So, while the Social Security tax is regressive, taken as a whole the Social Security system is progressive.)

State and Local Taxes   State and local governments get most of their income from the following sources:

1. Income taxes, which are generally somewhat progressive.

2. Sales taxes, which tend to be proportional (all people pay the same tax rate on what they spend) or slightly regressive. (Since poor people often spend a higher percentage of their incomes than rich people, poor people pay higher average sales taxes as a percentage of their incomes than rich people.)

3. Property taxes, which are taxes paid on the value of people's property (usually real estate, but sometimes also personal property like cars). Since people with higher incomes tend to have significantly more property than people with lower incomes, the property tax is considered to be somewhat progressive.

When all the taxes paid by individuals to all levels of governments are combined, the conclusion that most researchers come to is that little income redistribution takes place on the tax side. The progressive taxes are offset by the regressive taxes, so the overall tax system is roughly proportional. That is, on average the tax rates individuals pay are roughly equal.

Web Note 18.5
State Lotteries

Expenditure programs have been more successful than taxation for redistributing income.

EXPENDITURE PROGRAMS TO REDISTRIBUTE INCOME
Taxation has not proved to be an effective means of redistributing income. However, the government expenditure system has been quite effective. The federal government's expenditures that contribute to redistribution include the following.

Social Security   The program that redistributes the most money is the **Social Security system,** *a social insurance program that provides financial benefits to individuals who are elderly and disabled and to their eligible dependents and/or survivors.* Social Security also has a component called **Medicare,** which is a *multibillion-dollar medical insurance system.*

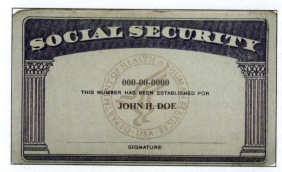
©zimmytws/iStockphoto/Getty Images

The amount of an individual's Social Security retirement, disability, or survivors' monthly cash benefits depends on a very complex formula, which is skewed in favor of lower-income workers. The program is not a pension program that pays benefits in proportion to the amount paid in. Many people will get much more than they paid in; some who never paid anything in will get a great deal; and others who paid in for years will get nothing. (No benefits are payable if you die before you retire and leave no survivors eligible for benefits due to your work.) On the whole, the program has been successful in keeping elderly people out of poverty. In addition, Social Security benefits have helped workers' survivors and individuals with disabilities.

Q-9 True or false? The U.S. Social Security system is only a retirement system.

Today, about 62 million people receive cash Social Security benefits, many of whom also receive Medicare payments. Total benefits paid, including Medicare, come to over $1.5 trillion each year.

Public Assistance   **Public assistance** programs are *means-tested social programs targeted to the poor, providing financial, nutritional, medical, and housing assistance.* (These programs are more familiarly known as *welfare payments.*) Public assistance programs exist in every state of the union, although the amount paid varies greatly from state to state. The main kinds of general public assistance are:

Temporary Assistance for Needy Families (TANF). Provides temporary financial assistance to needy families with children under age 19.

Supplemental Nutritional Assistance Program (SNAP). Provides nutritional assistance in the form of coupons redeemable at most food stores.

General assistance. State assistance to poor people when emergencies arise that aren't taken care of by any of the other programs.

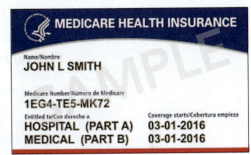

Source: USDA

By far the largest proportion of payments goes to needy families with dependent children, especially since these families are usually so poor that, in addition to qualifying for TANF, they meet the eligibility requirements for SNAP.

TANF was instituted by the Personal Responsibility and Work Opportunity Reconciliation Act of 1996 to replace Aid to Families with Dependent Children (AFDC). It has a number of provisions that distinguish it from earlier programs. One important provision is that it establishes a lifetime limit of no more than 60 months (not necessarily consecutive) of benefits. The purpose of the law is to direct welfare recipients to work, and another provision in the law requires welfare recipients to take a job within two years. The law also gives states significant latitude in determining benefits and eligibility criteria. These changes are major ones; they raise many questions about job training and child care. The effects of this law are discussed in the box "From Welfare to Work."

Medical Programs   Government also provides significant medical care assistance for lower-income individuals. About 9 million individuals are insured through government-created online insurance markets, with almost 90 percent receiving some government assistance. Another 74 million are covered under Medicaid and the Children's Health Insurance Program.

Source: Medicare.gov

Supplemental Security Income   Hundreds of thousands more people would be receiving public assistance if it weren't for **Supplemental Security Income (SSI),** *a federal program that pays benefits, based on need, to individuals who are elderly, blind, and disabled.* Although SSI is administered through the Social Security offices, it is unlike Social Security benefits because eligibility for SSI payments is based solely on need. Again unlike Social Security, the recipients pay nothing toward the cost of the program. To be eligible, though, people must have very low incomes and almost no resources except a home, if they are fortunate enough to own one, a wedding ring and engagement ring, and an automobile. Today, about $60 billion is paid in SSI benefits each year.

Unemployment Compensation   **Unemployment compensation** is *short-term financial assistance, regardless of need, to eligible individuals who are temporarily out of work.* It is limited financial assistance to people who are out of work through no fault of their own and have worked in a covered occupation for a substantial number of weeks in the period just before they became unemployed.

Normally a person can receive unemployment benefits for only about six months in any given year, and the amount of the benefit is always considerably less than the amount the person earned when working.

A person can't just quit a job and live on unemployment benefits. While receiving unemployment benefits, people are expected to actively search for work. Lower-income workers receive unemployment payments that are more nearly equal to their working wage than do higher-income workers, but there is no income eligibility test. Today, about $30 billion is paid in unemployment benefits each year, although this amount fluctuates with the state of the economy.

From Welfare to Work

In an effort to reduce the negative incentive effects of welfare, in 1996 Congress passed the Personal Responsibility and Work Opportunity Reconciliation Act. The act required recipients of welfare assistance to work after two years on assistance and limited welfare assistance to a total of five years over a lifetime. Part of the act was also designed to offset the taxation implicit in moving from welfare to work, which could be as high as 90 percent or more, since under the old law welfare recipients who earned income above a certain level often lost almost all their welfare benefits.

The act extended funding to the working poor; for example, it provided funding for child care to help mothers move into the workforce and extended Medicaid to include the first year of work. With the changes, the implicit tax on income was reduced to about 40 percent: For every dollar of additional income, people lost 40 cents of benefits.

Congress also promised monetary rewards to states that were successful in moving people off the welfare rolls.

This act played an important role in reducing the number of people on welfare by over 80 percent, in reducing the average stay on welfare from over eight to under four years, and in reducing the unemployment rate among single mothers.

The largest reduction occurred in the late 1990s and early 2000s, when the economy was booming and one could expect the number of welfare recipients to fall anyway. But the reductions continued after 2008 when many more people were pushed into poverty by a recession.

Advocates argue that the law significantly increased the incentives to get off and stay off welfare and therefore the law has been a success. Opponents argue that any success has been at the cost of significantly reducing the safety net, leaving many more people in extreme poverty than otherwise would have been the case.

Housing Programs   Federal and state governments have many different programs to improve housing or to provide affordable housing. While many of these programs are designed to benefit low-income persons, there are also programs for moderate-income persons and lower-income persons (people whose incomes are lower than moderate but higher than low).

The federal agency overseeing most of these programs, the Department of Housing and Urban Development (HUD), has been criticized for abuse and mismanagement. Hundreds of millions of dollars that could have benefited the poor went instead to developers of housing and other projects, to consultants, and to others who skimmed off money before—or instead of—building or rehabilitating housing. In part because of these problems, federal funding for housing was steadily reduced during the 1980s. Today, about $40 billion is allocated to housing programs each year.

How Successful Have Income Redistribution Programs Been?

Most government redistribution works through its expenditure programs, not through taxes.

After including the effect of both taxes and government programs on the redistribution of income, the after-transfer income is somewhat closer to being equally distributed. As you can see in Figure 18-7, government programs have a small effect on income equality. But because of the incentive effects of collecting and distributing the money, that redistribution has come at the cost of a reduction in the total amount of income earned by the society. The debate about whether the gain in equality of income is worth the cost in reduction of total income is likely to continue indefinitely.

While the direct methods of redistributing income get the most press and discussion, perhaps the most important redistribution decisions that the government makes involve an indirect method, the establishment and protection of property rights. Let's take an example: intellectual property rights. Intellectual property consists of things like a book you've written, a song you've composed, or a picture you've drawn. How

Web Note 18.6

A Look over Time

FIGURE 18-7   **Impact of Transfers and Taxes on Income**

As this chart shows, taxes and transfer programs have a modest impact on the distribution of income.

Source: Congressional Budget Office, "The Distribution of Household Income, 2014." cbo.gov. Data do not sum to 100 due to rounding.

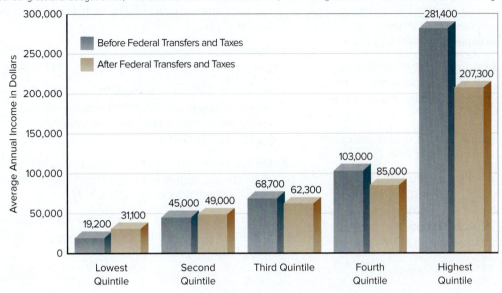

these property rights are structured plays a fundamental role in determining the distribution of income.

For example, if strict private property rights are given for, say, a design for a computer screen (e.g., a neat little trash can in the corners and icons of various files), any user other than the designer herself will have to pay for the right to use it. The designer (or the person who gets the legal right to the design) becomes very rich. If no property rights are given for the design, then no payment is made and income is much more equally distributed. Of course, without a promise of high returns to designing a computer screen device, fewer resources will be invested in finding the ideal design. While most people agree that some incentive is appropriate, there is no consensus on whether the incentives embodied in our current property rights structure are too large. I suspect that the trash can (recycling bin) design, while ingenious, would have been arrived at with a much smaller incentive.

The point of the above example is not that property rights in such ideas should not be given out. The point is that decisions on property rights issues have enormous distributional consequences that are often little discussed, even by economists. Ultimately, we can answer the question of whether income redistribution is fair only after we have answered the question of whether the initial property rights distribution is fair.

Q-10   Why are property rights important in the determination of whether any particular income distribution is fair?

The fairness of income depends on the fairness of property rights.

Conclusion

Much more could be said about the issues involved in income redistribution. But limitations of time and space pressure us to move on. I hope this chapter has convinced you that income redistribution is an important but difficult question. Specifically, I hope I have given you the sense that income distribution questions are integrally related to questions about the entire economic system. Supply and demand play a central role in the determination of the distribution of income, but they do so in an institutional and historical context. Thus, the analysis of income distribution must include that context as well as the analyst's ethical judgments about what is fair.

Summary

- The Lorenz curve is a measure of the distribution of income among families in a country. The farther the Lorenz curve is from the diagonal, the more unequally income is distributed.　(*LO18-1*)

- The official poverty measure is an absolute measure because it is based on the minimum food budget for a family. It is a relative measure because it is adjusted for average inflation.　(*LO18-1*)

- Economic and social mobility in the United States has decreased over the past decades.　(*LO18-1*)

- Income is less equally distributed in the United States than in some countries such as Sweden, but more equally distributed than in other countries such as Brazil. There is more income inequality among countries than income inequality within a country.　(*LO18-1*)

- Wealth is distributed less equally than income.　(*LO18-1*)

- Income differs substantially by class and by other socioeconomic characteristics such as age, race, and gender.　(*LO18-2*)

- Fairness is a philosophical question. People must judge a program's fairness for themselves.　(*LO18-3*)

- Income is difficult to redistribute because of incentive effects of taxes, avoidance and evasion effects of taxes, and incentive effects of redistribution programs.　(*LO18-4*)

- On the whole, the U.S. tax system is roughly proportional, so it is not very effective as a means of redistributing income.　(*LO18-4*)

- Government spending programs are more effective than tax policy in reducing income inequality in the United States.　(*LO18-4*)

Key Terms

income	progressive tax	Social Security system	unemployment
Lorenz curve	proportional tax	Supplemental Security	compensation
Medicare	public assistance	Income (SSI)	wealth
poverty threshold	regressive tax		

Questions and Exercises　connect

1. The Lorenz curve for Bangladesh looks like this:

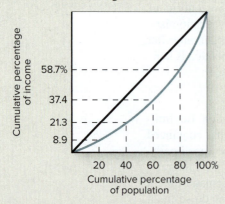

How much income do individuals in the top income quintile in Bangladesh receive?　(*LO18-1*)

2. What would the Lorenz curve for lawyers represent?　(*LO18-1*)

3. Why are we concerned with the distribution of income between whites and blacks, but not between redheads and blondes?　(*LO18-1*)

4. The accompanying table shows income distribution data for three countries:　(*LO18-1*)

| Income Quintile | Percentage of Total Income | | |
	India	Czech Republic	Mexico
Lowest 20%	8.6%	10.2%	4.4%
Second quintile	12.2	14.3	8.9
Third quintile	15.8	17.5	13.3
Fourth quintile	21.0	21.7	20.4
Highest 20%	42.4	36.3	53.0

a. Using this information, draw a Lorenz curve for each country.

b. Which country has the most equal distribution of income?

c. Which country has the least equal?

d. By looking at the three Lorenz curves, can you tell which country has the most progressive tax system? Why or why not?

5. Should poverty be defined absolutely or relatively? Why?   (LO18-1)

6. How does social mobility in the United States compare to that in Britain? Why do you think this is so?   (LO18-1)

7. Would the Lorenz curve for the world be more or less bowed out compared to the Lorenz curve for the United States?   (LO18-1)

8. How has the median income of women compared to men changed since 1980? What do you think is the cause?   (LO18-2)

9. Is the class system in the United States more like a pyramid, diamond, or pentagon? Why is this so?   (LO18-2)

10. Why did Bertrand de Juvenal argue for a high level of income inequality?   (LO18-3)

11. In what instance would John Rawls support greater income inequality?   (LO18-3)

12. In Taxland, the first $10,000 earned per year is exempt from taxation. Between $10,000.01 and $30,000, the tax rate is 25 percent. Between $30,000.01 and $50,000, it's 30 percent. Above $50,000, it's 35 percent. You're earning $80,000 a year.   (LO18-4)

a. How much in taxes will you have to pay?

b. What is your average tax rate?

c. What is your marginal tax rate?

13. Some economists have proposed making the tax rate progressivity depend on the wage rate rather than the income level. Thus, an individual who works twice as long as another but who receives a lower wage would face a lower marginal tax rate.   (LO18-4)

a. What effect would this change have on incentives to work?

b. Would this system be fairer than our current system? Why or why not?

c. If, simultaneously, the tax system were made regressive in hours worked so that individuals who work longer hours face lower marginal tax rates, what effect would this change have on hours worked?

Questions from Alternative Perspectives

1. In a recent study the top 20 percent of Americans had 49.7 percent of the income before taxes and transfers and 48.3 percent after taxes and transfers. The same figures for the bottom 20 percent were 3.4 percent and 4.3 percent, respectively.

a. How much do taxes and transfers "cost" the upper quintile?

b. How much discretionary income should they be willing to invest to change this situation?

c. How much discretionary income does the bottom quintile have to prevent such a change? (Institutionalist)

2. In the Old Testament, God promised riches to Israel if Israel kept God's commandments. But in the New Testament, Jesus says that it is easier for a camel to go through the eye of a needle than for a rich man to enter the kingdom of heaven.

a. Considering the wealth distribution in Figure 18-5, what does this suggest about Americans?

b. Should government do anything about it?

c. What do the Old and New Testament teachings suggest about what private individuals ought to do? (Religious)

3. In 2017 the poverty level for a family of four was $25,283.

a. If one-third of the total income of lower-income households is typically used for food, estimate the amount of money per day per person available for food for a person living at or below the poverty rate.

b. How much does that leave this family per month for everything else: rent, utilities, taxes, auto, medical, clothing, and education? (Radical)

4. Say you earn $200, and the government takes $75 from you in taxes to give to someone else.

a. How would you feel about that?

b. What would that transfer likely do to your incentive to work?

c. What would the government transfer of $75 likely do to the incentive to work of the person who receives the payment?

d. Would the effect be different if you voluntarily gave $75 to someone else? (Austrian)

5. Antipoverty programs in the United States since the mid-1990s have focused on welfare-to-work programs that compel welfare recipients to take paid jobs. Some economists argue that these programs place women who are not "ready for work" into jobs that are not "ready for mothers" and move them from the ranks of the welfare poor to the working poor.

a. What policies would be necessary to make U.S. antipoverty programs far more effective?

b. How could public policy be used to make jobs more "mother-ready" and more likely to lift these women above the poverty line? (Feminist)

Issues to Ponder

1. Some economists argue that a class distinction should be made between managerial decision makers and other workers. Do you agree? Why or why not?

2. If a garbage collector earns more than an English teacher, does that mean something is wrong with the economy? Why or why not?

3. List four conditions you believe should hold before you would argue that two individuals should get the same amount of income.
   a. How would you apply the conditions to your views on welfare?
   b. How would you apply the conditions to your views on how progressive the income tax should be?
   c. If the income tax were made progressive in wage rates (tax rates increase as wage rates increase) rather than progressive in income, would your conditions be better met? Why?

4. Is it ever appropriate for society to:
   Let someone starve?
   Let someone be homeless?
   Forbid someone to eat chocolate?

5. The dissident Russian writer A. Amalrik has written:

   The Russian people . . . have . . . one idea that appears positive: the idea of justice. . . . In practice, "justice" involves the desire that "nobody should live better than I do." . . . The idea of justice is motivated by hatred of everything that is outstanding, which we make no effort to imitate but, on the contrary, try to bring down to our level, by hatred of any sense of initiative, of any higher or more dynamic way of life than the life we live ourselves.

   What implications would such a worldview have for the economy?

6. If you receive a paycheck, what percentage of it is withheld for taxes? What incentive effect does that have on your decision to work?

7. "There are lies, damned lies, and statistics. Then, there are annual poverty figures." Both liberal and conservative economists believe U.S. poverty statistics are suspect. Here are some reasons:
   (1) They do not take into account in-kind benefits such as food stamps and tax credits.
   (2) They do not consider regional cost-of-living differences.
   (3) They do not take into account unreported income.
   (4) Food accounts for about one-seventh of a family's budget, not one-third.
   (5) Ownership of assets such as homes, cars, and appliances is not taken into account.
   a. What would the effect of correcting each of these be on measured poverty?
   b. Would making these changes be fair?

8. In "Why Higher Real Wages May Reduce Altruism for the Poor," Ball State economist John B. Horowitz considers whether redistribution of income is a public good or a public bad.
   a. How might income redistribution be considered a public good?
   b. How might income redistribution be considered a public bad?
   c. What is the likely effect of higher real wages on whether income redistribution is perceived to be a public good or bad?

9. There are many more poor people in the United States than there are rich people. If the poor wanted to, they could exercise their power to redistribute as much money as they please to themselves. They don't do that, so they must see the income distribution system as fair. Discuss.

Answers to Margin Questions

1. When drawing a Lorenz curve, you put the cumulative percentage of income on the vertical axis and the cumulative percentage of families (or population) on the horizontal axis. (*LO18-1*)

2. The U.S. definition of poverty is an absolute measure, but the way poverty is calculated means that some relativity is included in the definition. (*LO18-1*)

3. The United States has significantly more income inequality than Sweden and Japan, but significantly less than Brazil. (*LO18-1*)

4. In early capitalist society, the distributional fight was between workers and capitalists. In modern capitalist society, the distributional fight is more varied. For example, in the United States minorities are pitted against whites and males against females. (*LO18-2*)

5. No, it is not self-evident that greater equality of income would make society a better place to live. Unequal income distribution has its benefits. Still, most people would prefer a somewhat more equal distribution of income than what currently exists. (*LO18-3*)

6. What is fair is a very difficult concept. It depends on people's needs, people's wants, to what degree people are deserving, and other factors. Still, in the absence of any more information than is given in the question, I would divide the pie equally. *(LO18-3)*

7. No, one cannot reasonably assume other things remain constant. Redistributive programs have important side effects that can change the behavior of individuals and subvert the intent of the program. Three important side effects are substituting leisure for labor, a decrease in measured income, and attempts to appear more needy. *(LO18-4)*

8. As a general statement, "A progressive tax is preferable to a proportional tax" is false. A progressive tax may well be preferable, but that is a normative judgment (just as its opposite would be). Moreover, taxes have incentive effects that must be considered. *(LO18-4)*

9. False. The U.S. Social Security system includes many other aspects, such as disability benefits and survivors' benefits. *(LO18-4)*

10. The distribution of initial property rights underlies the distribution of income. Those with the property rights will reap the returns from those rights. Ultimately, we can answer the question whether income distribution is fair only after we have answered whether the initial property rights distribution is fair. *(LO18-4)*

CHAPTER 19

The Logic of Individual Choice: The Foundation of Supply and Demand

> The theory of economics must begin with a correct theory of consumption.
>
> —Stanley Jevons

After reading this chapter, you should be able to:

LO19-1 Discuss the principle of diminishing marginal utility and the principle of rational choice.

LO19-2 Explain the relationship between marginal utility and price when a consumer is maximizing total utility.

LO19-3 Summarize how the principle of rational choice accounts for the laws of demand and supply.

LO19-4 Name three assumptions of the theory of choice and discuss why they may not reflect reality.

©Fancy Collection/SuperStock RF

It's Friday night and you've managed to scrimp and save $50 to take a break from classes and buy two tickets, one for yourself and one for a friend, to see the rock concert at the field house. But then you think about it; maybe going to a movie and having a hot fudge sundae after for the two of you would make more sense. Or maybe a big steak dinner just for yourself. Or maybe ordering Chinese. Or maybe studying and giving the money to the homeless shelter. Choices, choices; they are around you all the time.

How individuals make choices is central to microeconomics. It is the foundation of economic reasoning and it gives economics much of its power. The first part of this chapter shows you that foundation and leads you through some exercises to make sure you understand the reasoning. The second part of the chapter relates that analysis to the real world, giving you a sense of when the model is useful and when it's not.

As you go through this chapter, think back to Chapter 1, which set out the goals for this book. One goal was to get you to think like an economist. This chapter, which formally develops the reasoning process behind economists' cost/benefit approach to problems, examines the underpinnings of how to think like an economist.

Rational Choice Theory

Different sciences have various explanations for why people do what they do. For example, Freudian psychology tells us we do what we do because of an internal fight between the id, ego, and superego plus some hang-ups we have about our bodies. Other psychologists tell us it's a search for approval by our peers; we want to be OK. Economists agree that these are important reasons but argue that if we want an analysis that's simple enough to apply to policy problems, these heavy psychological explanations are likely to get us all mixed up. At least to start with, we need an easier underlying psychological foundation. And economists have one—self-interest. People do what they do because it's in their self-interest.

Economists' traditional analysis of individual choice doesn't deny that most of us have our quirks. That's obvious in what we buy. On certain items we're penny-pinchers; on others we're big spenders. For example, how many of you or your parents clip coupons to save 40 cents on cereal but then spend $60 on a haircut? How many save 50 cents a pound by buying a low grade of meat but then spend $25 on a bottle of wine, $90 on dinner at a restaurant, or $75 for a concert ticket?

But through it all comes a certain rationality. Much of what people do reflects their rational self-interest. That's why economists start their analysis of individual choice with a relatively simple, but powerful, underlying psychological foundation.

Using that simple theory, two things determine what people do: **utility**—*the pleasure or satisfaction people get from doing or consuming something,* and the price of doing or consuming that something. Price is the tool the market uses to bring the quantity supplied equal to the quantity demanded. Changes in price provide incentives for people to change what they're doing. Through those incentives, the invisible hand guides us all. To understand economics, you must understand how price affects our choices. That's why we focus on the effect of price on the quantity demanded. We want to understand the way in which a change in price will affect what we do.

In summary, economists' theory of rational choice is a simple and powerful theory that shows how these two things—pleasure and price—are related.

> Utility is the pleasure or satisfaction that people get from doing or consuming something.

Thinking Like a Modern Economist

The Traditional Models as Stepping-Stones

A group of economists, called behavioral economists, have explored consistent deviations from rationality and self-interest, and in doing so they have expanded the building blocks of economics. But doing so has a cost—it complicates the model enormously, and a more complicated model is much more difficult to use. The advantage of using traditional building blocks is that doing so leads to black-and-white conclusions—and then lets you decide whether the model is or is not applicable.

Behavioral economists recognize the cost and are trying to characterize types of decisions that fit the traditional model and types of decisions that don't. Unfortunately, the work is still in an early stage and they have a long way to go. That's why, at this time, when it comes to teaching economics, almost all economists—including behavioral economists—agree that the best place to start is with models based on the traditional building blocks. And that's why this book is structured like it is—it focuses on models with the traditional building blocks, but lets you know that, in their research, modern economists are going beyond the traditional models.

Total Utility and Marginal Utility

In thinking about utility, it's important to distinguish between *total utility* and *marginal utility.* **Total utility** refers to *the total satisfaction one gets from consuming a product.* **Marginal utility** refers to *the satisfaction one gets from consuming one additional unit of a product above and beyond what one has consumed up to that point.* For example,

> It is important to distinguish between marginal and total utility.

FIGURE 19-1 (A, B, AND C) Marginal and Total Utility

Marginal utility tends to decrease as consumption of a good increases. Notice how the information in the table (a) can be presented graphically in two different ways. The two different ways are, however, related. The downward slope of the marginal utility curve (c) is reflected in the total utility curve bowed downward in (b). Notice that marginal utility relates to changes in quantity so the marginal utility line is graphed at the halfway point. For example, in (c), between 7 and 8, marginal utility becomes zero.

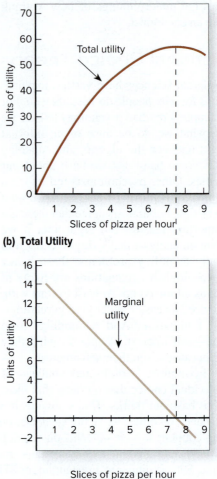

(b) **Total Utility**

(1) Number of Pizza Slices	(2) Total Utility	(3) Marginal Utility
0	0	
		14
1	14	
		12
2	26	
		10
3	36	
		8
4	44	
		6
5	50	
		4
6	54	
		2
7	56	
		0
8	56	
		−2
9	54	

(a) **Utility Table**

(c) **Marginal Utility**

Web Note 19.1

Utility and Pleasure

eating a whole pound of Beluga caviar might give you 4,700 units of utility.[1] Consuming the first 15 ounces may have given you 4,697 units of utility. Consuming the last ounce of caviar might give you an additional 3 units of utility. The 4,700 is total utility; the 3 is the marginal utility of eating that last ounce of caviar.

An example of the relationship between total utility and marginal utility is given in Figure 19-1. Let's say that the marginal utility of the first slice of pizza is 14, and since you've eaten only 1 slice, the total utility is also 14. Let's also say that the marginal utility of the second slice of pizza is 12, which means that the total utility of 2 slices of pizza is 26 (14 + 12). Similarly for the third, fourth, and fifth slices of pizza, whose marginal utilities are 10, 8, and 6, respectively. The total utility of your eating those 5 pieces of pizza is the sum of the marginal utilities you get from eating each of the 5 slices. The sixth row of column 2 of Figure 19-1(a) shows that sum.

[1]Throughout the book I choose specific numbers to make the examples more understandable and to make the points I want to make. Economists don't use actual numbers to discuss utility. At the principles level, they use such numbers to make the presentation easier. A useful exercise is for you to choose different numbers and reason your way through the same analysis. In this chapter's appendix, I go through the same analysis without using actual numbers.

Notice that marginal utility shows up between the rows. That's because it is the utility of *changing* consumption levels. For example, the marginal utility of changing from 1 to 2 slices of pizza is 12. The relationship between total and marginal utility also can be seen graphically. In Figure 19-1(b), we graph total utility (column 2 of the utility table) on the vertical axis and the number of slices of pizza (column 1 of the utility table) on the horizontal axis. As you can see, total utility increases up to 7 slices of pizza; after 8 slices it starts decreasing—after 8 pieces of pizza, you're so stuffed that you can't stand to look at another slice.

In Figure 19-1(c), we graph marginal utility (column 3 of the utility table) on the vertical axis and slices of pizza (column 1) on the horizontal axis. Notice how marginal utility decreases while total utility increases. When total utility stops increasing (between 7 and 8 slices), marginal utility is zero. Beyond this point, total utility decreases and marginal utility is negative. An additional slice of pizza will actually make you worse off.

Diminishing Marginal Utility

Now let's consider the shapes of these curves a bit more carefully: What are they telling us about people's choices? As we've drawn the curves, the marginal utility that a person gets from each additional slice of pizza decreases with each slice of pizza eaten. Economists believe that the shape of these curves is generally a reasonable description of the pattern of people's enjoyment. They call that pattern the **principle of diminishing marginal utility:**

> *As you consume more of a good, after some point, the marginal utility received from each additional unit of a good decreases with each additional unit consumed, other things equal.*

As individuals increase their consumption of a good, at some point, consuming another unit of the product will simply not yield as much additional pleasure as did consuming the preceding unit.

Consider, for example, that late-night craving for a double-cheese-and-pepperoni pizza. You order one and bite into it. Ah, pleasure! But if you've ordered a large pizza and you're eating it all by yourself, eventually you'll enjoy each additional slice less. In other words, the marginal utility you get is going to decrease with each additional slice of pizza you consume. That's the principle of diminishing marginal utility.

Notice that the principle of diminishing marginal utility does not say that you don't enjoy consuming more of a good; it simply states that as you consume more of the good, you enjoy the additional units less than you did the previous units. A fourth slice of pizza still tastes good, but it doesn't match the taste of the third slice. At some point, however, marginal utility can become negative. Say you had two large pizzas and only two hours in which to eat them. Eating the last slice could be pure torture. But in most situations, you have the option *not* to consume any more of a good. When consuming a good becomes torture (meaning its utility is negative), you simply don't consume any more of it. If you eat a slice of pizza (or consume an additional unit of a good), that's a good indication that its marginal utility is still positive.

Rational Choice and Marginal Utility

The analysis of rational choice is the analysis of how individuals choose goods within their budget in order to maximize total utility, and how maximizing total utility can be accomplished by considering marginal utility. That analysis begins with the premise that rational individuals want as much satisfaction as they can get from their available resources. The term *rational* in economics means, specifically, that people prefer more to less and will make choices that give them as much satisfaction as possible. The problem is that people face a budget constraint. They must choose among the alternatives. How do they do that?

Eating contests are proof that, at some point, utility becomes zero.

©Chris Hondros/Getty Images

Q-1 If the total utility curve is a straight line—that is, does not exhibit diminishing marginal utility—what will the marginal utility curve look like?

The principle of diminishing marginal utility states that, after some point, the marginal utility received from each additional unit of a good decreases with each additional unit consumed, other things equal.

Q-2 True or false? Consuming more of a good generally increases its marginal utility. Why?

Web Note 19.2

Diminishing Marginal Utility

Because people face a budget constraint, they must choose among alternatives.

SOME CHOICES   Let's start by considering three choices. (Answer each choice as you read it.)[2]

> *Choice 1:*   Between spending another dollar on a slice of pizza that gives you an additional 41 units of utility, or spending another dollar on a cup of coffee that gives you an additional 30 units of utility.
>
> *Choice 2:*   Between reading an additional chapter in this book that gives you an additional 200 units of utility at a cost of one hour of your time, or reading an additional chapter in psychology that gives you an additional 100 units of utility at a cost of 40 minutes of your time.
>
> *Choice 3:*   Between having your next date with that awesome guy Jerry, which gives you an additional 2,000 units of utility and costs you $70, or taking out plain Jeff on your next date, which gives you an additional 200 units of utility and costs you $10.

The correct choices, in terms of marginal utility, are (1) the pizza, (2) a chapter of this book, and (3) Jerry.

If you answered all three correctly, either you're lucky or you have a good intuitive understanding of the principle of rational choice. Now let's explore the principle of rational choice more thoroughly by considering each of the three examples.

Choice 1   Since the slice of pizza and the cup of coffee both cost $1, and the pizza gives you more units of utility than the coffee, the pizza is the rational choice. If you spend $1 on the coffee rather than the pizza, you're losing 11 units of utility and not making yourself as happy as you could be. You're being irrational. Any choice (for the same amount of money) that doesn't give you as much utility as possible is an irrational choice.

But now let's say that the price of coffee falls to 50 cents a cup so that you can buy two cups for the same price you previously had to pay for only one. Let's also say that two cups of coffee would give you 56 units of utility (not $2 \times 30 = 60$—remember the principle of diminishing marginal utility). Which would now be the more rational choice? The two cups of coffee, because their 56 units of utility are 15 more than you would get from that dollar spent on one slice of pizza.

Another way of thinking about your choice is to recognize that essentially what you're doing is buying units of utility. Obviously you want to get the most for your money, so you choose goods that have the highest units of utility per unit of cost. Let's see how this way of thinking about a decision works by considering our second choice.

Q-3 Which is the rational choice: watching one hour of CNN that gives you 20 units of utility or watching a two-hour movie that gives you 30 units of utility?

Choice 2   Here the two alternatives have a cost in time, not money. The analysis, however, is the same. You calculate the marginal utility (additional units of utility) of the choice facing you and divide that by the costs of the activity; that gives you the marginal utility per unit of cost. Then choose the activity that has the higher marginal utility per unit of cost or lower cost per unit of utility. When you do that, you see that this chapter gives you $3^1/_3$ units of utility per minute ($200/60 = 3^1/_3$), while the psychology chapter gives you $2^1/_3$ units of utility per minute. So you choose to read another chapter in this book.[3]

---

[2] To keep the analysis simple in this example, I consider either/or decisions. Below, I show how to extend the analysis to marginal choices.

[3] As I've pointed out before, I choose the numbers to make the points I want to make. A good exercise for you is to choose different numbers that reflect your estimate of the marginal utility you get from a choice, and see what your rational choices are.

Choice 3   Taking out Jerry gives you 28½ units of utility per dollar (2,000/$70), while taking out Jeff gives you 20 units of utility per dollar (200/$10). So you choose to take out Jerry.[4]

THE PRINCIPLE OF RATIONAL CHOICE   The **principle of rational choice** is as follows: *Spend your money on those goods that give you the most marginal utility (MU) per dollar.* The principle of rational choice is important enough for us to restate.

If $\dfrac{MU_x}{P_x} > \dfrac{MU_y}{P_y}$, choose to consume an additional unit of good *x*.

If $\dfrac{MU_x}{P_x} < \dfrac{MU_y}{P_y}$, choose to consume an additional unit of good *y*.

By substituting the marginal utilities and prices of goods into these formulas, you can always decide which good it makes more sense to consume. Consume the one with the highest marginal utility per dollar.

SIMULTANEOUS DECISIONS   So far in discussing our examples, we've considered the choices separately. But in real life, choices aren't so neatly separated. Say you were presented with all three choices simultaneously. If you make all three of the decisions given in the examples, are you being rational? The answer is no. Why? The pizza gives you 41 units of utility per dollar; taking out Jerry gives you 28½ units of utility per dollar. You aren't being rational; you aren't maximizing your utility. It would clearly make sense to eat more pizza, paying for it by cutting the date with Jerry short. (Skip the dessert at the end of the meal.)

But what about the other choice: studying psychology or economics? We can't compare the costs of studying to the costs of the other goods because, as I noted earlier, the costs of both studying alternatives are expressed in terms of time, not money. If we can assign a money value to the time, however, we can make the comparison. Let's say you can earn $6 per hour, so the value of your time is 10 cents per minute. This allows us to think about both alternatives in terms of dollars and cents. Since a chapter in economics takes an hour to read, the cost in money of reading a chapter is 60 minutes × 10 cents = $6. Similarly, the cost of the 40 minutes you'd take to read the psychology chapter is $4.

With these values, we can compare our studying decisions with our other decisions. The value in units of utility per dollar of reading a chapter of this book is

$$\frac{200}{\$6} = 33^{1}/_{3} \text{ units of utility per dollar}$$

So forget about dating Jerry with its 28½ units of utility per dollar. Your rational choice is to study this chapter while stuffing yourself with pizza.

But wait. Remember that, according to the principle of diminishing marginal utility, as you consume more of something, the marginal utility you get from it falls. So as you consume more pizza and spend more time reading this book, the marginal utilities of these activities will fall. Thus, as you vary your consumption, the marginal utilities you get from the goods are changing.

The principle of rational choice tells us to spend our money on those goods that give us the most marginal utility per dollar.

---

[4]In these examples, I am implicitly assuming that the "goods" are divisible. Technically, this assumption is needed for marginal utilities to be fully specified.

Maximizing Utility and Equilibrium

When do you stop changing your consumption? The principle of rational choice says you should keep adjusting your spending within your budget if the marginal utility per dollar (MU/P) of two goods differs. The only time you don't adjust your spending is when there is no clear winner. *When the ratios of the marginal utility to price of the two goods are equal,* you're maximizing utility; this is the **utility-maximizing rule:**

$$If \frac{MU_x}{P_x} = \frac{MU_y}{P_y}, \text{ you're maximizing utility.}$$

When you're maximizing utility, you're in equilibrium. To understand how you can achieve equilibrium by adjusting your spending, it's important to remember the principle of diminishing marginal utility. As we consume more of an item, the marginal utility we get from the last unit consumed decreases. Conversely, as we consume *less* of an item, the marginal utility we get from the last unit consumed *increases.* (The principle of diminishing marginal utility operates in reverse.)

Achieving equilibrium by maximizing utility (juggling your choices, adding a bit more of one and choosing a bit less of another) requires more information than I've so far presented. We need to know the marginal utility of alternative amounts of consumption for each choice and how much we have to spend on all those items. With that information, we can choose among alternatives, given our available resources.

An Example of Maximizing Utility

Table 19-1 offers an example in which we have the necessary information to make simultaneous decisions and maximize utility. In this example, we have $7 to spend on ice cream cones and Big Macs. The choice is between ice cream at $1 a cone and Big Macs at $2 apiece. In the table, you can see the principle of diminishing marginal utility in action. The marginal utility (MU) we get from either good decreases as we consume more of it. MU becomes negative after 5 Big Macs or 6 ice cream cones.

The key columns for your decision are the MU/P columns. They tell you the MU per dollar spent on each of the items. By following the rule that we choose the good with the higher marginal utility per dollar, we can quickly determine the optimal choice.

TABLE 19-1   Maximizing Utility

This table provides the information needed to make simultaneous decisions. Notice that the marginal utility we get from another good declines as we consume more of it. To maximize utility, adjust your choices until the marginal utility of all goods is equal.

	Big Macs ($P = $2)				Ice Cream ($P = $1)		
Q	TU	MU	MU/P	Q	TU	MU	MU/P
0	0			0	0		
		20	10			29	29
1	20			1	29		
		14	7			17	17
2	34			2	46		
		10	5			7	7
3	44			3	53		
		3	1.5			2	2
4	47			4	55		
		0	0			1	1
5	47			5	56		
		−5	−2.5			0	0
6	42			6	56		
		−10	−5			−4	−4
7	32			7	52		

Let's start by considering what we'd do with our first $2. Clearly we'd only eat ice cream. Doing so would give us 29 + 17 = 46 units of utility, compared to 20 units of utility if we spent the $2 on a Big Mac. How about our next $2? Again the choice is clear; the 10 units of utility per dollar from the Big Mac are plainly better than the 7 units of utility per dollar we can get from ice cream cones. So we buy 1 Big Mac and 2 ice cream cones with our first $4.

Now let's consider our fifth and sixth dollars. The *MU/P* for a second Big Mac is 7. The *MU/P* for a third ice cream cone is also 7, so we could spend the fifth dollar on either—if McDonald's will sell us half a Big Mac. We ask McDonald's if it will, and it tells us no, so we must make a choice between either two additional ice cream cones or another Big Mac for our fifth and sixth dollars. Since the marginal utility per dollar of the fourth ice cream cone is only 2, it makes sense to spend our fifth and sixth dollars on another Big Mac. So now we're up to 2 Big Macs and 2 ice cream cones and we have one more dollar to spend.

Now how about our last dollar? If we spend it on a third ice cream cone, we get 7 additional units of utility. If McDonald's maintains its position and only sells whole Big Macs, this is our sole choice since we only have a dollar and Big Macs sell for $2. But let's say that McDonald's wants the sale and this time offers to sell us half a Big Mac for $1. Would we take it? The answer is no. One-half of the next Big Mac gives us only 5 units of utility per dollar, whereas the third ice cream cone gives us 7 units of utility per dollar. So we spend the seventh dollar on a third ice cream cone.

With these choices and $7 to spend, we've arrived at equilibrium—the marginal utilities per dollar are the same for both goods and we're maximizing total utility. Our total utility is 34 from 2 Big Macs and 53 units of utility from the 3 ice cream cones, making a total utility of 87.

Why do these two choices make sense? Because they give us the most total utility for the $7 we have to spend. We've followed the utility-maximizing rule: Maximize utility by adjusting your choices until the marginal utilities per dollar are the same. These choices make the marginal utility per dollar between the last Big Mac and the last ice cream cone equal. The marginal utility per dollar we get from our last Big Mac is:

$$\frac{MU}{P} = \frac{14}{\$2} = 7$$

The marginal utility per dollar we get from our last ice cream cone is:

$$\frac{MU}{P} = \frac{7}{\$1} = 7$$

The marginal utility per dollar of each choice is equal, so we know we can't do any better. For any other choice, we would get less total utility, so we could increase our total utility by switching to one of these two choices.

Extending the Principle of Rational Choice

Our example involved only two goods, but the reasoning can be extended to the choice among many goods. Our analysis has shown us that the principle of rational choice among many goods is simply an extension of the principle of rational choice applied to two goods. That general principle of rational choice is to consume more of the good that provides a higher marginal utility per dollar.

When $\dfrac{MU_x}{P_x} > \dfrac{MU_z}{P_z}$, consume more of good *x*.

When $\dfrac{MU_y}{P_y} > \dfrac{MU_z}{P_z}$, consume more of good *y*.

The "good choice" is the one that provides the highest marginal utility per dollar.

©Milosh Kojadinovich/123RF

Choices at the Margin

Remember that an individual is maximizing utility if the marginal utilities per dollar for each good are equal:

$$\frac{MU_x}{P_x} = \frac{MU_y}{P_y}$$

If $MU_x/P_x < MU_y/P_y$, then good x isn't providing enough marginal utility to be in equilibrium, so reduce the amount of good x and increase the amount of good y. Because of diminishing marginal utility, doing this will raise the marginal utility of x and lower the marginal utility of y.

If $MU_x/P_x = MU_y/P_y$, but then the price of good x rises, good x will no longer provide enough marginal utility to be in equilibrium. MU_y/P_y will exceed MU_x/P_x. So again, reduce the amount of good x and increase the amount of good y to return to equilibrium.

Stop adjusting your consumption when the marginal utilities per dollar are equal.

So the *general utility-maximizing rule* is that you are maximizing utility when the marginal utilities per dollar of the goods consumed are equal.

When $\dfrac{MU_x}{P_x} = \dfrac{MU_y}{P_y} = \dfrac{MU_z}{P_z}$, you are maximizing utility.

When this rule is met, the consumer is in equilibrium; the cost per additional unit of utility is equal for all goods and the consumer is as well off as it is possible to be.

Notice that the rule does not say that the rational consumer should consume a good until its marginal utility reaches zero. The reason is that consumers don't have enough money to buy all they want. They face a budget constraint and do the best they can under that constraint—that is, they maximize utility. To buy more goods, a person has to work more, so she should work until the marginal utility of another dollar earned just equals the marginal utility of goods purchased with another dollar. According to economists' analysis of rational choice, a person's choice of how much to work is made simultaneously with the person's decision of how much to consume. So when you say you want a Porsche but can't afford one, economists ask whether you're working two jobs and saving all your money to buy a Porsche. If you aren't, you're demonstrating that you don't really want a Porsche, given what you would have to do to get it.

Rational Choice and the Laws of Demand and Supply

Now that you know the rule for maximizing utility, let's see how it relates to the laws of demand and supply. We begin with demand. The law of demand says that quantity demanded is inversely related to price. That is, when the price of a good goes up, the quantity we consume of it goes down.

The Law of Demand

According to the principle of rational choice, if there is diminishing marginal utility and the price of a good goes up, we consume less of that good. Hence, the principle of rational choice leads to the law of demand.

Now let's consider the law of demand in relation to our principle of rational choice. When the price of a good goes up, the marginal utility *per dollar* we get from that good goes down. So when the price of a good goes up, if we were initially in equilibrium, we no longer are. Therefore, we choose to consume less of that good. The principle of rational choice shows us formally that following the law of demand is the rational thing to do.

Let's see how. If

$$\frac{MU_x}{P_x} = \frac{MU_y}{P_y}$$

and the price of good y goes up, then

$$\frac{MU_x}{P_x} > \frac{MU_y}{P_y}$$

Our utility-maximizing rule is no longer satisfied. Consider the preceding example, in which we were in equilibrium with 87 units of utility (34 from 2 Big Macs and 53 from 3 ice cream cones) with the utility-maximizing rule fulfilled:

$$\frac{\overset{\text{Big Mac}}{14 \text{ units of utility}}}{\$2} = \frac{\overset{\text{Ice cream}}{7 \text{ units of utility}}}{\$1} = 7$$

If the price of an ice cream cone rises from \$1 to \$2, the marginal utility per dollar for Big Macs (whose price hasn't changed) exceeds the marginal utility per dollar of ice cream cones:

Big Mac > Ice cream

$$\frac{14}{\$2} > \frac{7}{\$2}$$

To satisfy our utility-maximizing rule so that our choice will be rational, we must somehow raise the marginal utility we get from the good whose price has risen. Following the principle of diminishing marginal utility, we can increase marginal utility only by *decreasing* our consumption of the good whose price has risen. As we consume fewer ice cream cones and more Big Macs, the marginal utility of ice cream rises and the marginal utility of a Big Mac falls.

This example can be extended to a general rule: If the price of a good rises, you'll increase your total utility by consuming less of it. When the price of a good goes up, consumption of that good will go down. Our principle of rational choice underlies the law of demand:

Quantity demanded rises as price falls, other things constant.

Or alternatively:

Quantity demanded falls as price rises, other things constant.

Q-5 If you are initially in equilibrium and the price of one good rises, how would you adjust your consumption to return to equilibrium?

Income and Substitution Effects

So far I haven't said precisely how much the quantity demanded would decrease with an increase in the price of an ice cream cone from \$1 to \$2. I didn't because of a certain ambiguity that arises when one talks about changes in nominal prices. To understand the cause of this ambiguity, notice that if the price of an ice cream cone has risen to \$2, with \$7 we can no longer consume 2 Big Macs and 3 ice cream cones. We've got to cut back for two reasons: First, we're poorer due to the rise in price. *The reduction in quantity demanded because the increase in price makes us poorer* is called the **income effect.** Second, the *relative* prices have changed. The price of ice cream has risen relative to the price of Big Macs. *The reduction in quantity demanded because relative price has risen* is called a **substitution effect.** Technically the law of demand is based only on the substitution effect.

Q-6 What are two effects that generally cause the quantity demanded to fall when the price rises?

To separate the two effects, let's assume that somebody compensates us for the rise in the price of ice cream cones. Since it would cost \$10 [(2 × \$2 = \$4) + (3 × \$2 = \$6)] to buy what \$7 bought previously, we'll assume that someone gives us an extra \$3 to compensate us for the rise in price. Since we are not any poorer because of the price change, this eliminates the income effect. We now have \$10, so we can buy 2 Big Macs and the 3 ice cream cones as we did before. If we do so, our total utility is once again 87 (34 units of utility from 2 Big Macs and 53 units of utility from 3 ice cream cones). But will we do so? We can answer that with the following table:

Big Macs ($P = \$2$)				Ice Cream ($P = \$2$)			
Q	TU	MU	MU/P	Q	TU	MU	MU/P
0	0			0	0		
		20	10			29	14.5
1	20			1	29		
		14	7			17	8.5
2	34			2	46		
		10	5			7	3.5
3	44			3	53		

We see that the second Big Mac gives us more *MU* per dollar than the third cone. What happens if we exchange an ice cream cone for an additional Big Mac, so instead of buying 3 ice cream cones and 2 Big Macs, we buy 3 Big Macs and 2 ice cream cones? The *MU* per dollar of Big Macs falls from 7 to 5 and the *MU* per dollar of the ice cream cone (whose price is now $2) rises from 3.5 to 8.5. Our total utility rises to 44 from 3 Big Macs and 46 from 2 ice cream cones, for a total of 90 units of utility rather than the previous 87. We've increased our total utility by shifting our consumption out of ice cream, the good whose price has risen. The price of ice cream went up and, even though we were given more money so we could buy the same amount as before, we did not; we bought fewer ice cream cones. That's the substitution effect in action: It tells us that when the relative price of a good goes up, the quantity purchased of that good decreases, *even if you're given money to compensate you for the rise.*

The Law of Supply

According to the principle of rational choice, if there is diminishing marginal utility and the price of supplying a good goes up, you supply more of that good.

The above discussion focused on demand and goods we consume, but this analysis of choice holds for the law of supply of factors of production, such as labor, that individuals supply to the market, as well as for demand. In supply decisions, you are giving up something—your time, land, or some other factor of production—and getting money in return. To show you how this works, let's consider one final example: how much labor you should supply to the market.

Say that working another hour at your part-time job pays you another $8 and that you currently work 20 hours per week. That additional income from the final hour of work gives you an additional 24 units of utility. Also assume that your best alternative use of that hour—studying economics—gives you another 24 units of utility. (You didn't know economics gave you so much pleasure, did you?) So what should you do when your boss asks you to work an extra hour? Tell her no, you are already satisfying the utility-maximizing rule $MU_s/W = MU_w/W$.

$$\frac{\text{Studying}}{24 \text{ units of utility}}{\$8} = \frac{\text{Working}}{24 \text{ units of utility}}{\$8}$$

The price of studying an additional hour is also your wage per hour because that wage is the opportunity cost of studying.

Q-7 Use the principle of rational choice to explain how you would change your quantity of work supplied if your employer raised your wage by $1 per hour.

But now say that your boss offers to raise your wage to $8.50 per hour for work you do over 20 hours. That means that both your wage at work and the price of studying have increased. But now you can get more goods for working that additional hour. Let's say that those additional goods raise the marginal utility you get from an additional hour of work to 32 additional units of utility. Now the marginal utility of working an additional hour exceeds the marginal utility of studying an additional hour:

$$\frac{\text{Studying}}{24 \text{ units of utility}}{\$8.50} < \frac{\text{Working}}{32 \text{ units of utility}}{\$8.50}$$

So you work the extra hour.

Now say your boss comes to you and asks what it would take to get you to work five hours more per week. After running the numbers through your computer-mind, you solve the utility-maximizing rule and tell her, "$12.00 an hour for overtime work and you've got your worker." Combining these hours and wages gives you the supply curve shown in the margin, which demonstrates the law of supply. As you have seen, factor supply curves can be derived from a comparison of marginal utilities for various activities in relation to work.

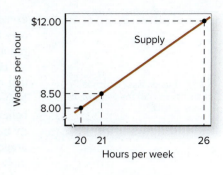

To see that you have the reasoning down, say that an exam is coming and you haven't studied. This will likely raise the marginal utility of studying sufficiently, so you will choose to work less, if you have a choice. What will that change do to your supply curve of labor?

If you answered that it will shift it in to the left, you're in good shape.

Opportunity Cost

Before we leave the principle of rational choice, let's consider how it relates to the opportunity cost concept that I presented in earlier chapters. *Opportunity cost* was the benefit forgone of the next-best alternative. Now that you've been through the principle of rational choice, you have a better sense of what is meant by opportunity cost of a forgone opportunity: It is essentially the marginal utility per dollar you forgo from the consumption of the next-best alternative.

To say $MU_x/P_x > MU_y/P_y$ is to say that the opportunity cost of not consuming good x is greater than the opportunity cost of not consuming good y. So you consume x.

When the marginal utilities per dollar spent are equal, the opportunity costs of the alternatives are equal. In terms of opportunity cost, the principle of rational choice can be stated in the following way: To maximize utility, choose goods until the opportunity costs of all alternatives are equal. In reality, people don't use the utility terminology, and, indeed, a specific measure of utility doesn't exist. But the choice based on the price of goods relative to the benefit they provide is used all the time. Instead of utility terminology, people use the "really need" terminology. They say they will work the extra hour rather than study because they *really need* the money. To say you are working because you "really need" the money is the equivalent of saying the marginal utility of working is higher than the marginal utility of other choices. So the general rule fits decisions about supply, even if most people don't use the word *utility*. The more you "really, really need" something, the higher its marginal utility.

The principle of rational choice states that, to maximize utility, choose goods until the opportunity costs of all alternatives are equal.

Q-8 If the opportunity cost of consuming good *x* is greater than the opportunity cost of consuming good *y*, which good has the higher marginal utility per dollar?

Applying Economists' Theory of Choice to the Real World

Understanding a theory involves more than understanding how a theory works; it also involves understanding the limits the assumptions underlying the theory place on the use of the theory. As I've noted above, behavioral economists are questioning some of the assumptions on which traditional economists' analysis of choice is based. These assumptions include: (1) Decisions are costless; (2) tastes are given; and (3) individuals maximize utility. Let's consider some of their questions. The first assumption we'll consider is the implicit assumption that decisions can be made costlessly.

The Cost of Decision Making

The principle of rational choice makes reasonably good intuitive sense when we limit our examples to two or three choices, as I did in this chapter. But in reality, we make hundreds of thousands of choices simultaneously. It simply doesn't make intuitive sense that we're going to apply rational choice to all those choices at once. That would exceed our decision-making abilities. This cost of decision making means that it is only rational to be somewhat irrational—to do things without applying the principle of rational choice. Thinking about decisions is one of the things we all economize on.

How real-world people make decisions in real-world situations is an open question that modern economists are spending a lot of time researching. Following the work of Nobel Prize–winning economist Herbert Simon, a number of economists have come to believe that to make real-world decisions, most people use *bounded rationality*—rationality based on rules of thumb—rather than using the principle of rational choice. They argue that many of our decisions are made with our minds on automatic pilot. This view of rationality has significant implications for interpreting and predicting economic events. For example, one rule of thumb is "You get what you pay for," which means that something with a high price is better than something with a low price. Put technically, we rely on price to convey information about quality. This reliance on price for information changes the inferences one can draw from the analysis, and can lead to upward-sloping demand curves.

A second rule of thumb that people sometimes use is "Follow the leader." If you don't know what to do, do what you think smart people are doing. Consider the clothes you're wearing. I suspect many of your choices of what to wear reflect this and the previous rule of thumb. Suppliers of clothing certainly think so and spend enormous amounts of money to exploit these rules of thumb. They try to steer your automatic pilot toward their goods. The suppliers emphasize these two rules ("You get what you pay for" and "Follow the leader") to convince people their product is the "in" thing to buy. If they succeed, they've got a gold mine; if they fail, they've got a flop. Advertising is designed to mine these rules of thumb.

In technical terms, the "Follow the leader" rule leads to *focal point equilibria*, in which a set of goods is consumed, not because the goods are objectively preferred to all other goods, but simply because, through luck, or advertising, they have become focal points to which people have gravitated. Once some people started consuming a good, others followed.

Given Tastes

A second assumption that behavioral economists are questioning is that our preferences are given and are not shaped by society. In reality, our preferences are determined not only by nature but also by our experiences—by nurture. Let's consider an example: Until it was recently banned,

Q-9 True or false? Bounded rationality violates the principle of rational choice.

Advertising is designed to mine rules of thumb.

Thinking Like a Modern Economist

Mental Accounting

If some of the analysis in this chapter doesn't sit well with you, you're not alone. It assumes that people make decisions on the margin and are able to make mental calculations easily. Behavioral economists, over the past 10 years, have been exploring exactly how people make decisions. The chapter considers a few of those explorations. Here's another.

Consider the following scenario. You buy a $100 ticket to a concert and lose it on the way. If you had another $100, would you buy a replacement ticket and still go to the concert? Most people answer "no." But consider this second scenario. You're on your way to buy a $100 concert ticket and you lose $100 in cash on the way. You still have enough cash to buy the ticket. Do you? Most people answer "yes."

Why the difference even though the financial situation is equivalent in both situations? Behavioral economists suggest that people make choices within particular mental categories, instead of over all categories. In the first scenario, the ticket was in the "concert" category. Adding another $100 places too much in that mental category. So people decline doing so. In the second scenario, the $100 cash wasn't in the "concert" category, so spending another spare $100 doesn't add to that "concert" category.

(Top) ©Alexander Kalina/Shutterstock; (bottom) ©Michael Burrell/Alamy Stock Photo

numerous major league baseball players chewed tobacco, but close to zero percent of college professors chewed tobacco. Why? Were major league baseball players somehow born with a tobacco-chewing gene while college professors were not? I doubt it. Tastes often are significantly influenced by society.

CONSPICUOUS CONSUMPTION   Another aspect of taste that has been described by economists is **conspicuous consumption**—*the consumption of goods not for one's direct pleasure, but simply to show off to others.* The term was created approximately 100 years ago by the famous institutional economist Thorstein Veblen. Veblen argued that, just as some animals strut around to show their abilities, humans consume to show that they can "afford it." For Veblen, mansions, designer clothing, and $300 appetizers were all examples of conspicuous consumption. He further argued that male industrialists (which were all industrialists at the time) were so busy with business that they didn't have time to show off enough, so they married a trophy spouse whose purpose was to spend their money in a way that showed off their wealth.

TASTES AND INDIVIDUAL CHOICE   One way in which economists integrate the above insights into economics is by emphasizing that the analysis is conducted on the assumption of "given tastes." As discussed above, in reality, economists agree that often forces besides price and marginal utility play a role in determining what people demand. They fully recognize that a whole other analysis is necessary to supplement theirs—an analysis of what determines taste.

Ask yourself what you ate today. Was it health food? Pizza? Candy? Whatever it was, it was probably not the most efficient way to satisfy your nutritional needs. The most efficient way to do that would be to eat only soybean mush and vitamin supplements at a cost of about $300 per year. That's less than one-tenth of what the average individual today spends on food per year. Most of us turn up our noses at soybean mush. Why? Because tastes are important.

I emphasize this point because some economists have been guilty of forgetting their simplifying assumption. Some economists in the 1800s thought that society's economic needs eventually would be fully met and that we would enter a golden age of affluence where all our material wants would be satisfied. They thought there would be surpluses of everything. Clearly that hasn't happened. Somehow it seems that whenever a need is met, it's replaced by a want, which soon becomes another need.

There are, of course, examples of wants being temporarily satisfied, as a U.S. company on a small island in the Caribbean is reported to have discovered. Employees weren't showing up for work. The company sent in a team of efficiency experts who discovered the cause of their problem: The firm had recently raised wages, and workers had decided they could get all they wanted (warm weather, a gorgeous beach, plenty of food, and a little bit of spending money) by showing up for work once, maybe twice, a week. Such a situation was clearly not good for business, but the firm found a solution. It sent in thousands of Sears catalogs (back when Sears sent catalogs), and suddenly the workers were no longer satisfied with what they already had. They wanted more and went back to work to get it. When they were presented with new possibilities, their wants increased. Companies know that tastes aren't constant, and they spend significant amounts of money on advertising to make consumers have a taste for their goods. It works, too.

Tastes are also important in explaining differences in consumption among countries. For example, a Japanese person wouldn't consider having a meal without rice. Rice has a ceremonial, almost mystical value in Japan. In many parts of the United States, supper means meat and potatoes. In Germany, carp (a large goldfish) is a delicacy; in the United States, many people consider carp inedible. In the United States, corn is a desirable vegetable; in parts of Europe, until recently, it was considered pig food.

Web Note 19.3
The Price of a Child

Somehow, whenever a need is met, it's replaced by a want, which soon becomes another need.

Web Note 19.4
Tastes and Choices

Q-10 Using the principle of rational choice, explain why a change in tastes will shift the demand curve.

Making Stupid Decisions

It is hard to make good decisions. You need lots of training—in math, in economics, in logic. Think of kids—do five-year-olds make rational decisions? Some dyed-in-the-wool utilitarians might argue that whatever decision one makes must, by definition, be rational, but such usage makes the concept tautological—true by definition.

When applying the theory of rational choice, most economists agree that some decisions people make can be irrational. For example, they will concede that five-year-olds make a lot of what most parents would call stupid (or irrational) decisions. By a stupid decision, they mean a decision with expected consequences that, if the child had logically thought about them, would have caused the child not to make that particular decision. But five-year-olds often haven't learned how to think logically about expected consequences, so even traditional economists don't assume decisions made by five-year-olds reflect the rational choice model.

In the real world, parents and teachers spend enormous effort to teach children what is rational, reasonable, and "appropriate." Children's decision-making process reflects that teaching. But parents and teachers teach more than a decision-making process; they also teach children a moral code that often includes the value of honor and selflessness. These teachings shape their children's decision-making process (although not always in the way that parents or teachers think or hope) and modify their preferences. So our decision-making process and our preferences are, to some degree, taught to us.

Recognizing that preferences and decision-making processes are, to some degree, taught, not inherent, eliminates the fixed point by which to judge people's decisions: Are they making decisions that reflect their true needs, or are they simply reflecting what they have been taught? Eliminating that fixed point makes it difficult to draw unambiguous policy implications from economists' model of rational choice.

To say we don't analyze tastes in the core of economic theory doesn't mean that we don't take them into account. Think back to Chapter 4, when we distinguished shifts in demand (the entire demand schedule shifts) from movements along the demand curve. Those movements along the demand curve were the effect of price. Tastes were one of the shift factors of demand. So economists do include tastes in their analysis; a change in tastes makes the demand curve shift.

Economists take into account changes in tastes as shift factors of demand.

Utility Maximization

Behavioral economics is the study of economic choice that is based on realistic psychological foundations.

A third assumption that behavioral economists question is that individuals maximize a utility function that involves getting more for themselves. In experiments, behavioral economists have found that many people don't behave that way—at least in laboratory experiments.

Let's consider one example: the **ultimatum game.** Say that two people are given the opportunity to split $10. One person is allowed to make the decision as to how to divide it. He can keep whatever portion he wants, say $9.90, and give 10 cents to the other, or he could give a 50–50 split. But in the ultimatum game, *the first person gets the money only if the other person accepts the offer. If the second person does not accept, they both get nothing.*

Three assumptions of the theory of rational choice are:

1. Decisions are costless.
2. Tastes are given.
3. Individuals maximize utility.

From a purely selfish rationality standpoint, the first individual would keep most of the money, giving only a small amount to the other. Moreover, since the other person comes out better if he accepts even the small amount, he should accept any offer (even one cent) because it makes him better off in terms of his income. So the prediction from the standard economic model is that the first person will keep most of the $10 and the second person will accept whatever amount is offered. But when people play this game, this is not what happens. Instead, generally the first person offers something close to 50–50, which is almost always accepted. However, in instances where the first person offers only a small amount, the offer is generally rejected. It seems that people have a sense of fairness in their decisions, and are willing to pay money (reduce their income) to enforce that sense of fairness.

In other experiments, behavioral economists have found a strong **status quo bias**— *an individual's actions are very much influenced by the current situation, even when that reasonably does not seem to be very important to the decision.* An example of this in the real world occurred when Sweden privatized its social security system. When privatizing retirement, Sweden offered its citizens 456 funds from which to choose to invest. Even though the Swedish government encouraged participants to actively choose their own portfolio, it also offered one of the funds as a default. Even with over 450 other funds from which to choose, 33 percent chose the default fund, a far higher percentage than would be expected if the fund had not been identified as the default.

Given that reality, arguing that people are rationally choosing among all alternatives is difficult. As we will discuss in Chapter 22, some behavioral economists have suggested that policy makers can take advantage of this status quo bias when they design policy by structuring programs so that choices are framed in ways that lead people to do what policy makers want them to do. Since individuals are freely choosing, they argue that such policy design does not violate consumer sovereignty.

There are many more such experiments and behavioral economic insights that are changing the face of modern economics. But these insights should be seen as complements to, rather than substitutes for, standard economic reasoning.

Conclusion

This chapter began with a discussion of the simplifying nature of the economists' analysis of rational choice. Now that you've been through it, you may be wondering if it's all that simple. In any case, I'm sure most of you would agree that it's complicated enough. When we're talking about formal analysis, I'm in total agreement.

But if you're talking about informal analysis and applying the analysis to the real world, most economists also would agree that this theory of choice is in no way acceptable. Economists believe that there's more to life than maximizing utility. We believe in love, anger, and doing crazy things just for the sake of doing crazy things. We're real people.

But, we argue, simplicity has its virtue, and often people hide their selfish motivations. Few people like to go around and say, "I did this because I'm a self-interested, calculating person who cares primarily about myself." Instead they usually emphasize other motives: "Society conditioned me to do it"; "I'm doing this to achieve fairness"; "It's my upbringing." And they're probably partially right, but often they hide and obscure their self-interested motives in their psychological explanations. The beauty of the simple traditional economic psychological assumption is that it cuts through many obfuscations (that's an obfuscating word meaning "smokescreens") and, in doing so, often captures a part of reality that others miss. Let's consider a couple of examples.

Why does government restrict who's allowed to practice law? The typical layperson's answer is "to protect the public." The traditional economic answer is that many of the restrictions do little to protect the public. Instead their primary function is to restrict the *number* of lawyers and thereby increase the marginal utility of existing lawyers and the price they can charge.

Why do museum directors almost always want to increase the size of their collections? The layperson's (and museum directors') answer is that they're out to preserve our artistic heritage. The traditional economic answer is that it often has more to do with maximizing the utility of the museum staff. (Economist William Grampp made this argument in a book about the economics of art. He supported his argument by

Economists use their simple self-interest theory of choice because it cuts through many obfuscations and, in doing so, often captures a part of reality that others miss.

pointing out that more than half of museums' art is in storage and not accessible to the public. Acquiring more art will simply lead to more art going into storage.)

Now in no way am I claiming that the traditional economic answer based on pure self-interest is always the correct one. But I am arguing that approaching problems by asking the question "What's in it for the people making the decisions?" is a useful approach that will give you more insight into what's going on than many other approaches. It gets people to ask tough, rather than easy, questions. After you've asked the tough questions, then you can see how to modify the conclusions by looking deeply into the real-world institutions.

All too often, students think of economics and economic reasoning as establishment reasoning. That's not true. Economic reasoning can be extremely subversive to existing establishments. But whatever it is, it is not subversive in order to be subversive, or proestablishment to be proestablishment. It's simply a logical application of a simple idea—individual choice theory—to a variety of problems.

Summary

- Total utility is the satisfaction obtained from consuming a product; marginal utility is the satisfaction obtained from consuming one additional unit of a product. (*LO19-1*)

- The principle of diminishing marginal utility states that after some point, the marginal utility of consuming more of the good will fall. (*LO19-1*)

- The principle of rational choice is:

  If $\dfrac{MU_x}{P_x} > \dfrac{MU_y}{P_y}$, choose to consume more of good x.

  If $\dfrac{MU_x}{P_x} < \dfrac{MU_y}{P_y}$, choose to consume more of good y.

  (*LO19-1*)

- The utility-maximizing rule says:

  If $\dfrac{MU_x}{P_x} = \dfrac{MU_y}{P_y}$, you're maximizing utility; you're indifferent between good x and good y. (*LO19-2*)

- Unless $MU_x/P_x = MU_y/P_y$, an individual can rearrange his or her consumption to increase total utility. (*LO19-2*)

- The law of demand can be derived from the principle of rational choice. (*LO19-3*)

- If you're in equilibrium and the price of a good rises, you'll reduce your consumption of that good to reestablish equilibrium. (*LO19-3*)

- The law of demand is based on the income effect and the substitution effect. The income effect is the reduction in quantity demanded when price rises because the price rise makes one poorer. The substitution effect is the reduction in quantity demanded when price rises because you substitute a good whose price has not risen. (*LO19-3*)

- The law of supply can be derived from the principle of rational choice. (*LO19-3*)

- If your wage rises, the marginal utility of the goods you can buy with that wage will rise and you will work more to satisfy the utility-maximizing rule. (*LO19-3*)

- Opportunity cost is essentially the marginal utility per dollar one forgoes from the consumption of the next-best alternative. (*LO19-3*)

- To apply economists' analysis of choice to the real world, we must carefully consider, and adjust for, the underlying assumptions, such as costlessness of decision making and given tastes. (*LO19-4*)

- The theory of choice assumes decision making is costless, tastes are given, and individuals maximize utility. (*LO19-4*)

- Behavioral economics is the study of economic choice that is based on realistic psychological foundations. (*LO19-4*)

- The ultimatum game suggests that people care about fairness as well as total income. The status quo bias suggests that actions are based on perceived norms. (*LO19-4*)

Key Terms

conspicuous consumption	principle of diminishing	status quo bias	ultimatum game
income effect	marginal utility	substitution effect	utility
marginal utility	principle of rational choice	total utility	utility-maximizing rule

Questions and Exercises ■ connect

1. Explain how marginal utility differs from total utility. (*LO19-1*)

2. According to the principle of diminishing marginal utility, how does marginal utility change as more of a good is consumed? As less of a good is consumed? (*LO19-1*)

3. Complete the following table of Scout's utility from drinking cans of soda and answer the questions below. (*LO19-1*)

Cans of Soda	Total Utility	Marginal Utility
0	—	
1	—	10
2	22	12
3	32	
4	—	8
5	—	4
6	44	
7	42	

a. At what point does marginal utility begin to fall?
b. Will Scout consume the seventh can of soda? Explain your answer.
c. True or false? Scout will be following the utility-maximizing rule by consuming two cans of soda. Explain your answer.

4. What key psychological assumptions do economists make in their theory of individual choice? (*LO19-1*)

5. The following table gives the price and total utility of three goods: A, B, and C.

		Total Utility							
Good	Price	1	2	3	4	5	6	7	8
A	$10	200	380	530	630	680	700	630	430
B	2	20	34	46	56	64	72	78	82
C	6	50	60	70	80	90	100	90	80

As closely as possible, determine how much of the three goods you would buy with $20. Explain why you chose what you did. (*LO19-2*)

6. The following table gives the marginal utility of John's consumption of three goods: A, B, and C. (*LO19-2*)

Units of Consumption	MU of A	MU of B	MU of C
1	20	25	45
2	18	20	30
3	16	15	24
4	14	10	18
5	12	8	15
6	10	6	12

a. Good A costs $2 per unit, good B costs $1, and good C costs $3. How many units of each should a consumer with $12 buy to maximize his or her utility?
b. How will the answer change if the price of B rises to $2?
c. How about if the price of C is 50 cents but the other prices are as in *a*?

7. The total utility of your consumption of widgets is 40; it changes by 2 with each change in widgets consumed. The total utility of your consumption of wadgets is also 40 but changes by 3 with each change in wadgets consumed. The price of widgets is $2 and the price of wadgets is $3. How many widgets and wadgets should you consume? (*LO19-2*)

8. Early Classical economists found the following "diamond/water" paradox perplexing: "Why is water, which is so useful and necessary, so cheap, when diamonds, which are so useless and unnecessary, so expensive?" Using the utility concept, explain why it is not really a paradox. (Difficult) (*LO19-2*)

9. State the law of demand and explain how it relates to the principle of rational choice. (*LO19-3*)

10. Suppose a small cheese pizza costs $10 and a calzone costs $5. You have $40 to spend. The marginal utility (*MU*) that you derive from each is as follows: (*LO19-3*)

Number	MU of Pizza	MU of Calzone
0		
1	60	30
2	40	28
3	30	24
4	20	20
5	10	10

a. How many of each would you buy?
b. Suppose the price of a calzone rises to $10. How many of each would you buy?
c. Use this to show how the principle of rational choice leads to the law of demand.

11. Your study partner tells you that if you are compensated for the impact on your budget of a rise in the price of a good, your purchase choices won't change. Is he right? Explain. (*LO19-3*)

12. State the law of supply and explain how it relates to opportunity cost. (*LO19-3*)

13. If the supply curve is perfectly inelastic, what is the opportunity cost of the supplier? (*LO19-3*)

14. There is a small but growing movement known as "voluntary simplicity," which is founded on the belief in a simple life of working less and spending less. Do Americans who belong to this movement follow the principle of rational choice? (*LO19-3*)

15. According to Thorstein Veblen, what is the purpose of conspicuous consumption? Does the utility derived from the consumption of these goods come from their price or functionality? Give an example of such a good. (*LO19-4*)

16. Say that the ultimatum game described in the chapter was changed so that the first individual could keep the money regardless of whether the offer was accepted by the second individual or not. (*LO19-4*)
a. What would you expect would likely happen to the offers?
b. What would happen to the acceptances?

Questions from Alternative Perspectives

1. The book seems to suggest that all decisions are economic decisions.
a. Would you agree?
b. How would tithing fit into the decision-making calculus? (*Religious*)

2. In his book *Why Perestroika Failed: The Politics and Economics of Socialist Transformation,* Austrian economist Peter Boettke argues that Soviet-style socialist countries had to fail because they could not appropriately reflect individuals' choices. What was his likely argument? (*Austrian*)

3. This textbook discusses the issue of decision making in reference to the individual, but generally households, not individuals, make decisions.
a. How do you think decisions are actually made about issues such as consumption and allocation of time within the household?
b. Does bargaining take place?
c. If so, what gives an individual power to bargain effectively for his or her preferences?

d. Do individuals act cooperatively within the family and competitively everywhere else? (*Feminist*)

4. Often, people buy a good to impress others and not because they want it.
a. What implications would such actions have for the application of economic analysis?
b. How many goods are bought because people want them and how many goods are bought because of advertising and conspicuous consumption? (*Post-Keynesian*)

5. Most people believe that marginal utility diminishes with each additional dollar of income (or one more dollar is worth more to a poor person than a rich one).
a. If that is true, how would you design an income tax that imposes an equal burden in lost utility on rich and poor households?
b. How would your answer differ if the marginal utility of income did not diminish?
c. How would your answer differ if your goal was to leave households with equal levels of utility from their last dollar of income? (*Radical*)

Issues to Ponder

1. How would the world be different than it is if the principle of diminishing marginal utility seldom held true?

2. True or false? It is sometimes said that an economist is a person who knows the price of everything but the value of nothing. Why?

3. Assign a measure of utility to your studying for various courses. Do your study habits follow the principle of rational choice?

4. Explain your motivation for four personal decisions you have made in the past year, using economists' model of individual choice.

5. Nobel Prize–winning economist George Stigler explains how the famous British economist Phillip Wicksteed decided where to live. His two loves were fresh farm eggs, which were more easily obtained the farther from London he was, and visits from friends, which decreased the farther he moved away from London. Given these two loves, describe the decision rule that you would have expected Wicksteed to follow.

6. Although the share of Americans who say they are "very happy" hasn't changed much in the last five decades, the number of products produced and consumed per person has risen tremendously. How can this be?

7. Give an example of a recent purchase for which you used a rule of thumb in your decision-making process. Did your decision follow the principle of rational choice? Explain.

8. Economic experiments have found that individuals prefer an outcome where no one is made better off to an outcome where the welfare of only some is improved if that improvement in welfare is unequally distributed. Why do you think this is so?

9. You are buying your spouse, significant other, or close friend a ring. You decide to show your reasonableness and buy a cubic zirconium ring that sells at ⅟₅₀ the cost of a mined diamond and that any normal person could not tell from a mined diamond just by looking at it. In fact, the zirconium will have more brilliance and fewer occlusions (imperfections) than a mined diamond.
    a. How will your spouse (significant other, close friend) likely react?
    b. Why?
    c. Is this reaction justified?

10. Joseph Gallo, the founder of the famous wine company that bears his name, said that when he first started selling wine right after Prohibition (laws outlawing the sale of alcohol), he poured two glasses of wine from the same bottle and put a price of 10 cents a bottle on one and 5 cents a bottle on the other. He let people test both and asked them which they wanted. Most wanted the 10-cent bottle, even though they were the same wine.
    a. What does this tell us about people?
    b. Can you think of other areas where that may be the case?
    c. What does this suggest about pricing?

Answers to Margin Questions

1. If the total utility curve is a straight line, the marginal utility curve will be flat with a slope of zero since marginal utility would not change with additional units. (LO19-1)

2. False. The principle of diminishing marginal utility is that as one increases consumption of a good, the good's marginal utility decreases. (LO19-1)

3. Given a choice between the two, the rational choice is to watch CNN for one hour since it provides the higher marginal utility per hour. (LO19-1)

4. False. You are maximizing total utility when the marginal utilities per dollar are the same for all goods. This does not have to be where marginal utility is zero. (LO19-2)

5. If I am initially in equilibrium, then $MU_x/P_x = MU_y/P_y = MU_z/P_z$ for all goods I consume. If the price of one good goes up, I will decrease my consumption of that good and increase the consumption of other goods until the equilibrium is met again where $MU_x/P_x = MU_y/P_y = MU_z/P_z$. (LO19-3)

6. The two effects are the income effect and the substitution effect. (LO19-3)

7. If offered one more dollar per hour, I would choose to substitute labor for leisure since the price of leisure (pay per hour of work) has increased. Following the principle of rational choice, I would work more to lower the marginal utility of work so that $MU_w/P_w = MU_l/P_l$. (LO19-3)

8. Good y has the higher marginal utility per dollar since the opportunity cost of consuming good x is the marginal utility per dollar of consuming good y. (LO19-3)

9. This could be true or false. It depends on how you interpret bounded rationality. If it is interpreted within a costless decision-making environment, it does violate the principle of rational choice since there is no reason to be less than rational. If, however, it is interpreted within a costly decision-making environment, then you can be making decisions within a range if the marginal cost of increasing the range of choices exceeds the marginal benefit of doing so. In that case bounded rationality is consistent with the principle of rational choice. Information is not costless. (LO19-4)

10. If a person is in equilibrium and a change in tastes leads to an increase in the marginal utility for one good, he will increase consumption of that good to reestablish equilibrium. A change in tastes will shift a demand curve because it will cause a change in quantity consumed without a change in the good's price. (LO19-4)

Indifference Curve Analysis

As I stated in the chapter, analyzing individual choice using actual numbers is unnecessary. In the chapter, I asked you to make a deal with me: You'd remember that actual numbers are unnecessary and I'd use them anyway. This appendix is for those who didn't accept my deal (and for those whose professors want them to get some practice in Graphish). It presents an example of a more formal analysis of individual choice.

Sophie's Choice

Sophie is a junk food devotee. She lives on two goods: chocolate bars, which cost $1 each, and cans of soda, which sell for 50 cents apiece. Sophie is trying to get as much pleasure as possible, given her resources. Alternatively expressed, Sophie is trying to maximize her utility, given a budget constraint.

By translating this statement of Sophie's choice into graphs, I can demonstrate the principle of rational choice without ever mentioning any specific amount of utility.

The graph we'll use will have chocolate bars on the vertical axis and cans of soda on the horizontal axis, as in Figure A19-1.

Graphing the Budget Constraint

Let's begin by asking: How can we translate her budget constraint (the $10 maximum she has to spend) into Graphish? The easiest way to do that is to ask what would happen if she spends her $10 all on chocolate bars or all on cans of soda. Since a chocolate bar costs $1, if she

spends it all on chocolate bars, she can get 10 bars (point A in Figure A19-1). If she spends it all on cans of soda, she can get 20 cans of soda (point B). This gives us two points.

But what if she wants some combination of soda and chocolate bars? If we draw a line between points A and B, we'll have a graphical picture of her budget constraint and can answer that question because a **budget constraint** is *a curve that shows us the various combinations of goods an individual can buy with a given amount of money*. The line is her budget constraint in Graphish.

To see that it is, say Sophie is spending all her money on chocolate bars. She then decides to buy one fewer chocolate bar. That gives her $1 to spend on soda, which, since those cans cost 50 cents each, allows her to buy 2 cans. Point C (9 chocolate bars and 2 cans of soda) represents that decision. Notice how point C is on the budget constraint. Repeat this exercise from various starting points until you're comfortable with the fact that the line does indeed represent the various combinations of soda and chocolate bars Sophie can buy with the $10. It's a line with a slope of $-\frac{1}{2}$ and intersects the chocolate-bars axis at 10 and the cans-of-soda axis at 20.

To be sure that you've got it, ask yourself what would happen to the budget constraint if Sophie got another $4 to spend on the two goods. Going through the same reasoning should lead you to the conclusion that the budget constraint will shift to the right so that it will intersect the cans-of-soda axis at 28 (point D), but its slope won't change. (I started the new line for you.) Make sure you can explain why.

Now what if the price of a can of soda goes up to $1? What happens to the budget line? (This is a question many people miss.) If you said the budget line becomes steeper, shifting in along the cans-of-soda axis to point E while remaining anchored along the chocolate-bars axis until the slope equals -1, you've got it. If you didn't say that, go through the same reasoning we went through at first (if Sophie buys only cans of soda . . .) and then draw the new line. You'll see it becomes steeper. Put another way, the absolute value of the slope of the curve is the ratio of the price of cans of soda to the price of chocolate bars; the absolute value of the slope becomes greater with a rise in the price of cans of soda.

FIGURE A19-1 **Graphing the Budget Constraint**

$$\text{Slope} = -\frac{P_{soda}}{P_{chocolate}} = -\frac{1}{2}$$

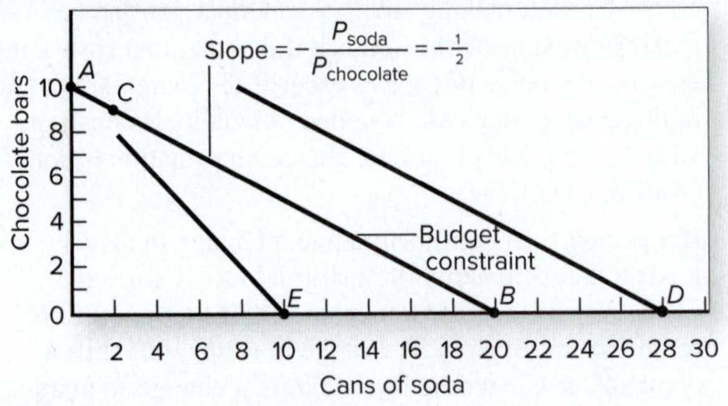

Graphing the Indifference Curve

Now let's consider the second part of Sophie's choice: the pleasure part. Sophie is trying to get as much pleasure as she can from her $10. How do we deal with this in Graphish?

To see, let's go through a thought experiment. Say Sophie had 14 chocolate bars and 4 cans of soda (point *A* in Figure A19-2). Let's ask her, "Say you didn't know the price of either good and we took away 4 of those chocolate bars (so you had 10). How many cans of soda would we have to give you so that you would be just as happy as before we took away the 4 chocolate bars?"

Since she's got lots of chocolate bars and few cans of soda, her answer is probably, "Not too many; say, 1 can of soda." This means that she would be just as happy to have 10 chocolate bars and 5 cans of soda (point *B*) as she would to have 14 chocolate bars and 4 cans of soda (point *A*). Connect those points and you have the beginning of a "just-as-happy" curve. But that doesn't sound impressive enough, so, following economists' terminology, we'll call it an **indifference curve**—*a curve that shows combinations of goods among which an individual is indifferent.* She's indifferent between points *A* and *B*.

If you continue our thought experiment, you'll get a set of combinations of chocolate bars and cans of soda like that shown in the table in Figure A19-2.

If you plot each of these combinations of points on the graph in Figure A19-2 and connect all these points, you have one of Sophie's indifference curves: a curve representing combinations of cans of soda and chocolate bars among which Sophie is indifferent.

Let's consider the shape of this curve. First, it's downward-sloping. That's reasonable; it simply says that if you take something away from Sophie, you've got to give her something in return if you want to keep her indifferent between what she had before and what she has now. The absolute value of the slope of an indifference curve is the **marginal rate of substitution**—*the rate at which one good must be added when the other is taken away in order to keep the individual indifferent between the two combinations.*

Second, it's bowed inward. That's because as Sophie gets more and more of one good, it takes fewer and fewer of another good to compensate for the loss of the good she incurred in order to get more of the other good. The underlying reasoning is similar to that in our discussion of the law of diminishing marginal utility, but notice we haven't even mentioned utility. Technically the reasoning for the indifference curve being bowed inward is called the **law of diminishing marginal rate of substitution**—which tells us that *as you get more and more of a good, if some of that good is taken away, then the marginal addition of another good you need to keep you on your indifference curve gets less and less.*

Even more technically, we can say that the absolute value of the slope of the indifference curve equals the ratio of the marginal utility of cans of soda to the marginal utility of chocolate bars:

$$\left| \text{Slope} \right| = \frac{MU_{soda}}{MU_{chocolate}} = \text{Marginal rate of substitution}$$

That ratio equals the marginal rate of substitution of cans of soda for chocolate bars. Let's consider an example. Say that in Figure A19-2 Sophie is at point *A* and that the marginal utility she gets from an increase from 4 to 5 cans of soda is 10. Since we know that she was willing to give up 4 chocolate bars to get that 1 can of soda (and thereby move from point *A* to point *B*), that 10 must equal the loss of utility she gets from the loss of 4 chocolate bars out of the 14 she originally had. So the marginal rate of substitution of cans of soda for chocolate bars between points *A* and *B* must be 4. That's the absolute value of the slope of that curve. Therefore, her *MU* of a chocolate bar must be about 2.5 (10 for 4 chocolate bars).

FIGURE A19-2 **Sophie's Indifference Curve**

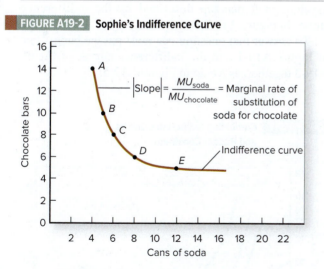

Chocolate Bars	Cans of Soda	
14	4	A
10	5	B
8	6	C
6	8	D
5	12	E

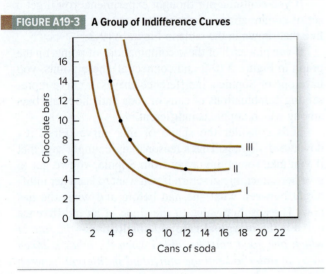

FIGURE A19-3   **A Group of Indifference Curves**

You can continue this same reasoning, starting with various combinations of goods. If you do so, you can get a whole group of indifference curves like that in Figure A19-3. Each curve represents a different level of happiness. Assuming she prefers more to less, Sophie is better off if she's on Curve II than if she's on Curve I, and even better off if she's on Curve III. Her goal in life is to get out to the furthest indifference curve she can.

To see whether you've followed the reasoning, ask yourself the following question: "Assuming Sophie prefers more of a good to less (which seems reasonable), can any two of Sophie's indifference curves cross each other as the ones in Figure A19-4 do?"

The answer is no, no, no! Why? Because they're indifference curves. If the curves were to cross, the

"prefer-more-to-less" principle would be violated. Say we start at point A: Sophie has 8 chocolate bars and 6 cans of soda. We know that since *A* (8 chocolate bars and 6 sodas) and *B* (6 chocolate bars and 8 cans of soda) are on the same indifference curve, Sophie is indifferent between *A* and *B*. Similarly with points *B* and *C*: Sophie would just as soon have 9 chocolate bars and 7 cans of soda as she would 6 chocolate bars and 8 cans of soda.

It follows by logical deduction that point *A* must be indifferent to *C*. But consider points *A* and *C* carefully. At point *C*, Sophie has 7 cans of soda and 9 chocolate bars. At point *A* she has 6 cans of soda and 8 chocolate bars. At point *C* she has more of both goods than she has at point *A*, so to say she's indifferent between these two points violates the "prefer-more-to-less" criterion. Ergo (that's Latin, meaning "therefore"), two indifference curves cannot intersect. That's why we drew the group of indifference curves in Figure A19-3 so that they do not intersect.

Combining Indifference Curves and Budget Constraints

Now let's put the budget constraint and the indifference curves together and ask how many chocolate bars and cans of soda Sophie will buy if she has $10, given the psychological makeup described by the indifference curves in Figure A19-3.

To answer that question, we must put the budget line of Figure A19-1 and the indifference curves of Figure A19-3 together, as we do in Figure A19-5.

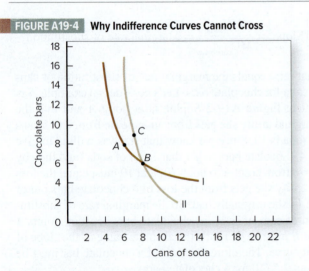

FIGURE A19-4   **Why Indifference Curves Cannot Cross**

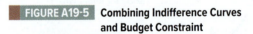

FIGURE A19-5   **Combining Indifference Curves and Budget Constraint**

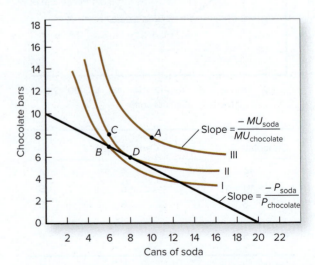

As we discussed, Sophie's problem is to get to as high an indifference curve as possible, given her budget constraint. Let's first ask if she should move to point A (8 chocolate bars and 10 cans of soda). That looks like a good point. But you should quickly recognize that she can't get to point A; her budget line won't let her. (She doesn't have enough money.) Well then, how about point B (7 chocolate bars and 6 cans of soda)? She can afford that combination; it's on her budget constraint. The problem with point B is the following: She'd rather be at point C since point C has more chocolate bars and the same amount of soda (8 chocolate bars and 6 cans of soda). But, you say, she can't reach point C. Yes, that's true, but she can reach point D. And, by the definition of *indifference curve*, she's indifferent between point C and point D, so point D (6 chocolate bars and 8 cans of soda), which she can reach given her budget constraint, is preferred to point B.

The same reasoning holds for all other points. The reason is that the combination of chocolate bars and cans of soda represented by point D is the best she can do. It is the point where the indifference curve and the budget line are tangent—the point at which the slope of the budget line $(-P_s/P_c)$ equals the slope of the indifference curve $(-MU_s/MU_c)$. Equating those slopes gives $(-P_s/P_c) = (MU_s/MU_c)$, or

$$MU_c/P_c = MU_s/P_s$$

This equation, you may remember from the chapter, is the equilibrium condition of our principle of rational choice. So by our Graphish analysis we arrived at the same conclusion we arrived at in the chapter, only this time we did it without using actual numbers. This means that even without a utilometer, economists' principle of rational choice is internally logical.

Deriving a Demand Curve from the Indifference Curve

Not only can we derive the principle of rational choice with indifference curve/budget line analysis, we also can derive a demand curve. To do so, ask yourself what a demand curve is. It's the quantity of a good that a person will buy at various prices. Since the budget line gives us the relative price of a good, and the point of tangency of the indifference curve gives us the quantity that a person would buy at that price, we can derive a demand curve from the indifference curves and budget lines. To derive a demand curve, we go through a set of thought experiments asking how many cans of soda Sophie would buy at various prices. We'll go through one of those experiments.

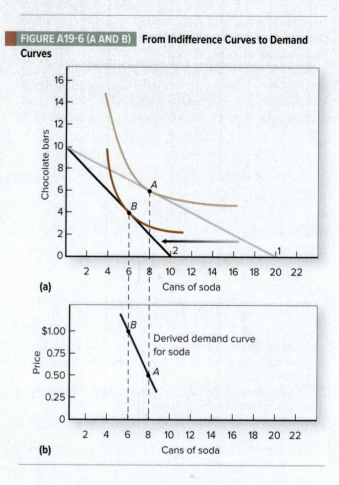

FIGURE A19-6 (A AND B)   **From Indifference Curves to Demand Curves**

We start with the analysis we used before when Sophie started with $10 and chose to buy 8 cans of soda when the price of a can of soda was 50 cents [point A in Figure A19-6(a)]. That analysis provides us with one point on the demand curve. I represent that by point A in Figure A19-6(b). At a price of 50 cents, Sophie buys 8 cans of soda.

Now say the price of a can of soda rises to $1. That rotates the budget line in, from budget line 1 to budget line 2 as in Figure A19-6(a). She can't buy as much as she could before. But we can determine how much she'll buy by the same reasoning we used previously. She'll choose a point at which her lower indifference curve is tangent to her new budget line. As you can see, she'll choose point B, which means that she buys 6 cans of soda when the price of a can of soda is $1. Graphing that point (6 cans of soda at $1 each) on our price/quantity axis in Figure A19-6(b), we have another point on our demand curve, point B. Connect these two together and you can see we're getting a downward-sloping demand curve, just as the law of demand said we would. To make sure you understand, continue the analysis for a couple of additional price changes. You'll see that the demand curve you derive will be downward-sloping.

There's much more we can do with indifference curves. We can distinguish income effects and substitution effects. (Remember, when the price of a can of soda rose, Sophie was worse off. So to be as well off as before, as is required by the substitution effect, she'd have to be compensated for that rise in price by an offsetting fall in the price of chocolate bars.) But let's make a deal. You tentatively believe me when I say that all kinds of stuff can be done with indifference curves and budget constraints, and I'll leave the further demonstration and the proofs for you to experience in the intermediate microeconomics courses.

Key Terms

budget constraint
indifference curve

law of diminishing marginal rate of
    substitution

marginal rate of substitution

Questions and Exercises

1. Zachary has $5 to spend on two goods: video games and hot dogs. Hot dogs cost $1 apiece while video games cost 50 cents apiece.
    a. Draw a graph of Zachary's budget constraint, placing video games on the *y* axis.
    b. Suppose the price of hot dogs falls to 50 cents apiece. Draw the new budget constraint.
    c. Suppose Zachary now has $8 to spend. Draw the new budget constraint using the prices from *b*.

2. Zachary's indifference curves are shown in the following graph. Determine on which indifference curve Zachary will be, given the budget constraints and prices in *a, b,* and *c* from question 1.

    a. Given a choice, which budget constraint would Zachary prefer most? Least?
    b. What is the marginal rate of substitution of hot dogs for video games at each of the combinations chosen with budget constraints *a, b,* and *c* in question 1?

3. What would an indifference curve look like if the marginal rate of substitution were zero? If it were constant?

4. What might an indifference curve look like if the law of diminishing marginal utility did not hold?

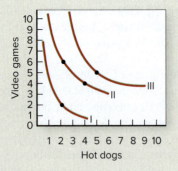

Game Theory, Strategic Decision Making, and Behavioral Economics

CHAPTER 20

After reading this chapter, you should be able to:

LO20-1 Explain what game theory is and give an example of a game and a solution to a game.

LO20-2 Discuss how strategic reasoning and backward induction are used in solving games.

LO20-3 Distinguish informal game theory from formal game theory.

LO20-4 Describe how the results of game theory experiments challenge some standard economic assumptions.

©Eli Reed/Dreamworks/Universal/Kobal/Shutterstock

In the movie *A Beautiful Mind,* economist John Nash and some friends walk into a bar with the idea of meeting some women. They see some women, one of whom is blonde, and discuss their strategy to meet them. Nash tells his friends that if each were to approach the problem on his own, they might all initially go for the blonde (whom they consider the most beautiful—OK, so it's a bit clichéish—movies generally are). Nash tells his friends:

> If everyone competes for the blonde, we block each other and no one gets her. So then we all go for her friends. But they give us the cold shoulder,

because no one likes to be second choice. Again, no winner. But what if none of us go for the blonde? We don't get in each other's way; we don't insult the other girls. That is the only way we win. That's the only way we all get a girl. (From *A Beautiful Mind: The Shooting Script*, Akiva Goldsman, © 2002.)[1]

In the movie this is Nash's eureka moment: Each person, acting in his or her own best interest, will not necessarily arrive at the best of all possible outcomes. Adam Smith is wrong.

Game Theory and the Economic Way of Thinking

The general reasoning process that Nash is portrayed as using captures a central element of the modern economic way of thinking.[2] That central element is *strategic thinking*. Whenever the decisions being analyzed involve interdependent decisions, the decision makers' strategy needs to be considered. Since all types of decisions are interdependent, the study of such interdependent decision-making processes is central to modern economics. In fact, in recent years an entire theory of strategic thinking, called **game theory**—*formal economic reasoning applied to situations in which decisions are interdependent*—has developed.

Game theory is a broad-based approach to understanding human interaction, and is not solely a tool used by economists. All social scientists—political scientists, sociologists, and anthropologists as well as economists—are using game theory more and more as a tool of analysis. Thus, you can see political scientists discussing war strategy and sociologists discussing social relationships in game theoretic terms. In many ways, game theory is the underlying model of the social sciences.

More and more, game theory is becoming the basic tool of modern economics, in many cases replacing supply and demand as economists' core model of choice. Today, when graduate students study microeconomics, they spend more time learning game theory than they spend learning the intricacies of supply and demand models. Game theory has become so important because it is a highly flexible tool that can be applied to many situations without making the restrictive assumptions of the supply/demand model.

Game Theory and Economic Modeling

Before we analyze some specific games, let's step back and reflect on modern economists' modeling method—their way of thinking—and consider where game theory fits within that method. Nobel Prize–winning economist Bob Solow has nicely summarized economists' way of thinking as follows: "You look at a problem; you create a simple model that captures its essence; you empirically test how well that model fits the data, and if it fits, you use that model as a guide to understanding the problem and devising a solution." This method sometimes gets lost as introductory students learn

Game theory is formal economic reasoning applied to situations in which decisions are interdependent.

Q-1 True or false? Game theory is inconsistent with supply/demand analysis. Explain your answer.

---

[1] I am only reporting, not condoning, the portrayal in the movie. I fully agree that Nash's EQ (emotional quotient) and sense of what is socially appropriate can be questioned. If you saw the movie, you probably agree, too.

[2] The reasoning attributed to Nash in the film can also be questioned. (Economists have pointed out that the movie gets the reasoning about the men's best strategy mixed up. Chalk up these inaccuracies to artistic license; it made for a better scene, so the filmmakers didn't care about its being wrong. Their reasoning was probably: Except for economists and mathematicians, no one will notice or care.)

how to apply the models that have already been developed, rather than learning how to develop their own models.

I suspect that oftentimes when you have learned a model, you sensed that it was a stretch to make the model fit real-world situations. Economists share that concern, and are continually tweaking the existing models and developing other models that help us understand real-world problems and issues. That's why game theory developed; it offers a new set of models with which to approach economic issues. Game theory models can be better tailored to fit the actual problem, and thus are more flexible than the standard models. The cost of that flexibility is that individual game theory models are not as broad as the standard models. A different game theory model must be developed for each different situation and for each different set of assumptions. So rather than having a single model with a single equilibrium solution, in game theory there are many models that often have multiple equilibrium solutions. Hence, game theory is really a framework—a method—rather than a finished set of models to mechanistically use in understanding real-world events.

> Game theory models are more flexible than the standard economic models.

The Game Theory Framework

To introduce you to the game theory framework, let's consider a variation of a story told by economists Avinash Dixit and Susan Skeath, in their excellent book on game theory, *Games of Strategy*. In it, four students, who all had A averages, had partied the night before the exam (yes, partying happens) and had slept through the exam. Since they were "A" students, and they felt the professor liked them, they decided to make up a sob story and convince her that they should be allowed to take the exam late. So they went to the professor all apologetic, explaining how they had meant to come to the exam, but when they were returning from visiting a sick brother of one of them (who lived 100 miles away), they had gotten a flat tire. Unfortunately, they had no spare, and it took them five hours to get the flat fixed, making them late for the exam. They knew it wasn't the best story but they figured it was worth a try.

To their surprise the professor agreed to let them take the exam two days later. So they studied hard, figuring they were a shoo-in for A's. The professor put them each in separate rooms and gave them the exam. The first page, worth 10 points, was an easy question, which they all were sure they aced. The second page, however, had just one question, but it was worth 90 points. The question was: "Which tire?"

This is an example of a **screening question,** *a question structured in such a way as to reveal strategic information about the person who answers.* If they had actually had a flat, the question would be easy to answer, and they would get their A's. But if they didn't have a flat (and didn't coordinate their stories beforehand), it is highly unlikely that they would all pick the same tire, and the professor would know that they were lying. Of course, if they had been bright, or had studied game theory, they would have expected that the professor would use such a screening device and would have figured out which tire to say went flat before they went in to take the exam. But of course, if the professor had taught them game theory, or knew they were even better-than-"A" students, she would have assumed that they would have coordinated their stories about which tire, and she would have worked out an even more elaborate testing strategy to get them to reveal the truth. Game theory studies such issues. Devising such strategies and understanding the strategic interaction of individuals when they take into account the expected reaction of others are the essence of game theory.

> A screening question is a question structured in such a way as to reveal strategic information about the person who answers.

You have already seen some of the games that comprise game theory—for example, the ultimatum game in the earlier chapter on individual choice. In the remainder of the chapter, we introduce you to some other games and game theory concepts.

The goal of the chapter is not to make you game theorists, but to give you a sense of the way in which economists think and try to understand the many puzzles that are out there.

The Prisoner's Dilemma

Web Note 20.1

Prisoner's Dilemma

Let's begin with the most famous of all games—the **prisoner's dilemma,** *a well-known two-person game that demonstrates the difficulty of cooperative behavior in certain circumstances.* The standard prisoner's dilemma can be seen in the following example: Two people suspected of committing a crime are brought into the police station and interrogated separately. They know that if neither of them confesses, the police have only enough evidence to charge each with a minor crime for which each will serve 6 months. The police know that too, but they also know that the criminals are guilty of a more serious felony. The police, however, have insufficient evidence to prosecute for the more serious crime. In order to make their case, the police offer each prisoner the following deal if he confesses to the more serious crime:

> If both you and the other prisoner confess, instead of being sentenced to the maximum 10 years in prison, the two of you will each serve only 5 years in jail. Further, if you confess but the other prisoner doesn't confess, in exchange for your serving as a witness for the prosecution, we will drop the charges for the lesser felony, and you will be set free. If, however, you don't confess and the other suspect does, you will be sentenced to the maximum 10 years in prison. If neither confesses, both will be charged with the lesser felony and serve 6 months.

A payoff matrix is a table that shows the outcome of every choice by every player, given the possible choices of all other players.

The choice each suspect faces is: Do I confess or not confess? The outcome of each choice can be presented in what is called a **payoff matrix**—*a table that shows the outcome of every choice by every player, given the possible choices of all other players*—shown in Figure 20-1. The payoff matrix shows the three elements of any game: the *players* (in this case, two of them, A and B), their possible *strategies* (in this case, to confess or not confess), and the contingent *payoffs* (in this case, their sentences) for each possible outcome.

What strategy will each choose? The combined best option for them, if they could coordinate their actions, is most likely for neither to confess; each gets a short sentence of 6 months. But will they choose that option if they use strategic reasoning? To see whether they do, consider the possibilities each faces. Prisoner A's choices are shown

---

FIGURE 20-1 Prisoner's Dilemma

This payoff matrix illustrates the prisoner's dilemma. If the prisoners could agree not to confess, each would get a light sentence. But each prisoner is offered the chance to go free if he confesses to the crime and agrees to serve as a witness against the other prisoner. With this incentive, both will likely confess and each will be sentenced to 5 years in jail.

	B Confesses	**B Does not confess**
A Confesses	Prisoner **A:** 5 years / Prisoner **B:** 5 years	Prisoner **A:** Goes free / Prisoner **B:** 10 years
A Does not confess	Prisoner **A:** 10 years / Prisoner **B:** Goes free	Prisoner **A:** 6 months / Prisoner **B:** 6 months

in the rows of Figure 20-1. The blue triangle shows Prisoner A's punishment and the green triangle shows Prisoner B's punishment for each possible outcome. Say that Prisoner A does not confess, putting us in the bottom row of the payoff matrix. He now uses the payoff matrix to consider what options Prisoner B faces. If Prisoner B also does not confess, they both get 6 months in jail (the bottom right corner of the matrix). But if Prisoner B confesses while Prisoner A has not confessed, then Prisoner B will go free. So Prisoner B's best strategy, if Prisoner A does not confess, is to confess; instead of serving a 6-month sentence, he goes free.

Now say that Prisoner A confesses, putting us in the top row of the payoff matrix. In this case, if Prisoner B does not confess, Prisoner B gets 10 years, and if he confesses, 5 years. Again, confessing is Prisoner B's best strategy. Prisoner A concludes that regardless of what he does, Prisoner B's best strategy is to confess, so Prisoner A has to assume that if Prisoner B is following his best options, Prisoner B will confess.

Q-2 In the payoff matrix in Figure 20-1, what is B's best strategy if A confesses?

The same reasoning holds for Prisoner B, so each of their optimal strategies (the ones that maximize the expected benefits) is to confess, placing them in the upper left corner of the matrix. Since neither can count on the other *not* to confess, which would lead to the combined best outcome for them, the optimal strategy will be for each to confess because each must assume the other will do the same. Confessing is the rational thing for each prisoner to do. That's why it's called the *prisoner's dilemma.*

Q-3 In the payoff matrix in Figure 20-1, what is B's best strategy if A does not confess?

Let's consider the reasoning and assumptions of game theory that led us to the outcome. First, we assumed that the prison sentences capture all the relevant costs and benefits of their decisions. Second, we assumed that no cooperation was possible. The prisoner's dilemma is an example of what is called a **noncooperative game**—*a game in which each player is out for him- or herself and agreements are either not possible or not enforceable*. If the prisoners could have trusted each other to choose the action that helps them both jointly, not only themselves, the optimal strategy is "not to confess," and they both get only a light sentence. Thus, if people's utility functions are interdependent so that each cares about the other person and him- or herself equally, or if the two of them can enter into binding contracts to act that way before they are questioned, then they can escape the dilemma. The "Code of Silence" that is often attributed to the Mafia is an example of such a binding contract; they know that they must do what is in the best interest of the group, or they will be "taken out."

Q-4 In the payoff matrix in Figure 20-1, if Prisoners A and B are in love and care for each other as they care for themselves, what is the expected outcome of the prisoner's dilemma game?

Such binding contracts are seldom possible, which makes the dilemma real for many prisoners, and for many individuals and firms. What is possible is what economists call **cheap talk**—*communication that occurs before the game is played that carries no cost and is backed up only by trust, and not any enforceable agreement*. If standard game theory assumptions hold, cheap talk does not influence the results, since the players cannot trust the other players to follow through on what they say. As Hollywood film producer Samuel Goldwyn said, and baseball star Yogi Berra is famous for repeating, "A verbal contract isn't worth the paper it's written on." But economists have shown that cheap talk might not be so cheap. In many experiments, cheap talk does influence the outcome of a game, especially ones where players have significant difficulty figuring out their optimal strategy. These empirical findings suggest that, to some degree, people do have interdependent utility functions, where each person cares about others as well as him- or herself.

Q-5 In formal game theory, should cheap talk influence the results?

Web Note 20.2

Golden Ball

Dominant Strategies and Nash Equilibrium

In analyzing the prisoner's dilemma, notice that the analysis is based on the assumption that the players figure out the other player's best strategy and build into his or her decision the assumption that the other player will choose that best strategy, while taking into account the fact that the first player is doing the same analysis in reverse. In

The Austan Goolsbee *Check-a-Box* Method for Finding Dominant Strategies and Nash Equilibria

Getting used to thinking in terms of payoff matrices is hard for some students, and economist Austan Goolsbee has pointed out a neat way of finding both *dominant strategies* and *Nash equilibria*. It works by marking the best strategies for each player. Here's how you do it:

1. Put a ✓ for each of B's best strategies.

2. Put an ✕ for each of A's best strategies.

3. Compare ✓'s and ✕'s:

    a. A column with two ✓'s or a row with two ✕'s is a dominant strategy.

    b. A box with both a ✓ and an ✕ is a Nash equilibrium.

Let's see how it works with an example. Start by looking at the choices facing individual A—confess or not confess—and ask yourself: What is her best strategy if B confesses? What is her best strategy if B does not confess?

- If B confesses, we are in column 1, and A's best strategy is to confess. Put an ✕ in the upper-left-hand box.

- If B does not confess (column 2), then A's best strategy is to confess, so put an ✕ in the upper-right-hand box.

Continue by asking the same questions for individual B.

- If A confesses, we are in the top row, and B's best strategy is to confess, so put a ✓ in the upper-left-hand box.

- If A does not confess (bottom row), B's best strategy is to confess. So put a ✓ in the lower-left-hand box.

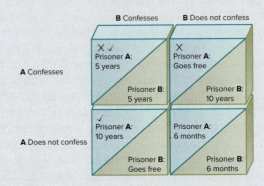

By looking at the pattern of ✓'s and ✕'s, you can make the following conclusions:

- Do any rows have two ✕'s? *Yes. Confessing is a dominant strategy for A.*

- Do any columns have two ✓'s? *Yes. Confessing is a dominant strategy for B.*

- Do any boxes have both a ✓ and an ✕? *Yes. Both A and B confessing is a Nash equilibrium.*

this prisoner's dilemma case, each player has a single best strategy. *A strategy that is preferred by a player regardless of the opponent's move* is called a **dominant strategy.**

A key concept in analyzing games is a concept called a Nash equilibrium, in honor of John Nash, who first proposed it as a solution concept for strategic games. Specifically, a **Nash equilibrium** is *a set of strategies for each player in the game in which no player can improve his or her payoff by changing strategy unilaterally.*[3] A Nash equilibrium is the predicted outcome of a noncooperative game if each player follows his best strategy and assumes that the other players are following their best strategies. The solution to the prisoner's dilemma is a Nash equilibrium.

Notice that the Nash equilibrium doesn't have to be the solution that is jointly best for all players. The solution that is jointly best for both prisoners in the prisoner's dilemma is that neither prisoner confesses. But without the possibility of enforceable cooperation, "not confessing" independently is not the best strategy for either prisoner.

> A Nash equilibrium is a set of strategies for each player in the game in which no player can improve his or her payoff by changing strategy unilaterally.

---

[3]The concept of a Nash equilibrium has a long history and goes back to August Cournot, a French economist in the 1800s, and is sometimes called a Cournot Nash equilibrium. Nash's specific contribution was to prove that all finite games have such equilibria.

An Overview of Game Theory as a Tool in Studying Strategic Interaction

There are many different assumptions that can be made about the nature of the strategic interaction, and in formal game theory, different assumptions about the nature of those interactions lead to different kinds of games. For example, in the prisoner's dilemma game discussion, we were careful to point out that cooperation was not allowed. In many real-world situations, cooperation is possible, so economists have also developed an analysis of **cooperative games**—*games in which players can form coalitions and can enforce the will of the coalition on its members.* The possibility for cooperation is often greater when a game will be repeated. Because players have the opportunity to communicate, reward, and punish one another in a repeated game, the outcome of a repeated game can often be different from the outcome of a game played just once.

Yet another assumption relates to the order in which players make their decisions. In **sequential games,** *players make decisions one after another, so one player responds to the known decisions of other players.* Sequential games stand in contrast to **simultaneous move games,** *where players make their decisions at the same time as other players without knowing what choices the other players have made.* Tic-tac-toe is an example of a sequential game; the prisoner's dilemma and rock-paper-scissors are examples of simultaneous move games.

Often in sequential games, the order makes a big difference. For example, some games have first-mover advantage; tic-tac-toe, for instance. Other games have second-mover advantage. Say Todd and Jenifer both attend the same school. Todd isn't wild about Jenifer, but Jenifer is wild about Todd. They both eat in the same dining hall, which has two tables. If Todd is the first mover, then he ends up sitting with Jenifer since she will always sit at the table with him. If Jenifer is the first mover and chooses a table, Todd will always sit at another table. In this game, the second mover has the advantage.

Web Note 20.3

Tic-Tac-Toe

Some Specific Games

Let's now discuss how game theory can be used as a tool to study strategic interactions by looking at specific games. Let's start with an easy game—tic-tac-toe. Tic-tac-toe is not a very interesting strategic game because it has a clear-cut answer that, I suspect, most of you know. Assuming people want to win and that they behave rationally—that is, they play a strategy that gives them the best chance of winning—tic-tac-toe will always end in a tie.

Formal game theory predicts that any tic-tac-toe game (or similar game) will end in a tie because formal game theory assumes all players (1) are fully forward-looking, (2) always behave in a manner that gives them the highest payoff, and (3) expect all other players to behave in that same manner. This is what we mean when we say that players are rational.

It is this assumption of rationality that allows us to give precise answers to game theoretic situations. Of course, people aren't always rational, and it is important to remember that formal game theory only provides a prediction about the outcome of a game. Actual behavior may deviate from the formal game theoretic predictions and modern behavioral economists use games in their experiments to discover where people's behavior is predictably irrational.

To compare the theoretical and empirical results, the real-world games that provide the empirical results must correspond to the assumptions of the theoretical model. Unfortunately, real-world games seldom do, which is why economists are turning more

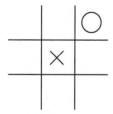

Formal game theory predicts that any tic-tac-toe game will end in a tie.

Behavioral economics examines the deviations between formal game theoretic predictions and actual outcomes of games.

Game Theory and Experimental Economics

Game theory has offered significant insight into the structure of economic problems but arrives at the conclusion that a number of alternative solutions are possible. A new branch of economics—experimental economics—has developed that offers insight into which outcome is most likely. Let's consider an example.

Based on experiments that involve games, economists have found that people believe that the other players in the game will work toward a cooperative solution. Thus, when the gains from cheating are not too great, often people do not choose the individual utility-maximizing position but instead choose a more cooperative strategy, at least initially. Such cooperative solutions tend to break down, however, as the benefits of cheating become larger. Additionally, as the number of participants gets larger, the less likely it is that the game will result in a cooperative rather than a competitive solution.

Experimental economists also have found that the structure of the game plays an important role in deciding the solution. For example, posted-price markets, in which the prices are explicitly announced, are more likely to

reach a collusive result than are nonposted- or uncertain-price markets, where actual sale prices are not known.

Experiments in game theory are used extensively in designing auctions for allocating such things as telecom licenses or oil leases. Seeing how these auctions were designed gives you a good sense of how game theory, experiments, and real-world experience are combined to design policy. The policy makers started with the results of the formal game and integrated those into the regulations of the actual bidding process. Then, game theorists pointed out how bidders could exploit loopholes in the regulations. Policy makers then modified the regulations and went through the process again, with game theorists pointing out potential loopholes. Eventually policy makers arrived at the best regulations they could design; then they turned to experimental economists who ran experimental auctions to see if the designs worked—much like airplane designs are tested in wind tunnels before they are actually built. Then the auctions were redesigned, and reconsidered by the game theorists, and, eventually, used as the regulations in auctions.

and more toward controlled experiments to test the predictions of games. These controlled experiments—either in the field, seeing what actually happens in real life when the games are played under various circumstances, or in the laboratory, where the game is structured to match the assumptions of the theory—are increasing, and the *experimental economics* branch of economics is increasing in importance. There is considerable debate about how much we can rely on such experiments since the controls are never, and often far from, perfect.

Strategies of Players

In backward induction, you begin with a desired outcome and then determine the decisions that will lead you to that outcome.

The analysis of games is often conducted by using a method called **backward induction,** where *you begin with a desired outcome and then determine the decisions that will lead you to that outcome.* With sequential decisions, you continue the backward induction until you arrive at the best strategy for your first move. The tic-tac-toe game is easy to analyze because it is a sequential game with a complete set of choices that can be determined by working backward from the desired outcome (winning the game) to the initial decision of where to place your X or O. Sometimes backward induction leads you to an optimal rollback strategy. *Optimal rollback strategies* are based on assuming your opponent follows her best strategy, which is based on assuming you follow your best strategy, which . . . Optimal rollback strategies are much harder to determine in simultaneous move games because you have to figure out what the person is *likely* to do when you are making your move. (As your hand flies out in a rock-paper-scissors game, you can't base your choice on your opponent's choice in the game.)

DOMINANT STRATEGY   As you saw in the prisoner's dilemma game, in some games, a player will prefer a strategy regardless of the opponent's move. No matter what choice one prisoner makes, assuming the other player is rational, the other prisoner's best strategy is to confess. As I discussed above, such a strategy is called a dominant strategy. So, even though the prisoner's dilemma is a simultaneous game, there is a dominant strategy, with both players "knowing" (given the assumptions of the model) what the other person will do.

A dominant strategy is a strategy that is preferred by a player regardless of the opponent's move.

MIXED STRATEGY   Many simultaneous games don't have a single dominant strategy. Again, consider rock-paper-scissors. Whether you choose rock, paper, or scissors depends on what your opponent chooses. What you don't want to happen is for your opponent to figure out a pattern in your choices. It makes sense to vary your choices randomly so that your opponent has no pattern on which to base his strategy. This strategy is called a **mixed strategy**—*a strategy of choosing randomly among moves.*

A mixed strategy is a strategy of choosing randomly among moves.

Even if a sequential game has an optimal solution, we may not be able to figure out that solution. Sequential move games can involve so many sequential moves that figuring out a rollback strategy is impossible. Chess is an example. Technically chess has a full rollback strategy—once the first move is made, if one has sufficiently powerful and fast computing ability, that person is the winner. But our computing ability is not sufficient to compute that rollback strategy; chess grand masters have defeated computers whose calculations were based on a rollback strategy. But computer chess moves do not have to be based solely on rollback strategies; they can be based on patterns ascertained by studying previous winning strategies. Computers whose strategy is based on a combination of rollback strategies *and* patterns of human play are able to beat grand masters in chess. Most games that people play in real life are far more complicated than chess, and thus require a combination of intuition, calculation, and common sense.

Chess is complicated.
©Kaikoro/Shutterstock

Strategies in games can change dramatically with just a single change in the rules. Consider the effect of moving from a game played only once to a game played repeatedly. Say you are playing the ultimatum game. As I discussed in an earlier chapter, in the ultimatum game, two players are offered $10 to split between the two of them, as long as they both agree to accept the money. One player is allowed to decide how to split the $10, and the other player has the choice of accepting the deal or not accepting the deal.

In a single-play ultimatum game, the optimal strategy, assuming people are concerned only with how much money they receive, is clear. The first player's optimal strategy is to give himself almost all the money, say $9.99, offering the second player 1 cent. The second player is clearly better off receiving the 1 cent rather than nothing, so his optimal strategy is to accept. In a repeated-play ultimatum game—a game that will be played a number of times with the same players—the strategy is not so clear-cut. By refusing the 1 cent, the second player can send a signal to the first player that if he wants to keep any of the money, he had better raise his offer. So repeated games offer more possibilities for implicit cooperation than do single-play games. The empirical evidence bears this out.

Q-6 In a single-play ultimatum game, what is the optimal strategy for the first player?

AN EXAMPLE OF STRATEGY: THE TWO-THIRDS GAME   Let's now consider another game, called the two-thirds game, that demonstrates how backward induction and rollback reasoning work. The two-thirds game is the following: You, and all members of your class, are to choose a number between 0 and 100. You win if the number you have chosen is two-thirds of the average chosen by the class. Before you proceed with reading the chapter, write down your choice.

What Game Is Being Played?

In analyzing a game, it is important to know how much players know about the game being played, and whether that knowledge is symmetrical—all players have equal information—or asymmetrical—one player has more information than the others. The implications of asymmetrical knowledge can be seen by considering a game played in the movie *The Princess Bride*. The game is a battle of wits, with the winner getting the heroine, Buttercup. In it, the hero, Westley, offers the villain, the Sicilian Vizzini, this challenge. Westley places two glasses of wine on the table and states that one contains a deadly poison. The game is for Vizzini to choose a glass, and then for them both to drink. Vizzini accepts the challenge. The scene goes as follows:

Westley: All right: where is the poison? The battle of wits has begun. It ends when you decide and we both drink, and find out who is right and who is dead.

At this point, Vizzini babbles on in order to get Westley to turn around; when Westley does so, Vizzini switches the glasses so that what Westley thinks is his glass is actually the glass that he thinks Vizzini is getting. By this move Vizzini figures he can win the game by changing it to a sequential game—he plans only to drink after Westley has drunk. Since he has switched the glasses, he figures that Westley will drink only if Westley believes that his is not the poisoned glass. Since the glasses are switched, that decision to drink will mean that Vizzini has the nonpoisoned glass, and thus Vizzini can drink safely. (He has switched the game into an asymmetric sequential game where he has the advantage.) The scene continues as follows:

Vizzini: Let's drink—me from my glass, and you from yours. [*Allowing Westley to drink first, he swallows his wine.*]

©Dmitry Travnikov/123RF

Westley: You guessed wrong.

Vizzini (roaring with laughter): You only think I guessed wrong—that's what's so funny! I switched glasses when your back was turned. You fool. You fell victim to one of the classic blunders. The most famous is "Never get involved in a land war in Asia." But only slightly less well known is this: "Never go in against a Sicilian when death is on the line."

[*He laughs and roars and cackles and whoops until he falls over dead.*]

[*At this point the heroine, Buttercup, enters the scene*]

Buttercup: To think—all that time it was your cup that was poisoned.

Westley: They were both poisoned. I spent the last few years building up an immunity to iocane powder.

The scene makes for some comic relief in the movie, but our interest is in the strategy. Given what Vizzini thought he knew, Vizzini's strategy was sound. But in this case, the game he thought he was playing was not the game he was playing. The game he was actually playing was a game in which he could only lose. This presents another lesson from game theory—often when another individual presents you with a choice, particularly one that seems especially beneficial, the choice you are making will often not be the choice you think you are making, and the game will often be rigged to your disadvantage (you don't have full information). Hence, the general rule of thumb: If it sounds too good to be true, most likely it is.

Source: *The Princess Bride* © 1987, Twentieth Century Fox Film Corporation.

Now, let's consider your reasoning. First, if you chose a number greater than 67, you were daydreaming rather than thinking. Even if all the other students chose 100, you would still lose, since 2/3 of 100 is 67. Now, let's say you thought a bit and assumed that people would choose randomly, which means that the average would be 50, and 2/3 of it would be 33. That would be a more likely answer, but John Nash wouldn't have thought much of it as an answer. Why? Because don't you think other people are as smart as you—and would use the same reasoning? That's the standard game theory assumption—that people will assume that others will use the best deductive reasoning possible. Making the assumption that people choose the best, we see that it makes sense to assume that people would not initially choose randomly, but instead would reason as you did—and choose 33, 2/3 of which would be 22, so it would make more sense to choose 22. However, even if you chose 22, you are still only partway toward thinking strategically.

I say partway to strategic thinking because 22 would not be the solution John Nash would have arrived at. He would have pointed out that if other people were following that same reasoning, they would have arrived at the same conclusion as you did, and would not have put down 22, but would have put down 2/3 of 22, or 14.7, so to choose any number higher than 14.7 is unreasonable. But that is not the end of the rollback reasoning. In fact, one can carry the reasoning back further and further, until finally the number you choose approaches zero. In fact, any number other than zero would lose to a smaller number. (This is the rollback strategy in action because the full set of choices is considered in light of the consequences for decisions of all players.) For this game, the Nash equilibrium is zero.

Q-7 What is the Nash equilibrium in the two-thirds game?

Informal Game Theory and Modern Behavioral Economics

Some games have no Nash equilibrium, and other games have an infinite number of them. Moreover, the probability of all people following their best strategy is highly unlikely, and thus, choosing the Nash equilibrium for the two-thirds game would almost always cause you to lose. (Actually, in first-time plays of the two-thirds game, the usual answer comes out with an average of about 30 to 40.) But then, if we play it again, after we have seen the answer to the first game, the average falls. Figure 20-2 shows the typical outcomes of multiple rounds of play. Initially the average guess is about 35, and it decreases with each additional time played.[4]

Notice that, as the game was played the second time, after the reasoning was explained, the average number chosen by students decreased, and hence moved toward the Nash equilibrium. These results demonstrate another aspect of game theory:

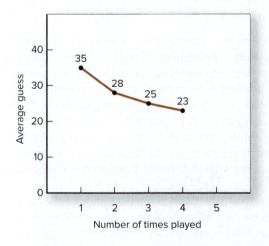

FIGURE 20-2 The Two-Thirds Game

Although when using an optimal rollback strategy the solution to the two-thirds game is zero, most people do not choose zero. Instead, as they play the game over and over again, their guesses fall from about 35 in the initial round to the 20s in the third and fourth rounds as this graph illustrates.

[4]For a discussion of evidence about playing the two-thirds game, see Virtudes Alba-Fernández, Pablo Brañas-Garza, Francisca Jiménez-Jiménez, and Javier Rodero-Cosano, "Teaching Nash Equilibrium and Dominance: A Classroom Experiment on the Beauty Contest," *Journal of Economic Education* 37, no. 3 (Summer 2006), pp. 305–22.

Players learn, which means that, in practice, repeated games often have different results than one-time games.

Even after the reasoning of the two-thirds game is fully explained to students, the average number they choose never reaches zero, so here we have an example of a game with a Nash equilibrium that, in practice, is not reached. One reason why the Nash equilibrium is not reached is that people's reasoning process is more complicated than assumed by Nash. People do not assume that all other people behave rationally; instead they are making complicated estimates of other people's behavior based on their past behavior and their sense of other people. This means that to apply game theory to real-world problems, game theory must be accompanied by a combination of reasoning, intuition, and empirical study about how people actually behave.

To apply game theory to real-world problems, game theory must be accompanied by a combination of reasoning, intuition, and empirical study about how people actually behave.

Informal Game Theory

While formal game theory can quickly become very complicated and mathematically intimidating, much of the power of game theory does not lie in its formal application, but rather in its informal application, which simply involves setting up a study of human interactions in a game theoretic or strategic framework. Informal game theory is often called *behavioral game theory* because it relies on empirical observation, not deductive logic alone, to determine the likely choices of individuals. Instead of assuming that people are high-powered calculating machines who can figure out their optimal strategy, no matter how complicated it may be (that's the Nash equilibrium), informal game theory looks at how people actually think and behave and is thus empirically based. Informal game theory doesn't provide definite answers; instead, it provides a framework for approaching questions.

This approach to game theory was developed by Nobel Prize winner Thomas Schelling, who argued that much of the power of game theory comes in the framework it provides for thinking about problems, rather than from formal solutions. The power of game theory comes from simply structuring a problem as a strategic interaction problem and writing down a payoff matrix. The box "The Segregation Game and Agent-Based Modeling" explores one of Schelling's informal models.

Real-World Applications of Informal Game Theory

In their book *The Art of Strategy,* economists Avinash Dixit and Barry Nalebuff describe a number of examples of real-world applications of informal game theory. Let's discuss a couple of them. The first involves the long-running TV show *Survivor*—a show that gains much of its interest by creating strategic problems for contestants that are mixed with games of skill. Each week one contestant is eliminated until two are left, at which time all the eliminated contestants get to vote on who will be the Sole Survivor and win the grand million-dollar prize. This means that contestants must be ruthless (think about how to get other people thrown off), but also be considered fair and nice so that they are not voted off in the final round. That's the show's hook.

The TV show *Survivor* is a game of strategy.

The situation Dixit and Nalebuff describe is probably the most famous episode of the show in which eventually the three players left were Rudy, a former Navy Seal, who was seen as honest and fair and was most people's favorite; Richard, a corporate consultant who was seen as a cold and calculating "pudgy nudist"; and Kelly, a 23-year-old river guide who was also seen as cold and calculating, although maybe a bit less than Richard, and definitely not pudgy. In the final challenge, the three of them had to stand on a pole with one hand on something called the immunity idol for as long as they could. The one who stayed on the longest would win the challenge and would get to decide which two went into the final.

The Segregation Game and Agent-Based Modeling

To see the power of economist Thomas Schelling's informal approach to game theory, let us consider one of his thought experiments that uses the game theory framework. In this example, the question he was interested in was why our society is so segregated when much of the population seems to have only slight tendencies toward segregation. As he was thinking of this question, he imagined a society with two types of individuals. Both types had only a slight preference for living next to individuals from their own group, but that preference was not strong. His question was: Would that slight preference lead to significant segregation on the aggregate level?

To answer the question, he created a model that consists of a grid. On this grid he assumed people have a slight preference for living next to people with their same characteristics. He then went through a variety of experiments that explored the impact of that slight preference. What he discovered was that a slight individual preference for living next to a person who is similar to oneself could lead to significant aggregate segregation. Schelling's "game" has been computerized and can be explored on the web (www.econ.iastate.edu/tesfatsi/demos/schelling/schellhp.htm).

As you play this game, notice that although the game has no single solution, it does give you insight into the process through which segregation comes about. When Schelling first devised his game, powerful computers were still in their infancy. That has now changed. Schelling's approach has led to a whole field of economics, called agent-based modeling, in which agents are "created" by the computer and then allowed to interact. The researchers then look at the resulting patterns of behavior and try to use those patterns to understand complex economic phenomena. Ultimately, such agent-based computational economics (ACE) modelers hope to create virtual economies, in which one can test the effects of policy in the "virtual economy" before one adopts it in practice. We are a long way from that goal, but it has already had some interesting uses. For example, Disneyland has used agent-based modeling to keep its lines as short as possible.

Both Kelly and Richard knew that if Rudy made it to the final, he would win since he was the other players' favorite. So they both wanted Rudy off. The problem for Richard was that he had an alliance with Rudy, and if he won the challenge and kicked Rudy off, he would have to violate the alliance and would likely lose to Kelly in the final show. Thus, the options from Richard's perspective:

- Rudy wins—Rudy would pick Richard to continue, but Rudy would beat Richard in the final.
- Kelly wins—Kelly would pick Richard to continue, and it is unclear who would win.
- Richard wins—Richard would either pick Rudy to continue, but then would lose in the final, or pick Kelly to continue, in which case, because he had broken his alliance with Rudy, he would almost certainly lose in the final voting.

Given these options, Dixit and Nalebuff point out that Richard has a dominant strategy—to lose, hoping that Kelly wins. Richard did precisely that—he quit the immunity challenge early; Kelly won the challenge, chose Richard to continue, and, in the final voting, Richard won the million-dollar prize. Rudy cast the deciding vote for Richard, even though Richard's losing on purpose had effectively cost Rudy the game.

A second example they give involves a proposal by American billionaire Warren Buffett to get a strict campaign finance reform bill passed. In an op-ed piece in the *New York Times,* Buffett proposed banning many types of campaign contributions that most people believe should be banned; such a ban would make it more difficult for incumbents to win elections. The problem is that incumbents are the ones who vote on campaign reform bills and they have little incentive to vote for effective campaign finance reform since that would make it hard for them to win elections. Thus, while incumbents want to portray themselves as being in favor of campaign finance reform, they don't really want the bill to pass. To get around the problem, Buffett put forward the following suggestion:

> Well just suppose some eccentric billionaire (not me, not me!) made the following offer: If the bill was defeated, this person—the EB—would donate $1 billion in an allowable manner (soft money makes all possible) to the political party that had delivered the most votes to getting it passed. Given this diabolical application of game theory, the bill would sail through Congress and thus cost our EB nothing (establishing him as not so eccentric after all).[5]

The proposal places both Democrats and Republicans in a prisoner's dilemma. Consider their options. If they vote against the bill and the bill is successful, they will deliver $1 billion to the other party, which will give the other party an enormous advantage in the next election, offsetting their advantage in fund-raising. Thus, there is no gain in opposing the bill for a party if the other party supports it. This means that the dominant strategy for both sides would be to support the bill. So the bill would pass.

As a bonus, Buffett noted that the effectiveness of the plan "would highlight the absurdity of claims that money doesn't influence Congressional votes." Unfortunately no eccentric billionaire has come forward with the offer, and with the continued increase in political party fund-raising, it will likely take an eccentric multibillionaire today to implement it.

There are many more applications of the ideas in informal game theory to the real world, and much of modern economic thinking involves posing problems as strategic games, analyzing the strategic decision-making problem facing both sides, and designing an institutional structure that achieves the goals one wants to achieve.

An Application of Game Theory: Auction Markets

■ Web Note 20.4

Googlenomics

Game theory has highlighted the importance of strategy in individuals' decision making. Looking at problems with this approach has resulted in extraordinarily powerful solutions to economic problems. Let's consider one example that was devised by Nobel Prize–winning economist William Vickrey.

He analyzed the strategies of people in a standard sealed-bid auction where participants do not know the value of other bids. In a standard auction, the person who bids the highest gets the good. Let's say that you are bidding on a computer that you really want, for which you would be willing to pay $500. In this auction, if you were fully rational and Nash-like, would you bid $500? The answer is no; that's not your best strategy; your best strategy is to lower your bid enough so that it is slightly higher than what you expect the next highest bidder to bid. If you believe that to be very low, you can do much better than paying your full price.

Q-8 How does a Vickrey auction differ from a standard sealed-bid auction?

Vickrey suggested what is now called the **Vickrey auction**—*a sealed-bid auction where the highest bidder wins but pays the price bid by the next-highest bidder.* He demonstrated that this second-highest-bid auction changes the strategy of the bidders, giving them an incentive to bid their true valuation for the good since by bidding his or her true value, a bidder will win the auction without paying the higher amount.

In a highest-bid auction, a bidder's strategy is to not bid the highest, but rather to bid slightly higher than the next-highest bidder. Say you would be willing to pay $500, but you think the next-highest bidder will bid only $220. You might bid $230 since if you bid $500 you would be paying $270 more than you had to pay. In a Vickrey

---

[5]Warren Buffett, *New York Times*, September 10, 2000. This material is copyrighted and used with permission of the author.

auction, your strategy changes. Since you are not paying your bid, but rather the second-highest bid, you could bid $500, and if the second-highest bidder bid only $220, you would pay only $220.

The advantage of the Vickrey auction becomes more apparent when you incorrectly guessed the second-highest bidder's bid. Say that second-highest bid was $300, but you thought it was going to be only $220, so you bid $250. In the standard auction, you would not win—the other bidder would win, even though you were willing to pay more for it. In the Vickrey auction bid, the person who wants it most wins. Vickrey auctions are now often used in auctions for oil lease rights, radio spectrums, and Google's online advertisement program AdWords.

Game Theory and the Challenge to Standard Economic Assumptions

While formal game theory relies upon precise definitions of rationality, informal game theory is used to explore what rationality is and the nature of individuals' utility functions. Modern behavioral economists use an approach that builds on the traditional economics that you've been presented with in earlier chapters—utility maximization, equilibrium, and efficiency—but instead of stopping there, and assuming that the theory has to be right, extends the theory to fit the observations in the real world, modifying the theory where necessary to achieve the fit. This means that instead of exploring the theoretical results of a formal model with a set of assumptions, behavioral economists use *experiments* in which people actually play the formal games to explore the validity of the assumptions in formal game theory and how they might be revised. Work in behavioral economics has led to significant advances in our understanding of the nature of preferences and choice.

For example, one of the basic assumptions of economics is that people are self-interested, and they do what benefits them. In some ways, this assumption is true by definition. One can assume that altruistic people help others because other people's welfare is a component of their utility function. Such a tautological approach to the analysis of choice is not especially helpful, since it is true by definition. Game theory allows us to explore the degree to which, and the nature in which, individuals are concerned with the welfare of others.

Fairness

Consider a variation of the ultimatum game called the trust game. As with the ultimatum game, the trust game has two players. The first player is given $10 and the choice about how to split it. The difference is that she can either keep it all for herself or "invest" some portion, which is tripled and given to the other player. The second person, called the "trustee," can either keep the now tripled amount or return some portion of it to the first person. At this point the game ends. The Nash equilibrium of this game—what would happen if people are concerned only with themselves, and are fully "rational"—is for the first player to keep the entire $10.

The rollback reasoning (beginning with the last choice) goes like this: The dominant strategy of the "trustee" is to keep any money that is shared since there is no opportunity for the first player to reciprocate. Knowing that, the dominant strategy for the first person is to share nothing in the first place. No gains from cooperation are possible.

Experimental evidence shows that, on average, individuals invest about $5 in cooperation and, on average, trustees return a little less than their investment. It is as if people want to trust and to reward trust. In other experiments, it has been found that

Web Note 20.5

The Dictator Game

people will even spend money of their own to punish others who do not respond "fairly" to offers. So, if people feel someone is being unfair, people will reduce their own income to make that person pay.

Endowment Effects

Web Note 20.6

Opting In or Opting Out?

The endowment effect is the tendency of people to value an item that they possess more than they would value that item if they did not possess it.

Another example of empirical work suggesting that people do not behave as the traditional model predicts concerns how people value things. Standard economic theory assumes that the value of something is independent of whether you own the item or not; that is, preferences are independent of endowment. To test whether this is true, Stanford neuropsychologist Brian Knutson did an experiment where he offered people either an iPod or $100. When given the opportunity to choose between the two, most people chose $100. But when participants were initially given an iPod, but then were offered $100 in exchange for the iPod, most chose to keep the iPod. This is called the **endowment effect**—*the tendency of people to value an item that they possess more than they would value that item if they did not possess it.* That ownership increases the value of a good is even confirmed by brain scans that show increased brain activity associated with fear of loss when a good is acquired. Experiments suggest that the traditional assumptions about economic behavior do not always reflect actual behavior.

Framing Effects

Framing effects are the tendency of people to base their choices on how the choice is presented.

Another finding of behavioral economics is the importance of **framing effects**—*the tendency of people to base their choices on how the choice is presented.* The classic example of framing effects was presented by Columbia psychologist Amos Tversky and Princeton psychologist Daniel Kahneman. They asked people how they would respond in the following situations regarding 600 people who were threatened by a disease. Subjects were given the following two undesirable options. In the first experiment, the options were: (A) a guarantee of saving 200 lives for sure but losing the others or (B) a 1/3 chance of saving all 600, but a 2/3 chance of saving no one. Most people chose A over B. Then, they offered the same people the following choices: (A) a guaranteed outcome of losing 400 lives for sure but saving the others or (B) a 2/3 chance of 600 dying and a 1/3 chance of no one dying. Most people chose B over A. Now consider the two sets of choices—they are exactly the same, but people responded differently if the choice was presented in the negative rather than the positive frame. This result has been widely duplicated, and framing effects are an important part of modern economics.

Q-9 If a firm wants to increase the number of employees who participate in a savings plan, should the enrollment form ask whether the employee wants an automatic withdrawal from a paycheck to retirement or an automatic deposit to retirement from a paycheck?

Behavioral Economics and the Traditional Model

There are many more such findings, and behavioral economists are attempting to integrate those findings with traditional economic reasoning. As they do this, the methods of economics are changing. As I stated above, game theory is growing enormously in importance. Why? Because game theory allows a wider range of assumptions than does standard theory—which allows us to state the economic result more precisely. But, as we saw in the example of the two-thirds game, game theory alone does not provide answers. Thus, economists are doing much more in the way of empirical work and incorporating experimental work into their methodology.

Experimental economics is a burgeoning field. It includes laboratory experiments in which assumptions of the economic model are carefully followed, to see how subjects actually respond, and field experiments, in which the precise conditions are not as carefully controlled, but subjects are provided a more realistic setting. Behavioral economists also use computer simulations and even brain scans. One of the branches of behavioral economics is called neuroeconomics, which relies on CAT scans of individuals' brains to study individual choices.

What comes out of behavioral economics is a much more nuanced view of humans. They are purposeful, rather than fully rational; they demonstrate enlightened self-interest rather than greed; and they are boundedly rational rather than fully "Nash-style" rational.

Behavioral economics provides a more nuanced view of human behavior than does standard economics.

The Importance of the Traditional Model: Money Is Not Left on the Table

The fact that people do not act as the traditional economic model predicts does not mean that the traditional assumptions and model are irrelevant—quite the contrary. People acting differently than they would if the standard rationality assumptions hold true creates potential profit opportunities for individuals to take advantage of people's actual behavior. It means that "money is being left on the table." Whenever "money is left on the table," we can expect firms and individuals who understand the economic model to develop businesses and schemes to take that money off the table—to transfer money from those who are acting "irrationally" to those who are acting "rationally." What this means is that the findings of behavioral economics make understanding the logic of the traditional model even more important than it would be if everyone acted according to its assumptions. If you don't understand it, you can expect to lose money to those who do. The point is that the traditional economic model doesn't require everyone, or even a majority of people, to behave in accordance with its assumptions for its predictions to come true. All it takes is a few people to behave rationally because those few can develop businesses and institutions that make people pay for their "irrationality" and lack of self-interest.

Whenever "money is left on the table," we can expect firms and individuals who understand the economic model to develop businesses and schemes to take that money off the table.

Q-10 If 90 percent of people operate as behavioral economics suggests, does that mean that the standard economic model is no longer applicable?

Advertising mutual funds is an example. Those advertisements emphasize past performance, and in selling actively managed mutual funds (which have higher management fees) firms strongly emphasize past performance, even though past performance of a mutual fund often has little or no predictive power of future earnings of that mutual fund. Often investment companies have many actively managed mutual funds, some of which do well in a specific time period, and some of which do poorly, just because of random variation. With a variety of such funds, they can always have some that have done better than average. When the mutual fund salesperson calls his clientele, he will push the actively managed funds that have done well, taking advantage of people's tendency to think that past history is more relevant to future behavior than it often is. Investment salespeople and fund managers make a good living selling such funds—that's the transfer of money from the unwise (in an economic sense) to the wise (in an economic sense). Most economists suggest that the way around this is to buy indexed mutual funds, which are mutual funds that contain a broad set of stocks that reflect the broader market and are not actively managed. These index funds have much smaller fees and avoid "leaving money on the table" that can be transferred to those who understand the economic model.

Conclusion

Let me now conclude. I hope that this chapter shows you that if you had concerns about whether the traditional models learned in earlier chapters fit reality, they were legitimate concerns. Economic models don't tell you how people should behave, or how they do behave. They aren't meant to do that. Instead, they give insights into how people behave, and how to think strategically. Any economic model must be used with judgment. As Alfred Marshall, an economist whose approach I have followed, said, "The economic model is not a tool that gives answers to questions; it is an apparatus of the mind that helps its possessor come to reasonable conclusions." The overall logic of the economic model provides insight even if most people do not behave as the assumptions predict. Money is not left on the table, and when people act differently than the economic model, we can expect people and firms to figure out ways to take advantage of their behavior.

Those concerns that you had about the relevance of the traditional economic models are also concerns that economists have, and are the basis of current research. In their research economists are pushing the boundaries of the traditional model and are developing new models to include such concerns. Don't think of economic theory as a static, unchanging theory; think of it as a dynamic theory, which is continually taking into account new discoveries and incorporating those discoveries into the model.

Summary

- Game theory is a highly flexible modeling approach that can be used to study a variety of situations in which decisions are interdependent. (*LO20-1*)

- A prisoner's dilemma game is one in which both players have a dominant strategy that leads them to a jointly undesirable outcome. (*LO20-1*)

- A payoff matrix provides a summary of each player's strategies and how the outcomes of their choices depend on the actions of other players. (*LO20-1*)

- A Nash equilibrium is an equilibrium of a game that results from a noncooperative game when each player plays his or her best strategy. With a Nash equilibrium, no player can improve his or her payoff by changing strategy unilaterally. (*LO20-1*)

- A dominant strategy is one that is preferred regardless of one's opponent's move. A mixed strategy is choosing randomly. (*LO20-1*)

- The strategies of players are different in simultaneous and sequential games. (*LO20-2*)

- Sometimes people follow a mixed strategy of choosing randomly among moves. (*LO20-2*)

- Behavioral economics examines deviations between formal game theoretic predictions and actual outcomes of games. (*LO20-3*)

- Insights from behavioral economics can be applied to real-world decision making such as in auctions. (*LO20-3*)

- Endowment and framing effects are examples of findings in behavioral economics that challenge the traditional model's predictions. (*LO20-4*)

- The traditional model remains relevant because it takes only a few people to realize that money has been left on the table for the results of the standard model to hold. (*LO20-4*)

Key Terms

backward induction
cheap talk
cooperative game
dominant strategy
endowment effect
framing effect
game theory
mixed strategy
Nash equilibrium
noncooperative game
payoff matrix
prisoner's dilemma
screening question
sequential game
simultaneous move game
Vickrey auction

Questions and Exercises ■ connect·

1. Define the prisoner's dilemma game. *(LO20-1)*
   a. What assumptions lead to the dilemma?
   b. What creates the possibility of escaping it?
   c. What does the standard model say about your answer to *b*? What does experimental economics say?

2. In the following payoff matrix, Player A announces that she will cooperate. *(LO20-1)*
   a. How is this likely to change the outcome compared to when neither cooperates?
   b. What does your answer to *a* suggest about the value of cheap talk?
   c. How could Player A make her pronouncement believable?

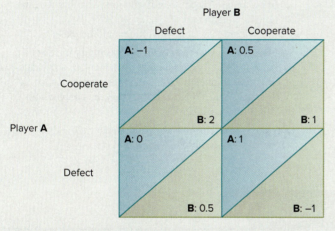

3. Is the solution to the prisoner's dilemma game a Nash equilibrium? Why? *(LO20-1)*

4. If a player does not have a dominant strategy, can the game still have a Nash equilibrium? *(LO20-1)*

5. Two firms have entered an agreement to set prices. The accompanying payoff matrix shows profit for each firm in a market depending upon whether the firm cheats on the agreement by reducing its prices. *(LO20-1)*
   a. What is the dominant strategy for each firm, if any?
   b. What is the Nash equilibrium, if any?

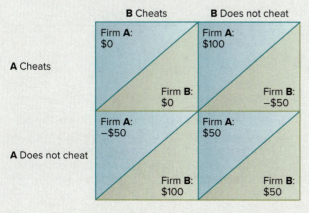

6. Two people are arrested and charged with the same crime. Each is given the opportunity to accuse the other of the crime. The payoff matrix shows how much time each will serve depending on who rats out whom. *(LO20-1)*
   a. What is the dominant strategy for each, if any?
   b. What is the Nash equilibrium, if any?

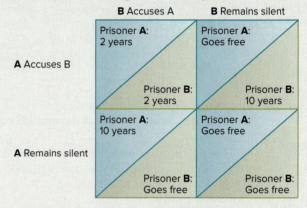

7. For each of the following, state whether Player A and Player B have a dominant strategy and, if so, what each player's dominant strategy is. *(LO20-1)*

   a.

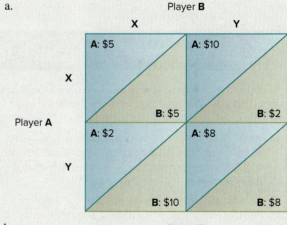

   b.

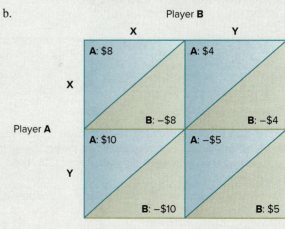

c.

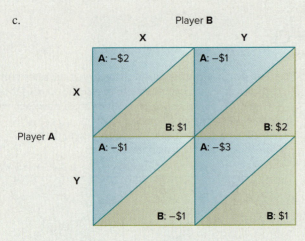

8. Would the results of the prisoner's dilemma game be different if it were a sequential rather than a simultaneous game? *(LO20-2)*

9. State whether each of the following situations is a simultaneous or sequential game. Explain your answer. *(LO20-2)*
   a. A congressional vote by roll call.
   b. The ultimatum game.
   c. The Civil War.
   d. The segregation game (requires reading the box "The Segregation Game and Agent-Based Modeling").

10. Can a player have a rollback strategy in a simultaneous move game? *(LO20-2)*

11. True or false? If a game has a Nash equilibrium, that equilibrium will be the equilibrium that we expect to observe in the real world. *(LO20-2)*

12. Why might the multiple-play ultimatum game have a different result than the single-play ultimatum game? *(LO20-2)*

13. Why do sellers generally prefer a Vickrey auction to a regular sealed bid if sellers don't receive the highest bid in the Vickrey auction? *(LO20-3)*

14. Say that you are bidding in a sealed-bid auction and that you really want the item being auctioned. Winning it would be worth $250 to you. Say you expect the next-highest bidder to bid $100. *(LO20-3)*
   a. In a standard "highest-bid" auction, what bid would a rational person make?
   b. In a Vickrey auction, what bid would he make?

15. When consumers were given the opportunity to select a package of ground beef labeled "75% lean" or a package of ground beef labeled "25% fat," most consumers chose "75% lean." Why? What concept from the chapter does this illustrate? *(LO20-4)*

16. Why does it take just a few people to act rationally for the standard model to hold? *(LO20-4)*

Issues to Ponder

1. How is the fact that employers look to see that applicants took difficult courses in college, even though the subject matter has no bearing on the work they will likely do, an example of screening?

2. How is investing in the stock market similar to playing the two-thirds game?

3. In 1950, economists Merrill Flood and Melvin Dresher devised an experiment to challenge the Nash equilibrium. They presented the following payoff matrix to two economists and asked them to play the following game 100 times in succession:

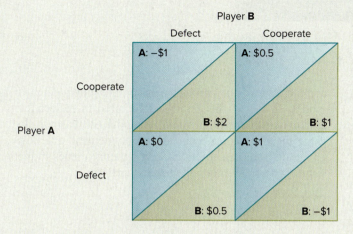

a. What is the Nash equilibrium of this payoff matrix?
b. Is the payoff matrix symmetric? If not, who has the advantage? Do you think this affected the strategy of the players? If so, how?
c. In 60 of the 100 games, the players cooperated. Why do you think this was so?
d. What do you suppose the players chose for the 100th play? Why?

4. In 1970 economist Martin Shubik proposed a game that involved auctioning off a one-dollar bill with the following rules:

   1. The highest bidder wins the dollar bill and pays his bid.

   2. The *second-highest* bidder also has to pay the amount of his last bid—and gets *nothing* in return.

   3. Each new bid has to be higher than the current high bid.

4. The game ends when there is no new bid within a specified time limit.
   a. When the dollar was auctioned off, do you suppose that the highest bid was less than or greater than a dollar? Why?
   b. Can a rational player ever allow himself to lose the auction once he has started bidding?
   c. Is it rational to begin bidding?

5. Suppose the two-thirds game described in the chapter were changed to the "average" game, so that the class had to guess a number between 0 and 100, and the person who wins is the person who guesses closest to the average number.
   a. What would the Nash equilibrium likely be?
   b. If your class played this "average" game, would you expect the equilibrium to approach the Nash equilibrium?
   c. If the equilibrium in playing the real-world game is not the Nash equilibrium, what might explain the difference?

6. Say that 90 percent of the people in a market demonstrate the endowment effect and 10 percent are "rational." Say that, initially, all people have equal wealth.
   a. How would you expect the wealth distribution to change over time?
   b. Would you expect the traditional model's predictions, which are based on the assumption of rationality, to be correct? Why?
   c. How might you determine the percentage of "rational" people needed for the standard model to give accurate aggregate predictions?

7. In a Vickrey auction how would a person's bid differ if she knew that the seller had someone at the auction submitting a bid for the seller?

Answers to Margin Questions

1. False. The two are not inconsistent. Game theory is a more flexible framework than supply/demand analysis because it can account for less restrictive assumptions compared to supply/demand analysis.   (*LO20-1*)

2. If A confesses, B's best strategy is also to confess. (*LO20-1*)

3. If A does not confess, B's best strategy is to confess. (*LO20-1*)

4. Assuming that love means they trust one another, both are more likely to choose to not confess. Each person is willing to do what is necessary to show his or her love and care for the other.   (*LO20-1*)

5. Because cheap talk carries no cost and is unenforceable, it is not expected to influence the results of a game. (*LO20-1*)

6. The optimal strategy for the first player of a single-play ultimatum game is to offer as little as possible to the second player because the second player is better off with any amount greater than zero.   (*LO20-2*)

7. The Nash equilibrium in the two-thirds game is zero. (*LO20-2*)

8. In a Vickrey auction, the highest bidder wins but pays the second-highest bid, while in a standard sealed-bid auction, the highest bidder wins and pays the highest bid.   (*LO20-3*)

9. Assuming positive framing effects, the question should be framed as a contribution to retirement rather than a withdrawal from a paycheck.   (*LO20-4*)

10. No, it does not. The remaining 10 percent of rational people will develop businesses to make the remaining 90 percent pay for their irrationality and lead the overall economy to the results of the traditional model.   (*LO20-4*)

Game Theory and Oligopoly

This chapter discussed game theory and its ability to shed light on a broader set of issues than the traditional model. You can see the power of game theory by applying it to oligopoly. As discussed in Chapter 15, oligopoly involves *strategic interaction* in which the firms take into account the decisions of the other firms. In all the other basic models—supply/demand, perfect competition, monopolistic competition, and monopoly—firms did not take into account the decisions of other firms. In those models, firms assumed that their decisions had no effect on other firms' decisions. In perfect competition and monopolistic competition, the argument justifying that assumption was that the firms were so small that their decisions didn't matter to others in the industry; in monopoly, the argument justifying that assumption was that the firm faced no competitors, so there was no other firm to consider. In oligopoly that wasn't the case, which meant that we could not develop a neat formal geometric model of firm behavior.

Game theory allows us to develop more precise models of oligopolistic markets, and of all situations that involve strategic interaction. Thus, game theory can be seen as a complement to, not a replacement for, the supply/demand model. In fact if the game is structured to reflect the assumptions of the supply/demand model, the reasoning in game theory is consistent with supply/demand analysis. Given the same assumptions, game theory comes to the same conclusions as supply/demand analysis.

Prisoner's Dilemma and a Duopoly Example

The easiest application of game theory to oligopoly involves the prisoner's dilemma. To keep the analysis easy, we will assume there are only two firms in the market, which makes the oligopoly what is called a **duopoly**—*an oligopoly with only two firms.* So let us consider the strategic decisions facing a "foam peanut" (packing material) company in a duopoly. Let us assume that the average total cost and marginal cost of producing foam peanuts are the same for both firms. These costs are shown in Figure A20-1(a).

FIGURE A20-1 (A AND B) **Firm and Industry Duopoly Cooperative Equilibrium**

In (**a**) I show the marginal and average total cost curves for either firm in the duopoly. To get the average and marginal costs for the industry, you double each. In (**b**) the industry marginal cost curve (the horizontal sum of the individual firms' marginal cost curves) is combined with the industry demand and marginal revenue curves. At the competitive solution for the industry, output is 8,000 and price is $500. As you can see in (**a**), at that price economic profits are zero. At the monopolistic solution, output is 6,000 and price is $600. As you can see in (**a**), ATC is $575 at an industry output of 6,000 (firm output of 3,000), so each firm's profit is $25 × 3,000 = $75,000 [the shaded area in (**a**)].

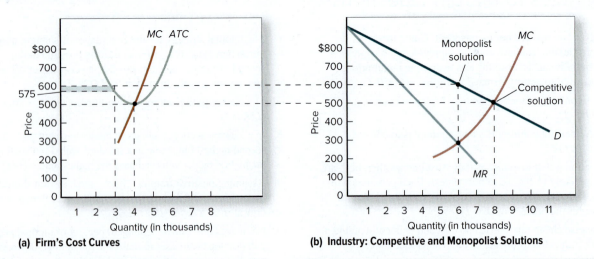

(a) **Firm's Cost Curves**

(b) **Industry: Competitive and Monopolist Solutions**

Assume that a production facility with a minimum efficient scale of 4,000 tons is the smallest that can be built. In Figure A20-1(b), the marginal costs are summed and the industry demand curve is drawn in a way that the competitive price is $500 per ton and the competitive output is 8,000 tons. The relevant industry marginal revenue curve is also drawn.

If the firms can coordinate their actions (fully collude), they will act as a joint monopolist setting total output at 6,000 tons where $MR = MC$ (3,000 tons each). As you can see in Figure A20-1(a), this gives each a price of $600 with a cost of $575 per ton, for a joint economic profit of $150,000, or $75,000 each. If the firms do not coordinate their actions, they will produce where the MC curve intersects the demand curve, setting output at 8,000 tons, producing 4,000 tons each. At this level of output, price is $500 a ton. With average costs of $500, neither earns an economic profit. The firms prefer fully colluding to the situation where they do not coordinate their actions (the competitive equilibrium), where they earn zero economic profit.

If they can ensure that they will both abide by the agreement, the monopolist output will be the joint profit-maximizing output. But the strategic reasoning doesn't end there. What if one firm reasons that it can earn more by cheating on the deal? What if one firm produces 4,000

tons (1,000 tons under the counter)? The additional 1,000 tons in output will cause the price to fall to $550 per ton. The cheating firm's average total costs fall to $500 as its output rises to 4,000, so its profit rises to $200,000. However, the noncheating firm's profit moves in the opposite direction. Its average total costs remain $575, but the price it receives falls to $550, so it loses $75,000 instead of making $75,000. The division of profits and output is shown in Figure A20-2.

In Figure A20-2(a), you can see that the firm that abides by the agreement and produces 3,000 units makes a loss of $75,000; its average total costs are $575 and the price it receives is $550. In Figure A20-2(b), you can see that the cheating firm makes a profit of $200,000; its average costs are $500, so it is doing much better than when it did not cheat. The combined profit of the cheating and the noncheating firms is $125,000 ($200,000 − $75,000 = $125,000), which is lower than if they cooperated. By cheating, the firm has essentially transferred $125,000 of the other firm's profit to itself and has reduced their combined profit by $25,000. Figure A20-2(c) shows how output is split between the two firms.

Once the other firm realizes that the first firm will benefit by cheating and cannot enforce the agreement, it will do better by cheating too. By cheating, it eliminates its loss and the other firm's profit. Output moves to the

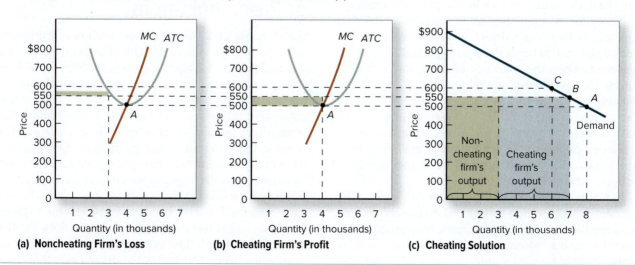

FIGURE A20-2 (A, B, AND C)   **Firm and Industry Duopoly Equilibrium When One Firm Cheats**

Figures (a) and (b) show the noncheating and the cheating firms' output and profit, respectively, while (c) shows the industry output and price. Say they both cheat. The price is $500 and output is 8,000 (4,000 per firm) [point A in (c)]. Both firms make zero profit. If neither cheats, the industry output is 6,000, the price is $600, and their ATC is $575. This outcome gives them a profit of $75,000 each and would place them at point C in (c). If one firm cheats and the other does not, the output is 7,000 and the industry price is $550 [point B in (c)]. The noncheating firm's $75,000 loss is shown by the shaded area in (a). The cheating firm's $200,000 profit is shown by the shaded area in (b).

(a) **Noncheating Firm's Loss**   (b) **Cheating Firm's Profit**   (c) **Cheating Solution**

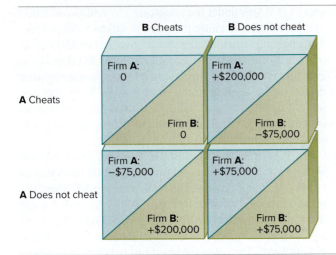

FIGURE A20-3   **The Payoff Matrix of Strategic Pricing Duopoly**

The strategic dilemma facing each firm in a duopoly can be shown in a payoff matrix that captures the four possible outcomes. A's strategies are listed vertically; B's strategies are listed horizontally. The payoffs of the combined strategies for both firms are shown in the four boxes of the matrix, with B's payoff shown in the green shaded triangles and A's payoff shown in the blue shaded triangles. For example, if A cheats but B doesn't, A makes a profit of $200,000, but B loses $75,000.

Their combined optimal strategy is to cartelize and achieve the monopoly payoff, with both firms receiving a profit of $75,000. However, each must expect that if it doesn't cheat and the other does cheat, it will lose $75,000. To avoid losing that $75,000, both firms will cheat, which leads them to the payoff in the upper-left corner—the competitive solution with zero profit for each firm.

competitive output, 8,000, and both of the firms make zero profit.

It is precisely to provide insight into this type of strategic situation that game theory was developed. It does so by analyzing the strategies of both firms under all circumstances and placing the combination in a payoff matrix.

Duopoly and a Payoff Matrix

The duopoly presented above is a variation of the prisoner's dilemma game. The results can also be presented in a payoff matrix that captures the essence of the prisoner's dilemma. In Figure A20-3, each square shows the payoff from a pair of decisions listed in the columns and rows.

The blue triangles show A's profit; the green triangles show B's profit. For example, if neither cheats, the result for both is shown in the lower-right square, and if they both cheat, the result is shown in the upper-left square.

Notice the dilemma they are in if cheating cannot be detected. If they can't detect whether the other one cheated and each believes the other is maximizing profit, each must expect the other one to cheat. But if firm A expects firm B to cheat, the relevant payoffs are in the first column. Given this expectation, if firm A doesn't cheat, it loses $75,000. So firm A's optimal strategy is to cheat. Similarly for firm B. If it expects firm A to cheat, its relevant payoffs are in the first row. Firm B's optimal strategy is to cheat. But if they both cheat, they end up in the upper-left square with zero profit.

In reality, of course, cheating is partially detectable, and even though explicit collusion and enforceable contracts are illegal in the United States, implicit collusive contracts are not. Moreover, in markets where similar conditions hold time after time, the cooperative solution is more likely since each firm will acquire a reputation

based on its past actions, and firms can retaliate against other firms that cheat. But the basic dilemma remains for firms and tends to push oligopolies toward a zero-profit competitive solution.

The push toward a zero-profit equilibrium can be seen in a price war between Amazon.com and Walmart.com. When Walmart dropped its free shipping minimum from $49 to $35, Amazon matched the minimum. Three months later Amazon beat Walmart's free shipping threshold by lowering its minimum to $25. Another example is in airline pricing. When a low-fare airline enters a market, the existing airlines generally match, or even go below, the low-fare airline's fare.

Low-Price Guarantees: The Advantage of Rules or Precommitment

Game theory also sheds light on institutional arrangements of oligopolistic firms. One that has now become standard practice for many oligopolistic firms is the low-price guarantee, in which a store states that it will guarantee that the price it charges is lower than the price at any other store in the area. To back up that guarantee, the store offers any customer who finds a lower price a "double the difference back guarantee." One's initial thought likely is that such low-price guarantees are good for consumers—they guarantee consumers low prices. But when considering the low-price guarantee within a game theoretic framework, that conclusion is not so clear.

Notice what the low-price guarantee does for the seller: It provides information about the pricing of competing firms, and warns the other firms that their competitor will have that information very quickly.

Second, consider what this low-price guarantee does to the other firm's strategy. With the low-price guarantee, it knows that if it tries to charge a lower price, the other store will quickly and automatically reduce its price to one even lower. So, it now makes little sense to try to compete on price. Paradoxically, the net effect of the "low-price guarantee" can be to raise the overall price that consumers pay.

Key Term

duopoly

Questions and Exercises

1. Netflix and Hulu each expect profit to rise by $100,000 in the coming year. Netflix, thinking that it would like its net profit to rise by more, considers advertising during the Super Bowl. An advertisement during the Super Bowl will cost $80,000. If Netflix advertises, and Hulu does not, it expects its profit to rise by $230,000 instead of $100,000, while Hulu's profit will rise by only $50,000. Netflix also knows that if it does not advertise, but Hulu does, its profit will rise by only $50,000 while Hulu's profit will rise by $230,000 instead of just $100,000. If both firms advertise, their profit will rise by the same as if neither had advertised, except each will have spent $80,000 for the ad.
   a. Develop the payoff matrix for the decision facing Netflix and Hulu.
   b. Is there a dominant strategy?
   c. If so, what is it?

2. Two firms, TwiddleDee and TwiddleDum, make up the entire market for widgets. They have identical costs. They are currently colluding explicitly and are making $2 million each. TwiddleDee has a new CEO, Mr. Notsonice, who is considering cheating and producing more than he has agreed to produce. He has been informed by his able assistant that if he cheats, he can increase the firm's profit by $1 million at the cost of TwiddleDum losing $1 million of its profits. If both cheat, their profits are $1.5 million each. (TwiddleDum faces the same option.) You have been hired to advise Mr. Notsonice.
   a. Construct a payoff matrix for him that captures the essence of the decision.
   b. If the game is played only once, what strategy would you advise?
   c. How would your answer to b change if the game were to be played many times?

Design elements: Web Note icon: ©McGraw-Hill Education; Real-World Application icon: ©McGraw-Hill Education; A Reminder icon: ©McGraw-Hill Education; Added Dimension icon: ©McGraw-Hill Education; Thinking Like a Modern Economist icon: ©NeydtStock/Shutterstock

CHAPTER 21

Thinking Like a Modern Economist

> Economics is what economists do.
>
> —Jacob Viner

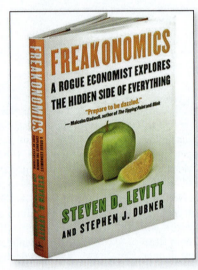

©Roberts Publishing Services

My son doesn't think much of economists. I know that it's rather common for kids not to have high regard for their parents, but it still hurts. A while ago, however, when I attended a conference at which I was on a panel with Steve Levitt, my ranking moved up. In fact my son asked me, "Can you get his autograph for me? He's cool." Steve Levitt's book, *Freakonomics* (written jointly with Stephen Dubner), had struck a chord with my son, and judging from its and its sequel's sales, with lots of other people as well.

I raise this issue here not to sell more copies of Levitt's book (he's sold plenty), but instead to introduce you to what modern economists do, and how what modern economists do relates to the supply and demand model. I include this chapter to disabuse you from thinking that the supply and demand model is the holy grail of economics. Remember Carlyle's comment, "Teach a parrot the words 'supply' and 'demand,' and you have an economist." He's wrong; as I stated in an earlier chapter, economists are not parrots, and to understand modern economics you have to know that modern economics uses supply and demand analysis only as a stepping-stone. It's an important stepping-stone, but still just a stepping-stone.

Freakonomics makes the point nicely because if you look in its index, you won't find any entries under *supply* or *demand*. The reason isn't because the indexer goofed—it's because Levitt didn't use the formal supply and demand model. Instead, he applied the general ideas behind supply and demand within a variety of other models; most of his conclusions derive from his creative ability to collect data and analyze them with statistical tools. His approach is typical of how modern applied economists approach problems—they collect data, or use data collected by others, and analyze them. The purpose of this chapter is to give you a sense of what modern economists do, and how what you will learn in principles of economics relates to what modern economists do.

A key lesson of this chapter is that *supply and demand is not the glue that holds modern economics together*. Rather, modeling is the glue. When you present a problem or question to an economist, he or she will automatically attempt to reduce that question to a **model**—*a simplified representation of the problem or question that captures the essential issues*—and then work with that model and empirical evidence to understand the problem. The modeling approach is the modern economics approach.

No single model characterizes modern economic models. Modern economists are a highly diverse group of social scientists. What ties them together is their training in modeling and their shared view that incentives are important, and that their models have to capture the importance of incentives.

Q-1 What is the glue that holds modern economics together?

The Nature of Economists' Models

Economists aren't the only people who use models. Most everyone does. An architect will often create a computer model or a small wooden model of a house he is building. Similarly, an engineer will test a new design with a model. So modeling alone does not distinguish an economist from other scientists and engineers. What does differentiate economists are:

1. The building blocks that economists use in their models, and

2. The structure of formal models that economists find acceptable.

By *building blocks* I mean the assumptions that form the basis of economic models. All economists' models hold that incentives are important, but they differ in how they picture people reacting to incentives. For example, you can assume that individuals are selfish, or that individuals care about other people; the models would be different in each instance. By *structure,* I mean the form of the model—for example, a model can be verbal, graphical (for example, the supply/demand model), algebraic with simple equations (for example, $q = 4 - 2P$), or algebraic with highly complex equations[1] [for example,

Building blocks are the assumptions of a model. The structure of a model is the form it takes—verbal, graphical, or algebraic.

$$\begin{pmatrix} \delta_t \bar{u}_k(t) \\ \delta_t \bar{v}_k(t) \end{pmatrix} = -k^2 \begin{pmatrix} D_u \bar{u}_k(t) \\ D_u \bar{v}_k(t) \end{pmatrix} + R' \begin{pmatrix} \bar{u}_k(t) \\ \bar{v}_k(t) \end{pmatrix}$$

requiring mind-spinning graduate-level mathematics]. The one-time crime drama *Numb3rs* on television was in many ways a description of how modern economists approach problems. In each episode the investigation included modeling the crime mathematically, which became critical to solving the crime. In fact, many of the show's episodes were built around models that modern economists have developed and use in their analyses.

Models don't have to be mathematical; economists also use more informal verbal or **heuristic models**—*models that are expressed informally in words*. Models can be physical or they can be virtual models embodied in computer simulations. Computer simulation models also can be interactive, where individuals become part of the model. For example, the online virtual world, Minecraft, can be thought of as a model of society, and its economy can provide insight for the real-world economy. Just like these models, economic models come in many different forms with many different building blocks.

Heuristic models are informal models expressed in words.

The building blocks and structures of models that economists use have evolved over time. Early economists tended to use a highly restricted set of building blocks and a narrow set of relatively simple (at least compared to their modern alternatives) formal models. **Modern economists** are *economists who are willing to use a wider range of models than did earlier economists.* A major change is that modern economists use a

---

[1]In case you were wondering, this is a reaction diffusion equation expressed in simplifying vector notation. What's a reaction diffusion equation? It's probably better not to ask.

Q-2 Are modern economists more likely to use inductive models than were earlier economists?

much more *inductive approach* to modeling. An **inductive approach** is *an approach to understanding a problem or question in which understanding is developed empirically from statistically analyzing what is observed in the data.* Models based on an inductive approach are developed by how well they fit the data. Earlier economists were much more likely to use a **deductive approach**—*an approach that begins with certain self-evident principles from which implications are deduced (logically determined).*

Scientific and Engineering Models

Models can have many purposes. There are models primarily designed to provide an understanding of what is happening for the sake of understanding—these are scientific models. Other models can be designed to provide insight into policy issues—these are applied-policy or engineering models. Still other models fall somewhere in between; there is no firm line distinguishing science from engineering. Most of the models presented within this book fall more within the applied-policy models. They are designed to provide insight into what is happening in a way that serves as a foundation for a discussion of policy.

Behavioral and Traditional Building Blocks

Traditional economists tend to use simple models based on assumptions of rationality and self-interest.

The traditional building blocks of microeconomics are the assumptions that people are rational and self-interested. What we have called **traditional economists** are *economists who study the logical implications of rationality and self-interest in relatively simple algebraic or graphical models such as the supply and demand model.* (Yes, it is true; by a mathematician's standards, supply and demand models are very simple models. But I agree with you; these simple models are often complicated enough.) Modern economists use supply and demand models, but they also use much more sophisticated models that integrate dynamics and strategic interactions into the analysis.

How much modern economists are willing to deviate from the traditional approach differs among modern economists. For example, some modern economists such as Nobel Prize winner Gary Becker advocate limiting economic models to these traditional building blocks. He wrote: "The combined assumptions of maximizing behavior [note: maximizing behavior is how economists interpret rationality], market equilibrium, and stable preferences, used relentlessly and unflinchingly, form the heart of the economic approach." Up until the end of the 1970s, Becker's view predominated among economists. Since the 1980s, however, a group of modern economists has been edging away from these traditional building blocks.

Web Note 21.1

Adam Smith and Self-Interest

Behavioral Economic Models

The study of models with alternative building blocks has grown so much in recent years that it has acquired a name: **behavioral economics**—*microeconomic analysis that uses a broader set of building blocks than the rationality and self-interest used in traditional economics.* Instead of deductively assuming rationality and self-interest, behavioral economists inductively study people's behavior and use those behaviors in their models. Based on these inductive studies, they argue that the assumptions of both rationality and self-interest should be broadened somewhat. Rationality should be broadened to **purposeful behavior**—*behavior reflecting reasoned but not necessarily rational judgment*—and self-interest should be broadened to **enlightened self-interest** in which *people care about other people as well as themselves.*

Q-3 If an economist argues that people tend to be purposeful and follow their enlightened self-interest, would you most likely characterize that economist as a behavioral or a traditional economist?

Behavioral economics is a leading field of research in economics today. The two important differences between traditional and behavioral building blocks are presented in Table 21-1.

TABLE 21-1 The Different Building Blocks of Traditional and Behavioral Models

Traditional Economics	Behavioral Economics
People are completely rational.	People behave purposefully.
People are self-interested.	People follow their enlightened self-interest.

One basic building block of behavioral economists is the assumption that people follow their enlightened self-interest. We saw this in a previous chapter with the work of economists Matt Rabin and Ernst Fehr who developed models that incorporate a sense of fairness. As discussed, they have found that when dividing a sum of money, people try to divide the sum fairly rather than giving it all to themselves, even though they could keep it all. In these modern models, the individuals would not be considered solely self-interested but, rather, enlightened self-interested; they care about fairness for its own sake. Another building block is that people act purposefully rather than rationally as defined in the traditional sense. In their models, behavioral economists Herbert Simon and Thomas Schelling have found that people will make choices based on rules of thumb such as "Do what you see others doing" without rationally weighing the costs and benefits of each decision. In their models they assume that people follow habit, which is purposeful behavior that reduces the costs of making decisions.

Building blocks affect how one interprets observations and influence the patterns one sees in the data. For example, say you observe a firm not taking advantage of its market position. Using traditional building blocks of rationality and self-interest, this would seem very strange. You would look for some hidden reason why the firm isn't taking advantage of that position and keep searching until you find the selfish motive underlying the behavior.

The assumptions of a model affect the patterns that one sees in the data.

Models based on behavioral building blocks, in which people and firms have goals beyond self-interest, allow researchers to consider the possibility that the firm is not taking advantage of its market position for reasons other than self-interest. Pharmaceutical companies, for example, sell AIDS drugs in African countries at prices far below market price. This could be because of political pressure, but it could also be out of a sense of fairness. A traditional economist would focus on the first; a behavioral economist would consider both possibilities and use empirical data to decide which it is. The point of this example is that an economist who is willing to use a wider set of building blocks sees different information in data than does an economist who uses the traditional building blocks. In modern economics there is a lively debate about what building blocks economists should use.

PREDICTABLE IRRATIONALITY   The key to understanding the difference between behavioral economics and modern traditional economics is to recognize that behavioral economists are not just arguing that people are irrational; they are arguing that people are *predictably irrational* and that actions that traditional economists call irrational might not be irrational when considered in context.[2] For a behavioral economist, rationality comes in many forms, and what's important is that the model captures how

For behavioral economists, universality is less important than the fact that the model captures how people actually behave.

---

[2]An entire book could be written on what is meant by rationality and self-interest, and in some ways, all types of behavior can be considered rational and selfish. So it can be argued that behavioral economists are not arguing that purposeful behavior includes irrational behavior, but only that it includes a different type of rationality than is allowed within traditional economics.

people actually behave. Capturing this real-world nature of humans requires giving up some of the universality and power of models based on the traditional assumptions. Behavioral models depend on context. Instead of having one model, one has a collection of models from which to choose for a variety of situations.

Let's consider an example of the difference. Say you are given a choice between two income streams. In the first scenario, you will earn $30,000 the first year, $27,000 the second, and $24,000 the third. In the second scenario, you will earn $24,000 the first year, $27,000 the second, and $30,000 the third. Which would you choose? A model based on traditional rationality predicts you would choose the first, since you will be able to save the additional $6,000 earned the first year, put it in the bank, and end up with more than $30,000 of income in the third year. Since you get more total income with the first stream of income ($24,000 plus the $6,000 from the first year, plus two years of interest on that $6,000), it is "rationally" preferred to the second. But when economists have asked people which stream of income they preferred, economists have found that most people choose the second stream, even when it is explained that they could be better off by choosing the first.

What's going on? Behavioral economists argue that most people recognize that they don't have complete self-control; people believe that they will spend the extra $6,000 earned in the first year rather than save it. Thus, while it may be possible for people to switch the first income stream into an income stream that is preferred to the second, they don't believe that they have the discipline to do so. Thus, they actually prefer the second to the first because it precommits them to saving, and thereby constrains them from doing something they believe they will do, but which they actually don't want to do. They have developed what is called a **precommitment strategy**—*a strategy in which people consciously place limitations on their future actions, thereby limiting their choices.* The behavior is irrational because people tend to choose the stream that results in less total income; it's predictable because in experiments time and time again, people make the same choice. This seemingly irrational choice is not unique to this example but occurs in a variety of contexts.

Q-4 Can adding a constraint on people make them better off?

ARE YOU PREDICTABLY IRRATIONAL?

Economist Dan Ariely, from whose book *Predictably Irrational* many of these examples have been developed, has created a test as a fun way to introduce people to these ideas and to determine whether they exhibit predictably irrational tendencies.

- Does how happy you are with your salary depend on how much you make relative to what your friends, family members, and neighbors make?

- When you are facing a decision to buy something, do you make your decision by considering the pleasure that this item will bring to you and contrast it with all the other possible things that you could buy for the same amount of money, now and in the future?

- Have you ever planned to skip the dessert at the end of a nice meal out, but once the server stopped by with the dessert cart, you ended up ordering the chocolate soufflé?

- Have you ever had a romantic partner in whom you started to lose interest, but when he or she all of a sudden began to grow more distant, your interest rekindled?

Most people answer these questions yes, no, yes, and yes. These answers are the opposite of what an economist using the traditional building blocks would predict people would answer. Behavioral economics says that we must develop additional economic models that take these predictable behaviors into account.

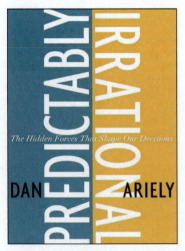

©Roberts Publishing Services

The Advantages and Disadvantages of Modern Traditional and Behavioral Models

While it may seem that economists would want models that most closely reflect people's behavior, that is not so obvious—models that precisely reflect people's actual behavior are extraordinarily complex and don't provide significant insight because they are impossible to generalize. For example, a pool player probably does not calculate the angles and spin of a ball to determine how to hit it, but it may make the most sense to assume that she does if one were modeling her behavior. That model may be easier to solve, and may be a better predictor of what will happen, than a model built on her actual behavior. Modern traditional economists emphasize the advantage of simplicity and ease of testing. Having one model means that you can test it and see if it fits reality. With many models, you have to do much more testing. For policy purposes, modern traditional economists argue that a single model that is easy to apply and test is the most useful model.

THE DIFFICULTY WITH BEHAVIORAL BUILDING BLOCKS: TESTING   Modern traditional economists point out that formally moving away from the traditional building blocks is difficult because models in which people follow their enlightened self-interest rather than self-interest and act purposefully rather than rationally lead to much less clear-cut models and results. By their nature, behavioral models depend on the specific context of the choices involved; so instead of a single model, there are many. These broader building blocks allow many more patterns to be discerned in the data. That's both an advantage and a disadvantage. It is an advantage because such models may more accurately reflect actual behavior; it is a disadvantage because it is hard to know which pattern to focus on.

©Courtesy of Robert Bloomfield's Mentanomics™

The behavioral economists' answer to this problem is that economists can use laboratory and field experiments, or what is called *experimental economics,* to test alternative building blocks and identify those that best describe how people actually behave. Let's consider an example: In an experiment, half the participants were given a mug and the other half were given a pen, each of approximately the same value. The participants were then allowed to exchange one for the other simply by returning the first item. Since who got the pen or the mug was random, the rationality building block would suggest that about half of each group would choose to trade the gift they had for the other. In fact, only 10 percent of each group chose to trade, suggesting that what one has influences what one wants—in contradiction to the traditional building block of rationality. A behavioral economist would then include **endowment effects** *(people value something more just because they have it)* in their building blocks for models. Endowment effects fit the broader "behaving purposefully" building block; they do not fit the narrower "rationality" building block.

Endowment effects—the observation that what one has affects what one wants—are an example of a modern behavioral economics building block.

Behavioral economists using *evolutionary models*—models of how an individual's preferences are determined on the basis of natural selection of what is useful for survival—argue that the endowment effect is hardwired into people's brains because it serves a very useful evolutionary function. It makes people happier with what they have, which decreases the social conflict over who gets what. The endowment effect probably makes it possible for parents to put up with their children, and to actually believe that they are close to perfect, even though, to an objective observer, they are far from perfect. In fact, without the endowment effect, we would probably have an online market in children where you could trade yours for someone else's.

 Web Note 21.2

Shipping-Then-Shopping

TRADITIONAL MODELS PROVIDE SIMPLICITY AND INSIGHT   Modern traditional economists don't agree with the direction that behavioral economics is heading in terms of giving up the old building blocks; they strongly prefer staying with the narrower building blocks of rationality and self-interest. The reason is the simplicity and clarity that come from models with these traditional building blocks; these traditional

Neuroeconomics and Microeconomics

Both traditional and behavioral economics generally assume that the most basic building block of economic analysis is the individual. Where the two groups differ is in the assumptions they make about how the individual behaves. Some economists, such as Caltech economist Colin Camerer and University of Zurich economist Ernst Fehr, have questioned whether economists should study building blocks more basic than the individual. They argue that individuals are made up of cells, and that behavior is the result of chemical and electrical processes in the brain. By studying these brain processes, we can better understand an individual's behavior. To do this they perform CT scans of people's brains under a variety of controlled conditions and see what part of the brain is reacting. Their work goes under the name *neuroeconomics*.

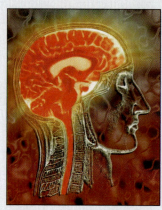
©Brand X Pictures/PunchStock

What they have found is that choice is a very complicated electrochemical phenomenon. For example, inconsistent decisions are often not the result of a mistake that would have been corrected if someone had pointed out the inconsistency, but, instead, the result of different electrochemical processes occurring in the brain. People are essentially hardwired to be inconsistent. In a sense, more than one "you" is making decisions. There are the "emotional you" when your emotions hold sway and the "rational you" when the rational side of your brain holds sway. Depending on which "you" is being affected, the choice that "you" prefer can be quite different. And when both you's are affected, the result is often confusion. (This is a reason why advertisers appeal to both emotion and rationality simultaneously.)

This supports the behavioral economists' argument that we need to use building blocks that are different from the traditional ones. It also opens up a whole new set of possibilities about controlling behavior, such as the precommitment savings strategy discussed in the text. Another example of that precommitment strategy is not keeping dessert in the refrigerator to avoid temptation. Such precommitment strategies allow the "rational you" to win out over the "emotional you."

Traditional models provide simple and clear results, which can highlight issues that behavioral models cannot.

models give clear-cut results that nicely highlight issues in ways that the modern building blocks do not. It was this view that was expressed by economist Gary Becker when he said that traditional building blocks, used unflinchingly, are the essence of the economic approach. He would argue that behavioral economists have flinched.[3]

Because Becker and other similarly minded economists taught at the University of Chicago, until recently, this unflinching approach was associated with what was called the *Chicago approach* to economics. Recently, however, a number of University of Chicago school economists such as Richard Thaler have begun using a broader set of building blocks, and, as I will discuss below, have been in the forefront of drawing policy implications from models based on modern building blocks.

Web Note 21.3

Predictably Irrational

BEHAVIORAL ECONOMIC MODELS REFLECT OBSERVED BEHAVIOR Behavioral economists' response to Becker and others who advocate sticking with the traditional building blocks is that they agree that the traditional model provides enormous insights,

---

[3]Some economists, called *evolutionary economists,* believe that even this group of building blocks does not go far enough. They advocate for thinking about individuals as reflecting their evolutionary tendencies and being shaped by the market into the type of individuals that traditional economists assume are their inherent natures. Others, called *econophysicists* because they are often trained as physicists, argue that for many aggregate issues individual behavior is irrelevant; what happens in the aggregate reflects statistical properties of interactions that are independent of agents and that are independent of the building blocks used within the model.

and that *they do not advocate discarding the supply/demand model or the traditional building blocks,* especially when teaching economics. Their argument is not that models built on the traditional building blocks—such as supply and demand—are irrelevant; it is simply that the traditional building blocks do not explain everything, and that attempts to use them to explain everything actually undermine our understanding of what models using the traditional building blocks do explain. Behavioral economists argue that empirical work has convincingly shown that people are predictably irrational in some of their behaviors, and modern economics must take that into account.

Eventually, the hope of modern economics is that economists will have a set of models that "explain" the decisions we observe, along with a guide that explains which models fit what situations. Alas, you're not going to get that guide in this book (or in any other textbook). Economists are just not there yet. In fact, we're far from it, and even those who use the new building blocks do not believe that the behavioral models are sufficiently developed to replace the traditional models as the pedagogical core of economics. That's why I focus on the traditional building blocks and the standard supply/demand model throughout the book. But that focus should not lead you to think of the supply/demand model and its assumptions as anything more than a beginning of an introduction to modern economics.

Q-5 Which are better—models based on traditional building blocks or models based on behavioral building blocks?

Behavioral and Traditional Informal (Heuristic) Models

As I stated above, economists have many types of models—verbal, empirical, and formal models. Modern economists use all of them. Thus, to understand modern economics, you need to know the various types and their advantages and disadvantages. Let's consider each briefly, starting with heuristic models.

Most of the time when laypeople hear about the results of an economist's analysis, they don't see the underlying formal model. Instead, all they see is a heuristic or verbal discussion that conveys the essence of the model. But if you search deeper into the discussion, you can generally extract the model and see whether the economist is using behavioral or traditional building blocks.

To show you the difference between heuristic models based on traditional building blocks and ones based on broader behavioral building blocks, let's consider some discussions in two popular books that apply economic reasoning to everyday events. That consideration will help clarify the difference between an economist using traditional building blocks and one using behavioral building blocks.

The Armchair Economist: Heuristic Models Using Traditional Building Blocks

Let's begin with a consideration of a model by University of Rochester economist Steven Landsburg. Landsburg calls himself an "armchair economist," by which he means that he provides heuristic models to explain everyday events. For the most part, Landsburg's heuristic models use traditional economic building blocks; he unflinchingly and happily pulls out unexpected implications from models built on those assumptions. Thus, Landsburg is an excellent example of a modern economist who sticks to traditional building blocks.

The particular model of his that I will consider deals with a sometimes taboo topic—sex. His model is designed to make the reader think, and to see how economic reasoning can come to counterintuitive conclusions. Coming to such highly counterintuitive ideas is seen as a strong plus for these models based on traditional building

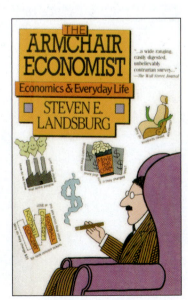

©Roberts Publishing Services

blocks because it gets people to think of questions in a different way than they normally do, and in the process provides important insights.

MORE SEX IS SAFER SEX   In one of his more provocative models (available on *Slate,* www.slate.com/id/2033), Landsburg considered the problem facing a hypothetical person named Martin, "a charming and generally prudent young man with a limited sexual history, who has been gently flirting with his coworker Joan." Landsburg described a situation in which Martin and Joan were both thinking that they might go home together after an office party that would be held the next day. However, on the way to the party, Martin notices a Centers for Disease Control and Prevention (CDC) subway advertisement advocating the virtues of abstinence. Feeling guilty about his thoughts, he decides to stay home rather than tempt himself. He is being virtuous.

Joan shows up at the party and, in Martin's absence, she hooks up with an "equally charming but considerably less prudent Maxwell." Maxwell is rather careless in practicing safe sex, and the end result of this hookup is that Joan ends up with AIDS—all because Martin was virtuous. (Economic models conveying these parables of the problems with being virtuous have a long history in economics, going back to Bernard Mandeville, who wrote *The Fable of the Bees* back in the 1700s.)

Landsburg then argued that this story demonstrates that Martin's withdrawal from the mating game made the mating game more dangerous for others. He argued that it follows that the world would have been better off (specifically, we could have slowed the spread of AIDS) if "the Martins of the world would loosen up a little." He then reported some empirical estimates by a Harvard professor that if everyone with fewer than about 2.25 partners per year had had a few more partners, we could actually have slowed the spread of AIDS. Landsburg argued the following: "To an economist, it's crystal clear why people with limited sexual pasts choose to supply too little sex in the present: their services are underpriced."

Landsburg's model was meant to shock, which it did. But it was also meant to hone people's reasoning ability, which it also did. It captured the economic insight that when the effects of one's decisions on others are not included in a person's decision-making process—that is, where there are externalities—the decision may not lead to the aggregate outcome that most people would prefer. But they were the decisions that Landsburg thought people would make. Landsburg's model was based on the traditional building block of strong self-interest.

Decisions about sexual activity may have externalities, and therefore what is best for the individuals involved may not be best for society.

WHY CAR INSURANCE COSTS MORE SOME PLACES THAN OTHERS   While Landsburg is traditional in his building blocks, he is not always traditional in the formal models he uses, and in some of the issues he has studied, he has gone far beyond the simple supply/demand model. For example, in another model, he considered the issue of why car insurance cost three times as much in Philadelphia, Pennsylvania, than in Ithaca, New York, even though the theft and accident rates were not significantly different between the two cities. The model he used is a "path-dependent tipping-point" model with two, rather than one, equilibria. In a tipping-point model, the model can arrive at quite different results depending on people's initial choice. The results are path-dependent, and without knowing the path, one cannot predict the equilibrium. Tipping-point models are a type of a broader group of models called **path-dependent models**—*models in which the path to equilibrium affects the equilibrium.* Path-dependent models require a knowledge of the relevant history to reach a conclusion. Were the supply/demand model a path-dependent model, it would not lead to a unique equilibrium price.

The argument Landsburg gave is the following. In the pricing of insurance, there is a feedback effect of the initial choices people make of whether to buy insurance that affects the cost of insurance. If a few people decide not to buy insurance, the costs of insurance

Can You Explain Landsburg's Provocative Insights?

The two arguments that I present in the text are examples of Landsburg's provocative approach, which is characteristic of modern traditional economists. Below are some of his other provocative conclusions based on traditional building blocks. See if you can figure out what the implicit model is that leads to that conclusion. If you can't figure out the model, or want to check your reasoning, his arguments can be found in his book *More Sex Is Safer Sex,* and brief summaries of his reasoning can be found among the library resources available via McGraw-Hill Connect®.

1. Daughters cause divorce.
2. A taste for revenge is healthier than a thirst for gold.
3. A ban on elephant hunting is bad news for elephants.

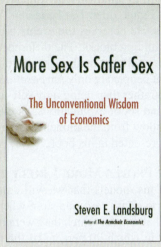

More Sex Is Safer Sex

The Unconventional Wisdom of Economics

Steven E. Landsburg
Author of *The Armchair Economist*

©Roberts Publishing Services

4. Disaster assistance is bad news for the people who receive it.
5. Malicious computer hackers should be executed.
6. The most charitable people support the fewest charities.
7. Writing books is socially irresponsible.
8. Elbowing your way to the front of the water-fountain line is socially responsible.

Many of these are presented a bit in jest (I think)—they are meant to shock and get you to think. But that is precisely how the best advocates of the traditional building blocks use their heuristic models based on traditional building blocks. The models provide you with a different view of an issue, and thereby increase your understanding of what's really going on.

to others who do buy insurance will be higher since, if they have an accident with an uninsured driver, their insurance will have to pay. Because insurance costs are higher, even more people drive without insurance, further increasing the rates for those who do buy insurance. Landsburg argued that that was what happened in Philadelphia. In Ithaca, however, the situation went the other way—many initially bought insurance, which meant that insurance costs for everyone were lower, which led others to buy insurance, which led to even lower rates. Both equilibria were self-reinforcing, and, once chosen, were very difficult to change without a major intervention by government.

Such government interventions go against Landsburg's (and most traditional economists') intuition. Traditional models based on the traditional building blocks without externalities almost inevitably lead to a laissez-faire policy. He states, "For ideological free marketers (like myself), theories (like this one) can be intellectually jarring. We are accustomed to defending free markets as the guarantors of both liberty and prosperity, but here's a case where liberty and prosperity are at odds: By forcing people to act against their own self-interest in the short run, governments can make everybody more prosperous in the long run. . . . Is it worth sacrificing a small amount of freedom for cheaper auto insurance? I am inclined to believe that the answer is yes, but the question makes me squirm a bit."

Here we see a heuristic model based on reasoning that people are rational and self-interested, as in the supply/demand model. But because it is not a supply/demand model with a single equilibrium, it leads to a quite nontraditional result of two possible equilibria. It also leads to a potential policy solution—one requiring all individuals to get insurance.

The Economic Naturalist: Heuristic Models Using Behavioral Building Blocks

Let's now turn to some models from another popular book, this one by Cornell economist Robert Frank, titled *The Economic Naturalist*. Frank's approach is very similar to Landsburg's. He observes the events around him and tries to understand them using economic building blocks. The difference between Frank and Landsburg is that Frank is much more willing than Landsburg to go beyond the traditional building blocks. He assumes that people are only *purposeful,* not rational, and that they follow *enlightened self-interest* rather than being only self-interested. This allows for a much wider range of models and set of explanations, as well as a much wider range of policy interventions that follow from the model. We can see the difference by considering two of the models he presented in his book.

WHY ARE PEOPLE MORE LIKELY TO RETURN CASH THAN A LAMPSHADE?

The first of his models that we will consider is designed to explain why people are more likely to return cash to a store when given too much change by a cashier than to return merchandise for which they were not charged. He began by reporting the results of a survey in which 90 percent of the respondents said they would return $20 to a store if given that amount extra in change, but only 10 percent said they would return a $20 lampshade if the cashier had neglected to charge for it. If people took only their own interests into account, they shouldn't return either.

He explained this difference in behavior by arguing that people took into account *who* would be hurt by the action. In the case of the cash, the "cashier will have to pay out of her own pocket." Thus, he reasoned most people would not want her to be penalized. In the case of the lampshade, it would be the store, not the individual, that would suffer the loss, and people were much less worried about hurting stores than they were about hurting people. Notice the difference in Frank's assumption as compared to Landsburg's. In Frank's model, people were somewhat self-interested (they kept the $20 lampshade), but not totally self-interested (they returned the $20). Using a model with traditional building blocks, the prediction would be that no one would return the money. Frank's behavioral model allowed for the possibility that individuals care about the impact of their actions on others.

WHY DON'T MORE PEOPLE WEAR VELCRO SHOES?

A second model found in Frank's book dealt with why people continue to wear shoes with shoelaces, even though Velcro shoes are more practical, and, according to Frank, "offer clear advantages over laces" because lace shoes can become untied, causing people to trip and fall. He argued that the reason why shoelaces were still predominant was that the very young (who don't know how to tie shoes) and the very old (who are too feeble to bend down and tie shoes) wear Velcro shoes, and therefore they became associated with what Frank calls "incompetence and fragility"—characteristics with which most people don't want to be associated.

Where this explanation deviated from the traditional building blocks was the rationality assumption. Using a technology that was less efficient than another (shoelaces over Velcro) was irrational, and thus doesn't make sense. The behavioral assumption in Frank's model was that people care about what other people think about them and thus take social issues, not just economic issues, into account when making their decisions. Behavioral economic models take social dimensions of problems into account; traditional economic models don't.

I should include an addendum (confession?) to this model; I've worn Velcro shoes for the last 30 years, much to the horror of my children, who asked me not to be seen

Behavioral models take social considerations into account; traditional models do not.

Can You Explain Frank's Observations?

The text recounts two heuristic models that are found in Robert Frank's *The Economic Naturalist*. In his review of Frank's book, Vanderbilt economist John Siegfried listed the questions that led to 10 other models in Frank's book. Below is Siegfried's list; I leave it to you to develop the model that would explain the questions.

1. Why does a light come on when you open a refrigerator, but not a freezer?
2. Why do dry cleaners charge more for women's shirts than for men's?
3. Why are brown eggs more expensive than white ones?
4. Why do women endure the discomfort of high heels?
5. Why are whales in danger of extinction, but not chickens?

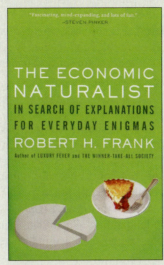

©Roberts Publishing Services

6. If we have Blockbuster video, why don't we have Blockbuster book?
7. Why is there so much mathematical formalism in economics?
8. Why do stores post signs saying that guide dogs are permitted inside?
9. Why do most U.S. department stores put men's fashions on the ground floor?
10. Why is it easier to find a partner when you already have one?

If you want to see the models Frank came up with, see his book *The Economic Naturalist*. Short summaries of the explanations Frank followed can be found among the library resources available via McGraw-Hill Connect®.

---

with them when I wear them. Why do I wear them? I suspect because of my training in traditional economic models. That training has shaped me so that I value efficiency for its own sake. By wearing Velcro shoes I am making a statement to society (I am as much a social creature as others) that I am not driven by social norms about dressing (anyone who has seen my standard attire can attest to the fact that I am not). I consciously do it (at least in the sense of not allowing my wife to put out the clothes she wants me to wear) and, to some degree, I revel in the looks I get because it means that I am free, and efficient, allowing me to consider others slaves of some designer. I tell my kids that some day the world will follow me. They tell me, "Don't hold your breath."

My behavior represents another dimension of behavior that behavioral economists have discovered. Studying a model and using its assumptions can lead you to adopt its assumptions as your own; thus, the models you choose to use to look at the world can influence your behavior. This means that studying economics may not only provide you with insights; it also may change you.

The Limits of Heuristic Models

I could go on with hundreds of these vignettes; they are entertaining, fun, and good practice for the mind. If my sole purpose were to entertain you, I'd include a lot more. But the principles course is meant to do more than entertain; it is meant to teach, and except when they are writing for laypeople, most economists see heuristic models as simply a stepping-stone to a more formal model. The reason is that heuristic models are not sufficiently precise, making their validity impossible to test. Think back to the heuristic models we presented and ask yourself how convinced you were by the arguments. Each was relatively easy to modify to come to a different conclusion.

Q-6 Does the author's tendency to wear Velcro shoes demonstrate that he is beyond social pressures?

477

For example, what if Joan had chosen not to hook up with anyone? Or what if she had seen the same abstinence ad as had Martin? Then the argument would have been reversed. Would that mean that the Martins of the world should have less sex? Or what if Velcro shoes suddenly became "in." Would that mean that the more practical solution wins out? So, while the heuristic models embodied in the vignettes are entertaining, it is a fair question to ask whether we really know anything more about the world after learning about the models than we did before. To a scientist the answer is no, we don't, at least in a scientific sense. That's why science is not based on heuristic models.

Empirical and Formal Models

Q-7 Why are economists very hesitant to base knowledge on heuristic models?

Scientists are very hesitant to base any knowledge on anecdotes or heuristic models, even highly convincing ones. The reason is that they have found that the human mind is extremely good at creating convincing stories that make sense within its own world view or frame, but not necessarily outside it. They have found that the human mind is what psychologists call a *fast pattern completer*. Heuristic models exploit this tendency in humans that gives people a sense of understanding, but not necessarily a scientific understanding. Scientists argue that to extend a heuristic model to true understanding, you have to quantify and empirically test your arguments.

The Importance of Empirical Work in Modern Economics

This leads us to a second important element of modern economics: It is highly empirical. That is, modern economics is based on experiments that can be replicated, or on statistical analysis of real-world observations. While the importance of empirical work has a long history in economics, going back to William Petty in the 1600s, up until the 1940s, economics primarily concentrated on deductive, not inductive, reasoning. That occurred because of the lack of data and the lack of computational power to analyze data.

With the development of **econometrics**—*the statistical analysis of economic data*—in the 1940s, that started to change. But because of limited data and computing power, empirical work in economics did not move to the forefront until the late 1980s when computer power had expanded enough to begin making such an empirical approach useful. At that point, induction started to supplement deduction as the economist's method for understanding the real world. Since the late 1980s this movement toward induction has accelerated, so that today it is fair to say that the development of computing power has fundamentally changed the way economic research is done.

Modern economics—models based on both traditional and behavioral building blocks—relies on experiments and statistical analysis of real-world observations.

The strong reliance on empirical work is true of all modern economists—both those who use traditional building blocks and those who use behavioral building blocks. Today, much empirical work in economics is not based on formal deductive models, but rather on heuristic models—relatively simple and informal models that capture a possible insight, such as those we discussed above by Frank and Landsburg.

The difference between an economic scientist's heuristic model and those of Frank and Landsburg presented above is that the economic scientist doesn't stop with the heuristic model, as did Frank's and Landsburg's presentations. He or she builds an empirical model around that heuristic model and supports the argument with empirical evidence. Essentially, what he or she does is take relationships found in the heuristic model and see if these relationships can be generalized subject to scientifically based statistical studies. Economists call this approach "letting the data speak." To let the data speak, you collect data and analyze them with statistical and econometric tools.

To analyze an issue with an **empirical model**—*a model that statistically discovers a pattern in the data*—researchers empirically study the relationship arrived at in their heuristic models. That's what Steve Levitt did with enormous creativity and success.

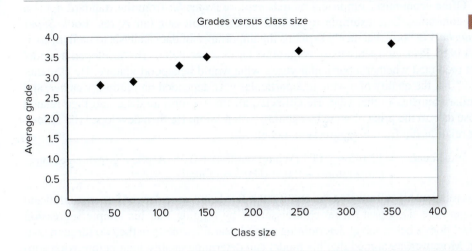

Grades versus class size

FIGURE 21-1 **Grades versus Class Size**

A regression finds a line that best fits a combination of points such as the one shown here. It appears from this scatter plot that class size is related to average grade.

He looked at a variety of issues: Do sumo wrestlers throw matches? Do basketball teams cheat? And why do drug dealers often live with their mothers? He looked at the data, created simple informal models and hypotheses, and used those models to structure his empirical study. For example, he reasoned that if who won sumo wrestling matches did not involve cheating, whether a wrestler was close to winning enough matches to raise his ranking would make no difference as to whether he won a match or not. But he reasoned further that if wrestlers are self-interested and rational, they will have an incentive to agree to quid pro quo arrangements to cheat and throw a match, allowing opponents to win a match in exchange for their throwing a future match. So now he had a testable hypothesis. His hypothesis was: *The closer a wrestler is to raising his rank, the more often his opponent will intentionally lose.* He then collected and statistically analyzed the data. What he discovered was that how close a wrestler was to elimination did make a difference, which allowed him to conclude that sumo wrestlers "cheat."

Do sumo wrestlers cheat?
©Nice One Productions/Corbis

REGRESSION MODELS A primary tool of an empirical economist is a **regression model,** *an empirical model in which one statistically relates one set of variables to another,* and the statistical tools that accompany it. For example, say you are wondering if a professor giving higher grades increases the number of students in his class. You would collect data about two variables—the grades he normally gives and enrollment in his classes—giving you a relationship shown in Figure 21-1. Then you would "run a regression," which essentially means that you use a statistical package to find a line that "best fits" the data, where "best fit" means making the distances between that line and the points as small as possible. If the "best fit" line is upward-sloping, as it would be here, then the regression model's answer to the question is a tentative yes, subject to all the things that were held constant and an assumption that causation goes from grades to enrollment.

The "goodness of fit" between the two variables is described by the **coefficient of determination,** which is *a measure of the proportion of the variability in the data that is accounted for by the statistical model.* The larger the coefficient of determination, the better the fit, and if it is a perfect fit, then every point will be on the "best fit" line. This isn't a statistics class so I won't go into further explanation, but that short description should give you a sense of how empirical regression models work. Regression models are the workhorses of much of what applied microeconomists do, and modern economists become almost magicians at pulling information out from data.

A regression model is a model that statistically relates one set of variables to another.

Often economists' empirical models explore issues far from the standard domain of economics. One example recounted in Yale professor Ian Ayres' book *Super Crunchers* (a book that nicely explains the importance of data analysis to modern society) is by Princeton University economist Orley Ashenfelter. He developed a model that predicted whether a particular year's wine would be a good vintage. He hypothesized that the quality of a wine in a particular year depended on rainfall, weather, and similar elements in that year. He collected all the appropriate data, and then related those data to the price of wine by running a regression. He then developed the following relationship from his regression model:

Wine quality = 12.145 + 0.001 (Winter rainfall) + 0.06 (Average growing-season
temperature) − 0.004 (Harvest rainfall)

This relationship tells us that the quality of a Bordeaux wine depends upon rainfall and temperature. He upset "wine connoisseurs" by arguing that his simple regression model does a better job at determining a good year for wine than they do through tasting. Moreover, he argued that his model can determine quality long before wine connoisseurs could even start tasting the wine. So when choosing a wine, forget about sniffing, swirling, and tasting; just get out your computer, collect the data, plug in the numbers, and solve the equation. Is he right? I'm no wine connoisseur, but the people I talk to (admittedly, they tend to be economists) believe that he is.

Another regression model has been used by baseball teams to determine how valuable a prospect is. Econometrically trained specialists collected data on young baseball recruits and ran regressions, finding how different skills are correlated with a team's success. When these specialists did this, they found that bases on balls were almost as important as hits. Thus, they argued that a person's ability to draw a walk should be one of the variables considered in choosing a recruit, something that previously wasn't done. They then used that regression model to predict which young recruit would most likely help a team win. The strategy worked, as discussed by Michael Lewis in *Moneyball;* after using the model, the Oakland Athletics won their division, despite their low payroll. Oakland's success did not go unnoticed; when the Boston Red Sox, a team with a high payroll, started using the model, they won the World Series.

These empirical models are sometimes called *data-mining models,* but I prefer to call them *pattern-finding models.* They play an important role in the modern microeconomist's tool kit and have become more important because of the enormous increase in computing power and statistical software. This increase in computer power allows economic researchers to find stable patterns in data much more easily than before. With sophisticated econometric software, computers can automatically find patterns and turn those patterns into models.

Summarizing: The development of computer power and these empirical models has led to an enormous change in how modern microeconomics is done. For example, when I asked top graduate students as part of an interview what differentiated an economist from another social scientist, they did *not* say that they differed from other social scientists in the building blocks they used. Instead, they said that the difference was the economist's reliance on formal empirical methods.[4]

SIMPLE DATA MODELS: CHARTS, GRAPHS, AND QUANTITATIVE ARGUMENTATION
As a principles student, you will likely not be developing regression models, but you will be building models based on data by developing a

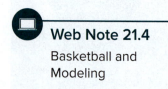

Web Note 21.4

Basketball and Modeling

Regression models can reveal all sorts of relationships from the effect of weather on the quality of wine to the contribution of a player's ability to draw a walk toward a team's season record.

---

[4]That may change in the future since other social sciences are becoming much more empirical as well, but for the next decade they will likely still lag behind economics.

chart or a graph that demonstrates how something is changing over time or a pattern that captures the co-movement of two variables. These charts and graphs might not have the full scientific look of a regression model, but they are often more useful. What characterizes the modern economic way of thinking is not the regression model per se, but using quantitative data to make an argument, often by presenting those data with a simple chart or graph.

The Role of Formal Models

Were economic modeling only a matter of data mining, empirical models would replace all other types of modeling, but it is not, and they haven't. Data, by themselves, have no meaning; they have to be interpreted and given meaning, and how one interprets the data depends on the model and the building blocks one has in mind. Either implicitly or explicitly, one's model guides how one organizes the data. That's why theory remains important, and an important part of this principles course is meant to give you practice in understanding the theoretical structure of economic thinking.

You can see the importance of theory by thinking about a magic eye picture—as you change your focus, what you see will change. (You can see a magic eye picture at www.magiceye.com.) A simpler example is the figure of the old woman shown here. Did you see an "old woman"? Most of you will have because that's how I described it. But what if I had said "beautiful young woman" rather than "old woman"? If I had, I suspect you might have seen the picture in a different light. The moral: Which pattern your eye sees in pictures, and even more so in data, depends on the implicit model or frame that you bring to the picture or the data. (If you see only one, keep looking; the eye of the "old woman" is the ear of the beautiful young woman.)

I raise this issue of framing because it highlights the difficulty of pulling information from an empirical model. Two different economists may well see different results even with the same empirical model. Let's consider an example of such a recent debate in economics. The debate concerns the deterrent effect of the death penalty.

In natural science one would determine whether the death penalty has a deterrent effect by doing a controlled experiment that isolates specific variables and changing one variable to see if it causes another to change. But in economics such controlled experiments are generally impossible. An economist can't suggest that we try out the death penalty to see what its deterrent effect would be. So instead of using controlled experiments, economists need to be creative and search for what they call a **natural experiment** (*an event created by nature that can serve as an experiment*) that may help shed light on an issue.

Doing such a study with existing data, economists Isaac Ehrlich and Joanna Shepherd have found a statistical relationship between the death penalty and the number of murders. In one statistical study, Ehrlich found that an increase in the number of executions by 1 percent is associated with a decrease in the murder rate by 0.5 percent, while Shepherd found that one execution deterred seven to eight murders. These statistical relationships have been contested by a number of economists. They pointed out that how the variables are specified and the equations mattered. For example, using the same data, economists John Donohue and Justin Wulfers came to quite different conclusions. They stated: "The view that the death penalty deters is still the product of belief, not evidence."

I'm not going to get into the debate here; I don't claim to know who is right. I recount it merely to give you a sense that given the limited ability economists have to conduct controlled experiments, letting the data speak will not necessarily provide the definitive answer. This means that economists, and other social scientists, must rely on their theoretical models to guide them in interpreting data and in drawing out policy implications from their work.

Original image from an anonymous German postcard, circa 1888

©Chronicle/Alamy Stock Photo

The same pattern can be interpreted in multiple ways. Economists rely on theoretical models to help them interpret the data.

Q-8 True or false? Debates in modern economics will be resolved by letting the data speak.

DIFFERENT TYPES OF FORMAL MODELS THAT ECONOMISTS USE

The above discussion leads us to a third characteristic of modern economics. Earlier economists used models with relatively simple relationships among variables; the supply/demand model is an example of such a simple model. Modern economists—both modern traditional and modern behavioral economists—still use simple models, but they also use models that allow for much more complex relationships among variables than do the simple models. These analytically sophisticated models cannot be expressed in the two-dimensional graphs used by earlier economists.

An example of the difference between earlier economists and modern economists can be seen by considering the "tipping-point" model that Landsburg used to analyze differences in car insurance prices. As I stated earlier, that model is a path-dependent model, which technically means that any decision feeds back into the model. In a path-dependent model, you can only know what will happen if you know the path the model takes. Mathematically, specifying path-dependent models is much more complicated than specifying supply/demand models; you have to use an advanced-calculus, differential-equations model rather than a standard algebraic model, or you have to solve it computationally.

The reason why formal models have evolved from simple models to more complex and highly technical mathematical models, again, is that technology has changed. In this case, the technology is mathematics. Today's economists are much better trained in mathematics than were earlier economists, which allows economists to go far beyond the interrelationships allowed in supply/demand models. With advances in mathematics, for example, you can have:

- Models with many equilibria, so it is difficult to know what an equilibrium is.

- Models in which not only are the variables related, but so too are the changes in variables and the changes in changes in variables.

- Models in which systemic equilibrium involves enormous continual change in the parts so that even though the system is in equilibrium, the individual parts are not.

- Models in which relationships are nonlinear on various levels, and in which an infinitely small change can lead to drastically different results.

The potential interrelationships that can be captured in modern formal models are almost unending, and when one studies the broad range of models with all these potential interrelationships, the number of potential outcomes in the economy is awesome. There is a formal theoretical model that can arrive at just about any possible conclusion.

Which theoretical model is right? Do you choose models with more complex building blocks, as argued by behavioral economists? Or do you choose models with more limiting traditional building blocks? Do you not worry about building blocks? Or do you just worry about which model best fits the empirical evidence? Such questions are the grist of the modern economists' debates. (And you thought we economists were boring people; if my kids only understood how wildly interesting these questions are—would you believe?)

THE TRADE-OFF BETWEEN SIMPLICITY AND COMPLETENESS

You might think that one should use the most complex model with the broadest building blocks because that would give you the broadest approach. But that doesn't necessarily follow. Each new interrelationship involves adding an additional level of technical difficulty, and the more complex the model, the harder it is to arrive at a conclusion. Thus, in their modeling, economists make a continual trade-off between simplicity and completeness. At the principles level, the choice is clear: KISS (Keep It Simple Stupid)

Q-9 Is the supply and demand model a path-dependent model?

rules, which is why the graphical supply/demand model is the workhorse of principles of economics. That's why, even though modern economics goes far beyond supply and demand, the principles course focuses on supply and demand and teaches students the traditional model.[5] Almost all economists agree that the supply/demand model is a really neat and useful model when used appropriately with sufficient caveats for introducing principles students to economic reasoning. It is the perfect calisthenics of the mind for moving on to models with more complicated behavioral building blocks.

Let me give an example of where the model one uses matters: the state of the U.S. aggregate economy in 2008. The question at issue was: Should we be worried about the economy going into a depression or not? The traditional aggregate-supply/aggregate-demand model, which was the standard textbook model at the time, suggested that we should not be concerned. In it, the economy is close to equilibrium, and policies exist to move it to equilibrium if it isn't. That isn't the case for some of the more complex formal models. In these more complex models, the aggregate economy could suddenly change depending on what people believe. You can have what is called a **self-confirming equilibrium**—*an equilibrium in a model in which people's beliefs become self-fulfilling*—so if people think the economy will go into a depression, it will. In some models, what people believe might not even matter; you can have *strange attractor models,* sometimes called **butterfly effect models**—*models in which a small change causes a large effect.* For example, a butterfly flapping its wings in China can cause the output of the U.S. economy to fall significantly. In these models, a small change could tip the economy into a low-growth, high-unemployment equilibrium that would be difficult to escape. In these models, therefore, we had reason to be seriously concerned about the U.S. economy going into a depression. Unfortunately, the slow growth since then suggests that the more complicated models were correct.

OTHER FORMAL MODELS There are many other types of formal models as well. For example, *set theory models* are models based only on formal logical relationships and are used by theoretical economists when doing abstract theory. Yet another model used by economists is a **game theory model**—*a model in which one analyzes the strategic interaction of individuals when they take into account the likely response of other people to their actions.* Game theory models, rather than supply/demand models, form the core of much of what is studied in graduate microeconomics today. Thus, the standard graduate microeconomics text has only three supply and demand diagrams in an entire 1,000-plus-page book.

More complicated models often yield no analytic solution—that is, you can't solve the set of equations to discover the equilibrium in the model. These complicated analytic models were unusable for a traditional economist because a model that you couldn't solve analytically didn't provide any insight. That isn't the case for a modern economist. If a modern economist can't solve a model analytically, he or she will estimate the solution by simulating the model with a computer. Computational power replaces analytic elegance. Thus, computer simulation is an important tool of modern

⬜ **Web Note 21.5**
Models in Movies

Game theory models analyze the strategic interaction among individuals.

---

[5] I discuss the justification for why the textbooks focus on the supply/demand model and the traditional model, even as the economists in their research have moved from them, in *The Stories Economists Tell* and a *Journal of Economic Education* article, "What Economists Teach and What We Believe." While the supply/demand model captures these ideas, for mathematically inclined students, as Harold Kuhn, a famous mathematical economist, once told his students, the lessons can be generalized into a set of constrained optimization models assuming convex functions, and if principles students were strongly mathematically inclined, many of the models could be presented in calculus format in one-twentieth the space.

economists (both those using behavioral and those using traditional assumptions), and in his or her research a modern economist will often go from struggling with analytically solving a model to simulating it on the computer, and then back to trying to solve it analytically.

Economists use a number of different types of computer simulations. The one described above was a simulation designed to solve a model with a specified set of equations that can't be solved analytically. In those types of simulations, the computer is a computational assistant that can arrive at estimated solutions to complicated analytic sets of equations. This approach is widespread. A more novel approach to computer simulation is designed to deal with problems that are so difficult that you don't even know how to specify the equations. How do economists model when they can't specify the equations that describe the relationships in the model? They use the computer to guide them in specifying the model itself.

This alternative approach to modeling is called the **agent-based computational economic (ACE) model**—*a culture dish approach to the study of economic phenomena in which agents* (encapsulated collections of data and methods representing an entity residing in that environment on the computer) *are allowed to interact in a computationally constructed environment and the researcher observes the results of that interaction.* (For more information about ACE models, see www.econ.iastate.edu/tesfatsi/ace.htm.) ACE modeling is fundamentally different from standard modeling. It is computer-based, and it has no equations that have to be solved. Instead, ACE researchers simply try to create virtual computer models that capture the essence of the interdependencies, and then observe the results. So rather than solve a model, you build a computer model with computer agents; you then run the model thousands of times and keep track of the results.

This is a fascinating new approach to modeling complex systems because it allows for all types of interactions. It has the possibility of fundamentally changing the way economists model and how they understand the economy because it allows researchers to consider much more complicated interactions than they could if they had to "solve" the model on their own. For example, ACE models can allow multiple equilibria and the possibility of many levels of path dependency—complications that are beyond traditional models. Recognizing that the models may reflect path dependency, the ACE modeler doesn't run the program once; he or she runs it thousands of times and sees the range of results. So just like engineers are now using virtual computer modeling to design planes and cars, economists are now using virtual computer models to understand how the economy works and to devise policies that might make it work better.

EMPIRICALLY TESTING FORMAL MODELS   With so many different models, one must ask: How do you decide which model to use? To decide, economists empirically test alternative models and try to see which one fits best. Essentially this reverses the process used in heuristic empirical modeling, where the data are collected and analyzed before the hypothesis is determined and are then used to determine the hypothesis. With empirically tested formal models, the hypothesis is formulated first—without knowledge of the data—and then the hypothesis is tested to see if the data fit the model. Obviously, formulating hypotheses without knowing the data is difficult, and thus economists try to test hypotheses on "out-of-sample" data—data that were not used in the formulation of the hypothesis. If they don't have such data, they try to develop the data, or something close to them, with experiments and clever observation of events.

Today, fitting the models to the data is much of what modern economists do. "Bringing the model to the data" is a phrase you hear all the time from modern economists. Economists are continually asking questions such as: "How does the model

The ACE model is like a petri dish of individual economic actors deployed with specific behaviors. Economists watch and study the relationships and behaviors that develop.

A REMINDER

Modern Traditional and Behavioral Economists

	Earlier Economics	Modern Economics	
		Modern Behavioral Economists	Modern Traditional Economists
Assumptions	Rationality	Purposeful behavior	Rationality
	Self-interest	Enlightened self-interest	Self-interest
Approach	Deduction	Induction and deduction; emphasis on experimental economics and empirical models	Induction and deduction; emphasis on empirical models
Types of models	Simple supply/demand models	All types including highly complex mathematical models and ACE models	All types including highly complex mathematical models and ACE models

work in out-of-sample data?" "Do we have a natural experiment that we can use to test the model?" "Can we develop a randomized experiment that will test the model?" "Can we design a lab experiment that will test the model?" and "Can we design a field experiment to test the model?"

Such empirical testing requires precision, which means that to truly bring the model to the data, one needs a formal model where all relationships are precisely specified, rather than a heuristic model where relationships are imprecise. Thus, the "empirical models" discussed earlier are quite different from the "empirically tested formal models" that form the foundation of economic science. Empirical models based on heuristic models are fine for policy analysis and for guiding real-world policy decisions that have to be made before one has a full scientific understanding of an issue. These models are absolutely necessary. But before one elevates the insights of the model to the level of full scientific knowledge, one needs much more precise models. As I stated at the beginning of the chapter, most of this book is concerned with engineering models, not scientific models, which is why we will not explore the intricacies of testing formal models.

The difference between the empirical models discussed earlier and the empirically tested formal models described here is a subtle, but important, difference. In a heuristic empirical model, one has only an informal model that lets the data speak first, as heard through your general worldview embodied in your building blocks. After you've heard the data, you can provide an explanation for what you have heard. That explanation will be based on your implicit formal model, *but the empirical model cannot be an explicit test of the model* since the actual model came from the data; there is no formal model to test. To empirically test a formal model or a formalized empirical model developed from a data set, the process is different. Here, one carefully develops the implications of the formal model as they relate to the issue. Then one empirically tests this model's implications against another set of data.

In a heuristic empirical model, one has only an informal model that lets the data speak first.

APPLICATION: WHY DID THE PRICE OF CHOCOLATE RISE?   To see how formal models can make a difference in how one thinks about real-world problems, let's consider an example of a puzzle that economists faced. This example gives you a sense of why modern economists have moved to these more complicated models and how the results of the two models differ—even with the same data. The puzzle is the following—the price of chocolate. From 2006 to 2009, the price of chocolate went up to $3,500 a ton from $1,500 a ton. The question is why.

You should be able to give the traditional economic analysis of what likely happened from the analysis of earlier chapters—that explanation would involve supply falling, demand rising, or a combination of the two. (A good exercise is to graph these to see why that would be the explanation.) In a principles course, that would be the right answer. For real-world researchers it is not enough. The problem is that the data don't reveal any apparent shifts in either supply or demand. So why did the price change when supply and demand did not?

Exploring the situation further, economists discovered that there was a structural change in the market. *Hedge funds*—investment funds representing rich investors which had few constraints on what they could buy—that had access to large amounts of credit were moving their investments out of real estate and into commodities over this time period. Chocolate was one of these commodities, but commodities whose prices rose also included oil and grains, both of which also experienced sudden large increases in price during this same time period. These hedge funds did not want the chocolate, and they did not buy chocolate and store it. Instead, they were buying what are called *chocolate futures*—the right to buy chocolate at a specified point in the future at a specified price—in large amounts. Specifically, they increased their demand for chocolate futures from 260 thousand tons to 706 thousand tons over a couple of years, which amounts to an increase from less than 10 percent to more than 20 percent of the total market demand. Prices of chocolate rose to their highest level in more than 30 years.

The question that policy makers posed to economists was whether this hedge fund activity in the futures market was the cause of the rise in the price of chocolate (and other commodities), and if it were the cause, would the rise in price be permanent or temporary? The supply/demand model doesn't directly answer that question. The answer requires an analysis that includes inventories and that captures the relationship between future expected prices—the futures prices of chocolates—and the current price of chocolate. That means that you need a model of intertemporal (across time periods) equilibrium with heterogeneous agents (agents that are not exactly alike).

You also need to figure out how the new behavioral economics building blocks might be playing a role in determining the outcome. For example, one key concept of behavioral economics is an anchor point. *Anchor points* are points toward which people gravitate. The existence of anchor points can lead to multiple equilibria for the model. It is possible that the hedge funds increased other participants' anchor point for chocolate prices, which in turn led them to increase their inventory of chocolate. The demand increases and ratifies the increase in price, even though there was no need for price to increase had the anchor point not changed. (I should also point out that hedge funds pay economists large amounts of money to model the economy and to decide where they should invest their funds. So if hedge funds were doing this, it may be because they hired a modern economist who developed a model that showed them how they might do it.)

One needs a more advanced formal model than the supply/demand model to deal with many real-world questions.

The analysis quickly becomes complicated, but what is clear is that one needs a more advanced formal model than the supply/demand model to deal with the question. Essentially, the answer economists arrived at was that the hedge fund purchases could have temporarily pushed up the price of chocolate, but did not do so permanently. Later, chocolate prices fell nearly 40 percent amid bumper crops and a continued decline in consumer demand due to a weak global economy. A similar run-up and price reversal occurred again between 2013 and 2017, although these price fluctuations were tied to the weather. Related puzzles exist in various markets, and economists are hard at work on them. The lesson of this example: Supply and demand are just the beginning for a modern economist.

Supply and demand are just the beginning for a modern economist.

What Difference Does All This Make to Policy?

Let me now turn to a consideration of what difference these modeling considerations have for policy. The answer is: a lot. Let me briefly distinguish the differences. An economist who concentrates on a single frame tends to be more consistent in his or her policy recommendation. In the past, the framework was that the market is likely the best way to deal with a problem, and that, left alone, the market will guide people toward doing the best they, and society, can, given the constraints. Steven Landsburg nicely summed up what a traditional economist expects in his discussion of the insurance markets.

Modern economists, with their multiple frames, are less sure of the conclusion that the market will solve every problem. They accept that the market has nice properties, but they also find that it has limitations. They know that there are many models where there exists a potential role for public policy in dealing with those limitations. That's why *for a modern economist who uses multiple frames, policy does not follow directly from a model*. As I discussed in the introductory chapter, models provide *theorems*—results that follow logically from a model—not *precepts*—general rules for public policy. Precepts are developed from theorems that follow from various models, along with knowledge of history and of limitations of the models.

Let's consider three examples where a modern economist's precepts might differ from a traditional economist's precepts.

Q-10 If a model tells you that price controls will reduce people's welfare, does it follow that economists will advise governments not to impose price controls?

How much emphasis should be given to benefits of economic growth?

The traditional economist's precept is that more is preferred to less, and that more output is generally good; thus, policies directed at achieving more growth make society better off. The behavioral economic precept is that growth should be questioned. They point out that people's happiness depends on their relative, not their absolute, income after an annual per capita income of about $75,000 is reached. That means that more growth will not necessarily benefit society, and suggests that more focus should be given to how the existing income is distributed, rather than just focusing on total income.

Should the government have done something about the dramatic rise in housing prices in the early 2000s?

The earlier precept is that no, government probably shouldn't have. The rise in housing prices that occurred represented people's valuation of the worth of the house. They may have made a mistake in this instance, but there is no reason to believe that the government would have gotten it right, and you can only tell whether houses are overvalued after the fact, not before.

The modern precept (based on dynamic models of interacting agents) for both modern traditional and behavioral economists is that financial bubbles, where prices of assets significantly exceed their sustainable prices, are possible, and that the housing market in the early 2000s had all the signs of a bubble, which means that the government might have usefully intervened. The bursting of the housing bubble was something that was predictable, and something that policy could have eliminated the need for.

Are people saving enough?

The earlier precept is that people make rational decisions and if they are choosing to save little, that reflects their desires and best estimates of their future needs. The behavioral economics precept is that how much people save depends on the institutional structure of the economy, and with so much of the institutional structure designed to get people to spend, people likely save far too little. But this does not mean that government has to tell people to save more. Instead, government can change the institutional structure so that people will save more. For example, when employees are choosing among savings plans at work the default option could be saving 15 percent of income. People would have to check a box if they don't want to save. By changing the default option on retirement savings plans, one can significantly change the amount people choose to save, leaving people free to make their own decision in both cases.

I could give many more such examples.

Conclusion

Modern economics goes far beyond supply and demand.

This has been a wide-ranging survey of what economists do, and what it means to think like a modern economist. Summarizing, briefly, modern economics goes far beyond supply and demand. Modern microeconomics is open to a wider range of building blocks and models, and is highly empirical. Thinking like a modern economist means approaching problems through modeling, and then relating the results of the model to the empirical evidence. Ultimately, the choice of models is made by empirically testing those models and choosing the one that does the best job of predicting.

The distinction between modern and traditional economists can be overdone. In many ways, the difference is just in when to put real-world complications into the model. Traditional economists use the traditional building blocks, and then adjust the model to fit the more complicated real world. That has the advantage of keeping the basic model clean and as simple as possible, but has the cost of not fitting many real-world situations. Modern economists use more complicated models so that fewer adjustments need to be made. The advantage is that the models better fit more real-world situations, but the disadvantage is that the models are not as clean and clear-cut as the traditional approach.

KISS reigns.

For teaching purposes, KISS reigns, and most economists, including me, continue to emphasize the traditional micro- and macroeconomic models. Modern insights are added as addenda and modifications.

Summary

- Modeling is the glue that holds economics together. But economists differ in the models that they use.   (*LO21-1*)

- A deductive approach is to begin with principles and logically deduce the implications of those principles.

An inductive approach is to develop a model based on patterns in observed data. Modern economists tend to approach models inductively, while traditional economists approach models deductively. (*LO21-1*)

- Behavioral economists replace the traditional assumption of rationality with purposeful behavior and replace self-interest with enlightened self-interested behavior. (*LO21-1*)

- While models based on modern building blocks often better fit observed behavior, they often do not generalize to contexts outside the one being studied. (*LO21-1*)

- Heuristic models are models expressed informally in words. They can be based on either traditional building blocks like the models of Landsburg or modern building blocks like the models of Frank. (*LO21-2*)

- The validity of models often is determined based on their ability to explain real-world data. Thus, models must be tested against the data. This is part of the scientific method. (*LO21-2*)

- An empirical model is a model that statistically discovers a pattern in the data. For such a model to be scientifically tested, it must be tested against another set of data. A regression model is an example of an empirical model. (*LO21-3*)

- Two types of models used by modern economists are game theory models and agent-based computational economic models. (*LO21-3*)

- Traditional economists tend to concentrate on a single frame and offer more policy recommendations based on the assumption of a well-functioning market. (*LO21-4*)

- Modern economists use multiple frames and carefully distinguish between theorems that follow from models and precepts that rely on theorems, but they also rely on judgments about history and institutions. (*LO21-4*)

Key Terms

agent-based computational economic (ACE) model
behavioral economics
butterfly effect model
coefficient of determination

deductive approach
econometrics
empirical model
endowment effects
enlightened self-interest
game theory model

heuristic model
inductive approach
model
modern economist
natural experiment
path-dependent model

precommitment strategy
purposeful behavior
regression model
self-confirming equilibrium
traditional economist

Questions and Exercises ■ connect

1. How is a model different from the reality that it represents? Give an example. (*LO21-1*)

2. How does an inductive approach to economics differ from a deductive approach? (*LO21-1*)

3. What are the two main building blocks for traditional economists? How do they differ from the building blocks of behavioral economists? (*LO21-1*)

4. How does enlightened self-interest differ from self-interest? (*LO21-1*)

5. One rule of thumb many people follow is "Eat until your plate is clean." How does this rule of thumb violate the rationality assumption? (*LO21-1*)

6. Name two advantages and two disadvantages of the traditional model. (*LO21-1*)

7. Name two advantages and two disadvantages of the behavioral model. (*LO21-1*)

8. In a study, when asked to choose between an iPod retailing for $100 and $100 cash, people were more likely to choose the money. But when they were given an iPod and then asked if they would trade it for $100, they were more likely to choose the iPod. (*LO21-2*)

   a. What effect does this reflect?

   b. Is this behavior rational?

9. What is a *heuristic model?* Can a heuristic model be traditional? Why or why not?　(*LO21-2*)

10. Why might government intervention make sense in a model of path dependency but not a supply/demand model?　(*LO21-2*)

11. According to economist Robert Frank, why are people more likely to return $20 they'd been given in error in change than a lampshade that had not been scanned at checkout? What does this say about traditional building blocks?　(*LO21-2*)

12. Why do economists rely more on empirical evidence today than they did 100 years ago?　(*LO21-3*)

13. What does it mean to "let the data speak"?　(*LO21-3*)

14. What is a regression?　(*LO21-3*)

15. What characteristics would you look for in data to use as a natural experiment?　(*LO21-3*)

16. What is an agent-based computational economic model?　(*LO21-3*)

17. Why are "out-of-sample" data important for testing inductive models?　(*LO21-3*)

18. True or false? Models provide both theorems and precepts. Explain your answer.　(*LO21-4*)

19. State whether each of the policy recommendations is an example of a modern economist's precepts or a traditional economist's precepts.　(*LO21-4*)
    a. More goods are preferred to fewer goods.
    b. Banks ought to be required to get approval for new financial instruments.
    c. Firms can decide what information to put on food labels because consumers will demand that relevant information be listed.
    d. Utility companies ought to provide consumers a chart comparing their electricity usage with the average in their neighborhood.

Questions from Alternative Perspectives

1. How might modeling itself frame an economist's analysis, making the economist unable to see basic truths about the way in which society subjugates women? *(Feminist)*

2. Was Mother Teresa rational? *(Religious)*

3. It is sometimes said that modern economists pose little questions that can be answered while sociologists pose large questions that cannot be answered. How might that description be related to the economist's modeling approach? *(Radical)*

4. The book talks as if modern economists have made a large break from traditional assumptions; many heterodox economists see the two as simply minor modifications of the same approach. In what way is that true? *(Austrian)*

5. If modern economics focuses on empirical models, does that mean that those aspects of life that cannot be quantified are shortchanged? *(Institutionalist)*

Issues to Ponder

1. What does it mean to assume that people are purposeful in their behavior instead of rational?

2. In one study, a group of Asian American women were asked to take a math exam. First they were divided into two groups. Before taking the test, individuals in the first group were asked their opinions about coed dorms while the second were asked their family history. Those who had been reminded by the questions that they were women performed worse than those who were reminded that they were Asian. How is this an example of predictably irrational behavior?

3. Is the supply/demand model a path-dependent model? Why or why not?

4. Can an economist who bases her models on traditional building blocks be a modern economist? Why or why not?

5. What might an economist do if he cannot solve a model analytically? (Give up is not an option.)

6. A student is given the option of selecting two homework schedules—one in which three five-page papers and one one-page paper are due at the end of the semester and another in which the first three papers are due the third, sixth, and ninth weeks of the semester and the last paper is due at the end.
   a. Why might a student choose the first option?
   b. Why might a student choose the second option?
   c. Which is the rational choice?

Answers to Margin Questions

1. Modeling, not supply and demand, is the glue that holds modern economics together. (*LO21-1*)

2. Because of technological changes in computing, modern economists are more likely to use inductive models compared to earlier economists, who gave more weight to deductive models. (*LO21-1*)

3. These are both assumptions associated with behavioral economists. (*LO21-1*)

4. It depends on what model you use. In a traditional model it cannot because people choose what is best for them. Thus a constraint upon choice must make them worse off. In a behavioral model, it may make them better off because people are not assumed to have complete self-control. (*LO21-1*)

5. It depends. Both have their advantages and disadvantages, and a choice can be made only when one knows the purpose of the model. (*LO21-1*)

6. No, it simply demonstrates that he is affected by them in different ways than are other people. (*LO21-2*)

7. Economists are hesitant to base knowledge on heuristic models because they are only suggestive, and are subject to people's tendency to be fast pattern completers. Science involves slow, and precise, pattern completion. The rules of scientific models are in many ways rules designed to slow people down and make sure the patterns they complete really do fit together. (*LO21-3*)

8. False. While it would be nice if that were the case, the data speak very softly and what one hears depends upon one's frame. Thus, in economics the data seldom provide definitive answers, and economists must rely on their theoretical models to guide them. (*LO21-3*)

9. No. In a path-dependent model the path to equilibrium affects the equilibrium. The supply/demand model assumes that is not the case. (*LO21-4*)

10. No. One derives theorems (logical implications) from models; policy is based on precepts. Thus, the fact that most economists oppose price controls is based on both a model and judgments about the appropriateness of that model. (*LO21-5*)

CHAPTER 22

Behavioral Economics and Modern Economic Policy

> Nobody's ever gone broke underestimating the intelligence of the general public.
>
> —H. L. Mencken

After reading this chapter, you should be able to:

LO22-1 Explain the relationship between behavioral economic policy and mechanism design.

LO22-2 Define *nudge* and *choice architecture* and explain how they are related to behavioral economic policy.

LO22-3 Discuss the problems of implementing nudges and how the behavioral economic frame changes how policy is viewed.

LO22-4 Discuss the concerns many traditional economists have about nudge and push policies.

When Dutch economist Aad Kieboom was put in charge of the men's restroom at the Amsterdam Airport, he instructed the builders to etch an image of a black housefly on each urinal. As we will see later in the chapter, that directive was an application of modern behavioral economic theory to policy. In this chapter, you will learn why it is, and many other ways in which behavioral economics changes the way economists approach policy.

I begin the chapter by putting the developments in behavioral economic policy in historical perspective, explaining why they developed. I then briefly review the policy implications of the traditional supply/demand models that have been the core of this book's presentation. Finally, I turn to the core of this chapter—behavioral economic policy and how it differs from more traditional economic policy.

©Roberts Publishing Services

Behavioral Economic Policy in Perspective

As discussed in the last chapter, behavioral economics is that branch of modern economics that broadens the assumptions about behavior from rationality and self-interest to purposeful behavior and enlightened self-interest. As behavioral economists have broadened the building blocks of their models, they have also started to explore the implications of those broader building blocks for policy. Thus, today a **behavioral economic policy**—*economic policy based upon models using behavioral economic building blocks that take into account people's predictable irrational behavior*—is emerging that complements traditional economic policy.

Behavioral Economics and Economic Engineering

Behavioral economic policy has developed as part of a broader change in the way that economists see their role in policy making. As their understanding of markets has increased, modern economists have moved more heavily into what might be called **economic engineering**—*economics devoted not only to studying markets but also to designing markets and other coordinating mechanisms*. Economic engineers don't just try to understand the way the economy works as economic scientists do. Economic engineers ask: Can we design mechanisms to better coordinate people's actions?

As modern economists have moved more toward engineering, they have begun to explore a broad range of mechanisms and institutions that solve coordination problems. These mechanisms and institutions are called **coordination mechanisms**—*methods of coordinating people's wants with other people's desires*. All markets are a type of coordination mechanism. There are auction markets, posted-price markets, and markets where firms set prices. Each of these mechanisms coordinates wants in a slightly different way. What this means is that there is not a single market solution, but hundreds of them. The economic policy debate is not about whether to have a market solution; the policy debate is what coordinating mechanism will best solve the problem at hand.

Economists began studying coordinating mechanisms by studying markets with money prices. They soon discovered that coordinating mechanisms that don't involve money prices can be modeled as if they do involve prices. To study these coordinating mechanisms, they developed formal models based on **shadow prices**—*prices that aren't paid directly, but instead are paid in terms of opportunity cost borne by the demander, and thus determine his or her choices indirectly*. In these shadow price models, every choice has an associated implicit shadow price, regardless of whether money is exchanged or not. Shadow price models convert opportunity costs to shadow prices.

Shadow price analysis is extremely powerful. For example, it allows you to take morals and social pressure into account in your model. Take stealing, for example. A shadow price of stealing is violating your moral code. If this shadow price is too high, you will choose not to steal. Shadow price models allow you to indirectly measure the price of violating your morals.

Let me give an example of the power of shadow price analysis. In his book *Freedomnomics: Why the Free Market Works and Other Half-Baked Theories Don't,* economist John Lott gives an example of the number of batters hit by a ball when up at bat in the American and National Leagues. Starting in 1973, more batters were being hit in the American League than in the National League. The question was why. Lott developed a shadow price model that determined the cost to a pitcher of throwing a beanball (a pitch aimed at the batter's head). He pointed out that in 1973, the American League instituted the designated hitter (pitchers were exempt from batting). The new rule meant that the pitcher no longer could be hit by a ball thrown by the opposing team's pitcher in retaliation. In his model for American League pitchers that rule change lowered the shadow price of throwing a beanball. The model gave him an explanation: The increase in beanballs in 1973 occurred because the cost of throwing a beanball fell for an American League pitcher. (Applying this insight to policy suggests that to reduce the number of beanballs, the league might raise the money price of pitching a beanball, perhaps by instituting a $10,000 fine for every hit batsman.) Shadow price analysis is central to the way in which economists think about the effect of incentives on an individual's actions and how institutions interact with incentives.

Q-1 How does economic engineering differ from economic science?

There is not a single market solution; there are hundreds of them.

Q-2 How does a shadow price differ from a normal price?

Shadow price analysis allows you to take morals and social pressures into account in your models.

Shadow price analysis has allowed economists to expand the scope of economics.

and thus not a strong nudge, despite the fact that labeling would be a government regulation. However, many economists oppose such labeling since most scientific tests have found that milk that comes from cows given the growth hormone rBST is no different from milk that does not; they argue that people's concern about rBST is itself predictably irrational—people cannot deal with complicated issues. Other economists argue that regardless of what science may conclude, if people believe that rBST milk is bad for them, they should be given the information needed to avoid milk with rBST; the regulation is simply providing feedback.

The problem is that placing the statement on the milk carton will likely raise people's concerns about the issue and lead some to choose higher-priced milk than they otherwise would. Should the government require such labeling or not, and if so, what other information should be included on the labels? Should people be informed of the antibiotic treatment cows receive, along with many other facts about how cow milk is produced? Where does one draw the line?

It Isn't Clear Government Knows Better

A third concern is that behavioral economic policies (whether true nudge policies or push policies) require government to decide, on the advice of behavioral economists, what is best for people, and what people truly want. For example, a "luxury tax," a policy that Frank and others advocate, involves determining what is a luxury and what is a necessity.

For example, Pennsylvania taxes bathing suits because it consider them luxuries. Even though policies to tax luxuries may seem to resonate with the sense of frustration that many of us feel about perceived excesses of modern society, implementing such a policy requires the government to decide which goods make people truly happy and which goods don't. Doing that isn't easy. If people truly cared about relative, not absolute, income, people would be happy to give up some percentage of their income as long as everyone else did so as well. They are not.

How can we be sure behavioral economists, or whoever is the decision maker about what nudges and pushes to implement, are right about what is best for people? Even if economists could agree that people do not always act in their own self-interest, it isn't clear government can determine what's in people's best interest either.

Government Policy May Make the Situation Worse

A fourth concern is that nudge policy substantially increases the potential for *government failure*—where government, in dealing with a problem, actually makes the problem worse. Will government have the willpower to limit its nudges to the set that behavioral economists, or some other group, determine is appropriate? Or will it use nudges in other ways—perhaps to win an election, or to benefit one group over another? Just as traditional economists are concerned with government failure in implementing traditional economic policies to correct for externalities, traditional economists are concerned with government failure in implementing nudge policies.

Traditional economists argue that accepting behavioral economic policy will start the government sliding along a slippery slope. Since the government has a monopoly on power, somehow that monopoly has to be kept in check if it is to benefit the people, not members of the government or its friends. For that reason, early Classical economists argued that government power had to be kept under control, even when the appropriate use of power could improve the situation, because one cannot assume that government will appropriately use its power. Because of the fear of an oppressive government, earlier economists felt that, for all its problems, the market with minimal government intervention was often the better alternative. Economics' laissez-faire set of policy precepts arose as part of a liberal tradition that was based upon certain

Web Note 22.4

Questioning Nudge Policies

Even if economists could agree that people do not always act in their own self-interest, it isn't clear government can determine what's in people's best interest either.

Q-10   What are four concerns about behavioral economic policies?

Traditional economists argue that accepting behavioral economic policy will start the government sliding along a slippery slope.

inalienable rights of the individual that government could not violate. These arguments fit in political philosophy and are outside the confines of this text, but they are the ones that a consideration of behavioral economic policy raises.

A Changing View of Economists: From Pro-market Advocates to Economic Engineers

I have defined economic efficiency as achieving a goal as cheaply as possible and said that economists advise government on how to achieve economic efficiency. The traditional economic model made a shorthand adjustment to interpret the goal of society as designing the economy to maximize people's consumption. Markets tend to do that, and hence the traditional economic model tended to support markets.

Traditional economics justified its concentration on maximizing people's consumption by arguing that people knew what they wanted better than anyone else, and their actions revealed their desires. Consumer sovereignty was not to be questioned. Behavioral economics questions consumer sovereignty and thus opens up a Pandora's box of issues that the traditional economic model keeps out of sight.

Behavioral economics is part of a broader movement in modern economics where economists see themselves as mechanism design engineers. They solve problems by building coordination mechanisms that achieve predetermined goals. Traditional economists' models focus on economic incentives and people's tendency to respond to price incentives. Behavioral economists' models modify that by taking into account people's tendency to be predictably irrational. In doing this, behavioral economics opens up the policy discussion of economics from the traditional economic view that prices and incentives matter to a broader view that *everything matters*. For a behavioral economist, modern economic policy making involves complicated issues, and we need to take into account those complications when designing policy.

Who can argue with the truism that everything matters? Who better than a traditional economist using a behavioral economist's argument. Behavioral economics tells us that people are not good at making decisions when issues are complicated. Economic policy involves very complicated decisions, and the general population and policy makers need a nudge to get them to make good decisions. The traditional model gives them that nudge by concentrating on the most important aspects of choice—price incentives—and not distracting the analysis as behavioral economics does by concentrating on the many irrationalities that people exhibit. Furthermore, the traditional model protects individual liberty and prevents the state from trying to shape people's wants. By taking the focus away from that most important incentive, models based on behavioral economic insights fail to give people that nudge to concentrate on the most important element—price incentives—and, therefore, are likely to do more harm than good.

I leave it to you to decide which argument is right.

> Behavioral economics questions consumer sovereignty and thus opens up a Pandora's box of issues that the traditional economic model keeps out of sight.

Conclusion

I am a big fan of complexity theory, which pictures the economy as a complex evolving system. But not only is the economy evolving, so too is the economics profession. This chapter gives you a sense of that evolution, and the implications of those changes for policy. As you can see, behavioral economics opens up a new set of policy questions and new ways of looking at the world through an economic lens. It shows you that economics is not a single lens, but a set of lenses that recognize that incentives are important, but also recognize that the way in which incentives work is far more complicated than any simple model can capture.

Summary

- Mechanism design is an engineering approach to economic problems in which one identifies a goal and then designs a mechanism such as a market, social system, or contract to achieve that goal.   (*LO22-1*)

- Behavioral economics is an outgrowth of the mechanism design approach to economics.   (*LO22-1*)

- Choice architecture is the context in which decisions are presented. A nudge is designed to influence choice architecture in a way that directs people to make choices that make them better off.   (*LO22-2*)

- Nudges are libertarian because people remain free to make choices. They are paternalistic because they change the structure of choices with the intention of influencing people's behavior in a way that improves their choices.   (*LO22-2*)

- Nudges can be useful for (1) choices where benefits and costs are separated by time, (2) complicated choices with many dimensions, and (3) infrequent choices.   (*LO22-2*)

- Two categories of nudge polices are (1) advantageous default option policies and (2) information and encouragement policies.   (*LO22-2*)

- A true nudge policy leaves everyone free to choose and does not have to be imposed through regulation or taxation. Push policies are government policies requiring firms or individuals to use certain types of nudges. They do not meet the libertarian criterion.   (*LO22-3*)

- Government regulation may be required if firms do not want to implement a nudge. Such nudges become pushes.   (*LO22-3*)

- Behavioral economic policy is controversial. It is not clear that government can decide what is best for people or, even if it knew what was best, would implement the policy. Government is subject to failure just as is the market.   (*LO22-4*)

Key Terms

behavioral economic
   policy
choice architecture
coordination mechanism

economic engineering
incentive compatibility
   problem
nudge

libertarian paternalistic
   policy
mechanism design

nudge policy
push policy
shadow price

Questions and Exercises connect

1. What is a coordination mechanism? Give an example.   (*LO22-1*)

2. True or false? For a market to have a coordination mechanism, money must be exchanged. Explain.   (*LO22-1*)

3. True or false? Only money prices affect incentives; shadow prices do not. Explain.   (*LO22-1*)

4. What is the incentive compatibility problem? Give an example.   (*LO22-1*)

5. What is the primary task of a mechanism design economist?   (*LO22-1*)

6. How did mechanism design lead to behavioral economics?   (*LO22-1*)

7. Can a model that includes just money price miss relevant prices? Why or why not?   (*LO22-1*)

8. How is choice architecture related to behavioral economics and mechanism design?   (*LO22-2*)

9. Behavioral economics is a new field in economics. Are nudges new too?   (*LO22-2*)

10. What is a nudge policy? Give an example.   (*LO22-2*)

11. How can a nudge be defined as libertarian?   (*LO22-2*)

12. In what way is nudge policy paternalistic? (*LO22-2*)

13. Two people are given the choice to participate in a retirement program in which the firm matches contributions. Person A is given a form on which she must check a box to opt into the retirement program. Person B is given a form on which she must check a box to opt out of the retirement program. According to studies, which person is more likely to participate? Or are both equally likely to participate? Explain your answer. (*LO22-2*)

14. What are three types of choices in which nudges are useful? (*LO22-2*)

15. Why is a nudge useful for choices where benefits and costs are separated by time? (*LO22-2*)

16. Why, in the traditional model, is a nudge unnecessary but potentially helpful in the behavioral model? (*LO22-2*)

17. Classify the following nudges as either a "potentially advantageous default nudge," an "information or encouragement nudge," or "not a nudge." (*LO22-2*)
    a. A firm redesigns its health enrollment form so that employees must explicitly choose to forgo health insurance.
    b. Your local city sends you an annual report of average water usage per resident with your actual usage along with tips for conserving water.
    c. Government raises the taxes on gasoline to reduce pollution.
    d. A consumer-advocacy group sets up a site with a side-by-side comparison of auto insurance cost based on estimated risk of drivers.

18. Government has provided a way for people to file their tax returns on the Internet to make filing easier and raise compliance. Is this an example of a libertarian paternalistic policy? Explain your answer. (*LO22-2*)

19. What distinguishes a nudge from a push? (*LO22-3*)

20. Why would push instead of nudge policies be required? (*LO22-3*)

21. Identify the following as either a nudge, a push, or neither. (*LO22-3*)
    a. The cover of your state tax forms reports that 90 percent of residents pay taxes on time.
    b. If your friends gain weight, you are likely to gain weight too.
    c. Amazon is required by government to set the default mail option as the standard mail rate.
    d. Government taxes in part to redistribute income.
    e. A health insurer issues participants credits for exercising and eating healthy foods that they can use to buy products.

22. How is conspicuous consumption an example of the importance of relative materialism to one's happiness? (*LO22-3*)

23. How might conspicuous consumption lower total happiness? (*LO22-3*)

24. What are four reasons to be cautious about nudges? (*LO22-4*)

25. Why aren't there many libertarian nudge policies? (*LO22-4*)

26. Assume that government proposes that all employees must be presented with the choice of opting out of a retirement saving program. What assumptions are necessary for this to be a true nudge? Are they reasonable assumptions? (*LO22-4*)

Questions from Alternative Perspectives

1. Behavioral economics seems to suggest that the "long-term self" rather than the "short-term self" is rational. How do we know that? *(Austrian)*

2. There is an implicit view in the chapter that if a policy meets the libertarian paternalistic goal, it is a good policy. Is that necessarily the case? *(Radical)*

3. How does behavioral economics undermine the standard supply/demand model? *(Institutionalist)*

4. Behavioral economics acknowledges that cultural norms impact people's behavior, something that feminist economists have long included in their analysis. What risks does nudge policy pose for using cultural norms to affect behavior of those in society who have comparatively less power? *(Feminist)*

Issues to Ponder

1. What mechanism might be developed to determine whether it is appropriate for government to give a nudge?

2. Why were more batters being hit in the American League than in the National League starting in 1973? (Be sure your answer uses shadow prices.)

3. To offset the effect of the designated hitter system, what might the American League do to reduce the number of beanballs thrown?

4. In which of the following cases might a nudge be helpful? Explain why or why not.
   a. Deciding what mortgage is affordable.
   b. Deciding whether to exercise or not on a particular day.

c. Deciding whether to fill your gas tank.
d. Deciding whom to marry.

5. Do we as a society focus too much on consumption, and, if so, how would one change that focus?

6. Describe five nudges that firms currently use to get you to do what they want you to do.

Answers to Margin Questions

1. Economic science tries to understand how the economy works; economic engineering tries to design mechanisms to better coordinate people's actions. *(LO22-1)*

2. A shadow price is an implicit price of an action whose value is measured in opportunity costs. It does not involve a payment to another person but is estimated by analyzing people's actions. *(LO22-1)*

3. Yes, it does. The goal of college is generally thought to be learning. Grading gives one an incentive to learn what is likely to be on the test, not what is necessarily the most useful or important knowledge. *(LO22-1)*

4. Economists' work in mechanism design led to a greater interest in behavioral economics because they discovered that people were predictably irrational, and that by taking that predictable irrationality into account, they could design more effective coordination mechanisms. *(LO22-1)*

5. False. They believe that people are sometimes irrational but are generally not irrational in a predictable way, and that if they are predictably irrational, that irrationality can be accounted for as an adjustment to the general model. *(LO22-1)*

6. He or she is more likely to be a behavioral economist. *(LO22-2)*

7. A policy designed to structure choices so that people make a certain choice is called a nudge policy. *(LO22-2)*

8. It depends. From the perspective of the firm, it definitely is not a nudge policy since the firm is being told what to do. It is a push policy. From the perspective of the individual, it can be seen as a nudge policy. *(LO22-3)*

9. Not necessarily. Increasing conspicuous consumption goods makes the owner of the good feel better off but makes others feel worse off, and thus does not necessarily make society as a whole better off. *(LO22-3)*

10. Four concerns are: (1) There are very few true nudge policies; (2) nudge policies quickly become complicated; (3) governments do not necessarily know what is best; and (4) nudge policies increase the potential for government failure. *(LO22-4)*

Microeconomic Policy, Economic Reasoning, and Beyond

> If an economist becomes certain of the solution of any problem, he can be equally certain that his solution is wrong.
>
> —H. A. Innis

©AL DRAGO/EPA-EFE/Shutterstock

After reading this chapter, you should be able to:

LO23-1 List three reasons why economists sometimes differ and sometimes agree in their views on social policy.

LO23-2 Explain the cost/benefit approach the typical economist takes to analyze regulations.

LO23-3 Describe three types of failure of market outcomes.

LO23-4 Explain why most economists are doubtful government can correct failure of market outcomes.

One important job of economists is to give advice to politicians and other policy makers on a variety of questions relating to social policy: How should unemployment be dealt with? How can society distribute income fairly? Should the government redistribute income? Would a program of equal pay for jobs of comparable worth (a pay equity program) make economic sense? Should the minimum wage be increased? These are tough questions.

In previous chapters, I discussed the formal frameworks that modern economists use to think about such issues. In this chapter I consider economic reasoning in a broader context.

The reason for doing so is that economic reasoning and the supply/demand model are tools, not rules. To draw policy implications from it, the supply/demand model has to be placed in context. Used in the proper context, the supply/demand model is enormously strong, something no one should be without. Used out of context, it can lead to conclusions that don't seem right, and that maybe are not right. Consider the assembly-line chicken production example in Chapter 12. Some of you may have felt that the assembly-line production of chickens was somehow not right—that the efficiency of the production process somehow did not outweigh the chickens' suffering. Yet the economic model, which focuses on efficiency, directs production toward that assembly line. This chapter considers when you might want to use economic reasoning, and when you might not.

The chapter is divided into two parts. The first part of the chapter extends the supply/demand model to a broader cost/benefit framework, tying together the discussion we had about economic reasoning in the introductory chapters with the chapters that developed the foundations of the supply/demand model. It shows you how economic reasoning is used in practice. The second part of the chapter turns economic reasoning back upon itself, considering not only the benefits (which are considerable) but also the costs of using economic reasoning. In doing so, I discuss how markets that are working perfectly may still lead to outcomes that are undesirable.

Economists' Differing Views about Social Policy

Economists' views on social policy differ widely because:

1. They have different underlying values.
2. They interpret empirical evidence differently.
3. They use different underlying models.

Economists have many different views on social policy because:

1. Economists' suggestions for social policy are determined by their subjective value judgments (normative views) as well as by their objective economic analyses.

2. Policy proposals must be based on imprecise empirical evidence, so there's considerable room for differences of interpretation not only about economic issues but also about how political and social institutions work. Economic policy is an art, not a science.

3. Policy proposals are based on various models that focus on different aspects of a problem.

All three reasons directly concern the role of ideology in economics. However, any policy proposal must embody both economic analysis and value judgments because the goals of policy reflect value judgments. When an economist makes a policy proposal, it's of this type: "If A, B, and C are your goals, then you should undertake policies D, E, and F to achieve those goals most efficiently." In making these policy suggestions, the economist's role is much the same as an engineer's: He or she is simply telling someone else how to achieve desired ends most efficiently. Ideally the economist is as objective as possible, telling someone how to achieve his or her goals (which need not be the economist's goals).

Web Note 23.1

Clash of the Economists

How Economists' Value Judgments Creep into Policy Proposals

Even though economists attempt to be as objective as possible, value judgments still creep into their analyses in three ways: interpretation of policy makers' values, interpretation of empirical evidence, and choice of economic models.

INTERPRETATION OF THE POLICY MAKER'S VALUES   In practice, social goals are seldom so neat that they can be specified A, B, and C; they're vaguely understood and vaguely expressed. An economist will be told, for instance, "We want to make the poor better off" or "We want to see that middle-income people get better housing." It isn't clear what *poor, better off,* and *better housing* mean. Nor is it clear how judgments should be made when a policy will benefit some individuals at the expense of others, as real-world policies inevitably do.

Faced with this problem, some academic economists have argued that economists should recommend only **Pareto optimal policies**—*policies that benefit some people and hurt no one.* The policies are named in honor of the famous Italian economist Vilfredo Pareto, who first suggested that kind of criterion for judging social change.[1] It's hard to object to the notion of Pareto optimal policies because, by definition, they improve life for some people while hurting no one.

I'd give you an example of a real-world Pareto optimal policy if I could, but unfortunately I don't know of any. Every policy inevitably has some side effect of hurting, or at least seeming to hurt, somebody. In the real world, Pareto optimal policies don't exist. Any economist who has advised governments on real-world problems knows that all real-world policies make some people better off and some people worse off.

But that doesn't mean that economists have no policy role. In their policy proposals, economists try to spell out the effects of a policy and whether the policy is consistent with the policy maker's value judgments. Doing so isn't easy because the policy maker's value judgments are often vague and must be interpreted by the economist. In that interpretation, the economist's own value judgments often slip in.

INTERPRETATION OF EMPIRICAL EVIDENCE   Value judgments also creep into economic policy proposals through economists' interpretations of empirical evidence, which is almost always imprecise. For example, say an economist is assessing the elasticity of a product's demand in the relevant price range. She can't run an experiment to isolate prices and quantities demanded; instead she must look at events in which hundreds of other things changed, and do her best to identify what caused what. In selecting and interpreting empirical evidence, our values will likely show through, try as we might to be objective. People tend to focus on evidence that supports their position. Economists are trained to be as objective as they can be, but pure objectivity is impossible.

Let's consider the example of a debate in which some economists proposed that a large tax be imposed on sales of disposable diapers, citing studies that suggested disposable diapers made up between 15 and 30 percent of the garbage in landfills. Others objected, citing studies that showed disposable diapers made up only 1 or 2 percent of the refuse going into landfills. Such differences in empirical estimates are the norm, not the exception. Inevitably, if precise estimates are wanted, more studies are necessary. (In this case, the further studies showed that the lower estimates were correct.) But policy debates don't wait for further studies. Economists' value judgments influence which incomplete study policy makers choose to believe is more accurate.

CHOICE OF ECONOMIC MODELS   Similarly with the choice of models. A model, because it focuses on certain aspects of economic reality and not on others, necessarily reflects certain value judgments, so economists' choice of models must also reflect certain value judgments. Albert Einstein once said that theories should be as simple as possible, but not more so. To that we should add a maxim: Scientists should be as objective and as value-free as possible, but not more so.

This book presents primarily mainstream economic models. This includes the standard supply/demand model and the new behavioral models. These models direct us to certain conclusions. Two other general models that some economists follow are a

Pareto optimal policies are policies that benefit some people and hurt no one.

Q-1 If someone suggests that economists should focus only on Pareto optimal policies, how would you respond?

Scientists should be as objective as possible, but not more so.

---

[1]Pareto, in his famous book *Mind and Society,* suggested this criterion as an analytic approach for theory, not as a criterion for real-world policy. He recognized the importance of the art of economics and that real-world policy has to be judged by much broader criteria than this.

Marxian (radical) model, which is *a model that focuses on equitable distribution of power, rights, and income among social classes,* and a **public choice model,** which is *a model that focuses on economic incentives as applied to politicians.* These two models, by emphasizing different aspects of economic interrelationships, sometimes direct us to other conclusions.

Q-2 How does a radical analysis of labor markets differ from a mainstream analysis?

Let's consider an example. Mainstream economic analysis directs us to look at how the invisible hand achieves harmony and equilibrium through the market. Thus, when mainstream economists look at labor markets, they generally see supply and demand forces leading to equilibrium. When Marxist economists look at labor markets, their model focuses on the tensions among the social classes, and they generally see exploitation of workers by capitalists. When public choice economists look at labor markets, they see individuals using government to protect their monopolies. Their model focuses on political restrictions that provide rents to various groups. Each model captures different aspects of reality. That's why it's important to be as familiar with as many different models as possible.

Each model captures different aspects of reality. That's why it's important to be as familiar with as many different models as possible.

The Need for a Worldview

John Maynard Keynes, an economist who gained fame in the 1930s, once said that economists should be seen in the same light as dentists—as competent technicians. He was wrong, and his own experience contradicts that view. In dealing with real-world economic policy, Keynes was no mere technician. He had a definite worldview, which he shared with many of the policy makers he advised. An economist who is to play a role in forming policy must be willing to combine value judgments and technical knowledge. That worldview determines how and when the economic model will be applied.

Agreement among Economists about Social Policy

Liberal and conservative economists agree on many policy prescriptions because they use the same models, which focus on incentives and individual choice.

Despite their widely varying values, both liberal and conservative economists agree more often on policy prescriptions than most laypeople think they do. They're economists, after all, and their models focus on certain issues—specifically on incentives and individual choice. They believe economic incentives are important, and most economists tend to give significant weight to individuals' ability to choose reasonably. This leads economists, both liberal and conservative, to look at problems differently than other people do.

Many people think economists of all persuasions look at the world coldheartedly. In my view, that opinion isn't accurate, but it's understandable how people could reach it. Economists are taught to look at things in an "objective" way that takes into account a policy's long-run incentive effects as well as the short-run effects. Many of their policy proposals are based on these long-run incentive effects, which in the short run make the policy look coldhearted. The press and policy makers usually focus on short-run effects. Economists argue that they aren't being coldhearted at all, that they're simply being reasonable, and that following their advice will lead to less suffering than following others' advice will. This is not to say that all advice economists give will lead to significant benefits and less suffering in the long run. Some of it may be simply misguided.

Q-3 When can "being mean" actually be "being nice"?

The problem economists face is similar to the one parents face when they tell their children that they can't eat candy or must do their homework before they can play. Explaining how "being mean" is actually "being nice" to a six-year-old isn't easy.

A former colleague of mine, Abba Lerner, was well known for his strong liberal leanings. The government of Israel asked him what to do about unemployment. He went to Israel, studied the problem, and presented his advice: "Cut union wages." The government official responded, "But that's the same advice the conservative economist gave us." Lerner answered, "It's good advice, too." The Israeli Labor government then went and did the opposite; it raised wages, thus holding on to its union support in the short run.

Another example comes from a World Bank economist. She had to advise a hospital in a developing country to turn down the offer of a free dialysis machine because the marginal cost of the filters it would have to buy to use the machine significantly exceeded the costs of lifesaving medicines that would save even more lives. Economic reasoning involves making such hard decisions.

The best way to see the consistency and the differences in economists' policy advice is to consider some examples. Let's start with a general consideration of economic views on government regulation.

Economists' Cost/Benefit Approach to Government Regulation

Say that 200 people die in a plane crash. Newspaper headlines trumpet the disaster while news magazines are filled with stories about how the accident might have been caused, citing speculation about poor maintenance and lack of government regulation. The publicity spreads the sense that "something must be done" to prevent such tragedies. Politicians quickly pick up on this, feeling that the public wants action. They introduce a bill outlawing faulty maintenance, denounce poor regulatory procedures, and demand an investigation of sleepy air controllers. In short, they strike out against likely causes of the accident and suggest improved regulations to help prevent any more such crashes.

Many regulations are formulated for political expediency and do not reflect cost/benefit considerations.

Economists differ in their views on government regulation of airlines and other businesses, but most find themselves opposing some of the supposedly problem-solving regulations proposed by politicians. They generally adopt a **cost/benefit approach** to problems—*assigning costs and benefits, and making decisions on the basis of the relevant costs and benefits*—that requires them to determine a quantitative cost and benefit for everything, including life. What's the value of a human life? All of us would like to answer, "Infinite. Each human life is beyond price." But if that's true, then in a cost/benefit framework, everything of value should be spent on preventing death. People should take no chances. They should drive at no more than 30 miles per hour with airbags, triple-cushioned bumpers, double roll bars—you get the picture.

Cost/benefit analysis is analysis in which one assigns costs and benefits to alternatives, and draws a conclusion on the basis of those costs and benefits.

It might be possible for manufacturers to make a car in which no one would die as the result of an accident. But people don't want such cars. Many people don't buy the auto safety accessories that are already available, and many drivers ignore the present speed limit. Instead, many people want cars with style and speed.

The Value of Life

Far from regarding human life as priceless, people make decisions every day that reflect the valuations they place on their own lives. The table below presents a number of estimates that various economists have made of some of those decisions.

Basis for Calculation	Value of Human Life
Automobile safety features	$5,020,000–7,130,000
Bicycle helmets	1,580,000–5,680,000
Smoke detector purchases	1,010,000–3,380,000
Seat belt usage	1,320,000
Car seats	1,100,000

Car crashes are evidence human life is not beyond price.

©Carolyn Franks/Shutterstock

Economists in the Courtroom

Valuing life is more than just an academic exercise. These valuations play an important role in court cases in which one individual sues another for having caused a wrongful death. How do you put a value on the person's life? The courts have to do that—determine how much the defendant will have to pay the plaintiff if the court decides it was a "wrongful death." A court can't simply say that a life is priceless; it relies on economic expert witnesses to provide values.

One way to value life is the method presented in the text—deduce how much people value life from their willingness to take risks. This sounds like a reasonable method, but it has problems that have been much discussed in the literature and in the courtroom. Some of these problems include: Small risk values are irrelevant to large risk issues; the variance of estimates is too high to give a reasonable estimate; anonymous lives

©Wavebreak Media Ltd/123RF

are irrelevant in specific cases; people's risk preferences differ; and people's decisions are not fully rational but reflect many other issues such as awareness of the problem and shock value. In fact, there is a whole branch of economics—forensic economics—that looks at such issues.

Another method economists use for valuing life is to calculate the lost earnings and pleasure that someone would have had in his or her remaining lifetime. But this method also has problems since it is difficult to specify either precisely. For example, is a depressed person's life worth less than a happy person's life? Is an investment banker's life worth more than a trainee's life? What is the appropriate discount rate to use to value earnings in different years? Courts have to sort through these many problems, and economists' testimony as expert witnesses often plays a key role in these cases.

These values are calculated by looking at people's revealed preferences (the choices people make when they must pay the costs). To find them, economists calculate how much people will pay to reduce the possibility of their death by a certain amount. If that's what people will pay to avoid death, the value of life can be calculated by multiplying the inverse of the reduction in the probability of death by the amount they pay. (What is relevant for these calculations is not the actual probabilities but the decision makers' estimate of the probabilities.)

For example, say someone will buy a smoke detector for $25 but won't buy one if it costs more than $25. Also say that the buyer believes that a smoke detector will reduce the chance of dying in a fire by 1/80,000. That means that to increase the likelihood of surviving a house fire by 1/80,000, the buyer will pay $25. That also means that the buyer is implicitly valuing his or her life at roughly $2,000,000 (80,000 × $25 = $2,000,000).

Alternatively, say that people will pay an extra $60 for a set of premium tires that reduces the risk of death by 1/100,000. As opposed to having a 3/100,000 chance per year of dying in a skid on the highway, people driving cars with premium tires have a 2/100,000 chance of dying (3/100,000 − 2/100,000 = 1/100,000). Multiplying 100,000 (the inverse of the reduction in probability) by $60, the extra cost of the set of premium tires, you find that people who buy these tires are implicitly valuing their lives at $6,000,000.[2] Another way of determining the value that society places on life is to

Q-4 If the text correctly describes the valuation individuals place on life with regard to smoke detector purchases and premium tire usage, how would you advise them to alter their behavior in order to maximize utility?

[2]For simplicity of exposition, I'm not considering risk preferences or other benefits of these decisions, such as lowering the chance of injury.

look at awards juries give for the loss of life. One study looking at such awards found that juries on average value life at about $3.5 million.

No one can say whether people know what they're doing in making these valuations, although the inconsistencies in the valuations people place on their lives suggest that to some degree they don't, or that other considerations are entering into their decisions. But even given the inconsistencies, it's clear that people are placing a finite value on life. Most people are aware that in order to "live" they must take chances on losing their lives. Economists argue that individuals' revealed preferences are the best estimate that society can have of the value of life, and that in making policy society shouldn't pretend that life is beyond value.

Placing a value on human life allows economists to evaluate the cost of a crash. Say each life is valued at $2 million. If 200 people die in a plane accident and a $200 million plane is destroyed, the cost of the crash is $600 million.

Right after the accident, or even long after the accident, tell a mother and father you're valuing the life of their dead daughter at $2 million and the plane at $200 million, and you'll see why economists have problems with getting their views across. Even if people can agree rationally that they implicitly place a value on their own lives, it's not something they want to deal with emotionally, especially after an accident. Using a cost/benefit approach, an economist must be willing to say, if that's the way the analysis turns out, "It's reasonable that my son died in this accident because the cost of preventing the accident by imposing stricter government regulations would have been greater than the benefit of preventing it."

Economists take the emotional heat for making such valuations. Their cost/benefit approach requires them to do so.

Comparing Costs and Benefits of Different Dimensions

After the marginal cost and marginal benefit data have been gathered and processed, one is ready to make an informed decision. Will the cost of a new regulation outweigh the benefit, or vice versa? Here again, economists find themselves in a difficult position in evaluating a regulation about airplane safety. Many of the costs of regulation are small but occur in large numbers. Every time you lament some "bureaucratic craziness" (such as a required weekly staff meeting or a form to be signed ensuring something has been done), you're experiencing a cost. But when those costs are compared to the benefits of avoiding a major accident, the dimensions of comparison are often wrong.

For example, say it is discovered that a loose bolt was the probable cause of the plane crash. A regulation requiring airline mechanics to check whether that bolt is tightened and, to ensure that they do so, requiring them to fill out a form each time the check is made might cost $1. How can we compare $1 to the $600 million cost of the crash? Such a regulation obviously makes sense from the perspective of gaining a $600 million benefit from $1 of cost.

But wait. Each plane might have 4,000 similar bolts, each of which is equally likely to cause an accident if it isn't tightened. If it makes sense to check that one bolt, it makes sense to check all 4,000. And the bolts must be checked on each of the 4,000 flights per day. All of this increases the cost of tightening bolts to $16 million per day. But the comparison shouldn't be between $16 million and $600 million. The comparison should be between the marginal cost ($16 million) and the marginal benefit, which depends on how much tightening bolts will contribute to preventing an accident.

Let's say that having the bolts checked daily reduces the probability of having an accident by 0.001. This means that the check will prevent one out of a thousand

Web Note 23.2
The Value of Life

Economists argue that individuals' revealed choices are the best estimate that society can have of the value of life, and that in making policy society shouldn't pretend that life is beyond value.

Cost/benefit analysis sometimes leads one to uncomfortable results.

accidents that otherwise would have happened. The marginal benefit of checking a particular bolt isn't $600 million (which it would be if you knew a bolt was going to be loose), but is

$$0.001 \times \$600 \text{ million} = \$600,000$$

That $600,000 is the marginal benefit that must be compared to the marginal cost of $16 million.

Given these numbers, I leave it to you to decide: Does this hypothetical regulation make sense?

Putting Cost/Benefit Analysis in Perspective

Q-5 Why should you be very careful about any cost/benefit analysis?

The numbers in our plane crash example are hypothetical. The numbers used in real-world decision making are not hypothetical, but they are often ambiguous. Measuring costs, benefits, and probabilities is difficult, and economists often disagree on specific costs and benefits. Costs have many dimensions, some more quantifiable than others. Cost/benefit analysis is often biased toward quantifiable costs and away from non-quantifiable costs, or it involves enormous ambiguity as nonquantifiable costs are quantified.

Cost/benefit analysis is often biased toward quantifiable costs.

The subjectivity and ambiguity of costs are one reason why economists differ in their views of regulation. In considering any particular regulation, some economists will favor it and some will oppose it. But their reasoning process—comparing marginal costs and marginal benefits—is the same; they differ only on the estimates they calculate.

The Problem of Other Things Changing

A major reason why economists come to different conclusions about policies involves the "other things equal" assumption discussed in Chapter 4. Supply/demand analysis assumes that all other things remain equal. But in a large number of issues it is obvious that other things do not remain equal. However, it is complicated to sort out how they change, and the sorting-out process is subject to much debate. The more macro the issue, the more other things change, and hence the more debate.

Q-6 When using marginal cost/marginal benefit analysis, do "other things remain constant"? Explain.

Let's consider the minimum wage example we discussed in earlier chapters. Suppose you can estimate the supply and demand elasticities for labor. Is that enough to enable you to estimate the number of people who will be made unemployed by a minimum wage? To answer that, ask yourself: Are other things likely to remain constant? The answer is: No; numerous things will change. Say the firm decides to replace these workers with machines. So it will buy some machines. But machines are made by other workers, and so the demand for workers in the machine-making industry will rise. So the decrease in employment in the first industry may be offset by an increase in employment elsewhere.

But there are issues on the other side too. For example, if other things change, workers who get the higher wage may not receive a net benefit. Say you had a firm that was paying a wage lower than the minimum wage but was providing lots of training, which was preparing people for much better jobs in the future. Now the minimum wage goes into effect. The firm keeps hiring workers, but it eliminates the training. Its workers actually could be worse off.

How important are such issues? That's a matter of empirical research, which is why empirical research is central to economics. Unfortunately, the data aren't very good, which is why there is so much debate about policy issues in economics.

There are many more examples of "other things changing," but the above should be sufficient to give you an idea of the problem.

The Cost/Benefit Approach in Context

Economics teaches people to be reasonable—sickeningly reasonable, some people would say. I hope that you have some sense of what I mean by that. The cost/benefit approach to problems (which pictures a world of individuals whose self-interested actions are limited only by competition) makes economists look for the self-interest behind individuals' actions, and for how competition can direct that self-interest into the public interest.

Economics teaches people to be "reasonable."

©bleakstar/Shutterstock

In an economist's framework,

- Well-intentioned policies often are prevented by individuals' self-interest-seeking activities.

- Policies that relieve immediate suffering often have long-run consequences that create more suffering.

- Politicians have more of an incentive to act fast—to look as if they're doing something—than to do something that makes sense from a cost/benefit point of view.

Economics teaches people to be "reasonable."

The marginal cost/marginal benefit approach is telling a story. That story is embodied in the supply/demand framework. Supply represents the marginal costs of a trade, and demand represents the marginal benefits of a trade. Equilibrium is where quantity supplied equals quantity demanded—where marginal cost equals marginal benefit. That equilibrium maximizes the combination of consumer and producer surplus and leads to an efficient, or Pareto optimal, outcome. The argument for competitive markets within that supply/demand framework is that markets allow the society to achieve **economic efficiency**—*achieving a goal, in this case producing a specified amount of output, at the lowest possible cost.* Alternatively expressed, the story is that, given a set of resources, markets produce the greatest possible output. When the economy is efficient, it is on its production possibility curve, producing total output at its lowest opportunity cost.

The marginal cost/marginal benefit story is embodied in the supply/demand framework.

The supply/demand framework is logical, satisfying, and (given its definitions and assumptions) extraordinarily useful. That's why we teach it. It gives students who understand it the ability to get to the heart of many policy problems. It tells them that every policy has a cost, every policy has a benefit, and if the assumptions are met, competition sees to it that the benefits to society are achieved at the lowest possible cost. Applied to policy issues, the framework gets you to face trade-offs that you would often rather avoid, and that you likely wouldn't see if you didn't use it. It is what "thinking like an economist" is all about.

Failure of Market Outcomes

A good story emphasizes certain elements and deemphasizes others to make its point. When the moral of the story is applied, however, we have to be careful to consider all the relevant elements—especially those that the story didn't emphasize. That's why in the second part of this chapter I will discuss some implicit assumptions that the supply/demand framework pushes to the back of the analysis and that therefore often don't get addressed in principles courses. I classify these as failures of market outcomes. A **failure of market outcome** occurs *when, even though the market is functioning properly (there are no market failures), it is not achieving society's goals.*

Q-7 True or false? The goal of society is efficiency.

Three separate types of failures of market outcomes will be considered:

1. *Failures due to distributional issues:* Whose surplus is the market maximizing?

2. *Failures due to rationality problems of individuals:* What if individuals don't know what is best for themselves?

Failure of market outcome occurs when, even though it is functioning properly, the market is not achieving society's goals.

Economic Efficiency and the Goals of Society

Economic efficiency means achieving a goal at the lowest possible cost. For the definition to be meaningful, the goal must be specified. Efficiency in the pursuit of efficiency is meaningless. Thus, when we talk about economic efficiency, we must have some goal in mind. In the supply/demand framework, we *assume* the goal is to maximize total utility given the income people have. Each of the three failures of market outcomes that we discuss in this section represents a situation in which the goals of society cannot be captured by a single measure—where society's goal is more complicated than to maximize total utility—and thus the assumed goal of efficiency (maximizing total utility) is not the only goal of society.

3. *Failures due to violations of inalienable or at least partially inalienable rights of individuals:* Are there certain rights that should not be for sale?

I'll discuss an example of each of the three failures of market outcomes and contrast them with market failures. Then I will conclude with a brief discussion of why, even though most economists recognize these failures of market outcomes, they still favor the use of markets for the large majority of goods that society produces.

Distribution

Say that the result of market forces is that some people don't earn enough income to be able to survive—the demand for their labor intersects the supply for their labor at a wage of 25 cents an hour. Also assume there are no market failures. (Information is perfect, trades have no negative externalities, and all goods are private goods.)

The market solution to a wage that is so low the worker can't survive is starvation—people who don't earn enough die. Not all low-wage workers must die, however. As some low-wage workers die, the supply of labor shifts back to the left, raising the wage for the survivors. This process takes time, but eventually all remaining workers will receive a subsistence wage. This is the long-run market solution. Implicit within the supply/demand framework is a Darwinian "survival of the fittest" approach to social policy. Most people would regard the market solution—starvation—as an undesirable outcome. Even though the market is doing precisely what it is supposed to be doing—equating quantity supplied and quantity demanded—most people would not find the outcome acceptable.

Implicit within the supply/demand framework is a "survival of the fittest" approach to social policy.

DISTRIBUTION OF TOTAL SURPLUS   Let me now relate this distributional issue to the supply/demand framework by considering distribution of consumer and producer surplus. For most discussions of economic policy, an implicit assumption is that the goal of policy is to create as much total surplus as possible. In a world of only one good and one person, that goal would be clear. But with many goods and many people, what is meant by total surplus in terms of social welfare can be unclear. One reason is that society does not value all surplus equally. In the above starvation example, *the reason most people do not like the market outcome is that they care about not only the size of the total surplus but also how total surplus is distributed.* The supply/demand framework does not distinguish among those who get producer and consumer surplus, and thus avoids that distribution issue.

EXAMPLES OF DISTRIBUTIONAL ISSUES   Let's consider two real-world examples where distributional issues are likely to play a significant role in value judgments about the market outcome. Our economy produces chocolate truffles that cost $1,000 a pound, but it does not provide a minimum level of health care for all. This happens because income distribution is highly unequal. The high income of the wealthy means there is demand for $1,000 a pound chocolate. Businesses establish production facilities to produce it (or any one of a million other luxury items), and it is sold on the market. Selling chocolate truffles at $1,000 a pound is efficient if one's goal is to maximize total consumer and producer surplus. However, given the distribution of income, it would be inefficient to produce health care for the poor. The poor just don't have sufficient income to demand it. Since they have little income, the poor are given little weight in the measure of consumer surplus.

A second example of where distribution of income likely makes a big difference in our normative judgments, and where we would likely not apply the consumer and producer surplus reasoning, concerns the demand for the HIV/AIDS drug cocktail. The cocktail can stop HIV/AIDS from killing people; thus, the desire for the HIV/AIDS cocktail among individuals with HIV/AIDS is high. The demand for the drug among those without HIV/AIDS is minimal.

In a few African countries, one-fifth or more of the population has HIV/AIDS. Since consumer surplus reflects desire, one might think that in Africa the consumer surplus from the desire for the HIV/AIDS drug cocktail would be enormous. But it isn't. Most people in Africa have relatively little income; in fact, most have so little income that they cannot afford the cocktail at all if it were priced at the U.S. price. In the supply/demand framework, those who cannot afford to purchase the drugs would get no consumer surplus from it. To supply the drugs to them would be inefficient. In the supply/demand framework you can only have a demand for a good if you have the desire *and* the income to pay for it. So, despite the fact that it is inefficient to provide HIV/AIDS drugs to low-income Africans, the prices of HIV/AIDS drugs to African nations were significantly reduced. Distributional issues trumped efficiency issues and new incidents of HIV/AIDS have been declining.

The point of these examples is not to convince you that the consumer surplus concept is useless. Far from it. For the majority of goods, it is a useful shorthand that demonstrates the power of competitive markets. The point of the examples is to show you the type of case where overriding the supply/demand framework in policy considerations may be socially desirable and efficient if society's goals include a particular distribution of consumer surplus. The sole purpose of society is not to maximize consumer and producer surplus. Society also has other goals. Once these other goals are taken into account, the competitive result may not be the one that is desired.

For many goods, maximizing total surplus is a useful shorthand.

Societies integrate other goals into market economies by establishing social safety nets (programs such as welfare, unemployment insurance, and Medicaid). When individuals earn less than a certain income, what they receive does not depend solely on what they earn in the market. How high to set a given social safety net is a matter of debate, but favoring the market outcome in most cases is not inconsistent with favoring a social safety net in others.

Consumer Sovereignty and Rationality Problems

John Drunk drinks more than is good for him; he just has to have another drink. He buys liquor voluntarily, so that means buying it makes him better off, right? Not necessarily. Even when they have full information, individuals sometimes do not do what is in their own best interest. If they don't do what's best for themselves, then the market solution—let people enter freely into whatever trades they want to—is not necessarily the best solution. Again, the market is working, but the outcome may be a failure.

Elasticity and Taxation to Change Behavior

A good way to see how economists view the difference between the effect of a sin tax and the effect of a tax to raise revenue is to ask: Would a policy maker rather have an elastic or an inelastic demand curve for the good being taxed? If the purpose is to raise revenue while creating only a minimal amount of deadweight loss, an inelastic demand is preferable. If the purpose is to change behavior, as it is in the example of an alcohol-dependent individual, a more elastic demand curve is better because a relatively small tax can cause a relatively large reduction in purchases.

Consider an example of taxation to reduce consumption. If government believes that smoking is bad for people, it can decrease the amount people smoke by placing a tax on cigarettes. If the demand for cigarettes is inelastic, then the tax will not significantly decrease smoking; but if the demand is elastic, then it will. If demand is inelastic, government may choose alternative methods of affecting behavior, such as advertising campaigns.

Now consider the case in which the government wants to raise revenue. In this case an inelastic demand would be better. That's why most states rely on general sales taxes for revenue—such taxes allow them to raise revenue with relatively little effect on the efficiency of the market.

The following table provides a quick review of when a tax will be most effective, given a particular goal of government.

Goal of Government	Most Effective When
Raise revenue, limit efficiency loss	Demand or supply is inelastic
Change behavior	Demand or supply is elastic

Q-8 A cocaine addict purchases an ounce of cocaine from a drug dealer. Since this was a trade both individuals freely entered, is society better off?

This problem is sometimes called *rationality failure of individuals.* The supply/demand framework starts with the proposition that individuals are completely **rational**—that *what individuals do is in their own best interest.* Reflecting on this, however, as we did in earlier chapters, we see that that is not always the case. Most of us are irrational at times; we sometimes can "want" something that we really "don't want." Think of smoking, chocolate, or any other of our many vices. We know those potato chips are bad for us, but they taste so good.

Even if we don't have serious addictions, we may have minor ones; often we don't know what we want and we are influenced by what people tell us we want. Businesses spend hundreds of billions of dollars every year on advertising in the United States to convince us that we want certain things. Individuals can be convinced they want something that, if they thought further about it, they would not want. The fact that individuals don't know what they want can be a second reason for government intervention—getting people to want what is good for them.

Let's look at an example: The U.S. government has taken the position that if people could be induced to stop smoking, they would be better off. **Sin taxes**—*taxes that discourage activities society believes are harmful (sinful)*—are meant to do just this. Based on the consumer surplus argument, a tax on smoking would create deadweight loss; it would reduce the combination of consumer and producer surplus. But in this case, government has decided that consumer surplus does not reflect individuals' welfare.

Notice the difference between the argument for taxes to change behavior (sin taxes) and the argument for taxes to raise revenue discussed in Chapter 7. When government wants to raise revenue, it takes into account how much deadweight loss is created by the tax. With sin taxes, government is trying to discourage the use of the good that is being taxed and does not take into account deadweight loss. When society takes the position that individuals' demands in the marketplace do not reflect their true welfare,

Where to Locate Polluting Industries

Larry Summers, an MIT-trained economist and former president of Harvard University, often carries economic reasoning to its logical conclusion, and talks about it in public, or at least lets it leak out to the public. These traits often get him in hot water. When Summers was chief economist at the World Bank, he signed a memo that argued that the World Bank should encourage more migration of dirty industries to the LDCs (least-developed countries). Part of the memo stated the following:

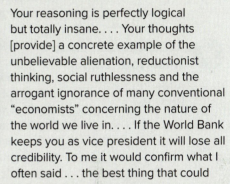

Transporting waste.
©Comstock Images/Alamy

> The measurements of the costs of health-impairing pollution depend on the forgone earnings from increased morbidity and mortality. From this point of view a given amount of health-impairing pollution should be done in the country with the lowest cost, which will be the country with the lowest wages. I think the economic logic behind dumping a load of toxic waste in the lowest-wage country is impeccable and we should face up to that.

Based upon cost/benefit analysis and calculations of the "value of life," this reasoning follows, but it is not necessarily the correct reasoning, nor is it reasoning that most people will accept. Here is the response it provoked from Brazil's secretary of the environment:

> Your reasoning is perfectly logical but totally insane. . . . Your thoughts [provide] a concrete example of the unbelievable alienation, reductionist thinking, social ruthlessness and the arrogant ignorance of many conventional "economists" concerning the nature of the world we live in. . . . If the World Bank keeps you as vice president it will lose all credibility. To me it would confirm what I often said . . . the best thing that could happen would be for the Bank to disappear.

I leave it to you to sort out which, if any, view is the correct one.

it is not at all clear that the market result is efficient. (See the box "Elasticity and Taxation to Change Behavior.")

Inalienable Rights

Nice Guy wants to save his son, who needs an operation that costs $300,000. He doesn't have that kind of money, but he knows that Slave Incorporated, a newly created company, has been offering $300,000 to the first person who agrees to become a slave for life. He enters into the contract, gets his money, and saves his son. Again, the market is working just as it is supposed to. There's no negative externality, and there's no information problem—Nice Guy knows what he's doing and Slave Inc. knows what it's doing. Both participants in the trade believe that it is making them better off.

Many people's view of the trade will likely be different; they would regard such a market outcome—an outcome that allows slavery—as a market outcome failure. That is why governments have developed laws that make such trades illegal.

As economist Amartya Sen pointed out (and won a Nobel Prize for doing so), most societies regard certain rights as inalienable. By definition, inalienable rights cannot be sold or given away. There can be no weighing of costs and benefits. For example, the right to freedom is an inalienable right, so slavery is wrong, and any trade creating slavery should not be allowed, regardless of any issues of consumer and producer surplus.

Q-9 True or false? If someone chooses to sell himself into slavery, the individual, and thus society, is better off.

THE NEED TO PRIORITIZE RIGHTS   To understand why market outcomes might be undesirable, we have to go back and consider markets in a broader perspective.

Markets develop over time as individuals trade to make themselves better off. But markets don't just come into existence—they require the development of property rights for both suppliers and consumers. Each side must know what precisely is being traded. So markets can exist only if there are property rights.

Property rights, in turn, are included in a broader set of rights that are part of society's constitution—the right to vote, the right to free speech, the right to the pursuit of happiness, the right to life. Property rights are subrights to the right to pursue happiness. If property rights conflict with other rights, society must make a judgment about which right has priority. Thus, within the written or unwritten constitution of a society, rights need to be prioritized.

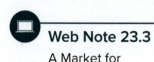

Web Note 23.3

A Market for Body Parts

EXAMPLES OF INALIENABLE RIGHTS   Let's consider a couple of examples. Say I come up to you with a gun and offer you this deal: Your money or your life. This can be viewed as a trade. Because I have the gun, I control whether you live or die. You control the money you have. If we make the "trade," you'll be better off because I don't shoot you and I'll be better off because I'll have more money. But it is not an acceptable trade because the right to your life was inalienable—no one but you owns it; I cannot claim to own it. So, even if the gun gave me the power over your life, it did not give me the right to it. Other moral prohibitions that are related to inalienable rights include those against prostitution, selling body parts, and selling babies.

My point is not that the moral judgments our society has made about these rights are correct; they may or may not be correct. Nor is my point that such trades should not be subjected to the market. My point is that society must make these judgments. Such issues are moral questions and therefore do not have to stand up to the consumer and producer surplus arguments. If something is wrong, it is wrong; whether it is efficient is irrelevant.

Moral judgments must be made about where markets should exist, and someone might decide that the market should be allowed everywhere (that is the libertarian view). Such moral judgments can override consumer surplus arguments about markets achieving efficiency. Consider again the efficient-chicken-farming example discussed in Chapter 12. If you believe that it is immoral to treat chickens the way "efficient" farming requires them to be treated, then the fact that the farming is efficient may be irrelevant to you.

Government Failure

Distributional issues, issues of rationality, and the existence of inalienable rights are representative of the types of problems that can arise even in perfectly functioning markets. For most economists these issues play a role in interpreting the policy results that follow from the economic model presented, even when there is no market failure. But it is important to remember that even these failures of market outcomes do not necessarily call for government action. The reason is government failure.

As I discussed in Chapter 8, if a failure is to be corrected, someone must formulate and enact the policy, and if we believe that government's attempt to correct a failure will do more harm than good, then we can still support the market as the lesser of two evils. For the government to correct the problem, it must:

1. Recognize the problem.
2. Have *the will* to do something positive about the problem.
3. Have *the ability* to do something positive about the problem.

Government seldom can do all three of these well. Often the result is that government action is directed at the wrong problem at the wrong time.

Probably the most vocal group of economists on the subject of government failure is *public choice economists*. This group, started by James Buchanan and Gordon Tullock, has pointed out that politicians are subject to the laws of supply and demand, like everyone else. Often the result of politics is that the redistribution that takes place does not go from rich to poor, but from one group of the middle class to another group of the middle class. Public choice economists argue that when the government enters the market, its incentives are not to achieve its goal in the least-cost manner; its incentives are to provide a policy that its voting constituency likes. The result is larger and larger government, with little benefit for society, and public choice economists advocate as little government intervention as possible regardless of whether there are market failures or failures of market outcomes.

Economic policy is, and must be, applied within a political context. This means that political elements must be taken into account. Politics enters into the determination of economic policy in two ways, one positive and one negative. Its positive contribution is that politicians take market failures and failures of market outcomes into account when formulating policy. Ultimately the political system decides what externalities should be adjusted for, what a desirable distribution is, what rights are above the market, and when people's revealed demand does not reflect their true demand. To the extent that the government's political decisions reflect the will of society, government is making a positive contribution.

> Economic policy is, and must be, applied in a political context.

The negative contribution is that political decisions do not always reflect the will of society.[3] The political reality is that, in the short run, people are often governed by emotion, swayed by mass psychology, irrational, and interested in their own rather than the general good. Politicians and other policy makers know that; the laws and regulations they propose reflect such calculations. Politicians don't get elected and reelected by constantly saying that all choices have costs and benefits. What this means is that while policy makers listen to the academic economists from whom they ask advice, and with whom in private they frequently agree, in practice they often choose to ignore that advice.

> Q-10 In what way does government positively contribute to economic policy? In what way does it negatively contribute to economic policy?

Because government attempts to adjust for failures of market outcomes are subject to short-run political pressures, the way in which economic reasoning influences policy can be subtle. Sometimes we see elaborate charades acted out: Politicians put forward bills that from a cost/benefit viewpoint don't make sense but that make the politicians look good. They hope the bills won't pass, but they also hope that presenting them will allow enough time to pass so that emotions can cool and a more reasonable bill can be put forward. Other times, compromise bills are proposed that incorporate as much cost/benefit policy as possible, but also appeal to voters' emotional sense. In short, economic policy made in the real world reflects a balancing of cost/benefit analysis and special interest desires.

Conclusion

Adam Smith, the creator of modern economics, was a philosopher; his economics was part of his philosophy. Before he wrote *The Wealth of Nations,* in which he set out his argument for markets, he wrote a book called *The Theory of Moral Sentiments,* in which he laid out his broader philosophy. That foundation, in turn, was part of the Scottish Enlightenment, which spelled out what was meant by a "good" society and how individuals' and society's rights should be considered. Any economic policy issue

---

[3]By even discussing the "will of society" I am avoiding a very difficult problem in political philosophy of what that will is, and how it is to be determined. I leave it to your political science courses to discuss such issues.

The Conventional Policy Wisdom among Economists

Where do economists come out on whether government can correct a failure of market outcomes? The easy answer is that they conclude that to make a policy decision, we must weigh the costs of the failures of market outcomes against the costs of government failure. But those costs are often poorly specified and difficult to estimate. Thus, policy considerations require subjective judgments. Let me give you my interpretation of how economists fit these broader considerations into their analysis.

Most economists downplay the distribution issues for the majority of goods, and use distribution in their policy consideration only for the extreme examples, such as those I presented in the text. They believe that it is far better to be open about the distributional goals and to give money directly to individuals, rather than to hide the redistribution by changing the pricing structure through subsidizing goods. Let's take an example: The European Union's agricultural policy currently provides large amounts of price supports for European agricultural production. To keep farmers in business, the prices of agricultural goods are kept high. If the social decision were to keep farmers in business, most economists, however, would prefer to see the EU provide direct subsidies to farmers. Then the policy of redistribution is clear to everyone, and is far less costly in terms of both efficiency and implementation.

The "rights argument" plays a role in all economists' policy arguments. Almost all economists oppose selling citizenship. All oppose slavery. All see economic policy as being conducted within a constitutional setting, and that means that inalienable rights come before market efficiency.

There are, of course, areas of ambiguity—allowing the regulated sale of body parts from individuals who have died is one such area. Let's consider it. There is currently a shortage of organs for transplants. When someone dies, from a medical perspective his or her organs can usually be "harvested" and used by someone else—but only if the deceased had signed a donor card. If the family of the deceased donor were given $5,000 for burial expenses, some economists argue, the shortage of transplant organs would disappear and everyone would be better off—the family could give the deceased a much nicer funeral and people needing the organs could live. My feeling is that economists are more open to such market solutions than the general public, but there is nothing in economics that requires such solutions.

The argument about problems arising from rationality issues is also accepted by most economists, but they downplay it for most nonaddictive goods. The reason is that while it is true that individuals may not know what they want, it is far less likely that the government will know better. Based on that view, on average, the acceptance of consumer sovereignty, and the market result, is probably warranted. Exceptions include children and some elderly individuals. How to deal with addictive goods is still very much in debate among economists, and there is no conventional wisdom.

must be interpreted within such a broad philosophical framework. Clearly, an introductory course in economics cannot introduce you to these broader philosophical and political issues. But it can point out to you their importance, and that economic policy arguments must fit within that broader context.

Economics provides the tools, not the rules, for policy.

This chapter was written to give you a sense of that broader context—economics provides the tools, not the rules, for policy. Cost/benefit analysis and the supply/demand framework are powerful tools for analyzing issues and coming up with policy conclusions. But to apply them successfully, one must think like a modern economist and apply them in the appropriate context.

Applying economics is much more than muttering "supply and demand." Economics involves the thoughtful use of economic insights and empirical evidence.

Nineteenth-century Scottish thinker Thomas Carlyle, who, as we saw in the introductory quotation to Chapter 4, argued that all you have to do is teach a parrot the words *supply* and *demand* to create an economist, was wrong. Economics involves the thoughtful use of economic insights and empirical evidence. If this chapter gave you a sense of the nature of that thoughtful application along with the core of economic reasoning, then it succeeded in its purpose.

Summary

- Economists differ because of different underlying value judgments, because empirical evidence is subject to different interpretations, and because their underlying models differ.   *(LO23-1)*

- Value judgments inevitably work their way into policy advice, but good economists try to be objective.   *(LO23-1)*

- Economists tend to agree on certain issues because their training is similar. Economists use models that focus on economic incentives and rationality.   *(LO23-1)*

- The economic approach to analyzing issues is a cost/benefit approach. If the marginal benefits exceed the marginal costs, do it. If the marginal costs exceed the marginal benefits, don't do it.   *(LO23-2)*

- People make choices every day that reveal the value that they place on their lives. The value of life is calculated by multiplying the inverse of the reduction in the probability of death by the amount individuals pay for that reduction.   *(LO23-2)*

- Collecting and interpreting empirical evidence is difficult, which contributes to disagreements among economists.   *(LO23-2)*

- The cost/benefit approach and the supply/demand framework deemphasize the possibility that market outcomes may be undesirable to society.   *(LO23-2)*

- Three failures of market outcomes are (1) failures due to distributional issues, (2) failures due to rationality problems of individuals, and (3) failures due to violations of inalienable rights.   *(LO23-3)*

- Although an implicit assumption in most policy discussions is that the goal of policy is to maximize consumer and producer surplus, society does care about how that total surplus is distributed.   *(LO23-3)*

- The supply/demand framework assumes that individuals are rational. Individuals are not always rational in practice. Their actions are swayed by addictions, advertising, and other pressures.   *(LO23-3)*

- Some rights, called inalienable rights, cannot be bought and sold. What rights are inalienable are moral judgments that do not have to stand up to the same cost/benefit framework.   *(LO23-3)*

- Economics provides the tools, not the rules, for policy.   *(LO23-4)*

- Economics involves the thoughtful use of economic insights and empirical evidence.   *(LO23-4)*

Key Terms

cost/benefit approach	failure of market outcome	Pareto optimal policy	rational
economic efficiency	Marxian (radical) model	public choice model	sin tax

Questions and Exercises ■ connect

1. Could anyone object to a Pareto optimal policy? Why?   *(LO23-1)*

2. Would it be wrong for economists to propose only Pareto optimal policies?   *(LO23-1)*

3. Would all economists oppose price controls? Why or why not?   *(LO23-1)*

4. In the early 1990s, the 14- to 17-year-old population fell because of low birthrates in the mid-1970s. Simultaneously the combined decisions of aging baby boomers to have kids resulted in an increase in the number of babies and hence in an increase in the number of parents needing babysitters. What effect will these two events likely have on: *(LO23-2)*

    a. The number of times parents go out without their children?

    b. The price of babysitters?

    c. The average age of babysitters?

    d. Should government require a minimum wage and age of babysitters?

5. Should the buying and selling of body organs be allowed? Why or why not?   *(LO23-2)*

6. In the 1970s legislators had difficulty getting laws passed requiring people to wear seat belts. Now not only do most people wear seat belts, but many cars have airbags too. Do people value their lives more today? *(LO23-2)*

7. Economist Steven D. Levitt estimated that, on average, for each additional criminal locked up in the United States, 15 crimes are eliminated. In addition, although it costs about $30,000 a year to keep a prisoner incarcerated, the average prisoner would have caused $53,900 worth of damage to society per year if free. If this estimate is correct, does it make economic sense to build more prisons? *(LO23-2)*

8. If one uses a willingness-to-pay measure in which life is valued at what people are willing to pay to avoid risks that might lead to death, the value of a U.S. citizen's life is $2.6 million, a Swede's life is worth $1.2 million, and a Portuguese's life is worth $20,000. *(LO23-2)*
   a. What policy implications does this value schedule have?
   b. Say you operate an airline. Should you spend more on safety precautions in the United States than you do in Portugal?

9. Economists Robin R. Jenkins, Nicole Owens, and Lanelle Bembenek Wiggins estimate the value of the lives of children by using parents' willingness to purchase bicycle helmets. Wearing a helmet reduces the probability of death from bicycling by 0.0000041. The annualized cost of a helmet is $6.51. *(LO23-2)*
   a. What economic concept is their study based on?
   b. Assuming helmets are worn 100 percent of the time, what is the value of life parents place on a child as revealed by their purchase of a bicycle helmet?

c. What happens to the value-of-life estimate if parents expect their children to wear the helmets less than 100 percent of the time?

10. What are three ways in which a well-functioning market might have undesirable results? *(LO23-3)*

11. Until recently, China had a strict one-child-per-family policy. For cultural reasons, families favor boys and there are now many more male than female children born in China. How is this likely to affect who pays the cost of dates in China in 15 to 20 years? Explain. *(LO23-3)*

12. As organ transplants become more successful, scientists are working on ways to transplant animal organs to humans. Pigs are the odds-on favorites as "donors" since their organs are about the same size as human organs. *(LO23-3)*
   a. What would the development of such organ farms likely do to the price of pigs?
   b. If you were an economic adviser to the government, would you say that such a development would be Pareto optimal (for humans)?
   c. Currently, there is a black market in human organs. What would this development likely do to that market?

13. Why are economists' views of politicians cynical? *(LO23-4)*

14. Anthony Zielinski, a former member of the Milwaukee Board of Supervisors, proposed that the county government sell the organs of dead welfare recipients to help pay off the welfare recipients' welfare costs and burial expenses. What was the likely effect of that proposal? Why? *(LO23-4)*

15. What is the basis for the opinions of public choice economists about government's ability to correct market failures? *(LO23-4)*

Questions from Alternative Perspectives

1. Even though a policy's stated goals may be laudable, its actual outcome can often cause serious problems.
   a. How much does it matter to an economist how closely a policy's goals match its outcome?
   b. How much does it matter to a politician? *(Austrian)*

2. In standard textbook economic analysis, institutions are often portrayed as creating market failures.
   a. Give an example of market failure caused by an institution not discussed in the text.
   b. What would a free market advocate likely say should be done about the failure?
   c. How would an Institutionalist likely respond? *(Institutionalist)*

3. The text deemphasizes the fact that people are social creatures who feel a need to conform to norms; Post-Keynesians emphasize norms.

   a. Who shapes these social norms?
   b. Does society as a whole benefit from these norms?
   c. How does the existence of these norms affect the analysis presented in the text about the way markets work? *(Post-Keynesian)*

4. Critics have pointed out a number of flaws in cost/benefit analysis: It assigns a dollar value to things that are not commodities such as human life; it places a price on public goods that we consume collectively (such as air quality); it downgrades the importance of the future through its discount rates; and it ignores distributional issues and issues of fairness.
   a. How reliable do you consider cost/benefit analysis as a policy analysis tool?
   b. Does cost/benefit analysis work better in some situations and worse in others? (Be sure to give

some examples and to explain your overall position.)
(Radical)

5. In his paper "Why Did the Economist Cross the Road? The Hierarchical Logic of Ethical and Economic Reasoning," economist Andrew Yuengert of Pepperdine University argues that "economists often give truncated justifications for their activities as economists out of fear that 'ethical' considerations will render their conclusions unscientific."
   a. Do you agree with this view?
   b. How might the presentation of economics change if economists did not have that fear? *(Religious)*

Issues to Ponder

1. In cost/benefit terms, explain your decision to take an economics course.

2. How much do you value your life in dollar terms? Are your decisions consistent with that valuation?

3. If someone offered you $1 million for one of your kidneys, would you sell it? Why or why not?

4. The technology is now developing so that road use can be priced by computer. A computer in the surface of the road picks up a signal from your car and automatically charges you for the use of the road.
   a. How could this technological change contribute to ending bottlenecks and rush-hour congestion? Demonstrate graphically.
   b. How will people likely try to get around the system?
   c. If people know when the prices will change, what will likely happen immediately before? How might this be avoided?

5. According to U.S. government statistics, the cost of averting a premature death differs among various regulations. Car seat belt standards cost $100,000 per premature death avoided, while hazardous waste landfill disposal bans cost $4.2 trillion per premature death avoided. If these figures are correct, should neither, one, the other, or both of these regulations be implemented?

6. Technology will soon exist such that individuals can choose the sex of their offspring. Assume that technology has now arrived and that 70 percent of the individuals choose male offspring.
   a. What effect will that have on social institutions such as families?
   b. What effect will it have on dowries—payments made by the bride's family to the groom—which are still used in a number of developing countries?
   c. Why might an economist suggest that if 70 percent male is the expectation, families would be wise to have daughters rather than sons?

7. In a study of hospital births, the single most important prediction factor of the percentage of vaginal births as opposed to caesarean (C-section) births was ownership status of hospitals—whether they were for-profit or nonprofit.
   a. Which had more C-sections, and why?
   b. What implications about the health care debate can you draw from the above results?
   c. How might the results change if the for-profit hospital received a fixed per-patient payment—as it would in a managed care system?

8. Why might an economist propose a policy that has little chance of adoption?

9. In the book *Why Not?* Yale professors Barry Nabalof and Ian Ayres suggest that computers that record driver behavior (similar to the black boxes in planes that record crashes) be installed in cars. In trials where such computers were installed in cars, crash rates fell by one-third.
   a. If these boxes cost $100 each, and their installation reduces the probability of a crash that costs an average of $30,000 in damage to persons and vehicles, do such boxes make sense?
   b. If they do make sense, what is a reason they are not installed?
   c. In what cars will they likely be installed first?
   d. What will their installation likely do to driving habits?

10. According to economists Henry Saffer of Kean University, Frank J. Chaloupka of the University of Illinois at Chicago, and Dhaval Dave of CUNY Graduate Center, using the criminal justice system to deter one person from using drugs costs $1,733, and using treatment centers costs $1,206.
    a. Which of the two programs would you recommend?
    b. What additional information do you need to determine whether either is worth pursuing?
    c. The authors estimated that the social cost to society of a person using drugs is $897. Based on this information alone, should the government spend the money on drug control?

11. Economists Michael Tanner and Stephen Moore of the Cato Institute recently calculated the hourly wage equivalent of welfare for a single mother with two children for each of the 50 United States. Their estimates ranged from $17.50 an hour for Hawaii to $5.33 in Mississippi. What do you suppose were their policy recommendations? What arguments can be made to oppose those prescriptions?

Answers to Margin Questions

1. I would respond that in the real world, Pareto optimal policies don't exist, and all real-world policies designed to make someone better off will make someone worse off. In making real-world policy judgments, one cannot avoid the difficult distributional and broader questions. It is those more difficult questions, which are value-laden, that make economic policy an art rather than a science. *(LO23-1)*

2. A radical analysis of the labor market differs from the mainstream analysis in that it emphasizes the tensions among social classes. Thus, a radical analysis will likely see exploitation built into the institutional structure. Mainstream analysis is much more likely to take the institutional structure as given and not question it. *(LO23-1)*

3. Oftentimes being "mean" in the short run can actually involve being "nice" in the long run. The reason is that often policy effects that are beneficial in the long run have short-run costs, and people focusing on those short-run costs see the policy as "mean." *(LO23-1)*

4. To maximize utility, one would expect that the marginal value per dollar spent should be equal in all activities. Thus, if the text is correct, it would suggest that you should be far less concerned about premium tire usage and far more concerned about whether your house has smoke detectors or not. *(LO23-1)*

5. Costs and benefits are ambiguous. Economists often disagree enormously on specific costs and benefits, or the costs and benefits are difficult or impossible to quantify. Thus, you should be extremely careful about using a cost/benefit analysis as anything more than an aid to your analysis of the situation. *(LO23-2)*

6. Other things do not always remain constant. The more macro the issue, the more things are likely to change. These changes must be brought back into the analysis, which complicates things enormously. *(LO23-2)*

7. False. Efficiency is achieving a goal as cheaply as possible. Stating efficiency as a goal does not make sense. *(LO23-3)*

8. No. The cocaine addict may be responding to the cravings created from the addiction, and not from any rational desire for more cocaine. Society may not be better off. *(LO23-3)*

9. False. Society may find that personal freedom is an inalienable right. Selling such a right may make society worse off. *(LO23-3)*

10. Government makes a positive contribution by adjusting for market failures and failures of market outcomes. Government may make a negative contribution because government is swayed by short-run political pressures. *(LO23-4)*

PART III

Macroeconomics

Unlike microeconomics, which has a definite focus and theory, macroeconomics, the study of the economy in the aggregate, has a focus and theory that is continually changing. That is in part because macroeconomic theory is less developed, and in part because the macroeconomic problems the economy is facing keep changing as well.

The general focus of macroeconomics is on unemployment, business cycles (fluctuations in output), growth, and inflation. Which of these problems gets specific focus depends on the policy problems facing the economy. In recent years, the focus has been on why the economy seems unable to get back on the growth trend that people had come to expect despite the economy being generally strong. These issues generate a lot of debate, and in the following chapters I provide you with the background necessary to understand that modern debate. Let's begin with a little history.

Macroeconomics emerged as a separate subject within economics in the 1930s, when the U.S. economy fell into the Great Depression. Businesses collapsed and unemployment rose until 25 percent of the workforce—millions of people—were out of work. The Depression changed the way economics was taught and the way in which economic problems were conceived. Before the 1930s, economics was microeconomics (the study of partial-equilibrium supply and demand). After the 1930s, the study of the core of economic thinking was broken into two discrete areas: microeconomics, as before, and a new field, macroeconomics.

Macroeconomic policy debates have centered on a struggle between two groups: Keynesian (pronounced KAIN-sian) economists and Classical economists. Should the government run a budget deficit or surplus? Should the government increase the money supply when a recession threatens? Should it decrease the money supply when inflation threatens? Can government prevent recessions? Keynesians generally answer one way; Classicals, another.

Classical economists generally oppose government intervention in the economy; they favor a laissez-faire policy.* Keynesians are more likely to favor government intervention in the economy. They feel a laissez-faire policy can sometimes lead to disaster. Both views represent reasonable economic positions. The differences between them are often subtle and result from their slightly different views of what government can do and slightly different perspectives on the economy. In the chapters that follow, I try to provide you with a sense of both Classical and Keynesian ideas, and their modern variations.

Section I, Macroeconomic Basics (Chapters 24 and 25), introduces the macroeconomic problems, terminology, and statistics used to track the economy's macroeconomic performance. Section II, Policy Models (Chapters 26 and 27), presents the core macroeconomic models and how they relate to current problems. Web Chapter 26W goes deeper into the multiplier model. Section III, Finance, Money, and the Economy (Chapters 28–30), looks at how money and the financial system fit into the macro model. These chapters discuss the Federal Reserve Bank (the Fed), monetary policy, and the financial crisis that hit the economy in 2007. That crisis resulted in the use of a number of unconventional policies by the Fed. that I discuss in Chapter 30. Section IV, Taxes, Budgets, and Fiscal Policy (Chapters 31 and 32), looks at the issues in fiscal policy and tax policy, and the debate about government deficits and debt, which have been expanding in recent years. Section V, Macroeconomic Problems (Chapters 33 and 34), looks specifically at the problems of unemployment and inflation. Finally, Section VI, International Macroeconomic Policy Issues (Chapters 35–38), discusses macroeconomic policy within an international context.

---

*Laissez-faire (introduced to you in Chapter 2) is a French expression meaning "Leave things alone; let them go on without interference."

CHAPTER 24

Economic Growth, Business Cycles, and Unemployment

> Remember that there is nothing stable in human affairs; therefore avoid undue elation in prosperity, or undue depression in adversity.
>
> —Socrates

After reading this chapter, you should be able to:

LO24-1 Discuss the history of macroeconomics, distinguishing Classical and Keynesian macroeconomists.

LO24-2 Define *growth* and discuss its recent history.

LO24-3 Distinguish a business cycle from structural stagnation.

LO24-4 Relate unemployment to business cycles and state how the unemployment rate is measured.

©leungchopan/Shutterstock

Like people, the economy has moods. Sometimes it's in wonderful shape—it's booming; at other times, it's depressed. Like people whose moods are often associated with specific problems such as headaches, sore backs, and itchy skin, the economy's moods are associated with specific problems such as lack of growth, business cycles, unemployment, and inflation. **Macroeconomics** is *the study of problems that affect the economy as a whole (lack of economic growth, recessions, unemployment, and inflation) and what to do about them.*

As of 2018 the U.S. economy was doing reasonably well. Unemployment was under 4 percent, and inflation was on target. Economic growth was a bit sluggish as it had been for the past decade, ever since the economy had experienced a major downturn in output in 2008. That downturn caused some to fear that the economy was falling into a depression like the one the United States faced in the 1930s. It didn't, in part because of the actions undertaken by the government. Those actions, and similar actions by governments in other countries throughout the world, which involved an increase in government debt, large deficits, and large increases in the money supply, were controversial. Critics argued that such policies might improve the economy in the short term but would create long-term problems. These debates are continuing. To understand the nature of the current policy debates, it is helpful to review the historical development of macroeconomics. We begin with the 1930s.

The Historical Development of Macroeconomics

In the 1930s, the U.S. economy fell into a deep recession that lasted for 10 years. It was a defining event that undermined people's faith in markets and was the beginning of macro's focus on the demand side of the economy. It is also where our story of macroeconomics begins.

During the Depression of the 1930s, output fell by 30 percent and unemployment rose to 25 percent. Not only was the deadbeat up the street unemployed but so were your brother, your mother, your uncle—the hardworking backbone of the country. These people wanted to work; if the market wasn't creating jobs for them, it was the market system that was at fault.

From Classical to Keynesian Economics

Macroeconomists before the Depression focused on the problem of growth (keeping the economy growing over the long run). Their policy recommendations were designed to lead to that growth. They avoided discussing policies that would affect the short-run prospects of the economy. In the 1930s that changed. Macroeconomists started focusing on short-run issues such as unemployment and economic ups and downs. To distinguish the two types of economics, the earlier economists who focused on long-run issues were called *Classical economists* and economists who focused on the short run were called *Keynesian economists.* Keynesian economists were named because a leading advocate of the short-run focus was John Maynard Keynes, the author of *The General Theory of Employment, Interest and Money,* and the originator of macroeconomics as a separate discipline from micro.

Classical Economics

Classical economists believed the market was self-regulating through the invisible hand (the pricing mechanism of the market). Short-run problems were temporary glitches; the Classical framework said that the economy would always return to its full capacity and a rate of unemployment consistent with the economy being at its potential. Thus, the essence of Classical economists' approach to problems was laissez-faire (leave the market alone). **Classical economists,** then, are *economists who believe that business cycles (ups and downs of the economy) are temporary glitches, and who generally favor laissez-faire, or nonactivist, policies.*

As long as the economy was operating relatively smoothly, the Classical analysis of the aggregate economy met no serious opposition. But when the Great Depression hit and unemployment became a serious problem, most Classical economists avoided the issue (as most people tend to do when they don't have a good answer). When pushed by curious students to explain how the invisible hand, if it was so wonderful, could have allowed the Depression, Classical economists used microeconomic supply and demand arguments. They argued that labor unions and government policies kept prices and wages from falling. The problem, they said, was that the invisible hand was not being allowed to coordinate economic activity.

During the Depression, unemployment lines were enormously long.

©Bettmann/Getty Images

Web Note 24.1

The Great Depression

Classical economists support laissez-faire policies.

Their laissez-faire policy prescription followed from their analysis: Eliminate labor unions and change government policies that held wages too high. If government did so, the wage rate would fall, unemployment would be eliminated, and the Depression would end.

Laypeople (average citizens) weren't pleased with this argument. (Remember, economists don't try to present pleasing arguments—only arguments they believe are correct.) But laypeople couldn't point to anything wrong with it. It made sense, but it wasn't satisfying. People thought, "Gee, Uncle Joe, who's unemployed, would take a job at half the going wage. But he can't find one—there just aren't enough jobs to go around at any wage." So most laypeople developed different explanations. One popular explanation of the Depression was that an oversupply of goods had glutted the market. Since firms couldn't sell the goods they had for sale, they cut production and laid off workers. All that was needed to eliminate unemployment was for government to hire the unemployed, even if only to dig ditches and fill them back up. The people who got the new jobs would spend their money, creating even more jobs. Pretty soon, the United States would be out of the Depression.

Classical economists argued against this lay view. They felt that the money to hire people would have to be borrowed. Such borrowing would use money that would have financed private economic activity and jobs, and would thus reduce private economic activity even further. The net effect would be essentially zero. Their advice was simply to have faith in markets.

Keynesian Economics

As the Depression deepened, the Classical "have-faith" solution lost support. Everyone was interested in the short run, not the long run. John Maynard Keynes put the concern most eloquently: "In the long run, we're all dead."

Keynes stopped asking whether the economy would eventually get out of the Depression on its own and started asking what was causing the Depression and what society could do to counteract these forces. By taking this approach, he created the macroeconomic framework that focuses on short-run issues such as business cycles and how to stabilize output fluctuations. **Keynesian economists** are *economists who believe that business cycles reflect underlying problems that can be addressed with activist government policies.*

While Keynes' ideas had many dimensions, the essence was that as wages and overall prices adjusted to sudden changes in overall spending (such as an unexpected decrease in household spending), the economy could get stuck in a rut.

If, for some reason, people stopped buying—decreased their demand in the aggregate—firms would decrease production, causing people to be laid off. These people would, in turn, buy even less—causing other firms to further decrease production, which would cause more workers to be laid off, and so on. Firms' supply decisions would be affected by consumers' buying decisions, and the economy would end up in a cumulative cycle of declining production that would end with the economy stuck at a low level of income. In developing this line of reasoning, Keynes provided a simple model of how unemployment could be caused by too little spending and how the economy could fall into a depression. The issue was not whether a more desirable equilibrium existed. It was whether a market economy, once it had fallen into a depression and was caught in a cumulative downward cycle, could get out of it on its own in an acceptable period of time.

In making his argument, Keynes carefully distinguished the adjustment process for a single market (a micro issue) from the adjustment process for the aggregate economy (a macro issue), arguing that the effects differ significantly when everyone does

Keynes focused on the short run, not the long run.

Q-1 Distinguish a Classical economist from a Keynesian economist.

Web Note 24.2

John Maynard Keynes

something versus when only one person does it. You were introduced to this problem in Chapter 4 under the name *fallacy of composition*.

The problem is neatly seen by considering an analogy to a football game. If everyone is standing, and you sit down, you can't see. Everyone is better off standing. No one has an incentive to sit down. However, if somehow all individuals could be enticed to sit down, all individuals would be even better off. Sitting down is a public good—a good that benefits others but one that nobody on his or her own will do. Keynesians argued that, in times of recession, spending benefits not just the person spending but everyone, so government should spend or find ways of inducing private individuals to spend. This difference between individual and economywide reactions to spending decisions creates a possibility for government to control, or at least significantly influence, aggregate expenditures and thereby control aggregate output.

> Keynesians argued that, in times of recession, spending is a public good that benefits everyone.

The Merging of Classical and Keynesian Economics

Within its own framework, Keynesian economics makes a lot of sense. But it leaves out some important issues. One is inflation. If, instead of an oversupply of goods, people spend more than is produced, there may be pressures for prices to rise and the economy may experience inflation. Microeconomics looks at the effect of price rises when prices of other goods remain constant. Put another way, it looks at the effect of *relative* price changes. But price increases for one good *can* lead to increases in the prices of other goods. The problem is, however, that if all people raise their prices by 10 percent, it is equivalent to nobody raising relative prices; all that will happen is the price level will rise. Classical economists had focused on inflation—an increase in the price of all goods—arguing that when aggregate demand (expenditures in the economy) exceeds aggregate supply (production in an economy), inflation will result. Keynesian economists had assumed the price level was constant.

When inflation became a serious problem, as it did in the 1970s, macroeconomics swung back to Classical economics and, over time, Keynesian economics lost influence. Keynesian economics wasn't addressing the problems of the times. Policy makers still used Keynesian policies, but they also used Classical policies. By the 1980s, the two types of economics had merged into a new conventional macroeconomics. At that point macroeconomics was neither Keynesian nor Classical but a combination of the two. That new conventional macroeconomics formed the core of modern macroeconomics until the downturn of 2008 when output declined, unemployment rose, and the U.S. economy did not recover as conventional economists had predicted it would. To everyone's disappointment, it seemed as if the U.S. economy had fallen into a **structural stagnation**—*a period of protracted slow growth with the economy not providing the type of jobs society expects from it.*

> Structural stagnation is a period of slow growth and high unemployment with the economy not providing the type of jobs society expects from it.

Concerns about structural stagnation continued even as the U.S. unemployment rate fell. Somehow, even though the overall economy was prospering, entire segments seemed stuck in a continual recession. Such concerns helped lead to the election of Donald Trump as president. He promised to "make America great again," and the promise resonated with many in the United States who felt that they had been left behind.

Politics as the Driving Force in Macro Policy

The Classical/Keynesian debates about structural stagnation and the appropriate macro policy often are seen as debates grounded in economic theory. In practice, they are generally grounded in political differences; support for policies depends on who is in power. For example, when Democrats were in power, Republicans were concerned with the long-run effects of deficits while the Democrats were far less concerned with deficits. Then, when the Republicans won the White House in 2016, their concern

The Author's Biases

Normally, I try to keep myself and my views out of policy discussions, or at least keep them relatively hidden. The positive spin on my doing that is that I'm a very open-minded economist and I want my textbook to be teachable by economists with many different views. (The economic self-interest spin on my doing so is that I want to sell my book, and showing my biases will cut sales since only those who share my biases will adopt it.)

Whatever my motives, I continue this "policy neutrality" approach in this edition, but the presentation of current macro policy issues involves so many difficult and unavoidable judgments about political and economic relationships that are unsettled within macroeconomics that I have come to the belief that in macro, it is necessary to admit my views, so that the reader can take them into account. So, here are my policy views.

I am a moderate macroeconomist who has collaborated with both Classical and Keynesian economists. I am associated with both and neither; I usually end up upsetting both sides, especially those who are dyed-in-the-wool one-or-the-other siders. I believe that both the Classical and Keynesian traditions offer important insights and policy makers must consider both.

Hyman Minsky
Courtesy of Levy
Economics Institute of
Bard College

These insights can be found not only in the conventional traditions but also in the writings of unconventional Keynesian and Classical macroeconomists who never signed on to the conventional views of what became known as Keynesians and Classicals. In fact, what the textbooks (including mine) present as Keynesian and Classical economics is a simplistic caricature of both. Both Classical and Keynesian policy views are far richer than their textbook representations. Both Classicals and Keynesians were always searching for a balance. For example, during the Great Depression, Keynes was enormously worried about deficits, and at various times opposed larger deficits. Similarly, in the depths of the Depression, various Classical economists agreed that the government should accept deficits and do whatever it could to eliminate unemployment. The necessary simplifications in textbooks inevitably lose such nuances of policy.

What this means for understanding the policy debate is that conventional views of Keynesians and Classicals need to be scrutinized and the unconventional views of both need to be considered as well. Unconventional Classical economists include *Austrian economists*—pro-market-oriented economists who have long argued that the conventional blend of Classical and Keynesian economics has undermined true Classical ideas. Unconventional Keynesian economists include *Post-Keynesian* and *Institutional economists*—more pro-government-control-oriented economists who have also long argued that the conventional blend of Classical and Keynesian economics has undermined true Keynesian ideas.

Friedrich von Hayek
©Hulton-Deutsch
Collection/Corbis/Getty
Images

What makes these two groups especially relevant to the current macro policy debate is that they both argued that conventional macro policies the U.S. government was following in the early 2000s would lead to the economic problems we are now facing. For example, Post-Keynesian economist Hyman Minsky argued that financial crashes, such as the one the United States experienced in 2007, were inevitable in a market economy, and were intricately tied to the workings of a capitalist economy. Similarly, Austrian economist Friedrich von Hayek had warned of financial crises if government became as involved in the economy as it had.

While both Austrian and Post-Keynesian economists foresaw the current macroeconomic problems, their solutions were quite different. Institutionalists and Post-Keynesians called for more government involvement in the economy; Austrians called for less. This leaves policy makers in a bind. Clearly, something was wrong with conventional macroeconomics, but there is no clear alternative model or policy that emerged from these unconventional views. My bottom line: Some problems just don't have simple solutions, especially when the solutions have to be implemented through a highly problematic political system.

about deficits and debt disappeared as they put forward a tax cut bill that significantly increased the deficit and long-run debt. Now it was the Democrats who were concerned about the dangers of deficits and debt. What to make of all this? Politics involves strategic rhetoric. Both sides use economic arguments when they lead to their desired policy, and tend to disregard them when they don't.

Two Frameworks: The Long Run and the Short Run

In analyzing macroeconomic issues, economists generally use two frameworks: a short-run and a long-run framework. Issues of growth are generally considered in a long-run framework. Business cycles are generally considered in a short-run framework. Inflation and unemployment fall within both frameworks.

What is the difference between the two frameworks? The long-run growth framework focuses on incentives for supply; that's why sometimes it is called *supply-side economics.* In the long run, policies that affect production or supply—such as incentives that promote work, capital accumulation (factors of production), and technological change—are key.

The short-run business-cycle framework focuses on demand. That is why short-run macro analysis is sometimes called *demand-side economics.* Much of the policy discussion of short-run business cycles focuses on ways to increase or decrease aggregate expenditures, such as policies to get consumers and businesses to increase their spending.[1]

The short-run/long-run distinction allowed Keynesians and Classicals to avoid major disagreements about models and policies. Conventional Keynesian-oriented economists mostly focused on the short-run framework and argued that this framework should guide policy. That short-run framework leads to the policy position that all we have to do to get the economy back to its potential is to have government stimulate the economy by increasing government spending enormously.

Conventional Classical-oriented economics mostly focused on the long-run framework and argued that the long-run model should guide policy. That is the framework that leads to the view that the economy will solve its own problems and that government spending will not help, but hurt, the economy.

In my view, both extremes are problematic, as is the stark division between the short-run and the long-run frameworks. Dividing up macro problems into short-run and long-run problems may be a useful teaching simplification, but such a sharp distinction between the two does not fit the real world. The policy debate between the two sides cannot be hidden by a framework that assigns the short run to Keynesian policy focusing on demand, and the long run to Classical policy that focuses on supply.

In reality the short run and the long run are not separate. The economy is simultaneously in the long run and short run, and any analysis of either must take both runs into account. This means that the short-run and long-run frameworks have to be blended into a composite framework in which both supply and demand influence long-run and short-run forces. In the long run we are all dead, but the long run is just a combination of short runs; they cannot be separated.

In this book, I attempt to blend the two together in an analysis of structural stagnation, in which an economy's short-run potential output is limited by structural limitations that most short-run models do not consider. In this blended framework, short-run expansionary government policy might cause a financial bubble rather than a solid recovery even with the economy at a high employment level. In this blended framework,

Q-2 From 2007 to 2012, employment in the United States declined by 4 million. The decline was in part due to a recession and in part due to U.S. firms outsourcing jobs to foreign countries. Is the decline in employment an issue best studied in the long-run framework or the short-run framework?

Dividing up macro problems into short-run and long-run problems may be a useful teaching simplification, but such a sharp distinction does not fit the real world.

In the long run we are all dead, but the long run is just a combination of short runs; they cannot be separated.

---

[1] A short-run/long-run distinction helps make complicated issues somewhat clearer, but it obscures other issues, such as: How long is the short run, and how do we move from the short run to the long run? Some economists argue that in the long run we are only in another short run, while others argue that since our actions are forward-looking, we are always in the long run.

The Power of Compounding

A difference in growth rates of 1 percentage point may not seem like much, but over a number of years, the power of compounding can turn these small differences in growth rates into large differences in income levels. Consider Eastern European countries compared to Western European countries. In 1950, real per capita income was about $2,000 in Eastern European countries and about $4,500 in Western European countries. Over the next 60 years, income grew 2.4 percent a year in Eastern European countries and 2.7 percent a year in Western European countries. One-third percentage point may be small, but it meant that in those 60 years, income in Western European countries rose to $22,000, while income in Eastern European countries rose by much less to only $8,400.

The reason small differences in starting points and growth rates over long periods of time can mean huge differences in income levels is *compounding*. Compounding means that growth is based not only on the original level of income but also on the accumulation of previous-year increases in income. Say your income starts at $100 and grows at a rate of 10 percent each year; the first year your income grows by $10, to $110. The second year the same growth rate increases income by $11, to $121. The third year income grows by $12.10, which is still 10 percent but a larger dollar increase. After 50 years, that same 10 percent annual increase means income will be growing by over $1,000 a year.

globalization and trade deficits play key limiting roles in determining policy, and the problems that can easily be solved in the short-run framework become almost impossible to solve without strong government policy to deal with both the long-run and the short-run nature of the problem.

So if you are looking for an easy answer to macroeconomic problems, you won't find it here. What you are going to get in this book is a somewhat sobering view of the state of the macroeconomy—not because there are no answers, but because the answers that will most likely solve the underlying problems involve difficult and risky policy choices that are politically difficult to institute.

We will be going over the various macroeconomic problems and policy goals in the following chapters, but here at the beginning, I want to provide you with a brief overview of the central issues. We will start with growth.

Growth

Since the end of World War II the U.S. economy generally has been growing or expanding. Economists measure growth with changes in total output over a long period of time. When people produce and sell their goods, they earn income, so when an economy is growing, both total output and total income are increasing. Such growth gives most people more income this year than they had last year. Since most of us prefer more to less, growth is easy to take.

U.S. economic output has grown at an annual 2.5 to 3.5 percent rate since World War I. What it will be in the future is uncertain.

The U.S. Department of Commerce traced U.S. economic growth in output since about 1890 and discovered that, on average, output of goods and services grew about 3.5 percent per year. In the 1970s and 1980s, growth was more like 2.5 percent. In the late 1990s and early 2000s, it was assumed again to be 3.5 percent. Even though it was assumed to be 3.5 percent, the actual growth rate since the early 2000s has been more like 2.0 to 2.5 percent, which leads to the question of whether the long-run growth rate has slowed. How one answers that question significantly influences what one believes to be the appropriate macro policy.

This 2.5 to 3.5 percent growth rate is sometimes called the *secular growth trend.* The long-run, or secular, growth trend represents the rise in **potential output**—*the* *highest amount of output an economy can sustainably produce and sell using existing production processes and resources.* Two points should be made about potential output. The first is that potential output is not a purely physical measure. For example, if workers are asking for a wage that is higher than any firm is willing to pay, those unwilling to work at the lower wage will not contribute to an economy's potential output. Similarly, a factory that is technologically obsolete does not contribute to potential output. The second point is that the production must be sustainable. If a level of output leads to accelerating inflation, or to a financial collapse, that level is not sustainable and hence does not meet the potential output definition. Much of the current policy debate reflects differences in opinion about what the level of potential output is.

Another measure of growth is changes in per capita output. **Per capita output** is *output divided by the total population.* When the population is growing, per capita growth is lower than overall growth. For example, if the population is growing at 1 percent and the economy is growing at 3 percent, per capita growth is 2 percent. Change in output per person is an important measure of growth because it gives us a measure of how the average person is affected by growth.

Q-3 Say that output in the United States is $15 trillion, and there are 300 million people living in the United States. What is per capita output?

Global Experiences with Growth

While per capita output has steadily grown, that trend has been highly variable for long periods of time, especially when you consider specific regions, as you can see in Figure 24-1. Consider China and India. They grew slowly until the 1990s, and then their growth rate increased substantially. Western Europe and Japan provide other examples. In the postwar era (after the end of World War II in 1945) Western European economies grew by an average 3.0 percent a year; Japan grew by 4 percent, but its growth rate fell considerably in the 1990s and has remained low. The U.S. economy grew at an annual per capita rate of 2.5 percent from 1940 to 1970, but its growth rate has slowed in recent years. This slowdown in growth is a major policy issue today.

FIGURE 24-1 Per Capita Growth Rates around the World

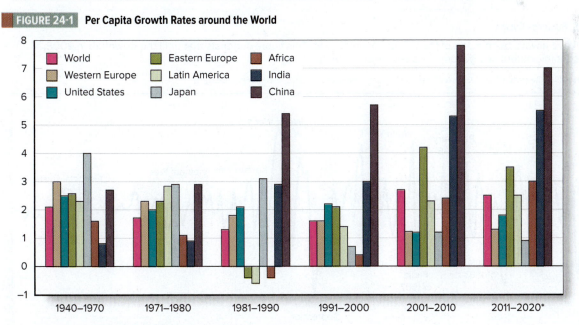

Source: World Economy, Historical Tables, Per Capita Growth, www.theworldeconomy.org.

*Estimates based on World Bank and government data and projections.

The Prospect for Future U.S. Growth

Past data are not necessarily good predictors of future events, and while predictions are always dangerous, it is worthwhile asking: How might the future differ from the past, and what do those differences suggest about future U.S. economic growth? One big difference is the current economic development of the Indian and Chinese economies, which is similar to the growth experienced by other Asian countries, such as Korea and Thailand, in the 1980s. As their economies became integrated into the global economy, production that could shift from the United States into India and China did. China's and India's growth rates grew and the U.S. growth rate fell. Over the coming years, as you can see in Figure 24-1, economic growth in India and China, even though it is slowing, is likely to significantly outpace growth in most economies throughout the world, particularly industrialized countries in Western Europe, the United States, and Japan.

Q-4 How does China's and India's integration into the global economy affect the prospect for U.S. growth?

What's different about China and India is their size; combined, they have a population of 2.7 billion, making their potential for growth significant. As they continue to develop into highly industrialized countries, the world economic landscape will change tremendously. Specifically, their development will likely place more and more pressures on U.S. firms in both services and manufacturing industries to become more competitive either by holding down wage increases and developing more efficient production methods or by moving their production facilities abroad. It will also be accompanied by greater demand for natural resources.

Business Cycles and Structural Stagnation

Even if the economy is on a steady long-run growth path, there are inevitably fluctuations around that trend. This phenomenon has given rise to the term *business cycle*. A **business cycle** is *a short-run, temporary upward or downward movement of economic activity, or real GDP, that occurs around the growth trend.* Figure 24-2 graphs the fluctuations in GDP for the U.S. economy since 1860.

A business cycle is the upward or downward movement of economic activity that occurs around the growth trend.

FIGURE 24-2   **U.S. Business Cycles**

Business cycles have always been a part of the U.S. economic scene. This figure suggests that until the downturn in 2008, fluctuations in economic output had become less severe since 1945.

Source: Historical Statistics of the United States, Colonial Times to 1970, and Bureau of Economic Analysis (www.bea.gov).

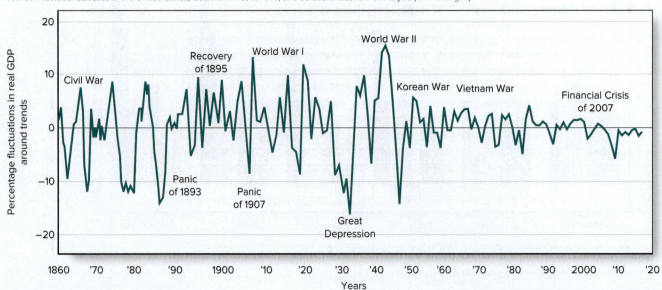

NBER Dating of the Business Cycle

In December 2008, the six members of the NBER Business Cycle Dating Committee issued this statement:

> The NBER's Business Cycle Dating Committee has determined that a peak in business activity occurred in the U.S. economy in December 2007. The peak marks the end of an expansion that began in November 2001 and the beginning of a recession. The expansion lasted 73 months; the previous expansion of the 1990s lasted 120 months. A recession is a significant decline in economic activity spread across the economy, lasting more than a few months, normally visible in production, employment, real income, and other indicators.

Technically, an economy is in a recession only after it has been declared to be in a recession by a group of economists appointed by the National Bureau of Economic Research (NBER). Because real output is reported only quarterly and is sometimes revised substantially, the NBER Dating Committee looks at monthly data such as industrial production, employment, real income, sales, and sometimes even people's perceptions of what is happening in the economy to determine whether a recession has occurred. In 2001, for example, the committee announced that a recession had begun in March even though, according to preliminary GDP figures, real output had not fallen for two consecutive quarters. (Revised figures, which came out more than six months later, showed that GDP had actually started falling earlier and fell for three quarters.) The fact that: (1) the NBER economists include many factors when determining a recession and (2) they base their decision on preliminary data, makes it difficult to provide an unambiguous definition of recession.

According to the NBER, the U.S. economy exited the recession in 2009, but the growth that followed was much slower than it had been in previous recessions. That growth has remained below what was normal, which is why the slowdown that began in 2007 is not seen by many as a normal recession, but rather as a structural stagnation. Even as the economy picked up steam in 2018, many areas of the United States felt that they were stuck in an ongoing recession, regardless of what the NBER stated.

As mentioned previously, until the late 1930s, economists—Classical economists—took such cycles as facts of life. They argued that the government should just accept that business cycles occur. Once the Great Depression hit, Keynesian economists argued that government could temper these economic fluctuations with policy actions. Which of these two views is correct is still a matter of debate.

Describing the Business Cycle

Much research has gone into measuring business cycles and setting official reference dates for the beginnings and ends of contractions and expansions. The National Bureau of Economic Research (NBER) is the organization that determines the government's official dates of contractions and expansions. In the postwar era (since mid-1945), the average business expansion has lasted about 59 months. A major expansion occurred from 1982 until mid-1990, when the U.S. economy fell into a recession. In mid-1991 it slowly came out of the recession and began a long expansion, which ended in March 2001. The recession ended in November 2001, and the economy expanded until December 2007 when the economy entered a deep recession. The economy began to expand in mid-2009, but its growth has been slow.

Business cycles have varying durations and intensities, but economists have developed a terminology to describe all business cycles and just about any place within a given business cycle. Since the press often uses this terminology, it is helpful to go over it. I do so in reference to Figure 24-3, which gives a visual representation of a business cycle.

Let's start at the top. The top of a business cycle is called the *peak*. Eventually the economy enters a *downturn* (at least it always has) and may enter a recession. A **recession** is generally considered to be *a decline in real output that persists for more*

543

FIGURE 24-3 **Business Cycle Phases**

Economists have many terms that describe the position of the economy on the business cycle. Some of them are given in this graph.

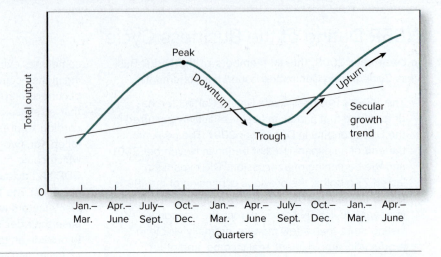

than two consecutive quarters of a year. The actual definition of a recession is more ambiguous than this generally accepted definition, as the box "NBER Dating of the Business Cycle" points out. The bottom of a recession or depression is called the *trough*. As total output begins to expand, the economy comes out of the trough; economists say it's in an *upturn*. As you can see in Figure 24-3, the four phases of the business cycle are a peak, a downturn, a trough, and an upturn.

The table below shows the duration and timing of business cycles since 1854 up until 2018 in the United States. The recession that began in December 2007 was the longest recession we had since World War II. Although it technically ended in June 2009, there was considerable debate about whether it actually ended then because unemployment remained high and growth remained significantly below the long-term trend. In 2018 the economy was picking up steam, leading to a debate about whether the U.S. economy was exiting its structural stagnation doldrums. Was the faster growth permanent or temporary? In part, how one answered that had to do with geography. Some areas were booming, while others remained mired in slow growth and recession. U.S. fiscal policy was highly stimulative with both a large tax cut and a large spending increase. What economists were waiting to see was whether, with unemployment low, that stimulus would lead to unacceptable increases in inflation.

Q-5 What are the four phases of the business cycle?

If prolonged contractions are a type of cold the economy catches, the Great Depression of the 1930s was double pneumonia.

	Duration (in months)	
Business Cycles	Pre–World War II (1854–1945)	Post–World War II (1945–2018)
Number (trough to trough)	22	11
Average duration (trough to trough)	50	66
Length of longest cycle	99 (1870–79)	128 (1991–2001)
Length of shortest cycle	28 (1919–21)	28 (1980–82)
Average length of expansions	29	59
Length of shortest expansion	10 (1919–20)	12 (1980–81)
Length of longest expansion	80 (1938–45)	120 (1991–2001)
Average length of recessions	21	11
Length of shortest recession	7 (1918–19)	6 (1980)
Length of longest recession	65 (1873–79)	18 (2007–2009)

Sources: National Bureau of Economic Research (http://nber.org) and *Survey of Current Business* (www.bea.doc.gov).

Structural Stagnation

The very concept *business cycle* conveys a sense that a fall in output is going to reverse itself, while the concept *growth trend* conveys a sense that the current growth rate will continue. The concept *cycle* conveys a sense that a fluctuation is a short-term event that will reverse itself. In reality, we never know for sure whether a cyclical downturn is a cycle or a change in the growth trend. This leads us to a third term, *structural stagnation.* As we discussed earlier in the chapter, structural stagnation is a downturn that leads to slow economic growth that prevents the economy from returning to its past trend for a long time unless the structure of the economy changes significantly. It is a short-term problem that extends into the long term.

Ending structural stagnation might require massive amounts of spending.

©Marcus Clackson/Getty Images

In a structural stagnation, many of the unemployed cannot get a job at the pay they were getting or in the field where they worked. To get a job they have to accept a lower wage or learn new skills. Unemployment is not due to temporary layoffs as it is in a business cycle; it is due to longer-term changes. Often, structural stagnation can lead workers to leave the labor force altogether and thus not show up in government statistics as being unemployed.

Structural stagnation might start as a business cycle but quickly turns into a long-term stagnation with no expectation of ending, or even that the government has the ability to pull the economy out of it without running stimulus policies such as massive deficits that carry the risk of causing serious long-term problems for the economy. In a structural stagnation the economy is stuck in a rut, with no easy way to get out.

Until recently most macroeconomic policy discussions assumed that the modern economy would experience only business cycles. Structural stagnation was not discussed in conventional macro. But the events since 2007 challenged that view, and in the financial crisis of 2008 many economists worried that the economy was falling into a **depression**—*a deep and prolonged recession*. The massive policy response of the U.S. government and central bank can only be understood with that perspective. Specifically, in its policy to deal with the financial crisis the government wasn't trying to smooth a business cycle around a growth trend. It was trying to save the economy from falling into a depression. And many economists (including me) believed that the strong government policies did keep the recession from falling into a depression.

A depression is a deep and prolonged recession.

As you can see no formal line indicates when a recession becomes a depression. This ambiguity has led to the joke: "When your neighbor is unemployed, it's a recession; when you're unemployed, it's a depression." If pushed for something more specific, I'd say that if unemployment exceeds 12 percent for more than a year, the economy is in a depression. Likewise no formal line indicates when a business cycle becomes structural stagnation. Again, if push came to shove, I'd say that if the economy doesn't return to its long-term growth rate within four years, the economy is experiencing structural stagnation. By that criterion, starting in 2008, the United States experienced a structural stagnation, not a typical business cycle.

This distinction between a business cycle and structural stagnation goes to the heart of the modern macro policy debates. Optimistic macroeconomists see the years after the 2008 recession as a long and severe, but nonetheless normal, business cycle. At some point, with sufficient expansionary conventional macroeconomic policies, the economy would return to its historical long-term growth trend. Less optimistic macroeconomists (like me) see the situation not as a business cycle but as a structural stagnation. They argue that the economy would not return to its historical long-run growth trend anytime soon, and that continued attempts to jump-start the economy with deficits are unsustainable in the long run. While such attempts might improve the economy

Q-6   Why is the distinction between a business cycle and structural stagnation important to policy?

in the short run, they might undermine the economy in the long run. They claim that without politically difficult-to-implement government action that addresses the longer-run structural problems, the growth rate will stay below its long-run average or will experience problematic structural imbalances.

Now that we have explored business cycles, let's turn to the other major problem currently facing the U.S. economy—unemployment and jobs.

Unemployment and Jobs

Both business cycles and growth are directly related to unemployment in the U.S. economy. Unemployment occurs when people are looking for a job and cannot find one. The **unemployment rate** is *the percentage of people in the economy who are both able to and looking for work, but who cannot find jobs.* When an economy is growing and is in an expansion, unemployment is usually falling; when an economy is in a recession, unemployment is usually rising, although often with a lag.

The relationship between the business cycle and unemployment is obvious to most people, but often the seemingly obvious hides important insights. Just why are the business cycle and growth related to unemployment? True, aggregate income must fall in a recession, but, logically, unemployment need not result. A different possibility is that all people, on average, work fewer hours.

Unemployment has not always been a problem associated with business cycles. In preindustrial societies, households—from farms to cottage craftspeople—produced goods and services. The entire family contributed to farming, weaving, or blacksmithing. When times were good, the family enjoyed a higher level of income. When times weren't so good, they still worked, but accepted less income for the goods they produced. When economic activity fell, people's income earned per hour (their wage) fell. Low income was a problem; but since people didn't become unemployed, **cyclical unemployment** *(unemployment resulting from fluctuations in economic activity)* was not a problem.

While cyclical unemployment did not exist in preindustrial society, **structural unemployment** *(unemployment caused by the institutional structure of an economy or by economic restructuring making some skills obsolete)* did. For example, scribes in Europe had less work after the invention of the printing press in the 1400s. Some unemployment would likely result; that unemployment would be called *structural unemployment.* But structural unemployment wasn't much of a problem for government, or at least people did not consider it government's problem. The reason is that those in the family, or community, with income would share it with unemployed family members.

Structural unemployment has many variations, and is relevant to today's economy. For example, the standard measure of the unemployment rate in the United States in 2018 fell below 4 percent, which is historically low; it certainly was much lower than it was in 2008 when concern about structural stagnation first surfaced. An employment rate of 4 percent generally is considered a sign that the economy has recovered. But that was not the case in 2018 because growth had remained low and many people could not find jobs commensurate with their education and training.

The reason the unemployment rate declined was in part because people were sufficiently discouraged that they had stopped looking for work and dropped out of the job market. (You have to be looking for a job to be considered unemployed.) So even though there were jobs, the types of jobs people were finding were often not the types of jobs that people were hoping for, nor were the jobs paying salaries that they hoped to be earning. Many college-educated students were taking jobs that did not require college degrees.

The unemployment rate is the percentage of people in the economy who are both able to and looking for work but who cannot find jobs.

Web Note 24.3

Defining Unemployment

Q-7 True or false? In a recession, structural unemployment is expected to rise.

FIGURE 24-4 **Unemployment Rate since 1900**

The unemployment rate has always fluctuated, with the average around 5 or 6 percent. Since the 1930s, fluctuations have decreased. In the mid-1940s, the U.S. government started focusing on the unemployment rate as a goal. Initially, it chose 2 percent as a target, but over time that gradually increased to somewhere around 5 percent. During the 2008–2009 recession, the unemployment rate increased to 10 percent and, in 2018, was under 4 percent.

Source: U.S. Bureau of Labor Statistics (www.bls.gov).

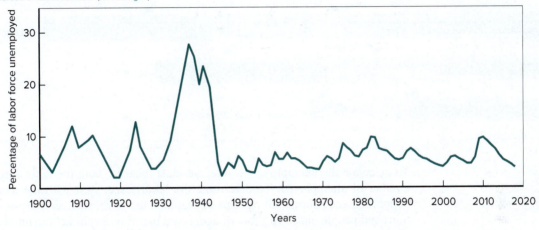

They were employed, but they were *underemployed*. This meant that, despite the relatively low unemployment rate, the economy was still considered stuck in a structural stagnation, and while the unemployment rate was low, the economy still had an employment problem.

How Is Unemployment Measured?

When there's debate about what the unemployment problem is, it isn't surprising that there's also a debate about how to measure it. When talking about unemployment, economists usually refer to a measure of the unemployment rate published by the U.S. Department of Labor's Bureau of Labor Statistics that includes all jobless persons who are available to take a job and have actively sought work in the past four weeks. Fluctuations in the official unemployment rate since 1900 appear in Figure 24-4. In it you can see that during World War II (1941–1945) unemployment fell from the high rates of the 1930s Depression to an extremely low rate, only 1.2 percent. You also can see that while the rate started back up in the 1950s, reaching 4 or 5 percent, it remained low until the 1970s, when the rate began gradually to rise again, peaking at 10.8 percent in 1983. In the 1990s and early 2000s, the unemployment rate fluctuated from a low of 3.8 percent in 2000 to a high of 10 percent during the 2008–2009 recession. In 2018, the unemployment rate fell below 4 percent.

> When there's debate about what the unemployment problem is, it isn't surprising that there's also a debate about how to measure it.

CALCULATING THE UNEMPLOYMENT RATE The U.S. unemployment rate is determined by dividing the number of people who are unemployed by the number of people in the **labor force**—*those people in an economy who are willing and able to work*—and multiplying by 100. For example, if the total unemployed stands at 8 million and the labor force stands at 160 million, the unemployment rate is:

$$\frac{8 \text{ million}}{160 \text{ million}} = 0.05 \times 100 = 5\%$$

> The unemployment rate is measured by dividing the number of unemployed individuals by the number of people in the civilian labor force and multiplying by 100.

FIGURE 24-5 **Unemployment/Employment Figures (in millions) in 2017**

This exhibit shows you how the unemployment rate is calculated. Notice that the labor force is not the entire population.

Source: Labor Force Statistics, Table A-1, Bureau of Labor Statistics (www.bls.gov). Data may not add up due to rounding.

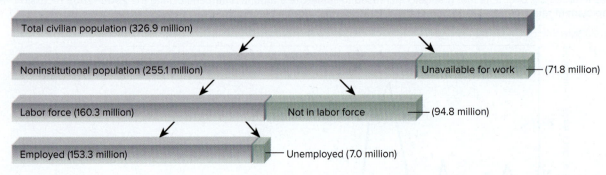

To calculate the unemployment rate, we must measure both the labor force and the number of unemployed. To determine the labor force, start with the total civilian population and subtract all persons unavailable for work, such as inmates of institutions and people under 16 years of age. From that figure subtract the number of people not in the labor force, including homemakers, students, retirees, those who are voluntarily idle, and individuals with disabilities. The result is the potential workforce, which is about 160 million people, or about 50 percent of the civilian population (see Figure 24-5). (The civilian population excludes about 1.3 million individuals who are in the armed forces.)

The number of unemployed can be calculated by subtracting the number of employed from the labor force. The Bureau of Labor Statistics (BLS) defines people as *employed* if they work at a paid job (including part-time jobs) or if they are unpaid workers in an enterprise operated by a family member. The BLS' definition of *employed* includes all those who were temporarily absent from their jobs the week of the BLS survey because of illness, bad weather, vacation, labor-management dispute, or personal reasons, whether or not they were paid by their employers for the time off.

In the fall of 2018 the number of unemployed individuals was about 6.0 million. Dividing this number by the labor force (162.2 million) gives us an unemployment rate of 3.7 percent.

Q-8 During some months, the unemployment rate declines, but the number of unemployed rises. How can this happen?

HOW ACCURATE IS THE OFFICIAL UNEMPLOYMENT RATE?

The unemployment rate that I have been using so far is the BLS' standard measure of unemployment and is the unemployment rate you see in the newspaper. The assumptions BLS makes in this standard measure have been a source of debate. For example, should *discouraged workers*—people who do not look for a job because they feel they don't have a chance of finding one—be counted as unemployed? Some Keynesian economists believe they should. Moreover, they question whether part-time workers who prefer full-time work, the *underemployed,* should be classified as employed.

The Keynesian argument is that there is such a lack of decent jobs and of affordable transportation to get to the jobs that do exist that many people become very discouraged and have simply stopped looking for work. Because the BLS measure of unemployment implicitly assumes that these people are voluntarily idle, and does not count them in their standard measure of unemployment, Keynesians argue that the BLS undercounts unemployment significantly. When discouraged workers *are* included, the number of unemployed rises significantly.

Alternative Measures of the Unemployment Rate

As mentioned in the text, the Bureau of Labor Statistics publishes a range of unemployment rates depending on who is considered unemployed. These various measures are referred to by the creative names U-1 through U-6 (U-3 is the standard measure). Their definitions are below along with a table that gives you an idea of how differences in definition impact what one considers to be the unemployment rate.

- U-1: persons unemployed 15 weeks or longer, as a percent of the civilian labor force;

- U-2: job losers and persons who completed temporary jobs, as a percent of the civilian labor force;

- U-3: total unemployed, as a percent of the civilian labor force (U-3 is the standard measure of the unemployment rate);

- U-4: total unemployed plus discouraged workers, as a percent of the civilian labor force plus discouraged workers;

- U-5: total unemployed, plus discouraged workers, plus all other marginally attached workers, as a percent of the civilian labor force plus all marginally attached workers; and

- U-6: total unemployed, plus all marginally attached workers, plus total employed part-time for economic reasons, as a percent of the civilian labor force plus all marginally attached workers.

	2006	2007	2008	2009	2010	2011	2012	2013	2014	2015	2016	2017
U-1	1.5	1.5	2.1	4.7	5.7	5.3	4.5	3.9	3.0	2.3	2.0	1.7
U-2	2.2	2.3	3.1	6.0	6.0	5.3	4.4	3.9	3.1	2.6	2.3	2.1
U-3	4.6	4.6	5.8	9.3	9.6	9.0	8.1	7.4	6.2	5.3	4.9	4.4
U-4	4.9	4.8	6.1	9.7	10.3	9.5	8.6	7.9	6.6	5.7	5.2	4.6
U-5	5.5	5.5	6.8	10.6	11.1	10.4	9.5	8.8	7.5	6.4	5.9	5.3
U-6	8.2	8.3	10.6	16.3	16.7	15.9	14.7	13.8	12.0	10.4	9.6	8.5

Classicals see the standard measure as likely overestimating unemployment. Classicals argue that being without a job often is voluntary. People may say they are looking for a job when they're not really looking. Many are working "off the books"; others are simply vacationing. Some Classicals contend that the way the BLS measures unemployment exaggerates the number of those who are truly unemployed. They argue that many so-called unemployed are just choosing not to work.

To address these concerns, the Bureau of Labor Statistics has developed a range of alternative measures of unemployment, classified as U-1 through U-6; U-1 and U-2 define unemployment more narrowly than the standard measure U-3; U-4, U-5, and U-6 define it more broadly. U-6, for example, includes all those counted as unemployed in the standard definition plus all marginally attached workers, plus total employed part-time for economic reasons. The unemployment rate thus broadly defined was 8.5 percent in 2017 compared to the standard rate of 4.4 percent. On the other side we have U-1, which includes only those who have been unemployed 15 weeks or longer. This narrowly defined unemployment rate was 1.7 in 2017. As you can see in the box "Alternative Measures of the Unemployment Rate" the unemployment rate varies considerably depending on what definition is used.

Despite its problems, the standard unemployment rate measure is a reasonable one that provides useful information about changes in the economy. Thus, in late 2007,

Q-9 In what way does the very concept of unemployment depend on value judgments?

Despite problems, the unemployment rate statistic still gives us useful information about changes in the economy.

when the economy went into a downturn and the standard unemployment rate rose from a low of 4.4 percent in early 2007 to a high of 10 percent during the recession, the unemployment problem clearly had worsened, no matter how you measure it. Keynesian and Classical economists agree that a changing standard unemployment rate tells us something about the economy, especially if interpreted in the light of other statistics. That's why it is used as a measure of the state of the economy.

Unemployment as a Social Problem

The Industrial Revolution changed the nature of work and introduced unemployment as a problem for society. This is because the Industrial Revolution was accompanied by a shift to wage labor and to a division of responsibilities. Some individuals (capitalists) took on ownership of the means of production and *hired* others to work for them, paying them an hourly wage. This change in the nature of production marked a significant change in the nature of the unemployment problem.

First, it created the possibility of cyclical unemployment. With wages set at a certain level, when economic activity fell, workers' income per hour did not fall. Instead, factories would lay off or fire some workers. That isn't what happened on the farm; when a slack period occurred on the farm, the income per hour of all workers fell and few were laid off.

Web Note 24.4

Unemployment and Spatial Mismatch

Second, the Industrial Revolution was accompanied by a change in how families dealt with unemployment. Whereas in preindustrial economies individuals or families took responsibility for their own slack periods, in a capitalist industrial society factory owners didn't take responsibility for their workers in slack periods. The pink slip (slang for the notice workers get telling them they are laid off) and the problem of unemployment were born in the Industrial Revolution.

Without wage income, unemployed workers were in a pickle. They couldn't pay their rent, they couldn't eat, and they couldn't put clothes on their backs. What was previously a family problem became a social problem. Not surprisingly, it was at that time—the late 1700s—that economists began paying more attention to the problem of unemployment.

When economists initially recognized unemployment as a problem, economists and society still did not view it as a social problem. It was the individual's problem. If people were unemployed, it was their own fault; hunger, or at least the fear of hunger, and people's desire to maintain their lifestyle, would drive them to find other jobs relatively quickly. Early capitalism had an unemployment solution: the fear of hunger.

Unemployment as Government's Problem

As capitalism evolved, capitalist societies no longer saw the fear of hunger as an acceptable answer to unemployment.

As capitalism evolved, the fear-of-hunger solution to unemployment became less acceptable. The government developed social welfare programs such as unemployment insurance and assistance to the poor. In the Employment Act of 1946, the U.S. government specifically took responsibility for unemployment. The act assigned government the responsibility of creating *full employment,* an economic climate in which just about everyone who wants a job can have one. Government was responsible for offsetting cyclical fluctuations and thereby preventing cyclical unemployment, and somehow dealing with structural unemployment.

Initially government regarded 2 percent unemployment as a condition of full employment. The 2 percent was made up of **frictional unemployment** *(unemployment caused by people entering the job market and people quitting a job just long enough to look for and find another one)* and of a few "unemployables," such as those addicted to alcohol or drugs, along with a certain amount of necessary structural and seasonal unemployment resulting when the structure of the economy

From Full Employment to the Target Rate of Unemployment

As I have emphasized throughout the book, good economists attempt to remain neutral and objective. It isn't always easy, especially since the language we use is often biased.

This problem has proved to be a difficult one for economists in their attempt to find an alternative to the concept of full employment. An early contender was the natural rate of unemployment. Economists have often used the word *natural* to describe economic concepts. For example, they've talked about "natural" rights and a "natural" rate of interest. The problem with this usage is that what's natural to one person isn't necessarily natural to another. The word *natural* often conveys a sense of "that's the way it should be." However, in describing as "natural" the rate of unemployment that an economy can achieve, economists weren't making any value judgments about whether

4 to 5 percent unemployment is what should, or should not, be. They simply were saying that, given the institutions in the economy, that is what is achievable. So a number of economists objected to the use of the word *natural*.

As an alternative, a number of economists started to use the term *nonaccelerating inflation rate of unemployment (NAIRU)*, but even they agreed it was a horrendous term. Thus, many avoided using it and shifted to the relatively neutral term *target rate of unemployment*.

The target rate of unemployment is the rate that one believes is attainable without causing undesirable side effects. It is not determined theoretically; it is determined empirically. Economists look at what seems to be achievable and is historically normal, adjust that for structural and demographic changes they believe are occurring, and come up with the target rate of unemployment.

changed. Any unemployment higher than 2 percent was considered either unnecessary structural or cyclical unemployment and was now government's responsibility; frictional unemployment and necessary structural unemployment were still the individual's problem.

By the 1950s, government had given up its view that 2 percent unemployment was consistent with full employment. It raised its definition of full employment to 3 percent, then to 4 percent, then to 5 percent unemployment. In the 1970s and early 1980s, government raised it further, to 6.5 percent unemployment. At that point the term *full employment* fell out of favor (it's hard to call 6.5 percent unemployment "full employment"), and the terminology changed. The term I will use in this book is *target rate of unemployment*, although you should note that it is also sometimes called the *natural rate of unemployment* or the *NAIRU* (the nonaccelerating inflation rate of unemployment). As discussed in the accompanying box, these terms are interchangeable. The **target rate of unemployment** is *the lowest sustainable rate of unemployment that policy makers believe is achievable given existing demographics and the economy's institutional structure*. After the downturn, their estimate of the target rate of unemployment rose; more recently, it has fallen.

Cyclical unemployment is related to business cycles—when the economy is in a recession cyclical unemployment rises, and when the economy is in an expansion unemployment falls. When the unemployment rate equals the target rate of unemployment, the economy is at potential output. When potential output rises above trend growth, the target rate of unemployment falls. Since the late 1980s the appropriate target rate of unemployment has been a matter of debate.

Q-10 How is the target rate of unemployment related to potential output?

The Future of Unemployment

As can be seen by the continued concern about jobs and employment despite the fall of the standard unemployment rate to below 4 percent, today there is still significant debate about government's role in dealing with unemployment, although now the focus is more on *under*employment, and the pay disparities among various types of jobs. The problem is that technological advances and globalization are creating some jobs that pay enormously high wages, and many more jobs that pay low wages, while eliminating many mid-level jobs that supported a strong middle class.

As technology continues to advance in information sciences, it is bringing about a mental revolution—a replacement of human thinking with machine thinking. This revolution has enormous implications for jobs. Many more good, high-paying middle-class jobs are likely to be eliminated; humans will be replaced by algorithms that do the job faster and cheaper. Just like the Industrial Revolution undermined high pay for mid-level physical strength jobs, and increased the pay for a few super athletes, this information revolution is undermining high pay for mid-level mental strength jobs— the type of jobs that the majority of college grads head into.

In the previous decade much of the loss of good jobs was due to globalization, as jobs moved out of the United States to countries where pay was lower. That will continue, but it will likely be overshadowed by good jobs being lost to computer algorithms and intelligent apps (or whatever these computer-based competitors to humans come to be called). Algorithms will replace humans because they process information faster and quicker.

This transformation has, of course, been ongoing. For example, at one time there were thousands of "calculator" jobs—jobs in which individuals would calculate solutions to equations and mathematical functions. These jobs were first replaced by mechanical calculators, and then by digital calculators dedicated to solving particular types of problems. There were scientific calculators, engineering calculators, and financial calculators, for example. Now such calculations are done by an app on a computer as an afterthought.

What had been good middle-class calculating jobs—you had to be smart to solve equations—became much lower-paid data-entry jobs (which were then outsourced during globalization) with a small number of highly paid jobs designing, organizing, and overseeing the creation of algorithms and managing the work. This is just one example of how algorithms have impacted employment. It happened in all types of industries, and will happen in an increasing number of them as what are called deep-learning algorithms, which find hidden patterns in data and do the heavy mental lifting of dealing with uncertain and complex patterns, become commonplace.

With deep-learning algorithms, humans' last claim to superiority in thinking is disappearing. That means that activities that form the basis of professional jobs, and of the upper middle class in the United States—activities that involve intuition and judgment, such as diagnosing a disease, financial advising, practicing law, teaching classes, driving cars, counseling—will no longer be most efficiently done by humans. In fact, in the coming decade most mid-level professional jobs will be able to be done more efficiently by algorithms in the same way that large-scale physical labor is currently done more efficiently by machines.

There will still be jobs for humans. Just as it is still efficient to have a couple of humans with shovels and brooms to clean up small amounts of dirt that the backhoe misses, and to handle the specific tasks that haven't yet been algorithmized, so too will it be necessary to handle the small mental jobs not done by algorithms. But the jobs will likely be different than the current professional jobs, in which the professional does the heavy thinking; they are more likely to be technician jobs. These new jobs will most likely require far less general training than they do now, since the algorithm will be doing the heavy mental lifting. Most humans will be doing jobs handling the shovels and brooms, cleaning up the mental tasks that fall through the cracks. Not all humans, of

Many more good high-paying middle-class jobs are likely to be eliminated; humans will be replaced by algorithms that do the job faster and cheaper.

Source: NASA/JPL-Caltech

With deep-learning algorithms, humans' last claim to superiority in thinking is disappearing.

course. We will still need humans to create and manage the algorithms, and these will be super high-paying jobs. But, in time, even these jobs will likely be more efficiently done by managing algorithms, and algorithms that create algorithms.

If the futurists who have painted the above gloomy picture are right, the future of humankind will involve significant change. It is a future in which we will be very concerned about jobs, but not so much for their role in producing output; rather for their role in distributing income and in giving people a sense of purpose in life. Purpose and jobs will be less connected than they are now for most professionals. In summary, the economy will experience significant transitions in the coming decades, and how society will handle these transitions is unclear. What is clear is that the issues go far beyond standard macroeconomics.

Conclusion

As should be clear from the discussion in this chapter, macroeconomic theory and policy are far less settled than are microeconomic theory and policy. The reason is that macroeconomic problems involve all microeconomic problems plus additional problems that relate to the complex interactions of the individuals in the economy—more than 327 million in the United States and 7.6 billion in the rest of the world. The appropriate macro policy will depend on how the problems are framed; a short-run problem is quite different from a long-run problem. Conventional macroeconomics "solves" the problems by developing separate policies for the short run and for the long run. That makes the macroeconomic presentation to students relatively easy.

The problem comes when you don't know whether you are in the short run or the long run. Currently the economy seems to be in an "in between" run, and the policy advice is much messier and more diverse.

Summary

- Economists use two frameworks to analyze macroeconomic problems. The long-run growth framework focuses on supply, while the short-run business-cycle framework focuses on demand. (*LO24-1*)

- Classical economists focus on long-run growth and use a laissez-faire approach. Keynesian economists focus on short-run fluctuations and use an activist government approach. (*LO24-1*)

- Modern conventional economics has been a blend of the Keynesian and Classical approaches. The problems the economy faces today do not fit either model. (*LO24-1*)

- Growth is measured by the change in total output over a long period of time and the change in per capita output. Per capita output is output divided by the population. (*LO24-2*)

- While the secular trend growth rate of the economy has been 2.5 to 3.5 percent, some expect it to fall. (*LO24-2*)

- Fluctuations of real output around the secular trend growth rate are called *business cycles.* (*LO24-3*)

- Phases of the business cycle include peak, trough, upturn, and downturn. (*LO24-3*)

- Structural stagnation is a cyclical downturn that is not expected to end anytime soon without major changes to the structure of the economy. (*LO24-3*)

- Whether the economy is experiencing structural stagnation or a recession has significant implications for macroeconomic policy. Conventional macroeconomic policies can pull an economy out of a recession, but not out of a structural stagnation. (*LO24-3*)

- Cyclical unemployment goes up and down with the business cycle. Structural unemployment is caused by the institutional structure of an economy and economic restructuring.   (*LO24-4*)

- The unemployment rate is calculated as the number of unemployed divided by the labor force. Unemployment rises during a recession and falls during an expansion.   (*LO24-4*)

- The official measure of unemployment is based on judgments about whom to count as unemployed. Keynesians believe that discouraged workers and those who have left the labor force entirely ought to

be counted as unemployed. Classicals believe that some counted as unemployed are choosing to be unemployed and should not be counted.   (*LO24-4*)

- The target rate of unemployment is the lowest sustainable rate of unemployment possible given existing institutions. It's associated with an economy's potential output. The higher an economy's potential output, the lower an economy's target rate of unemployment. (*LO24-4*)

- More and more jobs previously done by humans are now done by algorithms.   (*LO24-4*)

Key Terms

business cycle	frictional unemployment	per capita output	structural unemployment
Classical economists	Keynesian economists	potential output	target rate of
cyclical unemployment	labor force	recession	unemployment
depression	macroeconomics	structural stagnation	unemployment rate

Questions and Exercises connect

1. Classicals saw the Depression as a political problem, not an economic problem. Why?   (*LO24-1*)

2. Did Keynesian or Classical economics support laissez-faire policy?   (*LO24-1*)

3. Would Keynesian or Classical economists be more likely to emphasize the fallacy of composition? (*LO24-1*)

4. As the problem of inflation grew in the 1970s, did Keynesian or Classical economics grow in importance?   (*LO24-1*)

5. Is structural stagnation a Keynesian or a Classical theory?   (*LO24-1*)

6. In what way is potential output not purely a physical measure based on the number of workers and existing factories?   (*LO24-2*)

7. What are two ways in which long-term economic growth is measured?   (*LO24-2*)

8. What has happened to growth rates in Western Europe and the United States in recent years?   (*LO24-2*)

9. How does the U.S. per capita growth rate since 1940 compare to growth rates in other areas around the world?   (*LO24-2*)

10. Draw a representative business cycle, and label each of the four phases.   (*LO24-3*)

11. How does a structural stagnation differ from a recession? (*LO24-3*)

12. Which has the more pessimistic view of the problems facing the U.S. economy: structural stagnation theory or conventional business-cycle theory?   (*LO24-3*)

13. Distinguish between structural unemployment and cyclical unemployment.   (*LO24-4*)

14. What type of unemployment is best studied within the long-run framework?   (*LO24-4*)

15. What type of unemployment is best studied under the short-run framework?   (*LO24-4*)

16. Suppose the total labor force is 189 million of a possible 244 million working-age adults. The total number of unemployed is 15 million. What is the standard unemployment rate?   (*LO24-4*)

17. Does the standard unemployment rate underestimate or overestimate the unemployment problem? Explain. (*LO24-4*)

18. Using only a pencil and paper, who is most likely to calculate the square root of 4,959 to three decimal places more quickly—you or your grandparents? What does that tell you about jobs in the future?   (*LO24-4*)

19. How will concerns in the future about employment likely change with the information revolution?   (*LO24-4*)

Questions from Alternative Perspectives

1. It is unfair, but true, that bad things happen. Unfortunately, to attempt to prevent unavoidable bad things can actually make things worse, not better. How might the above ideas be relevant to how society deals with business cycles? *(Austrian)*

2. Wesley Mitchell, a founder of Institutional economics, said that to understand the business cycle, a distinction must be made between making goods and making money. All societies make goods. In the modern money economy, those who control the production and distribution of goods will allow economic activity to occur only if they can "make money." He used this line of reasoning to conclude that what drives the business cycle are business expectations; production, and thus increased employment today, will be allowed only if business expects to sell those goods at a profit tomorrow. Is his proposition reasonable? Explain. *(Institutionalist)*

3. Since the Great Depression, the United States has been able to avoid severe economic downturns.
   a. What macroeconomic policies do you think have allowed us to avoid another Great Depression?
   b. Would you classify those policies as being Classical or Keynesian?
   c. Are such policies still relevant today? *(Post-Keynesian)*

4. The text presents the target rate of unemployment as being about 4 percent. William Vickrey, a Nobel Prize–winning economist, argued that the target unemployment rate should be seen as being between 1 percent and 2 percent. Only an unemployment rate that low, he argued, would produce genuine full employment that guaranteed job openings for all those looking for work. Achieving a low unemployment rate would, according to Vickrey, bring about "a major reduction in the illness of poverty, homelessness, sickness, and crime."
   a. What is the appropriate target unemployment rate?
   b. Explain your position.
   c. What policies would you recommend to counteract the human tragedy of unemployment? *(Radical)*

5. In natural science, when theories fail, as conventional macroeconomics failed in the financial crisis and its aftermath, they are overthrown and replaced by new theories. Why has it been so difficult to overthrow conventional macroeconomics? *(All)*

Issues to Ponder

1. In H. G. Wells' *The Time Machine,* a late-Victorian time traveler arrives in England sometime in the future to find a new race of people, the Eloi, in their idleness. Their idleness is, however, supported by another race, the Morlocks, underground slaves who produce the output. If technology were such that the Elois' lifestyle could be sustained by machines, not slaves, is it a lifestyle that would be desirable? What implications does the above discussion have for unemployment?

2. If unemployment fell to 1.2 percent in World War II, why couldn't it be reduced to 1.2 percent today?

3. In 1991, Japanese workers' average tenure with a firm was 10.9 years; in 1991 in the United States the average tenure of workers was 6.7 years.
   a. What are two possible explanations for these differences?
   b. Which system is better?
   c. In the mid-1990s, Japan experienced a recession while the U.S. economy grew. What effect did this likely have on these ratios?

Answers to Margin Questions

1. A Classical economist takes a laissez-faire approach and believes the economy is self-regulating. A Keynesian economist takes an interventionist approach and believes that output can remain below what the economy is capable of producing. *(LO24-1)*

2. The change in employment is both a long-run and a short-run issue. It is a short-run issue because when the U.S. economy is in a recession, employment tends to decline.

It is a long-run issue because outsourcing is the result of changes in the institutional structure of the global economy caused by reduced trade barriers and reduced communications costs. *(LO24-1)*

3. To calculate per capita output, divide real output ($15 trillion) by the total population (300 million). This equals $50,000. *(LO24-2)*

4. The emergence of the Indian and Chinese economies as global competitors might lower U.S. growth in the coming decades because they present new competition to U.S. producers, who will have to adjust to global competition. *(LO24-2)*

5. The four phases of the business cycle are the peak, the downturn, the trough, and the upturn. *(LO24-3)*

6. Conventional economic policies that address business cycles won't work if the economy is experiencing structural stagnation. *(LO24-3)*

7. False. Structural unemployment is determined by the institutional structure of an economy, not by fluctuations in economic activity. *(LO24-4)*

8. If a sufficient number of people enter the labor force, the number of unemployed can rise at the same time that the unemployment rate falls. *(LO24-4)*

9. The unemployment rate depends on one's view about who should be counted as unemployed. Keynesians believe all people who want a job but cannot find one should be counted, even discouraged workers. Classicals believe that some people counted as unemployed choose not to work even if they report that they are looking. *(LO24-4)*

10. The target rate of unemployment is that rate achieved when actual output equals potential output. *(LO24-4)*

Measuring and Describing the Aggregate Economy

The government is very keen on amassing statistics. . . . They collect them, add them, raise them to the nth power, take the cube root and prepare wonderful diagrams. But you must never forget that every one of these figures comes in the first instance from the village watchman, who just puts down what he damn pleases.

—Sir Josiah Stamp (head of Britain's revenue department in the late 19th century)

After reading this chapter, you should be able to:

LO25-1 Calculate GDP using the expenditures and value-added approaches.

LO25-2 Calculate aggregate income and explain how it relates to aggregate production.

LO25-3 Distinguish real from nominal concepts.

LO25-4 Describe the limitations of using GDP and national income accounting.

©wrangler/Shutterstock

If in the 1500s you wanted to know how to do card tricks, juggle, eat fire, and make coins dance, you could find out how in a book by Luigi Paciolli, a close friend of Leonardo da Vinci.[1] Paciolli also wrote a book on accounting, or what was then called double-entry bookkeeping, and that book has been called the

---

[1]In case you're wondering, here's how Paciolli explained how to make a coin dance: "Take some magnetic powder and rub it on a quattrino [copper coin] before putting the coin in some vinegar. Then take a little bit of the magnetic powder between your thumb [and index finger] and tap the glass of water, where the coin is, and it will come up and go down . . . with your hand."

greatest technological invention in Western civilization. I won't go that far, but I will say that accounting—the process of identifying, measuring, and communicating information to permit judgments and decisions by the users—is central to the workings of the modern economy. If you are going to understand the macroeconomy, you need to know the accounting system macroeconomists use. That's what we cover in this chapter. So while you won't learn how to eat fire here, you will see how the terminology developed in the last chapter fits together into a coherent whole.

The chapter is divided into three parts. The first part deals with the macroeconomic statistics you are likely to see in the newspaper, GDP and its components, and how those components are related through an aggregate accounting system. The second part distinguishes between real and nominal (or money) concepts, which are used to differentiate and compare the economy over time. The third part discusses some shortcomings of the accounting system.

Aggregate Accounting

In the 1930s, it was impossible for macroeconomics to exist in the form we know it today because many concepts we now take for granted either had not yet been formulated or were so poorly formulated that it was impossible to talk rigorously about them. This lack of terminology to describe the economy as a whole was consistent with the Classical economists' lack of interest in studying the aggregate economy in the 1930s; they preferred to focus on microeconomics.

With the advent of Keynesian macroeconomics in the mid-1930s, development of a terminology to describe the macroeconomy became crucial. Measurement is a necessary step toward rigor. A group of Keynesian economists set out to develop a terminology and to measure the concepts they defined so that people would have concrete terms to use when talking about macroeconomic problems. Their work (for which two of them, Simon Kuznets and Richard Stone, received the Nobel Prize) set up an *aggregate* accounting system—a set of rules and definitions for measuring economic activity in the economy as a whole. That aggregate accounting system often goes by the name *national income accounting*.

Aggregate accounting provides a way of measuring aggregate production, aggregate expenditures, and aggregate income. Each can be broken down into subaggregates; aggregate accounting defines the relationship among these subaggregates.

This 17th-century engraving, "The Money Lender," shows that careful bookkeeping and accounting have been around for a long time.

©Fine Art Images/Heritage Images/Getty Images

Calculating GDP

Gross domestic product (GDP) is the aggregate final output of residents and businesses in an economy in a one-year period.

The previous chapter talked about total output. Economists call total output gross domestic product (GDP). **Gross domestic product (GDP)** is *the total market value of all final goods and services produced in an economy in a one-year period.* GDP is probably the single most-used economic measure. When economists, journalists, and other analysts talk about the economy, they continually discuss GDP, how much it has increased or decreased, and what it's likely to do.

Aggregate final output (GDP) consists of millions of different services and products: apples, oranges, computers, haircuts, financial advice, and so on. To arrive at total output, somehow we've got to add them all together into a composite measure. Say we produced 7 oranges plus 6 apples plus 12 computers. We have not produced 25 comapplorgs. You can't add apples and oranges and computers. You can only add like things (things that are measured in the same units). For example, 2 apples + 4 apples = 6 apples. If we want to add unlike things, we must convert them into like things. We do that by multiplying each good by its *price*. Economists call this *weighting the importance of each good by its price.* For example, if you have 4 pigs and 4 horses and you price pigs at $200 each and horses at $400 each, the horses are weighted as being twice as important as the pigs.

Multiplying the quantity of each good by its market price changes the terms in which we discuss each good from a quantity of a specific product to a *value* measure of that good. For example, when we multiply 6 apples by their price, 25 cents each, we get $1.50; $1.50 is a value measure. Once all goods are expressed in that value measure, they can be added together.

Take the example of 7 oranges and 6 apples. (For simplicity let's forget the computers, haircuts, and financial advice.) If the oranges cost 50 cents each, their total value is $3.50; if the apples cost 25 cents each, their total value is $1.50. Their values are expressed in identical measures, so we can add them together. When we do so, we don't get 13 orples; we get $5 worth of apples and oranges.

If we follow that same procedure with all the final goods and services produced in the economy in the entire year, multiplying the quantity produced by the market price per unit, we have all the goods and services an economy has produced expressed in units of value. If we then add up all these units of value, we have that year's gross domestic product.

The Components of GDP

Since anything produced will be bought by someone, we can measure output by the expenditure people make to buy that output. On the expenditure side, GDP is usually divided into four categories depending on who buys the output. The four expenditure categories that comprise GDP are consumption, investment, government spending, and net exports.

Web Note 25.1

GDP Data

Consumption is *spending by households on goods and services.* Consumption includes such things as food, shampoo, televisions, furniture, and the services of doctors and lawyers. This is the production in the economy that consumers buy. When you buy a smartphone, you are contributing to consumption expenditures.

Investment is *spending for the purpose of additional production.* Investment includes business spending on factories and equipment for production, the change in business inventories, and purchases by households of new owner-occupied houses. Investment is output that is used to produce goods and services in the future. You should take note that when economists speak of investment as they discuss aggregate accounting, they don't mean the kind of activity taking place when individuals buy stocks rather than consume goods—economists call such activity *saving.* So in economists' terminology when you buy a bond or stock rather than consuming, you are saving. When that savings is borrowed by businesses to buy factories, tractors, computers, or other goods or services that will increase their output, they are *investing.* The amount they spend on goods that will increase future output is what in aggregate accounting is called *investment.*

You might have been surprised to see the change in inventories and residential construction included in investment. Inventories are goods that have been produced, so they must be counted if one is going to include all produced goods, which is what GDP is designed to include; inventories represent goods to be sold in the future. They are a type of investment by the firm. Residential construction is part of investment because most of the housing services from a new house will be provided in the future, not the present.

Government spending is *goods and services that government buys.* When the government buys the services of an analyst, or buys equipment for its space program, it is undertaking economic activity. These activities are classified as government expenditures. In thinking about government expenditures, you should note that they include expenditures that involve government production. Although government generally does not sell its "production" but provides it free, aggregate accounting rules count government production at the government's cost of providing that output.

Many government payments do not involve production, so the government's budget is much larger than government spending included in GDP. The most important category of government spending that is not included in GDP is **transfer payments**—*payments to individuals that do not involve production by those individuals.* Transfer payments include Social Security payments and unemployment insurance among others. These payments are not part of GDP since there is no production associated with them.

Net exports is *spending on goods and services produced in the United States that foreigners buy (exports) minus goods and services produced abroad that U.S. citizens buy (imports).* (In economics and business, the word *net* is used to distinguish two offsetting flows: exports, which represent a spending flow into the country, and imports, which represent a spending flow out of the country.) The reason we have to use the "net concept" for exports is that GDP measures production *within* the geographic borders of a country. Because exports represent spending by foreigners for goods and services produced within the United States, exports are added. But because imports represent spending on goods and services produced outside the United States, they are subtracted. Our interest is in net spending so it is with the difference between imports and exports.

Summarizing: GDP measures aggregate final production taking place in a country. This production can be subdivided into expenditure categories, and all production must fit into one of the four categories. A shorthand way of expressing this division of GDP into expenditure categories is:

Q-1 Calculate GDP with the information below:

    Consumption = 60

    Investment = 20

    Government spending = 20

    Exports = 10

    Imports = 15

GDP = Consumption + Investment + Government spending + Net exports

or

$$GDP = C + I + G + (X - M)$$

Since all production is categorized into one or another of these four divisions, by adding up these four categories, we get total production of U.S. goods and services. Table 25-1 gives the breakdown of GDP by expenditure category for selected countries. Notice that, in all countries, consumption expenditures is the largest component of production.

TABLE 25-1   **Expenditure Breakdown of GDP for Selected Countries**

Country	GDP (U.S. $ in billions)	=	Consumption (% of GDP)	+	Investment (% of GDP)	+	Government Spending (% of GDP)	+	Exports (% of GDP)	−	Imports (−% of GDP)
United States	$19,485		69%		17%		17%		12%		15%
China	25,240		39		44		15		20		18
Germany	4,370		53		20		17		47		40
Japan	5,620		56		24		20		16		15
Mexico	2,570		65		24		12		37		39
Nigeria	1,170		79		15		7		13		14
Poland	1,190		59		20		18		54		50

Note: Percentages may not sum to 100 due to rounding. Values are for 2017, specified in U.S. dollars, adjusted for purchasing power parity.

Sources: World Economic Outlook Database, International Monetary Fund (www.imf.org); Central Intelligence Agency, *The World Factbook;* and National Income Accounts, OECD (http://stats.oecd.org); CIA World Factbook, accessed 6/29/18.

Two Things to Remember about GDP

In thinking about GDP, it is important to remember that (1) GDP represents a flow (an amount per year), not a stock (an amount at a particular moment of time); and (2) GDP refers to the market value of *final* output. Let's consider these statements separately.

GDP Is A FLOW CONCEPT   Say a student just out of college tells you she earns $8,000. You'd probably think, "Wow! She's got a low-paying job!" That's because you implicitly assume she means $8,000 per year. If you later learned that she earns $8,000 per week, you'd quickly change your mind. The confusion occurred because how much you earn is a flow concept; it has meaning only when a time period is associated with it: so much per week, per month, per year. A stock concept is an amount at a given point in time. No time interval is associated with it. Your weight is a stock concept. You weigh 150 pounds; you don't weigh 150 pounds per week.

GDP is a flow concept, the amount of total final output a country produces per year. The *per year* is often left unstated, but is essential. GDP is usually reported quarterly (every three months), but it is reported on an *annualized basis,* meaning the U.S. Department of Commerce, which compiles GDP figures, uses quarterly figures to estimate total output for the whole year.

The store of wealth, in contrast, is a stock concept. The stock equivalent to national income accounts are the **wealth accounts**—*a balance sheet of an economy's stock of assets and liabilities.* Table 25-2 shows a summary account of U.S. net worth from the wealth accounts for the United States in 2017. These are stock measures; they exist at a moment of time. For example, on December 31, 2017, the accounting date for these accounts, U.S. household and nonprofit net worth was $99.7 trillion.

Two important aspects to remember about GDP are:

1. GDP represents a flow.
2. GDP represents the market value of final output.

Web Note 25.2

Global Comparisons

TABLE 25-2   **U.S. National Wealth Accounts in 2017 (net worth)**

	Dollars (in trillions)		
Household and nonprofit net worth	$99.7		
Tangible wealth		$34.0	
Owner-occupied real estate			$27.9
Consumer durables			5.7
Other			0.4
Financial wealth		65.7	
Corporate equities			26.6
Noncorporate equities			11.8
Other (pension reserves, life insurance, etc.)			27.3
Government net financial assets	−19.1		
Federal		−16.7	
State and local		−2.4	
Total net worth	80.6		

Source: Financial Accounts of the United States - Z.1, Board of Governors of the Federal Reserve (www.federalreserve.gov/releases/z1). The value of the government's financial liabilities is greater than the value of its financial assets, which is why it shows up as a negative percentage.

Gross Output: A New Revolutionary Way to Measure the Economy?

GDP is a measure of *final output* in the economy. It tells us how much in the way of goods and services is available for consumption or investment. GDP is not designed to be a measure of *all* economic activity. Recently, the Bureau of Economic Analysis (BEA) started providing and publicizing a new quarterly measure that *is* designed to be a measure of all economic activity. The BEA calls it Gross Output. *Forbes* magazine editor, Steve Forbes, called this new Gross Output measure a "new revolutionary way to measure the economy." The difference between the two measures is that, unlike GDP, which nets out intermediate goods, Gross Output does not net out intermediate goods. That means that Gross Output is much larger than GDP; in 2017, Gross Output was about $34 trillion, compared to GDP of $19 trillion.

While Gross Output may be a useful measure if one's goal is to measure all economic transactions (rather than to measure only final output as GDP is designed to do), it is far from revolutionary, and the terminology used is likely to cause confusion. A far better name for what BEA calls "Gross Output" would be "Gross Economic Transactions." The problem is that "output" is generally used interchangeably with "production." To call something Gross Output makes one think that one is distinguishing it from some "net" concept. For example, the "gross" in *gross* domestic product is used to distinguish gross final output available for consumption and investment from net final output—*net* domestic product (NDP). You move from GDP to NDP by subtracting capital depreciation from GDP. Both GDP and NDP concepts eliminate intermediate goods.

Unlike gross domestic product, the term "gross" in Gross Output has nothing to do with whether depreciation is included or not. The "gross" in Gross Output distinguishes between a "gross" measure that includes all transactions in the economy and a "net" measure that excludes intermediary production.

GDP MEASURES FINAL OUTPUT As a student in my first economics class, I was asked how to calculate GDP. I said, "Add up the value of the goods and services produced by all the companies in the United States to arrive at GDP." I was wrong (which is why I remember it). Many goods produced by one firm are sold to other firms, which use those goods to make other goods. GDP doesn't measure total transactions in an economy; it measures **final output**—*goods and services purchased for their final use.* When one firm sells products to another firm for use in the production of yet another good, the first firm's products aren't considered final output. They're **intermediate products**—*products used as input in the production of some other product.* To count intermediate goods as well as final goods as part of GDP would be to double count them. An example of an intermediate good would be wheat sold to a cereal company. If we counted both the wheat (the intermediate good) and the cereal (the final good) made from that wheat, the wheat would be double counted. Double counting would significantly overestimate final output.

If we did not eliminate intermediate goods, a change in organization would look like a change in output. Say a firm that produced steel merged with a firm that produced cars. Together they produce exactly what each did separately before the merger. Final output hasn't changed, nor has intermediate output. The only difference is that the intermediate output of steel is now internal to the firm. Using only each firm's sales of goods to final consumers (and not sales to other firms) as the measure of GDP means that changes in organization do not affect the measure of output.

> GDP doesn't measure total transactions in an economy; it measures final output.

TWO WAYS OF ELIMINATING INTERMEDIATE GOODS   There are two ways to eliminate intermediate goods from the measure of GDP. One way is to calculate the final sales that make up GDP directly, either by measuring the expenditures on the products by final users or by measuring production specifically for final users. A second way to eliminate double counting is to follow the value-added approach. **Value added** is *the increase in value that a firm contributes to a product or service*. It is calculated by subtracting intermediate goods (the cost of materials that a firm uses to produce a good or service) from the value of its sales. For instance, if a firm buys $100 worth of thread and $10,000 worth of cloth and uses them in making a thousand pairs of jeans that are sold for $20,000, the firm's value added is not $20,000; it is $9,900 ($20,000 in sales minus the $10,100 in intermediate goods that the firm bought).

To avoid double counting, you must eliminate intermediate goods, either by calculating only final output (expenditures approach) or by using the value-added approach.

The table below provides another example.

Participants	(1) Cost of Materials	(2) Value of Sales	(3) Value Added	Row
Farmer	$ 0	$ 100	$100	1
Cone factory and ice cream maker	100	250	150	2
Middleperson (final sales)	250	400	150	3
Vendor	400	500	100	4
Totals	$750	$1,250	$500	5

It gives the cost of materials (intermediate goods) and the value of sales in the following scenario: Say we want to measure the contribution to GDP made by ice cream production of 200 ice cream cones at $2.50 each for total sales of $500. The vendor bought his cones and ice cream at a cost of $400 from a middleperson, who in turn paid the cone factory and ice cream maker a total of $250. The farmer who sold the cream to the factory got $100. Adding up all these transactions, we get $1,250, but that includes intermediate goods. Either by counting only the final value of the vendor's sales, $500, or by adding the value added at each stage of production (column 3), we eliminate intermediate sales and arrive at the contribution of ice cream production to GDP of $500.

Value added is calculated by subtracting the cost of materials from the value of sales at each stage of production. The aggregate value added at each stage of production is, by definition, precisely equal to the value of final sales, since it excludes all intermediate products. In the table illustrating our example, the equality of the value-added approach and the final-sales approach can be seen by comparing the vendor's final sales of $500 (row 4, column 2) with the $500 value added (row 5, column 3).

Calculating GDP: Some Examples

To make sure you understand what value added is and what makes up GDP, let's consider some sample transactions and determine what value they add and whether they should be included in GDP. Let's first consider secondhand sales: When you sell your two-year-old car, how much value has been added? The answer is none. The sale involves no current output, so there's no value added. If, however, you sold the car to a used-car dealer for $2,000 and he or she resold it for $2,500, $500 of value has been added—the used-car dealer's efforts transferred the car from someone

Q-2 If a used-car dealer buys a car for $2,000 and resells it for $2,500, how much has been added to GDP?

Is GDP Biased against Women?

Although in the example in the book the housespouse is a man, the reality is that most housespouses are women. The fact that GDP doesn't include the work of housespouses is seen, by some, as a type of discrimination against women who work without pay at home since their work is not counted as part of the domestic product. One answer for why it is not counted is that housework does not involve a market transaction and hence could not be measured. That makes some sense, but it does not explain why the services that houses provide to homeowners are estimated and included in GDP. Why can't housework also be estimated?

The answer is that it can be estimated, and my suspicion is that not including housespouses' services in GDP does represent the latent discrimination against women that was built into the culture in the 1930s when national income accounting was first developed. That latent discrimination against women was so deep that it wasn't even noticed. Anyone who has seen the movie *Rosie the Riveter,* which shows government programs to get women out from wartime employment and back into their role in the home, will have a good sense of the cultural views of people in the mid-1900s and earlier.

In thinking about whether GDP is biased against women, it is important to remember that the concepts we use are culturally determined and, over time, as cultural views change, the concepts no longer match our changed views. There is no escaping the fact that language is value-loaded. But so, too, is our attempt to point out the values in language. There are many other ways in which GDP reflects arbitrary choices and discrimination against groups. The major discussion of the fact that latent discrimination against women is embodied in GDP accounting itself reflects our current values, just as not including housespouses' work reflected earlier values.

who didn't want it to someone who did. I point this out to remind you that GDP is not only a measure of the production of goods; it is a measure of the production of goods *and services.*

Now let's consider a financial transaction. Say you sell a bond (with a face value of $1,000) that you bought last year. You sell it for $1,250 and pay $100 commission to the dealer through whom you sell it. What value is added to final output? You might be tempted to say that $250 of value has been added, since the value of the bond has increased by $250. GDP, however, refers only to value that is added as the result of production or services, not to changes in the values of financial assets. Therefore, the price at which you buy or sell the bond is irrelevant to the question at hand. The only value that is added by the sale is the transfer of that bond from someone who doesn't want it to someone who does. Thus, the only value added as a result of economic activity is the dealer's commission, $100. The remaining $1,150 (the $1,250 you got from the bond minus the $100 commission you paid) is a transfer of an asset from one individual to another, but such transfers do not enter into GDP calculations. Only production of goods and services enters into GDP.

Let's consider a different type of financial transaction: The federal government pays an individual Social Security benefits. What value is added? Clearly no production has taken place, but money has been transferred. As in the case of the bond, only the cost of transferring it—not the amount that gets transferred—is included in GDP. This is accomplished by including in GDP government expenditures on goods and services, but not the value of government transfer payments. Thus, Social Security payments, welfare payments, and veterans' benefits do not enter into calculations of GDP. That's why the federal government can have a $4.0 trillion budget but only $1.3 trillion ($4.0 trillion minus $2.7 trillion of transfer payments) is included in GDP.

Q-3 How can the federal government have a $4.0 trillion budget but have only $1.3 trillion of that included in GDP?

Finally, let's consider the work of a housespouse. (See the box "Is GDP Biased against Women?" for further discussion of this issue.) How much value does it add to economic activity in a year? Clearly if the housespouse is any good at what he or she does, a lot of value is added. Taking care of the house and children is hard work. Estimates of the yearly value of a housespouse's services range from $35,000 to $130,000, and some estimate that including housework in the national accounts would raise GDP more than 50 percent. Even though much value is added and hence, in principle, housespouse services should be part of GDP, by convention a housespouse contributes nothing to GDP. GDP measures only *market activities;* since housespouses are not paid, their value added is not included in GDP. This leads to some problems in measurement. For example, suppose a woman divorces her housespouse and then hires him to continue cleaning her house for $20,000 per year. That $20,000 value added, since it is now a market transaction, is included in GDP.

Caring for children is a demanding job.
Source: CDC/Cade Martin

The housespouse example shows one of the problems with GDP. It also has other problems, but these are best left for intermediate courses. What's important for an introductory economics student to remember is that numerous decisions about how to handle various types of transactions had to be made to get a workable measure.

> To arrive at the aggregate accounts, numerous decisions about how to handle various types of transactions have to be made to get a workable measure.

Some Complications

The above presentation of aggregate accounting makes it look as if measuring aggregate output is quite simple—just measure consumption, investment, government spending, and net exports. Add them together and you have GDP. Conceptually, it is that simple, but, in practice, complicated conceptual decisions and accounting adjustments have to be made to ensure that all final production is included and that no double counting takes place. This leads to complicated accounting rules and alternative measures to account for different methods of measuring different concepts. Let me briefly introduce you to two of them.

GROSS AND NET CONCEPTS   Notice that we use the term *gross* domestic product or GDP. *Gross* does not mean disgusting; it is a technical accounting term that distinguishes a concept that has not been adjusted for an offsetting flow. (Remember we used the term *net* in our discussion of the export component of GDP to distinguish a concept that is adjusted for an offsetting flow.) The complication is that during the production process, the machines and equipment wear out or simply become technologically obsolete. Economists call this wearing-out process **depreciation**—*the decrease in an asset's value.* Depreciation is part of the cost of producing a good; it is the amount by which plants and equipment decrease in value as they grow older. Much of each year's investment involves expenditures to replace assets that have worn out. For example, as you drive your car, it wears out. A car with 80,000 miles on it is worth less than the same type of car with only 1,000 miles on it. The difference in value is attributed to depreciation.

> Depreciation is the decrease in an asset's value over a specified time period. It is the difference between gross and net investment.

Because some production is used to replace worn-out plant and equipment (depreciation), this production is not available for purchase. To account for this, economists have created another aggregate term that adjusts for depreciation. That term is *net domestic product.* **Net domestic product (NDP)** is *GDP less depreciation:*

NDP = GDP − Depreciation

> NDP = GDP − Depreciation

Because depreciation affects capital available for production, depreciation shows up in the investment category of expenditures. Specifically, investment we have talked about so far is gross investment; **net investment** is *gross investment less depreciation.*

NDP takes depreciation into account. Since we want to measure output available for purchase, NDP is actually preferable to GDP as the expression of a country's domestic output. However, measuring true depreciation (the actual decrease in an asset's value) is difficult because asset values fluctuate. In fact, it's so difficult that, in the real world, accountants don't try to measure true depreciation, but instead use a number of conventional rules of thumb. In recognition of this reality, economists call the adjustment made to GDP to arrive at NDP the *capital consumption allowance* rather than *depreciation.* Since estimating depreciation is difficult, GDP rather than NDP is generally used in discussions of aggregate output.

NATIONAL AND DOMESTIC CONCEPTS   A second complication of measuring aggregate output is whether the aggregate output that one is referring to is output produced within the borders of the country or by the citizens and firms of the country.

Until 1992, the United States (unlike the rest of the world) used an accounting measure that focused on output produced by its firms and citizens. This was called *gross national product.* As economic issues have become global, aggregate accounting has been affected. In 1992, the United States followed the rest of the world and switched to gross domestic product as its primary measure of aggregate output.

Whereas gross domestic product measures the economic activity that occurs within the geographic borders of a country, the economic activity of the citizens and businesses of a country is measured by **gross national product (GNP)**—*the aggregate final output of citizens and businesses of an economy in a one-year period.* So the economic activity of U.S. citizens working abroad is counted in U.S. GNP but isn't counted in U.S. GDP. Similarly for the foreign economic activity of U.S. companies. However, the production of a Mexican or German person or business working in the United States isn't counted in U.S. GNP but is counted in U.S. GDP. Thus, GDP describes the economic output within the physical borders of a country while gross national product describes the economic output produced by the citizens of a country. To move from GDP to GNP we must add *net foreign factor income* to GDP. **Net foreign factor income** is defined as *the income from foreign domestic factor sources minus foreign factor income earned domestically.* Put another way, we must add the foreign income of our citizens and subtract the income of residents who are not citizens:

> GDP is output produced within a country's borders; GNP is output produced by a country's citizens.

$$GNP = GDP + \text{Net foreign factor income}$$

> **Q-4**   Which is higher: Kuwait's GDP or its GNP? Why?

For many countries there's a significant difference between GNP and GDP. For example, consider Kuwait. Its citizens and companies have significant foreign income—income that far exceeds the income of the foreigners in Kuwait. This means that Kuwait's GNP (the output of its citizens) far exceeds its GDP (the output produced in Kuwait). For the United States, however, foreign output of U.S. businesses and people for the most part offsets the output of foreign businesses and people within the United States. Kuwait's net foreign factor income has been large and positive, while that of the United States has been minimal. Most discussions today focus on GDP since it is the primary measure presented in government statistics, but it is important to know GNP since aggregate income is normally measured on a national basis.

Calculating Aggregate Income

Aggregate accounting also calculates the aggregate income—the total income earned by citizens and firms of a country. This aggregate income is divided into the following four categories.

COMPENSATION OF EMPLOYEES Employee compensation (the largest component of national income) consists of wages and salaries paid to individuals, along with fringe benefits and government taxes for Social Security and unemployment insurance.

RENTS Rents are the income from property received by households. Rents received by firms are not included because a firm's rents are simply another source of income to the firm and hence are classified as profits. In most years, the rent component of national income is small since the depreciation owners take on buildings is close to the income they earn from those buildings.

INTEREST Interest is the income private businesses pay to households that have lent the businesses money, generally by purchasing bonds issued by the businesses. (Interest received by firms doesn't show up in this category for the same reason that rents received by firms don't show up in the *rent* category.) Interest payments by government and households aren't included in national income since by convention they're assumed not to flow from the production of goods and services.

PROFITS Profits are the amount that is left after compensation to employees, rents, and interest have been paid out. (The national income accounts use accounting profits that must be distinguished from economic profits, which are calculated on the basis of opportunity costs.)

Q-5 Calculate aggregate income with the information below:

    Employee compensation = 140
    Rents = 4
    Interest = 12
    Profits = 42

In the United States, employment compensation and profits make up the largest share of total income, with employee compensation constituting 68 percent and profits constituting 23 percent. The remaining 9 percent are rents and interest. Most countries have similar divisions.

Equality of Aggregate Income, Output, and Production

Now that I have defined aggregate output, production, and income, let's consider how aggregate output and aggregate income are, by definition, always equal within the accounting framework. Accounting systems use double-entry bookkeeping, which requires that the opposite sides of the accounting ledger, often called T-accounts, equal each other. The table below shows a T-account with income on one side and output (production) divided into its component expenditures on the other.

National Income Equality

Output	Income
Consumption	Employee compensation
Investment	Rent
Government spending	Interest
Net exports	Profit

Accounting systems use double-entry booking, which requires that the opposite sides of the accounting ledger, T-accounts, equal each other.

For both sides to be equal, the components on each side have to be defined so that a component on one side mirrors a component on the other. Accounting thus provides a framework for thinking about the aggregate economy. This is the case with aggregate income accounting. By definition, whenever a good or service is produced (output) and purchased (expenditure), somebody receives an income for producing it. These definitions mean that aggregate income equals aggregate output equals aggregate production. The relationship can be expressed in the following identity:[2]

Output on one side, income on the other, otherwise blank.

$$\text{Aggregate income} \equiv \text{Aggregate production} \equiv \text{Aggregate output}$$

By definition aggregate income equals aggregate production.

---

[2]An *identity* is a statement of equality that's true by definition. In algebra, an identity is sometimes written as a triple equal sign ($\equiv$). It is more equal than simply equal. How something can be more equal than equal is beyond me, too, but I'm no mathematician.

In establishing this identity, many accounting decisions need to be made to ensure complete equality. For example, since production figures are collected on a domestic basis (measuring what is produced in the geographic confines of the United States) while income figures are collected on a national basis (measuring what citizens and firms of the United States earn), adjustments are needed to equalize them. Similarly, taxes placed on corporations have to be accounted for to ensure that they are treated in a way that will maintain the equality. There are many more decisions, but at this introductory level, they are best left alone, so that the main point—that aggregate income—the value of the employee compensation, rents, interest, and profits— equals aggregate production—the value of goods produced—doesn't get lost in the complications.

Profit is a residual that makes the income side equal the expenditure side.

How are these values kept exactly equal? The definition of profit is the key to the equality. Recall that *profit* is defined as what remains after all the firm's other income (employee compensation, rent, and interest) is paid out. For example, say a firm has a total output of $800 and that it paid $400 in wages, $200 in rent, and $100 in interest. The firm's profit is total output less these payments. Profit equals $800 − $700 = $100.

The accounting identity works even if a firm incurs a loss. Say that instead of paying $400 in wages, the firm paid $700, along with its other payments of $200 in rent and $100 in interest. Total output is still $800, but total payments are $1,000. Profits, still defined as total output minus payments, are negative: $800 − $1,000 = −$200. There's a loss of $200. Adding that loss to other income [$1,000 + (−$200)] gives total income of $800—which is identical to the firm's total output of $800. It is no surprise that total output and total income, defined in this way, are equal.

The aggregate accounting identity (Total output = Total income) allows us to calculate GDP either by adding up all values of final outputs through the expenditures and value-added methods, or by adding up the values of all earnings or income.

Adjusting for Global Dimensions of Production

When the aggregate accounting system was developed, international flows were not a central consideration for U.S. economic policy. But as globalization has expanded, international flows have become increasingly important. One of the most important issues has been net exports—a component of aggregate expenditures discussed earlier. Net exports, you will (I hope) remember, is the difference between foreign demand for U.S. goods and services and U.S. demand for foreign goods and services. This difference is also called the *balance of trade,* and in recent years, the United States has been running a large balance of trade deficits. So imports of goods and services have greatly exceeded exports of goods and services.

Inflation: Distinguishing Real from Nominal

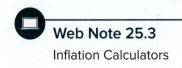

Web Note 25.3

Inflation Calculators

The GDP concept is often used to compare one year's output with another's. But doing so raises a problem: What happens if GDP increases, but the prices of all goods increase as well? Are we better off? The answer is not necessarily. For example, if all prices double and output doubles, we are not better off; we are simply paying higher prices for the same amount of goods. Put another way, we are experiencing **inflation**—*a continual rise in the overall price level.* Over time inflation can make a large difference in determining what happened to output. For example, compare U.S. GDP in 1932 ($58 billion) to GDP in 2017 ($19 trillion). Would it be correct to conclude the economy had grown 328 times larger? Again, the answer is no because there's been inflation.

When there is inflation, it is necessary to distinguish changes caused by inflation from changes that would have occurred had there been no inflation. The distinction is between *nominal measures*—measures that do not adjust for inflation or price level changes, and *real measures*—measures that adjust for inflation. We adjust for inflation by creating a **price index**—*a measure of the composite price of a specified group of goods*—that deflates the amount of inflation out of the nominal measure. This is why a price index for GDP can be called a deflator.

The deflator we will discuss first is the GDP deflator. It is the price index that includes the widest range of goods in the economy, and is the one used to distinguish **nominal GDP**—*the amount of goods and services produced measured at current prices* from **real GDP**—*the total amount of goods and services produced, adjusted for price-level changes.*

"Real" means "adjusted for inflation."

If GDP consisted of only one good, we wouldn't need a price index to determine the amount of inflation; we could simply look at what happened to the price of the good. For example, if the price of that one good goes up by 10 percent it would be obvious that there is 10 percent inflation. The need for a price index arises because GDP consists of millions of goods, each of whose prices change by differing amounts. Let's keep our analysis simple and consider a simple example in which GDP consists of only two goods. Say that the price of one good goes up by 4 percent and the price of the other goes up by 12 percent. If those are the only two goods that make up GDP, there has certainly been inflation, but how much is unclear. With just these two goods, the answer clearly has to be somewhere between 4 percent and 12 percent. But without knowing how important each good is in the economy, we can't say exactly how much inflation there has been.

Price indexes provide us with a way to determine inflation in an economy with a combination of goods. They do so by specifying what goods to include and by weighting each of the goods in the index by its relative importance, where relative importance is generally determined by the percentage of income spent on each good. Say, for example, that three-fourths of society's income is spent on the good whose price rose by 4 percent and one-quarter on the good whose price rose 12 percent. We multiply the share of income spent on each good by the rise in its price. Doing so gives us the amount of inflation, which in this case is 6 percent:

¼ × 12 percent + ¾ × 4 percent = 6 percent

The price index underlying these inflation numbers begins with a base year set at 100; price levels in every other time period are stated relative to that 100. In this example, because the price index is 100 in the base year and inflation is 6 percent, the price index rises to 106. There are a lot more technical issues involved in creating price indexes, which is why there are so many different measures of inflation. We will discuss some of those later in the chapter. For our purposes at this point, all you need to know is that a price index, and therefore inflation, can be calculated by weighting each good's price rise by the importance of that good to the economy as a whole.

Real versus Nominal GDP

Now let's look specifically at the **GDP deflator,** *the price index that includes all goods and services in the economy expressed relative to a base year of 100.* This is the deflator used to deflate nominal output by the rise in inflation to arrive at real output. Doing so gives us the output we would have had, had the price level remained constant.

Let's consider an example. Say nominal GDP rises by 10 percent from $16 trillion to $17.6 trillion. To determine how much of that 10 percent rise is real, we have to determine whether the price level has changed. Say that prices have risen by 5 percent. That means that the GDP deflator has increased from 100 to 105 (100 + 5). To calculate real GDP we deflate nominal GDP by dividing nominal GDP in the second year (the year when prices rose) by the GDP deflator and multiplying by 100:

$$\text{Real GDP} = \frac{\$17.6}{105} \times 100 = \$16.76 \text{ trillion.}$$

Real GDP, in this case, is $16.76 trillion, which is GDP that would have existed if the price level had not risen. In other words, real GDP rose not by $1.6 trillion, but by $760 million. The relationship between real GDP, nominal GDP, and the GDP deflator can be stated more generally,

Q-6 Nominal output has increased from $10 trillion to $12 trillion. The GDP deflator has risen by 15 percent. By how much has real output risen?

$$\text{Real GDP} = \frac{\text{Nominal GDP}}{\text{GDP deflator}} \times 100$$

Rearranging terms, we can also provide a formula for calculating the GDP deflator:

$$\text{GDP deflator} = \frac{\text{Nominal GDP}}{\text{Real GDP}} \times 100$$

To move from the GDP deflator to the rate of inflation, you calculate the change in the deflator from one year to another, divide the change in the deflator by the initial year's deflator, and multiply by 100.

$$\text{Inflation} = \frac{\text{Change in deflator}}{\text{Initial deflator}} \times 100$$

For example, if the initial deflator is 101 and the current deflator is 103, divide the difference, 2, by the initial deflator, 101, and multiply by 100. Doing so gives an inflation rate of 1.98 percent:

$$\text{Inflation} = \frac{103 - 101}{101} \times 100 = 1.98$$

For numbers close to 100, simply subtracting the two deflators ($103 - 101 = 2$) provides a reasonably good approximation to the rate of inflation.

The growth rate of nominal and real GDP can be calculated by the same method; you calculate the difference between the figures for the two years, divide that difference by the initial year figure, and multiply by 100. For example, if GDP rises from $20 trillion to $20.6 trillion, the difference is $600 billion. Dividing that by the initial year's GDP, $20 billion, and multiplying by 100 gives you a growth rate of 3 percent.

The growth rates of real GDP, nominal GDP, and inflation are related. Specifically:

% change in real GDP = % change in nominal GDP − Inflation

Doing that subtraction is what economists mean when they say that real GDP is equal to nominal GDP adjusted for inflation. We can see these relationships in the table below, which lists nominal GDP, the GDP deflator, and real GDP for recent years and their percentage changes from the previous year.

	Nominal GDP	GDP Deflator	Real GDP
2015 levels in billions	$18,219.3	104.8	$17,384.8
2016 levels in billions	18,707.2	105.9	17,665.0
% change from '15 to '16	2.7	1.1	1.6
2017 levels in billions	19,485.2	107.9	18,058.6
% change from '16 to '17	4.1	1.9	2.2

Notice that you can arrive at the growth rate in real GDP by subtracting inflation from the percentage change in nominal GDP. For example, from 2016 to 2017 real GDP rose by 2.2 percent, which equals the growth of nominal GDP, 4.1 percent, minus inflation of 1.9 percent.

Real GDP is what is important to a society because it measures what is *really* produced. Considering nominal GDP instead of real GDP can distort what's really happening. Let's say the U.S. price level doubled tomorrow. Nominal GDP would also double, but would the United States be better off? No.

We'll use the distinction between real and nominal continually in this course, so to firm up the concepts in your mind, let's go through another example. Consider Russia in 2016 and 2017, when nominal GDP rose from 61,098 billion rubles to 65,192 billion rubles while the GDP deflator rose from 100 to 103.7. Dividing nominal GDP in 2017 by the GDP deflator and multiplying by 100, we see that *real GDP* rose by only 3 percent. So much of Russia's growth was in prices.

Other Real-World Price Indexes

There are a variety of other price indexes that can be used to determine the amount of inflation. They differ from the GDP deflator in the goods that they include in the index and in some technical issues in how they determine the relative importance of each good. Three additional measures we'll consider here are the consumer price index, the personal consumption expenditure deflator, and the producer price index.

> An index shows prices at a particular time relative to base year prices.

Published monthly, the **consumer price index (CPI)** *measures the prices of a fixed basket of consumer goods, weighted according to each component's share of an average consumer's expenditures.* It measures the price of a fixed basket of goods rather than measuring the prices of all goods. It is the index of inflation most often used in news reports about the economy and is the index most relevant to consumers. Since different groups of consumers have different expenditures, there are different CPIs for different groups. One often-cited measure is the CPI for all urban consumers (the urban CPI)—about 87 percent of the U.S. population. The numbers that compose the urban CPI are collected at 87 urban areas and include prices from over 50,000 landlords or tenants and 23,000 business establishments.

> The consumer price index (CPI) is an index of inflation measuring prices of a fixed basket of consumer goods, weighted according to each component's share of an average consumer's expenditures.

Figure 25-1 shows the relative percentages of the basket's components. As you see, housing, transportation, and food make up the largest percentages of the CPI. To give you an idea of what effect the rise in price of a component of the CPI will have on the

> **Q-7** Say that health care costs make up 15 percent of total expenditures. Say they rise by 10 percent, while the other components of the price index remain constant. By how much does the price index rise?

FIGURE 25-1 Composition of CPI

The consumer price index is determined by looking at the prices of goods in the categories listed in this exhibit. These categories represent the rough percentages of people's expenditures.

Source: *CPI Detailed Reports,* Bureau of Labor Statistics (www.bls.gov).

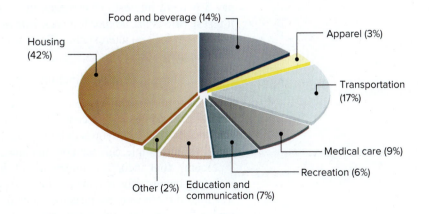

Food and beverage (14%)
Apparel (3%)
Housing (42%)
Transportation (17%)
Medical care (9%)
Recreation (6%)
Other (2%) Education and communication (7%)

CPI as a whole, let's say food prices rise 10 percent in a year and all other prices remain constant. Since food is about 14 percent of the total, the CPI will rise 14% × 10% = 1.4%. The CPI and GDP deflator indexes roughly equal each other when averaged over an entire year. (For more information on the CPI, go to www.bls.gov/cpi/cpifaq.htm.)

An alternative to the CPI is the personal consumption expenditure deflator. Whereas the CPI is a measure of prices of a fixed basket of goods, the **personal consumption expenditure (PCE) deflator** is *a measure of prices of goods that consumers buy that allows yearly changes in the basket of goods that reflect actual consumer purchasing habits.* The measure smooths out some of the problems associated with the CPI but otherwise is similar to it. Comparisons of alternative price indexes is a topic for advanced classes. At this point all you need to know is that indexes are simply composite measures; they cannot be perfect.

> The personal consumption expenditure (PCE) deflator allows yearly changes in the basket of goods.

Another price index that is often in the news is the **producer price index (PPI)**— *an index of prices that measures the average change in the selling prices received by domestic producers of goods and services over time.* This index measures price change from the perspective of the sellers, which may differ from the purchaser's price because of subsidies, taxes, and distribution costs and includes many goods that most consumers do not purchase. There are actually three different producer price indexes for goods at various stages of production—crude materials, intermediate goods, and finished goods. Even though the PPI doesn't directly measure the prices consumers pay, because it includes intermediate goods at early stages of production, it serves as an early predictor of consumer inflation since when costs go up, firms often raise their prices. (For more on the PPI, go to www.bls.gov/ppi/ppifaq.htm.)

Other Real and Nominal Distinctions

The distinction between real and nominal is a central distinction in economics that will come up again and again. So whenever you see the word *real,* remember:

> The "real" amount is the nominal amount adjusted for inflation.

> The "real" amount is the nominal amount divided by the price index. It is the nominal amount adjusted for inflation.

Economists' distinction between real and nominal concepts extends to other concepts besides output.

REAL AND NOMINAL INTEREST RATES   One important real and nominal distinction is between real and nominal interest rates. A **nominal interest rate** is *the rate you pay or receive to borrow or lend money.* Say you have a student loan on which you pay 5 percent interest. That means the nominal interest rate is 5 percent. The **real interest rate** is *the nominal interest rate adjusted for inflation.* In the case of interest rates, to get the real interest rate, all we have to do is subtract the inflation rate from the nominal interest rate:

> Real interest rate = Nominal interest rate − Inflation rate

> Real interest rate = Nominal interest rate − Inflation rate

Thus, if the nominal interest rate is 5 percent and the inflation rate is 3 percent, the real interest rate is 5 − 3 = 2 percent. The real interest rate is the amount that the loan actually costs you because you will be paying it off with inflated dollars. To see this, let's consider an example. Say the nominal interest rate is 5 percent and the inflation rate is 5 percent. Your income is increasing at the same rate as the balance on your loan, including interest. The real interest rate is 0 percent; it is equivalent to getting an interest-free loan if there were no inflation since in terms of real spending power, you will be paying back precisely what you borrowed.

REAL AND NOMINAL WEALTH   Another important real and nominal distinction is between **real wealth,** which is *the value of the productive capacity of the assets of an economy measured by the goods and services it can produce now and in the future,* and **nominal wealth,** which is *the value of those assets measured at their current market prices.* Prices of assets can go up for two reasons. They may rise because the productive capacity of that asset has risen. Say the price of a company's stock goes up because the company has just invented a new product. Because of that new invention, the economy's ability to produce has increased and society is richer. Such asset price rises represent increases in real wealth.

Asset prices can also rise without an increase in productive capacity. In such cases we have a rise in nominal wealth but not real wealth. We will call these kinds of price increases **asset price inflation**—*a rise in the price of assets unrelated to increases in their productive capacity.* Asset inflation does not involve a change in real assets—more buildings, factories, or changes in the productivity of the underlying assets. It is simply a higher price of assets. With asset price inflation, the price of assets rises, but there is no increase in real assets. The measured value of assets has increased, but the economy will not be able to produce more goods and services.

If we had a measure of asset inflation, we could adjust nominal wealth to find real wealth, just as we adjust nominal GDP for inflation to find real GDP. Unfortunately, because of the difficulties involved in determining whether or not the change in the price of an asset reflects changes in productive capacity of assets, we have no actual measure of asset inflation, which means we have no good measures for real wealth. We have to use very rough approximations. For example, when, say, real estate prices rise by 50 percent in five years when there is a 1 percent inflation in goods, but no significant change in population or in other relevant factors, then the presumption that society's real wealth in real estate has increased by very little is reasonable. We can surmise that much of the 50 percent increase is likely due to asset inflation, not a change in real wealth.

Even if we agree that there has been asset inflation, we still don't know whether the price of an asset is "too high." That's because we don't know whether the old price was too low, or whether the new price is now too high. We have to make judgments based on past trends. Let's take an example. The 1990s and early 2000s were marked by significant increases in the prices of assets, especially housing. Some economists argued that prior to the price increases, housing had been undervalued, so that the increase in prices was just helping assets "catch up" to a level that reflected their productive capacity. They turned out to be wrong: The increase in housing prices came to a sudden end in 2006 and nominal wealth in the economy fell by nearly 20 percent. By 2012, household nominal wealth recovered, not because housing prices had fully recovered, but because the prices of financial assets such as stocks had increased. It took another four years for housing prices, on average, to recover.

The fall in housing prices that occurred in this time period did not reduce the real wealth of society by anywhere near the amount of that fall, just as the rise didn't increase it. The reason is that few houses were destroyed by the fall in their prices. True, homeowners were worse off. But homeowners are not the entire picture. People who didn't own houses but were likely to buy one in the future (which includes many students) were better off by an offsetting amount because they would have to work less to buy a house in the future. The difference was that they didn't feel wealthier, even though they were, while the homeowners felt poorer. So psychologically, there was a loss in perceived aggregate wealth, even though real wealth did not change. Psychology can be extremely important for an economy, and the psychological effect of a bursting asset price bubble—a sudden fall in asset values—can throw an economy into a recession.

> It is useful to distinguish between real wealth—the actual productive capacity of the assets that make up the wealth, and nominal wealth—the value of the assets measured at current market prices.

> Asset price inflation is a rise in the price of assets unrelated to increases in their productive capacity.

Some Limitations of Aggregate Accounting

The quotation at this chapter's start pointed out that statistics can be misleading. I want to reiterate that here. Before you can work with statistics, you need to know how they are collected and the problems they present. If you don't, the results can be disastrous.

Here's a possible scenario: A student who isn't careful looks at the data and discovers an almost perfect relationship between imports and investment in a Latin American country. Whenever capital goods imports go up, investment of capital goods goes up by an equal proportion. The student develops a thesis based on that insight, only to learn after submitting the thesis that no data on investment are available for that country. Instead of gathering actual data, the foreign country's statisticians estimate investment by assuming it to be a constant percentage of imports. Since many investment goods are imported, this is reasonable, but the estimate is not a reasonable basis for an economic policy. It would be back to the drawing board for the student.

Limitations of aggregate accounting include the following:

1. GDP is not easily comparable among countries.

2. Measurement problems exist.

3. GDP measures market activity, not welfare.

4. Subcategories are often interdependent.

If you ever work in business as an economist, statistics will be your life's blood. Much of what economists do is based on knowing, interpreting, and drawing inferences from statistics. Statistics must be treated carefully. They don't always measure what they seem to measure. Though U.S. national income accounting statistics are among the most accurate in the world, they still have serious limitations including (1) GDP is not easily comparable among countries; (2) measurement errors exist; (3) GDP measures market activity, not welfare; and (4) subcategories are often interdependent.

Comparing GDP among Countries

One of the ways in which GDP can be misused is in comparing various countries' living standards. As you learned in the previous chapter, per capita GDP—GDP divided by population—gives us a sense of the relative standards of living of the people in various countries. But some of the comparisons should give you cause to wonder. That's because income is most often calculated at existing exchange rates (how much one currency costs in terms of another). For example, at existing exchange rates Bangladesh has per capita GDP of about $1,500, compared to U.S. per capita GDP of about $61,000, which means that the average U.S. citizen has about 41 times the income of the average Bangladeshi. How do people in Bangladesh survive?

Q-8 Why are GDP statistics not especially good for discussing the income of developing countries?

To answer that question, remember that GDP measures market transactions. In poor countries, individuals often grow their own food (subsistence farming), build their own shelter, and make their own clothes. None of these are market activities, and while they're sometimes estimated and included in GDP, if they are, they often are estimated inaccurately. Also, remember that GDP is an aggregate measure that values activities at the market price in a society. They certainly aren't estimated at the value of what these goods and services would cost in those countries. The relative prices of the products and services a consumer buys often differ substantially. In New York City, $2,500 a month gets you only a small studio apartment. In Bangladesh, $2,500 a month might get you a mansion with four servants. Thus, GDP can be a poor measure of the magnitude of relative living standards.

Purchasing power parity is a method of comparing income that takes the different relative prices among countries into account.

To avoid this problem in comparing per capita GDP, economists often calculate GDP using **purchasing power parity (PPP)**—*a method of comparing income that takes into account the different relative prices among countries.* Just how much of a difference the two approaches can make can be seen in the case of China. In 1992, the International Monetary Fund (IMF) changed from calculating China's GDP using the exchange rate approach to using the purchasing power parity approach. Upon doing so, the IMF calculated that China's per capita income rose from about $300 to well over $1,000—by over 400 percent in one year. When methods of calculation can make that much difference, one must use statistics very carefully.

GDP Measures Market Activity, Not Welfare

Another important limitation to remember is that GDP measures neither happiness nor economic welfare. GDP measures economic (market) activity. Real GDP could rise and economic welfare could fall. For example, say some Martians came down and let loose a million Martian burglars in the United States just to see what would happen. GDP would be likely to rise as individuals bought guns and locks and spent millions of dollars on protecting their property and replacing stolen items. At the same time, however, welfare would fall.

Welfare is a complicated concept. The economy's goal should not be to increase output for the sake of increasing output, but to make people better off or at least happier. But a pure happiness measure is impossible. Economists have struggled with the concept of welfare and most have decided that the best they can do is to concentrate their analysis on economic activity, leaving others to consider how economic activity relates to happiness. I should warn you, however, that there is no neat correlation between increases in GDP and increases in happiness.

Measurement Errors

GDP figures are supposed to measure all market economic activity, but they do not. Illegal drug sales, under-the-counter sales of goods to avoid income and sales taxes, work performed and paid for in cash to avoid income tax, nonreported sales, and prostitution are all market activities, yet none of them is included in GDP figures. Estimates of the underground, nonmeasured economy range from 1.5 to 20 percent of GDP in the United States and as high as 70 percent in Nigeria. That is, if measured U.S. GDP is $20 trillion, including the underground, nonmeasured activity would raise it to between $20.3 trillion and $24 trillion. If we were able to halt underground activity and direct those efforts to the aboveground economy, GDP would rise significantly. For instance, if we legalized prostitution and marijuana sales and quadrupled tax-collection mechanisms, GDP would rise. But that rise in GDP wouldn't necessarily make us better off. See the box "The Underground Economy and Undocumented Immigration" for further discussion.

A second type of measurement error occurs in adjusting GDP figures for inflation. Measurement of inflation involves numerous arbitrary decisions including how to weight various prices and how to adjust for changes in the quality of products. Let's take, for example, changes in the quality of products. If the price of a Toyota went up 5 percent from 2018 ($23,000) to 2019 ($24,150), that's certainly a 5 percent rise in price. But what if the 2019 Toyota had new self-driving features? Can you say that the price of cars rose 5 percent, or should you adjust for the improvement in quality? And if you adjust, how do you adjust? The economists who keep track of the price indexes used to measure inflation will be the first to tell you these questions have no one right answer. How these questions, and a million other similar questions involved in measuring inflation, are answered can lead to significant differences in estimates of inflation and hence in estimates of real GDP growth.

One Canadian study argued inflation could be either 5.4 or 15 percent, depending on how the inflation index was calculated. Which inflation figure you chose would make a big difference in your estimate of how the economy was doing.

Misinterpretation of Subcategories

Another limitation of aggregate accounting concerns possible misinterpretation of the components. In setting up the accounts, a large number of arbitrary decisions had to be made: What to include in "investment"? What to include in "consumption"? How to treat government expenditures? The decisions made were, for the most part, reasonable,

Web Note 25.4

Measuring Welfare

Web Note 25.5

The Underground Economy

Measurements of inflation can involve significant measurement errors.

Q-9 How can measurement errors occur in adjusting GDP figures for inflation?

The Underground Economy and Undocumented Immigration

In the text, I mentioned how the national income accounts fail to measure the underground economy and I gave some examples of underground activities. One underground activity that has become increasingly important involves undocumented immigration. Currently about 11 million people in the United States are undocumented immigrants, although the precise number isn't known since undocumented immigrants aren't especially forthcoming when the government comes around to do a census study.

©David McNew/Getty Images

Most people in the United States are affected by this group. You can see undocumented immigrants in a variety of lower-level jobs such as houseworkers, day laborers, construction workers, truckers, and farm laborers, among others. Many of these jobs are "on the books," which means that the undocumented immigrants become illegally documented by acquiring a forged identity, with a Social Security number. They end up paying taxes and contributing to measured output even though they are illegal. Others work "off the books" and, like the many U.S. citizens who work off the books, their contribution to output does not show up in the national income accounts. Such "off the books" transactions occur when restaurants don't ring up cash sales or when waiters forget to declare tips on their tax returns—they reduce their tax payments and make it look as if they have less income (and as if the economy has less production) than is the case.

How important is undocumented immigration to the underground economy? While a standard measure is that there are about 11 million undocumented immigrants in the United States and that the underground economy is about 10 percent the size of the U.S. economy, some economists have estimated that the true number of undocumented immigrants is closer to 18 to 20 million, and that the underground economy is much larger than 10 percent.

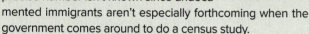

Q-10 How can some types of consumption increase our productive capacity of the economy by more than some types of investment?

but they weren't the only ones that could have been made. Once made, however, they influence our interpretations of events. For example, when we see that investment rises, we normally think that our future productive capacity is rising. But remember, that investment includes housing investment, which does not increase our future productive capacity. In fact, some types of consumption (say, purchases of personal computers by people who will become computer-literate and use their knowledge and skills to be more productive than they were before they owned computers) increase our productive capacity more than some types of investment.

Genuine Progress Indicator

The problems of aggregate accounting have led to a variety of measures of economic activity. One of the most interesting of these is the *Genuine Progress Indicator (GPI),* developed by Redefining Progress, which makes a variety of adjustments to GDP to better measure the progress of society rather than simply economic activity. The GPI makes adjustments to GDP for changes in other social goals. For example, if pollution worsens, the GPI falls even though GDP remains constant. Each of these adjustments requires someone to value these other social goals, and there is significant debate about how social goals should be valued. Advocates of the GPI agree that such valuations are difficult, but they argue that avoiding any such valuation, as is done with the GDP, implicitly values other social goals, such as having no pollution, at zero. Since some index will be used as an indicator of the progress of the economy, it is better to have an index that includes all social goals rather than an index of only economic activity.

By pointing out these problems, economists are not suggesting that aggregate accounting statistics should be thrown out. Far from it; measurement is necessary, and the GDP measurements and categories have made it possible to think and talk about the aggregate economy. I wouldn't have devoted an entire chapter of this book to aggregate accounting if I didn't believe it was important. I am simply arguing that aggregate accounting concepts should be used with sophistication, that is, with an awareness of their weaknesses as well as their strengths.

Measurement is necessary, and the GDP measurements and categories have made it possible to think and talk about the aggregate economy.

Conclusion

Used with that awareness, aggregate accounting is a powerful tool; you wouldn't want to be an economist without it. For those of you who aren't planning to be economists, it's still a good idea for you to understand the concepts of national income accounting. If you do, the business section of the newspaper will seem less like Greek to you. You'll be a more informed citizen and will be better able to make up your own mind about macroeconomic debates.

Summary

- Aggregate accounting is a set of rules and definitions for measuring activity in the aggregate economy. *(LO25-1)*

- GDP is the total market value of all final goods produced in an economy in one year. It's a flow, not a stock, measure of market activity. *(LO25-1)*

- GDP is divided up into four types of expenditures: *(LO25-1)*

  GDP = Consumption + Investment + Government spending + Net exports

- Intermediate goods can be eliminated from GDP in two ways: *(LO25-1)*
  1. By measuring only final sales.
  2. By measuring only value added.

- Net domestic product is GDP less depreciation. NDP represents output available for purchase because production used to replace worn-out plant and equipment (depreciation) has been subtracted. *(LO25-1)*

- GDP describes the economic output produced within the physical borders of an economy, while GNP describes the economic output produced by the citizens of a country. *(LO25-1)*

- The stock equivalent of the national income accounts is the national wealth accounts. *(LO25-1)*

- Aggregate income = Compensation to employees + Rent + Interest + Profit. *(LO25-2)*

- Aggregate income equals aggregate production because whenever a good is produced, somebody receives income for producing it. Profit is key to that equality. *(LO25-2)*

- Because the United States has a trade deficit, total expenditures by U.S. citizens are greater than production in the United States. *(LO25-2)*

- To compare income over time, we must adjust for price-level changes. After adjusting for inflation, nominal measures are changed to "real" measures. *(LO25-3)*

- Real GDP $= \dfrac{\text{Nominal GDP}}{\text{GDP deflator}} \times 100$ *(LO25-3)*

- The percentage change in real GDP equals the percentage change in nominal GDP minus inflation. *(LO25-3)*

- Inflation is a continual rise in the price level. The CPI, PPI, PCE deflator, and GDP deflator are all price indexes used to measure inflation. These indexes measure goods prices and do not include asset prices. *(LO25-3)*

- Real interest rate = Nominal interest rate − Inflation. *(LO25-3)*

- GDP has its problems: It's difficult to compare across countries; GDP does not measure economic welfare; it does not include transactions in the underground economy; the price index used to calculate real GDP is problematic; and subcategories of GDP are often interdependent. *(LO25-4)*

Key Terms

asset price inflation
consumer price index (CPI)
consumption
depreciation
final output
GDP deflator
government spending
gross domestic product
   (GDP)

gross national product
   (GNP)
inflation
intermediate products
investment
net domestic product (NDP)
net exports
net foreign factor income
net investment

nominal GDP
nominal interest rate
nominal wealth
personal consumption
   expenditure (PCE)
   deflator
price index
producer price index
   (PPI)

purchasing power parity
   (PPP)
real GDP
real interest rate
real wealth
transfer payments
value added
wealth accounts

Questions and Exercises connect

1. What's the relationship between a stock concept and a flow concept? *(LO25-1)*

2. What expenditure category of production is largest for most countries? *(LO25-1)*

3. How do wealth accounts differ from national income accounts? *(LO25-1)*

4. State whether the following actions will increase or decrease GDP: *(LO25-1)*
   a. The United States legalizes gay marriages.
   b. An individual sells her house on her own.
   c. An individual sells his house through a broker.
   d. Government increases Social Security payments.
   e. Stock prices rise by 20 percent.
   f. An unemployed worker gets a job.

5. If you add up all the transactions in an economy, do you arrive at GDP, GNP, or something else? *(LO25-1)*

6. The United States is considering introducing a value-added tax. What tax rate on value added is needed to get the same revenue as is gotten from an income tax rate of 15 percent? *(LO25-1)*

7. There are three firms in an economy: A, B, and C. Firm A buys $250 worth of goods from firm B and $200 worth of goods from firm C, and produces 200 units of output, which it sells at $5 per unit. Firm B buys $100 worth of goods from firm A and $150 worth of goods from firm C, and produces 300 units of output, which it sells at $7 per unit. Firm C buys $50 worth of goods from firm A and nothing from firm B. It produces output worth $1,000. All other products are sold to consumers. *(LO25-1)*
   a. Calculate GDP.
   b. If a value-added tax (a tax on the total value added of each firm) of 10 percent is introduced, how much revenue will the government get?
   c. How much would government get if it introduced a 10 percent income tax?
   d. How much would government get if it introduced a 10 percent sales tax on final output?

8. If the government increases transfer payments, what happens to aggregate output? *(LO25-1)*

9. Economists normally talk about GDP even though they know NDP is a better measure of economic activity. Why? *(LO25-1)*

10. Which will be larger, gross domestic product or gross national product? *(LO25-1)*

11. You've been given the following data:

Net exports	$ 4
Net foreign factor income	2
Investment	185
Government spending	195
Consumption	500
Depreciation	59

From these data, calculate GDP, GNP, and NDP. *(LO25-1)*

12. What is the largest component of aggregate income for most countries? *(LO25-2)*

13. Given the following data about the economy: *(LO25-2)*

Profit	$ 268
Consumption	700
Investment	500
Government spending	300
Net exports	275
Rent	25
Depreciation	25
Net foreign factor income	3
Interest	150
Compensation to employees	1,329

a. Calculate aggregate output (GDP) and aggregate income.
b. Compare the two calculations in *a*. Why are they not precisely equal?
c. Calculate GNP.
d. Calculate NDP.

14. You have been hired as a research assistant and are given the following data: (*LO25-2*)

Compensation to employees	$329
Consumption	370
Exports	55
Net foreign factor income	3
Government spending	43
Investment	80
Imports	63
Interest	49
Profit	96
Rent	14
Net investment	72

a. Calculate GNP, GDP, and aggregate income.
b. What is depreciation in this year?
c. What is NDP?

15. What income category keeps aggregate output and aggregate income equal? (*LO25-2*)

16. If an economy has a trade surplus, is domestic production higher or lower than domestic expenditures? Explain your answer. (*LO25-2*)

17. What makes it difficult to compare GDP over time? How is the problem addressed? (*LO25-3*)

18. Below are nominal GDP and GDP deflators for four years: (*LO25-3*)

Year	Nominal GDP (in billions)	GDP Deflator
Year 1	$18,000	100
Year 2	18,540	103
Year 3	19,467	104
Year 4	20,246	106

a. Calculate real GDP in each year.
b. Did the percentage change in nominal GDP exceed the percentage change in real GDP in any of the last three years listed?
c. In which year did society's welfare increase the most?

19. Fill in the missing values in the table below: (*LO25-3*)

Real Interest Rate	Nominal Interest Rate	Inflation
5	7	—
4	—	3
—	12	9

20. You find that real GDP per capita in Burundi is $800 while real GDP per capita in the United States is $50,000. What is misleading about these figures when comparing standards of living? (*LO25-4*)

21. When more and more women entered the labor force in the 1970s and 1980s, the economy's potential output rose. (*LO25-4*)
a. To the extent that real output rose because of their entry into the labor market, what was the effect on measured GDP?
b. What was the impact on welfare?

22. The Genuine Progress Indicator is an alternative measure to economic activity. (*LO25-4*)
a. Is the Genuine Progress Indicator a subjective measure of the economy? Explain your answer.
b. Is GDP a subjective measure? Explain your answer.

Questions from Alternative Perspectives

1. Your textbook points out that GDP fails to recognize much of the work done in the home, largely by women. Most estimates assign that work great economic value. For instance, one measure, developed by the UN's International Training and Research Institute, calculates that counting unpaid household production would add 30 to 60 percent to the GDP of industrialized countries and far more for developing countries.
a. Why do you think that work done at home is left out, but housing services are not?
b. Does it make any difference to how women are treated and thought about that work done at home is not counted in GDP?
c. If you were valuing the services of a housespouse, how would you go about measuring the value of those services? (*Feminist*)

2. In "Christianity and Economics: A Review of the Recent Literature," economist John Tiemstra states, "Taking good

(Continued)

to mean self-perceived happiness derived from economic consumption adopts an ethic that is foreign to biblical Christianity." Your textbook cautions that GDP is not the same as welfare.

a. What would you include in an index to measure the welfare of a society that takes into account Christian ethics?

b. What would you purposefully not include in that index? *(Religious)*

3. Explain the sense in which GDP accounting is an institution (see the *Oxford Dictionary of the English Language* for a precise definition of an institution).

a. How does GDP as an institution shape our understanding of the economic system?

b. Who benefits from using GDP accounting as a measure of welfare? *(Institutionalist)*

4. In the expenditure approach of GDP, should *G* (government purchases) be taken into account within the calculation the same way *C* (consumption) and *I* (investment) are measured? If not, is there something inherently different about the nature of private and public expenditures? *(Austrian)*

5. The government spends far too much money collecting and organizing statistics. If those statistics were necessary, the private market would collect them.

a. Explain the sense in which the above statement is true.

b. Who do you think is the major supporter of government collection of data? *(Austrian)*

6. Unlike GDP, the Genuine Progress Indicator measures the costs as well as the benefits of economic growth by accounting for how production and consumption create social ills such as inequality and create environmental problems that threaten future generations, such as global warming and the depletion of natural resources. GPI adjusts GDP downward to account for these costs, along with underemployment and the loss of leisure time. The result: The GPI rose from the 1950s through the early 1970s but has fallen since and today is still below its level in 1973.

a. In your opinion, does gross national product per capita or the Genuine Progress Indicator provide a better measure of economic progress?

b. Why? *(Radical)*

Issues to Ponder

1. Find consumption expenditures (as a percentage of GDP) for the following countries and explain what accounts for the differences. (Requires research.)
   a. Mexico
   b. Thailand
   c. Poland
   d. Nigeria
   e. Kuwait

2. People's perception of inflation often differs from actual inflation.
   a. List five goods that you buy relatively frequently.
   b. Looking in old newspapers (found in the library on microfiche), locate sales prices for these goods since 1950, finding one price every five years or so.

Determine the average annual price rise for each good from 1950 to today.
   c. Compare that price with the rise in the consumer price index.

3. If the United States introduces universal child care, what will likely happen to GDP? What are the welfare implications?

4. If society's goal is to make people happier, and higher GDP isn't closely associated with being happier, why do economists even talk about GDP?

5. In the early 2000s, some people, part of a renewed "Simplicity Movement," felt that accumulating material things reduced their happiness. Assuming they are truly happier with fewer material goods, what does this suggest about the connection between GDP and welfare?

Answers to Margin Questions

1. GDP is the sum of consumption, investment, and government spending plus the total of exports minus imports, in this case 95. *(LO25-1)*

2. Only the value added by the sale would be added to GDP. In this case, the value added is the difference between the purchase price and the sale price, or $500. *(LO25-1)*

3. The government budget includes transfer payments, which are not included in GDP. Only those government expenditures that are for goods and services are included in GDP. *(LO25-1)*

4. GDP measures the output of the residents of a country—the output within its geographic borders. GNP measures

the output of the citizens and businesses of a country. Kuwait is a very rich country whose residents have a high income, much of it from investments overseas. Thus, its GNP will be high. However, Kuwait also has large numbers of foreign workers who are not citizens and whose incomes would be included in GDP but not in GNP. In reality, Kuwait citizens' and businesses' foreign income exceeds foreign workers' and foreign companies' income within Kuwait, so Kuwait's GNP is greater than its GDP.   (*LO25-1*)

5. Aggregate income is the sum of employee compensation, rents, interest, and profits, in this case 198.   (*LO25-2*)

6. Real output equals the nominal amount divided by the price index. Since the price index has risen by 15 percent, real output has risen to $10.435 trillion ($12 trillion divided by 1.15). Real output has risen by $435 billion.   (*LO25-3*)

7. The price index will rise by $0.15 \times 0.1 = 1.5$ percent. (*LO25-3*)

8. In developing countries, individuals often grow their own food and take part in many activities that are not measured by the GDP statistics. The income figures that one gets from the GDP statistics of developing countries do not include such activities and, thus, can be quite misleading.   (*LO25-4*)

9. Measurement errors occur in adjusting GDP figures for inflation because measuring inflation involves numerous arbitrary decisions such as choosing a base year, adjusting for quality changes in products, and weighting prices.   (*LO25-4*)

10. Dividing goods into consumption and investment does not always capture the effect of the spending on productive capacity. For example, housing "investment" does little to expand the productive capacity of the economy. However, "consumption" of computers or books could expand the productive capacity significantly.   (*LO25-4*)

CHAPTER 26

The Keynesian Short-Run Policy Model: Demand-Side Policies

> The Theory of Economics . . . is a method rather than a doctrine, an apparatus of the mind, a technique of thinking which helps its possessor to draw correct conclusions.
>
> —J. M. Keynes

After reading this chapter, you should be able to:

LO26-1 Discuss the key insight of the *AS/AD* model and list both its assumptions and its components.

LO26-2 Describe the shape of the aggregate demand curve and what factors shift the curve.

LO26-3 Explain the shape of the short-run and long-run aggregate supply curves and what factors shift the curves.

LO26-4 Show the effects of shifts of the aggregate demand and aggregate supply curves on the price level and output in both the short run and long run.

LO26-5 Discuss the limitations of the macro policy model.

©AP Photo/Beth A. Keiser

In late 2007 and early 2008, the U.S. economy fell into a serious recession that many thought might lead to a depression. Faced with this serious recession, the U.S. government, with support from both Democrats and Republicans, implemented what are known as expansionary demand-side policies. The rationale was that if the government did not do so, firms would cut back production further. More employees would be laid off, reducing their income and their expenditures even further. This would lead to lower output and continue to push the economy into a prolonged recession or possibly even a depression. The tools that the government has to deal with a recession—monetary and fiscal policies (policies that we will discuss below)—affect the aggregate demand side of the economy.

The model that underlies these policies is the short-run macroeconomic model, also known as the aggregate supply/aggregate demand (*AS/AD*) model. Economists drew the ideas in this model from Keynes' contributions described in Chapter 24, so the model is often called the Keynesian model.

The Key Insight of the Keynesian *AS/AD* Model

The key idea of the Keynesian *AS/AD* model is that in the short run, the economy can deviate from what it is capable of producing, or its **potential output**—*the highest amount of output an economy can sustainably produce using existing production processes and resources*—and that government could correct such deviation with demand-side policies—**monetary policy,** *a policy of influencing the economy through changes in the money supply and interest rates,* and **fiscal policy,** *the deliberate change in either government spending or taxes (or more generally the deficit) to stimulate or slow down the economy.* We'll discuss more specifically what these policies mean and how they are implemented in later chapters, but I introduce them here so that I can better discuss them in both the short-run *AS/AD* demand-side framework of this chapter and the long-run supply-side framework of the next chapter.

The Keynesian model focuses on the use of monetary and fiscal policy.

Suppose the economy falls into a recession; that is, output falls below its potential. According to the *AS/AD* model, this could happen if aggregate demand falls for some unexplained reason. In response firms decrease output and lay off workers, which lowers people's income. Lower income leads consumers to cut expenditures further, which once again causes firms to decrease production. So the fall in aggregate demand creates a cycle that feeds on itself and can develop into a vicious downward spiral.

Web Note 26.1

Fiscal Policy

In the *AS/AD* model eventually this downward cycle of aggregate demand and production ends, settling at an equilibrium that is lower than the original income. That equilibrium might not be at the economy's potential output. Thus, for Keynes, there was a difference between **equilibrium output**—*the level of output toward which the economy gravitates in the short run because of the cumulative cycles of declining or increasing production*—and potential output. Keynes believed that at certain times the economy needed some help in reaching its potential output.

In the Keynesian model, there is a difference between equilibrium output and potential output.

Fixed Price Level

As mentioned in Chapter 24, Keynes distinguished between the forces operating in a single market and the forces operating in the aggregate economy. In a single market, when demand falls, firms reduce prices to bring the market back to equilibrium. You might think the same would be true for the aggregate economy, but Keynes correctly pointed out that it would not be the case for two reasons. First, social forces keep firms from reducing wages quickly, and falling product prices may create problems by causing expectations of further decreases; firms generally cut production long before they cut wages or prices. Cutting production could lead to the cumulative downward spiral of income discussed above. Second, even if firms cut wages and prices, if all firms did so, *relative* wages or prices would not fall. But it is relative wage and price changes that are needed to increase sales. Instead, such a general decrease in prices and wages would lead to **deflation** *(an overall decline in the price level in the economy).* This deflation would create problems of its own.

When prices are falling, profits decline, making entrepreneurs hesitant to start businesses, slowing the growth of the economy. Asset values (prices of assets such as houses, stocks, and bonds) may also decline, which means that the economy experiences not only a deflation in the general price level (price of goods and services); it also may experience asset price deflation (the fall in the prices of assets in which people hold their wealth). Since asset prices are much more volatile than goods prices, asset price deflation is much more common than deflation in the general price level of goods and services.

Asset price deflation is problematic for an economy; it reduces the value of collateral used to support consumer and producer loans and therefore spending. So both types of deflation undermine business and consumer confidence. Thus a general fall in prices cannot be relied upon to bring the aggregate economy into equilibrium without causing serious problems.

These inevitable side effects of a falling price level and a falling asset price level cause firms to decrease output more than the falling price level causes consumers to buy more. So deflation isn't an acceptable policy option. U.S. government policy makers of all political persuasions have agreed that deflation as a method of bringing aggregate supply and demand into equilibrium is unacceptable. It would destroy our economy. Because of the problems with deflation, Keynes argued that, when considering declines in demand, at least in the short run, the price level of goods can be considered essentially fixed. But a fixed price level leaves the economy with the problem of falling into an aggregate equilibrium that is not at the economy's potential output. The economy could get stuck in a prolonged recession with low income and high unemployment and no reasonable method for the market to escape from that undesirable equilibrium on its own. That's the essence of the Keynesian insight.

The Paradox of Thrift

We can see Keynes' insight working its way through the economy in the downturn that began in 2008. The economy went into a recession and people cut expenditures as they lost their jobs. Instead of consuming, they saved. As they increased savings, the economy started on a downward spiral. Income fell, and as it did savings fell, leading people to try to save more. If increased savings have feedback effects on income, the economy can find itself facing the *fallacy of composition:* When people try to save more, they actually save less. What is true for an individual is not necessarily true for the whole economy.

One might expect that people's savings would finance investment, which would offset the decline in consumption expenditures. But savings does not automatically get transferred into investment. Where does the savings go? In a downward spiral, it disappears. As output falls, people lose their jobs and are forced to save less than they had planned because they earn less income than they had planned. Thus the choice to increase the *percentage* of their income devoted to savings can lead income to fall, so that while the percentage devoted to savings increases, the absolute amount of savings decreases as income falls. Suppose income is $1,000 and the saving rate is 4 percent. We know that 4 percent of $1,000 is $40; if people increase their saving rate to 4.1 percent and that causes income to fall to $970, then their total savings does not increase to $41; it falls to $39.77 (4.1% × $970).

Attempts to increase total savings by increasing the percent of income saved may create the **paradox of thrift**—*when an increase in savings leads to a decrease in expenditures, decreasing supply, decreasing output, causing a recession, and lowering total savings.*

If the economy is in a position where the paradox of thrift holds, increasing savings will set in motion a cycle of declining expenditures and production. Eventually income will fall far enough so that once again saving and investment will be in equilibrium, but then the economy could be in an almost permanent recession, with ongoing unemployment. Keynesians believe that in this case the economy would need government's help to prop up aggregate expenditures. That is the essence of the Keynesian argument to support expansionary demand-side macro policy.

Notice that the Keynesian short-run framework gives a quite different view of saving than is often held by laypeople. In that conventional view of saving, saving is seen as something good; savings lead to investment, which in turn leads to growth. In the Keynesian short-run framework, that isn't the way it works.

In the Long Run, We're All Dead

When Keynes said "In the long run, we're all dead," he didn't mean that we can forget the long run. What he meant was that if the long run is so long that short-run forces do not let it come about, then for all practical purposes there is no long run. In that case, policy makers ought to focus on short-run problems.

Keynes believed that voters would not be satisfied waiting for market forces to bring about full employment. If something were not done in the short run to alleviate unemployment, he felt, voters would opt for fascism (as had the Germans) or communism (as had the Russians). He saw both alternatives as undesirable. For him, what would happen in the long run was academic.

Classicals, in contrast, argued that the short-run problems were not as bad as Keynes made them out to be and therefore should not be focused on to the exclusion of long-run problems.

Modern-day Classicals argue that while Keynes is dead, we are not, and the result of his short-run focus was long-run problems—specifically large government debts that threaten the long-run stability of the economy. Eventually, a society is going to have to deal with these debts, and while they may never have to pay them off, they will have to pay interest on them. Large government debts weaken an economy.

Up until 2008, Keynesian ideas had lost favor as people became concerned about the large debts the government was incurring. But when the financial crisis of 2008 hit, and the macroeconomy fell into a serious recession, Keynesian ideas came back into vogue. Somehow the long-run debt problem seems less important when the short-run problems are themselves threatening the stability of the society.

Three Things to Remember about the Keynesian Model

By the late 1950s, Keynesian economics had been accepted by most macroeconomists, and was taught almost everywhere in the United States. The model that initially was meant to capture Keynesian economics was called the multiplier model, and is the model I present in Chapter 26W. This multiplier model emphasizes aggregate output fluctuations and explores why those output fluctuations generally would not lead to wild fluctuations in output—depressions—and instead lead to smaller fluctuations—recessions. In the 1970s, that multiplier model was replaced by the aggregate supply/aggregate demand (*AS/AD)* model. It is that *AS/AD* model that I introduce you to in this chapter.

It is important to remember three things about the *AS/AD* model. The first is that it is a short-run model. It does not tell us what the long-run effects of any policy will be. The second is that it is a pedagogical model—designed to give students and policy makers a framework to organize their thinking about the macroeconomy. It is a rough-and-ready framework, not a model developed to capture all the dynamic forces operating in the economy. The third point is that in its standard presentation, the *AS/AD* model is not a model developed from first principles, as is the micro supply/demand model. That micro model starts with individual choices and relates those choices to equilibrium. The macro *AS/AD* model does not start with individual choices. Instead, it starts with aggregate relationships based on empirical observations about the way the aggregate economy works. It loosely relates those empirically observed aggregate relationships to decisions by firms and individuals. These dynamic forces are especially important when aggregate demand declines significantly, as happened in 2008 and 2009. (The multiplier model developed in Chapter 26W does a better job of highlighting those dynamic forces.)

The *AS/AD* model:

1. Is a short-run model.
2. Is a pedagogical tool.
3. Starts with aggregate relationships.

Instability caused by dynamic forces is especially important when aggregate demand declines significantly.

What the *AS/AD* model does do is provide a simple model that suggests a role for government in keeping feedback effects from spiraling an economy downward. It gives a good sense of how macroeconomists think about cyclical problems in the macro-economy. The *AS/AD* model is used by most macro policy economists to discuss mild short-run, cyclical fluctuations in output and unemployment. At the end of the chapter I will discuss some of the limitations of the *AS/AD* model in more depth.

The Components of the *AS/AD* Model

The *AS/AD* model consists of three curves. The curve describing the supply side of the aggregate economy in the short run is the short-run aggregate supply (*SAS*) curve, the curve describing the demand side of the economy is the aggregate demand (*AD*) curve, and the curve describing the highest sustainable level of output is the long-run aggregate supply (*LAS*) curve.

The first thing to note about the *AS/AD* model is that it is fundamentally different from the microeconomic supply/demand model. In microeconomics the price of a single good is on the vertical axis and the quantity of a single good on the horizontal axis. The reasoning for the shapes of the micro supply and demand curves is based on the concepts of substitution and opportunity cost. In the macro *AS/AD* model, the price level of all goods, not just the price of one good, is on the vertical axis and aggregate output, not a single good, is on the horizontal axis. The shapes of the curves are not directly based on opportunity cost or substitution.

The second thing to note about the *AS/AD* model is that it is a *historical model*. A historical model is a model that starts at a point in time and provides insight into what will likely happen when changes affect the economy. It does not try to explain how the economy got to its starting point; the macroeconomy is too complicated for that. Instead, the model starts from historically given price and output levels and, given the institutional structure of the economy, considers how changes in the economy are likely to affect those levels. What this means is that much of the discussion in this chapter is based on the economy's institutional realities and observed empirical regularities.

Let's now consider the three central components of the *AS/AD* model: the aggregate demand (*AD*) curve, the short-run aggregate supply (*SAS*) curve, and the long-run aggregate supply (*LAS*) curve.

The Aggregate Demand Curve

The **aggregate demand (*AD*) curve** is *a curve that shows how a change in the price level will change aggregate expenditures on all goods and services in an economy.* (Aggregate expenditures are the sum of consumption, investment, government expenditures, and net exports.) A standard *AD* curve is shown in Figure 26-1. Although the curve is called an aggregate demand curve, let me repeat that it is not the same as a microeconomic demand curve. The *AD* curve is more an equilibrium curve.[1] It shows the level of aggregate expenditures at every price level, implicitly taking into account some interactions among all producers and consumers in an economy.

The Slope of the *AD* Curve

As you can see, the *AD* curve is downward-sloping. A good place to begin understanding why it is downward-sloping is to remember the composition of aggregate demand.

---

[1]In a number of articles and in previous editions, I tried to change the terminology so that students would not be misled into thinking that the *AD* curve was a normal demand curve. But my changes did not catch on.

Knowing the difference between microeconomic supply and demand curves and macroeconomic aggregate demand and supply curves is very important.

Take the time to draw an *AD* curve, making sure to label the axes correctly.

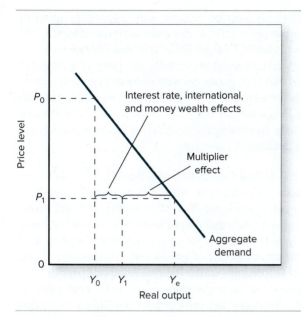

FIGURE 26-1 The Aggregate Demand Curve

The *AD* curve is a downward-sloping curve that looks like a typical demand curve, but it is important to remember that it is quite a different curve. The reason it slopes downward is not the substitution effect, but instead the interest rate effect, the international effect, and the money wealth effect. The multiplier effect strengthens each of these effects.

As I discussed in the chapter on aggregate accounting, aggregate expenditures (demand) is the sum of consumption, investment, government spending, and net exports. The slope of the *AD* curve depends on how these components respond to changes in the price level.

In principle, we would expect the *AD* curve to be vertical. Why? Because one of the definitional assumptions of economics is that the price level is simply what is called a *numeraire*. The price level is a reference point, and the actual value of that numeraire should not matter. To see why, say that all prices (including wages) doubled. How would people's choices change? They wouldn't. Instead of earning $10 an hour, you would now earn $20 an hour. All the goods you buy would cost twice as much too, so you wouldn't be better off or worse off. Only the reference point has changed. Thus, as a first approximation, we would expect that you would buy the same amount of real goods at every price level. That would make the *AD* curve vertical.

Macroeconomists have examined this proposition and have developed a number of explanations for why a falling price level increases aggregate expenditures in normal times. These explanations make the standard *AD* curve downward-sloping rather than vertical. I'll discuss three of these standard effects: the interest rate effect, the international effect, and the money wealth effect.

THE INTEREST RATE EFFECT   One explanation for why the aggregate demand curve slopes downward is called the **interest rate effect**—*the effect that a lower price level has on investment expenditures through the effect that a change in the price level has on interest rates.* The interest rate effect works as follows: A decrease in the price level will increase the purchasing power of the money in people's pockets and people will find they're holding more money than they need. So, they deposit the extra money at banks in some form, giving banks more money to loan out. As banks make more loans, interest rates will fall, which, in turn, will increase investment expenditures. Why? Because at lower interest rates businesses will undertake more investment projects. Since investment is one component of aggregate demand, the quantity of aggregate demand will increase when the price level falls.

In principle, we would expect the *AD* curve to be vertical.

The three standard reasons given for the downward-sloping *AD* curve are:

1. The interest rate effect;
2. The international effect; and
3. The money wealth effect.

THE INTERNATIONAL EFFECT   A second reason why aggregate quantity demanded increases with a fall in the price level is the **international effect,** which tells us that *as the price level falls (assuming the exchange rate does not change), net exports will rise.* As the price level in the United States falls, the price of U.S. goods relative to foreign goods goes down and U.S. goods become more competitive relative to foreign goods; thus, U.S. exports increase and U.S. imports decrease. Let's consider an example. In the mid-1990s, the Bulgarian currency was fixed to the German mark. Bulgaria's price level rose enormously, increasing the demand for German imports and reducing the quantity of aggregate demand in Bulgaria.

THE MONEY WEALTH EFFECT   A third explanation why the *AD* curve isn't vertical is called the money wealth effect. To understand this effect consider Figure 26-1. Say we start out at price P_0 and output Y_0 in Figure 26-1. (Remember, as I said above, in a historical model we start at a given price and output and determine what would happen if the price level rises or falls from that level.) Now, say that the price level falls to P_1. How will this affect the total amount of goods and services that people demand? The **money wealth effect** (sometimes called the *real balance effect*) tells us that *a fall in the price level will make the holders of money richer, so they buy more.* In other words, if the price level falls, the dollar bill in your pocket will buy more than before because the purchasing power of the dollar rises. You are, in effect, richer and as you get richer, other things equal, you will buy more goods and services. Since consumption expenditures are a component of aggregate demand, aggregate expenditures will increase, which is shown graphically by a movement along the *AD* curve. (To differentiate such movements along the *AD* curve from a shift in the *AD* curve, I call movements due to changes in the price level "changes in the quantity of aggregate demand.") Most economists do not see the money wealth effect as strong; they do, however, accept the logic of the argument.

So, in Figure 26-1 when we include the international effect, the interest rate effect, and the money wealth effect, a fall in the price level from P_0 to P_1 causes the quantity of aggregate demand to increase from Y_0 to Y_1.

THE MULTIPLIER EFFECT   The above three effects give us some explanation why the quantity of aggregate demand will increase with a fall in the price level. But the story about the slope of the aggregate demand curve doesn't end there. It also takes into account the **multiplier effect**—*the amplification of initial changes in expenditures.* It is important to recognize that when considering the demand curve in micro, we can reasonably assume that other things remain constant; in macro, other things change. Whereas the demand curve in micro includes only the initial change in quantity demanded, the aggregate demand curve includes the repercussions that these initial changes have throughout the economy. What I mean by *repercussions* is that the initial changes in expenditures set in motion a process in the economy that amplifies these initial effects.

> In micro other things can be assumed to remain constant, whereas in macro other things change.

To see how these repercussions will likely work in the real world, imagine that the price level in the United States rises. U.S. citizens will reduce their purchases of U.S. goods and increase their purchases of foreign goods. (That's the international effect.) U.S. firms will see the demand for their goods and services fall and will decrease their output. Profits will fall and people will be laid off. Both these effects will cause income to fall, and as income falls, people will demand still fewer goods and services. (If you're unemployed, you cut back your purchases.) Again production and income fall, which again leads to a drop in expenditures. This secondary cutback is an example of a repercussion. These repercussions *multiply* the initial effect that a change in the price level has on expenditures.

The multiplier effect amplifies the initial interest rate, international, and money wealth effects, thereby making the slope of the *AD* curve flatter than it would have been. You can see this in Figure 26-1. The three effects discussed above increase output from Y_0 to Y_1. The repercussions multiply that effect so that output increases to Y_e.

Economists have suggested other reasons why changes in the price level affect the quantity of aggregate demand, but these four should be sufficient to give you an initial understanding. Going through the same exercise that I did above for the interest rate, international, money wealth, and multiplier effects for a fall (rather than a rise) in the price level is a useful exercise.

Let's conclude this section with an example that brings out the importance of the multiplier effect in determining the slope of the *AD* curve. Say that the multiplier effect amplifies the interest rate, international, and money wealth effects by a factor of 2 and that the interest rate, international, and money wealth effects reduce output by 4 when the price level rises from 100 to 110. What will be the slope of the *AD* curve? Since the multiplier effect is 2, the total decline in output will be $2 \times 4 = 8$, so the slope will be $-10/8$, or -1.25.

> The slope of the *AD* curve is determined by:
> 1. The money wealth effect;
> 2. The interest rate effect;
> 3. The international effect; and
> 4. The multiplier effect.

> **Q-3** True or false? The slope of the *AD* curve is -1 if as the price level falls from 110 to 100, the international effect increases output by 10.

HOW STEEP IS THE *AD* CURVE? While all economists agree about the logic of the interest rate effect, the international effect, and the money wealth effect, most also agree that for small changes in the price level, the net effect is relatively small. So, even after the effect has been expanded by the multiplier, the *AD* curve has a very steep slope.[2] Unfortunately, statistically separating out the effects determining the slope of the *AD* curve from shifts in the *AD* curve is difficult because there is much noise—random unexplained movements—in the relationship between the price level and aggregate expenditures. It is that noise on the aggregate level that makes the economy so hard to predict, and accounts for the description of economic forecasting as "driving a car blindfolded while following directions given by a person who is looking out of the back window." In order to make the graphs easy to follow, they show a flatter *AD* curve than probably exists in reality.

> There is much noise in the relationship between the price level and aggregate expenditures.

Dynamic Price-Level Adjustment Feedback Effects

The interest rate, international, and money wealth effects, amplified by the multiplier effect, are all logically correct. But there are other forces in the economy that counteract these forces. At times these dynamic effects can overwhelm the standard effects and make the aggregate economy unstable, making expansions stronger and contractions larger. They can reduce or completely offset the stabilizing effects of a price-level adjustment in bringing about an aggregate equilibrium.

> At times dynamic effects can overwhelm the standard effects and make the aggregate economy unstable.

These forces are especially important when aggregate demand is declining and the price level needs to fall to bring about aggregate equilibrium. Here is the problem: Pressure for the price level to fall brings with it:[3]

- Expectations of falling aggregate demand.
- Lower asset prices, making society on average *feel* poorer, even though, theoretically, it is not *actually* poorer.

---

[2]Of the three, the international effect is probably the strongest, but its strength depends on whether fluctuations in the exchange rate offset it.

[3]These dynamic pressures are also at work in reverse when there are pressures for the price level to increase. But for increases, the pressures tend to reinforce the expansionary forces, and are usually seen as positive effects, especially when there is no fear of inflation.

- Financial panics, triggered by a decline in the value of financial assets, causing individuals and banks, who relied on those financial assets as collateral for loans, to require full payment on (to call in) those loans, which forces borrowers (mainly firms) to reduce production and lay off workers, decreasing aggregate demand further.

Each of these forces, which the standard model assumes away, works in an opposite direction to the standard effects that cause the quantity of aggregate demand to increase when the price level falls. If these dynamic forces are strong enough, aggregate demand will fall (shift in to the left) when the price level falls. In fact, for the *AD* curve to start a cumulative shifting back process, the price level doesn't even have to fall; there only has to be the *pressure* for the price level to fall. We will discuss these dynamic forces more in the chapter on financial crises and macro policy.

Shifts in the *AD* Curve

Next, let's consider what causes the *AD* curve to shift. A shift in the *AD* curve means that at every price level, total expenditures have changed. Anything other than the price level that changes the components of aggregate demand (consumption, investment, government spending, and net exports) will shift the *AD* curve. Five important shift factors of aggregate demand are foreign income, exchange rate fluctuations, the distribution of income, expectations, and government policies.

FOREIGN INCOME   A country is not an island unto itself. U.S. economic output is closely tied to the income of its major world trading partners. When our trading partners go into a recession, the demand for U.S. goods, and hence U.S. exports, will fall, causing the U.S. *AD* curve to shift in to the left. Similarly, a rise in foreign income leads to an increase in U.S. exports and a rightward shift of the U.S. *AD* curve.

Q-4 If a country's exchange rate rises, what happens to its *AD* curve?

EXCHANGE RATES   The currencies of various countries are connected through exchange rates. When a country's currency loses value relative to other currencies, its goods become more competitive compared to foreign goods. Foreign demand for domestic goods increases and domestic demand for foreign goods decreases as individuals shift their spending to domestic goods at home. Both these effects increase net exports and shift the *AD* curve out to the right. By the same reasoning, when a country's currency gains value, the *AD* curve shifts in the opposite direction. You can see these effects on the U.S.-Canadian border. In 2016, the U.S. dollar had a high value relative to the Canadian dollar, making Canadian goods cheaper for Americans. An iPad for $848 in the United States cost only $659 in Canada. This caused some Americans near the border to make buying trips to Canada.

DISTRIBUTION OF INCOME   Some people save more than others, and everyone's spending habits differ. Thus, as income distribution changes, so too will aggregate demand. One of the most important distributional effects concerns the distribution of income between wages and profits. Workers receive wage income and are more likely to spend the income they receive; firms' profits are distributed to stockholders or are retained by the firm. Since stockholders in the United States tend to be wealthy, and the wealthy save a greater portion of their income than the poor do, a higher portion of income received as profits will likely be saved. Assuming that not all saving is translated into investment, as the proportion of income going to profit increases, total expenditures are likely to fall, shifting the *AD* curve in to the left. Similarly, as wages (both as a proportion of total income and absolutely) increase, total expenditures are likely to rise, shifting the *AD* curve out to the right.

EXPECTATIONS   Another important shift factor of aggregate demand is expectations. Many different types of expectations can affect the *AD* curve. To give you an idea of the role of expectations, let's consider two expectational shift factors: expectations of future output and expectations of future prices. When businesspeople expect demand to be high in the future, they will want to increase their productive capacity; their investment demand, a component of aggregate demand, will increase. Thus, positive expectations about future demand will shift the *AD* curve out to the right.

Similarly, when consumers expect the economy to do well, they will be less worried about saving for the future, and they will spend more now—the *AD* curve will shift out to the right. Alternatively, if consumers expect the future to be gloomy, they will likely try to save for the future and will decrease their consumption expenditures. The *AD* curve will shift in to the left.

Another type of expectation that shifts the *AD* curve concerns expectations of future prices. If you expect the prices of goods to rise in the future, it pays to buy goods now that you might want in the future—before their prices rise. The current price level hasn't changed, but aggregate quantity demanded at that price level has increased, indicating a shift of the *AD* curve out to the right.

The effect of expectations of future price levels is seen more clearly in a hyperinflation. In most cases of hyperinflation, people rush out to spend their money quickly—to buy whatever they can to beat the price increase. So even though prices are rising, aggregate demand stays high because the rise in price creates an expectation of even higher prices, and thus the current high price is seen as a low price relative to the future. I said that an increase in expectations of inflation will "have a tendency to" rather than "definitely" shift the *AD* curve out to the right because those expectations of inflation are interrelated with a variety of other expectations. For example, an expectation of a rise in the price of goods you buy could be accompanied by an expectation of a fall in income, and that fall in income would work in the opposite direction, decreasing aggregate demand.

This interrelation of various types of expectations makes it very difficult to specify precisely what effect certain types of expectations have on the *AD* curve. But it does not eliminate the importance of expectations as shift factors. It simply means that we often aren't sure what the net effect of a change in expectations on aggregate demand will be.

MONETARY AND FISCAL POLICIES   One of the most important reasons why the aggregate demand curve has been so important in macro policy analysis is that often macro policy makers think that they can control it, at least to some degree. For example, if the government spends lots of money without increasing taxes, it shifts the *AD* curve out to the right; if the government raises taxes significantly and holds spending constant, consumers will have less disposable income and will reduce their expenditures, shifting the *AD* curve in to the left. Similarly, when the Federal Reserve Bank, the U.S. economy's central bank, expands the money supply, it can often lower interest rates, making it easier for both consumers and investors to borrow, increasing their spending, and thereby shifting the *AD* curve out to the right. This deliberate increase or decrease in aggregate demand to influence the level of income in the economy is what most policy makers mean by the term *macro policy*. Expansionary macro policy shifts the *AD* curve out to the right; contractionary macro policy shifts it in to the left.

MULTIPLIER EFFECTS OF SHIFT FACTORS   As I emphasized when I introduced the *AD* curve, you cannot treat the *AD* curve like a micro demand curve. This comes out most clearly when considering shifts in the curve caused by shift factors. The aggregate demand curve may shift by more than the amount of the initial shift factor because of the multiplier effect. The explanation is as follows: When government increases its spending, firms increase production, which leads to higher income. A fraction of that increase

Expectations of higher future income increase expenditures and shift the *AD* curve out.

Five important shift factors of *AD* are:

1. Foreign income.
2. Exchange rates.
3. The distribution of income.
4. Expectations.
5. Monetary and fiscal policies.

Deliberate shifting of the *AD* curve is what most policy makers mean by macro policy.

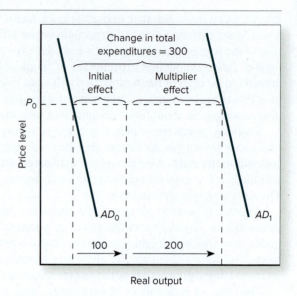

FIGURE 26-2 **Effect of a Shift Factor on the *AD* Curve**

The *AD* curve shifts out by more than the initial change in expenditures. In this example, exports increase by 100. The multiplier magnifies this shift, and the *AD* curve shifts out to the right by a multiple of 100, in this case by 300.

Change in total expenditures = 300

Initial effect

Multiplier effect

P_0

Price level

AD_0

AD_1

100

200

Real output

Q-5 If government spending increases by 20, by how much does the *AD* curve shift out?

in income is spent on more goods and services, shifting the *AD* curve even further out to the right. This leads firms to increase production again; income and expenditures also rise. Each round, the increase gets smaller and smaller until the increase becomes negligible. In the end the *AD* curve will have shifted by a multiple of the initial shift. Just how large that multiple is depends on how much the change in income affects spending in each round. Thus, in Figure 26-2, when an initial shift factor of aggregate demand is 100 and the multiplier is 3, the *AD* curve will shift out to the right by 300, three times the initial shift. The extra 200 shift is due to the multiplier effect.

To see that you are following the argument, consider the following two shifts: (1) a fall in the U.S. exchange rate, increasing net exports by 50, and (2) an increase in government spending of 100. Explain how the *AD* curve will shift in each of these cases and why that shift will be larger than the initial shift. If you are not sure about these explanations, review the multiplier effect discussion above.

The Aggregate Supply Curves

The other side of the aggregate economy is the supply side. We divide the supply side into short-run and long-run components. Let's first consider the short-run supply curve.

The Short-Run Aggregate Supply Curve

The **short-run aggregate supply (*SAS*) curve** is *a curve that specifies how a shift in the aggregate demand curve affects the price level and real output in the short run, other things constant*. A standard *SAS* curve is shown in Figure 26-3.

THE SLOPE OF THE *SAS* CURVE　As you can see, the *SAS* curve is upward-sloping, which means that in the short run, other things constant, an increase in output is accompanied by a rise in the price level. That is, when aggregate demand increases, the price level—the composite of all prices—rises. The shape of the *SAS* curve reflects two different types of markets in our economy: auction markets (which are the markets represented by the supply/demand model) and posted-price markets (in which prices are set by the producers and change only infrequently).

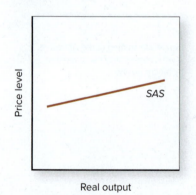

FIGURE 26-3 **The Short-Run Aggregate Supply Curve**

Price level

SAS

Real output

Why Are Prices Inflexible?

Why do firms adjust production instead of price? A number of reasons have been put forward by economists. One study by a group of economists led by Princeton economist Alan Blinder surveyed firms to find out which reasons firms believed were most important. The survey choices included strategic pricing, cost-based pricing rules, and implicit contracts.

1. **Strategic pricing.** About 90 percent of final goods markets in the United States are markets in which only a few major firms compete, each taking each other's reactions into account in their decisions. Although, under U.S. law, firms cannot get together and decide on a pricing strategy for the industry, they can informally coordinate their pricing procedures. If all firms can implicitly agree to hold their prices up when faced with decreased demand, they are not violating the law and will be better off than they would be if they acted in an uncoordinated fashion.

   They also won't increase prices when they experience an increase in demand because they fear that doing so will undermine the coordinated pricing strategy with other firms or they will lose market share when other firms don't raise prices.

   This is not to say that the U.S. economy is not competitive. Ask any businessperson and he or she will tell you that it is highly competitive. But firms often compete on fronts other than price.

2. **Cost-based pricing rules.** Strategic pricing is maintained by firms' tendency to use cost-based pricing rules. In a cost-plus-markup pricing procedure, firms set prices based on the costs of production. For a majority of firms, the most important costs are labor costs, which tend to be fixed by long-term wage contracts between workers and employers. (Unions, for example, typically negotiate wage contracts for three-year periods.) Thus, labor costs do not change with changes in demand, and, following a cost-plus-markup strategy, neither do prices.

3. **Implicit contracts.** Most firms have ongoing relationships with their customers. That means that they don't want to antagonize them. They have found that one way to avoid antagonizing customers is not to take advantage of them even when they could. In the Blinder survey, firms felt that they had implicit contracts with their customers to raise prices only when their costs changed, or when market conditions changed substantially.

The combination of these reasons leads to a large segment of the economy in which the prices do not significantly change as demand changes. For that reason, we generally don't see big changes in the overall price level. Of course, if costs, especially labor costs, start rising significantly, then prices will rise too. To the degree that demand changes affect costs, prices will respond, but, as a first approximation, it is generally acceptable to say that the price level does not significantly move in response to demand. That's why the short-run aggregate supply curve is not very steep.

In markets where prices are set by the interaction between buyers and sellers, none of whom have enough market power to set prices, there is little question why prices rise when demand increases as long as the supply curve for firms in the market is upward-sloping. But these auction markets make up only a small percentage of final goods markets. (They are much more common in markets for resources such as oil or farm products.) In most final goods markets, sellers set a price for their goods and buyers take these prices as given. These posted-price markets comprise 90 percent of the total final goods markets. In posted-price markets, firms set prices as a markup over costs. For example, if the markup is 40 percent and the cost of production is $10 per unit, the firm would set a price of $14.

Posted-price markets are often called **quantity-adjusting markets**—*markets in which firms respond to changes in demand primarily by changing production instead of changing their prices.* It would be wrong, however, to assume that prices in these markets are totally unresponsive to changes in demand. When demand increases, some firms will take the opportunity to raise their prices slightly, increasing their markup, and when demand falls, firms have a tendency to lower their prices slightly, decreasing their markup. This tendency to change markups as aggregate demand changes contributes to the upward slope of the *SAS* curve. So, the two reasons the *SAS* curve slopes upward are: (1) upward-sloping supply curves in auction markets and (2) firms' tendency to increase their markup when demand increases.

One reason I did not give for the upward slope of the *SAS* curve is changes in costs of production. That's because along an *SAS* curve, all other things, including input prices, are assumed to remain constant. Increases in input prices shift the *SAS* curve.

SHIFTS IN THE *SAS* CURVE   Notice that in the definition of the *SAS* curve, we have assumed that other things remain constant. As discussed above, this does not mean that other things *will* remain constant. It simply means that changes in other things, such as input prices, shift the *SAS* curve. For example, if input prices rise, the *SAS* curve shifts up; if input prices fall, the *SAS* curve shifts down. So a change in input prices, such as wages, is a shift factor of aggregate supply. An important reason why wages change is expectations of inflation. If workers expect prices to rise by 2 percent, they are likely to ask for at least a 2 percent rise in wages simply to keep up with inflation and maintain their real wage. If they expect the price level to fall by 2 percent, they are far more likely to be happy with their current wage. So the expectation of inflation is a shift factor that works through wages.

Another shift factor of aggregate supply is a change in the productivity of the factors of production such as labor. An increase in productivity, by reducing the amount of inputs required for a given amount of output, reduces input costs per unit of output and shifts the *SAS* curve down. A fall in productivity shifts the *SAS* curve up.

Two other shift factors are changes in import prices of final goods and changes in excise and sales taxes. Import prices are a shift factor because they are a component of an economy's price level. When import prices rise, the *SAS* curve shifts up; when import prices fall, the *SAS* curve shifts down. By raising the cost of goods, higher sales taxes shift the *SAS* curve up, and lower sales taxes shift the *SAS* curve down.

In summary, anything that changes production costs will be a shift factor of supply. Such factors include:

- Changes in input prices.
- Productivity.
- Import prices.
- Excise and sales taxes.

Economists spend a lot of time tracking these shift factors because they are central to whether the economy will have an inflation problem. Two of these—the wage component of input prices and labor productivity—are followed with special care because labor costs make up about two-thirds of total production costs.

The rule of thumb economists use when estimating how much the *SAS* curve will shift is that it will shift by the percentage change in wages and other factor prices minus changes in productivity. For example, if productivity rises by 3 percent and wages rise by 7 percent, we can expect the price level to rise by 4 percent for a given level of output. I show a shift up in the *SAS* curve in Figure 26-4. If wages and productivity rise by equal percentages, the price level will remain constant. If wages and other factor prices rise by less than the increase in productivity, the price level can fall, as recently happened in Japan. The relationship can be written as follows:

% change in the price level = % change in wages − % change in productivity

---

The two reasons the *SAS* curve slopes upward are:

1. Upward-sloping supply curves in auction markets.
2. Firms' tendency to increase their markup when demand increases.

Changes in input prices cause a shift in the *SAS* curve.

FIGURE 26-4   **Input Price Rise and the *SAS* Curve**

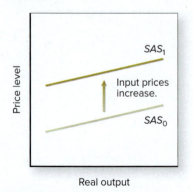

In the real world, we see shifts in the *SAS* curve in many areas. In 2007 and into mid-2008 oil prices more than doubled. That led to a sharp rise in the producer prices and a significant rise in factor prices, causing the *SAS* curve to shift up. Then, starting in 2014, oil and other commodity prices fell, causing the *SAS* curve to shift down. Another example occurred in England from 2016 to 2017 when the value of its currency, the pound, fell by 15 percent after the referendum to leave the European Union. That caused the price of imports measured in pounds to increase, which shifted its *SAS* curve up.

The Long-Run Aggregate Supply Curve

The final curve that makes up the *AS/AD* model is the **long-run aggregate supply (*LAS*) curve**—*a curve that shows the long-run relationship between output and the price level.* Whereas the *SAS* curve holds input prices constant, no prices are assumed held constant on the *LAS* curve. The position of the *LAS* curve is determined by potential output—the amount of goods and services an economy can produce when both labor and capital are fully employed. Figure 26-5(a) shows an *LAS* curve.

Notice that the *LAS* curve is vertical. Since at potential output all resources are being fully utilized, a rise in the price level means that the prices of goods and factors of production, including wages, rise. Consider it this way: If all prices doubled, including your wage, your real income would not change. Since potential output is unaffected by the price level, the *LAS* curve is vertical.

A RANGE FOR POTENTIAL OUTPUT AND THE *LAS* CURVE   Because our estimates of potential output are inexact, precisely where to draw the *LAS* curve is generally in debate. To understand policy debates, it is helpful to consider potential output to be a range of values. This range is bounded by a high level of potential output and a low level of potential output, as Figure 26-5(b) shows. The *LAS* curve can be thought of as being in the middle of that range.

This range is important because how close actual output (the position of the economy on the *SAS* curve) is to potential output is a key determinant of whether the *SAS* curve is expected to shift up or down. At points on the *SAS* curve to the left of the *LAS* curve (such as point *A*), resources are likely to be underutilized and we would expect factor prices (prices of inputs to production) to fall and, other things equal, the *SAS*

Q-6 If wages rise by 4 percent and productivity rises by 1 percent, by how much does the price level change?

The *SAS* curve holds input prices constant; no prices are assumed held constant on the *LAS* curve.

🖳 **Web Note 26.2**

Unemployed Machines

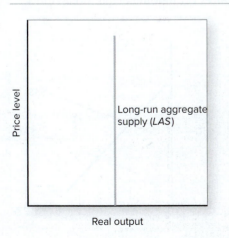

(a)

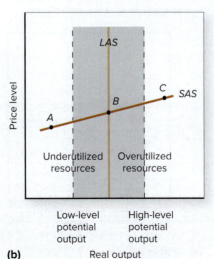

(b)

FIGURE 26-5 (A AND B)

The Long-Run Aggregate Supply Curve

The long-run aggregate supply curve shows the output that an economy can produce when both labor and capital are fully employed. It is vertical because at potential output a rise in the price level means that all prices, including input prices, rise. Available resources do not rise and thus neither does potential output.

curve to shift down. At points to the right of the *LAS* curve (such as point *C*), we would expect factor prices to be bid up and, other things equal, the *SAS* curve to shift up. Moreover, the further actual output is from potential output, the greater the pressure we would expect on factor prices to rise or fall. At the point of intersection between the *SAS* curve and the *LAS* curve (point *B*), other things equal, factor prices have no pressure to rise or fall.

In reality, whether factor prices will rise or fall in response to a change in demand is often in debate. That debate reflects the different estimates of potential output. Given the uncertainty of measured potential output, we would expect there to be a debate about whether the *SAS* curve will be shifting up or down. We will discuss these issues later. For now, all I want you to remember is that the *LAS* curve is an abstraction that reduces what is actually a range of potential output into a single value.

> Because the position of the *LAS* curve is determined by potential output, it shifts for the same reasons that potential output shifts.

SHIFTS IN THE *LAS* CURVE   Because the position of the *LAS* curve is determined by potential output, it shifts for the same reasons that potential output shifts: changes in capital, available resources, growth-compatible institutions, technology, and entrepreneurship. Increases in any of these increase potential output and shift the *LAS* curve out to the right. Decreases in any of these reduce potential output and shift the *LAS* curve in to the left. The position of the *LAS* curve plays an important role in determining long-run equilibrium and in determining whether policy should focus on long-run or short-run issues.

Equilibrium in the Aggregate Economy

Now that we have introduced the *SAS, AD,* and *LAS* curves, we'll consider short-run and long-run equilibrium and how changes in the curves affect those equilibria. I start with the short run.

In the short run, equilibrium in the economy is where the short-run aggregate supply curve and the aggregate demand curve intersect. Thus, one short-run equilibrium is shown by point *E* in Figure 26-6(a). If the *AD* curve shifts out to the right, from AD_0 to AD_1, equilibrium will shift from point *E* to point *F*. The price level will rise to P_1 and output will increase to Y_1. A decrease in aggregate demand will shift output and the price level down.

Figure 26-6(b) shows the effect on equilibrium of a shift up in the *SAS* curve. Initially equilibrium is at point *E*. An upward shift in the *SAS* curve from SAS_0 to SAS_1 increases the price level from P_0 to P_2 and reduces equilibrium output from Y_0 to Y_2.

FIGURE 26-6 (A AND B)

Equilibrium in the *AS/AD* Model

Short-run equilibrium is where the short-run aggregate supply and aggregate demand curves intersect. Point *E* in **(a)** is one equilibrium; **(a)** also shows how a shift in the aggregate demand curve out to the right changes equilibrium from *E* to *F*, increasing output from Y_0 to Y_1 and increasing price level from P_0 to P_1. In **(b)** a shift up in the short-run aggregate supply curve changes equilibrium from *E* to *G*.

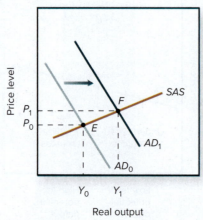

(a) Shift in *AD*

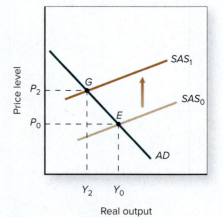

(b) Shift in *SAS*

FIGURE 26-7 (A AND B) Long-Run Equilibrium

Long-run equilibrium is where the *LAS* and *AD* curves intersect. Point *E* is long-run equilibrium. In (**a**) you can see how a shift in the aggregate demand curve changes equilibrium from *E* to *H*, increasing the price level from P_0 to P_1 but leaving output unchanged. The economy is in both short-run and long-run equilibrium when all three curves intersect in the same location. In (**b**) you can see the adjustment from recessionary and inflationary gaps to long-run equilibrium.

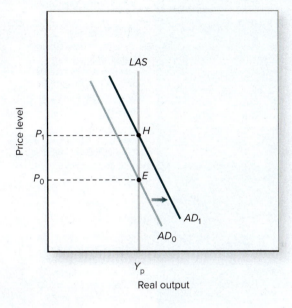

(a) **Shift in AD**

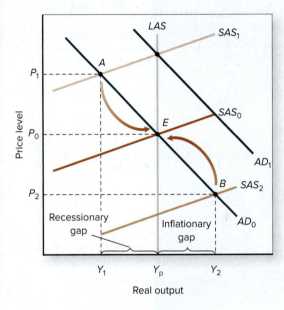

(b) **Movement to Long-Run Equilibrium**

Long-run equilibrium is determined by the intersection of the *AD* curve and the *LAS* curve, as shown by point *E* in Figure 26-7(a). Since in the long run output is determined by the position of the *LAS* curve, which is at potential output Y_p, the aggregate demand curve can determine only the price level; it does not affect the level of real output. Thus, as shown in Figure 26-7(a), when aggregate demand increases from AD_0 to AD_1, the price level rises (from P_0 to P_1) but output does not change. When aggregate demand decreases, the price level falls and output remains at potential. In the long run, output is fixed at potential output and the price level is variable, so aggregate output is determined not by aggregate demand but by potential output. Aggregate demand determines the price level.

> Long-run equilibrium is determined by the intersection of the *AD* curve and the *LAS* curve.

Integrating the Short-Run and Long-Run Frameworks

To complete our analysis, we have to relate the long run and short run. We start with the economy in both long-run and short-run equilibrium. As you can see in Figure 26-7(b), at point *E*, with output Y_p and price level P_0, the economy is in both a long-run equilibrium and a short-run equilibrium, since at point *E* the *AD* curve and *SAS* curve intersect at the economy's *LAS* curve. That is the situation economists hope for—that aggregate demand grows at just the same rate as potential output, so that growth and unemployment are at their target rates, with no, or minimal, inflation. In the conventional interpretation in the late 1990s and much of the early 2000s, the U.S. economy was in just such a position—potential output was increasing at the same rate that aggregate demand was increasing; unemployment was low, as was inflation.

> **Q-7** If the *SAS, AD,* and *LAS* curves intersect at the same point and wages are constant, what is likely to happen to output and the price level?

A Review of the *AS/AD* Model

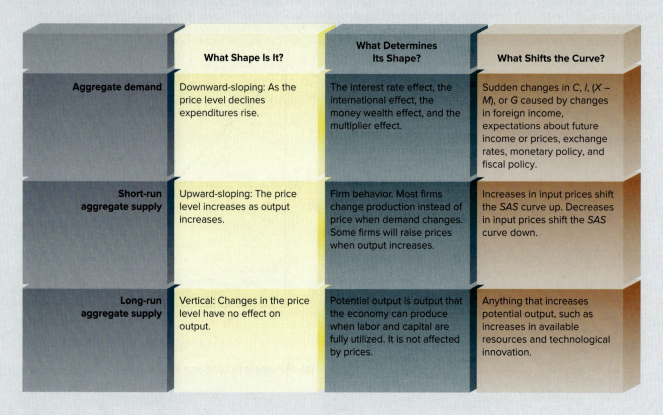

	What Shape Is It?	What Determines Its Shape?	What Shifts the Curve?
Aggregate demand	Downward-sloping: As the price level declines expenditures rise.	The interest rate effect, the international effect, the money wealth effect, and the multiplier effect.	Sudden changes in C, I, $(X - M)$, or G caused by changes in foreign income, expectations about future income or prices, exchange rates, monetary policy, and fiscal policy.
Short-run aggregate supply	Upward-sloping: The price level increases as output increases.	Firm behavior. Most firms change production instead of price when demand changes. Some firms will raise prices when output increases.	Increases in input prices shift the SAS curve up. Decreases in input prices shift the SAS curve down.
Long-run aggregate supply	Vertical: Changes in the price level have no effect on output.	Potential output is output that the economy can produce when labor and capital are fully utilized. It is not affected by prices.	Anything that increases potential output, such as increases in available resources and technological innovation.

The Recessionary Gap

Alas, the economy is not always at that point *E*. An economy at point *A* in Figure 26-7(b) is in a situation where the quantity of aggregate demand is below potential output and not all the resources in the economy are being fully used. The distance $Y_p - Y_1$ shows the amount of output that is not being produced but could be. This distance is often referred to as a **recessionary gap,** *the amount by which equilibrium output is below potential output.*

If the economy remains at this low level of output for a long time, costs and wages would tend to fall because there would be an excess supply of factors of production. As costs and wages fall, the price level also falls. Assuming the standard price-level effects are sufficiently strong, the short-run aggregate supply curve would shift down (from SAS_1 to SAS_0) until eventually the long-run and short-run equilibria would be reached at point *E*. But generally in our economy that does not happen.[4] Long before that happens, either the economy picks up on its own or the government introduces policies to expand output. That's why we seldom see declines in the price level. If the

Q-8 Demonstrate graphically both the short-run and long-run *AS/AD* equilibrium with a recessionary gap.

---

[4]If, as happened in the Great Depression in the 1930s and in Japan in the early 2000s, the economy stays below its potential output long enough, we would likely see the price level fall.

government expands aggregate demand, or some other shift factor expands aggregate demand, the *AD* curve shifts out to the right (to AD_1) eliminating the recessionary gap and keeping the price level constant.

The Inflationary Gap

An economy at point *B* in Figure 26-7(b) demonstrates a case where the short-run equilibrium is at a higher income than the economy's potential output. In this case, economists say that the economy has an **inflationary gap**—*aggregate expenditures above potential output that exist at the current price level, shown by* $Y_2 - Y_p$. Output cannot remain at Y_2 for long because the economy's resources are being used beyond their potential. Factor prices will rise and the *SAS* curve will shift up from SAS_2 to SAS_0; the new equilibrium is at point *E*.

When income exceeds potential output, there is an inflationary gap.

The Economy beyond Potential

How can resources be used beyond their potential? By overutilizing them. Consider the resources you put into classwork. Suppose that your potential is a B+. If you stay up all night studying and cram in extra reading during mealtimes, you could earn an A. But you can't keep up that effort for long. Eventually you'll get tired. The same is true for production. Extra shifts can be added and machinery can be run longer periods, but eventually the workers will become exhausted and the machinery will wear out. Output will have to return to its potential.

The result of this inflationary gap will be a bidding up of factor prices and a rise in costs for firms. When an economy is below potential, firms can hire additional factors of production without increasing production costs. Once the economy reaches its potential output, however, that is no longer possible. If a firm is to increase its factors of production, it must lure resources away from other firms. It will do so by offering higher wages and prices. But the firm facing a loss of its resources will likely respond by increasing its wages and other prices it pays to its employees and to other suppliers.

As firms compete for resources, their costs rise beyond increases in productivity, shifting up the *SAS* curve. This means that once an economy's potential output is reached, the price level tends to rise. In fact, economists sometimes look to see whether the price level has begun to rise before deciding where potential output is. Thus, in the late 1990s through 2018, economists kept increasing their estimates of potential output because the price level did not rise even as the economy approached, and exceeded, what they previously thought was its potential output.

If the economy is operating above potential, the *SAS* curve will shift up until the inflationary gap is eliminated. That, however, is usually not what happens. Either the economy slows down on its own or the government introduces aggregate demand policy to contract output and eliminate the inflationary gap.

©Stockbyte/Getty Images RF

If aggregate expenditures are above potential output, then increased demand for labor would put upward pressure on wages and subsequently on the overall level of prices.

Aggregate Demand Policy

A primary reason for government policy makers' interest in the *AS/AD* model is their ability to shift the *AD* curve with policy. As I mentioned above, they can do this with monetary or fiscal policy. Monetary policy involves the Federal Reserve Bank changing the money supply and interest rates. (Understanding the process requires a knowledge of the financial sector, which will be discussed at length in later chapters.) In this chapter I'll concentrate on *fiscal policy*—the deliberate change in either government spending or taxes to stimulate or slow down the economy. Fiscal policy is often discussed in terms of the government budget deficit (government expenditures less government revenue). If aggregate income is too low (actual income is below potential income), the appropriate fiscal policy is expansionary fiscal policy: Increase the

Fiscal policy is the deliberate change in either government spending or taxes to stimulate or slow down the economy.

FIGURE 26-8 (A AND B)   **Fiscal Policy**

Expansionary fiscal policy can bring an economy out of a recessionary gap, as shown in (**a**). If an economy is in an inflationary gap, contractionary fiscal policy can reduce real output to prevent inflation, as shown in (**b**).

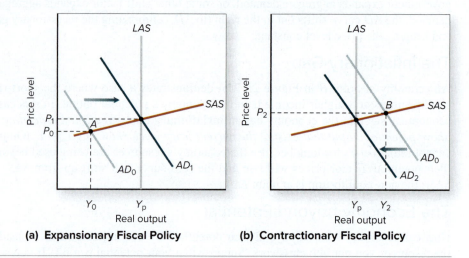

(a) **Expansionary Fiscal Policy**   (b) **Contractionary Fiscal Policy**

deficit by decreasing taxes or increasing government spending. Expansionary fiscal policy shifts the *AD* curve out to the right. If aggregate income is too high (actual income is above potential income), the appropriate fiscal policy is contractionary fiscal policy: Decrease the deficit by increasing taxes or decreasing government spending. Contractionary fiscal policy shifts the *AD* curve in to the left.

Let's go through a couple of examples. Say the economy is in a recessionary gap at point *A* in Figure 26-8(a). To eliminate the recessionary gap, government needs to implement expansionary fiscal policy. The appropriate fiscal policy would be to cut taxes or increase government spending, letting the multiplier augment those effects so that the *AD* curve shifts out to AD_1. This would raise the price level slightly but would eliminate the recessionary gap. Alternatively, say the economy is in an inflationary gap at point *B* in Figure 26-8(b). To prevent the inflation caused by the upward shift of the *SAS* curve, the appropriate fiscal policy is to increase taxes or cut government spending. Either of these actions will shift the *AD* curve in to AD_2. This lowers the price level slightly and eliminates the inflationary gap. So the best way to picture fiscal policy is as a policy designed to shift the *AD* curve to keep output at potential.

Q-9 If politicians suddenly raise government expenditures, and the economy is well below potential output, what will happen to prices and real income?

Some Additional Policy Examples

Now that we've been through the model, let's give you some practice with it by making you an adviser to the president. He comes to you for some advice. Unemployment is 12 percent and there is no inflation. History suggests that the economy is well below its potential output, so there is no need to worry about increasing factor prices. What policy would you recommend?

Pause for answer

The answer I hope you gave was expansionary fiscal policy, shifting the *AD* curve out from AD_0 to AD_1 to its potential income, as in Figure 26-9(a).

Now let's try a different scenario. Unemployment is 4 percent and it is believed that that 4 percent is the *target rate of unemployment*—the rate of unemployment that is consistent with potential output. But measures of consumer optimism suggest that a large rise in consumer expenditures is likely. What policy would you recommend?

Pause for answer

The answer I hope you gave is contractionary fiscal policy to counteract the expected rise in the *AD* curve before it occurs and prevent the economy from creating an

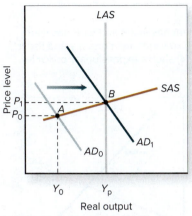

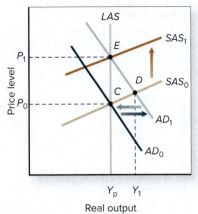

(a) Expansionary Fiscal Policy

(b) Economy above Potential

inflationary gap. What would happen without that fiscal policy is shown in Figure 26-9(b). The economy is initially at point *C,* where the price level is P_0 and output is Y_p. In the absence of offsetting policy, the increase in expenditures along with the multiplier would move the economy to point *D* at a level of output (Y_1) above potential, creating an inflationary gap. If left alone, factor prices will rise, shifting the *SAS* curve up until it reaches SAS_1. The price level would rise to P_1 and the real output would return to Y_p, point *E.* But, of course, that didn't happen because you recommended a policy of cutting government spending or raising taxes so that the *AD* curve shifts back to AD_0, keeping the equilibrium at point *C,* not point *E,* and avoiding any rise in prices. The economy remains at potential output at a constant price level, P_0.

To give you an idea of how fiscal policy has worked in the real world, we'll look at three examples: the effect of wartime spending in the 1940s, the recent recession in 2008, and fiscal policy in 2018.

FISCAL POLICY IN WORLD WAR II   In the 1940s the focus of U.S. policy switched from the Depression to fighting World War II. Fighting a war requires transferring civilian production to war production, so economists' attention turned to how to do so. Taxes went up enormously, but government expenditures rose far more, which resulted in a large government deficit. The result can be seen in Figure 26-10(a). The *AD* curve shifts out to the right by more than the increase in the deficit. As predicted, the U.S. economy expanded enormously in response to the expansionary fiscal policy that accompanied the war. One thing should bother you about this episode: If the economy exceeded its potential output, shouldn't the short-run aggregate supply curve have started to shift up, causing a serious inflation problem? It didn't because the wartime expansion was accompanied by wage and price controls, which prevented significant price-level increases, and by rationing.

Web Note 26.3

War Bonds

EXPANSIONARY POLICY DURING AND AFTER THE 2008 RECESSION   As a second example, let's consider the economy in 2008 and 2009, when output fell and unemployment rose. Policy makers and economists alike believed that the economy was going into a severe depression. The situation is shown in Figure 26-10(b). Aggregate demand had fallen from AD_0 to AD_1 and output was significantly below potential. The government went all out and ran extremely expansionary monetary and fiscal policy, shifting the *AD* curve out to AD_2 and preventing the economy from falling into a deeper recession, or even a depression.

FIGURE 26-10 (A AND B)   War Finance: Expansionary Fiscal Policy

During wars, government budget deficits have risen significantly. As they have, unemployment has fallen and GDP has risen enormously. You can see this in (a). The graph in (b) shows the situation in 2008 and 2009. Expansionary monetary and fiscal policy didn't bring the economy back to what was believed to be its potential. The graph in (c) shows expansionary policy in 2018 despite the reality that the economy did not call for it.

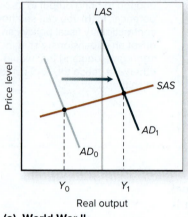

(a) World War II

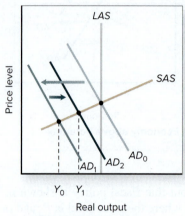

(b) 2008–2009 Recession

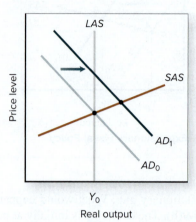

(c) Expansionary Policy in 2018

EXPANSIONARY POLICY IN 2018 As a third and final example let's take the U.S. economy in 2018. The economy kept growing, albeit slowly, after the 2008 recession. By 2018, the U.S. unemployment rate had fallen to about 4 percent, at or below what most economists saw as the target rate. Thus, the economy was seen as operating at, or possibly beyond, potential. Based on the *AS/AD* model, as shown in Figure 26-10(c), with the economy at potential output Y_0, a neutral fiscal policy was called for. That's not the policy the government implemented. Instead, it instituted large tax cuts and spending increases, shifting the *AD* curve out from AD_0 to AD_1; its fiscal policy was highly expansionary not because the economy called for it, but because politics did. This example conveys an important lesson about fiscal policy that we will discuss in later chapters. Often, probably even most often, policy is guided by political goals, not by economists' models.

Limitations of the *AS/AD* Model

The *AS/AD* model is simple and clear, which is why it has become the workhorse model of macro policy makers. However, these advantages come at a cost of assuming away many possible feedback effects that can significantly affect the macroeconomy and lead to quite different conclusions than the standard *AS/AD* model gives. So an important limitation of the *AS/AD* model is that it does not include many important feedback effects.

How Feedback Effects Complicate the *AS/AD* Model

The *AS/AD* model presents price-level fluctuations as being significantly more self-correcting than many macroeconomists believe they are, especially in response to decreases in aggregate demand. In Figure 26-11, I demonstrate how these feedback effects can cause serious problems for the economy, as they did in the recession the U.S. economy fell into in 2008.

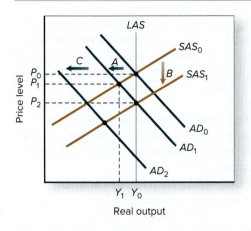

FIGURE 26-11 **Feedback Effects and the AS/AD Model**

The feedback effects of a declining price level on aggregate demand mean that as the SAS curve shifts down to return the economy to equilibrium, the aggregate demand curve shifts back to the left, leading the economy away from equilibrium.

The crisis began with the housing market turning from a booming market with housing prices rising quickly to a declining market with housing prices falling. Looking at the model in Figure 26-11, this would lead to a fall in aggregate demand back to the left from AD_0 to AD_1. One would think that the result of that decline in aggregate demand would be an initial fall in output from Y_0 to Y_1 and in the price level from P_0 to P_1 (arrow A). The SAS curve would then shift down from SAS_0 to SAS_1, bringing prices down to P_2 and the output level back up to Y_0 (arrow B). Deflation would move the economy along the aggregate demand curve and help bring the economy back to potential output. So the recession would be eliminated by deflation.

Unfortunately, a falling price level might create expectations that aggregate output will fall further, which will lead people to cut back on spending and firms to cut back on production, shifting the AD curve in to the left, to AD_2 (arrow C) in Figure 26-11. Aggregate demand may shift back by more than the falling price level increased the quantity of aggregate demand. The entire process may become a self-fulfilling vicious circle in which both prices and output continue to fall, leading the economy into a deep depression. It was fear of that vicious circle that led almost all economists to support expansionary fiscal policy in 2008.

Additional Complications That the AS/AD Model Misses

The AS/AD model makes the analysis of the aggregate economy look easy. All you do is determine where the economy is relative to its potential output and, based on that, choose the appropriate policy to shift the AD curve. Alas, it's much harder than that. Let me summarize some of the complications.

Policy is more complicated than the AS/AD model makes it seem.

PROBLEMS OF IMPLEMENTATION First, implementing fiscal policy—changing government spending and taxes—is a slow legislative process. Government spending and taxing decisions are generally made for political, not economic, reasons. Thus, there is no guarantee that government will do what economists say is necessary. And even if it does, the changes often cannot be completed in a timely fashion.

PROBLEMS OF MEASURING POTENTIAL OUTPUT A second problem is that we have no way of measuring potential output, so when we increase aggregate demand, we can't determine whether the SAS curve will be shifting up. Thus, the key to applying the policy is to know the location of the LAS curve, which is vertical at the economy's potential output. Unfortunately, we have no way of knowing that with certainty. Fortunately, we do have ways to get a rough idea of where it is.

Q-10 If politicians suddenly raise government expenditures and the economy is above potential income, what will happen to prices and real income in the long run?

Because inflation accelerates when an economy is operating above potential, one way of estimating potential output is to estimate the rate of unemployment below which inflation has begun to accelerate in the past. This is the target rate of unemployment. We can then estimate potential output by calculating output at the target rate of unemployment and adjusting for productivity growth. Unfortunately the target rate of unemployment fluctuates and is difficult to predict.

THE PROBLEMS OF OTHER INTERRELATIONSHIPS

A third problem was mentioned above. There are many other possible interrelationships in the economy that the model does not take into account. One is the effect of falling asset prices and a falling price level on expectations of aggregate demand.

When there are pressures for the price level to fall, there are also generally strong pressures for asset prices to fall. This fall in asset prices has three effects on aggregate demand. First, while the fall in asset prices is in part caused by falling expectations about the growth potential of the economy, the causation can also go the other way: The decrease in asset prices can decrease expectations about the growth of the economy. The expectation of lower economic growth tends to shift the *AD* curve back to the left. Second, falling asset prices decrease people's perception of the value of their wealth, which decreases aggregate demand. Third, falling asset prices potentially undermine the stability of the financial system, which can make production impossible since the financial system is essential for production. This last effect undermines aggregate production and shifts the *SAS* curve to the left. Running an economy with a financial system that has stopped working is a bit like running an automobile without oil. It can bring an economy to a sudden halt.

THE PROBLEM OF DYNAMIC INSTABILITY

Because of these effects, as we discussed earlier, the aggregate economy can become dynamically unstable, so a shock to the economy can set in motion a set of changes that will not be automatically self-correcting. Instead, falling output and asset prices lead to a vicious circle in which falling output and falling prices bring about further declines. The major concern of macro policy economists in 2008 and early 2009 was that the U.S. economy had fallen into precisely such a vicious circle.

Reality and Models

In summary, there are two ways to think about the effectiveness of fiscal policy: in the model and in reality. Models are great, and simple models, such as the one I've presented in this book that you can understand intuitively, are even greater. Put in the numbers and out comes the answer. Questions based on such models make great exam questions. But don't think that policies that work in a model will necessarily work in the real world.

The effectiveness of fiscal policy in reality depends on the government's ability to perceive a problem and to react appropriately to it. The essence of fiscal policy is government changing its taxes and its spending to offset any fluctuation that would occur in other autonomous expenditures, thereby keeping the economy at its potential level of income. If the model is a correct description of the economy, and if the government can act fast enough and change its taxes and spending in a *countercyclical* way, recessions can be prevented. This type of management of the economy is called **countercyclical fiscal policy**—*fiscal policy in which the government offsets any change in aggregate expenditures that would create a business cycle.* The term **fine-tuning** is used to describe such *fiscal policy designed to keep the economy always at its target or potential level of income.* With fine-tuning, the government responds to problems before they happen, and the aggregate economy runs smoothly.

A counter cyclical fiscal policy designed to keep the economy always at its target or potential level of income is called fine-tuning.

Today almost all economists agree the government is not capable of fine-tuning the economy. The modern debate is whether it is up to any tuning of the economy at all.

Almost all economists agree the government is not capable of fine-tuning the economy.

Conclusion

Let's conclude the chapter with a brief summary. In the 1930s macroeconomics developed as Classical economists' interest in growth and supply-side issues shifted to Keynesian economists' interest in business cycles and demand-side issues. To capture the issues about the effect of aggregate demand on the economy, economists developed the *AS/AD* model.

The *AS/AD* model summarizes the expected effects that shifts in aggregate supply and aggregate demand have on output and the price level. In the short run, outward shifts in the *AD* curve cause real output and the price level to rise. Inward shifts cause the opposite. If the economy is beyond potential output and the *LAS* curve, the *SAS* curve will shift up, causing the price level to increase and real output to decrease, until real output falls back to potential. The long-run equilibrium is where aggregate demand intersects the *LAS* curve. In the model, the government can, through fiscal policy, shift the *AD* curve in or out, thereby achieving the desired level of real output, as long as that desired level does not exceed potential output.

Unfortunately, potential output is hard to estimate, and implementing fiscal policy in a timely fashion is difficult, making macroeconomic policy more an art than a science.

Macro policy is more an art than a science.

Summary

- The key idea of the Keynesian *AS/AD* model is that in the short run the economy can deviate from potential output. The paradox of thrift is an important reason why. (*LO26-1*)

- The *AS/AD* model consists of the aggregate demand curve, the short-run aggregate supply curve, and the long-run aggregate supply curve. (*LO26-1*)

- The aggregate demand curve slopes downward because of the interest rate effect, the international effect, the money wealth effect, and the multiplier effect. (*LO26-2*)

- The short-run aggregate supply (*SAS*) curve is upward-sloping because, while for the most part firms in the United States adjust production to meet demand instead of changing price, some firms will raise prices when demand increases. (*LO26-3*)

- The long-run aggregate supply (*LAS*) curve is vertical at potential output. (*LO26-3*)

- The *LAS* curve shifts out when available resources, capital, labor, technology, and/or growth-compatible institutions increase. (*LO26-3*)

- Short-run equilibrium is where the *SAS* and *AD* curves intersect. Long-run equilibrium is where the *AD* and *LAS* curves intersect. (*LO26-4*)

- Aggregate demand management policy attempts to influence the level of output in the economy by influencing aggregate demand and relying on the multiplier to expand any policy-induced change in aggregate demand. (*LO26-4*)

- Fiscal policy—the change in government spending or taxes—works by providing a deliberate counter-shock to offset unexpected shocks to the economy. (*LO26-4*)

- A falling price level can have dynamic feedback effects on aggregate demand, perhaps more than offsetting the effect of the falling price level on the quantity of aggregate demand. (*LO26-5*)

- Macroeconomic policy is difficult to conduct because: (1) implementing fiscal policy is a slow process, (2) we don't really know where potential output is, (3) there are interrelationships not included in the model, and (4) the economy can become dynamically unstable. (*LO26-5*)

- We must estimate potential output by looking at past levels of potential output and by looking at where the price level begins to rise. (*LO26-5*)

Key Terms

aggregate demand (*AD*)
  curve
countercyclical fiscal policy
deflation
equilibrium output
fine-tuning

fiscal policy
inflationary gap
interest rate effect
international effect
long-run aggregate
    supply (*LAS*) curve

monetary policy
money wealth effect
multiplier effect
paradox of thrift
potential output
quantity-adjusting markets

recessionary gap
short-run aggregate
   supply (*SAS*) curve

Questions and Exercises   connect

1. According to Keynesians how could the economy's output deviate from its potential? *(LO26-1)*

2. Why might deflation be a problem for an economy? *(LO26-1)*

3. Why does the paradox of thrift suggest that government needs to intervene in a recession? *(LO26-1)*

4. Why, in principle, would one expect the *AD* curve to be vertical? *(LO26-2)*

5. Explain how a rise in the price level affects aggregate quantity demanded with the: *(LO26-2)*
   a. Interest rate effect.
   b. International effect.
   c. Money wealth effect.

6. What are five factors that cause the *AD* curve to shift? *(LO26-2)*

7. What dynamic feedback effects can offset the interest rate, international, and money wealth effects? *(LO26-2)*

8. What will likely happen to the slope or position of the *AD* curve in the following circumstances? *(LO26-2)*
   a. The exchange rate changes from fixed to flexible.
   b. A fall in the price level doesn't make people feel richer.
   c. A fall in the price level creates expectations of a further-falling price level.
   d. Income is redistributed from rich people to poor people.
   e. Autonomous exports increase by 20.
   f. Government spending decreases by 10.

9. What are two factors that cause the *SAS* curve to shift? *(LO26-3)*

10. What will likely happen to the *SAS* curve in each of the following instances? *(LO26-3)*
    a. Productivity rises 3 percent; wages rise 4 percent.
    b. Productivity rises 3 percent; wages rise 1 percent.
    c. Productivity declines 1 percent; wages rise 1 percent.
    d. Productivity rises 2 percent; wages rise 2 percent.

11. Why is the *LAS* curve vertical? *(LO26-3)*

12. What will happen to the position of the *SAS* curve and/or *LAS* curve in the following circumstances? *(LO26-3)*
    a. Available factors of production increase.
    b. A civil war occurs.
    c. Wages that were fixed become flexible, and aggregate demand increases.

13. If an economy is in short-run equilibrium that is below potential, what forces will bring the economy to long-run equilibrium? *(LO26-4)*

14. Moore's law states that every 18 months, the computing speed of a microchip doubles. *(LO26-4)*
    a. What effect does this likely have on the economy?
    b. Explain your answer using the *AS/AD* model.

15. Congratulations! You have been appointed an economic policy adviser to the U.S. president. You are told that the economy is significantly below its potential output and that the following will happen next year: World income will fall significantly and the price of oil will rise significantly. (The United States is an oil importer.) *(LO26-4)*
    a. What will happen to the price level and output? Using the *AS/AD* model, demonstrate your predictions graphically.
    b. What policy might you suggest to the government?

16. What fiscal policy actions would you recommend in the following instances? *(LO26-4)*
    a. The economy begins at potential output, but foreign economies slow dramatically.
    b. The economy has been operating above potential output and inflationary pressures rise.
    c. A new technology is invented that significantly raises potential output.

17. How can a falling price level destabilize an economy? *(LO26-5)*

18. Why is knowing the level of potential output important to designing appropriate fiscal policy? *(LO26-5)*

19. Why is macro policy more difficult than the simple model suggests? *(LO26-5)*

20. Why is countercyclical fiscal policy difficult to implement? *(LO26-5)*

Questions from Alternative Perspectives

1. Austrian economist Murray Rothbard has argued that government intervention during 1929 made what could have been a 1-year recession set off by the stock market crash into a 12-year depression. He believed that by creating confusing signals, government intervention kept investors from gaining knowledge of what investments to avoid.
   a. Is Rothbard's explanation of the Depression consistent with the *AS/AD* model?
   b. If one agrees with Rothbard, how would one's proposed policies to deal with recessions differ from those presented in the book? *(Austrian)*

2. In the 1950s, Michael Hubert King, an oil geologist, mathematically determined that when 50 percent of oil reserves have been extracted, annual oil output would inexorably decline. He looked at the rate of oil discovery in the United States and predicted that domestic oil production would peak in 1969.
   a. Use the *AS/AD* model and the production possibility curve to describe what happens if oil production declines.
   b. What will a decline in oil production do to the question of "distribution," both within and between nations? *(Institutionalist)*

3. Post-Keynesian economist Hyman Minsky predicted many of the problems that have recently befallen the U.S. economy. Given that he was right and conventional macroeconomists were wrong, why do textbooks continue to present the conventional macro analysis, rather than present the Post-Keynesian macro analysis? *(Post-Keynesian)*

4. Draw an *AS/AD* diagram from the Keynesian viewpoint. Assume the initial equilibrium in your diagram is just at the level of potential output. Then reduce the level of aggregate demand in your diagram. Now stare at this diagram.
   a. Can you identify the excess capacity or depression in the diagram and what caused it?
   b. What should be done to return the economy to a full-employment level of output?
   c. What does this exercise suggest about the distinction between economic theorizing (or positive economics) and policy recommendations (normative economics)?
   d. Is one more value-laden than the other? *(Radical)*

Issues to Ponder

1. The opening quotation of the chapter refers to Keynes' view of economic theory.
   a. What do you think he meant by it?
   b. How does it relate to the emphasis on the "other things constant" assumption?
   c. Do you think Keynes' interest was mainly in positive economics, the art of economics, or normative economics? Why?

2. If the economy were close to high potential output, would policy makers present their policy prescriptions to increase real output any differently than if the economy were far from potential output? Why?

Answers to Margin Questions

1. When people try to increase the proportion of income they save, they decrease consumption, which causes income to fall as long as that saving is not translated back into the spending stream. If total income falls sufficiently far, the higher percentage being saved can be associated with a lower absolute amount of saving. *(LO26-1)*

2. In the Keynesian view, saving can lead to a decrease in expenditures and a reduction in equilibrium output. In the layperson's view, saving leads to investment, which leads to growth. *(LO26-1)*

3. False. The multiplier magnifies the initial effect. The rise in expenditures will be greater than 10, making the *AD* curve flatter than a slope of −1. *(LO26-2)*

4. A rise in a country's exchange rate will make domestic goods more expensive to foreigners and foreign goods less expensive to domestic residents. It will shift the *AD* curve in to the left because net exports will fall. (*LO26-2*)

5. The *AD* curve will shift out by more than 20 because of the multiplier. (*LO26-2*)

6. The price level rises by 3 percent (4% − 1%). (*LO26-3*)

7. If the *AD*, *SAS*, and *LAS* curves intersect at the same point, the economy is in both long-run and short-run equilibrium. Nothing will happen to the price level and output. (*LO26-4*)

8. If there is a recessionary gap, the *SAS* and *AD* curves intersect to the left of potential output at a point such as *A* in the figure below. At that level of output there will be pressure for factor prices to fall, pushing the *SAS* curve down. Unless the *AD* curve shifts out (as it usually does), the *SAS* curve will shift down and output will rise until output equals potential output and the economy is in both long-run and short-run equilibrium at a point such as *B*. (*LO26-4*)

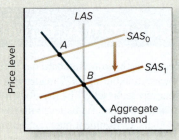

9. If the economy is well below potential, I would predict that output will rise and the price level will rise only slightly. (*LO26-5*)

10. If the economy is above potential output, I would predict that factor prices will rise, shifting the *SAS* curve up. The expansion in government expenditures will shift the *AD* curve out even further beyond potential output, putting even more pressure on factor prices to rise. My answer, therefore, is that the price level will rise very quickly and real output will fall until it equals potential output. (*LO26-5*)

The Multiplier Model

> Keynes stirred the stale economic frog pond to its depth.
>
> —Gottfried Haberler

CHAPTER 26W

This web chapter can be found in McGraw-Hill Connect®

©Science & Society Picture Library/SSPL/Getty Images

After reading this chapter, you should be able to:

LO26W-1 State the components of the multiplier model and explain the difference between induced and autonomous expenditures.

LO26W-2 Show how equilibrium income is determined in the multiplier model both graphically and using the multiplier equation.

LO26W-3 Demonstrate how, through the multiplier process, fiscal policy can eliminate recessionary and inflationary gaps.

LO26W-4 List seven reasons why the multiplier model might be misleading.

The Classical Long-Run Policy Model: Growth and Supply-Side Policies

> Queen Elizabeth owned silk stockings. The capitalist achievement does not typically consist in providing more silk stockings for queens but in bringing them within the reach of factory girls in return for steadily decreasing amounts of effort.
>
> —Joseph Schumpeter

©Francisco Diez Photography/Getty Images

Growth matters. In the long run, growth matters a lot. Given the importance of growth, it is not surprising that modern economics began with a study of growth. In *The Wealth of Nations,* Adam Smith noted that what was good about market economies was that they raised society's standard of living. He argued that people's natural tendency to exchange and specialize was the driving force behind growth. Specialization and trade, and the investment and capital that made these possible, were responsible for the wealth of nations.

As we discussed in an earlier chapter, through the 1920s, long-run growth remained an important focus of economics. Then, in the 1930s, the world economy fell into a serious depression. It was at that time that modern macroeconomics developed as a separate subject with a significant focus on short-run business cycles. It asked the questions: "What causes depressions?" and "How does an economy get out of one?" Short-run macroeconomics became known as Keynesian economics, and remained the standard macroeconomics through the 1960s. Keynesian economics continued to focus on fluctuations around the growth trend.

In the 1970s, as the memories of the Great Depression faded, the pendulum started to swing back again toward a focus on long-run growth, which had been the focus of Classical economists. Thus, the focus on growth is often seen as a new Classical revival. In this chapter we discuss economists' views of growth and the policies that economists advise governments to follow to keep growth high.

General Observations about Growth

Let's begin our consideration with some general observations about growth.

Growth and the Economy's Potential Output

Long-run growth occurs when the economy produces more goods and services from existing production processes and resources. The study of growth is the study of why that increase comes about. In discussing growth, economists use the term *potential output* (the highest amount of output an economy can sustainably produce from existing production processes and resources) introduced in an earlier chapter. Potential output conveys a sense of the growth that is possible. (Recall that *potential output* can also be called *potential income* because, in the aggregate, income and output are identical.) One way to think about growth and potential output is to relate them to the production possibility curve presented in Chapter 2. That curve gave us a picture of the choices an economy faces given available resources. When an economy is at its potential output, it is operating on its production possibility curve. When an economy is below its potential output, it is operating inside its production possibility curve. The analysis of growth focuses on the forces that increase potential output, in other words, that shift out the production possibility curve.

Why do we use potential output in macro rather than the production possibility curve? Because macro focuses on aggregate output—GDP—and does not focus on the choices of dividing up GDP among alternative products as does micro and the production possibility curve. But the concept is the same. Potential output is a barrier beyond which an economy cannot expand without either increasing available factors of production or increasing **productivity** *(output per unit of input)*.

Long-run growth analysis focuses on supply; it assumes demand is sufficient to buy whatever is supplied. That assumption is called **Say's law** *(supply creates its own demand),* named after a French economist, Jean Baptiste Say, who first pointed it out. The reasoning behind Say's law is as follows: People work and supply goods to the market because they want other goods. The very fact that they supply goods means that they demand goods of equal value. According to Say's law, aggregate demand will always equal aggregate supply.

In the short run, economists consider potential output fixed; they focus on how to get the economy operating at its potential if, for some reason, it is not. In the long run, economists consider an economy's potential output changeable. Growth analysis is a consideration of why an economy's potential shifts out, and growth policy is aimed at increasing an economy's potential output.

Notice that this focus is different from the Keynesian model in the last chapter, which took potential output as given and focused on aggregate demand, assuming that the short-run quantity of aggregate supply would expand to meet demand, at least up

Butter (vertical axis) / Guns (horizontal axis)

The analysis of growth focuses on forces that shift out the production possibility curve.

Q-1 How does long-run growth analysis justify its focus on supply?

Web Note 27.1

Is Growth Good?

Demand, Keynesian Economics, and Growth

The presentation in this chapter is the generally accepted analysis of growth. It focuses on the supply-side sources of growth. But because empirical relationships in growth are so difficult to discern, groups of economists raise a variety of different issues. One such group, which has its origins in Keynesian ideas, argues that demand and supply are so interrelated in macro that demand has to be considered as a source of growth. The argument goes as follows: Firms produce only if they expect there to be demand for their product. If they expect demand to be growing, they will try new projects and in the process will learn by doing and develop new technology. Both of these activities shift the production function out and

thereby create growth. So while it looks like a supply-side issue, it is the demand side that leads the supply side: By increasing demand, one can increase long-run supply.

True, they argue, increasing aggregate demand is only a short-run phenomenon, but since the long run is simply a set of successive short runs, the short run influences the long-run path that the economy follows. They are not separable, and, under the right conditions, demand-side policies should be considered as one way to increase supply. As economist Abba Lerner, one of the early Keynesian advocates of this view, has put it, *"In the long run we are simply in another short run."*

to the economy's potential income. Figure 27-1 summarizes the different views. Figure 27-1(a) shows the Keynesian view where aggregate demand can be below potential output at point *A* and government policy is to shift the aggregate demand curve to the right. Figure 27-1(b) shows the Classical view where the economy is always at long-run equilibrium. Point *A* is one possibility. Classical policy focuses on shifting the long-run aggregate supply curve to the right, to increase output (arrow 1). As that happens in the Classical view, aggregate demand will follow (arrow 2) since supply creates its own demand.

Republican and Democratic rhetoric often matches this distinction. Republicans tend to associate themselves with Classical economics. They call themselves supply-siders and argue that policy should focus on expanding potential income (the supply side). Democrats tend to associate themselves with Keynesians and argue that policy should focus on managing aggregate demand (the demand side). But when the models don't fit what politicians want at the time, both sides modify the models.

FIGURE 27-1 (A AND B)

The Demand-Side and Supply-Side Models

The Keynesian view is shown in (a), where the economy's output can vary from potential output. In this case the economy is below potential at point *A*. Government policy focuses on expansionary policy to shift the aggregate demand curve. The Classical view is shown in (b), where the economy is always at potential. The focus of government policy is on the supply side; its goal is to shift the long-run aggregate supply curve to the right (shift 1). Because supply creates its own demand, the AD curve also shifts to the right (shift 2).

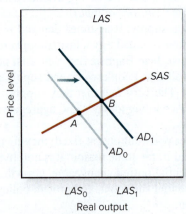

(a) Keynesian View

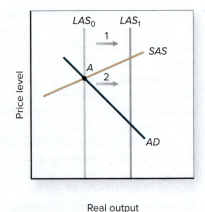

(b) Classical View

The Benefits and Costs of Growth

Economic growth (per capita) allows everyone in society, on average, to have more. Thus, it isn't surprising that most governments are generally searching for policies that will allow their economies to grow. Indeed, one reason market economies have been so successful is that they have consistently channeled individual efforts toward production and growth. Individuals feel a sense of accomplishment in making things grow and, if sufficient economic incentives and resources exist, individuals' actions can lead to a continually growing economy.

Politically, growth (or predictions of growth) allows governments to avoid hard distributional questions of who should get what part of our existing output: With growth there is more to go around for everyone. A growing economy generates jobs, so politicians who want to claim that their policies will create jobs generally predict those policies will create growth.

Of course, material growth comes with costs: pollution, resource exhaustion, and destruction of natural habitat. These costs lead some people to believe that we would be better off in a society that deemphasized material growth. (That doesn't mean we shouldn't grow emotionally, spiritually, and intellectually; it simply means we should grow out of our material goods fetish.) Many people believe these environmental costs are important, and the result is often an environmental-economic growth stalemate. An example is fracking (technically hydraulic fracturing) in which water and chemicals are pumped into the ground to extract natural gas and oil. This new technology was a boon to economic growth in the United States and helped pull the U.S. economy out of a recession, as U.S. oil and gas production increased significantly.

Just because fracking increased economic growth does not mean that it is desirable. Fracking comes with potentially serious environmental costs. Many environmentalists oppose the process, arguing that fracking hurts the environment and could pollute groundwater. Economics cannot say which side is right; it can only spell out the costs and benefits.

> Politically, growth (or predictions of growth) allows governments to avoid hard questions.

> Economics cannot say whether fracking advocates or environmental advocates are right; it can only spell out the costs and benefits.

The Importance of Growth for Living Standards

In 2004, Nobel Prize winner Robert Lucas wrote, "Of the tendencies that are harmful to sound economics, the most seductive, and in my opinion most poisonous, is to focus on questions of distribution. . . . The potential for improving the lives of poor people by finding different ways of distributing current production is *nothing* [his italics] compared to the apparently limitless potential of increasing production." For Lucas, and many other economists, growth, not distribution or business cycles, is the most important macroeconomic issue.

All economists agree that growth makes an enormous difference for living standards. Take Spain and Peru as examples. In the 1950s, per capita real income was the same in each country, but their growth rates differed. From 1950 to 2016, Spain's income grew at an average rate of 3.9 percent per year while Peru's grew at an average rate of 1.5 percent per year. Because of the differences in growth rates, Spain's per capita income is now about $31,500 and Peru's per capita income is about $6,100.

Other examples are South Korea and North Korea. In the 1950s, their incomes were identical. Because of differing growth rates, South Korea's per capita income has risen to about $40,000, while North Korea's per capita income is about $1,700. Why? Because North Korea had a 0.6 percent growth rate while South Korea had averaged a 5.4 percent annual growth rate. The moral of these stories: In the long run, growth rates matter a lot.

Small differences in growth rates can mean huge differences in income levels because of *compounding*. Compounding means that growth is based not only on the

> Growth in income improves lives by fulfilling basic needs and making more goods available to more people.

Is Growth Good?

The discussion in the chapter emphasizes the generally held view among economists that growth is inherently good. It increases our incomes, thereby improving our standard of living. But that does not mean that all economists support unlimited growth. Growth has costs, and economics requires us to look at both costs and benefits. For example, growth may contribute to increased pollution—reducing the quality of the air we breathe and the water we drink, and endangering the variety of species in the world. In short, the wrong type of growth may produce undesirable side effects, including global warming and polluted rivers, land, and air.

New technology, upon which growth depends, also raises serious moral questions: Do we want to replace sexual reproduction with cloning? Will a brain implant be an improvement over 12 years of education? Will selecting your baby's genetic makeup be better than relying on nature? Just because growth *can* continue does not mean that it *should* continue. Moral judgments can be made against growth. For example, some argue that growth changes traditional cultures with beautiful handiwork, music, and dance into cultures of gadgets where people have lost touch with what is important. They argue that we have enough gadgets cluttering our lives and that it is time to start focusing on noneconomic priorities.

This moral argument against growth carries the most weight in highly developed countries—countries with per capita incomes of at least $20,000 a year. For developing countries, where per capita income can be as low as $500 per year, the reality is the choice between growth and poverty or even between growth and starvation. In these countries it is difficult to argue against growth.

One final comment: The benefits of growth do not have to be just higher incomes and more gadgets. They could also include more leisure activities and improved working conditions. In the 19th century, a 12-hour workday was common. Today the workday is 8 hours, but had we been content with a lower income, the workday could now be 2 hours, with the remainder left for free time. We'd have less growth in GDP, but we'd have a lot more time to play.

---

original level of income but also on the accumulation of previous-year increases in income. For example, say you start with $10,000. At a 7 percent interest rate that $10,000 after 10 years will be more than $20,000; after 20 years it will be more than $40,000; after 30 years it will be more than $80,000; and after 50 years it will be more than $320,000. So if you are worried about your retirement, it pays to start saving early at as high an interest rate as you can get. The longer you save, and the higher the interest rate you receive, the more you end up with.

$$\frac{\text{Number of years}}{\text{to double}} = \frac{72}{(\text{Rate of growth})}$$

Q-2 If an economy is growing at 4 percent a year, how long will it take for its income to double?

Another way to see the effects of the difference in growth rates is to see how long it would take income to double at different growth rates. The rule of 72 tells you that. The **rule of 72** states: *The number of years it takes for a certain amount to double in value is equal to 72 divided by its annual rate of increase.* For example, if Argentina's income grows at a 1 percent annual rate, it will double in 72 years (72/1). If France's income grows at a 3 percent annual rate, it will double in only 24 years (72/3).

Markets, Specialization, and Growth

Growth began when markets developed, and then, as markets expanded, growth accelerated. Why are markets so important to growth? To answer that question, let's go back to Adam Smith's argument for markets. Smith argued that markets allow **specialization** *(the concentration of individuals on certain aspects of production)* and **division of labor** *(the splitting up of a task to allow for specialization of production).* According to Smith, markets create an interdependent economy in which individuals can take advantage of the benefits of specialization and trade for their other needs. In doing so, markets increase productivity—and, in turn, improve the standard of living.

Q-3 Why do markets lead to growth?

You saw in Chapter 2 how comparative advantage and specialization increase productivity. If individuals concentrate on the production of goods for which their skills and other resources are best suited and trade for those goods for which they do not have a comparative advantage, everyone can end up with more of all goods. To see this even more clearly, consider what your life would be like without markets, trade, and specialization. You would have to grow all your food, build your own living space, and provide all your own transportation. Simply to exist under these conditions, you'd need a lot of skills, and it is unlikely that you'd become sufficiently adept in any one of them to provide yourself with anything other than the basics. You'd have all you could do to keep up.

Now consider your life today with specialization. Someone who specializes in dairy farming produces the milk you consume. You don't need to know how it is produced, just where to buy it. How about transportation? You buy, not build, your car. It runs somehow—you're not quite sure how—but if it breaks down, you take it to a garage. And consider your education: Are you learning how to grow food or build a house? No, you are probably learning a specific skill that has little relevance to the production of most goods. But you'll most likely provide some good or service that will benefit the dairy farmer and auto mechanic. You get the picture—for most of the things you consume, you don't have the faintest idea who makes them or how they are made, nor do you need to know.

For most of the things you consume, you don't have the faintest idea who makes them or how they are made, nor do you need to know.

Economic Growth, Distribution, and Markets

Markets and growth are often seen as unfair with regard to the distribution of income. Is it fair that markets give some individuals so much (billions to Mark Zuckerberg) and others so little ($7.25 an hour to Joe Wall, who has a minimum wage job and two kids)? Such questions are legitimate and need to be asked. But in answering them we should also remember the quotation from Joseph Schumpeter that opened this chapter: Even if markets and growth do not provide equality, they tend to make everyone, even the poor, better off. The relevant question is: Would the poor be better off with or without markets and growth?

Even though growth isn't evenly distributed, it generally raises the incomes of the poor.

There are strong arguments, based on historical evidence, that people are better off with markets. Consider the number of hours an average person must work to buy certain goods at various periods in U.S. history. A century ago it took a worker 1 hour and 41 minutes to earn enough to buy a pair of stockings; today it takes less than 15 minutes of work. Figure 27-2 gives a number of other examples. As you can see from the figure, growth has made average workers significantly better off; to get the same amount, they have to work far less now than they did in the past. Growth also has made new products available. For example, before 1952 air conditioners were not available at any price.

The reality is that, judged from an *absolute* standard, the poor benefit enormously from the growth that markets foster. Markets, through competition, make the factors of production more productive and lower the cost of goods so that more goods are available to everyone. Today, the U.S. poverty level for a family of four is about $25,300. If we go back 100 years in U.S. history, and adjust for inflation, that $25,300 income would put a family in the upper middle class. Markets and growth have made that possible.

The above argument does not mean that the poor always benefit from growth; many of us judge our well-being by relative, not absolute, standards. Growth often reduces the share of income earned by the poorest proportion of society, making the poor *relatively* worse off. So, if one uses relative standards, one could say that the poor have become worse off over certain periods. Moreover, it is not at all clear that markets require the large differentials in pay that have accompanied growth in market economies. If such large differentials did not exist, and growth had been at the same rate, the poor would be even better off than they are.

Just because the poor benefit from growth does not mean they might not be better off if income were distributed more in their favor.

FIGURE 27-2   Cost of Goods in Hours of Work

Growth in the U.S. economy in the past century has reduced the number of hours the average person needs to work to buy consumer goods.

Source: Federal Reserve Bank of Dallas, *Time Well Spent* (1997 annual report). Updated by author.

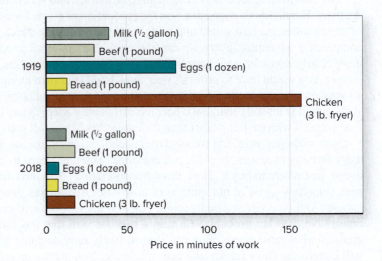

Per Capita Growth

When thinking about growth, it is important to distinguish between increases in total output and increases in per capita output, or total output divided by the total population. If there is **per capita growth,** the country is *producing more goods and services per person*. For example, say the real output of the economy is $4 billion and there are 1 million people. Each person, on average, has $4,000 to spend. Now say that output increases by 50 percent but that population also increases by 50 percent. In this case *output* has grown but *per capita output* has not; each person still has only $4,000 to spend. A number of countries have found themselves in such situations. Take the country of Bahrain as an example. In 2017, income grew by 3.9 percent, but its population grew at a higher rate of 4.7 percent, meaning that per capita income fell 0.8 percent. In that same year, the U.S. economy grew by 2.3 percent, but its population grew only 0.8 percent so that, on average, per capita income grew 1.5 percent.

If you know the percentage change in output and percentage change in population, you can approximate per capita growth:

Per capita growth = % change in output − % change in population

Here are some additional examples showing per capita growth, real growth, and population growth for various countries in 2017:

Q-4 Which country has experienced higher growth per capita: country A, whose economy is growing at a 4 percent rate and whose population is growing at a 3 percent rate, or country B, whose economy is growing at a 3 percent rate and whose population is growing at a 1 percent rate?

Country	Per Capita GDP Growth	=	Real GDP Growth	−	Population Growth
Canada	1.8		3.0		1.2
Chile	0.7		1.5		0.8
China	6.3		6.9		0.6
Denmark	1.5		2.2		0.7
South Africa	0.1		1.3		1.2
United States	1.5		2.3		0.8

Source: The World Bank. 2018. *World Development Indicators.* © The World Bank (https://data.worldbank.org). License: Creative Commons Attribution license (CC BY 3.0 IGO) (http://creativecommons.org/licenses/by/3.0/igo/) Accessed 10/8/2018.

Some economists have argued that per capita income is not what we should be focusing on; they suggest that it would be better to look at median income. (Remember, income and output are the same.) Per capita income measures the average, or *mean,* income. The *median* income, in contrast, is the income level that divides the population in equal halves. Half the people earn more and half the people earn less than the median income. In 2017, median income per household in the United States was $61,372. Half of all households earned less than that, and half earned more.

Why focus on median income? Because it partially takes into account how income is distributed. If the growth in income goes to a small minority of individuals who already receive the majority of income, the mean will rise but the median will not. Let's consider an example where there is a large difference between the two measures. Say that the incomes of five people in a five-person economy are $20,000; $20,000; $30,000; $120,000; and $450,000. The median income is $30,000 (the middle income with two above and two below); the mean income is $128,000. Now say that the economy grows but that the two richest people get all the benefits, raising their incomes to $150,000 and $500,000, respectively. The median income remains $30,000; the mean income rises to $144,000. Unfortunately, statistics on median income are often not collected, so I will follow convention and focus on the mean, or per capita, income.

Whether you're looking at per capita income or at median income, growth provides more goods and services for the people in an economy, allowing society to sidestep the more difficult issues of how those goods are distributed. That's why policy makers are interested in knowing what makes an economy grow.

Q-5 How would increases in income have to be distributed for the median to remain constant and the mean income to rise?

The Sources of Growth

Economists generally single out five important sources of growth:

1. Growth-compatible institutions.
2. Investment and accumulated capital.
3. Available resources.
4. Technological development.
5. Entrepreneurship.

Let's consider each in turn.

Web Note 27.2

A Measure of Ignorance

Growth-Compatible Institutions

Throughout this book I have emphasized the importance of economic institutions and that having the right institutions is vital for growth. Consider China. Until 1980 it grew at an average annual rate of 3 percent. After 1980, when it changed its institutional structure from a command-and-control to a more market-oriented economy, it started its rapid growth that averaged about 9 percent per year. Growth-compatible institutions—institutions that foster growth—must have incentives built into them that lead people to put forth effort and discourage people from spending a lot of their time in leisure pursuits or creating impediments for others to gain income for themselves.

When individuals get much of the gains of growth themselves, they have incentives to work harder. That's why markets and private ownership of property play an important role in growth. In the former Soviet Union, individuals didn't gain much from their own initiative and, hence, often spent their time in pursuits other than those that would foster measured economic growth. Another growth-compatible institution is the corporation, a legal institution that gives owners limited liability and thereby encourages large enterprises (because people are more willing to invest their savings when their potential losses are limited).

Q-6 Why is private property a source of growth?

Some developing countries follow a type of mercantilist policy in which government must approve any new economic activity. Some government officials get a large portion of their income from bribes offered to them by individuals who want to undertake economic activity. Such policies inhibit economic growth. Many regulations, even reasonable ones, also tend to inhibit economic growth because they inhibit entrepreneurial activities.

Peruvian economist Hernando de Soto has given some vivid examples of how the lack of formal property rights limits development. He points out that because of regulations it takes an average of 500 working days to legalize a bakery in Cairo. He has many similar examples. Excessive regulations combined with bribery and corruption are important reasons why people don't legalize their businesses. In some ways, whether a business is legal or not is not of concern: Both legal and illegal businesses provide goods. But legality impacts growth; illegal or semilegal businesses must stay small to remain below the government's radar, and because the owners have no property rights, they do not have access to business loans to grow. Similarly, squatters only informally own their residence; their lack of formal ownership is a barrier to getting loans to improve their living space, which keeps them in the vicious cycle of poverty. De Soto points out that the poor have informal control of trillions of dollars of assets but can't get loans on those assets to advance their economic futures in the normal market economy. The lack of property rights and the regulations doom the poor to remain in poverty.

The above argument is not an argument against all regulation; some regulation is necessary to ensure that growth is of a socially desirable type. The policy problem is in deciding between necessary and unnecessary regulation.

Informal property rights limit borrowing by the poor, and hence limit growth.

Investment and Accumulated Capital

A second important source of growth is capital and investment. In *Nickled and Dimed: On (Not) Getting By in America,* Barbara Ehrenreich explores how minimum wage workers manage to scrape by. What they don't have time or income for is saving—putting together a nest egg to invest. Lacking savings, they often remain mired in poverty, just scraping by. The same argument holds for society as a whole; societies that can't afford to save will not grow either. Investment is absolutely necessary for growth. Somehow, the society as a whole has to manage to save (forgo consumption) if it wants to grow.

Some economists even argue that it is the savers, not the "givers," who are the beneficent people. University of Rochester economist Steven Landsburg makes the argument most explicitly. He argues that misers—the people who could deplete the world's resources but choose not to—are the true philanthropists. He writes that "nobody is more generous than the miser" and that when Scrooge gave up his miserly ways, the world was worse off, not better off. (As with all such provocative statements, the issues are complicated, and there is a deeper question about the justness of the institutional structure and whether that institutional structure could be changed to channel more income to the "nickled and dimed" while maintaining the level of saving. But those issues quickly go beyond the principles level.)

Actually, it isn't saving that is important for growth; it's investment, and, for saving to be helpful, some method of translating savings into investment must exist in the society. Financial markets provide a method, which is why financial markets are an important aspect of macro. The role of financial markets in transferring savings into investment is captured in the loanable funds market shown in Figure 27-3.

Savings is the supply of loanable funds; it is an upward-sloping curve because, as the interest rate rises, more people are willing to save more. Investment is the demand

Web Note 27.3

Loans That Change Lives

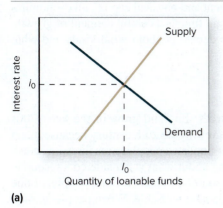

(a)

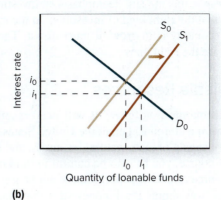

(b)

The Loanable Funds Market

The interest rate equilibrates the supply and demand for loanable funds as shown in (**a**). When the supply of loanable funds (savings) increases as shown in (**b**), the interest rate falls from i_0 to i_1, and the quantity of loanable funds demanded (investment) increases from I_0 to I_1.

for loanable funds that will be used by businesses to buy goods and services. It is a downward-sloping curve because, as the interest rate falls, it pays businesses to borrow more and invest more. Notice in this market that the interest rate is key; it equilibrates the supply and demand for loanable funds as shown in Figure 27-3(a). When the supply of loanable funds (savings) increases, as shown in Figure 27-3(b), the interest rate falls from i_0 to i_1, and the quantity of loanable funds demanded (investment) increases from I_0 to I_1. Thus, societies interested in growth look carefully at the interest rate in the economy. (The interest rate that is important to this market is the real interest rate—the nominal interest rate minus the rate of inflation.)

Before the 1970s, capital accumulation (where capital was thought of as just *physical capital*) and investment were seen as the key elements in growth. Physical capital includes both private capital—buildings and machines available for production—and public capital—infrastructure such as highways and water supply. The *flow* of investment leads to the growth of the *stock* of capital. While physical capital is still considered a key element in growth, it is now generally recognized that the growth recipe is far more complicated. One of the reasons physical capital accumulation has been deemphasized is that empirical evidence has suggested that capital accumulation doesn't necessarily lead to growth. For instance, before its demise, the former Soviet Union invested a lot and accumulated lots of capital goods, but its economy didn't grow much because its capital was often internationally obsolete. A second reason is that products change, and buildings and machines useful in one time period may be useless in another (e.g., a six-year-old computer often is worthless). The value of the capital stock depends on its future expected earnings, which are very uncertain. Capital's role in growth is extraordinarily difficult to measure with accuracy.

A third reason capital accumulation was deemphasized is that it has become clear that capital includes much more than machines. In addition to physical capital, modern economics includes **human capital** (*the skills that are embodied in workers through experience, education, and on-the-job training, or, more simply, people's knowledge*) and **social capital** (*the habitual way of doing things that guides people in how they approach production*) as types of capital. The importance of human capital is obvious: A skilled labor force is far more productive than an unskilled labor force. Social capital is embodied in institutions such as the government, the legal system, and the fabric of society. In a way, anything that contributes to growth can be called a type of capital, and anything that slows growth can be called a destroyer of capital. With the concept of capital including such a wide range of things, it is difficult to say what is not capital, which makes the concept of capital less useful.

Q-7 If the demand for loanable funds increases, what will likely happen to the interest rate?

Q-8 What are three types of capital?

Despite this modern deemphasis on investment and physical capital, all economists agree that the right kind of investment at the right time is a central element of growth. If an economy is to grow, it must invest. The debate is about what kinds and what times are the right ones.

Available Resources

If an economy is to grow, it will need resources. England grew in the late 1700s because it had iron and coal; the United States grew in the 20th century because it had a major supply of many natural resources, and it imported people, a resource it needed.

Of course, you have to be careful in thinking about what is considered a resource. A resource in one time period may not be a resource in another. For example, at one time oil was simply black gooey stuff that made land unusable. When people learned that the black gooey stuff could be burned as fuel, oil became a resource. What's considered a resource depends on technology. If solar technology is ever perfected, oil will go back to being black gooey stuff. So creativity can replace resources, and if you develop new technology fast enough, you can overcome almost any lack of existing resources. Even if a country doesn't have the physical resources it needs for growth, it can import them—as did Japan following World War II.

The enormous growth of China has involved an increase in the demand for physical resources such as oil, iron ore, and copper—throughout the world. This has led both the United States and China to work toward securing continued access to sufficient physical resources in the future. China, in particular, has made deals with Latin American and African countries to lend them money with the proviso that they provide natural resources to China in the future.

In 2007 and 2008 the large demand for resources pushed up the price of oil. Grain prices doubled and oil prices rose to more than $150 a barrel. Many noneconomists were predicting that the price of oil could only rise because world oil reserves were being depleted. Economists were not so sure. They had seen such predictions before, and those predictions had always been wrong, as happened in this case. The price of oil in 2016 fell to under $30 a barrel before it rose again to about $70 a barrel. The reason that prices of natural resources don't continue to rise is that the high price of oil brings about changes. Specifically, it reduces the quantity demanded as people figure out ways to skimp on using oil. The high price also creates incentives to develop alternative technologies. Here are just a few of the options being explored:

- Geothermal energy—the recoverable heat in rock under the United States equals 2,000 years' worth of energy.
- Algae-produced fuel—algae ponds are being created that produce "cellulosic ethanol," giving an almost inexhaustible source of energy.
- Wind power—as windmills become more efficient, a larger percentage of energy can come from wind.
- Plug-in cars—electric cars use half the energy of gasoline engine cars.
- Fuel cells—hydrogen-powered fuel cells offer new ways to provide power.
- Sugarcane-based ethanol—this is far more efficient than corn-based ethanol.
- Nuclear—the potential for almost unlimited energy.

If all these options are possible, why haven't they been developed? The reason is that when the price of oil is high, there is no guarantee that it will remain high. At $150 a barrel, developing alternatives to oil makes attractive investments. At $70 a barrel, they are far less attractive, and at $30 a barrel, without large government subsidies, they make no sense whatsoever. As long as the possibility exists that the price of oil will

What is a resource depends on the production processes of an economy and technology.

remain low, alternative energy development is an unattractive investment from an individual investor's perspective. (Since the use of oil has other negative consequences, such as contributing to global warming, from a society's perspective that might not be the case.)

Greater participation in the market is another means by which to increase available resources. In China at the end of the 20th century, for example, many individuals migrated into the southern provinces, which had free trade sectors. Before they migrated they were only marginally involved in the market economy. After they migrated they became employed in the market economy. This increased the labor available to the market, helping push up China's growth rate. In the United States beginning in the 1950s, the percentage of women entering the workforce increased, contributing to economic growth.

High oil prices led to the development of electric cars.
©Martin Pickard/Getty Images

Increasing the labor force participation rate is not a totally costless way of increasing growth. We lose whatever people were doing before they joined the labor force (which was, presumably, something of value to society). Our aggregate income accounting figures, which are measures of market activity, simply do not measure such losses.

Technological Development

Advances in technology shift the production possibility curve out by making workers more productive. Technological advances increase their ability to produce more of the things they already produce but also allow them to produce new and different products. While in some ways growth involves more of the same, a much larger aspect of growth involves changes in **technology**—*the way we make goods and supply services*—and changes in the goods and services we buy. Think of what this generation buys—music downloads, smartphones, cars, computers, fast food—and compare that to what the preceding generation bought—LP records, cars that would now be considered obsolete, and tube and transistor radios. (When I was 11, I saved $30—the equivalent of about $250 now—so I could afford a six-transistor Motorola radio; personal computers didn't exist.)

Contrast today's goods with the goods the next generation might have available: video brain implants (little gadgets in your head to receive sound and full-vision broadcasts—you simply close your eyes and tune in whatever you want, if you've paid your cellular fee for that month); fuel-cell-powered cars (gas cars will be considered quaint but polluting); and instant food (little pills that fulfill all your nutritional needs, letting your video brain implant supply all the ambiance). Just imagine! You probably can get the picture, even without a video brain implant.

How does society get people to work on developments that may change the very nature of what we do and how we think? One way is through economic incentives; another is with institutions that foster creativity and bold thinking—such as this book; a third is through institutions that foster hard work. There are, of course, trade-offs. For example, the Japanese educational system, which emphasizes hard work and discipline, doesn't do as good a job at fostering creativity as the U.S. educational system does, and vice versa.

Important advances in biotechnology, computers, and communications initially developed in the United States, and those developments helped fuel U.S. growth. Those new industries were much slower to develop in another important U.S. competitor, the European Union, which is one important reason why EU countries have grown far more slowly than has the United States in recent years.

Growth isn't just getting more of the same thing. It's also getting some things that are different.

Five sources of growth are:

1. Growth-compatible institutions.
2. Capital accumulation.
3. Available resources.
4. Technological development.
5. Entrepreneurship.

Growth and Terrorism

Terrorist attacks worldwide have risen dramatically since the terrorist attacks of September 11, 2001, in the United States. When talking about the costs of terrorism, many focus on the short-term effects—the tremendous cost in destruction of property and loss of life. But terrorism also affects long-term growth in ways that may be less dramatic yet are even more costly. Studies suggest that terrorist attacks:

9/11 Twin Towers
©Robert J Fisch/Flickr Open/Getty Images

- Destroy infrastructure and physical and human capital.
- Increase the cost of borrowing.
- Increase uncertainty.

- Disrupt household and business spending.
- Reallocate government spending from investment to national security.

Each of these effects contributes to slower growth by reducing the sources of growth. The terrorist attacks acted like sand in the wheels of trade, reduced expenditures on capital, lowered productivity, and reduced start-ups by entrepreneurs. The end result was hundreds of billions of dollars of lost output. The cost has been especially great for many Islamic countries, making it difficult for these countries to tie into the global economy.

Entrepreneurship

Entrepreneurship is the ability to get things done. That ability involves creativity, vision, willingness to accept risk, and a talent for translating that vision into reality. Entrepreneurs have been central to growth in the United States. They have created large companies, produced new products, and transformed the landscape of the economy. Examples of entrepreneurs include Thomas Edison, who revolutionized the generation and use of electricity in the late 1800s; Henry Ford, who revolutionized transportation in the early 1900s; Bill Gates, who led Microsoft as it transformed and dominated the computer industry; Mark Zuckerberg, who created Facebook and transformed the social networking culture; and Jeff Bezos, whose Amazon company transformed consumer shopping. When a country's population demonstrates entrepreneurship, it can overcome deficiencies in other ingredients that contribute to growth.

Turning the Sources of Growth into Growth

The five sources of growth cannot be taken as givens. Even if a country has all five ingredients, it may not have them in the right proportions. For instance, when Nicolas Appert discovered canning (storing food in a sealed container in such a way that it wouldn't spoil) in the early 19th century, the economic possibilities of society expanded enormously. But if, when the technological developments occurred, the savings at the time were not sufficient to finance the investment, the result would not have been growth. It is finding the right combination of the sources of growth that plays a central role in the growth of any economy.

Capital and Investment

Economists' thinking about the sources of growth, and how they can be turned into economic growth, has changed over time. Early economists—Classical economists—

focused on savings and investment as sources of growth. The Classical economists' major policy conclusion was: The more capital—physical inputs to production—an economy has, the faster it will grow. This focus on capital is what caused market economies to be called *capitalist economies*. Since investment leads to an increase in capital, Classical economists focused their analysis, and also their policy advice, on how to increase investment. The way to do that was for people to save:

Saving ⇒ Investment ⇒ Increase in capital ⇒ Growth

According to this **Classical growth model** *(a theory of growth that emphasizes the role of capital in the growth process)* if society wants its economy to grow, it has to save; the more saving, the better. Saving is good for both private individuals and governments because it is good for the economy. Thus, Classical economists objected to government deficits, which occur when government spends more than it collects in taxes. This view of deficits and saving was directly challenged by Keynes. Given the state of the economy and political debates today, we will have a lot more to say about these issues throughout the course.

The early economists believed that eventually growth in capitalist countries would slow down because of what they called the law of diminishing marginal productivity. The **law of diminishing marginal productivity** states that *as more and more of a variable input is added to an existing fixed input, eventually the additional output produced with that additional input falls.* The law was developed in the 1800s, when farming was the major activity of the economy. Economists such as Thomas Malthus emphasized the limitations that the fixed amount of land placed on growth and predicted that as the population grew, to grow the needed food farmers would have to farm increasingly less productive land. The result would be a smaller harvest per worker. Malthus applied this reasoning to all production with a fixed input. This model is known as the Classical growth model.

The predictions of the Classical growth model did not pan out. Per capita output did not stagnate; instead, it grew because of technological progress (think the invention of the cotton gin, for example) and increases in capital (think more farm equipment). Both more than offset the effects of the law of diminishing marginal productivity and eventually economists no longer saw land, or even capital, as the primary determinant of growth. Instead, they changed their focus to technology. In economists' current thinking, growth depends most on *technological innovation*. If technology grows, capital can be found to develop it. Without growth in technology, investment will not generate sustained growth.

Although capital isn't the primary determinant of growth, it does have a role to play. Technology requires investment and is embedded in capital. Take the telephone, which requires a kind of capital—landlines—to transmit voice. Today voice can be transmitted by a different type of capital—satellite. The technological innovation that has led to cell phones is embedded in voice-transmission capital. This technology would never have been used unless investment was available to both develop the technology and implement it with the purchase of new capital.

Technology

This new emphasis on the role of technology has led economists to develop a different path to growth:

Technological advance ⇒ Investment ⇒ Further technological advance ⇒ Growth

To distinguish this different focus from the model developed by Classical economists, it is called **new growth theory**—*a theory of growth that emphasizes the role*

For Classical economists, saving led to investment and to growth.

The law of diminishing marginal productivity states that as more and more of a variable input is added to an existing fixed input, eventually the additional output produced with that additional input falls.

In economists' current thinking, growth depends most on technological innovation.

Q-9 According to new growth theory, what is the primary source of growth?

Is the 21st Century the Age of Technology or One of Many Ages of Technology?

Sometimes newspapers write as if the importance of technology to the economy in the 21st century is a new phenomenon. It is not. Technology has been changing our society for the last two centuries, and it is not at all clear that the technological changes we are currently experiencing are any more revolutionary than those experienced by other generations in the last 200 years. For example, in terms of its impact on people's lives and communications in general, the Internet is small potatoes compared to the phone system.

One economist who recognized the importance of technology was Joseph Schumpeter. Schumpeter emphasized the role of the entrepreneur. He argued that entrepreneurs create major technological changes that drive the economy forward.

According to Schumpeter, the economy's growth depends on these entrepreneurs, and the industries they are in will be the leading industries, pulling the rest of the economy along after them. The accompanying figure lists five waves of technological innovation that have driven our economy. As you can see, in the late 1700s, steam power and iron manufacturing were the driving forces. In the 1860s, railroads were the dynamic industry. Later, electronics, automobiles, and chemicals drove our economy. In the 1980s through the early 21st century, computers and biotechnology have been the leading industries.

First wave 1785–1835	Second wave 1836–1885	Third wave 1886–1935	Fourth wave 1936–1985	Fifth wave 1986–?
Steam power Iron manufacturing	Railroad construction Mobile steam power Steam shipping	Chemicals Electricity Telegraph Telephone Automobiles	Electronics Drugs Oil Air transport Nuclear power	Artificial intelligence Telecommunications Biotechnology Computers Nanotechnology

Time

of technology in the growth process. New growth theory's central argument is that increases in technology do not just happen. Technological advance is the result of what the economy does—it invests in research and development (e.g., drug companies researching new ways to fight disease); makes advances in pure science (e.g., the human genome project); and works out new ways to organize production (e.g., just-in-time inventory techniques). Thus, in a sense, investment in technology increases the technological stock of an economy just as investment in capital increases the capital stock of an economy. Investment in technology is called research and development; firms hire researchers to explore options. Some of those options pay off and others do not, but the net return of that investment in technology is an increase in technology.

If investment in technology is similar to investment in capital, why does new growth theory separate the two? The reason is twofold. First, increases in technology are not as directly linked to investment as are increases in capital. Increases in investment require increases in saving, that is, building the capital. Increases in technology can occur with little investment and saving if the proverbial lightbulb goes off in someone's head and that person sees a new way of doing something.

Second, increases in technology often have enormous *positive spillover effects*, especially if the new technology involves common knowledge and is freely available to all. A technological gain in one sector of production gives people in other sectors of production new ideas on how to change what they are doing, which gives other people new ideas. Ideas spread like pool balls after the break. One hits another, and soon all the nearby balls have moved. Put in technical economic terms, technological change often has significant **positive externalities**—*positive effects on others not taken into account by the decision maker.* Through those externalities, what is called general-purpose technological change can have a much larger effect on growth than can an increase in capital.

The positive externalities result from the *common knowledge* aspect of technology because the idea behind the technology can often be used by others without payment to the developer. Using the same assembly line for different car models is just one example of a technological advance that has become incorporated into common knowledge. Any manufacturer can use it.

Basic research is not always freely available; it is often protected by **patents**—*legal protection of a technological innovation that gives the owner of the patent sole rights to its use and distribution for a limited time.* (If the development is an idea rather than a good, it can be copyrighted rather than patented, but the general concept is the same.) Patents turn innovations into private property. The Microsoft Windows operating system is an example of a technology that is owned, and hence is not common knowledge. The ideas in technologies that are covered by patents, however, often have common knowledge elements. Once people have seen the new technology, they figure out sufficiently different ways of achieving the same end while avoiding violating the patent.

LEARNING BY DOING   As the new growth theorists have analyzed technology, they have also focused on another aspect of economic processes—an individual's tendency to **learn by doing,** or to *improve the methods of production through experience.* As people do something, they become better and better at it, sometimes because of new technologies, and sometimes simply because they learned better ways to do it just from practice. Thus, as production increases, costs of production tend to decrease over time. The introduction of new technology is sometimes the result of learning by doing.

Learning by doing changes the laws of economics enormously. It suggests that production has positive externalities in learning. If these positive externalities overwhelm diminishing marginal productivity, as new growth theory suggests they do, the predictions about growth change. In the Classical theory, growth is limited by diminishing marginal productivity; in the new theory, growth potential is unlimited and can accelerate over time. It's a whole new world out there—one in which, holding wants constant, scarcity decreases over time. In new growth theory, per capita income can grow forever, and the dismal science of economics becomes the optimistic science.

TECHNOLOGICAL LOCK-IN   One of the questions new growth theory raises is: Does the economy always use the "best" technology available? Some say no and point to examples of technologies that have become entrenched in the market or locked in to new products despite the availability of more efficient technologies. This is known as *technological lock-in.*

One proposed example of technological lock-in goes under the name QWERTY, which is the upper-left six keys on the standard computer keyboard. Economist Paul David argues that the design of this keyboard was chosen to slow people's typing so that the keys in old-style mechanical typewriters would not lock up. He further argues that developments in word processing have since eliminated the problem the QWERTY keyboard was designed to solve (we don't use mechanical typewriters anymore). But

The common knowledge aspect of technology creates positive externalities, which new growth theory sees as the key to growth.

Learning by doing overcomes the law of diminishing marginal productivity because learning by doing increases the productivity of workers.

once people started choosing this keyboard, it was too costly for manufacturers to develop another.

This interpretation of history has been disputed by other economists, who argue that the QWERTY keyboard is not significantly less efficient than other keyboard arrangements and that, if it were, competition would have eliminated it. Sometimes this counterargument almost seems to state that the very fact that a technology exists means that it is the most efficient. Most economists do not go that far; they argue that even if the QWERTY keyboard is not a highly inefficient technology, other examples of lock-in exist. Beta format videos of the 1970s were preferable to VHS, the Windows operating system is inferior to many alternatives, the English language doesn't compare to Esperanto, and U.S. measurement systems are quite inefficient compared to the metric system.

Q-10 In what way does the Internet demonstrate network externalities?

One reason for technological lock-in is the existence of *network externalities*—an externality in which the use of a good by one individual makes that technology more valuable to other people. Telephones exhibit network externalities. A single telephone is pretty useless. Whom would you call? Two telephones are more useful, but as more and more people get telephones, the possible interactions (and the benefits of telephones) increase exponentially. Network externalities can make switching to a superior technology expensive or nearly impossible. The Windows operating system is another example of a product that exhibits network externalities that have made it difficult for other operating systems to develop.

Growth Policies

Exactly what these theories mean for growth and growth policies is the subject of much debate among economists. But there is some agreement about general policies that are good for growth. These include:

- Encouraging saving and investment.
- Formalizing property rights and reducing bureaucracy and corruption.
- Providing more of the right kind of education.
- Promoting policies that encourage technological innovation.
- Promoting policies that allow taking advantage of specialization.

Most economists would agree that each of these is good for growth. Unfortunately, the devil is in the details, and the policy problem is translating these general policies into specific politically acceptable policies.

What makes choosing a growth policy so difficult is that that choice must be made in terms of a continually changing economic environment; what made sense in the past may not make sense now. Consider the question of what is the right kind of education. In the 1990s, vocational training was discouraged because manufacturing jobs were being lost to outsourcing, robots, and machines. U.S. students were encouraged to pursue education that focused on academic knowledge.

The United States is still losing manual labor jobs to lower-wage countries, robots, and machines. But simultaneously, the Chinese and Indian workforce is becoming much more educated so that they compete with U.S. workers for higher and higher skilled jobs. Simultaneously, developments in artificial intelligence and deep learning (two methods of machine learning) are replacing what were considered highly skilled mental labor jobs (such as a doctor's ability to diagnose a patient's problems) with a computer app.

Short-Run Supply-Side Macro Policy

Some politicians argue that the best way to get the economy moving in the short run is to cut taxes on the rich since the rich are what they call job creators. As a long-run policy to encourage growth, economists have differing views about whether such cuts in taxes are appropriate. The empirical evidence is inconclusive.

As a short-run policy, however, there is much greater agreement among economists: Tax cuts for the rich are not an especially good way to create jobs. The reason is that in the short run, demand-side effects rule. Supply-side effects rule in the long run, impacting the economy over many years.

Here's the reason why tax cuts for the rich are not likely to have much impact on jobs in the short run. Tax cuts for the rich tend not to be spent as much as tax cuts for the poor. Thus, the tax cuts are more likely to go into savings, and not increase demand for goods. So, while a tax cut for the rich would have some demand-side effect, it would be smaller than if the tax cut were given to the poor or if it were spread out evenly among all people.

Another problem with expecting a tax cut for the rich to create jobs in the United States even if it were to increase aggregate demand is that in order to invest and create jobs in the United States any good businessperson will look at total costs of producing in the United States versus the total costs of producing elsewhere. So if a policy maker wants to stimulate job creation in the United States, he or she would have to either increase the costs of producing abroad or decrease the costs of producing here. Policies that do that include cutting wages, reducing regulatory burdens, and lowering costs in other ways. Cutting taxes on the rich doesn't affect their decision about whether to produce here or abroad unless the tax cut is available only if they produce goods here, and a cut in the income tax would not do that.

One recent technological breakthrough that has been stimulating growth in the United States involves a new technology that allows the extraction of large amounts of natural gas from the ground. That new technology lowers the cost of producing output in the United States relative to producing abroad, and hence increases the attractiveness of producing in the United States. For industries that are energy-intensive, energy costs can make a big difference, and that discovery has contributed to the recent economic expansion in the United States.

What this means is that the appropriate education is changing as well, and that the skills and knowledge most desired in the workforce will likely be quite different in the future than the past. The type of jobs being created within the U.S. economy involves a blend of vocational and academic training; they are jobs that work with the technology. For example, medical technicians who can use diagnosis apps, rather than doctors who diagnose, will be needed. Machinists who can use an app rather than actually doing the machining will be needed. This means that growth policies today will be different from those in the past.

Conclusion

Growth happens, or at least it generally has happened in market economies. But that doesn't mean it happens on its own. While saying precisely why growth happens is beyond economists at this point, economists have identified important sources of growth. These include capital accumulation, available resources, growth-compatible institutions, technological development, and entrepreneurship. What economists haven't been able to determine yet is how they all fit together to bring about growth, and the general feeling is that there is no single way of putting them together—what works likely changes over time. As the competition for natural resources increases and the growth dynamic moves to China and India, the United States will likely find it difficult to keep up its previous growth rate.

There is no single way of putting all the sources of growth together—what works likely changes over time.

627

Summary

- Growth is an increase in the amount of goods and services an economy can produce when both labor and capital are fully employed. *(LO27-1)*

- Growth increases potential output and shifts the production possibility curve out, allowing an economy to produce more goods. *(LO27-1)*

- Markets allow specialization and division of labor, which increases productivity and leads to growth. *(LO27-2)*

- Per capita growth means producing more goods and services per person. It can be calculated by subtracting the percentage change in the population from the percentage change in output. *(LO27-2)*

- Five sources of growth are: (1) growth-compatible institutions, (2) capital accumulation, (3) available resources, (4) technological development, and (5) entrepreneurship. *(LO27-3)*

- The loanable funds market translates savings into investment that is necessary for growth. The interest rate equilibrates saving and investment. *(LO27-3)*

- The Classical growth model focuses on the role of capital accumulation in the growth process. The law of diminishing productivity limits growth of per capita income. *(LO27-4)*

- New growth theory emphasizes the role of technology in the growth process. *(LO27-4)*

- Advances in technology have overwhelmed the effects of diminishing marginal productivity. *(LO27-4)*

- Policies that are good for growth are policies that: (1) encourage saving and investment, (2) formalize property rights, (3) provide the right kind of education, (4) encourage technological innovation, and (5) take advantage of specialization. *(LO27-4)*

Key Terms

Classical growth model	learn by doing	positive externality	social capital
division of labor	new growth theory	productivity	specialization
human capital	patent	rule of 72	technology
law of diminishing marginal productivity	per capita growth	Say's law	

Questions and Exercises ![McGraw Hill Education] connect

1. Outline some of the benefits and costs to society when it experiences growth. *(LO27-1)*

2. Assume that per capita income is growing at different rates in the following countries: Nepal, 1.3 percent; Kenya, 1.7 percent; Singapore, 7.6 percent; Egypt, 3.9 percent. How long will it take for each country to double its income per person? *(LO27-1)*

3. What roles do specialization and division of labor play in economists' support of free trade? *(LO27-2)*

4. Who most likely worked longer to buy a dozen eggs: a person living in 2019 or a person living in 1910? Why? *(LO27-2)*

5. Calculate real growth per capita in the following countries: *(LO27-2)*
   a. Democratic Republic of Congo: population growth = 3.0 percent; real output growth = −1.8 percent.

   b. Estonia: population growth = −0.4 percent; real output growth = 4.2 percent.
   c. India: population growth = 2.0 percent; real output growth = 6.0 percent.
   d. United States: population growth = 0.5 percent; real output growth = 2.5 percent.

6. In what ways do informal property rights limit growth? *(LO27-3)*

7. How can an increase in the U.S. saving rate lead to higher living standards? *(LO27-3)*

8. Demonstrate graphically how the loanable funds market translates savings into investment. What equilibrates saving and investment? *(LO27-3)*

9. Using the demand and supply of loanable funds, demonstrate the effect of the following on the interest rate. As a

result, what would you expect to be the impact of the change on growth? (*LO27-3*)

a. Government increases spending.

b. Businesses become more productive.

c. The people as a whole save more.

10. Name three types of capital and explain the differences among them. (*LO27-3*)

11. How does growth through technology differ from growth through the accumulation of physical capital? (*LO27-3*)

12. On what law of production did Thomas Malthus base his prediction that population growth would exceed growth in goods and services? (*LO27-4*)

13. Why hasn't Thomas Malthus' prediction come true? (*LO27-4*)

14. Classical growth theory and new growth theory both contribute to economists' understanding of how the sources of growth lead to economic growth. (*LO27-4*)

a. How are they the same?

b. How do they differ?

15. Explain how each of the following is expected to affect growth: (*LO27-4*)

a. Increase in technology.

b. Positive externalities.

c. Patents.

d. Learning by doing.

e. Technological lock-in.

16. What are spillover effects and how do they affect growth? (*LO27-4*)

17. What are network externalities and how do they lead to growth? (*LO27-4*)

18. In the early 20th century, worker productivity in the Horndal iron works plant in Sweden increased by 2 percent per year over a 15-year period even though the firm did not invest in new capital. What might be the cause for the increase in productivity? (*LO27-4*)

19. England once offered a prize to the person who invented an accurate clock that could be used on a ship. England then made the technology freely available. Do such policies lead to greater growth than leaving innovation to the market? Defend your answer. (*LO27-4*)

Questions from Alternative Perspectives

1. *Capitalism* was a derogatory term coined by Karl Marx to deride the riches of those who accumulated capital. He said that the accumulation of capital helps the rich get richer while simultaneously making the poor get poorer.

a. Have the poor become poorer under capitalism?

b. Based on the growth model presented in the text, what would you expect to happen to poor people's income when society accumulates capital? *(Austrian)*

2. Ecological economists believe that economic possibilities are constrained by natural laws (for example, the laws of thermodynamics, biological assimilation, and the limiting factor). Unlimited material growth from a finite resource base—spaceship earth—is therefore impossible. How many "earths" would it take for everyone to live like U.S. citizens? (To help answer this question, you might visit and take the test at www.footprintcalculator.org.) *(Institutionalist)*

3. Many Keynesians believe the best way to deal with growth is to have government promote an industrial policy that focuses on the development of technological change using tax credits, government research funding, and the transfer of technological knowledge from the military to the civilian sector.

a. Would such a policy be consistent with the new growth theory?

b. Would those believing in the Classical growth model support such a policy? *(Post-Keynesian)*

4. There is a furious debate among economists about the relationship between equality (or inequality) and economic growth. Based on the observation that developing countries often experience increasing inequality during their initial periods of rapid growth, some economists emphasize the role of inequality in establishing incentives to work, save, and invest. The experience of the East Asian economies that grew rapidly after reducing their levels of inequality (through land reform and other means) led other economists to argue that greater equality leads to faster economic growth. The reasons they cite are numerous: more political stability, greater access to credit, higher levels of spending on education, and wider land ownership.

a. How do these arguments about the positive link between equality and economic growth fit with your textbook's list of the sources of economic growth?

b. What do you think is the relationship between equality (or inequality) and economic growth? *(Radical)*

5. Christians believe that everything ultimately belongs to God. Is that belief consistent with economists' belief that property rights are necessary for growth? *(Religious)*

Issues to Ponder

1. a. If you suddenly found yourself living as a poor person in a developing country, what are some things that you now do that you would no longer be able to do? What new things would you have to do?
    b. Answer the questions again assuming that you are living in the United States 100 years ago.

2. Have the poor benefited more or less from economic growth than the rich?

3. What problem would a politician face when promoting policies to encourage saving?

4. DePaul University professor Ludovic Comeau Jr. hypothesizes that the length of time that a country has had a democratic political structure contributes positively to growth. In what way can a political structure be capital?

Answers to Margin Questions

1. The long-run growth analysis justifies its focus on supply by assuming that aggregate supply will create an equal level of aggregate demand. This is known as Say's law.   (*LO27-1*)

2. Using the rule of 72 (divide 72 by the growth rate of income), we can calculate that it will take 18 years for income to double when its growth rate is 4 percent a year.   (*LO27-1*)

3. Markets allow specialization and the division of labor, which increase productivity; greater productivity leads to growth.   (*LO27-2*)

4. Country B is experiencing the higher growth in income per capita. To calculate this, subtract the population growth rates from the income growth rates for each country. Country A's per capita growth rate is 1 percent (4 − 3) and country B's per capita growth rate is 2 percent (3 − 1).   (*LO27-2*)

5. The increases would have to be distributed so that no one whose income is below the median receives enough to bring his or her income above the median.   (*LO27-2*)

6. Private property provides an incentive for people to produce by creating the possibility of benefiting from their efforts.   (*LO27-3*)

7. With the demand for loanable funds shifting out, the interest rate will likely rise.   (*LO27-3*)

8. Three types of capital are physical capital, human capital, and social capital.   (*LO27-3*)

9. New growth focuses on technology.   (*LO27-4*)

10. The Internet connects over 4 billion people around the globe and reduces communication costs. The benefit of one person using the Internet is virtually nonexistent. The benefit of the Internet rises as more people use it because the higher usage increases the amount of information available on the Internet and increases the ability of each user to communicate.   (*LO27-4*)

The Financial Sector and the Economy

CHAPTER 28

After reading this chapter, you should be able to:

LO28-1 Discuss the functions and measures of money.

LO28-2 Define *banks* and explain how they create money.

LO28-3 Explain why the financial sector is so important to macroeconomic debates.

LO28-4 Explain the role of interest rates in an economy.

The Bulls and Bears in the Market by William Holbrook Beard
©Pictures Now/Alamy Stock Photo

The financial sector is exciting (as suggested in this famous painting *The Bulls and Bears in the Market*); it is also central to almost all macroeconomic debates. This central role is often not immediately obvious to students. In thinking about the economy, students often focus on the *real sector*—the market for the production and exchange of goods and services. In the real sector, real goods or services such as shoes, operas, automobiles, and textbooks are exchanged. That's an incomplete view of the economy. The *financial sector*—the market for the creation and exchange of financial assets such as money, stocks, and bonds—plays a central role in organizing and coordinating our economy; it makes modern economic society possible. A car won't run without oil; a modern economy won't operate without a financial sector.

As I've noted throughout this book, markets make specialization and trade possible and thereby make the economy far more efficient than it otherwise would be. But the efficient use of markets requires a financial sector that facilitates and lubricates those trades. Let's consider an example of how the financial sector facilitates trade. Say you walk into a store and buy a T-shirt. You shell out a 20-dollar bill and the salesperson hands you the T-shirt. Easy, right? Right—but why did the salesperson give you a T-shirt for a little piece of paper? The answer to that question is: Because the economy has a financial system that has convinced him that that piece of paper has value. To convince him (and you) of that requires an enormous structural system, called the financial sector, underlying the T-shirt transaction and all other transactions. That financial system makes the transaction possible; without it the economy as we know it would not exist.

The modern financial sector is highly sophisticated. It disperses credit throughout the economy in highly diverse ways. One way is through what is called *securitization*. When a bank makes you a loan, often that loan is securitized, which means that it is packaged with other loans into a large security whose value depends on all the loans that comprise the security. This large security is then broken up into smaller denomination securities and sold. This combining and breaking apart allows a person to buy a security whose value is based on the combination of all those loans that make it up, not one particular loan.

Spreading the risk through securitization is a central feature of modern financial markets.

Why package loans in this way? Because it spreads the risk of default—failure to pay back a loan—making owning the loans safer than it otherwise would be. Spreading the risk through securitization is a central feature of modern financial markets. The risk that securitizing loans cannot reduce is something called *systemic risk*—the risk that all or many of the loans all default together. As we will see in later chapters, the U.S. financial sector discovered that risk in 2008.

The Definition and Functions of Money

Money is a financial asset that makes the real economy function smoothly by serving as a medium of exchange, a unit of account, and a store of wealth.

Let's start our consideration of the financial sector by looking at the definition and function of money.

At this point you're probably saying, "I know what money is; it's currency—the dollar bills I carry around." In one sense you're right: Currency is money. But in another sense you're wrong; currency is just one example of money. In fact, a number of short-term financial assets are included as money. To see why, let's consider the definition of money: **Money** is *a highly liquid financial asset that's generally accepted in exchange for other goods, is used as a reference in valuing other goods, and can be stored as wealth.* In today's economy most of what economists call money is not currency but exists in the form of electronic holdings—an accounting entry in a computer.

To be *liquid* means to be easily changeable into another asset or good. When you buy something with money, you are exchanging money for another asset. So any of your assets that are easily spendable are money. Social customs and standard practices are central to the liquidity of money. The reason you are willing to hold money is that you know someone else will accept it in trade for something else. Its value is determined by its general acceptability to others. If you don't believe that, try spending yuan (Chinese money) in the United States. If you try to buy dinner with 100 yuan, you will be told, "No way—give me money."

©Datacraft Co Ltd/Getty Images

The U.S. Central Bank: The Fed

So is there any characteristic other than general acceptability that gives value to money? Consider the dollar bill that you know is money. Look at it. It states right on the bill that it is a Federal Reserve note, which means that it is an IOU (a liability) of the **Federal**

Reserve Bank (the Fed)—*the U.S. central bank, whose liabilities (Federal Reserve notes) serve as cash in the United States.* Individuals are willing to accept the Fed's IOUs in return for real goods and services, which means that Fed notes are money.

What, you ask, is a central bank? To answer that question, we had better first consider what a bank is. A **bank** is *a financial institution whose primary function is accepting deposits for, and lending money to, individuals and firms.* (There are more complicated definitions and many types of banks, but that will do for now.) If you have more currency than you want, you take it to the bank and it will "hold" the extra for you, giving you a piece of paper (or a computer entry) that says you have that much currency held there ("hold" is in quotation marks because the bank does not actually hold the currency). What the bank used to give you was a bank note, and what you used to bring in to the bank was gold, but those days are gone forever. These days what you bring is that Federal Reserve note described above, and what you get is a paper receipt and a computer entry in your checking or savings account. Individuals' deposits in these accounts serve the same purpose as does currency and are also considered money.

Which brings us back to the Federal Reserve Bank, the U.S. central bank. It is a bank that has the right to issue notes (IOUs). By law these Federal Reserve Bank notes are acceptable payment for people's taxes, and by convention these notes are acceptable payment to all people in the United States, and to many people outside the United States. IOUs of the Fed are what most of you think of as cash.

To understand why money is more than just cash, it is helpful to consider the functions of money in more detail. Having done so, we will consider which financial assets are included in various measures of money.

> The Federal Reserve Bank is the U.S. central bank; it has the right to issue notes that you think of as cash.

Functions of Money

As I stated above, money is an asset that can be quickly exchanged for any other asset or good. Money serves three functions:

> **Q-1** What are the three functions of money?

1. A medium of exchange.
2. A unit of account.
3. A store of wealth.

To get a better understanding of what money is, let's consider each of its functions in turn.

MONEY AS A MEDIUM OF EXCHANGE The easiest way to understand why money is used as a medium of exchange is to imagine what an economy would be like without money. Say you want something to eat at a restaurant. Without money you'd have to barter with the restaurant owner for your meal. *Barter* is a direct exchange of goods and/ or services. You might suggest bartering one of your papers or the shirt in the sack that you'd be forced to carry with you to trade for things you want. Not liking to carry big sacks around, you'd probably decide to fix your own meal and forgo eating out. Bartering is simply too difficult. Money makes many more trades possible because it does not require a double coincidence of wants by two individuals, as simple barter does.

> **Web Note 28.1**
>
> Gold

The use of money as a medium of exchange makes it possible to trade real goods and services without bartering. Instead of carrying around a sack full of diverse goods, all you need to carry around is a wallet full of money. You go into the restaurant and pay for your meal with money; the restaurant owner can spend (trade) that money for anything she wants.

Money doesn't have to have any inherent value to function as a medium of exchange. All that's necessary is that everyone believes that other people will accept it in exchange for their goods. This neat social convention makes the economy function more smoothly.

> Money doesn't have to have any inherent value to function as a medium of exchange.

MONEY AS A UNIT OF ACCOUNT
A second use of money is as a unit of account, that is, a measure of value. Money prices are actually relative prices. A money price, say 25 cents, for a pencil conveys the information of a relative price—1 pencil = ¼ of 1 dollar—because money is both our unit of account and our medium of exchange. When you think of 25 cents, you think of ¼ of a dollar and of what a dollar will buy. The 25 cents a pencil costs has meaning only relative to the information you've stored in your mind about what money can buy. If a hamburger costs $3.00, you can compare hamburgers and pencils (1 pencil = ¹⁄₁₂ of a hamburger) without making the relative price calculations explicitly.

Having a unit of account makes life much easier. For example, say we had no unit of account and you had to remember the relative prices of all goods. With three goods you'd have to memorize that an airplane ticket to Miami costs 6 lobster dinners in Boston or 4 pairs of running shoes, which makes a pair of shoes worth 1½ lobster dinners.

Memorizing even a few relationships is hard enough, so it isn't surprising that societies began using a single unit of account. If you don't have a single unit of account, all combinations of 100 goods will require that you remember millions of relative prices. If you have a single unit of account, you need know only 100 prices. A single unit of account saves our limited memories and helps us make reasonable decisions based on relative prices.

Money is used as a unit of account at a point in time, and it's also a unit of account *over time*. For example, money is a standard of deferred payments such as on college loans that many of you will be making after graduation. The value of those loan payments depends on how the money prices of all other goods change over time.

Money is a useful unit of account only as long as its value relative to the average of all other prices doesn't change too quickly. For example, in hyperinflation all prices rise so much that our frame of reference for making relative price comparisons is lost. Is 25 cents for a pencil high or low? If the price level increased 448,000 percent (as it did in late 2017 in Venezuela) or over 230 million percent (as it did in 2008 in Zimbabwe), 25 cents for a pencil would definitely be low, but would $100 be low? Without a lot of calculations we can't answer that question. A relatively stable unit of account makes it easy to answer.

Given the advantages to society of having a unit of account, it's not surprising that a monetary unit of account develops even in societies with no central bank or government. For example, in a prisoner of war camp during World War II, prisoners had no money, so they used cigarettes as their unit of account. Everything traded was given a price in cigarettes. The exchange rates on December 1, 1944, were:

1 bar of soap: 2 cigarettes

1 candy bar: 4 cigarettes

1 razor blade: 6 cigarettes

1 can of fruit: 8 cigarettes

1 can of cookies: 20 cigarettes

As you can see, all prices were in cigarettes. If candy bars rose to 6 cigarettes and the normal price was 4 cigarettes, you'd know the price of candy bars was high.

MONEY AS A STORE OF WEALTH
When you save, you forgo consumption now so that you can consume in the future. To bridge the gap between now and the future, you must acquire a financial asset. This is true even if you squirrel away currency under the mattress. In that case, the financial asset you've acquired is simply the currency itself. Money is a financial asset. (Think of it as a bond that pays no interest.) So a third use of money is as a store of wealth. As long as money is serving as a medium

Money is a useful unit of account only as long as its value relative to other prices doesn't change too quickly.

In hyperinflation, all prices rise so much that our frame of reference is lost.

As long as money is serving as a medium of exchange, it automatically also serves as a store of wealth.

The Cryptocurrency Bubble

Cryptocurrencies, such as Bitcoin and Ethereum, are much in the news. Some hail them as a revolutionary new technology that will replace money as we know it. Others, such as JPMorgan Chase CEO Jamie Dimon, call them a Ponzi scheme and a fraud. Which view is correct? The answer is complicated. The new technology behind the buzz around cryptocurrencies involves bookkeeping and accounting. Unlike current bookkeeping methods, the accounting for cryptocurrencies records and verifies exchanges by creating multiple digital entries distributed across a range of ledgers. Each record is known as a block, and each block is linked to other blocks in a different ledger in a chain. That's why the technology involved is called "blockchain" or "distributed ledger" technology. Because each transaction is listed on a large number of different independent servers and verified by an algorithm process that involves solving complicated math problems (called mining), the transactions can be secured and verified without involving banks, corporations, or government. Blockchain technology has major potential to change contracting and bookkeeping methods in the future.

But that future is a long way off and isn't what is behind much of the activity in cryptocurrencies today. What is driving much of the activity in cryptocurrencies is

©Carlos Amarillo/Shutterstock

the ability of companies to sell people cryptocurrency coins, which are a type of digital token that costs almost nothing to create. These "coins" are backed by nothing, other than some vague innuendo that somehow they will be revolutionary and the "new gold." While Bitcoin and Ethereum are the most well known, hundreds of companies sell cryptocurrencies, pulling in millions of dollars. Most have little chance of being anything other than worthless. That's what Dimon meant when he called them a fraud.

Part of the veiled promise of cryptocurrencies involves the sense that we are moving away from a cash economy, which we are, and even from a credit/debit card economy, which we also are, to a digital pay economy in which payments can be made with the swipe of a finger on an app. In a decade the economy will be largely cashless

and credit card–less. But that change to a digital currency world has nothing necessarily to do with crypto technology. Cashless transactions can be, and are, done far more cheaply and far more quickly with current bookkeeping and accounting technology than with the blockchain technology associated with cryptocurrencies. Consider M-Pesa, the phone-based money transfer service by Vodafone, which is a major provider of digital transactions throughout Africa. M-Pesa allows users to deposit money into an account stored on an app on a smartphone and transfer available funds to other users. People use M-Pesa to buy and sell goods and services as well as provide and repay loans.

Cryptocurrencies are different. None of the so-called cryptocurrencies meet, nor are they likely to meet, the definition of money anytime soon. They are not an easy medium of exchange—try spending a Bitcoin to buy your lunch. The only place where people use cryptocurrencies in transactions in any significant way has been on the dark web. The reason cryptocurrencies are preferred to dollar, credit, or cashless bank transactions on the dark web is not because the transaction is fast and cheap; it is because the illegal transactions using cryptocurrencies can be better hidden from government. Cryptocurrencies are also not a unit of account—the unit of account in the United States remains the dollar.

About the only aspect of the definition of money that cryptocurrencies meet is as a store of value. Thus, a far better name for cryptocurrencies would be crypto assets. Even here, they are not an especially good store of value since their value has fluctuated and will likely continue to fluctuate. Think of them as an alternative to Old Master paintings, Beanie Babies, commemorative coins, and stamps. If you can convince people they want them, and that others will want them in the future, their price can rise enormously. But since these assets are based on stories and dreams, their price can fall quickly. Beanie Babies that were once worth thousands of dollars now sell for 50 cents. Crypto assets have all the characteristics of assets that form the basis of bubbles.

of exchange, it automatically also serves as a store of wealth. The restaurant owner can accept your money and hold it for as long as she wants before she spends it. (But had you paid her in fish, she'd be wise not to hold it more than a few hours.)

You might wonder why people would hold money that pays no interest. Put another way: Why do people hold a government bond that pays no interest? The reason is that money, by definition, is highly liquid—it is more easily translated into other goods than are other financial assets. Since money is also the medium of exchange, it can be spent instantaneously (as long as there's a shop open nearby). Our ability to spend money for goods makes money worthwhile to hold even if it doesn't pay interest.

Alternative Measures of Money

According to the definition of *money,* what people believe is money and what people will accept as money are determining factors in deciding whether a financial asset is money. Consequently, it's difficult to measure *money* unambiguously. A number of different financial assets serve some of the functions of money and thus have claims to being called *money.* To handle this ambiguity, economists have developed different measures of money and have called them M_1 and M_2. Each is a reasonable concept of money. Let's consider their components.

M_1 consists of *currency in the hands of the public plus checking account balances.* Clearly, currency in the hands of the public (the dollar bills and coins you carry around with you) is money, but how about your checking account deposits? The reason they're included in this measure of money is that just about anything you can do with currency, you can do with a check or debit card. You can store your wealth in your checking account; you can use a check or debit card as a medium of exchange (indeed, for some transactions you have no choice but to use a check), and your checking account balance is denominated in the same unit of account (dollars) as is currency. If it looks like money, acts like money, and functions as money, it's a good bet it's money. Indeed, checking account deposits are included in all measures of money.

Currency and checking account deposits make up the components of M_1, the narrowest measure of money. Figure 28-1 presents the relative sizes of M_1's components.

M_2 is made up of *M_1 plus savings and money market accounts, small-denomination time deposits (also called CDs), and retail money funds.* The relative sizes of the components of M_2 are given in Figure 28-1.

These forms of financial assets are counted as money because they serve the functions of money. For example, savings accounts are readily spendable—all you need do is go to the bank and draw out money.

M_2's components include more financial assets than M_1. All its components are highly liquid and play an important role in providing lending capacity for commercial banks. What makes the M_2 measure important is that economic research has shown that M_2 is the measure of money often most closely correlated with the price level and economic activity.

Distinguishing between Money and Credit

You might have thought that credit cards would be included in one of the measures of *money.* But I didn't include them. In fact, credit cards are nowhere to be seen in a list of the components of money. Credit cards are not money. Credit cards aren't a financial liability of the bank that issues them. Instead, credit cards create a liability for their users (money owed to the company or bank that issued the card) and the banks have a financial asset as a result.

Let's consider how a credit card works. You go into a store and buy something with your credit card. You have a real asset—the item you bought. The store has a financial

Q-2 Why do people hold money rather than bonds when bonds pay higher interest than money?

Web Note 28.2

E-Currency

M_1 is a measure of the money supply; it consists of currency in the hands of the public plus checking accounts.

If it looks like money, acts like money, and functions as money, it's a good bet it's money.

M_2 is a measure of the money supply; it consists of M_1 plus other relatively liquid assets.

Q-3 Which would be a larger number, M_1 or M_2? Why?

Credit cards are not money.

FIGURE 28-1 Components of M₂ and M₁

The two most-used measures of the money supply are M₁ and M₂. The two primary components of M₁ are currency in the hands of the public and checking accounts. M₂ includes all of M₁, plus savings and money market accounts, retail money funds, and small-denomination time deposits.

Source: *H.6 Money Stock Measures* (www.federalreserve.gov).

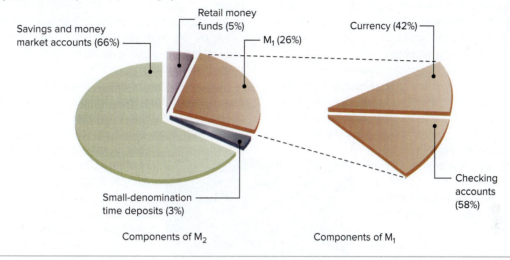

Savings and money market accounts (66%)

Retail money funds (5%)

M₁ (26%)

Currency (42%)

Small-denomination time deposits (3%)

Checking accounts (58%)

Components of M₂

Components of M₁

asset—an account receivable. The store sells that financial asset at a slight discount to the bank and gets cash in return. Either the bank collects cash when you pay off your financial liability or, if you don't pay it off, the bank earns interest on its financial asset (often at a high rate, from 12 to 18 percent per year). Credit cards are essentially prearranged loans.

Q-4 Are credit cards money?

A debit card serves the same function as a checkbook—think of it as a computer checkbook. It allows you to spend money in your bank account (to debit your account) and thus makes your bank account more liquid. But just as the physical checkbook is not money, neither is the debit card itself. However, the endorsed check torn from the checkbook and used to make a purchase is money, and so is the paperless debit card transaction. Debit cards are starting to be replaced by apps such as Venmo on smartphones and watches. In the far future apps will be embedded in our bodies. You'll just pick up what you want in a "store" and you are charged for it, assuming you have enough money in your account. Monetary transactions will be hidden and instantaneous. With money, the transaction does not involve getting a loan, even for a short time. Credit cards are different. With credit, the transaction involves a loan.

The distinction between credit and money is the following: Money is a financial asset of individuals and a financial liability of banks. Credit is savings made available to be borrowed. Credit is not an asset of the borrowing public.

Credit cards and credit impact the amount of money people hold. When preapproved loan credit is instantly available (as it is with a credit card), there's less need to hold money. (If you didn't have a credit card, you'd carry a lot more currency.) With credit immediately available, liquidity is less valuable to people. So credit and credit cards do make a difference in how much money people hold, but because they are not financial liabilities of banks, they are not money. Because of the importance of easy credit to our economy in modern financial sectors, measures of access to credit and credit availability are as important as are measures of money.

REAL-WORLD APPLICATION

Characteristics of a Good Money

The characteristics of a good money are that its supply be relatively constant, that it be limited in supply (sand wouldn't make good money), that it be difficult to counterfeit, that it be divisible (have you ever tried to spend half a horse?), that it be durable (raspberries wouldn't make good money), and that it be relatively small and light compared to its value (watermelon wouldn't make good money either). All these characteristics were reasonably (but not perfectly) embodied in gold. Many other goods have served as units of account (shells, wampum, rocks, cattle, horses, silver), but gold historically became the most important money, and in the 17th and 18th centuries gold was synonymous with money.

©Roman Malanchuk/123RF

But gold has flaws as money. It's relatively heavy, easy to counterfeit with coins made only partly of gold, and, when new gold fields are discovered, subject to fluctuations in supply. These flaws led to gold's replacement by paper currency backed only by trust that the government would keep its commitment to limit its supply.

Paper money can be a good money if somehow people can trust the government to limit its supply and guarantee that its supply will be limited in the future. That trust has not always been well placed.

Most societies today supplement paper money such as dollar bills with digital money that exists as debit and credit entries recorded on the computer. Both digital money and paper money are vulnerable to fraud. Digital money can be created by criminals who electronically change debit and credit entries, which is why banks spend billions of dollars on computer security and encryption technology each year. Paper money can be counterfeited. For example, in World War II, Germany planned to counterfeit a significant amount of British pounds and drop them in Britain to disrupt the British economy. It didn't succeed; by the time the Germans had printed the notes, they didn't have the aircraft to fly them over and drop them in Britain.

Counterfeiting continues today. For example, you may have noticed that some of the currency you carry has changed its look in recent years. That's because counterfeiters with new technology could create almost perfect counterfeit copies of the older designs. In 1989, authorities found some counterfeit U.S. $100 bills that had the right mix of cotton and linen and that had been manufactured on the very expensive Intaglio press, the same kind of press used to print real dollar bills. They called these counterfeit notes "supernotes." To stop the counterfeiters of the supernotes, the United States redesigned the U.S. currency, adding security measures such as color-shifting ink, watermarks, a security thread, an ultraviolet glow, and microprinting. Counterfeiters copied these newly designed bills, which forced U.S. authorities to redesign U.S. paper currency in 2013. Authorities will have to continue to redesign currency periodically in order to keep ahead of counterfeiters.

So far, counterfeiting is still relatively unimportant in the United States. But in some developing countries, merchants and even banks are hesitant to accept large-denomination U.S. currency, which means that counterfeiting in those countries is undermining the usefulness of the dollar as money.

Banks and the Creation of Money

Modern financial sectors are highly complex, with many different types of financial assets.

Modern financial sectors are highly complex, with many different types of financial assets (assets such as stocks or bonds, whose benefit to the owner depends on the issuer of the asset meeting certain obligations) and financial liabilities (obligations by the issuer of the financial asset). To make the financial sector understandable to students, it is useful to simplify and talk about a single financial institution—a bank—and a single concept—money—and to discuss how the amount of money can be expanded and contracted. That's what I do here. But you should remember that the discussion is simply an example of the way in which financial sectors expand and contract the amount of credit in the economy.

Banks are financial institutions that borrow from people (take in deposits) and use the money they borrow to make loans to other individuals. Banks make a profit by charging a higher interest rate on the money they lend out than they pay for the money they borrow. Individuals keep their money in banks, accepting lower interest rates, because doing so is safer and more convenient than the alternatives.

Banking is generally analyzed from the perspective of **asset management** *(how a bank handles its loans and other assets)* and **liability management** *(how a bank attracts deposits and what it pays for them)*. When banks offer people "free checking" and special money market accounts paying 1 percent, they do so after carefully considering the costs of those liabilities to them.

To think of banks as borrowers as well as lenders may seem a bit unusual, but borrowing is what they do. When you own a savings account or a checking account, the bank is borrowing from you, paying you a zero (or low) interest rate. It then lends your money to other people at a higher interest rate.

It is important to think of banks as both borrowers and lenders.

How Banks Create Money

Banks are centrally important to macroeconomics because they create money. How do banks create money? The process is simple—so simple it seems almost magical to many.

The key to understanding how banks create money is to remember the nature of financial assets: Financial assets can be created from nothing as long as an offsetting financial liability is simultaneously created. Since money is any financial asset that can be used as a medium of exchange, unit of account, and store of value, money can be created rather easily. The asset just needs to serve the functions of money. Seeing how dollar bills are created is the easiest way to begin examining the process. Whenever the Fed issues an IOU to you or someone else, it creates money.[1] Similarly, other banks create money by creating financial assets that serve the functions of money. As we saw when we considered the measures of money, bank checking accounts serve those functions, so they are money, just as currency is money. When a bank places the proceeds of a loan it makes to you in your checking account, it is creating money. You have a financial asset that did not previously exist.

Banks "create" money because a bank's liabilities are defined as money. So when a bank incurs liabilities, it creates money.

THE FIRST STEP IN THE CREATION OF MONEY   To see how banks create money, let's consider what would happen if you were given a freshly printed $100 bill. Remember, the Fed created that $100 bill simply by printing it. The $100 bill is a $100 financial asset of yours and a financial liability of the Fed, which issued it.

If the process of creating money stopped there, it wouldn't be particularly mysterious. But it doesn't stop there. Let's consider what happens next as you use that money.

THE SECOND STEP IN THE CREATION OF MONEY   The second step in the creation of money involves the transfer of money from one form to another—from currency to a bank deposit. Say you decide to put the $100 bill in your checking account. To make the analysis easier, let's assume that your bank is a branch of the country's only bank, Big Bank. All money deposited in branch banks goes into Big Bank. After you make your deposit, Big Bank is holding $100 in currency for you, and you have $100 more in your checking account. You can spend it whenever you want simply by writing a check. So Big Bank is performing a service for you (holding your money and keeping track of your expenditures) for free. Neat, huh? Big Bank must be run by a bunch of nice people.

About 95 percent of all bills printed each year replace worn-out notes. The remaining 5 percent represent new currency in circulation.

©AP Photo/Doug Mills

---

[1] As we'll see when we discuss the Fed in more detail, dollar bills aren't the Fed's only IOUs.

But wait. You and I know that bankers, while they may be nice, aren't as nice as all that. There ain't no such thing as a free lunch. Let's see why the bank is being so nice.

BANKING AND GOLDSMITHS

To see why banks are so nice, let's go way back in history to when banks first developed.[2] At that time, gold was used for money and people carried around gold to make their payments. But because gold is rather heavy, it was difficult to use for big purchases. Moreover, carrying around a lot of gold left people vulnerable to being robbed by the likes of Robin Hood. So they looked for a place to store their gold until they needed some of it.

FROM GOLD TO GOLD RECEIPTS

The natural place to store gold was the goldsmith shop, which already had a vault. For a small fee, the goldsmith shop would hold your gold, giving you a receipt for it. Whenever you needed your gold, you'd go to the goldsmith and exchange the receipt for gold.

Pretty soon most people kept their gold at the goldsmith's, and they began to wonder: Why go through the bother of getting my gold out to buy something when all that happens is that the seller takes the gold I pay and puts it right back into the goldsmith's vault? That's two extra trips.

Consequently, people began buying goods by using the receipts the goldsmith gave them to certify that they had deposited $100 (or whatever) worth of gold in his vault. At that point, gold was no longer the only money—gold receipts were also money since they were accepted in exchange for goods. However, as long as the total amount in the gold receipts directly represented the total amount of gold, it was still reasonable to say, since the receipts were 100 percent backed by gold, that gold was the money supply.

Q-5 Most banks prefer to have many depositors rather than one big depositor. Why?

GOLD RECEIPTS BECOME MONEY

Once this process of using the receipts rather than the gold became generally accepted, the goldsmith found that he had substantial amounts of gold in his vault. All that gold, just sitting there! On a normal day, only 1 percent of the gold was claimed by "depositors" and had to be given out. Usually on the same day an amount at least equal to that 1 percent came in from other depositors. What a waste! Gold sitting around doing nothing! So when a good friend came in, needing a loan, the goldsmith said, "Sure, I'll lend you some gold receipts as long as you pay me some interest." When the goldsmith made this loan, he created more gold receipts than he had covered in gold in his vault. He created money.

Pretty soon the goldsmith realized he could earn more from the interest he received on loans than he could earn from goldsmithing. So he stopped goldsmithing and went full-time into making loans of gold receipts. At that point, the number of gold receipts outstanding significantly exceeded the amount of gold in the goldsmith's vaults. But not to worry; since everyone was willing to accept gold receipts rather than gold, the goldsmith had plenty of gold for those few who wanted actual gold.

It was, however, no longer accurate to say that gold was the country's money or currency. Gold receipts were also money. They met the definition of *money*. These gold receipts were backed partially by gold and partially by people's trust that the goldsmiths would pay off their deposits on demand. The goldsmith shops had become banks.

Money is whatever meets the definition of money.

BANKING IS PROFITABLE

The banking business was very profitable for goldsmiths. Soon other people started competing with them, offering to hold gold for free. After all, if they could store gold, they could make a profit on the loans to other

---

[2]The banking history reported here is, according to historians, apocryphal (more myth than reality). But it so nicely makes the point that I repeat it anyhow.

people (with the first people's money). Some even offered to pay people to store their gold.

The goldsmith story is directly relevant to banks. People store their currency in banks and the banks issue receipts—checking accounts—that become a second form of money. When people place their currency in banks and use their receipts from the bank as money, those receipts also become money because they meet the definition of *money:* They serve as a medium of exchange, a unit of account, and a store of wealth. So money includes both currency that people hold and their deposits in the bank.

Which brings us back to why banks hold your currency for free. They do it not because they're nice, but because when you deposit currency in the bank, your deposit allows banks to make profitable loans they otherwise couldn't make.

The Process of Money Creation

With that background, let's go back to your $100, which the bank is now holding for you. You have a checking account balance of $100 and the bank has $100 currency. As long as other people are willing to accept your check in payment for $100 worth of goods, your check is as good as money. In fact, it is money in the same way gold receipts were money. But when you deposit $100, no additional money has been created yet. The form of the money has simply been changed from currency to a checking account or demand deposit.

Now let's say Big Bank lends out 90 percent of the currency you deposit, keeping only 10 percent as **reserves**—*currency and deposits a bank keeps on hand or at the Fed or central bank, to manage the normal cash inflows and outflows.* This 10 percent is the **reserve ratio** *(the ratio of reserves to total deposits)*. Banks are required by the Fed to hold a percentage of deposits; that percentage is called the *required reserve ratio*. Banks may also choose to hold an additional percentage, called the *excess reserve ratio*. The reserve ratio, then, is the sum of the required reserve ratio and the excess reserve ratio. Thus, the reserve ratio is at least as large as the required reserve ratio, and is generally significantly larger since the Fed pays interest on reserves, encouraging banks to hold large amounts of excess reserves.

So, like the goldsmith, Big Bank lends out $90 to someone who qualifies for a loan. The person that the bank loaned the money to now has $90 currency and you have $100 in a demand deposit, so now there's $190 of money, rather than just $100 of money. The $10 in currency the bank holds in reserve isn't counted as money since the bank must keep it as reserves and may not use it as long as it's backing loans. Only currency held by the public, not currency held by banks, is counted as money. By making the loan, the bank has created $90 in money.

Of course, no one borrows money just to hold it. The borrower spends the money, say on a new sweater, and the sweater store owner now has the $90 in currency. The store owner doesn't want to hold it either. She'll deposit it back into the bank. Since there's only one bank, Big Bank discovers that the $90 it has loaned out is once again in its coffers. The money operates like a boomerang: Big Bank loans $90 out and gets the $90 back again.

The same process occurs again. The bank doesn't earn interest income by holding $90, so if the bank can find additional credible borrowers, it lends out $81, keeping $9 (10 percent of $90) more in reserve. The story repeats and repeats itself, with a slightly smaller amount coming back to the bank each time. At each step in the process, money (in the form of checking account deposits) is being created.

DETERMINING HOW MANY DEMAND DEPOSITS WILL BE CREATED What's the total amount of demand deposits—money in checking and savings accounts—that will ultimately be created from your $100 when individuals hold no currency? To

The reserve ratio is the ratio of currency (or deposits at the central bank) to deposits a bank keeps as a reserve against currency withdrawals.

answer that question, we continue the process over and over: $100 + 90 + 81 + 72.9 + 65.6 + 59 + 53.1 + 47.8 + 43.0 + 38.7 + 34.9$. Adding up these numbers gives us \$686. Adding up \$686 plus the numbers from the next 20 rounds gives us \$961.08.

As you can see, that's a lot of adding. Luckily there's an easier way. Economists have shown that you can determine the amount of money that will eventually be created by such a process by multiplying the initial \$100 in money that was printed by the Fed and deposited by $1/r$, where r is the reserve ratio (the percentage banks keep out of each round including both the required and excess reserve ratios). In this case the reserve ratio is 10 percent, or .10.

Dividing,

Q-6 If banks hold 20 percent of their deposits as reserves, what is the money multiplier?

$$\frac{1}{r} = \frac{1}{.10} = 10$$

so the amount of demand deposits that will ultimately exist at the end of the process is

$$(10 \times \$100) = \$1,000$$

The \$1,000 is in the form of checking account deposits (demand deposits). The entire \$100 in currency that you were given, and that started the whole process, is in the bank as reserves, which means that \$900 (\$1,000 − \$100) of money has been created by the process.

CALCULATING THE MONEY MULTIPLIER   We will call the ratio $1/r$ the **money multiplier**—*the measure of the amount of money ultimately created per dollar deposited in the banking system, when people hold no currency*. It tells us how much money will ultimately be created by the banking system from an initial inflow of money:

The money multiplier is the measure of the amount of money ultimately created per dollar deposited by the banking system. When people hold no currency, it equals 1/r.

Amount of money created = Multiplier × New deposit

In our example, $1/.10 = 10$. Had the bank kept out 20 percent each time, the money multiplier would have been $1/.20 = 5$. If the reserve ratio were 5 percent, the money multiplier would have been $1/.05 = 20$. The higher the reserve ratio, the smaller the money multiplier, and the less money will be created.

The higher the reserve ratio, the smaller the money multiplier.

AN EXAMPLE OF THE CREATION OF MONEY   To make sure you understand the process, let's consider an example. Say that the reserve ratio is 20 percent and that John Finder finds \$10,000 in currency, which he deposits in the bank. Thus, he has \$10,000 in his checking account and the bank has \$8,000 (\$10,000 − \$2,000 in reserves) to lend out. Once it lends that money to Fred Baker, there is \$8,000 of additional money in the economy. Fred Baker uses the money to buy a new oven from Mary Builder, who, in turn, deposits the money back into the banking system. Big Bank lends out \$6,400 (\$8,000 − \$1,600 in reserves).

Now the process occurs again. Table 28-1 shows the effects of the process for five rounds, starting with the initial \$10,000. Each time the bank lends the money out, the money returns like a boomerang and serves as reserves for more loans. After five rounds we reach a point where total demand deposits are \$33,616, and the bank has \$6,723 in reserves. This is approaching the \$50,000 we'd arrive at using the money multiplier:

$$\frac{1}{r}(\$10,000) = \frac{1}{.2}(\$10,000) = 5(\$10,000) = \$50,000$$

If we carried it out for more rounds, we'd actually reach what the formula predicted.

Note that the process ends only when the bank holds all the currency in the economy, and the only money held by the public is in the form of demand deposits. Notice

TABLE 28-1 **The Money-Creating Process**

In the money-creating process, the currency keeps coming back to the banking system like a boomerang. With a 20 percent reserve requirement, ultimately (1/.2) × $10,000 = $50,000 will be created. In this example, you can see that after five rounds, much of the creation of deposits will have taken place. As you carry out the analysis further, the money creation will approach the $50,000 shown in the last line.

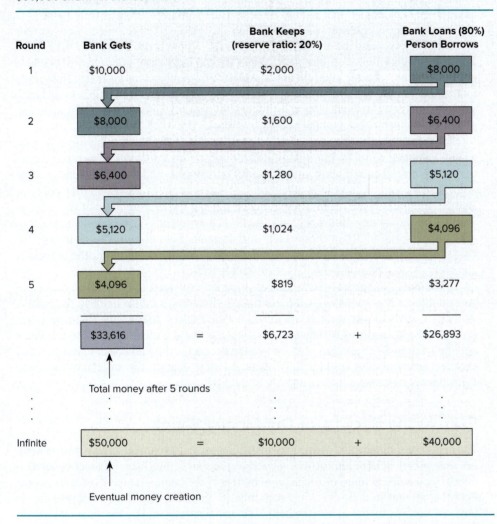

Round	Bank Gets		Bank Keeps (reserve ratio: 20%)		Bank Loans (80%) Person Borrows
1	$10,000		$2,000		$8,000
2	$8,000		$1,600		$6,400
3	$6,400		$1,280		$5,120
4	$5,120		$1,024		$4,096
5	$4,096		$819		$3,277
	$33,616	=	$6,723	+	$26,893

Total money after 5 rounds

| Infinite | $50,000 | = | $10,000 | + | $40,000 |

Eventual money creation

also that the total amount of money created depends on the amount banks hold in reserve. Specifically, an economy can support a supply of money equal to reserves times the money multiplier.

To see that you understand the process, say that banks suddenly get concerned about the safety of their loans, or can't find anyone to whom they want to loan. So they decide to keep **excess reserves**—*reserves held by banks in excess of what banks are required to hold.* What will happen to the money multiplier and the total amount of money in the economy? If you answered that it will decrease, you've got it. Excess reserves decrease the money multiplier as much as required reserves do. I mention this example because this very thing happened in the banking system in 2008. Banks became concerned about the safety of their loans; they started holding large excess reserves, and the money multiplier decreased.

Excess reserves are reserves held by banks in excess of what they are required to hold.

The Relationship between Reserves and Total Money

The preceding discussion explains how the banking system can expand the money supply far beyond the amount initially added by the Fed. As a bank makes loans, it keeps some cash and central bank reserves—often called *high-powered money*—as reserves to ensure that it has the cash if the depositor wants it. Ultimately, the reserves and the amount the bank has in deposits are related. If the banking system is fully loaned out and has no excess reserves, and people hold no cash, the relationship between the amount of reserves and the amount of money in the system is determined by the Federal Reserve Bank's reserve requirement. When people hold cash, and when banks hold excess reserves, then the central bank's reserve requirement no longer determines the total amount of money. In that case the money supply is determined by banks and individuals' decisions as well. The total money supply becomes what economists call *endogenous*—determined by the system as a whole, not solely by the central bank.

The fact that the money supply is determined endogenously doesn't mean that we cannot calculate a money multiplier after the fact. If we know what the reserve ratio (including both required reserves and excess reserves) is, and how much cash people hold, then we can, in principle, calculate the total amount of money in the economy. But the multiplier is the result of the process; it is not the driving force of the process. That's why the money multiplier isn't used much anymore. With both the amount of cash people hold and the excess reserves that banks hold continually changing, the money multiplier is not a fixed value and can be determined only after the process is complete. At that point it is no longer especially useful.

In summary, the process of money creation isn't difficult to understand as long as you remember that money is simply a bank's financial liability held by the public. Whenever banks create financial liabilities for themselves, they create financial assets for individuals, and those financial assets are money. Unfortunately for the Fed's attempt to control the amount of money in the economy, the Fed doesn't control either excess reserves or cash held by individuals. As these change, the amount of money in the economy can change independently of the Fed's actions.

Faith as the Backing of Our Money Supply

The creation of money and the money multiplier are easy to understand if you remember that money held in the form of a checking account (the financial asset created) is offset by an equal amount of financial liabilities of the bank. The bank owes its depositors the amount in their checking accounts. Its financial liabilities to depositors, in turn, are secured by the loans (the bank's financial assets) and by the financial liabilities of people to whom the loans were made. Promises to pay underlie any modern financial system.

The initial money in the story about the goldsmiths was gold, but it quickly became apparent that using gold certificates as money was far more reasonable. Therefore, gold certificates backed by gold soon replaced gold itself as the money supply. Then, as goldsmiths made more loans than they had gold, the gold certificates were no longer backed by gold. They were backed by promises to get gold if the person wanted gold in exchange for the gold certificate. Eventually the percentage of gold supposedly backing the money became so small that it was clear to everyone that the promises, not the gold, underlay the money supply.

The same holds true with banks. Initially, currency (Federal Reserve IOUs) was backed by gold, and banks' demand deposits were in turn backed by Federal Reserve IOUs. But by the 1930s the percentage of gold backing money grew so small that even the illusion of the money being backed by anything but promises was removed.

All that backs the modern money supply are bank customers' promises to repay loans and the guarantee of the government to see that the banks' liabilities to individuals will be met.

Why Is the Financial Sector Important to Macro?

In thinking about the financial sector's role, remember the following insight: *For every real transaction, there is a financial transaction that mirrors it*. For example, when you buy an apple, the person selling the apple is buying 50 cents from you by spending his apple. The financial transaction is the transfer of 50 cents; the real transaction is the transfer of the apple.

As long as the financial system is operating smoothly, you hardly know it's there; but should that system break down, the entire economy would be disrupted and would either stagnate or fall into a recession or even into a depression. That's what almost happened in 2008 in the United States when people lost faith in the existing financial institutions, and the financial sector was coming to a grinding halt. It was much like running a car without oil. Oil is only a small percentage of the car, but I can tell you from sad experience that you can run a car without oil only for about 10 miles before the entire engine seizes up. In October 2008, there was serious concern that was about to happen to the U.S. economy and the economy would totally seize up because of a meltdown of the financial sector. Only fast action by authorities prevented that from happening.

As I will discuss in a later chapter, in response to concern about such a seizing up, the U.S. government undertook unprecedented actions to try to prevent that by "bailing out" banks and other financial institutions with hundreds of billions of dollars. To understand that bailout, you have to understand the role of the financial sector in the economy. That's why it is necessary to give you an overview of the financial sector as part of your foundation of macroeconomics. Thus, although in this book I don't have a separate section on the steel sector or even the technology sector of the economy, I do have a separate section on money, banking, and the financial sector of the economy.

The financial sector has two roles. First, it facilitates trade, making it possible for normal business to happen—that's its role as a lubricant to the economy. The second, related, role of the financial sector is to transfer saving—outflows from the spending stream in hundreds of different forms—back into spending. Flows from the spending stream are channeled into the financial sector as saving when individuals buy *financial assets* from a person issuing the asset, who has a corresponding financial liability. (Financial assets and liabilities are discussed in detail in the appendix to this chapter.)

Think of this role of the financial sector as a gigantic channeling device, something like that shown in Figure 28-2. If the financial sector expands the spending flow too much, you get inflationary pressures in either goods or assets. If it contracts the spending flow too much, you get a recession. And if it transfers just the right amount, you get a smoothly running economy.

The Role of Interest Rates in the Financial Sector

Interest rates, as defined in an earlier chapter, are the prices that are charged or paid for the use of a financial asset. They are key variables in the financial sector. There are many interest rates in the economy—mortgage interest rates, interest rates on credit cards, interest rates on government bills, interest rates on corporate bonds, and many more—and they differ in many ways. There are different interest rates for different risk levels of loans, for different lengths of loans, and for different types of loans. To take

The financial sector is central to almost all macroeconomic debates because behind every real transaction, there is a financial transaction that mirrors it.

Q-7 Joe, your study partner, says that since goods and services are produced only in the real sector, the financial sector is not important to the macroeconomy. How do you respond?

For every financial asset, there is a financial liability.

The financial sector channels saving back into spending.

Web Note 28.3

Interest Rates

FIGURE 28-2   The Financial Sector as a Conduit for Savings

Financial institutions channel saving—outflows from the spending stream from various entities (government, households, and corporations)—back into the spending stream as loans to various entities (government, households, and corporations). To emphasize the fact that savings take many forms, a breakdown of the type of savings for one entity, households, is shown on the left. The same is done for loans on the right, but for corporations. Each of these loans can itself be broken down again and again until each particular loan is identified individually. The lending process is an individualistic process, and each loan is different in some way from each other loan.

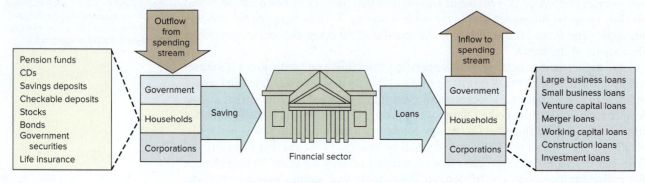

account of the length of the loan economists distinguish between short-term interest rates and long-term interest rates. To take account of different riskiness economists discuss risk premiums on loans.

In normal times in introductory economics we don't talk about risk premiums since they add another dimension of difficulty. But in recent years, they cannot be avoided since the risk premiums on loans have changed suddenly. Consider Greece in 2011 when people began to believe that the Greek government wouldn't be paying back its loans. Suddenly, the risk premium on Greek bonds shot up, from almost zero to 25 percent, so that the interest rate on Greek bonds rose from what it would have been without this risk—5 percent—to 30 percent.

Q-8   True or false? A high-risk premium makes default more likely. Explain.

Initially, that didn't affect Greece much since the high interest rate was only on new bonds. But as old, lower-interest-rate bonds became due, and had to be paid back, Greece would have had to issue new bonds at the higher interest rates. Greece couldn't afford to do so, and it would have been forced to default (not meet its debt obligation) without getting an outside loan that didn't have such high interest rates. Eventually, it got a loan from the European Union, but that loan came with an agreement that existing bondholders would not be fully paid back, and that Greece would raise taxes and cut government spending significantly. Private lenders agreed to not being fully paid back because the alternative was that they would get even less if the EU did not make the loan. So in 2012 Greece temporarily managed to escape a full economic collapse, but that possibility remained high since it was not clear that Greece had the political power to raise taxes and lower spending by as much as was required. In 2015 Greece attempted to renegotiate the deal and once again the interest rate on Greek debt shot up, and Greece found itself on the verge of financial collapse. Only another loan from the European Union prevented that collapse. That loan expired in 2018 when the financial community believed that Greece had reduced its budget deficit sufficiently; once again private institutions and individuals were willing to make direct loans to Greece.

This Greek experience captures an important element of the financial system: The financial system is based on expectations of future risk and economic conditions. Perceptions of risk can change suddenly, and when they do, expectations can create serious problems for the financial sector.

Long- and Short-Term Interest Rates

When talking about interest rates, it is useful to distinguish long-term interest rates from short-term interest rates. The long-term interest rate is the price paid for the use of financial assets with long repayment periods. Examples are mortgages and government bonds. The market for these long-term financial assets is called the *loanable funds market*. The short-term interest rate is the price paid for the use of financial assets with shorter repayment periods such as savings deposits and checking accounts. These short-term financial assets are called *money* as we discussed above. So, the long-term interest rate is determined in the loanable funds market, and the short-term interest rate is determined in the money market. Ideally, interest rate fluctuations will channel any flow of income escaping from the economy—what economists call saving—back into the economy through loans to consumers, or loans to businesses that they spend on new investment. This is why interest rates are so important to the economy. Unfortunately, interest rates do not always do a good job.

Q-9 Why are interest rates important to the economy?

To get at the problems that can develop when they do not do a good job, macroeconomics simplifies the flow of saving into investment by assuming only two types of financial assets exist: money and bonds. Some saving is translated back into investment by financial intermediaries through financial assets such as bonds, loans, and stocks. It is these financial assets to which the loanable funds market refers.[3] Savings held by individuals as money are assumed not to make their way back into the loanable funds market, and therefore not into investment. This means that some savings escape the circular flow. Compared to the complicated maze of interconnected flows that exists in reality, this is an enormous simplification, but it captures a potentially serious problem and possible cause of fluctuations in the economy.

The Demand for Money and the Role of the Interest Rate

Let's now consider the potential problems that may develop in the macroeconomy as people shift their holdings between financial assets and money. To do that, we must first ask: Why do people hold money? This is a relevant question because, by assumption, money doesn't pay any interest, whereas other financial assets do pay interest, so to hold money people are forgoing interest payments.[4]

Web Note 28.4

Stash Your Cash

Why People Hold Money

The only reason people would be willing to hold money is if they get some benefit from doing so, so we need to examine that benefit. The first benefit is easy: Money allows you to buy things. You can *spend* money; you can't spend bonds. You can change a financial asset into spendable money, but that takes time and effort. *The need to hold money for spending* is called the **transactions motive.** Second, you hold money for emergencies. For example, if your car breaks down, you'll need cash to get it towed. Knowing that there will always be unforeseen needs, you might carry $20 cash in addition to what you would otherwise carry. *Holding money for unexpected*

Q-10 What are three reasons people hold money?

---

[3]With a different interest rate for each different type of financial asset, you may be wondering which interest rate we are talking about. The answer is that we are talking about an average of the many different interest rates. Since that average interest rate is generally not easily calculable, often the interest rate on 10-year bonds is used as a proxy for the interest rate on all loanable funds.

[4]As discussed above, in today's economy, many components of money pay interest, but they pay a lower interest than do other financial assets. The analysis I present here applies to the differential rate of interest paid between money and longer-term financial assets or, more generally, to differential interest rates paid by various financial assets; we assume zero interest on money simply to keep the presentation as simple as possible.

This 18th-century etching by Robert Goez, *The Speculator,* captures a popular view of financial activities. It shows a man reduced to rags by bad speculation.

©Heritage Images/Hulton Archive/Getty Images

expenses and impulse buying is called the **precautionary motive** for holding money. The third reason for holding money is called the speculative motive. The **speculative motive** is *holding cash to avoid holding financial assets whose prices are falling*. It comes about because the price of financial assets such as bonds varies in value as the interest rate fluctuates. For example, if you expect the price of a bond (or any financial asset) to fall, that bond is not something you would want to be holding because you will be losing money by holding it; you'd rather be holding money. Your money holdings might not be earning any interest, but at least their value isn't falling like the price of the asset. In a sense, you are speculating about what the future value of the bond will be. That's why it's called the speculative motive for holding money. You hold money rather than longer-term financial assets so you don't lose if asset prices fall. (Of course, if asset prices are expected to rise, then you want to reduce your holdings of money and increase your asset holdings.)

Let's consider an example of bond price fluctuations. (Remember, bonds are often used as the reference asset for all financial assets when people provide loanable funds.) Say you have a one-year $1,000 bond that pays an interest rate of 4 percent a year, and that 4 percent is the interest rate in the economy. The bond sells for $1,000 and will provide $40 interest for the year. You're happy earning that 4 percent (that's the best you can do) so you buy the bond for $1,000. Now say that the day after you buy the bond, the interest rate in the economy rises to 6 percent. Since new bonds pay more interest than the bonds you bought, people will buy the new bonds and pay less for your bonds. That is, the price of that 4 percent $1,000 bond that you bought for $1,000 will fall, in this case to $981.13. (See the box "Interest Rates and the Price of Bonds" for a further explanation.) In one day, your bond has fallen in value by $18.87, an amount that far exceeds the interest you earned on the bond for that day. In this case, you would have preferred to have held cash instead of the bond because the cash would not have fallen in value. Holding cash in the expectation of falling bond prices is the speculative demand for money.

Most professional bond speculators, who often carry portfolios of millions and even billions of dollars of bonds, make their money on changes in the prices of bonds, not on the interest payments of bonds. The reason is that although the changes in annualized interest rates on any particular day are generally small—so small that they are measured in basis points, each of which is one one-hundredth of a percentage point—even those small changes in interest rates swamp the income made on the interest rate payments for the day.

In the real world, interest rates fluctuate all the time, and bond investors are continually looking for clues about whether the interest rates are going to rise or fall. When they expect bond prices to rise, they get rid of their cash and buy bonds; when they expect bond prices to fall, they get out of bonds and into cash.

Taking all three of these motives—transactions, precautionary, and speculative—into account, you can see that it makes sense to hold some money even though it is costing you something in forgone interest to do so—and the lower the interest rate, the greater the quantity of money demanded.

The Many Interest Rates in the Economy

As I stated earlier, the economy doesn't have just a single interest rate; it has many, just as there are many types of financial assets. (With recent developments in financial markets, the variety of financial assets grows every year.) Each of these financial assets will have an implicit interest rate associated with it (the implicit interest rate of an asset that pays no interest is the expected percentage change in the price of that asset, so if the asset price is expected to rise by 10 percent, its implicit interest rate is 10 percent).

Interest Rates and the Price of Bonds

In the example in the text, you may have thought that if the interest rate in the economy rose from 4 percent to 6 percent, and you had bought the $1,000 bond paying 4 percent, you would just sell it for $1,000 and buy the 6 percent bond. Would that you could, but that's not the way the bond market works. You only get your $1,000 back when the bond matures. If you wanted your money before that time, you would have to sell it to someone else, but the price of the 4 percent bond would have fallen as soon as the interest rate in the economy rose. More generally, we have the following relationship:

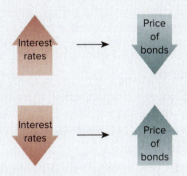

As an example, say that you buy a $1,000, one-year bond with a coupon rate (the fixed rate of interest paid on the bond) of 4 percent when the economy's interest rate is 4 percent. The price of that bond is determined by the formula

$$P = \frac{(1,000 + 40)}{1 + r}$$

where r is the interest rate in the economy and the numerator is the face value of the bond and the interest it pays. Since the bond's interest rate is the same as the interest rate for other savings instruments, you pay $1,000 for that bond. Now say that the economy's interest rate falls to 2 percent so that all new bonds being offered pay only 2 percent. That makes your bond especially desirable since it pays a higher interest rate. The price of the bond rises:

$$P = \frac{1,040}{1.02} = 1,019.61$$

People would be willing to pay up to $1,019.61. Alternatively, if the economy's interest rate rises to 6 percent, as it did in the example in the text, your bond will be less desirable and people would be willing to pay only $981.13. In summary, when the interest rate falls, the price of existing bonds rises, and when the interest rate rises, the price of existing bonds falls.

The longer the length of the bond to maturity, the more the price varies with the change in the interest rate. (For a further discussion of this inverse relationship, see the present value discussion in the appendix to this chapter.)

In such a multiple-asset market, which is what we have in the real world, the potential for the interest rate in the loanable funds market (which can be thought of as a composite market for all these varied financial assets) to differ from the interest rate in the market for a particular asset is large. The result can be a financial asset market bubble.

Let's take an example: the housing market in the early 2000s. During that period, housing prices were rising 10 to 15 percent per year (more than 50 percent in some areas) and were expected to continue to rise. That meant that the implicit rate of interest paid by houses was 10 to 15 percent (minus the costs of buying and selling the house). The interest rate that one could borrow at—the mortgage rate—was about 5.5 percent, which meant that it made sense to borrow as much as one possibly could and buy as many houses or as big a house as one could. And that's what many people did. As they did, housing prices rose, and the expectations were confirmed, which led to more and more people buying houses for speculative purposes. The strong housing market, because it led to additional construction and expenditures related to house buying, pulled the real economy along and helped the real economy expand. As long as one expected the housing prices to rise at a higher rate than the interest rate at which one could borrow, the strategy of buying as many houses as one could made good sense.

In 2006, people lowered their expectations of housing price appreciation, and started expecting housing prices to fall. So, many of those who had purchased houses with the intention of selling them at a higher price began to sell their houses more

In a multiple-asset market, which is what we have in the real world, the potential for the interest rate in the loanable funds market to differ from the interest rate in the market for a particular asset can be large. The result can be a financial asset market bubble.

aggressively so that they could return to holding their financial assets in cash before housing prices really fell. The demand for housing decreased substantially, and the equilibrium price of housing available for sale fell. The result was a financial crisis—and its aftermath—that is sufficiently important that it gets an entire chapter devoted to it.

Conclusion

We'll stop our introduction to money and the financial sector here. As you can see, money is central to the operation of the macroeconomy. If money functions smoothly, it keeps the outflow from the expenditure stream (saving) and the flow back into the expenditure stream at a level that reflects people's desires. Money can be treated simply as a mirror of people's real desires. When money doesn't function smoothly, it can cause serious problems.

When money doesn't function smoothly, it can cause serious problems.

Summary

- Money is a highly liquid financial asset that serves as a unit of account, a medium of exchange, and a store of wealth. *(LO28-1)*

- There are various measures of money. The two most important are M_1 and M_2. M_1 consists of currency in the hands of the public, plus checking account balances. M_2 is M_1 plus savings and money market accounts, small-denomination time deposits, and retail money funds. *(LO28-1)*

- Since money is what people believe money to be, creating money out of thin air is easy. How banks create money out of thin air is easily understood if you remember that money is simply a financial liability of a bank. Banks create money by loaning out deposits. *(LO28-2)*

- The money multiplier is $1/r$. It tells you the amount of money ultimately created per dollar deposited in the banking system. *(LO28-2)*

- The financial sector is the market where financial assets are created and exchanged. It channels flows out of the circular flow and back into the circular flow. *(LO28-3)*

- Interest rates play a crucial role in channeling savings back into the economy as investment. *(LO28-4)*

- People hold money for three reasons: (1) the transactions motive, (2) the precautionary motive, and (3) the speculative motive. The demand for money is inversely related to the interest rate paid on money. *(LO28-4)*

- Dramatically higher interest rates paid on particular assets compared to other financial assets can cause bubbles, which can cause problems for an economy. *(LO28-4)*

Key Terms

asset management	liability management	money multiplier	speculative motive
bank	M_1	precautionary motive	transactions motive
excess reserves	M_2	reserve ratio	
Federal Reserve Bank (the Fed)	money	reserves	

Questions and Exercises ■ connect

1. If dollar bills (Federal Reserve notes) are backed by nothing but promises and are in real terms worthless, why do people accept them? (*LO28-1*)

2. What are the three functions of money? (*LO28-1*)

3. For each of the following, state whether it is considered money in the United States. Explain why or why not. (*LO28-1*)
   a. A check you write against deposits you have at Bank USA.
   b. Brazilian reals.
   c. The available credit you have on your Mastercard.
   d. Reserves held by banks at the Federal Reserve Bank.
   e. Federal Reserve notes in your wallet.
   f. Gold bullion.
   g. Grocery store coupons.

4. What function is money serving when people compare the price of chicken to the price of beef? (*LO28-1*)

5. How does inflation affect money's function as a store of wealth? (*LO28-1*)

6. What are two components of M_2 that are not components of M_1? (*LO28-1*)

7. Categorize the following as components of M_1, M_2, both, or neither. (*LO28-1*)
   a. State and local government bonds.
   b. Checking accounts.
   c. Money market accounts.
   d. Currency.
   e. Stocks.
   f. Corporate bonds.

8. State the immediate effect of each of the following actions on M_1 and M_2: (*LO28-1*)
   a. Barry writes his plumber a check for $200. The plumber takes the check to the bank, keeps $50 in cash, and deposits the remainder in his savings account.
   b. Maureen deposits the $1,000 from her CD in a money market mutual fund.
   c. Sylvia withdraws $50 in cash from her savings account.

9. Why was character George Bailey in the film *It's a Wonderful Life* right when he stated on the day of a bank run that depositors could not withdraw all their money from the bank? (*LO28-1*)

10. Assuming individuals hold no currency, calculate the money multiplier for each of the following reserve ratios: 5 percent, 10 percent, 20 percent, 25 percent, 50 percent, 75 percent, and 100 percent. (*LO28-2*)

11. If the U.S. government were to raise the reserve requirement to 100 percent, what would likely happen to the interest rate banks pay on deposits? Why? (*LO28-2*)

12. While Jon is walking to school one morning, a helicopter flying overhead drops a $100 bill. Not knowing how to return it, Jon keeps the money and deposits it in his bank. If the bank keeps 5 percent of its money in reserves: (*LO28-2*)
    a. How much money can the bank initially lend out?
    b. After this initial transaction, by how much is the money in the economy changed?
    c. What's the money multiplier?
    d. How much money will eventually be created by the banking system from Jon's $100?

13. True or false? Policy makers in practice use the money multiplier to determine the amount of reserves needed to achieve the desired money supply. Explain. (*LO28-2*)

14. If financial institutions don't produce any tangible real assets, why are they considered a vital part of the U.S. economy? (*LO28-3*)

15. What are two roles of the financial sector? (*LO28-3*)

16. The financial sector channels saving into spending. (*LO28-3*)
    a. What is the risk of the financial sector expanding the spending flow too much?
    b. What kept this from happening in the United States from 2000 to 2007?

17. State whether the following is an example of the transactions, precautionary, or speculative motive for holding money: (*LO28-4*)
    a. I like to have the flexibility of buying a few things for myself, such as a latte or a snack, every day, so I generally carry $10 in my pocket.
    b. I never know when my car will break down, so I always keep $50 in my pocket.
    c. When the stock market is falling, money managers generally hold more in cash than when the stock market is rising.
    d. Any household has bills that are due every month.

18. If people expect interest rates to rise in the future, how will they change the quantity of money they demand? Explain your answer. (*LO28-4*)

19. In what market are short-term interest rates determined? (*LO28-4*)

Questions from Alternative Perspectives

1. The U.S. government has a monopoly on U.S. dollars.
   a. Could money be supplied privately?
   b. Has money ever been supplied privately? If so, how do you suppose people knew its value? *(Austrian)*

2. The Federal Reserve's Board of Governors is arguably the most powerful policy-making body in the United States.
   a. Since its inception, how many women have served on the Board of Governors?
   b. What do most of the current members of the Board of Governors have in common? www.federalreserve.gov/aboutthefed/bios/board/ *(Feminist)*

3. In Institutional economists' view, money not only serves as a medium of exchange, a unit of account, and a store of wealth; it also operates as an idea that shapes human understanding and interaction. Construct a list of examples during a day's interactions where money operates as an idea whereby people interact or attempt to understand a situation. For example, a friend might say, "Sherry is dating Herbert; she can do better than that!" *(Institutionalist)*

4. The chapter talks about the role that depositors and banks play in the "creation" of money.
   a. Do you think this role is consistent with the view that the money supply is only determined exogenously by the central bank?
   b. How could depositors and banks endogenously determine the money supply? *(Post-Keynesian)*

5. While *riba* (interest) is banned in Islam, profit sharing is not. An Islamically sound banking practice could be a system in which depositors deposited money under a principle of profit sharing and the bank provided funds on the same principle with a markup as payment for their financial services.
   a. How does this system differ from a system based on interest?
   b. How might the system of interest be exploitative and a system based on profit sharing not be exploitative? *(Religious)*

Issues to Ponder

1. Money is to the economy as oil is to an engine. Explain.

2. A number of U.S. localities circulate their own currency with names like "Ithaca Hours" and "Dillo Hours." Doing so is perfectly legal. These currencies are used as payment for rent, wages, goods, and so on. Are these currencies money? Explain.

3. Economist Michael Bryan reports that on the island of Palau, the Yapese used stone disks as their currency. The number of stones in front of a person's house denoted how rich he or she was.
   a. Would you expect these stones to be used for small transactions?
   b. An Irish American trader, David O'Keefe, was shipwrecked on the island, and thereafter returned to the island with a boatload of stones. If they were identical to the existing stones, what would that do to the value of the stones?

   c. If O'Keefe's stones could be distinguished from the existing stones, how would that change your answer to *b*?
   d. An anthropologist described the stones as "a memory of contributions"—the more stones a person has, the more that person has contributed to the community. Could the same description be used to describe our money?

4. U.S. paper currency is made with several features that are difficult to counterfeit, including a security thread, color-shifting ink, microprinting, a portrait, a watermark, and a fine-line printing pattern. As duplication technology, however, continually improves and more and more counterfeits are circulated, what will happen to the following?
   a. The value of money circulated.
   b. The volume of cashless transactions.
   c. The amount of money the U.S. Treasury spends to introduce additional security measures.

Answers to Margin Questions

1. The three functions of money are: (1) medium of exchange, (2) unit of account, and (3) store of wealth. *(LO28-1)*

2. Money provides liquidity and ease of payment. People hold money rather than bonds to get this liquidity and hold down transaction costs. *(LO28-1)*

3. M_2 would be the larger number since it includes all of the components of M_1 plus additional components. (*LO28-1*)

4. Credit cards are not money. Credit cards are a method by which people borrow. (*LO28-1*)

5. Banks operate on the fact that they will have some money flowing in and some money flowing out at all times. When the number of withdrawals and deposits is large, on average, they will offset one another, allowing banks to make loans on the average amount that they are holding. If there is one big depositor at a bank, this is less likely to happen, and the bank must hold larger reserves in case that big depositor withdraws that money. (*LO28-2*)

6. The money multiplier is $1/r$, which is equal to $1/.2 = 5$. (*LO28-2*)

7. I would respond by saying that the financial sector is central to the macroeconomy. It facilitates the trades that occur in the real sector. (*LO28-3*)

8. True. A higher risk premium increases the interest payments associated with a loan. To the extent that income used to pay that loan stays the same, higher expenses leave less to pay off the loan, making default more likely. (*LO28-4*)

9. Savings that escape the circular flow can cause fluctuations in the economy. Interest rates help translate the flow of savings into investment, which make their way back into the spending stream. (*LO28-4*)

10. People hold money to spend (transactions motive), for unexpected expenses and impulse buying (precautionary motive), and to avoid holding financial assets whose prices are falling (speculative motive). (*LO28-4*)

APPENDIX

A Closer Look at Financial Assets and Liabilities

Financial Assets and Financial Liabilities

To understand the financial sector and its relation to the real sector, you must understand how financial assets and liabilities work and how they affect the real economy.

An *asset* is something that provides its owner with expected future benefits. There are two types of assets: real assets and financial assets. Real assets are assets whose services provide direct benefits to their owners, either now or in the future. A house is a real asset—you can live in it. A machine is a real asset—you can produce goods with it.

Financial assets are *assets, such as stocks or bonds, whose benefit to the owner depends on the issuer of the asset meeting certain obligations.* **Financial liabilities** are *liabilities incurred by the issuer of a financial asset to stand behind the issued asset.* It's important to remember that *every financial asset has a corresponding financial liability;* it's that financial liability that gives the financial asset its value. In the case of bonds, for example, a company's agreement to pay interest and repay the principal gives bonds their value. If the company goes bankrupt and reneges on its liability to pay interest and repay the principal, the asset becomes

worthless. The corresponding liability gives the financial asset its value.

For example, a **stock** is *a financial asset that conveys ownership rights in a corporation.* It is a liability of the firm; it gives the holder ownership rights that are spelled out in the financial asset. An equity liability such as a stock usually conveys a general right to dividends, but only if the company's board of directors decides to pay them.

A debt liability conveys no ownership right. It's a type of loan. An example of a debt liability is a bond that a firm issues. A **bond** is *a promise to pay certain amounts of money at specified times in the future.* A bond is a liability of the firm but an asset of the individual who holds the bond. A debt liability such as a bond usually conveys legal rights to interest payments and repayment of principal.

Real assets are created by real economic activity. For example, a house or a machine must be built. Financial assets are created whenever somebody takes on a financial liability or establishes an ownership claim. For example, say I promise to pay you $1 billion in the future. You now have a financial asset and I have a financial liability. Understanding that financial assets can be created by a simple agreement between two people is fundamentally important to understanding how the financial sector works.

Valuing Stocks and Bonds

A financial asset's worth comes from the stream of income it will pay in the future. With financial assets such as bonds, that stream of income can be calculated rather precisely. With stocks, where the stream of income is a percentage of the firm's profits, which fluctuate significantly, the stream of future income is uncertain and valuations depend significantly on expectations.

Let's start by considering some generally held beliefs among economists and financial experts. The first is that an average share of stock in a company in a mature industry sells for somewhere between 15 and 20 times its normal profits. The second is that bond prices rise as market interest rates fall, and fall as market interest rates rise. The first step in understanding where the beliefs come from is to recognize that $1 today is not equal to $1 next year. Why? Because if I have $1 today, I can invest it and earn interest (say 10 percent per year), and next year I will have $1.10, not $1. So if the annual interest rate is 10 percent, $1.10 next year is worth $1 today; alternatively, $1 next year is worth roughly 91 cents today. A dollar two years in the future is worth even less today, and dollars 30 years in the future are worth very little today.

Present value is *a method of translating a flow of future income or savings into its current worth.* For example, say a smooth-talking, high-pressure salesperson is wining and dining you. "Isn't that amazing?" the salesperson says. "My company will pay $10 a year not only to you, but also to your great-great-great-grandchildren, and more, for 500 years—thousands of dollars in all. And I will sell this annuity—this promise to pay money at periodic intervals in the future—to you for a payment to me now of only $800, but you must act fast. After tonight the price will rise to $2,000."

Do you buy it? My rhetoric suggests that the answer should be no—but can you explain why? And what price *would* you be willing to pay?

To decide how much an annuity is worth, you need some way of valuing that $10 per year. *You can't simply add up the $10 five hundred times.* Doing so is wrong. Instead you must *discount* all future dollars by the interest rate in the economy. Discounting is required because a dollar in the future is not worth a dollar now.

If you have $1 now, you can take that dollar, put it in the bank, and in a year you will have that dollar plus interest. If the interest rate you can get from the bank is 5 percent, that dollar will grow to $1.05 a year from now. That means if the interest rate is 5 percent, if you have 95 cents now, in a year it will be worth nearly a dollar ($0.9975 = $0.95 + 5% × $0.95 to be exact).

Reversing the reasoning, $1 one year in the future is worth a little bit more than 95 cents today. So the present value of $1 one year in the future at a 5 percent interest rate is 95 cents.

A dollar *two* years from now is worth even less today. Carry out that same reasoning and you'll find that if the interest rate is 5 percent, $1 two years from now is worth approximately 90 cents today. Why? Because you could take 90 cents now, put it in the bank at 5 percent interest, and in two years have almost $1.

The Present Value Formula

Carrying out such reasoning for every case would be a real pain. But luckily, there's a formula and a table that can be used to determine the present value (*PV*) of future income. The formula is

$$PV = A_1/(1 + i) + A_2/(1 + i)^2 + \cdots + A_n/(1 + i)^n$$

where

A_n = the amount of money received n periods in the future

i = the interest rate in the economy (assumed constant)

Solving this formula for any time period longer than one or two years is complicated. To deal with it, people either use a business calculator or a present value table such as the one in Table A28-1.

Table A28-1(a) gives the present value of a single dollar at some time in the future at various interest rates. Notice a couple of things about the chart. First, the further into the future one goes, the lower the present value. Second, the higher the interest rate, the lower the present value. At a 12 percent interest rate, $1 fifty years from now has a present value of essentially zero.

Table A28-1(b) is an annuity table; it tells us how much a constant stream of income for a specific number of years is worth. Notice that as the interest rate rises, the value of an annuity falls. At an 18 percent interest rate, $1 per year for 50 years has a present value of $5.55. To get the value of amounts other than $1, simply multiply the entry in the table by the amount. For example, $10 per year for 50 years at 18 percent interest is 10 × $5.55, or $55.50.

As you can see, the interest rate in the economy is a key to present value. *You must know the interest rate to know the value of money over time.* The higher the current (and assumed constant) interest rate, the more a given amount of money in the present will be worth in the future. Or, alternatively, the higher the current interest rate, the less a given amount of money in the future will be worth in the present.

TABLE A28-1 (A AND B) **Sample Present Value and Annuity Tables**

	Interest Rate							Number of Years	Interest Rate						
Year	3%	4%	6%	9%	12%	15%	18%		3%	4%	6%	9%	12%	15%	18%
1	$0.97	$0.96	$0.94	$0.92	$0.89	$0.87	$0.85	1	$ 0.97	$ 0.96	$ 0.94	$ 0.92	$0.89	$0.87	$0.85
2	0.94	0.92	0.89	0.84	0.80	0.76	0.72	2	1.91	1.89	1.83	1.76	1.69	1.63	1.57
3	0.92	0.89	0.84	0.77	0.71	0.66	0.61	3	2.83	2.78	2.67	2.53	2.40	2.28	2.17
4	0.89	0.85	0.79	0.71	0.64	0.57	0.52	4	3.72	3.63	3.47	3.24	3.04	2.85	2.69
5	0.86	0.82	0.75	0.65	0.57	0.50	0.44	5	4.58	4.45	4.21	3.89	3.60	3.35	3.13
6	0.84	0.79	0.70	0.60	0.51	0.43	0.37	6	5.42	5.24	4.92	4.49	4.11	3.78	3.50
7	0.81	0.76	0.67	0.55	0.45	0.38	0.31	7	6.23	6.00	5.58	5.03	4.56	4.16	3.81
8	0.79	0.73	0.63	0.50	0.40	0.33	0.27	8	7.02	6.73	6.21	5.53	4.97	4.49	4.08
9	0.77	0.70	0.59	0.46	0.36	0.28	0.23	9	7.79	7.44	6.80	6.00	5.33	4.77	4.30
10	0.74	0.68	0.56	0.42	0.32	0.25	0.19	10	8.53	8.11	7.36	6.42	5.65	5.02	4.49
15	0.64	0.56	0.42	0.27	0.18	0.12	0.08	15	11.94	11.12	9.71	8.06	6.81	5.85	5.09
20	0.55	0.46	0.31	0.18	0.10	0.06	0.04	20	14.88	13.59	11.47	9.13	7.47	6.26	5.35
30	0.41	0.31	0.17	0.08	0.03	0.02	0.01	30	19.60	17.29	13.76	10.27	8.06	6.57	5.52
40	0.31	0.21	0.10	0.03	0.01	0.00	0.00	40	23.11	19.79	15.05	10.76	8.24	6.64	5.55
50	0.23	0.14	0.05	0.01	0.00	0.00	0.00	50	25.73	21.48	15.76	10.96	8.30	6.66	5.55

(a) Present Value Table (value now of $1 to be received x years in the future)
The present value table converts a future amount into a present amount.

(b) Annuity Table (value now of $1 per year to be received for x years)
The annuity table converts a known stream of income into a present amount.

Some Rules of Thumb for Determining Present Value

Sometimes you don't have a present value table or a business calculator handy. For those times, there are a few rules of thumb and simplified formulas for which you don't need either a present value table or a calculator. Let's consider two of them: the infinite annuity rule and the rule of 72.

THE ANNUITY RULE To find the present value of an annuity that will pay $1 for an infinite number of years in the future when the interest rate is 5 percent, we simply divide $1 by 5 percent (.05). Doing so gives us $20. So at 5 percent, $1 a year paid to you forever has a present value of $20. The **annuity rule** is that *the present value of any annuity is the annual income it yields divided by the interest rate.* Our general annuity rule for any annuity is expressed as

$$PV = X/i$$

That is, the present value of an infinite flow in income, X, is that income divided by the interest rate, i.

Most of the time, people don't offer to sell you annuities for the infinite future. A typical annuity runs for 30,

40, or 50 years. However, the annuity rule is still useful. As you can see from the present value table, in 30 years at a 9 percent interest rate, the present value of receiving $1 a year forever is $10.27 so we can use this infinite flow formula as an approximation of long-lasting, but less than infinite, flows of future income. We simply subtract a little bit from what we get with our formula. The longer the time period, the less we subtract. For example, say you are wondering what $200 a year for 40 years is worth when the interest rate is 8 percent. Dividing $200 by 0.08 gives $2,500, so we know the annuity must be worth a bit less than $2,500. (It's actually worth $2,411.)

The annuity rule allows us to answer the question posed at the beginning of this section: How much is $10 a year for 500 years' worth right now? The answer is that it depends on the interest rate you could earn on a specified amount of money now. If the interest rate is 10 percent, the maximum you should be willing to pay for that 500-year $10 annuity is $100:

$$\$10/.10 = \$100$$

If the interest rate is 5 percent, the most you should pay is $200 ($10/.05 = $200). So now you know why you should have said no to that super salesperson who offered it to you for $800.

The Press and Present Value

The failure to understand the concept of present value often shows up in the popular press. Here are three examples.

> Headline: **COURT SETTLEMENT IS $40,000,000**
>
> Inside story: The money will be paid out over a 40-year period.
>
> Actual value: $11,925,000 (8 percent interest rate).

> Headline: **DISABLED WIDOW WINS $25 MILLION LOTTERY**
>
> Inside story: The money will be paid over 20 years.
>
> Actual value: $13,254,499 (8 percent interest rate).

> Headline: **BOND ISSUE TO COST TAXPAYERS $68 MILLION**
>
> Inside story: The $68 million is the total of interest and principal payments. The interest is paid yearly; the principal won't be paid back to the bond purchasers until 30 years from now.
>
> Actual value: $20,000,000 (8 percent interest rate).

Such stories are common. Be on the lookout for them as you read the newspaper or watch the evening news.

THE RULE OF 72   A second rule of thumb for determining present values of shorter time periods is the **rule of 72,** which states:

> *The number of years it takes for a certain amount to double in value is equal to 72 divided by the rate of interest.*

Say, for example, that the interest rate is 4 percent. How long will it take for your $100 to become $200? Dividing 72 by 4 gives 18, so the answer is 18 years. Conversely, at a 4 percent interest rate the present value of $200 eighteen years in the future is about $100. (Actually it's $102.67.)

Alternatively, say that you will receive $1,000 in 10 years. Is it worth paying $500 for that amount now if the interest rate is 9 percent? Using the rule of 72, we know that at a 9 percent interest rate it will take about eight years for $500 to double:

$$72/9 = 8$$

So the future value of $500 in 10 years is more than $1,000. It's probably about $1,200. (Actually it's $1,184.) So if the interest rate in the economy is 9 percent, it's not worth paying $500 now in order to get that $1,000 in 10 years. By investing that same $500 today at 9 percent, you can have $1,184 in 10 years.

The Importance of Present Value

Many business decisions require such present value calculations. In almost any business, you'll be looking at flows of income in the future and comparing them to present costs or to other flows of money in the future.

Generally, however, when most people calculate present value, they don't use any of the formulas. They go to their computer, press in the numbers to calculate the present value, and watch while the computer displays the results.

Let's now use our knowledge of present value to explain the two observations at the beginning of this section: (1) An average share of stock sells for between 15 and 20 times its normal profits and (2) bond prices and interest rates are inversely related. Since all financial assets can be broken down into promises to pay certain amounts at certain times in the future, we can determine their value with the present value formula. If the asset is a bond, it consists of a stream of income payments over a number of years and the repayment of the face value of the bond. Each year's interest payment and the eventual repayment of the face value must be calculated separately, and then the results must be added together.

If the financial asset is a share of stock, the valuation is a bit less clear since a stock does not guarantee the payment of anything definite—just a share of the profits. No profits, no payment. So, with stocks, expectations of profits are of central importance. Let's consider an example: Say a share of stock is earning $1 per share per year and is expected to continue to earn that long into the future. Using the annuity rule and an interest rate of 6.5 percent, the present value of that future stream of expected earnings is about 1/.065, or a bit more than $15. Assuming profits are expected to grow slightly, that would mean that the stock should sell for somewhere around $20, or 20 times its profit per share, which is the explanation to economists' view that an average stock sells for about 15 times normal profits.

Do Financial Assets Make Society Richer?

Financial assets are neat. You can call them into existence simply by getting someone to accept your IOU. *Remember, every financial asset has a corresponding financial liability equal to it.* So when individuals in a country increase their financial assets by $1 trillion, they are also increasing their financial liabilities by $1 trillion. An optimist would say a country is rich. A pessimist would say it's poor. An economist would say that financial assets and financial liabilities are simply opposite sides of the ledger and don't indicate whether a country is rich or poor. You have to go beyond financial assets and liabilities.

To find out whether a country is rich or poor, you must look at its *real assets.* If financial assets increase the economy's efficiency and thereby increase the amount of real assets, they make society better off. This is most economists' view of financial assets. If, however, they decrease the efficiency of the economy (as some economists have suggested some financial assets do because they focus productive effort on financial gamesmanship), financial assets make society worse off.

The same correspondence between a financial asset and its liability exists when a financial asset's value changes. Say stock prices fall significantly. Is society

poorer? The answer is: It depends on the reason for the change. Let's say there is no known reason. Then, while the people who own the stock are poorer, the people who might want to buy stock in the future are richer since the price of assets has fallen. So in a pure accounting sense, society is neither richer nor poorer when the prices of stocks rise or fall for no reason.

But there are ways in which changes in the value of financial assets might signify that society is richer or poorer. For example, the changes in the values of financial assets might *reflect* (rather than cause) real changes. If suddenly a company finds a cure for cancer, its stock price will rise and society will be richer. But the rise in the price of the stock doesn't cause society to be richer. It reflects the discovery that made society richer. Society would be richer because of the discovery even if the stock's price didn't rise.

There's significant debate about how well the stock market reflects real changes in the economy. Classical economists believe it closely reflects real changes; Keynesian economists believe it doesn't. But both sides agree that the changes in the real economy, not the changes in the price of financial assets, underlie what makes an economy richer or poorer.

To see the answer to the second—bond prices and interest rates are inversely related—say the interest rate rises to 10 percent. Then the value of the stock or bond that is earning a fixed amount—in this case $1 per share—will go down to $10. Interest rate up, value of stock or bond down. This is the explanation of the second observation.

There is nothing immutable in the above reasoning. For example, if promises to pay aren't trustworthy, you don't put the amount that's promised into your calculation; you put in the amount you actually expect to receive. That's why when a company or a country looks as if it's going to default on loans or stop paying dividends, the value of its bonds and stock will fall considerably. For example, in the early 2000s, many people thought Argentina would default on its bonds. That expectation caused the price of Argentinean bonds to fall and interest rates to rise more than 30 percentage points.

Of course, the expectations could go in the opposite direction. Say that the interest rate is 10 percent, and that you expect a company's annual profit, which is now $1 per share, to grow by 10 percent per year. In that case, since expected profit growth is as high as the interest rate, the current value of the stock is infinite. It was such expectations of future profit growth that fueled the Internet stock craze in the late 1990s and caused the valuation of firms with no current profits (indeed, many were experiencing significant losses) at multiples of sales of 300 or more. Financial valuations based on such optimistic expectations are the reason most economists considered the stock market in Internet stocks to be significantly overvalued in the late 1990s and correctly predicted the fall in prices that occurred in 2001 and 2002.

Key Terms

annuity rule	financial assets	present value	stock
bond	financial liabilities	rule of 72	

Questions and Exercises

1. If the government prints new $1,000 bills and gives them to all introductory students who are using the Colander text, who incurs a financial liability and who gains a financial asset?

2. Is the currency in your pocketbook or wallet a real or a financial asset? Why?

3. Joe, your study partner, has just said that, in economic terminology, when he buys a bond he is investing. Is he correct? Why?

4. Joan, your study partner, has just made the following statement: "A loan is a loan and therefore cannot be an asset." Is she correct? Why or why not?

5. How much is $50 to be received 50 years from now worth if the interest rate is 6 percent? (Use Table A28-1.)

6. How much is $50 to be received 50 years from now worth if the interest rate is 9 percent? (Use Table A28-1.)

7. Your employer offers you a choice of two bonus packages: $1,400 today or $2,000 five years from now. Assuming a 6 percent rate of interest, which is the better value? Assuming an interest rate of 10 percent, which is the better value?

8. Suppose the price of a one-year bond with a $100 face value that pays 10 percent interest is $98.
   a. Are market interest rates likely to be above or below 10 percent? Explain.
   b. What is the bond's yield or return?
   c. If market interest rates fell, what would happen to the price of the bond?

9. Explain in words why the present value of $100 to be received in 10 years would decline as the interest rate rises.

10. A 6 percent bond will pay you $1,060 one year from now. The interest rate in the economy is 10 percent. How much is that bond worth now?

11. You are to receive $100 a year for the next 40 years. How much is it worth now if the current interest rate in the economy is 6 percent? (Use Table A28-1.)

12. You are to receive $200 in 30 years. About how much is it worth now? (The interest rate is 3 percent.)

13. A salesperson calls you up and offers you $200 a year for life. If the interest rate is 9 percent, how much should you be willing to pay for that annuity?

14. The same salesperson offers you a lump sum of $20,000 in 10 years. How much should you be willing to pay? (The interest rate is still 9 percent.)

15. What is the present value of a cash flow of $100 per year forever (a perpetuity), assuming:
    The interest rate is 10 percent.
    The interest rate is 5 percent.
    The interest rate is 20 percent.
    a. Working with those same three interest rates, what are the future values of $100 today in one year? How about in two years?
    b. Working with those same three interest rates, how long will it take you to double your money?

16. State whether you agree or disagree with the following statements:
    a. If stock market prices go up, the economy is richer.
    b. A real asset worth $1 million is more valuable to an individual than a financial asset worth $1 million.
    c. Financial assets have no value to society since each has a corresponding liability.
    d. The United States has much more land than does Japan. Therefore, the value of all U.S. land should significantly exceed the value of land in Japan.
    e. U.S. GDP exceeds Japan's GDP; therefore, the stock market valuation of U.S.-based companies should exceed that of Japan-based companies.

Monetary Policy

> There have been three great inventions since the beginning of time: fire, the wheel and central banking.
>
> —Will Rogers

CHAPTER 29

Fed Chairman Jerome Powell
Source: U.S. Federal Reserve

After reading this chapter, you should be able to:

LO29-1 Explain how monetary policy works in the *AS/AD* model.

LO29-2 Discuss how monetary policy works in practice.

LO29-3 Discuss the tools of conventional monetary policy.

LO29-4 Discuss the complex nature of monetary policy and the importance of central bank credibility.

The chair of the U.S central bank—the Federal Reserve Bank, or "the Fed"—is often called the second most important person in government. He or she is in charge of maintaining the financial health of the economy. Thus, when the financial sector almost seized up in the fall of 2008, the Fed stepped in and undertook policies to try to prevent it from collapsing. Those policies were part of its "lender of last resort" function in times of financial crisis.

It isn't only in financial crises that the Fed is important. In normal times, it is responsible for the country's monetary policy, and in this chapter I discuss the Fed's role and monetary policy in normal conditions. (In the next chapter I discuss the Fed's role in a financial crisis and the debate about its recent unconventional policy.)

How Monetary Policy Works in the Models

Monetary policy is *a policy of influencing the economy through changes in the banking system's reserves that influence the money supply, credit availability, and interest rates in the economy.* Unlike fiscal policy, which is controlled by the government directly, monetary policy is controlled by the U.S. central bank, the Fed. Monetary policy works through its influence on credit conditions and

FIGURE 29-1 (A AND B) **The Effect of Monetary Policy in the *AS/AD* Model**

Expansionary monetary policy shifts the *AD* curve to the right; contractionary monetary policy shifts the *AD* curve to the left. In **(a)** we see how monetary policy affects both real output and the price level. If the economy is at or above potential, as in **(b)**, expansionary monetary policy will cause input costs to rise, which will eventually shift the *SAS* curve up enough so that real output remains unchanged. The only long-run effect of expansionary monetary policy when the economy is above potential is to increase the price level.

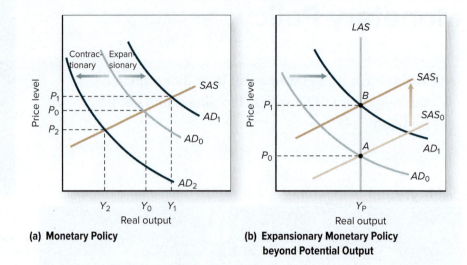

(a) Monetary Policy

(b) Expansionary Monetary Policy beyond Potential Output

the interest rate in the economy. In Figure 29-1(a), I show how it works in the standard macro model. Expansionary monetary policy shifts the *AD* curve out to the right and contractionary monetary policy shifts it in to the left. Changes in nominal income will be split between changes in real income and changes in the price level.

If the economy is significantly above potential output, once long-run equilibrium is reached, monetary policy affects only nominal income and the price level, as shown in Figure 29-1(b). Real output remains unchanged. Suppose the economy begins at potential output Y_P (point A), and expansionary monetary policy shifts the *AD* curve from AD_0 to AD_1. Because the economy is beyond potential, rising input price pressures very quickly shift the *SAS* curve up from SAS_0 to SAS_1. Once the long-run equilibrium has been reached, the price level has risen from P_0 to P_1 and real output returns to potential output (point B). So, beyond potential output, expansionary monetary policy does not affect real output.

The general rule is: Expansionary monetary policy increases nominal income. The increase in prices may not entirely offset the rise in nominal income and real income may rise. Its effect on real income depends on how the price level responds:

$$\%\Delta\text{Real income} = \%\Delta\text{Nominal income} - \%\Delta\text{Price level}$$

Thus, if nominal income rises by 5 percent and the price level rises by 2 percent, real income will rise by 3 percent.

Q-1 Demonstrate the effect of expansionary monetary policy in the *AS/AD* model.

Let's see how monetary policy works in the standard model where it serves as one of the key tools of macro policy. It works by changing aggregate expenditures, thereby shifting the aggregate demand curve out to the right or in to the left. Monetary policy affects aggregate demand indirectly by changing short-term and long-term interest rates. Here's how: Expansionary monetary policy adds reserves to banks. When banks have more reserves, they will be more inclined to lend those reserves. It's better to earn 4 percent interest on a loan than 1.25 percent interest from the Fed. To attract borrowers, banks will have an incentive to reduce their interest rates on loans. Later in the chapter we will talk about the way in which the process actually works, but for now simply recognize that when the Fed increases reserves in the banking system, banks have an incentive to lower interest rates. As interest rates fall, investment expenditures rise, which shifts the aggregate demand curve to the right, as we saw in Figure 29-1. The opposite happens when the Fed reduces reserves, and therefore money, in the economy.

Expansionary monetary policy is monetary policy aimed at reducing interest rates and raising the level of aggregate demand.

Summarizing, **expansionary monetary policy** is *a policy that increases the money supply and decreases the interest rate*. It tends to *increase* both investment and output.

Contractionary monetary policy works in the opposite direction. **Contractionary monetary policy** is *a policy that decreases the money supply and increases the interest rate.* It tends to *decrease* both investment and output.

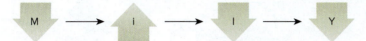

Contractionary monetary policy is monetary policy aimed at increasing interest rates and thereby restraining aggregate demand.

How Monetary Policy Works in Practice

Models make it all look so easy. Would that it were so easy. The reality of monetary policy is much messier and more complicated, and in this section, I discuss some of the institutional details that make monetary policy so complicated. I begin with a short summary of the structure and workings of the Federal Reserve Bank of the United States.

Monetary Policy and the Fed

Monetary policy is conducted by a country's **central bank**—*a type of banker's bank whose financial obligations underlie an economy's money supply.* The central bank in the United States is the Fed. If commercial banks (the banks you and I use) need to borrow money, they go to the central bank. If there's a financial panic and a run on banks, the central bank is there to make loans to the banks until the panic goes away. Since its IOUs (I owe you's) are cash, the Fed can create money simply by issuing an IOU. It is this ability to create money that gives the central bank the power to control monetary policy. (A central bank also serves as a financial adviser to government. As is often the case with financial advisers, the government sometimes doesn't like the advice and doesn't follow it.)

It is the central bank's ability to create money that gives it the power to control monetary policy.

In many countries, such as Great Britain, the central bank is a part of the government, just as this country's Department of the Treasury and Department of Commerce are part of the U.S. government. In the United States, the central bank is not part of the government in the same way. The box "Central Banks in Other Countries" gives you an idea of some differences.

Structure of the Fed

The Fed is not just one bank; it is composed of 12 regional banks along with the main Federal Reserve Bank, whose headquarters are in Washington, D.C. The Fed is governed by a seven-member Board of Governors. Members of the Board of Governors, together with the president of the New York Fed and a rotating group of four presidents of the other regional banks, are voting members of the **Federal Open Market Committee (FOMC),** *the Fed's chief body that decides monetary policy.* All 12 regional bank presidents attend, and can speak at, FOMC meetings. The financial press and business community follow their discussions closely. There are even Fed watchers whose sole occupation is to follow what the Fed is doing and to tell people what it will likely do.

Q-2 What group of the Fed decides monetary policy?

The president of the United States appoints each governor for a term of 14 years, although most governors choose not to complete their terms. The president also designates one of the governors to be the chairperson of the Fed for a four-year term. A chairperson can serve multiple terms, and the Fed chairperson is sometimes referred to as the second most powerful person in Washington (the most powerful being the president of the United States).

Web Note 29.1

Other Central Banks

The Fed's general structure reflects its political history. Figure 29-2 demonstrates that structure. Notice in Figure 29-2(a) that most of the 12 regional Fed banks are in

FIGURE 29-2 (A AND B)   The Federal Reserve System

The Federal Reserve System is composed of 12 regional banks. It is run by the Board of Governors. The Federal Open Market Committee (FOMC) is the most important policy-making body.

Source: The Board of Governors of the Federal Reserve System (www.federalreserve.gov).

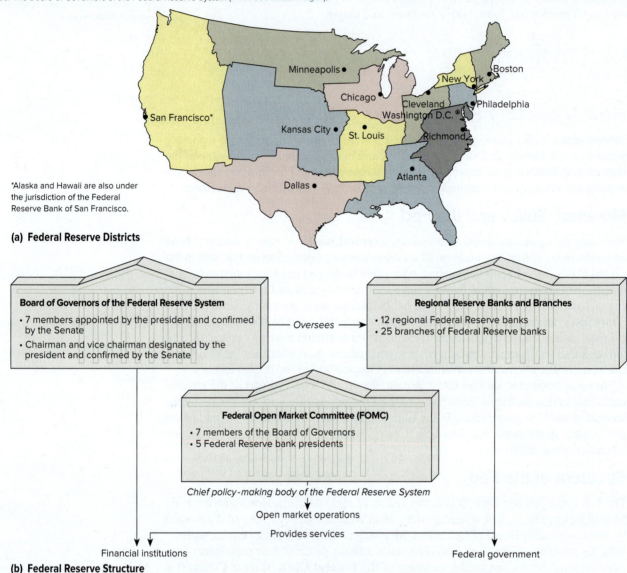

*Alaska and Hawaii are also under the jurisdiction of the Federal Reserve Bank of San Francisco.

(a) Federal Reserve Districts

Board of Governors of the Federal Reserve System
- 7 members appointed by the president and confirmed by the Senate
- Chairman and vice chairman designated by the president and confirmed by the Senate

Oversees →

Regional Reserve Banks and Branches
- 12 regional Federal Reserve banks
- 25 branches of Federal Reserve banks

Federal Open Market Committee (FOMC)
- 7 members of the Board of Governors
- 5 Federal Reserve bank presidents

Chief policy-making body of the Federal Reserve System

Open market operations

Provides services

Financial institutions   Federal government

(b) Federal Reserve Structure

the East and Midwest. The South and West have only three banks: Atlanta, Dallas, and San Francisco. The reason is that in 1913, when the Fed was established, the West and South were less populated and less important economically than the rest of the country, so fewer banks were established there.

As these regions grew, the original structure remained because no one wanted to go through the political wrangling that restructuring would bring about. Instead, the southern and western regional Feds established a number of branches to handle their banking needs.

Even though each of the 12 geographic districts has a separate regional Federal Reserve bank, these regional banks have little direct power over the banking system.

Central Banks in Other Countries

In the United States, the central bank is the Fed, and much of this chapter is about its structure. But the Fed is only one of many central banks in the world. Let's briefly introduce you to some of the others.

The People's Bank of China

The People's Bank of China (PBOC) was established in 1948, shortly after the communist victory and the establishment of the People's Republic of China, by nationalizing all Chinese banks and incorporating them into a single bank. (The former Chinese central bank, named the Central Bank of China, was relocated to Taipei in 1949 and is the central bank for Taiwan.) From 1949 to 1978, the PBOC was the only bank in the People's Republic of China.

In the 1980s the commercial banking functions of the PBOC were split off into state-owned independent banks, and the PBOC began focusing on central bank functions such as monetary policy and regulation of the financial sector. In 1995, it was restructured and consciously modeled after the U.S. Fed. It opened nine regional branches and focused its operations on foreign reserve issues, monetary policy, and financial regulation.

European Central Bank

In the late 1990s a number of European Union countries formed a monetary union, creating a common currency called the euro, and a new central bank called the European Central Bank (ECB), whose structure is still evolving. As of 2019, the governing council had 25 members, composed primarily of heads of central banks in countries that had adopted the euro.

According to its charter, the primary objective of the ECB is different from the Fed's; the ECB is focused solely on maintaining price stability, as was the former German central bank, the Bundesbank, after which it was modeled. Some economists have considered the ECB an expansion of the Bundesbank for the entire EU.

That view has changed over the past decade, as the ECB struggled with a severe recession and the Greek debt crisis. In that decade, its focus has changed from only maintaining price stability to a focus similar to the Fed, which includes trying to expand economic activity. Instead of seeing its target as zero inflation, it has been trying to encourage some inflation in the belief that doing so will expand economic growth. The changes have not been uniformly seen as positive, and there is dissension within the governing council.

People's Bank of China
©AStock/Corbis

The Bank of England

The Bank of England is sometimes called the Old Lady of Threadneedle Street (because it's located on that street, and the British like such quaint characterizations). It does not use a required reserve mechanism. Instead, individual banks determine their own needed reserves, so any reserves they have would, in a sense, be excess reserves. Needless to say, bank reserves tend to be much lower in England than they are in the United States.

How does the Old Lady control the money supply? Until recently, with the equivalent of open market operations and with informal directives to banks, what might be called "tea control." Since England has only a few large banks, the Old Lady passed on the word at tea as to which direction she thought the money supply should be going and the banks complied. Alas for sentimentalists, "tea control" is fading in England, as are many quaint English ways.

The Bank of Japan

Like the People's Bank of China, the Bank of Japan is quite similar to the Fed. It uses primarily open market operations to control the money supply. Reserve requirements are similar to the Fed's, but because it allows banks a longer period in which to do their averaging, and Japan does not have the many small banks that the United States does (it is small banks that often hold excess reserves in the United States), excess reserves tend to be lower in Japan than in the United States. The Japanese financial system exhibits more interdependence between the central bank, commercial banks, and industry than does the U.S. system, which means that Japanese companies get more of their funding from commercial banks, which in turn borrow more from the Bank of Japan than U.S. commercial banks borrow from the Fed. The financial position of many Japanese commercial banks was questionable over the past decade, and the Bank of Japan worked with the banks to restructure loans without causing a breakdown of the financial system. More recently, like most central banks, it has focused on policies to increase growth and create more inflation.

Clearly, there's more to be said about each of these central banks, but this brief introduction should give you a sense of both the similarities and the diversities among the central banks of the world.

How Independent Should the Central Bank Be?

The Fed is relatively independent, but not all central banks are. One of the big debates in the early 2000s concerned how independent the central bank should be. Advocates of central bank independence argued that independence allows central banks to make the hard political decisions that a government influenced by political pressures cannot make. Increasing interest rates hurts—it slows down the economy and causes unemployment. But if the economy is above its sustainable level, it needs to be slowed down, or inflation will accelerate. As former Fed chair William Martin said, "The job of the Federal Reserve is to take away the punch bowl just when the party is getting good." Independence, such as exists with the U.S. central bank, gives the Fed the ability to do that.

In some developing countries, the central bank is part of the government—and economists have found that when that is the case, the punch bowl tends to remain out longer. The result is that the money supply is more expansionary, and there tend to be higher levels of inflation.

There are many dimensions of independence—one is *goal independence* and another is *policy instrument independence*. Goal independence is having the freedom to determine what ultimate goals, such as low unemployment or low inflation, take priority. Policy instrument independence is having the freedom to determine how to achieve those goals. Many economists point out that goal independence is not necessarily a good thing. In a democracy, goals are determined in the political process, and in a well-functioning democracy, the central bank is accountable for achieving the goals set by the political process, and does not set the goals itself. Once the goals are set, then one can talk about policy instrument independence.

Alan Blinder, former vice chair of the Fed, put it this way:

> The independence of the Fed means, to me, two things. First, that we have very broad latitude to pursue our goals as we see fit; we decide what to do in pursuit of those goals.
>
> Second, it means that once our monetary policy decisions are made, they cannot be reversed by anybody in the U.S. government—except under extreme circumstances. (Congress would have to pass a law limiting the power of the Fed.) But although we are free to choose the means by which we achieve our goals, the goals themselves are given to us by statute, by the U.S. Congress. And that is how it should be in a democracy.

In the United States, the Fed has policy instrument independence, but not goal independence. By federal law, the goals of the Federal Reserve Bank are "maximum employment," "stable prices," and "moderate long-term interest rates." Those are different goals than the goals of the European Central Bank (ECB); the ECB's goal is only "stable prices." These different goals, however, blend together as conventional wisdom changes. For example, in the 1980s and 1990s, central banks argued that the best way to achieve maximum employment was to provide a system of stable prices and to prevent inflation. Thus, the ECB's and the Fed's differing mandates were seen as leading to the same policy—one designed to focus almost solely on inflation. More recently, conventional wisdom has changed, as concern about the contractionary effects of deflation, or even slow inflation, has replaced concern about inflation. This has led the Fed to focus more on employment goals, and on policies that stimulate the economy, particularly in the years after the 2008 recession. The ECB has followed suit and has undertaken expansionary policies, trying to increase the level of inflation, even though those policies don't directly follow from its mandated goal.

District banks and their branch banks handle administrative matters and gather information about business and banking conditions in their geographic regions for the Fed.

Duties of the Fed

Web Note 29.2

The Fed

In legislation establishing the Fed, Congress gave it six explicit functions:

1. Conducting monetary policy (influencing the supply of money and credit in the economy).
2. Supervising and regulating financial institutions.
3. Serving as a lender of last resort to financial institutions.

4. Providing banking services to the U.S. government.

5. Issuing coin and currency.

6. Providing financial services (such as check clearing) to commercial banks, savings and loan associations, savings banks, and credit unions.

In normal times, the most important of these functions is monetary policy. In times of financial crisis, the "lender of last resort" function is the most important. In this chapter I focus on monetary policy in normal times. In the next chapter, when I discuss the Fed's reaction to the financial crisis of 2008 and 2009, I will focus more on the "lender of last resort" function.

The Tools of Conventional Monetary Policy

You've already seen that monetary policy shifts the *AD* curve. Let's now consider how it does so in practice. To do so, we need to look more specifically at the institutional structure of the banking system and the role of the Fed in that institutional structure.

Think back to our discussion of the banking system in the last chapter. Banks take in deposits, make loans, and buy other financial assets, keeping a certain percentage of reserves for those transactions. Those reserves are IOUs of the Fed— either vault cash held by banks or deposits at the Fed. *Vault cash, deposits at the Fed, plus currency in circulation* make up the **monetary base.** The monetary base held at banks serves as legal reserves of the banking system. By controlling the monetary base, the Fed can influence the amount of money in the economy and the activities of banks. The money supply is determined directly by the monetary base (the amount of IOUs that the Fed has outstanding), and, indirectly, by the amount of credit that banks extend.

Allowable reserves are either banks' vault cash or deposits at the Fed.

Open Market Operations

The primary way that the Fed changes the amount of reserves in the system is through **open market operations**—*the Fed's buying and selling of Treasury bills and Treasury bonds* (the only type of asset that, until recently, the Fed held in any appreciable quantity). These open market operations are the primary tool of monetary policy in normal times.

The Fed's buying and selling of government securities is called open market operations.

When the Fed buys Treasury bills and Treasury bonds, it pays for them with IOUs that serve as reserves for banks. These IOUs don't have to be a written piece of paper. They may simply be a computer entry credited to a bank's account at the Fed.

Because the IOUs that the Fed uses to buy a government security serve as reserves to the banking system, with the simple act of buying a Treasury bond and paying for it with its IOU, the Fed can increase the money supply (since this creates reserves for the bank). To increase the money supply, the Fed goes to the bond market, buys a bond, and pays for it with its IOU. The individual or firm that sold the bond now has an IOU of the Fed. When the individual or firm deposits the IOU in a bank—presto!—the reserves of the banking system are increased. If the Fed buys bonds, it increases the monetary base. The total money supply rises by the increase in the monetary base times the money multiplier.

When the Fed sells Treasury bonds, it collects back some of its IOUs, reducing banking system reserves and decreasing the money supply. Thus,

To expand the money supply, the Fed buys bonds.

To contract the money supply, the Fed sells bonds.

Web Note 29.3

The FOMC

Q-3 When the Fed buys bonds, is it expanding or contracting the money supply?

Inside an FOMC Meeting

Let's go inside one of the eight annual Federal Open Market Committee (FOMC) meetings to gain some insight into how the Fed actually conducts monetary policy. The meeting consists of FOMC members and top Fed staff sitting around a large table debating what should be done. There's been enormous preparation for the meeting. The economists on the Federal Reserve staff have tracked the economy, and have made economic forecasts. Based on their studies, they've briefed the FOMC members, and the high-level staff get to sit in on the meeting. (Getting to sit in on the meeting is seen as a real perk of the job.)

The information they've put together is gathered in two books, which are distinguished by colors. The *Beige Book* is prepared by each of the 12 regional Federal Reserve banks and summarizes regional business conditions based on local surveys and conversations with local business people. The *Tealbook* is prepared by the staff of the Federal Reserve in Washington, D.C.; it presents a two-year forecast of the U.S. economy as a whole and analyzes three possible monetary policy options. The Fed releases the *Tealbook* to the public five years after it is first published.

The meeting begins with a summary of monetary policy actions since the committee last met, followed by a forecast of the economy. The Fed governors and regional bank presidents also present their forecasts. Once current economic conditions and forecasts are discussed, the director of monetary affairs presents the three monetary policy proposals in the *Tealbook*. Then there is open discussion of the various policy proposals. The committee meeting ends with a vote on what policy to follow, along with a policy directive on what open market operations to execute. At that point, the FOMC also makes a public announcement regarding current policy actions as well as what future actions it may take. For example, consider the following statement issued by the FOMC:

> The Federal Open Market Committee decided today to keep its target for the federal funds rate at 5¼ percent. Recent indicators have been mixed and the adjustment

Source: U.S. Federal Reserve

in the housing sector is ongoing. Nevertheless, the economy seems likely to continue to expand at a moderate pace over coming quarters. Recent readings on core inflation have been somewhat elevated. Although inflation pressures seem likely to moderate over time, the high level of resource utilization has the potential to sustain those pressures. In these circumstances, the Committee's predominant policy concern remains the risk that inflation will fail to moderate as expected. Future policy adjustments will depend on the evolution of the outlook for both inflation and economic growth, as implied by incoming information.

The announcement was made at about 2:15 p.m. and within the next hour, the interest rate in the economy fell and the stock market shot up, with the Dow Jones Industrial Average rising 1.3 percent, as you can see in the graph below.

MINUTE-BY-MINUTE

Dow Jones Industrial Average

Yesterday's close: **12,447.57, up 1.3%**

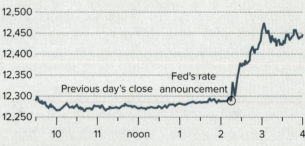

Source: WSJ Market Data Group.

Why did this happen? The statement did not announce a change of interest rates. It said only that future policy adjustments are uncertain. What caused the change was what was not said in the statement. Previous statements had said that the Fed was leaning toward raising interest rates. This one did not, which led many in the stock market to believe that the Fed might lower interest rates in the future. Since traders saw that as good for the stock market, they bought stocks, pushing their prices up.

Understanding open market operations is essential to understanding monetary policy as it is actually practiced in the United States. So let's go through some examples.

Open market operations involve the purchase or sale of Treasury bills and bonds. When the Fed buys bonds, it deposits the funds in its accounts at a bank. Bank cash reserves rise. Banks don't like to hold excess reserves, so they generally lend out the excess, thereby expanding the deposit base of the economy. The money supply rises by the money multiplier times the amount of bonds the Fed purchases. Thus, an open market purchase is an example of *expansionary monetary policy* (monetary policy that tends to reduce interest rates and raise income) since it raises the money supply (as long as the banks strive to minimize their excess reserves).

An open market sale has the opposite effect. Here, the Fed sells bonds. In return for the bond, the Fed receives a check drawn against a bank. The bank's reserve assets are reduced (since the Fed "cashes" the check and takes the money away from the bank), and the money supply falls. That's an example of *contractionary monetary policy* (monetary policy that tends to raise interest rates and lower income).

> An open market purchase is an example of expansionary monetary policy since it raises the money supply.

Reserves and the Money Supply

As I discussed in the previous chapter, the total amount of money created from a given amount of currency depends on the percentage of deposits that a bank keeps in reserves (the bank's reserve ratio). By law, the Fed controls the minimum percentage of deposits banks keep in reserves by controlling the reserve requirement of all U.S. banks. That minimum is called the **reserve requirement**—*the percentage the Federal Reserve Bank sets as the minimum amount of reserves a bank must have*. Recall, raising the reserve requirement lowers the money supply; lowering the reserve requirement raises the money supply.

> Raising the reserve requirement lowers the money supply and vice versa.

Before 2008 the reserve rate was essentially the reserve requirement. By raising the requirement the Fed could decrease the money supply; by lowering it the Fed could increase it.

To see why that worked, consider what would happen if the government raised the reserve requirement. Some banks would be short of reserves. What does a bank do if it comes up short of reserves? It can borrow from another bank that has excess reserves in what's called the Federal funds market. (The rate of interest at which these reserves can be borrowed is called the *Fed funds rate*. As I will discuss below, in normal times this Fed funds rate is a significant indicator of monetary policy.)

> In normal times the Fed funds rate is a significant indicator of monetary policy.

Another option that the bank has if it is short of reserves is to stop making new loans and to keep as reserves the proceeds of loans that are paid off. Still another option is to sell Treasury bonds to get the needed reserves. (Banks often hold some of their assets in Treasury bonds so that they can get additional reserves relatively easily if they need them.) Treasury bonds are sometimes called *secondary reserves*. They do not count as bank reserves—only IOUs of the Fed count as reserves. But Treasury bonds can be easily sold and transferred into cash, which does count as reserves. Banks use all these options.

The reason the Fed can use the reserve requirement to decrease the money supply is that while these options are open to the individual banks, they are not open to the entire system of banks. The total amount of reserves available is controlled by the Fed, and if the entire banking system is short of reserves, the banking system will have to figure out a way either to reduce the need for reserves or to borrow reserves from the Fed.

The ability of the Fed to use the reserve requirement to control the money supply changed in 2008 when banks began holding large amounts of excess reserves. The additional reserves that the Fed put into the banking system went into excess reserves and did not increase the money supply. Essentially, the money multiplier fell enough to offset any increase in reserves. Such a situation is called a **liquidity trap**—*a situation*

> **Q-4** In recent years, why hasn't the Fed's increasing reserves led to an increase in the money supply?

Using the Money Multiplier in Practice

The money multiplier has been a staple of the macro principles course since its inception, and it remains an important concept in understanding how the monetary base is related to the aggregate supply of money in the economy. But recent changes in the financial system have made the operational use of the multiplier less important. For the most part, central banks don't determine how much to change the monetary base to get a desired change in the money supply using an assumed fixed multiplier. Instead, they adjust the monetary base to target either a desired amount of bank credit in the economy or a short-term interest rate.

The money multiplier relationship continues to be true by definition, but it is not the operational concept that it once was. The reasons include the decrease in the reserve requirement (in many countries, required reserves are zero); financial innovations that have increased the ways in which individuals can hold money; the increase in the amount of cash that individuals hold; and the decline in the stability of the relationship between the money supply and output. Each of these makes it harder to use the money multiplier as an operational variable, which is why much of the monetary policy discussion today focuses more on the interest rate than on the money supply.

in which additional reserves go into excess reserves and not the money supply. In a liquidity trap banks don't increase lending when the Fed increases reserves because the banks believe that it would be better to retain the increase in reserves rather than make new loans. When banks are not lending, the Fed cannot increase the money supply in a conventional way—by increasing reserves. It is like pushing on a string. As much as the Fed pushes the string on one end, the other end doesn't budge. You can see in Figure 29-3 that this is just what happened in 2008 when excess reserves increased enormously.

Excess reserves continued to increase until about 2014 and have remained high even though the economy has expanded significantly and banks are making loans. These excess reserves make the reserve requirement of little importance. An important reason why banks hold more excess reserves is that beginning in 2011 the Fed began to pay interest on excess reserves held by banks, making it far less costly for banks to hold them. In 2018 that rate was 1.5 percent. By changing this rate, the Fed can influence the amount of reserves in the system and hence the money supply, thus giving the Fed a new policy tool.

Web Note 29.4

Paying Interest on Reserves

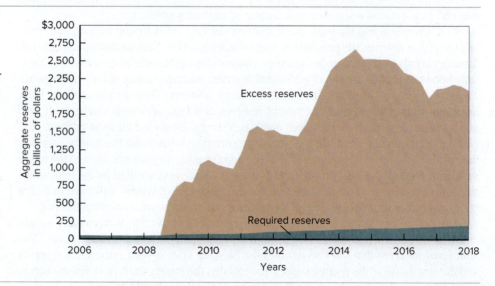

FIGURE 29-3 **Banking Reserves**

Beginning in 2008, commercial banks began holding significant excess reserves, making conventional monetary policy tools less effective.

If the Fed wants to decrease the money supply, it can raise the interest rate paid on reserves; if the Fed wants to increase the money supply, it can lower the rate. The Fed can even make this rate negative, essentially taxing banks on their excess reserves. Thus, the excess reserve interest rate tool allows the Fed to increase the money supply even when market interest rates are close to zero. Since it is when interest rates are close to zero that conventional expansionary monetary policy (buying bonds) becomes particularly ineffective, this change can be useful when the economy is in a liquidity trap. The Fed has not yet aggressively tried to use excess reserve interest rate policy, but it may in the future. Instead, it has introduced a number of other unconventional tools that I will discuss in the next chapter.

If the Fed wants to decrease the money supply, it can raise the interest rate paid on reserves; if the Fed wants to increase the money supply, it can lower the rate.

Borrowing from the Fed and the Discount Rate

As I stated at the beginning of the chapter, a central bank is a banker's bank, and if the entire banking system is short of reserves, banks can go to the Federal Reserve and take out a loan. The **discount rate** is *the rate of interest the Fed charges for loans it makes to banks.* An increase in the discount rate makes it more expensive for banks to borrow from the Fed; a decrease in the rate makes it less expensive for banks to borrow. So, an increase in the discount rate discourages banks from borrowing and contracts the money supply; a decrease in the discount rate encourages the banks to borrow and increases the money supply.

The discount rate is the rate of interest the Fed charges for loans it makes to banks.

The Fed Funds Market

To get an even better sense of the way monetary policy works, let's look at it from the perspective of a bank. The bank will review its books, determine how much in reserves it needs to meet its reserve requirement, and see if it has excess reserves or a shortage of reserves.

Say your bank didn't make as many loans as it expected to, so it has a surplus of reserves (excess reserves). Say also that another bank has made a few loans it didn't expect to make, so it has a shortage of reserves. The bank with surplus reserves can lend money to the bank with a shortage, and it can lend it overnight as **Fed funds**—*loans of excess reserves banks make to one another.* At the end of a day, a bank will look at its balances and see whether it has a shortage or surplus of reserves. If it has a surplus, it will call a Federal funds dealer to learn the **Federal funds rate**—*the interest rate banks charge one another for Fed funds.* Say the rate is 6 percent. The bank will then agree to lend its excess reserves overnight to the other bank for the daily equivalent of 6 percent per year. It's all done electronically, so there's no need actually to transfer funds. In the morning the money (plus overnight interest) is returned. The one-day interest rate is low, but when you're dealing with millions or billions, it adds up.

The Federal funds rate is the interest rate banks charge one another for overnight reserve loans.

The Federal funds market, the market in which banks lend and borrow reserves, is highly efficient. The Fed can reduce reserves, and thereby increase the Fed funds rate, by selling bonds. Alternatively, when the Fed buys bonds, it increases reserves, causing the Fed funds rate to fall. Generally, large city banks are borrowers of Fed funds; small country banks are lenders of Fed funds.

Q-5 If most banks are short of reserves, what will happen to the Fed funds rate?

Figure 29-4 shows the Fed funds rate and the discount rate since 1990. Notice that the Fed funds rate tended to be slightly above the discount rate until 2003, when the Fed changed its operating procedures and began setting the discount rate slightly above the Fed funds rate. As you can see, in 2001 and 2002 the Fed funds rate fell from 6 to 1.25 percent as the Fed followed an expansionary monetary policy. In mid-2004 the Fed began to raise the Fed funds rate. Then, in 2008, the financial crisis led the Fed to lower the Fed funds rate to almost zero. Starting in 2017, the Fed began raising the Fed funds target rate, as it moved to return to conventional monetary policy. In mid-2018 the target Fed funds rate was 2 and the Fed was expected to raise it to about 2.5 by the end of 2018.

The financial crisis led the Fed to lower the Fed funds rate to almost zero.

FIGURE 29-4   **The Fed Funds Rate and the Discount Rate**

The Federal Reserve Bank follows expansionary or contractionary monetary policy by targeting a lower or higher Fed funds rate. The discount rate generally follows the Fed funds rate closely. Before 2003, it was kept lower than the Fed funds rate. Since 2003, the discount rate has been set slightly above the Fed funds rate target.

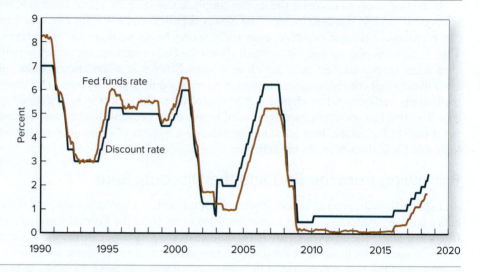

OFFENSIVE AND DEFENSIVE ACTIONS

Economists keep a close eye on the Federal funds rate in determining the state of monetary policy. It has become an important intermediate target of the Fed in determining what monetary policy to conduct. Remember, the Fed sets minimum reserve requirements, but the actual amount of reserves available to banks is influenced by the amount of cash people hold and excess reserves that banks may choose to hold. That changes daily. For example, say there's a storm, and businesses don't make it to the bank with their cash. Bank reserves will fall even though the Fed didn't do anything. The Fed can, and does, offset such changes—by buying and selling bonds. Such actions are called *defensive actions.* They are designed to maintain the current monetary policy. These defensive actions are to be contrasted with *offensive actions,* which are actions meant to make monetary policy have expansionary or contractionary effects on the economy.

Q-6   There's been a big storm and cash held by individuals has increased. Should the Fed buy or sell bonds? Why?

Monetary policy affects interest rates such as the Federal funds rate. The Fed looks at the Federal funds rate to determine whether monetary policy is tight or loose.

THE FED FUNDS RATE AS AN OPERATING TARGET

How does the Fed decide whether its buying and selling of bonds is having the desired effect? It has to look at other targets—and in recent years the Federal funds rate has been the operating target of the Fed. Thus, the Fed determines whether monetary policy is tight or loose depending on what is happening to the Federal funds rate. An increasing rate means that monetary policy is tight; a decreasing rate means monetary policy is loose. In practice, it targets a range for that rate, and buys and sells bonds to keep the Federal funds rate within that range. If the Federal funds rate rises above the Fed's target range, it buys bonds, which increases reserves and lowers the Federal funds rate. If the Federal funds rate falls below the Fed's target range, it sells bonds, which decreases reserves and raises the Federal funds rate.

The Complex Nature of Monetary Policy

While the Fed focuses on the Fed funds rate as its operating target, it also has its eye on its four ultimate targets: stable prices, acceptable employment, sustainable growth, and moderate long-term interest rates. But those ultimate targets are only indirectly affected by changes in the Fed funds rate, so the Fed watches what are called *intermediate targets:* consumer confidence, stock prices, interest rate spreads, housing starts, and a host of others. Intermediate targets are not always good guides for the Fed's ultimate targets. The Federal Reserve Bank of San Francisco once had an exhibit of an electronic video

REAL-WORLD APPLICATION

Will the Reserve Requirement Be Eliminated?

The Financial Services Regulatory Relief Act of 2006 allowed the Fed to reduce the reserve ratio to zero and to pay interest on reserves that banks maintain at the Fed. As discussed in the text, in November of 2008 the Fed started paying interest on reserves, but it has not yet eliminated the reserve requirement. In practice, however, its importance as a monetary tool has been largely eliminated.

If the Fed decides to reduce the reserve requirement to zero, it will be following the practices of central banks of other industrialized nations such as Canada, the United Kingdom, New Zealand, and Japan. The reason the Fed is adjusting its policy tools is that financial institutions have changed. More and more financial transactions take place outside the banking system, and distinguishing banks from other financial institutions has become harder and harder.

Essentially, if the Fed reduces the reserve requirement to zero, all reserves will become excess reserves. When that happens, the interest rate paid on reserve balances will become a key element in the determination of reserves and hence of the money supply. Thus, the Fed will be able to affect reserves through the discount rate, open market operations, and the interest rate paid on reserves.

The transition to the new system will likely involve some changes in the amount of reserves held by banks, but it is unlikely to have a significant effect on the actual conduct of monetary policy. In practice, central banks conduct monetary policy largely by targeting short-term interest rates through open market operations. If the system changes, the Fed will establish a relationship between the discount rate (the rate the Fed charges banks for lending reserves), the interest rate on reserves, and the targeted Fed funds rate. Which of these will become the lead indicator of Fed policy will depend on the relative differentials that the Fed chooses for these interest rates.

game in its lobby.[1] The object of the game was to hit a moving target with a dart from a moving arm. With both the arm and the target moving, most visitors missed the target.

The game was there to demonstrate the difficulties of implementing monetary policy. Monetary policy "shoots from a moving arm." Ultimately, policy actions of the Fed influence output and inflation, but the influence is not direct, and many other factors also influence output and inflation.

In reality, the Fed's problem is even more complicated than the video game suggests. A more telling game would be one modeled after a Rube Goldberg machine. If you hit the first moving target, it releases a second dart when hit. That second dart is supposed to hit a second moving target, which in turn releases a third dart aimed at yet another moving target. Given the complicated path that monetary policy follows, it should not be surprising that the Fed often misses its ultimate targets. Small wonder that the Fed often doesn't have the precise effect it wants.

Web Note 29.5

A Moving Arm

The following diagram summarizes the tools and targets of the Fed:

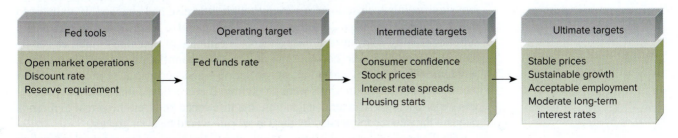

---

[1]Because of security concerns, central bank lobbies are now generally off limits to the public and this exhibit is no longer accessible.

The Taylor Rule

Former U.S. Treasury economist John Taylor has summarized a rule that, in the late 1990s and early 2000s, described Fed policy relatively well. The rule, which has become known as the **Taylor rule,** can be stated as follows: *Set the Fed funds rate at 2 percent plus current inflation if the economy is at desired output and desired inflation. If the inflation rate is higher than desired, increase the Fed funds rate by 0.5 times the difference between desired and actual inflation. Similarly, if output is higher than desired, increase the Fed funds rate by 0.5 times the percentage deviation.*

Formally the Taylor rule is:

Fed funds rate = 2 percent + Current inflation

+0.5 × (actual inflation less desired inflation)

+0.5 × (percent deviation of aggregate output from potential)

Q-7 If inflation is 1 percent, the Fed wants 2 percent inflation, and output is 2 percent below potential, what would the Taylor rule predict for a Fed funds rate target?

Let's consider some examples. Say that inflation is 2.5 percent, the Fed's target rate of inflation is 2 percent, and the aggregate output exceeds potential output by 1 percent. That means that the Fed would set the Fed funds rate at 5.25 percent [2 + 2.5 + 0.5 (2.5 − 2) + 0.5(1)]. The first row in the table below shows the calculations. The second row shows another example with lower current inflation.

Federal Funds Rate	=	2 Percent	+	Current Inflation	+	0.5(Actual less targeted inflation)	+	0.5(Deviation from potential output)
5.25	=	2	+	2.5	+	0.5(2.5 − 2)	+	0.5(1)
4.5	=	2	+	2	+	0.5(2 − 2)	+	0.5(1)

Web Note 29.6

The Taylor Rule

Notice that the Taylor rule depends on one's estimate of potential output. Because conventional macroeconomists see potential output as significantly higher than do macroeconomists who believe that the economy is experiencing a structural stagnation, they would tend to target a lower Fed funds rate than would a structural stagnation macroeconomist.

The Fed has never slavishly followed the Taylor rule. For example, in late 2000 and early 2001, the economy was 1 percent over potential output by most estimates, and inflation was 2 percent, which was equal to the target rate. The Taylor rule predicted that the Fed would set the Fed funds rate at 4.5 percent. (See the calculations in row 2 of the table.) Instead, it targeted a 5.5 percent rate because it was especially concerned about the economy overheating. Then right after September 11, the Fed became concerned about the economy going into a severe recession and it lowered the Fed funds rate significantly—close to zero—even though little else had changed. It maintained that low interest rate from 2002 through 2018 compared to what the Taylor rule would suggest, even by conventional macro theory's estimate of potential output, as can be seen in Figure 29-5. The Fed chose to do this because inflation did not seem to be a problem—the fear was deflation, not inflation—and because it wanted to avoid a recession that many economists were predicting. If one believed that the U.S. economy was experiencing a structural stagnation, the difference between the actual Fed funds rate and the rate recommended by the Taylor rule would be even greater.

The Fed policy during this time period goes to the heart of the debate about policy today. The issue was that, while there was not inflation in goods, asset prices were rising

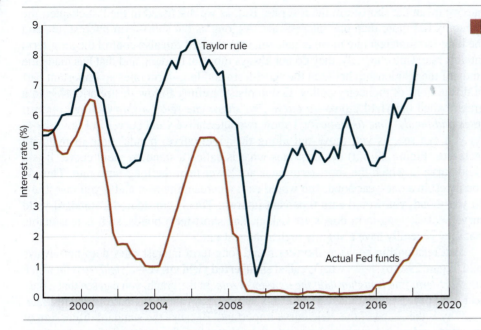

quickly, which might have been a financial bubble. One of the most important bubbles was in the housing market. Critics of Fed policy argued that these financial bubbles were being fueled by the low interest rates and the availability of credit encouraged by a historically low Fed funds rate. As you can see in Figure 29-5, in 2002 through 2004 the Fed set the interest rate far below what the Taylor rule suggested. In 2005, however the Fed began to worry about inflation and began to raise the Fed funds rate closer to where the Taylor rule suggested it should be. Soon thereafter the housing bubble started to burst. The higher interest rates of 2006 and 2007 did not last, and, as the economy fell into a deep recession and financial crisis, the Fed significantly lowered interest rates to essentially zero, and did anything it could to increase the money supply in unconventional ways. We will discuss this episode in the next chapter.

As the economy began to pick up in 2011, the Taylor rule called for a significant rise in the Fed funds rate as you can see in Figure 29-5. Again, the Fed did not follow the Taylor rule and kept the Fed funds rate at close to zero up until 2016. As the economy picked up steam in 2017 and 2018, the Taylor rule called for a Fed Funds rate of almost 8 percent, but the Fed kept the Fed Funds rate at below 2 percent. As should be clear, the Fed does not slavishly follow the Taylor rule. The episode is a good example of how the Fed uses models. It has a model for normal times, and it has another model for crises. The art of monetary policy is deciding which type of situation the economy is in.

CONTROLLING THE INTEREST RATE   Notice how the Taylor rule focuses the discussion of monetary policy on the interest rate (specifically, the Fed funds rate), not the money supply. On the surface, this may seem inconsistent with the discussions of monetary policy that focused on the money supply, but it is not. It is simply a difference in focus. The Fed does control the amount of money in the economy, but it uses that control to target an interest rate, not to control the money supply.

LIMITS TO THE FED'S CONTROL OF THE INTEREST RATE   The above discussion makes it sound as if the Fed can control the interest rate, and it can, if by interest rate we mean the short-term interest rate. But, as we discussed in the last chapter, the economy has more than one interest rate. As long as the short-term interest rate and the long-term interest rate move in tandem, then the Fed can also control the long-term interest rate. Unfortunately, they do not always move in tandem, and that has made the study of the relationship between the short-term and long-term rates an important part of discussions of monetary policy. Economists carefully follow this relationship in a graph called the **yield curve**—*a curve that shows the relationship between interest rates and bonds' time to maturity*. I show two alternative yield curves in Figure 29-6. As you can see, as you move out along the yield curve, bonds' time to maturity increases. Figure 29-6(a) demonstrates what is called a standard yield curve. It is a yield curve in which the short-term rates are lower than the long-term rate. Thus, if you invest in a one-year bond, you would earn 4 percent interest, and if you invest in a 30-year bond, you would earn 6 percent interest. This is considered a standard yield curve because long-term bonds are riskier than short-term bonds, so it is reasonable that they generally have a slightly higher interest rate.

That relationship between short-term and long-term interest rates does not always hold. Figure 29-6(b) shows what is called an **inverted yield curve**—*a yield curve in which the short-term rate is higher than the long-term rate*. In the graph, you can see that a one-year bond pays 6 percent interest and a 30-year bond pays a lower, 4 percent, interest rate.

Why is the shape of the yield curve important? Because the standard discussion of monetary policy is based on the assumption that when the Fed pushes up the short-term rate, the long-term rate moves up as well. If the long-term rate doesn't move with the short-term rate, then investment won't respond, and conventional monetary policy won't have any significant effect on investment and therefore on the economy. Think of the issue as one of pushing a pea along a plate with a noodle. If the noodle is dry, you can do it easily, but if the noodle is wet, when you move one end, the other end doesn't move.

As financial markets have become more liquid, and as technological changes in financial markets have provided firms with many alternative sources of credit, the Fed has

The yield curve is a curve that shows the relationship between interest rates and bonds' time to maturity.

Q-8 What is the difference between a standard yield curve and an inverted yield curve?

As financial markets have become more liquid, and as technological changes in financial markets have provided firms with many alternative sources of credit, the Fed has found that its ability to control the long-term rate through conventional monetary policy has lessened.

FIGURE 29-6 (A AND B)   The Yield Curve

The standard yield curve shown in (**a**) is upward-sloping: As the time to maturity increases, so does the interest rate. An inverted yield curve shown in (**b**) is downward-sloping: As the time to maturity increases, the interest rate decreases.

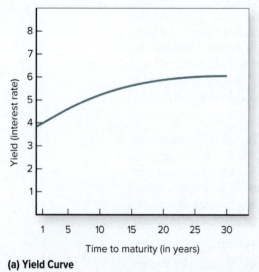

(a) Yield Curve

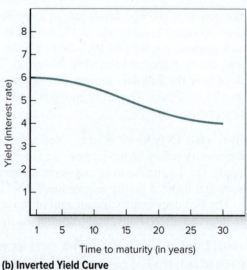

(b) Inverted Yield Curve

found that its ability to control the long-term rate through conventional monetary policy has lessened. When it uses contractionary monetary policy, as opposed to shifting the entire yield curve up, the policy simply causes an inverted yield curve. That's why policy makers pay close attention to the yield curve. Conventional expansionary monetary policy pushes the short-term interest rate down, but initially leaves the long-term interest rate almost unchanged.

The monetary influence is not completely gone; economists have found that if the Fed is willing to push the short-term rate high enough, it is able to pull the long-term rate with it, but the Fed's control of the long-term rate with conventional monetary policy is more like the control parents have over their kids—they can influence (and hope) but cannot control. That is why it has turned to the unconventional monetary policy that we will discuss in the next chapter.

Maintaining Policy Credibility

Policy makers are very concerned about establishing policy credibility. The reason is that policy makers believe that it is necessary to prevent inflationary expectations from becoming built into the economy. They fear that if inflationary expectations become built into the economy, the long-term interest rate, which is the rate that primarily influences investment, will be pushed up, making the yield curve steeper and requiring even stronger contractionary monetary policy to eliminate the inflation. To see why the long-term rate will rise because of inflationary expectations, it is important to remember that the long-term interest rate has two components: a real interest rate component and an inflationary expectations component, which means that you must distinguish the real interest rate from the nominal interest rate.

You learned about this real/nominal interest rate distinction in an earlier chapter. Recall, *nominal interest rates* are the rates you actually see and pay. When a bank pays 7 percent interest, that 7 percent is a nominal interest rate. What affects the economy is the real interest rate. *Real interest rates* are nominal interest rates adjusted for expected inflation.

For example, say you get 7 percent interest from the bank, but the price level goes up 7 percent. At the end of the year you have $107 instead of $100, but you're no better off than before because the price level has risen—on average, things cost 7 percent more. What you would have paid $100 for last year now costs $107. (That's the definition of *inflation.*) Had the price level remained constant, and had you received 0 percent interest, you'd be in the equivalent position of receiving 7 percent interest on your $100 when the price level rises by 7 percent. That 0 percent is the *real interest rate.* It is the interest rate you receive after adjusting for inflation.

The real interest rate cannot be observed because it depends on expected inflation. To calculate the real interest rate, you must subtract what you believe to be the expected rate of inflation from the nominal interest rate:[2]

Real interest rate = Nominal interest rate − Expected inflation rate

Q-9 If the nominal interest rate is 10 percent and expected inflation is 3 percent, what is the real interest rate?

---

[2]This is an equation that works best for small amounts of inflation.

For example, if the nominal interest rate is 7 percent and expected inflation is 4 percent, the real interest rate is 3 percent. The relationship between real and nominal interest rates is important both for your study of economics and for your own personal finances.

What does this distinction between nominal and real interest rates mean for monetary policy? It adds yet another uncertainty to the effect of monetary policy. In the *AS/AD* model, we assumed that expansionary monetary policy lowers the interest rate and contractionary monetary policy increases the interest rate. However, if the expansionary monetary policy leads to expectations of increased inflation, expansionary monetary policy can increase nominal interest rates (the ones you see) and leave real interest rates (the ones that affect borrowing decisions) unchanged. Why? Because of expectations of increasing inflation. Lenders will want to be compensated for the inflation (which will decrease the value of the money they receive back) and will push the nominal interest rate up to get the desired real rate of interest.

MONETARY REGIMES   The distinction between nominal and real interest rates and the possible effect of monetary policy on expectations of inflation has led most economists to conclude that a monetary regime, not a monetary policy, is the best approach to policy. A **monetary regime** is *a predetermined statement of the policy that will be followed in various situations.* A monetary policy, in contrast, is a response to events; it is chosen without a predetermined framework.

Monetary regimes are now favored because rules can help generate the expectations that even though in certain instances the Fed is increasing the money supply, that increase is not a signal that monetary expansion and inflation are imminent. A monetary regime involves feedback rules. In the conventional rules, if inflation is above its target, the Fed raises the Federal funds rate (by selling bonds, thereby decreasing the money supply) in an attempt to slow inflation down. If inflation is below its target, and if the economy is going into a recession, the Fed lowers the Fed funds rate (by buying bonds, thereby increasing the money supply). The Taylor rule discussed above is an example of a general feedback rule.

PROBLEMS WITH MONETARY REGIMES   Establishing an explicit monetary regime to hold down expectations of inflation is not without its problems. Inevitably, special circumstances arise where it makes sense to deviate from the regime. The problem is analogous to the problem faced by parents. All parenting manuals tell parents to maintain credibility and to set fair and firm rules. Most parents attempt to do so. But as all, or at least most, parents know, sometimes exceptions are necessary. Not all contingencies can be planned for. So I suspect that both parents and monetary policy makers will consistently emphasize their firm rules and state that they will follow them no matter what, but that inevitably they will trade some credibility for some short-term gain, or in the belief that the initial rule did not take into account the particular situation that arose.

To make its commitment to a monetary regime clear to the public, even as it deviates slightly from that commitment in specific instances, the Fed has been trying, over the past

Q-10 How does the distinction between nominal and real interest rates add uncertainty to the effect of monetary policy on the economy?

A monetary regime is a predetermined statement of the policy that will be followed in various situations.

A REMINDER ✔

Conventional Wisdom about Conventional Monetary Policy

Expansionary	Contractionary
Advantages	**Advantages**
1. Interest rates may fall. 2. Economy may grow. 3. Decreases unemployment.	1. Helps fight inflation. 2. Trade deficit may decrease.
Disadvantages	**Disadvantages**
1. Inflation may worsen. 2. Trade deficit may increase.	1. Risks recession. 2. Increases unemployment. 3. Slows growth. 4. May help cause short-run political problems. 5. Interest rates may rise.

decade, to increase the degree of *transparency* that accompanies its monetary policy decisions. Specifically, the Fed is releasing the minutes of its FOMC meetings much sooner after the meetings adjourn than it did in the past, and is going out of its way to explain its decisions. The hope is that the greater degree of transparency will demonstrate the Fed's general resolve to fight inflation, and show that any possible deviation from that resolve can be explained by special circumstances.

Conclusion

The above discussion should give you a good sense that conducting monetary policy in normal times is not a piece of cake. It takes not only a sense of the theory but also a feel for the economy. (See the Reminder box "Conventional Wisdom about Conventional Monetary Policy" on the previous page for a summary of the standard view of monetary policy.) In short, the conduct of monetary policy is not a science. It does not allow the Fed to steer the economy as one might steer a car. It does work well enough to allow the Fed to *influence* the economy, much as an expert rodeo rider rides a bronco bull. Sometimes the bull ride can be extremely bumpy, as we will see in the next chapter.

The Fed can influence, not steer, the economy.

Summary

- Monetary policy is the policy of influencing the economy through changes in the banking system's reserves that affect the money supply. (*LO29-1*)

- In the *AS/AD* model, contractionary monetary policy works as follows: (*LO29-1*)

  $M \downarrow \rightarrow i \uparrow \rightarrow I \downarrow \rightarrow Y \downarrow$

- Expansionary monetary policy works as follows: (*LO29-1*)

  $M \uparrow \rightarrow i \downarrow \rightarrow I \uparrow \rightarrow Y \uparrow$

- The Federal Open Market Committee (FOMC) makes the actual decisions about monetary policy. (*LO29-2*)

- The Fed is a central bank; it conducts monetary policy for the United States and regulates financial institutions. (*LO29-2*)

- The Fed changes the money supply through open market operations: To expand the money supply, the Fed buys bonds. To contract the money supply, the Fed sells bonds. (*LO29-3*)

- When the Fed buys bonds, the price of bonds rises and interest rates fall. When the Fed sells bonds, the price of bonds falls and interest rates rise. (*LO29-3*)

- A change in reserves changes the money supply by the change in reserves times the money multiplier. (*LO29-3*)

- The Federal funds rate is the rate at which one bank lends reserves to another bank. It is the Fed's primary operating target. (*LO29-3*)

- The Taylor rule is a feedback rule that states: Set the Fed funds rate at 2 percent plus current inflation plus one-half the difference between actual and desired inflation plus one-half the percent difference between actual and potential output. (*LO29-4*)

- The yield curve shows the relationship between interest rates and bonds' time to maturity. (*LO29-4*)

- The Fed's direct control is on short-term interest rates; its effect on long-term interest rates is indirect. Fed policy intended to shift the yield curve might instead change its shape, and therefore not have the intended impact on investment and output. (*LO29-4*)

- Nominal interest rates are the interest rates we see and pay. Real interest rates are nominal interest rates adjusted for expected inflation: Real interest rate = Nominal interest rate − Expected inflation. (*LO29-4*)

- Because monetary policy can affect inflation expectations as well as nominal interest rates, the effect of monetary policy on interest rates can be uncertain. This uncertainty has led the Fed to follow monetary regimes. (*LO29-4*)

Key Terms

central bank
contractionary monetary
   policy
discount rate
expansionary monetary
   policy

Fed funds
Federal funds rate
Federal Open Market
   Committee (FOMC)
inverted yield curve

liquidity trap
monetary base
monetary policy
monetary regime

open market operations
reserve requirement
Taylor rule
yield curve

Questions and Exercises   connect

1. Demonstrate the effect of contractionary monetary policy in the *AS/AD* model. (*LO29-1*)

2. Demonstrate the effect of expansionary monetary policy in the *AS/AD* model when the economy is: (*LO29-1*)
   a. Below potential output.
   b. Significantly above potential output.

3. Is the Fed a private or a public agency? (*LO29-2*)

4. Why are there few regional Fed banks in the western part of the United States? (*LO29-2*)

5. What are the six explicit functions of the Fed? (*LO29-2*)

6. How does the Fed use open market operations to increase the money supply? (*LO29-3*)

7. Write the formula for the money multiplier. If the Fed eliminated the reserve requirement, what would happen to the money multiplier and the supply of money? (*LO29-3*)

8. How can the Fed use the interest rate paid on reserves as a policy tool? (*LO29-3*)

9. When is an economy in a liquidity trap? (*LO29-3*)

10. If a bank is unable to borrow reserves from the Fed funds market to meet its reserve requirement, where else might it borrow reserves? What is the name of the rate it pays to borrow these reserves? (*LO29-3*)

11. What is meant by the *Federal funds rate*? (*LO29-3*)

12. If the Fed buys bonds, what would you expect to happen to the Fed funds rate? (*LO29-3*)

13. If the Federal Reserve announces a change in the direction of monetary policy, is it describing an offensive or defensive action? Explain your answer. (*LO29-3*)

14. Suppose the Fed decides it needs to pursue an expansionary policy. Assume the reserve requirement is 10 percent, and there are no excess reserves. Show how the Fed would increase the money supply by $3 million through open market operations. (*LO29-3*)

15. Some individuals have suggested raising the required reserve ratio for banks to 100 percent. (*LO29-3*)
    a. What would the money multiplier be if this change were made? Assume people hold no cash.

b. What effect would such a change have on the money supply?
c. How could that effect be offset?

16. The Fed wants to increase the money supply (which is currently $5,000) by $350. The money multiplier is 4, and people hold no cash. For each 1 percentage point the discount rate falls, banks borrow an additional $10. Explain how the Fed can achieve its goals using the following tools: (*LO29-3*)
    a. Change the reserve requirement.
    b. Change the discount rate.
    c. Use open market operations.

17. Say that investment increases by $20 for each interest rate drop of 1 percent. Say also that the expenditures multiplier is 3. If the money multiplier is 4, and each 5-unit change in the money supply changes the interest rate by 1 percent, what open market policy would you recommend to increase income by $240? (*LO29-3*)

18. Congratulations! You have been appointed adviser to the Federal Reserve Bank. (*LO29-3*)
    a. The Federal Open Market Committee decides that it must increase the money supply by $50. Committee members tell you the reserve ratio is 0.2. They ask you what directive they should give to the open market desk. You tell them, being as specific as possible, using the money multiplier.
    b. They ask you for two other ways they could have achieved the same end. You tell them.
    c. Based on the *AS/AD* model, tell them what you think the effect on the price level of your policy will be.

19. What is the relationship between tools, operating targets, intermediate targets, and ultimate targets? (*LO29-4*)

20. What are examples of tools, operating targets, and ultimate targets? (*LO29-4*)

21. The table below gives the Fed funds rate target at the end of each year shown.

Year	Federal Funds Target Rate
1	5.00%
2	5.25
3	4.25
4	0.25

Using these figures, describe how the monetary policy directions changed from Year 1 through Year 4. (*LO29-4*)

22. Target inflation is 2 percent; actual inflation is 3 percent. Output equals potential output. What does the Taylor rule predict will be the Fed funds rate? (*LO29-4*)

23. State the Taylor rule. What does the rule predict will happen to the Fed funds rate in each of the following situations? (*LO29-4*)
    a. Inflation is 2 percent, the inflation target is 3 percent, and output is 2 percent below potential.
    b. Inflation is 4 percent, the inflation target is 2 percent, and output is 3 percent above potential.
    c. Inflation is 4 percent, the inflation target is 3 percent, and output is 2 percent below potential.

24. What is an inverted yield curve? (*LO29-4*)

25. Are you more likely to see an inverted yield curve when the Fed is implementing contractionary or expansionary monetary policy? (*LO29-4*)

26. Why would policy makers pay attention to the shape of the yield curve? (*LO29-4*)

27. Does it matter to policy makers how people form expectations? (*LO29-4*)

28. Fill in the blanks in the following table: (*LO29-4*)

	Real Interest Rate	Nominal Interest Rate	Expected Inflation
a.	5	?	2
b.	?	3	4
c.	3	6	?
d.	?	5	1

29. How does a monetary regime differ from a policy? (*LO29-4*)

30. How might an inflation target policy impair the ability of the Fed? (*LO29-4*)

31. How are transparency and credibility related? (*LO29-4*)

Questions from Alternative Perspectives

1. Fischer Black, an economist who designed a famous options pricing model, argued that because of developments in financial markets, central banks would soon have no ability to control the economy with monetary policy, and that the price level would be indeterminant rather than determined by the money supply. What do you think his argument was? (*Austrian*)

2. The quotation at the beginning of this chapter, and those for almost all the chapters, is from a man, not a woman.
   a. Does this suggest anything about the author's viewpoint or about the economics profession?
   b. Should we be concerned about the lack of quotations from women? (*Feminist*)

3. Monetary policy is difficult when interest rates are low. For example, in the early 2000s the Bank of Japan lowered the interest rate to 0.01 percent with little effect on investment.
   a. Why is it difficult for monetary policy to be effective when interest rates are very low?
   b. How might institutions be changed to make monetary policy effective under these circumstances? (*Institutionalist*)

4. Monetarists believe that money is neutral in that it has no real effect on interest rates, output, or employment. Keynes, alternatively, believed that money is not neutral in both the short and long runs. For Keynesians, money supply can affect real decision making, providing liquidity when firms need it. How would a belief in the nonneutrality of money affect the policy discussion in the book? (*Post-Keynesian*)

5. As radical economists see it, when it comes to making monetary policy, the Fed consistently puts the interests of bondholders ahead of people seeking work. It regularly moves to protect the value of their stocks and bonds by keeping inflation low even at the expense of maintaining employment growth.
   a. In your opinion, does the Fed use monetary policy to direct the economy to everyone's benefit?
   b. Should the Fed serve the interests of the holders of financial assets or the interests of workers? (*Radical*)

Issues to Ponder

1. "The effects of open market operations are somewhat like a stone cast in a pond." Discuss the first three ripples after a splash.

2. You can lead a horse to water, but you can't make it drink. How might this adage be relevant to expansionary (as opposed to contractionary) monetary policy?

3. In November 2008 the Fed began to pay interest on reserves held at the bank.
   a. What effect would you expect this to have on excess reserves?
   b. Did banks generally favor or oppose this action?
   c. Would central banks generally favor or oppose this action?

   d. What effect did this probably have on interest rates paid by banks?

4. Why would a bank hold Treasury bills as secondary reserves when it could simply hold primary reserves—cash?

5. The "Check 21" Act, which allows banks to transfer check images instead of paper checks, speeds up check processing. When the act was implemented, what was the likely effect on:
   a. Float (duplicate money because a check has been deposited but not yet deducted from the payer's account).
   b. Variability of float.
   c. Defensive Fed actions.

Answers to Margin Questions

1. Expansionary monetary policy makes more money available to banks for lending. Banks lower their interest rates to attract more borrowers. With lower interest rates, businesses will borrow more money and increase investment expenditures. The multiplier shifts the AD curve to the right by a multiple of the increase in investment expenditures. Real output increases to Y_1, and the price level rises to P_1. What ultimately happens to output and the price level depends on where the economy is relative to potential.   (*LO29-1*)

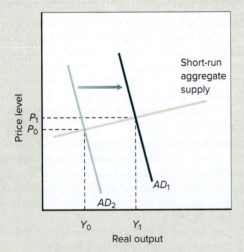

2. The Federal Open Market Committee (FOMC) decides on monetary policy. (*LO29-2*)

3. When the Fed buys bonds, it is expanding the money supply. (*LO29-3*)

4. In recent years banks' holdings of excess reserves have increased enormously. The Fed's increasing reserves will translate into an increase in the money supply only if banks lend those reserves. (*LO29-3*)

5. It will rise. (*LO29-3*)

6. The Fed should buy bonds to offset the unintended decline in reserves. (*LO29-3*)

7. The Taylor rule predicts a Fed funds rate target of 1.5 percent. (*LO29-4*)

8. In a standard yield curve, bonds with greater time to maturity pay higher interest rates. In an inverted yield curve, bonds with greater time to maturity pay *lower* interest rates. (*LO29-4*)

9. The real interest rate is 7 percent, the nominal interest rate (10) less expected inflation (3). (*LO29-4*)

10. If there is no inflation, the real interest rate is also the nominal rate. This equality makes the effect of monetary policy on real interest rates clearer since policy makers would know what the effect of any policy would be on the real interest rate. Inflation adds the uncertainty about whether a change in the interest rate is a change in the real interest rate, or a change in expectations of inflation, and therefore, just a change in the nominal interest rate. (*LO29-4*)

Financial Crises, Panics, and Unconventional Monetary Policy

CHAPTER 30

After reading this chapter, you should be able to:

LO30-1 Explain why financial crises are dangerous and why most economists see a role for the central bank as a lender of last resort.

LO30-2 Explain the role of leverage and herding in financial bubbles and how central bank policy can contribute to a financial bubble.

LO30-3 Explain why regulating the financial sector and preventing financial crises is so difficult.

LO30-4 Discuss monetary policy in the post–financial crisis period.

©Chris Hondros/Getty Images

In 2008, the world financial system nearly stopped working. Banks were on the verge of collapse, the stock market dropped precipitously, and the U.S. economy fell into a serious recession and possible structural stagnation. In response, central banks and governments across the world took extraordinary steps—buying banks, buying financial assets, guaranteeing deposits, and guaranteeing loans to try to calm the crisis. Initially central banks thought that the problems would be temporary, but after the initial short-term problems were handled, longer-term problems emerged; economies throughout the world were faced with sluggish growth and higher unemployment than they found acceptable, and central banks feared that if they returned to conventional monetary policy, the economies would crash. In response, what started as a highly unconventional monetary policy became the new normal, with very low and even negative interest rates, quantitative easing, and worry about inflation being too low, the new standard features of monetary policy. Only a decade later are central banks around the world moving back to a more traditional monetary policy. In this chapter, we consider unconventional monetary policy and the problems involved with unwinding it, and moving back to a more conventional monetary policy. Specifically, we consider: (1) financial panics and the Fed's role as a lender of last resort, (2) the difficulty of preventing financial crises and the structural problems they create, (3) the problems of regulating the financial sector, and (4) the debate about unconventional monetary policies and how best to unwind them.

The Central Bank's Role in a Crisis

Why is there so much concern about the financial sector and fear about a credit crisis? Firms in the financial sector got themselves into this mess; they should get out of it on their own. After all, the financial sector is only a small part of the entire economy. The answer why is simple: We worry about the financial sector not because it is big or small, but because all the other sectors need the financial sector to do business. While oil is a relatively minor part of a working engine, it is absolutely essential. While the failure of other big sectors such as the auto industry would be painful, it would not bring all other sectors crashing down as a financial-sector collapse would. That's why one of the roles of a central bank is to be a **lender of last resort**—*lending to banks and other financial institutions when no one else will.*

When credit is not available, the real economy can quickly come to a halt. It's not like the slow effect of a contractionary demand shock. It is fast, like a heart attack. The fear in October 2008 was that the financial crisis on Wall Street could cause the entire economy to seize, spreading the problem from Wall Street (the financial sector) to Main Street (the real sector), creating not a recession but a depression like the Great Depression of the 1930s.

Think about what would happen if *your* credit dried up. Say that even though you're every bit as trustworthy as before, you suddenly find you can no longer borrow money. No more spending with a credit card. Paying for some of your expenses might still work just fine—you could buy groceries with cash at the local grocery store. Others would be more difficult. Without credit, you'd have to pay all your bills before you get the product. No more loans to buy a car; you'll have to save $20,000 first. No more checks since businesses couldn't be assured the check would clear. Some things would be downright impossible; forget about buying anything on the Internet. Paying for college? No problem . . . if you've already saved up enough to pay up front and in full.

The situation is even worse for companies. While they might not use credit cards, just like you, they borrow for their short-term needs, such as buying the raw materials for production and paying their workers. If their credit line disappears, companies would essentially be forced to close because they couldn't pay their workers. When workers lose their jobs, they will cut their spending, causing other workers to lose their jobs as well. A downward spiral of output will result. That's why a severe financial crisis can bring the entire real economy to a halt.

Luckily that didn't happen. As soon as the crisis hit, the Fed put aside its standard cautious approach to monetary policy and undertook a wide variety of unprecedented actions. It acted as the lender of last resort—providing loans to financial institutions that it determined were **solvent**—*having sufficient assets to cover their long-run liabilities*—but were not sufficiently **liquid**—*having assets that could readily be converted into cash and money at non-fire-sale prices.* Without liquid assets banks couldn't pay their short-run liabilities, such as interest on money they had borrowed.

Q-1 Why do we worry about the financial sector more than the automobile sector?

Credit is a necessary part of the U.S. economy.

In the financial crisis, the Fed acted as a lender of last resort loaning to solvent, but illiquid banks.

To prevent a financial collapse, the Fed took the banks' long-run illiquid assets such as mortgages, business loans, and Treasury bonds as collateral, and loaned the banks money to pay their short-run liabilities. By doing so the Fed provided liquidity to the financial market.

Similarly, the Treasury dropped all its standard practices and bailed out financial firms, and Congress instituted strong expansionary fiscal policy. The hope was that such actions would be enough to prevent the financial meltdown that would turn a serious recession into a second Great Depression. The policy succeeded; the United States and world economies avoided a financial meltdown.

Anatomy of a Financial Crisis

Even though every financial crisis is different, all generally have similar elements and 2008 was no exception. A financial crisis begins with the creation of an **asset price bubble**—*unsustainable rapidly rising prices of some type of asset* (such as stocks or houses). Price increases in a bubble are unsustainable because they do not reflect an increase in the real productive value of the asset. In the early 2000s, the bubble was in the housing market.

> A bubble is an unsustainable rapidly rising price of some type of asset.

The key to a bubble is **extrapolative expectations**—*expectations that a trend will accelerate.* It works like this: Initially, the market experiences a shock, which causes prices to rise. In a standard aggregate supply/aggregate demand model, the initial rise in price is the end of the story. The rise in prices brings the market back into equilibrium. But in a financial bubble, the initial rise in price leads people to expect further price increases. In anticipation of these price increases, people buy goods and assets, causing aggregate demand to shift out to the right, which leads prices to rise further, fulfilling expectations, and people to expect even more price increases. In a bubble, expectations feed back on themselves, and prices rapidly spiral upward. This is how it works:

Web Note 30.1
Bubble Analysis

> In a bubble, expectations feed back on themselves, and prices rapidly spiral upward.

> Rise in price → Expectations of a further rise in price → Rise in demand at the current price → Rise in price → Expectations of a further rise in price . . . and so on

The Financial Crisis: The Bubble Bursts

In 2005, after rising precipitously for a number of years, housing prices started to level off. Most standard economists talked about prices settling into a permanently high plateau. But by 2006 housing prices began to fall precipitously—and it became clear that the boom in housing prices in the early 2000s had been a financial bubble. As soon as that was recognized, the bubble burst and everyone wanted to get out of housing and housing-related assets before the price of their houses fell further.

The bursting of the bubble involves the same process that leads to the bubble—extrapolative expectations; it just works in reverse. The price stops rising, which reverses the expectations of rising prices into falling prices. People begin selling their assets, which leads prices to fall even more. People expect prices to fall even further, which leads more people to sell . . . and so on. Those whose loans exceeded the value of their assets (commonly called being underwater) are forced to sell or to default on their loans. Those defaults lead to expectations of further price declines, which bring about further defaults.

Foreclosures rose considerably after the housing bubble burst in 2006.

©Andy Dean Photography/Alamy

> The bursting of a bubble involves the same process that leads to the bubble—extrapolative expectations; it just works in reverse.

Thinking Like a Modern Economist

Tulipmania, the South Sea Bubble, and Behavioral Economics

Financial bubbles have been a fixture in economies for centuries. Two of the most famous financial bubbles are Tulipmania and the South Sea bubble.

The height of Tulipmania occurred in Holland between November 1636 and February 1637. It centered on, you guessed it, tulips—a relatively newly introduced popular flower. Over three months, tulip bulb prices are estimated to have risen by several thousand percent, all without any tulips actually changing hands—tulips don't even *grow* between November and February. Instead, speculators tried to make money by buying and reselling *promises* to deliver tulip bulbs the following May, after they had flowered. Contracts for some particularly rare bulbs were reportedly trading for prices equivalent to 20 years of a typical workman's wages, and for a full 12 acres of land. Trading was purely speculative; people bought tulip contracts with the full intention of "flipping" them for a profit well before May. The bubble burst in February when people realized that at the current prices, no one would be willing to pay the outrageous prices for an actual *tulip*.

Another financial bubble was the South Sea bubble of the early 1700s. The South Sea bubble started when rumors spread that the South Sea Company—a company granted a monopoly on trade with South American colonies by the British government—would be enormously profitable. When the stock price of the South Sea Company doubled, others noticed and wanted to get in on the profit, pushing the price up further. The price of its stock rose almost tenfold between January and August of 1720. (The rise was helped along by various shady dealings between the company and members of the British Parliament.)

Source: Reprint of 1841/1852 editions of *Extraordinary Popular Delusions and the Madness of Crowds* by Charles Mackay, LL.D.

How could people afford to buy this stock at such high prices? They borrowed and were allowed to leverage their purchases. (Pay me 10 percent now and the remaining 90 percent next week.) As long as the stock price was rising, that wasn't a problem. When it was time to pay the remaining 90 percent, the stockholder could sell the stock at a higher price, repay the loan, and pocket the difference.

But then, suddenly, the rumors reversed. The stock prices started falling and everyone called in their loans. To pay their loans, people tried to sell stock that no one wanted to buy; stock prices plummeted and the bubble burst even more quickly than it had formed.

Behavioral economics and standard economics explain these bubbles differently. Standard economics works hard to provide a rational explanation for financial bubbles. It has a theory of what might be called rational bubbles. For example, some economists have argued that the high prices of tulips and of South Sea Company stock were plausible in light of the scarcity and novelty of certain bulbs and imperfect information about the profitability of trade with the Americas. If bubbles are rational, they should be considered an unavoidable aspect of modern society.

Modern behavioral economists disagree. They argue that bubbles form precisely because people *aren't* fully rational in the way that economists define rationality—they are subject to herd mentality. That is, they are predictably irrational. Moreover, economists argue that in an unpredictable world, there is no one rational course of action, and the future is always in some sense unknown. This difference is important because if behavioral economists are right, then there *is* a potential role for policy to reduce the severity and occurrence of bubbles.

Compared with the stock market crash of 1929, in 2007 housing prices declined slowly. While financial assets can be sold quickly—at the click of a mouse—houses cannot. Houses generally are listed with a real estate agent; buyers look at a number of houses before deciding; then the price is negotiated. Even when people are not paying their mortgage, banks can't just kick people out of their houses; they must foreclose, and that process can take years.

Despite all the difficulties with the housing market, the financial crisis was not directly precipitated by the housing market crisis. It was a crisis in the market for mortgage-backed securities. **Mortgage-backed securities** are *securities that are derivatives of mortgages in which thousands of mortgages are packaged with other mortgages into a bundle of mortgages and sold on the securities market.* These securities are related to housing because their value depends on the value of mortgages, which in turn depends on the ability of homeowners to pay their mortgages, which in turn depends on housing prices.

When the housing market crashed and people stopped paying their mortgages, these mortgage-backed securities lost much of their value. Panic ensued because, like homeowners who had borrowed significant sums to buy their houses, many financial institutions had purchased these securities with mostly borrowed money. Some used **leverage**—*the practice of buying an asset with borrowed money*—to buy those securities and were leveraged at a 30-to-1 ratio, which meant that for every dollar they invested, they had borrowed $30. As the market for mortgage-backed securities dried up, the banks found themselves in a pickle. Those financial institutions that had loaned money to banks wanted their cash, and the banks didn't have it. They had assets to pay their lenders; they just weren't liquid. They didn't have sufficient time to sell those assets and didn't want to have to sell them at fire-sale prices. In economic jargon, the banks were *illiquid,* not insolvent. That means that at non-fire-sale prices the banks had sufficient assets to meet their long-term obligations but they didn't have funds to meet their short-term obligations. Without some source of liquidity, they would all go bankrupt. Without liquidity banks stopped lending, and the economy started falling into a recession. To prevent that recession from turning into a depression, the Fed stepped in as lender of last resort.

> Leverage is the practice of buying an asset with borrowed money.

The Fed as the Lender of Last Resort

The Fed engaged in a type of financial triage—taking care of the most damaged banks with emergency measures, doing whatever it could to keep people and firms buying and selling securities. The Fed and the U.S. government took unprecedented actions to try to prevent a modern version of the "bank run" that had thrown the U.S. economy into the Great Depression of the 1930s. Ben Bernanke, the chair of the Fed, knew what could happen—he'd studied the 1930s and saw the parallels. Fearing the worst, he put aside all conventional monetary theory and policy, and started financial triage to prevent a complete meltdown of the U.S. financial system.

The specifics were hotly debated; some economists and policy makers felt it was too much, others felt it was too little, but just about all agreed that a policy in which the Fed acts as the lender of last resort is good in principle. The important point is that all these policies were emergency policies and have to be seen as such. Their goal was clear—to prevent a financial meltdown. The political consensus was based on general agreement that a financial meltdown would throw the economy into a depression. (We will discuss problems with these emergency policies below.)

> Just about all economists agreed that a policy in which the Fed acts as the lender of last resort is good in principle.

The Role of Leverage and Herding in a Crisis

Financial bubbles are important in a discussion of Fed policy because bubbles are most likely to occur when credit—financial instruments for borrowing—is easily available. With easily available credit people can borrow to invest, increasing leverage. The larger the percentage bought with borrowed funds, the larger the leverage. The reason Fed policy is important to bubbles is that the Fed significantly influences credit availability in an economy. So while the Fed's quick action in dealing with the financial crisis is laudable, it may very well have played a significant part in creating the bubble in the first place.

While the Fed's quick action in dealing with the financial crisis is laudable, it may very well have played a significant part in creating the bubble in the first place.

Leverage

To understand the power of leverage, consider the decision of a person buying a stock. Say you can buy a share of stock at $2 and you believe that its price will rise to $3 within a year. If you sell the stock after its price rises, you will earn a 50 percent return. While a 50 percent return is pretty good, if you use leverage, you can do even better. What if instead of buying a single $2 stock, you borrow $198 at 10 percent interest and buy 100 shares for $200? When the stock price goes up to $3, you could sell your stock for $300, pay back the $198 you borrowed plus $19.80 in interest, leaving you with a profit of $80.20—about a 4,000 percent return! That's the power of leverage. When you can expect returns like that, why hold back? You'd want to get as much money into the stock market as possible. With everyone buying more stocks, their prices rise, and rise, and rise, very quickly.

Leverage works with all assets and is a central part of any bubble.

Leverage works with all assets and is a central part of any bubble. Bubbles can happen in houses, mortgages, bonds, paintings, baseball cards, antiques—you name it. As long as the price is rising more than the rate of interest at which you can borrow, leverage is a way to get rich quickly. Because expansionary monetary policy increases the degree of leverage in the economy both by lowering interest rates and by making credit more easily available, monetary policy can encourage the development of a financial bubble.

Leverage contributes to a bubble by increasing the ability of people to finance the purchase of goods, services, and financial instruments, despite what might otherwise seem like high prices.

Leverage contributes to a bubble by increasing the ability of people to finance the purchase of goods, services, and financial instruments, despite what might otherwise seem like high prices. It is here where the debate about potential output described in a previous chapter comes in. In the standard macro model, which uses goods price rises as a signal to estimate potential output, until an economy experiences rising inflation, the economy is seen as not exceeding potential output. Because inflation remained low throughout the early 2000s, the Fed increased the money supply substantially—far more than suggested by the standard Taylor rule, as described in the previous chapter, and far far more than would be needed if the economy were in a structural stagnation. Both the Taylor rule and economists who believed the economy was experiencing structural stagnation suggested that much tighter monetary policy in the early 2000s was needed. What led the Fed to increase the money supply was the fact that increases in the money supply did not push up goods prices, since they were held down by world prices. Instead it made the U.S. economy awash in credit, which allowed enormous increases in leverage in financial markets.

Herding

Q-2   What are two central ingredients to the development of a financial bubble?

The other part of the formation of a financial bubble involves what psychologists and behavioral economists call herding. **Herding** is *the human tendency to follow the crowd*. When people around you see how much others are profiting by buying and selling assets, they want to profit too. They become convinced that the price of the asset is going to rise. When that happens, everyone buys more of the asset on credit, which increases economywide risk enormously. That's what happened in the housing market in the 2000s.

Through the middle of the first decade of the 2000s, times were good in the housing and construction markets, with housing prices rising nationally at historically high rates. *Flip That House* and similar TV programs showcased people making tens of thousands of dollars by buying a house with very little or no down payment, and selling that house with enormous profit just months later. It seemed as if you could get rich quick just by owning a house. Low interest rates and innovative mortgages (mortgages with zero down payment and no proof of income or creditworthiness) meant people who previously couldn't qualify for a mortgage could buy houses. Some people bought five or six houses, which they couldn't afford, but which they planned to sell before they had to repay the mortgage.

Homeownership rates rose to historic highs of nearly 70 percent. The feeling was that you simply couldn't lose on buying a house as an investment. As long as house prices kept rising, flipping houses and stretching into a mortgage made sense. With rising housing prices, people felt more wealthy—spending more and saving less because their "houses were their savings." When the value of your house is rising by $30,000 a year, you can take out a home equity loan. Whether you save an extra $1,000 or not doesn't seem all that important. All these actions increased the risk of significant problems occurring in the economy if housing prices didn't continue to rise, and left the economy vulnerable to the housing bubble bursting.

But that's not all. Leverage by homeowners was nothing compared with the leverage in the financial sector built on top of the housing market. As mentioned previously, investment banks and hedge funds had figured out how to create securities whose values were *linked* to the performance of these mortgages. These securities were leveraging the already highly leveraged mortgages, creating a financial asset built on double—and in many cases even triple or quadruple—leverage.

When the financial bubble burst, the U.S. economy was on the verge of a financial meltdown. Luckily, that didn't happen. By 2009 and 2010, it was clear that the U.S. economy had avoided a financial meltdown, but the economy wasn't in good shape. While it wasn't in a depression, it was stagnating. Unemployment was about 10 percent and growth was anemic.

With the threat of a financial meltdown out of the way, economists turned to other issues: Why had the financial system come so close to failing? Why didn't existing regulations prevent the asset price bubble? What new regulations could keep another bubble from occurring? What should the Fed do now to get the economy back on its long-run growth path? Let's start by considering the regulation problem.

The Problem of Regulating the Financial Sector

An engineer who designs a bridge that almost collapses would be questioned thoroughly. How did the collapse happen and what can be done to see that it doesn't happen again? So it is appropriate to question economists: How did economists not only let the economic collapse happen, but once the signs of a bubble were clear why didn't they warn society that a financial crisis was about to happen?

Economists answer these questions in various ways. Some emphasize that policy makers were swayed by political interests and wrangling, not by empirical evidence and economic theory. Politicians, not economists, are to blame for the financial crisis. These economists point out that a number of economists recognized the problems and suggested reforms, but policy makers failed to pass new regulations. Moreover, those regulations that were instituted weren't executed correctly. The then Fed chair Ben

Web Note 30.2
Herding Tendencies

Excess leverage played a major role in the financial crisis.

Bernanke expressed this view when he wrote, "The recent financial crisis was more a failure of economic engineering and economic management than of what I have called economic science."

Other economists are not as sure that economic theory can be absolved of blame. The problem is that in standard economic theory, financial bubbles aren't supposed to happen. People are supposed to be rational and rational people don't make such major mistakes. In standard economic thinking the prices of assets are considered the best estimate of those future prices, which is called the **efficient market hypothesis**—*all financial decisions are made by rational people and are based on all relevant information that accurately reflects the value of assets today and in the future.* Rational people will recognize that asset prices are rising too quickly.

The efficient market hypothesis has an important implication for monetary policy: Since bubbles can't happen, monetary policy makers didn't have to pay attention to the rising housing prices that occurred in the early 2000s. It wasn't housing price inflation; the real value of housing was rising. The efficient market hypothesis said that asset markets, such as housing, could be left on autopilot. With asset prices set on automatic, monetary policy could focus on goods market inflation as an indicator of whether monetary policy was too expansionary. As mentioned above, in the standard *AS/AD* model, when there was little inflation and no threat of accelerating inflation, monetary policy could be expansionary. That was the view that guided conventional macroeconomic theory. Policy makers didn't worry about the financial crisis because conventional economic theory was telling them they didn't have to worry about it. So for unconventional economists, conventional economists are to blame. Ben Bernanke is wrong; it was a failure of economic science.

The events of 2008 changed the view that markets are rational for many economists, including some of the leading advocates of the former conventional model. For example, another previous Fed chair, Alan Greenspan, stated, "I made a mistake in presuming that the self-interests of organizations, specifically banks and others, were such that they were best capable of protecting their own shareholders and their equity in the firms." He continued by saying that his conventional worldview was "not working." He stated, "That's precisely the reason I was shocked, because I have been going for 40 years or more with very considerable evidence that it was working exceptionally well."

It was at that point that alternative views about the problems in the economy started to gain in acceptance. These alternative views held that while people were individually rational, they could be collectively irrational, following herding behavior. This meant that asset prices were subject to bubbles, and monetary policy and regulation would have to be designed to prevent asset price bubbles as well as prevent goods market inflation. This made conducting monetary policy and designing financial regulation much more difficult. It is a process that requires institutional knowledge, judgment, and educated common sense that is on the lookout for bubbles. Policy cannot be based on fully predetermined rules.

One of the commonsense implications of this alternative view was that when monetary policy is too expansionary, and world prices are holding goods market inflation down because of globalization, excess liquidity from monetary policy could be channeled into asset price bubbles. This was the structural stagnationist's viewpoint. Many economists, including behavioral economists, heterodox economists, Post-Keynesian economists, Austrian economists, and more, had been arguing that bubbles could and did exist for years. One in particular, Hyman Minsky, a Post-Keynesian economist, developed a psychological theory that predicted asset price bubbles as almost inevitable in a capitalist economy.

The efficient market hypothesis assumes that all financial decisions are made by rational people and are based on all relevant information that accurately reflects the value of assets today and in the future.

For unconventional economists, economic science is to blame for the financial crisis.

When society can be collectively irrational, as unconventional economists believe to be the case, monetary policy is much more difficult; it requires institutional knowledge, judgment, and educated common sense.

So a wide variety of economists of quite different political persuasions accepted that bubbles were possible. Where they differed was in how bubbles should be dealt with; these debates are continuing.

Regulation, Bubbles, and the Financial Sector

The assumption that the market on its own can be collectively irrational creates the need for regulation, or an institutional structure that will prevent that collective irrationality from developing. The question is how that should be done. After the financial crisis led to a financial meltdown in 1929 and the Great Depression, the United States instituted strong controls over the financial sector. These regulatory controls were designed to prevent the financial markets from freezing up again in the future. Government set up rules for banks—what they could and could not do; it also set up a system of **deposit insurance**—*a system under which the federal government promises to reimburse an individual for any losses due to bank failure*—which would help prevent future bank runs. These rules were strong and were meant to see that a financial crisis would not happen again.

To implement the deposit insurance program, the government created the **Federal Deposit Insurance Corporation (FDIC)**—*a government institution that guarantees bank deposits of up to $250,000.* That guarantee discouraged bank runs, but it also created a *moral hazard problem*—a problem that arises when people's actions do not reflect the full cost of their actions. Specifically, with deposit insurance, people could put their money into a bank that offered high interest rates even though the bank made excessively risky loans. If the bank ran out of money because its loans went bad, the federal government would cover the loss. Depositors could earn high interest assured they would not lose their money.

To offset the moral hazard problem that deposit insurance would create, government: (1) established strict regulations of banks, (2) separated banks from other financial institutions, and (3) designed systems so that necessary financial transactions that were central to the operation of the economy stayed within banks. These were included in a number of financial laws passed in the 1930s, the most important of which was known as the **Glass-Steagall Act**—*an act of Congress passed in 1933 that established deposit insurance and implemented a number of banking regulations including prohibiting commercial banks from investing in the securities market.* The intent was to keep commercial banks from speculating in the stock market or in other risky financial asset markets.

With the institution of these new regulations, the United States had a highly regulated commercial banking system. The point of the regulations was to make commercial banking boring—and therefore safe. People called commercial banking the "3-6-3 business"—borrow at 3 percent, lend at 6 percent, and be on the golf course by 3 p.m. Banks couldn't invest in equities and were prohibited from paying interest on deposits. Both these restrictions reduced the ability of banks to engage in risky behavior. These regulations were implemented as a result of the Depression, in the belief that the government could never again let banks go under—they were too important to fail. And if they were too important to fail, they had to be regulated to address the moral hazard problems.

It isn't only deposit insurance that can create a moral hazard. Any type of guarantee, or expectation of bailout, can do the same thing. An example can be seen by considering the effects of subsidizing loans for homeowners facing foreclosure, or even of reducing the principal of loans that homeowners owe. Suppose that, in 2005, you had prudently decided not to buy a house because you believed that houses were already significantly overpriced. Your foolish friend, on the other hand, bought into the "house

Q-3 What is a lender of last resort and how does it relate to moral hazard?

Any type of guarantee, or expectation of a bailout, can create a moral hazard.

prices always rise" myth and decided to buy a big McMansion that he could not really afford. You were prudent and your friend was foolish, and he's underwater on his house and facing foreclosure. Now suppose the government comes along and bails him out, or lowers the balance on his loan since it doesn't want him to face foreclosure. What's the outcome? He ends up with a nice house and you end up with nothing. Who's foolish now?

The belief that the government will bail out people and firms when they make stupid decisions helped create the crisis in the first place, and any bailout now will likely lead people to expect a bailout in the future. They will then choose to follow riskier strategies than they otherwise would have, potentially creating even larger problems in the future. So the bailout rewards precisely the wrong type of behavior, and hence creates a moral hazard problem for future decisions. To offset those moral hazard problems, either strict regulation is needed, or the possibilities of bailouts have to be taken off the table. For individuals, this regulation would mean strict requirements about down payments and the income level needed to buy a home. For firms it would mean financial regulations and limitations on what firms too important to fail can and cannot do. That's what the Glass-Steagall Act did.

> The belief that the government will bail out people and firms when they make stupid decisions helped create the crisis in the first place.

The Law of Diminishing Control

> **Q-4** What causes diminishing control of regulations?

If we had regulations in the 1930s, why didn't those regulations protect us in 2008? An important reason is that over time the regulations designed in the 1930s became less and less effective. The reason can be called the **law of diminishing control,** which holds that *any regulation will become less effective over time as individuals or firms being regulated will figure out ways to circumvent those regulations through innovation, technological change, and political pressure.* This means that even if the initial regulations do what they are supposed to do, over time they will become less effective. In banking, the financial sector simply moved its risky operations, which the regulations were meant to prevent, outside the banking sector. So while the regulations contained risk by keeping the "core" of the banking system within a well-regulated commercial banking sector, they did not contain risk in the broader financial sector. It is a bit like the drinking laws for minors in the United States. On most campuses, the laws don't stop underage drinking; they just push it into the dorms or private homes.

> Trying to regulate banks is a bit like trying to regulate drinking by minors. The regulation doesn't stop it; it just pushes the problem somewhere else.

NEW FINANCIAL INSTITUTIONS AND INSTRUMENTS   An example of financial innovation that circumvented bank regulation was the creation of NOW (negotiable order of withdrawal) accounts in the 1970s. Under the Glass-Steagall Act only commercial banks could offer checking accounts, but they couldn't pay interest on those deposits. Savings banks had the benefit of being able to pay interest on deposits, but couldn't offer checking accounts. In the 1970s, savings banks got around the regulation by issuing what were called NOW accounts. With a NOW account a customer could direct the savings bank to send funds to a third party. These withdrawal notices looked almost identical to checks from a commercial bank. But since the funds were legally considered to be savings accounts, savings banks avoided regulations prohibiting interest on checking accounts. Money flowed out of commercial banks and into savings banks. Other financial institutions developed products such as money market accounts and mutual fund accounts, which also let depositors write checks on their accounts. These accounts included not just cash but bonds and even stocks. Regulations no longer solved the problem of preventing the financial sector from paying interest on the new accounts that were the equivalent of checking accounts.

REGULATIONS COVERED FEWER FINANCIAL INSTRUMENTS   The development of new financial instruments described above is just one example. Such changes occurred in just about every aspect of the law. By the 1980s, it was clear that the Glass-Steagall Act was no longer preventing activities it was meant to prevent. It simply moved the practice outside the banking system and into other financial institutions.

As new financial instruments developed, regulated commercial banks lost business to unregulated financial institutions. Thus, what had been a protective umbrella over the financial system that is necessary for a smoothly functioning economy provided cover for a smaller and smaller segment of the financial industry. The commercial banking system was still regulated, but the "financial oil" increasingly flowed through the less regulated parts of the financial infrastructure. This shift was compounded by the fact that financial markets were becoming global, and the U.S. regulations controlled only U.S. financial institutions. Many U.S financial institutions could legitimately threaten to move to those countries that offered the least regulation. (Think of it as a child of divorced parents who plays one parent off the other to get the most lenient rules.) This reduced the ability of the United States to strictly regulate many financial institutions.

POLITICAL PRESSURE TO REDUCE REGULATIONS   Politics is another reason regulation becomes less effective; when regulation successfully eliminates or reduces the problems, people begin to forget that the regulation was necessary in the first place. Instead, the groups being regulated view regulations as unnecessary restrictions and will lobby to dismantle them. With the Great Depression fresh in everyone's memory, people in the 1930s favored regulation to avert repeating the Depression. But as decades passed and societal memories of the Great Depression faded, so did that view. Regulation and regulators were increasingly viewed by many as undesirable hindrances to the free market and all its magic. That was the view that Alan Greenspan referred to in the earlier quote. The belief that the market could self-regulate meant that relatively low-paid regulators were faced with the nearly impossible task of balancing the pressures of innovation that made the regulations obsolete against the need to get *some* regulation within an atmosphere that saw regulation as preventing the U.S. economy from growing.

Politics also had to deal with an inherent problem of regulation—the **too-big-to-fail problem**—*the problem that large financial institutions are essential to the workings of an economy, requiring government to step in to prevent their failure.* The too-big-to-fail problem is another example of the moral hazard problem. If individuals in the financial sector recognize the financial sector's importance to the economy and know that the government will be forced to bail them out, they change their behavior, just like kids change their behavior when they know that their parents will bail them out. They do stupid things. The problem with kids, and with large banks, is that when you threaten them that you aren't going to bail them out, the threat isn't credible. It takes resolve that I, and most governments, don't have. (Note to my children: Mom has that resolve.) Unless one has that resolve, no threat will be credible, which means that kids and businesses (with soft parents and soft governments) will continue to do stupid things; they won't take the full consequences of their actions into account.

In response to the crisis, in 2010 the United States passed the **Dodd-Frank Wall Street Reform and Consumer Protection Act**—*a new financial regulatory structure to limit risk taking and require banks to report their holdings so that regulators could assess risk-taking behavior.* The Dodd-Frank law attempts to minimize the too-big-to-fail problem. If a company is at risk of default, a process is put in place to liquidate the corporation, limiting the impact on the economy. The hope is that these regulations will protect the U.S. economy from future financial meltdowns. The law once again

By the 1980s it was clear that the Glass-Steagall Act was no longer preventing activities it was meant to prevent.

When regulation successfully eliminates or reduces the problems, people begin to forget that the regulation was necessary in the first place.

Q-5 What did government do to address the too-big-to-fail problem?

Cryptomania

The law of diminishing control tells us that new ways of getting around regulations will always be developing, reducing the value of regulations over time. One new development in finance involves what are called cryptocurrencies—which as I discussed in Chapter 28 are best thought of as crypto assets, since they don't meet the requirement of being a currency. They are more like a stock—a

©spaxiax/Shutterstock

bundle of rights that are specified when you buy the asset. With stocks you get a percentage of the profits. With cryptocurrency you get a token, often with no specific rights, or only a highly ambiguous set of rights to some activity that is loosely related to the blockchain technology that underlies cryptocurrencies. By calling these assets a currency or a token, not a stock, the originators of cryptocurrencies are attempting to avoid the regulation that stock offerings must meet. That is now changing. Governments have increased regulation of initial coin offerings and are beginning to interpret them more as stock offerings (which are highly regulated).

Just about all financial advisers advise their clients who don't have money to throw away to stay out of the crypto asset market. But many clients don't follow that advice, and billions of dollars are generated by initial coin offerings, with more offerings springing up every day. After all, from the issuer's perspective, if you can get someone to give you $10,000 for a virtual token that costs, perhaps, 10 cents to make, offers little in the way of rights to the

buyer, and is largely unregulated, it's a good business deal for the issuer. Want to buy a Colandercryptotext coin? Only $200, and $200 will be devoted to thinking about how textbooks can incorporate blockchain technology. (*Hint*: Not a good idea.)

Why do people buy crypto assets? The answer is psychological. When a person hears stories about how the price of Bitcoin went from $14 to $20,000, and how cutting-edge blockchain technology will change the world he is tempted to get a "piece of the action." Add to that the mystical, seductive allure of the name *cryptocurrency*—along with a sense of Bitcoin's association with the dark web (un-indexed portions of the web, much of which is dedicated to illegal activities), and high-pressure salespeople telling you that if you don't buy soon you will be left behind, and you can understand why some investors are hooked, just as they have been hooked in the past by the South Sea bubble and Tulipmania.

Some people, mainly the issuers, but also some investors, will make money in crypto assets. Blockchain technology is revolutionary and in the coming decades likely will be useful in recording contracts. And even if the company eventually flops, you can still make money by buying crypto assets if the hype increases and you find someone who will pay more for them than you paid. But when the bubble bursts, people will push for government regulation.

limits banks' ability to invest in securities, consolidates regulatory agencies to improve their effectiveness, expands oversight to some nonbank financial institutions, and creates new tools for dealing with financial crises. Unfortunately, few economists believe that the new law, even before the law of diminishing marginal control has set in, has resolved the financial regulation problem. Legal and financial scholars on all sides of the political spectrum have criticized the law as both insufficient to prevent another financial crisis in some aspects and overly restrictive of financial institutions in others. With the election of President Trump in 2016, the policy focus turned to deregulation. The number of banks that were subject to Dodd-Frank requirements was decreased significantly, and regulations on others were reduced.

General Principles of Regulation

Economics does not identify ideal regulations, but it does provide some general guidelines. The basic guideline is that along with the freedom to undertake activities in the market comes the responsibility for one's actions. If firms (or kids) are not, and cannot be, made responsible for the negative consequences of their actions, there is a role for regulations to restrict the set of actions firms are permitted to take. Regulation is necessary if a bailout is in the cards. (As I tell my kids—the golden rule of economics is: Him who pays the bills makes the rules.)

The question policy makers face in trying to design the rules and regulations for our economy in the future is: Can a government influenced by special interests institute the right type of regulation? Economists come to different answers on this question, which is why they have different views of regulation.

Let's close our discussion of regulation with three general precepts about dealing with financial crises that most economists would sign on to. They are:

- *Set as few bad precedents as possible.* Policies that keep the economy alive might create long-run problems. Recognize these problems, and try to offset them as best you can.
- *Deal with moral hazard.* If a firm or individual is to be unregulated, it should be subject to the consequences of its actions. This leads to a corollary: If a firm or individual is considered too big to fail, it has to be regulated. Notice that this rule does not say that government should or should not regulate. It just says that it has to be consistent.
- *Deal with the law of diminishing control.* Regulation has to be considered a process, not a one-time decision. The economy is a dynamic changing entity, subject to the law of diminishing control, which means that when new business practices and financial instruments change, rules must change. Expect innovation and establish a method of changing those regulations to adapt to the changing situation without weakening the regulations.

Monetary Policy in the Post–Financial Crisis Era

Now let us turn to the question: What monetary policy should the Fed follow after it has fulfilled its lender of last resort role and avoided a financial crisis? In other words, what is the Fed's appropriate monetary policy role in a post–financial crisis era?

Coming out of a financial crisis, the Fed was carrying a large number of loans to banks and other financial institutions that it made to provide the banks with liquidity. As the threat of a financial meltdown subsided, that role had ended. The standard practice would be for the Fed to wind down policies as the lender of last resort, and revert back to conventional monetary policies. A number of economists called on the Fed to do precisely that. But with the economy in a deep recession, those policies would have been highly politically unpopular because they would slow down the recovery.

The argument for unwinding those positions despite the high unemployment was that this was not your typical recession—it was structural stagnation that reflected structural problems caused by globalization, and the 5 to 6 percent growth rate needed until the economy returned to trend was not in the cards. The structural problems that structural stagnationists see as the cause of the slow growth could not be solved by monetary policy. To maintain expansionary monetary policy essentially meant continuing the policies that caused the financial bubble in the first place by expanding credit in the economy enormously. If the economy is in a structural stagnation,

The basic guideline of regulation is that along with the freedom to undertake activities in the market comes responsibility for one's actions.

Regulation is necessary if a bailout is in the cards.

Q-6 What are the three principles of regulation?

After the financial crisis subsided, the standard practice would have been for the Fed to wind down its lender-of-last-resort loans. It did not do that because the economy was in a deep recession.

other approach? Which method the firm chooses makes a big difference in whether its current budget will be in surplus or deficit.

Accounting is central to the debate about whether we should be concerned about a deficit.

Accounting is central to the debate about whether we should be concerned about a deficit. Say, for example, that the government promises to pay an individual $1,000 ten years from now. How should government treat that promise? Since the obligation is incurred now, should government count as a current expense an amount that, if saved, would allow it to pay that $1,000 later? Or should government not count the amount as an expenditure until it actually pays out the money? The **Social Security system**—*a social insurance program that provides financial benefits to individuals who are elderly and disabled and to their eligible dependents and/or survivors*—is based on promises to pay, and thus the accounting procedures used for Social Security play an important role in how big the measure of the government's budget deficit actually is.

Many Right Definitions

Many accounting questions must be answered before we can determine the size of a budget deficit. Some have no right or wrong answer. For others, the answers vary according to the wording of the question. For still others, an economist's "right way" is an accountant's "wrong way." In short, there are many ways to measure expenditures and receipts, so there are many ways to measure surpluses and deficits.

There are many ways to measure expenditures and receipts, so there are many ways to measure deficits and surpluses.

To say that there are many ways to measure deficits is not to say that all ways are correct. Pretending to have income that you don't have is wrong by all standards. Similarly, inconsistent accounting practices—such as measuring an income flow sometimes one way and sometimes another—are wrong. Standard accounting practices rule out a number of "creative" but improper approaches to measuring deficits. But even eliminating these, numerous reasonable ways of defining deficits remain, which accounts for some of the debate.

Deficits and Surpluses as Summary Measures

The point of the previous discussion is that a deficit is simply a summary measure of a budget. As a summary, a surplus or deficit figure reduces a complicated set of accounting relationships to one figure. To understand what that summary measure is telling us, you've got to understand the accounting procedures used to calculate it. Only then can you make an informed judgment about whether a deficit is something to worry about. What's important is not whether a budget is in surplus or deficit but whether the economy is healthy.

Deficit and surplus figures are simply summary measures of the financial health of the economy. To understand the summary, you must understand the methods that were used to calculate it.

Structural and Cyclical Deficits and Surpluses

Web Note 31.1

What Is Austerity?

The discussion of fiscal policy in earlier chapters emphasized the effect of the deficit on total income. But when thinking about such policies, it is important to remember that many government revenues and expenditures *depend* on the level of income in the economy. For example, say that the multiplier is 2 and the government is running expansionary policy. Say that the government increases its spending by $100 (increasing the budget deficit by $100), which causes income to rise by $200. If the tax rate is 20 percent, tax revenues will increase by $40 and the net effect of the policy will be to increase the budget deficit by $60, not $100. So as income changes, the deficit changes.

One implication of this feedback effect of changes in income on the deficit is the need to distinguish a deficit caused by a recessionary fall in income and a deficit brought about by government policy actions. Economists' method of distinguishing these is to differentiate between *structural deficits* and *cyclical deficits*.

To differentiate between a budget deficit being used as a policy instrument to affect the economy and a budget deficit that is the result of income deviating from its potential, economists ask the question: "Would the economy have a budget deficit if it were at its potential level of income?" If it would, that portion of the budget deficit is said to be a **structural deficit**—*the part of a budget deficit that would exist even if the economy were at its potential level of income*. In contrast, if an economy is operating below its potential, the actual deficit will be larger than the structural deficit. In such an economy, that part of the total budget deficit is a **cyclical deficit**—*the part of the deficit that exists because the economy is operating below its potential level of output*. The cyclical deficit is also known as the passive deficit. When an economy is operating above its potential, it has a cyclical surplus.

The structural deficit is the deficit that remains when the cyclical elements of the deficit have been removed.

The actual deficit is always made up of the structural deficit and the cyclical deficit:

Actual deficit = Structural deficit + Cyclical deficit

This distinction is important for policy because economists believe that an economy can eliminate a cyclical budget deficit through growth in income, whereas it can't grow out of a structural deficit. Because the economy can't grow out of them, structural budget deficits are of more concern to policy makers than are cyclical budget deficits.

Let me give an example. Say potential income is $20 trillion and actual income is $19.8 trillion, a shortfall of $200 billion. Say also that the actual budget deficit is $250 billion and the marginal tax rate is 25 percent. If the economy were at its potential income, tax revenue would be $50 billion higher and the deficit would be $200 billion. That $200 billion is the structural deficit. The $50 billion (25 percent multiplied by the $200 billion shortfall) is the cyclical portion of the deficit.

Q-3 An economy's actual income is $1 trillion; its potential income is also $1 trillion. Its actual deficit is $100 billion. What is its cyclical deficit?

As you can see from this example, assuming government spending doesn't change with income, you can calculate the cyclical deficit in the following way:

Cyclical deficit = Tax rate × (Potential output − Actual output)

Once you know the cyclical deficit, you can also calculate the structural deficit:

Structural deficit = Actual deficit − Cyclical deficit

Cyclical deficit = Tax rate × (Potential output − Actual output)

Structural deficit = Actual deficit − Cyclical deficit

Often there is significant debate about what an economy's potential income level is, and hence there is disagreement about what percentage of a deficit is structural and what percentage is cyclical. Nonetheless, the distinction is often used and is important to remember.

Nominal and Real Deficits and Surpluses

Another distinction that economists make when discussing the budget deficit and surplus picture is the real/nominal distinction. A **nominal deficit** is *the deficit determined by looking at the difference between expenditures and receipts.*[1] It's what most people think of when they think of the budget deficit; it's the value that is generally reported. The **real deficit** is *the nominal deficit adjusted for inflation*. To understand this distinction, it is important to recognize that inflation wipes out debt (accumulated deficits less accumulated surpluses). How much does it wipe out? Consider an example: If inflation is 4 percent per year, the real value of all assets denominated in dollars is declining by 4 percent each year. If you had $100, that $100 would be worth 4 percent less at the end of the year—the equivalent of $96 without inflation. By the same reasoning, when there's 4 percent inflation, the value of the debt is declining 4 percent each year. If a country has a debt of $2 trillion, 4 percent inflation will eliminate $80 billion of the real value of the debt each year.

Q-4 Explain how inflation can wipe out debt.

Inflation reduces the value of the debt. That reduction is taken into account when the real deficit is calculated.

---

[1]In this section I will discuss deficits only. Since a surplus is a negative deficit, the discussion can be easily translated into a discussion of surpluses.

The larger the debt and the larger the inflation, the more debt will be eliminated by inflation. For example, with 10 percent inflation and a $2 trillion debt, $200 billion of the debt will be eliminated by inflation each year. With 10 percent inflation and a $4 trillion debt, $400 billion of the debt would be eliminated.

If inflation is wiping out debt, and the deficit is equal to the increases in debt from one year to the next, inflation also affects the deficit. Economists take this into account by differentiating nominal deficits from real deficits.

We can calculate the real deficit by subtracting from the nominal deficit the decrease in the value of the government's total outstanding debts due to inflation. Specifically:[2]

Real deficit = Nominal deficit − (Inflation × Total debt)

Let's consider an example. Say that the nominal deficit is $300 billion, inflation is 4 percent, and total debt is $4 trillion. Substituting into the formula gives us a real deficit of $140 billion [$300 billion − (0.04 × $4 trillion) = $300 billion − $160 billion = $140 billion].

This insight into debt is directly relevant to the budget situation in the United States. For example, back in 1990, the nominal U.S. deficit was about $221 billion, while the real deficit was about one-third of that—$79 billion; in 2017 the U.S. government deficit was about $665 billion; there was 1.8 percent inflation and a total debt of about $20.2 trillion. That means the real deficit was $302 billion. The table below shows the U.S. nominal and real deficits and surpluses for selected years. (In this table surpluses are designated with minus signs. Consider them to be negative deficits.) As you can see, in most years, the government has had both nominal and real deficits.

(Billions of Dollars)	1980	1990	2000	2010	2017
Nominal deficit/surplus*	74	221	−236	1,294	665
Minus Inflation × Total debt	86	142	125	163	363
Government debt	930	3,233	5,674	13,561	20,206
Inflation (%)	9.3	4.4	2.2	1.2	1.8
Equals Real deficit/surplus	−12	79	−361	1,131	302

*Deficits are shown as positive values and surpluses as negative values.

Source: Congressional Budget Office and *The Economic Report of the President.*

Because the United States has had both debt and inflation for the years shown, the real deficits are smaller than the nominal deficits and the real surpluses are greater than the nominal surpluses.

The lowering of the real deficit by inflation is not costless to the government. Persistent inflation becomes built into expectations and causes higher interest rates. When inflationary expectations were low, as they were in the 1950s, the U.S. government paid 3 or 4 percent on its bonds that financed the debt. In 1990, when inflationary expectations were high, the government paid 8 or 9 percent interest, which is about 5 percentage points more than it paid in the 1950s. With its $3.2 trillion debt, this meant that the United States was paying about $160 billion more in interest than it

Real deficit = Nominal deficit − (Inflation × Total debt)

Q-5 The nominal deficit is $40 billion, inflation is 2 percent, and the total debt is $4 trillion. What is the real deficit?

The lowering of the real deficit by inflation is not costless to the government.

---

[2]This is an approximation for low rates of inflation. When inflation becomes large, total debt is multiplied by Inflation/(1 + Inflation), rather than just by inflation.

Social Security and the U.S. Deficit

If you listened to *Car Talk* on PBS, you know that Tom and Ray Magliozzi often left listeners with a puzzler. In economics we also have puzzlers, and here's one of them for you to ponder. If debt is accumulated deficits, then the change in the debt in a particular year should be the size of the deficit or surplus. So if the U.S. debt was $8,951 billion as it was in 2007, and the deficit in 2008 was $459 billion, then the U.S. debt in 2008 should be $459 + $8,951 = $9,410 billion. When we look at the data, however, we see that debt in 2008 was $9,986 billion. Why was this?

Car Talk made you wait a week for the answer, but we don't have a week, so here's the answer. The deficit that the government reports is the deficit on what is called the unified budget, which consists of "off-budget" accounts (government trust funds, including the Social Security system) and "on-budget" accounts (most other government tax revenues and expenditures). The debt the government reports, however, does not include other government accounts, such as the Social Security system account, which

at the time were running surpluses. The only asset that Social Security could hold was government bonds. So it was buying government debt (bonds) with its surplus revenues, building up a trust fund of assets to pay benefits to future retirees. In effect, the government on-budget account owed the Social Security and other trust funds $4.2 trillion.

So the answer to the puzzler is that the reported government debt is only on the on-budget accounts while the reported deficit is on the unified account. Since the government is reporting different concepts, there is no reason that the debt in one year plus the deficit should equal the debt in the following year unless the Social Security and other government trust accounts are in balance. More recently, the trust fund has stopped growing as much, since Social Security expenditures approximately equal Social Security taxes. So there is far less difference between the unified budget and the nonunified budget.

would have had to pay if no inflation had been expected and the nominal interest rate had been 3 rather than 8 percent. That reduced the amount it could spend on current services by $160 billion. In other words, $160 billion of the 1990 nominal U.S. deficit existed because of the rise in interest payments necessary to compensate bondholders for the expected inflation. As inflationary expectations and nominal interest rates fell through the 1990s and early 2000s, the difference between the real and nominal deficit (surplus) decreased, but the inflation that remained left bondholders requiring a small inflation premium, meaning that interest rates paid by government were higher than they otherwise would have been. As long as inflationary expectations remained low, these low interest rates could continue. But in 2018 higher inflationary expectations were starting to push up long-term interest rates.

Q-6 Why is inflation not a costless way for government to lower the real debt?

Defining Debt and Assets

Let's now look more closely at debt. **Debt** is *accumulated deficits minus accumulated surpluses.* Whereas deficits and surpluses are flow measures (they are defined for a period of time), debt is a stock measure (it is defined at a point in time). For example, say you've spent $30,000 a year for 10 years and have had annual income of $20,000 for 10 years. So you've had a deficit of $10,000 per year—a flow. At the end of 10 years, you will have accumulated a debt of $100,000 (10 × $10,000 = $100,000)—a stock. (Spending more than you have in income means that you need to borrow the extra $10,000 per year from someone, so in later years much of your expenditure will

Debt is accumulated deficits minus accumulated surpluses. Whereas *deficit* is a flow concept, *debt* is a stock concept.

707

Generational Accounting

As I have emphasized in the text, different accounting procedures shed light on slightly different issues. Each provides a different perspective of the financial situation, and the combination of them provides you with a full understanding of the issues. One accounting procedure that some economists use is generational accounting. Generational accounting shows government deficits in terms of each generation's net lifetime tax payments and benefits received. Economists Larry Kotlikoff and Alan Auerbach have shown that our current system of taxation and transfers results in an intergenerational transfer of resources from younger to older generations. With the older generation becoming larger as the baby boomers age, these transfers are likely to put a severe strain on the tax system and the political foundations of our tax and transfer policies over the next couple of decades.

Q-7 Distinguish between *deficit* and *debt*.

be for interest on your previous debt.) If a country has been running more surpluses than deficits, the accumulated surpluses minus accumulated deficits are counted as part of its assets.

Debt Management

Web Note 31.2

Public Debt 101

The U.S. government, through its Treasury Department, must continually sell new bonds to refinance the bonds that are coming due, as well as sell new bonds when running a deficit. This makes for a very active market in U.S. government bonds, and the interest rate paid on government bonds is a closely watched statistic in the economy. If the government runs a surplus, it can either retire some of its previously issued bonds by buying them back or simply not replace the previously issued bonds when they come due.

THE NEED TO JUDGE DEBT RELATIVE TO ASSETS   Debt is also a summary measure of a country's financial situation. As a summary measure, debt has even more problems than deficit. Unlike a deficit, which is the difference between expenditures and revenue, and hence provides both sides of the ledger, debt by itself is only half of a picture. The other half of the picture is assets. For a country, assets include its skilled workforce, natural resources, factories, housing stock, and holdings of foreign assets. For a government, assets include not only the buildings and land it owns but also, and more importantly, a portion of the assets of the people in the country, since government gets a portion of all earnings of those assets in tax revenue.

Q-8 Why is debt only half the picture of a country's financial situation?

To get an idea of why the addition of assets is necessary to complete the debt picture, consider two governments: one has debt of $3 trillion and assets of $50 trillion; the other has only $1 trillion in debt but only $1 trillion in assets. Which is in a better financial position? The government with the $3 trillion debt is because its debt is significantly exceeded by its assets. Assets represent the ability of a country to pay off its debt. The point is simple: To judge a country's debt, we must view its debt in relation to all its assets.

To judge a country's debt, we must view its debt in relation to its assets.

This need to judge debt relative to assets adds an important caveat to the long-run position that government budget deficits are bad. When the government runs a deficit, it might be spending on projects that increase its assets. If the assets are valued at more than their costs, then the deficit is making the society better off. Government investment can be as productive as private investment or even more productive.

Government investment can be as productive as private investment or even more productive.

To distinguish between expenditures that are building up assets and those that are not, many businesses have separate capital and expenditures budgets. When they run deficits on their capital account we do not say that they are spending recklessly; we say that they are investing in the future, and generally we applaud that investment. We say they are running a deficit only in reference to their expenditures budget. While the U.S. government budget separates out investment from noninvestment expenditures, it does not have a separate capital account; it reports a consolidated budget, so it does not take into account the asset accumulation or the depreciation of its assets in determining its deficit.

Why aren't government finances generally discussed in relation to separate current and capital budgets? Because it is extraordinarily difficult to determine which government expenditures are investment. A business's investments will earn income that allows the business to pay off those investments. Most government goods earn no income; they are supplied free to individuals and are paid for by taxes. Impossible-to-answer questions arise such as: Are expenditures on new teachers an investment in better knowledge? Or: Are expenditures on a poverty program an investment in a better social environment? There are no unambiguous answers to these and similar questions; government accountants believe it is best to avoid such questions altogether.

ARBITRARINESS IN DEFINING DEBT AND ASSETS   Like income and revenues, assets and debt are subject to varying definitions. Say, for example, that an 18-year-old is due to inherit $1 million at age 21. Should that expected future asset be counted as an asset now? Or say that the government buys an aircraft for $1 billion and discovers that it doesn't fly. What value should the government place on that aircraft? Or say that a country owes $1 billion, due to be paid 10 years from now, but inflation is ongoing at 20 percent per year. The inflation will reduce the value of the debt when it comes due by so much that its current real value will be $134 million—the approximate present value of $1 billion in 10 years with 20 percent inflation. It will be like paying about $134 million today. Should the country list the debt as a $1 billion debt or a $134 million debt?

As was the case with income, revenues, and deficits, there's no single answer to how assets and debts should be valued. So even after you take assets into account, you still have to be careful when deciding whether or not to be concerned about debt.

The arbitrariness of the debt figure can be seen by considering the holdings of U.S. debt more carefully. In 2017, the U.S. government had a total of $20.2 trillion in debt. As you can see in Figure 31-1, only 60 percent of this amount was held by the public.

> Assets and debt are subject to varying definitions.

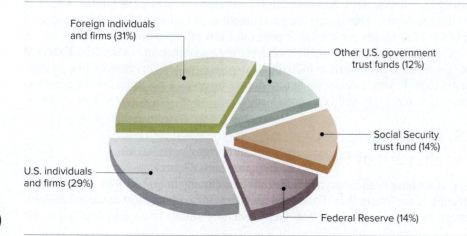

Foreign individuals and firms (31%)

Other U.S. government trust funds (12%)

Social Security trust fund (14%)

U.S. individuals and firms (29%)

Federal Reserve (14%)

FIGURE 31-1   Ownership of U.S. Government Debt

This pie chart shows that the debt is held by U.S. citizens, foreign citizens, financial institutions, and other government entities including state and local governments.

Source: *Treasury Bulletin*, U.S. Department of the Treasury (www.fiscal.treasury.gov).

The government holds about 40 percent of its own debt.

(Thirty-one percent was held by foreign individuals and 29 percent was held by U.S. individuals.) The other 40 percent was debt owed by the government to itself. (Twenty-six percent of the total government debt was held by government trust funds and another 14 percent was held by the Federal Reserve, which is semi-independent of the government, but whose assets belong to the government.) That means that 40 percent of the total government debt is simply debt owed by one part of the federal government to another part of the government. If we net out the assets and the debt of government, this 40 percent vanishes and the total federal debt decreases from about $20.2 trillion to $12.1 trillion.

The largest portion of the internally held government debt is held by the Social Security trust fund. By law the Social Security system is required to hold all its assets in the form of nonmarketable government bonds. In the early 2000s, Social Security revenues exceeded expenditures and the percentage of government debt held by government trust funds was increasing. That, however, ended in 2018, so the percentage of debt held by government agencies will be decreasing.

Difference between Individual and Government Debt

Three reasons government debt is different from individual debt are:

1. The government lives forever; people don't.

2. The government can print money to pay its debt; people can't.

3. The government owes much of its debt to itself—to its own citizens.

The final point I want to make concerns differences between government debt and individual debt. There are three primary differences:

1. The government lives forever; people don't.

2. The government can print money to pay its debt; people can't.

3. The government owes much of its debt to itself—to its own citizens.

First, government is ongoing. Government never has to pay back its debt. An individual's life span is limited; when a person dies, there's inevitably an accounting of assets and debt to determine whether anything is left to go to heirs. Before any part of a person's estate is passed on, all debts must be paid. The government, however, doesn't ever have to settle its accounts.

Second, government has an option that individuals don't have for paying off a debt. Specifically, it can pay off a debt by creating money. As long as people will accept a country's currency, a country can always exchange money (non-interest-bearing debt) for bonds (interest-bearing debt).

Q-9   Why do economists distinguish between internal and external debt?

Third, total government debt includes **internal debt** (*government debt owed to other governmental agencies or to its own citizens*). Paying interest on the internal debt involves a redistribution among citizens of the country, but it does not involve a net reduction in income of the average citizen. For example, say that a country has $5 trillion in internal debt. Say also that the government pays $250 billion in interest on its debt each year. That means the government must collect $250 billion in taxes, so people are $250 billion poorer; but it pays out $250 billion in interest to them, so, on average, people in the country are neither richer nor poorer because of the debt. **External debt** (*government debt owed to individuals in foreign countries*) is more like an individual's debt. Paying interest on external debt involves a net reduction in domestic income. U.S. taxpayers will be poorer; foreign holders of U.S. bonds will be richer.

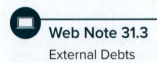

Web Note 31.3

External Debts

U.S. Government Deficits and Debt: The Historical Record

Now that we have been through the basics of deficits and debt, let's look at the historical record. Since World War II, the U.S. government has run almost continual deficits, although by today's standards they were generally small. Total debt doubled in the

30 years from 1946 to 1975 and grew more quickly beginning in the mid-1970s, rising by a multiple of 40 to $21 trillion in 2018.

Most economists are much more concerned with deficits and debt relative to GDP than with the absolute figures. Figure 31-2 graphs the budget deficit and debt as a percentage of GDP. From this perspective, as you can see in Figure 31-2(a), deficits as a percentage of GDP did not rise significantly in the 1970s and the 1980s, as they did when we considered them in absolute terms. And it's the same with debt. As you can see in Figure 31-2(b), debt relative to GDP has not been continually increasing. Instead, from the end of World War II in the mid-1940s until the end of the 1970s, the U.S. debt-to-GDP ratio decreased significantly. Starting in the early 1980s, the ratio began to increase. This increase continued until the mid-1990s, when the ratio started to fall. But in 2008, it started to rise significantly and in 2019 it was over 100 percent.

Economists prefer the "relative to GDP" measure because it better measures the government's ability to handle the deficit; a nation's ability to pay off a debt depends on its productive capacity (the asset side of the picture). GDP serves the same function for government as income does for an individual. It provides a measure of how much debt, and how large a deficit, government can handle. So when GDP grows, so does the debt the government can reasonably carry, and many economists use a constant debt-to-GDP ratio as a benchmark for judging neutral fiscal policy.

> Deficits and debt relative to GDP provide measures of a country's ability to pay off a deficit and service its debt.

The Debt Burden

Most of the decrease in the debt-to-GDP ratio in U.S. history occurred through growth in GDP. Growth in GDP can occur in two ways: through inflation (a rise in nominal but not real GDP) or through real growth. Both ways reduce the problem of the debt. As I discussed above, inflation wipes out the value of existing debt; with inflation, there can be large nominal budget deficits but a small real deficit.

When an economy experiences real growth, the ability of the government to incur debt is increased; the economy becomes richer and, being richer, can handle more debt. As noted in an earlier chapter, real growth in the United States has averaged

> Q-10 What annual deficit could a $5 billion economy growing at a real annual rate of 5 percent have without changing its debt-to-GDP ratio?

FIGURE 31-2 (A AND B) **U.S. Budget Deficits and Debt Relative to GDP**

The size of the deficits and the size of the debt look somewhat different when considered relative to the GDP. Notice specifically how the total debt-to-GDP ratio declined substantially from the 1950s to the 1980s and how it increased in the 1980s and early 1990s. It declined slightly in the late 1990s and rose substantially beginning in 2008. [In (a), deficits are stated as negative values.]

Source: *The Economic and Budget Outlook,* Congressional Budget Office (www.cbo.gov); U.S. Bureau of the Census, *Historical Statistics,* and estimates.

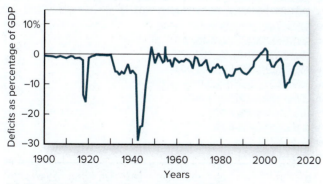

(a) Budget Deficits as Percentage of GDP

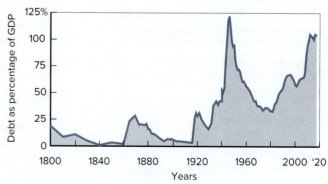

(b) Debt as Percentage of GDP

about 2.5 to 3.5 percent per year, which means that U.S. debt can grow at a rate of about 3 percent without increasing the debt-to-GDP ratio. But for debt to grow, government must run a deficit, so a constant debt-to-GDP ratio in a growing economy is consistent with a continual deficit.

How much of a deficit are we talking about? U.S. federal government debt in 2018 was about $21 trillion and GDP was about $20 trillion, so the government debt-to-GDP ratio was about 105 percent. A real growth rate of 2.5 percent means that real GDP is growing at about $500 billion per year. That means that government can run a deficit of $500 billion a year without increasing the debt-to-GDP ratio. For those who believe that the total U.S. government debt is already too large relative to GDP, this argument (that the debt-to-GDP ratio is remaining constant) is unsatisfying. They argue that the debt-to-GDP ratio should fall.

U.S. Debt Relative to Other Countries

As you can see in Figure 31-3, when judged relative to other countries, the United States' debt-to-GDP position is lower than some countries, but at over 100 percent, higher than most. It is at a level where many economists believe that the United States will soon have to start worrying about the debt level influencing bondholders' decisions.

You will also notice that Japan's debt level is much higher than that of the United States, which might make you think that the United States has more flexibility to run deficits than economists generally think. But those who have studied the issue point out that Japan is in a quite different position from the United States. An important reason is that Japan's citizens save a lot more than do U.S. citizens. Almost all the Japanese debt is internally held. Much of the U.S. debt is held externally, which means that a default by the United States will have major international consequences for the global financial system. But if either country were to have another financial crisis, and was required to increase debt enormously to prevent a financial meltdown, the already high debt may limit its ability to do so.

Interest Rates and Debt Burden

Considering debt relative to GDP is still not quite sufficient to give an accurate picture of the debt burden. How much of a burden a given amount of debt imposes

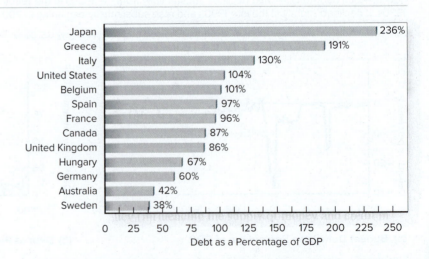

FIGURE 31-3 U.S. Debt Compared to Foreign Countries' Debt

The U.S. debt does not appear so large when compared to the debts of some other countries in the early 2000s.

Source: World Economic Outlook Database, International Monetary Fund (www.imf.org).

Japan 236%
Greece 191%
Italy 130%
United States 104%
Belgium 101%
Spain 97%
France 96%
Canada 87%
United Kingdom 86%
Hungary 67%
Germany 60%
Australia 42%
Sweden 38%

Debt as a Percentage of GDP

depends on the interest rate that must be paid on that debt. The annual debt service is the interest rate on debt times the total debt.

In 2017, the U.S. government paid approximately $260 billion in interest. A larger debt would require even higher interest payments. The interest payment is government revenue that can't be spent on defense or welfare; it's a payment for past expenditures. Ultimately, the interest payments are the burden of the debt. That's what people mean when they say a deficit is burdening future generations.

Over the past 50 years, the interest rate has fluctuated considerably; when it has risen, the debt service has increased; when it has fallen, debt service has decreased. Figure 31-4 shows the federal interest payments relative to GDP. This ratio increased substantially in World War II and then again in the 1970s and early 1980s. In the mid-1990s it declined, and has fluctuated since then. It is currently about 1.4 percent.

At current low interest rates, the United States can afford its current debt in the sense that it can afford to pay the interest on that debt. In fact, as I discussed above, it could afford a much higher debt-to-GDP ratio since U.S. government bonds are still considered one of the safest assets in the world. Currently no one is worried about the U.S. government defaulting. The U.S. debt can likely be increased by trillions of dollars without problems.

But there are limits, and with the expansionary fiscal policy of significant tax cuts and spending increases, the United States seems to be pushing that limit. At some point, the United States will reach a tipping point, where confidence in the United States' willingness to pay its bondholders ends. That can happen suddenly, which is why it is often called a tipping point. If that tipping point is reached, as mentioned earlier, investors will require a risk premium and the interest rate that the United States pays will rise and increase interest payments. If that problem arises, the Fed cannot necessarily solve the problem by buying up the bonds, because as the Fed buys up bonds, increasing the money supply, people may fear high inflation, which will raise the nominal interest rate even further since they will demand an inflation premium for their bonds. A vicious cycle of interest rate and deficit increases could develop. Such an event is highly unlikely in the near future.

The annual debt service is the interest rate on the debt times the total debt.

FIGURE 31-4 **Federal Interest Payments Relative to GDP**

Interest payments as a percentage of GDP remained relatively constant until the 1970s, after which they rose significantly due to high interest rates and large increases in debt. In the late 1990s, they fell as interest rates fell and surpluses reduced the total debt.

Source: *The Economic and Budget Outlook*, Congressional Budget Office (www.cbo.gov).

How long the United States can continue its current expansionary fiscal policies, without causing a new financial crisis, is unclear.

When considering the nature of the debt, one must consider the term structure of the debt. About 50 percent of the U.S. debt is due within 5 years. This means that if interest rates rise, the U.S. Treasury will be forced to refinance debt that comes due at the higher interest rates. To reduce this potential problem some have called for the government to issue more long-term bonds, so it will face less of a problem of refinancing. But doing so would push up the current long-term interest rate, which would likely slow U.S. growth to an even lower level than what it currently is. In fact, the Fed currently is a large buyer of 30-year bonds and is specifically attempting to keep these long-term interest rates down.

Conclusion

Whether a budget is in surplus or deficit is not especially important. What is important is the health of the economy.

This has been a relatively short chapter, but the points in it are important. Deficits, debts, and surpluses are all accounting measures. Whether a budget is in surplus or deficit is not especially important. What is important is the health of the economy. The economic framework tells us that if the economy is in a normal recession, you shouldn't worry much about deficits—they can actually be good for the economy. If you are in an economic boom, then the macroeconomic arguments for deficits are significantly reduced. Booms are a good time to get a country's financial house in order, maintaining, and possibly increasing, the country's capacity to run large deficits in recessions.

Politically, economic arguments are hard to follow, and economists' advice is usually not followed, creating political fights about imposing fiscal austerity in an economy when it is in a recession and is about to go bankrupt without outside help. That was the situation in Greece in the early 2000s. All economists agreed that the recession was the worst time to impose austerity, but those who favored the austerity policy argued that they had no choice since when the Greek economy was booming, instead of using that boom to get its fiscal affairs in order, Greece ran large deficits and made commitments that it could not keep.

Summary

- A deficit is a shortfall of revenues under payments. A surplus is the excess of revenues over payments. Debt is accumulated deficits minus accumulated surpluses.   (*LO31-1*)

- Deficits and surpluses are summary measures of a budget. Whether a budget deficit is a problem depends on the budgeting procedures that measure it.   (*LO31-1*)

- A cyclical deficit is that part of the deficit that exists because the economy is below or above potential: (*LO31-1*)

  Cyclical deficit = Tax rate × (Potential output − Actual output)

- A structural deficit is that part of a budget deficit that would exist even if the economy were at its potential level of income.   (*LO31-1*)

  Structural deficit = Actual deficit − Cyclical deficit

- A real deficit is a nominal deficit adjusted for the effect of inflation: (*LO31-2*)

  Real deficit = Nominal deficit − (Inflation × Debt)

- Because the United States has mostly had inflation and debt, its real deficit has been lower than its nominal deficit.   (*LO31-2*)

- A country's debt must be judged in relation to its assets. What is counted as a debt and as an asset can be arbitrary. (*LO31-3*)

- Government debt and individual debt differ in three major ways: (1) Government is ongoing and never needs to repay its debt, (2) government can pay off its debt by printing money, and (3) most of government debt is internal—owed to its own citizens. (*LO31-3*)

- Deficits, surpluses, and debt should be viewed relative to GDP because this ratio better measures the government's ability to handle the deficit and pay off the debt. Compared to some countries, the United States has a low debt-to-GDP ratio. (*LO31-4*)

- Since 2008, the United States has run significant deficits and the debt-to-GDP ratio has risen to over 100 percent. Unless the United States lowers the deficit it may face another financial crisis. (*LO31-4*)

Key Terms

cyclical deficit	external debt	nominal deficit	structural deficit
debt	fiscal austerity	real deficit	surplus
deficit	internal debt	Social Security system	

Questions and Exercises **connect**

1. "Budget deficits should be avoided, even if the economy is below potential, because they reduce saving and lead to lower growth." Does this policy directive follow from the short-run or the long-run framework? Explain your answer. (*LO31-1*)

2. Your income is $40,000 per year; your expenditures are $45,000. You spend $20,000 of that $45,000 for tuition. Is your budget in deficit or surplus? Why? (*LO31-1*)

3. Suppose a country's debt is $630 billion before Year 1. Using the information below (in billions of dollars), fill in the blanks for its budget balance and debt for the following years: (*LO31-1*)

	Revenues	Expenditures	Debt
Year 1	$203	$202	$___
Year 2	215	___	626
Year 3	227	221	___
Year 4	___	230	619
Year 5	258	243	___

4. What are the two ways government can finance a budget deficit? (*LO31-1*)

5. If the structural budget deficit is $100 billion and the actual deficit is $300 billion, what is the size of the cyclical deficit? (*LO31-1*)

6. If the actual budget deficit is $100 billion, the economy is operating $200 billion above its potential, and the marginal tax rate is 20 percent, what are the structural deficit and the cyclical deficit? (*LO31-1*)

7. Say the marginal tax rate is 30 percent and that government expenditures do not change with output. Say also that the economy is at potential output and that the deficit is $200 billion. (*LO31-1*)
   a. What is the size of the cyclical deficit?
   b. What is the size of the structural deficit?
   c. How would your answers to *a* and *b* change if the deficit were still $200 billion but output were $200 billion below potential?
   d. How would your answers to *a* and *b* change if the deficit were still $200 billion but output were $100 billion above potential?
   e. Which is likely of more concern to policy makers: a cyclical or a structural deficit?

8. Calculate the real deficit or surplus in the following cases: (*LO31-2*)
   a. Inflation is 10 percent. Debt is $3 trillion. Nominal deficit is $220 billion.
   b. Inflation is 2 percent. Debt is $1 trillion. Nominal deficit is $50 billion.
   c. Inflation is −4 percent. (Price levels are falling.) Debt is $500 billion. Nominal deficit is $30 billion.
   d. Inflation is 3 percent. Debt is $2 trillion. Nominal surplus is $100 billion.

9. Inflation is 20 percent. Debt is $2 trillion. The nominal deficit is $300 billion. What is the real deficit? *(LO31-2)*

10. How would your answer to question 9 differ if you knew that expected inflation was 15 percent? *(LO31-2)*

11. Assume a country's nominal GDP is $600 billion, government expenditures less debt service are $145 billion, and revenue is $160 billion. The nominal debt is $360 billion. Inflation is 3 percent and interest rates are 6 percent. *(LO31-2)*
    a. Calculate debt service payments.
    b. Calculate the nominal deficit.
    c. Calculate the real deficit.

12. List three ways in which individual debt differs from government debt. *(LO31-3)*

13. If all of the government's debt were internal, would financing that debt make the nation poorer? *(LO31-3)*

14. Assume that a country's real growth is 2 percent per year, while its real deficit is rising 5 percent a year. *(LO31-3)*
    a. Can the country continue to afford such deficits indefinitely?
    b. What problems might it face in the future?

15. Why is who holds the debt an important factor when comparing debt-to-GDP ratios among countries? *(LO31-4)*

16. Why is debt service an important measure of whether debt is a problem? *(LO31-4)*

17. How can a debt that is too high lead to an even higher debt? *(LO31-4)*

18. What might keep the Fed from buying up more bonds if the debt gets too high? *(LO31-4)*

Questions from Alternative Perspectives

1. International issues aside, what limits government's ability to undertake monetary or fiscal policy? *(Austrian)*

2. To help understand the distributional consequences of the tax cuts advocated by many conservative politicians, answer the following:
    a. What income groups have the largest marginal propensity to consume: high or low income?
    b. If your goal were to minimize the deficit cost of a tax stimulus, who should receive the tax cuts? Who received the tax cuts?
    c. What will the tax cut do, relatively speaking, to the debt?
    d. Is there a pattern here? *(Institutionalist)*

3. After President George W. Bush's election in 2000, he proposed cutting taxes.
    a. Would you consider that proposal to follow the short-run or long-run framework, or a combination of the two?
    b. From your response, how should President Bush have dealt with the U.S. deficit to be consistent with the school of thought that you chose? *(Post-Keynesian)*

4. Over 40 countries in the world now report what has been called a "women's budget," analyzing public expenditures and revenue from a gender perspective.
    a. What might be an example of a gender effect on the expenditure side of the budget?
    b. On the revenue side?
    c. Why are these effects important to consider? *(Feminist)*

Issues to Ponder

1. Two economists are debating whether the target rate of unemployment is 4 percent or 6 percent. Mr. A believes it's 4 percent; Ms. B believes it's 6 percent. One says the structural deficit is $40 billion; the other says it's $20 billion. Which one says which? Why?

2. "The debt should be of concern." What additional information do you need to undertake a reasonable discussion of this statement?

3. You've been hired by Creative Accountants, economic consultants. Your assignment is to make suggestions about how to structure a government's accounts so that the current deficit looks as small as possible. Specifically, they want to know how to treat the following:
    a. Government pensions.
    b. Sale of land.
    c. Social Security taxes.
    d. Proceeds of a program to allow people to prepay taxes for a 10 percent discount.
    e. Expenditures on F-52 bombers.

4. How can a government that isn't running a deficit still get itself into financial trouble?

Answers to Margin Questions

1. A policy of austerity may throw an economy into a recession, lowering both government revenue and GDP. Both of these would tend to increase the debt-to-GDP ratio. (*LO31-1*)

2. The U.S. government sells bonds to finance deficit spending. (*LO31-1*)

3. Since the economy is at its potential income, its cyclical deficit is zero. All of its budget deficit is a structural deficit. (*LO31-1*)

4. Inflation reduces the value of the dollars with which the debt will be repaid and hence, in real terms, wipes out a portion of the debt. (*LO31-2*)

5. The real deficit equals the nominal deficit minus inflation times the total debt. Inflation times the total debt in this case equals $80 billion (0.02 × $4 trillion). Since the nominal deficit is $40 billion, the real deficit is actually a surplus of $40 billion ($40 billion − $80 billion = −$40 billion). (*LO31-2*)

6. Inflation is not a costless way for the government to reduce the real deficit because inflation can push up interest rates. Higher interest rates can make its interest payments higher than they otherwise would be, leaving less to spend on other things. (*LO31-2*)

7. Deficit is a flow concept, the difference between income and expenditures. Debt—accumulated deficits minus accumulated surpluses—is a stock concept. (*LO31-3*)

8. To get a full picture of a country's financial situation, you have to look at assets as well as debt since a large debt for a country with large assets poses less of a problem. The greater its assets the more a country is able to pay off its debts. (*LO31-3*)

9. Paying interest on internal debt redistributes income among citizens in a country. Paying interest on external debt reduces domestic income. (*LO31-3*)

10. A $5 billion economy growing at a real annual rate of 5 percent could have an annual deficit of $250 million (0.05 × $5 billion) and not increase its debt-to-GDP ratio. (*LO31-4*)

The Fiscal Policy Dilemma

After reading this chapter, you should be able to:

LO32-1 Summarize the Classical view of sound finance.

LO32-2 Summarize the Keynesian view of functional finance.

LO32-3 List six assumptions of the *AS/AD* model that lead to potential problems with the use of fiscal policy.

LO32-4 Explain how automatic stabilizers work.

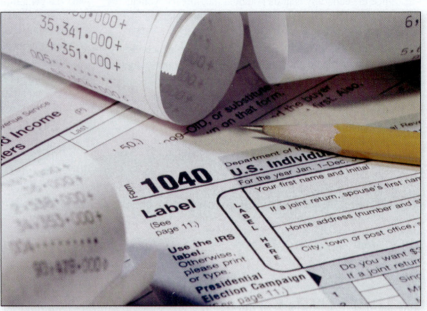

©Elizabeth Simpson/Getty Images

Modern economies face a major policy dilemma. In a serious recession, such as the one that the world economies entered into in 2008, almost all economists agree that governments need to run expansionary fiscal policy—that is, deficits. That follows from the standard macro policy models. In the long run, however, almost all economists agree that governments need to maintain a solid financial situation, which means that governments need to balance their budgets, or perhaps even run surpluses to offset some of the past deficits they built up trying to prevent recessions. The reason is not that deficits are inherently bad. Deficits reduce government's future borrowing capacity; if governments build up "too large" debt, they will likely find it harder to finance their debt in the future. A government that cannot easily finance its debt will either go bankrupt or have to resort to inflationary finance, with the central bank financing the government by printing money. Neither is good for any economy.

So the fiscal policy dilemma is what to do in periods of structural stagnation when both deficits and a balanced budget are called for. When an economy falls into a structural stagnation, the effectiveness of expansionary demand-side policy is limited. International conditions, political considerations, and institutional issues make it impossible for fiscal policy to achieve a sustainable growth rate consistent with the type of jobs and pay acceptable by most people. This chapter addresses that dilemma. In it, I provide a brief discussion of the evolution of economists' thinking about fiscal policy and how we arrived at the modern fiscal policy precepts that guide our thinking about modern fiscal policy.

Classical Economics and Sound Finance

Let's begin by looking at how economists' views of public finance and fiscal policy have changed over time. Before the 1930s, economists generally supported a policy that was described as "sound finance." **Sound finance** was *a view of fiscal policy that the government budget should always be balanced except in wartime.* Economists held this view based on a combination of political and economic grounds, but primarily on political grounds. (Before 1930, economic analysis and political analysis were not as separate as they are today, and it is hard to separate out positions held on political as opposed to economic grounds.) The reason politics was important is that the Classical liberal tradition, which was the dominant tradition of economists at the time, viewed government with suspicion, so any policy that would make it easier to increase government spending during peacetime was seen as undesirable.

Ricardian Equivalence Theorem: Deficits Don't Matter

Although Classical economists believed in the principle of sound finance, they also recognized that pure economic arguments for balancing the budget were weak or nonexistent. For example, David Ricardo, one of the most famous economists in the 19th century, pointed out that, in a purely theoretical sense, government spending financed by selling government bonds (the government running a budget deficit) was no different from government spending financed by taxes (the government running a balanced budget). The reason was that if the government ran deficits, it would have to increase taxes in the future both to pay the interest on the bonds and to repay the bonds when they came due. Those future taxes would make the taxpayers poorer in the same way that paying taxes now would make them poorer. Assuming people can borrow and save, and thereby shift spending between now and the future, people would save more now to pay for those future taxes. So, there is no reason why financing spending with a deficit should affect the aggregate level of income differently than financing spending with taxes. The difference between the two is simply a matter of who does the borrowing. It followed that a government deficit would not lead to an expansion of output in the economy. This *theoretical proposition that deficits do not affect the level of output in the economy because individuals increase their savings to account for expected future tax payments to repay the deficit* has become known as the **Ricardian equivalence theorem.**

Despite economists' recognition of the logical truth of the Ricardian equivalence theorem, most economists, including Ricardo, felt that, in practice, deficits could affect output and that it mattered a lot, politically, whether government financed its spending by bonds (ran deficits) or by taxes (balanced the budget). Based on their political ideology, economists of the time strongly pushed government to finance its spending with taxes, not bonds. Hence, their principle of sound finance. They supported the principle of sound finance because they felt that, politically, requiring government to follow the principle of sound finance made increasing government spending more difficult and brought home to the politicians the central economic lesson that there is no free lunch. They argued that adhering to a policy of sound finance forced government to face the costs of a spending decision simultaneously with the benefits

Although Classical economists believed in the principle of sound finance, they also recognized that the pure economic arguments for balancing the budget were weak or nonexistent.

 Web Note 32.1

When Do Deficits Matter?

Q-1 Does the Ricardian equivalence theorem lead to a policy of sound finance?

When it comes near you, it stops with a jerk. A door is opened, and an occupant asks whether you would like a lift. You look into the car and before you can control yourself you cry out, "Why, there's no steering wheel." Want a ride?

For Lerner, the aggregate economy was subject to wild fluctuations and it needed a steering wheel to guide it. Fiscal policy was that steering wheel. Notice that the focus here is only on the government steering the economy; there is no discussion of politics or whether the recession is major or minor as there was in the nuanced view of sound finance. Lerner's functional finance had no nuances about policy.

Functional finance nicely fits the *AS/AD* model you learned in Chapter 26. In these models, there was a desired level of output—potential output around which the economy fluctuated. However, by using its fiscal (and monetary) policy steering wheel, the government could increase or decrease either expenditures or taxes, thereby shifting the *AD* curve to the right or left to steer the economy to the desired level of output. (A good review exercise is to go through various changes in government spending and taxes in the *AS/AD* model.)

So in functional finance, the economist's answer to the question, what to do if there is a recession, is to run a deficit to return the economy to its potential output. Policy followed directly from the model.

Assumptions of the *AS/AD* Model

Lerner's stark presentation of functional finance did not last long as a guiding principle for practical macro public finance and fiscal policy. The reason was that the model made a number of assumptions that, in practice, did not hold, and the model did not deal with the difficult practical and political problems of implementing fiscal policy. These problems don't mean that functional finance models are wrong; they simply mean that for fiscal policy to work, the policy conclusions drawn from the model must be modified to reflect the real-world problems. Let's consider how the reality might not fit the model. The *AS/AD* model assumes:

1. Financing the deficit doesn't have any offsetting effects. (In reality, it often does.)
2. The government knows what the situation is—for instance, the size of the multiplier effect, and other exogenous variables. (In reality, the government must estimate them.)
3. The government knows the economy's potential income level—the highest level of income that doesn't cause accelerating inflation. (In reality, the government may not know what this level is.)
4. The government has flexibility to change spending and taxes. (In reality, government cannot change them quickly.)
5. The size of the government debt doesn't matter. (In reality, the size of the government debt often does matter.)
6. Fiscal policy doesn't negatively affect other government goals. (In reality, it often does.)

Let's consider each assumption a bit further.

Financing the Deficit Has No Offsetting Effects

One of the limitations of the functional finance approach embodied in the *AS/AD* model is that it assumes that financing the deficit has no offsetting effects on income. Some economists argue that that is not the case, that the government financing of deficit spending will offset the deficit's expansionary effect.

In functional finance, the focus is only on the government steering the economy; there is no discussion of politics or nuance.

In functional finance, if there is a recession, the government should run a deficit.

Six assumptions of the *AS/AD* model that could lead to problems with fiscal policy are:
1. Financing the deficit doesn't have any offsetting effects.
2. The government knows what the situation is.
3. The government knows the economy's potential income level.
4. The government has flexibility in changing spending and taxes.
5. The size of the government debt doesn't matter.
6. Fiscal policy doesn't negatively affect other government goals.

The *AS/AD* model assumes that saving and investment can differ, and that the government can increase its expenditures without at the same time causing private expenditures to decrease. Some economists object to that assumption. They believe the interest rate equilibrates saving and investment. They argue that when the government borrows to finance the deficit, that borrowing will increase interest rates and crowd out private investment.

Interest rate **crowding out**—*the offsetting of a change in government expenditures by a change in private expenditures in the opposite direction*—occurs as follows: When the government runs a budget deficit, it must sell bonds (that is, it must borrow) to finance that deficit. To get people to buy and hold the bonds, the government must make them attractive. That means the interest rate the bonds pay must be higher than it otherwise would have been. This tends to push up the interest rate in the economy, which makes it more expensive for private businesses to borrow, so they reduce their borrowing and their investment. That private investment is crowded out by expansionary fiscal policy. Hence the name *crowding out*. Increased government spending crowds out private spending.

> Crowding out is the offsetting effect on private expenditures caused by the government's sale of bonds to finance expansionary fiscal policy.

Crowding out is shown in Figure 32-1. If financing government spending were not an issue, expansionary fiscal policy would shift the *AD* curve to the right by a multiple of the increase in government spending, increasing income from Y_0 to Y_1. However, financing the deficit increases interest rates and decreases investment. This shifts the *AD* curve to the left to AD_2. Income falls back to Y_2. How much it shifts back is a matter of debate; it depends upon how responsive investment is to changes in the interest rate. The more investment is responsive to changes in the interest rate, the greater the crowding out.

> **Q-5** If interest rates had no effect on investment or consumption, how much crowding out would occur?

Because of crowding out, the net expansionary effect of fiscal policy is smaller than it otherwise would have been. Some economists argue that crowding out can totally offset the expansionary effect of fiscal policy, so the net effect is zero, or even negative, since they consider private spending more productive than government spending. Larger deficits decrease the pool of savings available for private investment.

The crowding out effect also works in reverse with contractionary fiscal policy. Say the government runs a budget surplus. That surplus will slow the economy since it shifts the *AD* curve back to the left. But it also means the U.S. Treasury (the U.S.

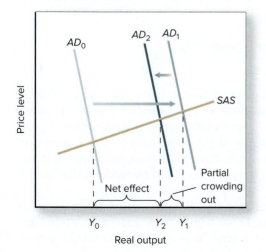

FIGURE 32-1 Crowding Out

An increase in government spending will expand income, but it will also cause interest rates to rise, reducing aggregate demand as shown. This is called *interest rate crowding out*. The net effect of fiscal policy depends on the degree of crowding out that takes place.

government department that issues bonds to finance the deficit) can buy back some of its outstanding bonds, which will have a tendency to push bond prices up and interest rates down. Lower interest rates will stimulate investment, which in turn will have an offsetting expansionary effect on the economy. So when we include financing the deficit in our consideration of fiscal policy, the shift in *AD* from the surplus is partially offset.

Q-6 Demonstrate graphically what would happen if government expenditures policy stimulated private investment.

How much financing will offset fiscal policy is a matter of debate. The empirical evidence about the degree of crowding out is mixed and has not resolved the debate. The degree of crowding out seems to change over time. Both sides see some crowding out occurring when the debt is financed by selling bonds. The closer to the potential income level the economy is, the more crowding out is likely to occur.

Even as the U.S. government has run large budget deficits in recent years, the U.S. interest rate has not risen substantially. The reasons why include the Fed's policy of buying bonds to hold down interest rates, and foreign governments' and foreign private individuals' willingness to finance the U.S. deficit by purchasing U.S. bonds. If their willingness stops, the U.S. interest rate could rise substantially.

The Government Knows the Situation

The numbers I use to demonstrate fiscal policy in the *AS/AD* model were chosen arbitrarily. In reality, the numbers used in models must be estimated or based on preliminary figures subject to revision. Most economic data are published quarterly, and it usually takes six to nine months of data to indicate, with any degree of confidence, the state of the economy and which way it is heading. Thus, we could be halfway into a recession before we even know it is happening. For example, in 2001, the data showed a decline in GDP in only one quarter (three months). Later reports revised the decline to three consecutive quarters. (Data are already three months old when published; then we need two or three quarters of such data before we have enough information to work with.)

In an attempt to deal with this problem, the government relies on large macroeconomic models and a variety of leading indicators such as housing starts and the consumer confidence index to predict what the economy will be like six months or a year from now. As part of the input to these complex models, the government must predict economic factors that determine the size of the multiplier. These predictions are imprecise, so the forecasts are imprecise. Economic forecasting is still an art, not a science.

Economists' data problems limit the use of fiscal policy for fine-tuning. There's little sense in recommending expansionary or contractionary policy until you know what policy is called for.

Economists' data problems limit the use of fiscal policy for fine-tuning.

The Government Knows the Economy's Potential Income Level

Web Note 32.2

What's the Speed Limit?

The problem of not knowing the level of potential income is related to the problem we just discussed. The target rate of unemployment and the potential level of income are not easy concepts to define. At one time it was thought 3 percent unemployment meant full employment. Some time later it was generally thought that 6.5 percent unemployment meant full employment. (About that time economists stopped calling the potential level of income the *full-employment* level of income). More recently, they see full employment to be closer to 4 percent.

Any variation in potential income can make an enormous difference in the policy prescription that could be recommended. To see how big a difference, let's translate a 1 percent change in unemployment into a change in income. Using a rough estimate, let's say that a 1 percentage point fall in the target unemployment rate is associated with a 2 percent increase in potential income. If that is the case, in 2018, with income at about $20 trillion, a 1 percentage point fall in the target unemployment rate would be associated with increased potential income of about $400 billion.

Now let's say that one economist believes 4.5 percent is the long-run achievable target rate of unemployment, while another believes it's 3 percent. That's a 1.5 percentage point difference. Since a 1 percent decrease in the unemployment rate means an increase of $380 billion in potential income, their views of the income level we should target differ by over $570 billion (1.5 × $380 = $570). Both views are reasonable. Looking at the same economy (the same data), one economist may call for expansionary fiscal policy while the other may call for contractionary fiscal policy.

In practice, differences in estimates of potential income often lead to different policy recommendations. Empirical estimates suggest that the size of the multiplier is somewhere between 1.5 and 2.5. Let's say it's 2.0. That means autonomous expenditures (initial changes before the multiplier) must be predicted to increase or decrease by more than $285 billion before an economist who believes the target rate of unemployment is 3 percent would agree with the same policy recommendation put forward by an economist who believes the rate is 4.5 percent. Since almost all fluctuations in autonomous investment and autonomous consumption are less than this amount, there's no generally agreed-on policy prescription for most fluctuations. Some economists will call for expansionary policy; some will call for contractionary policy; and the government decision makers won't have any clear-cut policy to follow.

> Differences in estimates of potential income often lead to different policy recommendations.

You might wonder why the range of potential income estimates is so large. Why not simply see whether the economy has inflation at the existing rate of unemployment and income level? Would that it were so easy. Inflation is a complicated process. Seeds of inflation are often sown years before inflation results. The main problem is that establishing a close link between the level of economic activity and inflation is a complicated statistical challenge to economists, one that has not yet been satisfactorily met. That leads to enormous debate as to what the causes are. In recent years globalization has added another complication. Because globalization keeps the price level down, the inflation rate may not rise even when an economy is exceeding its potential.

> Q-7 Why don't economists have an accurate measure of potential income?

Almost all economists believe that outside some range (perhaps 3 percent unemployment on the low side and 10 percent on the high side), too much spending causes inflation and too little spending causes a recession. That 3 to 10 percentage point range is so large that, in most cases, the U.S. economy is in an ambiguous state where some economists are calling for expansionary policy and others are calling for contractionary policy.

> In most cases, the U.S. economy is in an ambiguous state where some economists are calling for expansionary policy and others are calling for contractionary policy.

Once the economy reaches the edge of the range of potential income or falls outside it, the economists' policy prescription becomes clearer. For example, in the Depression, when the *AS/AD* model was developed, unemployment was 25 percent—well outside the range. Should the economy ever go into such a depression again, economists' policy prescriptions will be clear. The call will be for expansionary fiscal policy. Most times the economy is within the ambiguous range, so there are disagreements among economists.

The Government Has Flexibility in Changing Spending and Taxes

For argument's sake, let's say economists agree that contractionary policy is needed and that's what they advise the government. Will the government implement it? And, if so, will it implement contractionary fiscal policy at the right time? The answer to both questions is: probably not. Just consider 2018 when unemployment was low, and both the U.S. economy and the world economy seemed to be finally emerging from the

> Even if all economists agree that contractionary policy is needed and that's what they advise government, it is unlikely that government will institute contractionary policy.

Fighting the Vietnam War Inflation

Because of the lags associated with fiscal policy, often, fiscal policy's effect comes at the wrong time and affects the economy in the wrong way. For example, one time that economists were united in their views on appropriate fiscal policy was during the Vietnam War, from the early 1960s until 1975, when the economy was pushed to its limits. In 1965, President Lyndon B. Johnson's economic advisers started to argue strongly that a tax increase was needed to slow the economy and decrease inflationary pressures. President Johnson wouldn't hear of it. He felt a tax increase would be political suicide. Finally in mid-1968, after Johnson had decided not to run for reelection, a temporary

The Vietnam War led to inflationary pressures.

Source: National Archives and Records Administration [17331472]

income tax increase was passed. By then, however, many economists felt that the seeds of the 1970s inflation had already been sown. In 2018 the situation was the same. Economists called for fiscal restraint and government instituted expansionary policy, likely sowing the seeds for future problems.

structural stagnation they had fallen into for a decade. This would have been the time for government to focus on putting its fiscal house in order by reducing or eliminating the deficit so that it would have more capacity to run deficits when they were needed. What did the United States do? It cut taxes and increased spending, pushing deficits above $1 trillion. Economists' call for fiscal restraint went unheard.

Calls for expansionary fiscal policy have their problems, even if the calls are unanimous. Putting fiscal policy in place takes time and has serious implementation problems.

Numerous political and institutional realities in the United States today make implementing fiscal policy difficult. Government spending and taxes cannot be changed instantaneously. The budget process begins more than a year and a half before the government's fiscal year begins, so realistically at least two years are needed to implement fiscal policy. In the recent political climate, even this slow formal budget process has broken down, making it impossible to pass long-term budget bills. Over the past 20 years, more and more spending measures have been approved by continuing resolutions that get tangled with political wrangling rather than being part of a comprehensive spending plan. That is not a very responsive steering wheel.

Moreover, nearly two-thirds of the government budget is mandated by government programs, such as Medicare and Social Security, and by interest payments on government debt. Even the remaining one-third, called discretionary spending, is difficult to change. Defense programs are generally multiyear spending commitments. Discretionary spending also includes appropriations to fund established government agencies such as the Department of Agriculture, the Department of Transportation, and the Internal Revenue Service. Changing their budgets is politically difficult.

Politicians face intense political pressures; their other goals may conflict with the goals of fiscal policy. For example, few members of Congress who hope to be reelected would vote to raise taxes in an election year. Similarly, few members would vote to

> Numerous political and institutional realities make it a difficult task to implement fiscal policy.

slash defense spending when military contractors are a major source of employment in their districts, even when there's little to defend against. Squabbles between Congress and the president may delay initiating appropriate fiscal policy for months, even years. By the time the fiscal policy is implemented, what may have once been the right fiscal policy may have ceased to be right, and some other policy may have become right.

Imagine trying to steer a car at 60 miles an hour when there's a five-second delay between the time you turn the steering wheel and the time the car's wheels turn. Imagining that situation will give you a good sense of how fiscal policy works in the real world.

Real-world fiscal policy is similar to steering a car with a five-second delay from turning the steering wheel to turning the wheels.

The Size of the Government Debt Doesn't Matter

There is no inherent reason why adopting functional finance policies should have caused the government to run deficits year after year and hence to incur ever-increasing debt—accumulated deficits less accumulated surpluses. Activist functional finance policy is consistent with running deficits some years and surpluses other years. In practice, the introduction of activist functional finance policy has been accompanied by many deficits and few surpluses, and by a large increase in government debt.

There are two reasons why activist government policies have led to an increase in government debt. First, early activist economists favored large increases in government spending as well as favoring the government's using fiscal policy. These early activist economists justified increasing spending without increasing taxes by its expansionary effect on aggregate output. A second reason is political. Politically it's much easier for government to increase spending and decrease taxes than to decrease spending and increase taxes. Due to political pressure, expansionary fiscal policy has predominated over contractionary fiscal policy.

Most economists believe that a country's debt becomes a problem once it approaches somewhere around 90 or 100 percent of a country's GDP. That's not a fixed percentage but is a rough guide of when countries in the past have experienced problems. It is when people will begin to worry about whether the government will default on its bonds or will be forced to inflate its way out of its debt problem.

Most economists believe that a country's debt becomes a problem somewhere around 90 to 100 percent of a country's GDP.

Since the total value of U.S. bonds issued is over 100 percent of GDP and the total bonds held by the public (nongovernmental agencies) is about 75 percent of GDP, concern about how much more the U.S. government can borrow to continue to stimulate the economy, regardless of the state of the economy, has been increasing. Those who believe government should continue to use expansionary fiscal policy point out that U.S. bonds are still highly desirable to the public. They point out that the interest rates on Treasury bonds are exceptionally low, suggesting that people still see the U.S. government as highly creditworthy. Others respond that the low interest rates reflect a Fed policy designed to hold those interest rates down, and that as the Fed begins to raise short-term interest rates, long-term interest rates may rise, making it more difficult for the government to finance the debt.

They also point out that the bond market depends heavily on expectations and that those expectations can change quickly, particularly in a globalized world. If those who buy U.S. government bonds begin to worry about a U.S. government default (the United States cannot pay bondholders) or a rise in inflation, interest rates will rise quickly. As a result the government's budget deficit will rise, because it has to pay the higher interest rate on its borrowing. Since much of the U.S. government debt is short-term, a rise in the interest rate can quickly make the deficit problem worse. A worsening deficit problem could further increase the expectations of default or inflation, pushing interest rates and the deficit even higher. If interest rates on all government bonds rose from 2 percent to 6 percent, the U.S. deficit would rise by more than $800 billion merely to pay the added interest. The cycle of expectations can spiral out of control quickly.

The bond market depends heavily on expectations that can change quickly.

Q-8 Approximately what is the ratio of total U.S government debt compared to U.S. GDP?

Fiscal Policy Doesn't Negatively Affect Other Government Goals

A society has many goals; achieving potential income is only one of them. It's not surprising that those goals often conflict. When the government runs expansionary fiscal policy, the trade deficit tends to increase because as the economy expands and income rises, exports remain constant but imports rise. If a nation's international considerations do not allow a balance of trade deficit to become larger, as is true in many countries, those governments cannot run expansionary fiscal policies—unless they can somehow prevent this trade deficit from becoming larger.

Summary of the Problems

So where do these six problems leave fiscal policy? While they don't eliminate its usefulness, they severely restrict it. Fiscal policy is a sledgehammer, not an instrument for fine-tuning. When the economy seems to be headed into a depression, the appropriate fiscal policy is clear. This was the case in 2008 and 2009. Similarly, when an economy has a hyperinflation, the appropriate policy is clear. But in less extreme cases, there will be debate on what the appropriate fiscal policy is—a debate economic theory can't answer conclusively.

These practical problems in running deficits have led modern economists to a much more nuanced view of deficit finance than found in the functional finance view. The modern view held by applied macro policy economists is that deficits can stimulate aggregate output, but they also agree with earlier Classical economists that there are political reasons for not letting budgets get too unbalanced, and for not relying on governments to control spending and taxes to achieve the desired level of output. As a tool, except in a potential depression, discretionary fiscal policy is not very helpful. But that does not mean that modern macro policy economists have discarded fiscal policy altogether. Instead of advocating standard discretionary fiscal policy in which government responds to fluctuations in income with changes in government spending and taxes, modern economists advocate building fiscal policy into institutions.

Building Fiscal Policies into Institutions

Economists quickly recognized the political problems with instituting discretionary countercyclical fiscal policy. To avoid these problems, they suggested policies that built fiscal policy into U.S. institutions so that it wouldn't require any political decisions. They called a built-in fiscal policy an **automatic stabilizer**—*a government program or policy that will counteract the business cycle without any new government action.* Automatic stabilizers include welfare payments, unemployment insurance, and the income tax system.

How Automatic Stabilizers Work

To see how automatic stabilizers work, consider the unemployment insurance system. When the economy is slowing down or is in a recession, the unemployment rate will rise. When people lose their jobs, they will reduce their consumption, starting the multiplier process, which decreases income. Unemployment insurance immediately helps offset the decrease in individuals' incomes as the government pays benefits to the unemployed. Thus, government spending increases, and part of the fall in income is stopped without any explicit act by the government. Automatic stabilizers also work in reverse. When income increases, government spending declines automatically.

Fiscal policy is a sledgehammer, not an instrument for fine-tuning.

Practical problems in running deficits have led modern economists to a much more nuanced view of deficit finance than found in the functional finance view.

An automatic stabilizer is any government program or policy that will counteract the business cycle without any new government action.

Web Note 32.3

Improving Automatic Stabilizers

Another automatic stabilizer is our income tax system. Tax revenue fluctuates as income fluctuates. When the economy expands, tax revenues rise, slowing the economy; when the economy contracts, tax revenues decline, stimulating the economy. Let's go through the reasoning why. When the economy is strong, people have more income and thus pay higher taxes. This increase in tax revenue reduces consumption expenditures from what they would have been and moderates the economy's growth. When the economy goes into a recession, the opposite occurs.

State Government Finance and Procyclical Fiscal Policy

Automatic stabilizers are sometimes offset by other institutional structures that work as a type of automatic *destabilizer*. Examples of such destabilizers are states' constitutional provisions to maintain balanced budgets. These provisions mean that whenever a recession hits, states are faced with declining tax revenue. To maintain balanced budgets, the states must cut spending, increase tax rates, or both. For example, during the 2008 recession, state governments struggled to balance their budgets by cutting expenditures on education, transportation, health care, and a variety of other programs while raising income and sales taxes. These actions deepened the recession. Similarly, during the 10-year expansion in the 1990s and early 2000s, state revenue rose; states increased spending and decreased tax rates. The expansionary effect of these changes further increased total income. The result is what economists call **procyclical fiscal policy**—*changes in government spending and taxes that increase the cyclical fluctuations in the economy instead of reducing them.*

The procyclical nature of state government spending demonstrated itself in 2008 when the U.S. economy fell into a deep recession. In order to keep their budgets balanced, state governments began implementing massive spending cutbacks and tax increases, both of which worsened the recession. These cutbacks were reduced somewhat by temporary federal government assistance, but it was unclear how long that assistance could continue since the federal government was running massive unsustainable deficits.

To reduce the procyclical nature of state financing, economists have suggested states establish *rainy-day funds*—reserves kept in good times, to be used to offset declines in revenue during recessions. Large rainy-day funds (which some economists have called rainy-season funds) would decrease the destabilizing aspect of state government spending. But politics usually keeps rainy-day funds small; the funds are targets that are just too tempting for spending proposals or tax cuts.

Large rainy-day funds would decrease the destabilizing aspect of state government spending.

An alternative way of building countercyclical policies into institutions would be for states to use a five-year rolling-average budgeting procedure (with a built-in underlying trend rate of increase) as the budget they are required to balance. With a rolling-average budget, revenues available for spending would be determined from a growth-adjusted average of revenues for the past five years. When revenues increase substantially in a year, the surplus available to be spent would build up only slowly and would therefore be much less politically tempting to raid. When revenues fall, the measured deficit would grow much more slowly, and the constitutional budget-balancing requirements would be much less procyclical.

Balancing a rolling-average budget, rather than the current-year budget, would counterbalance the balanced-budget requirement and would remove much of the procyclical aspect of current state budgeting procedures. In fact, if the federal government started using a similar five-year rolling-average budget, it too could build a more reasonable fiscal policy into its accounting procedures and reduce the need for discretionary stimulus packages.

Austerity and the Greek Deficit Problem

The potential problems of running large government deficits were discovered by Greece in 2011, when it essentially defaulted on its loans. Early in 2010, the Greek government had revealed that its fiscal situation was much worse than reported. Bondholders became worried and interest rates rose. To pay these higher interest rates and to restore investor confidence, Greece announced spending cuts and tax increases. The Greek people protested and investors became even more worried, which caused interest rates to rise even further; the yield on old Greek bonds rose to over 25 percent, which meant that any new unsecured borrowing that the government needed would have to pay that rate. The situation spiraled into higher and higher interest rates, deeper and deeper spending cuts, and increases in taxes.

Greeks riot over austerity.
©ARIS MESSINIS/AFP/Getty Images

It was clear that Greece needed more and more new loans to keep the economy from collapsing. The problem was that no one wanted to lend more money to Greece because it wasn't expected to repay existing loans, let alone pay off new ones. After Greece implemented budget austerity measures, the European Union, of which Greece was part, loaned Greece enough to keep it afloat for another year or two. Simultaneously, the EU negotiated with private Greek bondholders to essentially write off more than half the amount Greece owed. As part of those negotiations, the EU required even greater budget discipline and austerity—increasing taxes, cutting public sector employment, cutting wages of government employees, raising the retirement age, and many more cutbacks than it had already implemented. The budget austerity measures pushed the Greek economy into a deeper recession, lowering tax revenues and increasing unemployment even higher. The result was rioting in the streets of Athens.

The public's dislike of the austerity policy that the European Central Bank (ECB) and IMF had forced on Greece as a condition for new loans led in 2014 to their ousting the government that had agreed to that austerity program. It was replaced by a new anti-austerity government that said it would not be bound by those austerity measures. That led to more negotiations, with the ECB and IMF eventually giving Greece a take-it-or-leave-it ultimatum: Accept austerity or no more loans. Faced with this ultimatum, the new Greek government capitulated, and agreed to phase in most of the imposed austerity measures. In response the ECB and IMF gave Greece the first part of a new loan, which prevented Greece from defaulting. It also phased in loans as Greece implements the required austerity. Each phase caused demonstrations and outrage at both the government and the IMF.

Is this the future for the United States? Probably not. The United States and Greece differ in two significant ways. First, the United States has a much bigger economy and is too big to fail (just like the large U.S. banks were too big to fail in the United States in 2008). If the United States fails, the world economy is likely to fail. Pulling out of U.S. bonds will lead to a world financial crisis. This means that the international community will have stronger incentives to prevent the United States from defaulting than it had with Greece. Second, the United States has its own central bank. (Greece gave up its currency and central bank when it joined the European Union.) The Fed can always buy government bonds—its own escape hatch, so to speak. So even if the United States faces a situation like that of Greece, the problems will not play out in the same way.

To say that the United States is different from Greece is not to say that if the world economy loses faith in the U.S. government's commitment and ability to repay its loans, the United States won't face serious problems. The current interest rate that the United States pays on its loans is exceptionally low by historical standards, and that low interest rate is helping to hold down the U.S. deficit. If interest rates rise considerably, the result would be an increase in the U.S. deficit and the need for spending cuts or tax increases.

Neither of these will be politically popular. People will say, "We are increasing taxes and cutting spending to pay off rich bondholders while cutting social benefits to the poor. That's unfair." This will likely lead to political fights about whether a default on bonds is preferable on equity grounds. It is precisely these issues that led to the riots in Greece.

The Negative Side of Automatic Stabilizers

Automatic stabilizers may seem like the solution to the economic woes we have discussed, but they, too, have their shortcomings. One problem is that when the economy is first starting to climb out of a recession, automatic stabilizers will slow the process, rather than help it along, for the same reason they slow the contractionary process. As income increases, automatic stabilizers increase government taxes and decrease government spending, and as they do, the discretionary policy's expansionary effects are decreased. Another problem is that in a downturn, the automatic stabilizers are increasing spending, thus making it harder for government to reduce its deficit. This helps slow the recession, but if the problem is that the debt has become so large that bondholders fear default, automatic stabilizers can increase that fear.

Despite these problems, most economists believe that automatic stabilizers have played an important role in reducing normal fluctuations in our economy. They point to the kind of data we see in Figure 32-2, which up until 2008 showed a significant decrease in fluctuations in the economy. Other economists aren't so sure; they argue both that the apparent decrease in fluctuations is an optical illusion and that problems that built up during the period of reduced fluctuations led to the financial crisis that began in 2008. As usual, economic data are sufficiently ambiguous to give both sides strong arguments. The jury is still out.

Q-9 What effect do automatic stabilizers have on the size of the multiplier?

Conclusion

Taking all the qualifications into account, the modern macro policy precepts involve a blend of functional and sound finance. Modern economists' answer to the question "What should the government do about a recession?" is generally: Do nothing in terms of specific tax or spending policy, but let the automatic stabilizers in the economy do the adjustment. The reason for not undertaking specific policies is not a lack of concern about recession, but because, theoretically, the effect a deficit would have is unclear and, practically and politically, implementing control via fiscal policy at the right time is very difficult. The "do-nothing" approach reflects the sound finance precept. There are two important exceptions. The first is if the economy is falling into a severe recession or depression, then the majority of economists believe that government should run expansionary fiscal policy, unless the country's debt situation makes that impossible. If that is the case, the country must choose between default and depression. The other exception is experiencing a

Q-10 According to modern economists, what should government do if there is a recession, a hyperinflation, and a depression?

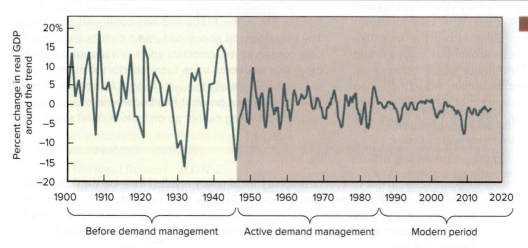

FIGURE 32-2   **Decrease in Fluctuations in the Economy**

Compared to the early 1900s, fluctuations in the economy have decreased; this suggests that policy makers have done something right.

Sources: Federal Reserve Historical Charts, Economic Report of the President (www.doc.gov), and author estimates.

average of four years. Even when the unemployment rate stays constant, there are still enormous amounts of flux in the labor market as millions of individuals quit jobs and take new ones and as people enter and exit the job market. For example in May 2018 the unemployment rate remained unchanged from the month before at 4 percent. But that month about 3.5 million workers quit jobs, another 2 million or so left for other reasons, and a total of 5.7 million started new jobs. So while total employment and unemployment remained roughly constant, many of the unemployed at the beginning of the month were not the same people who were unemployed at the end of the month.

The Debate about the Nature and Measurement of Unemployment

There is an ongoing debate about whether unemployment is voluntary or involuntary. The reality is that even in a recession, most educated people can either find a job or create one. The problem is that the jobs they can find or create pay far less and are far less desirable than the jobs they want. Here's an example: In 2009 more than half of students who graduated with a humanities degree either were unemployed or worked at a job that didn't require a college degree. Even new PhDs in these disciplines often don't have much better prospects. It's even worse for those who have dropped out of college or high school. As college-educated people look for jobs that don't require a college education, they will squeeze out those who don't have that education. It is like a game of musical chairs, and the people with the least education usually end up without the chair.

How many fewer chairs than people looking for chairs depends on the state of the economy. The stronger the economy, the more jobs available. In 2012 there were about four people looking for every job available. In 2018, when unemployment fell to under 4 percent, the ratio fell to just under 1. There were more job vacancies than people unemployed. However, many of the available jobs were ones that few people found acceptable, and workers looking for jobs didn't have the skills needed for the good acceptable jobs available. What this means is that if everyone is going to have an acceptable job, some people are going to have to create one for themselves.

Entrepreneurship and Unemployment

Creating a job for yourself isn't that far-fetched. Even teenagers can create jobs—babysitting, dog walking, washing cars, or teaching the technically challenged older generation how to use a smartphone or an iPad. Truly entrepreneurial people will never be unemployed; they will simply create jobs for themselves. Most of us are not that entrepreneurial, and the reality is that in today's economy high school dropouts, and increasingly college dropouts, are having a hard time finding what they consider an acceptable job.

In Chapter 24 I discussed how unemployment was measured. In the remainder of this chapter I take a closer look at some microeconomic concepts of unemployment, unemployment's relationship to potential output, and the debate about what the target level of unemployment should be. I conclude by considering the policy debate about unemployment through a discussion of a plan to eliminate all involuntary unemployment by providing a guaranteed job for everyone.

Microeconomic Categories of Unemployment

In the decades after World War II, unemployment was seen primarily as cyclical unemployment, and the focus of macroeconomic policy was on how to eliminate that cyclical unemployment with monetary and fiscal policy. Today, economists believe that's not enough. Unemployment has many dimensions, and different types of unemployment are susceptible to different types of policies.

The labor market is like a game of musical chairs, and the people with the least education usually end up without the chair.

Q-1 What does entrepreneurship have to do with unemployment?

Web Note 33.1

Defining Unemployment

FIGURE 33-1 **Unemployment by Microeconomic Subcategories, 2017**

Unemployment isn't all the same. This figure gives you a sense of some of the subcategories of unemployment.

Source: *Employment and Earnings*, Bureau of Labor Statistics (www.bls.gov). Data may not add up due to rounding and definitional differences.

Today's view is that you don't use a sledgehammer to pound in finishing nails, and you don't use macro policies to deal with certain types of unemployment; instead you use micro policies. To determine where microeconomic policies are appropriate as a supplement to macroeconomic policies, economists break unemployment down into a number of categories and analyze each category separately. These categories include how people become unemployed, demographic characteristics, duration of unemployment, and the reason for unemployment (see Figure 33-1).

The nature of unemployment has changed over time in a number of ways. For example, today fewer and fewer jobs are available to those without a high school diploma. In the past the unemployment rate was lower for men; now it's lower for women. Another measure of the changing nature of unemployment is the duration of unemployment, as shown in Figure 33-2. As you can see, in the downturn in 2008 the duration of unemployment increased significantly. While it came down after the

Some microeconomic categories of unemployment are: how people become unemployed, demographic unemployment, duration of unemployment, and unemployment by industry.

Q-2 How did the nature of unemployment change in the downturn of 2008?

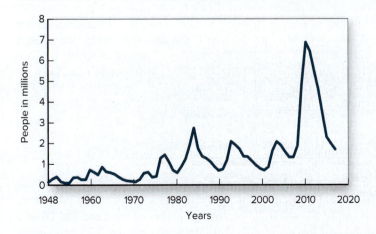

FIGURE 33-2 **Number of People Unemployed for More Than 27 Weeks**

Significantly more people were unemployed for more than 27 weeks in the 2008 recession compared to previous recessions because fewer people were able to find a comparable job at comparable pay to the one they lost. The wage they desired was higher than the wage they would have to accept to take a job.

Source: Bureau of Labor Statistics (www.bls.gov).

recession ended, it remained above its historic average. This means fewer unemployed people were finding and accepting another job soon after being unemployed. Some couldn't find work; more people were unable to find the type of job they had at the pay they were getting. It isn't that the government wasn't trying to lower unemployment; the government was running as expansionary monetary and fiscal policy as it dared (or at least as much as was politically feasible), and still the long-term unemployment rate only decreased slowly.

Unemployment and Potential Output

The unemployment rate provides an indication of how much labor is available to firms to increase production and thus provides a sense of what is the level of potential income. When unemployment falls below the target rate of unemployment, it is like driving your car 90 miles an hour. True, the marks on your speedometer might go up to 150, but a top speed of 75 is probably more prudent. Beyond 120 (assuming that's where your car is red-lined), the engine is likely to blow up (unless you have a Maserati). The achievable unemployment rate differs among countries and depends on labor institutions, labor laws, the country's exchange rate, and worker productivity. Thus, as is the case with cars, maximum speeds can differ among economies and can change over time.

Economists relate the target unemployment rate to the target level of potential output. That level of potential output in the United States is assumed to grow at the secular (long-term) trend rate of 2.25 to 3.5 percent per year.

Currently economists believe that an unemployment rate of about 4 percent is consistent with potential output. This, combined with the assumed underlying trend growth rate of 2.25 to 3.5 percent, gives them a reference point for estimating potential output. If unemployment remains constant, then real output should grow at the underlying trend rate. If unemployment falls, then output should grow by more than that.

The relationship between changes in output and unemployment is generally captured by **Okun's rule of thumb,** which states that *a 1 percentage point rise in the unemployment rate will tend to be associated with a 2 percent fall in output from its trend and vice versa.*

This means, for example, if the trend growth rate is 3 percent and the unemployment rate rises by 2 percentage points, output will actually fall by 1 percent (3 percent − 2 × 2 percent). In terms of number of workers, a 2 percentage point increase in the unemployment rate means about 3 million additional people are out of work than would be if the economy had stayed on its growth path. These figures are rough, but they give you a sense of the implications of the relationship.

What makes estimating this relationship difficult is that increases in productivity and increases in the number of people choosing to work fluctuate. Changes in either can cause output and employment to grow, even if the unemployment rate doesn't change. I point this out because in the 1980s the number of people choosing to work increased substantially, significantly increasing the labor participation rate. Then, in the early 2000s, as many large firms structurally adjusted their production methods to increase worker productivity, unemployment sometimes rose even as output rose. Thus, when the labor participation rate and productivity change, an increase in unemployment doesn't necessarily mean a decrease in employment or a decrease in output, and the relationship between output and unemployment can deviate from Okun's rule of thumb.

In the downturn starting in late 2007, government economists used Okun's rule of thumb to predict what would happen to unemployment as a result of the downturn. During that downturn output fell about 7.5 percentage points below trend and Okun's rule of thumb suggested that the unemployment rate would rise by 3.75 percentage

Okun's rule of thumb holds that a 1 percentage point rise in the unemployment rate will tend to be associated with a 2 percent fall in output below its trend and vice versa.

Q-3 If economic output falls 2 percent below its trend, what does Okun's rule predict happens to the unemployment rate?

points, from 5 percent to about 8.75 percent. Instead, unemployment rose to 10 percent, higher than predicted. The president's former chief economic adviser suggested that the fear associated with the potential financial breakdown led firms to cut employment much more than they normally would have because they were preparing for a possible depression. Because the remaining workers had to work harder, this increased productivity, which allowed the economy to keep growing, even if only slightly, as the unemployment rate rose.

Is Unemployment Structural or Cyclical?

Okun's rule of thumb is designed to explain cyclical unemployment. **Cyclical unemployment** is *temporary unemployment that can be expected to end as the economy recovers.* A person being temporarily laid off as a server because fewer people are going to restaurants in a recession is an example of cyclical unemployment. It can be resolved by expansionary fiscal and monetary policy. **Structural unemployment** is *long-term unemployment that occurs because of changes in the structure of the economy.* A person who loses his job as a stenographer because his job is replaced by voice recognition software is an example of structural unemployment. Structural unemployment cannot be resolved by expansionary monetary and fiscal policy. If a person is structurally unemployed, before he or she can find a job at the same pay, he or she will have to retrain. The distinction between structural and cyclical is not watertight. What starts out to be cyclical unemployment may well end up being structural unemployment, as the firms that lay off workers in a recession don't hire them back.

Most of the policy discussion about unemployment in conventional macroeconomics has been about cyclical unemployment, and most of that policy discussion has concerned monetary and fiscal policy. Expansionary macro policy is designed to deal with cyclical unemployment. If the U.S. economy is entering a period of structural stagnation, then that discussion and policy are no longer sufficient; the unemployment is structural—caused by a mismatch of the skills and wages desired by workers and the skills and wages firms are willing and able to pay. Macro policies won't solve structural unemployment.

Most of the policy discussions of unemployment in conventional macroeconomics have been about cyclical unemployment, not structural unemployment.

To give you an idea of what I mean by structural unemployment, consider a worker who has been laid off in the automobile industry. He was getting $28 an hour plus generous benefits such as a retirement plan and health insurance. Then he loses his job. In its place, the best job the economy can provide with the skills he has is a job for $10 an hour without benefits. Until a worker is willing to accept that lower-paying job, he is structurally unemployed. Expansionary monetary and fiscal policy won't solve his problem.

Q-4 How is the reservation wage related to structural unemployment?

An important determinant of whether someone takes a job is his or her **reservation wage**—*the wage a person requires before accepting a job.* The higher the reservation wage, the more likely one is to be unemployed. In today's globalized economy a U.S. worker's reservation wage tends to be higher than the reservation wage of many workers in developing countries. This means that many of the jobs U.S. workers used to do have been outsourced or given to new immigrants to the United States who are willing to work harder for less pay. Having had a good-paying job makes it psychologically difficult to lower one's reservation wage. For high school dropouts, globalization often means that they are lucky when they can pick up a minimum wage job washing dishes, cleaning rooms in a motel, working the midnight shift, or picking produce on a farm.

The wage for flipping hamburgers is below some people's reservation wage.
©Ken Wolter/Shutterstock

Another aspect that keeps reservation wages in the United States high are the costs associated with taking a job and the availability of income-support programs. People who are unemployed with kids to take care of—and child care costs $10 an hour—or those without transportation to a job might end up with lower take-home income if

Web Note 33.2

Low-Wage Jobs

they accept a low-paying job. This makes it essentially impossible for them to take the job as long as they can otherwise get enough to live on through food stamps and welfare support from friends, family, or government. So the available support for people without a job plays an important role in where one sets one's reservation wage.

Yet another aspect of structural unemployment is geographic. The job situation is never uniform across the United States; some parts of the country will have jobs while others have none. This also creates geographically imposed structural unemployment, because some people don't want to relocate to take a job. In 2012, for example, North Dakota, which had a natural gas boom, had numerous unfilled jobs, even as other parts of the country had significant unemployment. When oil prices fell in 2015, many of those jobs ended.

Why Has the Target Rate of Unemployment Changed over Time?

Why has the target rate of unemployment changed over time? One reason is demographics: As you saw in Figure 33-1, different age groups have different unemployment rates, and as the population's age structure changes, so does the target rate of unemployment. As we said, the market is one of continual change. Because younger people change jobs more frequently, a younger workforce will mean overall job change will be higher, leading to higher structural unemployment.

A second reason the target rate of unemployment changes is our economy's changing social and institutional structure. For example, women today comprise a greater percentage of the labor force than they did earlier. In the 1950s, the traditional view was that "a woman's place is in the home." At that time about one-third of women participated in the labor market. Usually only one family member—the husband—had a job. If he lost his job, the family had no income, and the main income earner (the husband) had to accept whatever job was available. Today about 60 percent of working-age women are in the labor force, and in 80 percent of all married-couple families, both husband and wife work. In a two-earner family, if one person loses a job, the family doesn't face immediate starvation. The other person's income carries the family over, allowing the one who lost a job to spend more time looking for one.

Third, government institutions have also changed. Unemployment benefits (created in 1911) and public welfare (created in 1939) were established to reduce suffering associated with unemployment and change people's responses to unemployment. People today are pickier about what jobs they will take than they were in the 1920s and 1930s. People don't want just any job; they want a *fulfilling* job with a decent wage. As people have become choosier about jobs, a debate has raged over the extent of government's responsibility for unemployment.

Technological change is a fourth reason. Automation, artificial intelligence, deep-learning apps, and other advancements are continually changing the nature of jobs—making previous skills obsolete and requiring workers to develop new skills. Often the new jobs that technology creates will pay less and seem less fulfilling than the jobs they replace.

Q-5 What are five reasons why the target rate of unemployment has changed in the United States?

Globalization is a fifth reason. The structural changes associated with globalization, which was characterized by large U.S. trade deficits and large U.S. capital account inflows that held the value of the dollar up, tend to increase the target rate of unemployment for the United States. As jobs move abroad, people must find new jobs that are globally competitive to remain employed in the tradable sector. The U.S. unemployment rate did not rise as jobs moved abroad because government ran highly expansionary monetary and fiscal policies that created additional jobs in the nontradable sector to

Web Note 33.3

Trump and Free Trade

replace the jobs lost in the tradable sector. Policy makers targeted a high potential output and a low target unemployment rate because low-priced imports removed the inflation signal that they previously had about the target level of unemployment being too low.

Both globalization and technological change require structural change. Consider globalization: Goods that used to be produced in the United States are now produced abroad by workers earning lower pay, which means that workers in tradable sectors in the United States either have to lower their reservation wages and accept much lower pay, or have to move to another sector where the United States has a comparative advantage. For a 50-year-old worker, that is easier said than done. A factory worker might have to retrain to become a computer specialist, or accept that the best she can do now is work for $11 an hour at Walmart with far fewer benefits than her previous $22-an-hour job. The lower the level of education, the lower the pay and the more likely one is to be unemployed, as you can see in Figure 33-3.

Globalization and technological change require structural change.

Globalization, Immigration, and Jobs

As I have emphasized throughout this book, the current U.S. unemployment problem can be understood only in reference to the world economy. The jobs experience of U.S. workers has depended in large part on whether the job is in a *tradable sector*—a sector such as manufacturing, where the production can be relatively easily shifted to a foreign country—or a *nontradable sector*—a sector such as education, where it cannot.

Another sector affected by globalization is what might be called the *immigration sector*—production that can be undertaken by non-U.S., largely unskilled immigrants (legal or illegal) from other countries willing to work in the United States for wages slightly more than those offered in their country. The U.S. government has helped develop this sector with programs such as the Temporary Agricultural Program that allow foreign workers to come to the United States on a temporary basis to fill jobs that Americans won't take. With free trade and movement across borders, wages in the tradable and immigrant sectors must be competitive, and will eventually equalize.

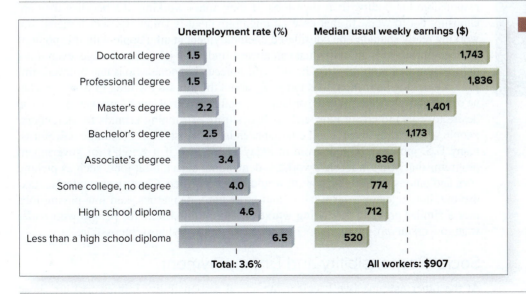

FIGURE 33-3 Unemployment Rates and Earnings by Educational Attainment, 2017

The lower the level of education, the lower the pay and the more likely one is to be unemployed.

Note: Data are for persons age 25 and over. Earnings are for full-time wage and salary workers.

Source: U.S. Bureau of Labor Statistics, Current Population Survey.

	Unemployment rate (%)	Median usual weekly earnings ($)
Doctoral degree	1.5	1,743
Professional degree	1.5	1,836
Master's degree	2.2	1,401
Bachelor's degree	2.5	1,173
Associate's degree	3.4	836
Some college, no degree	4.0	774
High school diploma	4.6	712
Less than a high school diploma	6.5	520
	Total: 3.6%	All workers: $907

The importance of immigration cannot be overestimated. Millions of people have immigrated into the United States to fill jobs. Why do U.S. firms hire them? For the same reason that they move production facilities outside the United States—firms get more for less. Immigration isn't entirely bad for U.S. workers. While without immigration the average pay of U.S. workers would have been higher, U.S. output would have been lower and many more businesses would have moved production facilities out of the United States. To the degree that U.S. workers wouldn't take many of the jobs filled by immigration, keeping these jobs in the United States created higher-paying complementary jobs in the United States that U.S. citizens could take.

Q-6 Has globalization affected jobs more in the tradable or nontradable sector?

The overall effect of globalization on unemployment across sectors has been to lower wages and raise unemployment in both the tradable and immigration sectors with very little change in wages or unemployment in the nontradable sector. As we will discuss in Chapter 37, globalization has even raised wages and employment in some nontradable sectors, particularly those related to facilitating international trade.

Framing the Debate about Voluntary and Involuntary Unemployment

Any discussion of unemployment quickly becomes intertwined with normative judgments about individual and government responsibility.

Any discussion of unemployment quickly becomes intertwined with normative judgments about individual and government responsibility. That is inevitable because the concept of unemployment is not, and cannot be, a completely scientific or technical concept. Whether a person is considered unemployed depends on one's framework.

To see the importance of frameworks, consider the picture in the margin. Is it a picture of an old woman with a large nose and a feather in her hair? Or is it a picture of a beautiful woman in a fur coat? Depending on how you look at it, it could be either. As psychologists have long pointed out, what you see depends on how you frame the picture; both are possibilities. (The ear of the beautiful woman is the eye of the old woman.) The same is the case with unemployment.

©Chronicle/Alamy Stock Photo

Individual Responsibility and Unemployment

At one extreme (we'll call it the individual responsibility framework) individuals are responsible for finding their own jobs. If they aren't working, it's because they are choosing not to work. In that case all unemployment is voluntary, which means not working really shouldn't be considered unemployment at all. People with this point of view emphasize that an individual can always find *some* job at *some* wage, even if it's only selling apples on the street for 40 cents apiece. Someone who is unemployed simply isn't looking hard enough, is too picky about the job, isn't willing to work for what he or she considers too-low pay, or lacks the entrepreneurial spirit (motivated by a true desire to work) to create jobs such as babysitting or running errands for neighbors. People who hold this view point out that even in the worst of the economic downturns, many U.S. jobs go unfilled. Even in today's economy, if it weren't for government programs that bring in foreign workers, demanding agricultural jobs, such as picking corn and onions for $10.50 an hour, would be left unfilled. Chicken slaughtering, taxi driving, housecleaning, farm labor, and other hard, dangerous, and low-paying jobs face a similar problem of finding workers. Within this frame for people who *really* want to work at *any* job or at *any* pay, unemployment is almost impossible.

Social Responsibility and Unemployment

Q-7 What is the difference between the individual responsibility and social responsibility views about unemployment?

At the other extreme (we'll call it the social responsibility framework) are those who believe that society owes people jobs commensurate with their training and job experience at a respectable wage. They see individuals with enormous skills and training who have studied for years but who cannot find a job—at least one using those skills. They see unskilled workers being asked to accept dangerous jobs that don't pay a living wage. They see people who would like to work much more than they do, but who have to accept part-time work. They see people who have become so discouraged that they are no longer even looking for a job. Under the official measure, these discouraged workers are not even counted as unemployed; in the social responsibility frame, they should be. They point out that in recent years, despite the improving economy and decrease in the unemployment rate, between 40 and 50 percent of recent college graduates cannot find jobs in their field, and that many cannot even find jobs that require college degrees. They end up in jobs such as waiting tables that don't use their degrees. The problem is made all the worse by the fact that the majority of college graduates have college loans to repay.

People who subscribe to this framework point out that except in significant economic expansions, the number of unemployed exceeds the number of job openings. In 2015, when unemployment was 5.3 percent, there were about one-and-a-half unemployed workers for each job opening. In 2018, when unemployment was under 4 percent, there were still slightly more job openings than people seeking jobs, and many available jobs were not ones that most people would find acceptable.

The Tough Policy Choices

The current definition and measure of unemployment is a combination of individual and social responsibility frameworks. By current measurements and definitions, approximately 6.2 million people were unemployed in mid-2018. This number would be challenged by both frameworks. According to an "individual responsibility" measure an accurate number of unemployed would be closer to 1 million; according to the "social responsibility" measure an accurate number would be closer to 30 million. As you can see, the differences are huge.

Any policy has to be implemented through the political system, which means that politicians must deal with these difficult normative issues and integrate them with the more objective aspects of the analysis. This integration is difficult and is not easily reduced into simple arguments that can be captured in the sound bites that the press often picks up. Politics significantly influences the debate and leads politicians to avoid discussing the difficult choices that need to be made. It is not that politicians do not recognize the need to make these difficult choices. It's that politicians on both sides believe they won't be reelected if they tell voters the reality. Somehow, within the U.S. political system, politicians fear facing and making the difficult decisions that need to be made.

It is not that politicians do not recognize the need to make difficult policy choices; it is that they believe they won't be reelected if they do.

Both sides' economic arguments have some validity, and the likely solution will involve a compromise between the two as well as honesty about the implications of the resulting policies. Any actual government jobs policy requires costs to society—in either increased taxes or suffering in terms of lost jobs and income. These costs need to be a central part of the debate and resulting solutions, and that discussion can come about only if both sides directly address normative differences in their views.

The United States isn't the only country facing tough political decisions related to unemployment. For example, Europe developed a tradition of government taking responsibility for providing people with jobs. But the policy had costs. It discouraged job market mobility and discouraged individuals from taking low-paying jobs. While many felt the system was fair, the unemployment rate in European countries remained high until they changed their labor laws. In southern European countries such as Greece and Spain, unemployment remained at close to 20 percent. In addition, the programs were expensive and because people are not willing to pay the taxes necessary to maintain them, many European countries have been trying to reduce or eliminate them and transfer more responsibility to the individual.

Summary of the Debate

Whether an economy has an unemployment problem depends on how you look at it. Within the individual responsibility framework, the United States doesn't really have a problem. Within the government responsibility framework, the problem is much more serious than statistics suggest. Unemployment can be understood only in relation to the pay and nature of the job. Talking about unemployment without reference to those two elements is like talking about language without words. Since people have very different views about the standard against which to judge pay and the nature of unemployment, they have different views about the jobs problem. These differences are not differences in economic theory or in how the economy works; they are differences in moral judgments. Economic theory is not directly tied to any particular moral judgments.

What positive economics does have to say about the jobs policies is that any solution must come to grips with unpleasant choices. That means that those who want to frame the unemployment problem as a government responsibility must take into account that government intervention in the market will slow the structural change and increase the number of unemployed, and therefore will be enormously expensive. They must answer how the program is to be funded. Those who favor framing unemployment as an individual responsibility must be able to explain how to make society willing to accept the suffering that goes along with that approach.

Any jobs policy must come to grips with unpleasant choices.

A Guaranteed-Job Proposal: Government as Employer of Last Resort

Oftentimes the best way to understand a problem is to consider a policy proposal that attempts to deal with that problem. So let us now turn to a proposal that "solves" the U.S. unemployment problem. The proposal is the following:

Web Note 33.4

Job-Guarantee Programs

> The government will provide a minimum job at a wage of $10 per hour for every eligible citizen.

The goal of the program is to provide a safety net for people who truly want to work and cannot find a job. If this proposal were implemented, the government could argue that the jobs problem had been solved because anyone who wanted a job could get one. No longer would there be more unemployed than vacancies. There would be at least one vacancy for every person unsuccessfully looking for work. This program also weeds out those people who really aren't looking for work.

Implementing such a proposal involves specifying who would be eligible for the program and the nature of the job—what the person would do, how the jobs would be monitored, where the jobs would be located, and many more similar aspects. The costs of the program would vary with each of these decisions; the more inclusive and expansive these decisions are, the greater the cost.

The program I will outline is a bare-bones proposal. It is designed that way to keep the costs as low as possible and still claim to provide a job to everyone who wants one. Although the proposal may not be politically acceptable, it highlights the many dimensions of the unemployment and jobs problem. It attempts to find a middle way between those who believe that government should have a responsibility to the unemployed and those who believe in letting the market work, not relying on government to provide jobs.

The Design and Characteristics of the Program

The guaranteed job in this program will consist of a variety of mental and physical tasks that can be easily monitored. They might consist of mental tasks such as copying a dictionary, keyboarding practice, doing arithmetic exercises, doing exercises in word processing and spreadsheets, or reading and summarizing reports. The physical tasks might include exercising such as doing jumping jacks, digging holes and filling them back up, moving weights, and other similar types of activities. The job will require the worker to work the standard number of hours per week—variations of an eight-hour day—and meet the normal job requirements that private and government firms impose on their employees—dress code and behavior codes such as showing up on time, demonstrating the appropriate attitude, and being responsible.

Whenever possible, the job would help a person learn new skills to increase productivity, and the program would provide a certificate for mastering the skills— credentials that would help their holders find better-paying jobs in the private market. For example, for those who have not graduated from high school, the activities might prepare them to get their GED.

The government will contract with firms and organizations to monitor and mentor the workers in a set of specified activities. These firms would be paid a small stipend and be allowed to have the person work for them at no cost for up to two hours a day. Organizations that might do this include small retail firms, nongovernmental organizations, or governmental organizations such as schools that have space and the ability to undertake this monitoring.

The guaranteed-jobs program guarantees the same minimum job to everyone regardless of previous job or training. It does not attempt to provide people with a job commensurate with their training or previous job. It's meant for people who *really* want a job. The program doesn't help those who aren't willing to accept a minimum job. For example, the government doesn't guarantee someone with an English PhD a job as an English professor. Just like everyone else, it guarantees him or her a minimal job like digging holes. This is the personal-responsibility aspect—it incorporates the view that people unwilling to participate in this jobs program don't really want to work.

Both this program and current government programs dealing with unemployment are designed to provide a social safety net, but they differ in important respects. This program concentrates the safety net for the least well off—those most in need of income. Existing programs are meant for those who are recently unemployed (in 2018 up to about 26 weeks after becoming unemployed) and who have earned a minimum amount of wages over a specified period. The current program covers people both who truly cannot find a job and who can't find a job with their minimum job requirements. This alternative guaranteed-minimum-job program would not help this second group. It would cover those who are ineligible for insurance because their employment history was not long enough or their unemployment insurance had expired. Whether the program could substitute for unemployment insurance, or supplement it, depends on what one believes is the role for government's safety net. The broader the safety net, the less is available for those who need it most.

Ideally all people would be eligible for the guaranteed program, but practically, eligibility will likely have to be limited. For example, it might make sense to restrict eligibility to nonstudents; otherwise the program would likely be overwhelmed by students wanting summer work. To be feasible, the program will also likely have to be limited to citizens; if open to immigrants, it would also likely be far too costly. The general principle: The looser the eligibility requirement, the more costly the program.

Q-8 Why doesn't the guaranteed-jobs program provide jobs commensurate with a person's training?

Why Don't the Guaranteed Jobs Do Something Useful?

Q-9 Why don't the guaranteed jobs provide activities directly useful to society?

The jobs that this program provides would involve activities useful for the individual but not directly productive to society. The only output would be self-improvement. The reason for choosing jobs that are primarily productive to individuals, not society, is so that the guaranteed jobs do not compete with jobs of existing institutions whose role *is* to provide useful output to society, as opposed to just the individual. Any attempt to make the guaranteed jobs have an output useful for society would mean that they would compete with existing institutions, creating opposition to the program. The goal of this proposal is not to replace the market or existing governmental and nongovernmental organizations. The goal is simply to supplement them—to make sure that there are sufficient low-wage jobs for anyone who wants to work in such a job.

These guaranteed jobs may be more desirable than some existing minimum wage jobs and less desirable than other existing minimum wage jobs. To the degree that jobs in the marketplace are less desirable than guaranteed jobs, people will quit their minimum wage private jobs to take these guaranteed jobs. This effectively puts a floor on both the wage and desirability of the jobs that institutions will have to provide to keep their workers. It has the same effect as having a legal minimum wage because workers will demand this wage from private employers or quit, and work in the minimum jobs program. Some regular jobs could pay less than minimum wage if the regular job has attractive aspects, such as providing more relevant training or the promise of advancement. Truly undesirable jobs will have to pay significantly more than the minimum job wage to lure workers away from the minimum program jobs.

The introduction of this minimum jobs program will make it possible to eliminate the federal minimum wage for workers eligible for the minimum job. In fact, it's better than a minimum wage law because the minimum jobs program would affect both wages and the nature of jobs available. Thus, if a private sector job offers training benefits (as many internships do, where, often, students work for free), someone may choose to take that job rather than a guaranteed minimum job because the overall package is preferable, even if the wage is lower.

Conservative economists argue that the minimum wage law creates unemployment because it reduces the quantity of workers firms are willing to hire and increases the quantity of people looking for work. Further, it prevents some firms from offering jobs that provide training, and therefore are attractive to workers and would benefit the firm. The minimum job does not have these problems. It would not keep private firms from offering a below–minimum wage job that has significant learning and advancement benefits. Firms not offering jobs that were sufficiently desirable in terms of both wages and type of job would not get workers. They would either have to raise the wage above the minimum or make the job more desirable in other ways. The jobs program would set a minimum job, not a minimum wage. Because of this, the minimum job program is preferable in many ways to a minimum wage program.

Q-10 How is the minimum jobs proposal better than a minimum wage law?

In fact, at a pay of $10 an hour, it is highly unlikely that these guaranteed jobs will attract significant numbers of workers from other low-wage jobs if the jobs are full-time and if full-time students are not eligible for the program. The reason is that many minimum wage jobs have other attributes that make them more desirable than the guaranteed job. For example, about one-half of workers in minimum wage (or less) jobs are food service workers who often receive additional income in the form of tips and other payments. People in these jobs would be unlikely to switch because they would lose those tips. While the number of full-time eligible workers who would find this program desirable would likely be small, it would provide for those most in need of a job.

Previous Government Jobs Programs

The minimum jobs proposal is both similar to and different from earlier government jobs programs. In the United States the most important of these was the Works Progress Administration (WPA), established during the 1930s to hire people directly to build public buildings, roads, highways, parks, and bridges. (It built a total of 78,000 bridges and 651,000 miles of roads!) Workers were paid $15 to $90 a month. (In today's dollars that's about $250 to $1,500 a month.) The WPA also funded tap-dancing lessons and the painting of murals in public spaces. The WPA was a product of the Depression, when the private sector failed to provide anywhere near enough jobs. It ended with the advent of World War II as unemployment fell and jobs were available for everyone in the war effort.

Source: Library of Congress Prints and Photographs Division [LC-USZC2-837]

An affordable modern-day WPA for the United States is unlikely. Much of the construction done at that time has been mechanized. To build today you need a few people who know how to operate the machines, not a lot of people with strong backs willing to work hard. Most modern construction jobs pay well beyond $10 an hour. For example, government now mandates that all construction companies that work on government construction projects pay union wages. The $15 to $90 a month paid to workers in the 1930s, even adjusted for inflation, wouldn't come close to union wages. Were the minimum job program to pay union wages, it would be inundated with people quitting their existing jobs to come to work at the government minimum job. The program would be unaffordable.

Variations of guaranteed-job proposals have been implemented throughout the world. Argentina developed a program for heads of households that offered part-time work. India instituted a National Rural Employment Guarantee Act that promised government public works employment for workers. However, all recent programs have run into problems because the jobs they provided competed with existing jobs, the pay was beyond what government was willing to pay, or the "jobs" were more desirable than alternative low-paying private sector jobs, leading to corruption and nonmarket rationing of the government jobs. None provided a guaranteed job for everyone.

Paying for the Program

Even this limited program will not be cheap. To get a rough estimate of how much it might cost, let's first consider the cost of one job. A job paying $10 an hour for 40 hours a week costs a bit over $20,000 per person per year. Add to that $5,000 for administration and monitoring, and it comes to $25,000 per job. Let's next consider how many people would be taking these jobs.

In mid-2018, some 6.2 million people were unemployed. Of these probably only a small number of those currently eligible for unemployment insurance would choose to participate in the government jobs program. Even many of the long-term unemployed would choose not to participate, preferring instead to be supported by their family, friends, or savings. So it is reasonable to assume that about 30 percent of the measured unemployed, or 2 million, would choose to participate. Assuming no students, Social Security recipients, or noncitizens are eligible, probably another 1.5 million workers who are currently not counted as unemployed or who are in less desirable jobs would find this guaranteed job attractive and would choose to participate. Adding the two makes a total of 3.5 million people, which means that were the program in place in 2018, the program would cost about $88 billion a year.

Eighty-eight billion dollars is not cheap, and this is for a bare-bones program; a more inclusive program would be more costly. But $88 billion is doable, considering that the government currently spends hundreds of billions of dollars to create jobs. To the degree that the program enhances workers' skills, the plan should slowly decrease the number of people who rely on the program. As the economy expands, the private sector will increase its hiring, and people will move from these minimum guaranteed jobs into better-paying jobs. To the degree that this happens, over time, the program costs will decline. Should the economy fall into a recession, the program will expand.

Would Such a Plan Ever Be Implemented?

There is a reason most existing government programs are designed as they are—to help both the middle class and the least well off.

To say that the program is doable is not to say that it is a program the government will implement. There is a reason most existing government programs are designed as they are—to help both the middle class and the least well off. The least well off are not a well-organized voting bloc, and thus programs specifically tailored to help them have only a small political constituency.

Much of the current debate about unemployment is not about providing a minimum job; rather it is about providing people with a level of job that they expect.

While the plan may not be politically possible, it provides an excellent teaching tool to highlight the policy issues about jobs. It focuses on the current debate about jobs, much of which is not just about providing a minimum job, but about keeping people at the level of job they expect. This is why structural stagnation is such a problem and is associated with high unemployment rates. Dealing with globalization requires major structural changes. People who had done well before suddenly do not anymore. There are major differences in normative views about how government should handle such structural changes—differences that economic theory cannot resolve.

The differences between normative views are revealed by asking whether this program, if implemented, solves the unemployment problem. If you believe it does, and you define employment as having a minimally acceptable job (and what is considered a minimum acceptable job does not depend on one's education), then you are following an individualist normative view. If you believe that it will not, and it is government's responsibility to provide a job commensurate with people's training and past jobs, the program does not solve the unemployment problem; you are following a more social responsibility normative frame. But such a social responsibility viewpoint is logical only if society is willing to pay for such a program. It would require much higher taxes on everyone than we have currently. To date our society has not been willing to pay the higher taxes. Even so, it has attempted to follow a social responsibility frame. Wanting something and not wanting to pay for it are inconsistent, and in the coming decade one, the other, or both will be forced to give way.

Conclusion

I began this chapter with a story about my son finding a job. He has advanced in that job, and is now hiring people, and seeing how hard it is to find the right person for a job. Modern jobs involve multiple dimensions and interaction with fellow workers and managers. The skills needed are often not measurable skills; they do not relate closely to what one learns in the educational system. Many of the needed skills are learned on the job, at home, and in life.

The problem that people often call "an unemployment problem" generally goes beyond providing a minimum job and raises issues that go far beyond economics.

The problems that people call "unemployment" involve broader issues of social justice, fairness of the system, and the degree to which what one gets should be associated with the job one has. These issues go far beyond economics alone; they involve social philosophy, psychology, and cultural issues. Thus, in many ways the question of unemployment is not a question that economists can answer. It is a question society must answer through its political system. Unfortunately, our political system does not seem to be doing an especially good job dealing with these hard issues that must be answered before any serious attempt to deal with the unemployment problem can work.

Expanding aggregate demand can decrease unemployment, but little of that aggregate demand actually flows down to those most in need. Thus, if one's concern about social justice is a concern about the least well off, alternative approaches, such as a direct method to guarantee a job to anyone who wants one, may have to be considered.

Summary

- The microeconomic approach to unemployment divides unemployment into categories and looks at those individual components. (*LO33-1*)

- Okun's rule of thumb states that a 1 percentage point change in the unemployment rate will tend to be associated with a 2 percent deviation in output from its trend in the opposite direction. (*LO33-2*)

- Cyclical unemployment is the result of temporary declines in economic output and can be addressed with expansionary policy, whereas structural unemployment requires structural changes in an economy. (*LO33-2*)

- The target rate of unemployment has changed because the workforce is younger, more women have entered the workforce, government has expanded income-support programs, and globalization has affected certain job sectors. (*LO33-2*)

- At the extremes, those who believe that employment is a responsibility of the individual believe there is virtually no unemployment. Those who believe it is a social responsibility believe that government ought to provide everyone a job commensurate with his or her skills. A solution to the unemployment problem requires a compromise between the two. (*LO33-3*)

- One proposal that "solves" the unemployment problem is for government to provide a minimum job for every eligible citizen. This program doesn't provide a job for everyone, such as those looking for a job like the one they lost. It provides "jobs" only for those who really need one. (*LO33-4*)

- The benefit of a government guaranteed-jobs program is that everyone who wants to work is employed. The problem is that such a program costs money. (*LO33-4*)

Key Terms

cyclical unemployment   Okun's rule of thumb   reservation wage   structural unemployment

Questions and Exercises   ̶ connect

1. What happened to the duration of unemployment during the 2008–2009 recession and what is the likely reason? (*LO33-1*)

2. During the past few recessions, government ran expansionary policies, but the duration of unemployment has risen. What does this suggest about the change in structural unemployment over this time period? (*LO33-2*)

3. If unemployment rises by 2 percentage points, what will likely happen to output in the United States relative to its growth trend? (Use Okun's rule of thumb.) (*LO33-2*)

4. Categorize each of the following as cyclical or structural unemployment: (*LO33-2*)
   a. An autoworker is laid off during a recession until car sales pick up.
   b. A steelworker loses his job because steel is now produced in foreign countries with lower wages.
   c. A compositor loses her job because the work is now outsourced to India.
   d. An unemployed person turns down job offers that do not pay the wages of his previous job.

5. What is a reservation wage and how is it related to structural unemployment? (*LO33-2*)

6. Name five reasons why the target rate of unemployment has fluctuated over the past 40 years. *(LO33-2)*

7. Why does the concept of unemployment involve normative judgments? *(LO33-3)*

8. Will someone who believes that unemployment is an individual's responsibility believe that the current measure of unemployment over- or underestimates the level of unemployment? Explain. *(LO33-3)*

9. College degrees are usually associated with higher wages. Does that association mean that what one learns in college increases college students' productivity? *(LO33-3)*

10. Since a jobs program puts people to work, would it impose costs on society? *(LO33-4)*

11. How does the safety net in the proposed guaranteed-jobs program differ from the current safety net? *(LO33-4)*

12. In what ways would the guaranteed-jobs program outlined in the text be more expensive if it provided useful jobs for society? *(LO33-4)*

13. Why does the author suggest that students be ineligible for the guaranteed-jobs program even though many students are in need? *(LO33-4)*

Questions from Alternative Perspectives

1. Some economists believe the target rate of unemployment is about 6 to 7 percent. William Vickrey, a Nobel Prize–winning economist, argued that the target unemployment rate should be seen as being between 1 percent and 2 percent. Only an unemployment rate that low, he argued, would produce genuine full employment that guaranteed job openings for all those looking for work. Achieving a low unemployment rate would, according to Vickrey, bring about "a major reduction in the illness of poverty, homelessness, sickness, and crime."
   a. What is the appropriate target unemployment rate?
   b. Explain your position.
   c. What policies would you recommend to counteract the human tragedy of unemployment? *(Radical)*

2. The text treats the unemployed as if both sexes are equally considered full persons within a capitalist market economy. The historic public/private split of employment for women, however, denies women full rights in the marketplace. Evidence of this is that women earn about 85 percent of what men earn. This reality needs to be taken into account with any guaranteed-jobs program.

How might the jobs program suggested in the text be modified to take into account these differences? *(Feminist)*

3. The type of employment available to different workers is inherently tied to income distribution. With globalization, the market favors those with access to higher education, which tends to be those people with accumulated family assets as well as inherent ability.
   a. Is the income distribution within the United States that results from globalization fair?
   b. Is the global income distribution that results from globalization fair? *(Post-Keynesian)*

4. Economists such as Frédéric Bastiat believed in natural liberty, which is based on a belief that a God has naturally ordered the world for the benefit of all. According to these economists, saving was a virtue because it potentially led to increased consumption in the future, a belief that Keynes asserted is based on a belief in one's immortality. Does this mean that Bastiat and Keynes would differ in their views about how to address the unemployment problem? How? *(Religious)*

Issues to Ponder

1. If you had no income and no one to help you, could you create a job for yourself? How would you go about doing it?

2. Does government owe everyone a job who wants one?

3. What could government do to reduce structural unemployment?

4. What changes in the guaranteed-jobs program might be made to fit your moral sensibilities about governmental responsibilities?

5. What changes in the guaranteed-jobs program might be made to make it more politically acceptable?

Answers to Margin Questions

1. Entrepreneurship creates jobs; if someone is entrepreneurial he or she can never be unemployed. (*LO33-1*)

2. After the downturn of 2008, the duration of unemployment increased significantly, creating a larger pool of people experiencing long-term unemployment. (*LO33-1*)

3. It predicts the unemployment rate will rise by 1 percentage point. (*LO33-2*)

4. A high reservation wage keeps people from accepting low-wage jobs and therefore increases the unemployment rate until people's reservation wages decline. (*LO33-2*)

5. The target rate of unemployment has risen because the workforce is younger, more women have entered the workforce, government has expanded income-support programs, technology is continually changing the nature of jobs, and globalization has affected certain job sectors. (*LO33-2*)

6. The tradable sector is more affected by globalization. It lowers wages in this sector and raises unemployment. (*LO33-3*)

7. The individual responsibility view is that anyone who wants a job can either find one or create one. Employment is the responsibility of the individual. The social responsibility view is that government should provide everyone who wants a job with a job at a respectable wage that is commensurate with his or her skills. Employment is the responsibility of society. (*LO33-3*)

8. Providing a guaranteed job commensurate with a person's training would cost too much. The program is for people who really want a job regardless of their training. (*LO33-4*)

9. If a job is useful to society, the program would be replacing a job that would be created in the market. The purpose of the program is to supplement the market. (*LO33-4*)

10. The proposal puts a floor on the wage as well as on the nature of the job. People would be willing to accept a better job, such as those providing job training, even if it pays lower wages. (*LO33-4*)

CHAPTER 34

Inflation, Deflation, and Macro Policy

> The first few months or years of inflation, like the first few drinks, seem just fine. Everyone has more money to spend and prices aren't rising quite as fast as the money that's available. The hangover comes when prices start to catch up.
>
> —Milton Friedman

After reading this chapter, you should be able to:

LO34-1 Know the difference between goods inflation and asset inflation.

LO34-2 List and discuss the costs and benefits of inflation.

LO34-3 Summarize the inflation process and the quantity theory of money.

LO34-4 Define the Phillips curve relationship between inflation and unemployment.

Politicians tend to get reelected when the economy is doing well. Thus, it should not surprise you that political pressures exert a strong bias toward lowering taxes, increasing spending, and expanding the money supply, all of which tend to expand the economy in the short run. In the past what has prevented politicians and the Fed from implementing expansionary policies is inflation, or at least the fear of generating an accelerating inflation. Recently, however, for the United States that relationship between expansionary policy and inflation has been much weaker than in the past, at least for goods price inflation. Because expansionary monetary and fiscal policy have not led to inflation, policy makers have felt able to increase spending, cut taxes, and increase the money supply enormously.

©Bettmann/Getty Images

The disconnect between inflation and expansionary monetary and fiscal policy removes a constraint on expansionary policy, and some economists argue that the fear of inflation no longer limits policy. Other economists are less optimistic. They point out that goods price inflation is not the only type of inflation. There can also be asset price inflation. **Asset price inflation** occurs when *the prices of assets rise more than their "real" value*. Assets include gold, houses, artwork, collectibles, land, stocks, bonds, and many other items that people hold as a store of wealth. The prices of these assets are not included in standard measures of inflation because standard measures focus on goods and services, not assets. Asset inflation is important because it is an asset price bubble that encourages society to believe the illusion that it is wealthier than it actually is—and a bursting asset price bubble can wreak havoc on an economy, as the U.S. economy experienced in 2008.

If expansionary monetary and fiscal policies are causing an asset price bubble, the expansionary macro policy could be causing problems even though the standard measures of inflation are not increasing significantly. So how inflation is measured goes to the heart of the current policy debate. Some economists argue that the expansionary monetary policy in the 2000s contributed to the financial bubble that burst in 2008. Further, they see the continued increases in the money supply as preventing, or at least slowing, the structural changes that the economy needs to undergo. They argue that even if the expansionary monetary policy doesn't lead to goods price inflation, it leads to higher asset prices than are consistent with a sustainable level of growth. It creates an illusion of wealth. The continued expansionary monetary policy is just delaying the full extent of the asset price adjustment that must occur for the economy to get back on track. Other economists argue that the only significant problem that expansionary monetary policy can cause is inflation, so we don't have to worry about monetary policy being too expansionary until we start to see signs of inflation.

To understand these debates, you need to understand inflation, so in this chapter I explore inflation in more detail. I first consider the definition of inflation and how it is measured, expanding on the discussion of inflation in Chapter 25. Then I discuss the costs of inflation both in terms of the current standard definition—a rise in the price level for goods and services—and in terms of an older definition—a rise in the money supply that includes the effect of increases in the money supply on asset price inflation. After that I turn to two relationships used to discuss inflation—the quantity theory of money and the Phillips curve relationship.

Q-1 What is the difference between an asset price inflation and a goods price inflation?

Defining Inflation

Let's start with the definition of inflation. In earlier chapters we defined inflation as a continual rise in the price level, and we focused on measuring inflation with the GDP deflator, which is the most inclusive measure of goods and services that we have. We mentioned that there are a number of other measures of goods and services inflation that focus on personal consumption goods, consumer goods, and producer goods. But generally, these alternative goods inflation measures move in tandem, so distinguishing among them is not especially important for the recent debates about monetary policy.

Asset Price Inflation and Deflation

The distinction between goods inflation and asset inflation, however, is important. The reason is that asset prices and goods prices don't always move in tandem and can diverge significantly for long periods of time. These are periods of asset price bubbles. For example, goods prices could remain essentially constant, but asset prices could rise by 30 percent. Such different movements can continue for a number of years, as was the case in the housing market and other asset markets in the United States during the early 2000s. Using the goods market measure of inflation, such an asset price rise is not seen as an inflation (except to the extent that the rental value of housing changes with the price of housing, which it often doesn't).

Economists before the 1940s would have been much more likely to call such a rise in asset prices an inflation as long as it is accompanied by an increase in the money supply or credit. That's because they defined inflation as an increase in the money supply, not as an increase in any particular price index. They noted that increases in prices

Asset prices and goods prices don't always move in tandem and can diverge significantly for long periods of time.

generally follow an increase in the money supply, but instead of focusing on what was happening to any particular set of prices, they focused on the money supply and the amount of credit in the economy. By inflation, they meant easy credit—credit that is readily available to people to spend and invest. While, as we will see, economists' measure of goods inflation has significantly improved since the 1940s, they have not yet developed an index of asset prices or of asset inflation.

ESTIMATING ASSET PRICE INFLATION AND DEFLATION   One reason economists have not developed a measure of asset price inflation is that it's difficult to know when increases in asset prices reflect an increase in their real value and when they are just increases in prices without an increase in real value. In individual cases estimating an asset's real value is essentially impossible, but for the aggregate of assets it is easier since, based on accounting rates over the long run, real wealth should increase at a similar rate as real output. So by looking at the ratio of asset values (as captured by net worth) to nominal GDP (which includes both increases in output and increases in prices of goods) we can estimate whether asset price inflation is occurring beyond the level of goods price inflation. For example, if nominal output is increasing 6 percent a year, nominal wealth should be increasing at about the same rate in what economists call the steady-state equilibrium. This means that the ratio of nominal wealth to nominal GDP can serve as a rough estimate of whether there is asset price inflation in excess of goods price inflation. When that ratio is increasing, asset inflation is likely occurring.

Figure 34-1 shows nominal total net worth relative to nominal GDP compared to its postwar (1945–1955) average, with that average normalized to 1. If the increases in asset prices reflect real increases in the value of assets associated with real growth and goods price inflation, this ratio should be relatively constant as it was up until 1995. If the measure rises, then the increases in the price of assets likely represent asset inflation above and beyond inflation measured by goods prices. If it falls, then there is likely asset deflation.

> One reason economists have not developed a measure of asset price inflation is that it's difficult to know when increases in asset prices reflect an increase in their real value.

FIGURE 34-1   **Ratio of Household Net Worth to GDP**

Starting in the 1990s asset prices rose significantly above their historic norms, increasing the ratio of net worth to GDP far above its historic norm.

Source: Bureau of Economic Analysis and Federal Reserve Bank.

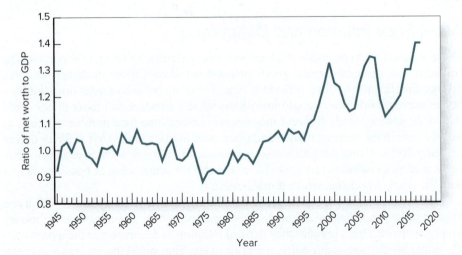

Notice that the ratio was relatively stable from 1945 to 1995. Then, in the late 1990s, that ratio started rising precipitously, suggesting that starting in the late 1990s assets were overvalued by 20 percent compared to the historic norm. This was precisely the time that globalization and the U.S. trade deficit started rising precipitously.

During the 2001 recession, as we experienced asset price deflation, asset prices fell back closer to their historic norm. In 2001 government responded to this fall in asset prices by implementing expansionary monetary and fiscal policy, which changed the asset deflation to an asset inflation once again. By 2007 the valuation of assets was over 30 percent above its historic norms. Then with the financial crisis asset prices dropped significantly, and the economy fell into a serious recession. The government responded by running expansionary monetary policy, pushing asset prices up. In 2018 the asset-price-to-GDP ratio significantly exceeded the level it had been before the financial crisis of 2008. This led some economists to predict that another financial crisis is likely to occur in the future.

> The net worth to GDP ratio increased substantially in the late 1990s, suggesting that the economy was experiencing asset inflation.

DOES ASSET INFLATION MATTER?

Let's now consider whether asset inflation matters to an economy by considering the problems it might create.

One of the problems of asset inflation for an economy is that it (and the low interest rates that accompany it) can lead to serious misallocation of resources from conservative to risky investments, since risk-preferring borrowers will want to take advantage of rising asset prices and cautious borrowers, who fear that asset prices are too high, will not want to borrow. So asset price inflation strongly encourages and rewards risk taking. An example in the early 2000s is that people built and bought houses not to live in but to hold and sell, hoping to make a quick profit.

Another problem is that asset price inflation gives people the illusion that their real wealth has increased much more than it really has, causing them to spend more than they would have, and take on more debt than they would have otherwise. On the upside this increased spending increases aggregate demand, which increases the economic growth rate, which brings government more tax revenue, which means that government is able to increase its spending without increasing its deficit. These are all seen as highly positive results; asset inflation makes the society feel wonderful. The problem isn't the upside stimulant; the problem is the downside—what happens once asset inflation turns into asset deflation.

> On the upside, asset inflation makes the society feel wonderful; the problem is the downside.

ASSET PRICE DEFLATION

The problem with asset inflation is that it cannot last; it is based on the illusion that the real value of assets has risen when, in fact, their real value has not. Asset price inflation is an alternative name for a financial bubble, and bubbles are, at some point, followed by an asset price deflation. This deflation reverses many of the positive effects of the asset price inflation and creates additional problems as well. When asset deflation hits, it hits suddenly and hard, as the United States saw in 2008.

While discussions of inflations are usually conducted in reference to goods prices, discussions of deflation usually are conducted in reference to asset prices. The reason is twofold. First, we haven't seen significant amounts of goods price deflation, and even as asset prices are falling precipitously, there is generally some small amount of goods price inflation. So historically what we see are asset price deflations, not goods price deflations.

The second reason is that an asset price deflation can create serious problems for the economy. If asset price inflation leads to pleasure and asset price deflation leads to pain, then maybe, on average, the two even out. This is generally not thought to be the case; most economists see the pain caused by the asset price deflation as exceeding the pleasure caused by the asset price inflation. The reason has to do with the costs connected to reversing decisions people make when experiencing an asset inflation.

> **Q-2** Why are discussions of deflations usually conducted in reference to asset prices?

For example, in the 2000s because the prices of houses were rising, millions of people bought them with the expectation that prices would rise even further. When housing prices fell, those people faced foreclosure and the prospect of living out of their cars. Millions of other people took out second and third mortgages to use some of the presumed equity in their house to take a trip or buy a boat. So the illusion that they were wealthier than they were led them to spend more than they would have otherwise. With asset deflation, they had already spent the borrowed money and now had to pay it back, which might mean they didn't have enough to buy food or medical care; thus asset deflation might drive them into bankruptcy. Without the asset inflation providing people with the illusion of wealth, they never would have taken the trip or bought the house in the first place. But they can't reverse past purchases. For people whose actions are affected by an asset inflation, the consequences of an asset deflation that simply reverses the effect of an asset inflation can be very serious.

The same illusion can lead firms to make poor decisions when faced with asset inflation. Perhaps they bought an office building they didn't really need, or paid workers more than they could have afforded. When deflation hits, they find that they cannot remain in business. In that case not only does the firm suffer; employees suffer too. Once an asset deflation occurs, firms will find that they can no longer borrow, and that they have to pay off past debts. Some firms are likely to go bankrupt since they don't have the assets to cover their liabilities. If they are forced to close, their employees will lose their jobs. Because deflation undermines the financial health of firms, it can quickly turn into a financial crisis that brings the economy to a standstill. At that point, the government finds it necessary to step in and prop up asset prices, as it did in 2008, to prevent a collapse of the entire economy. So most economists see asset deflations as something to be carefully avoided.

The Costs and Benefits of Inflation

Inflation has costs, but not the costs that most people associate with it.

Inflation has costs and benefits, but not the costs and benefits that most laypeople associate with it. So a careful discussion of inflation's costs and benefits is warranted. The "cost" that most laypeople associate with inflation is not a cost at all. Specifically, most people believe inflation makes society poor, but this isn't the case. True, whenever prices go up the people who buy the goods whose price has risen cannot buy as much as before. They are poorer. But the economy is made up of both consumers and sellers. For every consumer hurt by a price rise there is a seller who is made better off by an offsetting amount. The change in prices hasn't made society richer or poorer; it has redistributed wealth from buyers to sellers.

The Costs of Inflation

The costs of inflation that economists focus on are more subtle. They include what are called informational, institutional, and distributional costs. Let us briefly consider each.

INFORMATIONAL COSTS OF INFLATION   As we discussed in Chapter 28, one of the important functions of money is that it serves as a unit of account, just as a pound serves as a unit of account for measuring weight in the United States. Ideally, units of account don't change over time, allowing us to compare quantities over time. With an unchanging measure, if you weighed 118 pounds last year and this year you weigh 130 pounds, you know you gained weight. So you can use your conception of what a pound is to make comparisons over time. That's what a unit of account does.

The same is true of the unit of account function for money. An unchanging unit of account (zero inflation) makes it possible to convey the information with a price much more easily if there is no inflation than when there is. Inflation and deflation undermine the information provided by prices. Consider a person who wants to buy a house who laments the high cost of housing, pointing out that it has doubled in 10 years. But if goods inflation averaged 7 percent a year over the past 10 years, a doubling of housing prices should be expected. In fact, with 7 percent inflation, on average all prices double every 10 years. That means the individual's wages have probably also doubled, so he or she is no better off and no worse off than 10 years ago. The price of housing relative to other goods, which is the relevant price for making decisions, hasn't changed. With millions of goods in an economy, when there's inflation, it's hard for people to know what is and what isn't a relative price change. People's minds aren't computers, so inflation reduces the amount of information that prices can convey and causes people to make choices that do not reflect relative prices.

INSTITUTIONAL COSTS OF INFLATION   A second cost of inflation is often called the *institutional cost of inflation*. People rely on government to provide a stable infrastructure within which to make decisions and enter into contracts. Part of that infrastructure is the unit of account. People and businesses rely on government to provide a relatively stable unit of account. A constant unit of account, which exists when there is no inflation, serves as the basis for long-term contracts. Inflation, especially unexpected inflation, can undermine that contractual infrastructure and thereby cause people to lose faith in government and possibly undermine long-term growth. The existence of inflation means government is not fulfilling its institutional role.

People rely on government to provide a stable infrastructure within which to make decisions and enter into contracts.

DISTRIBUTIONAL COSTS OF INFLATION   A third cost of inflation can be its distributional effects. As we stated above, on average, inflation's distributional costs largely offset each other; winners are offset by losers. If you are rooting for one group, and they are largely losers, then you might say that there are distributional costs of inflation because you care more about the losers than the winners. (As I discuss below, it could also go the other way; the inflation could redistribute income to people you are rooting for. In that case you might say that there are distributional benefits of inflation.) To make such decisions one must look more carefully at the distributional effects of inflation.

Distributional Effects of Goods Inflation   Who wins and who loses in an inflation? The answer is simple: The winners are people who can raise their wages or prices and still keep their jobs or sell their goods. The losers are people who can't raise their wages or prices or who lose their jobs because their wage is too high. Consider a worker who has entered a contract to receive 4 percent annual wage increases for three years. If the worker expected inflation to be 2 percent at the time of the agreement, she was expecting her real wage to rise 2 percent each year. If instead inflation is 6 percent, her real wage will *fall* 2 percent. The worker loses, but the firm gains because it can charge 4 percent more for its products than it anticipated. The worker's wage was fixed by contract, but the firm could raise its prices. On average, winners and losers balance out; inflation does not make the population richer or poorer. Most people, however, worry about their own situation, not what happens to the average person.

Q-3   True or false? Inflation makes an economy poorer. Explain your answer.

Lenders and borrowers, because they often enter into fixed nominal contracts, are also affected by inflation. If lenders make loans at 5 percent interest and expect inflation to be 2 percent, they plan to earn a 3 percent real rate of return on their loan. If, however, inflation turns out to be 4 percent, lenders will only earn a 1 percent real rate of return, and borrowers, who were expecting to pay a real interest rate of 3 percent, end up paying only 1 percent. Lenders will lose; borrowers will gain. In other words, unexpected inflation redistributes income from lenders to borrowers.

The composition of the group winning or losing from inflation changes over time. For example, before 1975, people on Social Security and pensions lost out during inflation since Social Security and pensions were, on the whole, fixed in nominal terms. Inflation lowered recipients' real income. Starting in 1975 Social Security payments and many pensions were changed to adjust automatically for changes in the cost of living, so Social Security recipients are no longer losers. Their real income is independent of inflation. (Actually, because of the adjustment method, some say that Social Security recipients now gain from inflation since the adjustment more than compensates them for the rise in the price level.)

Distributional Effects of Asset Price Inflation   Let's now consider what happens when the money supply doesn't lead to goods price inflation, but does lead to asset price inflation. People who bet on rising asset prices are helped and those who did not are hurt. Specifically, those who might be called cautious savers are hurt and risky savers are helped. Asset price inflation redistributes wealth from cautious individuals to less cautious individuals.

On the borrowing side, the same effects occur. Cautious borrowers are hurt since they likely see the asset prices as being too high, and choose not to borrow even though the interest rates are low. Less cautious borrowers are helped because they borrow at low interest rates, and receive high returns when the asset they bought with the borrowed money increases in value.

In summary, the increase in the money supply that affects asset prices can have significant distributional effects on wealth even when it does not result in higher goods prices.

The Benefits of (Low) Inflation

If inflation only had costs, we would expect that the goal of societies would be to prevent inflation. But if you listen to the news, and look at the past, zero inflation is not always a policy goal. So there must be some benefits of inflation. These benefits can explain the fact that societies have continually experienced inflation.

Until recently, the benefits of inflation were seldom discussed. The implicit goal of society was to have zero inflation. Generally, the costs of achieving zero inflation were seen as too high, so societies were willing to accept a small amount of inflation. It wasn't something that they wanted, but they would put up with it. The United States, for example, accepted goods inflation as long as it stayed under about 2.5 percent. This goal was built into discussions of conventional monetary policy. So in conventional monetary policy, governments tried to keep inflation as low as they could below 2.5 percent. This 2.5 percent target was an upper bound for inflation. It was the highest rate of inflation policy makers would accept. If inflation was lower than 2.5 percent, policy makers would congratulate themselves as having done better than they expected.

Since the financial crisis of 2008, and the introduction of unconventional monetary policy, that view about an inflation target as being an upper bound for inflation has changed. Inflation targets are no longer seen as an upper bound, but as a rate of inflation to aim for, not a target to stay under. So if the inflation target is 2 percent, and inflation is 1 percent, policy makers don't congratulate themselves; they look for ways to increase inflation.

To see why policy makers' thinking has changed, we need to consider the benefits of small amounts of inflation. The best way to explain it is with an analogy to weight.

Margin notes:

Unexpected inflation redistributes income from lenders to borrowers.

Asset price inflation redistributes wealth from cautious individuals to less cautious individuals.

Since the financial crisis of 2008, and the introduction of unconventional monetary policy, the view about an inflation target as being an upper bound for inflation has changed.

We like to eat, but we don't like to gain weight. Say we had inflation in our weight unit of account, so that 1 pound next year is equal to 1.25 pounds this year. If, in the first year, the scale said you weighed 200 pounds, you could gain 50 pounds without the scale saying you weighed a single pound more. The scale would say you weighed 200 pounds both years. You might even convince yourself that your weight hasn't increased. (Psychologists call this type of thinking cognitive dissonance.) We feel better about ourselves by keeping our weight gain hidden within the changing unit of account.

We don't do that with weight, but we do that with clothing sizes. A size 6 dress today is much larger than a size 6 dress twenty years ago, because dressmakers long ago recognized that people like to think that they fit into smaller dress sizes. So each year they slightly increased (inflated) dress sizes so that larger people could fit into small-sized dresses. A changing unit of account helps us maintain our illusions.

Inflation's ability to allow people to maintain illusions underlies many of the benefits of inflation; it explains why many policy makers see the benefits of low inflation as offsetting the costs. Inflation allows us to keep illusions that we are better off than we really are. Such illusions "grease the system" allowing changes that, if they had to be directly faced, would not be acceptable, but if they can be hidden by the small amounts of inflation, are acceptable. Let's consider three benefits of small amounts of inflation:

INFLATION CAN FACILITATE RELATIVE PRICE CHANGES   People don't like to see their wages and prices of goods they sell fall. But for relative price changes to occur with a constant unit of account (no inflation), some prices must fall to allow others to rise. Inflation allows some nominal wages and prices to stay constant or rise, but for those same wages and prices to fall in real terms. For example, say your nominal wage goes up by 3 percent, and the price level rises by 6 percent. The result would be identical to a situation in which your nominal wage fell by 3 percent with the price level remaining constant. But, for most of us, the inflationary alternative is easier to accept than the constant price alternative. We can have the illusion that our wages are not falling. Inflation allows such money illusions and thus allows relative price changes to occur a bit more easily than they otherwise would.

ALLOWING MORE EXPANSIONARY MONETARY POLICY   The benefits of inflation are especially apparent when policy makers are trying to stimulate economic growth when interest rates are zero or close to zero. With conventional monetary policy, policy makers face a **zero interest rate lower bound**—*a limit on how much interest rates can fall*. With unconventional monetary policy they do not.

The argument for a zero interest rate lower bound is the following: If the nominal interest rate falls below zero, people will simply shift to holding cash which pays zero interest since zero interest is better than a negative interest. The nominal interest rate cannot fall significantly below zero. (It can fall a bit below zero since holding large amounts of wealth in cash has costs.)

Because the real interest rate equals the nominal interest rate minus inflation, inflation provides a way around the zero lower bound. While the nominal interest rate cannot fall below zero, the real interest rate can, as long as inflation is greater than the nominal interest rate. For example, with 2 percent inflation and a zero interest rate, the real interest rate is −2 percent. The higher the level of inflation, the lower the real interest rate relative to the nominal interest rate. Inflation allows policy makers to achieve negative interest rates, which allows monetary policy to be more expansive than it otherwise could be. Inflation is a way around the zero lower bound. It is because of these benefits that within unconventional monetary policy, the inflation target is seen as a target to be achieved, rather than a target to stay under.

Q-4   What is meant by a zero lower bound?

INFLATION AS A PLACEBO   As we stated above one can see the distributional effects of inflation as either a cost or a benefit depending on whether one favors or opposes the distributional effects of inflation. From a policy maker's point of view, however, the distributional effects of inflation are often a compelling argument for having some inflation. Unexpected inflation helps debtors and hurts lenders of fixed interest rate debt, since the dollars that are paid back are worth less when there is inflation. Since debtors include businesses and entrepreneurs, policy makers can favor the distributional consequences of inflation because these consequences encourage investment and therefore business activity and economic growth.

Goods inflation also keeps the economy away from asset deflation. Since assets often serve as collateral for loans, significant asset deflation can throw an economy into a financial crisis, as occurred in 2007 when the prices of housing assets fell substantially. Inflation pushes up the value of assets, giving society the illusion that it is richer, which encourages people to invest and start new businesses. As they do, the illusion creates a growing economy, and what started as an illusion becomes a reality. It works a bit like a placebo effect in medicine. The illusion of taking a medicine—even one that has no clinical benefit—actually helps cure the patient.

The Danger of Accelerating Inflation

As you can see, low inflation has benefits, and those benefits have led policy makers to not try to achieve zero inflation, but to target inflation at 2 to possibly 3 percent. Why not higher? The reason is that placebos work only so far. Inflation's benefits involve taking advantage of monetary illusions, and as any magician knows, once the illusion is lost, the trick no longer works. Once the illusion disappears, small amounts of inflation can generate expectations of higher inflation, which can cause inflation to build up and compound itself. A 3 percent inflation becomes a 6 percent inflation, which in turn becomes a 12 percent inflation. Once inflation hits 5 percent or 6 percent, it's definitely no longer a little thing. Inflation of 10 percent or more is significant. At that rate, it begins to undermine money's role as a unit of account and undermine the institutional foundations of contracts.

Expectations of inflation were very much on the minds of policy makers in early 2007 when the economy experienced commodity price shocks, which pushed the inflation rate to over 4 percent. If people had seen the price increase as a one-time event and accepted the decrease in their real income that it implied, it would not have generated an ongoing inflation. But if the increase became built into expectations, it would have led to other price increases and resulted in accelerating inflation. That didn't occur since the economy fell into a severe recession in late 2007, which reversed the price increases in commodity prices, and replaced policy makers' concern about goods inflation with concern about preventing a depression.

While there is no precise definition for hyperinflation, we may reasonably say that goods inflation has become **hyperinflation** *when inflation hits triple digits—100 percent or more per year.* The United States has been either relatively lucky or wise because it has not experienced hyperinflation since the Civil War (1861–1865). Other countries, such as Brazil, Zimbabwe, Venezuela, and Argentina, have not been so lucky. These countries have experienced hyperinflation. But even with inflation at these levels, some of these economies have continued to operate and, in some cases, continued to do well.

In hyperinflation people try to spend their money quickly, but they still use the money. Let's say the U.S. price level is increasing 1 percent a day, which is a yearly

Hyperinflation in Zimbabwe
©REUTERS/Howard Burditt

Hyperinflation is exceptionally high inflation of, say, 100 percent or more per year.

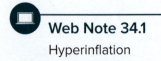

Web Note 34.1

Hyperinflation

inflation rate of over 3,600 percent.[1] Is an expected decrease in value of 1 percent per day going to cause you to stop using dollars? Probably not, unless you have a good alternative. You will, however, avoid putting your money into a savings account unless that savings account somehow compensates you for the expected inflation (the expected fall in the value of the dollar), and you will try to ensure that your wage is adjusted for inflation. In hyperinflation, wages, the prices firms receive, and individual savings are all in some way adjusted for inflation. Hyperinflation leads to economic institutions with built-in expectations of inflation. For example, usually in a hyperinflation the government issues indexed bonds whose value keeps pace with inflation. This doesn't mean alternatives to money aren't used at times. In 2016, for example, a securities firm in Venezuela offered bonuses for good performance to be paid in chicken eggs.

Once these adjustments have been made, substantial inflation will not necessarily destroy an economy, but it certainly is not good for it. Such inflation tends to break down confidence in the monetary system, the economy, and the government.

The Inflation Process and the Quantity Theory of Money

Expectations of inflation play a key role in the inflationary process. When expectations of inflation are high, people tend to raise their wages and prices, causing inflation. So, in fact, expectations can become self-fulfilling. Because of the importance of expectations in perpetuating, and perhaps even in creating, inflation, economists have looked carefully at how individuals form expectations. Almost all economists believe that the expectations that people have of inflation are in some sense rational, by which I mean they are based on the best information available, given the cost of that information. But economists differ on what is meant by rational and thus on how those expectations are formed. Some economists argue that rational people will expect the same inflation that is predicted by the economists' model. That is, they form **rational expectations**—*the expectations that the economists' model predicts.* If inflation was, say, 2 percent last year and is 4 percent this year, but the economists' model predicts 0 percent inflation for the coming year, individuals will rationally expect 0 percent inflation.

Other economists argue that rational expectations cannot be defined in terms of economists' models. These economists instead focus on the process by which people develop their expectations. One way people form expectations is to look at conditions that already exist, or have recently existed. Such expectations are called **adaptive expectations**—*expectations based in some way on the past.* Thus, if inflation was 2 percent last year and 4 percent this year, the prediction for inflation will be somewhere around 3 percent. Adaptive expectations aren't the only type that people use. Sometimes they use **extrapolative expectations**—*expectations that a trend will accelerate.* For example, say that inflation was 2 percent last year and 4 percent this year; extrapolative expectations would predict 6 percent or more inflation next year. These are only three of the many reasonable ways people form expectations. Because there is no one economic model that predicts the economy perfectly, there is no way of specifying one rational expectation; there are only reasonable expectations. Individuals use various ways of forming expectations, often shifting suddenly from one way to another.

Expectations of inflation play a key role in the inflationary process.

Web Note 34.2
Forecasting Inflation

Q-5 Name three different types of expectations.

---

[1] Why over 3,600 percent and not 365 percent? Because of compounding. On the second day the increase is on the initial price level *and* the 1 percent rise in price level that occurred the first day. When you carry out this compounding for all 365 days, you get over 3,600 percent.

Because expectations can change quickly, the inflationary outlook can change suddenly. As of 2018, there had not been significant goods inflation in the United States for over a decade even when the money supply increased significantly. But, as the unemployment rate fell to under 4 percent many economists were concerned that inflation could increase above its target, presenting the Fed with the choice of whether to deal with the inflation even though doing so might increase the unemployment rate.

Productivity, Inflation, and Wages

Two key measures that policy makers use to determine whether inflation may be coming are changes in productivity and changes in wages. Together these measures determine whether or not the short-run aggregate supply curve will be shifting up. The rule of thumb is that wages can increase by the amount that productivity increases without generating any inflationary pressure:

Inflation = Nominal wage increase – Productivity growth

For example, if productivity is increasing at 2 percent, as it did in the early 2000s, wages can go up by 2 percent without generating any inflationary pressure. Let's consider another example—the mid-1970s, when productivity growth slowed to 1 percent while wages went up by 6 percent. Using our rule of thumb, inflation was 5 percent (6 percent – 1 percent).

You probably recognize this relationship from an earlier chapter. This is the same relationship that explains how the short-run aggregate supply curve shifts. When nominal wages increase by more than the growth of productivity, the *SAS* curve shifts up as shown in Figure 34-2, resulting in inflation. When nominal wages increase by less than the growth of productivity, the *SAS* curve shifts down, resulting in deflation (a sustained fall in the price level).

The Quantity Theory of Money and Inflation

Economists' longest existing theory of inflation is the quantity theory of money, which is a theory that goes back to the 1600s.

The quantity theory of money can be summed up in one sentence: *Inflation is always and everywhere a monetary phenomenon.* If the money supply rises, the price level will rise. If the money supply doesn't rise, the price level won't rise. A quantity theory advocate argues: Forget all the other explanations of inflation—they just obscure the connection between money and inflation.

Inflation = Nominal wage increase – Productivity growth

FIGURE 34-2 **Nominal Wages, Productivity, and Inflation**

When nominal wages increase by more than the growth of productivity, the *SAS* curve shifts up, resulting in inflation. When nominal wages increase by less than the growth of productivity, the *SAS* curve shifts down, resulting in deflation.

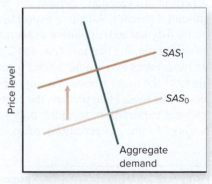

THE EQUATION OF EXCHANGE   The quantity theory of money centers on the **equation of exchange,** *an equation stating that the quantity of money times the velocity of money equals the price level times the quantity of real goods sold.* This equation is:

$$MV = PQ$$

where:

- M = Quantity of money
- V = Velocity of money
- P = Price level
- Q = Quantity of real goods sold

In the quantity theory model, inflation is caused by growth in the money supply. It focuses on the equation of exchange: $MV = PQ$

Q is the real output of the economy (real GDP) and P is the price level, so PQ is the economy's nominal output (nominal GDP). V, the **velocity of money,** is *the number of times per year, on average, a dollar gets spent on goods and services.* Put another way, velocity is the amount of income per year generated by a dollar. Since $MV = PQ$, MV also equals nominal output. Thus, if there's $100 of money in the economy and velocity is 20, nominal GDP is $2,000. We can calculate V by dividing nominal GDP by the money supply. Let's take the United States as an example. In the United States in 2016, nominal GDP was approximately $19 trillion and M was approximately $3,100 billion (using M_1), so velocity (GDP/M) was about 6, meaning each dollar in the economy circulated enough to support approximately $6 in total income.

VELOCITY IS CONSTANT   The equation of exchange is a tautology, meaning it is true by definition. What changes it from a tautology to the quantity theory are three assumptions. The first assumption is that velocity remains constant (or changes at a predictable rate). Money is spent only so fast; how fast is determined by the economy's institutional structure, such as how close individuals live to stores, how people are paid (weekly, biweekly, or monthly), and what sources of credit are available. (Can you go to the store and buy something on credit, that is, without handing over cash?) This institutional structure changes slowly, quantity theorists argue, so velocity won't fluctuate very much. Next year, velocity will be approximately the same as this year.

Three assumptions of quantity theory:
1. *Velocity is constant.*
2. *Real output is independent of money supply.*
3. *Causation goes from money to prices.*

If velocity can be predicted, the quantity theory can be used to predict how much nominal GDP will grow if we know how much the money supply grows. For example, if the money supply goes up 6 percent and velocity is predicted to be constant, the quantity theory of money predicts that nominal GDP will go up by 6 percent.

REAL OUTPUT IS INDEPENDENT OF THE MONEY SUPPLY   The second assumption is that Q is independent of the money supply. That is, Q is autonomous, meaning real output is determined by forces outside those forces in the quantity theory. If Q grows, it is because of factors that affect the real economy. Thus, according to the quantity theory of money, policy discussions of the real economy should focus on the real economy—the supply side of the economy, not the demand or monetary side.

Something that is determined outside the model is called autonomous.

This assumption makes analyzing the economy a lot easier than if the financial and real sectors are interrelated and if real economic activity is influenced by financial changes. It separates two puzzles: how the real economy works and how the price level and financial sector work. Instead of having two different jigsaw puzzles all mixed up, each puzzle can be worked separately. The quantity theory doesn't say there aren't interconnections between the real and financial sectors, but it does say that most of these interconnections involve short-run considerations. The quantity theory is primarily concerned with the long run.

CAUSATION GOES FROM MONEY TO PRICES With both V (velocity) and Q (quantity of output) assumed unaffected by changes in M (money supply), the only thing that can change as money changes is P (price level). Given the two assumptions so far, either prices or money could be the driving force. The quantity theory makes the additional assumption that causation goes from money to prices.

With these three assumptions, the equation of exchange becomes the quantity theory of money:

$$M\overline{V} \to P\overline{Q}$$

In its simplest terms, the **quantity theory of money** says that *the price level varies in response to changes in the quantity of money.* Another way to write the quantity theory of money is: $\%\Delta M \to \%\Delta P$. If the money supply goes up 20 percent, prices go up 20 percent. If the money supply goes down 5 percent, the price level goes down 5 percent.

WHICH WAY DOES THE CAUSATION GO? According to the quantity theory of money, changes in the money supply cause changes in the price level. The direction of causation goes from left to right:

$$MV \to PQ$$

More institutionally focused economists see it the other way around. Increases in prices force government to increase the money supply or cause unemployment. The direction of causation goes from right to left:

$$MV \leftarrow PQ$$

According to these critics of the quantity theory, the source of inflation is in the price-setting process of firms. When setting prices, firms and individuals find it easier to raise prices than to lower them and do not take into account the effect of their pricing decisions on the price level.

The Declining Influence of the Quantity Theory

In recent times the quantity theory has been out of favor for two reasons. First, the velocity of money has not been constant, and second, the connection between increases in money supply growth and goods inflation has broken down.

VELOCITY IS NOT CONSTANT The problem with velocity can be seen in Figure 34-3. For the quantity theory to be useful we need velocity to be relatively constant or increasing or decreasing in a predictable way. As you can see in Figure 34-3(a), velocity has been anything but constant. This means that at times when the money supply decreased, inflation did not change or went up, and most recently, when the money supply increased, inflation fell and has remained low.

Other things equal, a rise in the velocity of money has the same effect as an increase in the money supply. When velocity increases so will the price level, and when it decreases the price level will also decrease. So, the velocity of money can either offset or add to the effect of money supply changes on the price level. Right before the financial crash, both the money supply and velocity increased. Since 2008 velocity has decreased enormously, offsetting much of the effect of the increase in the money supply.

BREAKDOWN IN THE CONNECTION BETWEEN MONEY AND INFLATION A second reason the quantity theory has lost favor is related to the first. It is that money and goods inflation are no longer closely connected. For example, notice in Figure 34-3(b) the money supply has been increasing even as inflation has remained low.

The Keeper of the Classical Faith: Milton Friedman

One of the most important economists of the 20th century was University of Chicago economist Milton Friedman. In macroeconomics, Friedman is best known for his support of the quantity theory.

By most accounts, Friedman was a headstrong student. He didn't simply accept the truths his teachers laid out. If he didn't agree, he argued strongly for his own belief. He was very bright, and his ideas were generally logical and convincing. He needed to be both persistent and intelligent to maintain and promote his views in spite of strong opposition.

Throughout the Keynesian years of the 1950s and 1960s, Friedman stood up and argued for the quantity theory, keeping it alive. During this period, Classical economics was called *monetarism,* and because

Nobel Prize winner Milton Friedman
©Chuck Nacke/The LIFE Images Collection/Getty Images

Friedman was such a strong advocate of the quantity theory, he was considered the leader of the monetarists.

Friedman argued that fiscal policy simply didn't work. It led to expansions in the size of government. He also opposed an activist monetary policy. The effects of monetary policy, he said, were too variable for it to be useful in guiding the economy. He called for a steady growth in the money supply, and argued consistently for a laissez-faire policy by government.

Friedman has made his mark in both microeconomics and macroeconomics. In the 1970s, his ideas caught hold and helped spawn a renewal of the quantity theory. He was awarded the Nobel Prize in Economics in 1976.

AN ADJUSTED QUANTITY THEORY? Even though the traditional quantity theory is no longer directly applicable, its general point remains relevant. That general point is that when real output is increasing by 3 percent a year, money times velocity can increase by only 3 percent per year if there is not to be inflation. Thus, if velocity is increasing substantially there can be inflationary pressures even if the money supply is

Even though the quantity theory is no longer directly applicable, its general point remains relevant.

FIGURE 34-3 (A AND B)   Inflation, the Money Supply, and the Velocity of Money

Velocity has not been constant, as shown in (**a**), which complicates the relationship between the money supply and inflation, as you can see in (**b**). Inflation has sometimes risen significantly without a rise in the money supply, and has fallen significantly even as the money supply has increased.

Source: Federal Reserve Bank of St. Louis (CPI inflation, M_1, and M_1 velocity).

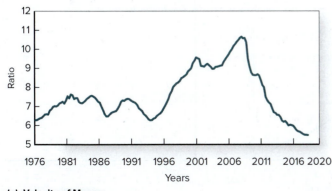

(a) **Velocity of Money**

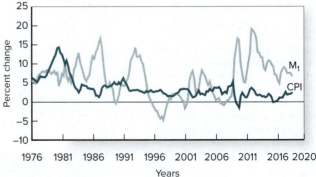

(b) **Money Supply and CPI**

constant, and if velocity is decreasing substantially there can be deflationary pressures even though the money supply is constant. When velocity fluctuates, policy makers must look at both velocity and the money supply to determine what is happening on the monetary side of the economy, and they must adjust their monetary policy to account for the fluctuating velocity.

If that monetary side of the economy (money times velocity) is increasing at a rate faster than the real economy is growing, say at 3 percent, then the monetary pressure is causing inflationary pressure in some sector of the economy. But that inflationary pressure need not show up directly in goods price inflation; it can end up in asset price inflation. An example is the case of the United States in recent years where globalization and the large continuing trade deficit placed significant downward pressure on tradable goods and services prices. At the same time, the monetary side of the quantity theory equation (money times velocity) grew significantly faster than the real side but we did not have significant goods inflation because international competition was holding down wages and prices in the tradable goods sector of the economy. But we did have what proved to be an unsustainable increase in asset prices that led to a financial meltdown. So if we had included asset prices in our view of inflation, monetary policy was inflationary during that time period, just as the quantity theory said it would be. The same situation has occurred in the early teens. Money supply has increased, asset prices have increased, but goods inflation has not. The debate is whether that will lead to another financial crisis.

Inflation and the Phillips Curve Trade-Off

The traditional short-run Phillips curve is a downward-sloping curve showing the relationship between inflation and unemployment when expectations of inflation are fixed.

Inflation has traditionally been discussed in relation to unemployment in what is called the Phillips curve. The traditional **short-run Phillips curve** is *a downward-sloping curve showing the relationship between inflation and unemployment when expectations of inflation are constant*. In a Phillips curve diagram, unemployment is measured on the horizontal axis; inflation is on the vertical axis. The short-run Phillips curve shows us the possible short-run combinations of those two phenomena. It tells us that when unemployment is low, say 4 percent, inflation tends to be high, say 4 percent [point *A* in Figure 34-4(a)]. It also tells us that if we want to lower inflation, say to 1 percent, we must be willing to accept high unemployment, say 7 percent [point *B* in Figure 34-4(a)].

FIGURE 34-4 **The Phillips Curve Trade-Off**

The Phillips curve depicts a trade-off between inflation and unemployment. In the short-run Phillips curve shown in (**a**), there is a trade-off between inflation and unemployment. In the long-run Phillips curve shown in (**b**) there is assumed to be no trade-off, which means that the long-run Phillips curve is vertical.

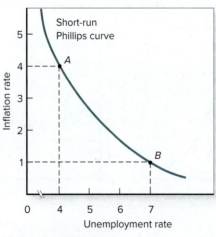

(a) Short-Run Phillips Curve

(b) Long-Run Phillips Curve

Inflation, Nominal Income, and Asset Inflation Targeting

One of the big debates about Fed policy concerns whether the Fed should have an explicit target. The most generally discussed target is a goods price inflation target. With inflation targeting, the Fed commits itself to tightening the money supply and raising interest rates if inflation exceeds a certain level. Advocates of inflation targeting argue that it provides better assurances for investors that the central bank will fight inflation, and thus holds inflationary expectations down. They point to the success of countries such as New Zealand, which introduced inflation targeting in 1989 when a law was passed that required the Reserve Bank of New Zealand to keep consumer price inflation between 0 and 3 percent a year, a target agreed on by the government and the central bank. After averaging 10 percent a year in the 1980s, New Zealand's inflation rate fell in the early 1990s and averaged below 3 percent per year thereafter. Advocates of inflation targeting argue that this experience, and others like it, show that inflation targeting helps central banks establish credibility in their resolve to fight inflation.

©Tashatuvango/Shutterstock

Critics of inflation targeting argue that explicit inflation targeting has serious problems. Inflation is hard to measure, and the standard measures of inflation do not include asset inflation. Thus a monetary policy can lead to significant asset inflation, and still meet the target. The target could also work the other way. An inflation target could force the central bank to raise interest rates and cut money supply growth when there was no need to do so. They argue that it is better to have a *general inflation goal,* which can be adjusted for the particular situation, and that

the general inflation target should include a consideration of the components of the price rise and of whether increases in nominal wealth are exceeding increases in real wealth. Until recently the inflation target was considered an upper bound on inflation. The goal was to have 2 percent inflation or less. More recently, the inflation target has been considered a target so that if inflation is zero, for example, the Fed will attempt to raise inflation to its 2 percent target.

A variation of inflation targeting that has recently been proposed is *nominal income targeting.* In nominal income targeting the Fed targets a specific increase in nominal income—say 5 percent—and does not try to separate out which part of it is inflation. If real income increases at 3 percent, then nominal income targeting would be the equivalent of a 2 percent inflation target. If real income does not grow by 3 percent, then the nominal income target would allow for a higher inflation. If real income growth were greater, the inflation component of the nominal income target would be lower. The potential problem with such a policy is that it might allow, and perhaps even encourage, asset price inflation.

Many other variations of targets are possible. For example, one could have a combined goods inflation and asset inflation target, where the inflation target of, say, 2 percent was combined with a net-worth-to-GDP ratio target, to reduce the likelihood of the Fed feeding an asset bubble. Such a target would call for much more contractionary monetary policy in asset price booms, and more expansionary monetary policy in asset deflations.

Up until the 1970s the short-run Phillips curve seemed to match the empirical evidence, but then in the early 1970s the empirical short-run Phillips curve relationship seemed to break down. The data no longer seemed to show a trade-off between unemployment and inflation. Instead, when unemployment was high, inflation was also high. This phenomenon is termed **stagflation**—*the combination of high and accelerating inflation and high unemployment.* Since that time, the Phillips curve has been ephemeral—sometimes seeming as if it were reappearing, and then disappearing again.

Web Note 34.3

The Phillips Curve

The Long-Run and Short-Run Phillips Curves

Economists have explained this constantly changing relationship between inflation and unemployment by incorporating expectations of inflation into the analysis. They argue that actual inflation depends both on supply and demand forces and on how much inflation people expect. If people expect a lot of inflation, they will ask for higher nominal wage and price increases. To incorporate expectations into the Phillips curve it is necessary to distinguish between a short-run Phillips curve, shown in Figure 34-4(a), and a long-run Phillips curve, shown in Figure 34-4(b). Economists explain the difference between the short-run and the long-run Phillips curves by different assumptions about expectations.

At all points on a short-run Phillips curve, expectations of inflation (the rise in the price level that the average person expects) are fixed. Thus, on the short-run Phillips curve, expectations of inflation can differ from actual inflation. As expectations of infla-tion change, the short-run Phillips curve shifts. When expected inflation rises, the short-run Phillips curve shifts up, and when expected inflation falls, the short-run Phillips curve shifts down. In contrast, at all points on the long-run Phillips curve, expectations of inflation are equal to actual inflation. The **long-run Phillips curve** is thought to be *a vertical curve at the unemployment rate consistent with potential output.* It shows the trade-off between inflation and unemployment (or complete lack thereof) when expecta-tions of inflation equal actual inflation. Economists argue that expectations of inflation explain why the short-run Phillips curve relationship broke down in the 1970s.

Let's consider how expectations of inflation can explain high inflation and high unemployment in reference to the Phillips curve graph. Say the economy starts with a 5.5 percent unemployment rate consistent with potential output. At this unemployment rate there is no inflation. (Wages can still be going up by the rate of productivity growth, say it's 3 percent, but the price level is not rising.) Further assume that indi-viduals are expecting zero inflation; that is, if they get a 3 percent wage increase, they expect their real income to rise by 3 percent. This starting point is represented by point *A* in Figure 34-5, on which we graph both the short-run and long-run Phillips curves.

Let's say the economy starts at point *A*—zero inflation and unemployment of 5.5 percent, the target rate. As you can see, point *A* in Figure 34-5 is also on both the

The long-run Phillips curve is vertical; it shows the lack of a trade-off between inflation and unemployment when expectations of inflation equal actual inflation. Expectations of inflation do not change along a short-run Phillips curve.

FIGURE 34-5   **The Inflationary Process and the Phillips Curve**

In the short run, the economy can expand beyond the target rate of unemployment by accepting more inflation. This shows up as a movement along the short-run Phillips curve from point *A* to point *B*. That is not, however, a sustainable equilibrium. As the higher inflation becomes built into expectations, there will be pressure to raise wages and prices even more than 4 percent, which will push up inflation and inflationary expectations, shifting the short-run Phillips curve up (arrow 1). Only when that pressure is removed and unemployment is allowed to increase back to its target rate (arrow 2) will the upward shift stop. The eventual equilibrium will be an equilibrium such as point *C,* which is on both the long-run and short-run Phillips curves.

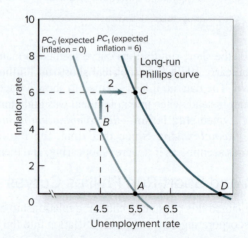

long-run and short-run Phillips curves. This means that point *A* is a sustainable combination of inflation and unemployment—the situation can continue indefinitely. The only sustainable combination of inflation and unemployment rates on the short-run Phillips curve is where it intersects the long-run Phillips curve because that is the only unemployment rate consistent with the economy's potential income.

MOVING OFF THE LONG-RUN PHILLIPS CURVE   Now let's say that the government decides to run expansionary monetary or fiscal policy in an effort to reduce unemployment below 5.5 percent. Such a policy would decrease unemployment (say to 4.5 percent) but increase inflation. This is shown as a movement along the short-run Phillips curve from point *A* to point *B*. That is not, however, a sustainable equilibrium. Inflation is higher than expected, and the people are being fooled. For example, workers who were expecting zero inflation, which made them happy with a 3 percent raise, now find that there was 4 percent inflation, so now they will find that their real wage actually fell. As the higher inflation becomes built into expectations, there will be pressure to raise wages and prices, which will push up inflation even more than 4 percent.

As expectations of inflation increase, the short-run Phillips curve will begin shifting up as shown by the upward arrow at point *B* (arrow 1). This pressure on inflation to rise will continue as long as the unemployment is below the unemployment rate consistent with potential output, which in this case is assumed to be 5.5 percent. Only when that pressure is removed by allowing the economy to move back to a rate of unemployment consistent with potential output (shifting the short-run Phillips curve to the right along arrow 2, to a point such as point *C* in Figure 34-5) will the upward pressure stop. At point *C* the economy will be at a sustainable equilibrium where the unemployment rate equals the target rate and inflation expectations equal actual inflation.

In the Phillips curve model, the general relationship is the following: Any time unemployment is lower than the target level of unemployment consistent with potential output, inflation and expectations of inflation will be increasing. That means that the short-run Phillips curve will be shifting up. The short-run Phillips curve will continue to shift up until output is no longer above potential. Thus, any level of inflation is consistent with the target level of unemployment if the cause of that inflation is expectations of inflation. Economists used these expectations of inflation to explain the U.S. experience of high inflation and unemployment in the 1970s. The economy had been pushed beyond its potential, which had caused inflation to accelerate. (This explanation was supplemented with discussions of supply-side inflationary pressures caused by the large rise in oil prices that occurred at that time.)

Q-10 If the economy is at point *A* on the short-run Phillips curve below, what prediction would you make for unemployment and inflation?

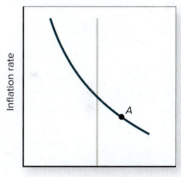

Global Competition and the Phillips Curve

Global competition holds U.S. inflation down, and it has done so in the past decade. As a result, the typical downward-sloping short-run Phillips curve has not seemed to be relevant. This experience can be depicted as an essentially flat short-run Phillips curve. With a flat short-run Phillips curve, increases in income and decreases in unemployment do not lead to increases in inflation and hence to increases in inflationary expectations. As long as the world price level is below the domestic price level, a decline in the unemployment rate will not lead to an increase in domestic prices. In this case, the short-run Phillips curve is horizontal as shown by PC_2 in Figure 34-6. With a standard short-run Philips curve, PC_1, expansionary policy moves the economy from point *A* to *B*, unemployment falls, inflation rises, and inflation expectations eventually put pressure on prices and wages to rise. It is unsustainable and eventually the economy will return to the original unemployment rate. A short-run Phillips curve that takes globalization into account, PC_2, allows the economy to move from point *A* to *C*

FIGURE 34-6   The Inflation Process with Globalization

When the world price level is below the domestic price level, and the country can run unlimited trade deficits, a decline in the unemployment rate need not lead to inflation. Inflation is held down by globalization. The standard short-run Phillips curve (PC₁) changes to a flat short-run Phillips curve (PC₂).

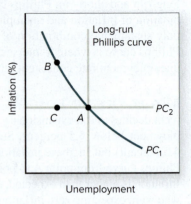

without increases in either inflation or inflation expectations. This position is sustainable as long as the international conditions allow it, with large flows of capital from abroad financing the trade deficit. In this case, government can use expansionary policy without leading to goods market inflation. Instead it may lead to an asset price inflation. The downside of asset price inflation is that if and when the asset price bubble ultimately bursts, the economy will likely experience a financial crisis and an accompanying recession.

Conclusion

Inflation is not an easy topic. It is made more challenging by definitional and measurement problems that make it difficult to know precisely what type of inflation one is talking about. Should we define inflation in terms of goods prices, or more broadly in terms of both asset and goods prices? These definitional choices make a big difference in how we view policy. If one judges inflation in terms of both goods and asset prices, then the period up until the financial bubble burst was a more inflationary time period than it seemed. If one judges inflation only in terms of increases in the price of goods, it was not.

Summary

- At one time, inflation was measured as an increase in the money supply.   *(LO34-1)*

- Inflation can occur for both goods and assets. Goods inflation is easier to measure than is asset inflation.   *(LO34-1)*

- It is difficult to determine how much of an increase in the value of assets is the result of inflation or of increased productive capacity. This is one reason asset prices are not included in measured inflation.   *(LO34-1)*

- The usefulness of standard goods market price indexes for judging policy is limited because they do not include the prices of assets.   *(LO34-1)*

- The winners in inflation are people who can raise their wages or prices and still keep their jobs or sell their goods. The losers are people who can't raise their wages or prices. On average, winners and losers balance out.   *(LO34-2)*

- Asset inflation hurts people who save with safe assets and helps those who save in risky assets.   *(LO34-2)*

- Inflation has both costs and benefits. Conventional monetary policy emphasizes informational, institutional, and distributional costs.   *(LO34-2)*

- In unconventional monetary policy, the benefits of low inflation receive more emphasis.   *(LO34-2)*

- Low inflation greases the wheels of the economy, provides beneficial placebo effects, and provides a way of getting around the zero interest rate lower bound. *(LO34-2)*

- A basic rule of thumb to predict inflation is: Inflation equals nominal wage increases minus productivity growth. *(LO34-3)*

- The equation of exchange is $MV = PQ$; it becomes the quantity theory when velocity is constant, real output is independent of the money supply, and causation goes from money to prices. The quantity theory says that the price level varies in direct response to changes in the quantity of money. That is,

  $\%\Delta M \rightarrow \%\Delta P$ *(LO34-3)*

- According to the quantity theory of money, policy analysis about the real economy is based on the supply side of the economy, not the demand side. *(LO34-3)*

- The lack of a clear relationship between money growth and inflation as well as the variability of velocity undermines the quantity theory of money. *(LO34-3)*

- The short-run Phillips curve holds expectations constant. It is generally seen as downward-sloping and shifts up when expectations of inflation rise and shifts down when expectations of inflation fall. *(LO34-4)*

- The long-run Phillips curve allows expectations of inflation to change; it is generally seen as vertical. *(LO34-4)*

- Globalization can lead to a flat short-run Phillips curve. In this case, expansionary policy can reduce unemployment without causing goods inflation. *(LO34-4)*

Key Terms

adaptive expectations	hyperinflation	rational expectations	velocity of money
asset price inflation	long-run Phillips curve	short-run Phillips curve	zero interest rate lower
equation of exchange	quantity theory of money	stagflation	bound
extrapolative expectations			

Questions and Exercises ■ connect

1. What is asset price inflation? Why does it matter? *(LO34-1)*

2. True or false? Inflation, on average, makes people neither richer nor poorer. Therefore it has no cost. Explain. *(LO34-2)*

3. What are three costs of inflation that economists focus on? *(LO34-2)*

4. When would policy makers change from an inflation target being an upper bound to a target to aim for? When would this policy fail to produce the expected result? *(LO34-2)*

5. How does inflation allow central banks to run more expansionary monetary policy? *(LO34-2)*

6. What is meant by a placebo effect and how is it related to unconventional monetary policy? *(LO34-2)*

7. Why do lenders tend to lose out in an unexpected inflation? *(LO34-2)*

8. What are the benefits of a small amount of inflation? *(LO34-2)*

9. What are the distributional effects of asset inflation caused by an increase in the money supply? *(LO34-2)*

10. Why have policy makers changed their focus from keeping inflation from getting too high to keeping inflation from getting too low? *(LO34-2)*

11. Why is a zero interest rate lower bound important to policy making? *(LO34-2)*

12. If you base your expectations of inflation on what has happened in the past, what kind of expectations are you demonstrating? *(LO34-3)*

13. If productivity growth is 3 percent and wage increases are 5 percent, what would you predict inflation would be? *(LO34-3)*

14. What three assumptions turn the equation of exchange into the quantity theory of money? *(LO34-3)*

15. What does the quantity theory predict will happen to inflation if the money supply rises 10 percent? *(LO34-3)*

16. Assume the money supply is $800, the velocity of money is 8, and the price level is $2. Using the quantity theory of money: (*LO34-3*)
    a. Determine the level of real output.
    b. Determine the level of nominal output.
    c. Assuming velocity remains constant, what will happen if the money supply rises 20 percent?
    d. If the government established price controls and also raised the money supply 20 percent, what would happen?

17. What are two reasons why the quantity theory of money is problematic? (*LO34-3*)

18. Draw a short-run Phillips curve. What does it say about the relationship between inflation and unemployment? (*LO34-4*)

19. Draw a long-run Phillips curve. What does it say about the relationship between inflation and unemployment? (*LO34-4*)

20. If people's expectations of inflation didn't change, would the economy move from a short-run to a long-run Phillips curve? (*LO34-4*)

21. Congratulations. You've just been appointed finance minister of Inflationland. Inflation has been ongoing for the past five years at 5 percent. The target rate of unemployment, 5 percent, is also the actual rate. (*LO34-4*)
    a. Demonstrate the economy's likely position on both short-run and long-run Phillips curves.
    b. The president tells you she wants to be reelected. Devise a monetary policy strategy for her that might help her accomplish her goal.
    c. Demonstrate that strategy graphically, including the likely long-run consequences.

22. European Central Bank (ECB) governing council member Erkki Liikanen was quoted as saying, "The stronger we get the productivity growth . . . the more room we will get in monetary policy (to keep interest rates low)." (*LO34-4*)
    a. Demonstrate his argument using the *AS/AD* model.
    b. Demonstrate his argument using the Phillips curve model.

Questions from Alternative Perspectives

1. According to the quantity theory of money, the government controls inflation through the supply of money.
    a. Does that mean that the government can stop inflation if it wants to do so?
    b. What reasons might government have not to stop inflation? *(Austrian)*

2. The book of Leviticus in the Bible states, "You shall do no injustice in judgment, in measurement of length, weight, or volume. You shall have just balances, just weights, a just ephah, a just hin. I am the Lord your God, who brought you out of the land of Egypt." When the Israelites began using shekels for money, a just weight meant that the silver coin had a particular weight and therefore an intrinsic value.
    a. If U.S. currency is not backed by gold, how do we know the dollar is a "just weight"?
    b. How is inflation an injustice in measurement?
    c. Who bears the injustice of inflation? *(Religious)*

3. When it comes to understanding inflation, and even other aspects of the business cycle, ecological economists will often emphasize the role of energy, and especially oil, in shaping macroeconomic outcomes. To decide how important oil prices are in shaping macroeconomic outcomes such as inflation, do the following:
    a. Graph the average annual CPI inflation rate from 1970 to the 2000s (www.bls.gov has the data); graph the world price of oil over the same time period (www.eia.gov has these data); overlay the graphs (this is sometimes called "teardrop analysis") and move them forward and backward a bit to create leads and lags. What kind of pattern do you see?
    b. Use the *AS/AD* model to analyze the impact of an oil shock on the economy.
    c. What is the necessary consequence of using fiscal policy to stimulate the economy after a supply-side oil shock? What conclusions do you draw from the analysis? *(Institutionalist)*

4. This chapter discusses causes of inflation.
    a. Do you believe the cause of inflation is to be found in the institutional structure of wage- and price-setting institutions or in excess demand for goods and services?
    b. If you believe inflation is caused by wage- and price-setting institutions, what type of policy would you recommend?
    c. If you believe that inflation is caused by excess demand, would your policy recommendations be the same? *(Post-Keynesian)*

5. Radicals see the trade-off between inflation and unemployment as one that pits inflation-phobic investors—out to protect the value of their assets and the corporate profits in which they invest—against workers who are out for employment and wage growth. Lower unemployment rates and more jobs bolster the bargaining power of workers, pushing up wages, which either leads to inflation or eats into corporate profit margins. The trade-off changed in the 1990s as globalization put workers in no position to push for higher wages even as unemployment rates declined. Compare this explanation of change in the trade-off between unemployment and inflation during the 1990s with the one in your textbook.
    a. Where do they agree and where do they differ?
    b. Which do you find more convincing? *(Radical)*

Issues to Ponder

1. In the early 1990s when Argentina was experiencing hyperinflation, the government stopped increasing the money supply and fixed the exchange rate of the Argentine austral at 10,000 to the dollar. It then renamed the Argentine currency the "peso" and cut off four zeros so that one peso equaled one dollar. Inflation slowed substantially. After this was done, the following observations were made. Explain why these observations did not surprise economists.
   a. The golf courses were far less crowded.
   b. The price of goods in dollar-equivalent pesos in Buenos Aires, the capital of the country, was significantly above that in New York City.
   c. Consumer prices—primarily services—rose relative to other goods.
   d. Luxury auto dealers were shutting down.

2. A recent study revealed that 40 percent of all grades given in college were in the A range. Some economists argue that such grade inflation should be dealt with in the same way that price inflation should be dealt with—by creating a fixed standard and requiring all grades to be specified relative to that standard. One way to accomplish this is to index the grades professors give: Specify on the grade report both the student's grade and the class average, and deflate (or inflate) the grade to some common standard. What are the advantages and disadvantages of such a proposal?

3. True or false? The short-run Phillips curve is just a figment of economists' imagination.

4. Wayne Angell, a former Fed governor, stated in an editorial, "The Federal Reserve should get back on track getting inflation rates so low that inflation would no longer be a determining factor in household and business investment decisions." Mr. Angell believes inflation lowers long-term growth.
   a. Is Wayne Angell most likely a quantity theorist or an institutionally focused economist? Explain your answer.
   b. How does inflation affect household decisions and, consequently, growth?

Answers to Margin Questions

1. Asset inflation is the rise in the price of assets such as stocks and houses in excess of changes in their real values. Goods inflation is the rise in the price of goods and services. (LO34-1)

2. Asset deflation presents more problems for the economy than does goods inflation. (LO34-1)

3. False. Inflation does not make an economy poorer. It redistributes income from those who do not raise their prices to those who do raise their prices. (LO34-2)

4. A zero lower bound refers to the fact that nominal interest rates cannot fall significantly below zero. (LO34-2)

5. Three types of expectations are rational expectations, adaptive expectations, and extrapolative expectations. (LO34-3)

6. The equation of exchange, $MV = PQ$, is a tautology. What changes it to the quantity theory are three assumptions about the variables, specifically that velocity remains constant, that real output is determined separately, and that the causation flows from money to prices. With these assumptions added, the equation of exchange implies that changes in the money supply are reflected in changes in the price level—which is what the quantity theory of money says. (LO34-3)

7. According to the quantity theory of money, the Fed should decrease the growth of the money supply to lower inflation. (LO34-3)

8. According to the quantity theory, the direction of causation goes from money to prices ($MV \rightarrow PQ$)—increases in the money supply lead to increases in the price level. According to institutionally focused economists, the direction of causation goes from prices to money ($MV \leftarrow PQ$)—increases in the price level are ratified by government, which increases the money supply. (LO34-3)

9. The relationship between the money supply and inflation does not always hold and the velocity of money is not constant.   (*LO34-3*)

10. If the economy is at point *A* on the Phillips curve below, inflation is below expected inflation and unemployment is higher than the target rate of unemployment. If this were the only information I had about the economy I would expect the economy to shift back to a point on the long-run Phillips curve, as inflation and expectations of inflation fall, shifting the short-run Phillips curve down and to the left.   (*LO34-4*)

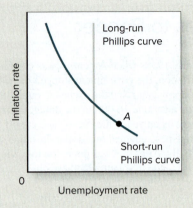

International Financial Policy

> A foreign exchange dealer's office during a busy spell is the nearest thing to Bedlam I have struck.
>
> —Harold Wincott

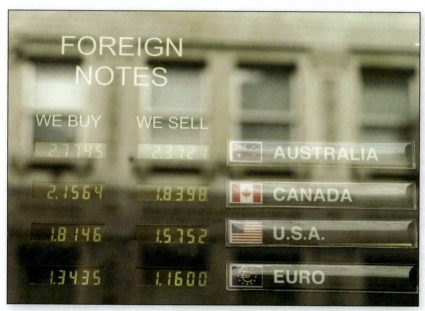

CHAPTER 35

©AP Photo/Sang Tan

After reading this chapter, you should be able to:

LO35-1 Summarize the balance of payments accounts and explain the relationship between the current account and the financial and capital account.

LO35-2 Explain how exchange rates are determined and how government can influence them.

LO35-3 Discuss the problem of determining the appropriate exchange rate.

LO35-4 Differentiate various exchange rate regimes and discuss the advantages and disadvantages of each.

Throughout the book we've seen that exchange rates and international considerations are fundamental to a country's economy and that they play a major role in its macroeconomic policy. In this chapter we consider international financial issues more directly. I begin by looking at the balance of payments account and the relationship between the current account and the financial and capital account. Then we consider exchange rates and the important role they play in the macro economy; I discuss the problems of determining the appropriate exchange rate and the advantages and disadvantages of alternative exchange rate regimes. Finally, I conclude with a discussion of the euro and the problems it has been experiencing as an example of how exchange rate regimes make a major difference in how an economy functions.

The Balance of Payments

The best door into an in-depth discussion of exchange rates and international financial considerations is a discussion of **balance of payments** (*a country's record of all transactions between its residents and the residents of all foreign nations*). These include a country's buying and selling of goods and services (imports and exports) and interest and profit payments from previous

TABLE 35-1 The Balance of Payments Account in Billions of Dollars, 2017

Current account

Merchandise

1.	Exports	1,553.4			
2.	Imports	−2,360.9			
3.	Balance on merchandise trade		−807.5		
	Services				
4.	Exports	797.7			
5.	Imports	−542.5			
6.	Balance on services		255.2		
7.	Balance of trade			−552.3	
8.	Net investment income		221.7		
9.	Net transfers		−118.6		
10.	Invest. trans. balance			103.1	
11.	**Balance on current account**				−449.2

Financial and capital account

12.	Net financial and capital derivatives		23.1	
13.	Net U.S. acquisition of foreign financial assets		−1,182.7	
14.	Net foreign acquisitions of U.S. financial assets		1,537.7	
15.	**Balance on financial and capital account**			378.1
16.	Statistical discrepancy			71.1
17.	**Balance of payments**			0.0

Source: International Transactions, Bureau of Economic Analysis (www.bea.gov).

The balance of payments is a country's record of all transactions between its residents and the residents of all foreign countries.

investments, together with all the capital inflows and outflows. Table 35-1 presents the 2017 balance of payments accounts for the United States. These accounts record all payments made by foreigners to U.S. citizens and all payments made by U.S. citizens to foreigners in those years.

Goods the United States exports must be paid for in dollars so, in order to buy U.S. exports, foreigners must exchange their currencies for dollars. Exports involve a flow of payments into the United States, so they have a plus sign in the balance of payments accounts. Similarly, U.S. imports must be paid for in foreign currency; they involve a flow of dollars out of the United States, and thus they have a minus sign. Notice that the bottom line of the balance of payments is $0. By definition, the bottom line (which includes all supplies and demands for currencies, including those of the government) must add up to zero whenever a currency is freely tradable for other currencies.

As you can see in Table 35-1, the balance of payments account is broken down into the current account and the financial and capital account. The **current account** (lines 1–11) is *the part of the balance of payments account in which flows of payments related to goods and services are listed*. It includes exports and imports, which are what we normally mean when we talk about the trade balance. The **financial and capital account** (lines 12–15) is *the part of the balance of payments account in which flows of payments related to the buying and selling of financial and capital assets are listed*. If a U.S. citizen buys a German stock, or if a Japanese company buys a U.S. company, the transaction shows up on this account.

The current account is the part of the balance of payments account that lists all short-term flows of payments.

The financial and capital account is the part of the balance of payments account that lists all long-term flows of payments.

The U.S. government can influence the exchange rate (the rate at which one currency trades for another) by buying and selling *official reserves* (government holdings of foreign currencies), or by buying and selling other international reserves, such as gold. Such buying shows up in the financial and capital account as a subcomponent of net U.S. acquisitions of foreign financial assets (line 13). We don't separate it out here because in recent years U.S. international reserve transactions have been relatively small. Foreign governments can also influence the U.S. exchange rate by buying and selling reserves. Such buying and selling is included in net foreign acquisitions of U.S. financial assets (line 14).

To get a better idea of what's included in these accounts, let's consider each of them more carefully.

The Current Account

Looking at Table 35-1, you can see that the current account is composed of the merchandise (or goods) account (lines 1–3), the services account (lines 4–6), the net investment income account (line 8), and the net transfers account (line 9).

Starting with the merchandise account, notice that in 2017 the United States imported $2,360.9 billion worth of goods and exported $1,553.4 billion worth of goods. *The difference between the value of goods exported and the value of goods imported* is called the **balance of merchandise trade.** Looking at line 3, you can see that the United States had a balance of merchandise trade deficit of $807.5 billion in 2017.

The merchandise trade balance is often discussed in the press as a summary of how the United States is doing in the international markets. It's not a good summary. Trade in services is just as important as trade in merchandise, so economists pay more attention to the combined balance of goods and services.

Thus, the **balance of trade**—*the difference between the value of goods and services exported and imported*—(line 7) becomes a key statistic for economists. Notice that in 2017 most of the U.S. trade deficit resulted from an imbalance in the merchandise account. The services account worked in the opposite direction. In 2017 the services account reduced the trade deficit by $255.2 billion. Such services include tourist expenditures and insurance payments by foreigners to U.S. firms. For instance, when you travel in Japan, you spend yen, which you must buy with dollars; this is an outflow of payments, which is a negative contribution to the services account.

There is no reason that in a particular year the goods and services sent into a country must equal the goods and services sent out, even if the current account is in equilibrium, because the current account also includes payments from past investments and net transfers. When you invest, you expect to make a return on that investment. The payments to foreign owners of U.S. capital assets are a negative contribution to the U.S. balance of payments. The payment to U.S. owners of foreign capital assets is a positive contribution to the U.S. balance of payments. These payments on investment income are a type of holdover from past trade and services imbalances. So even though they relate to investments, they show up on the current account.

The final component of the current account is net transfers, which include foreign aid, gifts, and other payments to individuals not exchanged for goods or services. If you transfer $1,000 to your aunt in Mexico, it shows up with a minus sign here.

Adding up the pluses and minuses on the current account, we arrive at line 11, the current account balance. Notice that in 2017 the United States had a deficit of $449.2 billion (line 11). That means that, in the current account, the supply of dollars greatly exceeded the demand for dollars. If the current account represented the total supply of and demand for dollars, the value of the dollar would have fallen. But it doesn't represent the total. There is also the financial and capital account.

The balance of trade is the difference between the value of goods and services exported and imported.

Q-1 If you, a U.S. citizen, are traveling abroad, where will your expenditures show up in the balance of payments accounts?

Payments on investment income show up on the current account.

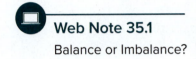

Web Note 35.1

Balance or Imbalance?

The Financial and Capital Account

The financial and capital account measures the flow of payments between countries for financial assets such as stocks, bonds, and ownership rights to real estate. Table 35-1 breaks it into three subcategories: (1) the net financial and capital derivatives account (line 12), which is relatively small and includes the buying and selling of some esoteric financial instruments that are best left to upper-level courses; (2) net U.S. acquisitions of foreign financial assets (such as bonds, stocks, and ownership rights to real estate) (line 13); and (3) net foreign acquisitions of U.S. financial assets (line 14). The combination of these three flows makes up the balance on the financial and capital account. As you can see this balance in 2017 was $378.1 billion, which means there was a net foreign acquisition of U.S. assets, which translates into a net demand for $378.1 billion U.S. dollars by foreigners stemming from the financial and capital account.

In thinking about what determines a currency's value, it's important to remember both the demand for dollars to buy goods and services and the demand for dollars to buy assets.

Because the supply of dollars going out of a country and the demand for dollars coming into a country must be equal if a country has a convertible currency—that is, a currency that is freely exchanged for other currencies—we'd expect the current account deficit (which represents a net demand for dollars) to completely offset the balance on the financial and capital account. Adding the two balances (line 11 + line 15), we see that it does not. There is a $71.1 billion difference. Since by accounting definition the two must be equal, there must have been some measurement errors. Economic accountants resolve the problem by adjusting for those measurement errors (line 16). After adjusting for these measurement errors, the balance of payments (line 17) is zero.

What Is Meant by a Balance of Payments Deficit or Surplus?

The data on financial and capital flows in Table 35-1 combine government and private demand for assets. When economists say that a country is running a balance of payments deficit or surplus, they are separating out government's sale and purchases of foreign financial assets from private purchases or sales of U.S. financial assets. This means that the private balance of payments (without government) may be in surplus or in deficit, as long as that private imbalance is offset by a government imbalance in the other direction. So when one says that a country is running a balance of payments deficit, one actually means that the private sector is running a balance of payments deficit. Where there is a private balance of payments deficit, the private sector's supply of a country's currency is greater than the private sector's demand for that currency. But as long as there is free trading in the currency, the government must offset the difference; it buys its currency in the foreign exchange market (paying for it with foreign currency it has stored up) thereby making the quantity of currency supplied equal to the quantity of currency demanded.

While the current and financial accounts offset each other, there is a difference between the long-run effects of the demand for dollars to buy currently produced goods and services and the demand for dollars to buy assets.

While the supply of and demand for dollars reflected in the current and financial accounts offset each other, there is a difference between the long-run effects of the demand for dollars to buy currently produced goods and services (from the current account) and the demand for dollars to buy assets (the financial and capital account). Assets earn profits or interest, so when foreigners buy U.S. assets, they earn income from those assets just for owning them. As discussed above, the net investment income from foreigners' previous asset purchases shows up on line 8 of the current account.

If assets earned equal rates of returns in the United States and abroad, we would expect that when foreigners own more U.S. assets than U.S. citizens own foreign assets, net investment income from assets (line 10) would be negative. Similarly, if U.S. citizens own more foreign assets than foreigners own U.S. assets, net investment income should be positive. Why is this? Because net investment income is the difference between the returns on U.S. assets held abroad and foreign assets held in the United States.

The Exorbitant Privilege Puzzle

In 1985, the United States became a net debtor nation, which means that it owed other countries more than it was owed by other countries. Most economists, me included, believed that the result would be that net investment income (line 8 of Table 35-1) would switch from positive to negative. It didn't happen right away, which was a puzzle. We economists explained the puzzle by the differing compositions of the debt, and the undervaluation of the U.S. holdings abroad. We pointed out that much U.S. investment involved direct foreign investment—think of it as equity investment, and much foreign

©Ieva Geneviciene/Shutterstock

investment in the United States involved bond financing, which paid lower interest. Moreover, the U.S. investment was made earlier and, because of accounting conventions, was valued far below what its true value was. These are reasonable explanations, but we thought the explanations were temporary, and that within a decade, or possibly two, U.S. net transfers would become negative.

The problem is that more than three decades later, investment income is still positive even as the United States is in an even greater debtor position, meaning we still have to use these temporary explanations for an unexpected outcome. Our "reasonable" explanations are not so reasonable for this ongoing phenomenon, unless we can explain why foreigners are willing to hold dollar assets that pay so much less than what they could earn by investing elsewhere. The phenomenon has acquired the name the "exorbitant privilege puzzle": Why does the United States get to pay far less for its borrowings than other countries?

Part of the explanation is that the U.S. dollar remains the closest thing to a reserve currency that the world has, which increases the demand for U.S. cash holdings and for dollar-denominated deposits. Another likely explanation involves political safety of assets. If you worry your government is going to take away your assets, as many of the rich people in developing countries do, you'd prefer to hold them somewhere else where they would be safe, such as the United States. With these additions, the puzzle is partially solved, but it suggests that political risk and safety play a much larger role in people's decision making than economists' international trade and finance models allow. Models that don't take political safety and reserve currency status into account are missing important elements.

Since the 1980s, the inflow of capital into the United States has greatly exceeded the outflow of capital from the United States. As a result, the United States has become a net debtor nation; the amount foreigners own in the United States now exceeds the amount U.S. citizens own abroad by about $8 trillion. So we would expect that U.S. investment income would be highly negative. But looking at line 8 of Table 35-1, we see that was not the case. The reason? Foreigners' returns from investments in the United States have been low, and many of the foreign assets owned by U.S. citizens abroad are undervalued.

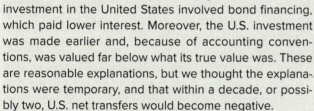

Q-2 How can net investment income be positive if a country is a net debtor nation?

Exchange Rates

Let's now consider how exchange rates are determined. In Figure 35-1, I present the forex (foreign exchange) market supply and demand curves for the Chinese yuan, with quantity of yuan on the quantity axis and price of yuan in terms of dollars on the price axis. At the market equilibrium at point *A,* one yuan costs 20 cents. Since the quantity of yuan supplied to the market equals the quantity of yuan demanded, the balance of payments is zero. Let's say now that Chinese consumers decide they want to buy more American goods. Since they must pay for those goods in U.S. dollars, they will supply yuan to the forex market. The supply curve of yuan shifts out from S_0 to S_1 and its price falls to 16 cents per yuan. If the price of yuan remained at 20 cents, the quantity of yuan supplied would exceed the

Web Note 35.2

The Dollar: High or Low?

FIGURE 35-1   **Exchange Rate Determination**

As long as you keep quantities and prices *of what* straight, the standard, or fundamental, analysis of the determination of exchange rates is easy. Just remember that if you're talking about the supply of and demand for yuan, the price will be measured in dollars and the quantity will be in yuan.

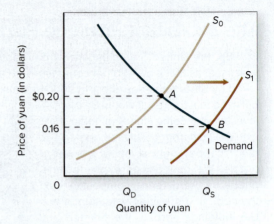

quantity of yuan demanded, and China's balance of payments would be in deficit. But assuming that the Chinese currency is fully convertible, the balance of payments (including both government and private demands and supplies of currencies) cannot be in deficit. It must be zero. The decline in price of the yuan eliminates the deficit.

The source of the increase in supply of yuan does not have to come from the private sector. It could also come from government, which could decide to supply yuan to the forex market to buy dollars. This is what has been happening for most of the past decade. This sustained Chinese government supply of yuan in the financial and capital account has allowed China to run a trade surplus (which allows the United States to run a trade deficit) at a lower value of the yuan than would have been the case had the exchange rate been determined by only the current account and private flows in the financial and capital account.

Fundamental Forces Determining Exchange Rates

Now that we have been through the determination of exchange rates within a supply and demand framework, let's summarize some of the fundamental forces that determine the supply of and demand for currencies, and hence cause them to shift. These fundamental forces include a country's income, a country's prices, the interest rate in a country, and the country's trade policy. That means that changes in a country's income, changes in a country's prices, and changes in interest rates can cause the supply of and demand for a currency to shift. Let's consider how they do so.

CHANGES IN A COUNTRY'S INCOME   The demand for imports depends on the income in a country. When a country's income falls, demand for imports falls. Hence, demand for foreign currency to buy those imports falls, which means that the supply of the country's currency to buy the foreign currency falls. How important is this relationship? Very important. For example, in the early 2000s, strong economic growth in the United States relative to its primary trading partners led to increased imports, which increased the supply of U.S. dollars. The increase in supply tended to lower the price of the dollar relative to foreign currencies.

CHANGES IN A COUNTRY'S PRICES   The United States' demand for imports and foreign countries' demand for U.S. exports depend on prices of U.S. goods compared to prices of foreign competing goods. If the United States has more inflation than other countries, foreign goods will become relatively cheaper, U.S. demand for foreign currencies will tend to increase, and foreign demand for dollars will tend to decrease. This rise in U.S. inflation will shift the dollar supply outward and the dollar demand inward.

CHANGES IN INTEREST RATES People like to invest their savings in assets that will yield the highest return. Other things equal, a rise in U.S. interest rates relative to those abroad will increase demand for U.S. assets. As a result, demand for dollars will increase, while simultaneously the supply of dollars will decrease as fewer Americans sell their dollars to buy foreign assets. A fall in the U.S. interest rate or a rise in foreign interest rates will have the opposite effect.

SOME EXAMPLES To make sure that you've understood the analysis, let's consider some examples. First, the U.S. economy goes into recession with interest rates remaining constant—what will likely happen to exchange rates? Second, the Mexican economy has runaway inflation—what will likely happen to the exchange rate for pesos? And third, the interest rate on yen-denominated assets increases—what will likely happen to the exchange rate value of the yen? If you answered: The value of the dollar will rise, the value of the peso will fall, and the value of the yen will rise, you're following the argument. If those weren't your answers, a review is in order.

Exchange Rate Dynamics

The supply/demand analysis may have made it look like exchange rates are driven by fundamentals. Unfortunately, that is not always the case. In day-to-day trading, fundamentals can be overwhelmed by expectations of how a currency will change in value. The supply and demand curves for currencies can shift around rapidly in response to rumors, expectations, and expectations of expectations. As they shift, they bring about large fluctuations in exchange rates that make trading difficult and have significant real effects on economic activity.

Let me outline just one potential problem. Say you expect the price of the currency to fall one-half of 1 percent tomorrow. What should you do? The correct answer is: Sell that currency quickly. Why? One-half of 1 percent may not sound like much, but, annualized, it is equivalent to a rate of interest per year of 617 percent. Based on that expectation, if you're into making money (and you're really sure about the fall), you will sell all of that currency that you hold, and borrow all you can so you can sell some more. You can make big money if you guess small changes in exchange rates correctly. (Of course, if you're wrong, you can lose big money.) This means that if the market generally believes the exchange rates will move, those expectations will tend to be self-fulfilling. Self-fulfilling expectations undermine the argument in favor of letting markets determine exchange rates: When expectations rule, the exchange rate may not reflect actual demands and supplies of goods. Instead, the exchange rate can reflect expectations and rumors. The resulting fluctuations serve no real purpose, and cause problems for international trade and the country's economy. Let's consider an example.

Suppose that a firm decides to build a plant in the United States because costs in the United States are low. But suppose also that the value of the dollar then rises significantly; the firm's costs rise significantly too, making it uncompetitive. When currencies fluctuate, companies find it harder to make good decisions on where to produce.

In a real-world example, from July to September 1997, the value of the Thai baht fell nearly 40 percent. Goodyear (Thailand), which had been one of the five most profitable companies on the Stock Exchange of Thailand, suddenly faced a 20 percent rise in the costs of raw materials because it paid for those raw materials in dollars. It also faced a decline in tire prices because the demand for tires had fallen 20 to 40 percent when the Thai economy contracted. Within just two months, a highly profitable venture had become unprofitable. Other firms were closing shop because they were unable to pay the

Q-3 Why don't most governments leave determination of the exchange rate to the market?

Fundamental Forces and Exchange Rates

The fundamental forces affecting exchange rates were covered a number of chapters ago, so let's review them. The four forces are (1) changes in a country's income, (2) changes in a country's prices, (3) changes in interest rates, and (4) changes in trade policy. Increased trade barriers tend to push up the value of a country's currency. Here are the effects for the other three:

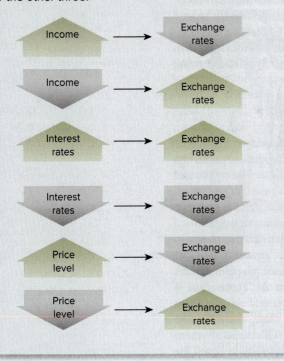

A country fixes the exchange rate by standing ready to buy and sell its currency anytime the exchange rate is not at the fixed exchange rate.

A country can maintain a fixed exchange rate above its market price only as long as it has the reserves.

Q-4 In general, would it be easier for the United States to push the value of the dollar down or up? Why?

interest on loans that were denominated in dollars. In summary, large fluctuations make real trade difficult and cause serious real consequences.

The problems caused by fluctuating exchange rates have led to calls for government to intervene and either stabilize or fix its exchange rate directly by buying or selling its currency. It can increase the value of its currency by buying its currency, assuming it has international reserves to buy it with. Alternatively, it can decrease the value of its currency by selling its currency. This ability of a country to buy and sell its currency means that, assuming it has sufficient reserves, a country can fix its currency at a specific level.

CURRENCY SUPPORT Let's now consider an example of currency support, in this case the euro. Let's say that the European Union's central bank wants to keep the price of the euro higher than it otherwise would be. Suppose that, given the interaction of private supply and demand forces, the equilibrium value of the euro is $1.00 a euro, but the European Union wants to maintain a value of $1.20 a euro. This is shown in Figure 35-2. At $1.20 a euro, quantity supplied exceeds quantity demanded. The European Union must buy the surplus, $Q_2 - Q_1$, using official reserves (foreign currency holdings). In doing so, it shifts the total demand for euros to D_1, making the equilibrium market exchange rate (including the European government's demand for euros) equal to $1.20. This process is called **currency support**—the *buying of a currency by a government to maintain its value at above its long-run equilibrium value.* It is a direct exchange rate policy. If a government has sufficient official reserves, or if it can convince other governments to lend it reserves, it can fix the exchange rate at the rate it wants, no matter what the private level of supply and demand is. In reality, governments have no such power to support currencies in the long run since their official reserves are limited. For example, in 2002 the Argentinean government tried to keep its currency fixed to the U.S. dollar, but it ran out of official reserves and was forced to let its currency decline in value.

A country has more power to prevent the value of its currency from rising since it can create its own money. As discussed above, that's what happened with the Chinese yuan in the early 2000s. China supplied yuan to the forex market to buy dollars, thereby meeting the demand for yuan created by the demand for Chinese exports. Since China can create all the yuan it wants, it can hold the value of the yuan below its equilibrium price much more easily than it can hold it above its equilibrium price.

If one country wants to hold the value of its currency down and another wants to hold the value of its currency up, they have a large incentive to cooperate. Of course, cooperation requires an agreement on the goals, and often countries' goals conflict. In the case of China and the United States, their goals differed. Both wanted to hold the value of their currencies low, which was impossible. One role of the various international economic organizations is to provide a forum for reaching agreement on exchange rate goals and a vehicle through which cooperation can take place.

CURRENCY STABILIZATION A more viable long-run exchange rate policy is **currency stabilization**—the *buying and selling of a currency by the government to*

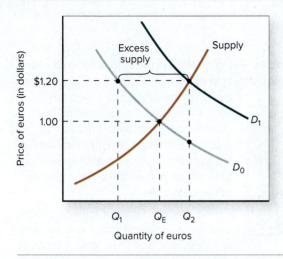

FIGURE 35-2 **A Demonstration of Direct Exchange Rate Policy**

If the government chooses to hold the exchange rate at $1.20, when the equilibrium is $1.00, there is an excess supply given by $Q_2 - Q_1$. The government purchases this excess (using official reserves) and closes the difference, thus maintaining equilibrium.

offset temporary fluctuations in supply and demand for currencies. In currency stabilization, the government is not trying to change the long-run equilibrium; it is simply trying to keep the exchange rate at that long-run equilibrium. The government sometimes buys and sometimes sells currency, so it is far less likely to run out of reserves.

Successful currency stabilization requires the government to choose the correct long-run equilibrium exchange rate. A policy of stabilization can become a policy of support if the government chooses too high a long-run equilibrium. Unfortunately, government has no way of knowing for sure what the long-run equilibrium exchange rate is.

In most cases given the small level of official reserves compared to the enormous level of private trading, significant amounts of stabilization are impossible. Instead, governments use *strategic currency stabilization*—buying and selling at strategic moments to affect expectations of traders, and hence to affect their supply and demand. Such issues are discussed in depth in international finance courses.

> Strategic currency stabilization is the process of buying and selling at strategic moments to affect the expectations of traders, and hence affect their supply and demand.

Influencing Exchange Rates with Monetary and Fiscal Policy

Governments can also influence exchange rates—both directly, as would be the case if the Chinese central bank sold yuan and bought dollars, increasing the supply of yuan and pushing the value of the yuan down, and indirectly through monetary and fiscal policy. Let's consider that indirect approach.

MONETARY POLICY'S EFFECT ON EXCHANGE RATES   Monetary policy affects exchange rates in three primary ways: (1) through its effect on the interest rate, (2) through its effect on income, and (3) through its effect on price levels and inflation.

The Effect on Exchange Rates via Interest Rates   Expansionary monetary policy pushes down the U.S. interest rate, which decreases the financial inflow into the United States, decreasing the demand for dollars, pushing down the value of the dollar, and decreasing the U.S. exchange rate. Contractionary monetary policy does the opposite. It raises the U.S. interest rate, which tends to bring in financial capital flows from abroad, increasing the demand for dollars, increasing the value of the dollar, and increasing the U.S. exchange rate. This interest rate effect is the dominant short-run effect, and it often overwhelms the other effects.

To see why these effects take place, consider a person in Japan in the early 2000s, when the Japanese interest rate was close to 0 percent. He or she reasoned, "Why

> **Q-5**   What effect does the lowering of a country's interest rates have on exchange rates?

> The interest rate effect on exchange rates is the dominant short-run effect.

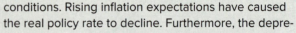
Iceland's Monetary Woes

In 2006, the inflation rate in Iceland exceeded its target inflation rate, and investors became worried. The financial press began to issue comments such as this: "The negative outlook has been triggered by a material deterioration in Iceland's macro-prudential risk indicators, accompanied by an unsustainable current account deficit and soaring net external indebtedness." A group of developed countries, the Organisation for Economic Co-operation and Development (OECD), warned that the failure to bring inflation down could damage the country's international credibility, and that "in the absence of swift and vigorous policy action, financial market stability could be at risk."

©Stockbyte/Getty Images

In response to these and other warnings, foreign exchange traders began selling króna, Iceland's currency. The króna's value started to decline, which led the Central Bank of Iceland to tighten the money supply and raise interest rates. In 2006 the Central Bank of Iceland issued the following statement:

> Economic developments since the end of March indicate that a considerable increase in the policy rate may be required to maintain sufficiently tight monetary

conditions. Rising inflation expectations have caused the real policy rate to decline. Furthermore, the depreciation of the króna has eased conditions in the traded goods sector. The current policy rate hike is intended to respond to these developments. Attaining the inflation target within an acceptable period of time is the firm intention of the Central Bank.

The Central Bank of Iceland continued raising interest rates substantially, to 12 percent and then to 13.5 percent, stating that "further rises were unavoidable." In mid-2007, the interest rate was about 15 percent while inflation had decreased to less than 6 percent.

That temporarily resolved the short-run problem, but it did not resolve the longer-run problem of massive external indebtedness of all Icelandic banks. In 2008, when the global credit crisis hit the world economy, that indebtedness caused all the Icelandic banks to fail, and the Icelandic government had nowhere near the money needed to support them. This led to a freezing up of the exchange markets for the króna, and Iceland was forced to take large loans from other countries to help reestablish a viable banking system. It took until 2015 for the Icelandic economy to recover.

---

should I earn 0 percent return in Japan? I'll save (buy some financial assets) in the United States where I'll earn 3 percent." If the U.S. interest rate is higher due to contraction in the money supply, other things equal, the advantage of holding one's financial assets in the United States will become even greater and more people will want to save here. People in Japan hold yen, not dollars, so in order to save in the United States they must buy dollars. Thus, a rise in U.S. interest rates increases demand for dollars and, in terms of yen, pushes up the U.S. exchange rate. This example illustrates that it is relative interest rates that govern the flow of financial assets.

Countries are continually taking into account the effect of monetary policy on exchange rates. For example, in 2014 the European Central Bank increased its money supply, significantly lowering interest rates, thereby lowering the value of the euro in order to make European exports more attractive.

The Effect on Exchange Rates via Income   Monetary policy also affects income in a country. As money supply rises, income expands; when money supply falls, income contracts.[1] This effect on income provides another way in which the money supply affects

---

[1] When there's inflation, it's the rate of money supply growth relative to the rate of inflation that's important. If inflation is 10 percent and money supply growth is 10 percent, the rate of increase in the real money supply is zero. If money supply growth falls to, say, 5 percent while inflation stays at 10 percent, there will be a contractionary effect on the real economy.

the exchange rate. When income rises, imports rise while exports are unaffected. To buy foreign products, U.S. citizens need foreign currency, which they must buy with dollars. So when U.S. imports rise, the supply of dollars to the foreign exchange market increases as U.S. citizens sell dollars to buy foreign currencies to pay for those imports. This decreases the dollar exchange rate. This effect through income and imports provides a second path through which monetary policy affects the exchange rate: Expansionary monetary policy causes U.S. income to rise, imports to rise, and the U.S. exchange rate to fall via the income path. Contractionary monetary policy causes U.S. income to fall, imports to fall, and the U.S. exchange rate to rise via the income path.

The Effect on Exchange Rates via Price Levels   A third way in which monetary policy can affect exchange rates is through its effect on prices in a country. Expansionary monetary policy pushes up the U.S. price level. As the U.S. price level rises relative to foreign prices, U.S. exports become more expensive, and goods the United States imports become relatively cheaper, decreasing U.S. competitiveness. This increases demand for foreign currencies and decreases demand for dollars. Thus, via the price path, expansionary monetary policy pushes down the dollar's value for the same reason that an expansion in income pushes it down.

Contractionary monetary policy puts downward pressure on the U.S. price level and slows down any existing inflation. As the U.S. price level falls relative to foreign prices, U.S. exports become more competitive and the goods the United States imports, relatively more expensive. Thus, contractionary monetary policy pushes up the value of the dollar via the price path.

The Net Effect of Monetary Policy on Exchange Rates   Notice that all these effects of monetary policy on exchange rates are in the same direction. Expansionary monetary policy pushes a country's exchange rate down; contractionary monetary policy pushes a country's exchange rate up. Summarizing these effects, we have the following relationships for expansionary and contractionary monetary policy:

Q-6   What effect would contractionary monetary policy have on a country's exchange rates?

Monetary policy affects exchange rates through the interest rate path, the income path, and the price-level path, as shown in the accompanying diagram.

Expansionary monetary policy

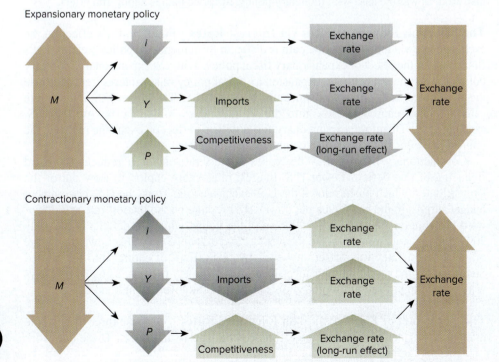

Contractionary monetary policy

There are, of course, many provisos to the relationship between monetary policy and the exchange rate. For example, as the exchange rate falls, the price of imports goes up and there is some inflationary pressure from that rise in price and hence some pressure for the price level to rise as well as fall. Monetary policy affects exchange rates in subtle ways, but if an economist had to give a quick answer to what effect monetary policy would have on exchange rates, it would be:

Expansionary monetary policy lowers exchange rates. It decreases the relative value of a country's currency.

Contractionary monetary policy increases exchange rates. It increases the relative value of a country's currency.

FISCAL POLICY'S EFFECT ON EXCHANGE RATES   The effect of fiscal policy on exchange rates is not so clear. The reason why can be seen by considering its effects on income, the price level, and interest rates.

The Effect on Exchange Rates via Income   Expansionary fiscal policy expands income and therefore increases imports, increasing the trade deficit and lowering the exchange rate. Contractionary fiscal policy contracts income, thereby decreasing imports and increasing the exchange rate. These effects of expansionary and contractionary fiscal policy via the income path are similar to the effects of monetary policy, so if it's not intuitively clear to you why the effect is what it is, it may be worthwhile to review the more complete discussion of monetary policy's effect presented previously.

The Effect on Exchange Rates via Price Levels   Let's next turn to the effect of fiscal policy on exchange rates through prices. Expansionary fiscal policy increases aggregate demand and increases prices of a country's exports; hence, it decreases the competitiveness of a country's exports, which pushes down the exchange rate. Contractionary fiscal policy works in the opposite direction. These are the same effects that monetary policy had. And, as was the case with monetary policy, the price path is a long-run effect.

The Effect on Exchange Rates via Interest Rates   Fiscal policy's effect on the exchange rate via the interest rate path is different from monetary policy's effect. Let's first consider the effect of expansionary fiscal policy. Whereas expansionary monetary policy lowers the interest rate, expansionary fiscal policy raises interest rates because the government sells bonds to finance that budget deficit. The higher U.S. interest rate causes foreign capital to flow into the United States, which pushes up the U.S. exchange rate. Therefore, expansionary fiscal policy's effect on exchange rates via the interest rate effect is to push up a country's exchange rate.

Contractionary fiscal policy decreases interest rates since it reduces the bond financing of that deficit. Lower U.S. interest rates cause capital to flow out of the United States, which pushes down the U.S. exchange rate. Thus, the U.S. government budget surplus in the late 1990s put downward pressure on the interest rate and downward pressure on the exchange rate value of the dollar, while the deficits in the early 2000s put upward pressure on the interest rate and exchange rate. That upward pressure on the interest rates was offset, however, by large flows of capital into the United States not for the return on their investment, but for safety reasons, as many investors were attempting to get out of other assets and into U.S. government bonds.

The Net Effect of Fiscal Policy on Exchange Rates   Of these three effects, the interest rate effect and the income effect are both short-run effects. These two work

---

Expansionary monetary policy lowers exchange rates. It decreases the relative value of a country's currency.

Contractionary monetary policy increases exchange rates. It increases the relative value of a country's currency.

Q-7   What is the net effect of expansionary fiscal policy on the exchange rate?

in opposite directions, so the net effect of fiscal policy on the exchange rate is, in general, ambiguous, although in specific instances either the interest rate effect or the income effect may swamp the other. The following diagram summarizes these three effects.

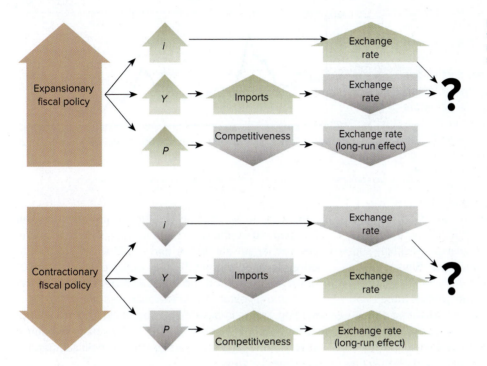

Fiscal policy affects exchange rates through the income path, the interest rate path, and the price-level path, as shown in the accompanying diagram.

As you can see, it's unclear what the effect of expansionary or contractionary fiscal policy will be on exchange rates.

The Problems of Determining the Appropriate Exchange Rate

To intervene effectively in foreign exchange markets, the government must know the appropriate exchange rate to target. If the government targets the wrong exchange rate, its interventions can cause more problems than they solve. Unfortunately, the government can only guess the appropriate long-run rate since no definitive empirical measure of this rate exists. The long-run equilibrium must be estimated. If that estimate is wrong, a sustainable stabilization policy becomes an unsustainable deviation from long-run equilibrium policy. Thus, a central issue in exchange rate intervention policy is estimating the long-run equilibrium exchange rate.

To intervene effectively in foreign exchange markets, the government must know the appropriate exchange rate to target.

Purchasing Power Parity and Real Exchange Rates

Purchasing power parity is one way economists have of estimating the long-run equilibrium rate. **Purchasing power parity (PPP)** is *a method of calculating exchange rates that attempts to value currencies at rates such that each currency will buy an equal basket of goods.* It is based on the idea that the exchange of currencies reflects

Purchasing power parity is a method of calculating exchange rates that attempts to value currencies at rates such that each currency will buy an equal basket of goods.

Determining the Causes of Fluctuations in the Dollar's Value

As you can see on the graph, the dollar's value has fluctuated considerably since 1973. A good exercise to see if you understand movements in the value of the dollar is to try to choose which factors caused the fluctuation.

Let's start with the relatively small fluctuations in the mid-1970s. These probably reflected expectational bubbles—in which speculators were more concerned with short-run fluctuations than long-run fundamentals—while the dollar's low value in 1979 and 1980 reflected high inflation, relatively low real interest rates, and the booming U.S. economy during this period.

The rise of the dollar in the early 1980s reflected higher real U.S. interest rates and the falling U.S. inflation rate, although the rise was much more than expected and probably reflected speculation, as did the sudden fall in the dollar's value in 1985. Similarly, the fluctuations in the late 1980s and early 1990s reflected both changing interest rates in the United States and changing foreign interest rates, as well as changing relative inflation rates.

In the late 1990s and early 2000s the value of the dollar rose substantially. Part of the explanation for this lies in the weakness of the Japanese economy, which led the Japanese central bank to increase the Japanese money supply, thereby lowering the Japanese interest rate. That weakness also was reflected in the fall in the prices of Japanese stocks. That fall led investors to shift out of

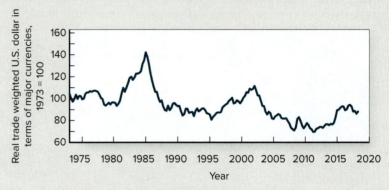

Source: Board of Governors, Federal Reserve System (www.federalreserve.gov).

Japanese stocks and into U.S. stocks, thereby increasing the demand for the dollar, and pushing up the U.S. effective exchange rate. In the early 2000s, the value of the dollar declined as the U.S. trade deficit expanded. In 2011, however, it began rising when Europe lowered interest rates and investors became concerned about the risk of holding assets in developing countries. The value of the dollar began to decline in 2017 as European economies strengthened and investors reacted to political turmoil in the United States.

As you can see, after the fact we economists are pretty good at explaining the movements in the exchange rates. Alas, before the fact we aren't so good because often speculative activities make the timing of the movements unpredictable.

---

the exchange of real goods. If you are able to exchange a basket of goods from country X for an equivalent basket of goods from country Z, you should also be able to exchange the amount of currency from country X that is needed to purchase country X's basket of goods for the amount of currency from country Z that is needed to purchase country Z's basket of goods. For example, say that the yen is valued at 100 yen to $1. Say also that you can buy the same basket of goods for 1,000 yen that you can buy for $7. In that case, the purchasing power parity exchange rate would be 143 yen to $1 (1,000/7 = 143) compared to an actual exchange rate of 100 yen to $1. An economist would say that at 100 to the dollar the yen is overvalued—with 100 yen you could not purchase a basket of goods equivalent to the basket of goods you could purchase with $1.

Table 35-2 shows various calculations for purchasing power parity for a variety of countries. The second column shows the 2018 actual exchange rates. The third column shows purchasing power parity exchange rates. The fourth column shows the difference

Web Note 35.3

The Big Mac Index

TABLE 35-2 Actual and Purchasing Power Parity Exchange Rates for 2018

Country	Actual Exchange Rate (currency per dollar)	PPP Exchange Rate (currency per dollar)	Under (−)/ Over (+) valuation
Switzerland	0.96	1.23	28.1
Sweden	8.02	9.30	16.0
United States	1.00	1.00	0.0
Brazil	3.23	3.13	−3.1
United Kingdom	0.72	0.60	−16.7
Japan	110.73	71.97	−35.0
China	6.43	3.86	−40.0
Turkey	3.80	2.04	−46.3
South Africa	12.26	5.86	−52.2
Russia	56.75	24.62	−56.6

Source: www.economist.com/content/big-mac-index.

between the two, or the 2018 distortion in the exchange rates (if you believe the PPP exchange rates are the correct ones).

Criticisms of the Purchasing Power Parity Method

For many economists, estimating exchange rates using PPP has serious problems. If the currency is overvalued and will eventually fall, why don't traders use that information and sell that currency now, making it fall now? After all, they are out to make a profit. So if there is open trading in a currency, any expected change in the exchange rate will affect exchange rates now. If traders don't sell now when there are expectations that a currency's overvaluation will eventually make its value fall, they must believe there is some reason that its value won't, in fact, fall.

Critics argue that the difficulty with PPP exchange rates is the complex nature of trade and consumption. They point out that the PPP will change as the basket of goods changes. This means that there is no one PPP measure. They also point out that, since all PPP measures leave out asset demand for a currency, the measures are missing an important element of the demand. Critics ask: Is there any reason to assume that in the long run the asset demand for a currency is less important than the goods demand for a currency? Because the asset demand for a currency is important, critics of PPP argue that there is little reason to assume that the short-run actual exchange rate will ever adjust to the PPP exchange rates. And if that rate doesn't adjust, then PPP does not provide a good estimate of the equilibrium rate. These critics further contend that the existing exchange rate is the best estimate of the long-run equilibrium exchange rate.

Purchasing power parity exchange rates may or may not be appropriate long-run exchange rates.

Real Exchange Rates

Regardless of one's view of the usefulness of purchasing power parity, the concept gets at the importance of prices in the determination of exchange rates. Say, for example, that the price level in the United States goes up by 10 percent while the price level in Europe stays constant. In such a situation, we would expect some change in the exchange rate—the most likely effect would be that the U.S. dollar falls by 10 percent relative to the euro. To capture the distinction between changes in exchange rates caused by changes in price levels and changes in exchange rates caused by other things, economists differentiate between nominal and real exchange

A real exchange rate is an exchange rate adjusted for differential changes in the price level.

rates. A **real exchange rate** is *an exchange rate adjusted for differential changes in the price level.* A nominal exchange rate is the exchange rate you see in the papers— it is the rate you'd get when exchanging currencies.

Let's consider the above example: The U.S. price level rises by 10 percent, the European price level remains constant, and the nominal U.S. exchange rate falls by 10 percent. In that case, the real exchange rate will have remained constant. More generally, the change in the real exchange rate (foreign/domestic or in this case euro/dollar) can be approximately calculated by adding the difference in the rates of inflation between the two countries (Domestic inflation − Foreign inflation) to the percentage change in the nominal exchange rate.

Q-8   If U.S. inflation is 2 percent, the European Union's inflation rate is 4 percent, and the nominal U.S. dollar exchange rate rises by 3 percent relative to the euro, what happens to the real exchange rate of the dollar?

$$\begin{bmatrix} \%\Delta\ \text{real} \\ \text{exchange rate} \end{bmatrix} = \begin{bmatrix} \%\Delta\ \text{nominal} \\ \text{exchange rate} \end{bmatrix} + \begin{bmatrix} \text{Domestic} \\ \text{inflation} \end{bmatrix} - \begin{bmatrix} \text{Foreign} \\ \text{inflation} \end{bmatrix}$$

For example, say the U.S. price level had risen by 8 percent and Europe's had remained constant, but the U.S. nominal exchange rate had fallen by 10 percent. In that case, we would say that the real U.S. exchange rate had fallen by 2 percent.

$\%\Delta$ real exchange rate $= -10 + (8 - 0) = -2$ percent

Advantages and Disadvantages of Alternative Exchange Rate Systems

The problems of stabilizing exchange rates have led to an ongoing debate about whether a fixed exchange rate, a flexible exchange rate, or a combination of the two is best. This debate nicely captures the macro issues relevant to exchange rate stabilization, so in this section I consider that debate. First, a brief overview of the three alternative regimes:

Three exchange rate regimes are:

1. Fixed exchange rate: The government chooses an exchange rate and offers to buy and sell currencies at that rate.
2. Flexible exchange rate: Determination of exchange rates is totally left up to the market.
3. Partially flexible exchange rate: The government sometimes affects the exchange rate and sometimes leaves it to the market.

Fixed exchange rate: *The government chooses a particular exchange rate and offers to buy and sell its currency at that price.* For example, suppose the U.S. government says it will buy euros at 0.95 euro per dollar. In that case, we say that the United States has a fixed exchange rate of 0.95 euro to the dollar.

Flexible exchange rate: *The government does not enter into foreign exchange markets at all, but leaves the determination of exchange rates totally up to currency traders.* The price of its currency is allowed to rise and fall as private market forces dictate.

Partially flexible exchange rate: *The government sometimes buys or sells currencies to influence the exchange rate, while at other times letting private market forces operate.* A partially flexible exchange rate is sometimes called a dirty float because it isn't purely market-determined or government-determined.

Fixed Exchange Rates

The advantages of a fixed exchange rate system are:

1. Fixed exchange rates provide international monetary stability.
2. Fixed exchange rates force governments to make adjustments to meet their international problems.

The disadvantages of a fixed exchange rate system are:

1. Fixed exchange rates can become unfixed. When they're expected to become unfixed, they create enormous monetary instability.
2. Fixed exchange rates force governments to make adjustments to meet their international problems. (Yes, this is a disadvantage as well as an advantage.)

Let's consider each in turn.

FIXED EXCHANGE RATES AND EXCHANGE RATE STABILITY The advantage of fixed exchange rates is that firms know what exchange rates will be, making trade easier. However, to maintain fixed exchange rates, the government must choose an exchange rate and have sufficient official reserves to support that rate. If the rate it chooses is too high, its exports lag and the country continually loses official reserves. If the rate it chooses is too low, it is paying more for its imports than it needs to and is building up official reserves. Notice that, in principle, any trader could establish a fixed exchange rate by guaranteeing to buy or sell a currency at a given rate. Any "fix," however, is only as good as the guarantee, and to fix an exchange rate would require many more resources than an individual trader has; only governments have sufficient resources to fix an exchange rate, and often even governments run out of resources.

A major difficulty of fixing an exchange rate is that as soon as the country gets close to its official reserves limit, foreign exchange traders begin to expect a drop in the value of the currency, and they try to get out of that currency because anyone holding that currency when it falls will lose money. For example, in 2015, Malaysia's currency, the ringgit, fell substantially following a reported drop in its official reserves. False rumors of an expected depreciation or decrease in a country's fixed exchange rate can become true by causing a "run on a currency," as all traders sell that currency. Thus, at times fixed exchange rates can become highly unstable because expectation of a change in the exchange rate can force the change to occur. As opposed to small movements in currency values, under a fixed rate regime these movements occur in large, sudden jumps.

> Fixed exchange rates provide international monetary stability and force governments to make adjustments to meet their international problems. (This is *also* a disadvantage.) If they become unfixed, they create monetary instability.

FIXED EXCHANGE RATES AND POLICY INDEPENDENCE Maintaining a fixed exchange rate places limitations on a central bank's actions. In a country with fixed exchange rates, the central bank must ensure that the international quantities of its currency supplied and demanded are equal at the existing exchange rate.

Say, for example, that the United States and the Bahamas have fixed exchange rates: $1 B = $1 U.S. The Bahamian central bank decides to run an expansionary monetary policy, lowering the interest rate and stimulating the Bahamian economy. The lower interest rates will cause financial capital to flow out of the country, and the higher income will increase imports. Demand for Bahamian dollars will fall. To prop up its dollar and to maintain the fixed exchange rate, the Bahamian government will have to buy its own currency. It can do so only as long as it has sufficient official reserves of other countries' currencies.

Because most countries' official reserves are limited, a country with fixed exchange rates is limited in its ability to conduct expansionary monetary and fiscal policies. It loses its freedom to stimulate the economy in response to a recession. That's why, when a serious recession hits, many countries are forced to abandon fixed exchange rates. They run out of official reserves and let their exchange rate fall. They choose to direct their monetary policy at achieving their domestic goals rather than achieving their international policy goals.

> Because most countries' official reserves are limited, a country with fixed exchange rates is limited in its ability to conduct expansionary monetary and fiscal policies.

Flexible Exchange Rates

The advantages and disadvantages of a flexible exchange rate (exchange rates totally determined by private market forces) are the reverse of those of fixed exchange rates. The advantages are:

1. Flexible exchange rates provide for orderly incremental adjustment of exchange rates rather than large, sudden jumps.

2. Flexible exchange rates allow government to be flexible in conducting domestic monetary and fiscal policies.

The disadvantages are:

1. Flexible exchange rates allow speculation to cause large jumps in exchange rates, which do not reflect market fundamentals.

2. Flexible exchange rates allow government to be flexible in conducting domestic monetary and fiscal policies. (This is a disadvantage as well as an advantage.)

Let's consider each in turn.

FLEXIBLE EXCHANGE RATES AND EXCHANGE RATE STABILITY   Advocates of flexible exchange rates argue as follows: Why not treat currency markets like any other market and let private market forces determine a currency's value? There is no fixed price for TVs; why should there be a fixed price for currencies? The opponents' answer is based on the central role that international financial considerations play in an economy and the strange shapes and large shifts that occur in the short-run supply and demand curves for currencies.

When expectations shift supply and demand curves around all the time, there's no guarantee that the exchange rate will be determined by long-run fundamental forces. The economy will go through real gyrations because of speculators' expectations about other speculators. Thus, the argument against flexible exchange rates is that they allow far too much fluctuation in exchange rates, making trade difficult.

Flexible exchange rate regimes provide for orderly incremental adjustment of exchange rates rather than large sudden jumps, and allow governments to be flexible in conducting domestic monetary and fiscal policies. (This is also a disadvantage.)

FLEXIBLE EXCHANGE RATES AND POLICY INDEPENDENCE   The policy independence arguments for and against flexible exchange rates are the reverse of those given for fixed exchange rates. Individuals who believe that national governments should not have flexibility in setting monetary policy argue that flexible exchange rates don't impose the discipline on policy that fixed exchange rates do. Say, for example, that a country's goods are uncompetitive. Under a fixed exchange rate system, the country would have to contract its money supply and deal with the underlying uncompetitiveness of its goods. Under a flexible exchange rate system, the country can maintain an expansionary monetary policy, allowing inflation simply by permitting the value of its currency to fall.

Advocates of policy flexibility argue that it makes no sense for a country to go through a recession when it doesn't have to; flexible exchange rates allow countries more flexibility in dealing with their problems. True, policy flexibility may lead to inflation, but inflation is better than a recession.

Partially Flexible Exchange Rates

Faced with the dilemma of choosing between these two unpleasant policies, most countries have opted for a policy in between: partially flexible exchange rates. With such a policy, they try to get the advantages of both fixed and flexible exchange rates.

When policy makers believe there is a fundamental misalignment in a country's exchange rate, they will allow private forces to determine it—they allow the exchange rate to be flexible. When they believe that the currency's value is falling because of speculation, or that too large an adjustment in the currency is taking place, and that that adjustment won't achieve their balance of payments goals, they step in and stabilize the exchange rate, either supporting or pushing down their currency's value. Countries that follow a currency stabilization policy have partially flexible exchange rates.

Partially flexible exchange rate regimes combine the advantages and disadvantages of fixed and flexible exchange rates.

If policy makers are correct, this system of partial flexibility works smoothly and has the advantages of both fixed and flexible exchange rates. If policy makers are incorrect, however, a partially flexible system has the disadvantages of both fixed and flexible systems.

Which View Is Right?

Which view is correct is much in debate. Most foreign exchange traders I know tell me that the possibility of government intervention increases the amount of private speculation in the system. In the private investors' view, their own assessments of what exchange rates should be are better than those of policy makers. If private investors knew the government would not enter in, private speculators would focus on fundamentals and would stabilize short-run exchange rates. When private speculators know government might enter into the market, they don't focus on fundamentals; instead they continually try to outguess government policy makers. When that happens, private speculation doesn't stabilize; it destabilizes exchange rates as private traders try to guess what the government thinks.

Q-9 Does government intervention stabilize exchange rates?

Many of my economics colleagues who work for the Fed aren't convinced by private investors' arguments. They maintain that some government intervention helps stabilize currency markets. I don't know which group is right—private foreign exchange traders or economists at the Fed. But to decide, it is necessary to go beyond the arguments and consider how the various exchange rate regimes have worked in practice. The appendix to this chapter gives you an introduction into the history of exchange rate regimes.

Advantages and Disadvantages of a Common Currency: The Future of the Euro

If you think of countries with a fixed exchange rate as being in a marriage between currencies, you can think of a common currency (a shared currency among different countries) as a marriage for life, from which escape is almost impossible. All the business and legal contracts and institutions are structured around the common currency, and moving away from that will cause a legal morass. But common currencies also offer advantages, and there is no clear-cut economic rule about which exchange rate system is better.

In 2002 twelve European nations consummated a fixed exchange rate regime established under a European Union (EU) plan for monetary union and adopted the euro as their common currency. Later, more, but not all, European countries joined, with 28 countries belonging to the European Union as of 2018. (In 2016, the United Kingdom voted to leave the European Union, and in 2019 was in the midst of negotiating its withdrawal.) Of these, 19 use the euro as their currency, as indicated in Figure 35-3 with the euro symbol (€). Their experience provides a good example of both the advantages and disadvantages of moving from a fixed exchange rate system to a common currency.

The European countries that adopted the euro did so for a number of reasons, some political and some economic. Regardless of the reasons they did so, the euro will have significant effects on international finance and trade over the next decade.

ADVANTAGES OF THE EURO First, let's consider the advantages the EU countries get from adopting a common currency. The first advantage is that, politically, a common currency ties the countries closely together. World Wars I and II started from fights among European countries. An important motive behind the increasing integration of Europe—from initial creation of a common market, to the establishment of the European Union with reduced border controls, to the establishment of the monetary union—has been to prevent large-scale war within Europe from ever happening again. Many feel that political reasons drove the countries toward an economic and monetary union.

There were, however, also economic advantages. One was that monetary union reduced the cost of trading among countries by eliminating the need to exchange currencies and thereby provided an incentive to increase trade within the European Union. A second advantage was price transparency. With a single currency, consumers and

Web Note 35.4

Multinational Money

FIGURE 35-3   **Map of EU Countries That Use the Euro**

Countries that use the euro are Austria, Belgium, Cyprus, Estonia, Finland, France, Germany, Greece, Ireland, Italy, Latvia, Lithuania, Luxembourg, Malta, the Netherlands, Portugal, Slovakia, Slovenia, and Spain.

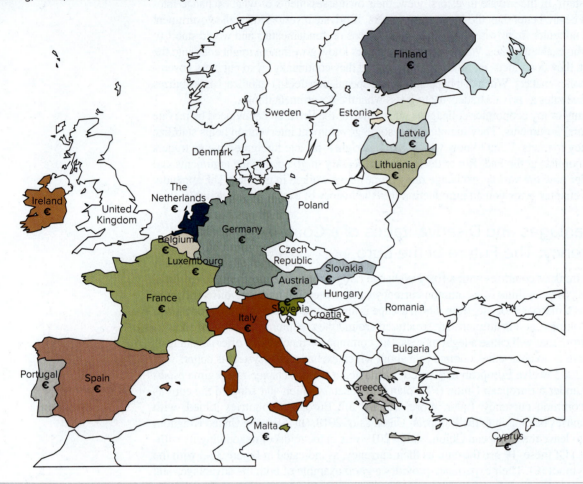

Four economic advantages of a common currency are that it:

1. Eliminates the cost of exchanging currencies.
2. Facilitates price comparisons.
3. Creates a larger market.
4. Increases the demand for the currency as a store of wealth.

businesses can more easily see price differentials, resulting in greater competition. For example, instead of having to compare a pair of German shoes priced at 60 marks with an Italian pair priced at 48,000 lire, a consumer just needs to compare 30 euros with 25 euros. A third advantage is that the common currency made it more likely that companies will think of Europe as a single market. As firms focused on producing for the European market, European consumers gained more clout and Europe, along with the United States, became the reference market when new goods were planned. It also allowed European firms to take advantage of economies of scale (lower costs as production rises) when producing for the European market. Finally, the importance of the euro led individuals throughout the world to hold their assets denominated in euros, increasing the demand for euros as a store of wealth. That lowered the relative interest rate for Europeans.

With an international reserve currency, the EU could create euros and exchange them for other currencies to buy products without increasing its domestic money supply, therefore lowering the possibility of inflation. (The increased money was held by foreigners. For the EU, it would be like getting an interest-free loan.) Because the U.S. dollar has been the world's reserve currency, the United States has been getting those interest-free loans, which is one of the reasons the United States has been able to run continual large trade deficits. If the euro partially replaces the dollar as the world reserve currency, there will likely be a large fall in demand for the dollar and a decrease in its value relative to other exchange rates.

During the first few years after the creation of the euro, most countries that adopted it did well. This was especially true of the southern countries—Portugal, Italy, Greece, and Spain. With a stable currency, they were able to borrow internationally at much lower interest rates than before. Northern countries, such as Germany, also did well since they now had a ready market for their goods, which did not push up the value of their currency as it would have had they not been part of the eurozone. It all worked well as long as lenders (primarily European banks) were willing to lend money to consumers and governments of the southern countries. The result was a boom in the southern countries built on increased debt. As their governments expanded their spending without increasing taxes correspondingly (they were able to now borrow cheaply), their economies went on a growth spurt.

Joining the eurozone also brought with it obligations—the government deficits they were allowed to run were limited. These obligations, however, were not strongly enforced for a variety of reasons: Governments did not report deficits accurately, the EU simply chose not to enforce the penalties when deficits exceeded agreed-upon levels, or deficits were run by regional entities (similar to local governments in the United States) that did not face debt restrictions but were implicitly guaranteed by the national government. The initial introduction of the euro was marked by fast growth in the poorer countries and slow but steady growth in the northern, larger countries such as Germany.

DISADVANTAGES OF THE EURO   A common currency has disadvantages as well as advantages. The major disadvantages of a common currency are: (1) loss of national identity, (2) increased economic ties among member countries, and (3) loss of independent monetary policy for member countries. Let's consider the disadvantages.

One involves national identity. A country's currency is a symbol of a country to its people, and giving it up means losing part of that identity. Loss of nationalism is one reason Britain did not adopt the euro.

A second related disadvantage is that a common currency closely ties the economies together. This means that countries have a harder time ignoring the economic problems of other member countries because their banks will be interconnected, and a problem in one country can quickly spread to other countries.

A third major disadvantage of a common currency is that members will no longer have independent monetary policies. So if an external shock hurts one region worse than another, the region hit hardest cannot increase its money supply to offset the effect of the shock on output. Ireland in 2004 to 2006 is an example. Its economy was growing quickly while Germany's economy was contracting. Because the two countries shared the same interest rate and monetary policy, Germany could not run expansionary monetary policy and Ireland could not run contractionary monetary policy. They had to share the same monetary policy.

A more serious variation of this problem occurred in Greece after the 2008 financial crisis when Greece's economy entered a deep recession, driving unemployment close to 30 percent. If Greece had had its own currency, it could have printed drachma (its currency before the euro), lowering interest rates, thereby lowering the relative value of its currency, expanding exports and stimulating the Greek economy. But it could not do that because it had the euro as its currency. Also, since it had agreed to limit its government deficits, it could not run expansionary fiscal policy. Politically, these limits, which Greece had agreed to into in order to get the advantages of being part of the eurozone, were no longer acceptable to the voting public. The Greek government

Major disadvantages of a common currency are:

1. Loss of national identity.
2. Increased economic ties among member countries.
3. Loss of independent monetary policy for member countries.

Q-10 How did Greece's adoption of the euro as its currency make its recent problems more difficult to solve?

that had tried to implement these limits was voted out of office. A new government was voted in, which refused to go along with the limits the previous government had agreed to, and Greece came close to being dropped from the eurozone and forced to return to the drachma. Such a move would have been an administrative mess, and both sides worked hard to find face-saving compromises. By 2017, Greece was able to issue bonds again, and the bailout program was scheduled to end in 2018.

Because of these recent problems, there has been much concern about the stability of the eurozone, and it remains an experiment that will be followed carefully over the next decade.

Conclusion

This chapter began with a quotation suggesting that a foreign exchange dealer's office can be the nearest thing to bedlam that there is. Seeing some order within that bedlam is not easy, but understanding the balance of payments and its relation to the determination of exchange rates is a good first step. And it is a step worth taking. With international transportation and communication becoming easier and faster and other countries' economies growing, the U.S. economy will become more interdependent with the global economy in the upcoming decades, making understanding these issues more and more necessary to understanding macroeconomics.

Summary

- The balance of payments is made up of the current account and the financial and capital account. *(LO35-1)*

- Exchange rates in a perfectly flexible exchange rate system are determined by the supply of and demand for a currency. *(LO35-2)*

- The fundamental forces that affect exchange rates are changes in income, prices, interest rates, and trade policies. These forces are often overwhelmed by expectations. *(LO35-2)*

- A country can stabilize or fix its exchange rate by either directly buying and selling its own currency or adjusting its monetary and fiscal policy to achieve its exchange rate goal. *(LO35-2)*

- It is easier technically for a country to bring down the value of its currency than it is to support its currency. *(LO35-2)*

- Expansionary monetary policy, through its effect on interest rates, income, and the price level, tends to lower a country's exchange rate. *(LO35-2)*

- Fiscal policy has an ambiguous effect on a country's exchange rate. *(LO35-2)*

- It is extraordinarily difficult to correctly estimate the long-run equilibrium exchange rate; one method

of doing so is the purchasing power parity approach. *(LO35-3)*

- A real exchange rate is an exchange rate adjusted for differences in inflation: *(LO35-3)*

  %Δ real exchange rate = %Δ nominal exchange rate + [Domestic inflation − Foreign inflation]

- Fixed exchange rates provide international monetary stability but can create enormous monetary instability if they become unfixed. Fixed exchange rates force governments to make adjustments to meet their international problems. *(LO35-4)*

- Flexible exchange rates allow exchange rates to make incremental changes, but are also subject to large jumps in value as a result of speculation. *(LO35-4)*

- Flexible exchange rates give governments flexibility in conducting domestic monetary and fiscal policy. *(LO35-4)*

- A common currency has advantages and disadvantages. Members of the eurozone have experienced both. Its most recent experience has been Greece's default of its debt. *(LO35-4)*

Key Terms

balance of merchandise
  trade
balance of payments
balance of trade
currency stabilization

currency support
current account
financial and capital
  account

fixed exchange rate
flexible exchange rate
partially flexible
  exchange rate

purchasing power parity
  (PPP)
real exchange rate

Questions and Exercises ![Mc Graw Hill] **connect**

1. If a country is running a balance of trade deficit, will its current account be in deficit? Why? (*LO35-1*)

2. When someone sends 100 British pounds to a friend in the United States, will this transaction show up on the financial and capital account or current account? Why? (*LO35-1*)

3. Support the following statement: "It is best to offset a financial and capital account surplus with a current account deficit." (*LO35-1*)

4. Support the following statement: "It is best to offset a financial and capital account deficit with a current account surplus." (*LO35-1*)

5. State whether the following will show up on the current account or the financial and capital account: (*LO35-1*)
   a. IBM's exports of computers to Japan.
   b. IBM's hiring of a British merchant bank as a consultant.
   c. A foreign national living in the United States repatriates money.
   d. Ford Motor Company's profit in Hungary.
   e. Ford Motor Company uses that Hungarian profit to build a new plant in Hungary.

6. Will the following be suppliers or demanders of U.S. dollars in foreign exchange markets? (*LO35-1*)
   a. A U.S. tourist in Latin America.
   b. A German foreign exchange trader who believes that the dollar exchange rate will fall.
   c. A U.S. foreign exchange trader who believes that the dollar exchange rate will fall.
   d. A Costa Rican tourist in the United States.
   e. A Russian capitalist who wants to protect his wealth from expropriation.
   f. A British investor in the United States.

7. If currency traders expect the government to devalue a currency, what will they likely do? Why? (*LO35-2*)

8. Draw the fundamental analysis of the supply and the demand for the British pound in terms of dollars. Show what will happen to the exchange rate with those curves in response to each of the following events: (*LO35-2*)
   a. The U.S. price level rises.
   b. The United States reduces tariffs.

c. The UK economy experiences a boom.
d. The U.S. interest rates rise.

9. The government of Never-Never Land, after much deliberation, finally decides to switch to a fixed exchange rate policy. It does this because the value of its currency, the neverback, is so high that the trade deficit is enormous. The finance minister fixes the rate at $10 a neverback, which is lower than the equilibrium rate of $20 a neverback. (*LO35-2*)
   a. What traditional macro policy options could accomplish this lower exchange rate?
   b. Using the laws of supply and demand, show graphically how possible equilibria are reached.

10. Draw the schematics to show the effect of expansionary monetary policy on the exchange rate. (*LO35-2*)

11. What effect on the U.S. trade deficit and exchange rate would result if Japan ran an expansionary monetary policy? (*LO35-2*)

12. What would be the effect on the U.S. exchange rate if Japan ran a contractionary fiscal policy? (*LO35-2*)

13. What effect will a combination of expansionary fiscal policy and contractionary monetary policy have on the exchange rate? (*LO35-2*)

14. If a country's actual exchange rate is 20 units per dollar and its purchasing power parity exchange rate is 25, is its currency under- or overvalued? Explain your answer. (*LO35-3*)

15. Ms. Economist always tries to travel to a country where the purchasing power parity exchange rate is lower than the market exchange rate. Why? (*LO35-3*)

16. If U.S. inflation is 4 percent, Japan's inflation is 1 percent, and the nominal U.S. dollar exchange rate falls by 3 percent relative to the yen, what happens to the real exchange rate? (*LO35-3*)

17. How is forcing governments to make adjustments to meet their international problems both an advantage and disadvantage of fixed exchange rates? (*LO35-4*)

18. Which is preferable: a fixed or a flexible exchange rate? Why? (*LO35-4*)

19. A *Wall Street Journal* article, "As Fear of Deficits Falls, Some See a Larger Threat," describes the following threat of a high U.S. budget deficit:

(Continued)

The investors who finance our deficits by buying Treasury bonds and bills, especially the foreigners who buy a larger share of them than ever, will question our ability to repay them, and balk at lending more—triggering a big drop in the dollar and much higher interest rates. *(LO35-4)*

a. Why would a drop in foreign confidence in the U.S. ability to repay debt lead to a drop in the dollar and much higher interest rates?

b. In what way are higher interest rates and a lower value of the dollar bad for the U.S. economy?

20. In mid-1994 the value of the dollar fell sufficiently to warrant coordinated intervention among 17 countries. Still, the dollar went on falling. One economist stated, "[The intervention] was clearly a failure. . . . It's a good indication something else has to be done." Why would the United States and foreign countries want to keep up the value of the dollar? *(LO35-4)*

21. In the early 2000s, China was running a large current account surplus. *(LO35-4)*

a. What did this suggest about its financial and capital account?

b. China's private balance of payments was in surplus. What does this suggest about its exchange rate regime?

c. What actions was the Chinese central bank likely undertaking in the foreign exchange markets? Demonstrate the situation with supply and demand graphs.

d. If the Chinese central bank pulled out of the foreign exchange market, what would likely happen to the yuan?

22. What are four economic advantages of the euro for Europe? *(LO35-4)*

23. What are three disadvantages of the euro for Europe? *(LO35-4)*

Questions from Alternative Perspectives

1. If all currencies were on a gold standard, there would be no exchange rates between currencies and we would not face the difficulties presented by fluctuating exchange rates.
   a. What would be the benefit of having all currencies on a gold standard?
   b. What would be the cost? *(Austrian)*

2. According to economist Gary North in *Priorities and Dominion: An Economic Commentary on Matthew,* in the book of Matthew, Jesus teaches about the rate of exchange between earthly wealth and eternal wealth.
   a. Would Jesus argue for a high or low exchange rate for earthly riches? Explain your answer.
   b. Do wealthy people believe the exchange rate is high or low?
   c. Do you believe the perceived exchange rate falls or rises as one approaches death? *(Religious)*

3. Most traders in currencies are men.
   a. Why is this?
   b. Why has it remained even though there is supposed to be no discrimination in employment?
   c. The language of traders is often quite coarse; does this fact provide a possible answer to both *a* and *b*?
   d. Did you think of the observation in *c* before you read it? *(Feminist)*

4. Nobel Prize–winning economist James Tobin has suggested that a method of decreasing unwanted sudden capital flows among countries would be to place a small tax on such flows. Post-Keynesian economist Paul Davidson argued against doing so because it won't solve the problem, suggesting that it is like using a pebble when a boulder is needed. What might Davidson's argument be? *(Hint:* It is related to the role of expectations.) *(Post-Keynesian)*

5. Most economists favor lowering barriers to trade. But even among mainstream economists there is far less support for financial liberalization—the removal of government regulation of financial and capital markets—than for trade liberalization. "It is a seductive idea," says free-trader Jagdish Bhagwati, "but the claims of enormous benefit from free capital mobility are not persuasive." In addition, capital market liberalization entails substantial risks because it strips away the regulations intended to control the flow of short-term loans and contracts in and out of a country. The IMF, on the other hand, remains an unabashed supporter of free financial markets, arguing that they are a precondition for a developing country attracting long-term foreign investment.
   a. Who has it right?
   b. Is financial liberalization a good or bad policy, especially for developing countries? *(Radical)*

Issues to Ponder

1. In the early 1980s, the U.S. economy fell into a recession (the government faced the problem of both a high federal deficit and a high trade deficit, called the twin deficits), and the dollar was very strong. Can you provide an explanation for this sequence of events?

2. During the 1995–1996 Republican presidential primaries, Patrick Buchanan wrote an editorial in *The Wall Street Journal* beginning, "Since the Nixon era the dollar has fallen 75 percent against the yen, 60 percent against the mark." What trade policies do you suppose he was

promoting? He went on to outline a series of tariffs. Agree or disagree with his policies.

3. In an op-ed article, Paul Volcker, former chair of the Board of Governors of the Federal Reserve, asked the following question: "Is it really worth spending money in the exchange markets, modifying monetary policy, and taking care to balance the budget just to save another percentage or two [of value of exchange rates]?" What's your answer to this question?

4. If you were the finance minister of Never-Never Land, how would you estimate the long-run exchange rate of your currency, the neverback? Defend your choice as well as discuss its possible failings.

5. Dr. Dollar Bill believes price stability is the main goal of central bank policy. Is the doctor more likely to prefer fixed or flexible exchange rates? Why?

6. One of the basic laws of economics is the law of one price. It says that given certain assumptions one would

expect that if free trade is allowed, the prices of goods in multiple countries should converge. This law underlies purchasing power parity.
   a. What are three assumptions likely to be?
   b. Should the law of one price hold for labor also? Why or why not?
   c. Should it hold for capital more so or less so than for labor? Why or why not?

7. Should Canada, the United States, and Mexico adopt a common currency? Why or why not?

8. If expansionary monetary policy immediately increases inflationary expectations and the price level, how might the effect of monetary policy on the exchange rate be different from that presented in this chapter?

9. In Figure 35-2, a foreign government chooses to maintain an equilibrium market exchange rate of U.S. $1.00 per unit of its own currency. Discuss the implications of the government trying to maintain a higher fixed rate—say at $1.20.

Answers to Margin Questions

1. The expenditures of a U.S. citizen traveling abroad will show up as a debit on the services account. As tourism or traveling, it is a service. (*LO35-1*)

2. Net investment income is the return a country gets on its foreign investment minus the return foreigners get on their investment within a country. A country is a net debtor nation if the value of foreign investment within a country exceeds the value of its investment abroad. A country can be a net debtor nation and still have positive net investment income if its foreign investment is undervalued at market values (valuation is generally done at book value), or if its foreign investment earns a higher rate of return than foreigners' investment within that country. (*LO35-1*)

3. In the short run, normal market forces have a limited, and possibly even perverse, effect on exchange rates, which is why most governments don't leave determination of exchange rates to the market. (*LO35-2*)

4. In general, it would be easier for the United States to push the value of the dollar down because doing so requires selling dollars and the United States can print more dollars to sell. To push the dollar up requires official reserves. (*LO35-2*)

5. A fall in a country's interest rate will push down its exchange rate. (*LO35-2*)

6. Contractionary monetary policy pushes up the interest rate, decreases income and hence imports, and has a tendency to decrease inflation. Therefore, through these paths, contractionary monetary policy will tend to increase the exchange rate. (*LO35-2*)

7. The net effect of expansionary fiscal policy on exchange rates is uncertain. Through the interest rate effect it pushes up the exchange rate, but through the income and price level effects it pushes down the exchange rate. (*LO35-2*)

8. The real exchange rate of the dollar relative to the euro rises 1 percent. (*LO35-3*)

   %Δ real exchange rate = %Δ nominal exchange rate + [Domestic inflation − Foreign inflation] = 3 + (2 − 4) = 1

9. There is much debate about whether government intervention stabilizes exchange rates—private traders tend to believe it does not; government economists tend to believe that it does. (*LO35-4*)

10. As a member of the eurozone, Greece could not use monetary policy to expand its economy. It could also not let its currency depreciate so that its economy could become competitive. Finally, had Greece had its own currency, lenders would not have let Greece get into the debt problem in the first place. (*LO35-4*)

History of Exchange Rate Systems

A good way to give you an idea of how the various exchange rate systems work is to present a brief history of international exchange rate systems.

The Gold Standard: A Fixed Exchange Rate System

Governments played a major role in determining exchange rates until the 1930s. Beginning with the Paris Conference of 1867 and lasting until 1933 (except for the period around World War I), most of the world economies had a system of relatively fixed exchange rates under what was called a **gold standard**—*a system of fixed exchange rates in which the value of currencies was fixed relative to the value of gold and gold was used as the primary reserve asset.*

Under a gold standard, the amount of money a country issued had to be directly tied to gold, either because gold coin served as the currency in a country (as it did in the United States before 1914) or because countries were required by law to have a certain percentage of gold backing their currencies. Gold served as currency or backed all currencies. Each country participating in a gold standard agreed to fix the price of its currency relative to gold. That meant a country would agree to pay a specified amount of gold on demand to anyone who wanted to exchange that country's currency for gold. To do so, each country had to maintain a stockpile of gold. When a country fixed the price of its currency relative to gold, it essentially fixed its currency's price in relation to other currencies also on the gold standard as a result of the process of arbitrage.

Under the gold standard, a country made up the difference between the quantity supplied and the quantity demanded of its currency by buying or selling gold to hold the price of its currency fixed in terms of gold. How much a country would need to buy and sell depended on its balance of payments deficit or surplus. If the country ran a surplus in the balance of payments, it was required to sell its currency—that is, buy gold—to stop the value of its currency from rising. If a country ran a deficit, it was required to buy its currency—that is, sell gold—to stop the value of its currency from falling.

The gold standard enabled governments to prevent short-run instability of the exchange rate. If there was a speculative run on its currency, the government would buy its currency with gold, thereby preventing the exchange rate from falling.

802

But for the gold standard to work, there had to be a method of long-run adjustment; otherwise countries would have run out of gold and would no longer have been able to fulfill their obligations under the gold standard. The **gold specie flow mechanism** was *the long-run adjustment mechanism that maintained the gold standard.* Here's how it worked: Since gold served as official reserves to a country's currency, a balance of payments deficit (and hence a downward pressure on the exchange rate) would result in a flow of gold out of the country and hence a decrease in the country's money supply. That decrease in the money supply would contract the economy, decreasing imports, lowering the country's price level, and increasing the interest rate, all of which would work toward eliminating the balance of payments deficit.

Similarly a country with a balance of payments surplus would experience an inflow of gold. That flow would increase the country's money supply, increasing income (and hence imports), increasing the price level (making imports cheaper and exports more expensive), and lowering the interest rate (increasing capital outflows). These would work toward eliminating the balance of payments surplus.

Thus, the gold standard determined a country's monetary policy and forced it to adjust any international balance of payments disequilibrium. Adjustments to a balance of payments deficit were often politically unpopular; they often led to recessions, which, because the money supply was directly tied to gold, the government couldn't try to offset with expansionary monetary policy.

The gold specie flow mechanism was called into play in the United States in late 1931 when the Federal Reserve, in response to a shrinking U.S. gold supply, decreased the amount of money in the U.S. economy, deepening the depression that had begun in 1929. The government's domestic goals and responsibilities conflicted with its international goals and responsibilities.

That conflict, which was rooted in the after-effects of World War I and the Depression, led to partial abandonment of the gold standard in 1933. At that time the United States made it illegal for individual U.S. citizens to own gold. Except for gold used for ornamental and certain medical and industrial purposes, all privately owned gold had to be sold to the government. Dollar bills were no longer backed by gold in the sense that U.S. citizens could exchange dollars for a prespecified amount of gold. Instead, dollar bills were backed by silver, which meant that any

U.S. citizen could change dollars for a prespecified amount of silver. In the late 1960s, that changed also. Since that time, for U.S. residents, dollars have been backed only by trust in the soundness of the U.S. economy.

Gold continued to serve, at least partially, as international backing for U.S. currency. That is, other countries could still exchange dollars for gold. However, in 1971, in response to another conflict between international and domestic goals, the United States totally cut off the relationship between dollars and gold. After that, a dollar could be redeemed only for another dollar, whether it was a U.S. citizen or a foreign government that wanted to redeem the dollar.

The Bretton Woods System: A Fixed Exchange Rate System

As World War II was coming to an end, the United States and its allies met to establish a new international economic order. After much wrangling, they agreed upon a system called the **Bretton Woods system,** *an agreement about fixed exchange rates that governed international financial relationships from the period after the end of World War II until 1971.* It was named after the resort in New Hampshire where the meeting that set up the system was held.

The Bretton Woods system established the International Monetary Fund (IMF) to oversee the international economic order. The IMF was empowered to arrange short-term loans between countries. The Bretton Woods system also established the World Bank, which was empowered to make longer-term loans to developing countries. Today the World Bank and IMF continue their central roles in international financial affairs.

The Bretton Woods system was based on mutual agreements about what countries would do when experiencing balance of payments surpluses or deficits. It was essentially a fixed exchange rate system. For example, under the Bretton Woods system, the exchange rate of the dollar for the British pound was set at slightly over $4 to the pound.

The Bretton Woods system was not based on a gold standard. When countries experienced a balance of payments surplus or deficit, they did not necessarily buy or sell gold to stabilize the price of their currency. Instead they bought and sold other currencies. To ensure that participating countries would have sufficient reserves, they established a stabilization fund from which a country could obtain a short-term loan. It was hoped that this stabilization fund would be sufficient to handle all short-run adjustments that did not reflect fundamental imbalances.

In those cases where a misalignment of exchange rates was determined to be fundamental, the countries involved agreed that they would adjust their exchange rates. The IMF was empowered to oversee an orderly adjustment. It could authorize a country to make a one-time adjustment of up to 10 percent without obtaining formal approval from the IMF's board of directors. After a country had used its one-time adjustment, formal approval was necessary for any change greater than 1 percent.

The Bretton Woods system reflected the underlying political and economic realities of the post–World War II period in which it was set up. European economies were devastated; the U.S. economy was strong. To rebuild, Europe was going to have to import U.S. equipment and borrow large amounts from the United States. There was serious concern over how high the value of the dollar would rise and how low the value of European currencies would fall in a free market exchange. The establishment of fixed exchange rates set limits on currencies' relative movements; the exchange rates that were chosen helped provide funds for the rebuilding of Europe.

In addition, the Bretton Woods system provided mechanisms for long-term loans from the United States to Europe that could help sustain those fixed exchange rates. The loans also eliminated the possibility of competitive depreciation of currencies, in which each country tries to stimulate its exports by lowering the relative value of its currency.

One difficulty with the Bretton Woods system was a shortage of official reserves and international liquidity. To offset that shortage, the IMF was empowered to create *a type of international money* called **special drawing rights (SDRs).** But SDRs never became established as an international currency and the U.S. dollar kept serving as official reserves for individuals and countries. To get the dollars to foreigners, the United States had to run a deficit in its current account. Since countries could exchange the dollar for gold at a fixed price, the use of dollars as a reserve currency meant that, under the Bretton Woods system, the world was on a gold standard once removed.

The number of dollars held by foreigners grew enormously in the 1960s. By the early 1970s, those dollars far exceeded in value the amount of gold the United States had. Most countries accepted this situation; even though they could legally demand gold for their dollars, they did not. But Charles de Gaulle, the nationalistic president of France, wasn't pleased with the U.S. domination of international affairs at that time. He believed Europe deserved a much more prominent position. He demanded gold for the dollars held by the French central bank, knowing that the United States didn't have enough gold to meet his demand. As a result of his and other countries' demands, on August 15, 1971, the United States ended its policy of exchanging gold for dollars at $35 per ounce. With that change, the Bretton Woods system was dead.

The Present U.S. System: A Partially Flexible Exchange Rate System

International monetary affairs were much in the news in the early 1970s as countries groped for a new exchange rate system. The makeshift system finally agreed on involved partially flexible exchange rates. Most Western countries' exchange rates are allowed to fluctuate, although at various times governments buy or sell their own currencies to affect the exchange rate.

Under the present partially flexible exchange rate system, countries must continually decide when a balance of payments surplus or deficit is a temporary phenomenon and when it is a signal of a fundamental imbalance. If they believe the situation is temporary, they enter into the foreign exchange market to hold their exchange rate at what they believe is an appropriate level. If, however, they believe that the balance of payments imbalance is a fundamental one, they let the exchange rate rise or fall.

While most Western countries' exchange rates are partially flexible, certain countries have agreed to fixed exchange rates of their currencies in relation to rates of a group of certain other currencies. Other currencies are fixed relative to the dollar (not by the United States but by the other countries).

Deciding what is, and what is not, a fundamental imbalance is complicated, and such decisions are considered at numerous international conferences held under the auspices of the IMF or governments. A number of organizations such as the Group of Seven focus much discussion on this issue. Often the various countries meet and agree, formally or informally, on acceptable ranges of exchange rates. Thus, while the present system is one of partially flexible exchange rates, the range of flexibility is limited.

Key Terms

Bretton Woods system	gold specie flow mechanism	gold standard	special drawing rights (SDRs)

Macro Policy in a Global Setting

CHAPTER 36

©Francis Joseph Dean/Shutterstock

After reading this chapter, you should be able to:

LO36-1 Discuss why there is significant debate about what U.S. international goals should be.

LO36-2 Describe the paths through which monetary and fiscal policy affect the trade balance.

LO36-3 Summarize the reasons why governments try to coordinate their monetary and fiscal policies.

LO36-4 Explain how restoring U.S. competitiveness will likely affect U.S. policy in the future.

Throughout previous chapters I have emphasized the importance of global issues in domestic macro policy. In this chapter, I pull together what we have learned about monetary and fiscal policy, comparative advantage, trade deficits, and exchange rates, and talk about macro policy in a global setting. To begin, I need to discuss our international macro goals.

The Ambiguous International Goals of Macroeconomic Policy

Macroeconomic international goals are less straightforward than domestic goals. There is general agreement about the domestic goals of macroeconomic policy: We want low inflation, low unemployment, and high growth. There's far less agreement on what a country's international goals should be.

Most economists agree that the international goal of U.S. macroeconomic policy is to maintain the U.S. position in the world economy. But there's enormous debate about what achieving that goal means. Do we want a high or a low exchange rate? Do we want a balance of trade surplus? Or would it be better to have a balance of trade deficit? Or should we not even pay attention to the balance of trade? Let's consider the exchange rate goal first.

The Exchange Rate Goal

The U.S. exchange rate has fluctuated significantly over the past 30 years. There is a debate over whether a country should have a high or a low exchange rate. A high exchange rate for the dollar makes foreign currencies cheaper, lowering the price of imports. Lowering import prices places competitive pressure on U.S. firms and helps to hold down inflation. All of this benefits U.S. residents' living standard. But a high exchange rate encourages imports and discourages exports and can cause a balance of trade deficit that can exert a contractionary effect on the economy by decreasing aggregate demand for U.S. output. So a high exchange rate also has a cost to U.S. residents. It has contributed to the structural stagnation the U.S. economy has recently experienced.

A low exchange rate has the opposite effect. It makes imports more expensive and exports cheaper and can contribute to inflationary pressure. But, by encouraging exports and discouraging imports, it can cause a balance of trade surplus and exert an expansionary effect on the economy.

Many economists argue that a country should have no activist exchange rate policy because exchange rates are market-determined prices that are best left to the market. These economists question whether the government should even worry about the effect of monetary policy and fiscal policy on exchange rates. According to them, government should simply accept whatever exchange rate exists and not consider it in conducting monetary and fiscal policies.

Q-1   What effect does a low exchange rate have on a country's exports and imports?

Web Note 36.1

Putting Exchange Rates First

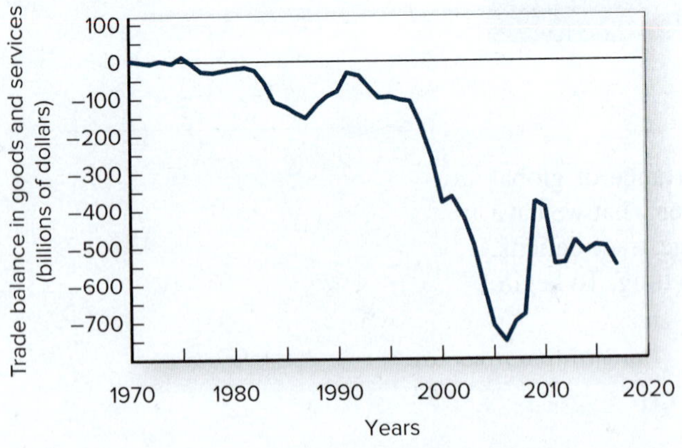

The Trade Balance Goal

Figure 36-1 shows the U.S. trade balance over the past 45 years. You can see that the United States has consistently run a trade deficit over that period, and that that trade deficit has generally increased. A deficit in the trade balance (the difference between imports and exports) means that, as a country, we're consuming more than we're producing. Imports exceed exports, so we're consuming more than we could if we didn't run a deficit. A surplus in the trade balance means that exports exceed imports—we're producing more than we're consuming. Since consuming more than we otherwise could is kind of nice, it might seem that a trade deficit is preferred to a trade surplus.

But wait. A trade deficit isn't without costs, and a trade surplus isn't without benefits. We pay for a trade deficit by selling off U.S. assets to foreigners—by selling U.S. companies, factories, land, and buildings to foreigners, or selling them financial assets such as U.S. dollars, stocks, and bonds. All the future interest and profits on these assets will go to foreigners, not U.S. citizens. That means eventually, sometime in the future, we will have to produce more than we consume so we can pay them *their* profit and interest on *their* assets. Thus, while in the short run a trade deficit allows more current consumption, in the long run it presents potential problems.

FIGURE 36-1   **The Trade Balance**

Trade balance in goods and services (billions of dollars) vs. Years

100, 0, −100, −200, −300, −400, −500, −600, −700

1970, 1980, 1990, 2000, 2010, 2020

Running a trade deficit is good in the short run but presents problems in the long run.

The U.S. Trade Deficit and the Value of the Dollar

The U.S. trade deficit that started back in the 1970s and has continued into the 2000s has confounded many analysts. Why has it remained so high? Why are other countries willing to give the United States many more real goods and services than they require in return? The answer is that they want to buy U.S. assets. There are a number of reasons why. First, the value of U.S. assets has increased. For example, Japan's stock market and real estate markets were falling while the U.S. stock market was rising, which gave Japanese investors a strong incentive to invest in the United States. Second, the United States is considered a safe haven—a solid economy that is safer than any other. If you want safety, you buy U.S. government bonds. Third, Japan and China have been buying large amounts of dollars in order to prevent the value of the dollar from falling relative to their currencies. At some point, however, the demand for U.S. assets is expected to end and the U.S. trade deficit will have to fall. In 2006 and 2007, the value

©Daisuke Morita/Getty Images

of the dollar fell substantially relative to many other currencies, but then in 2008 it rose as the international financial crisis made safety, not the return on investment, the overriding factor in individuals' decisions about where to hold their assets. That rise reversed slightly between 2009 and 2011 but then resumed until 2017, when the value of the dollar began to decline. So financial flows into the United States have dominated over trade flows. That has put downward pressure on U.S. exports and encouraged imports. So the U.S. trade deficit remains high.

Eventually, those financial flows will slow, and cause a fall in the price of the dollar, which will lower the relative price of U.S. exports and increase the cost of imports, which will lead to a lower trade deficit. Because people don't want to hold assets in currencies whose values are falling, this fall could be much more sudden than policy makers would like, creating serious questions about whether they can do anything to prevent it.

As long as a country can borrow, or sell assets, a country can have a trade deficit. But if a country runs a trade deficit year after year, eventually the long run will arrive and the country will run out of assets to sell and run out of other countries from which to borrow. When that happens, the trade deficit problem must be faced. Trade deficits can also cause short-run problems. A trade deficit means that there is less demand for U.S. goods, which will lead to higher unemployment and slower growth in the United States. Thus a country's potential output will be lower with a trade deficit than it would be without one. If the country attempts to prevent that higher unemployment with expansionary monetary and fiscal policy, the result will not be inflation as long as global competition is holding down prices, but it might be a financial bubble, which, when it crashes, will lead to a difficult period of structural adjustment.

The debate about whether a trade deficit should be of concern to policy makers involves whether long-run effects should be anticipated and faced before they happen and whether structural problems need to be addressed.

Opinions differ greatly. Some say not to worry—just accept what's happening. These "not-to-worry" economists argue that the trade deficit will end when U.S. citizens don't want to borrow from foreigners anymore and foreigners don't want to buy any more of our assets. They argue that the inflow of financial capital (money coming into the United States to buy our assets) from foreigners is financing new investment that will make the U.S. economy strong enough in the long run to reverse the trade deficit without serious disruption to the U.S. economy. They believe the economy will soon return to high growth. So why deal with the trade deficit now, when it will take care of itself in the future?

Q-2 Why do some people argue that we should not worry about a trade deficit?

Others argue that, yes, the trade deficit will eventually take care of itself, but the accompanying economic distress associated with structural adjustment will be great. By dealing with the problem now, the United States can avoid a highly unpleasant solution in the future.

Both views are reasonable, which is why there's no consensus on what a country's trade balance goal should be.

International versus Domestic Goals

Domestic goals generally dominate international goals.

In the real world, when there's debate about a goal, that goal is generally less likely to guide policy than goals about which there's general agreement. Since there's general agreement about our country's domestic goals (low inflation, low unemployment, and high growth), domestic goals generally dominate the U.S. political agenda.

Even if a country's international goals weren't uncertain, domestic goals would likely dominate the political agenda. The reason is that inflation, unemployment, and growth affect a country's citizens directly. Trade deficits and exchange rates affect them indirectly—and in politics, indirect effects take a backseat. However, as countries' economies become more integrated, international issues intersect more and more with domestic issues.

Often a country responds to an international goal only when the international community forces it to do so. For example, in the 1980s when Brazil couldn't borrow any more money from other countries, it reluctantly made resolving its trade deficit a key goal. Similarly, when other countries threatened to limit Japanese imports, Japan took steps to increase the value of the yen and decrease its trade surplus. More recently China faced international pressure to let its exchange rate rise. When a country is forced to face certain economic facts, international goals can become its primary goals. As countries become more economically integrated, these pressures from other countries become more important. If the U.S. government budget and trade deficits become unsustainable, the United States may find that it is forced to take international issues more significantly into account.

Balancing the Exchange Rate Goal with Domestic Goals

In the last chapter we talked about monetary and fiscal policy's effect on the exchange rate. In it we saw that while fiscal policy's effect on exchange rates was ambiguous, monetary policy has a predictable effect: Expansionary monetary policy tends to push the exchange rate down; contractionary monetary policy tends to push the exchange rate up.[1] What this means is that in principle, the government can control the exchange rate with monetary policy. The problem with doing so is that monetary policy also affects the domestic economy—contractionary monetary policy decreases income and jobs. Contractionary monetary policy is not a policy that countries generally want to follow.

The way in which monetary policy affects the exchange rate is by affecting the supply and demand for the country's currency. To review this, let's consider the case of Europe that we examined in the previous chapter. That case is shown in Figure 36-2. Europe's problem here is that it wants the exchange rate for the euro to be $1.20, not $1.00. The EU has three options for raising the value of the euro: Decrease the private

---

[1] We don't discuss fiscal policy as a control policy for exchange rates because fiscal policy has an ambiguous effect on the exchange rate, as the interest rate effect of fiscal policy pushes the exchange rate one way and the income effect pushes it another. (See the previous chapter if you are not clear on this effect.)

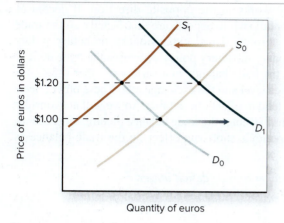

FIGURE 36-2 **Targeting an Exchange Rate with Monetary and Fiscal Policy**

To increase the exchange rate value of the euro, the European Central Bank (ECB) could run contractionary monetary policy to increase interest rates and increase the private demand for euros or induce a recession and decrease the private supply of euros, or a combination of the two.

supply of euros (shifting the supply curve in from S_0 to S_1), increase the private demand for euros (shifting the demand curve out from D_0 to D_1), or use some combination of the two. Let's see how it could accomplish its goal with monetary policy.

To increase the demand for euros, the EU must create policies that increase the private foreign demand for EU assets, or for EU goods and services. In the short run, the European Central Bank (ECB) can increase the interest rate by running contractionary monetary policy. A higher interest rate increases the foreign demand for the EU's interest-bearing assets. The problem with this approach is that to maintain an exchange rate at a certain level, a country must give up any attempt to target its interest rate to achieve domestic goals. To put it another way: A country can achieve an interest rate target or an exchange rate target, but generally it cannot achieve both at the same time.

Contractionary monetary policy also slows down the domestic economy and induces a recession. This recession decreases the demand for imports and thereby decreases the private supply of euros. Governments are usually loath to use this contractionary policy because politically induced recessions are not popular. It is because of the constraints that fixed exchange rates, or any policy designed to hold its exchange rate up, place on domestic monetary and fiscal policy that many countries choose flexible, or at least partially flexible, exchange rate regimes.

Q-3 If a country wants to fix its exchange rate at a rate that is higher than the market rate, what monetary or fiscal policy must it use?

Q-4 If a country runs a contractionary monetary policy, what effect will that likely have on its exchange rate?

Monetary and Fiscal Policy and the Trade Deficit

Since a major policy issue for the United States in the coming years is likely to be its large trade deficit, and the pressures that will likely decrease that deficit, let's now turn to a consideration of how monetary and fiscal policy affect the trade deficit. We begin with monetary policy.

Monetary Policy's Effect on the Trade Balance

When a country's international trade balance is negative (a trade deficit), the country is importing more than it is exporting. When a country's international trade balance is positive (a trade surplus), the country is exporting more than it is importing.

Monetary policy affects the trade balance primarily through its effect on income. Specifically, expansionary monetary policy increases income. When income rises, imports rise, while exports are unaffected. As imports rise, the trade balance shifts in the direction of deficit. So expansionary monetary policy shifts the trade balance toward a deficit.

Q-5 What effect will contractionary monetary policy have on the trade balance?

Contractionary monetary policy works in the opposite direction. It decreases income. When income falls, imports fall (while exports are unaffected), so the trade balance shifts in the direction of surplus. Thus, expansionary monetary policy increases the trade deficit; contractionary monetary policy decreases the trade deficit.

Monetary policy will also affect the trade balance in a variety of other ways—for example, through its effect on the price level and the exchange rate. These other effects tend to be more long-run effects and tend to offset one another. So we will not consider them here. While many complications can enter the trade balance picture, most economists would summarize monetary policy's short-run effect on the trade balance as follows:

Expansionary monetary policy makes a trade deficit larger.

Contractionary monetary policy makes a trade deficit smaller.

Expansionary monetary policy makes a trade deficit larger.

Contractionary monetary policy makes a trade deficit smaller.

Expansionary monetary policy

$M \rightarrow Y \rightarrow$ Imports $\rightarrow$ Trade deficit

Contractionary monetary policy

$M \rightarrow Y \rightarrow$ Imports $\rightarrow$ Trade deficit

Fiscal Policy's Effect on the Trade Balance

Fiscal policy, like monetary policy, works on the trade deficit primarily through its effects on income. (Again, there are other paths by which fiscal policy affects the trade deficit, but this one is the largest since changes in income are quickly reflected in a change in imports.) So if asked for a quick answer, economists would say that contractionary fiscal policy decreases a trade deficit.

Summarizing the effects of expansionary and contractionary fiscal policy schematically, we have:

Q-6 What is the effect of expansionary fiscal policy on the trade deficit?

Expansionary fiscal policy $\rightarrow Y \rightarrow$ Imports $\rightarrow$ Trade deficit

Contractionary fiscal policy $\rightarrow Y \rightarrow$ Imports $\rightarrow$ Trade deficit

Contractionary fiscal policy decreases a trade deficit.

International Phenomena and Domestic Goals

So far, we've focused on the effect of monetary and fiscal policies on international goals. But often the effect is the other way around: International phenomena change and significantly influence the domestic economy and the ability to achieve domestic goals.

For example, say that Japan ran contractionary monetary policy. That would increase the Japanese exchange rate and increase Japan's trade surplus, which means it would decrease the U.S. exchange rate and increase the U.S. trade deficit, both of which would affect U.S. domestic goals.

Alternatively, let's consider how the current situation is likely to play out for the United States in the coming decade. Currently, the United States is running a large trade deficit, which will be difficult to sustain. If the United States chooses to reduce that trade deficit with monetary or fiscal policy, it will have to run contractionary monetary and fiscal policy, keeping the economy from growing as fast as it otherwise would. That is not a politically attractive option, which is an important reason why the United States has not chosen to deal with the trade deficit with monetary or fiscal policy.

But what if other countries stop buying the large amount of dollar-denominated assets that they are currently buying? The dollar exchange rate will fall, possibly precipitously, unless the trade deficit is reduced. In the long run, that fall in the exchange rate will improve the competitiveness of the U.S. economy, decrease imports, and increase exports. But in the short run, the dollar's decline will place the U.S. economy in a bind, since it will push up prices of imports, creating inflationary pressure, and make Americans worse off. Too fast a decline will likely create severe financial problems that can reverberate through the world economy. If the value of the dollar declines precipitously, other countries will pressure the U.S. government to cut its trade deficit by implementing contractionary monetary and fiscal policy. These policies will be imposed by creditor countries as a requirement for temporary loans to the United States.

Web Note 36.2

Coordinating Policies

Q-7 If other countries stop buying large amounts of dollar-denominated assets, what will likely happen to the value of the dollar?

International Goals and Policy Alternatives

The following table provides a summary of how alternative policy actions achieve international goals:

International Goal	Policy Alternatives
Lower exchange rate	• Contractionary foreign monetary policy • Expansionary domestic monetary policy
Lower trade deficit	• Contractionary domestic fiscal policy • Expansionary foreign fiscal policy • Contractionary domestic monetary policy • Expansionary foreign monetary policy

You can see in the table why coordination of monetary and fiscal policies is much in the news, since a foreign country's policy can eliminate, or reduce, the need for domestic policies to be undertaken.

International Monetary and Fiscal Coordination

Governments try to coordinate their monetary and fiscal policies because their economies are interdependent.

As I have stated, unless forced to do so because of international pressures, most countries don't let international goals guide their macroeconomic policy. But for every effect that monetary and fiscal policies have on a country's exchange rates and trade balance, there's an equal and opposite effect on the combination of other countries' exchange rates and trade balances. When one country's exchange rate goes up, by definition another country's exchange rate must go down. Similarly, when one country's balance of trade is in surplus, another's must be in deficit. This interconnection means that other countries' fiscal and monetary policies affect the United States, while U.S. fiscal and monetary policies affect other countries, so pressure to coordinate policies is considerable.

Coordination Is a Two-Way Street

Q-8 If domestic problems call for expansionary monetary policy and international problems call for contractionary monetary policy, what policy will a country likely adopt?

Policy coordination—*the integration of a country's policies to take account of their global effects*—of course, works both ways. If other countries are to take the U.S. economy's needs into account, the United States must take other countries' needs into account in determining its goals. Say, for example, the U.S. economy is going into a recession. This domestic problem calls for expansionary monetary policy. But expansionary monetary policy will increase U.S. income and U.S. imports and lower the value of the dollar. Say that, internationally, the United States has agreed that it must work toward eliminating the U.S. trade deficit in the short run. Does it forsake its domestic goals? Or does it forsake its international commitment? If the economy is forced to address the trade deficit, it will have no choice but to make the structural adjustments necessary to reduce the trade deficit and bring it into balance. These are the types of questions that policy makers face.

Each country will likely do what's best for the world economy as long as it's also best for itself.

There's no one right answer to these questions. It depends on political judgments (how long until the next election?), judgments about what foreign countries can do if the United States doesn't meet its international commitments, and similar judgments by foreign countries about the United States.

Despite the complications, the above discussion gives you an understanding of many events that may have previously seemed incomprehensible. To show you the relevance of what I have said about international considerations, let's look at three situations.

Let's consider the example of Argentina in the early 2000s. In the early 1990s, Argentina established a fixed exchange rate between the peso and the U.S. dollar and promised to maintain that exchange rate under all circumstances. Numerous international investors relied on that promise. In the late 1990s, the Argentinean economy went into recession and domestic political pressures called for expansionary aggregate demand policy. Maintaining the fixed exchange rate required contractionary aggregate demand policy. The internal political pressures won, and Argentina abandoned its fixed exchange rate in early 2002.

A second concerns Switzerland. In 2011 Switzerland had established a fixed exchange rate with the euro in an attempt to hold down the value of the Swiss franc to make its exports more competitive. This meant that Switzerland had to increase its money supply, using that newly created money to buy euros. In 2014, the euro was experiencing difficulties and the eurozone was lowering its interest rates, which meant Switzerland had to buy even more euros as large numbers of people sold euro-denominated financial assets and bought Swiss assets. To offset the effect of the increased demand for the Swiss franc, the Swiss central bank lowered interest rates to close to zero, and some Swiss bonds even paid negative

©Maryna Pleshkun/Shutterstock

interest rates, which means that investors *paid,* rather than received, interest on the bonds they held. In 2015, Switzerland abandoned its fixed exchange rate, and the day it did so, the value of the Swiss franc rose more than 40 percent against the euro. This meant that Swiss companies had a much harder time selling their products abroad. The Swiss economy slowed for a few years and only resumed stronger growth in 2018.

The third example is China in 2015. In the previous decade, China was under pressure from many countries, including the United States, to switch from an export-led growth policy to a domestic consumption-led growth policy. The new growth policy involved increasing government expenditures on social goods and increasing the real value of the yuan through domestic inflation and entering the exchange market directly by selling dollars. These policies helped reduce the U.S. trade deficit by making Chinese exports more expensive.

There are many more examples, but these three should give you a good sense of the relevance of the issues.

Crowding Out and International Considerations

Let's reconsider the issue of crowding out that we considered in an earlier chapter, only this time we'll take into account international considerations. Say a government is running a budget deficit and the central bank has decided it won't increase the money supply to help finance the deficit. (This happened in the 1980s with the Fed and the U.S. government.) What will be the result?

The basic idea of crowding out is that the budget deficit will cause the interest rate to go up. But wait. There's another way to avoid the crowding out that results from financing the deficit: Foreigners could buy the debt at the existing interest rate. This is called *internationalizing the debt,* and that is what happened to the U.S. economy in recent years.

There have been massive inflows to the United States of financial capital from abroad. These inflows held down the U.S. interest rate even as the federal government ran large budget deficits. Thus, large U.S. budget deficits didn't push up interest rates because foreigners, not U.S. citizens, were buying U.S. debt.

But, as we discussed, internationalization of the U.S. debt is not costless. While it helps in the short run, it presents problems in the long run. Today about 50 percent of privately held U.S. government debt is held by foreigners. Foreign ownership of U.S. debt means that the United States must pay foreigners interest each year on that debt. To do so, the United States must export more and import less than it otherwise would, which means that the United States must consume less than it produces at some time in the future. As you can see, the issues quickly become complicated.

Globalization, Macro Policy, and the U.S. Economy

We began this book stating that the United States operates in a global economy and that policy today must consider global issues. As a conclusion to the chapter, let's pull our various discussions together and review the likely problems that international

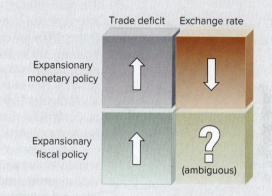
Q-9 How does internationalizing the debt reduce crowding out?

While internationalizing a country's debt may help in the short run, in the long run it presents potential problems since foreign ownership of a country's debt means the country must pay interest to those foreign countries and that debt may come due.

Web Note 36.3

Interconnection

considerations are creating for the U.S. economy over the coming decades. I start with some general points about the relationship of international issues to macro policy.

International Issues and Macro Policy

The first point is that the more globally connected a country is, the less flexibility it has with its monetary and fiscal policy. Global issues restrict the use of monetary and fiscal policy to achieve domestic goals. How much they do so, and the manner in which they do so, depend on the country's exchange rate regime, which leads to our second point: How fast a country must respond to international pressure depends on the exchange rate regime it follows. If an economy sets fixed exchange rates, its monetary and fiscal policies are much more restricted than they are with flexible exchange rates. The reason is that the amount of currency stabilization that can be achieved with direct intervention is generally quite small since a country's foreign reserves are limited. When this is the case, to keep its currency fixed at the desirable level, it must adjust the economy to the exchange rate. Specifically, it must undertake policies that will change either the private supply of its currency or the private demand for its currency. It can do so by traditional macro policy—monetary and fiscal policy—influencing the economy, or by trade policy to affect the level of exports and imports. This means that if monetary and fiscal policies are being used to achieve exchange rate goals, they cannot also be used to achieve domestic goals.

Q-10 If a country has a fixed exchange rate, does it have more or less flexibility in choosing its monetary and fiscal policy to achieve domestic goals?

A third point is that with flexible exchange rates, countries have more freedom with monetary and fiscal policy, but then they have to accept whatever happens to their exchange rate, and there are often strong political forces that do not want to do that. That is the position in which the United States will find itself if foreigners significantly reduce their demand for U.S. assets.

A fourth point is that an alternative to using monetary and fiscal policy to guide the economy toward meeting its international goals is trade policy designed to affect the level of exports and imports. Specific use of tariffs and quotas is limited by international conventions, but indirect policies to affect imports and exports are used all the time. For example, U.S. tax laws can be designed to make it more costly for companies to produce abroad. Implicit subsidies can be given for exports, and implicit constraints can be placed on imports. We can expect such programs to continue and to expand in the coming decade as the United States attempts to reduce its trade deficit by means other than a fall in the exchange rate of the dollar, which is the alternative path to reducing its trade deficit.

A fifth point is that macro policy is short-run policy, which must be conducted within a longer-range setting of the country's overall **competitiveness**—*the ability of a country to sell its goods to other countries.* That longer-range setting for the United States in the coming decade is not likely to be conducive to expansionary macro policy, which is a change from the past. Following World War II, the long-run setting did allow expansionary macro policy. The United States had a strong competitive position and a trade surplus even though the value of the dollar was high. (During that time, the United States had a fixed exchange rate; see the appendix to the previous chapter for a brief history of the period.)

In the 1970s, economic development and investment abroad reduced U.S. competitiveness. Fortunately for the United States, foreign individuals and countries had an enormous demand for U.S. assets. (The capital and financial account surplus discussed in the last chapter reflects that demand.) Had foreign individuals and countries not wanted to increase their holdings of U.S. assets, the long-run setting for macro policy would have been far less conducive to expansionary macro policy. The trade deficit would have lowered the value of the dollar, which would have offset the declining U.S. competitiveness. If this had happened, however, and the United States had also wanted to hold the value of the dollar up, U.S. monetary and fiscal policy would have had to have been contractionary.

Much of the discussion in this chapter is based on the assumption that the standard monetary and fiscal tools are strong enough for policy makers to achieve their goals. This may not be the case since there are limits to what can be achieved with monetary and fiscal policy. For example, currently, many people believe the U.S. economy is in a period of slow growth—structural stagnation—and conventional fiscal and monetary policies, even though exceptionally strong by historical measures, have not been strong enough to achieve the type of jobs and growth that policy makers want and have targeted. This suggests that policy makers will have to either develop new tools or reduce their targets to what the economy can achieve. These new tools will likely involve more international coordination to offset destabilizing monetary flows and exchange rates and structural changes in the economy to make institutions better able to deal with global competition.

Restoring International Trade Balance to the U.S. Economy

As I have emphasized throughout previous chapters, when we think about the likely future direction of the U.S. economy, we have to integrate the theory of comparative advantage into our discussion because it provides the long-run setting within which short-run policy is conducted. The theory of comparative advantage focuses on the case where trade is balanced—where the comparative advantages of both countries in various goods are balanced. If that is not the case, economic theory assumes something will adjust to bring them into balance.[2] But when the demand for a country's assets is large, those adjustments do not have to take place. That's what happened to the United States. The large and increasing demand for U.S. assets allowed U.S. production in a variety of goods and services to lose their competitiveness. U.S. comparative advantage was not in produced goods but in assets; the demand for its assets meant that the United States needed a smaller demand for its goods and services to maintain a balance of payments equilibrium. Thinking only in terms of goods and services, at current exchange rates, the United States doesn't have a comparative advantage in as many different goods and services as do other countries. That's what it means to be running a trade deficit. As long as other countries are willing to accept U.S. currency or U.S. assets in payment for the goods that they produce, the United States can continue to run a trade deficit at the current exchange rate.

We've seen downward pressure on the value of the dollar, but the real value of the dollar compared to the Chinese yuan has a ways to fall to bring about a trade balance, in part because their central banks have bought dollars to stop their own currencies from appreciating. (A good review of the last chapter is to discuss, using supply and demand curves, how the Central Bank of China can prevent the appreciation of the yuan.)

At some point, foreigners will not be willing to accumulate more U.S. currency or assets and foreign government support will likely slow. When and if this happens, assuming nothing else changes, the dollar will depreciate, especially relative to the yuan, until the United States regains comparative advantage in enough goods to create

> As long as other countries are willing to accept U.S. currency or U.S. assets in payment for the goods that they produce, the United States can continue to run a trade deficit at the current exchange rate.

---

[2]When David Ricardo first developed the comparative advantage argument, he discussed how, if there were trade imbalances between the two countries, those imbalances would be quickly eliminated by changes in the two countries' price levels as money flowed from the deficit country to the surplus country. When he was writing, countries based their currencies on gold, and it was probably a reasonable assumption. Today, capital markets are much more developed, and capital flows in the opposite direction can offset the need for quick adjustment based on imbalances of trade.

a balance in the balance of payments without the inflow of foreign financial assets. Until that happens, we can expect further outsourcing of U.S. jobs and weak U.S. economic growth.

The fall in the value of the dollar is not absolutely certain. Many events could temporarily change the situation. For example, political uncertainty in China could slow the process enormously, and even possibly reverse it temporarily. Similarly, large inflation in China would serve the same purpose as a rise in its exchange rates, and eliminate the need for the value of the dollar to fall. Even if those events don't happen, a sudden collapse of the U.S. exchange rate is not likely to be in the cards because the collapse of the U.S. economy that would accompany it is not in the interest of other countries. Global economies are interconnected; if the U.S. economy were to collapse, so would other world economies. Thus, we can expect foreign governments to step in to support the dollar and slow its fall if the private demand for U.S. assets decreases. Just as the United States does not want its currency to fall too precipitously, China does not want its currency to rise too quickly. This suggests that international pressures on U.S. macro policy will keep U.S. growth slower than what it otherwise would be and place continual downward pressure on U.S. wages for workers producing an expanding number of tradable goods.

Global economies are interconnected; if the U.S. economy were to collapse, so would other world economies.

Conclusion

It's time to conclude the chapter and our consideration of global macro policy. Both have been just an introduction. You shouldn't think of them as any more than that. In no way has this brief chapter exhausted the international topics relevant to macro policy. But the chapter has, I hope, made you better aware of the international dimensions of our economic goals—and of the problems that international issues pose for macro policy—and the book has made you aware of the central insights of economics. That awareness is absolutely necessary if you are to understand the ongoing debates about economic policy.

Summary

- The international goals of a country are often in dispute. (*LO36-1*)

- Domestic goals generally dominate international goals, but countries often respond to an international goal when forced to do so by other countries. (*LO36-1*)

- Expansionary monetary policy, through its effect on income, increases a country's trade deficit. (*LO36-2*)

- Contractionary fiscal policy tends to decrease a country's trade deficit. (*LO36-2*)

- For every effect that monetary and fiscal policies have on a country's exchange rate and trade balance, there is an equal and opposite effect on the combination of foreign countries' exchange rates and trade balances. Therefore, countries try to coordinate their policies. (*LO36-3*)

- International financial inflows can reduce crowding out. (*LO36-3*)

- Internationalizing a country's debt means that at some time in the future the country must consume less than it produces. (*LO36-3*)

- The United States has lost its competitiveness in the production of many goods. Unless foreigners continue to demand U.S. assets, the U.S. trade deficit will put downward pressure on the dollar and U.S. policy makers will face implementing contractionary policies, trade restrictions, or structural adjustments to improve U.S. comparative advantage. (*LO36-4*)

Key Terms

competitiveness   policy coordination

Questions and Exercises ■ connect

1. Is it better to have a low or high exchange rate? (*LO36-1*)

2. Is it better to have a trade deficit or a trade surplus? (*LO36-1*)

3. Why can't a country target both its interest rate and exchange rate? (*LO36-1*)

4. What effect on the U.S. trade deficit would result if China and Japan ran an expansionary monetary policy? (*LO36-2*)

5. What would be the effect on the U.S. trade deficit if China and Japan ran a contractionary fiscal policy? (*LO36-2*)

6. Draw the schematics to show the effect of expansionary monetary policy on the trade deficit. (*LO36-2*)

7. You observe that over the past decade a country's trade deficit has risen. (*LO36-2*)
   a. What monetary or fiscal policies might have led to such a result?
   b. You also observe that interest rates have steadily risen along with a rise in the exchange rate. What policies would lead to this result?
   c. Could another explanation be that people in other countries wanted to hold lots of that country's debt?

8. Congratulations! You have been appointed as an adviser to the IMF. A country that has run trade deficits for many years now has difficulty servicing its accumulated international debt and wants to borrow from the IMF to meet its obligations. The IMF requires that the country set a target trade surplus. (*LO36-2*)
   a. What monetary and fiscal policies would you suggest the IMF require of that country?
   b. What would be the likely effect of that plan on the country's domestic inflation and growth?
   c. How do you think the country's government will respond to your proposals? Why?

9. Congratulations! You've been hired as an economic adviser to the government of a country that has perfectly flexible exchange rates. State what monetary and fiscal policy you might suggest in each of the following situations, and explain why you would suggest those policies. (*LO36-2*)
   a. You want to lower the interest rate, decrease inflationary pressures, and lower the trade deficit.

   b. You want to lower the interest rate, decrease inflationary pressures, and lower the trade surplus.
   c. You want to lower the interest rate, decrease unemployment, and lower the trade deficit.
   d. You want to raise the interest rate, decrease unemployment, and lower the trade deficit.

10. Is the United States justified in complaining about Japan's and China's use of an export-led growth policy? Why or why not? (*LO36-3*)

11. In the 1990s, Japan's economic recession was much in the news. (*LO36-3*)
    a. What would you suspect was happening to its trade balance during this time?
    b. What policies would you guess other countries (such as those in the Group of Eight) were pressuring Japan to implement?

12. According to a study done at JPMorgan Chase, as world trade increased from about 12 percent of world output in the 1970s to about 25 percent of world output in the early 2000s, global differences in growth rates decreased, from around 3 percent in the 1970s to about 1 percent in the early 2000s. (*LO36-3*)
    a. If that is true, would one expect more or less stabilization coming from trade with other countries?
    b. What does this convergence of growth rates suggest about the possibility of a global recession?
    c. If a global recession occurred, what policy recommendation would you put forward?

13. How does internationalizing the debt reduce crowding out? (*LO36-3*)

14. What are the costs of internationalizing the debt? (*LO36-3*)

15. Countries must choose an exchange rate policy. (*LO36-4*)
    a. Why is currency stabilization limited through direct purchases?
    b. What are a country's other options?

16. Why are there strong political forces to manage exchange rates? (*LO36-4*)

(Continued)

17. Domestic policy as it relates to a country's currency is related to the state of the economy. *(LO36-4)*
    a. Why didn't the United States have to implement contractionary policy following World War II even though the value of the dollar was high?
    b. Why didn't a decline in U.S. competitiveness in the 1970s require the United States to run contractionary policy?

    c. Why is the trade deficit creating a challenge to domestic policy today?

18. Why don't foreign countries want the U.S. dollar to fall precipitously? *(LO36-4)*

Questions from Alternative Perspectives

1. In developed countries, the usefulness of an activist monetary and fiscal policy is highly questionable. Why is it even more questionable in developing countries? *(Austrian)*

2. The United States has been consuming more than it has been producing for more than 30 years, making it the largest debtor nation in the world. Deuteronomy 28:43–44 warns against such indebtedness to foreigners: "Aliens residing among you shall ascend above you higher and higher, while you shall descend lower and lower. They shall lend to you but you shall not lend to them; they shall be the head and you shall be the tail."
    a. Is the trade deficit bad even if it can continue indefinitely?
    b. Are there biblical precepts against living beyond one's means that suggest any trade deficit is bad?
    c. In what way is the Deuteronomist saying true for America today? *(Religious)*

3. In 2015, the U.S. federal budget deficit (how much greater government spending was than taxes) was about 2.5 percent of GDP. That year the trade deficit (how much imports surpassed exports) was about 3 percent of GDP. Also in 2015, investment in the U.S. economy exceeded U.S. private savings by about 5 percent of GDP.
    a. What is the relationship among these three balances?
    b. What do they tell us about who financed the U.S. budget deficit in 2015?
    c. What do they suggest about the extent of crowding out of private investment in the U.S. economy in 2015? *(Institutionalist)*

4. The U.S. trade deficit was about $531 billion, or 3 percent of GDP, in 2015. Some economists argue that this gap is truly frightening because the current account deficit is the amount of money the United States must attract from abroad. If foreign investors stop buying U.S. bonds and stocks, then skyrocketing interest rates, plummeting stock values, and an economic downturn will surely follow. Others see the gaping current account deficit as a sign of economic vitality. The flipside of a large trade deficit is, after all, a surplus of capital flowing into your country.
    a. Is the U.S. current account deficit a sign of impending disaster or a sign of economic health or something in between?
    b. How has this unprecedented shortfall affected the U.S. economy and how will it affect our economic future? *(Post-Keynesian)*

5. What has happened to world income inequality is a matter of sharp dispute. Many analysts claim that world incomes converged in the second half of the 20th century, leading to a sharp reduction in world inequality. Many others report that the gap between the poorest and the richest people and countries has continued to widen over the last two decades. When a friend who writes about global inequality sorted through these studies, he came to this conclusion: "The wide range of different results of respected studies of world inequality in the last two decades casts doubt on the idea that world inequality has sharply and unambiguously declined or increased during the epoch of neoliberalism." Assuming the friend has read them correctly and fairly, what do these studies imply about the globalization process? *(Radical)*

Issues to Ponder

1. Look up the current U.S. exchange rate relative to the yen. Would you suggest raising it or lowering it? Why?

2. Look up the current U.S. trade balance. Would you suggest raising it or lowering it? Why?

3. What would likely happen to exchange rates if one country has a comparative advantage in production of most goods and the financial and capital account was balanced?

Answers to Margin Questions

1. A low exchange rate value of a country's currency will tend to stimulate exports and curtail imports.   *(LO36-1)*

2. A trade deficit means a country is consuming more than it is producing. Consuming more than producing is pleasant. It also means that capital is flowing into the country, which can be used for investment. Proponents also argue that the inflow of financial capital from foreigners would finance new investment that would make an economy strong enough in the long run to reverse the trade deficit. So why worry?   *(LO36-1)*

3. To increase the value of its currency, a country can increase the private demand for its currency by implementing contractionary monetary policy or it could decrease private supply of its currency by implementing contractionary monetary and fiscal policy.   *(LO36-1)*

4. Contractionary monetary policy will likely lead to an increase in its exchange rate.   *(LO36-1)*

5. Contractionary monetary policy will tend to decrease income, decreasing imports and decreasing the trade deficit.   *(LO36-2)*

6. The effect of expansionary fiscal policy on the trade deficit is to increase the trade deficit.   *(LO36-2)*

7. If other countries stop buying dollar-denominated assets, the value of the dollar will likely fall.   *(LO36-3)*

8. Generally, when domestic policies and international policies conflict, a country will choose to deal with its domestic problems. Thus, it will likely use expansionary monetary policy if domestic problems call for that.   *(LO36-3)*

9. Because foreigners buy U.S. bonds that finance the U.S. debt, the demand for bonds is higher than it otherwise would be and the interest rate is lower than it otherwise would be.   *(LO36-3)*

10. If a country has a fixed exchange rate, it has less flexibility in choosing its monetary and fiscal policies to achieve domestic goals.   *(LO36-4)*

Structural Stagnation and Globalization

CHAPTER 37

> Illusions commend themselves to us because they save us pain and allow us to enjoy pleasure instead. We must therefore accept it without complaint when they sometimes collide with a bit of reality against which they are dashed to pieces.
>
> —Sigmund Freud

After reading this chapter, you should be able to:

LO37-1 Differentiate a structural stagnation from a standard recession.

LO37-2 Demonstrate using the *AS/AD* model how globalization can mask inflationary pressures caused by expansionary policies.

LO37-3 Describe the structural problems caused by globalization.

LO37-4 Outline the policy choices that policy makers have to deal with structural stagnation.

In December 2007 the U.S. economy fell into a downturn that initiated a prolonged period of slow growth and stagnation; it wasn't a depression, but it wasn't a normal recession either. As in a typical downturn in a business cycle, unemployment rose and output fell, but unlike a typical downturn, the economy did not seem to recover even when the government ran expansionary demand-side macro policy. If the recession had been part of a typical business cycle, expansionary policy *would have* pulled aggre-

©zimmytws/Shutterstock

gate output back to its growth trend. It is now 2018, and the economy has come out of its recession, but there is still debate whether it has returned to its long-term growth path. It is as if the economy has contracted a chronic disease that is preventing it from returning to its long-run growth trend. *Time* magazine called this prolonged period of slow growth the "wimpy recovery" that did not end.

Economists are still debating why the economy is growing more slowly than expected, and in this chapter, I provide one explanation—the **structural stagnation hypothesis**—*a hypothesis about the macro economy that sees the recent problems of the U.S. economy as directly related to the structural problems caused by displacement due to globalization and technological change.* This structural stagnation hypothesis provides a possible explanation for why the economy is experiencing slower growth than we would like, and why so many complain about the nature of the growth that is occurring. In this chapter we will focus on the displacement problems caused by globalization, and only briefly discuss the related displacement problems of technological change.

In some ways the structural stagnation hypothesis is conventional—structural issues are what microeconomics focuses on. But in macro it is less conventional to focus on structural issues. Thus, your professor may have a different take on some or all aspects of the issues presented in this chapter. This is as it should be. Macroeconomic theory, as it relates to recent events, is unsettled; it is very much in flux. To present it any other way is to be disingenuous. There are conflicting interpretations even among economists of what is happening in the U.S. economy and what should be done about it.

Regardless of whether or not one agrees with the structural stagnation hypothesis presented in this chapter, it is useful as a tool for learning. It is an example of the economic way of thinking—how economic reasoning blends different economic ideas and concepts from both microeconomics and macroeconomics into plausible explanations for current events. The second part of economic reasoning, the empirical testing of the ideas, is what is covered in higher-level economics courses.

The Structural Stagnation Hypothesis

According to the structural stagnation hypothesis, the slow growth and stagnation the United States experienced in the first decades of the 21st century had both long-run and short-run causes. The long-run cause is intricately related to globalization, exchange rates, and the trade deficit. The short-run cause is intricately tied to the aftermath of the financial crisis that occurred in 2007, and now in 2018 has generally subsided as the immediate financial problems in the United States have been resolved. The two are related because one of the causes of the financial crisis was that government was avoiding dealing with the problems created by the economic displacement caused by globalization and technological change. The government is still trying to avoid dealing with these longer-run problems, which creates the possibility of another financial crisis.

According to the structural stagnation hypothesis, structural stagnation has both long-run and short-run causes.

Standard business cycles are cycles that can be resolved with standard monetary and fiscal policy. As the economy goes into recession, the government runs deficits and expansionary monetary policy, pulling the economy out of recession. The government might get the timing wrong, but the guidance from economists for what to do in a recession is standard and should be familiar to you. A standard recession is a short-run problem dealt with using short-run policies.

In a structural stagnation, those short-run policies may work to bring the economy out of recession, but they won't return the economy to its long-run growth path because of structural problems. Structural problems have to be dealt with using long-run structural policies. Short-run policy can temporarily mask, but cannot solve, long-run structural problems. In fact, it can make the long-run problems worse.

Why the Assumed Underlying Growth Trend Is Important for Policy

The biggest change that the structural stagnation hypothesis makes to standard macro theory involves the economy's assumed underlying growth rate during a recovery. The standard macro policy assumption is that after a downturn, an economy will quickly get back to its long-run trend growth rate of 3 to 3.5 percent. Structural stagnation assumes that the adjustment will take much longer, and that returning to a 3 to 3.5 long-term growth trend will require dealing with the structural changes that precipitated the downturn. The hallmark of structural stagnation is slow growth, an economy that doesn't create the type of jobs people want or are qualified for, and a general dissatisfaction with the economy's performance even if there is low unemployment and low inflation.

The biggest change that the structural stagnation hypothesis makes to standard macro theory involves the economy's assumed underlying growth rate in a recovery.

Business Cycles in History

Before Keynesian economics came to dominate macroeconomic discussions, economists talked about business cycles. They developed numerous categories to describe cycles of various lengths—Juglar cycles, Jevons cycles, Kitchin cycles, Kuznets cycles, Kondratief cycles, and many more. Students could spend a whole course learning all the cycles, each having different explanations for causes and length. (For example, Kondratief cycles were 50-year cycles that could come in sync or out of sync with other cycles that could make it stronger or weaker.)

With the rise of Keynesian economics and modern macroeconomics, as well as better statistical measurement, these "named" cycle theories were abandoned and economists talked about generic random fluctuations, not predictable cycles with different lengths and different characteristics. They saw fluctuations as being caused by random fluctuations in demand. Because the shocks were random, empirical predictability of any predetermined cycle couldn't be supported. After World War II, most

macroeconomists expected recessions to be short because we now had a remedy—expansionary government demand-side policy. In the conventional view, we might not be able to totally eliminate business cycles, but we could make them milder and prevent them from turning into long drawn-out stagnations. Most economists shared this highly optimistic view—that the macroeconomic problem of drawn-out stagnations was solved. They did not see a major depression as a possibility. Even Keynesian critic Robert Lucas stated, "The central problem of depression-prevention [has] been solved, for all practical purposes."

The optimism of macroeconomists came in for a rude shock in 2007, the start of a prolonged downturn. This has led to renewed interest in these earlier discussions of the reasons for longer and shorter cycles. In the new view, macroeconomic fluctuations can have different causes; one cannot treat all fluctuations with the same medicine. Instead, the treatments must be tailored to the causes of the fluctuation.

This difference between the assumptions of standard macro policy and structural stagnation is important because the assumed growth rate for the economy plays a central role in policy advice. You can see the importance of the assumed growth rate in Figure 37-1. In it the straight-line trend growth rate is assumed to be 3 percent, the rate that existed throughout most of U.S. history since World War II and the growth rate assumed by economists who subscribe to the standard macro model. The curved line

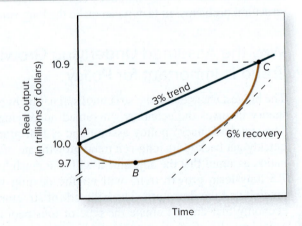

FIGURE 37-1 **Expansions to Maintain Trend Growth**

In a typical recovery, economic expansion must significantly exceed the trend growth rate to make up for the decline and catch up with the rise in potential output.

shows a standard recession and recovery. The recession begins at point *A* and pulls the economy below the trend growth rate until it hits the trough at point *B*. At this point, the economy begins to recover until real output returns to potential output (along the long-term growth path) at point *C*. What's important to note is that, for the economy to return to its growth path, the rate at which the economy expands during the recovery must be greater than the trend rate. That's because it must make up for the resulting gap between actual output and potential output.

Figure 37-1 also shows the faster growth needed numerically to eliminate the gap created by the recession. Suppose real economic output is $10 trillion (point *A*) and the economy falls by 3 percent in one year, to $9.7 trillion (point *B*). For the economy to recover within two years (point *C*), it would have to increase at an annual rate of about 6 percent per year. The economy needs to grow by more than the 3 percent decline during the recession to make up for the decline in output during the recession *and* the rise in potential—in this case the $0.3 trillion *plus* the $0.9 trillion for a total of $1.2 trillion.

Q-1 Why must an economy grow faster in a recovery than it declined during a recession to return to its long-term growth trend?

Most policy makers were expecting such a robust recovery in 2008 when they ran highly expansionary fiscal policy—a $1 trillion-plus annual government deficit—and highly expansionary monetary policy in response to the recession. The expectation was that the economy would initially expand at a high annual rate of 6 percent for two or three years, which would get it back on its 3 percent long-term growth trend. During this period, they didn't worry too much about the high budget deficit because the strong recovery would allow the economy to "grow out of the deficit." By that they meant that the deficits as a percentage of GDP would decline when both tax revenues and GDP rose quickly in the expansion. Once the economy recovered, they did not see a need for ongoing deficits and highly expansionary monetary policy to keep stimulating the economy. And that would have been the case if it were a standard recession. But it wasn't.

The standard macroeconomists didn't worry much about the high budget deficit because they expected that a strong recovery would allow the economy to "grow out of the deficit."

After contracting by 0.1 percent in 2008 and 2.5 percent in 2009 (the economy hit its trough in June 2009), the economy rose only 2.6 percent in 2010 and slowed to 1.6 percent in 2011. Further, the unemployment rate remained stubbornly high, jumping from 4.7 percent just before the financial crisis in 2007 to 10 percent in the fall of 2009 and falling only 2 percentage points to 8.2 percent by mid-2012. This is why the economy was said to have experienced a jobless recovery. It was this situation that led the Fed to adopt unconventional monetary policy designed to further expand the economy. Eventually, in 2016, the unemployment rate fell below 5 percent, but many of the new jobs were low-wage jobs, not the type of jobs people wanted. In 2018, the U.S. economy finally started heating up and approached what many considered its potential; unemployment fell to below 4 percent and the labor participation rate began rising. Even then, the Fed was hesitant to undo the unconventional expansionary monetary policy that it had instituted during the recession, for fear of creating another recession.

The reality is that economists just don't know what the underlying growth trend is, and that underlying growth rate has enormous implications for policy. Given our limited state of knowledge of that growth trend, policy depends on rough guesses rather than on precise science. Those who support expansionary fiscal policy argue that potential output is high, and the U.S. economy is significantly below potential income. Those who oppose expansionary fiscal policy see the level of potential output as lower. When pushed, both sides see the output gap as highly speculative, which is why output gaps have been called FROGS (Frivolously Related Output Gaps) by the Institute of International Finance (a global association of firms in the finance industry that argued for European countries to implement much more expansionary fiscal policy).

Structural Stagnation as a Cause of the Slow Recovery

The failure of standard monetary and fiscal policy to generate the 6 to 7 percent temporary growth that policy makers expected after the 2008 recession led economists to search for reasons why, and structural stagnation was one explanation. This explanation is pessimistic about the sustainable demand-side growth prospects for the United States. As mentioned above, according to structural stagnationists, the U.S. economy is experiencing structural changes that will keep it from returning to a sustained 3 percent growth trend in the near term. Further, according to this hypothesis, the structural stagnation problem began in the mid-1990s. It lowered the growth trend for the U.S. economy below what had been assumed for the past decade. If this hypothesis is correct, the demand-side government policy in the early 2000s was too expansionary and led to the 2007 financial crisis. The hypothesis also suggests that the recovery since that time, which has not dealt with structural causes of the recession and slow growth, has made the U.S. economy prone to another financial crisis. According to the structural stagnation hypothesis, if the United States wants to avoid another financial crisis, it will have to learn to live with a slower sustained growth rate of about 2.25 percent.

Structural Stagnation's Implications for Macro Policy

You can see the different policy implications of the standard 3 percent trend growth assumption and the structural stagnation 2.25 percent growth trend assumption in Figure 37-2. The trend growth rate is a central difference between the standard theory and the structural stagnation hypothesis. Both assume a 3 percent growth trend up until 1995 and an eventual return to the 3 percent growth trend in the future. The difference is that the structural stagnationists believe that the United States will likely never recoup the full loss of output during the structural stagnation.

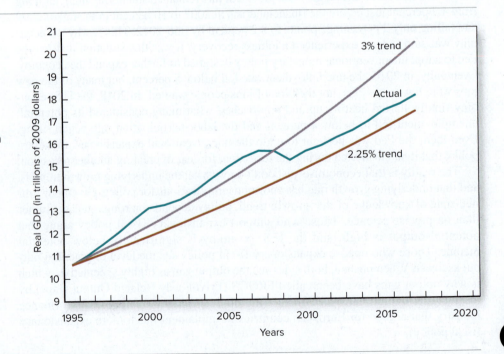

FIGURE 37-2 **Policy Implications of Structural Stagnation**

If the long-run growth path falls, but policy makers do not adjust their estimates for the fall, they will target a higher potential output than is sustainable and eventually create problems for an economy. One of the problems this "too high targeting" creates is a financial bubble.

Where the theories differ substantially is what the trend path of the economy should have been from the onset of the pressures of globalization in the late 1990s and the following decades, or when the structural problems are resolved. Standard-model economists are the optimists; they believe in a continued 3 percent growth trend, as shown by the purple line throughout this time period. Structural stagnationists are the pessimists; they believe the trend line fell closer to 2.25 percent in the late 1990s and 2000, as shown by the orange line. They argue that the trend will start to return to a long-run 3 percent trend only when the structural problems have been resolved. So, the best we should have been hoping for in the 2000s was a 2.25 percent growth trend. That small difference in targeted trend makes an enormous difference in one's view of whether demand-side policy during this period was too expansionary.

> The assumed trend growth rate is a central difference between the standard theory and the structural stagnation hypothesis.

In the early 2000s, the economy grew by over 3 percent a year and inflation remained low. So, all looked well. Advocates of the structural stagnation hypothesis believe, however, that what was in fact happening was that the economy was operating significantly above its sustainable level of potential output during this entire period. The result of trying to keep the economy above its potential was an unsustainable financial bubble. That bubble burst in late 2007, pushing the economy back down toward its actual growth trend. As you can see with a 2.25 percent growth trend, the recession that resulted from the financial crisis was simply pulling the economy back down toward its true potential growth trend.

The issue is long-run sustainability, not whether the U.S. economy might grow faster than 2.25 percent if the government runs expansionary macro policy as it did in 2018. The structural stagnation hypothesis holds that while faster growth can be achieved with expansionary monetary and fiscal policy, it is not necessarily desirable to do so. The faster growth runs a high risk of causing new financial bubbles and additional problems, just as the expansionary macro policy in the early 2000s did. According to the structural stagnation hypothesis, expansionary fiscal and monetary policies hide the underlying structural problems by inflating asset prices and creating an illusion of increased wealth. The bottom line: If the structural stagnation hypothesis is true, as the United States undergoes the structural changes that are required by globalization, it should accept slow growth and work on solving its structural problems.

> If the structural stagnation hypothesis is true, the United States will likely experience a decade of slow growth and high unemployment.

Structural, Not Secular, Stagnation

Economists in the 1940s after the Great Depression had a quite different argument for why an economy would experience prolonged slow growth after World War II. Their argument is called the **secular stagnation theory,** *a theory in which advanced countries such as the United States would eventually stop growing because investment opportunities would be eliminated.* This theory is associated with Alvin Hansen and economists in the 1940s who introduced Keynesian economics to the United States. The central tenet of Hansen's secular stagnation theory was that eventually all investment opportunities will be met. Without new investment opportunities, the investment component of aggregate demand will wither, and along with it economic growth. Eventually economic growth for all economies throughout the world would decline, and growth would stop.

Some economists, such as Larry Summers, have called the recent slowdown in growth—what I have called *structural* stagnation—*secular* stagnation, using the *secular stagnation* term as a catchall for "a prolonged period of below-trend economic growth or no growth at all." That is a misleading name because historically, as I discussed above, the term *secular stagnation* associated with Alvin Hansen's theory didn't mean just a period of slow growth; it meant a future of permanent slow growth, which economists called the stationary state. In this stationary state, profitable investment opportunities would no longer exist. The reason the term *secular stagnation* doesn't fit the existing situation is that Hansen was proved wrong—investment opportunities did not dry up and technological advances have continually created new investment opportunities.

The term *secular stagnation* and Summers' explanation for it—that, at a positive interest rate, savings are greater than investment due to the lack of investment opportunities—has been challenged by numerous economists. For example, economist Robert Gordon pointed out that investment opportunities haven't disappeared. He suggests that there were other explanations for the slow growth—what he called "headwinds." These other reasons include demography—people have gotten older; education—gains from education have been used up; inequality—gains from productivity have gone to the rich; and government debt—the rise in government debt makes current public services unsustainable. He suggests simply calling secular stagnation *slow growth*.

I have followed a different route and have called the slow growth that the U.S. economy is experiencing structural stagnation. *Structural stagnation* is a generic term for slow growth. It can include many different causes, including all those that Gordon identifies. Thus, it is consistent with both Gordon's and Summers' explanations. But it is also consistent with another explanation that I will highlight in this chapter. This explanation does not assume that low global investment will slow global growth, or that the world growth trend will fall. Instead, it focuses on the effect of **globalization**—*the increasing economic connections among economies around the world that increase competition among countries*—on U.S. growth. According to the structural stagnation hypothesis, globalization causes structural problems that primarily affect advanced economies, particularly the United States and European economies. Dealing with these structural problems of globalization will keep their economic growth below world economic growth into the foreseeable future as much of world economic growth takes place in developing countries.

Another structural adjustment that the United States is facing involves job displacement by the information revolution discussed in earlier chapters. While technological advances increase global growth, they do not do so evenly; some countries will grow fast while others grow slowly. Similarly, within countries, technological advances will spur growth in some parts of the economy and leave others to languish. For example, technological advances may replace some lower- and middle-class jobs for which people have training with a few highly specialized and highly paid jobs for which most people don't have training. The result can be an increase in income and wealth inequality, and a reduction in demand for goods typically bought by lower- and middle-income individuals and even less overall demand for goods since the rich are more likely to spend their money on nonreproducible assets whose value increases, but which don't create many new jobs. So technological change can lead to less overall demand for produced goods. Government can make up for some of that lower demand in the short run by increasing its deficit, but that deficit does not resolve the underlying structural problem. To keep the discussion manageable, I will focus on the globalization part of structural problems.

Q-2 What is the structural stagnation hypothesis' explanation for slowing growth?

The *AS/AD* Model with Globalization

For the structural stagnation hypothesis to fit the U.S. experience, it must explain how globalization led to structural problems and what those structural problems are. Let's first consider how the structural stagnation hypothesis sees globalization affecting potential output. We do so in Figure 37-3, which presents the **globalized *AS/AD* model**—*a modified* AS/AD *model with an added world supply curve that highlights the effect that globalization can have on an economy.*

The globalized *AS/AD* model adds a world supply curve to the standard *AS/AD* model to capture the effect that globalization issues can have on an economy.

FIGURE 37-3(A, B, AND C)   The Globalized *AS/AD* Model

The model in (**a**) is the standard *AS/AD* model with an economy in both short-run and long-run equilibrium. The globalized *AS/AD* model in (**b**) has a flat world aggregate supply curve. In this figure, the economy is also in short-run and long-run equilibrium because all the curves meet at the same location. The current situation in the United States is shown in (**c**) with a world supply curve that is below what would have been the equilibrium price in the standard *AS/AD* model.

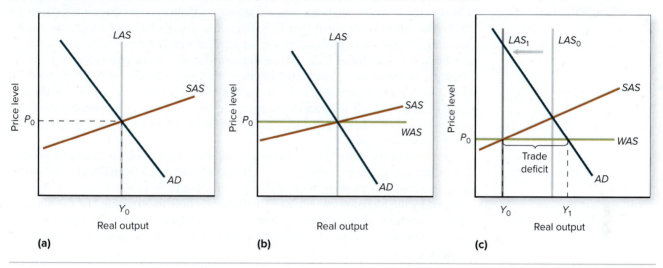

(a)   (b)   (c)

Let's begin with the standard *AS/AD* model shown in Figure 37-3(a). The economy is in short-run equilibrium where the *SAS* and *AD* curves intersect and is in long-run equilibrium when the *SAS*, *AD*, and *LAS* curves all intersect. The situation shown in Figure 37-3(a) is of an economy that is in both short-run and long-run equilibrium because the *SAS* and *AD* curves meet at potential output denoted by the *LAS* curve.

In this standard *AS/AD* model the U.S. aggregate demand curve represents the demand for domestic output—the amount that U.S. consumers will demand from domestic producers at each price level. Similarly, the U.S. aggregate supply curve is the amount of goods that U.S.-based firms will supply at each price level. In the globalized *AS/AD* model we modify the definitions slightly and define the *AD* curve as the *demand for output,* not just the *demand for domestic output.* This allows us to highlight the structural effects of a trade imbalance.[1]

To see how the world economy affects the *AS/AD* model, we must add an additional curve—the world supply curve. Figure 37-3(b) adds the **world supply curve**— *the amount of tradable goods that other countries in the world will supply to the country at a given price level and exchange rate.* (Throughout this discussion I will discuss goods, but it should be clear that *goods* also includes services.) I include the exchange rate in the definition because the exchange rate will change the price of imported goods. Specifically, as explained in Chapter 9, when the domestic exchange rate falls, the price of imports rises and the world aggregate supply curve shifts up;

Q-3   How is the globalized *AS/AD* model different from the standard *AS/AD* model?

---

[1]The difference between the standard *AS/AD* model and the globalized *AS/AD* model is that the standard *AS/AD* model does not highlight the effect of imbalanced trade on potential output and unemployment. This means that it doesn't highlight how much aggregate demand is supplied by U.S. production and how much is supplied by foreign production. The difference—net exports— does not show up in the standard *AS/AD* model. This alternative model highlights the role of net exports in the economy.

Web Note 37.1

Globalization and
Inflation

when the domestic exchange rate rises, the price of imports falls and the world aggregate supply curve shifts down.

The world supply curve is flat because we assume that, for all practical purposes, foreign producers can supply an infinite amount of tradable goods at the world price. What this means is that the world supply curve sets a price ceiling for U.S. goods, and all U.S. producers of tradable goods must match the world price. For example, if China is the low-cost producer, and a company in China can produce a television for $600, that $600 is the most that U.S. firms can charge for equivalent televisions. Similarly, if the cost in India of answering a call at a call center is $2 a call, that $2 is the highest price that a U.S. call center can charge for an equivalent service. If domestic producers don't match world prices, they won't be able to sell their goods in the United States or abroad. That equivalency follows from the law of one price—equivalent goods sell for equivalent prices. (When we say an equivalent good we mean price after adjusting for transportation costs and other aspects of goods that make them comparable.)

Notice that the definition of the world supply curve specified "tradable goods." That's because the world supply curve affects only those goods in direct competition with international producers—tradable goods. Nontradable goods are not directly affected by the global price. (Below, I will discuss how the tradable and the nontradable sectors have quite different experiences with globalization and how these experiences cause structural problems for the economy. For now we assume all goods are tradable.)

Figure 37-3(b) shows a world supply curve that intersects at the short- and long-run equilibrium—where the *LAS, SAS,* and *AD* curves meet. In this case net exports (exports minus imports) are zero. While some of the goods that the United States purchases are imported, those imports are exactly offset by exports. Since the world price level equals the U.S. price level at equilibrium, globalization by itself does not change the results of the standard model.

Q-4 If the world supply curve is below the domestic economy's long-run equilibrium price level, what is true about its trade balance?

But what happens if the world price is lower than the equilibrium price? In that case there would be a trade deficit, as there has been in the United States over the past 20 years. In Figure 37-3(c) I demonstrate this case. The world price level is P_0, so we draw the world supply curve as a horizontal line at P_0. The world supply curve intersects the domestic aggregate supply curve at Y_0 and intersects the aggregate demand curve at Y_1. Consumers buy Y_1, Y_0 of which is supplied by domestic producers. The remaining demand ($Y_1 - Y_0$) is met by foreign producers.

Globalization Can Limit Potential Output

Notice that a world price for goods below the U.S. price of goods enables U.S. consumers to consume more than they had previously. But it also makes it harder for U.S. producers to sell their goods, which means that, due to structural reasons, international competitive forces put a limit on domestic potential output, in this case at LAS_1. This fall in potential output may seem strange. After all, the number of workers hasn't declined and neither has the number of factories. So the United States could continue to produce just as much as it could before.

If potential output were determined only by the physical existence of workers and factories, potential output *would not* have fallen. But according to the structural stagnation hypothesis, potential output depends on more than physical productive capacity; it depends on the wages, technology, and global competitive conditions. If a worker wants $30 an hour and the economy only has a $10 job for him, that worker won't take the job and will not contribute to potential output. He is structurally unemployed, and his existence does not contribute to potential output unless he is willing to lower his wage to a level at which he can find a job that is sustainable in the global economy. Similarly with a factory. If its technology is no longer globally competitive, it does not contribute to potential output; it might just as well be boarded up. So if there isn't sustainable demand for U.S. inputs to production at their going wage or price, those inputs don't contribute to potential output.

In the short run, the effect of globalization (which involves the introduction of countries with lower costs in most goods at existing exchange rates) on the U.S. economy is to lower the U.S.'s potential output until the United States structurally adjusts and U.S. producers are competitive with foreign producers without a trade deficit. Notice that I am not saying that globalization hurts society. While globalization can lower potential output, it also increases the amount a country can consume if aggregate demand can be held at its current position. The gap between a country's potential output and its consumption is directly related to its trade deficit—the further apart the two are from one another, the greater the trade deficit.

According to the structural stagnation hypothesis, the difference between Figure 37-3(b) and Figure 37-3(c) represents the changing macro problem facing the United States in the early 2000s. Until the 1990s, Figure 37-3(b) was a reasonable description of the U.S. economy. But when China's and India's 2.7-billion-people economies started to be integrated into the world economy, that changed. Before then, although there were certainly issues with globalization, international trade was a small part of the U.S. economy. The trade deficit was small because the United States was the low-cost producer for a variety of goods that had no serious global competitors. These U.S. low-cost sectors offset other high-cost sectors where foreign producers provided the low-cost goods. Before the 1990s, international issues could be added as a secondary issue in the discussion of macro policy. That is no longer the case.

According to the structural stagnation hypothesis, Figure 37-3(c) is a better description of the situation facing the United States since the late 1990s, and it is the model that can highlight the structural problems that the United States is now facing. It is a model in which U.S. potential output has been lowered by the forces of globalization and the United States runs a consistently large trade deficit because its exchange rate has not adjusted to equalize trade flows. Just as some countries, such as China, experienced export-led growth, the United States experienced *import-led stagnation*.

According to the structural stagnation hypothesis, the U.S. trade deficit has a significant impact on employment—a $550 billion trade deficit translates into millions of fewer jobs for the United States than if there was no trade deficit and everything else was identical. Simply put, the trade deficit translates into higher unemployment and lower potential output until these displaced workers find new jobs in different fields that are competitive in the globalized economy.

> If there isn't sustainable demand for U.S. inputs to production at their going wage or price, those inputs don't contribute to potential output.

> A trade deficit translates into higher unemployment and lower potential output until those displaced workers find new jobs in different fields that are competitive in the globalized economy.

International Adjustment Forces

In the globalized *AS/AD* model what is supposed to happen is that international and domestic adjustments will be set in motion to eliminate the trade deficit, as discussed in Chapter 9. These forces include: (1) changes in exchange rates, (2) changes in relative wages and costs of production, and (3) changes in aggregate demand.

One adjustment is for the U.S. exchange rate to fall, which would shift the world supply curve up, reducing both domestic spending and how much of that spending is met with foreign production. The downward pressure on the exchange rate is supposed to continue until exports and imports are equal. This fall in the exchange rate would create some inflationary pressures in the United States as import prices rise and global prices are no longer holding down U.S. prices, but a large enough exchange rate fall would eliminate the structural unemployment caused by globalization.

Three factors that will eliminate the trade deficit are:

1. Changes in exchange rates.
2. Changes in relative wages and costs of production.
3. Changes in aggregate demand.

A second adjustment is for U.S. wages and costs of production to fall in response to high unemployment and a lack of international demand for U.S. goods. This fall in costs would shift down the short-run aggregate supply curve. A fall in U.S. wages and costs of production will have the side effect of decreasing U.S. consumption since falling wages and costs mean workers have less income to spend.

A third adjustment is for aggregate demand to fall, as those workers and other factors that became unemployed because of the global competition reduce their demand for goods and services. As you can see, these three adjustments come with negative side effects. The upside is that given enough time, these adjustments will bring the economy back to a global and domestic equilibrium.

Why the Adjustments Did Not Occur

If international adjustments had happened, U.S. growth and potential output would have fallen temporarily until the adjustments were complete. But, according to the structural stagnation hypothesis, that didn't happen. One reason why was that government held up aggregate demand to hold unemployment down. That expansionary aggregate demand fueled a financial bubble (unsustainable rise in asset prices) and allowed private aggregate demand to remain high despite the structural problems. By expanding aggregate demand, the United States avoided making the adjustments to a long-run sustainable equilibrium. The trade deficit and the willingness of foreigners to loan the United States money allowed it to avoid facing the difficult structural issues involved in adjusting to a new sustainable long-run equilibrium. The large trade deficit continued from the 1990s until today. So even after 30 years the international adjustment forces still have not eliminated the U.S. trade deficit [see Figure 37-3(c)].

You might ask how an increase in aggregate demand could be effective in holding down unemployment when all demand for tradables would go into global, not domestic, markets. In the globalized *AS/AD* model any increase in aggregate demand will simply lead to increased imports and an even larger trade deficit. But as I said, all goods are not tradable. Some of the increase in aggregate demand during the 1990s and early 2000s went to increased production in the nontradable sector, which is shielded from direct global competition. With a sufficiently large increase in aggregate demand, those who became unemployed in the tradable sector could shift to jobs in the nontradable sector, keeping the overall unemployment low. If the nontradable sectors grow enough, these sectors can temporarily absorb the unemployment caused by globalization. Unfortunately, if the growth in the nontradable sector is dependent on a financial bubble or unsustainable deficits, it is not a permanent solution.

According to the structural stagnation hypothesis, the problem with this expansionary macro policy is that it prevented the structural adjustments, which would have been induced by higher unemployment, from bringing the economy back into international equilibrium without a trade deficit. Instead of workers accepting pay cuts, or learning additional skills that would have retained globally competitive jobs in the United States by making the U.S. tradable sector globally competitive, government policy enabled workers to take the easier path of working at the newly available jobs in the nontradable sector such as education, government, health care, locally produced services, and retail sales jobs.

Aggregate Demand Increases No Longer Cause Accelerating Inflation

Notice the difference for inflation between this globalized *AS/AD* model and the standard *AS/AD* model. In the standard *AS/AD* model, any increase in aggregate demand above potential output will cause inflation. Potential output presents an upward limit to expansionary aggregate demand. When aggregate demand exceeds potential output, excess demand will cause wages and prices to rise, causing the *SAS* curve to begin shifting up as the higher prices become built into people's expectations, leading to higher wage demands. As prices rise, overall real spending falls. If government tries to keep real spending from falling, inflation will accelerate; equilibrium with output higher than potential is unsustainable. You should be able to go through this analysis, explaining why unsustainable inflation would occur. (If you can't, you should review the argument in Chapter 26.)

In the structural stagnation hypothesis' globalized *AS/AD* model, the economy can exceed potential output without generating accelerating inflation because the world price level puts a cap on the domestic price level. Because inflation is the primary signal to policy makers that the economy has exceeded potential output, policy makers aren't forced to run contractionary policy to bring the economy back to its potential. In fact, the government can run highly expansionary macro policies, shifting output and employment from the manufacturing tradable sector to the nontradable sectors, creating the illusion that the economy is doing great. According to the structural stagnation hypothesis this was the situation in the early 2000s.

But there is a problem with this strategy. In a globalized economy, in which a country can run large trade deficits, expansionary macro policy does not cause inflation, but it can cause other serious short-run structural problems. Instead of causing inflation in goods, the increased demand is channeled into increased imports and increases in demand for real and financial assets. Thus, it pushes up the price of assets, such as land and housing, creating a financial bubble. The prices of these assets do not directly show up in the price indexes, such as the GDP deflator, created to measure inflation, since they measure the price of goods, not assets. This rise in asset prices makes asset holders, such as homeowners, feel richer, which further increases aggregate demand. People feel safe spending a lot because their houses have so greatly increased in value. Thus the effect of the expansionary fiscal policy is amplified by increases in the percentage of income that consumers spend.

According to the structural stagnation hypothesis, the low price of global goods and the ability to run large trade deficits gives policy makers a false sense of security that the economy can continue 3 percent growth, even when a better estimate of globalized constrained growth would be 2.25 percent growth. In short, this structural change in the inflation process, which channeled aggregate demand into asset price inflation, not goods inflation, masked the need in the U.S. economy for real structural adjustment.

Q-5 Why were policy makers able to run expansionary policy without causing inflation in the early 2000s?

In a globalized economy in which a country can run large trade deficits, expansionary macro policy does not cause inflation but it can cause other serious short-run structural problems.

Summary: Globalization and Structural Imbalances

What this globalized *AS/AD* model and the structural stagnation hypothesis suggest is that in a globalized world where international adjustment forces work slowly, a country's potential output becomes harder to estimate, and the normal inflationary signals that the economy has exceeded potential will not work. So the economy may seem to be doing fine in the aggregate, but festering underneath can be serious structural imbalances between the tradable sector and the nontradable sector, and between the goods market and asset market. Eventually these structural problems will have to be dealt with in order for the economy to reach a long-run sustainable equilibrium in which both domestic and international forces are in equilibrium. That is the problem that the United States is now grappling with.

Structural Problems of Globalization

The model just described is general. What it doesn't do is convey a real feel for what the structural problems of globalization are. We do that now. Let's begin by looking at jobs. What globalization means for employment is that the jobs and skills of millions

Web Note 37.2

Globalization and
Unemployment

of Americans are now no longer needed. Those jobs can be done more cheaply abroad. For people whose jobs have disappeared, unemployment isn't just a matter of finding a similar job at a similar pay. These people must find another job that requires different training, or that doesn't need much training, but pays a much lower wage.

To remain employed in the tradable sector the unemployed will have to: (1) find new jobs that they can do more cheaply than anyone else in the world because they have a needed specialized skill, (2) be willing to accept lower wages, or (3) have access to better technology and capital than do workers in other countries, making them more productive. Finding a job in the nontradable sector will be easier because they compete with only U.S. citizens or immigrants. But most of the jobs available to displaced workers are unlikely to pay as well as the jobs they had before. So globalization means that someone who had a $20 an hour job with benefits now works a $10 an hour job without benefits. These are the lucky ones. Others can't find a job at all. With structural stagnation, the jobs problem requires creating globally competitive jobs. To increase the number of sustainable globally competitive jobs will require structural changes that either improve the skills of those searching for jobs or decrease their wage aspirations.

It was structural problems such as described above that led to the election of President Donald Trump in 2016. He conveyed a concern about the effects of globalization in a way that other politicians didn't. Concern is one thing; devising workable policies to deal with the structural problems is another, and Trump's economic policy focused more on expansionary macro policy and tariff policy than it did on dealing directly with the structural problems in the U.S. economy.

Structural Change in the Nontradable Sector

Q-6 Which sector is most affected by globalization—the tradable or nontradable sector? Why?

Not everyone is faced with choosing between not working and lowering wage aspirations or changing skills. The nontradable sector still offers good paying jobs, especially those paid for by government. Many of these government jobs (or government-supported jobs) provide better benefits and higher wages than do available private jobs in the tradable sector, which has to worry about its global competitiveness. But U.S. taxpayers have not been willing to pay the high taxes necessary to fund these jobs. So, according to the structural stagnation hypothesis, the United States has run government deficits or hidden the costs of government employment by not fully funding the promised pensions and future benefits, so that they do not show up in the budget, making the actual budget deficits much larger than the reported budget deficits. The inability to continue these large U.S. budget deficits will put strong pressure on government in the coming decade to cut government employee wages, benefits, and employment.

The inability to continue large U.S. budget deficits will put strong pressure on government in the coming decade to cut government employee wages, benefits, and employment.

The pressure to lower wages in the nontradable sector is made all the more real by the fact that the nontradable sector affects the cost of living of those in the tradable sector. Workers with $10 an hour jobs in the tradable sector cannot afford to buy the services that support $30 an hour nontradable jobs—at least not without government subsidies. The situation is different for a factory worker in China. The Chinese worker earns $5 an hour and pays $8 to see a doctor. Compare that to the U.S. worker earning $10 an hour who has to pay $75 to see a doctor. So globalization along with expansionary fiscal policy reduces the spending power of those working in the tradable sector in two ways, lower wages and higher cost of living, which translates into lower demand for nontradable goods. So the same downward pressure on wages that is occurring in the tradable sector will work its way to the nontradable sector. But it will occur slowly, and will not be an easy adjustment. According to the structural stagnation hypothesis the reality is that significant structural change is needed to make the

Globalization along with expansionary fiscal policy reduces the spending power of those working in the tradable sector in two ways: lower wages and higher costs of living.

Why Are the Structural Problems of Globalization So Much Greater Now?

The world economy has been opening up for years. Why have the structural problems become so significant now? The answer is that the imbalances have been building up for decades but did not manifest themselves until recently because of government policies and institutional realities that limited global trade. The institutional realities include politics, international capital restrictions, and high costs of communication and transportation. Political forces include a global fight with communism that limited the countries that were part of the global economy (communist countries such as China did not trade with market economies).

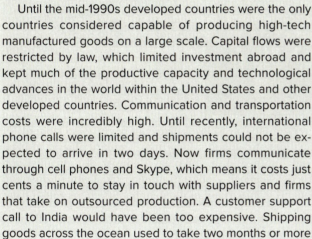

©EQRoy/Shutterstock

Until the mid-1990s developed countries were the only countries considered capable of producing high-tech manufactured goods on a large scale. Capital flows were restricted by law, which limited investment abroad and kept much of the productive capacity and technological advances in the world within the United States and other developed countries. Communication and transportation costs were incredibly high. Until recently, international phone calls were limited and shipments could not be expected to arrive in two days. Now firms communicate through cell phones and Skype, which means it costs just cents a minute to stay in touch with suppliers and firms that take on outsourced production. A customer support call to India would have been too expensive. Shipping goods across the ocean used to take two months or more

on a cargo ship; now it takes hours on a jet plane. Large shipments have declined in price with the development of standard containers. So before the 1980s few goods were in the competitive tradable sector. That allowed the United States to develop an institutional structure for its economy with little regard to international issues.

Institutional changes in the United States widened the doors to trade. These changes included the rise of big-box discount stores such as Walmart. Foreign producers could sell in bulk to a few national chains, and these retailers could use their market power to negotiate lower prices. (Compare this to the diffuse retail system in Europe that has made an expansion of Chinese goods into European markets much slower than it has been in the United States.)

The trade situation started to change in the late 1980s, but it was only in the early 2000s, as India and China entered the global economy *en force,* that globalization had a significant impact on the U.S. economy. Their entrance created the same kind of problems experienced with Japan in the 1970s and 1980s, but of a much greater magnitude. Japan has a population of about 127 million compared to India and China's 2.7 billion. In summary, the size of the productive capacities of India and China combined with these institutional and technological changes makes the global competition from Japan in the 1970s seem like a small wave compared to a tsunami from India and China starting in the late 1990s.

United States internationally competitive, and that structural change likely involves both a decrease in the relative wages of the nontradable sector and additional cuts in pay for those in the tradable sector relative to Chinese and Indian workers.

Given the difficulty of making these structural changes, it is understandable that politicians have avoided facing up to them. Telling people difficult changes need to be made does not get someone reelected. But globalization means that eventually the adjustments will have to be made. The long-run equilibrium will involve eliminating the trade deficit, which will require that the United States increase its competitiveness in a variety of sectors. That means that the cost of producing in the United States has to fall, relative to the cost of producing outside the United States.

Telling people that difficult changes need to be made does not get someone reelected.

Globalization and Income Distribution

According to the structural stagnation hypothesis, one of the primary reasons why the structural problems of globalization are not dealt with is that they involve the difficult

One of the primary reasons why the structural problems of globalization are not dealt with is that they involve difficult policy issues of fairness and income redistribution.

Q-7 How has globalization impacted the distribution of income in the United States?

Web Note 37.3

Training Programs

The group that did worst in the globalization process was U.S. workers and businesses involved in the actual manufacture of commodities.

political issues of fairness and income redistribution. Globalization affects different groups of the economy differently. We will distinguish three groups: (1) the international traders, and workers associated with them, who have done phenomenally well from globalization; (2) the unskilled and not highly skilled in the tradable sector who are most hurt by globalization because they either have lost jobs or had wages significantly reduced; and (3) those in nontradable sectors, who are only indirectly affected by globalization. The latter have been made better off by the benefits of lower prices of goods but have been made worse off because of the indirect competition for jobs from those who have lost jobs in the tradable sector.

For international traders—financiers and import/export companies—globalization has been a boon, creating enormous demand for their services and for the services of those who sell to them. So the demand for high-level U.S. international trading services remained high, even as the demand for U.S. products fell. Demand was rising for high-level business organization and services and falling for U.S. products. Most of the jobs in this "organizers of international trade sector" were high-paying white-collar jobs, which required high levels of education. Jobs for those with only a high school education were disappearing. The result was an enormous change in the distribution of income. The success of this sector also created a periphery of jobs that serviced this high-income sector. High-end luxury goods, expensive restaurants, and similar businesses did well, but generally the lower middle class was not in this group.

Paradoxically, the fact that globalization provided these high-paying jobs for the United States meant that the trade deficit was smaller than it otherwise would have been. International forces kept the U.S. exchange rate from falling as much as it would have had these organizational gains from trade not gone to U.S. citizens. To see the reason why this reduced the total number of jobs, consider that for the trade balance not to change, for every $200,000 job that globalization creates, more than six $30,000 jobs must be lost.

The group that did worst was U.S. workers and businesses involved in the actual manufacture of **commodities**—*homogeneous goods that could be produced in a variety of countries by workers without any special skills and shipped at a low cost.* Commodities such as motherboards, LED screens, and generic shoes and socks are the ultimate tradable goods, and a standard rule in business is that there is no profit in commodities. There are also no wage differentials across countries in the production of commodities, which means that either the wages of workers in these sectors fell to the global wage level or the workers lost their jobs entirely.

A third group affected by globalization are skilled workers in the nontradable sector. These are workers producing goods or services that cannot be produced outside the United States because of legal, technical, or physical restrictions. While workers in these sectors do not directly face global competition, they do indirectly as described above. As unemployment in the tradable sector rises, the unemployed compete for jobs in the nontradable sector. This competition holds wages and prices down in this sector as well, but much less so than in the tradable sector. How well this group does depends on the state of aggregate demand. Up until recently, they have done relatively well, as government has held up aggregate demand.

As we stated earlier, structural problems can also be caused by technological change. It makes skills obsolete and can channel significant income to a few high-skilled individuals who design and have acquired control of the new technology, while holding down wages for middle-skilled and low-skilled individuals. That can change the composition and size of the consumption component of aggregate demand. Aggregate demand can be kept up by increasing the debt of middle- and lower-skilled individuals, but that makes the wealth distribution even more uneven, and cannot continue forever without causing a financial bubble. Concern about such technological issues will likely grow and might even overtake concern about globalization in the coming decades.

Remembering the Benefits of Globalization

While structural change is difficult and is the inevitable result of globalization, the costs of structural changes do not mean that globalization is bad, or that it should not have happened. Globalization is simply competition on the global level. Globalization is both inevitable and beneficial. If you think back to the globalized *AS/AD* model, the other side of globalization is an increase in consumption of tradable goods at low prices. Because of globalization, tradable goods have become much cheaper.

Globalization has also increased specialization as production is divided into smaller segments (some of which are outsourced), which lowers costs and stimulates technological development. As Adam Smith long ago pointed out in his famous example of the manufacturing of pins, more specialization means workers can focus on specific tasks and significantly increase productivity. Not only does specialization allow firms to spread costs over an expanded production; it also increases the amount of learning by doing, which also lowers costs. Globalization expands trade, and it is trade that has allowed the world economy to grow. So globalization increased the overall world growth rate and increased U.S. consumption even as U.S. potential output was reduced.

The nature of the competitive process, of which globalization is a part, is to continually create structural problems in a process that economic historian Joseph Schumpeter called *creative destruction*. Creative destruction is part of any dynamic and growing economy.

Throughout the postwar era, the United States has benefited enormously from globalization. Because global trade has allowed the specialization of production and opening of new consumer markets abroad, the U.S. trend growth rate is higher than what it would have been. So, according to the structural stagnation hypothesis, the problem isn't globalization per se or even the structural problems it creates. The problem is that the United States tried to have the benefits of globalization without facing up to the difficult structural changes that accompany globalization and the resulting trade deficits.

> The costs of structural change do not mean globalization is bad or that it should not have happened. Globalization is simply competition on the global level. It is both inevitable and beneficial.

> The problem is that the United States tried to have the benefits of globalization without facing up to the difficult structural changes that accompany globalization and the resulting trade deficits.

The Future of Globalization

According to the structural stagnation hypothesis, the globalization process described in the globalized *AS/AD* model is not a one-shot event. It is an ongoing process in which developing countries compete in more and more activities. Thus, even though the process of integrating China and India into the world economy began in the late 1990s, it is likely to continue for another 20 or 30 years as China and India move up the **value-added chain**—*the movement of trade from natural resources to low-skill manufacturing to increasingly complicated goods and services.*

To understand the value-added chain, think of the story of comparative advantage that I discussed in earlier chapters. Initially, trade begins with low-cost and low-tech items that are heavily labor-intensive, but not heavily technological or capital-intensive. This is the bottom of the value-added chain. Then as producers in a developing country learn by doing and become more skilled, they move up to production that is a bit more capital- and technological-intensive, as Japan and Korea did in the 1970s and 1980s. Over time foreign producers keep moving up to increasingly complicated production methods and technology, and eventually, they find themselves able to compete on all aspects of manufacturing. Ultimately, they arrive at the top of the value-added chain, where they are the international traders organizing trade.

Once a country reaches international trader status, it experiences enormous gains from trade—far more than the gains for manufacturing even high-technology goods. It

> **Q-8** What is the value-added chain and how does it relate to globalization?

is the international traders who create many of the high-wage professional jobs in advertising, research, finance, and law. So when the international traders come from your country, you get disproportionate gains from trade, as the United States has for the past 70 years. As countries move up the value-added chain, ultimately the pressures of globalization will feed back on the traders, and international traders will find themselves globalized as well. That is a long way in the future.

In the meantime the United States has done extremely well at the high end of the value-added chain. Its comparative advantages in high-value-added production and organizing trade have helped the United States do well from globalization while at the same time eliminating many U.S. jobs. To see what is going on, consider the iPad, which is imported from China. Of the $500 cost of an iPad, about $300 goes to U.S. firms and workers in the form of profits, distribution expenses, advertising, and research and development. So the sale of every iPad creates profits for shareholders and some very high-paying jobs for a few in the United States while eliminating a much greater number of lower-paying manufacturing and lower-skilled jobs.

As China and India become more integrated in the world economies, other low-cost countries will replace them on the low-cost end of production, and China and India will challenge the United States on higher- and higher-level production activities. The picture of globalization conveyed in the globalized *AS/AD* model will continue for decades as developing countries move up the value-added chain.

Policies to Deal with Structural Stagnation

According to the structural stagnation hypothesis the structural effects of globalization accompanied by large trade deficits are chronic, and are likely to continue for a decade or more. The reason is that globalization is an ongoing process, and policy makers cannot do much about it. Structural change is difficult, but required. Any solution will involve some combination of the following: a rise in foreign goods prices (lower U.S. exchange rates), a rise in foreign labor costs (higher wages or lower productivity), a fall in domestic labor costs (lower wages or higher productivity), or trade restrictions that raise foreign goods prices. The policies to deal with structural stagnation will be policies that bring those changes about.

In terms of the globalized *AS/AD* model shown in Figure 37-4, the policies will involve shifting the world supply curve up [arrow *A* in Figure 37-4(a)] or the domestic aggregate supply down [arrow *B* in Figure 37-4(b)]. Notice that either of these policies reduces the structural constraints on production in the economy and shifts out the U.S. economy's globalized constrained potential output.

Shifting the World Supply Curve Up

Let's start by considering policies that will shift the world supply curve up.

DECREASING THE EXCHANGE RATE   One of the policies that almost all agree will help the U.S. structural stagnation problem is for the U.S. exchange rate—the price of dollars measured in foreign currency—to fall relative to its competitors. The U.S. exchange rate has fallen over the past decade, reducing the structural stagnation problem compared to what it would have been. But the continuing trade deficit is a signal that it did not eliminate the problem. In the standard *AS/AD* model a fall in the exchange rate in response to a trade deficit would occur much faster than it has, so that structural stagnation would not be a problem. But, for a variety of reasons, the exchange rate did not fall sufficiently.

As countries move up the value-added chain, the pressures of globalization will ultimately feed back on the traders, and international traders will find themselves globalized as well. That is a long way in the future.

The picture of globalization conveyed in the globalized *AS/AD* model will continue for decades as developing countries move up the value-added chain.

Web Note 37.4
Growth and Politics

In the globalized *AS/AD* model, policies involve shifting the world supply curve up or the domestic aggregate supply curve down.

Q-9   What policies solve the structural stagnation problem by shifting the world supply curve up?

Policies to Shift the *SAS* Curve Down or the World Supply Curve Up

Policies that address structural stagnation will either shift the world supply curve up from
WAS_0 to WAS_1 as shown in (**a**) or the *SAS* curve down from SAS_0 to SAS_1 as shown in (**b**).

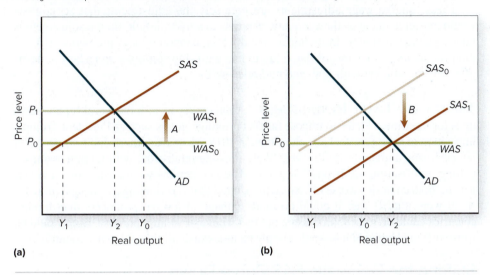

(a)

(b)

One reason was that China's policy to keep the value of its currency, the yuan, low
by buying U.S. dollars and dollar-denominated assets has helped prevent the value of
the U.S. dollar from falling. China and the United States have had ongoing talks about
these policies, with the United States arguing that China should stop preventing its
currency from rising. However, China has continued to follow policies designed to
keep the value of the yuan low.

The question of exchange rate adjustment is a question about the speed of
adjustment. It is not clear that the United States would be a lot better off if China were
to suddenly end its support of the dollar. The result would likely be a dramatic fall in
the U.S. exchange rate, and upward pressure on the price level in the United States.
Were this to occur too fast, it could possibly lead to the accelerating inflation that has
been prevented by the low world supply price. If the U.S. government responds to that
inflationary pressure by decreasing aggregate demand, as it has committed itself to do,
it will keep the U.S. economy in stagnation for an extended period even as the value of
the dollar falls. If that happened we wouldn't have only structural stagnation; we would
have **stagflation**—*the combination of stagnation and inflation*—as we had in the
1970s.

> The question of exchange rate adjustment is a question about the speed of adjustment.

DIFFERENTIAL WAGE GROWTH   Rising wages in other countries relative to U.S.
wages would also shift the world supply curve up, which has happened in the past
decade. For example, U.S. wages in manufacturing have been stagnant, and in real
terms have not risen, while Chinese wages have gone up by as much as 12 percent a
year. What this means is that each year, production costs in China have risen relative to
the United States. Because wages differ by area and type of job, comparisons are
difficult, but in 2018 in a number of industries, wage differentials between U.S. and
Chinese workers have decreased somewhat, so those differences are no longer driving
the decision about where to produce. Supply chain issues dominate. Since so much
manufacturing is currently done in China, it is easier to keep production there than to
move it to the United States, even if wage savings are not substantial. Wages in other

countries have not risen anywhere near as much as in China, and low-wage manufacturing more and more is moving to countries other than China such as India, Bangladesh, Vietnam, and some African countries. So, in the coming years, U.S. workers will likely face competition at many different wage levels.

These relative wage adjustments are precisely the adjustments that economists would expect to occur as the economy responds to a trade deficit. So the adjustment is taking place, but slowly. In the meantime the U.S. economy faces problems of structural stagnation, which means that it has to live with slower growth and a lack of desirable jobs for workers with low- and mid-level skills.

TARIFFS AND TRADE RESTRICTIONS   Another way to shift the world supply curve up is for the United States to impose tariffs on foreign goods such as President Trump's imposition of tariffs on steel and aluminum in 2018. Most economists don't support such policies. Any attempt to do this will likely provoke retaliation, with foreign countries putting an offsetting tariff on U.S. goods. The two actions would offset one another, leaving both countries worse off. Since the United States is running a trade deficit, if the result were a tariff war, it could do more damage to foreign producers than foreign countries could do to U.S. producers, but that would serve little purpose. Both would be worse off; the United States would simply be less worse off than the other countries.

While tariffs would also shift the world supply curve up, most economists don't support such a policy because of their side effects.

Shifting the Domestic *SAS* Curve Down

Let's now turn to a second set of policies that the United States might follow—shifting the *SAS* curve down. Doing so will lower costs in the United States and thereby increase the internationally constrained potential output curve.

Q-10 What policies solve structural stagnation by shifting the short-run aggregate supply curve down?

LOWER WAGES   The most obvious of policies to shift the *SAS* curve down is to lower U.S. wages. When workers in the tradable sectors lose their jobs, eventually they lower their **reservation wage**—*the lowest wage that a person needs to receive to accept a job*—to a level that gets them a job. That is the market's solution to structural unemployment. It isn't pretty or pleasant, but it works. Over the last 30 years, real wages in the United States have been relatively flat as more and more U.S. workers have accepted that the best they can do is a relatively low-wage job.

The problem is that our society does not like that solution. It seems unfair that some people have to suffer from globalization while others benefit. So while a policy of cutting wages would work, it is unlikely to gain much political support. Moreover, the cutting-wage solution would have side effects. Lower wages means lower consumption, so it will slow the growth of domestic demand. But if other solutions don't work, wages will be forced to fall. If the U.S. government needs an international bailout because bondholders don't want to buy its bonds at an interest rate the United States is willing and able to pay, one of the likely requirements bondholders will impose will be cutting government wages.

REDUCE UNEMPLOYMENT INSURANCE   The United States has many policies designed to lessen the pain caused by unemployment and to hold wages up, not push them down. Reducing these policies would help in the adjustment process. Unemployment insurance is an example. Unemployment insurance, or any policy to mitigate the pain of unemployment, reduces the role that unemployment plays in bringing wages down by allowing workers to keep holding out for a higher-wage job. Thus, by eliminating unemployment insurance, one could speed up the adjustment. But as was the case with lowering wages, such a policy would be accompanied by significant hardships to people who are bearing the large share of the costs of globalization already.

Unemployment insurance, or any policy to reduce the pain of unemployment, reduces the role that unemployment plays in the adjustment process.

INCREASING U.S. PRODUCTIVITY BY IMPROVING TRAINING OR INCREASING RESOURCE PRODUCTION Another policy that one often hears about is retraining workers, and that clearly can help. Unfortunately, direct job-relevant training in the United States is often either expensive compared to similar job-relevant training abroad or is significantly subsidized through government support of the training or government-subsidized loans to students, which means that it pushes up government deficits. If increased training is to lead to high-paying jobs in tradable sectors, it has to make U.S. workers more competitive than foreign workers, whose training often costs far less. Currently, our educational sector is not especially efficient—ranking 26th in the world in achievement—and is far more costly than just about any other educational system. It has advantages in fostering creativity much better than do foreign educational systems, but it also has problems. Any gains in training will have to be relative gains—other countries are pouring enormous resources into additional training, so U.S. training will have to increase simply to keep up.

> If increased training is to lead to high-paying jobs in tradable sectors, it has to make U.S. workers more competitive than foreign workers, whose training often costs far less.

Another way to increase productivity is to increase a country's available nontradable low-cost resources. In this dimension the United States has some positive attributes. For example, the United States has some of the most productive farmland in the world, and as the world economy grows, the comparative advantage of the United States in agriculture is likely to grow because agricultural production is not labor-intensive and the United States has rich soil. Agriculture will likely be a long-term inherent comparative advantage.

The positive resource shock caused by the development of new fracking technology in the extraction of natural gas also contributed to the growth of the U.S. economy. This new technology significantly lowered the price of natural gas and hence energy in the United States. This technology lowered energy costs by less outside the United States because natural gas could not be easily exported. Thus it lowered the cost of producing in the United States relative to abroad. This low energy cost offset other cost advantages of other countries even at existing exchange rates. These positives helped pull the U.S. economy back toward its 3 percent growth trend, but as of 2018 there was still debate about whether the U.S. economy had reached a point where 3 percent growth was sustainable.

The Problems with the Standard Political Solution

The list of policies just discussed does not include many proposals that one hears from politicians. The policies I listed are what might be called "suffer-as-best-you-can" policies; they offer gain through pain, not gain without pain. Pain is not something that politicians like to discuss. Few politicians are going to say that what is needed is for U.S. wages to fall relative to foreign wages. They will be more likely to advocate for a policy that seems to offer only advantages without acknowledging the costs. By hiding the pain part of the proposals, most political policies provide the illusion of an effective policy but do not offer a serious solution to the structural problems facing the United States.

> By hiding the pain part of the policy proposals, most political parties provide the illusion of an effective policy but do not offer a serious solution to the structural problems facing the United States.

Conclusion

I began this chapter with a quotation from Sigmund Freud—"Illusions commend themselves to us because they save us pain and allow us to enjoy pleasure instead. We must therefore accept it without complaint when they sometimes collide with a bit of reality against which they are dashed to pieces." According to the structural stagnation hypothesis, just as individuals attempt to avoid unpleasant truths, so too do societies. The United States has maintained a policy stance over the past decade that reflects an illusion: Globalization, combined with large trade and government deficits and large private sector borrowing, comes at no cost. The current difficulty the United States is experiencing is the result of those earlier decisions based on this illusion.

TABLE 38-1 Statistics on Selected Developing, Middle-Income, and Developed Countries

Country	Physicians (per 1,000)	Daily Calorie Intake	Life Expectancy	Infant Mortality (per 1,000)	Labor Force in Agriculture (%)	Labor Force in Industry (%)	Adult Literacy Rate (%)	Cellular Phones (per 100)	GDP per Capita ($)
Developing									
Bangladesh	0.47	2,450	73	28	47	13	73	83	4,200
Ethiopia	0.03	2,131	66	41	73	7	49	50	2,100
Haiti	0.26	2,091	64	51	38	12	61	60	1,800
Middle-income									
Brazil	1.85	3,263	75	14	10	40	93	118	15,500
Iran	1.49	3,094	76	13	16	35	87	100	20,000
Armenia	2.80	2,260	75	12	36	17	100	117	9,100
Thailand	0.47	2,784	76	11	32	17	93	174	17,800
Developed									
Japan	2.37	2,726	84	2	3	26	99	131	42,700
Sweden	4.19	3,179	82	2	2	12	99	128	51,300
United States	2.57	3,682	79	6	1	20	99	123	59,500

Sources: The World Bank. 2018. *World Development Report 2018: Digital Dividends.* ©World Bank. License: Creative Commons Attribution license (CC BY 3.0 IGO) and *CIA World Factbook.* (CC BY 3.0 IGO). GDP per capita is adjusted for purchasing power parity.

Purchasing power parity exchange rates are calculated by determining what a specified basket of consumer goods will cost in various countries.

To allow for these differences, some economists have looked at the domestic purchasing power of money in various countries and have adjusted the comparisons accordingly. Rather than comparing incomes by using exchange rates, they use **purchasing power parity (PPP)**—*a method of comparing income by looking at the domestic purchasing power of money in different countries.* That is, purchasing power parity equalizes the cost of an identical basket of goods among countries. Using purchasing power parity, the World Bank found that income differences among countries are cut by half. In other words, when one uses the World Bank's PPP method of comparison, it's as if the people in developing countries had much more income than they had when their incomes were compared using market exchange rates.

A similar adjustment can be made with the life expectancy rates. A major reason for the lower life expectancies in developing countries is their high infant mortality rates. Once children survive infancy, however, their life expectancies are much closer to those of children in developed countries. Say life expectancy at birth is 50 years and that 10 percent of all infants die within their first year. As a person grows older, at each birthday the person's life expectancy is higher. So if a child lives to the age of 3 years, then at that point the child has an actual life expectancy of close to 60 years, rather than 55 years.

Growth versus Development

Growth occurs because of an increase in inputs, given a production function; development occurs through a change in the production function.

Economists use the term *developing,* rather than *growing,* to emphasize that the goals of these countries involve more than simply an increase in output; these countries are changing their underlying institutions. Put another way, these economies are changing their production functions; they are not increasing inputs given a production function. Thus, *development* refers to an increase in productive capacity and output brought about by a change in the underlying institutions, and *growth* refers to an increase in output brought about by an increase in inputs.

The distinction can be overdone. Institutions, and hence production functions, in developed as well as in developing countries are continually changing, and output changes are a combination of changes in production functions and increases in inputs. For example, over the past 40 years the major Western economies have been **restructuring** their economies—*changing the underlying economic institutions*—as they work to compete better in the world economy. As they restructure, they change their methods of production, their laws, and their social support programs. Thus, in some ways, they are doing precisely what developing countries are doing—developing rather than just growing. As the United States continues to face greater globalization, it will be forced to make more and more structural adjustments and face slower growth as those adjustments are made. Despite the ambiguity, the distinction between growth and development can be a useful one if you remember that the two blend into each other.

The reason economists separate out developing economies is that these economies (1) have different institutional structures and (2) weight goals differently than do Western developed economies. These two differences—in institutional structure and in goals—change the way in which the lessons of abstract theory are applied and discussed.

Q-2 Why does restructuring in developed countries suggest that the distinction between growth and development can be overdone?

While the lessons of abstract theory do not change when we shift our attention to developing economies, the institutions and goals change enormously.

Differing Goals

When discussing macro policy within Western developed economies, I did not dwell on questions of normative goals of macroeconomics. Instead, I used generally accepted goals in the United States as the goals of macro policy—achieving low inflation, low unemployment, and an acceptable growth rate—with a few caveats. You may have noticed that the discussion focused more on what might be called stability goals—achieving low unemployment and low inflation—than it did on the acceptable growth rate goal. I chose that focus because growth in Western developed countries is desired because it holds unemployment down, and because it avoids difficult distributional questions, as much as it is desired for its own sake. Our economy has sufficient productive capacity to provide its citizens, on average, with a relatively high standard of living. The problem facing Western societies is as much seeing that all members of those societies share in that high standard of living as it is raising the standard.

In developing countries, goals are weighted differently. Growth and development are primary goals. When people are starving and the economy isn't fulfilling people's basic needs—adequate food, clothing, and shelter—a main focus of macro policy will be on how to increase the economy's growth rate through development so that the economy can fulfill those basic needs.

There are differences in normative goals between developing and developed countries because their wealth differs. Developing countries face basic economic needs whereas developed countries' economic needs are considered by most people to be normatively less pressing.

Differing Institutions

Developing countries differ from developed countries not only in their goals but also in their macroeconomic institutions. These macroeconomic institutions are qualitatively different from institutions in developed countries. Their governments are different; their financial institutions—the institutions that translate savings into investment—are different; their fiscal institutions—the institutions through which government collects taxes and spends its money—are different; and their social and cultural institutions are different. Because of these differences, the way in which we discuss macroeconomic policy is different.

One of the differences concerns very basic market institutions—such as Western-style property rights and contract law. In certain groups of developing countries, most notably sub-Saharan Africa, these basic market institutions don't exist; instead, communal property rights and tradition structure economic relationships. How can one talk about

Economies at different stages of development have different institutional needs because the problems they face are different.

market forces in such economies?[1] On a more mundane level, consider the issue of monetary policy. Talking about monetary policy via open market operations (the buying and selling of bonds by the central bank) is not all that helpful when there is no market for government bonds, as is the case in many developing countries.

Let's now consider some specific institutional differences more carefully.

POLITICAL DIFFERENCES AND LAISSEZ-FAIRE   Views of how activist macroeconomic policy should be necessarily depend on the economy's political system. One of the scarcest commodities in developing countries is socially minded leaders. Not that developed countries have any overabundance of them, but most developed countries have at least a tradition of politicians seeming to be fair and open-minded, and a set of institutionalized checks and balances that limit leaders from using government for their personal benefit. In many developing countries, those institutionalized checks and balances on governmental leaders often do not exist.

> In many developing countries, institutional checks and balances on government leaders often do not exist.

Let's consider a few examples. First, let's look at Saudi Arabia, which, while economically rich, maintains many of the institutions of a developing country. It is an absolute monarchy in which the royal family is the ultimate power. Say a member of the royal family comes to the bank and wants a loan that, on economic grounds, doesn't make sense. What do you think the bank loan officer will do? Grant the loan, if the banker is smart. Thus, despite the wealth of the country, it isn't surprising that many economists believe the Saudi banking system reflects that political structure. In late 2017 the new crown prince of Saudi Arabia established an anticorruption committee that led to the arrest of hundreds of Saudi princes. They were held in a luxury hotel until they agreed to transfer some of their wealth back to the state. Whether the crackdown was implemented to root out corruption or to gain political power or wealth for the new crown prince is unclear.

A second example is South Sudan, which was seen as having enormous possibilities for economic growth when it was granted independence in the early 2000s because of its oil riches. It didn't develop. Instead, it disintegrated into political and economic chaos, with little to no investment and growth. Unfortunately there are many other similar examples.

Because of the structure of government in many developing countries, many economists who, in Western developed economies, favor activist government policies may well favor Classical laissez-faire policies for the same reasons that early Classical economists did—because they have a profound distrust of the governments. That distrust, however, must have limits. As I discussed in Chapter 3, even a laissez-faire policy requires some government role in setting the rules. So there is no escaping the need for socially minded leaders.

THE DUAL ECONOMY   A second institutional difference between developed and developing countries is the dual nature of developing countries' economies. Whereas it often makes sense to talk about a Western economy as a single economy, it does not for most developing countries. A developing country's economy is generally characterized by a **dual economy**—*the existence of two sectors: a traditional sector and an internationally oriented modern market sector.*[2]

> **Q-3**   What is meant by the term *dual economy*?

---

[1] One can, of course, talk about economic forces. But, as discussed in Chapter 1, economic forces become market forces only in a market institutional setting.

[2] I discuss these two sectors as if they were separate, but in reality they are interrelated. Portions of the economy devoted to the tourist trade span both sectors, as do some manufacturing industries. Still, there is sufficient independence of the two sectors that it is reasonable to treat them as separate.

Often, the largest percentage of the population participates in the traditional economy. It is a local currency, or no currency, sector in which traditional ways of doing things take precedence. The second sector—the internationally oriented modern market sector—is often indistinguishable from a Western economy. Activities in the modern sector are often conducted in foreign currencies, rather than domestic currencies, and contracts are often governed by international law. This dual-economy aspect of developing countries creates a number of dilemmas for policy makers and affects the way they think about macroeconomic problems.

For example, take the problem of unemployment. Many developing countries have a large subsistence-farming economy. Subsistence farmers aren't technically unemployed, but often so many people farm on the land that, in economic terms, their contribution to output is minimal or even negative, so for policy purposes one can consider the quantity of labor that will be supplied at the going wage unlimited. But to call these people unemployed is problematic. These subsistence farmers are simply outside the market economy. In such cases, one would hardly want, or be able, to talk of an unemployment problem in the same way we talk about it in the United States.

FISCAL STRUCTURE OF DEVELOPING ECONOMIES

A third institutional difference concerns developing countries' fiscal systems. To undertake discretionary fiscal policy—running a deficit or surplus to affect the aggregate economy—the government must be able to determine expenditures and tax rates, with a particular eye toward the difference between the two. As discussed in an earlier chapter, discretionary fiscal policy is difficult for Western developed countries to undertake; it is almost impossible for developing economies.

In the traditional sector of many developing countries, barter or cash transactions predominate, and such transactions are especially difficult to tax. Often, the governments in these economies don't have the institutional structures with which to collect taxes (or, when they have the institutional structure, it is undermined by fraud and evasion), so their taxing options are limited; that's why they often use tariffs as a primary source of revenue.

> Often developing countries do not have the institutional structures with which to collect taxes.

Similar problems exist with government expenditures. Many expenditures of developing countries are mandated by political considerations—if the government doesn't make them, it will likely be voted out of office. Within such a setting, to talk about activist fiscal policy—choosing a deficit for its macroeconomic implications—even if it might otherwise be relevant, is not much help since the budget deficit is not a choice variable, but instead is a result of other political decisions.

> Many government expenditures in developing countries are mandated by political considerations.

The political constraints facing developing countries can, of course, be overstated. The reality is that developing countries do institute new fiscal regimes. Take, for example, Mexico. In the early 1980s, Mexico's fiscal problems seemed impossible to solve, but in the late 1980s and early 1990s, Carlos de Salinas, a U.S.-trained economist, introduced a fiscal austerity program and an economic liberalization program that lowered Mexico's budget deficit and significantly reduced its inflation. But such changes are better called a **regime change**—*a change in the entire atmosphere within which the government and the economy interrelate*—rather than a **policy change**—*a change in one aspect of government's actions, such as monetary policy or fiscal policy*. Regimes can change suddenly. In Mexico, soon after President Salinas left office, his brother was implicated in a murder and drug scandal. Foreign investors became worried and pulled money out of Mexico. The peso fell, inflation and interest rates rose, and the Mexican economy fell into a serious recession. In one day, the regime of confidence had changed to a regime of uncertainty and confusion, full of questions about what policy actions the Mexican government would take.

> A regime change is a change in the entire atmosphere within which the government and the economy interrelate; a policy change is a change in one aspect of government's actions.

More recently, Mexico got back on a growth regime. Between 2012 and 2013, the Mexican Congress led by then-president Enrique Peña Nieto implemented sweeping

M-Pesa and Leapfrogging

With the introduction of mobile money such as M-Pesa, a number of cash-based economies have leapfrogged developed countries that rely on traditional banking mechanisms such as checks and credit cards, and led the way in the development of mobile money—money balances held on one's phone, rather than in a traditional bank. M-Pesa is one of the best known of these mobile monies. First introduced in 2007 in Kenya and Tanzania, M-Pesa is a form of electronic money that can be used to pay for goods and services. So, rather than carrying around cash, people can just pay with their mobile phone. M-Pesa provides liquidity and access to financial services to people who would otherwise have little access to the financial market.

©Dai Kurokawa/Epa/Shutterstock

Mobile money such as M-Pesa can be an engine of growth for developing countries. According to one study, income for households in Kenya that used M-Pesa rose by as much as 30 percent. In Kenya, about 25 percent of all transactions flow through M-Pesa and in sub-Saharan Africa, mobile money accounts exceed bank accounts.

M-Pesa is an example of leapfrogging technology. It occurs when a developing country skips a step in development and jumps ahead of developed countries because it is not encumbered with an intermediate technology. Mobile phones are another example. In the 1970s and 1980s, one of the comparative advantages of developed countries was a phone system consisting of landline phones connected by telephone lines. Every developed country family had a home phone. Developing countries did not. Then came mobile phones; developed countries were slow to move to mobile phones because their landlines worked well. Developing countries went immediately to mobile phones and are leading the way in making novel uses of their mobile phone systems. They have leapfrogged developed countries. Leapfrogging such as the adoption of M-Pesa is seen by some as providing real hope for countries to overcome years of underdevelopment.

reforms that opened markets to competition, strengthened the rule of law and regulatory oversight, and restructured its fiscal policy. These reforms contributed to steady economic growth and relatively low unemployment and inflation during his tenure in office. Toward the end of that tenure, however, with President Trump's push to renegotiate or end NAFTA, and with the election of Andrés Manuel López Obrador in 2018, it was unclear what economic development path Mexico would choose.

FINANCIAL INSTITUTIONS OF DEVELOPING ECONOMIES   I spent three chapters discussing the complex financial systems of developed countries because you had to understand those financial systems in order to understand macro policy. While some parts of that discussion carry over to developing countries, other parts don't since financial systems in developing countries are often quite different from those in developed countries.

The primary difference arises from the dual nature of developing countries' economies. In the traditional part of developing economies, the financial sector is embryonic; trades are made by barter, or with direct payment of money; trades requiring more sophisticated financial markets, such as mortgages to finance houses, just don't exist.

In the modern international part of developing economies, that isn't the case. Developing countries' international financial sectors are generally as sophisticated as Western financial institutions. A currency trading room in Ecuador or Nigeria looks similar to one in New York, London, or Frankfurt. That modern financial sector is integrated into

> The primary difference between financial institutions in developing countries and developed countries arises from the dual nature of developing countries' economies.

A Real, Real-World Application: The Traditional Economy Meets the Internet

San Juana Hernandez, of Acuna, Mexico, wanted to borrow some money to paint her grocery store and order some more goods to stock. Marco Apaza, of La Paz, Bolivia, needed some money to expand his sporting goods wholesale business and to build an addition on his parents' home, where he lives, so that he has a bit more room. They needed only small amounts—under $1,000 each. In the traditional economy, the possibilities for loans didn't exist; banks generally don't make the type of small loans that they needed, and there were no good methods of providing the loans. But both got their loans, in part because I loaned them some of the money. How did I do it from up here in Vermont? I went to the website Kiva.org, found their loan requests (along with thousands of others), and sent some money via PayPal. Kiva combined my

Courtesy of Kiva.org

money with that of another 40 or so people, and made the loans to them.

This innovative program allows a type of international micro credit, in which individuals throughout the world can make small loans to individuals in developing countries. The people go to a microfinance agency in their home city, which checks them out to see that they are legitimate borrowers, and which then posts their loan requests on the Kiva website. Individuals with money to lend can go to the website and choose to make loans to whomever they want. There is no guarantee that the loans will be paid back, but the experience to date about repayments has been, as it has with most micro credit lending, very good. Such programs show that technology can help break down the barrier between the traditional and the market sector.

the international economy (with pay rates that often approach or match those of the West). This dual nature of developing countries' financial sectors constrains the practice of monetary policy and changes the regulatory and control functions of central banks.

The above is one of many institutional examples of differences that exist and that change the nature of the macro problem. What's important is not so much the specifics of the example but, rather, the general point it brings home. Economies at different stages of development have different institutional, and policy, needs. Institutions with the same names in different countries can have quite different roles. Such institutions can differ in subtle ways, making it important to have specific knowledge of a country's institutions before one can understand its economy and meaningfully talk about policy.

It is important to have specific knowledge of a country's institutions before one can understand its economy and meaningfully talk about policy.

Monetary Policy in Developing Countries

Now that I've discussed some of the ways in which financial institutions differ in developing countries, let's consider some issues of central banking and monetary policy for those economies.

Central Banks Are Less Independent

The first thing to note about central banking in developing countries is that its primary goal is often different from a central bank's primary goal in developed countries. The reason is that, while all central banks have a number of goals, at the top of them all is the goal of keeping the economy running. In normal times Western central banks have the luxury of assuming away the problem of keeping the economy running—inertia, institutions, and history hold Western industrial economies together, and keep them running. Central banks in developing countries can't make that assumption.

On the whole, developing emerging countries have experienced higher inflation. In the early 2000s, however, inflation has been relatively low for most countries, and the IMF is predicting that it will remain low.

Source: World Economic Outlook Database, International Monetary Fund, www.imf.org.

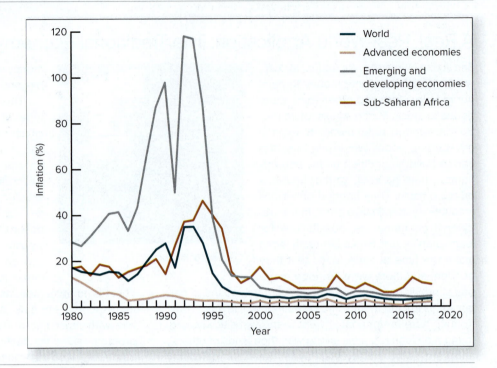

Central banks in developing countries generally have far less independence than do central banks in developed countries.

Q-4 If everyone knows that the cause of inflation in developing countries is the creation of too much money, why don't these countries stop inflation?

What this means in practice is that central banks in developing countries generally have far less independence than do central banks in developed countries. With a political and fiscal system that generates large deficits and that cannot exist without these deficits, the thought of an independent monetary policy goes out the window.

A second difference concerns the institutional implementation of monetary policy. In a developing country, a broad-based domestic government bond market often does not exist. So if the government runs a deficit and is financing it domestically, the central bank usually must buy the bonds, which means that it must increase the money supply. As you know, increasing the money supply leads to higher inflation. And developing countries on the whole have experienced high inflation, as Figure 38-1 shows. Central banks recognize that increasing the money supply will cause inflation, but often central banks feel as if they have no choice because of the political consequences of not issuing the money.

As I discussed above, often, in developing countries, the government's sources of tax revenue are limited, and the low level of income in the economy makes the tax base small. A government attempting to collect significantly more taxes might risk being overthrown. Similarly, its ability to cut expenditures is limited. If it cuts expenditures, it will almost certainly be overthrown. With new tax sources unavailable and with no ability to cut expenditures, the government uses its only other option to meet its obligations—it issues debt. And, if the central bank agrees with the conclusion that the government is correct in its assessment that it has no choice, then if the central bank doesn't want the government to be overthrown, it has no choice but to monetize that debt (print money to pay that debt). Sometimes the central bank's choices are even more limited; dictators simply tell the central bank to provide the needed money, or be eliminated.

Issuing money to finance budget deficits may be a short-term solution, but it is not a long-term solution. It is an accounting identity that real resources consumed by the economy must equal the real resources produced or imported. If the government deficit doesn't increase output, the real resources the government is getting because the central bank is monetizing its debt must come from somewhere else. Where do those real resources come from? From the **inflation tax**—*an implicit tax on the holders of cash and the holders of any obligations specified in nominal terms.* Inflation works as a type of tax on these individuals.

Faced with the prospect of a collapse of government, the central banks generally choose to keep the governments operating (which isn't surprising since they are often branches of the government). To do that, they increase the money supply enormously, causing hyperinflation in many of these countries. These hyperinflations soon take on a life of their own. The expectation of accelerating inflation creates even more inflationary pressure as individuals try to spend any money they have quickly, before the prices go up. This increases velocity, nominal demand for goods, and inflationary pressures.

One problem with using an inflation tax is that in an inflation, the government is not the only recipient of revenue; any issuer of fixed-interest-rate debt (the borrower) denominated in domestic currency also gains. And the holder of any fixed-interest-rate debt (the lender) denominated in domestic currency loses. This income redistribution caused by an inflation can temporarily stimulate real output, but it can also undermine the country's financial institutions.

The point of the above discussion is that the central banks know that issuing large quantities of money will cause inflation. What they don't know, and what the policy discussions are about, is which is worse: the inflation or the unpleasant alternatives. Should the central bank bail out the government? There are legitimate questions about whether countries' budget deficits are absolutely necessary or not. It is those assessments in which the debate about developing countries' inflation exists; the debate is not about whether the inflation is caused by the issuance of too much money.

Opponents of any type of bailout point out that any "inflation solution" is only a temporary solution that, if used, will require ever-increasing amounts of inflation to remain effective. Proponents of bailouts agree with this argument but argue that inflation buys a bit more time, and the alternative is the breakdown of the government and the economy. Because of the unpleasant alternative, the fact that inflation is only a temporary solution doesn't stop developing countries' leaders from using it. They don't have time for the luxury of long-run solutions and are often simply looking for policies that will hold their governments together for a month at a time.

Focus on the International Sector and the Exchange Rate Constraint

Another difference between the monetary policies of developed and developing countries concerns the policy options they consider for dealing with foreign exchange markets. Developed countries are generally committed to full exchange rate convertibility. With full exchange rate convertibility, individuals can exchange their currency for any other country's currency without significant government restrictions.

Developing countries seldom have fully convertible currencies. Individuals and firms in these countries face restrictions on their ability to exchange currencies—sometimes general restrictions and sometimes restrictions that depend on the purpose for which they wish to use the foreign exchange.

VARIOUS TYPES OF CONVERTIBILITY   Since convertibility plays such a central role in developing countries' macro policies, let's review the various types of

Inflation works as a tax on holders of obligations specified in nominal terms.

Q-5 In an inflation, who else, besides government, gets revenue from an inflation tax?

The fact that inflation is only a temporary solution doesn't stop developing countries' leaders from using it.

Web Note 38.1

Restoring Convertibility

convertibility. The United States has **full convertibility**—*individuals may change dollars into any currency they want for whatever legal purpose they want.* (There are, however, reporting laws about movements of currency.) Most Western developed countries have full convertibility.

Q-6 Distinguish between convertibility on the current account and full convertibility.

A second type of convertibility is **convertibility on the current account**—*a system that allows people to exchange currencies freely to buy goods and services, but not to buy assets in other countries.* The third type of convertibility is **limited capital account convertibility**—*a system that allows full current account convertibility and partial capital account convertibility.* There are various levels of restrictions on what types of assets one can exchange, so there are many types of limited capital account convertibility.

Almost no developing country allows full convertibility. Why? One reason is that they want to force their residents to keep their savings and investment in their home country, not abroad. Why don't their citizens want to do that? Because when there is a chance of a change in governments—and government seizure of assets as there often is in developing countries—rich individuals generally prefer to have a significant portion of their assets abroad, away from the hands of their government.

Almost no developing country has full convertibility.

These limits on exchange rate convertibility explain a general phenomenon found in most developing countries—the fact that much of the international part of the dual economy in developing countries is "dollarized"—contracts are framed, and accounting is handled, in dollars, not in the home country's currency. Dollarization exists almost completely in the international sectors of countries that have nonconvertible currencies, and largely in the international sectors of countries where the currency is convertible on the current account but not on the capital account. This dollarization exists because of nonconvertibility, or the fear of nonconvertibility. Thus, ironically, nonconvertibility increases the focus on dollarized contracts in the international sector, and puts that sector beyond effective control by the central bank.

Nonconvertibility does not halt international trade; it merely makes it more difficult.

Nonconvertibility does not halt international trade—it merely complicates it by adding another layer of uncertainty and bureaucracy to the trading process. Each firm that is conducting international trade must see that it will have sufficient foreign exchange to carry on its business. Developing governments will often want to encourage this international trade, while preventing outflows of their currencies for other purposes.

When developing countries have partially convertible exchange rates, exchange rate policy—buying and selling foreign currencies in order to help stabilize the exchange rate—often is an important central bank function. This is such an important function because trade in most of these countries' currencies is *thin*—there is not a large number of traders or trades. When trading is thin, large fluctuations in exchange rates are possible in response to a change in a few traders' needs. Even the uncertainties of the weather can affect traders. Say an expected oil tanker is kept from landing in port because of bad weather. The financial exchange—paying for that oil—that would have taken place upon landing does not take place, and the supply/demand conditions for a country's currency could change substantially. In response, the value of the country's currency could rise or fall dramatically unless it were stabilized. The central bank often helps provide exchange rate stabilization.

CONDITIONALITY AND THE BALANCE OF PAYMENTS CONSTRAINT

In designing their policies, developing countries often rely on advice from the International Monetary Fund (IMF). One reason is that the IMF has economists who have much experience with these issues. A second reason is that, for these countries, the IMF is a major source of temporary loans that they need to stabilize their currencies.

These loans usually come with conditions that the country meet certain domestic monetary and fiscal stabilization goals. Specifically, these goals are that government deficits be lowered and money supply growth be limited. Because of these requirements, the IMF's loan policy is often called **conditionality**—*the making of loans that are subject to specific conditions.* The IMF's goals have been criticized by economists such as Joseph Stiglitz, who argues that the contractionary monetary and fiscal policies often required by conditionality tend to be procyclical and only worsen the recession. The IMF responds that in a developing country, the long-run fiscal and monetary goals must take precedence to establish a basis for development.

Even a partially flexible exchange rate regime presents the country with a **balance of payments constraint**—*limitations on expansionary domestic macroeconomic policy due to a shortage of international currency reserves.* Attempts to expand the domestic economy with expansionary monetary policy continually push the economy to its balance of payments constraint. To meet both its domestic goals and international balance of payments constraints, many developing countries turn to loans from the IMF, not only for the exchange rate stabilization reasons discussed above but also for a more expansionary macro policy than otherwise would be possible. Because of the IMF's control of these loans, macro policy in developing countries is often conducted with one eye toward the IMF, and sometimes with a complete bow.

> The basis for most IMF loans is conditionality.

> The balance of payments constraint consists of limitations on expansionary domestic macro policy due to a shortage of international reserves.

The Need for Creativity

The above discussion may have made it seem as if conducting domestic macro policy in developing countries is almost hopelessly dominated by domestic political concerns and international constraints. If by macro policy one means using traditional monetary and fiscal policy tools as they are used in standard ways, that's true. But macro policy, interpreted broadly, is much more than using those tools. It is the development of new institutions that expand the possibilities for growth. It is creating a new production function, not operating within an existing one. Macro policy, writ large to include the development of new institutions, can be enormously effective. To undertake such policies requires an understanding of the role of institutions, the specific nature of the problem in one's country, and creativity.

Obstacles to Economic Development

What stops countries from developing economically? Economists have discovered no magic potion that will make a country develop. We can't say, "Here are steps 1, 2, 3, 4. If you follow them you'll grow, but if you don't follow them you won't grow."

What makes it so hard for developing countries to devise a successful development program is that social, political, and economic problems blend into one another and cannot be considered separately. The institutional structure that we take for granted in the United States often doesn't exist in those countries. For example, economists' analysis of production assumes that a stable government exists that can enforce contracts and supply basic services. In most developing countries, that assumption can't be made. Governments are often anything but stable; overnight, a coup d'état can bring a new government into power, with a whole new system of rules under which businesses have to operate. Imagine trying to figure out a reasonable study strategy if every week you had a new teacher who emphasized different things and gave totally different types of tests from last week's teacher. Firms in developing countries face similar problems.

Web Note 38.2

Development Economics

Seven problems facing developing
countries are:

1. Political instability.

2. Corruption.

3. Lack of appropriate institutions.

4. Lack of investment.

5. Inappropriate education.

6. Overpopulation.

7. Health and disease.

While economists can't say, "Here's what you have to do in order to grow," we have been able to identify some general obstacles that all developing countries seem to face:

1. Political instability.

2. Corruption.

3. Lack of appropriate institutions.

4. Lack of investment.

5. Inappropriate education.

6. Overpopulation.

7. Health and disease.

I consider each in turn.

Political Instability

A student's parents once asked me why their son was doing poorly in my economics class. My answer was that he could not read well and he could hardly write. Until he could master those basics, there was no use talking about how he could better learn economics.

Roughly the same reasoning can be applied to the problem of political instability in developing countries. Unless a country achieves political stability (acceptance within a country of a stable system of government), it's not going to develop economically, no matter what it does.

All successful development strategies
require a stable government.

All successful development strategies require a stable government. A mercantilist or a socialist development strategy requires an elaborate government presence. A market-based strategy requires a much smaller government role, but even markets need a stable environment to function, and for contracts to be made with confidence.

Many developing countries don't have that stability. Politically they haven't established a tradition of orderly governmental transition. Coups d'état or armed insurrections always remain possible.

One example is South Sudan, which gained its independence from the Sudan in 2011. Many Western countries invested significant sums to rebuild its infrastructure, but within two years, civil war broke out as political factions fought for power. While the civil war has officially ended, the country continues to be beset by internal violence. About 3.5 million South Sudanese are either internally displaced from their homes or live as refugees in neighboring countries.

Even countries whose governments aren't regularly toppled face threats of overthrow, and those threats are sufficient to prevent individual economic activity. To function, an economy needs some rules—any rules—that will last.

Q-7 Why does political instability
present an economic problem for
developing countries?

The lack of stability is often exacerbated by social and cultural differences among groups within a country. Political boundaries often reflect arbitrary decisions made by former colonial rulers, not the traditional cultural and tribal boundaries that form the real-life divisions. The result is lack of consensus among the population as a whole as well as intertribal suspicion and even warfare.

For example, Nigeria is a federation established under British colonial rule. It comprises three ethnic regions: the northern, Hausa Fulan, region; the western, Yoruba, region; and the eastern, Ibo, region. These three regions are culturally distinct and so are in continual political and military conflict. Nigeria has experienced an endless cycle of military coups, attempts at civilian rule, and threats of secession by the numerically smaller eastern region. Had each region been allowed to remain separate, economic development might have been easier; but partially because the British lumped the regions together and called them a country, political instability often undermines economic development.

THE INFLUENCE OF POLITICAL INSTABILITY ON DEVELOPMENT   Do these political considerations affect economic questions? You bet. As I will discuss shortly, any development plan requires financial investment from somewhere—either external or internal. Political instability closes off both sources of investment funds.

Any serious potential investor takes political instability into account. Foreign companies considering investment in a developing country hire political specialists who analyze the degree of risk involved. Where the risk is too great, foreign companies simply don't invest.

Political instability also limits internal investment. Income distribution in many developing countries is highly skewed. There are a few very rich people and an enormous number of very poor people, while the middle class is often small.

Whatever one's view of the fairness of such income inequality, it has a potential advantage for society. Members of the wealthy elite in developing countries have income to spare, and their savings are a potential source of investment funds. But when there is political instability, that potential isn't realized. Fearing that their wealth may be taken from them, the rich often channel their investment out of their own country so that, should they need to flee a revolution, they'll still be able to live comfortably. Well-off people in developing countries provide major inflows of investment into the United States and other Western countries.

Q-8 True or false? Income inequality leads to higher levels of savings by the rich and therefore has significant advantages for developing countries. Explain your answer.

POLITICAL INSTABILITY AND UNEQUAL DISTRIBUTION OF INCOME   The highly skewed distribution of income in most developing countries contributes in another way to political instability. It means that the poor majority has little vested interest in maintaining the current system. A coup? Why not? What have they got to lose? The economic prospects for many people in developing countries are so bleak that they are quite willing to join or at least support a guerrilla insurgency that promises to set up a new, better system. The resulting instability makes development almost impossible.

Corruption

Bribery, graft, and corruption are ways of life in most developing countries. In Egypt it's called *baksheesh* (meaning "gift of money"); in Mexico it's called *la mordida* ("the bite"). If you want to park in a parking spot in Mexico City, you'd better pay the police officer, or your car will get a ticket. If you want to take a photograph of the monument to Ramses II in front of the Cairo railroad station, you'd better slip the traffic officer a few bucks, or else you may get run over.

When rights to conduct business are controlled and allocated by the government, economic development can be hindered.

Without a well-developed institutional setting and a public morality that condemns corruption, economic forces function in a variety of areas that people in developed countries would consider inappropriate. In any country, the government has the right to allow imports, to allow development, to determine where you can park your car, to say whether you can take photographs of public buildings, to decide who wins a lawsuit, and so forth. In developing countries, however, those rights can be, and often are, sold. The litigant who pays the judge the most wins. How about the right to import? Want to import a new machine? That will be 20 percent of the cost, please.

Web Note 38.3

Transparency

Such graft and corruption quickly become institutionalized to the degree that all parties involved feel they have little choice but to take part. Government officials say that graft and bribery are built into their pay structure, so unless they take bribes, they won't have enough income to live on. Businesspeople say that if they want to stay in business, they have to pay bribes. Similarly, workers must bribe business in order to get a job, and labor leaders must be bribed not to cause trouble for business.

I'm not claiming that such payments are wrong. Societies decide what is right and wrong; economists don't. The term *bribery* in English has a pejorative connotation.

Societies decide what is right and wrong; economists don't.

Q-9   In what way do bribes limit development?

In many other languages, the terms people use for this type of activity don't have such negative connotations.

But I am claiming that such payments—with the implied threat that failure to pay will have adverse consequences—make it more difficult for a society's economy to grow. Knowing that those payments must be made prevents many people from undertaking actions that might lead to growth. For example, a friend of mine wanted to build a group of apartments in the Bahamas, but when he discovered the payoffs he'd have to make to various people, he abandoned the whole idea.

Limiting an activity makes the right to undertake that limited activity valuable to the person doing the limiting. When bribery is an acceptable practice, it creates strong incentives to limit an ever-increasing number of activities—including many activities that could make a country grow.

Lack of Appropriate Institutions

Almost all economists agree that, to develop, a country needs to establish markets if it wants economic growth. Markets require the establishment of property rights. In *The Mystery of Capital,* Hernando de Soto argued that developing countries' main problem is that their assets, such as houses, do not have the legal standing to be used as collateral or to be bought and sold easily, so markets cannot work. Unfortunately, establishing property rights is a difficult political process. That is the problem for a number of African countries: how to establish property rights with an undeveloped political process.

Markets do not just exist; they are created, and their existence is meshed with the cultural and social fabric of the society.

Creating markets is not enough. The markets must be meshed with the cultural and social fabric of the society. Thus, questions of economic development inevitably involve much more than supply and demand. They involve broader questions about the cultural and social institutions in a society.

Let me give an example of cultural characteristics not conducive to development. Anyone who has traveled in developing countries knows that many of these countries operate on what they call " _____ time," where the "_____" is the name of the particular country one is in. What is meant by "_____ time" is that in that country, things get done when they get done, and it is socially inappropriate to push for things to get done at specific times. Deadlines are demeaning (many students operate on "_____ time").

As a self-actualizing mentality, "_____ time" may be a high-level mental development, but in an interdependent economic setting, "_____ time" doesn't fit.

As a self-actualizing mentality, "_____ time" may be high-level mental development, but in an interdependent economic setting, "_____ time" doesn't fit. Economic development requires qualities such as extreme punctuality and a strong sense of individual responsibility. People who believe their being two minutes late will make the world come to an end fit far better with a high-production country than do people who are more laid back. The need to take such cultural issues into account explains why development economics tends to be far less theoretical and far more country- and region-specific than other branches of economics.

Lack of Investment

Even if a country can overcome the political, social, and institutional constraints on development, there are also economic constraints. If a country is to grow, it must somehow invest, and funds for investment must come from savings. These savings can be either brought in from abroad (as private investment or foreign government aid) or generated internally (as domestic savings). Each source of investment capital has its problems.

INVESTMENT FUNDED BY DOMESTIC SAVINGS   In order to save, a person must first have enough to live on. With per capita incomes of $400 per year, poor people in

Development and the Failure of the Doha Round

Say you are a cotton farmer in Africa. Since your labor costs are much lower than U.S. labor costs, you figure you can compete, even though U.S. technology and capital far exceed yours. Taking technology and labor into account, you figure you have a 20 percent cost advantage, so that even taking into account higher shipping costs, your cotton is cost competitive. Unfortunately for you, that cost advantage disappears because U.S. cotton farmers have a benefit that you don't have—they get substantial subsidies from the U.S. government, which allows them to sell at lower prices. It isn't only in cotton, and it isn't only in the United States that the subsidies undermine your ability to compete on the world market. Farmers get help in a large number of agricultural goods, and the European and Japanese governments also give their farmers large subsidies. African and other developing nations argue that these subsidies undermine their ability to compete on the world market, and to develop their economies. They argue that they don't want foreign aid as much as they want a level playing field so that they can compete.

©ASSOCIATED PRESS

It was precisely such arguments that led the World Trade Organization to organize the Doha round of trade negotiations. It was designed to reduce tariffs and other trade barriers that developing countries place on developed countries' goods, and in return reduce subsidies and other assistance that developed countries give to their own agricultural production. These trade negotiations, which started in 2001, were suspended in 2006 because political pressures kept the United States and European Union from being able to reduce farm subsidies, which the developing countries argued was needed to create a level playing field in trade of agricultural goods. The Doha round talks officially ended in 2016.

Some analysts argue that the failure of the Doha round sounded the death knell of multilateral trade agreements and that future trade agreements will be negotiated among groups of countries. These pacts, they argue, will not involve least developed countries, except those countries whose economies are sufficiently large, such as China and India, to impact the economies of developed countries, nor will the pacts take their interests into consideration. With the election of President Trump, even smaller bilateral and trilateral trade agreements have come under scrutiny, with his claims that past agreements have been unfair to the United States.

developing countries don't have a whole lot left over to put into savings. Instead, they rely on their kids, if they live, to take care of them in their old age. As for the rich, the threat of political instability often makes them put their money into savings abroad, as I discussed before. For the developing country, it's as if the rich didn't save. In fact, it's even worse because when they save abroad, the rich don't even spend the money at home as do poor people, so the rich generate less in the way of short-run income multiplier effects in their home country than do the poor.

That leaves the middle class (small as it is) as the one hope these countries have for domestic savings. For them, the problem is: Where can they put their savings? Often these countries have an underdeveloped financial sector; there's no neighborhood bank, no venture capital fund, no government-secured savings vehicle. The only savings vehicle available may be government savings bonds. But savings bonds finance the government deficit, which supports the government bureaucracy, which is limiting activities that could lead to growth. Few middle-class people invest in those government bonds. After all, what will a government bond be worth after the next revolution? Nothing!

Some governments have taxed individuals (a type of forced savings) and channeled that money back into investment. But again, politics and corruption are likely to

With per capita incomes of as low as $400 per year, poor people in developing countries don't have a lot left over to put into savings.

interfere. Instead of going into legitimate productive investment, the savings—in the form of "consulting fees," outright payoffs, or "sweetheart contracts"—go to friends of those in power. Before you get up on your high horse and say, "How do the people allow that to happen?" think of the United States, where it's much easier to prevent such activities but where scandals in government spending are still uncovered with depressing regularity.

INVESTMENT FUNDED FROM ABROAD   The other way to generate funds for investment is from external savings, either foreign aid or foreign investment.

FOREIGN AID   The easiest way to finance development is with **foreign aid** *(funds that developed countries lend or give to developing countries)*. The problem is that foreign aid generally comes with strings attached; funds are earmarked for specific purposes. For example, most foreign aid is military aid; helping a country prepare to fight a war isn't a good way to help it develop.

As you can see in the table below, the United States gives about $34 billion (about $103 per U.S. citizen) per year in foreign aid.

Country	Development Aid 2017 (millions of U.S. dollars)	Percent of GDP
Sweden	$ 5,380	1.01%
United Kingdom	18,425	0.70
Germany	23,844	0.66
France	11,057	0.43
Austria	1,188	0.30
Italy	5,605	0.29
Canada	4,090	0.26
Japan	11,864	0.23
United States	34,638	0.18

Source: OECD Data, Net ODA, OECD Publishing, Paris. https://data.oecd.org/oda/net-oda.htm.

Total foreign aid from all countries comes to about $24 per person in developing countries.

For the 6.1 billion people in developing countries, total foreign aid from all countries comes to about $24 per person. That isn't going to finance a lot of economic development, especially when much of the money is earmarked for military purposes.

FOREIGN INVESTMENT   If a global or multinational company believes that a country has a motivated, cheap workforce; a stable government supportive of business; and sufficient **infrastructure investment**—*investment in the underlying structure of the economy,* such as transportation or power facilities—it has a strong incentive to invest in the country. That's a lot of ifs, and generally the poorest countries don't measure up. What they have to offer instead are raw materials that the global corporation can develop.

Countries at the upper end of the group of developing countries (such as Mexico and Brazil) may meet all these requirements, but large amounts of foreign investment often result in political problems as citizens of these countries complain about imperialist exploitation, outside control, and significant outflows of profits. Developing countries have tried to meet such complaints by insisting that foreign investment come in the form of joint development projects under local control, but that cuts down the amount that foreign firms are willing to invest.

When the infrastructure doesn't exist, few firms will invest no matter how cheap the labor or how stable the government.

When the infrastructure doesn't exist, as is the case in the poorest developing countries, few firms will invest in that country, no matter how cheap the labor or how stable the government. Firms require infrastructure investment such as transportation facilities, energy availability, and housing and amenities for their employees before they will consider investing in a country. And they don't want to pay to establish this infrastructure themselves.

COMPETITION FOR INVESTMENT AMONG DEVELOPING COUNTRIES The world is made up of about 30 highly industrial countries and about 160 other countries at various stages of development. Global companies have a choice of where to locate, and often developing countries compete to get the development located in their country. In their efforts to get the development, they may offer tax rebates, free land, guarantees of labor peace, or loose regulatory environments within which firms can operate.

This competition can be keen, and can result in many of the benefits of development being transferred from the developing country to the global company and ultimately to the Western consumer since competition from other firms will force the global company to pass on the benefits in the form of lower prices.

> Competition for global company investment often leads to the benefits of that investment being passed on to the Western consumer.

An example of the results of such competition can be seen in the production of chemicals. Say a company is planning to build a new plant to produce chemicals. Where does it locate? Considering the wide-ranging environmental restrictions in the United States and Western Europe, a chemical company will likely look toward a developing country that will give it loose regulation. If one country will not come through, the chemical firm will point out that it can locate elsewhere. Concern about Mexico's relatively loose environmental regulatory environment was one of the sticking points of U.S. approval of NAFTA.

FOCAL POINTS AND TAKEOFF The scope of competition among developing countries can be overstated. Most companies do not consider all developing countries as potential production and investment sites. To decide to produce in a developing country requires a knowledge of that country—its legal structure, its political structure, and its infrastructure. Gaining this information involves a substantial initial investment, so most companies tend to focus on a few developing countries about which they have specific knowledge, or that they know other companies have chosen as development sites. (If company X chose it, it must meet the appropriate criteria.)

Because of this informational requirement, developing countries that have been successful in attracting investment often get further investment. Eventually they reach a stage called **economic takeoff**—*a stage when the development process becomes self-sustaining.* Other developing countries fall by the wayside. This means that economic development is not evenly spread over developing countries, but rather is concentrated in a few.

Inappropriate Education

The right education is a necessary component of any successful development strategy. The wrong education is an enormous burden. Developing countries tend to have too much of the wrong education and too little of the right education.

> The right education is a necessary component of any successful development strategy. The wrong education is an enormous burden.

Often educational systems in developing countries resemble Western educational systems. The reason is partly the colonial heritage of developing countries and partly what might be described as an emulation factor. The West defines what an educated person is, and developing countries want their citizens to be seen as educated. An educated person should be able to discuss the ideas of Vladimir Nabokov, the poetry of Lord Byron, the intricacies of chaos theory, the latest developments in fusion technology, the nuances of the modern Keynesian/Classical debate, and the dissociative properties of Andy Warhol's paintings. So saith Western scholars; so be it.

Sustainable Development Goals

In 2000, leaders from around the world gathered at the United Nations and adopted the UN Millennium Declaration that set specific goals to combat poverty, hunger, disease, illiteracy, environmental degradation, and discrimination against women, to be achieved by 2015. The goals came to be known as the Millennium Development Goals (MDGs). They included:

1. Cut extreme poverty and hunger in half.
2. Achieve universal primary education.
3. Empower women and promote equality between women and men.
4. Reduce under-five mortality by two-thirds.
5. Reduce material mortality by three-quarters.
6. Reverse the spread of disease, especially HIV/AIDS and malaria.
7. Ensure environmental sustainability.
8. Create a global partnership for development, with targets for aid, trade, and debt relief.

No one argued about the desirability of achieving these goals, but economists did debate how to achieve them. Economist Jeffrey Sachs, one of the strong supporters of the MDGs, wrote a book called *The End of Poverty* where he argued that extreme poverty, defined as living on less than $1.50 a day, could be eliminated by 2025 by doubling foreign aid and using that aid to address the multiplicity of problems extremely poor countries face, from the very simple problem of lacking mosquito nets to prevent malaria to more complicated issues of drinkable water. Sachs argued that we can eliminate extreme poverty and disease if we just try.

Not all economists agree with Sachs. Economist William Easterly wrote a book called *The White Man's Burden* where he argued that extreme poverty is caused by a complicated interplay of politics, society, technology, geography, and economic systems; therefore, the cures are also necessarily complicated. He argued that we have doubled foreign aid in the past with no measurable result, and that Sachs' "End of Poverty program" would lead to

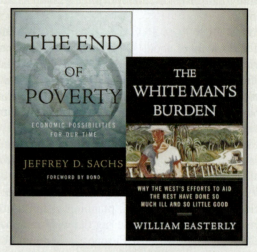

Book covers of *The End of Poverty* by Jeffrey D. Sachs, The Penguin Press, and *The White Man's Burden* by William Easterly, The Penguin Press. Photo: ©Roberts Publishing Services

little success. Easterly is not opposed to eradicating poverty, but he promoted a slower piecemeal approach that would: (1) allow policy makers and economists to evaluate the success of specific programs, (2) hold institutions accountable for how funds are spent, and (3) be based on a good understanding of which programs work.

The year 2015 came and went and, while some progress was made in achieving these goals, it was clear that many would not be reached. The answer was to create a new set of goals, and the MDGs were replaced with a broader set of 17 Sustainable Development Goals (SDGs) that apply to both developing and developed countries. These goals are to be achieved by 2030 and include variations of the MDGs along with numerous other goals such as "make cities and human settlements inclusive, safe, resilient and sustainable."

These are nice-sounding phrases and goals, but even supporters agreed that there is little likelihood of their being met, and that they will likely fade in memory as the years pass.

Put bluntly, that type of education is almost irrelevant to economic growth and may be a serious detriment to growth for a majority of the population. Basic skills—reading, writing, and arithmetic, taught widely—are likely to be more conducive to growth than is high-level education. When education doesn't match the needs of the society, the degrees—the credentials—become more important than the knowledge learned. The best jobs go to those with the highest degrees, not because the individuals holding the degrees are better able to do the job, but simply because they hold the credentials. **Credentialism,** in which *the degrees, or credentials, become more important than the knowledge learned,* serves to preserve the monopoly position of those who manage to get the degree.

If access to education is competitive, credentialism has its advantages. Even irrelevant education, as long as it is difficult, serves a screening or selection role. Those individuals who work hardest at getting an education advance and get the good jobs. Since selecting hardworking individuals is difficult, even irrelevant education serves this selection role.

But developing countries' current educational practices may be worse than irrelevant. Their educational systems often reflect Western culture, not their own cultures. The best students qualify for scholarships abroad, and their education in a different tradition makes it difficult for them to return home.

In my studies in Europe and the United States, I've come to know a large number of the best and the brightest students from developing countries. They're superb students and they do well in school. But as they near graduation, most of them face an enormously difficult choice. They can return to their home country—to material shortages, to enormous challenges for which they have little training, and to an illiterate society whose traditional values are sometimes hostile to the values these new graduates have learned. Or they can stay in the West, find jobs relevant to their training, enjoy an abundance of material goods, and associate with people to whom they've now learned to relate. Which would you choose?

The choice many of them make results in a **brain drain** (*the outflow of the best and brightest students from developing countries to developed countries*). Many of these good students don't return to the developing country. Those who do go home take jobs as government officials, expecting high salaries and material comforts far beyond what their society can afford. Instead of becoming the dynamic entrepreneurs of growth, they become impediments to growth.

There are, of course, many counterexamples to the arguments presented here. Many developing countries try to design their educational system to fit their culture. And many of the dynamic, selfless leaders who make it possible for the country to develop do return home. As with most issues, there are both positive and negative attributes to the way something is done. I emphasize the problems with educational systems in developing economies because the positive attributes of education are generally accepted. Without education, development is impossible. The question is how that education should be structured.

Credentialism serves to preserve the monopoly position of those who manage to get the degree.

Many good students from developing countries who study abroad don't return to the developing country.

Q-10 How could too much education cause problems for development?

Overpopulation

Two ways a country can increase per capita income are:

1. Decrease the number of people in the country (without decreasing the total income in the country).
2. Increase the income (without increasing the population).

In each case, the qualifier is important because income and population are related in complicated ways: People earn income; without people there would be no income. But often the more people there are, the less income per person there is because the resources of the country become strained.

A country's population can never be higher than can be supported by the natural resources that it has, or can import. But that doesn't mean that overpopulation can't be an obstacle to development. Nature has its own ways of reducing populations that are too large: Starvation and disease are the direct opposite to development. That control system works in nature, and it would work with human societies. The problem is that we don't like it.

Thomas Carlyle gave economics the name the *dismal science* as he was verbally sparring about a number of issues with economists of his period. The name stuck with economics in large part because of the writings of Thomas Malthus, who in the early 1800s said that society's prospects are dismal because population tends to outrun the means of subsistence. (Population grows geometrically—that is, at an increasing rate; the means of subsistence grow arithmetically—that is, at a constant rate.) The view was cemented into economic thinking in the law of diminishing marginal productivity: As more and more people are added to a fixed amount of land, the output per worker gets smaller and smaller.

Through technological progress, most Western economies have avoided the fate predicted by Malthus because growth in technology has exceeded growth in population. In contrast, many developing economies have not avoided the Malthusian fate because diminishing marginal productivity has exceeded technological change, and limited economic growth isn't enough to offset the increase in population. The result is a constant or falling output per person.

That doesn't mean that developing countries haven't grown economically. They have. But population growth makes per capita output growth small or negative.

Population grows for a number of reasons, including:

1. As public health measures are improved, infant mortality rates and death rates for the population as a whole both decline.

2. As people earn more income, they believe they can afford to have more children.

3. In rural areas, children are useful in working the fields.

What to do? Should the government reduce the population growth rate? If it should, how can it do so? Various measures have been tried: advertising campaigns, free condoms, forced sterilization, and economic incentives. For example, until recently, in China the government imposed severe economic penalties on couples who have more than one child, while providing material incentives, such as a free television, to couples who agree not to have more than one child.

China's vigorous population control campaign has had a number of effects. First, it created so much anger at the government that in rural areas the campaign was dropped. Second, it led to the killing of many female babies because, if couples were to have only one baby, strong cultural and economic pressures existed to ensure that the baby was a male. Third, it led to an enormous loss of privacy. Dates of women's menstrual periods were posted in factories, and officials would remind them at appropriate times that they should take precautions against getting pregnant. Only a very strong government could impose such a plan. The policy also created a generational imbalance in the population, with a large cohort of elderly and much smaller cohorts of younger individuals. In 2015 China replaced its one-child policy with a two-child policy in an attempt to help offset that generational imbalance.

Even successful population control programs have their problems. In Singapore a population control campaign was so successful among educated women that the government became concerned that its "population quality" was suffering. It began a selective campaign to encourage college-educated women to have children. They issued "love tips" to men (since some college-educated women complained that their male companions were nerds and had no idea how to be romantic) and offered special monetary bonuses to college-educated women who gave birth to children. As you might imagine, the campaign provoked a backlash, and it was eventually dropped by the government.

Individuals differ substantially in their assessment of the morality of these programs, but even if one believes that population control is an appropriate government concern, it does not seem that such programs will be successful, by themselves, in limiting population growth.

Many developing economies have not avoided the Malthusian fate because diminishing marginal productivity has exceeded technological change.

Even successful population control programs have their problems.

Health and Disease

Before a country can hope to develop, it must have a reasonably healthy population. If you are sick, it's hard to think, to work, or even to do standard daily tasks like growing food. In many developing countries, large portions of the population are undernourished or sick. Disease hits young children particularly hard. Millions of children die from pneumonia, diarrhea, malaria, and measles, all of which, because of the children's general malnutrition, are often aggravated by intestinal worms. Older individuals suffer from HIV/AIDS, tuberculosis, and malaria.

These diseases make it difficult for people to work, or even to take care of their kids, and create a vicious cycle. You're sick, you can't work, and so you and your family become victims of malnutrition. You get even more prone to disease, and less able to work and contribute to development. Thus, maintaining public health is more than a humanitarian issue; it is a key development issue.

What to do? Most of these diseases can be alleviated with drugs, but developing the infrastructure to provide these drugs is often difficult or impossible, even when the money for the drugs becomes available. Thus, one must not only get the drugs but also create the cultural and physical environment in which those drugs can be effective. Drug companies have little incentive to work on developing low-cost medicines to treat diseases in developing countries because the people there don't have much money to pay for them, so the return would be low. Instead, pharmaceutical companies focus their research on providing high-priced drugs to be sold in rich countries. Drug companies created anti-AIDS drugs, but their focus was on markets in wealthy developed countries. Only later, and under significant social and political pressure, did they start offering treatment for HIV/AIDS at low cost to developing countries.

Web Note 38.4

Fighting Disease

Conclusion

At this point in my course, I inevitably throw my hands up and admit that I don't know what makes it possible for a country to develop. Nor, judging from what I have read, do the development experts. The good ones (that is, the ones I agree with) admit that they don't know; others (that is, the ones I don't agree with) simply don't know that they don't know.

My gut feeling is that there are no definitive general answers that apply to all developing countries. The appropriate answer varies with each country and each situation. Each proposed solution to the development problem has a right time and a right place. Only by having a complete sense of a country, its history, and its cultural, social, and political norms can one decide whether it's the right time and place for this or that policy.

Economic development is a complicated problem because it is entwined with cultural and social issues.

Summary

- Per capita income in developing countries is less than 1/100 of per capita income in the United States. Societies, however, should not be judged by income alone. *(LO38-1)*

- While policies in developed countries focus on stability, developing countries struggle to provide basic needs. *(LO38-2)*

- Development refers to an increase in productive capacity and output brought about by a change in underlying institutions, while growth refers to an increase in output brought about by an increase in inputs. *(LO38-2)*

- Many developing countries have serious political problems that make it impossible for government to take an active, positive role in the economy. *(LO38-2)*

C

Capitalism   An economic system based on the market in which the ownership of the means of production resides with a small group of individuals called capitalists.

Cartel   A combination of firms that acts as if it were a single firm.

Cartel Model of Oligopoly   A model that assumes that oligopolies act as if they were monopolists that have assigned output quotas to individual member firms of the oligopoly so that total output is consistent with joint profit maximization.

Central Bank   A type of bankers' bank whose financial obligations underlie an economy's money supply.

Cheap Talk   Communication that occurs before the game is played that carries no cost and is backed up only by trust, and not any enforceable agreement.

Choice Architecture   The context in which decisions are presented.

Classical Growth Model   A model of growth that focuses on the role of capital accumulation in the growth process.

Classical Economists   Macroeconomists who generally favor laissez-faire, or nonactivist, policies.

Coefficient of Determination   A measure of the proportion of the variability in the data that is accounted for by the statistical model.

Commodities   Homogeneous goods that can be produced in a variety of countries without any special skills and shipped at a low cost.

Comparable Worth Laws   Laws mandating comparable pay for comparable work.

Comparative Advantage   The ability to be better suited to the production of one good than to the production of another good.

Competitiveness   The ability of a country to sell its goods to other countries.

Complements   Goods that are used in conjunction with other goods.

Concentration Ratio   The value of sales by the top firms of an industry stated as a percentage of total industry sales.

Conditionality   The making of loans that are subject to specific conditions.

Conspicuous Consumption   The consumption of goods not for one's direct pleasure, but simply to show off to others.

Constant Returns to Scale   A situation in which long-run average total costs do not change with an increase in output. Also: Output will rise by the same proportionate increase as all inputs.

Consumer Price Index (CPI)   A measure of prices of a fixed basket of consumer goods, weighted according to each component's share of an average consumer's expenditures.

Consumer Sovereignty   The principle that the consumer's wishes determine what's produced.

Consumer Surplus   The difference between what consumers would have been willing to pay and what they actually pay. Also, the value the consumer gets from buying a product less its price.

Consumption   Spending by households on goods and services.

Contestable Market Model   A model of oligopoly in which barriers to entry and barriers to exit, not the structure of the market, determine a firm's price and output decisions.

Contractionary Monetary Policy   Monetary policy that decreases the money supply and increases interest rates.

Contractual Legal System   The set of laws that govern economic behavior.

Convertibility on the Current Account   An exchange rate system that allows people to exchange currencies freely to buy goods and services, but not to buy assets in other countries.

Cooperative Game   A game in which players can form coalitions and can enforce the will of the coalition on its members.

Coordinate System   A two-dimensional space in which one point represents two numbers.

Coordination Mechanisms   Methods of coordinating people's wants with other people's desires.

Corporate Takeover   An action in which another firm or a group of individuals issues a tender offer (that is, offers to buy up the stock of a company) to gain control and to install its own managers.

Corporation   A business that is treated as a person, legally owned by its stockholders. Its stockholders are not liable for the actions of the corporate "person."

Cost Minimization Condition   A situation where the ratio of marginal product to the price of an input is equal for all inputs.

Cost/Benefit Approach   Assigning costs and benefits, and making decisions on the basis of the relevant costs and benefits.

Countercyclical Fiscal Policy   Fiscal policy in which the government offsets any change in aggregate expenditures that would create a business cycle.

Credentialism   When the academic degrees, or credentials, become more important than the knowledge learned.

Cross-Price Elasticity of Demand   The percentage change in demand divided by the percentage change in the price of a related good.

Crowding Out   The offsetting of a change in government expenditures by a change in private expenditures in the opposite direction.

Currency Appreciation   A change in the exchange rate so that one currency buys more units of a foreign currency.

Currency Depreciation   A change in the exchange rate so that one currency buys fewer units of a foreign currency.

Currency Stabilization   Buying and selling of a currency by the government to offset temporary fluctuations in supply and demand for currencies.

Currency Support   Buying of a currency by a government to maintain its value at above its long-run equilibrium value.

Current Account   The part of the balance of payments account in which all short-term flows of payments are listed.

Cyclical Deficit   The part of the deficit that exists because the economy is operating below its potential level of output.

Cyclical Unemployment   Temporary unemployment resulting from fluctuations in economic activity.

D

Deadweight Loss   The loss of consumer and producer surplus from a tax.

Debt   Accumulated deficits minus accumulated surpluses.

Deductive Approach   An approach that begins with certain self-evident principles from which implications are deduced (logically determined).

Deficit   A shortfall of revenues under payments.

Deflation   A continual fall in the price level.

Demand   A schedule of quantities of a good that will be bought per unit of time at various prices, other things constant.

Demand Curve   The graphic representation of the relationship between price and quantity demanded.

Demerit Good or Activity   A good or activity that government believes is bad for people even though they choose to use the good or engage in the activity.

Deposit Insurance   A system under which the federal government promises to reimburse an individual for any losses due to bank failure.

Depreciation   A measure of the decline in value of an asset that occurs over time through use. Also: A decrease in the value of a currency.

Depression   A deep and prolonged recession.

Derived Demand   The demand for factors of production by firms, which depends on consumers' demands.

Derived Demand Curve for Labor   A curve that shows the maximum amount of labor, measured in labor-hours, that a firm will hire.

Direct Regulation   A program in which the amount of a good people are allowed to use is directly limited by the government.

Direct Relationship   A relationship in which when one variable goes up, the other goes up too.

Discount Rate   The rate of interest the Fed charges for loans it makes to banks.

Diseconomies of Scale   Situation when the long-run average total costs increase as output increases.

Division of Labor   The splitting up of a task to allow for specialization of production.

Dodd-Frank Wall Street Reform and Consumer Protection Act   An act of Congress passed in 2010 establishing a regulatory structure to limit risk taking and require banks to report their holdings so that regulators can assess risk-taking behavior.

Dominant Strategy   A strategy that is preferred by a player regardless of the opponent's move.

Dual Economy   The existence of two sectors: a traditional sector and an internationally oriented modern market sector.

Duopoly   An oligopoly with only two firms.

E

Econometrics   The statistical analysis of economic data.

Economic Decision Rule   If the marginal benefits of doing something exceed the marginal costs, do it. If the marginal costs of doing something exceed the marginal benefits, don't do it.

Economic Efficiency   Achieving a goal at the lowest possible cost.

Economic Engineering   Economics devoted not only to studying markets, but also to designing markets and other coordinating mechanisms.

Economic Force   The necessary reaction to scarcity.

Economic Model   A framework that places the generalized insights of a theory in a more specific contextual setting.

Economic Policy   An action (or inaction) taken by government to influence economic actions.

Economic Principle   A commonly held economic insight stated as a law or general assumption.

Economic Profit   Explicit and implicit revenue minus explicit and implicit cost. Also, a return on entrepreneurship above and beyond normal profits.

Economic Takeoff   A stage when the development process becomes self-sustaining.

Economically Efficient   A method of production that produces a given level of output at the lowest possible cost.

Economics   The study of how human beings coordinate their wants and desires, given the decision-making mechanisms, social customs, and political realities of the society.

Economies of Scale   Situation when long-run average total costs decrease as output increases.

Economies of Scope   Situation when the costs of producing products are interdependent so that it's less costly for a firm to produce a good when it's already producing another.

Efficiency   Achieving a goal as cheaply as possible. Also: Using as few inputs as possible.

Efficiency Wages   Wages paid above the going market wage to keep workers happy and productive.

Efficient   Achieving a goal at the lowest cost in total resources without consideration as to who pays those costs.

Efficient Market Hypothesis   The assumption that all financial decisions are made by rational people and are based on all relevant information that accurately reflects the value of assets today and in the future.

Effluent Fees   Charges imposed by government on the level of pollution created.

Elastic   The percentage change in quantity is greater than the percentage change in price ($E > 1$).

Empirical Model   A model that statistically discovers a pattern in the data.

Endowment Effect   People value something more just because they have it.

Enlightened Self-Interest   People care about other people as well as themselves.

Entrepreneur   An individual who sees an opportunity to sell an item at a price higher than the average cost of producing it.

Entrepreneurship   The ability to organize and get something done. Also: Labor services that involve high degrees of organizational skills, concern, oversight responsibility, and creativity.

Equation of Exchange   An equation stating that the quantity of money times the velocity of money equals the price level times the quantity of real goods sold.

Equilibrium   A concept in which opposing dynamic forces cancel each other out.

Equilibrium Output   The level of output toward which the economy gravitates in the short run because of the cumulative cycles of declining or increasing production.

Equilibrium Price   The price toward which the invisible hand drives the market.

Equilibrium Quantity   The amount bought and sold at the equilibrium price.

Excess Demand   Situation when quantity demanded is greater than quantity supplied.

Excess Reserves   Reserves held by banks in excess of what banks are required to hold.

Excess Supply   Situation when quantity supplied is greater than quantity demanded.

Exchange Rate   The price of one country's currency in terms of another currency.

Excise Tax   A tax that is levied on a specific good.

Expansionary Monetary Policy   Monetary policy that increases the money supply and decreases the interest rate.

Expenditures Multiplier   A number that tells how much income will change in response to a change in autonomous expenditures.

Experimental Economics   A branch of economics that studies the economy through controlled laboratory experiments.

External Debt   Government debt owed to individuals in foreign countries.

Externality   An effect of a decision on a third party not taken into account by the decision maker.

Extrapolative Expectations   Expectations that a trend will accelerate.

F

Failure of Market Outcome   A situation in which, even though the market is functioning properly (there are no market failures), it is not achieving society's goals.

Fallacy of Composition   The false assumption that what is true for a part will also be true for the whole.

Fed Funds   Loans of excess reserves banks make to one another.

Federal Deposit Insurance Corporation (FDIC)   A government institution that guarantees bank deposits up to $250,000.

Federal Funds Market   The market in which banks lend and borrow reserves.

Federal Funds Rate   The interest rate banks charge one another for Fed funds.

Federal Open Market Committee (FOMC)   The Fed's chief body that decides monetary policy.

Federal Reserve Bank (the Fed)   The U.S. central bank whose liabilities (Federal Reserve notes) serve as cash in the United States.

Final Output   Goods and services purchased for their final use.

Financial and Capital Account   The part of the balance of payments account in which all long-term flows of payments are listed.

Financial Assets   Assets, such as stocks or bonds, whose benefit to the owner depends on the issuer of the asset meeting certain obligations.

Financial Liabilities   Liabilities incurred by the issuer of a financial asset to stand behind the issued asset.

Fine-Tuning   Fiscal policy designed to keep the economy always at its target or potential level of income.

Firm   An economic institution that transforms factors of production into goods and services.

First-Mover Advantage   Benefits gained from being the first to gain a significant share of a market.

Fiscal Austerity   Increasing taxes and decreasing spending.

Fiscal Policy   The deliberate change in either government spending or taxes to stimulate or slow down the economy. Also, the changing of taxes and spending to affect the level of output in the economy.

Fixed Costs   Costs that are spent and cannot be changed in the period of time under consideration.

Fixed Exchange Rate   When the government chooses a particular exchange rate and offers to buy and sell its currency at that price.

Flexible Exchange Rate   When the government does not enter into foreign exchange markets at all, but leaves the determination of exchange rates totally up to market forces.

Foreign Aid   Funds that developed countries lend or give to developing countries.

Framing Effect   The tendency of people to base their choices on how the choice is presented.

Free Rider Problem   Individuals' unwillingness to share in the cost of a public good.

Free Trade Association   A group of countries that have reduced or eliminated trade barriers among themselves.

Frictional Unemployment   Unemployment caused by people entering the job market and people quitting a job just long enough to look for and find another one.

Full Convertibility   An exchange rate system in which individuals may change dollars into any currency they want for whatever legal purpose they want.

Functional Finance   A theoretical proposition that governments should make spending and taxing decisions on the basis of their effect on the economy, not on the basis of some moralistic principle that budgets should be balanced.

G

Game Theory   Formal economic reasoning applied to situations in which decisions are interdependent.

Game Theory Model   A model in which one analyzes the strategic interaction of individuals when they take into account the likely response of other people to their actions.

GDP Deflator   An index of the price level of aggregate output, or the average price of the components of GDP, relative to a base year.

General Agreement on Tariffs and Trade (GATT)   A regular international conference to reduce trade barriers held from 1947 to 1995. It has been replaced by the World Trade Organization (WTO).

General Rule of Political Economy   When small groups are helped by a government action and large groups are hurt by that same action, the small group tends to lobby far more effectively than the large group.

Glass-Steagall Act   An act of Congress passed in 1933 that established deposit insurance and implemented a number of banking regulations.

Global Corporation   A corporation with substantial operations on both the production and sales sides in more than one country.

Globalization   The increasing economic connections among economies around the world that increase competition among countries.

Globalized *AS/AD* Model   A modified *AS/AD* model with an added world supply curve that highlights the effect that globalization can have on an economy.

Gold Specie Flow Mechanism   The long-run adjustment mechanism that maintained the gold standard.

Gold Standard   The system of fixed exchange rates in which the value of currencies was fixed relative to the value of gold and gold was used as the primary reserve asset.

Good/Bad Paradox   The phenomenon of doing poorly because you're doing well.

Government Failure   A situation in which the government intervention in the market to improve market failure actually makes the situation worse.

Government Spending   Goods and services that government buys.

Grandfather   To pass a law affecting a specific group but providing that those in the group before the law was passed are exempt from some provisions of the law.

Graph   A picture of points in a coordinate system in which points denote relationships between numbers.

Gross Domestic Product (GDP)   The total market value of all final goods and services produced in an economy in a one-year period.

Gross National Product (GNP)   The aggregate final output of citizens and businesses of an economy in a one-year period.

H

Herding   The human tendency to follow the crowd.

Herfindahl Index   An index of market concentration calculated by adding the squared value of the individual market shares of all firms in the industry.

Heuristic Model   A model that is expressed informally in words.

Households   Groups of individuals living together and making joint decisions.

Human Capital   The skills that are embodied in workers through experience, education, and on-the-job training, or, more simply, people's knowledge.

Hyperinflation   Inflation that hits triple digits—100 percent or more per year.

I

Impartial Spectator Tool   Placing oneself in the position of a third-person examiner and judge of a situation rather than as a participant.

Implicit Collusion   A type of collusion in which multiple firms make the same pricing decisions even though they have not explicitly consulted with one another.

Implicit Costs   Costs associated with a decision that often are not included in normal accounting costs.

Incentive Compatibility Problem   A problem in which the incentive facing the decision maker does not match the incentive needed for the mechanism to achieve its desired ends.

Incentive-Compatible Contract   A contract in which the incentives of each of the two parties to the contract are made to correspond as closely as possible.

Incentive Effect   How much a person will change his or her hours worked in response to a change in the wage rate.

Income   Payments received plus or minus changes in the value of a person's assets in a specified time period.

Income Effect   The reduction in quantity demanded because price increases make us poorer.

Income Elasticity of Demand   The percentage change in demand divided by the percentage change in income.

Indifference Curve   A curve that shows combinations of goods among which an individual is indifferent.

Indivisible Setup Cost   The cost of an indivisible input for which a certain minimum amount of production must be undertaken before the input becomes economically feasible to use.

Induced Expenditures   Expenditures that change as income changes.

Inductive Approach   An approach to understanding a problem or question in which understanding is developed empirically from statistically analyzing what is observed in the data.

Inefficiency   Getting less output from inputs that, if devoted to some other activity, would produce more output.

Inefficient   Achieving a goal in a more costly manner than necessary.

Inelastic   The percentage change in quantity is less than the percentage change in price ($E < 1$).

Infant Industry Argument   The argument that with initial protection, an industry will be able to become competitive.

Inferior Good   Good whose consumption decreases when income increases.

Inflation   A continual rise in the overall price level.

Inflation Tax   An implicit tax on the holders of cash and the holders of any obligations specified in nominal terms.

Inflationary Gap   A difference between equilibrium income and potential income when equilibrium income exceeds potential income. That is, aggregate expenditures above potential output that exist at the current price level.

Infrastructure Investment   Investment in the underlying structure of the economy.

Inherent Comparative Advantage   Comparative advantage that is based on factors that are relatively unchangeable.

Institutions   The formal and informal rules that constrain human behavior.

Interest   The income paid to savers—individuals who produce now but don't consume now.

Interest Rate Effect   The effect that a lower price level has on investment expenditures through the effect that a change in the price level has on interest rates.

Intermediate Products   Products used as input in the production of some other product.

Internal Debt   Government debt owed to other governmental agencies or to its own citizens.

International Effect   As the price level falls (assuming the exchange rate does not change), net exports will rise.

Interpolation Assumption   The assumption that the relationship between variables is the same between points as it is at the points.

Inverse Relationship   A relationship between two variables in which when one goes up, the other goes down.

Inverted Yield Curve   A yield curve in which the short-term rate is higher than the long-term rate.

Investment   Spending for the purpose of additional production.

Invisible Hand   The price mechanism; the rise and fall of prices that guide our actions in a market.

Invisible Hand Theorem   A market economy, through the price mechanism, will tend to allocate resources efficiently.

Isocost Line   A line that represents alternative combinations of factors of production that have the same costs.

Isoquant Curve   A curve that represents combinations of factors of production that result in equal amounts of output.

Isoquant Map   A set of isoquant curves that show technically efficient combinations of inputs that can produce different levels of output.

J

Judgment by Performance   To judge the competitiveness of markets by the performance (behavior) of firms in that market.

Judgment by Structure   To judge the competitiveness of markets by the structure of the industry.

K

Keynesian Economists   Economists who believe that business cycles reflect underlying problems that can be addressed with activist government policies.

L

Labor Force   Those people in an economy who are willing and able to work.

Labor Market   The factor market in which individuals supply labor services for wages to other individuals and to firms that need (demand) labor services.

Labor Productivity   The average output per worker.

Laissez-Faire   An economic policy of leaving the coordination of individuals' actions to the market.

Land Bank Program   A program in which government supports prices by giving farmers economic incentives to reduce supply.

Law of Demand   Quantity demanded rises as price falls, other things constant. Also can be stated as: Quantity demanded falls as price rises, other things constant.

Law of Diminishing Control   Whenever a regulatory system is set up, individuals or firms being regulated will figure out ways to circumvent those regulations.

Law of Diminishing Marginal Productivity   As more and more of a variable input is added to an existing fixed input, eventually the additional output produced with that additional input falls. Also, increasing one input, keeping all others constant, will lead to smaller and smaller gains in output.

Law of Diminishing Marginal Rate of Substitution   As you get more and more of a good, if some of that good is taken away, then the marginal addition of another good you need to remain on the same indifference curve gets less and less.

Law of One Price   The wages of workers in one country will not differ significantly from the wages of (equal) workers in another institutionally similar country.

Law of Supply   Quantity supplied rises as price rises, other things constant. Also can be stated as: Quantity supplied falls as price falls, other things constant.

Lazy Monopolist   A monopolist that does not push for efficiency, but merely enjoys the position it is already in.

Learning by Doing   As we do something, we learn what works and what doesn't, and over time we become more proficient at it. Also: To improve the methods of production through experience.

Lender of Last Resort   Lending to banks and other financial institutions when no one else will.

Leverage   Borrowing to make financial investments.

Liability Management   How a bank attracts deposits and what it pays for them.

Libertarian Paternalistic Policy   A policy that leaves people free to choose, but nonetheless guides them toward a choice that a paternalistic observer would see as good for them.

Limited Capital Account Convertibility   An exchange rate system that allows full current account convertibility and partial capital account convertibility.

Line Graph   A graph where the data are connected by a continuous line.

Linear Curve   A curve that is drawn as a straight line.

Liquid   Having assets that can readily be converted into cash and money.

Liquidity   One's ability to convert an asset into cash.

Liquidity Trap   A situation in which additional reserves that the Fed puts into the banking system go into excess reserves and do not increase the money supply.

Long-Run Aggregate Supply (*LAS*) Curve   A curve that shows the long-run relationship between output and the price level.

Long-Run Decision   A decision in which a firm chooses among all possible production techniques.

Long-Run Phillips Curve   A vertical curve at the unemployment rate consistent with potential output. (It shows the trade-off [or complete lack thereof] when expectations of inflation equal actual inflation.)

Lorenz Curve   A geometric representation of the share distribution of income among families in a given country at a given time.

Luxury   A good that has an income elasticity greater than 1.

M

M₁   Currency in the hands of the public, checking account balances, and traveler's checks.

M₂   M₁ plus savings and money market accounts, small-denomination time deposits (also called CDs), and retail money funds.

Macroeconomic Externality   An externality that affects the levels of unemployment, inflation, or growth in the economy as a whole.

Macroeconomics   The study of the economy as a whole, which includes inflation, unemployment, business cycles, and growth.

Marginal Benefit   Additional benefit above the benefits already derived.

Marginal Cost (*MC*)   Additional cost over and above the costs already incurred. Also: Increase (decrease) in total cost from increasing (or decreasing) the level of output by one unit. Also: The change in total cost associated with a change in quantity.

Marginal Factor Cost   The additional cost to a firm of hiring another worker.

Marginal Physical Product (*MPP*)   The additional units of output that hiring an additional worker will bring about.

Marginal Product   The additional output that will be forthcoming from an additional worker, other inputs constant.

Marginal Productivity Theory   Factors are paid their marginal revenue product (what they contribute at the margin to revenue).

Marginal Propensity to Expend (*mpe*)   The ratio of the change in aggregate expenditures to a change in income.

Marginal Rate of Substitution   The rate at which one good must be added when the other is taken away to keep the individual indifferent between the two combinations. Also: The rate at which one factor must be added to compensate for the loss of another factor to keep output constant.

Marginal Revenue (*MR*)   The change in total revenue associated with a change in quantity.

Marginal Revenue Product (*MRP*)   The marginal revenue a firm expects to earn from selling an additional worker's output.

Marginal Social Benefit   The marginal private benefit of consuming a good plus the benefits of the positive externalities resulting from consuming that good.

Marginal Social Cost   The marginal private costs of production plus the cost of the negative externalities associated with that production.

Marginal Utility   The satisfaction one gets from consuming one additional unit of a product above and beyond what one has consumed up to that point.

Market Demand Curve   The horizontal sum of all individual demand curves.

Market Economy   An economic system based on private property and the market in which, in principle, individuals decide how, what, and for whom to produce.

Market Failure   A situation in which the invisible hand pushes in such a way that individual decisions do not lead to socially desirable outcomes.

Market Force   An economic force that is given relatively free rein by society to work through the market.

Market Incentive Plan   A plan requiring market participants to certify that they have reduced total consumption—not necessarily their own individual consumption—by a specified amount.

Market Niche   An area in which competition is not working.

Market Supply Curve   The horizontal sum of all individual supply curves. Also: Horizontal sum of all the firms' marginal cost curves, taking account of any changes in input prices that might occur.

Marxian (Radical) Model   A model that focuses on equitable distribution of power, rights, and income among social classes.

Mechanism Design   Identifying a goal and then designing a mechanism such as a market, social system, or contract to achieve that end.

Medicare   A multibillion-dollar medical insurance system.

Merit Good or Activity   A good or activity that government believes is good for you, even though you may not choose to consume the good or engage in the activity.

Microeconomics   The study of individual choice, and how that choice is influenced by economic forces.

Minimum Efficient Level of Production   The amount of production that spreads out setup costs sufficiently for a firm to undertake production profitably.

Minimum Wage Law   A law specifying the lowest wage a firm can legally pay an employee.

Mixed Strategy   A strategy of choosing randomly among moves.

Model   A simplified representation of the problem or question that captures the essential issues.

Modern Economists   Economists who are willing to use a wider range of models than did earlier economists.

Monetary Base   Vault cash, deposits at the Fed, plus currency in circulation.

Monetary Policy   A policy of influencing the economy through changes in the banking system's reserves that influence the money supply and credit availability in the economy.

Monetary Regime   A predetermined statement of the policy that will be followed in various situations.

Money   A highly liquid financial asset that's generally accepted in exchange for other goods, is used as a reference in valuing other goods, and can be stored as wealth.

Money Multiplier $1/r$ where r is the percentage of deposits banks hold in reserve.

Money Wealth Effect   A fall in the price level will make the holders of money richer, so they buy more.

Monitoring Costs   Costs incurred by the organizer of production in seeing to it that the employees do what they're supposed to do.

Monitoring Problem   The need to oversee employees to ensure that their actions are in the best interest of the firm.

Monopolistic Competition   A market structure in which many firms sell differentiated products; there are few barriers to entry.

Monopoly   A market structure in which one firm makes up the entire market.

Monopsony   A market in which a single firm is the only buyer.

Moral Hazard Problem   A problem that arises when people don't have to bear the negative consequences of their actions.

Mortgage-Backed Securities   Financial assets whose flow of income comes from a combination of mortgages.

Movement along a Demand Curve   The graphical representation of the effect of a change in price on the quantity demanded.

Movement along a Supply Curve   The graphical representation of the effect of a change in price on the quantity supplied.

Multiplier-Accelerator Model   A model in which changes in output are accelerated because changes in investment depend on changes in income (rather than on the level of income).

Multiplier Effect   The amplification of initial changes in expenditures.

Multiplier Equation   An equation that tells us that income equals the multiplier times autonomous expenditures.

Multiplier Model   A model that emphasizes the effect of fluctuations in aggregate demand, rather than the price level, on output.

N

Nash Equilibrium   A set of strategies for each player in the game in which no player can improve his or her payoff by changing strategy unilaterally.

Natural Experiment   A naturally occurring event that approximates a controlled experiment where something has changed in one place but has not changed somewhere else. That is, an event created by nature that can serve as an experiment.

Natural Monopoly An industry in which a single firm can produce at a lower cost than can two or more firms. Also: An industry in which significant economies of scale make the existence of more than one firm inefficient.

Necessity A good that has an income elasticity less than 1.

Negative Externality The adverse effect of a decision on others not taken into account by the decision maker. When the effects of a decision not taken into account by the decision maker are detrimental to others.

Net Domestic Product (NDP) The sum of consumption expenditures, government expenditures, net exports, and investment less depreciation. That is, GDP less depreciation.

Net Exports Spending on goods and services produced in the United States that foreigners buy (exports) minus goods and services produced abroad that U.S. citizens buy (imports).

Net Foreign Factor Income Income from foreign domestic factor sources minus foreign factor income earned domestically.

Net Investment Gross investment less depreciation.

Network Externality The phenomenon that the greater use of a product increases the benefit of that product to everyone without them paying for it.

New Growth Theory A theory that emphasizes the role of technology rather than capital in the growth process.

Nominal Deficit The deficit determined by looking at the difference between expenditures and receipts.

Nominal GDP GDP calculated at existing prices.

Nominal Interest Rate The interest rate you actually see and pay when borrowing, or receive when lending.

Nominal Wealth The value of the assets of an economy measured at their current market prices.

Noncooperative Game A game in which each player is out for him- or herself and agreements are either not possible or not enforceable.

Nonlinear Curve A curve that is drawn as a curved line.

Nonrecourse Loan Program A program in which government "buys" goods in the form of collateral on defaulting loans.

Normal Good Good whose consumption increases with an increase in income.

Normal Profit The amount the owners of a business would have received in the next-best alternative. Also: Payments to entrepreneurs as the return on their risk taking.

Normative Economics The study of what the goals of the economy should be.

North American Industry Classification System (NAICS) An industry classification that categorizes industries by type of economic activity and groups firms with like production processes.

Nudge A deliberate design of the choice architecture that alters people's behavior in predictably positive ways.

Nudge Policy Policy in which government structures choices so that people are free to choose what they want, but also more likely to choose what is best for them.

O

Okun's Rule of Thumb A 1 percentage point change in the unemployment rate will be associated with a 2 percent deviation in output from its trend in the opposite direction.

Oligopoly A market structure in which there are only a few firms and firms explicitly take other firms' likely response into account; there are often significant barriers to entry.

Open Market Operations The Fed's buying and selling of government securities.

Operation Twist Selling short-term Treasury bills and buying long-term Treasury bonds without creating more new money.

Opportunity Cost The benefit you might have gained from choosing the next-best alternative.

Optimal Policy A policy in which the marginal cost of a policy equals the marginal benefit of that policy.

P

Paradox of Thrift An increase in saving can lead to a decrease in expenditures, decreasing output and causing a recession.

Pareto Optimal Policy A policy that benefits some people and hurts no one.

Partially Flexible Exchange Rate When the government sometimes buys or sells currencies to influence the exchange rate, while at other times the government simply accepts the exchange rate determined by supply and demand forces, that is, letting private market forces operate.

Partnership A business with two or more owners.

Patent The legal protection of a technical innovation that gives the person holding it sole right to use that innovation. (*Note:* A patent is good for only a limited time.)

Path-Dependent Model A model in which the path to equilibrium affects the equilibrium.

Payoff Matrix A table that shows the outcome of every choice by every player, given the possible choices of all other players.

Per Capita Growth Producing more goods and services per person.

Per Capita Output Real GDP divided by the total population.

Perfectly Competitive Market   A market in which economic forces operate unimpeded.

Perfectly Elastic   Quantity responds enormously to changes in price ($E = \infty$).

Perfectly Inelastic   Quantity does not respond at all to changes in price ($E = 0$).

Permanent Income Hypothesis   A proposition that expenditures are determined by permanent or lifetime income.

Personal Consumption Expenditure (PCE) Deflator   A measure of prices of goods that consumers buy that allows yearly changes in the basket of goods that reflect actual consumer purchasing habits.

Pie Chart   A circle divided into "slices of pie," where the undivided pie represents the total amount and the pie slices reflect the percentage of the whole pie that the various components make up.

Policy Change   A change in one aspect of government's actions, such as monetary policy or fiscal policy.

Policy Coordination   The integration of a country's policies to take account of their global effects.

Political Forces   Legal directives that direct individuals' actions.

Positive Economics   The study of what is and how the economy works.

Positive Externality   The positive effect of a decision on others not taken into account by the decision maker. Also, when the effects of a decision not taken into account by the decision maker are beneficial to others.

Potential Output   Output that would materialize at the target rate of unemployment. Also, the highest amount of output an economy can sustainably produce from existing production processes and resources.

Poverty Threshold   The income below which a family is considered to live in poverty.

Precautionary Motive   Holding money for unexpected expenses and impulse buying.

Precepts   Policy rules that conclude that a particular course of action is preferable.

Precommitment Policy   Committing to continue a policy for a prolonged period of time.

Precommitment Strategy   A strategy in which people consciously place limitations on their future actions, thereby limiting their choices.

Present Value   A method of translating a flow of future income or savings into its current worth.

Price Ceiling   A government-imposed limit on how high a price can be charged. In other words, a government-set price below the market equilibrium price.

Price-Discriminate   To charge different prices to different individuals or groups of individuals.

Price Elasticity of Demand   The percentage change in quantity demanded divided by the percentage change in price.

Price Elasticity of Supply   The percentage change in quantity supplied divided by the percentage change in price.

Price Floor   A government-imposed limit on how low a price can be charged. In other words, a government-set price above equilibrium price.

Price Index   A number set at 100 in the base year that summarizes what happens to a weighted composite of prices of a selection of goods (often called a market basket of goods) over time.

Price Stabilization Program   A program designed to eliminate short-run fluctuations in prices, while allowing prices to follow their long-run trend line.

Price Support Program   A program designed to maintain prices at levels higher than the market prices.

Price Taker   A firm or individual who takes the price determined by supply and demand as given.

Principle of Diminishing Marginal Utility   As you consume more of a good, after some point, the marginal utility received from each additional unit of a good decreases with each additional unit consumed, other things equal.

Principle of Rational Choice   Spend your money on those goods that give you the most marginal utility (MU) per dollar.

Prisoner's Dilemma   A well-known game that demonstrates the difficulty of cooperative behavior in certain circumstances.

Private Good   A good that, when consumed by one individual, cannot be consumed by another individual.

Private Property Right   Control a private individual or firm has over an asset.

Procyclical Fiscal Policy   Changes in government spending and taxes that increase the cyclical fluctuations in the economy instead of reducing them.

Producer Price Index (PPI)   An index of prices that measures average change in the selling prices received by domestic producers of goods and services over time.

Producer Surplus   Price the producer sells a product for less the cost of producing it.

Production   The transformation of factors into goods and services.

Production Function   The relationship between the inputs (factors of production) and outputs.

Production Possibility Curve (PPC)   A curve measuring the maximum combination of outputs that can be obtained from a given number of inputs.

Production Table   A table showing the output resulting from various combinations of factors of production or inputs.

Productive Efficiency   Achieving as much output as possible from a given amount of inputs or resources.

Productivity   Output per unit of input.

Profit What's left over from total revenues after all the appropriate costs have been subtracted. That is, Total revenue − Total cost. Also: A return on entrepreneurial activity and risk taking.

Profit-Maximizing Condition $MR = MC = P$.

Progressive Tax A tax whose rates increase as a person's income increases.

Property Rights The rights given to people to use specified property as they see fit.

Proportional Tax A tax whose rates are constant at all income levels, no matter what a taxpayer's total annual income is.

Public Assistance Means-tested social programs targeted to the poor and providing financial, nutritional, medical, and housing assistance.

Public Choice Economist An economist who integrates an economic analysis of politics with an analysis of the economy.

Public Choice Model A model that focuses on economic incentives as applied to politicians.

Public Good A good that if supplied to one person must be supplied to all and whose consumption by one individual does not prevent its consumption by another individual. That is, a good that is nonexclusive and nonrival.

Purchasing Power Parity (PPP) A method of calculating exchange rates that attempts to value currencies at rates such that each currency will buy an equal basket of goods. Also, a method of comparing income by looking at the domestic purchasing power in different countries.

Purposeful Behavior Behavior reflecting reasoned but not necessarily rational judgment.

Push Policy A regulatory or tax policy to get firms or individuals to use "appropriate" nudges.

Q

Quantitative Easing A policy of buying a wide range of financial assets from banks and other financial institutions in order to stimulate the economy.

Quantity-Adjusting Markets Markets in which firms respond to changes in demand primarily by changing production instead of changing their prices.

Quantity Demanded A specific amount that will be demanded per unit of time at a specific price, other things constant.

Quantity Supplied A specific amount that will be supplied at a specific price, other things constant.

Quantity Theory of Money A theory that the price level varies in response to changes in the quantity of money.

Quasi Rent Any payment to a resource above the amount that the resource would receive in its next-best use.

Quota A quantity limit placed on imports.

R

Rational An adjective used to describe behavior individuals undertake in their own best interest.

Rational Expectations Expectations that the economists' model predicts. Also: Forward-looking expectations that use available information. Also: Expectations that turn out to be correct.

Rational Expectations Model A model in which all decisions are based on the expected equilibrium in the economy.

Real-Business-Cycle Theory A theory that fluctuations in the economy reflect real phenomena—simultaneous shifts in supply and demand, not simply supply responses to demand shifts.

Real Deficit The nominal deficit adjusted for inflation.

Real Exchange Rate The nominal exchange rate adjusted for differential inflation or differential changes in the price level.

Real Gross Domestic Product (real GDP) The market value of final goods and services produced in an economy, stated in the prices of a given year. Also: Nominal GDP adjusted for inflation.

Real Interest Rate Nominal interest rate adjusted for expected inflation.

Real Wealth The value of the productive capacity of the assets of an economy measured by the goods and services it can produce now and in the future.

Recession A decline in real output that persists for more than two consecutive quarters of a year.

Recessionary Gap The amount by which equilibrium output is below potential output.

Regime Change A change in the entire atmosphere within which the government and the economy interrelate.

Regression Model An empirical model in which one of variables is statistically related to another.

Regressive Tax A tax whose rates decrease as income rises.

Regulatory Trade Restrictions Government-imposed procedural rules that limit imports.

Rent The income from a factor of production that is in fixed supply.

Rent Control A price ceiling on rents, set by government.

Rent Seeking The restricting of supply in order to increase the price suppliers receive.

Rent-Seeking Activity Activity designed to transfer surplus from one group to another.

Reservation Wage The lowest wage that a person needs to receive to accept a job.

Reserve Ratio The ratio of reserves to total deposits.

Reserve Requirement The percentage the Federal Reserve Bank sets as the minimum amount of reserves a bank must have.

Reserves Currency and deposits a bank keeps on hand or at the Fed or central bank, enough to manage the normal cash inflows and outflows.

Resource Curse The paradox that countries with an abundance of resources tend to have lower economic growth and more unemployment than countries with fewer natural resources.

Restructuring Changing the underlying economic institutions.

Reverse Engineering The process of a firm buying other firms' products, disassembling them, figuring out what's special about them, and then copying them within the limits of the law.

Ricardian Equivalence Theorem The theoretical proposition that deficits do not affect the level of output in the economy because individuals increase their savings to account for expected future tax payments to repay the deficit.

Rule of 72 The number of years needed for a certain amount to double in value is equal to 72 divided by its annual rate of interest.

S

Sanction A restriction on the imports or exports of a country's goods.

Say's Law A law that states that supply creates its own demand.

Scarcity The goods available are too few to satisfy individuals' desires.

Screening An action taken by an uninformed party that induces the informed party to reveal information.

Screening Question A question structured in a way to reveal strategic information about the person who answers.

Secular Stagnation Theory A theory in which advanced countries such as the United States would eventually stop growing because investment opportunities would be eliminated.

Self-Confirming Equilibrium An equilibrium in a model in which people's beliefs become self-fulfilling.

Sequential Game A game where players make decisions one after another, so one player responds to the known decisions of other players.

Shadow Price A price that isn't paid directly, but instead is paid in terms of opportunity cost borne by the demander, and thus determines his or her action indirectly.

Shift in Demand The graphical representation of the effect of anything other than price on demand.

Shift in Supply The graphical representation of the effect of a change in a factor other than price on supply.

Short-Run Aggregate Supply (SAS) Curve A curve that specifies how a shift in the aggregate demand curve affects the price level and real output in the short run, other things constant.

Short-Run Decision A decision in which the firm is constrained in regard to what production decisions it can make.

Short-Run Phillips Curve A downward-sloping curve showing the relationship between inflation and unemployment when expectations of inflation are constant.

Shutdown Point The point below which the firm will be better off if it temporarily shuts down than it will if it stays in business.

Signaling An action taken by an informed party that reveals information to an uninformed party and thereby partially offsets adverse selection.

Simultaneous Move Game A game where players make their decisions at the same time as other players without knowing what choice the other players have made.

Sin Tax A tax that discourages activities society believes are harmful (sinful).

Slope The change in the value on the vertical axis divided by the change in the value on the horizontal axis.

Social Capital The habitual way of doing things that guides people in how they approach production.

Social Forces Forces that guide individual actions even though those actions may not be in an individual's selfish interest.

Social Security System A social insurance program that provides financial benefits to individuals who are elderly and disabled and to their eligible dependents and/or survivors.

Socialism An economic system based on individuals' goodwill toward others, not on their own self-interest, and in which, in principle, society decides what, how, and for whom to produce.

Sole Proprietorship A business that has only one owner.

Solvent Having sufficient assets to cover long-run liabilities.

Sound Finance A view of fiscal policy that the government budget should always be balanced except in wartime.

Special Drawing Rights (SDRs) A type of international money.

Specialization The concentration of individuals on certain aspects of production.

Speculative Motive Holding cash to avoid holding financial assets whose prices are falling.

Stagflation The combination of high and accelerating inflation and high unemployment.

Status Quo Bias An individual's actions are very much influenced by what the current situation is, even when that reasonably does not seem to be very important to the decision.

Stock A financial asset that conveys ownership rights in a corporation. Also, certificate of ownership in a company.

Strategic Bargaining Demanding a larger share of the gains from trade than you can reasonably expect.

Strategic Decision Making   Taking explicit account of a rival's expected response to a decision you are making.

Strategic Trade Policy   Threatening to implement tariffs to bring about a reduction in tariffs or some other concession from the other country.

Structural Deficit   The part of a budget deficit that would exist even if the economy were at its potential level of income.

Structural Stagnation   A period of protracted slow growth and high unemployment.

Structural Stagnation Hypothesis   A hypothesis about the macro economy that sees the recent problems of the U.S. economy as directly related to the structural problems caused by displacement due to globalization and technological change.

Structural Unemployment   Unemployment caused by the institutional structure of an economy or by economic restructuring making some skills obsolete.

Substitute   A good that can be used in place of another good.

Substitution Effect   The reduction in quantity demanded because relative price has risen.

Sunk Cost   Cost that has already been incurred and cannot be recovered.

Supplemental Security Income (SSI)   A federal program that pays benefits, based on need, to individuals who are elderly, blind, and disabled.

Supply   A schedule of quantities a seller is willing to sell per unit of time at various prices, other things constant.

Supply Curve   A graphical representation of the relationship between price and quantity supplied.

Surplus   An excess of revenues over payments.

T

Target Rate of Unemployment   The lowest sustainable rate of unemployment that policy makers believe is achievable given existing demographics and the economy's institutional structure.

Tariff   A tax that governments place on internationally traded goods.

Tax Incentive Program   A program using a tax to create incentives for individuals to structure their activities in a way that is consistent with the desired ends.

Taylor Rule   The rule is: Set the Fed funds rate at 2 percent plus current inflation if the economy is at desired output and desired inflation. If the inflation rate is higher than desired, increase the Fed funds rate by 0.5 times the difference between desired and actual inflation. Similarly, if output is higher than desired, increase the Fed funds rate by 0.5 times the percentage deviation.

Team Spirit   The feelings of friendship and being part of a team that bring out people's best efforts.

Technical Efficiency   A situation in which as few inputs as possible are used to produce a given output.

Technological Change   An increase in the range of production techniques that leads to more efficient ways of producing goods as well as the production of new and better goods.

Technological Lock-In   The prior use of a technology makes the adoption of subsequent technologies difficult.

Technology   The way we make goods and supply services.

Theorems   Propositions that are logically true based on the assumptions in a model.

Third-Party-Payer Market   A market in which the person who receives the good differs from the person paying for the good.

Too-Big-to-Fail Problem   The belief that large financial institutions are essential to the workings of an economy, requiring government to step in to prevent their failure.

Total Cost   The explicit payments to the factors of production plus the opportunity cost of the factors provided by the owners of the firm.

Total Revenue   The amount a firm receives for selling its product or service plus any increase in the value of the assets owned by the firm.

Total Utility   The total satisfaction one gets from consuming a product.

Trade Adjustment Assistance Programs   Programs designed to compensate losers for reductions in trade restrictions.

Trade Deficit   When imports exceed exports.

Trade Surplus   When exports exceed imports.

Traditional Economists   Economists who study the logical implications of rationality and self-interest in relatively simple algebraic or graphical models such as the supply and demand model.

Transactions Motive   The need to hold money for spending.

Transfer Payments   Payments to individuals by government that do not involve production by those individuals.

Transferable Comparative Advantage   Comparative advantage based on factors that can change relatively easily.

U

Ultimatum Game   A game in which the person gets the money only if the other person accepts the offer. If the second person does not accept, they both get nothing.

Unemployment Compensation   Short-term financial assistance, regardless of need, to eligible individuals who are temporarily out of work.

Unemployment Rate   The percentage of people in the economy who are willing and able to work but who cannot find jobs.

Unit Elastic   The percentage change in quantity is equal to the percentage change in price ($E = 1$).

Utility   The pleasure or satisfaction that one expects to get from consuming a good or service.

Utility-Maximizing Rule   Utility is maximized when the ratios of the marginal utility to price of two goods are equal.

V

Value Added   The increase in value that a firm contributes to a product or service.

Value-Added Chain   The movement of trade from natural resources to low-skill manufacturing to increasingly complicated goods and services.

Value of Marginal Product (*VMP*)   An additional worker's marginal physical product multiplied by the price at which the firm could sell that additional product.

Variable Costs   Costs that change as output changes.

Velocity of Money   The number of times per year, on average, a dollar goes around to generate a dollar's worth of income.

Vickrey Auction   A sealed-bid auction where the highest bidder wins but pays the price bid by the next-highest bidder.

W

Wealth   The value of the things individuals own less the value of what they owe.

Wealth Accounts   A balance sheet of an economy's stock of assets and liabilities.

Welfare Loss Triangle   A geometric representation of the welfare cost in terms of misallocated resources caused by a deviation from a supply/demand equilibrium.

World Supply Curve   The amount of tradable goods that other countries will supply to a country at a given price level and exchange rate.

World Trade Organization (WTO)   An organization whose functions are generally the same as GATT's were—to promote free and fair trade among countries.

X

X-inefficiency   The underperformance of a firm that has a monopoly position. The firm operates far less efficiently than it could technically.

Y

Yield Curve   A curve that shows the relationship between interest rates and bonds' time to maturity.

Z

Zero Interest Rate Lower Bound   A limit on how much interest rates can fall.

Zoning Laws   Laws that set limits on the use of one's property.

A

Ads (noun)   Short for "advertisements."

Ain't (verb)   An informal form of "isn't," sometimes used to emphasize a point although the speaker knows that "isn't" is the correct form.

All the Rage (descriptive phrase)   Extremely popular, but the popularity is likely to be transitory.

American League (name of an organization)   An association of baseball teams. The United States has two baseball associations—the other is the National League.

Andy Warhol (proper name)   American artist who flourished in the period 1960–1980. He was immensely popular and successful with art critics and the intelligentsia, but, above all, he gained worldwide recognition in the same way and of the same quality as movie stars and athletes do. His renown has continued even after his death.

Automatic Pilot (noun)   To be on automatic pilot is to be acting without thinking.

B

Baby Boom (noun)   Any period when more than the statistically predicted number of babies are born. Originally referred to a specific group: those born in the years 1945–1964.

Baby Boomers (descriptive phrase)   Americans born in the years 1945 through 1964. An enormous and influential group of people whose large number is attributed to the "boom" in babies that occurred when military personnel, many of whom had been away from home for four or five years, were discharged from military service after the end of World War II.

Back to the Drawing Board (descriptive phrase)   To start all over again after having your plan or project turn out to be useless.

Backfire (verb)   To injure a person or entity who intended to inflict injury.

Bailed Out (descriptive phrase)   To be rescued. It has other colloquial meanings as well, but they do not appear in this book.

Bailout (noun)   The action of having been bailed out. (See also "Bailed Out.")

Balloon (verb)   To expand enormously and suddenly.

Barista (noun)   The name given to a worker at a "high-class" coffee shop.

Bases on Balls (descriptive phrase)   A strategy in the game of baseball. If a pitcher throws a long enough succession of defective throws, the batter gets to run—or walk—to first base without having hit any balls.

Bean (noun)   A person's head; also a person's mind or intellectual ability. ("Bean" is American slang for "head.")

Beanball (noun)   A ball thrown with the intention of hitting the opponent on the head.

Bear Market (noun)   Stock market dominated by people who are not buying (i.e., are hibernating). Opposite of a bull market, where people are charging ahead vigorously to buy.

Bedlam (noun)   Chaotic and apparently disorganized activity. Today the word is not capitalized. A few hundred years ago in England, the noun meant the Hospital of St. Mary's of Bethlehem, an insane asylum. The hospital was not in Bethlehem; it was in London. "Bedlam" was the way "Bethlehem" was pronounced by the English.

Beluga Caviar (noun)   The best, most expensive, caviar.

Benchmark (noun)   A point of reference from which measurement of any sort may be made.

Better Mousetrap (noun)   Comes from the proverb "Invent a better mousetrap and the world will beat a path to your door."

Bidding (or Bid) (verb sometimes used as a noun)   Has two different meanings. (1) Making an offer, or a series of offers, to compete with others who are making offers. Also the offer itself. (2) Ordering or asking a person to take a specified action.

Big Bucks (noun)   Really, really large sum of money.

Big Mac (proper noun)   Brand name of a kind of hamburger sold at McDonald's restaurants.

Bind (noun)   To "be in a bind" means to be in a situation where one is forced to make a difficult decision one does not want to make—where any decision seems as if it would be wrong, or at least undesirable, where all choices appear bad, but a decision is necessary.

Blow Off (verb)   To treat as inconsequential; to deal superficially with something.

Blue-Collar (adjective)   Description of manufacturing work, contrasted with white-collar or administrative work.

Blue-Collar America (noun)   That portion of the U.S. population that works in manufacturing and in manual labor jobs.

Boggled (adjective)   All mixed up; confused almost to the point of hopelessness.

Booming (adjective)   Being extraordinarily and quickly successful.

Boost (verb and noun)   To give a sudden impetus, or boost, to something or someone.

Bootstrap (verb)   Addressing a problem with the few tools that are available, whether related and tested or not.

Boston Red Sox (compound noun)   A U.S. baseball team.

Botched (adjective)   Operated badly; spoiled.

Bottleneck (noun)   Situation in which no action can be taken because a large number of people or actions are confronted by a very small opening or opportunity.

Brainteaser (noun)   Question or puzzle that intrigues the brain, thus "teasing" it to answer the question or solve the puzzle.

Brick-and-Mortar (adjective)   A company that has a physical presence such as a building. Brick-and-mortar contrasts with companies with a presence only on the Internet.

Brief (noun)   Formal written document prepared by a lawyer supporting a legal argument or case. More generally, any careful argument or strongly held opinion, written or oral.

Bring Home (verb)   To emphasize or convince.

Broke (adjective)   (1) To "go broke" or to "be broke" is to become insolvent, to lose all one's money and assets. (2) Usually not as bad as to have gone broke—just to be (hopefully) temporarily out of money or short of funds.

Bronco Bull   A bull ridden in a rodeo. The rider's objective is to stay on the bull until he wrestles it to the ground or is thrown off. (See also "Rodeo.")

Buck Rogers (proper name)   American comic strip character popular in the first three-quarters of the 20th century.

Bucks (noun)   American slang for "dollars."

Buffalo (adjective, as used in this book)   "Buffalo chicken wings" are a variety of tempting food developed in, and hence associated with, the city of Buffalo. (Not all chicken wings are Buffalo chicken wings.)

Busch Stadium (name of a stadium)   Anheuser-Busch is a firm that produces widely consumed brands of beer. Its home offices are in St. Louis. It bought naming rights to Busch Stadium in St. Louis, MO.

Bust (noun) (as in "housing bust")   A sudden decline in the price of an asset. (Opposite of boom.)

C

Cachet (noun)   Prestige, distinction, high quality. This word is borrowed from French and is pronounced "ca-SHAY."

Call (verb)   In sports refereeing, one meaning of "to call" is for the referee to announce his or her decision on a specific point.

Calvin Coolidge (proper name)   President of the United States 1923–1929.

Catch (noun)   An event that stops or impedes an action. (Note: "Catch" can be either a noun or a verb. Its many definitions take up 5 or 6 column inches in a dictionary.) A proviso; an unexpected complication.

Caveat (noun)   In English, this noun means "caution" or "warning." It comes from Latin, where it is a whole little sentence: "Let him beware."

Center Stage (noun)   A dominant position.

Central Park West (proper noun)   A fashionable and expensive street in New York City.

CEO (noun)   Abbreviation of "chief executive officer."

Charade (noun)   A pretense, usually designed to convince someone that you are doing something that you are definitely not doing.

Charleston (noun)   A social dance requiring two people. It was popular in the 1920s and 1930s.

Cherry (noun)   A small red fruit. Also a particularly excellent representative of a member of a class or grouping.

Chit (noun)   Type of IOU or coupon with a designated value that can be turned in toward the purchase or acquisition of some item. See also "IOU."

Chump Change (noun)   Insignificant amount of money earned by or paid to a person who is not alert enough to realize that more money could rather easily be earned.

Clear-cut (adjective)   Precisely defined.

Clip Coupons (verb)   To cut coupons out of newspapers and magazines. The coupons give you a discount on the price of the item when you present the item and the coupon at the cashier's counter in a store. It can also mean collecting interest on bonds. (In earlier times, bonds had coupons attached. The holders clipped them and sent them in to the bond issuer to collect the bond's interest.)

Clout (noun)   Influence or power.

Coffer (noun)   A box or trunk used to hold valuable items; hence, "coffer" has come to mean a vault or other safe storage place to hold money or other valuable items.

Coined (verb)   Invented or originated.

Coldhearted (adjective)   Without any sympathy; aloof; inhuman.

Command-and-Control (adjective)   A top-down organizational structure, where decisions are made at the top and transmitted down to lower levels.

Come Through (verb)   Satisfy someone's demands or expectations.

Cookie Monster (proper noun)   Character in the television show *Sesame Street*. (See also "Elmo.")

Co-opted (adjective)   Overwhelmed.

Cornrows (noun)   Hairstyle in which hair is braided in shallow, narrow rows over the entire head.

Corvette (noun)   A type of expensive sports car.

Costco (proper noun)   Name of a chain of big stores selling groceries and other items at a sharp discount. Usually the items are packaged in large quantities—for example, 50-pound bags of flour.

Couch (verb)   To construct and present an argument.

Crack (noun)   A strong form of cocaine.

Cry over spilt milk (expression)   To be remorseful for something that has already happended and cannot be changed.

D

Deadbeat (noun)   Lazy person who has no ambition, no money, and no prospects.

Deadweight (noun)   Literally, the unrelieved weight of any inert mass (think of carrying a sack of bricks); hence, any oppressive burden.

Decent (adjective)   One of its specialized meanings is "of high quality."

Doodle (noun and verb)   Idle scribbles, usually nonrepresentational and usually made while actively thinking about something else, such as during a phone conversation or sitting in a class.

Doritos (proper noun)   Brand name of a type of snack in chip form. The label lists its principal ingredient as corn, but it contains at least 30 other ingredients, many of them chemical.

Down Pat (descriptive phrase)   To have something down pat is to know it precisely, accurately, and without needing to think about it.

Dr. Seuss Book (noun)   A book by a favorite U.S. children's author.

Draw a Walk (descriptive phrase)   In the game of baseball, the ability to cause the pitcher to throw a series of defective pitches to the batter, thus allowing the batter to advance to first base without having actually hit a ball.

Drop in the Bucket (noun)   Insignificant quantity compared to the total amount available.

Dyed-in-the-Wool (adjective)   Irretrievably convinced of the value of a particular course of action or of the truth of an opinion. Literally, wool that is dyed after it is shorn from the sheep but before it is spun into thread.

E

Elmo (proper noun)   Character in the television show *Sesame Street*. (See also "Cookie Monster.")

'Em (pronoun)   Careless way of pronouncing "them." Written out, it reproduces the sound the speaker is making.

Emotional Quotient (EQ) (noun)   The ability to relate to others. It is a play on the concept IQ or intelligence quotient. There is no EQ measure or test.

Esperanto (noun)   An artificial language invented in the 1880s, intended to be "universal." It is based on words from the principal European languages, and the theory was that all speakers of these European languages would effortlessly understand Esperanto. It never had a big following and today is almost unknown.

Establishment (noun and adjective)   Noun: the prevailing theory or practice. Adjective: something that is used by people whose views prevail over other people's views.

Eureka Moment (noun)   "Eureka" is Greek for "I have found it!" Means having a sudden insight. Aristophanes is said to have cried out "Eureka," jumped out of his bath, and run down the street crying "Eureka!" when it struck him suddenly that the weight of water displaced by a submerged body is the same as the weight of the body being displaced.

F

Fake (verb)   To fake is to pretend or deceive; to try to make people believe that you know what you're doing or talking about when you don't know or aren't sure.

Fiberglas (proper noun)   A brand of insulating material.

Fire (verb)   To discharge an employee permanently. It's different from "laying off" an employee, an action taken when a temporary situation makes the employee superfluous, but the employer expects to take the employee back when the temporary situation is over.

Fix (verb)   To prepare, as in "fixing a meal." This is only one of the multiplicity of meanings of this verb.

Fleeting (adverb)   This word's usage is elegant and correct, but rare. It means transitory or short-lived.

Flipside (noun)   The other side of a two-sided object or of a two-sided argument or situation. Origin: In the days before tape and DVD, music was recorded on large disks, made of vinyl or other material. Both sides of the disk were used, thus—the flipside.

Flop (noun)   A dismal failure.

Follow Suit (verb)   To do the same thing you see others do. Comes from card games where if a card of a certain suit is played, the other players must play a card of that suit, if they have one.

Follow the Leader (noun)   Name of a children's game. Metaphorically, it means to do what others are doing, usually without giving it much thought.

Form Follows Function (description)   A phrase borrowed from architecture, where it means that the architect determines what a building is to be used for, and then designs the building to meet the demands of that use, or function.

Fourth Sector (noun)   An additional sector in the U.S. economy in addition to the typical three: government, private business, and nonprofit.

Free Lunch (descriptive phrase)   Something you get without paying for it in any way. Usually applied negatively: There is no "free lunch."

Front (noun and verb)   Activity undertaken to divert attention from what it is.

Funky (adjective)   Eccentric in style or manner.

G

Gadget (noun)   Generic term for any small, often novel, mechanical or electronic device or contrivance, usually designed for a specific purpose. For instance, the small wheel with serrated rim and an attached handle used to divide a pizza pie into slices is a gadget.

Gas-Guzzling (adjective) Describes motor vehicles that use a noneconomical or excessive amount of gasoline.

Gee (expletive) Emphatic expression signaling surprise or enthusiasm.

Get You Down (descriptive phrase) Make you depressed about something or make you dismiss something altogether. (Do not confuse with "get it down," which means to understand fully.)

G.I. Joe (noun) A toy in the form of a boy (as "Barbie" is a girl). The original meaning was "government issue"—i.e., an item such as a uniform issued by the U.S. government to a member of the U.S. armed forces, and, by extension, the person to whom the item was issued.

Giveaways (noun) Something, usually valuable, that you confer without receiving anything tangible in return. In this book, it refers to Congress enacting tax cuts that are insignificant to all but people who are already rich.

Glitch (noun) Trivial difficulty.

GM (noun) The General Motors automobile company.

Go-Cart (noun) A small engine-powered vehicle that is used for racing and recreation.

Gold Mine (noun) Metaphorically, any activity that results in making you a lot of money.

Good and Ready (descriptive phrase) Really, really ready.

Good Cop/Bad Cop (noun) Alternating mood shifts. It comes from the alleged practice of having two police officers interview a suspect—one officer is kind and coaxing while the other is mean and nasty. This is supposed to make the suspect feel that the nice cop is a safe person to confide in.

Gooey (adjective) Sticky or slimy.

Goofed (verb) Past tense of the verb *goof,* meaning to make a careless mistake.

GOP This acronym stands for "Grand Old Party." The GOP is the Republican political party.

Got It Made (descriptive phrase) Succeeded.

Greek (noun) See "Like Greek."

Grind (noun) Slang for necessary intense effort that may be painful but will likely benefit your understanding.

Groucho Marx (proper name) A famous U.S. comedian (1885–1977).

Gung-ho (adjective) Full of energy and eager to take action.

Guns and Butter (descriptive phrase) Metaphor describing the dilemma whether to devote resources to war or to peace.

Guzzle, Guzzler (verb and noun) Verb: to consume something greedily, wastefully, and rapidly. Noun: an object (or a person) that guzzles.

H

Haggling (noun) Bargaining, usually in a petty and confrontational manner.

Handout (noun) Unearned offering (as distinct from a gift); charity.

Hangover (noun) The queasy feeling, usually accompanied by a headache, that can afflict a person who has gotten drunk. The feeling can last for hours after the person is no longer actually drunk.

Hard Hit (adjective) Affected in a negative way, often severely.

Hard Liquor (noun) Alcoholic beverages with a high content of pure alcohol. Beer and wine are not "hard liquor," but most other alcoholic drinks are.

Hassle (noun and verb) Noun: unreasonable obstacle. Verb: to place unreasonable obstacles or arguments in the way of someone.

Hawking (adjective) Selling aggressively and widely.

Heat (noun) Anger, blame, outrage, and pressure to change.

Hefty (adjective) Large; substantial.

Here's the Crunch (introductory phrase) Emphasizes an expression of the reality of the situation. Precedes a description of the situation.

Hero Sandwich (noun) A type of very large sandwich.

High Horse, Getting on Your (descriptive phrase) Adopting a superior attitude; looking down (from your high horse) on other people's opinions or actions.

Highfalutin (adjective) American slang term meaning pretentious, self-important, supercilious.

Hitting the Mark (expression) Achieving your purpose.

Holds Its Own (descriptive phrase) Refuses to give up, even in the face of adversity or opposition.

Holy Grail (noun) A desired outcome; According to medieval legend it was the cup used by Jesus at the Last Supper.

Home Free (descriptive phrase) Safe and successful.

Hook (noun) Strategy to engage your attention.

Hot Air (descriptive phrase) An empty promise. Also, bragging.

Hot Dog (noun) A type of sausage.

I

"In" (preposition sometimes used as an adjective) Placed within quotation marks to show it is used with a special meaning. In this book, "in" is used as an adjective, to indicate "fashionable or popular, usually just for a short period." To be "in" means to be associated with highly desirable people (the "in" people).

In a Pickle (descriptive phrase) To be in trouble.

In Sync (descriptive phrase) Moves in tandem with something that it should move with.

In the Cards (descriptive phrase)   Destined to happen.

Incidentals (noun)   Blanket term covering the world of small items a person uses on a daily basis as the need happens to arise—that is, needed per incident occurring. Examples are aspirin, combs, and picture postcards.

IOU (noun)   A nickname applied to a formal acknowledgment of a debt, such as a U.S. Treasury bond. Also an informal but written acknowledgment of a debt. Pronounce the letters and you will hear "I owe you."

iPod (proper name)   A compact digital music player designed by Apple Inc.

It'll (contraction)   "It will."

Ivory Tower (adjective/noun)   Aloofness from life. Comes from a fairy tale about a princess who lived in an ivory tower where she had everything she needed and absolutely nothing to disturb her.

J

Jarring (adjective)   Extremely surprising and unexpected occurrence, usually slightly unpleasant.

JetBlue (proper name)   A low-cost U.S. airline, which is actively entering new markets.

Junk Food (noun)   Food that tastes good but has little nutritional value and lots of calories. It is sometimes cheap, sometimes expensive, and it's quick and easy to buy and eat.

Just Say No (admonition)   Flatly refuse. This phrase became common in the 1980s after Nancy Reagan, the wife of the then-president of the United States, popularized it in a campaign against the use of addictive drugs.

K

Ketchup (noun)   Spicy, thick tomato sauce used on, among other foods, hot dogs.

Knockoff (noun)   A cheap imitation.

L

Laetrile (noun)   Substance derived from peach pits, thought by some people to be a cure for cancer.

Laid Back (adjective)   Casual; calm; free from worry and feelings of pressure.

Lay Off (verb)   To discharge a worker temporarily.

Leads (noun)   Persons or institutions that you think will be interested in whatever you have to sell. Also, the information you have that makes you think someone or something is worth pursuing.

Leaps and Bounds (expression)   A large amount.

Left the Nest (descriptive phrase)   To have left one's parental home, usually because one has grown up and become self-sufficient.

Lemon (noun)   Slang term for an object that is irreparably faulty. It's usually something for which you have paid a substantial amount of money and by whose performance you feel cheated.

Levi's (noun)   Popular brand of jeans.

Like Greek (descriptive phrase)   Incomprehensible (because, in the United States, classical Greek is considered to be a language that almost no one learns).

Lion's Share (noun)   By far the best part of a bargain.

Lobby (verb and noun)   Verb: to attempt by organized effort to influence legislation. Noun: an organized group formed to influence legislation. A lobbyist is a member of a lobby.

Lousy (adjective)   Incompetent or distasteful.

M

Make a Killing (expression)   To be highly successful in negotiations.

Make It (verb)   To succeed in doing something; for instance, "make it to the bank" means to get to the bank before it closes.

Mall (noun)   Short for "shopping mall." A variety of stores grouped on one piece of land, with ample parking for all the mall's shoppers and often with many amenities such as covered walkways, playgrounds for children, fountains, and so on.

Mastercard (proper noun)   Brand name of a widely issued credit card.

Mazuma (noun)   U.S. slang term for money. It was used in the first half of the 20th century but is now rare, to say the least.

MBA (noun)   An academic degree: master of business administration.

Medicaid (proper noun)   Health insurance program for low-income people. It is administered jointly by the U.S. government and the individual states.

Medicare (proper noun)   U.S. government health insurance program for people who are disabled or age 65 and over. There is no means test.

Messed Up (adjective)   Damaged or badly managed.

Mind your Ps and Qs (expression)   Be careful of the details.

Mob (noun)   Organized criminal activity. Also, the group to which organized criminals belong.

Mother of Necessity   A witty remark that reverses the terms of a famous saying, "Necessity is the mother of invention."

Mousetrap (noun)   Producing a better mousetrap is part of the saying, "Make a better mousetrap and the world will beat a path to your door." Metaphorically, producing a better mousetrap stands for doing anything better than it has previously been done.

Musical Chairs (noun)   A U.S. child's game where people walk around a circle of chairs with one fewer chair than there are participants while the music is playing. When the music stops, participants scramble to sit in an empty chair. The last person standing is out of the game.

N

NA (abbreviation)   "Not available."

NATO (noun)   North American Treaty Organization. Western alliance for joint economic and military cooperation. It includes the United States, Canada, and several European nations.

Nanite (noun)   Microscopic mechanism that could hypothetically be injected into living organisms to mend or control them.

National League (name of an organization)   An association of U.S. baseball teams. The United States has two baseball associations—the other is the American League.

Nature of the Beast (descriptive phrase)   Character of whatever you are describing (need not have anything to do with a "beast").

Nerd (noun)   An insignificant and uninteresting person or a person so absorbed in a subject that he or she thinks of nothing else and is therefore boring.

Nickel-and-Dimed (adjective)   Worried over every expenditure, even of tiny sums like nickels and dimes; also having the last tiny sum of money extracted.

Nirvana (noun)   This word is adopted from Buddhism. Its religious meaning is complicated, but it is used colloquially to mean salvation, paradise, harmony, perfection.

No Way (exclamation)   Emphatic expression denoting refusal, denial, or extreme disapproval.

Nobel Prize (adjective/noun)   A prestigious money prize awarded annually from a fund set up in 1901 by the will of Alfred Nobel, the inventor of dynamite. The prizes are in several categories: physics, chemistry, physiology and medicine, literature, and economics. Nobel also established the Nobel Peace Prize, distinguished by the word "peace."

Not to Worry (admonition; also, when hyphenated, used as an adjective)   Don't worry; or it's nothing to worry about.

Nudge (noun and verb)   Noun: a little push. Verb: to give a little push.

O

Oakland Athletics (adjective/noun)   A U.S. major league baseball team.

Occupy Movement (proper noun)   A protest movement against income inequality that started with an occupation of Zuccotti Park in Wall Street, New York City.

Off the Books (descriptive phrase)   Illegal.

Off-the-Cuff (adjective)   A quick, unthinking answer for which the speaker has no valid authority (comes from the alleged practice of writing an abbreviated answer on the cuff of your shirt, to be glanced at during an examination).

Oliver Wendell Holmes Jr. (proper name)   A justice of the U.S. Supreme Court, famous for his wit, his wisdom, his literary ability, his advocacy of civil rights, and his long life (1841–1935).

On Her (His) Own (descriptive phrase)   By herself (himself); without any help.

On the Books (descriptive phrase)   Legal.

On the Dole (descriptive phrase)   Receiving official government assistance such as unemployment, compensation, and welfare.

On Their Toes (descriptive phrase)   Alert; ready for any eventuality.

Op-Ed (adjective)   Describes an article that appears on the "op-ed" page of a newspaper, which is **OP**posite the **ED**itorial page.

Out of Sync (descriptive phrase)   Does not move in tandem with something that it should move with.

P

Pain, Real (noun)   This real pain is not a real pain; rather, it is something—anything—that gives you a lot of trouble and that you dislike intensely. For instance, some people think balancing a checkbook is a real pain.

Pandora's Box (complex noun)   An allusion to a Greek myth. To release a cloud of troubles. Pandora, a figure in Greek mythology, was given a box but told not to open it. She could not resist, and she opened it. It was filled with all the problems of the universe, which escaped to plague us forever.

Park Avenue (noun)   An expensive and fashionable street in New York City.

Part and Parcel (noun)   An integral element of a concept, action, or item.

Payola (noun)   A slang term, meaning a bribe, either of money or a favor, given to someone to do something that is to your advantage—something that the person would not do for you unless he or she received a payola.

Peanuts (noun)   Slang for a small amount, usually money but sometimes anything with a small value.

Peer Pressure (descriptive phrase)   Push to do what everyone else in your particular group is doing.

Perks (noun)   Short for "perquisites."

Pickle (noun)   Dilemma.

Picky (adjective)   Indulging in fine distinctions when making a decision.

Pie (noun)   Metaphor for the total amount of a specific item that exists.

Piece of Cake (descriptive phrase)   Simple; easy to achieve without much effort or thought.

Piecemeal (adverb)   To do something bit by bit instead of all at once.

Pitcher (noun)   In the game of baseball, the player who throws—or "pitches"—the ball to the player who is waiting to strike it.

Poorhouse (noun)   Public institution where impoverished individuals were housed. These institutions were purposely dreary and unpleasant. They no longer officially exist, but they have a modern manifestation: shelters for homeless people.

Pop-Tart (noun)   Brand name of a type of junk food. It's a sweet filling enclosed in pastry that you pop into the toaster and when the pastry is hot, it pops out of the toaster.

Populist (noun and adjective)   Noun: a member of a political party that purports to represent the rank and file of the people. Adjective: a political party, a group, or an individual that purports to represent rank-and-file opinion.

Pound (noun)   Unit of British currency.

Powers That Be (expression)   People or institutions that have power such that there is nothing one can do to influence those people or institutions—or at least nothing easy.

Practice Makes Perfect (expression)   The grammar of this phrase is illogical but the meaning is clear.

Presto! (exclamation)   Immediately.

Proxy (noun)   A stockholder can give a "proxy" to the firm. It is an authorization that permits the firm's officials to vote for the proposition that the stockholder directs them to vote for. By extension, proxy means a substitute.

Ps and Qs   See under *Mind*.

Pub (noun)   Short for "public house," a commercial establishment where alcoholic drinks are served, usually with refreshments and occasionally with light meals.

Q

Quack (noun)   An imposter; an ignorant practitioner.

Queen Elizabeth (proper noun)   Here the author means Queen Elizabeth the first (reigned in England from 1558 to 1603).

Quip (noun and verb)   Noun: a jocular remark. Verb: to make a jocular remark.

Quote (noun)   Seller's statement of what he or she will charge for a good or service.

R

R&D (noun)   Research and development.

Rainy Day (noun)   Period when you (hopefully) temporarily have an income shortage.

Rainy Day Fund (descriptive phrase)   Money set aside when you are doing well financially—that is, in a financially sunny period—to use in case you have a period when you are doing less well financially—that is, when you run into a financially rainy period.

Red Flag (noun)   A red flag warns you to be very alert to a danger or perceived danger. (Ships in port that are loading fuel or ammunition raise a red flag to signal danger.)

Red-Handed (adjective)   Indisputably guilty. Comes from being found at a murder or injury scene with the blood of the victim on one's hands.

Red-Lined (adjective)   On a motor vehicle's tachometer, a red line that warns at what speed an engine's capacity is being strained.

Relief (noun)   This term was an informal one, applied specifically to the financial assistance people in the United States received from the government during the Great Depression (1929 until about 1941). It arose because of a government program administered by the Works Progress Administration (WPA), formed to create jobs, and hence to employ people who otherwise would have been unemployed.

Renege (verb)   Go back on; fail to keep an agreement. Also, in a card game, to fail to play the suit you have contracted to play.

Resort (noun)   An expensive hotel with extensive grounds, swimming pools, and many attractive activities.

Right On! (exclamation)   Expression of vigorous, often revolutionary, approval and encouragement.

Ring Up (verb)   Before the introduction of computer-type machines that record each payment a retail customer makes—say at the supermarket or a restaurant—a "cash register" was used. When you pressed the keys representing the amount offered by the customer, a drawer sprang open and a bell rang.

Ritzy (adjective)   Very expensive, fashionable, and ostentatious. Comes from the entrepreneur Caesar Ritz, a Swiss developer of expensive hotels, active in the first quarter of the 20th century. Upscale, fancy. Has overtones of ostentation.

Robin Hood (proper name)   Semifictional English adventurer of the 12th or 13th century. He "stole from the rich and gave to the poor."

Rock Bottom (noun)   To reach the absolute limit of one's endurance or resources.

Rodeo (noun)   Entertainment where a person rides a bull that is wildly trying to throw the rider off. Horses are often exhibited similarly.

Rough-and-Ready (expression)   Quick decision made because it's easy. It is a type of compromise or improvisation.

Rube Goldberg (proper name)   A famous cartoonist whose cartoons depicted complicated methods of doing simple things.

Rule of Thumb (complex noun)   Judgment based on practical experience rather than on scientific knowledge. Comes from the habit of using the space between the tip to the first joint of your thumb as being about an inch—good enough for the task at hand but not precise.

S

Saks (proper name)   A midsize department store that sells expensive, fashionable items. There are very few stores in the Saks chain, and Saks stores are considered exclusive.

Savvy (adjective)   Slang term meaning very knowledgeable. Adaptation of the French verb *savoir,* meaning "to know."

Scab (noun)   Person who takes a job, or continues in a job, even though workers at that firm are on strike.

Scalp (verb)   To buy a ticket legally and then resell it at a very high profit to an individual who wants it very badly but can't buy it legally because all the tickets have already been sold to others.

Scraps (noun)   Little pieces of leftover food. Also, little pieces of anything that is left over: for example, steel that is salvaged from a wrecked car.

Scrooge (proper name)   Character in Charles Dickens' *A Christmas Carol,* an English story written in the mid-1850s. He was unbelievably miserly and disagreeable (but in the story he reformed).

Sears Catalog (noun)   Sears, Roebuck and Co. is a large but shrinking chain of stores that sells a wide variety of goods. Before shopping malls, interstate highways, and the Internet, Sears used to have a huge mailing list to which it sent enormous catalogs. A person receiving such a catalog would have information about, and access to, thousands of items, many of which the person might not have known existed before the catalog provided the prospect.

Seizes Up (verb)   To come to a sudden and complete stop that you cannot easily repair or alleviate.

Set Up Shop (verb)   To go into business.

Shady (adjective)   Questionable, a little bit or more than a little bit dishonest.

Shell Out (verb)   To pay money, often somewhat more than you want to pay for the item in question.

Shivering in Their Sandals (descriptive phrase)   Adaptation of standard English idiom *shivering in their shoes,* which means being afraid.

Shoo-in (noun)   Highly probable (as in "you are a shoo-in" to get an A).

Shorthand (noun)   Any of several systems of abbreviated writing or writing that substitutes symbols for words and phrases. Shorthand was widely used in business until the introduction of mechanical and electronic devices for transmitting the human voice gradually made shorthand obsolete. Today it means to summarize very briefly or to substitute a short word or phrase for a long description.

Show-off (verb and noun)   To be blatant and vulgar in displaying a possession or accomplishment. The person who is a show-off is displaying conspicuous consumption.

Show Up (verb)   To put in an appearance, to arrive.

Significant Other (noun)   A person with a close relationship with an individual, often a romantic interest.

Silk Stockings (noun)   Silk stockings for women denoted luxury and extravagance, almost like caviar or pearls. With the development of nylon in 1940, silk stockings for anyone, let alone the queens or factory girls mentioned in this book, joined the dinosaurs in oblivion.

Sixpence (noun)   A British coin that is no longer in use. It represented six British pennies; its U.S. equivalent in the 2000s would be about a nickel.

Skin of One's Teeth (descriptive phrase)   To succeed by the skin of one's teeth means to just barely succeed. A micromeasure less and one would not have succeeded.

Skyrocket (verb and noun)   Verb: to rise suddenly and rapidly. Noun: the type of fireworks that shoot into the sky and explode suddenly in a shower of brilliant sparks.

Slow as Molasses (descriptive phrase)   Very slow. Molasses is a thick, sweet syrup made from sugar cane (known as "treacle" in the United Kingdom) that pours with agonizing slowness from its container.

Small Potatoes (noun)   An expression meaning insignificant or trivial.

Smoke Screen (noun)   Metaphorically, anything used intentionally to hide one's true intentions.

Smoking Gun (noun)   This term has come to stand for any indisputable evidence of guilt or misdeeds.

Snitch (verb)   To engage in petty theft. (This verb has another meaning, which is to betray a person by divulging a secret about that person. If you do that, you are not only snitching, you are a snitch.)

Snitch a Sandwich (expression)   Grab a sandwich in an inobtrusive manner that is almost unnoticeable.

Snowball (verb)   To increase rapidly, like a ball of wet snow that grows and grows when it is rolled rapidly in more wet snow.

Soft Drink (noun)   Nonalcoholic carbonated beverage.

Solid Steady (noun)   A friend whom one has agreed to go out with in an almost exclusive relationship.

Sourpuss (noun)   Dour; sulky; humorless. Derives from *sour,* which is self-explanatory, and *puss,* a slang word for "face."

Speakeasy (noun)   A bar—a place to drink alcoholic beverages—that is operating illegally without a license.

They were common in the United States during Prohibition, a period (1919–1933) when the manufacture and sale of alcoholic beverages were prohibited by an amendment to the U.S. Constitution and lifted when that Constitutional amendment was revoked.

Spending a Penny (descriptive phrase)   Spending any money at all. Do not confuse with usage in England, where the phrase means to go to the bathroom.

Spoils (noun)   Rewards or advantages gained through illegal or unethical activity.

Squash (verb)   To crush or ruin.

Squirrel Away (verb)   To hide or conceal in a handy but secret place (as a squirrel stores nuts).

Star Trek **(title)**   Famous U.S. TV and movie series about life in outer space.

Stay on Their Toes (idiom)   To be alert.

Steady (noun)   A person to whom you are romantically committed and with whom you spend a lot of time, especially in social activities.

Stealth Gains (noun)   Gains that occur unbeknownst to you.

Sticky (adjective)   Resistant to change, as if glued on.

Strike a Chord (expression)   To convey an idea in a way that connects with someone.

Strings Attached (descriptive phrase)   A gift that comes with strings attached comes with certain conditions set forth by the donor.

Sucker (noun)   A gullible person.

Super Bowl (noun)   Important football game played annually that attracts millions of viewers (most of them see the game on TV).

Swap (verb and noun)   Verb: to trade one thing for another. Noun: the trade itself.

Sweetheart Contract (noun)   A contract where one party to the contract is given all, or almost all, the advantage; specifically, a contract between an employer and the workers' union where the employer gains the advantage and the contract on the workers' side has been arranged by a union official who secretly gives up advantages for the workers in return for significant advantage for the official.

Switch Gears (verb/noun)   Change your strategy.

T

Tables Were Turned (descriptive phrase)   The advantage of one side over the other reverses so that now the winner is the loser and the loser is the winner.

Tacky (adjective)   In very poor taste.

Taco Technician (noun)   A name given to a worker at a fast-food restaurant specializing in Mexican foods.

Take a Flier (expression)   To take a chance; to undertake a risky action in the hope that you will be lucky.

Take the Heat (verb)   To accept all criticism of one's action or inaction, whether or not one is actually the person that should be blamed.

Take Title (verb)   Legal term meaning to acquire ownership.

Tea Control (noun)   A method of resolving differences by informal but powerful social mechanisms, such as inviting your opponents to tea and settling matters while passing teacups and plates of cake around.

Temp (noun)   Worker whose job is temporary and who accepts the job with that understanding.

Time-and-a-Half (noun)   In labor law, 150 percent of the normal hourly wage.

To Be in Hot Water (descriptive phrase)   To be in trouble.

To Be Watertight (descriptive phrase)   To be in perfect working order.

Ton (noun)   A ton weighs 2,000 pounds and an English ton (often spelled "tonne") weighs 2,240 pounds. In this book, the term is used most frequently to mean simply "a large quantity."

Tough (adjective)   Very difficult.

Trendy (adjective)   A phenomenon that is slightly ahead of traditional ways and indicates a trend. Something trendy may turn into something traditional, or it may fade away without ever becoming mainstream.

Trophy Spouse (noun)   A spouse (usually the wife) who is young, beautiful, and perhaps famous and/or rich who has been married to an older—sometimes much older—very successful and rich person, usually after divorcing one or more previous spouses. The trophy spouse is just that—a trophy. (See also "show-off.")

Truck (verb)   To exchange one thing for another. This was Adam Smith's definition in 1776 and it is still one of the meanings of the verb.

Truth (noun)   When capitalized (other than at the start of a sentence), true beyond any doubt (as opposed to "truth"— the best truth we have at the moment).

Tune In (verb)   To become familiar with.

Turf (noun)   Territory, especially the figurative territory of a firm.

Turn of the Century (expression)   The few years at the end of an expiring century and the beginning of a new century. For example: 1998–2002.

Turn Up One's Nose (verb)   To reject.

Twinkies (noun)   Brand name of an inexpensive small cake.

U

Under the Table (descriptive phrase)   To accept money surreptitiously in order to avoid paying taxes on it or to conceal the income for other reasons. Also, to proffer such money to avoid having it known that you are making a particular deal.

Underwater Homeowners (noun) Homeowners who owe more on their mortgages than their houses are worth.

Union Jack (noun) Nickname for the British flag.

Up at Bat (expression) From the sport of baseball. A player (the "batter") who is in the position ("home plate") where a player from the opposing team (the "pitcher") will throw the ball to him. The player to whom the ball is thrown is "up at bat." Thus, to be up at bat can mean being ready to meet an impending emergency or other situation.

Up in Arms (adjective) Furious and loudly protesting. Comes from the use of *arms* to stand for *firearms*.

V

Vanity License Plate (descriptive phrase) One-of-a-kind motor vehicle license plate issued to your individual specification. It might have your name, your profession, or any individual set of letters and numbers you choose that will fit on the plate.

Vignette (noun) Short story that uses a few words to illustrate or reinforce a point.

Village Watchman (descriptive phrase) Before modern communication technology, in small communities local news was gathered and reported by an official, the village watchman or town crier, who walked around collecting facts and gossip.

W

Wadget (noun) Term used by economists to stand for any manufactured good except goods designated as widgets. (See also "widget.")

Walmart (proper name) A very large store that sells thousands of inexpensive items. There are thousands of Walmarts in the United States and the company has expanded into foreign markets.

Wampum (noun) String of beads made of polished shells, formerly used by North American Indians as money.

Wash (noun) Process or event that neutralizes an "either/or" situation; in fact, eliminates the argument or erases the event.

Whatever (noun) Designates an unspecified generic item or action when the speaker wants to let you know that it doesn't matter whether you know the exact item or place.

Wheaties (proper noun) Name of a brand of dry breakfast cereal.

White Elephant (noun) Property requiring expensive care but yielding little profit; trinket without value to most people but esteemed by a few. There are real white elephants, which are albinos. They are rare and therefore expensive and high-maintenance.

Whopper (proper noun) Brand name of a kind of hamburger sold at Burger King restaurants.

Widget (noun) The opposite of a wadget. (See also "wadget.")

Wild About (descriptive phrase) Extremely enthusiastic about undertaking a particular action or admiring a particular object or person.

Wind Up (descriptive phrase) To discover that you have reached a particular conclusion or destination.

With It (descriptive phrase) Highly popular.

With-It (adjective) Current in one's knowledge.

Workhorse (noun) Common, everyday method of accomplishing a task—nothing fancy. A "workhorse" in actuality is a strong horse of no particular beauty or attraction but is useful for pulling heavy loads in situations where using a machine is impractical.

Working Off the Books (descriptive phrase) Being paid wages or fees that are not reported to the tax or other authorities by either the payer or the payee.

World Series (complex noun) At the end of the baseball season the two opposing teams left after the season's contests have eliminated all the other teams play each other. The winner in this "World Series" wins the season.

World War I (proper noun) 1914–1918. The United States did not enter until 1917.

World War II (proper noun) 1938–1945. The United States did not enter until 1941.

Wound Up (past tense of verb wind up) To have found oneself in a particular situation after having taken particular actions.

Wreak Havoc (verb) Cause severe devastation.

Writ Large (adjective) Strongly emphasized; defined broadly. ("Writ" is an obsolete form of the word "written.")

Writing on the Wall (descriptive phrase) To see the writing on the wall is to realize that a situation is inevitably going to end badly. It comes from the biblical story that Nebuchadnezzar, king of Babylon, saw a fatal prediction written on a wall.